Rice

Kittery Maine

Public Library

1888

Webster's American Military Biographies

Webster's American Military Biographies

Edited by
Robert McHenry

Dover Publications, Inc., New York

Published in Canada by General Publishing Company, Ltd., 30 Lesmill
Road, Don Mills, Toronto, Ontario.
Published in the United Kingdom by Constable and Company, Ltd., 10
Orange Street, London WC2H 7EG.

This Dover edition, first published in 1984 by special arrangement with
Merriam-Webster, Inc., 47 Federal Street, Springfield, Massachusetts 01101,
is an unabridged and unaltered republication of their edition published
in 1978.

Manufactured in the United States of America
Dover Publications, Inc., 31 East 2nd Street, Mineola, N.Y. 11501.

Library of Congress Cataloging in Publication Data
Main entry under title:

Webster's American military biographies.

Reprint. Originally published: Springfield, Mass. : G. & C. Merriam
Co., c1978.
1. Soldiers—United States—Biography.   2. United States. War
Dept.—Biography.   3. United States. Dept. of Defense—Biogra-
phy.   4. United States—History, Military—Biography.   I. McHenry,
Robert.   II. G. & C. Merriam Company.   III. Title: American military
biographies.
[U52.W4   1984]   355'.092'2 [B]   84-8004
ISBN 0-486-24758-9

Contents

INTRODUCTION

Page ix

BIOGRAPHIES

Page 1

ADDENDA

Page 498

Introduction

"Don't fire until you see the white of their eyes!"

"I'll try, sir."

"Damn the torpedoes! Full speed ahead!"

"Hold the fort! I am coming."

"You may fire when you are ready, Gridley."

"I shall return."

"Nuts!"

Nearly every reader will recognize most of these famous quotations. To a surprising degree our understanding of America's wars and military history generally is epitomized in the form of such colorful, dramatic phrases. But behind every one of these and the dozens more that may spring to mind there stands a real person, a man or woman who lived what is now to us history and whose own story is the rich substance that is only suggested by the few words we now remember. It is such stories that make up this book.

Webster's American Military Biographies presents in alphabetical order 1033 full biographies of persons who have contributed signally to the military history of the nation. The word "military," it should be quickly pointed out, is used here in an extended sense covering those things pertaining to all the armed forces, regular and irregular, on land or sea or in the air. Indeed, it is used as an even larger umbrella than that, for included among the 1033 are not only the battlefield heroes and the great commanders, but also the frontier scouts, nurses, Indian leaders, historians, explorers, shipbuilders, and inventors of better gunpowder and of better staff organizations. There are also astronauts, a few spies, three cartoonists, and the men who built the Panama Canal. Some of the people in these biographies became President, some went off to command the Peruvian navy or the Egyptian army, and some died in disgrace or obscurity. All left stories that are part of our heritage.

In compiling these biographies the goal has been to provide full and accurate information on each subject and to present it in an attractive and useful form. At an average length of 450 words, these biographies are not merely lists of titles, offices, dates, and the like. In each biography the birth date and place (where known) and some words on education and other early experiences are followed by an outline of the subject's entire career. Emphasis is given to his or her particular contribution or significance, often in considerable detail, and where useful the historical or institutional context is sketched in such a way as to make the story as meaningful as possible. Major published works, especially autobiographical ones, are noted, as are outstanding honors and awards. And finally, the death date and place are given, or, in the case of a living subject, a mention of current activities.

A few terms and conventions that appear in many biographies call for some explanation. One of the most confusing practices in the army in the 19th century was the conferring of brevet ranks. These were quasi-commissions at grades higher than the recipient's permanent or regular rank. They entitled the recipient to wear the uniform and the insignia of the higher rank and, under certain never clearly defined circumstances, to command in that rank. Brevets were awarded for various causes, primarily as a reward for meritorious service but also for longevity or for political reasons, and for many years graduates of the Military Academy began their service as brevet second lieutenants and were commissioned only later. After the 1870s brevets were eliminated, and medals became the army's tokens of honor. The marine corps has also used brevet ranks, often in order to complete tables of organization in provisional tactical units.

In times of war the permanent and professional Regular Army has always needed to be reinforced by a larger temporary force of citizen-soldiers, and some confusions arise from the changing terminology associated with this process. Early on the army was joined in war by units of the various state militias, which had their own commanders, their own tactics, and often their own notions of whom to fight and where. There was often also a distinction between the standing militia and the volunteer militia organized for specific federal service. Later the militia system faded and was gradually replaced by the enrollment of volunteers in a federal volunteer army, organized like the Regular Army and generally commanded at top levels by regular officers serving in volunteer ranks higher than their regular ranks. This system was employed from the War of 1812 through the Spanish-American War and found its fullest elaboration in the Civil War, when it was not impossible for a man to have been a regular first lieutenant in March 1861, colonel of a volunteer regiment by March 1863, and a brevet major general of both regulars and volunteers by March 1865. All permutations of regular, volunteer, and brevet ranks have been distinguished in these biographies.

In World War I the "Army of the United States" consisted principally of an expanded Regular Army and units of the National Guard; for all practical purposes there was no volunteer component in the old sense, enlistees and draftees being assigned to expanded permanent regular units (divisions 1 through 8) or to the newly organized divisions of the "National Army" (divisions 76 through 93). (Divisions 26 through 42 were National Guard.) In the standing or the National Army divisions, many or most commands were held by regular officers serving temporarily at higher ranks. In World War II and since, officers have continued to serve in temporary ranks (Army of the United States) higher than their permanent ranks (Regular Army).

In many biographies of naval figures from the age of sail, the number of guns mounted by warships is often noted when a combat engagement makes a comparison useful. Thus the phrase "aboard the *Constellation*, 36," notes that the *Constellation* mounted 36 guns in her main batteries. In a similar manner the captain of a ship may sometimes be noted "aboard the *Constellation*, Capt. Truxtun." While it is naval custom to refer to the commanding officer of a vessel as "captain" regardless of his actual rank, for clarity the actual rank is generally used in this book. A related confusion is sometimes created by the term "commodore." Until 1862 the term designated not a rank but the position of command of a squadron; the officer so designated held the rank of captain, which was then the highest in the navy. From 1862 to 1899 commodore was an actual rank, the next one above captain and below rear admiral. After 1899 the term is used mainly to refer to a captain other than the commanding officer aboard a naval vessel.

An extensive Addenda section begins on page 498. It features a number of lists of officials and commanders of the military and naval establishments from 1776, tables of major commanders in the principal modern wars, and, most importantly, a unique set of chronologies whereby the reader interested in a particular war, battle, expedition, or period can be directed to the biographies most relevant to that interest. It is hoped that this sort of index to the contents of Webster's American Military Biographies will prove more useful than the conventional kind. A more detailed explanation of this material is found on page 498.

Many persons on the Merriam staff have contributed to the completion of this book: Frederick C. Mish, joint editorial director, and Michael G. Belanger, assistant editor, each of whom read and checked details of the manuscript; Julie Anne Collier, assistant editor, and James G. Lowe, associate editor, who proofread every page; and Barbara Quimby, who under the direction of Evelyn G. Summers of the Merriam clerical staff valiantly undertook to transcribe reams of impossible handwriting into a typescript. All have been mentioned in dispatches.

Robert McHenry
Editor

A

Abbot, Henry Larcom (1831–1927), army officer and engineer. Born in Beverly, Massachusetts, on August 13, 1831, Abbot was the older brother of Francis Ellingwood Abbot, an influential religious radical. On graduating from West Point in 1854, Henry Abbot was commissioned in the engineers and assigned to duty with the Pacific coast railway survey. For several years from 1857 he was associated with Capt. Andrew A. Humphreys in a study of flood control and navigation improvement on the Mississippi River; their *Report upon the Physics and Hydraulics of the Mississippi River,* 1861, was a lasting contribution to the field. During the Civil War Abbot saw varied service. He was wounded at the first battle of Bull Run, served as an engineer with Gen. George B. McClellan on the Peninsula and as chief topographical engineer with the New Orleans expedition under Gen. Nathaniel P. Banks, and commanded the 1st Connecticut Heavy Artillery of which he had been appointed colonel in the spring of 1863, and the siege artillery before Richmond, Virginia. In the course of the war he was brevetted seven times, rising by March 1865 to brigadier general in the regular army and major general of volunteers; he reverted to his regular rank of major afterward. Placed in command of the engineer battalion at Willett's Point, New York, he organized there the Engineer School of Application, a combined advanced training and research facility for military engineers. He devoted much of his time to the improvement of coastal defenses by means of submarine mines and of other forms of ordnance and equipment, serving as well on numerous engineering boards. He was promoted to lieutenant colonel in March 1880 and to colonel in October 1886, and he retired at that rank in 1895; in 1904 Congress voted him rank of brigadier general, retired. As a civilian consulting engineer Abbot drew plans for the harbor at Manitowoc, Wisconsin, and served on the technical committee of the New French Panama Canal Company. He later was a member of the board of engineers appointed by President Theodore Roosevelt to plan the American canal in Panama. He was on the graduate engineering faculty of George Washington University from 1905 to 1910. Among Abbot's published works were *Early Days of the Engineer School of Application,* 1904, and *Problems of the Panama Canal,* 1905, as well as many technical reports, and he was a contributor to the *Encyclopaedia Britannica.* He died on October 1, 1927, in Cambridge, Massachusetts.

Abert, John James (1788–1863), army officer and engineer. Born on September 17, 1788, in Shepherdstown, Virginia (now West Virginia), Abert graduated from West Point in 1811, having served as an assistant in mathematics while still a student. He resigned from the army, however, and worked as a clerk in the War Department until winning admission to the bar in 1813. In 1814 he entered volunteer service, was in the battle of Bladensburg, August 24, and in November of that year was reappointed to the army with the rank of major in the topographical engineers. For fifteen years he was engaged in surveys of the Atlantic coast, canal construction, harbor and river improvement, and coastal defense, in association with Ferdinand R. Hassler, founder of the U.S. Coast Survey. In February 1829 he became head of the Topographical Bureau, which two years later, June 1831, was made an independent branch of the War Department. In July 1838 the topographical engineers became a staff corps of the army, and Abert was duly promoted to colonel. After a time in the early 1830s in which he was assigned to oversee the program of Indian removal beyond the Mississippi, Abert devoted himself to the exacting task of organizing and directing the continent-wide work of the bureau and overseeing the collation and publication of its reports. At a time when the West was largely unknown, he had charge of planning its scientific exploration and description. Abert retired in the rank of colonel in September 1861. He was a founder of the National Institute of Science, Washington, D.C., which was later absorbed by the Smithsonian Institution. He died in Washington, D.C., on January 27, 1863.

Abrams, Creighton Williams, Jr. (1914–1974), army officer. Born in Springfield, Massachusetts, on September 15, 1914, Abrams graduated from West Point in 1936 and was commissioned in the cavalry. After service with the 1st Cavalry Division at Fort Bliss, Texas, he was assigned to the newly created 1st Armored Division in 1940. He was promoted to first lieutenant in June 1939 and to captain in October 1940. Early in 1941 he was transferred to the 4th Armored Division, and, advancing to temporary major in February 1942 and temporary lieutenant colonel in September of the same year, in September 1943 he became commander of the 37th Tank Battalion. The 4th Division landed in Normandy in July 1944, and from then until the end of the war in Europe

Abrams commanded alternately the 37th and the divisional combat command. Attached for the most part to Gen. George S. Patton's Third Army, the 37th was in the vanguard of the sweep across central France and into southern Germany. Abrams's battalion led the relief of Gen. Anthony C. McAuliffe's 101st Airborne Division at Bastogne in December 1944, and by early May 1945 had crossed into Czechoslovakia. General Patton publicly acknowledged Abrams's mastery of tank warfare. Much decorated, Abrams was promoted to colonel (temporary) in 1945. His service in subsequent years included a variety of staff and field assignments. In 1949 he graduated from the Command and General Staff College and in 1953 from the Army War College. During the Korean War he served as chief of staff of the I Corps, the X Corps, and the IX Corps in succession. He was promoted to brigadier general (temporary) in February 1956, to major general (temporary) in May 1960, in which grade he commanded the 3rd Armored Division in Germany in 1960–1962, and to lieutenant general (temporary) in August 1963, commanding the V Corps. In September 1964 he was named vice chief of staff and promoted to general (temporary). In May 1967 he was appointed deputy commander of the United States Military Assistance Command in Vietnam, and in June 1968 he succeeded Gen. William Westmoreland as commander, MACV. Abrams remained in that post for four years, during which he attempted to implement the "Vietnamization" policy of training Vietnamese troops ultimately to take over sole conduct of the war with the communist forces of North Vietnam. The goal was still far from achieved when he was named chief of staff of the army in July 1972. Abrams held that post until his death on September 4, 1974, in Washington, D.C.

Ainsworth, Frederick Crayton (1852–1934), army officer. Born in Woodstock, Vermont, on September 11, 1852, Ainsworth graduated from the medical department of the University of the City of New York (later New York University) in 1874 and in November of that year enlisted in the Army Medical Corps as an assistant surgeon. He was stationed at various posts in Alaska and the Southwest for many years, gaining promotion to captain surgeon in November 1879. In 1885 he was called to serve as recorder of the Army Examining Board, and in 1886 he was placed in charge of the Record and Pension Division in the surgeon general's office. His great success in reorganizing and streamlining the work of that formerly chaotic division brought him considerable attention from the public and from Congress, ever sensitive to veteran- and pension-related matters. In 1889 the division was made a War Department division, taking over certain functions of the adjutant general's office. Ainsworth, promoted to

major surgeon in February 1891, resigned that commission in May 1892 to take a line commission as colonel and chief of the Record and Pension Office. As his responsibilities grew, so also did his influence; promoted to brigadier general in March 1899, he was appointed military secretary over an again enlarged department in April 1904 with rank of major general, and in March 1907 he took over the title as well as what remained of the office of adjutant general. He exercised that office jealously and sometimes arbitrarily until February 1912, when, faced with suspension from duty and a court-martial on grounds of insubordination at the instance of Secretary of War Henry L. Stimson, arising from Ainsworth's dispute with the chief of staff, Gen. Leonard Wood—Ainsworth was strongly opposed to the newly adopted General Staff idea—he requested and was granted retirement. Prominent among his achievements was his overseeing the bulk of the work of publishing *The War of the Rebellion: A Compilation of the Official Records of the Union and Confederate Armies, 1880–1901.* Ainsworth died on June 5, 1934, in Washington, D.C.

Alden, Ichabod (1739–1778), Revolutionary army officer. Born in Duxbury, Massachusetts, on August 11, 1739, Alden was a great-grandson of John Alden of the *Mayflower* pilgrims. In 1775 he was appointed lieutenant colonel of the Plymouth militia regiment, and he saw service in the siege of Boston with the 25th Continental Infantry. In November 1776 he became colonel of the 7th Massachusetts, which was assigned to garrison duty at Cherry Valley, New York, an important and prosperous settlement in the upper Susquehanna Valley. Alden had at his disposal between 200 and 300 men but had little knowledge of warfare and none of Indian methods, a fatal shortcoming in a frontier post. Early in November 1778 he received warning that an attack on Cherry Valley threatened, but he took few precautionary measures. On November 11 a force of about 600 Indians led by Joseph Brant and some 200 Tories and British known as Butler's Rangers, under Maj. Walter Butler, having captured Alden's scouts, fell upon the settlement without warning. Thirty people, including 16 soldiers, were killed, and 71 were taken prisoner, most of whom were later released. The settlement itself was completely destroyed except for the fort, where survivors gathered afterward. During the attack Alden was killed attempting to reach the fort from one of the outlying houses. The Cherry Valley Massacre, in part an Indian retaliation for their defeat at Oriskany, provoked in turn the punitive expedition of 1779 under Gen. John Sullivan.

Alden, James (1810–1877), naval officer. Born on March 31, 1810, in Portland, Maine (then still a part of Massachusetts), Alden was a direct descendant of

John Alden of the original Plymouth colony. In 1828 he was appointed midshipman in the navy. He was promoted to lieutenant in February 1841, while taking part in the 1838–1842 South Sea Exploring Expedition under Lt. Charles Wilkes, in the course of which he distinguished himself in the rescue of a landing party from hostile Fiji Islanders. During 1844 –1846 he made a second world cruise on the *Constitution*. In the Mexican War he participated, under Commodore David Conner and Commodore Matthew C. Perry, in the capture of Veracruz, Tuxpan, and Tabasco. He was promoted to commander in September 1855, saw action, as captain of the *Active,* a Coast Survey steamer, against Indians on Puget Sound in 1855–1856, and at the outbreak of the Civil War was in command of the steamer *South Carolina,* with which he reinforced Fort Pickens, Florida, and fought an engagement at Galveston, Texas. He commanded the sloop of war *Richmond,* part of Flag-Officer David G. Farragut's West Gulf Squadron, in the passage of Fort Jackson and Fort St. Philip and the capture of New Orleans in April 1862 and in subsequent operations at Port Hudson. In January 1863 he was promoted to captain. In August 1864 he was in command of the ironclad *Brooklyn,* which, with the *Tecumseh,* formed the van of Farragut's attack on Mobile Bay. When the *Tecumseh* suddenly struck a torpedo (as underwater mines were then known) and sank and lookouts on the *Brooklyn* simultaneously sighted buoys ahead believed to mark more torpedoes, Alden, in indecision, stopped and then backed the *Brooklyn.* Under the action of wind and her single screw propeller, the ship turned broadside in the narrow channel, throwing the entire column into confusion. It was at that moment that Farragut made his famous sprint in the *Hartford,* and uttered his more famous curse. Alden's action was the subject of some controversy, but Farragut took the generous view and no stain was left upon his record. He later took part in the attacks on Fort Fisher, December 24–25, 1864, and January 15, 1865, under Adm. David D. Porter. He was promoted to commodore in July 1866, put in command of the Mare Island, California, navy yard in 1868, named chief of the Bureau of Navigation in 1869, and promoted to rear admiral in 1871. After a tour as commander of the European Squadron he retired in 1872. Alden died in San Francisco on February 6, 1877.

Alexander, Edward Porter (1835–1910), Confederate army officer. Born in Washington, Georgia, on May 26, 1835, Alexander graduated from West Point in 1857, was commissioned in the engineers, and served on the faculty of the Military Academy for the next three years except for a brief period with the Mormon expedition in 1858. In 1859 he conducted tests of the signaling system proposed by Dr. Albert J. Myer of the Medical Corps, aiding

thereby in the perfection of the "wigwag" system. In 1860 he was posted to Washington Territory and then to Alcatraz Island, but at the outbreak of the Civil War he resigned. In June 1861 he accepted a captain's commission in the Confederate army. Placed on the staff of Gen. P. G. T. Beauregard as engineer and chief of signal service, he was soon promoted to major and made chief of ordnance for the Army of Northern Virginia. In November 1862 he took command of an artillery battalion in Gen. James Longstreet's Corps and the following month was promoted to colonel. His batteries were of great effect in the battles of Fredericksburg, December 13, 1862, Chancellorsville, May 2–4, 1863, where his artillery accompanied Gen. Thomas J. Jackson's flanking move, and Gettysburg, July 1–3, 1863, where he was responsible for softening up the Union line preparatory to Gen. George E. Pickett's desperate attack. In February 1864 he advanced to brigadier general and command of all artillery in Longstreet's Corps. He continued to serve in that capacity through Spotsylvania, Cold Harbor, and the siege of Petersburg, and he was at Appomattox, where he advised Lee not to surrender. From 1866 to 1869 Alexander was on the engineering faculty of the University of South Carolina, and in later years he was president of a number of business organizations, including several southern railroads. He was a government director of the Union Pacific Railroad in 1885–1887, and in 1891 he served as engineer-arbitrator in the boundary dispute between Nicaragua and Costa Rica. Among his writings were *Railway Practice,* 1887, *Catterel Ratterel (Doggerel),* 1888, and *Military Memoirs of a Confederate,* 1907, an important study of the operations of the Army of Northern Virginia. Alexander died in Savannah, Georgia, on April 28, 1910.

Alexander, William (1726–1783), "Lord Stirling," Revolutionary army officer. Born in New York City in 1726, Alexander was the son of a self-exiled Scottish Jacobite who had become wealthy in the New World. He added to the family fortune as a merchant. His service as aide and secretary to Gov. William Shirley early in the French and Indian War required him to visit London in 1756, and while there he laid claim to the title of earl of Stirling. The fifth earl had died without issue in 1739, and Alexander claimed collateral descent. A Scottish jury upheld him, but the House of Lords in 1762 denied his claim; nonetheless, he thereafter styled himself, and was generally known as, Lord Stirling. He was a figure of considerable consequence, holding various public offices and extensive private interests. He was also a patriot, and early in the conflict that led to the Revolution he raised a grenadier company. In November 1775 he was appointed colonel of the 1st New Jersey Regiment of militia. In January 1776 he led a force of volunteers in the capture of a British armed transport ship off Sandy Hook, for which he was commissioned brigadier general in the Continental army in March and put in command of New York City. In preparing for the defense of the city he had a number of fortifications built, including Fort Lee and Fort Washington on opposite sides of the Hudson to the north of the city (now in Fort Lee, New Jersey, and Harlem), and Fort Stirling on Brooklyn Heights. He was later superseded in command by Gen. John Sullivan and then by Gen. Israel Putnam, who by August had some 5000 largely untrained troops—nearly a third of the American army—on Long Island. The British forces landed at Gravesend Bay from Staten Island by Gen. Sir William Howe on August 22 numbered more than 20,000. Lord Stirling, with fewer than 2000 troops, was to hold the unfortified coast road at Gowanus Bay. When the attack began on August 27, he successfully held off a column under Gen. Grant for some hours, but a threat on his left from another force under Gen. Charles Cornwallis forced him to send most of his brigade in retreat toward Brooklyn. He remained with a small command to cover the retreat, suffered terrible casualties in doing so, and was captured by Gen. De Heister of the Hessian troops. He was exchanged shortly thereafter and took part in the general retreat of the American army. He fought well at Trenton, December 26, and in February 1777 was advanced to major general. He suffered a defeat at Metuchen in June 1777 but redeemed himself by his conduct at Brandywine, September 11, Germantown, October 4, and especially Monmouth, June 27, 1778, where he commanded the left wing. After this last battle he presided over the court-martial of Gen. Charles Lee. In August 1779 he provided invaluable support to Maj. Henry "Light Horse Harry" Lee's attack on Paulus Hook, and in January 1780 he mounted an ineffectual expedition to Staten Island. Thereafter his service consisted in the main of garrison duty, primarily at Albany, where he died on January 15, 1783.

Allen, Ethan (1738–1789), Revolutionary army officer. Born on January 21, 1738, in Litchfield, Connecticut, Allen was prevented from completing his education by the death of his father in 1755, after which he assumed responsibility for his family. During his youth he became intrigued by the ideas of a rationalist philosopher, Thomas Young, and later wrote a book based on them, *Reason, the Only Oracle of Man*, 1784. After serving in the French and Indian War in 1757, he acquired, with his four brothers, large land holdings in the region, then known as the New Hampshire Grants, that was to become the state of Vermont. Jurisdiction over the Grants was disputed by New York and New Hampshire. Eager to control the region themselves, the Allens formed in 1770, with Ethan as "colonel commandant," the Green

Mountain Boys, a group that harassed New Yorkers in the area and eventually grew so notorious that Gov. Tryon of New York offered a £100 reward for Ethan's capture. Allen had plans to petition the king to confer separate status on the disputed area, but the outbreak of the Revolution interrupted his efforts. In April 1775 he was instructed by the Connecticut Assembly to capture Fort Ticonderoga, and on May 10, with the able assistance of Col. Benedict Arnold and a body of militia, Allen and his patriot band succeeded triumphantly. The British garrison was called upon by Allen to surrender "in the name of Jehovah and the Continental Congress," and it did so. Skenesborough and Crown Point, the only other major points on Lake Champlain, were taken soon afterwards. Emboldened by this success, he proposed and took part in an ill-conceived expedition against Montreal in September 1775; he was promptly captured and imprisoned by the British. In May 1778 he was released in exchange for a British prisoner. The brevet rank of colonel in the Continental army was conferred on him when he was released from prison, but he returned to his own affairs in Vermont, where he was made major general of militia. His *Narrative of Colonel Ethan Allen's Captivity*, 1779, omitted mention of Arnold's aid in capturing Fort Ticonderoga. With his brothers, he resumed his activities in behalf of the region and, whether seriously or as a tactical move in the continuing dispute with New York and Congress, discussed a plan of his former captors, the British in Canada, to annex Vermont to Canada or, at the least, to aid Vermont to obtain separate status. (The Green Mountain Boys had meanwhile continued to serve the Revolution under Col. Seth Warner.) He died in Burlington on February 11, 1789. Two years later Vermont achieved statehood, and under its tax laws the Allens lost all of their land.

Allen, Henry Tureman (1859–1930), army officer. Born in Sharpsburg, Kentucky, on April 13, 1859, Allen graduated from West Point in 1882 and was commissioned in the cavalry. After six years of service in the West, including command of an exploring expedition in Alaska in 1885–1886, he returned to West Point as an instructor from 1888 to 1890, receiving promotion to first lieutenant in June 1889. From 1890 to 1895 he was military attaché in Russia and during 1897–1898 held a similar post in Germany. In the Spanish–American War he served as a major and assistant adjutant general (from June 1898), seeing action in the campaign against Santiago, Cuba, and distinguishing himself in Gen. Henry Lawton's capture of El Caney. After a bout of yellow fever and another short stay in Germany, he went to the Philippine Islands to aid in the suppression of the insurrection there. He was briefly governor of Leyte in April–June 1901, advancing to lieutenant colonel of volunteers in May. He was mustered out of volunteer service in June, reverting to permanent rank of captain, and in July he began organizing the Philippine constabulary, a paramilitary police force intended to replace the American military force in the islands. He remained head of the constabulary until 1907, holding from January 1903 the temporary rank of brigadier general. Promoted to major of regulars in April 1907, he returned to duty in the United States. He was promoted to lieutenant colonel in August 1912 and to colonel of the 8th Cavalry in July 1916, taking part in that year in the Mexican Punitive Expedition under Gen. John J. Pershing. In May 1917 he advanced to brigadier general and in August to temporary major general in command of the 90th Division. After training at Camp Travis, Texas, he took the 90th to France in June 1918 and beginning in August saw action in the Toul sector and in the St. Mihiel and Meuse–Argonne offensives. After the armistice he was commander successively of the VIII Corps, the IX Corps, and the VII Corps. In July 1919 he was named commander of the American occupation forces in Germany. For four years he managed that difficult task with great skill and equally great success. In March 1920 he was promoted to permanent major general. Early in 1923 he returned to the United States, and in April he retired. His experiences in Germany were published in *My Rhineland Journal*, 1923, and *The Rhineland Occupation*, 1927. Allen died on August 30, 1930, in Buena Vista Spring, Pennsylvania.

Allen, Henry Watkins (1820–1866), Confederate army officer and public official. Born on April 29, 1820, in Prince Edward County, Virginia, Allen grew up there and, after 1833, in present-day Lafayette County, Missouri. After two years at Marion College in Ely, Missouri, he moved to Grand Gulf, Mississippi, where he taught school, studied law, and was admitted to the bar. He suspended his practice briefly to respond to Pres. Sam Houston's appeal for volunteers for the Texas army in 1842. After the death of his wife he left Mississippi for Louisiana, settling in 1852 in West Baton Rouge. He was elected to the legislature the next year, and, despite his going to Harvard to study law and then sailing suddenly to Italy to join Garibaldi's forces (he arrived too late), he was reelected in absentia for a second term. (He later described his European visit in *The Travels of a Sugar Planter*, 1861.) At the outbreak of the Civil War Allen, by that time a popular figure in the state, enlisted as a private and was quickly commissioned lieutenant colonel of the 4th Louisiana Regiment. He advanced to colonel in March 1862. He was a brave and capable commander; he was in action at Shiloh and Vicksburg and commanded a brigade in Gen. J. C. Breckinridge's unsuccessful attack on Baton Rouge in August 1862, where he received a wound that rendered him unfit for further field duty. He was

nonetheless promoted to brigadier general in September 1863. Immediately afterward he was elected governor of Louisiana, emerging, in his year and a half in the post, as the best administrator in the Confederacy. To relieve the widespread suffering of the people, he set up a system of state stores and factories which made and distributed needed goods and helped to restore the value of the state's money. He rigidly controlled exports and imports, bringing in necessities from Mexico and banning luxuries; the sale of alcoholic beverages was stopped and an active program of relief for the needy and for disabled soldiers was established. After Gen. Robert E. Lee's surrender in April 1865, Gen. Edmund Kirby-Smith, Confederate commander of the Trans-Mississippi Department, was prepared to continue his resistance, particularly since his army at that time was as strong as or stronger than it had ever been. Allen, however, finally persuaded Kirby-Smith to surrender, thus preventing the death and destruction that would otherwise have been inevitable. Following the surrender Allen fled to Mexico and started an English-language newspaper. However, his popularity in Louisiana remained such that late in 1865, in spite of his fugitive status, he was widely suggested for governor. His health having suffered greatly from his battle wounds, he died in Mexico City on April 22, 1866.

Allen, Terry de la Mesa (1888–1969), army officer. Born on April 1, 1888, at Fort Douglas, Utah, where his father was stationed, Allen entered West Point in 1907 but was forced to leave before graduating. In 1912 he took a degree from Catholic University of America and in November of that year won a commission as second lieutenant of cavalry. After duty on the Mexican border with the 14th Cavalry and graduation from Mounted Service School, Fort Riley, Kansas, he was promoted to first lieutenant in July 1916 and to captain in May 1917. Shortly after arriving in France in June 1918 he employed a stratagem to obtain an infantry officer's school certificate and in August was at the front with the 358th Infantry Regiment of the 90th Division under Gen. Henry T. Allen. He served with much distinction and earned the nickname "Terrible Terry." After occupation duty, during which he advanced to major, he returned to post duty and graduated from Cavalry School, Fort Riley, Kansas, in 1922 and Command and General Staff School, Fort Leavenworth, Kansas, in 1924. More routine garrison duty, principally in the South, was punctuated by attendance at the Army War College in 1934–1935 and promotion to lieutenant colonel in August of the latter year. From 1935 to 1939 he was an instructor at the Cavalry School. In October 1940 he was promoted to temporary brigadier general in command of the 3rd Cavalry Brigade at Fort Riley, and in April 1941 he took command of the 2nd Cavalry Division there. Promoted to temporary major general in June 1942, he took over the 1st Infantry Division in August, and after a period of training he led it into the North African campaign. Landing at Oran, Algeria, with the VII Corps on November 8, 1942, the 1st fought through the entire campaign to the occupation of Tunis in May 1943. On July 10, 1943, Allen led his division ashore in the van of the Seventh Army's (Gen. George S. Patton) invasion of Sicily, where he displayed to advantage his characteristic audacity in tactics. He was relieved in September 1943 and assigned to train the 104th Infantry Division at Camp Adair, Oregon. There were hints of a personality clash, possibly with Gen. Patton, in the transfer. Allen became the only general to train and lead two different divisions in World War II when he landed with the 104th in France in September 1944. The division fought on the northern flank, generally a part of Gen. William H. Simpson's Ninth Army under the British 21st Army Group, from Belgium and the Netherlands into Germany at Aachen. The 104th took Köln on March 5, 1945, participated in the encirclement of the Ruhr pocket, and in mid-April took Halle. In June the division was shipped home. Allen retired in August 1946; he lived in El Paso, Texas, until his death on September 12, 1969.

Allen, William Henry (1784–1813), naval officer.

Born on October 21, 1784, in Providence, Rhode Island, Allen was appointed a midshipman in the navy in April 1800. He made several cruises to the Mediterranean over the next few years and in October 1804 was promoted to lieutenant. In 1807 he was third lieutenant of the frigate *Chesapeake* under command of Commodore James Barron. When the *Chesapeake* was attacked by the British *Leopard* on June 22, 1807, Allen was mortified by Barron's failure to defend his ship. Before the *Chesapeake*'s colors were struck, he later reported, he himself fired the only shot at the *Leopard*. The following day he drew up a letter, signed by six officers, demanding the arrest and trial of Barron. In 1809 he became first lieutenant of the frigate *United States* under Commodore Stephen Decatur. In the famous fight with the British *Macedonian* on October 25, 1812, Allen played a conspicuous role, and he afterward took command of the captured frigate, and brought it to port in spite of its heavily damaged condition; he thereby won promotion to the rank of master commandant. In 1813 he took command of the sloop of war *Argus*, 20 guns, and after carrying the new American minister to France he took up station in the Irish Sea to do what damage he could to British shipping. The damage amounted to 27 ships captured. On August 14 he met the brig *Pelican*, 21 guns. The fight was brief and Allen was mortally wounded. Taken prisoner, he was conducted to Mill Prison, Plymouth, where he died on August 18, 1813.

Almond, Edward Mallory (1892–   ), army officer.

Born in Luray, Virginia, on December 12, 1892, Almond graduated from Virginia Military Institute in 1915 and in November 1916 took a commission in the infantry, receiving promotion to first lieutenant on the same day. He was promoted to captain in July 1917. He served with the 4th Division (Gen. John L. Hines and Gen. George H. Cameron) in France from June 1918 into the occupation period, receiving temporary rank of major in October 1918. He taught military science at Marion Institute, Alabama, from 1919 to 1923 and after attending the Infantry School, Fort Benning, Georgia, in 1924 he taught there until 1928, in August of which year he was promoted to major. He graduated from the Command and General Staff School, Fort Leavenworth, Kansas, in 1930, and after a tour of duty in the Philippines he attended the Army War College, graduating in 1934. From 1934 to 1938 he was attached to the intelligence division of the General Staff. Promoted to lieutenant colonel in September 1938, he completed the course at the Navy War College in 1940 and in January 1941 was assigned to staff duty at the VI Corps headquarters in Providence, Rhode Island. Almond was promoted to temporary ranks of colonel in October 1941 and brigadier general in March 1942, when he was named assistant commander of the 93rd Infantry Division in Arizona. In July 1942 he took command of the new 92nd Division (Negro), which he organized and, following its activation in October, trained in Alabama and Arizona (he was given rank of temporary major general in September 1942) until August 1944, when he took it overseas for service in Italy. The 92nd attacked the Ligurian coast toward Massa and for months fought a seesaw battle up and down the Serchio valley. In April 1945 a major drive to the north was spearheaded by the famed 442nd Regiment (Nisei), a unit of the 92nd; La Spezia was taken, the Germans' Gothic Line flanked, and the way to the Po valley across the mountains opened. By the time of the German surrender on May 2, the 92nd held the coast north to Genoa. Almond returned to the United States in August 1945, was placed in command of the 2nd Division at Camp Swift, Texas, in September, and was promoted to permanent rank of colonel in December. In June 1946 he was transferred to Gen. Douglas MacArthur's headquarters staff in Tokyo, becoming deputy chief of staff, Far East Command, in January 1947. Promoted to permanent rank of major general in January 1948 (rank dating from September 1944), he became chief of staff, Far East Command, in February 1949. In September 1950, soon after the outbreak of the Korean War, he was named to command the newly created X Corps, assembled from two skeleton divisions and assorted other elements, to execute MacArthur's plan for an amphibious assault at Inch'on, midway up the west coast of the Korean peninsula. The landing, conducted by naval forces under Adm. Arthur D. Struble, took place on September 15. The X Corps quickly took Seoul, the South Korean capital, and having linked up with Gen. Walton H. Walker's Eighth Army pushing northward, trapped some 120,000 North Korean troops. In October the X Corps moved by sea around the peninsula and landed unopposed at Wonsan, on the east coast of North Korea. Incorporating the Republic of Korea I Corps into his command, Almond pushed north and reached the Chinese border at the Yalu River by November 21. Massive Chinese counterattacks from November 25 forced United Nations forces to withdraw, and by December 11 the X Corps had concentrated in the port of Hungnam, whence it embarked for Pusan, in South Korea, a huge operation involving 105,000 troops, nearly as many refugees, and all matériel, and was incorporated into the Eighth Army. Reentering the line in east-central Korea, the X Corps was a central anchor in the UN defense and gradual advance back across the 38th parallel. Almond was promoted to temporary lieutenant general in February 1951, and he remained in command of the X Corps until July. He was then placed in command of the Army War College, a post he held until his retirement in January 1953. He lived thereafter in Anniston, Alabama, where he was an executive in an insurance company and had numerous civic interests.

Anders, William Alison (1933–   ), air force officer and astronaut. Born on October 17, 1933, in Hong Kong, Anders was the son of an American naval officer stationed in China. He graduated from the Naval Academy in 1955 and took a commission in the air force. Over the next eight years, in addition to becoming an expert pilot, he took advanced training in nuclear engineering, earning a master's degree from the Air Force Institute of Technology. In 1963 his scientific background qualified him for astronaut training. As the Apollo moon-landing project was formulated, Anders was designated pilot of the LM, landing module, on the *Apollo VIII* mission, originally intended as the first landing. Delays in the LM testing schedule, however, forced the National Aeronautics and Space Administration to downgrade *Apollo VIII* to a moon-orbital mission, with Anders redesignated flight systems engineer. On December 21, 1968, the mission began with lift-off from Cape Kennedy, bearing Anders, flight commander Frank Borman, and navigator James A. Lovell, Jr., who became the first men to leave earth's gravity. The entire mission was an uneventful success, and during 10 orbits 70 miles above the moon on December 24 much valuable photographic and other scientific information was gathered. On December 27 *Apollo VIII* splashed down in the Pacific Ocean and was recovered by the carrier *Yorktown*. Promoted to colonel upon his return to earth, Anders served on the back-

up crew for *Apollo XI,* the actual lunar landing mission in July 1969, and then resigned from the air force to become executive secretary of the National Aeronautics and Space Council. In 1973 he was named to the Atomic Energy Commission by President Nixon, and in October 1974, on appointment by President Gerald R. Ford, he became chairman of the Nuclear Regulatory Commission, successor to the AEC. Among his numerous honors were the Collier Trophy, the Hubbard Medal, the Harmon Trophy, and Air Force and NASA Distinguished Service medals.

Anderson, George Whelan, Jr. (1906–   ), naval officer and diplomat. Born on December 15, 1906, in Brooklyn, New York, Anderson graduated from the Naval Academy in 1927 and in 1930 completed aviation training at the Pensacola Naval Air Station, Florida. From 1930 to 1933 he was attached to the aviation units aboard the *Concord* and then the *Raleigh* of the Atlantic Fleet. After a time with the flight test division at the naval air station at Norfolk, Virginia, he served in 1935–1937 on the carrier *Lexington* and in 1937–1939 on the *Yorktown.* For a short time in 1939–1940 he was assigned to a unit of Patrol Wing 4 at Seattle, Washington, and then until 1943 he was in the plans division of the Bureau of Aeronautics. In April 1943 he was ordered to sea on the new *Yorktown.* Between November 1943 and March 1944 he served on the staff of the air commander, Pacific Fleet, and from March 1944 to April 1945 as assistant to the deputy commander of the Pacific Fleet and Pacific Ocean Areas. After a short time on the staff of the U.S. Fleet commander he served in 1946–1948 on the U.S.–Canadian Permanent Joint Board on Defense and on the Brazil–U.S. Defense Commission. In 1948–1949 he commanded the carrier *Mindoro,* and on graduating from the National War College in 1950 he was named fleet operations officer of the Sixth Fleet in the Mediterranean. Later in that year he was assigned to the NATO staff under Gen. Dwight D. Eisenhower. He commanded the carrier *Franklin D. Roosevelt* in 1952–1953, and from 1953 to 1955 was special assistant to Adm. Arthur W. Radford, chairman of the Joint Chiefs of Staff, advancing to rear admiral in August 1954. In 1955 he took command of Fleet Air Wing 1 and of the Taiwan Patrol Force, and in May 1957, promoted to vice admiral, he became chief of staff of the Pacific Command. In July 1958, voluntarily reverting to rear admiral for a time, he commanded Carrier Division 6 and Task Force 60 in support of the marine landings in Lebanon. In September 1959 he took command of the Sixth Fleet and the attached Naval Striking and Support Forces, Southern Europe. In August 1961 Anderson became chief of naval operations with the rank of admiral. On his retirement in August 1963 he was named by President John F. Kennedy to be U.S.

ambassador to Portugal, a post he held until March 1966. In March 1969 he was named to the President's Foreign Intelligence Advisory Board, of which he became chairman in April 1970. He also had numerous business interests.

Anderson, Joseph Reid (1813–1892), Confederate army officer and industrialist. Born in Botetourt County, Virginia, on February 6, 1813, Anderson graduated from West Point in 1836. He was commissioned a second lieutenant of artillery but was soon transferred to the Corps of Engineers. He assisted in the construction of Fort Pulaski, Georgia, before resigning his commission in September 1837. After a brief period as assistant engineer for the state of Virginia, he became chief engineer of the Valley Turnpike Company. In 1841 he became an agent for the Tredegar Iron Works in Richmond and by 1848 was the owner. While directing the growing company, which manufactured locomotives for Southern railroads as well as ordnance and machinery for the federal government, he became interested in public affairs, serving in the legislature from 1852 to 1855. When secession appeared imminent in 1860 Anderson contracted to supply ordnance to several Southern state militias and in September 1861 obtained a brigadier general's commission in the Confederate army. He took part in the Peninsular campaign and performed creditably in command of a brigade of Gen. Ambrose P. Hill's division in the battles of Mechanicsville, Gaines's Mill, and Frazier's Farm, June 26, 27, and 30, 1862. He was wounded at Frazier's Farm. In July 1862 he resigned his commission to return to the Tredegar Works, whose importance to the Confederacy was such as to have been largely responsible for Richmond's becoming the capital. For most of the war, Tredegar was virtually the only producer of heavy artillery for the Confederacy and also manufactured most of the other Confederate ordnance, along with railroad and naval equipment. In the face of seemingly insuperable difficulties with manpower, materials, transportation, and money, Anderson maintained Tredegar's output until the fall of Richmond in April 1865. The works were confiscated and held by the U.S. government until 1867, when the company was reorganized with Anderson as president. He retained that post, except during 1876–1878 when Tredegar was in receivership, until his death on one of the Isles of Shoals, New Hampshire, on September 7, 1892.

Anderson, Richard Heron (1821–1879), Confederate army officer. Born on October 7, 1821, in Statesburg, Sumter County, South Carolina, Anderson graduated from West Point in 1842 and was commissioned in the dragoons. After service in the West he took part, as a second lieutenant in the 2nd Dragoons, in Gen. Winfield Scott's march from Vera-

cruz to Mexico City in 1847. For his conduct at San Augustin he was brevetted first lieutenant. He advanced to regular first lieutenant in July 1848 and to captain in March 1855. He served variously at Carlisle Barracks, Pennsylvania, in Kansas, and from 1859 at Fort Kearny, Nebraska. In March 1861, on the secession of South Carolina, he resigned his commission and accepted appointment as colonel of the 1st South Carolina Infantry. After supporting the siege of Fort Sumter and being promoted to brigadier general in July 1861, he joined Gen. Braxton Bragg at Pensacola, Florida. Aside from leading a surprise night attack on a Union camp on Santa Rosa Island, October 8, he saw little action until the spring of 1862, when he took command of a brigade in Gen. James Longstreet's division. He particularly distinguished himself at Seven Pines (Fair Oaks), May 31, and in the Seven Days' Battles, June 26–July 2, following which he was promoted to major general and given command of a division. Subsequently he took part in the second battle of Manassas (Bull Run), August 29–30; the capture of Harpers Ferry in September; the battle of Sharpsburg (Antietam), where he was wounded, September 17; and the battle of Chancellorsville, May 2–4, 1863. At Gettysburg, July 1–3, Anderson's division, then part of Gen. Ambrose P. Hill's Corps, took Seminary Ridge on the second day of battle and later advanced, only briefly, to Cemetery Ridge. In May 1864 Anderson was given temporary rank of lieutenant general and command of the corps of the wounded Longstreet. His prompt occupation of Spotsylvania Court House after a night march on May 7 prevented Grant from gaining a very advantageous position; on May 8 he repulsed an attack by Gen. Gouverneur K. Warren's V Corps and Gen. John Sedgwick's VI Corps. He commanded the corps through Cold Harbor and the rest of the Richmond campaign and in October relinquished it to Longstreet, returning to his regular rank and his division. In the general Confederate retreat in April 1865 Anderson suffered his only defeat. Discovered by cavalry scouts sent out by Sheridan, Anderson found himself under unexpected and very heavy attack at Sailors' (or Sayler's) Creek on April 6. After extricating himself he rejoined the main body of the army, but a reorganization left him without command shortly before the final surrender. After the war he returned to South Carolina and held the post of state inspector of phosphates until his death in Beaufort on June 26, 1879.

Anderson, Robert (1805–1871), army officer. Born near Louisville, Kentucky, on June 14, 1805, to a prominent Virginia family, Anderson graduated from West Point in 1825 and was commissioned in the artillery. For a time he was secretary to his brother, the U.S. minister to Colombia; he then assumed military duty. In the Black Hawk War in 1832 he was colonel of the Illinois volunteers, and in the Seminole War of 1836–1838 in Florida he was brevetted captain for his conduct. That rank was made permanent in 1841. He served in Gen. Winfield Scott's army in the Mexican War, receiving a brevet to major for Molino del Rey, September 8, 1847, where he was wounded. In 1857 he advanced to major. In November 1860 he was selected, partly by reason of his southern birth and proslavery inclinations, for the delicate task of commanding the forts in the harbor of Charleston, South Carolina. Originally headquartered in Fort Moultrie, he complained to the War Department that the post could not be held with the few men he had, but he received neither reinforcements nor other instructions. He remained there until South Carolina declared its secession from the Union in December 1860, whereupon, on his own initiative, he moved his garrison to the more defensible Fort Sumter. Anderson maintained a conciliatory attitude toward the Charleston authorities, refusing to surrender the fort but refusing also to aid the *Star of the West*, a federal supply ship that was shelled by shore batteries and driven off when it attempted to enter the harbor with reinforcements on January 9, 1861. His situation grew steadily more desperate, but on April 11 he again refused to surrender. The next morning the South Carolina guns began firing on Fort Sumter, and by the afternoon of the 13th it was no longer possible for the besieged garrison to remain. Anderson wrote to Secretary of War Simon Cameron a few days later: "Having defended Fort Sumter for thirty-four hours, until the quarters were entirely burned, the main gates destroyed by fire, the gorge walls seriously impaired, the magazine surrounded by flames and its door closed from the effects of the heat, four barrels and three cartridges of powder only being available and no provisions remaining but pork, I accepted the terms of evacuation offered by General Beauregard . . . and marched out of the fort on Sunday afternoon, being the 14th instant, with colors flying and drums beating, bringing away company and private property, and saluting my flag with fifty guns." Promoted to brigadier general in May 1861, he commanded the Department of Kentucky until his health broke in October of that year. He retired in October 1863 from active service but in February 1865 was brevetted major general. On April 14, 1865, he was sent to raise the Union flag over recaptured Fort Sumter. He died while on a European journey, in Nice, France, on October 26, 1871.

Anderson, Thomas McArthur (1836–1917), army officer. Born on January 21, 1836, near Chillicothe, Ohio, Anderson graduated from St. Mary's College, Maryland, in 1855 and three years later from the Cincinnati Law School, whereupon he was admitted to the bar and entered practice in Cincinnati.

In April 1861 he enlisted as a private in the 6th Ohio Volunteers; a short time later, through the influence of his uncle, Gen. Robert Anderson of Fort Sumter fame, he was commissioned second lieutenant of the 5th Cavalry (regulars). Soon promoted to captain, he served through the Civil War with the 12th Infantry, being twice wounded and twice brevetted, to major for his conduct in the Wilderness and to lieutenant colonel for Spotsylvania Court House. After the war he remained in the army, rising to colonel commanding the 14th Infantry. In 1898, with temporary rank of brigadier general, he commanded the first troops to reach the Philippines after Adm. George Dewey's victory in Manila Bay. Arriving on July 17 with some 2000 men, he occupied Cavite, the vital naval base in the bay, and on August 13, when the U.S. ground forces had grown to about 15,000, constituting Gen. Wesley Merritt's VIII Corps, Anderson led the first of them into the city of Manila. In command of the 1st Division he saw action in the battles of Santana, San Pedro, Passe, and Guadalupe in the early months of the Philippine Insurrection. Promoted to brigadier general in March 1899, he retired in January 1900. He lived in Vancouver, Washington, until his death in Portland, Oregon, on May 8, 1917.

Andrews, Frank Maxwell (1884–1943), army officer and airman. Born on February 3, 1884, in Nashville, Tennessee, Andrews graduated from West Point in 1906 and was commissioned in the cavalry. For ten years he saw routine service, including tours of duty in the Philippines, 1906–1907, and Hawaii, 1911–1913, but in 1917 he transferred to the aviation section of the Signal Corps. He completed pilot training at Rockwell Field, California, in July 1918, served at various airfields in the South during the rest of World War I, advancing to temporary rank of lieutenant colonel, and in 1919–1920 was attached to the office of the chief of the reorganized Air Service. From 1920 to 1923 he served with the army occupation forces in Germany as head of the air service, executive officer, and civil affairs officer. He was stationed at Kelly Field, Texas, in 1923–1927, the last two years as commander of the 10th School Group and later also of the Advanced Flying School. He graduated from the Air Corps Tactical School, Langley Field, Virginia, in 1928; from the Command and General Staff School, Fort Leavenworth, Kansas, in 1929; and, after three years in the office of the chief of the Air Corps, from the Army War College in 1933. He commanded the 1st Pursuit Group at Selfridge Field, Michigan, briefly before joining the General Staff in October 1934. In the reorganization of the Air Corps in March 1935 Andrews, promoted to temporary brigadier general, was named commander of the newly created General Headquarters Air Force, a unified tactical combat command based at Langley Field. Subsequently he advanced to temporary major general. The successful molding of GHQ Air Force into an offensive combat force operating under the army's highest command level was a major achievement and created a model that was to prove invaluable in World War II. Andrews, persistent in his belief in the necessity of a large, modern air arm, also played a large role in the development of the B-17 bomber. In March 1939, his term as commander of GHQ Air Force over, he reverted to colonel; but in August, again promoted to temporary brigadier general, he was appointed assistant chief of staff of the army for training and operations by Gen. George C. Marshall. Promoted to temporary major general in October 1940, he was named the next month to command of the newly organized Panama Canal Air Force (later the Caribbean Air Force and then the Sixth), based in the Canal Zone. In September 1941 he was promoted to temporary lieutenant general and moved up to command of the Caribbean Defense Command, becoming the first air officer ever to hold theater command. In November 1942 he was ordered to the Middle East as commander of all U.S. army forces in that theater, and in February 1943 he relinquished that post to Gen. Dwight D. Eisenhower, taking Eisenhower's former post as commander of U.S. army forces in Europe. A short time later, on May 3, 1943, Andrews was killed in an airplane accident in Iceland. Andrews Air Force Base, Maryland, was later named for him.

Andrews, Garnett (1837–1903), Confederate army officer. Born in Washington, Georgia, on May 15, 1837, Andrews graduated from the law school of the University of Georgia in 1861 and was immediately commissioned first lieutenant in the 1st Georgia Regulars. Over the next three years he served in Virginia and North Carolina and was twice wounded. In 1864, by then a lieutenant colonel, he was charged with raising a regiment from the foreigners among Federal prisoners. At first designated the "Second Foreign Legion" and later the 8th Confederate Battalion of Infantry, the regiment was popularly known as the "Galvanized Yankees." On April 11, 1865, he was ordered to occupy and hold Salisbury, North Carolina, against Gen. George Stoneman's attempt there to seize trains carrying officials and treasure from the Confederate capital at Richmond. On April 12 Andrews and his 600 "Galvanized Yankees" held off Stoneman's entire division for the required time. The bloody battle occured three days after the surrender of Lee at Appomattox, news of which had not yet reached them, and was the last engagement of the war involving troops of the Army of Northern Virginia. In the hand-to-hand combat Andrews was seriously wounded. After the war he practiced law in Yazoo City, Mississippi, where also he commanded the Yazoo Rifles militia company. He served in the legislature in 1879–1880. In 1882 he moved to Chat-

tanooga, Tennessee, where he continued his law practice and served as mayor in 1891–1893. Andrews died there on May 6, 1903.

Andrews, James J. (1829?–1862), Union agent. Born about 1829 in Hancock County, Virginia (now West Virginia), Andrews grew up there and in southwestern Missouri. Little is known of his youth. In 1859 he moved to Flemingsburg, Kentucky, and was working there as a housepainter when the Civil War began. Early in the war he apparently engaged in some lucrative trafficking in various commodities across Union-Confederate lines and also apparently served as a source of information about Confederate forces and plans. Early in 1862 he conceived a bold plan to capture a train on the vital Western and Atlantic line between Marietta, Georgia, and Chattanooga, Tennessee, and to wreak as much destruction on the line as possible. The success of such a blow would isolate Tennessee from Confederate armies and supply lines and insure its taking by Union forces. The Confederacy's east-west communications could also be disrupted, with incalculable results. Andrews proposed the plan to Gen. Ormsby M. Mitchel and then to Gen. Don Carlos Buell and won approval of it. A first attempt failed through poor planning, but on April 7, 1862, Andrews and 21 volunteers left Shelbyville, Tennessee, in small groups, made their way to Chattanooga, and boarded a train for Marietta. On the 12th they boarded a northbound train at Marietta, taking care to buy tickets to various destinations so as not to arouse suspicions. At Big Shanty (now Kennesaw), Georgia, while the crew and passengers were at breakfast, Andrews and his men went to work: one commandeered the engine (the *General*), one cut the bell rope, others uncoupled all but three boxcars from the train. Having checked the switch ahead, Andrews jumped aboard and, in full view of several regiments of Confederate soldiers camped nearby, pulled away from the station. A few miles up they stopped to cut telegraph wires and pile ties on the track. The *General* was sidetracked at one point and lost time while two freights passed, and soon afterwards it was discovered that they were being pursued. The alarm had spread quicker than Andrews had planned, and the engine *Texas* was gaining on them. Andrews had his men tear up track, but the pursuers continued to close the gap by taking up track behind them and laying it in front. One by one Andrews released his boxcars, but the *Texas* slowed, caught them, and pushed them onto sidetracks. Andrews dropped more ties on the road, to little effect. Finally he cut loose his last boxcar, afire, on the bridge at Oostenaula, but heavy rains had soaked the timbers of the bridge and it did not burn. Andrews was unable to stop to refuel because of the close pursuit and after 90 miles, only 20 miles short of Chattanooga, the *General* stopped. The men jumped off and ran into the woods, but within days all had been captured. Andrews and seven others were court-martialed and on June 7, 1862, hanged in Atlanta. Eight of the other 14 men escaped prison in October, and the 6 remaining were paroled in March 1863. On March 25 those 6 became the first men to receive the newly created Medal of Honor; 13 others (Andrews and 2 other civilians were ineligible) were awarded the Medal of Honor at later dates.

Armistead, George (1780–1818), army officer. Born on April 10, 1780, in New Market, Caroline County, Virginia, Armistead was commissioned second lieutenant in the army in January 1799. He rose to first lieutenant in April of the same year, to captain in November 1806, and to major in March 1813. He distinguished himself in the capture of Fort George, near the mouth of the Niagara River, by Col. Winfield Scott on May 27, 1813. Later he was transferred to Baltimore, which in August 1814 was sorely threatened by British troops and fleet. Armistead, with about 1000 men, was ordered to hold Fort McHenry, the principal defense of the harbor. The British troops advancing on Baltimore from Washington, D.C., brushed aside the militia and regulars opposed to them, although their commander, Gen. Robert Ross, was killed, and on September 13 were in sight of the fort. The fleet, meanwhile, had proceeded up the Patapsco River, but, owing in part to shallow water, which held the larger ships off, it was unable to subdue Fort McHenry by bombardment. The effort to do so, however, inspired Francis Scott Key, held prisoner aboard one of Adm. Sir George Cockburn's ships, to write his famous poem. Armistead held the fort until, on September 14, the British retired. For this action he was brevetted lieutenant colonel and honored by the citizens of Baltimore with a silver service. He died in Baltimore on April 25, 1818.

Armistead, Lewis Addison (1817–1863), Confederate army officer. Born in New Bern, North Carolina, on February 18, 1817, Armistead was the son of a member of the second class to graduate from West Point and a nephew of George Armistead, defender of Fort McHenry. He entered West Point in 1834 but left two years later. In July 1839 he was nevertheless commissioned second lieutenant in the 6th Infantry. He was promoted to first lieutenant in March 1844. During the Mexican War he saw action in Gen. Winfield Scott's army at Contreras, Churubusco, and Molino del Rey and was twice brevetted for gallant conduct. Promoted to captain in March 1855, he spent several years in frontier duty, again distinguishing himself in battle with Indians near Fort Mojave, Colorado, in 1859. In May 1861 he resigned from the army and entered Confederate service as colonel of the 57th Virginia. In April 1862,

after several months of duty in West Virginia and North Carolina, he was promoted to brigadier general. He commanded a brigade in the Peninsula campaign in March–July, and at Sharpsburg (Antietam) on September 17 he was wounded. In July 1863, his brigade attached to Gen. George E. Pickett's division, he took part in the battle of Gettysburg. On the third day of battle, July 3, he was in the center of the desperate rush on Cemetery Ridge known as Pickett's Charge. Two other brigade commanders in the first line of the advance were killed crossing the open space before the ridge, but Armistead, raising his cap upon swordpoint, survived the deadly Federal fire long enough to lead about 100 men (out of 15,000) to the stone wall atop the ridge. There, facing Gen. John Gibbon's division, he was mortally wounded; and he fell within Union lines, at the spot marking the "high tide of the Confederacy."

Armstrong, John (1717–1795), Revolutionary army officer. Born in County Fermanagh, Ireland, on October 13, 1717, Armstrong emigrated to America and settled in what is now Cumberland County, Pennsylvania. His work as a surveyor included laying out the town of Carlisle. In January 1756 he was made captain of militia and in May lieutenant colonel. The long conflict known as the French and Indian War had made itself felt in that region in the form of scalping raids by a band of Delaware Indians living in a town called Kittanning on the Allegheny River. On September 8, 1756, Armstrong led 300 men from Fort Shirley in a night raid that destroyed the town, rescued many white prisoners, and captured stores supplied by the French. For that action Armstrong was greatly honored. In 1756 he built Fort Loudon, near the town of that name, and in 1757 Fort Raystown (later Fort Bedford), near Bedford, Pennsylvania. In 1758 he commanded the Pennsylvania troops taking part in the expedition under Gen. John Forbes and Col. George Washington against Fort Duquesne. In March 1776 he was commissioned brigadier general in the Continental army. After a time in South Carolina he returned to Pennsylvania and, by then a major general of Pennsylvania, militia, commanded the militia at Brandywine and Germantown, though without conspicuous success. In April 1777 he resigned from the army in a dispute over rank. He served thereafter in various civil capacities and was a delegate to Congress in 1779–1780 and 1787–1788. He died in Carlisle on March 9, 1795.

Armstrong, John (1755–1816), army officer and explorer. Born in New Jersey on April 20, 1755, Armstrong served with distinction in the Pennsylvania militia during the Revolution and in 1783–1784 was an officer in the force sent to quiet the Pennsylvania–Connecticut land-claims dispute in the Wyoming Valley of Pennsylvania. In August 1784 he was given an army commission and sent to the Ohio frontier. In 1785–1786 he commanded Fort Pitt and during that period began the exploits and adventures that were to make him a near-legendary figure. In 1790 he was chosen to make secret explorations into Spanish territory to the west; little is known of his trip beyond the fact that he went alone and that, although he intended to follow the Missouri River and cross the Rockies, as Meriwether Lewis and William Clark were to do 14 years later, he was forced by Indian wars to turn back some distance beyond St. Louis. He then explored much of what is now Indiana. Later in the same year he took part in Gen. Josiah Harmar's expedition to pacify the Indians in the Maumee Valley. He commanded the regulars in the first battle, October 18, and his brave stand and subsequent escape after the militia deserted added to his reputation. He also took part in Gen. Arthur St. Clair's 1791 expedition against the Indians. In 1793 he resigned from the army and settled in Columbia, near Cincinnati, and three years later became treasurer of the Northwest Territory. In 1814 he moved to Armstrong's Station in what is now Indiana and died there on February 4, 1816.

Armstrong, John (1758–1843), Revolutionary army officer and public official. Born in Carlisle, Pennsylvania, on November 25, 1758, Armstrong was the youngest son of John Armstrong (1717–1795) of the Pennsylvania militia. He entered the College of New Jersey (now Princeton) but left in 1775 to take part in the Revolution. He served with Gen. Hugh Mercer and Gen. Horatio Gates and was a major on Gates's staff at the end of the war. When Congress failed to appropriate money to pay its soldiers, discontent spread rapidly through the camps of the Continental army, particularly among the officers, and in March 1783, in the army camp at Newburgh, New York, Armstrong circulated the unsigned "Newburgh Letters," urging the men to reject further promises and to take decisive action to force Congress to meet its obligations. The threat of revolt was ended by Gen. George Washington's speech to his officers on March 15. Armstrong returned to Pennsylvania and was appointed secretary to the state's Supreme Executive Council. In 1784 he commanded a militia force sent to the Wyoming Valley of Pennsylvania to quell a dispute over land claims between Pennsylvania and Connecticut settlers, and in spite of, or perhaps because of, his unfair treatment of the Connecticut party, he soon became state adjutant general. He was elected to Congress in 1787. Two years later he moved to New York and, by his marriage to Alida, the sister of Robert R. Livingston, formed an alliance with the dominant political force in the state, among the leaders of which were George and De Witt Clinton. In 1800 the Republican victory of the Livingston–Clinton group brought Armstrong

a vacated Senate seat. He was elected to a new term beginning in March 1801 but resigned in February 1802 in favor of De Witt Clinton. He resumed the seat in November 1803 when Clinton became mayor of New York City. He resigned again in June 1804 to succeed Livingston as U.S. minister to France. During six years in Paris he enjoyed little success and in fact failed in 1810 to perceive a course of events which led to war with England two years later. Armstrong was given a brigadier general's commission and command of New York City in July 1812, shortly after the declaration of war with Great Britain, and in January 1813 was appointed secretary of war by President James Madison. His administration of the War Department was mixed, but on balance it was a failure; he did well in promoting and supporting such young, energetic officers as Winfield Scott and Andrew Jackson and he introduced into the department for the first time a staff—known as the General Staff— of competent officials to serve as adjutant and inspector general, commissary general, quartermaster general, and so on. On the other hand, his grasp of tactics was deficient, and in that, as in insisting upon taking the field himself, he shared responsibility for the disastrous Montreal campaign under the rivalrous generals Wade Hampton and James Wilkinson in the autumn of 1813, and especially for the fall of the city of Washington after the fiasco at Bladensburg, Maryland, under Gen. William H. Winder on August 24, 1814. He resigned under pressure in September 1814 and retired to his home in Red Hook, New York, where he died on April 1, 1843.

Armstrong, Neil Alden (1930–   ), naval officer and astronaut. Born on August 5, 1930, near Wapakoneta, Ohio, Armstrong early developed an interest in aviation and received his pilot's license on his sixteenth birthday. In 1947 he entered Purdue University as a naval air cadet. Two years later he was called to active duty; during service in the Korean War he flew 78 combat missions and was awarded the Air Medal three times. Returning to Purdue, he graduated in 1955 and joined the staff of the National Advisory Committee for Aeronautics as a civilian test pilot. During the next seven years he tested several new types of aircraft, including F-100, F-102, and F-104 fighter planes and the X-15 rocket plane, and in 1962 was accepted into the astronaut training program of the National Aeronautics and Space Administration (NASA). His first space flight came on March 16, 1966, when he commanded *Gemini VIII;* with Maj. David R. Scott he performed the first manual docking maneuver in space and successfully dealt with trouble in the thruster-control system that threatened to wreck the mission. On July 16, 1969, in command of *Apollo XI,* Armstrong, with astronauts Edwin Aldrin and Michael Collins, set out on the first lunar-landing mission. Four days later he piloted the lunar landing module *Eagle* to the moon's surface, landing at the edge of the Sea of Tranquility. When he descended a ladder and set foot on the moon as an automatic television camera beamed the event back to earth, he spoke the words, "That's one small step for a man, one giant leap for mankind." Armstrong and Aldrin, who had followed him onto the moon, set up scientific observations on the lunar surface before returning to the *Eagle* with a quantity of moon material for later study. The next day they rocketed back to the command ship *Columbia,* which had remained in lunar orbit, and began the return trip. After splashdown in the Pacific on July 24 they were met and congratulated by President Richard M. Nixon on board the aircraft carrier *Hornet* before beginning an 18-day period of quarantine to guard against the possible consequences of dangerous microorganisms that they might have come in contact with on the moon. In 1970 Armstrong was appointed chairman of the Peace Corps National Advisory Council. In the same year he retired from the astronaut corps to become an administrator of NASA. He resigned the next year to join the faculty of the University of Cincinnati as professor of aerospace engineering. In spite of his extraordinary achievement and the many honors it brought him Armstrong remained a modest and, indeed, retiring figure.

Arnold, Benedict (1741–1801), Revolutionary army officer and traitor. Born in Norwich, Connecticut, on January 14, 1741, to an eminent Rhode Island family, Arnold ran away at sixteen served with the colonial militia in the French and Indian War. He soon became disenchanted and deserted. On his return home he completed an apprenticeship to a druggist and in 1762 moved to New Haven, Connecticut, where he operated a drug and book shop. The business prospered, and he began investing in merchant voyages in the Canadian and West Indian trade. In April 1775 Arnold, who had been for some months captain of the local militia, set out immediately with his men on hearing of the battle of Lexington. When he reached Cambridge, Massachusetts, he proposed to the Committee of Safety an expedition to Fort Ticonderoga to capture ordnance stored there. He was commissioned colonel and dispatched on the mission, but soon encountered Col. Ethan Allen, sent by Connecticut for the same purpose; they agreed to joint command of the merged expedition, although Allen assumed a measure of precedence. Ticonderoga was taken on May 10, and Arnold embarked with his men on a rapid trip up Lake Champlain and captured St. Johns, Quebec. He then returned to Connecticut briefly, in part to attend to his personal affairs and in part because his successes had been somewhat ignored by Massachusetts authorities and by Congress. He was soon in Cambridge again, where he proposed to Gen. George Washington a march on Quebec city.

He left with 1100 men in September 1775; 200 men turned back early in the expedition, and 200 more died during an epic march along the Kennebec and Chaudière rivers through the Maine woods. He reached Quebec on November 8, scaled the cliffs, and encamped on the Plains of Abraham, his force too small and exhausted to attack. On December 2 he was joined by a second force of 300 men under Gen. Richard Montgomery, who had advanced from Ticonderoga, capturing Montreal en route. The attack on Quebec on the snowy night of December 31, 1775, was a failure; Montgomery was killed, and Arnold, severely wounded, settled in for a siege, during which he was promoted by Congress to brigadier general (January 1776). In the spring he was forced to retire by the approach of British reinforcements under Gen. Carleton bound for Quebec and thence Albany, but he fought a brilliant retreat, building a fleet of boats and inflicting heavy losses on a superior enemy force in a battle on Lake Champlain (October 11–13, 1776) and thus succeeded in forestalling the invasion of New York. Spending the winter of 1776–1777 at home, Arnold came close to resigning his commission when, in February, Congress for political reasons promoted five brigadiers who were junior to him to major general. Washington prevailed upon him to remain in the army. On April 25, 1777, he hurried to the scene of Col. William Tryon's attack on Danbury, Connecticut, and, with militia under Gen. Gold S. Silliman and Gen. David Wooster, harried Tryon's British regulars at Ridgefield. That exploit forced Congress to promote him to major general, although his seniority was not restored. Washington had again to intervene personally to keep Arnold from resigning. In July he marched north to join Gen. Philip J. Schuyler and the Northern Army above Albany to meet a British advance from Canada. With remarkable quickness, and by force of his reputation as much as of arms, he raised the siege of Fort Stanwix, sending Col. Barry St. Leger into hasty retreat back up the Mohawk valley, and swung back to Saratoga to join Gen. Horatio Gates (Schuyler's successor) in the two battles that ended Gen. John Burgoyne's advance. Arnold commanded the left wing in the battle of Freeman's Farm, September 19, and performed brilliantly in the battle on Bemis Heights on October 7, where he was seriously wounded. His seniority was at last restored by Congress, and, after recuperating from his wound, he was placed in command of Philadelphia in June 1778. There he led a highly social life and, in his attempts to keep up with the previous British occupiers of the city, incurred heavy debts, for his pay as a Continental officer could not support him in that style. He still had enemies in Congress, and they managed to bring a number of charges of impropriety against him; always sensitive to the slightest criticism, he responded to the charges with indignation. His marriage in

April 1779 to Margaret (Peggy) Shippen, the daughter of a wealthy merchant who had earlier moved easily in Loyalist circles, probably increased his already growing disaffection with the American cause, for in May 1779 he initiated a secret correspondence with Sir Henry Clinton, the British commander in chief, in which he offered military information in return for a considerable sum of money. This first phase of the famous traitorous correspondence lasted only for a few months, ending in the fall of 1779 when Arnold apparently had reason to believe that the charges still pending against him would be dropped or nullified. He was finally court-martialed in December 1779 and most of the charges were dropped, but on two minor ones he had to undergo a mild reprimand by Washington. Evidently infuriated by this rebuke, he reopened the correspondence with Clinton in May 1780, providing much valuable information, the extent of which was not known until the relevant British military papers were brought to the United States in the 1920s. In June Arnold learned that he was to be appointed commandant at West Point, and in July he proposed to betray that vital American fort to Clinton for £20,000. In September 1780 Maj. John André was sent by Clinton under a false flag of truce to arrange the details with Arnold. But André was captured, more or less by accident, the plot was discovered through some papers hidden in his stocking, and Arnold fled to New York City on a British warship. André, who had disobeyed Clinton's orders and attired himself in civilian clothes, was hanged as a spy. Given the rank of brigadier general of provincial troops by the British, Arnold commanded marauding expeditions into Virginia in December 1780 and into Connecticut in September 1781. On the latter occasion he burned New London, an act that was never forgiven by his one-time neighbors, colleagues, and friends; the raid was marked also by the massacre of Fort Griswold, for which Arnold was not directly responsible. In December 1781 he sailed for England. Given a small pension, he was widely scorned even in that country as a traitor and became deeply embittered. He engaged without success in trade in Canada and the West Indies until his death in London on June 14, 1801. His wife, who also had a small pension, remained his loyal friend and supporter until the end.

Arnold, Henry Harley (1886–1950), army and air force officer. Born on June 25, 1886, in Gladwyne, Pennsylvania, Arnold graduated from West Point in 1907 and was commissioned in the infantry. He served two years in the Philippines and two more at Governors Island, New York, and in April 1911 he transferred to the aeronautical division (in July 1914 redesignated the aviation section) of the Signal Corps. In June of that year he received his pilot's certificate after taking instruction from Orville

Wright in Dayton, Ohio. For nearly a year he was an instructor at the army's first aviation school at College Park, Maryland. In September 1911 he flew the first U.S. airmail; on June 1, 1912, he established a world altitude record of 6540 feet in a Burgess–Wright plane; and in October 1912 he won the first Mackay Trophy for aviation. After a few months in the office of the chief signal officer and promotion to first lieutenant in April 1913 Arnold was returned for a time to infantry duty. Promoted to captain in May 1916, he was then attached to the aviation school at San Diego, California. He advanced to temporary major in June. In February 1917 he was ordered to the Panama Canal Zone to organize and command an air service there. In May he was called to staff duty in Washington, D.C., overseeing the army's aviation training schools until the end of World War I and advancing to temporary colonel in August 1917. From 1919 to 1924 he served in various posts in the Pacific states, including that of air officer of the IX Corps area and, in 1922–1924, that of commander of the Rockwell Air Depot, Coronado, California. On July 6, 1924, he set a new speed record, 113 mph average, between Rockwell and San Francisco. In 1925 Arnold was named chief of the information division of the Air Corps; he commanded Marshall Field at Fort Riley, Kansas, in 1926–1928, graduated from Command and General Staff School, Fort Leavenworth, Kansas, in 1929, and commanded the Fairfield Air Depot, Ohio, in 1929–1930. Promoted to lieutenant colonel in February 1931, he commanded the 1st Bomb Wing and the 1st Pursuit Wing as well as the base at March Field, California. In 1934 he won a second Mackay Trophy for his command of a flight by ten Martin B-10 bombers from Bolling Field, D.C., to Fairbanks, Alaska, and back during July–August. Promoted to temporary brigadier general in February 1935, he took command of the 1st Wing, GHQ Air Force (the newly created combat force under Gen. Frank M. Andrews) the next month, still at March Field. In December 1935 he was named assistant chief of the Air Corps, and in September 1938 he became chief of the Air Corps with the rank of temporary major general. Long a champion of the concept of air power—he had supported Col. William Mitchell's campaigning in that cause—Arnold employed considerable ingenuity in maximizing the Air Corp's combat readiness on sharply limited prewar budgets. A program of sending future pilots to civilian training schools was begun, only afterwards receiving formal congressional sanction under the Civil Aeronautics Authority in 1939. Similarly Arnold used his influence with manufacturers to urge them to begin preparing for greatly stepped-up production of the latest models. By the time the United States entered World War II in December 1941 the productive capacity of the aircraft industry had increased sixfold from 1939, and pilot training capacity had kept pace. In October 1940 Arnold was made acting deputy chief of staff of the army for air matters. In June 1941 he was continued as chief of the renamed Army Air Forces. Promoted to temporary lieutenant general in December 1941 (he had become permanent brigadier general in December 1940 and major general in February 1941), he was designated commanding general, AAF, in the War Department reorganization of March 1942 that raised the air arm to coordinate status with the other two major commands, Army Ground Forces and Army Service Forces. He was advanced to temporary general in March 1943. During the war he served on the Joint Chiefs of Staff and the Allied combined chiefs, helping to plan overall strategy for the war and in particular contributing to the strategies and organization that early established Allied control of the air in all theaters. In a step that looked toward the eventual creation of an independent air force, he organized in April 1944 the Twentieth Air Force, a global strategic bombing force flying B-29's, under his direct command as agent for the Joint Chiefs (Gen. Curtis E. LeMay was field commander of the Twentieth for most of the war). In December 1944 he was one of four army leaders promoted to five-star rank of general of the army (George C. Marshall, Douglas MacArthur, and Dwight D. Eisenhower were the others). "Hap" Arnold turned over command of the AAF to Gen. Carl Spaatz in March 1946 and formally retired in June to a farm near Sonoma, California. In May 1949 he was named general of the air force, the first such commission ever made. He was the author of a series of books for boys on aviation and, with Gen. Ira C. Eaker, of *This Flying Game*, 1936, *Winged Warfare*, 1941, and *Army Flyer*, 1942; in 1949 he published *Global Mission*, an autobiography. Arnold died in Sonoma, California, on January 15, 1950.

Ashe, John (1720?–1781), Revolutionary militia officer. Born probably in 1720 in Grovely, Brunswick County, North Carolina, Ashe was of a prominent family and was apparently well educated. He served in the militia in the French and Indian War (1755–1763), and as speaker of the colonial assembly from 1762 to 1765 was outspoken in his support for the colonial cause. As the Revolution approached, he served on the committee of correspondence in North Carolina and then on the committee of safety. In 1775 he led a force of 500 men in the destruction of Fort Johnson, near Wilmington. Made a colonel of militia later in that year, he raised and equipped a regiment at his own expense. In April 1776 he was made brigadier general of militia. In 1778 he was dispatched to assist Gen. Benjamin Lincoln in the defense of Charleston, South Carolina. Early the following year Lincoln sent him at the head of some 1200 troops to drive the British force under Col. Campbell out of Augusta, Georgia. On March 4,

however, at Briar Creek, he allowed himself to be flanked and surprised by Col. Prevost's army. The battle was a rout—150 or more of Ashe's men killed and a like number captured to 16 British casualties—and effectively ended resistance in Georgia. A court of inquiry censured him for lack of vigilance. He returned to Wilmington, North Carolina, and was captured with the town in 1781. He contracted smallpox in prison and died in Sampson County, shortly after being paroled, on October 24, 1781.

Ashford, Bailey Kelly (1873–1934), army officer and physician. Born in Washington, D.C., on September 18, 1873, Ashford took a medical degree from Georgetown University in 1896 and, after enlisting in the army medical service in November 1897, graduated from the Army Medical School in 1898. He was sent immediately to Puerto Rico in July of that year for service in the Spanish–American War, and he remained there afterward. In addition to his routine duties he undertook an investigation into the widespread incidence of tropical anemia on the island, particularly among agricultural workers. In November 1899 he announced his discovery that the disease was caused by a parasite, *Necator americanus*, commonly known as the hookworm. After further research he organized in 1904 the Puerto Rico Anemia Commission, which embarked on a campaign to eradicate the disease. After ten years of effort the annual death rate from hookworm disease was reduced to a tenth of its former figure; the death rate from all causes fell by a third. Out of this work grew the subsequent campaign against the hookworm in the southern United States. He had meanwhile been promoted to captain in November 1902, major in April 1908, and lieutenant colonel in July 1916. He advanced to colonel in May 1917 and in June–October was divisional surgeon with the 1st Division. From November 1917 to November 1918 he served in France as head of battle training for medical officers of the American Expeditionary Force. He returned after the war to Puerto Rico. He became professor of mycology and tropical medicine when Columbia University, through the Puerto Rico School of Medicine, took over in 1926 the Institute of Tropical Medicine and Hygiene, which he had founded. He was also head of the medical service of University Hospital, San Juan. In poor health in his later years, Ashford died in San Juan on November 1, 1934.

Atkinson, Henry (1782–1842), army officer. Born in North Carolina in 1782, Atkinson entered the army in July 1808; of his childhood and youth there is no record. Commissioned a captain upon enlistment in the 3rd Infantry, he advanced to colonel of the 45th Infantry in April 1814, during the War of 1812, and in May 1815 he was placed in command of the 6th Infantry Regiment. In 1819 Secretary of War

John C. Calhoun proposed that a strong expeditionary force be sent to the Yellowstone country as a demonstration, to the Indians and the British traders there, of U.S. interest. Atkinson was put in charge but, largely through lack of funds and proper equipment, the trip ended at Old Council Bluffs in what is now Nebraska, where Camp Missouri (later Fort Atkinson and then Fort Calhoun) was established. From there Maj. Stephen H. Long set out on his famous expedition to the Rockies in 1820. In May 1820, while stationed in St. Louis, Atkinson was promoted to brigadier general in joint command of the Western Department, but the army reorganization of the following year reduced him to rank of colonel and brevet brigadier general. In 1825 he led a second expedition to the West and this time succeeded in reaching the mouth of the Yellowstone, treating with a number of Indian tribes along the way and also meeting trader William H. Ashley, who was returning from the first rendezvous of the "mountain men," as his fur trappers were known. The two parties joined for the return to St. Louis. In 1826 Atkinson chose the site for Jefferson Barracks, an army post south of St. Louis, and the following year he sent Col. Henry Leavenworth to establish a post—Fort Leavenworth —on the Kansas frontier. Later in 1827 he traveled north to Prairie du Chien (in what is now Wisconsin) to pacify the Winnebago Indians. Atkinson commanded the 400 regulars and 900 volunteers in the Black Hawk War in 1832 and was field commander during the decisive battle at Bad Axe, in what is now Wisconsin, on August 2. In 1840 he was in charge of the removal of the Winnebagos from Wisconsin to Iowa, where the next year Fort Atkinson was built. He returned to Jefferson Barracks, St. Louis, where he died on June 14, 1842.

Attucks, Crispus (1723?–1770), Revolutionary patriot. Born about 1723, Attucks is believed to have been a mulatto, but little of certainty is known of his early life. He may well have been a runaway slave from nearby Framingham, for an advertisement for a slave named Crispus was published in a Boston newspaper in 1750. He may also have been at some time a sailor. All that is definitely known of him concerns the Boston Massacre on March 5, 1770. Toward evening on that day a crowd of colonists gathered on King (now State) Street and began taunting a small group of British soldiers, commanded by Capt. Thomas Preston, who had rushed to rescue a lone sentry from the mob. Tension mounted rapidly, and when one of the soldiers was struck the others, without orders, opened fire. Attucks, described as a huge man "whose looks was enough to terrify any person," was shot, and he died almost immediately. Of the five victims of the fray, Attucks was the only one whose name was widely remembered, in part possibly because of the irony of the fact that one of

the first men to shed blood in the cause of American independence was one whose personal rights were not secure and would not have been secure after the Revolution. A statue of him by Augustus Saint-Gaudens was unveiled on Boston Common in 1888.

Averell, William Woods (1832–1900), army officer and inventor. Born in Cameron, New York, on November 5, 1832, Averell graduated from West Point in 1855 and was commissioned in the mounted rifles. After two years at Jefferson Barracks, Missouri, and completion of the course at the Cavalry School for Practice in Carlisle, Pennsylvania, he was ordered to duty in the Southwest, where he took part in numerous skirmishes with Indians and was wounded. He was on leave from 1859 to May 1861, when he was promoted to first lieutenant. He took part in the battle of Bull Run (Manassas) on July 21, 1861, and the next month was appointed colonel of the 3rd Pennsylvania Volunteer Cavalry. Until March 1862 he commanded the cavalry defenses of Washington, D.C. He took part in all the major battles of the Peninsula campaign in 1862, receiving promotion to captain of regulars in July and to brigadier general of volunteers in September. Through the winter of 1862–1863 he led a great many raids and scouting forays in northern Virginia, taking part in the battle of Fredericksburg, December 13, and during February–May 1863 he commanded the 2nd Cavalry Division, Army of the Potomac. On March 17 he led his 2100 cavalry troops across the Rappahannock at Kelly's Ford, Virginia, and fought a sharp engagement with Confederate cavalry under Gen. Fitzhugh Lee that became celebrated as the war's first purely cavalry battle, and a brilliant one. (Among the casualties was the South's dashing Maj. John Pelham.) Brevetted major of regulars for that action, Averell took part in Gen. George Stoneman's raid on Richmond, Virginia, in April–May and was subsequently transferred to West Virginia, where he effectively ended the operations of Gen. John D. Imboden and other Confederate raiders and won a brevet to lieutenant colonel of regulars at Droop Mountain, November 6. In December he launched a cavalry raid into Virginia, reaching as far as Salem; he destroyed several miles of railroad, interrupting the supply line of the Confederate forces besieging Gen. Ambrose E. Burnside at Knoxville, Tennessee, and captured a large amount of supplies intended for Gen. James Longstreet. He was brevetted colonel of regulars for that exploit. During 1864 he led the 2nd Cavalry Division under Gen. Philip H. Sheridan in the Shenandoah valley. In March 1865 he was brevetted brigadier general for services and major general for the battle of Moorfield, Virginia (August 7, 1863). He resigned from the army in May 1865 and during 1866 –1869 was U.S. consul general at Montreal. Later he went into business, having invented a system of conduit for electrical wiring and a successful form of asphalt paving. In August 1888 he was placed on the army retired list as a captain. He died in Bath, New York, on February 3, 1900.

B

Babcock, Orville E. (1835–1884), army officer. Born on December 25, 1835, in Franklin, Vermont, Babcock graduated from West Point in 1861 and was commissioned in the engineers. He was promoted to first lieutenant in November of that year. He performed various engineering duties early in the Civil War and in 1862 joined the staff of Gen. William B. Franklin. He was promoted to captain in June 1863 and in that year was present at the surrender of Vicksburg and took part in the campaign in eastern Tennessee leading to the siege of Knoxville. In January 1864 he was named acting chief engineer of the Department of the Ohio, and in March he was made aide-de-camp to Gen. Ulysses S. Grant with the rank of lieutenant colonel. He served Grant in a number of useful capacities and was much relied upon for observation and the carrying of high-level orders. In March 1865 he was brevetted brigadier general. After the close of the war he continued in his association with Grant, then commanding general of the army, and in July 1866 was promoted to colonel. When Grant was inaugurated President in 1869, Babcock became his private secretary. In 1869 he was sent to Santo Domingo as part of Grant's plan to annex the island. In 1871 he was appointed to the additional post of superintendent of public buildings and grounds for the city of Washington, in which capacity he oversaw the construction of such works as the Washington aqueduct and the Anacostia bridge. In December 1875 Babcock was charged by a St. Louis grand jury with complicity in the "Whisky Ring," a conspiracy of distillers and Internal Revenue Service officials to evade taxes. Babcock demanded a court-martial but instead was tried before a civil court. In spite of his friendship with some of the conspirators and his having received costly gifts from a principal one, he was acquitted in February 1876. The loyal Grant had treated the scandal as an attack on himself, which in part it may have been, and made a deposition asserting his secretary's innocence. Babcock returned to his duties briefly, but soon thereafter he retired. He died on June 2, 1884, drowning at Mosquito Inlet, Florida.

Bacon, Nathaniel (1647–1676), colonial leader. Born on January 2, 1647, in the county of Suffolk, England, Bacon was a kinsman of Francis Bacon. He studied at Cambridge and at Gray's Inn. In 1673 he emigrated to Virginia, established two plantations, and within a year was appointed to the governor's council. He was soon at odds with Gov. Sir William Berkeley, principally because Berkeley was reluctant to authorize reprisals against the Indians who were raiding frontier settlements and Bacon was strongly in sympathy with the inhabitants who demanded action. In 1676 an expeditionary force was organized in defiance of Berkeley, and Bacon was chosen to lead it. Raids were launched against the Pamunkey, Susquehanna, and Occaneechi tribes, while Berkeley denounced Bacon and his followers as rebels. The colonists, who by this time were demanding governmental reforms as well as protection from the Indians, forced the governor to back down, however, and through the weight of public opinion Bacon returned to the council in June 1676. He soon organized another raiding party and was again denounced by Berkeley, from whom he had extorted a commission to conduct a campaign against the Indians. Bacon and his supporters then occupied Jamestown, the capital, and Berkeley fled. When Bacon left the town to move again against Pamunkey villages, the governor returned. Bacon led his force back to Jamestown in September and, after a sharp battle, burned it while the governor once again fled. By this time Bacon was in control of virtually all of Virginia; he withdrew to Green Spring to consolidate his power and prepare for an attack on Berkeley's royalist stronghold in Accomac County, but in October 1676 he died suddenly. His followers soon dispersed and Bacon's Rebellion quickly collapsed.

Bailey, Anna Warner (1758–1851) "Mother Bailey," patriot. Born in Groton, Connecticut, in October (probably the 11th) 1758, Anna Warner was orphaned and reared by an uncle. On September 6, 1781, a large British force under the turncoat Gen. Benedict Arnold landed on the coast near Groton and stormed Fort Griswold. American casualties were very high, and among them was Anna Warner's uncle, Edward Mills. She walked several miles to the scene of battle, found her uncle after much difficulty, and learned that he was mortally wounded. At his request she hurried home, saddled a horse for her aunt, and herself carried her infant cousin back for a last meeting of the family. This feat soon became a favorite tale of the Revolution. Anna Warner later married Capt. Elijah Bailey, postmaster of Groton. In 1813, during the second war with Great Britain, Mother Bailey appeared among the Groton soldiers aiding in the defense of New London against a blockading British fleet. On learning of a shortage, she contributed her flannel petticoat—her "martial petticoat," as it came to be known—for use as cartridge wadding. Mother Bailey died in Groton on January 10, 1851.

Bailey, Joseph (1825–1867), army officer and engineer. Born in Pennsville, Ohio, on May 6, 1825, Bailey grew up there and in Illinois. By the time he settled in Kilbourn City, Wisconsin, in 1847, he had studied civil engineering and begun to earn a living at it. In 1861 he raised a company of infantry for the 4th Wisconsin, being mustered into federal volunteer service as a captain in July, and in April 1862 he took part in the occupation of New Orleans by Gen. Benjamin F. Butler. In December 1862 he was made acting engineer of the defenses of New Orleans. He was promoted to major in May 1863 and to lieutenant colonel in July, and in August, when the regiment became one of cavalry, he retired for a time to Wisconsin for recruiting work. In February 1864 he returned to New Orleans, and the next month he took part in the joint army–navy Red River campaign under Gen. Nathaniel P. Banks and Adm. David D. Porter. When the expedition faltered on the upper river, following the battle of Pleasant Hill, April 9, and fell back in some disorder to Alexandria, Louisiana, it was discovered that the river had fallen too low for the gunboats and transports to pass the rapids. Porter was at the point of arranging to destroy the flotilla, a terrible loss to the vital Mississippi Squadron, when Bailey suggested building a wing dam to raise the river. Regular engineers disparaged the notion, but he persisted and finally won permission to make the attempt. Nearly 3000 men worked in shifts around the clock at the immense job. Logs were laid from one side, stone-filled cribs from the other; brick-filled coal barges held the center, where the current was ten miles an hour. Nearly 1000 feet of river was dammed, leaving a 66-foot gap in the center through which the boats were to pass. By May 9, nine days after work began, the river behind the dam was up nearly six feet, and Porter was able to send four gunboats through. By the 12th the entire fleet was saved. Bailey's promotion to colonel came during the work on the dam; in June he was brevetted brigadier general and given a sword by Porter, a purse by other officers, and the thanks of Congress. In November he advanced to brigadier general of volunteers, and in March 1865 he was brevetted major general of volunteers for his conduct in the Mobile campaign under Gen. Edward R. S. Canby. In July 1865 he resigned from the army and settled in Vernon County, Missouri, where the following year he was elected sheriff. On March 21, 1867, he was shot from behind and killed by two outlaws whom he had arrested and was escorting unassisted to the county seat.

Bailey, Theodorus (1805–1877), naval officer. Born in Chateaugay, New York, on April 12, 1805, Bailey entered the navy as midshipman in January 1818. His first cruise, in 1820–1821, was on the sloop of war *Cyane*, suppressing the slave trade off the coast of Africa. Receiving promotion to lieutenant in March 1827, he served later on the *Franklin* and circled the globe aboard the *Vincennes* and again on the *Constellation*. In 1846 he took command of the storeship *Lexington*. At the outbreak of the Mexican War he conveyed a company of artillery from New York around the Horn to Monterey, California. He took active part in the war on the Pacific coast, and on January 12, 1848, in the final naval action of the war, he blockaded and then captured the town of San Blas in Baja California. In March 1849 Bailey was promoted to commander; his promotion to captain in December 1855 came during a three-year cruise in command of the *St. Mary's* of the Pacific Squadron, during which he improved American relations with various groups of islanders and in 1856 quelled an outbreak of rioting in Panama. In 1861 he took command of the steam frigate *Colorado*, West Gulf Blockading Squadron, before Pensacola. In April 1862 he was second in command to Flag-Officer David G. Farragut in the attack on New Orleans. The *Colorado* being too heavy to cross the bar into the Mississippi, Bailey transferred to the gunboat *Cayuga*, Lt. N. B. Harrison, and early on April 24 led the first division past Fort Jackson and Fort St. Philip, from which heavy fire was received. He met the Confederate river fleet, which he fought for a time unsupported, and then silenced the Chalmette batteries, the last defense of the city. When the Union fleet was in full command of the river, Farragut sent Bailey, accompanied only by Lt. G. H. Perkins, to enter the city, brave a hostile mob, receive the surrender, and raise the U. S. flag over the mint. In his report Bailey described the battle in the river as "a contest between iron hearts in wooden vessels and ironclads with iron beaks—and the iron hearts won." He had taken part in the attack in spite of weakened health; he was then placed on light duty for some months, receiving promotion to commodore in July. In November he took command of the East Gulf Blockading Squadron, which in his 18 months in that post captured 150 blockade runners. In September 1864 he was given command of the Portsmouth, New Hampshire, navy yard; he was promoted to rear admiral in July 1866, and in October of that year he retired. Bailey died on February 10, 1877, in Washington, D.C.

Bainbridge, William (1774–1833), naval officer. Born in Princeton, New Jersey, on May 7, 1774, Bainbridge received a thorough schooling and at the age of fifteen went to sea on a merchant ship. Before he was twenty he was in command of his own vessel. In 1796, while engaged in trade between Europe and the

West Indies at a time when England was conducting an undeclared war at sea against the United States, Bainbridge made a name for himself and for his vessel, the *Hope*, by defeating a British privateer with twice his firepower that had attacked his ship without warning. Later, after one of his men had been impressed and taken aboard a heavily armed British cruiser, he immediately seized a replacement from a British merchantman. In 1798, when the Department of the Navy was organized in the face of the need to defend shipping against the French and the Barbary pirates, Bainbridge was commissioned lieutenant and given command of the 14-gun schooner *Retaliation*. Captured by the French frigates *L'Insurgente* and *Volontier* in the West Indies in September 1798, he was imprisoned for a time on Guadeloupe. Upon his release he was promoted to master commandant and given the brig *Norfolk*. His success in defending a large convoy of merchant craft bound from the West Indies to the United States led to his promotion to captain, then the highest rank in the navy, in May 1800. That same year, in command of the frigate *George Washington*, he undertook the extremely difficult mission of bearing tribute to Algiers, and while scoring diplomatic gains for the United States he rescued several French citizens from slavery. He commanded the *Essex* briefly in 1801–1802 and in May 1803 took command of the frigate *Philadelphia*, joining in August Commodore Edward Preble's squadron operating against Tripoli in the war against the Barbary pirates. On October 31, while chasing a Tripolitan corsair into the poorly charted harbor, his ship ran aground, and he and the crew were taken prisoner. It was at his suggestion that the *Philadelphia* was burned in a daring raid into the harbor by Lt. Stephen Decatur in February 1804. Released in June 1805 after having taken an important part in the peace negotiations with Tripoli, Bainbridge reentered the merchant service. He was recalled to active naval duty as a commodore during 1808–1810 to command the frigate *President*, and again at the outbreak of the War of 1812, when he became commandant of the Charlestown navy yard. He succeeded Isaac Hull as commander of the *Constitution*, 44 guns, fresh from its victory over the *Guerrière*, and in December he won a notable victory over the British frigate *Java*, 49, being twice wounded during the battle. In February 1813 he returned to the Charlestown yard and supervised the building of the ship of the line *Independence*, 74. He made two more voyages to the Mediterranean, in 1815 (aboard the *Independence*), when he relieved Commodore Stephen Decatur as commander of the U.S. squadron there, and 1820 (on the great *Congress*, 80), helping to maintain there a strong American guard against a resumption of piracy by the Barbary states. In 1817 at Charlestown he organized the first school for U.S. naval officers. His later years were spent in command of various naval yards

and in service on the Board of Naval Commissioners, of which he was president in 1832–1833. In March 1820 he served as Stephen Decatur's second in the latter's duel with James Barron. Bainbridge died in Philadelphia on July 27, 1833.

Baker, Edward Dickinson (1811–1861), army officer and public official. Born on February 24, 1811, in London, Baker came with his family to the United States in 1815, settling in Philadelphia. The family moved to New Harmony, Indiana, in 1825 and to Belleville, Illinois, a short time later. Baker studied law, was admitted to the bar in 1830, and after serving in the Black Hawk War in 1832 he opened a legal practice in Springfield in 1835. Politics followed naturally; he served, 1837–1840, in the lower house and, 1840–1844, in the upper house of the Illinois legislature, and in 1844 he was elected to Congress, having beaten his friend Abraham Lincoln for the Whig nomination. At the outbreak of the Mexican War he hurried back to Illinois, raised a volunteer regiment, and marched it to join Gen. Zachary Taylor. He then returned briefly to Washington in December to make an effective speech, in uniform, to Congress. Resigning his seat, he rejoined his regiment, the 4th Illinois; he distinguished himself at Cerro Gordo and took over command of the Illinois volunteers brigade from the wounded Gen. James Shields. Soon after his return to law practice in 1848 he moved to Galena, Illinois, from which he was elected again to Congress in that year. In 1851 he was briefly interested in a Panamanian railroad project. In 1852 he moved to California, where his continued efforts on behalf of the Whig Party, and later the Republican Party, while futile in that solidly Democratic state, attracted the attention of party men in Oregon. At their invitation he moved there early in 1860 and later in that year was elected to a vacant seat in the Senate. As the only Republican senator from the Pacific states, as a prominent friend of Lincoln, and as an orator of note, Baker quickly gained considerable influence and popularity in Washington. In April 1861 he accepted an invitation to command a regiment known as the "California," although it was recruited mainly in Pennsylvania and New York and was formally the 71st Pennsylvania Volunteers. He declined offers of brigadier and major general's rank in order to retain his seat in the Senate (his colonelcy being no bar). On October 21, 1861, Baker, commanding a brigade, was killed in a skirmish with Confederate troops at Ball's Bluff, Virginia, and his brigade was badly defeated. What had begun as a simple reconnaissance and turned into an unfortunate but militarily inconsequential engagement soon became a major political controversy. Northern apprehension and the growing exasperation with the absence of decisive action in the field, together with Baker's popularity in the Senate, prompted the formation in

December of the joint Committee on the Conduct of the War, called at first only to investigate the Ball's Bluff affair but destined to play a large role in the war. General Charles P. Stone, Baker's division commander, saw his career ruined as a result of the event.

Baker, George (1915–1975), cartoonist. Born on May 22, 1915, in Lowell, Massachusetts, Baker grew up there, in Rockford, Illinois, and in Chicago. After attending an art school briefly he became a commercial artist. In 1937, on the brink of joining a West Coast minor-league baseball team, he instead took a job with the Walt Disney studios in Hollywood. He worked on a number of Disney cartoon features until 1941, when he was drafted into the army. Assigned to duty at Fort Monmouth, New Jersey, he was attached to the Signal Corps to do animations for information films; while there he toyed with a cartoon series depicting army life as seen from the bottom of the heap. A few of his strips were published in *Life*, and in 1942, when *Yank*, a weekly magazine aimed principally at enlisted men, was organized, he became an original member of the staff. Baker's cartoon series, starring a well-meaning but thoroughly inept private known only as "The Sad Sack," became *Yank*'s most enduring and popular feature. Followed by an estimated 10 million servicemen throughout the world, the Sad Sack's adventures reflected and magnified the experiences of every enlisted man who ever faced red tape, KP, sergeants, officers, and duty details. The Sack, who never spoke a word, became probably the best known fictional figure of the war (his only competitors being Bill Mauldin's Joe and Willie) and was credited with being one of the army's most effective morale builders. Collections of strips from *Yank* were published in 1944 and 1946, and after his discharge at the end of the war Baker continued to draw the Sad Sack for a newspaper syndicate, later producing a comic book series as well. He died in Los Angeles on May 7, 1975.

Balchen, Bernt (1899–1973), pilot, explorer, and air force officer. Born on October 23, 1899, in Tveit, Norway, Balchen was in his youth a champion boxer, skier, and cyclist. He studied at the Norwegian Royal Naval Aviation School and in 1924 was commissioned a flight lieutenant. In 1925 he was in command of the successful aerial search for explorers Roald Amundsen and Lincoln Ellsworth, who had failed in an attempt to fly over the North Pole. The following year he assisted in the preparation of a base in Spitsbergen from which the two explorers were to try again. Originally included in the flight crew, Balchen was left behind when it became necessary to lighten the load in the airship; as it happened, Lt. Commander (ret.) Richard E. Byrd was also preparing for a polar flight from Spitsbergen, and Balchen was able to give valuable aid to Byrd's pilot, Floyd Bennett—he advised waxing the plane's skis, thereby solving a problem that had threatened to postpone the attempt. In return Byrd invited Balchen to the United States, where he accompanied a cross-country exhibition of the polar airplane. He then joined the Fokker Aircraft Corp. of New Jersey as a test pilot. His exploits in the air were many, including a daring landing in the surf on the French coast in June 1927 at the conclusion of a flight with Byrd and others across the Atlantic. He rejoined Byrd in 1928 for the latter's expedition to the Antarctic, and on November 29, 1929, he piloted Byrd over the South Pole in a 1600-mile flight that was a miracle of flying skill. He was naturalized a U.S. citizen in 1931. During 1933–1935 he was chief pilot with Ellsworth's Antarctic expedition. He then returned to Norway, but he was in the United States when his country was invaded by Germany in 1940 and he thereupon joined the British Royal Air Force, ferrying aircraft from San Diego to Singapore. In September 1941 he received a captain's commission in the Army Air Corps and was sent to Greenland to establish Bluie West Eight, the northernmost U.S. air base. While in Greenland he led several missions to rescue downed American airmen and one to destroy a secret German weather base. By early 1944 he was a colonel and was transferred to Europe, where he organized a ferry service to fly arms, medicine, radio equipment, and Allied agents from Scotland to the Norwegian and Danish undergrounds and smuggle thousands of Norwegians and nearly a thousand interned U.S. airmen from Sweden back to Britain. The unarmed B-24 aircraft that Balchen used flew 110 such missions, usually in bad weather and at wave level. In 1946 he was placed on the reserve list, and he returned to Norway as director of Royal Norwegian Airlines. In 1948, at his own request, he was recalled to active duty with the U.S. Air Force and sent to command the 10th Rescue Squadron at Fort Richardson, Alaska. He retired in 1956 and lived in later years in Chappaqua, New York. He died in Mount Kisco, New York, on October 17, 1973.

Ballou, Charles Clarendon (1862–1928), army officer. Born on June 13, 1862, in Orange County, New York, Ballou graduated from West Point in 1886 and was commissioned in the infantry. He was promoted to first lieutenant in April 1893. In 1898 he graduated from the Infantry and Cavalry School, Fort Leavenworth, Kansas. In the Spanish–American War he served from July to October 1898 as a major in the 7th Illinois Infantry Volunteers, posted at Fort Niagara, New York. Promoted to captain in March 1899, he served as regimental quartermaster with the 12th Infantry in the Philippines in that year, seeing action in several skirmishes with insurrectionists. In 1900–1902 he was stationed at Fort Slocum, New York. Over the next 15 years he saw routine duty, including 4 tours in the Philippines, and received promotions to major in June 1909, lieutenant colonel in February 1915, and colonel in July 1916. In 1917 he graduated from the Army War College. In June 1917, shortly after the United States entered World War I, he was made commander of the Colored Officers' Training Camp at Fort Des Moines, Iowa. In August he was promoted to temporary brigadier general, and in September he took command of the 163rd Depot Brigade at nearby Camp Dodge. In October he was named to command the 92nd Infantry Division (Negro), advancing to temporary major general the next month. He took the 92nd to France in July 1918 and led it in the Meuse–Argonne offensive of September–November as part of Gen. Robert L. Bullard's Second Army. In October Ballou was moved up to command of the VI Corps, retaining command of the 92nd. In November, shortly after the armistice, he took command of the 89th Division, remaining with it in occupation duty until February 1919. Subsequently he commanded briefly Camp Dodge; in 1919–1920 he commanded Fort Logan, Colorado, taking command in Denver on the declaration of martial law following labor riots in August 1920; and in 1920–1923 he commanded Ft. George Wright, Washington. From August 1923 until his retirement in June 1926 he had charge of the general recruiting service in New York City. Ballou died in Spokane, Washington, on July 23, 1928.

Banks, Nathaniel Prentiss (1816–1894), public official and army officer. Born on January 30, 1816, in Waltham, Massachusetts, Banks was largely self-educated. He read widely, practiced public speaking, and after a brief dalliance with the Boston stage took up the study of law. He was admitted to the bar in 1839 but never practiced, instead taking a job in the Boston customhouse and, for three years, publishing in Waltham the weekly *Middlesex Reporter*. After several unsuccessful campaigns he won election to the Massachusetts house of representatives in 1849 and served for four years, the last two as speaker. In 1853 he presided over the state constitutional convention and in the same year entered the U.S. House of Representatives as a Democrat. He was reelected in 1854 on the "Know-Nothing" (American Party) ticket and thereupon waged a long and arduous battle for the speakership of the House, winning it on the 133rd ballot. He conducted that office in an eminently fair and tactful manner and was widely respected for his parliamentary skill. He was elected to a third term in 1856. In 1857 he was elected governor of Massachusetts as a moderate Republican. During his three years in that office he was an efficient administrator, and he is often given credit for making possible the immediate response of his successor, John A. Andrew, to President Lincoln's call for troops in 1861. By that time Banks had gone to Chicago to

replace George B. McClellan as president of the Illinois Central Railroad, but he soon resigned to accept an army commission as major general of volunteers in May 1861; he was put in command of the Department of Annapolis. Early in 1862, in command of the V Corps detached from Gen. George B. McClellan's Army of the Potomac, he faced Gen. Thomas J. (Stonewall) Jackson in the Shenandoah valley and was forced to retreat, fighting an effective defensive battle at Winchester on May 25. Later, the V Corps being attached to Gen. John Pope's Army of Virginia, he attacked and was outfought by Jackson at Cedar Mountain on August 9. After a brief period in command of the defense of Washington, D.C., he was sent to New Orleans in November 1862 to succeed Gen. Benjamin F. Butler as commander of the Department of the Gulf. In May 1863 he captured Alexandria and, after two unsuccessful assaults, May 25 and 27, laid siege to Port Hudson, which surrendered after the fall of Vicksburg in July, thus earning Banks a congressional commendation. Later in the year he conducted some largely fruitless operations on the Texas coast south to Brownsville. In 1864 he commanded an ill conceived joint expedition up the Red River with a river fleet under Adm. David D. Porter, an expedition aimed less at Confederate forces than indirectly at the French in Mexico. The combined force suffered serious reverses at Sabine Crossroads on April 8 and at Pleasant Hill the next day at the hands of Gen. Richard Taylor. Banks was forced to withdraw and Porter's fleet escaped only with great difficulty and largely through the ingenious dam building of Col. Joseph Bailey. His authority soon superseded by that of Gen. Edward R. S. Canby, Banks resigned in August 1865, returned to Waltham, and was immediately elected again, as a Republican, to the House of Representatives. He served in Congress until his defeat on the Liberal Republican ticket in 1872. He was then elected to the Massachusetts senate but was returned to the U.S. House as a Democrat in 1874 and as a Republican in 1876. From 1879 to 1888 he served as federal marshal for Massachusetts and in 1888 was once again elected to the House as a Republican. Ill health forced his retirement from public life in 1891, and he died in Waltham on September 1, 1894.

Barbey, Daniel Edward (1889–1969), naval officer. Born in Portland, Oregon, on December 23, 1889, Barbey graduated from the Naval Academy in 1912 and saw his first sea duty aboard the cruiser *California*. As duties at sea and ashore alternated over the next 30 years, he commanded at various times the destroyer *Lea*, the tanker *Ramapo*, and the battleship *New York*. During 1937–1940, with rank of captain, he had charge of the War Plans Section of the Bureau of Navigation, and there pictures of operations in the Chinese–Japanese war kindled his interest in amphibious warfare. Early in 1941 he was named chief of staff and aide to the commander of the Service Force and Amphibious Force, Atlantic Fleet, and he began serious investigation of the requirements for landing large quantities of equipment and numbers of troops on hostile beaches. Establishing the Amphibious Warfare Section in the Navy Department, he organized the work of devising equipment, methods, and combat doctrine. Under his supervision the LSD (Landing Ship, Dock) was developed, along with the smaller vessels that it was designed to carry and discharge—the LST (Landing Ship, Tank), LCI (Landing Craft, Infantry), and other beaching craft, and his own invention, the "duck," (DUKW), an amphibious truck. In December 1942 Barbey was promoted to rear admiral and the following month was named commander of the VII Amphibious Force of the Seventh Fleet (from November 1943 under Adm. Thomas C. Kinkaid), with responsibility for all amphibious operations in Gen. Douglas MacArthur's Southwest Pacific area. In two and a half years his forces accomplished the landing of more than a million men and one and a half million tons of equipment in 56 amphibious assaults throughout the Pacific. These included operations in the Trobriand Islands, begun June 30, 1943; in Papua New Guinea during August 1943-March 1944; on Morotai in the Moluccas, September 15, 1944; at Tacloban, Leyte, October 20, 1944, where his Northern Attack Force landed the army's X Corps; and in Lingayen Gulf, Luzon, January 9, 1945 (in the last two Barbey operated alongside Adm. Theodore S. Wilkinson's III Amphibious Force). Barbey was promoted to vice admiral in June 1944. In November 1945 he took command of the Seventh Fleet and oversaw the repatriation of more than two million Japanese in China and Korea as well as the landing of Nationalist Chinese troops in northern areas formerly held by Japan. In 1946 Barbey became commander of Atlantic Amphibious Forces, and later he was commander of the Caribbean Sea Frontier and the 13th Naval District. He retired from the navy in May 1951 and for six years served as civil defense director for the state of Washington. He lived in Olympia, Washington, and died at the Bremerton Naval Hospital on April 11, 1969.

Barlow, Francis Channing (1834–1896), army

officer and public official. Born on October 19, 1834, in Brooklyn, New York, Barlow grew up mainly in Brookline, Massachusetts. He graduated from Harvard in 1855, took up the study of law in New York City, and in 1858 was admitted to the bar. In April 1861 he enlisted as a private in the 12th New York Infantry, which was sent to the defense of Washington, D.C. By the expiration of his three-month enlistment he had been promoted to first lieutenant. In November he took a commission as lieu-

tenant colonel of the 61st New York. He advanced to colonel during the siege of Yorktown in Gen. George B. McClellan's Peninsular campaign early in 1862, and for his gallantry at Fair Oaks (Seven Pines), May 31, he was awarded command of a brigade in Gen. O. O. Howard's XI Corps. At Antietam (Sharpsburg) on September 17 he distinguished himself again in the Bloody Lane, receiving a serious wound. On September 19 he was appointed brigadier general of volunteers. Barlow returned to duty in time to take part in the Union defeat at Chancellorsville, May 2–4, 1863, and on July 1 he was again severely wounded in the fighting on the north of Gettysburg. He lay paralyzed behind Confederate lines until the battle ended two days later. In April 1864 he again returned to duty, taking command of a division of Gen. Winfield S. Hancock's II Corps. During the battle of Spotsylvania Court House, Barlow's was one of two divisions to make a successful dawn attack on a Confederate salient on May 12, taking more than 3000 prisoners including two generals. For this action he was brevetted major general, the honor coming while he was on an extended European trip for his health. He rejoined the II Corps in April 1865 and led his division in the running battle leading to Lee's surrender; his capture of a vital bridge over Appomattox Creek near Farmville contributed signally to the immobilization of the Confederate army, and for it he was appointed major general in command of the II Corps in May. He was mustered out shortly thereafter and returned to New York, resigning his commission officially in November. He was elected New York secretary of state in that month and served until 1868, when President Grant appointed him U.S. marshal for the southern district of New York. In 1869 he was again elected secretary of state, and in 1870 he was elected attorney general, in which post he initiated the prosecution of the Tweed Ring. He left office in 1874. In 1876 he took part in the investigation of voting irregularities in the Hayes–Tilden presidential election. Barlow died in New York on January 11, 1896.

Barlow, John Whitney (1838–1914), army offi-

cer and engineer. Born in Perry, New York, on June 26, 1838, Barlow graduated from West Point in 1861 and was commissioned in the 2nd Artillery. He joined the forces in the field in time to take part in the battle of Bull Run (Manassas) in July. In the Peninsular campaign in the spring of 1862 he distinguished himself at Hanover Court House, May 27, holding off an entire division with a single gun, and was brevetted captain. He was transferred to the topographic engineers in July and to the engineers corps in March 1863; he was promoted to captain in July 1863. In 1864 he was attached to Gen. William T. Sherman's army before Atlanta, serving in July–August as chief engineer of the XVII Corps and being brevetted major. From November 1864 he was in charge of the defenses of Nashville, under the overall command of Gen. George H. Thomas, where his conduct during the decisive battle with Gen. John B. Hood's Army of Tennessee, December 15–16, earned him brevet rank of lieutenant colonel. After the war Barlow performed a variety of engineering duties. In 1871 he was in command of a detachment of engineers that, in conjunction with a group from the Geological Survey of the Territories under Ferdinand V. Hayden, made the first federally sponsored expedition into the region that would the next year be designated Yellowstone National Park, in large part owing to the report of the Barlow-Hayden group. During 1886–1890 he was engaged in navigation canal work at Muscle Shoals, Alabama, and during 1892–1896 he was senior U.S. commissioner in a joint U.S.–Mexican engineering party that surveyed and marked the border from El Paso to the Pacific coast. Barlow advanced in rank to major in 1879, lieutenant colonel in 1884, colonel in 1895, and brigadier general and chief of engineers in 1901. The day after the last promotion, May 2, 1901, he retired at his own request. He died on February 27, 1914, while visiting Jerusalem.

Barnett, George (1859–1930), marine officer. Born on December 9, 1859, in Lancaster, Wisconsin, Barnett graduated from the Naval Academy in 1881, and after two years of sea duty he was commissioned in the marine corps as a second lieutenant in July 1883. He became a first lieutenant in September 1890. In 1897 he was appointed fleet marine officer in the European Squadron, and the next year, promoted in August to captain, he served as marine officer aboard the *New Orleans* in the blockade of the Spanish fleet at Santiago, Cuba. He advanced to major in March 1901 and lieutenant colonel in February 1905, the latter promotion coming during his tour in command of the 1st Marine Brigade in the Philippine Insurrection. In 1906–1907, under Col. Littleton W. T. Waller, he took part in the pacification operation in Cuba, and from 1908 to 1910 he commanded the marine guard at the American legation in Peking, China. Promoted to colonel in October 1910, he took command of the marine barracks at the Philadelphia navy yard. In February 1914 he was appointed temporary major general and commandant of the corps, a post he held for six difficult years. The first Naval Academy graduate to command the corps, he became in 1915 the first marine commandant to sit on the navy's General Board. He directed the expansion and training of the corps for World War I duty, his service earning him reappointment as commandant in 1918 at the expiration of the normal four-year term. Among the new facilities he acquired for the corps during the war was the San Diego barracks. His permanent rank was raised to brigadier general in 1916. In June 1920 he became commander of the marine Department of the Pacific, with headquarters in San Francisco, and in March 1921 he was given permanent rank of major general. Barnett retired in December 1923 and died in Washington, D.C., on April 28, 1930.

Barney, Joshua (1759–1818), naval officer. Born in Baltimore on July 6, 1759, Barney went to sea at the age of thirteen. At fifteen, when the captain of the ship on which he was serving died suddenly in mid-Atlantic, he took command, successfully completed the voyage and handled the business details upon reaching port, and returned to Baltimore. He joined the Continental navy in October 1775; the next year he was aboard the sloop *Hornet* in Commodore Esek Hopkins's squadron at the capture of New Providence in the Bahamas and performed with sufficient distinction to earn a commission as lieutenant in June 1776. He served on a number of ships during the Revolution, captured many prizes, and was three times captured and imprisoned by the British, the last time for a year in England, whence he escaped to France and then to America. In 1782 he took command of the Pennsylvania ship *Hyder-Ally*, 16 guns, a small converted merchant vessel, and set out to convoy a merchant fleet down Delaware Bay; at Cape May on April 8 he was set upon by a much more heavily armed British force. Barney covered the retreat of the merchantmen and then brilliantly outmaneuvered and captured the much larger *General Monk*, 20 guns, an action for which he was widely celebrated. In November 1782 he sailed the *General Monk* to France with dispatches. Barney retired from active service in May 1784 and for ten years engaged in various enterprises. In 1794 he was listed third on the captains' list in the reorganized navy and was about to be sent against the Barbary pirates; instead he balked at what he considered an insultingly low rank and resigned. He returned to the merchant service until 1796, when he accepted a commission in the French navy; he served for six years and then returned to Baltimore. During the War of 1812 he equipped and commanded a number of privateer vessels that operated against British shipping. In July 1814 he was called to aid in the defense of Washington, D.C. With a fleet of armed barges he held off the advance of Adm. Sir George Cockburn's fleet, bearing Gen. Robert Ross's army, up Chesapeake Bay for some weeks and, when the enemy eventually eluded him and threatened the capital, he abandoned the barges and marched his small force of about 500 sailors and marines back to Bladensburg, Maryland, and placed his men, armed with a few ship's guns mounted on carriages, at the center of Gen. William H. Winder's position. The battle on August 24 was a serious defeat for the Americans, who were saved from utter disgrace only by the valiant resistance offered by Barney's small command. Barney, wounded in the battle, was taken prisoner. He later served as port officer at Baltimore and then retired to an estate in Kentucky. He died in Pittsburgh on December 1, 1818.

Barron, James (1768–1851), naval officer. Born on September 15, 1768, probably in Norfolk, Virginia, Barron was the son of a merchant captain, and as his father's apprentice he saw some naval action late in the Revolution. He continued to follow the sea after the war and in March 1798 was commissioned a lieutenant in the navy and assigned to the *United States* under Commodore John Barry. The next year he was promoted to captain and given command successively of the *Essex,* the *President,* Commodore Richard Dale's flagship, and the *New York* in Commodore Richard V. Morris's squadron, serving in the Mediterranean until 1805. In 1807, with the rank of commodore, he assumed command of the hastily activated *Chesapeake,* 38 guns, and was en route to the Mediterranean when on June 22, off Cape Henry, Virginia, he was stopped by the British frigate *Leopard,* 50 guns, which demanded the return of several alleged deserters from the British navy who were claimed to be aboard. When Barron refused to allow a search of his ship the *Leopard* opened fire with devastating effect; Barron's unprepared and ill trained men were thrown into confusion and he surrendered the ship to prevent its complete destruction. Before the *Chesapeake* struck her colors, a single shot was gotten off by Lt. William Henry Allen. American casualties came to 21, including Barron. The *Leopard* then seized four men, at least two of whom were American citizens, and left the *Chesapeake* to limp home to Hampton Roads severely damaged. The incident inflamed the American public and proved to be the most serious of the period preceding the declaration of war in 1812. Barron, court-martialed in January 1808 largely at the instance of Lt. Allen, was found guilty of negligence in the affair but was acquitted of charges of cowardice and was suspended from duty for five years, during which time he served in the French navy. When he returned to active U.S. service, he found himself blocked from promotion and sea duty; his frustration grew until, in 1820, he accused Commodore Stephen Decatur of leading an intrigue against him and challenged him to a duel. Decatur was killed in the exchange on March 22, and Barron, badly wounded, found himself universally condemned. For the rest of his life he was on inactive status, and, at his death in Norfolk, on April 21, 1851, he was the senior but probably the most unpopular officer in the navy.

Barron, Samuel (1809–1888), Confederate naval officer. Born in Hampton, Virginia, on November 28, 1809, Barron was the son and namesake of a distinguished commodore and, most likely for that reason, was admitted into the navy at two years of age. He entered upon his duties in 1820 and served in various capacities, advancing to lieutenant in March 1827, commander in July 1847, and captain in September 1855. His commands included the *John Adams,* 1849–1853 and the steam frigate *Wabash,* whose crew included Midshipman George Dewey, 1858–1859. In April 1861 he resigned from the navy (his resignation was refused and he was recorded as dismissed) and accepted a captain's commission in the Confederate States navy. He helped organize coastal defense, taking particular responsibility for the Virginia and North Carolina coastline. On August 28–29, 1861, at the attack of a Union squadron under Flag-Officer Silas H. Stringham on Hatteras Inlet, a vital point for privateers based in Pamlico Sound, Barron had overall charge of the defense of Fort Hatteras and Fort Clark. When they fell he was taken prisoner and held in New York until exchanged the next year. In November 1862 he was appointed to command of the naval forces in Virginia waters, and the following summer he went to England to oversee the fitting-out of two ironclad rams ordered by the Confederate government. Those vessels being seized by British authorities, he traveled in November 1863 to Paris, where he remained as "Flag-Officer Commanding Confederate States Naval Forces in Europe," until February 1865. Resigning his commission, he took up farming in Essex County, Virginia, and died on February 26, 1888.

Barry, John (1745?–1803), Revolutionary naval officer. Born in County Wexford, Ireland, about 1745, Barry went to sea at an early age and by 1760 had settled in Philadelphia. A successful merchant captain, he also became an ardent patriot and in March 1776 was commissioned captain in the Continental navy and placed in command of the brig *Lexington.* A month later he captured the British tender *Edward* in the navy's first successful engagement at sea. He later commanded the *Effingham,* but his ship was kept in Philadelphia by the British blockade of Delaware Bay; during that period he fought with the army in Philadelphia and at Trenton and Princeton. In the winter of 1777–1778 he was forced to scuttle the *Effingham* to keep it from the hands of the British occupying Philadelphia, but he was able to lead a daring boat foray down the Delaware and capture a British schooner, several transports, and many supplies. In September 1778 he sailed the *Raleigh,* 32 guns, out of Boston but lost it shortly thereafter in a battle against the combined forces of the *Experiment,* 50, and the *Unicorn,* 20, in Penobscot Bay. Two years later he was placed in command of the *Alliance,* 32. On his first voyage, while conveying John Laurens to France, he captured a number of prizes on the way and on May 29, on the return voyage, defeated the *Atalanta,* 16, and the *Trepassy,* 14, in a grueling four-hour battle off Newfoundland, during which he was badly wounded. After the American victory at Yorktown, Barry made a second trip to France, this time to carry the Marquis de Lafayette home. In 1782 he put out for the West Indies on his final wartime cruise; he captured several prizes and four British ships of the line and on March 10, 1783, during his return from Havana with a load of bullion, repelled an attack by three frigates, damaging one of them severely in the last Revolutionary naval engagement of note. Barry returned to the merchant trade briefly and then retired. In 1794 he was recalled, named senior captain of the navy, and assigned to the frigate *United States,* 44 guns, then under construction by Joshua Humphreys in Philadelphia. The ship was launched in May 1797, and in the summer of 1798, during a period of undeclared naval war with France, Barry was sent with her to the West Indies as commander of all U.S. ships in those waters. He remained in that post until May 1799. After a trip to France carrying diplomatic envoys he assumed command of the naval station at Guadeloupe in the West Indies. He returned home to Philadelphia in 1801 and was senior officer of the navy when he died on September 13, 1803, in that city.

Barton, Clara (1821–1912), founder of the American Red Cross. Born on December 25, 1821, in Oxford, Massachusetts, Clarissa Harlowe Barton was the youngest of five children. She was educated at home and grew up willful and independent, with a love for outdoor sports. She began a career of teaching at the age of fifteen. In 1850–1851 she attended the Liberal Institute at Clinton, New York, and in 1852 she established in Bordentown, New Jersey, a free school that soon became so large that the townsmen would no longer allow a woman to run it. Rather than subordinate herself to a male principal, she resigned. She was employed by the U.S. Patent Office from 1854 to 1857 and again in 1860. In 1861 she showed characteristic initiative in organizing facilities to recover soldiers' lost baggage and in securing medicine and supplies for men wounded in the first battle of Bull Run. She gained permission to pass through the battle lines to distribute supplies, search for the missing, and nurse the wounded. She carried on this work through the remainder of the Civil War, traveling with the army as far south as Charleston in 1863. In June 1864 she was formally appointed superintendent of nurses for the Army of the James. In 1865 she organized a program to investigate the cases of soldiers listed as missing. During 1866–1868 she spoke widely about her Civil War work. In 1869 she went abroad for her health but soon was busy in relief work in the Franco–Prussian War. Learning of the activities of the International Red Cross recently organized in Geneva, Switzerland, she campaigned and lobbied vigorously, after her return to the United States in 1873 and another period of convalescence, with the result that the United States became a signatory of the Geneva Convention in March 1882. In 1881 she organized the American Association of the Red Cross, known from 1893 as the American National Red Cross, and served as its president until 1904. She devoted herself entirely to the organization, soliciting contributions and taking the field with relief workers even as late as the Spanish–American War in Cuba, when she was seventy-seven. She was jealous of any interference, however, and supervised the organization's activities so closely that finally charges of authoritarianism were brought against her by members of her executive council. The Red Cross had been chartered by Congress in 1900, and the rebelling faction used that lever to force her resignation in 1904. Despite the arbitrariness of her administrative methods, her achievements remained, not the least of which was, in 1884, her successful advocacy of the "American amendment" to the Geneva Convention, a provision that permitted the Red Cross to provide relief in times of natural disasters and calamities as well as in wartime. In addition to many pamphlets and books on the Red Cross she wrote *The Story of My Childhood,* 1907. Clara Barton died in Glen Echo, Maryland, on April 12, 1912.

Barton, William (1748–1831), Revolutionary militia officer. Born in Warren, Rhode Island, on May 26, 1748, Barton was working as a hatter when the Revolution began. At the news of Bunker Hill he took up his musket and enlisted with the Rhode Island forces, quickly advancing to the rank of major by August 1776. In the spring of 1777 Brig. Gen. Richard Prescott became commander of the British occupation forces on the island of Rhode Island, and from his headquarters near Newport he made his presence oppressively felt. Barton conceived the idea of capturing Prescott and exchanging him for the imprisoned American Gen. Charles Lee. Handpicking 40 men from his regiment, he set out with 4 whaleboats, oars muffled, from Tiverton, which had become a refuge for Rhode Island patriots and armed forces, on the night of July 4, 1777. The party proceeded to Bristol, to Warwick Neck on the mainland, and then down Narragansett Bay, passing unobserved by three British frigates, and on the night of July 9 landed on the western shore of the island of Rhode Island, not far from Newport. They crept inland, overcame a sentinel posted outside Prescott's farmhouse headquarters, and burst in upon the sleeping general. Not allowing him even time to dress (a circumstance that, skillfully misinterpreted, added spice to the humor with which Prescott was subsequently handled by the London press), Barton and his men made away with Prescott to Warwick and then to Gen. George Washington's headquarters in New Jersey. The Prescott–Lee exchange was duly made in April 1778. The exploit won Barton honors from the Rhode Island General Assembly and from Congress, and in November 1777 he was promoted to lieutenant colonel. He served through the remainder of the war, being wounded during the British retreat from Warren in 1778. In 1790 he served in the Rhode Island constitutional ratifying convention. In 1811 he refused to pay a judgment on a tract of land in Vermont that he had acquired (possibly by congressional grant) and was detained in Danville, Vermont, until the Marquis de Lafayette, hearing of Barton's plight during his visit to the United States in 1825, paid the judgment and had him released. Barton returned to Providence, Rhode Island, and died there on October 22, 1831.

Bates, John Coalter (1842–1919), army officer. Born on August 26, 1842, in St. Charles County, Missouri, Bates was the son of Edward Bates, President Lincoln's attorney general. He attended Washington University for a time and in May 1861 joined the army, receiving a first lieutenant's commission in the 11th Infantry. He served with the Army of the Potomac throughout the Civil War; promoted to captain in 1863, he was brevetted major in August 1864 and lieutenant colonel in April 1865, the latter for his service as aide-de-camp to Gen. George G. Meade for two years. Bates remained in the army after Appomattox, spending the next 30-odd years at various posts in the West and advancing to major in May 1882, lieutenant colonel in October 1886, and colonel of the 2nd Infantry in April 1892. In May 1898, at the outbreak of the Spanish–American War, he was appointed brigadier general of volunteers and given command of what became known as Bates' Independent Brigade, nominally of the 3rd Division of Gen. William R. Shafter's V Corps. He was in command of the base at Siboney, Cuba, for a short time after landing on June 25, and on July 1 he joined Gen. Henry W. Lawton's 2nd Division for the attack on El Caney. During the last days of the campaign against Santiago in July he was promoted to major general of volunteers and put in command of the 3rd Division. In January–May 1899 he was again in Cuba as commander of the Department of Santa Clara. In April his major general's commission expired, and he was reappointed brigadier general of volunteers. He was then sent to the Philippines to command the 1st Division of Gen. Elwell S. Otis's VIII Corps, responsible for the Jolo and Mindanao districts. In August he negotiated a treaty with the sultan of Sulu wherein the latter recognized American sovereignty (he had never recognized Spanish). He was promoted to major general of volunteers once again in January 1900. In February 1901 he became regular brigadier general and in July 1902 major general. In January 1906 he was named chief of staff of the army with rank of lieutenant general. He was retired at his own request

on April 14, 1906. Bates died in San Diego on February 4, 1919.

Beach, Edward Latimer (1918–   ), naval officer and author. Born in New York City on April 20, 1918, Beach was the son and namesake of a naval officer and writer of boys' books on navy life. He graduated from the Naval Academy in 1939 and, after sea duty aboard the *Chester* and the *Lea,* attended submarine school in 1941. Throughout World War II he served on submarines, the *Trigger* 1942–1944 and the *Tirante* 1944–1945. From June 1945 he was in command of the *Piper,* the last submarine to return from patrol at war's end. Beach received numerous citations and decorations for his war service. While on duty at the Navy Department he began to write of his experiences, and after a tour in command of the submarine *Amberjack,* 1948–1949, and a period as naval aide to Gen. Omar Bradley, chairman of the Joint Chiefs of Staff, 1949–1951, his first book was published as *Submarine!,* 1952. During 1952–1953 he was again at sea in command of the new *Trigger,* and from 1953 to 1957 he was naval aide to President Eisenhower. In 1955 he published a novel about wartime submarine duty, *Run Silent, Run Deep,* that was a best-seller and was made into a popular motion picture. Beach was promoted to captain in 1956. He commanded a tanker briefly after leaving the White House staff and was then attached to the nuclear submarine development program of the Atomic Energy Commission. Early in 1960 he took command of the nuclear submarine *Triton,* which during February –May made a record 84-day submerged cruise, circumnavigating the globe along the track of Magellan's historic voyage, more than 41,000 miles without surfacing. He remained with the *Triton* until 1961. Beach retired from the navy in December 1966; he was at the time attached to the staff of the chief of naval operations, Adm. David L. McDonald.

Beaumont, William (1785–1853), army surgeon. Born on November 21, 1785, in Lebanon, Connecticut, Beaumont was apprenticed in 1810 to a Vermont surgeon and was licensed to practice medicine two years later. He served as a surgeon's mate in the 6th Infantry during the War of 1812, and after four years of private practice in Plattsburgh, New York, he enlisted for a second time in 1819 and was sent to Fort Mackinac in Michigan Territory as post surgeon. In June 1822 he treated a young Canadian trapper, Alexis St. Martin, for a gunshot wound that had both exposed and punctured the stomach, leaving a flap through which the interior could be seen. He restored the man to health but was unable to close the wound. About 1825 it occurred to Beaumont to take advantage of St. Martin's condition to study the action of the stomach in a living man. Soon after he began his observations, however, St. Martin ran away and it was not until 1829 that Beaumont, then at Fort Crawford, in Wisconsin Territory, located him and persuaded him to return. There, and later in Washington, D.C., Beaumont pursued his investigations, with the support of the surgeon general of the army, Joseph Lovell. To his earlier findings—on the movements of the stomach during digestion, the relative digestibility of various foods, and the ability of gastric juice to digest food even outside the body—he added further knowledge of the nature of the gastric juice itself. A collaborator, Professor Robley Dunglison of the University of Virginia, determined that the principal constituent was free hydrochloric acid and suggested the presence of another chemical (much later shown to be pepsin) that then defied analysis. Beaumont's work was summed up in his classic *Experiments and Observations on the Gastric Juice and the Physiology of Digestion*, 1833. In 1834 St. Martin, having borne years of Beaumont's experiments and even having submitted to enlistment in the army in 1832, returned to Canada and thereafter refused to participate in further experiments; in the same year Beaumont was transferred to St. Louis. He resigned from the army in 1840 and carried on a private practice until his death in St. Louis on April 25, 1853. St. Martin outlived him by twenty years.

Beauregard, Pierre Gustave Toutant (1818–1893), Confederate army officer.

Born near New Orleans on May 28, 1818, Beauregard graduated from West Point in 1838 and was commissioned in the engineers. For several years he was engaged in work on fortifications in various places. In the Mexican War he saw action at Veracruz, Cerro Gordo, Contreras, and Mexico City and was twice rewarded by brevet promotions. He was promoted to captain in March 1853. He was then stationed in Louisiana until his appointment as superintendent of West Point. He served less than a week in that post in January 1861, being reassigned following his declaration of intent to follow his native state should it secede. He resigned his commission in February 1861 to become a brigadier general in the Confederate army. Placed in command of Charleston, South Carolina, he gave the order for the firing on Fort Sumter on April 12. He was then made second in command, under Gen. Joseph E. Johnston, of the Confederate forces in Virginia, having command of an army assembled near the important rail center at Manassas, while Johnston was with a second army in the Shenandoah valley. On the approach of Union forces under Gen. Irvin McDowell in July, Johnston hurried to Manassas, deferring to Beauregard's familiarity with the territory in planning troop deployment and movement. On July 21 McDowell attacked across Bull Run Creek, but tentatively and without conviction. Both armies were untrained, but the Confederates, with the advantage of defensive position, repulsed the attack, and, though their staff work was poor, took advantage of the Union's even poorer organization to turn a Union fallback into a panic-stricken rout. Beauregard, in personal command of the Confederate left, was prominent in the field, had a horse shot out from under him, and was a hero of the day. Promoted to full general, he joined Gen. Albert S. Johnston in Tennessee in 1862 and on April 6 at Pittsburg Landing (Shiloh) succeeded to command of the Army of Mississippi upon Johnston's death. He was compelled to give up the field the next day on the approach of fresh Union forces under Gen. Don Carlos Buell; he fell back to Corinth, Mississippi, and thence southward. Falling ill, he turned over his command to Gen. Braxton Bragg. In August he took charge of the coastal defense of Georgia and South Carolina and through 1863 and into 1864 successfully repelled Union attacks, particularly at Charleston. Beauregard was then sent to defend Richmond against the Army of the James under Gen. Benjamin F. Butler, whom he defeated at Drewry's Bluff, May 12–16, and then finally against Gen. Ulysses S. Grant, against whom he set up defenses at Petersburg. He turned his forces over to Gen. Robert E. Lee at that point, served again for a time in the West, and at the end of the war was with Gen. Joseph E. Johnston's Army of Tennessee in the Carolinas. After the war he was for five years president of the New Orleans, Jackson & Mississippi Railway and thereafter served variously as manager of the Louisiana lottery, commissioner of public works for New Orleans, and state adjutant general. He wrote numerous books and articles on military affairs, including *Principles and Maxims of the Art of War*, 1863; *Report on the Defense of Charleston*, 1864; and *A Commentary on the Campaign and Battle of Manassas*, 1891. Beauregard died in New Orleans, Louisiana, on February 20, 1893.

Bee, Barnard Elliott (1824–1861), Confederate army officer.

Born early in 1824 in Charleston, South Carolina, Bee moved with his family to Texas in 1835. He graduated from West Point in 1845, was commissioned in the 3rd Infantry, and was off almost immediately to the Mexican War. He saw action under Gen. Zachary Taylor at Palo Alto, May 8, 1846, and Resaca de la Palma, May 9, and under Gen. Winfield Scott at Cerro Gordo, where he was brevetted first lieutenant, April 18, 1847, Chapultepec, where he was brevetted captain, September 13, and Mexico City. After the war he was on frontier duty, advancing to first lieutenant in 1851 and to captain in the new 10th Infantry in 1855, but in March 1861 he resigned his commission and was appointed a major and then in June a brigadier general in the Confederate army. On July 21 he was in command of a brigade of Gen. Joseph E. Johnston's army at the first battle of Manassas (Bull Run); his inexperienced men faced the heaviest part of the first Union attack at the Henry house, and, in a desperate effort to maintain their courage, Bee pointed to a nearby brigade and its commander, crying "Let us determine to die here, and we will conquer. There is Jackson's Brigade, standing like a stone wall. Rally behind the Virginians!" The second sentence gave Gen. Thomas J. Jackson the nickname by which he was afterwards known. Bee managed to hold his command together, even though nearly all his officers had been killed, until reinforcements were brought up. He was seriously wounded a short time later and died the next day, July 22, 1861.

Beecher, Frederick Henry (1841–1868), army officer. Born in New Orleans on June 22, 1841, Beecher was a grandson of the famed clergyman Lyman Beecher. He graduated from Bowdoin College in 1862 and immediately entered the army. He served with the Army of the Potomac and was twice severely wounded; after Gettysburg he was transferred to the veteran reserve corps until he recuperated. In 1864 he was commissioned second lieutenant in the regular army, and in July 1866, having remained in the army after the close of the Civil War, he advanced to first lieutenant. On duty on the western frontier, he was selected by Maj. George A. Forsyth of the 9th Cavalry as second in command of a party of 50 scouts from Fort Harker and Fort Hays, Kansas, ordered by Gen. Philip H. Sheridan to operate against the Indians of the region. Late in 1868 the party was patrolling on the Arickaree Fork of the Republican River just over the border into Colorado Territory. At dawn on September 17 they were attacked by a band of nearly 1000 Indians—Cheyenne, Sioux, and Arapaho—under chief Roman Nose. Retreating to a small sandy island in the river bed, the scouts dug in. In the first charge of the Indians Forsyth was wounded and Beecher was killed, as was Roman Nose. Four more of the soldiers died during three days of fighting and several more under siege. Their horses killed, and without food, their only hope was for messengers sent out under cover of night to find help. On the ninth day they were rescued by a company of black troopers of the 10th Cavalry from Fort Wallace, Kansas. The engagement became widely known as the Battle of Beecher Island.

Bell, James Franklin (1856–1919), army officer. Born near Shelbyville, Kentucky, on January 9, 1856, Bell graduated from West Point in 1878 and was commissioned in the cavalry. His first post was with the 7th Cavalry at Fort Abraham Lincoln, Dakota Territory. Frontier duty was broken by an assignment as instructor of military science and tactics at Southern Illinois Normal University, 1886–1889, and he was absent on leave from his regiment at the time of the Wounded Knee massacre in December 1890. Promoted to first lieutenant in the latter year, he took part in the campaign around Pine Ridge, South Dakota, in 1891 and later in that year joined the staff of the Cavalry and Light Artillery School, Fort Riley, Kansas. Bell was detailed to the staff of Gen. James W. Forsyth, Department of California, in 1894; to Fort Apache, Arizona Territory, in 1897; and to the Department of Columbia as judge advocate in 1898. A few months later, appointed major of volunteers, he was ordered to the Philippines with Gen. Wesley Merritt's VIII Corps. Promoted to regular captain in March 1899, he served with great distinction during the insurrection, part of the time as chief of scouts under Gen. Arthur MacArthur. In July he was appointed colonel of the 36th Infantry Volunteers, and on September 9, 1899, he earned the Medal of Honor in charging a Filipino patrol. In December 1899 he was appointed brigadier general of volunteers; he subsequently commanded various districts on Luzon and served for a time as provost marshal general for Manila. He was promoted to brigadier general in the regular army in February 1901; in July 1903 he returned to the United States to take command of the General Service and Staff College at Fort Leavenworth, Kansas. From April 1906 to April 1910 Bell was chief of staff of the army, with rank of major general from January 1907. From 1911 to 1914 he commanded the Philippine Department. Subsequent commands were of the 2nd Division, at Texas City, Texas, 1914–1915; Western Department, 1915–1917; and Eastern Department from 1917. The last command was interrupted by a training assignment with the newly formed 77th Division in 1917 and an observation mission to France in 1917–1918. Bell died on January 8, 1919, in New York City.

Bellinger, Patrick Neison Lynch (1885–1962), naval officer. Born on October 8, 1885, in Cheraw, South Carolina, Bellinger graduated from the Naval Academy in 1907. He early took an interest in aviation and in 1912 was among the first group of seven navy pilots to be certified. In April 1914, during the occupation of Veracruz, Mexico, he flew reconnaissance missions off the *Mississippi* and became the first navy pilot to come home with enemy bullet holes in his airplane. He set an altitude record of 10,000 feet in 1915 and experimented constantly with bombing techniques, catapult takeoffs at sea, and flight instruments. During World War I he commanded the naval air station at Hampton Roads, Virginia, and there began preparing for a transatlantic flight. The attempt was delayed until 1919, but on May 8 three Glenn Curtiss-built planes took off from Rockaway, Long Island. Bellinger, then a lieutenant, piloted the NC-1, accompanied by Lt. Marc A. Mitscher; forced down in a fog 100 miles west of the Azores, they were picked up by a Greek steamer shortly before the plane sank in a heavy sea. (The NC-3 also went down; the NC-4, piloted by Lt. Albert C. Read, completed the flight.) By 1940 Bellinger had advanced to the rank of rear admiral in command of Patrol Wing 2 based in Honolulu. He was the senior air officer present at the Japanese attack on Pearl Harbor and himself sent out the first radio alert: "Air raid, Pearl Harbor—this is no drill." In May 1942 he took command of all patrol wings in the Pacific, and in August he became chief of staff to the commander in chief of the U.S. fleet, Adm. Ernest J. King. In March 1943 Bellinger was given command of the Atlantic Fleet Air Force, with primary responsibility for antisubmarine patrols throughout the Atlantic. He was promoted to vice admiral in October. He retired in 1949 and died in Clifton Forge, Virginia, on May 30, 1962.

Bennett, Floyd (1890–1928), aviator. Born near Warrensburg, New York, on October 25, 1890, Bennett left school at seventeen and became an automobile mechanic and part owner of a service garage. In 1917 he enlisted in the navy and signed up for aviation training, but although he became a capable pilot he was retained in the service only as an aviation mechanic. His chance came in 1925 when he was assigned to duty with Lt. Cmdr. Richard E. Byrd's naval aviation group attached to D. B. MacMillan's expedition to Greenland in that year. Both his character and his ability caught the attention of his commander, and he soon became Byrd's close friend and personal pilot. Together they planned a flight over the North Pole; and on a second expedition in the next year they carried out the plan, flying a three-engine Fokker monoplane, the *Josephine Ford*, from Spitsbergen to the Pole and back on May 9. Both men were awarded the Medal of Honor for their feat, one of the rare peacetime awards of that highest honor. Byrd was promoted to commander and Bennett, by special act of Congress, to warrant machinist. Bennett and Byrd then began preparing for an air crossing of the Atlantic in their plane, the *America.* But Bennett suffered serious injuries when the *America* crashed on its first test flight in April 1927 and the attempt was delayed, opening the way for Charles A. Lindbergh to make the first transatlantic flight. Bennett was appointed second in command of Byrd's 1928–1930 expedition to the South Pole, most of the details of which he had planned. Before the expedition set out, he and Berndt Balchen set out to salvage the *Bremen,* first aircraft to cross the Atlantic westwards, which had gone down off the coast of Labrador. On the way he fell ill and died in Quebec on April 25, 1928. He was mourned throughout the United States as a national hero.

Benning, Henry Lewis (1814–1875), public official and Confederate army officer. Born on April 2, 1814, in Columbia County, Georgia, Benning settled in Columbus, Georgia, after graduating from Frank-

lin College (now the University of Georgia) in 1834. In 1835 he was admitted to the bar. He early became convinced that the secession of the southern states from the Union was necessary for the protection of slavery, though he differed from many other secessionists in favoring a strong central government for the seceded states. He was a delegate to the Southern convention at Nashville in 1850, introducing a resolution, subsequently passed, that called for the restoration of the Missouri Compromise line and in effect repudiating the Compromise of 1850. He was unable to secure Georgia's ratification of the resolution, which he believed would lead ultimately to secession. In 1851 he was defeated as a Southern-Rights Democratic candidate for Congress. From 1853 to 1859 he was a justice of the state supreme court, which he declared in one opinion to be coequal with the U.S. Supreme Court. In 1860 he served as vice-president of the Democratic convention at Baltimore which nominated Stephen A. Douglas. In 1861 he was prominent in the Georgia convention called to adopt an ordinance of secession. Shortly thereafter Benning raised a regiment in Columbus and served as its colonel, later being promoted to brigadier general. He fought with distinction through the Civil War, particularly distinguishing himself at Sharpsburg (Antietam); at Chickamauga, where he had two horses shot from under him and rode a third bareback into the battle again; at Gettysburg; and at Petersburg. He was wounded in the Wilderness campaign. After the war he returned to the practice of law in Columbus, where he died on July 10, 1875. In October 1918, during the mobilization for World War I, a new army base was established near Columbus and named Fort Benning in his honor; it remained thereafter the home of the Infantry School.

Benson, William Shepherd (1855–1932), naval officer. Born in Bibb County, Georgia, on September 25, 1855, Benson graduated from the Naval Academy in 1877. He saw his first sea duty on the *Hartford* in the South Atlantic Squadron. He subsequently served aboard the old *Constitution,* the *Yantic* during the Arctic expedition of Lt. Adolphus W. Greely, the *Dolphin* in 1888–1889, and the *Chicago* in 1898–1899. He advanced in rank to ensign in 1881, lieutenant in 1893, lieutenant commander in 1900, commander in 1905, and captain in July 1909. During 1909–1910 he was chief of staff of the Pacific Fleet, at the same time commanding the *Albany.* From 1911 to 1913 he commanded the great *Utah,* largest warship in the world. His assignments ashore included various posts at the Naval Academy, including instructor in 1890–1893 and 1896–1898 and commandant of midshipmen in 1907–1908, and command of the Philadelphia navy yard from 1913 to 1915. In May 1915 he was appointed to the newly created post of chief of naval operations (CNO), with the task of creating, within limits set by the civilian administration (Secretary of the Navy Josephus Daniels, Assistant Secretary Franklin D. Roosevelt) a central staff, somewhat akin to the army's General Staff, for coordinating the navy's training, supply, and planning. Benson, who was promoted to rear admiral in May and to admiral the following year, contributed greatly to the improved efficiency and battle-readiness of the navy. During his time as CNO significant steps were taken toward developing aircraft and submarine forces for the navy. He was abroad in 1917 and again in 1918 as the American naval representative in Allied war planning councils, and in 1919 he was the naval adviser to the American delegation at the Versailles peace treaty conference. He retired at the rank of rear admiral on reaching the statutory age of 64 in September 1919. From 1920 to 1928 he served as chairman of the U.S. Shipping Board, and from 1920 to 1921 he was a trustee of the Emergency Fleet Corporation. He published *The Merchant Marine* in 1923. From 1921 to 1925 he was first president of the National Council of Catholic Men. Benson was advanced to the rank of admiral on the retired list in June 1930; he died in Washington, D.C., on May 20, 1932.

Benton, James Gilchrist (1820–1881), army officer. Born on September 15, 1820, in Lebanon, New Hampshire, Benton graduated from West Point in 1842 and was assigned to the Ordnance Corps. After six years duty at the Watervliet arsenal, New York, he was promoted to first lieutenant in March 1848. Following a brief period in Washington, D.C., he was stationed at arsenals in Harpers Ferry, San Antonio, and Charleston between 1849 and 1853. He was again in Washington until 1857, working on the design of a rifled barrel for refitting the smoothbore muskets then manufactured at the national armory in Springfield, Massachusetts. In July 1856 he was promoted to captain. From 1857 to 1861 he was an instructor of ordnance and gunnery at West Point, publishing in the latter year *A Course of Instruction in Ordnance and Gunnery.* From April 1861 to 1863 he was assistant to Gen. J. W. Ripley, the chief of ordnance, in Washington, and in September 1863 he was promoted to major and given command of the Washington arsenal. He was brevetted lieutenant colonel and colonel in March 1865. From June 1866 until his death Benton commanded the Springfield armory. He contributed largely to the development and supervised the production of the Springfield rifle models of 1866, 1868, 1873, and 1879 and invented a number of useful devices for use in ordnance work, including the Benton electro-ballistic pendulum for testing powder, a thread velocimeter and an electro-ballistic "chronograph" for measuring the velocity of shells, a spring dynamometer, improved calipers for inspecting shells, a cap-filling device, and others. None of his

inventions was patented, in his belief that the government deserved full benefit of them. He was promoted to lieutenant colonel in June 1874 and colonel in May 1875. Benton died in Springfield, Massachusetts, on August 23, 1881.

Bernard, Simon (1779–1839), military engineer. Born on April 22, 1779, in Dôle, France, Bernard graduated from the École Polytechnique, Paris, in 1797 and was commissioned a lieutenant of engineers. He served under Napoleon in the Army of the Rhine and in the northern Italian campaign of 1796–1797 and was promoted to captain in 1800. His successful completion of a secret reconnoitering mission in Austria in 1805 brought him to the attention of the emperor, who gave him command of the topographical bureau. From 1810 to 1812 he was engaged in the fortification of Antwerp, and in 1813 he became colonel and aide-de-camp to Napoleon. Soon after his defense of Torgau in that year he was promoted to lieutenant general of engineers. During Napoleon's exile Bernard served Louis XVIII as brigadier general, and on Napoleon's return he rejoined him, remaining with him to the end at Waterloo. He again entered royal service and soon obtained permission to go to the United States. In the aftermath of the War of 1812 Congress was much concerned with the low state of coastal defenses, and in April 1816 it appropriated a large sum for a thorough survey of the nation's requirements. A few days afterward a resolution was passed empowering President Madison to commission Bernard "assistant in the corps of engineers . . . with the rank of brigadier general by brevet." This somewhat anomalous commission, granted in November 1816, led to considerable friction in the engineering corps, culminating in the resignation of two senior officers in 1818. Bernard, together with Maj. Joseph G. Totten, constituted a permanent board of engineering for coastal defense, to which other army and navy officers were attached as needed. They worked out a comprehensive system of defense involving fortifications, canals, and roads, for which Congress, at the urging of Secretary of War John C. Calhoun, made large appropriations. Bernard's major work was the design of Fort Monroe, the greatest fortified work in the nation, which was begun in 1819 at Old Point Comfort, Virginia, and completed in 1847. In 1830 Bernard returned to France, was appointed lieutenant general by Louis Philippe, and charged with preparing the defenses of Paris. He served as inspector general of engineers and as minister of war in 1834 and from 1836 to 1839. He died in Paris on November 5, 1839.

Bickerdyke, Mary Ann Ball (1817–1901), hospital worker. Born on July 19, 1817, in Knox County, Ohio, Mary Ann Ball grew up in the houses of various relatives. In Cincinnati in 1847 she married a widower, Robert Bickerdyke; the couple moved in 1856 to Galesburg, Illinois, where Bickerdyke died in 1859. Mrs. Bickerdyke supported herself by the practice of "botanic" medicine. Soon after the outbreak of the Civil War she volunteered to accompany and distribute a collection of supplies taken up for the relief of wounded soldiers at a makeshift army hospital in Cairo, Illinois. On her arrival there she found conditions to be primitive in the extreme, and she set to work immediately at cleaning, cooking, and caring for the men. She became matron when a general hospital was organized there in November 1861. Following the fall of Fort Donelson in February 1862 she made a number of forays onto the battlefield to search for wounded, and her exploits began to attract general attention. Her alliance with the U.S. Sanitary Commission began about that time. Mrs. Bickerdyke soon attached herself to the staff of Gen. Ulysses S. Grant, by whom she was given a pass for free transportation anywhere in his command; she used it unsparingly in order to be at the front, where her services were most needed. From Shiloh through the campaigning in Tennessee, Kentucky, and Mississippi she worked prodigies of organization, scavenging supplies and equipment, establishing mobile laundries and kitchens, and endearing herself to the wounded and sick as "Mother" Bickerdyke. To incompetent officers and physicians she was brutal, succeeding in having several dismissed, and she retained her position largely through the influence of Grant, Gen. William T. Sherman, and others who properly valued her work. Late in 1862 and again in 1864 she made speaking tours of midwestern and northern cities on behalf of the Sanitary Commission. At other times she remained in the field, with Sherman's Army of the Tennessee from Vicksburg through Tennessee to Georgia and again from Wilmington, North Carolina, to Beaufort, where she was at work at war's end. During 1866–1867 she worked with the Chicago Home for the Friendless, and in 1867, in connection with a plan to settle veterans on Kansas farmland, she opened a boarding house in Salina with backing from the Kansas Pacific Railroad. The venture failed in 1869, and in 1870 she went to New York City to work for the Protestant Board of City Missions. In 1874 she returned to Kansas, where her sons lived, and made herself conspicuously useful in relieving the victims of locust plague. In 1876 she removed to San Francisco, where she secured through Sen. John A. Logan, another wartime patron, a position at the U.S. Mint. She also devoted considerable time to the Salvation Army and similar organizations. She worked tirelessly on behalf of veterans, making numerous trips to Washington to press pension claims, and was herself granted a pension of $25 a month by Congress in 1886. She returned to Kansas in 1887 and died in Bunker Hill on November 8, 1901.

Biddle, James (1783–1848), naval officer. Born on February 18, 1783, in Philadelphia, Biddle entered the navy as a midshipman in 1800 and was assigned to the *President* under Commodore Thomas Truxtun. He was retained in the service despite a reduction of the navy in the following year and served on the *Constellation* of Commodore Richard V. Morris's squadron in the Mediterranean in 1802. In 1803, during the war against the Barbary states, he was transferred to Capt. William Bainbridge's *Philadelphia* and was aboard when the ship ran aground off Tripoli in October; with Bainbridge and the rest of the crew he was imprisoned for a year and a half. Promoted to lieutenant and given command of a coastal gunboat upon his release, he was on duty against West Indian privateers until 1807, when he took a leave of absence and sailed to China on a merchant vessel. Returning to active service, he engaged in enforcement of the embargo against foreign commerce and then, from 1809 (when the embargo was repealed), served on the *President* and other warships. His first command was the sloop *Syren* in 1810. In 1812 he was appointed first lieutenant of the sloop *Wasp* under Master Commandant Jacob Jones; after the *Wasp's* celebrated capture of the more heavily armed British *Frolic* on October 18 he was detached to bring the prize into port, but both the *Frolic* and the *Wasp* were taken by the 74-gun *Poictiers* and he was imprisoned in Bermuda until March 1813. Promoted to master commandant and given the sloop *Hornet*, 20 guns, Biddle escaped the British blockade of New London, Connecticut, and set sail for Tristan da Cunha. On March 23, 1815, he engaged and destroyed the *Penguin*, 19, and then, in the last naval encounter of the War of 1812, made a skillful escape from a much larger British ship of the line in April 1815. Promoted to captain while at sea, he returned to a hero's welcome in New York City. In 1817, commanding the sloop of war *Ontario*, he was sent to the Columbia River to lay formal claim to the Oregon Territory. En route he engaged in highly successful diplomacy with Spanish authorities in Chile and Peru. He arrived at the mouth of the Columbia River in August 1818 and laid claim by nailing a lead plate, suitably inscribed, to a tree (the region did not actually become part of the United States for 30 years). For the next 25 years he saw duty in South American waters, the Caribbean, and the Mediterranean, and also served as head of the Naval Asylum in Philadelphia. He was the first commander of the West India Squadron when it was established in 1822 to patrol against pirates. In 1845, as commodore of the East India Squadron, he helped negotiate the first treaty between China and the United States, establishing a legation in Canton and acting as U.S. commissioner there until April 1846. He then attempted unsuccessfully to open relations with Japan. After briefly commanding Pacific coast naval forces during the Mexican War, January–July 1847, he relinquished them to Commodore William B. Shubrick and resumed his interrupted return to Philadelphia, where he died on October 1, 1848.

Biddle, Nicholas (1750–1778), naval officer. Born in Philadelphia on September 10, 1750, Biddle went to sea in the merchant service at the age of thirteen. He had acquired much experience, including that of shipwreck, by the time he entered the British navy in 1770. In 1773 he left that service in order to join an arctic expedition of the Royal Geographic Society under Capt. Constantine John Phipps (later the second Baron Mulgrave); in the expedition he met young Horatio Nelson, who had done likewise. At the end of the voyage, with the revolt of the American colonies looming, he returned home and offered his services. In August 1775 he took command of the *Franklin,* a riverboat outfitted by the state of Pennsylvania for the defense of the Delaware River. In December he was one of five Continental navy captains commissioned by Congress and was given the *Andrew Doria,* a small brig of 14 guns, in which he took part in the capture of New Providence Island, Bahamas, in February 1776 by the Continental fleet under Esek Hopkins. He then cruised the North Atlantic in search of prizes, and he took so many, including two armed troop transports encountered off the coast of Newfoundland, that on his return to port it was said that only 5 of his 130 crewmen were still aboard the *Andrew Doria,* the rest having been put aboard prizes. In June 1776 he took command of the newly completed frigate *Randolph,* 32 guns, and in February 1777 he set out from Philadelphia for Martinique. The discovery that the masts had been made of rotten wood obliged him to put into Charleston, South Carolina, for repairs. These made, he made a cruise of the West Indies, returning to Charleston with four prizes including the *True Briton,* 20. The *Randolph* was blockaded in Charleston harbor for several months, but on February 12, 1778, Biddle stood out to sea accompanied by the *General Moultrie,* 18, *Notre Dame,* 16, *Polly,* 16, and *Fair American,* 14, all provided him by the state of South Carolina. On March 7, sailing near Barbados, the small fleet fell in with the British two-decker *Yarmouth,* 64 guns. The fight lasted twenty minutes. Biddle was badly wounded early and directed the battle from a chair on deck. The smaller boats could not get in range, except for the *General Moultrie,* which fired into the *Randolph* by mistake. Though heavily outweighed, the *Randolph* inflicted severe damage on the *Yarmouth* before she suddenly blew up, killing Biddle and all but 4 of the *Randolph's* 315 officers and men.

Biddle, William Phillips (1853–1923), marine officer. Born on December 17, 1853, in Philadelphia, Biddle graduated from the University of Pennsylvania in 1875 and was commissioned a second lieu-

tenant in the marine corps. He advanced to first lieutenant in 1884 and to captain in 1894. He was in command of the detachment of marines aboard the cruiser *Olympia,* Commodore George Dewey's flagship, at the battle of Manila Bay in May 1898. Promoted to major in 1899, in 1900 he commanded the 1st Regiment, 1st Marine Brigade, in the Peking Relief Expedition during the Boxer rebellion. He was in command of the marine barracks at Cavite, the naval base in Manila Bay, Philippines, until 1903, in which year he was promoted to lieutenant colonel. During 1903–1904 he commanded his regiment in Panama, then in the throes of revolution, and from 1904 to 1906 he had charge of the marine barracks in Philadelphia, advancing to the rank of colonel in 1905. He commanded the 1st Brigade in Manila, 1906–1908, and the marine barracks in New York, 1908–1909; he was again in Panama, 1909–1910. In February 1911 Biddle was promoted to major general and commandant of the marine corps. He held that post for three years, until his retirement in February 1914. He returned to active duty at the San Diego naval base during World War I. He died in Nice, France, on February 25, 1923.

Black Hawk (1767–1838), Indian leader. Born in 1767 in the Sauk village on the Rock River near the present Rock Island, Illinois, Makataimeshekiakiak, or Black Sparrow Hawk, succeeded his father as a chief of the Sauk about 1788. He resented the Americans as dispossessors of the Spanish, with whom his people had traded since 1769. His hatred grew when members of the Sauk and Fox tribes were persuaded by William Henry Harrison, governor of Indiana Territory, to sign the treaty of 1804, ceding all of their lands east of the Mississippi River to the United States. In the War of 1812 he aided the British, serving under the command of the Shawnee chief Tecumseh, and then, with encouragement from the British, attempted to rally other tribes against the Americans to halt westward expansion. His rival Sauk chief, Keokuk, had accepted American rule and under the treaty of 1804 and subsequent ones confirming it had moved to lands in Iowa. In April 1832 Black Hawk led about 1000 of his people back to resettle their disputed homeland in Illinois, hoping to plant crops and avoid the settlers. Alarmed at the "invasion," Gov. John Reynolds summoned federal troops, which arrived at Rock River under the command of Gen. Henry Atkinson. Expected aid from the Winnebago and other tribes failed to materialize, and two Indian envoys were dispatched to confer with Atkinson. They were shot by Illinois volunteers; thus began the so-called Black Hawk War. Retreating northward through the Rock River valley, the Indians were slaughtered in the battle at Bad Axe River, in Wisconsin, on August 2, 1832. Black Hawk was captured and imprisoned. He was taken to meet

President Andrew Jackson in 1833, and in the same year he dictated an autobiography that is considered to be a classic statement of Indian resentment against white interlopers. Meanwhile a new treaty in September 1832 marked the first cession of Indian land in Iowa. In 1834 he was given over to the custody of Keokuk, in whose village near the Des Moines River in Iowa he died, on October 3, 1838.

Blakely, Johnston (1781–1814), naval officer. Born in October 1781 in County Down, Ireland, Blakely came with his family to America in 1783 and settled in Wilmington, North Carolina. He entered the University of North Carolina in 1797, but the death of his father and subsequent financial difficulties forced him to give up college; in February 1800 he entered the navy as a midshipman. He served in the Mediterranean Squadron, on the *President*, the *John Adams*, and the *Congress*, during the Tripolitan War and in February 1807 was promoted to lieutenant. During 1811–1813 he commanded the *Enterprise*. In July 1813 he was promoted to master-commandant and given command of the sloop of war *Wasp*, 22 guns. He sailed from Portsmouth, New Hampshire, in May 1814, captured several prizes, and in the English Channel on June 28 fell in with the British brig *Reindeer*, 18. In a sharp action the *Reindeer* attempted three times to board, her captain being killed on the third attempt, whereupon she surrendered. She was so badly damaged that Blakely burned her. He put into L'Orient, France, to refit and in August returned to sea. After taking more prizes he fell in with the brig *Avon*, 18, on September 1 and in a brisk night engagement compelled her to surrender. But before he could take possession, he was forced off by the approach of three British vessels. The *Avon* nonetheless sank a short time later. Bearing south, Blakely took more prizes and on September 21 captured the brig *Atalanta* and sent her home with a prize crew. The *Wasp* was at that time just east of Madeira; on October 9, 1814, she was spoken by a Swedish vessel some 900 miles further south, but nothing was ever heard of her again. As a result of his victory over the *Avon*, news of which was brought into Savannah early in November by the *Atalanta*, Blakely was promoted to captain on November 24 and was also voted a medal and the thanks of Congress for the victory over the *Reindeer*, all before his loss was known.

Blanchfield, Florence A. (1884–1971), nurse and army officer. Born in Shepherdstown, West Virginia, on April 1, 1884, Florence Blanchfield was educated at business college in Pittsburgh and at the University of California and Columbia University. In 1906 she graduated from the South Side Training School for Nurses in Pittsburgh. After additional training at the Johns Hopkins Hospital, she entered

upon a succession of posts in Pittsburgh, in the Canal Zone in 1913, at the United States Steel plant in Bessemer, Pennsylvania, and as superintendent of nurses at Suburban General Hospital in Bellevue, Pennsylvania in 1916. In August 1917 she enlisted in the Army Nurse Corps, and she served in France until 1919. Subsequently she was assigned to army hospitals in Michigan, California, the Philippines, Washington, D.C., Georgia, Missouri, and China; she served for a time also in the office of the surgeon general. In March 1942 she was given a commission as lieutenant colonel to serve as assistant to Col. Julia Flikke, superintendent of the Army Nurse Corps. Because their ranks were found to be without legal basis, they were paid as major and lieutenant colonel, respectively, and when Blanchfield succeeded Flikke as superintendent in 1943, she made it one of her concerns to secure full rank, as opposed to relative rank (which consisted of the formality but not the pay or benefits of full rank), for army nurses. During World War II she supervised the worldwide work of some 60,000 nurses on all fronts. Her case for full rank was won on a temporary basis in 1944, and in April 1947 both the army and navy revised regulations to permit women to hold full rank. Colonel Blanchfield thereupon received from Gen. Dwight D. Eisenhower the first regular army commission to be awarded a woman. She retired in that year, living thereafter in Arlington, Virginia. She died in Washington, D.C., on May 12, 1971.

Bliss, Tasker Howard (1853–1930), army officer and diplomat. Born on December 31, 1853, in Lewisburg, Pennsylvania, Bliss transferred in his second year from the University of Lewisburg (now Bucknell University) to West Point, from which he graduated in 1875. After a year of service with the 1st Artillery he returned to West Point as an instructor, remaining for four years and receiving promotion to first lieutenant in July 1880, and then served at various army posts. In 1884–1885 he was adjutant of the Artillery School, Fort Monroe, Virginia. From 1885 to 1888 he taught military science at the Naval War College and in 1888 became aide-de-camp to the commanding general of the army, John M. Schofield, holding the position until the latter's retirement in 1895. Though still only a captain (from December 1892), he then became a special assistant to the secretary of war and in 1897 military attaché at the U.S. legation in Madrid. At the outbreak of the Spanish–American War in April 1898 he was recalled, promoted to major, and appointed chief of staff of Gen. James H. Wilson's 1st Division in the Puerto Rico campaign. In May 1898 he was appointed lieutenant colonel of volunteers. Late in 1898 he was placed in charge of the corrupt Cuban customs service and there established high standards of honesty and efficiency. In April 1901 he became brigadier general of volunteers. In 1902 he was called to Washington to serve on the War College Board, appointed to advise Secretary of War Elihu Root on the establishment of a general staff system. Later in the year, having been promoted to regular brigadier general in July, he returned to Cuba to negotiate a reciprocity treaty for Secretary of State John M. Hay. He became first commandant of the newly established Army War College in February 1903, and two years later he began four years of service in the Philippines, the last as commander of the entire division. Upon his return to the United States in 1909 he was again, June–December, commandant of the Army War College, and then served as commanding officer of various army departments and divisions (California, 1910–1911; West, 1911; East, 1911–1913; South, 1913–1915) and from February 1915 as assistant chief of staff of the army, receiving in November 1915 promotion to major general. In May 1917, shortly after the United States entered World War I, Bliss became assistant to Gen. Hugh L. Scott, chief of staff, and was acting chief much of the time until September, when he became chief of staff, taking rank as full general a month later. He was retained in that post beyond regular retirement age by special order of President Woodrow Wilson. Exercising his great administrative abilities to their utmost, he transformed the army from a small peacetime organization into a huge war machine, receiving invaluable aid in that task from his deputy (and successor), Gen. Peyton C. March. In addition he represented the United States on the supreme war council of the Allies, lending strong support there to the unified-command plan, the use of U.S. troops as a separate force, Wilson's Fourteen Points, and the idea of the League of Nations. In May 1918 he was relieved as chief of staff and given brevet rank of general in retirement. At the war's end he was a delegate to the Versailles Peace Conference. He served as governor of the Soldiers' Home in Washington from 1920 to 1927. Bliss died in Washington, D.C., on November 9, 1930.

Bomford, George (1780–1848), army officer. Born in New York City in 1780, Bomford was graduated from West Point in 1805 and commissioned a second lieutenant of engineers. From 1805 to 1808 he was assistant engineer on the fortifications in New York harbor, advancing to first lieutenant in 1806 and captain in 1808. From that year until 1810 he was engaged in similar work on Chesapeake Bay, and from 1810 to 1812 he was superintending engineer on Governors Island in New York harbor. In 1812 he was promoted to major and assigned to ordnance work, first as assistant commissary general of ordnance and then again in the engineers. He quickly became the foremost expert on ordnance in the country. He devised a bomb cannon, a heavy gun having characteristics of both the howitzer and the mortar, and

named it the "columbiad" after the poem by Joel Barlow. Columbiads remained standard artillery weapons until the Civil War. In February 1815 Bomford was promoted to lieutenant colonel. In 1821 the Ordnance Department became part of the Artillery Corps; Bomford headed the department from June of that year until May 1832, when he was promoted to colonel and placed in command of the newly organized, independent Ordnance Corps. From February 1842 he was also inspector of arsenals, ordnance, arms, and munitions of war. He had numerous business interests and for many years owned the estate near Washington, D.C., that had formerly been Joel Barlow's, whose wife and Bomford's were sisters. Bomford died while on a foundry inspection trip in Boston on March 25, 1848.

Bong, Richard Ira (1920–1945), army officer and airman. Born on September 24, 1920, in Superior, Wisconsin, Bong left Wisconsin State Teachers' College (now the University of Wisconsin-Superior) in May 1941, during his junior year, to enlist in the Army Air Corps. Commissioned second lieutenant in January 1942 on the completion of pilot training, he spent some months as a flight instructor before being sent to the Fifth Air Force in the Southwest Pacific in September 1942. He was soon a flight leader in his squadron, flying a P-38 "Lightning" against the Japanese and compiling a remarkable record of enemy aircraft shot down. During a second combat tour, February–May 1944, he served as assistant operations officer of the Fifth Air Force Fighter Command and continued as the leading American ace in the Pacific. He was promoted to major in April 1944. In October 1944 he returned for a third tour. Although he was assigned to gunnery instruction, he continually volunteered for combat missions, several of them under particularly hazardous conditions over Borneo and Leyte Gulf. During October–November alone he shot down at least 8 Japanese aircraft, bringing his total to 40. For his gallantry as the foremost American fighter pilot of the war, Bong was awarded the Medal of Honor in December 1944. In June 1945 he was assigned to duty as a test pilot for the air technical service command in Los Angeles; he was killed on August 6, 1945, in the crash of a jet-propelled P-80 aircraft he was testing near Los Angeles, California.

Bonneville, Benjamin Louis Eulalie de (1796–1878), army officer. Born in or near Paris on April 14, 1796, Bonneville was the son of a prominent French radical. Among the close friends of the family were the Marquis de Lafayette, the Marquis de Condorcet, and especially Thomas Paine, whom they followed to the United States in 1803. Bonneville graduated from West Point in 1815, was commissioned in the artillery, and after a few years of routine military assignments was sent to the frontier post of Fort Smith, Arkansas Territory, in 1821. Later transferred to Fort Gibson in what is now Oklahoma, he was put on detached duty in 1825 as aide to the visiting Lafayette; promoted to captain in October, he returned to Fort Gibson in 1826 after accompanying Lafayette back to France and remained there until 1830. After securing financial backing in New York City he took a leave of absence from the army in 1832 for the stated purpose of exploration in the West. With a company of more than a hundred men he established himself on the Green River in Wyoming and attempted to break into the fur trade. Lack of experience was largely responsible for his failure, and in 1835 he returned to the East to find that he had been dismissed from the army for overstaying his leave. Over some protest he won reinstatement from President Andrew Jackson in April 1836. Promoted to major in July 1845, he served in the Mexican War, seeing action at Veracruz, Cerro Gordo, and Molino del Rey, and for his actions at Contreras and Churubusco, August 19–20, 1847, received brevet rank of lieutenant colonel. He was promoted to regular lieutenant colonel in May 1849 and to colonel in February 1855. During 1856–1857 and 1858–1860 he commanded the army post at Santa Fe. He retired for disability in September 1861 but soon returned to active duty, with recruiting and garrison assignments in Missouri through the Civil War. Given the brevet rank of brigadier general in March 1865, he retired permanently in October 1866 and returned to Fort Smith, where he died on June 12, 1878. Bonneville's fame rested on his journals, edited by an enthusiastic Washington Irving and published in 1837 as *The Adventures of Captain Bonneville, U.S.A., in the Rocky Mountains and the Far West.* Later critics pointed out that, in his assumed role of explorer, Bonneville discovered little, owing in large part to the fact that his "exploration" expedition was in reality a commercial venture. Nonetheless he had at least conducted the first wagons over South Pass, later a landmark of the Oregon Trail; in addition, an exploring party sent out by Bonneville under J. R. Walker made the first crossing of the Sierra Nevadas into California and discovered the "Big Trees" (Sequoias).

Boone, Joel Thompson (1889–1974), physician and naval officer. Born on August 29, 1889, in St. Clair, Pennsylvania, Boone graduated from Mercersburg Academy in 1909 and from Hahnemann Medical College, Philadelphia, in 1913. In April 1914 he took a commission as lieutenant (junior grade) in the naval reserve medical corps, and after attending Naval Medical School he was commissioned lieutenant (junior grade) in the regular navy in May 1915. He served with a marine battalion sent to Haiti in 1915 and in 1916 was assigned to the battleship *Wyoming.* In August 1917 he was attached to the 6th

Marine Regiment, which became an element of the army's 2nd Division in combat in France. Boone advanced to assistant divisional surgeon, distinguishing himself at Belleau Wood in June 1918 and winning the Medal of Honor at Vierzy on July 19 in braving extremely heavy fire to dress wounds in an unprotected field, then twice making his way through explosive and gas barrages to replenish his supplies. After brief occupation duty he returned to the United States in February 1919 and was assigned to staff work in the Bureau of Medicine and Surgery. In May 1922 he was named medical officer aboard the presidential yacht *Mayflower* and as associate physician to President Warren G. Harding attended him during his last illness in 1923. He retained his post under President Coolidge and President Hoover, becoming chief White House medical officer in April 1929 and official physician to the White House, with temporary rank of captain, on creation of that title in May 1931. During the Hoover administration Boone instituted the well known "Medicine Ball Cabinet" as a fitness regimen for the President. In April 1933 he returned to regular duty, serving as force medical officer of the Fleet Marine Force, San Diego, from 1936 to 1938, aboard the carrier *Saratoga* in 1938–1939 and on the *Argonne* in 1940, and as senior medical officer at the San Diego Naval Air Station from 1940 to 1943. From May 1943 to April 1945 he commanded the naval hospital in Seattle, receiving promotion to commodore in March 1945, and in April he became fleet medical officer of Adm. William F. Halsey's Third Fleet. He was present at the Japanese surrender ceremony aboard the *Missouri* on September 2, 1945. Promoted to rear admiral (rank dating from May 1942), he became district medical officer, Eleventh Naval District, San Diego, in January 1946 and in April was named medical officer of the Western Sea Frontier. In addition he made numerous inspections and recommendations as medical adviser to the federal coal mines administrator in 1946–1947. In 1948 he was assigned to duty in the Department of Defense, and in March 1950 he became inspector general of the Naval Medical Bureau. Boone retired in the rank of vice admiral in November 1950; from January 1951 to February 1955 he was chief medical director of the Veterans' Administration. He died on April 2, 1974.

Borman, Frank (1928–   ), air force officer and astronaut. Born on March 14, 1928, in Gary, Indiana, Borman grew up from the age of five in Tucson, Arizona. He graduated from West Point in 1950, took his commission in the air force, and became a pilot in 1951. After duty with various fighter squadrons in the Philippines and the United States he resumed his education, taking an M.A. in aeronautical engineering from California Institute of Technology in 1957. From that year until 1960 he was an instructor in thermodynamics and fluid mechanics at West Point. After completing test pilot training at Edwards Air Force Base, California, in 1960, he became an instructor there. In September 1962 he was one of the second group of men to be chosen for astronaut training by the National Aeronautics and Space Administration (NASA). Promoted to colonel in 1965, he made his first space flight in December of that year in command of *Gemini 7*, with James A. Lovell, which in its record 14 days in orbit performed a rendezvous with *Gemini 6* (Walter M. Schirra and Thomas P. Stafford). Borman served on the board of review that investigated the disastrous fire in an Apollo test vehicle that killed three astronauts in January 1967. On December 21, 1968, *Apollo VIII* blasted off from Cape Kennedy, commanded by Borman, with William A. Anders and Lovell completing the crew. Early on December 24 the three became the first men to leave earth's gravity field, and later in the day they entered lunar orbit. In the midst of their photographic and scientific work they made a television broadcast to viewers on earth on Christmas Eve, during which Borman led in a reading from Genesis, a decision that occasioned some controversy. *Apollo VIII* splashed down in the Pacific on schedule on December 27 and was recovered by the carrier *Yorktown*. In January 1969 Borman left the astronaut corps and became NASA deputy director of flight operations. In 1970 he retired from the air force and from NASA and joined Eastern Air Lines as senior vice-president for operations. He became president of Eastern in 1975. In that post he achieved a remarkable improvement in the airline's performance and made himself the firm's chief public representative in advertisements.

Bouquet, Henry (1719–1765), British army officer. Born in 1719 in Rolle, Switzerland, Bouquet entered the service of Holland in 1736, later served Sardinia, and in 1748 was in Holland again as lieutenant colonel of the Swiss Guards. Early in 1756 he was persuaded to enter the British army as lieutenant colonel in a regiment of Royal Americans to be raised mainly in Pennsylvania. Promoted to colonel (rank valid only in America) in January 1758, he was second in command of the expedition of Gen. John Forbes against Fort Duquesne. It was Bouquet who advanced the idea of cutting a new road, subsequently known as Forbes' Road, through to the western country, prevailing over the objections of George Washington and others who preferred Braddock's trail, and he contributed greatly to the success of the expedition. The road remained for decades the major highway to the Ohio valley. Bouquet also built Fort Ligonier during the expedition. In February 1762 he was brevetted colonel and in the same year naturalized in both Maryland and Pennsylvania. Soon after the outbreak of Pontiac's War in May 1763 Bouquet left Philadelphia in command of 500 Royal Americans and Highlanders to the relief of Fort Pitt. On the evening of August 5, at Bushy Run, near the site of Braddock's defeat, he was attacked by a body of Delawares and Shawnees. Fighting ended at nightfall, but in the morning resumed. Bouquet then demonstrated his virtually unique understanding of the tactical requirements of warfare in America and the value of his concentrated drilling. Maneuvering by companies rather than battalions, he drew the Indians into an exposed position, then routed them by a bayonet charge from ambush. The victory was complete, and the siege of Fort Pitt was lifted four days later. In October 1764 he led a smaller but also successful pacification expedition up the Great Trail from the Ohio to the forks of the Muskingum and imposed a treaty of peace on the Indians. In reward for his services he was promoted to brigadier general in 1765 and given command of all troops in the southern colonies. He died of a fever at Pensacola, in what was then the British province of West Florida, on September 2, 1765.

Bowie, James (1796–1836), Texas revolutionary leader. Born in Logan County, Kentucky, in 1796, Bowie moved with his family to Missouri in 1800 and to Louisiana in 1802. From 1814 he engaged in various enterprises, on his own or with his brothers— lumbering, slave trading, and raising sugarcane—and became something of a figure in New Orleans society. On September 19, 1827, in an affray that became widely known as the "Sandbar Duel," Bowie killed a man with his knife, a weapon reputedly made from a blacksmith's rasp. He went to Texas in 1828, possibly because of his role in the duel. Settling in San Antonio (then called Bexar), he became a Mexican citizen in 1830 and the following year married the daughter of the vice-governor, acquiring in the meantime extensive land holdings. Despite these attachments to Mexico, he sided with the American colonists as agitation for Texan independence developed. He was in the early engagement at Nacogdoches in August 1832 and at the beginning of the revolution in 1835 was a member of the Committee of Safety. He took part in the battle at Mission Concepción, October 28, and the Grass Fight, November 26, and in December was commissioned a colonel in the revolutionary army. Early in 1836 he joined the garrison under Col. William B. Travis at the Alamo. He fell ill during the siege and was discovered dead on his cot when General Santa Anna's troops took the stronghold on March 6, 1836. The bowie knife—a stout hunting knife that became widely popular—is believed to have been named after him, although its invention is sometimes credited to his brother Rezin.

Boyd, Belle (1844–1900), Confederate spy. Born on May 9, 1844, in Martinsburg, Virginia (now West Virginia), Isabelle, known as Belle, Boyd attended

Mount Washington Female College, Baltimore, from 1856 to 1860 and had entered society in the national capital when the Civil War broke out. Returning then to Martinsburg, she joined in fund-raising activities on behalf of the Confederacy. When the town was occupied by Union forces in July 1861, she associated freely with officers, gleaning bits of military information which she sent by messenger to Confederate authorities. The interception of one of these messages brought her only a reprimand. Within a few months she was appointed a courier for Gen. P. G. T. Beauregard and Gen. Thomas J. Jackson. After being arrested and briefly detained in Baltimore in early 1862, she went to live with an aunt in Front Royal, Virginia. There, she later wrote, she eavesdropped on Gen. James Shields and his staff and then made a fifteen-mile night ride through lines to deliver the intelligence thus gained. Her most noted service came in May 1862 when she learned that Jackson, who was planning to recapture the town, could by speeding his advance prevent Union forces from destroying the bridges out of town in their retreat. She ran into the field between opposing lines, her "dark blue dress and fancy white apron" making her a conspicuous target, and waved the Confederates on. Whether or not she materially aided the attack, she later claimed to have been thanked by Jackson. In July, after the Union retaking of Front Royal, she was arrested and held for a month in Old Capitol Prison in Washington, D.C. By the time she was exchanged south, she was a heroine throughout the Confederacy. In June 1863 she returned to Martinsburg and the next month was again arrested. Released in December, she was banished south. In March 1864 she sailed on a blockade runner from Wilmington, North Carolina, with dispatches for Confederate agents in England. The ship was captured, and Miss Boyd was taken to Boston and then banished to Canada. She made her way from there to London, where she married the naval officer who had had charge of her captured vessel (he was subsequently disciplined for neglect of duty). After he died early in 1865, she published her two-volume memoir, *Belle Boyd, in Camp and Prison.* In 1866 she turned to the stage, making her debut in *The Lady of Lyons* in Manchester and then returning to the United States to make a tour of the South. She appeared in New York in *The Honeymoon* in 1868. She retired in 1869, but in 1886, her third marriage having brought her into financial difficulties, she began a career as a lecturer on her own exploits. She died on a speaking tour in Kilbourn (now Wisconsin Dells), Wisconsin, on June 11, 1900.

Boyington, Gregory (1912–   ), marine officer. Born on December 4, 1912, in Coeur d'Alene, Idaho, Boyington graduated from the University of Washington in 1934 and in June 1936 enlisted in the marine corps. He became a pilot in 1937 and by 1941 was a lieutenant and flight instructor at Pensacola, Florida. In September of that year he resigned from the marines to join Gen. Claire L. Chennault's American Volunteer Group—the "Flying Tigers"—in China. During his service in that group he shot down six Japanese fighters, thus qualifying as an ace. In mid-1942 he returned to the United States and in September rejoined the marines, taking a reserve major's commission. For several months Boyington served mainly in administrative duties in the Pacific area, but in August 1943 he was allowed to form a squadron from among replacement and inactivated pilots. Squadron 214, based on Espiritu Santo in the New Hebrides Islands, went into action in September with Boyington—nicknamed "Pappy" by his men—as commanding officer. In 84 days of combat, the 49 pilots of 214 shot down 98 Japanese planes over Kahili, Bougainville, and Rabaul in the Central Solomons, damaging or destroying on the ground over 130 more, together with large numbers of small surface craft. The "Blacksheep" became one of the most celebrated fighting units in the war, and Pappy Boyington one of the most colorful commanders. On his last mission, January 3, 1944, he shot down 3 enemy aircraft, bringing his total, including his Flying Tiger score, to 28, the highest of the war among marine pilots and fourth highest among all U.S. pilots. He was shot down himself that day, and after surviving two hours of strafing he was picked up by a Japanese submarine and carried to Japan. He remained in a prison camp for 20 months. While his whereabouts, even his survival, were still uncertain, he was awarded the Medal of Honor in April 1944 and subsequently promoted to lieutenant colonel. Released after the war, he returned to a hero's welcome in September 1945. He retired as a colonel in August 1947. For several years his fortunes declined, owing in large part to alcohol. That phase passed, however, and in 1958 he published a book of memoirs, *Baa Baa Black Sheep,* that enjoyed considerable success and was later made into a motion picture. Boyington continued to live quietly in California, having outlived his own often quoted maxim, "Show me a hero, and I'll show you a bum."

Bradley, Omar Nelson (1893–   ), army officer. Born on February 12, 1893, in Clark, Missouri, Bradley graduated from West Point in 1915 and was commissioned in the infantry. He served with the 14th Infantry at various posts in Washington and Arizona, receiving promotions to first lieutenant in July 1916, to captain in May 1917, and to temporary major in June 1918. After a few months at Camp Grant, Illinois, he was made professor of military science and tactics at South Dakota State College in September 1919. He reverted to captain in January 1920 but was promoted to permanent major in July. Later in that year he became an instructor at West

Point, remaining there until 1924. He graduated from the Infantry School, Fort Benning, Georgia, in 1925 and, after three years at Schofield Barracks, Hawaii, from the Command and General Staff School, Fort Leavenworth, Kansas, in 1929. From 1929 to 1933 he was an instructor at the Infantry School, and, after graduating from the Army War College in 1934, he was again an instructor at West Point until 1938, advancing to lieutenant colonel in June 1936. In June 1938 Bradley was ordered to duty with the General Staff, and, promoted to brigadier general in February 1941, he was commandant of the Infantry School from March 1941 to February 1942. Advancing to temporary major general, he then commanded the 82nd Infantry (later Airborne) Division at Camp Claiborne, Louisiana, and, from June 1942 to January 1943, the 28th Infantry Division at Camp Livingston, Louisiana. A short time later he was ordered to North Africa, where he was an aide to Gen. Dwight D. Eisenhower until April, when he took command of the II Corps from Gen. George S. Patton. The II Corps captured Bizerte, Tunis, on May 8. Promoted to temporary lieutenant general in June, Bradley led the II Corps, then part of Gen. Patton's Seventh Army, in the landing near Scoglitti, Sicily, on July 10. In September he was called to England to assist in the planning, under Gen. Eisenhower, of the cross-channel invasion. In October he was named commander of the provisional First United States Army Group (FUSAG) for that purpose. In January 1944 he took command of the First Army, which, constituting the Allied right wing, landed at Utah and Omaha beaches, Normandy, on D-Day, June 6. Late in July the First Army made the crucial breakthrough at St. Lô that released the Allied forces from the Cotentin Peninsula. In August FUSAG was superseded by the 12th Army Group. As commander at that level Bradley had responsibility for the First Army, now under Gen. Courtney H. Hodges, and the Third, under Gen. Patton, which together carried the center and right (central and southern) of the Allied advance across Europe; from September 1944 for the Ninth, under Gen. William H. Simpson, operating from Brest south along the French coast; and from January 1945 for the Fifteenth, under Gen. Leonard T. Gerow, also concentrated on the French coast. At its peak the 12th Army Group numbered some 1.3 million men, the largest force ever commanded by an American field commander. In March 1945 Bradley was promoted to general. The 12th was inactivated in July 1945. From August of that year to December 1947 Bradley headed the Veterans Administration. In February 1948 he succeeded Eisenhower as chief of staff of the army, holding that post until August 1949, when he became the first chairman of the permanent Joint Chiefs of Staff. He was promoted to general of the army in September 1950. In 1951 he published *A Soldier's Story*, a memoir, and in August 1953 he retired.

Thereafter he engaged in various business pursuits, serving from 1958 as chairman of the Bulova Watch Company.

Bradstreet, John (1711?–1774), British and colonial army officer. Born about 1711, either in England or in Nova Scotia, Bradstreet was in any case in the latter place at an early age and by 1735 had become an ensign in the British army. He was a lieutenant stationed at Canso, Nova Scotia, when, at the beginning of King George's War, that town was captured by the French in 1744; and during his imprisonment in Louisbourg he became knowledgeable about the fort and its weaknesses. On his release he went to Boston and convinced Gov. William Shirley that an expedition against Louisbourg would be successful. Such an expedition was mounted under William Pepperrell, Bradstreet serving as a subordinate officer. In September 1745 he was promoted to captain and a year later made lieutenant governor of St. John's, Newfoundland, a sinecure he retained for the rest of his life. During 1755–1756, the first year of the French and Indian War, he was engaged in strengthening the garrison at Oswego and organizing supply lines in upper New York; in the course of his highly successful work he beat back several French attacks. In March 1757 he took command of a company of Col. Henry Bouquet's Royal Americans, and in December he was raised to lieutenant colonel and made deputy quartermaster general in America. He took part in Gen. James Abercrombie's unsuccessful attack on Fort Ticonderoga in July 1758 and then led an expedition of his own planning against Fort Frontenac (Kingston, Ontario). With 3000 men he made his way in boats previously prepared and on August 27 captured the fort, which he promptly burned to the ground. In 1759 he served under Gen. Jeffrey Amherst in the campaign against Ticonderoga and Crown Point. In February 1762 he was made colonel in America. In Pontiac's War in 1764 he commanded the more northern of the two armies (Col. Henry Bouquet's was the other) sent west against the Indians; his arrival at Detroit in August ended the 15-month siege of that post. He negotiated a treaty with the Indians there in September. In 1772 he succeeded by seniority to the rank of major general. Bradstreet died in New York City on September 25, 1774.

Bragg, Braxton (1817–1876), Confederate army officer. Born in Warrenton, North Carolina, on March 22, 1817, Bragg graduated from West Point in 1837 and was commissioned in the 3rd Artillery. He took part in the Seminole War from 1837 to 1841 and served with distinction under Gen. Zachary Taylor in the Mexican War. He was brevetted captain at Fort Texas, May 8, 1846, and major at Monterrey, September 20–24. His performance at Buena Vista, February 23, 1847, was particularly notable and won him his third brevet of the war, to lieutenant colonel. His promotion to permanent captain came in June 1846, and he advanced to major in March 1855. In January 1856 he resigned from the army and settled on a plantation in Louisiana, where he also served as commissioner of public works. Five years later, in February 1861, he was called to service as a brigadier general in the Confederate army. After a time engaged in coastal defense he was promoted to major general in January 1862, and in March he took command of the II Corps in Gen. Albert S. Johnston's newly formed Army of Mississippi. He took part in the battle of Pittsburg Landing (Shiloh), April 6–7, and a few days later was promoted to general. In June he took command of the Army of Mississippi (redesignated the Army of Tennessee in November) from Gen. P. G. T. Beauregard. Hoping to secure Kentucky for the Confederacy, he moved north. He retired from an indecisive engagement with Gen. Don Carlos Buell at Perryville, October 8, however, having let himself become engaged in political matters while Buell was in a very vulnerable position, and thus lost an initial advantage. He retired from another with Gen. William S. Rosecrans at Murfreesboro (Stones River), December 31, 1862–January 3, 1863, where he inflicted heavy damage on the Army of the Cumberland before withdrawing. Despite severe criticism of his inability to press his advantages Bragg retained the favor of Confederate president Jefferson Davis and thereby his command. He won a notable victory over Rosecrans at Chickamauga, September 18–20, 1863, with the reinforcement of Gen. James Longstreet's corps from Virginia, but, unable to pursue vigorously owing to extremely heavy casualties, he hesitated and soon thereafter was routed by Gen. Ulysses S. Grant at Chattanooga, whence Rosecrans had retired after Chickamauga and been superseded, on November 24–25. In December Bragg surrendered his command to Gen. Joseph E. Johnston and became military adviser to Jefferson Davis. After the war he returned to civil engineering and for four years was commissioner of public works in Alabama. He died in Galveston, Texas, on September 27, 1876.

Brant, Joseph (1742–1807), Indian leader. Born in 1742 on the banks of the Ohio River in what is now Ohio, Brant was the son of a Mohawk chief and was known to the Indians as Thayendanegea. He was educated at Eleazar Wheelock's Indian charity school (which was the forerunner of Dartmouth) in Lebanon, Connecticut. In 1763, soon after leaving school, he served in the French and Indian War as one of the Iroquois contingent aiding the British against Chief Pontiac. For a time he worked with an Anglican missionary translating various religious works into the Mohawk tongue. In 1774 he became secretary to the superintendent of Indian affairs and when the Revolution broke out remained loyal to the British. After

a visit to England, during which he was presented at court, he was commissioned a captain by the British and assumed leadership of the Indians in the Mohawk valley region, directing devastating raids on settlements on the New York–Pennsylvania frontier. He fought ferociously at the head of the Indian forces attached to Col. Barry St. Leger's column at the battle of Oriskany on August 6, 1777, and at the Cherry Valley Massacre on November 11, 1778, he led the Indian contingent attached to Maj. Walter Butler's force. Although Brant constantly frustrated attempts by other Indian leaders, notably Red Jacket, to secure an early peace with the Americans, at the war's end he took the lead in pacifying the Indian frontier. He devoted himself thereafter to missionary work and to attempting to secure the welfare and safety of his people. After failing in efforts to obtain a settlement of the Iroquois Nations' land claims in the United States he turned to the British; on a second visit to England in 1786 he obtained funds to purchase lands in Canada at present-day Brantford, Ontario, and to erect the first Episcopal church in Upper Canada. He died at his own Ontario estate on November 24, 1807.

Braun, Wernher von (1912–1977), rocket engineer. Born on March 23, 1912, in Wirsitz, Germany (now Wyrzysk, Poland), von Braun as a youth became fascinated with the possibilities of using rockets to explore outer space and in 1930 joined the Verein für Raumschiffahrt, a group of amateur rocket enthusiasts in Berlin. He studied engineering at technological institutes in Zurich and Berlin, took his degree from the latter in 1932, and later in the same year became chief of a rocket research station established by the German army. Two years later he was awarded a Ph.D. by the University of Berlin. In 1936 German Führer Adolf Hitler became interested in rockets as potential weapons and ordered construction of a large research facility at Peenemünde, where von Braun and his group continued their work with greatly improved resources. By 1938 a first model of the liquid-fueled Vergeltungswaffe Zwei (V-2, "revenge weapon two") had been developed. Over the next six years it was enlarged and improved until it was capable of carrying a warhead weighing nearly a ton more than 190 miles in 5 minutes. V-2 launchings against London and Antwerp began in September 1944 and eventually numbered more than 3500. Other developments by the Peenemünde group included jet-assisted takeoff units, a supersonic antiaircraft missile, and preliminary work on what was to have become an intercontinental ballistic missile. Shortly before the end of the war von Braun and a large number of his colleagues fled before advancing Soviet armies and surrendered to U.S. forces. In 1945 he came to the United States and became technical director of the army's proving grounds for missiles at

White Sands, New Mexico. In 1950 he was made director of the missile research facility at Huntsville, Alabama. Under his supervision the Redstone, Jupiter-C, Jupiter, Juno, and Pershing rockets were developed. He continued to press for a program of space exploration and wrote numerous papers, articles, and books on the subject, including *Conquest of the Moon*, 1953, with Fred Whipple and Willy Ley, and *Exploration of Mars*, 1956. He became a U.S. citizen in 1955. Lack of government support retarded progress on the development of an earth satellite until the launching of *Sputnik I* by the Soviet Union in October 1957 provided the necessary impetus. In January 1958 the Huntsville group orbited *Explorer I*, the first U.S. satellite. Two years later the group became part of the National Aeronautics and Space Administration (NASA); von Braun remained director of the renamed George C. Marshall Space Flight Center at Huntsville and worked on the development of new launch vehicles, notably the huge *Saturn V* employed in the Project Apollo program for a manned moon landing. Others among his published works were *First Men to the Moon*, 1960, and *Space Frontier*, 1967. From 1970 to 1972 he served as deputy administrator of NASA; in the latter year he retired to enter private industry, becoming a vice-president of Fairchild Industries. Von Braun died in Alexandria, Virginia on June 16, 1977. For three decades von Braun's name had been virtually synonymous with rocket development.

Breckinridge, John Cabell (1821–1875), public official and Confederate army officer. Born on January 21, 1821, near Lexington, Kentucky, Breckinridge graduated from Centre College of Kentucky in 1839, studied at the College of New Jersey (now Princeton), and then took up law at Transylvania University in Lexington; he was admitted to the Kentucky bar in 1841. He entered practice in Frankfort, moved to Burlington, Iowa, where he lived for two years, and then returned to Kentucky. In 1847 he was commissioned major of the 3rd Kentucky Volunteer Regiment and served briefly in the Mexican War; his principal work in Mexico was as counsel to Gen. Gideon J. Pillow in the latter's dispute with Gen. Winfield Scott. In 1849 he was elected to the state legislature as a Democrat and two years later won a seat in the House of Representatives from a normally Whig district. Reelected to a second term, he remained in Congress from March 1851 to March 1855, when, despite having established a national reputation and become the leader of the Kentucky Democrats, he returned to his law practice. The next year, however, he was nominated for vice-president as James Buchanan's running mate and was elected with Buchanan. His conduct as presiding officer of the Senate in those very difficult years was highly creditable. His popularity in his home state was such that in 1859 he was elected to the Senate for the term to begin two years later. In 1860, when Southern Democrats withdrew from the national convention in protest against the nomination of Stephen A. Douglas, a splinter convention was held in Baltimore, and Breckinridge was nominated for the presidency. Although reluctant at first, he soon began to campaign vigorously on a moderate Unionist platform, and he won 72 electoral votes from 11 states. After the election of Abraham Lincoln he continued to preside over the Senate and to work for a compromise solution to the sectional problem until March 1861. After taking his Senate seat in July in that year's special session he attempted to maintain the neutrality of Kentucky while voting against Lincoln's war measures. In September military rule was established in Kentucky; Breckinridge fled to the Confederacy and in December was expelled from the Senate. By that time he had already, in November, been commissioned a brigadier general in the Confederate army; he commanded the reserves at Pittsburg Landing (Shiloh), April 6–7, 1862, and in August 1862 was promoted to major general. In the summer of 1862 he commanded the defenses of Vicksburg; in August he unsuccessfully attacked Baton Rouge and then fortified Port Hudson against the Union advance up the Mississippi. Later he joined Gen. Braxton Bragg's Army of Tennessee. At Murfreesboro (Stones River), December 31–January 3, 1863, he commanded a division of Gen. William J. Hardee's corps. In May 1863 he was with Gen. Joseph E. Johnston at Jackson, Mississippi. At Chickamauga, September 18–20, and Chattanooga, November 24–25, he led a division of Gen. Daniel H. Hill's corps of Bragg's army. In 1864 he was in the Shenandoah valley. On May 15 he joined Gen. John D. Imboden in defeating Gen. Franz Sigel at New Market; on June 1–3 he took part under Gen. Robert E. Lee in the battle of Cold Harbor; and in July he took part in Gen. Jubal A. Early's raid on Washington, D.C. In September he succeeded Gen. John H. Morgan as commander of the Department of Southwest Virginia. In that post he saw action in numerous small engagements and on December 15–16 in the more important battle of Nashville. In February 1865 he was appointed Confederate secretary of war by Jefferson Davis. After Lee's surrender in April he fled south with other high-ranking Confederate officials. He escaped to Cuba and then to England, where he remained until an amnesty proclamation in 1868 made it possible for him to return to Lexington. He resumed his law practice there and was active in railroad development in the state. He died in Lexington on May 17, 1875.

Brereton, Lewis Hyde (1890–1967), army and air force officer. Born on June 21, 1890, in Pittsburgh, Brereton grew up there and in Annapolis, Maryland. After two years at St. John's College he entered the Naval Academy, graduating in 1911. He quickly seized an opportunity to exchange his ensign's commission for one as second lieutenant in the army, and after a year in the coast artillery he transferred in 1912 to the aviation section of the Signal Corps. Qualified as an aviator in 1913, he served a tour with the field artillery, was promoted to first lieutenant, and in 1916 was assigned to the 2nd Aero Squadron in the Philippines. He spent a time in the office of the chief signal officer in Washington, D.C., and completed advanced aviation training before being sent to France in 1917. In March 1918 he took command of the 12th Aero Squadron, which saw much combat; in October he became operations officer of the air service, AEF, and was subsequently chief of staff of the air service, Third Army, in occupied Germany. Subsequently he was, with rank of major, air attaché at the U.S. embassy in Paris from 1919 to 1922. For two years he was an instructor in aviation, and in 1924 he took command of the 2nd Bombardment Group, Langley Field, Virginia. Brereton was long associated with Col. William Mitchell in the development of military aviation; they were jointly credited with inventing the technique of "dive-bombing," and Brereton served as a defense counsel at Mitchell's court-martial in 1925. He graduated from the Command and General Staff School, Fort Leavenworth, in 1928 and then joined the 88th Observation Squadron. From 1931 to 1935 he was on duty in the Canal Zone, and in the latter year, promoted to lieutenant colonel, he joined the faculty of the Command and General Staff School. He was promoted to temporary colonel in 1936. In 1940 he became temporary brigadier general in command of the 17th Bomb Wing and in July 1941, promoted to major general, of the Third Air Force (Tampa, Florida). In November he took command of the Far Eastern Air Force in the Philippines, under the overall command of Gen. Douglas MacArthur. His force was virtually destroyed on the ground by the Japanese in December, but with what material he was able to salvage in the retreat to Java he carried on air war against the enemy over the Java Sea, the Strait of Macassar, Burma, and the Andaman islands. In March 1942 he was ordered to India to organize the Tenth Air Force. In June he was transferred to the Middle East as commander of the Middle East Air Force, soon redesignated the Ninth Air Force, flying support for the British Eighth Army against Field Marshal Rommel in the North Africa campaign. In that post Brereton planned the massive Allied air strikes carried out against the petroleum refining complex at Ploesti, Romania, in August 1943. From January to September 1943 he was commander of all U.S. army forces in the Middle East. Promoted to temporary lieutenant general in April 1944, he was named commander of the First Allied Airborne Army in August 1944, with headquarters in England. In September the First carried out a massive airborne invasion of the Netherlands, in conjunction with the British Second Army, in Operation Market–Garden, a bold attempt to seize bridges and a launching area around Arnhem, Nijmegen, and Veghel, for a move into northern Germany. For many reasons the operation, under overall command of British Gen. Bernard Montgomery, was a conspicuous failure. In December 1944 the First dropped supplies to Gen. Anthony C. McAuliffe's besieged 101st Airborne Division at Bastogne. In March 1945 it dropped American and British troops near Wesel to help seize a bridgehead over the Rhine. Brereton continued in his post until the inactivation of the First in May 1945. From 1946 to 1948 he was senior air member of the military liaison committee of the Atomic Energy Commission and served also on the Inter-Allied Armistice Commission for Aviation. In 1948 he retired from the air force, to which he had moved in September 1947, and served afterwards as president of the Overseas Service Corporation. *The Brereton Diaries,* his war memoirs, appeared in 1946. He died in Washington, D.C., on July 19, 1967.

Bristol, Mark Lambert (1868–1939), naval officer. Born in Glassboro, New Jersey, on April 17, 1868, Bristol graduated from the Naval Academy in 1887. He was commissioned an ensign in May 1889 and served on the *Texas,* Capt. John W. Philip, at the battle of Santiago in the Spanish–American War. He specialized in ordnance, the modernization of naval gunnery techniques, and aeronautics. In 1904 he headed the torpedo branch of the Bureau of Ordnance. He was aboard fleet flagship *Connecticut* in the world cruise of the Battle Fleet under Adm. Charles S. Sperry in 1907–1909. In 1909–1911 he was inspector at the naval torpedo station at Newport, Rhode Island, and in 1911 he had his first sea command on the *Monterey.* He commanded the *Albany* on China station in 1912–1913. Promoted to captain in July 1913, he was named director of naval aeronautics at a time when the navy had just nine pilots. In 1916 he took command of the armored cruiser *North Carolina,* in which during the early part of the American participation in World War I he convoyed troops to Europe. In January 1918 he transferred to the battleship *Oklahoma.* In July he advanced to temporary rank of rear admiral (made permanent in July 1921), and in October he took command of the U.S. Naval Base, Plymouth, England. During November–December 1918 he served on the International Armistice Commission for Belgium. Bristol was appointed commander of a naval detachment in the eastern Mediterranean in January 1919; his headquarters in Constantinople became the point of diplomatic contact between the United States and the Ottoman Empire, whose formal relations had been broken in 1917. In August he was appointed high commissioner to Turkey, and for eight years he maintained American presence and interests through the turbulence of the empire's dissolution. He directed American relief operations among Greek and Armenian refugees, Turkish Christians, White Russians, and other groups and in numerous ways made himself a figure respected by all sides. When formal relations were reestablished in May 1927, Bristol was given command of the Asiatic Fleet with temporary rank of admiral, holding that post until 1929. In March 1930 he became chairman of the navy's General Board. He retired in May 1932 and lived in Washington, D.C., until his death there on May 13, 1939.

Brooke, John Mercer (1826–1906), Confederate naval officer. Born on December 18, 1826, in an army camp on Tampa Bay, Florida, Brooke was the son of an army officer. He entered the navy as a midshipman in March 1841 and saw his first sea duty aboard the *Delaware* under Commander David G. Farragut. He entered the Naval Academy in 1845 and graduated two years later. During 1849–1850 he served under Lt. Samuel P. Lee in hydrographic survey work, and from 1851 to 1853 he worked under Lt. Matthew F. Maury at the Depot of Charts and Instruments in Washington, D.C. There he invented a deep-sea sounding apparatus, an achievement that brought him international attention. During 1854–1858 he was attached to the North Pacific and Bering Straits Surveying and Exploring Expedition, under Commodore Cadwalader Ringgold and then Commodore John Rodgers, and while engaged in that work was promoted to lieutenant in September 1855. In 1858 he commanded the schooner *Fenimore Cooper* in a survey of a California–China route. The ship was wrecked in a storm on the Japanese coast and Brooke returned to the United States in 1860 aboard a Japanese corvette, providing navigation instruction en route. In April 1861 he resigned from the navy and took a commission in the Virginia state navy, subsequently entering the Confederate States navy. In June he proposed a plan for reconstructing the *Merrimac,* which had been burned to the waterline when Union forces abandoned the Norfolk naval yard. He urged that she be converted to an ironclad, mounting inclined metal shields on a deck with submerged ends. Together with Confederate naval constructor John L. Porter and chief engineer W. P. Williamson he worked out final designs and plans and then took responsibility for the manufacture of the armor plate and the guns at the Tredegar Iron Works in Richmond. The completed vessel was launched on its famous career as the C.S.S. *Virginia* in March 1862. From March 1863 Brooke was chief of the Bureau of Ordnance and Hydrography, where he developed the "Brooke" gun, a reinforced cast-iron rifle of considerable power. In 1866 he was appointed professor of physics and astronomy at the Virginia Military Institute, remaining there until his retirement in 1899. He was joined on the faculty by his old commander,

Maury, in 1868. Brooke died in Lexington, Virginia, on December 14, 1906.

Brown, George Scratchley (1918–), air force officer. Born on August 17, 1918, in Montclair, New Jersey, Brown attended the University of Missouri for a year before entering West Point, from which he graduated in 1941, taking his commission in the Army Air Corps. During World War II he was a bomber pilot in the 93rd Bombardment Group (flying B-24s), attached to the Eighth Air Force. He distinguished himself particularly in the last of the Ploesti raids in August 1943. By October 1944 he had risen to temporary rank of colonel. After a year as assistant operations officer of the 2nd Air Division he returned to the United States in May 1945. His subsequent assignments included command of the 56th Fighter Wing at Selfridge Air Force Base, Michigan, in 1951–1952, and chief of operations of the Fifth Air Force in Korea, 1952–1953. After completing the course at the National War College in 1957 he was appointed executive officer to the chief of staff of the air force, Gen. Thomas D. White. In August 1959 he was promoted to temporary brigadier general. From December 1959 to August 1963 he was military assistant to the secretary of defense, advancing to temporary major general in April 1963, after which he returned to line commands. In 1964–1966 he commanded Joint Task Force II, a weapons system test unit at Sandia Base, New Mexico. Promoted to temporary lieutenant general in August 1966, he was named assistant to Gen. Earle G. Wheeler, chairman of the Joint Chiefs of Staff. In August 1968, promoted to general, he took command of the Seventh Air Force, based in Saigon, South Vietnam, and responsible for the entire southwest Asia region. From September 1970 to July 1973 he was commander of Air Force Systems Command. In July 1973 Brown was named by President Richard M. Nixon to a term as chief of staff of the air force; his nomination was confirmed despite controversy over the issue of falsified reports from his office that hid secret bombing missions in Cambodia in 1969–1970. In July 1974 he became chairman of the Joint Chiefs of Staff, again on Nixon's nomination. In that post he frequently aroused controversy by public and private comments on the extent of Jewish influence in business, the news media, and Congress and on other sensitive topics.

Brown, Jacob Jennings (1775–1828), army officer. Born on May 9, 1775, in Bucks County, Pennsylvania, Brown was descended from a line of Quaker farmers. After some years spent teaching school in New Jersey, doing surveying in Ohio, and again teaching, in New York City, he served for a time as secretary to Alexander Hamilton. In 1800 he took up farming on a large estate on the shore of Lake Ontario in western New York, founding the town of Brownville. He became active in the state militia and at the outbreak of the War of 1812 had been for two years a brigadier general. Placed in command of the New York frontier, he successfully repelled British attacks at Ogdensburg on October 3, 1812, and Sackett's Harbor on May 26, 1813, and was consequently appointed brigadier general in the regular army in July 1813. After taking part in the disastrous Montreal campaign under Gen. James Wilkinson that autumn he was promoted to major general in January 1814 and given command at Niagara, replacing Wilkinson. With Gen. Winfield Scott leading one of his brigades of regulars, Brown undertook a campaign into Canada in July 1814, crossing the Niagara River and taking Fort Erie on July 3. Scott won a sharp engagement at Chippewa on July 5, and, after waiting in vain for promised naval support from Commodore Isaac Chauncey to materialize, the army proceeded to Lundy's Lane, where a battle producing heavy casualties on both sides ensued on July 25. Although the British position was taken and the commander, Gen. Riall, captured, Brown, himself badly wounded, was forced to retire and to give up his ultimate objective, the capture of York (now Toronto). The battle nonetheless was one of the most famous of the war. After returning to Fort Erie, Brown's forces repulsed a British attack in August and later, by a highly successful sortie, broke a month-long siege. The northern campaign, the Americans' only really satisfactory one in the war, soon came to an end. Brown became the senior officer of the army in June 1815 and on June 1, 1821, was appointed to the newly created post of commanding general, a post he held until his death on February 24, 1828, in Washington, D.C.

Browning, John Moses (1855–1926), inventor. Born in Ogden, Utah, on January 21, 1855, Browning was the son of a Mormon gunsmith. He early displayed a talent for mechanics and invention, constructing his first gun from scrap at the age of thirteen. In 1879 he patented a breech-loading, single-shot rifle and sold it for a substantial royalty to the Winchester Repeating Arms Company. He went on to design numerous other firearms for various manufacturers; among them were a repeating rifle patented in 1884, a repeating shotgun for Winchester, the Remington automatic-loading shotguns and rifles, the Stevens rifles, and the Colt automatic pistols. His guns were also manufactured by his own company, organized with his brother as the J. M. & M. S. Browning Company. In 1890 the U.S. army adopted his Colt-made machine gun and later, during the Spanish–American War, used his "Peacemaker" machine gun. His Colt automatic pistol, introduced in 1911, was also bought by the army for use during World War I, along with a heavy water-cooled machine gun. The machine gun, in a .50-caliber model

firing up to 1250 rounds per minute, was also adapted for use in aircraft. Introduced too late for use in World War I but a standard army shoulder weapon for 40 years thereafter was the 1918 model .30-caliber Browning Automatic Rifle, the famed BAR. The army subsequently adopted his air-cooled .30-caliber light machine gun, used through World War II, and several other weapons. No Browning design ever failed, an astounding record. Browning was much honored for his inventions. While on a business trip he died near Liège, Belgium, on November 26, 1926.

Buchanan, Franklin (1800–1874), Confederate naval officer. Born in Baltimore on September 17, 1800, Buchanan was commissioned a midshipman in the navy in January 1815 and saw his first sea duty under Commodore Oliver Hazard Perry aboard the *Java*. He served mostly in the Mediterranean for five years, sailed on a merchantman to China while on a leave of absence, and was then engaged in pirate patrol in the West Indies for six years, receiving promotion to lieutenant in January 1825. For the next 20 years he served on a series of ships in duty stations around the world and in September 1841 advanced to the rank of commander. From 1842 to 1845 he commanded the frigate *Mississippi* and then the sloop *Vincennes*. In August 1845, having submitted a plan of organization for the new U.S. Naval Academy at Annapolis, he was appointed first superintendent of the school by Secretary of the Navy George Bancroft. He spent two years setting the academy, which opened formally on October 10, 1845, upon its course. He then petitioned for active duty in the Mexican War, receiving command of the sloop *Germantown* in March 1847 and taking part in the capture of Veracruz and other coastal towns under Commodore David Conner and Commodore Matthew C. Perry. He returned to shore duty for a time after the war but in 1852 was given command of the steam frigate *Susquehanna*, Commodore Perry's flagship in the expedition to Japan. Promoted to captain in September 1855, Buchanan served in various capacities, including commander of the Washington navy yard, until April 1861, when, in the belief that Maryland would secede from the Union, he resigned. An attempt to retract his resignation a short time later failed and he was dismissed. He then entered the Confederate navy as a captain in September 1861 and in February 1862 took command of the Chesapeake Bay Squadron aboard his flagship, the ironclad *Virginia* (formerly the *Merrimac*, the name by which it continued to be best known). On March 8, 1862, he attacked the Union squadron that was blockading Hampton Roads, sinking the *Cumberland*, under Lt. George U. Morris, in a bloody fight that left the *Virginia* in damaged condition, and then destroying the *Congress*, on which his brother was serving, and other vessels, but sustaining a serious wound that kept him out of the next day's historic engagement with the *Monitor*. In August he was made admiral and ranking officer of the Confederate navy. Sent to take command at Mobile Bay, he was aboard his flagship, the armored ram *Tennessee*, when Adm. David G. Farragut attacked on August 5, 1864; outnumbered and outgunned, the *Tennessee* was taken and Buchanan was wounded and captured. Released from prison in February 1865, he settled in his home in Talbot County, Maryland, and died there on May 11, 1874.

Buckner, Simon Bolivar (1823–1914), Confederate army officer. Born on April 1, 1823, near Munfordville, Kentucky, Buckner graduated from West Point in 1844 and was commissioned in the 2nd Infantry. Assigned first to duty at Sackett's Harbor, New York, and then as an instructor at West Point, he sought active duty in the Mexican War and distinguished himself at Churubusco August 20, 1847, and Molino del Rey, September 8, winning brevets to first lieutenant and then to captain. Thereafter he served again at West Point, at New York harbor, and in the West, advancing to first lieutenant in December 1851 and to captain in November 1852 before resigning from the army in March 1855. He lived in Chicago for a time, acquiring and managing large real-estate holdings, and in 1858 moved to Louisville, Kentucky. As the likelihood of civil war grew, he became deeply concerned with the effect it would have on the state, which was officially neutral. In 1860 the legislature approved his plan for a large, well trained militia and appointed him major general. He succeeded in organizing an able home guard to defend Kentucky's neutrality and in June 1861 secured from Gen. George B. McClellan recognition of the state's position. When federal forces invaded the western part of Kentucky, he sought their withdrawal from McClellan and then from President Abraham Lincoln; he did not succeed, but Lincoln offered him a brigadier general's commission, which he refused. Soon afterward Confederate forces also entered Kentucky and again he tried in vain to secure their removal and again he refused an offer of a commission. Buckner relinquished command of the militia in July because the state government had become partial to the Union; he was already leaning toward the Confederacy when the legislature officially abandoned neutrality. He forthwith accepted an appointment as brigadier general in the Confederate army in September 1861 and joined the command of Gen. Albert S. Johnston. Early in 1862 he was sent to the relief of Fort Donelson, where he found the situation hopeless. The ranking officers, Gen. John B. Floyd and Gen. Gideon J. Pillow, in turn relinquished command and escaped, leaving Buckner to the inevitable; on February 16 he was forced to surrender the fort, 15,000 troops, and considerable stores to his old friend, Gen. Ulysses S. Grant. Imprisoned until August, he returned to duty then and was promoted to major general on the staff of Gen. Braxton Bragg, operating in Tennessee and Kentucky. He later built fortifications at Mobile, rejoined Bragg in time to command a corps in the battle of Chickamauga, September 18–20, and in September 1864 was made lieutenant general in command of the District of Louisiana. At the war's end he entered the newspaper and insurance businesses in New Orleans; in 1868 he returned to Kentucky and became editor of the *Louisville Courier*. The recovery of confiscated properties in Kentucky and Chicago established him as a wealthy man, and he devoted himself to his business interests until 1887, when he was elected governor of Kentucky. Upon leaving office in 1891 and serving in the state constitutional convention that year he retired to his Munfordville estate. In 1896 he was nominated for vice-president by the Gold Democrats, a splinter party. The last surviving Confederate lieutenant general, Buckner died at home on January 8, 1914.

Buckner, Simon Bolivar, Jr. (1886–1945), army officer. Born on July 18, 1886, in Munfordville, Kentucky, Buckner was the son of Confederate Gen. Simon B. Buckner. He attended Virginia Military Institute for two years, 1902–1904, before entering West Point, from which he graduated in 1908. Commissioned in the infantry, he was stationed over the next nine years successively in Texas, the Philippines, Kentucky, Texas again, Washington, D.C., and the Philippines once more, advancing to first lieutenant in 1914 and to captain in May 1917. In the latter year he was transferred to the aviation section of the Signal Corps, and he commanded training units at Kelly Field, Texas, advancing to temporary major, until October 1918. After a few months of staff and recruiting work he became an instructor at West Point in 1919, remaining there until 1923 and receiving promotion to permanent major in July 1920. Buckner graduated from the Infantry School, Fort Benning, Georgia, in 1924 and from the Command and General Staff School, Fort Leavenworth, Kansas, in 1925. He remained at the latter as an instructor until entering the Army War College in 1928; graduating in 1929, he was on the staff of the college for three years. Promoted to lieutenant colonel in April 1932, he was again an instructor at West Point in 1932–1933 and commandant of cadets in 1933–1936. In August 1936 he was attached to the 23rd Infantry at Fort Sam Houston, Texas. He was promoted to colonel in January 1937 and in May took command of the 66th Infantry at Fort George Meade, Maryland. During 1938–1939 he was assigned to duty with the Civilian Conservation Corps in Alabama. He became chief of staff of the 6th Infantry Division in October 1939. In July 1940 he was ordered to Alaska to take command of all army troops there, then loosely organized as the

Alaska Defense Force, with headquarters at Fort Richardson, near Anchorage. By February 1941 his forces were thoroughly reorganized as the Alaska Defense Command (redesignated the Alaskan Department in November 1943). Buckner was promoted to brigadier general in October 1940 and to major general (temporary) in August 1941. In June 1942 aircraft of the Alaska Command joined those of the navy in driving off a Japanese landing force bound for Dutch Harbor on Unalaska Island in the eastern Aleutians. Japanese troops did get ashore on Attu and Kiska to the west, but in May–June 1943 two regiments and a battalion of infantry and a regiment and a battalion of artillery from Buckner's command successfully retook the islands. Promoted to lieutenant general in May 1943, Buckner remained in Alaska until March 1944. In June 1944 he was ordered to Schofield Barracks, Hawaii, to organize and command the Tenth Army. Composed of the XXIV Corps, under Gen. John R. Hodge, and the marine III Amphibious Corps, under Gen. Roy S. Geiger, the Tenth Army went into combat on Okinawa in the Ryukyus, where, after preliminary landings on March 26 and 31, 1945, to secure support positions, the main force was landed on the Hagushi beaches of the southwest coast on April 1 by Adm. R. Kelly Turner's Fifth Amphibious Force. The Okinawa campaign was the most stubbornly fought of the Pacific theater and was not won until June 21. Three days before, on June 18, 1945, Buckner was killed by a Japanese artillery shell. Nakagusuku Wan, a naval anchorage on the southeast coast of Okinawa, was renamed Buckner Bay in his honor.

Buell, Don Carlos (1818–1898), army officer. Born on March 23, 1818, near Marietta, Ohio, Buell grew up there and in Lawrenceburg, Indiana. He graduated from West Point in 1841, was commissioned in the 3rd Infantry, and promptly took part in the Seminole War. Promoted to first lieutenant in June 1846, he served under generals Zachary Taylor and Winfield Scott in the Mexican War, winning brevets to captain and major for action at Monterrey, September 20–24, 1846, and Contreras and Churubusco, August 19–20, 1847. He was later assigned to duty with the adjutant general and other staff positions and at the outbreak of the Civil War was a lieutenant colonel. Appointed brigadier general of volunteers in May 1861, he was sent in November 1861 to take command of the newly constituted Army of the Ohio in Louisville, Kentucky. He argued against Gen. George B. McClellan's plan to strike into eastern Tennessee, pointing out the lack of available lines of communication, and continued to hesitate until Gen. Henry W. Halleck sent Gen. Ulysses S. Grant up the Tennessee and Cumberland rivers against Fort Henry in February 1862. Buell, in a supporting action, moved into Bowling Green and, following Grant's success at Fort Donelson, occupied Nashville later in the month. Placed under the command of Halleck in March and later in the month promoted to major general of volunteers, Buell was then ordered to join Grant's Army of the Tennessee at Savannah, Tennessee. He arrived there with fresh troops just in time to join battle at Shiloh on April 6; throwing his full force into the fierce contest the next day, he was able to drive Gen. P. G. T. Beauregard from the field. He accompanied Halleck to Corinth, Mississippi, and was then sent to repair the railroad to Chattanooga. During that operation he was much harassed by Confederate raiders, particularly those of Col. John Hunt Morgan. Learning that Chattanooga had been occupied by Gen. Braxton Bragg, he turned north to Murfreesboro. From there he continued north in a race against Bragg to reach Kentucky; arriving in Bowling Green he found Bragg's troops between him and his base in Louisville. He bided his time until Bragg sacrificed his advantage by moving off to Frankfort to set up a Confederate government. Buell moved to Louisville to regroup and then turned back to fight. A small but sharp battle ensued at Perryville on October 8. Bragg withdrew with heavy casualties, the hope of securing Kentucky to the Confederacy gone; but Buell failed to pursue him vigorously. He was abruptly replaced by Gen. William S. Rosecrans and kept inactive for a year and a half while his conduct was investigated. At length he resigned both his volunteer and regular commissions in May and June 1864. He retired to Kentucky and engaged in business until his death in Rockport on November 19, 1898.

Buffalo Bill *see* Cody, William Frederick

Buford, Abraham (1749–1833), Revolutionary militia officer. Born in Culpeper County, Virginia, on July 31, 1749, Buford raised a company of minutemen in 1775. He rose to major in November 1776, lieutenant colonel in April 1777, and colonel in May 1778. In September 1778 he took command of the 11th Virginia Infantry. Early in 1780 he set out south to relieve Charleston, South Carolina, then under siege. On hearing of the fall of the city on May 12 to Cornwallis's army, Buford turned back, with instructions to remove or burn military stores in North Carolina. Cornwallis dispatched a force of nearly 300 cavalry under Col. Banastre Tarleton to intercept Buford. Buford's force of about 350 men was overtaken at the Waxhaws, near the North Carolina border, on May 29. Under a flag of truce Tarleton demanded surrender, all the while deploying his men for attack. Buford refused to capitulate, whereupon Tarleton launched a furious mounted attack on the unprepared and unmounted Virginians. The exhausted soldiers soon threw down their arms, but their pleas for quarter were ignored; 113 of Buford's men were killed outright, 150 were wounded too badly to be moved, and 53 were taken prisoner. The British lost 20 men. The phrase "Tarleton's quarter" became proverbial for butchery. Buford and a handful of men escaped, and he later commanded the 3rd Virginia. After the war he moved to Kentucky, where he located his land grants in the bluegrass region. He died in Scott County, Kentucky, on June 30, 1833.

Buford, John (1826–1863), army officer. Born in Woodford County, Kentucky, on March 4, 1826, Buford graduated from West Point in 1848 and was commissioned in the 1st Dragoons. In 1849 he was transferred to the 2nd Dragoons and began a period of frontier duty. He was promoted to first lieutenant in July 1853. He took part in the punitive expedition under Gen. William S. Harney against the Sioux in retaliation for the Grattan Massacre and came to the attention of his immediate superior, Col. Philip St. G. Cooke, at the battle of Ash Hollow (Nebraska) on September 3, 1855. He was a member of the Mormon expedition under Col. Albert S. Johnston in 1857–1858 and performed outstanding work as regimental quartermaster. In 1861 he went to Washington, D.C., and in November was promoted to major and placed on the inspector general's staff. In July 1862 he was appointed brigadier general of volunteers and placed in command of the reserve cavalry brigade in Gen. John Pope's Army of Virginia. He saw action at Madison Court House, August 9, checked Longstreet briefly at Thoroughfare Gap on August 28, and was severely wounded at the second battle of Bull Run (Manassas) on August 30. In September he was appointed chief of cavalry of the Army of the Potomac, a staff position under Gen. George McClellan and then Gen. Ambrose Burnside. On the creation of a separate cavalry corps under Gen. George Stoneman in February 1863 Buford resumed command of the reserve brigade. He took part in the cavalry raid toward Richmond in May 1863, covered Gen. Joseph Hooker's retreat from the disaster at Chancellorsville, and, when Lee began his second invasion of the North in June, fought a series of running engagements with Gen. J. E. B. Stuart's cavalry, at Aldie Gap, Upperville, Middleburg, and Ashby's Gap. On June 30 and July 1 he engaged the advance units of Gen. Ambrose P. Hill's Corps before Gettysburg, effectively delaying superior Confederate forces until relieved. He took part in the pursuit of Lee back into Virginia, seeing action at Westminster, Boonsboro, Beaver Creek, Funkstown, Manassas Gap, Chester Gap, Morton's Ford, and Rixeyville. In November 1863 he was transferred to command of the cavalry of the Army of the Cumberland. His health failing, he took a leave of absence in Washington, D.C., and died there on December 16, 1863, having received promotion to major general of volunteers only hours before.

Bulkeley, John Duncan (1911–   ), naval officer. Born in New York City on August 19, 1911, Bulkeley graduated from the Naval Academy in 1933. He served tours on the *Indianapolis*, the *Sacramento*, and the *Saratoga*. By 1941 he had advanced to the rank of lieutenant. In February of that year he took command of Submarine Chaser Division 1, and in September he was ordered to the Philippines in command of Motor Torpedo Boat Squadron 3, consisting of six vessels. When the initial Japanese attacks of December 8 (December 7 in Hawaii) ended, nearly all American naval and air forces in the Philippines were destroyed, and much of what survived was ordered out shortly thereafter. The defense of the islands devolved upon a few P-40 aircraft and Bulkeley's PT boats, a task made seemingly impossible by the unavailability of spare parts, repair facilities, and, before long, even proper fuel. By dint of determination and ingenuity he kept his squadron operating for more than four months under these conditions, repelling Japanese landing parties, destroying great numbers of transports, armed cruisers, and aircraft, and even operating against land forces. When the American ground forces had withdrawn onto the Bataan peninsula and the situation was becoming desperate, Squadron 3 made a daring dash out of Manila harbor on the night of March 11 bearing Gen. Douglas MacArthur and a small party to safety. Squadron 3 continued to operate in Philippine waters until April. For his gallantry and leadership Bulkeley was awarded the Medal of Honor. Promoted to lieutenant commander, he took part in the landings in the Trobriand Islands in July 1943. Bulkeley commanded the PT boats patrolling the beaches during the Allied landing in Normandy, June 6, 1944. At the landing of Gen. Alexander M. Patch's Seventh Army by Adm. H. Kent Hewitt's Western Naval Task Force on the south coast of France on August 15, 1944, Bulkeley, then a commander, was captain of the destroyer *Endicott*, which sank two German corvettes attempting to escape from the harbor at Toulon. He remained in the navy after the war, rising to the rank of rear admiral in June 1963, in which year he was named commander of the naval base at Guantánamo, Cuba. In 1967 he became president of the navy's Board of Inspection and Survey. He retired in 1975. One of the best known naval combat commanders of World War II, Bulkeley was also one of the most highly decorated.

Bullard, Robert Lee (1861–1947), army officer. Born on January 5, 1861, near Opelika, Alabama, Bullard was christened William Robert but in his boyhood took the name Robert Lee in honor of the Confederate commander. After a year at the Agricultural and Mechanical College of Alabama (now Auburn University) he entered West Point, graduating in 1885 and taking a commission in the infantry. The next dozen years he spent mainly in garrison duty in the Southwest, receiving promotions to first lieutenant in April 1892 and to captain in June 1898. Shortly after the outbreak of the Spanish–American war, in June 1898, he was appointed major of an independent battalion of Alabama volunteers, and in August he was promoted to colonel of volunteers in command of the 3rd Alabama (Negro), which took part in the Cuba campaign, and then the 39th Volunteer Infantry, with which he served in the Philippine Insurrection in 1900–1901. He returned to the regulars in May 1901 as a major and remained in the Philippines until 1904, serving as a district governor on Mindanao. In October 1906 he was promoted to lieutenant colonel in the 8th Infantry. During 1906–1909 he was in the provisional military government in Cuba. He was promoted in March 1911 to colonel in command of the 26th Infantry, graduated from the Army War College in 1912, and was sent to help guard the Mexican border in 1915, assuming command also of the National Guard forces sent there the following year. Promoted to brigadier general in June 1917, he took a brigade of Gen. William L. Sibert's 1st Division to France. In August he advanced to temporary major general and commandant of the infantry officer specialist schools established in France by Gen. John J. Pershing. In December he returned to the 1st Division as its commander and with it, on May 28, 1918, made the first American divisional offensive of the war, against Cantigny, which he captured and held. In July he moved up to command of the III Corps, which participated in the Aisne–Marne offensive in July–August, and in the great Meuse–Argonne offensive beginning in September. During that offensive Pershing organized the Second Army, which Bullard took over as temporary lieutenant general in October. In May 1919 he returned from occupation duty to the United States, with permanent rank of major general dating from November 1918, and took command of the II Corps area with headquarters at Fort Jay, Governors Island, New York. He retired in January 1925. His *Personalities and Reminiscences of the War* was published that year, and he was afterwards a prolific writer of newspaper and magazine articles on military affairs. He was president of the National Security League from 1925. In June 1930 he was promoted to lieutenant general on the retired list by act of Congress. Bullard died at Fort Jay, New York, on September 11, 1947.

Bullard, William Hannum Grubb (1866–1927), naval officer. Born in Media, Pennsylvania, on December 6, 1866, Bullard graduated from the Naval Academy in 1886. He was commissioned an ensign in July 1888 and promoted to lieutenant (junior grade) in September 1896. In the Spanish–American War he served on the *Columbia,* which patrolled the Atlantic coast and later transported troops to Puerto Rico. Promoted to lieutenant in March 1899 and to lieutenant commander in January 1905, he saw further sea duty on the *Maine* in 1905–1907. He had already become a specialist in electrical engineering and published his *Naval Electricians' Test and Hand Book,* 1904, when he joined the faculty of the Naval Academy in 1907, reorganizing the electrical engineering department there. He was promoted to commander in February 1909. During 1911–1912 he was commandant of the San Francisco naval station. In the latter year, promoted in July to captain, he was appointed superintendent of the naval radio service, a post he held for four years and in which he contributed greatly to the development of radio technology and regulation. In 1916 he took command of the battleship *Arkansas,* which in 1918 was in the American naval division attached to the British Grand Fleet; he was promoted to temporary rank of rear admiral in July of that year, the rank becoming permanent in October 1919. Bullard commanded American forces in the eastern Mediterranean for a time and served on the Inter-Allied Commission which arranged the armistice with Austria–Hungary and accepted surrender of its fleet. He took part also in international conferences on radio communication and from 1919 to 1921 was naval director of communications. After a period, 1921–1922, in command of the Yangtze Patrol Force he retired in September 1922. He was appointed chairman of the Federal Radio Commission (a forerunner of the Federal Communications Commission) by President Coolidge on its creation in March 1927. Bullard died on November 24, 1927, in Washington, D.C.

Bulloch, James Dunwody (1823–1901), naval officer and Confederate agent. Born near Savannah, Georgia, on June 25, 1823, to a family long prominent in the state, Bulloch entered the navy in 1839. He saw sea duty aboard the *United States,* the *Decatur,* and the *Delaware* in the next few years and in 1849–1851 served with the Coast Survey. He later commanded the *Georgia* on mail service. Having advanced only to lieutenant, he left the navy for commercial employment in New York. On May 9, 1861, he accepted appointment from Stephen Mallory, Confederate secretary of the navy, as Confederate naval agent abroad. He immediately sailed for England and began arranging for the purchase and construction of ships for the Confederacy. He was responsible for all the Confederate cruisers obtained in Britain except for the *Georgia,* purchased in Scotland by Matthew F. Maury. Early in 1862 the *Florida* was launched, and in May the *Alabama,* destined for a spectacular career raiding Union shipping. In that year he ordered two powerful ironclads, known as the Laird rams, from the shipbuilding firm of that name. Apprehensions over these potential blockade breakers led to increased diplomatic pressure by the U.S. government on British authorities to stop the activities of Bulloch and other agents. In March 1863 he removed his operation to Paris for the remainder of the war. Union diplomacy succeeded, and the Laird rams never reached the Confederacy. After the war Bulloch entered mercantile business in Liverpool. In 1884 he published *The Secret Service of the Confederate States in Europe.* He died on January 7, 1901. His half-sister, Martha Bulloch, was the mother of Theodore Roosevelt.

Bundy, Omar (1861–1940), army officer. Born in New Castle, Indiana, on June 17, 1861, Bundy attended Asbury College (now DePauw University) for a year and then entered West Point, graduating in 1883 and receiving a commission in the 2nd Infantry. He saw frontier service against the Crow Indians in Montana in 1887 and the Sioux in South Dakota in 1890–1891, receiving promotion to first lieutenant in May 1890. He advanced to captain in the 6th Infantry in April 1898, and during the Spanish–American War he took part in the battle of El Caney, July 1, 1898, and the subsequent siege of Santiago, where he was brevetted major. From 1899 to 1902 he was in the Philippines, serving in the field against the insurrectionists and later on staff duty in Visayas and Iloilo. After three years attached to the General Service and Staff College at Fort Leavenworth, Kansas, during which he was promoted to major in July 1904, he returned to the Philippines in 1905. He distinguished himself in March 1906 in leading a column against a Moro stronghold at Mount Dajo, on Jolo Island. He returned to the United States in 1907 and served at various posts, advancing to lieutenant colonel in March 1911, until entering the Army War College, from which he graduated in 1913. In July 1914 he was promoted to colonel in command of the 16th Infantry, based in El Paso, Texas, and in October 1915 he was appointed adjutant of the Southern Department. Bundy was promoted to brigadier general in May 1917 and ordered to France in command of the 1st Brigade, 1st Division. In August he was given temporary rank of major general. After a period in charge of setting up training areas in France for incoming AEF troops, he took command in November 1917 of the 2nd Division, which was sent up to a quiet sector of the front in March 1918. On June 1, 1918, the 2nd Division was rushed to the front west of Chateau-Thierry on the north bank of the Marne to meet the brunt of the German Aisne offensive. Holding firm for two days against furious German assault, the 2nd saved the last Allied line before Paris and allowed retreating French troops time to regroup. Beginning on June 6, elements of the 2nd, particularly the attached marine 4th Brigade under Gen. John A. Lejeune, counterattacked in Belleau Wood, taking the villages of Bouresches and Vaux. By July 1 the German offensive had been reversed, at a cost of nearly 10,000 American casualties. In August Bundy was appointed to command of the VI Corps, and in September he moved to the VIII Corps. In November he returned to the United States, taking command of Camp Lee, Virginia. In September 1920 he was placed in command of the VII Corps area at Fort Crooks, Nebraska. In March 1922, with rank of major general, he became commander of the Philippine Division. After two years in that post he was transferred to command of the V Corps area at Columbus, Ohio. Bundy retired in June 1925; he died in Washington, D.C., on January 21, 1940.

Burke, Arleigh Albert (1901–   ), naval officer. Born on October 19, 1901, in Boulder, Colorado, Burke graduated from the Naval Academy in 1923. After duty on the *Arizona* and the *Procyon* he resumed his studies in 1929 at the Academy and at the University of Michigan, taking a master's degree in engineering from the latter in 1931. Specializing in ordnance, he was assigned to the Bureau of Ordnance between tours on the *Chester* and the *Craven.* In 1939 he took command of the destroyer *Mugford,* attached to the Atlantic Fleet. From 1940 to 1943 he was again on shore duty with the Bureau of Ordnance. In May 1943 Burke was promoted to captain and named commander of Destroyer Squadron 23 operating in the Pacific. At the assault of Bougainville and nearby Buka in the Solomon Islands, October–November 1943, he made two spectacular dashes at high speed, sinking a large number of Japanese vessels by the high level of gunnery he had obtained in the squadron and earning for himself the nickname "Thirty-One Knot" Burke. In 1945 he was for a time chief of staff to Adm. Marc A. Mitscher, commander of Task Force 58, with temporary rank of commodore. From late 1945 to 1947 he was chief of staff of the Atlantic Fleet, and from 1947 to 1949 he was attached to the office of the chief of naval operations. In July 1950 he was promoted to rear admiral after some controversy over his participation in the "admirals' revolt," a dispute between the navy and the air force over strategic weapons priorities. He was named commander of Cruiser Division 5, then concentrated around Korea, and for some months in 1951 he served on the Military Armistice Commission there. He was director of the strategic plans division of the Navy Department in 1952–1954 and commander of Cruiser Division 6, Atlantic Fleet, in 1954–1955. In August 1955 Burke became chief of naval operations with rank of vice admiral after nomination by President Dwight D. Eisenhower, advancing to that post over more than 90 senior officers. He held the post longer than any predecessor, until his retirement in August 1961. He lived thereafter in Maryland; he had numerous business interests, including several directorships of major companies, and was a director of the Freedoms Foundation.

Burnham, Frederick Russell (1861–1947), scout and explorer. Born near Mankato, Minnesota, on May 11, 1861, Burnham grew up there and from the age of nine in Los Angeles, then but a town. At thirteen he became a messenger for Western Union, and he later worked as a hunter, hired gun, Indian fighter, and deputy sheriff, all the while consciously training himself in all the subtle arts of the scout. In 1893 he traveled to southern Africa, a region that had long excited his imagination, and became a scout for the British South Africa Company in Matabeleland (southern Rhodesia). In the Matabele (Ndebele) rebellion of that year his heroic though unsuccessful attempt to rescue a besieged British force under Maj. Wilson brought him renown; it increased in 1896, in the second Matabele uprising, when he tracked a supposed oracle-god, M'Limo, to his sacred cave and killed him. Burnham also led numerous exploring expeditions, discovering ancient ruins and copper and coal deposits and adding significantly to knowledge of the interior. He sought unsuccessfully for the mines of King Solomon written of by his friend, H. Rider Haggard. He left Africa in 1897 and until 1899 engaged in gold prospecting and mining in the Klondike. He returned to Africa at the outbreak of the Boer War at the request of Field Marshal Lord Roberts, who made him chief scout for the British Army in the field. In the war he became associated with Col. Robert Baden-Powell. He was twice captured and was wounded in an unsuccessful raid against a vital railway. In June 1900 he went to London, where he was given the rank of major and numerous honors and dined with Queen Victoria. From 1901 to 1904 he was again in Africa, exploring along the Volta river and the territory east of Lake Victoria. He discovered Lake Magadi and its rich soda deposits in what is now southern Kenya. He returned to the United States in 1904. In 1908 he found, on one of several archaeological expeditions he led into Mexico, rich Mayan ruins. In 1919, with John Hays Hammond, he organized the Burnham Exploration Company, which developed oil fields in California. In later years he lived on a cattle ranch in the High Sierras. Burnham wrote of his adventurous life in *Scouting on Two Continents,* 1926, and *Taking Chances,* 1944. He died in Santa Barbara, California, on September 1, 1947.

Burnside, Ambrose Everett (1824–1881), army officer and public official. Born on May 23, 1824, in Liberty, Indiana, Burnside graduated from West Point in 1847 and was assigned to the artillery but was too late to see major action in the Mexican War. He served at various posts until October 1853, when he resigned from the army. For a few years he operated a gun factory in Bristol, Rhode Island, turning out a breech-loading carbine of his own invention, but bankruptcy forced him to close it in 1857. Through the influence of George B. McClellan he was offered a position with the Illinois Central Railroad and continued there until April 1861, when he recruited the 1st Rhode Island Regiment of volunteers and as its colonel took it to Washington. Following the first battle of Bull Run (Manassas), July 21, in which he commanded a brigade, he was commissioned in August a brigadier general of volunteers. In January 1862 he led a seaborne expeditionary force with naval forces under Flag-Officer Louis M. Goldsborough that captured several strongholds, including Roanoke Island on February 7 and New Bern on March 14, along with ordnance and prisoners, on the North Carolina coast and eliminated the Confederate fleet in Albemarle and Pamlico sounds. Promoted to major general of volunteers in March 1862, he was then sent to join the Army of the Potomac, his command designated the IX Corps. In September he commanded the right wing, consisting of his own IX and Gen. Joseph Hooker's I Corps, in the battles of South Mountain on the 14th, pushing Gen. Robert E. Lee's forces back to Sharpsburg, and Antietam on the 17th, his incomplete success at the latter resulting mainly from a confusion of command. In November he was chosen by President Abraham Lincoln to succeed McClellan as commander of the Army of the Potomac; he had twice before declined the job. He imposed a new (and ultimately unwieldy) tactical organization on the army, dividing it into Right, Center, and Left Grand Divisions, each of two corps plus cavalry, under Gen. Edwin V. Sumner, Gen. Hooker, and Gen. William B. Franklin. Carrying his plan—to cross the Rappahannock at Fredericksburg in order to race Lee to Richmond—over the objections of Hooker and Lincoln, he suffered on December 13 a heavy defeat due to administrative delay, the results of good Confederate intelligence, and his own poor judgment. The next month he was replaced by Hooker and in March 1863 was transferred to command of the Department and a new Army of the Ohio. There he took strong action against persons and newspapers critical of the government, most notably Clement L. Vallandigham, whom he had imprisoned; but this, like most of his measures of that period, was overruled by Lincoln. In July he stopped Gen. John Hunt Morgan's cavalry raid into Ohio and then marched into eastern Tennessee, successfully clearing it of Confederate forces at Cumberland Gap and in November holding Knoxville against Gen. James Longstreet, who was thus prevented from reinforcing Gen. Braxton Bragg at Chattanooga. In January 1864 he returned to his old IX Corps, which remained an independent command but was attached by Gen. Ulysses S. Grant to Gen. George G. Meade's Army of the Potomac. With it he took part in the many battles of the Wilderness campaign. After several successful showings, however, he again met failure at Petersburg, where his attempt to assault Confederate lines after breaching the fortifications with a mine on July 30 resulted in a rout. A court of inquiry called by Gen. Meade found him to blame; he left active service as a consequence and in April 1865 resigned. He became an officer of several railroad companies and served three terms, 1866–1869, as governor of Rhode Island. In 1874 Burnside was elected to the Senate, serving until his death in Bristol, Rhode Island, on September 13, 1881. Also in 1874 he succeeded John A. Logan as national commander of the Grand Army of the Republic. His name came to be applied to the style of side-whiskers he wore; the term was later anagrammatized to "sideburns."

Burrows, William (1785–1813), naval officer. Born on October 6, 1785, in Kinderton (now part of Philadelphia), Burrows was the son of Lt. Col. William W. Burrows, first commandant of the marine corps. He entered the navy with a midshipman's warrant in November 1799 and in January 1800 made his first voyage aboard the *Portsmouth* bound for France. In 1803 he joined the *Constitution* and, with rank of acting lieutenant given him by Commodore Edward Preble, served on it through the Tripolitan War. He returned home in 1807 and the following year commanded gunboat *119* in the Delaware river flotilla on duty to enforce the embargo. He subsequently served on the *President* and the *Hornet*. Dissatisfied with his progress in rank, he tendered his resignation but instead was given a year's furlough, during which he sailed on a merchant ship to India and China. The vessel was captured by the British on the return voyage, and Burrows was held for a time in Barbados. On his return to the United States he resumed active duty as captain of the sloop of war *Enterprise*, 14 guns. Sailing from Portsmouth, New Hampshire, early in September 1813, he fell in with the British brig *Boxer*, 12, on September 5 off the Maine coast. In a 45-minute action he used his slight superiority in gunpower with great skill and compelled the *Boxer* to surrender. Captain Blythe of the *Boxer* was cut in two by chain shot, and Burrows, mortally wounded in the fight, lived only long enough to receive the surrender. The two captains were buried side by side in Portland, Maine. The victory of the *Enterprise* was the first American success at sea since the loss of the *Chesapeake* in June and went far to restore the nation's morale.

Burrows, William Ward (1758–1805), marine officer. Born on January 16, 1758, in Charleston, South Carolina, Burrows studied law in Charleston and later in London. He returned to the United States in 1775 and during the Revolution fought as a member of the South Carolina militia. Afterwards he took up the practice of law in Philadelphia. On July 11, 1798, an act of Congress established the United States Marine Corps as a branch of the navy, and the

next day Burrows was appointed major commandant of the corps by President John Adams. The reorganization and rapid strengthening of the navy in 1798, a process in which the creation of the marine corps played a major part, was a response to a state of undeclared war with France, a war fought on the high seas for the most part. Detachments of marines were assigned to ships and shore stations and took part in virtually every engagement. With the end of the war in September 1800 the corps, numbering nearly 900 men, was drastically reduced. Burrows was required to recruit upwards of 500 new marines following the outbreak of the Tripolitan War in 1801. Before the conclusion of that war he retired as commandant in March 1804, having been promoted to lieutenant colonel some time before; he died in Washington, D.C., in 1805. His son, William Burrows, became a distinguished naval officer.

Bush, Vannevar (1890–1974), electrical engineer and public official. Born on March 11, 1890, in Everett, Massachusetts, Bush grew up there and in nearby Chelsea. He graduated from Tufts College in 1913 and, while working first for the General Electric Company, then as a civilian in the inspection department of the navy, and from 1914 as an instructor in mathematics at Tufts, he pursued graduate studies at both Harvard and the Massachusetts Institute of Technology (MIT), receiving a doctorate in engineering from each in 1916. He remained at Tufts as an assistant professor of electrical engineering until 1917, when he undertook antisubmarine research for the navy. In 1919 he was appointed associate professor of electrical power transmission at MIT, where he remained until 1938, from 1923 as full professor and from 1932 as vice-president and dean of the School of Engineering. He had also been from 1917 to 1922 a consulting engineer for the American Radio and Research Corporation and in the latter year had joined in founding the American Appliance Corporation, later the Raytheon Manufacturing Company. In addition to his academic duties at MIT Bush carried on a fertile and highly varied program of research that led to the invention of such disparate devices as improved vacuum tubes, a justifying typewriter, a network analyzer, and, most importantly, a differential analyzer, which was a pioneering form of analog computer built in 1928 and the direct progenitor of later devices in the field. In 1938 Bush was named president of the Carnegie Institution of Washington. In the same year he became a member of the National Advisory Committee for Aeronautics, of which he was chairman from 1939 to 1941. In 1940 he assumed a leading role in mobilizing the U.S. scientific community for the impending war by prevailing upon President Franklin D. Roosevelt to create the National Defense Research Committee (NDRC), of which he was named chairman, and the following year he became chairman of the newly established Office of Scientific Research and Development (OSRD), which absorbed the NDRC. As head of the OSRD until its dissolution in 1946 Bush directed the vast array of research projects undertaken by the government as a vital part of the war effort, including, until its transfer to the Army Corps of Engineers in 1943, the Manhattan Project for the development of the atomic bomb. After the war he served as chairman of the Joint Research and Development Board of the army and navy in 1946–1947 and of its successor body, the Research and Development Board, in 1947–1948. He remained active thereafter as an adviser to many governmental agencies and boards on matters of scientific manpower, organization, and policy. He left the presidency of the Carnegie Institution in 1955, becoming a trustee three years later; he was also a trustee of the Carnegie Corporation of New York from 1939 to 1955 and honorary chairman of the corporation of MIT from 1959. The recipient of a great many honors and awards, Bush published several nontechnical works, including *Science: The Endless Frontier*, 1945; *Endless Horizons*, 1946; *Modern Arms and Free Men*, 1949; *Science Is Not Enough*, 1967; and *Pieces of the Action*, 1970. He died in Belmont, Massachusetts, on June 28, 1974.

Bushnell, David (1742?–1824), inventor. Born in Saybrook, Connecticut, probably in 1742, Bushnell grew up on a farm and remained there until the death of his father freed him to pursue his education. He entered Yale and graduated in 1775. By that time the idea of an underwater gunpowder mine had occurred to him. Returning to Saybrook, he expanded on the notion and soon built a small one-man submarine boat. Powered by two screw propellers cranked from inside, having manually controlled inlet valves and outlet pumps for descending and ascending, and equipped with rudimentary phosphorus-lit instruments, the vessel was crude, difficult to operate, and ungainly in appearance (rather like a top), fully warranting its name, *Bushnell's Turtle* (later it was often called the *American Turtle*). The *Turtle* was armed with an ingenious detachable gunpowder mine with an auger bit; operated from inside, the bit allowed the mine to be screwed to the hull of an enemy ship below the waterline. A clock device was intended to delay the explosion while the *Turtle* escaped. Manned by Sgt. Ezra Lee, the *Turtle* went up against the British frigate *Eagle*, 64 guns, in New York harbor in August 1776, but the frigate's copper sheathing foiled the auger. The *Turtle* did manage the several hours required in the attempt, however, without serious difficulty. In 1777 the intrepid Lee tried again with the frigate *Cerberus* at New London; he loosed the mine, but its line was caught by a crewman aboard a prize schooner alongside and when he hauled it in it exploded, killing three sailors and de-

stroying the schooner but not the *Cerberus*. Subsequent attempts in Boston harbor and at Philadelphia also failed. The *Turtle* was nonetheless the first American submarine and probably the first to be used anywhere in warfare. In January 1778 Bushnell built a large number of crude mines and floated them down the Delaware River in an attempt to destroy British shipping around Philadelphia. Only one of the devices exploded, killing four British seamen in a boat, but the British were made so anxious by the occurrence that in panic they began shooting at every floating object on the river. The occasion was subsequently satirized by Francis Hopkinson in his poem "The Battle of the Kegs." Bushnell finally gave up and joined the Continental army as an engineer; for a few months before his discharge late in 1783 he was in command of the detachment of engineers at West Point. He then apparently went to France for several years. He turned up in Georgia in 1795 under an assumed name; he taught school for a time and then took up the practice of medicine in Warrenton, where he died in 1824.

Butler, Benjamin Franklin (1818–1893), army officer and political leader. Born in Deerfield, New Hampshire, on November 5, 1818, Butler graduated from Waterville (now Colby) College in 1838 and two years later was admitted to the bar. He built up a large practice in Lowell, Massachusetts, and entered politics, serving in the state assembly in 1853 and the state senate in 1859. A Democrat, he was a strong supporter of labor and a defender of immigrants. He was a delegate to the 1860 Democratic national convention and was one of the group that bolted to nominate John C. Breckinridge. When the Civil War began, Butler, called to service as a brigadier general of the Massachusetts militia, strongly supported the Union. In May 1861 he occupied Baltimore; in the same month he was commissioned major general of volunteers and given command of Fort Monroe in Virginia. While in this post, he declared escaped slaves to be "contraband" of war, a use of the word which persisted through the war. On June 10 he lost an engagement, the first major one of the war, with Col. John B. Magruder's forces at Big Bethel, Virginia. In August he sailed with a squadron commanded by Flag-Officer Silas H. Stringham that captured Fort Clark and Fort Hatteras at Hatteras Inlet, North Carolina. In May 1862, after leading the land forces in support of Adm. David Farragut's naval assault on the city, he became military commander of New Orleans. Although he improved the city's sanitation and kept order, he aroused the hatred of the populace. He strained relations with foreign consuls, executed a citizen for lowering the Union flag, was suspected of financial irregularities and, in his infamous Order No. 28, warned that any disrespect or contempt shown his men by a female would be taken as evidence of the latter's moral disrepute and treated accordingly. Having been declared an outlaw by the Confederate government, he was recalled from that post in December 1862. Held inactive for nearly a year, he was given command late in 1863 of the Department of Virginia and North Carolina, a command subsequently designated the Army of the James. Following his defeat by Gen. P. G. T. Beauregard at Drewry's Bluff, May 12–16, 1864, he allowed himself to be bottled up at Bermuda Hundred, unable to render any assistance to the Army of the Potomac in the Richmond–Petersburg campaign. After failing in an expedition against Fort Fisher, North Carolina, in December, undertaken in conjunction with Adm. David D. Porter, he was removed from command by Gen. Ulysses S. Grant in January 1865. From 1867 to 1875 and from 1877 to 1879 he was a member of the House of Representatives, first as a Radical Republican and then as a Greenbacker. He was one of the managers of the impeachment trial of President Andrew Johnson and became a strong supporter of President Ulysses S. Grant. He was the Democratic governor of Massachusetts in 1882, a post for which he had tried four times before on various tickets. He was defeated for reelection in 1883. The next year he was the Greenback–Labor and Anti-Monopoly nominee for President. He died on January 11, 1893, in Washington, D.C.

Butler, John (1728–1796), Loyalist and Indian agent. Born in 1728 in New London, Connecticut, Butler moved with his family to the Mohawk valley of New York in 1742. With the rank of captain he served under Gen. (later Sir) William Johnson in the expedition against Crown Point in 1755 and later under Gen. James Abercrombie at Ticonderoga and with Col. John Bradstreet in the capture of Fort Frontenac in 1758. He rejoined Johnson in 1759 for the Montreal campaign, becoming commander of the Indian allies. He remained an associate of Johnson's until the latter's death. At the outbreak of the Revolution Butler and his son, Walter N. Butler, fled to Canada. Named deputy superintendent of Indian affairs at Niagara, he was active in the irregular partisan warfare that disturbed the Mohawk valley during 1775–1776. In 1777 he assembled a mixed force of Indians and Loyalists and joined Col. Barry St. Leger's march down the Mohawk, sharing in the latter's defeat by Gen. Nicholas Herkimer at Oriskany on August 6. Recruiting a battalion of rangers among Loyalists at Niagara, he set out in the spring of 1778 to invade the Wyoming Valley of Pennsylvania, leading about 1100 men including his own Butler's Rangers, a detachment of the King's Royal Regiment of New York, and a number of Iroquois Indians. On July 3 he met the 300-odd ragtag defenders of the valley under Lt. Col. Zebulon Butler outside Forty Fort; all but 60 of the defenders were killed. The

survivors of the battle fled to Forty Fort and surrendered the next day. Maj. Butler was unable to restrain his Indians from burning and pillaging, and, though the atrocities were later often exaggerated, the event became known as the Wyoming Massacre. (The event was virtually repeated in November by his son Walter at Cherry Valley.) In 1779 he was defeated by Gen. John Sullivan at Newtown on August 29. In 1780, promoted to lieutenant colonel, he joined Sir John Johnson (Sir William's son) in raids on the Mohawk and Schoharie valleys. His possessions in New York having been confiscated, Butler remained in Niagara after the Revolution, serving as Indian agent and enjoying a considerable pension from the British government. He died at Niagara in May 1796.

Butler, Smedley Darlington (1881–1940), marine officer. Born in West Chester, Pennsylvania, on July 30, 1881, Butler failed in an attempt to enlist in the army at the outbreak of the Spanish–American War, but in May 1898, aged sixteen, he did manage to secure a second lieutenant's commission in the marine corps by misstating his age. He saw no action in the war, arriving in Cuba after the cessation of hostilities. Discharged in February 1899, he was recommissioned a first lieutenant in April of that year. He was then ordered to the Philippines for service against the insurrectionists. In 1900, under Maj. Littleton W. T. Waller, he took part in the Peking Relief Expedition against the Boxers and twice distinguished himself in rescuing wounded comrades. He was twice wounded himself, at Tientsin, July 13, and Peking, August 14, and brevetted captain in February 1901. After duty at the marine barracks at Philadelphia and elsewhere, he commanded a small marine force from the transport *Panther* that rescued a U.S. consular agent from rebels in Honduras in February 1903. In 1904 he joined the 1st Marine Regiment in the Philippines. After recovering from a serious illness he was again in Philadelphia from 1906, receiving promotion to major dating from May of that year. From 1909 to 1914 he commanded a battalion stationed in Panama, and from there he was sent to Corinto, Nicaragua, in August 1912 to suppress a revolt. In September his force was absorbed into the large one under Col. Joseph H. Pendleton. In January 1914 Butler was assigned to duty with the Atlantic Fleet, and in April 1914 he won a Medal of Honor for his role in the capture of Veracruz, Mexico, during the Huerta–Carranza civil war. In August 1915 he commanded a battalion in the marine force under Col. Waller sent to Haiti, and in November he led a detachment of marines in capturing the reputedly impregnable Haitian stronghold of Fort Rivière from Caco bandits and thereby won a second Medal of Honor. Promoted to lieutenant colonel, Butler was given the task of organizing a native Haitian gendarmerie in December 1915, and he commanded it in the rank of major general. Though an outstanding leader of troops and an officer of boundless energy and courage (known widely as "Old Gimlet-Eye"), Butler saw no combat during World War I, instead commanding Camp Pontanezen near Brest, France, with temporary rank of brigadier general, from October 1918 to July 1919. He was promoted to colonel in March 1919 and to brigadier general in March 1921, the latter while commanding the marine camp at Quantico, Virginia, converting it from a wartime cantonment into a permanent base. During 1924–1925 he took leave of absence to serve as director of public safety for the city of Philadelphia; the blunt methods that perfectly suited the marine corps, however, were less successful in civil affairs. In February 1926 he resumed active service as commander of the marine barracks at San Diego, California. Following the Nanking incident in March 1927, in which foreign nationals and consulates in that city were attacked, he commanded the marine expeditionary force sent to China during 1927–1929, displaying remarkable diplomatic skills in that tense situation. In July 1929 he was promoted to major general. Butler's relations with his superiors had often been marked by friction, a condition exacerbated by his occasionally indiscreet remarks on public affairs. Consequently, he was passed over when the post of marine commandant opened in 1930, in spite of his being the senior major general available; he thereupon requested and was granted retirement in October 1931. The following year he ran unsuccessfully for the U.S. Senate from Pennsylvania as a Prohibition candidate. In 1935 he published *War Is a Racket*, and in later years wrote and spoke often in favor of military preparedness and neutrality. He died in Philadelphia on June 21, 1940.

Butler, Walter N. (?–1781), Loyalist. Born near Johnstown, New York, Butler was the son of Col. John Butler. He studied law for a time in Albany but fled with his father to Canada at the beginning of the Revolution. In 1777, with rank of lieutenant, he marched with his father under Col. Barry St. Leger down the Mohawk valley, encouraging the Loyalists remaining in the region to rise up. He was captured and court-martialed as a spy, but friends who had known him in Albany successfully interceded on his behalf, and he later escaped back to Niagara. In 1778, by then a captain, he won approval of a plan for an attack on Cherry Valley, in the upper Susquehanna valley of New York, by Butler's Rangers, led by himself, and a band of Indian allies under Joseph Brant, together totalling some 500 men. The attack was made on November 11; Brant's Indians were particularly ferocious, and in all 30 settlers, many of them women and children, were killed, 71 were taken prisoner, and all the buildings outside the fort were burned. While he later claimed to have done all he could to restrain his Indian forces, the event inevita-

bly became known as the Cherry Valley Massacre. Together with the earlier Wyoming Massacre at his father's hands, the work at Cherry Valley led directly to Gen. John Sullivan's expedition the next year. Most of the Cherry Valley prisoners were soon released, but a few were held hostage and Butler later exchanged them for his mother and the younger Butler children, who had been held in Albany. In October 1781 he took part in another raid by Loyalists, Indians, and British regulars on the Mohawk settlements; during the retreat on October 30 he was killed.

Butler, William Orlando (1791–1880), army officer and public official. Born in Jessamine County, Kentucky, on April 19, 1791, Butler was of a family long distinguished in military affairs. He graduated from Transylvania University in 1812 and began the study of law, but at the outbreak of war with England in that year he enlisted in the army. He served as a private under Gen. James Winchester in the relief of Fort Wayne and, having been commissioned ensign in the 17th Infantry, was in the battles of January 18 and 22, 1813, at the Raisin River; in the second of these he distinguished himself and was wounded and captured, escaping the massacre carried out by the Indian allies of the British. Exchanged after a period of harsh imprisonment, he returned to Kentucky, was commissioned captain, and led a company in Gen. Andrew Jackson's capture of Pensacola. At New Orleans he led the attack on the British under Gen. Pakenham on December 23, 1814, that checked the British advance and allowed the Americans time to prepare defenses at Chaumette. He also took part in the great battle on January 8, 1815. Brevetted major, he became aide-de-camp to Jackson in 1816, but in 1817 he resigned from the army and resumed the study of law. Establishing his practice in Carrollton, Kentucky, he enjoyed considerable success and served in the legislature, 1817–1818, and in Congress, 1839–1843. He ran unsuccessfully as a Democrat for governor in 1844. In June 1846 he reentered the army to serve in the Mexican War and was appointed major general of volunteers. Joining Gen. Zachary Taylor in Texas, he took part in the campaign in northern Mexico, and at Monterrey, September 20–24, 1846, he distinguished himself in charging a Mexican battery. He was wounded there, and after recuperating he joined Gen. Winfield Scott in time to be present at the capture of Mexico City on September 14, 1847. In 1848 he succeeded Scott as commander of the army in Mexico. Shortly before his return home later that year he was nominated for the vice-presidency on the Democratic ticket with Lewis Cass; they lost to the Whig candidates, Zachary Taylor and Millard Fillmore. Resuming his law practice, he failed of election to the Senate in 1851 and in 1855 declined appointment as governor of Nebraska Territory. In February 1861, on the eve of the Civil War, he was a delegate to the Washington Peace Conference. Butler died in Carrollton, Kentucky, on August 6, 1880.

Butler, Zebulon (1731–1795), Revolutionary army officer. Born January 23, 1731, in Ipswich, Massachusetts, Butler grew up there and in Lyme, Connecticut. During the French and Indian War he rose to the rank of captain by 1760 and in 1762 took part in the siege and capture of Havana, Cuba. In 1769 he led a band of Connecticut settlers to the Wyoming Valley of Pennsylvania and became a leader in the Yankee–Pennamite War over the conflicting claims of Connecticut and Pennsylvania to the area. During 1774–1776 he represented the area, designated as "Westmoreland township," in the Connecticut legislature. In December 1775 he repulsed a body of 500 Pennsylvanians under Col. Plunkett, sheriff of Northumberland County, at the Nanticoke Gap. Butler was commissioned colonel of the Connecticut line at the outbreak of the Revolution, and in 1776 he became a lieutenant colonel in the Continental army. He served under Gen. George Washington through the New Jersey campaign and in March 1778 was promoted to colonel. In June 1778, while home on leave, he received warning of the approach of a force of rangers, Loyalists, and Indians under Maj. John Butler. Col. Butler gathered the families of the region inside Forty Fort. On July 3 he allowed himself to be overruled by a council of war and led the 300-odd defenders, mostly untrained militia, out of the fort to engage the invaders. Flanked by the Indians and outnumbered four to one, the defenders were slaughtered. Butler and a few regulars made it back into the fort, whence he fled to escape capture. He soon returned as commandant in the valley and was there during the punitive expedition led against the Indians by Gen. John Sullivan in 1779. In 1780 he was assigned to duty at West Point. He died in Wilkes-Barre, Pennsylvania, on July 28, 1795.

Buttrick, John (1715–1791), Revolutionary militia officer. Born in 1715 at a place unknown, Buttrick was a major of militia in Concord, Massachusetts, in 1775. On April 19, after the desultory engagement with minutemen on Lexington Green, the British troops sent out from Boston under Maj. Pitcairn proceeded to Concord to search out secret military stores. The provincial militia gathered to the number of about 450 and under Buttrick marched to the North Bridge, which was held by about 100 British. On their approach, the British began taking up the planking on the bridge. Buttrick called on them to stop, but instead they fired on the provincials, killing two. Buttrick cried out "Fire, fellow soldiers, for God's sake, fire!" His men did so and advanced over the bridge, driving off the British. The battle at North Bridge was remembered as one of the most famous of the Revolution and was immortalized by Ralph Waldo Emerson in 1837 in the lines "By the rude bridge that arched the flood,/ Their flag to April's breeze unfurled,/ Here once the embattled farmers stood,/ And fired the shot heard 'round the world." Buttrick died in Concord on May 16, 1791.

Byrd, Richard Evelyn (1888–1957), naval officer, aviator, and explorer. Born in Winchester, Virginia, on October 25, 1888, Byrd was a direct descendant of William Byrd, planter and councillor of colonial Virginia. After attending Virginia Military Institute and the University of Virginia he entered the Naval Academy, from which he graduated in 1912. Active service followed for three years; forced to retire in 1915 because of old leg injuries, Byrd returned to duty and entered the navy's aviation branch in 1917, winning his pilot's wings in 1918. During World War I, with temporary rank of lieutenant commander, he commanded a navy air patrol squadron based in Canada and was active afterward in promoting the development of naval aviation. He was largely responsible for the creation of the Bureau of Aeronautics, and he invented several important aids to aerial navigation. He helped plan the 1919 transatlantic flight of the navy NC flying boats. In 1924 he commanded a small naval flying group attached to D. B. MacMillan's Arctic expedition; the next year he went back with a second expedition and on May 9, 1926, with Floyd Bennett as his copilot in the *Josephine Ford,* made the first flight over the North Pole, a round trip from Spitsbergen. The feat won both men the Medal of Honor, and Byrd was awarded the Distinguished Service Medal and promoted to commander. In June of the following year, with Bernt Balchen and two others, Byrd piloted a multiengined aircraft across the Atlantic (he had earlier given special training to Charles A. Lindbergh and, but for equipment difficulties, would probably have beaten him in the race for first crossing). With the status of popular hero combined with considerable skill in public relations, Byrd had little difficulty in securing private sponsors for an expedition to the Antarctic in 1928–1930. The expedition reached the Bay of Whales on the Antarctic coast in December 1928 and established its base, "Little America"; vast new land areas were discovered on that trip, and on November 29, 1929, Byrd, Balchen, and two others took off from Little America and made the first flight over the South Pole. Soon afterward he was promoted to rear admiral, retired. From 1933 to 1935 he was in command of a second expedition in Antarctica, during which much more unknown territory was mapped. For five months in the southern winter of 1934 he was alone in a weather observation shack far south of the main base and, nearly dying there of carbon monoxide poisoning, he suffered from impaired health thereafter. In 1939–1940, under the aegis of the newly established U.S. Antarctic Service, he led another survey expedition that added still more territory to the map. During World War II he was on the staff of Adm. Ernest J. King, chief of naval operations. In 1946–1947 he was again in Antarctica in command of a huge navy-sponsored expedition called Operation High Jump and made a second flight over the pole. In 1955 he was placed in charge of Operation Deep Freeze, a major scientific and exploratory expedition sent to the Antarctic under navy auspices as part of the program of the International Geophysical Year, 1957–1958. Byrd accompanied the task force to Antarctica, made a last flight over the pole in January 1956, and returned to the United States. Failing health prevented his rejoining the expedition, and he died in Boston on March 11, 1957. Several books by Byrd achieved wide popularity: *Skyward*, 1928; *Little America*, 1930; *Discovery*, 1935; and *Alone*, 1938.

C

Callaghan, Daniel Judson (1890–1942), naval officer. Born in San Francisco on July 26, 1890, Callaghan graduated from the Naval Academy in 1911 and saw his first sea duty on the *California*, with which he took part in the pacification of Nicaragua in 1912. He subsequently served on the *Truxtun* and the *New Orleans* and in various shore assignments. In 1938, by which time he held the rank of commander, he was named naval aide to President Franklin D. Roosevelt. He remained in that post for three years, returning to sea in 1941 as captain in command of the cruiser *San Francisco*. He was at Pearl Harbor at the time of the Japanese attack on December 7, 1941, but the *San Francisco* was not damaged and was soon at sea. Shortly thereafter Callaghan was named chief of staff to Adm. Robert L. Ghormley, naval commander in the Southwest Pacific area. By the autumn of 1942 the *San Francisco* was in the thick of the Solomons campaign, taking part in the battle of Cape Esperance, off Guadalcanal, on October 11. On November 12–13 Callaghan, by then promoted to rear admiral, was in command of a task force of cruisers and destroyers standing off Guadalcanal toward Savo Island after escorting troop transports. The *San Francisco* had lost its radar mast to a Japanese airplane. The task force came up into a Japanese fleet of battleships, cruisers, and destroyers, far outnumbering his forces. By dint of tactical and gunnery skill he outfought the Japanese; the *San Francisco* sank a cruiser and a destroyer and then turned to engage a battleship. A shell from the battleship struck the bridge of the *San Francisco*, killing Callaghan and his staff. The damage inflicted on the Japanese fleet was so heavy as to seriously disrupt the attempt to reinforce ground forces on Guadalcanal; the American loss was two cruisers and four destroyers. Callaghan, the third flag officer killed in the war, was posthumously awarded the Medal of Honor.

Cameron, George Hamilton (1861–1944), army officer. Born in Ottawa, Illinois, on January 8, 1861, Cameron graduated from West Point in 1883 and was commissioned in the 7th Cavalry. He saw duty in Nebraska and Kansas and from 1888 to 1895 was an instructor at West Point, receiving promotion to first lieutenant in March 1891. After a time in garrison duty in the Pacific northwest he was ordered to the Philippines in August 1898, where he saw action under Gen. Henry W. Lawton against the insurrectionists until 1901. He advanced to captain in March 1899. For five years he was on the staff of the Cavalry and Light Artillery School, Fort Riley, Kansas, and, after a second brief tour in the Philippines, he was assistant commandant of the Mounted Service School (it had been renamed in 1906) at Fort Riley from 1907 to 1910, becoming major of the 14th Cavalry in November 1909. After a third tour in the Philippines, 1910–1912, and graduation from the Army War College in 1914 he was promoted to lieutenant colonel in April 1914 and colonel in July 1916 while attached to the General Staff. In August 1917 he was promoted to temporary brigadier general, and in September he was placed in command of a western states National Guard infantry brigade, activated as the 40th Division, at Camp Kearny, California. In November he was promoted to temporary major general, and in December he was transferred to command of the 4th Division at Camp Greene, North Carolina, taking it overseas in June 1918 in time to participate in the Aisne–Marne operations. In August Cameron was raised to command of the V Corps, which was immediately sent into combat as the west (left) wing of the Allied attack on the St. Mihiel salient. In the expanded offensive from late September along the Meuse River and through the Argonne Forest, the V Corps anchored the center of the advance. He remained commander of the V Corps until October. After his return to the United States Cameron was commander of Camp Gordon, Georgia, and then commander of the reorganized Cavalry School, Fort Riley, from May 1919 to September 1921. After three years as chief of staff of the reserve 76th Division in Hartford, Connecticut, Cameron retired in July 1924 to Fishers Island, New York. He died in Staunton, Virginia, on January 28, 1944.

Campbell, William (1745–1781), Revolutionary militia officer. Born in 1745 in Augusta County, Virginia, Campbell moved west to the Holston valley about 1767 and married the sister of Patrick Henry. He became prominent in the frontier militia, serving as a captain in Lord Dunmore's War against the Shawnee, Ottawa, and other Indians in 1774. He served also as a justice of the peace for Fincastle and later Washington counties. Quick to join the patriot cause in 1775, he led a company to join Patrick Henry's regiment in Williamsburg in September, and in July 1776 he took part in the expulsion of Lord Dunmore, the royal governor. Late in that year he resigned from active duty in order to return home and help guard the Indian frontier. In 1777 he was appointed lieutenant colonel of militia; in 1778 he was appointed a commissioner to run the Virginia–Cherokee border. In 1780, promoted to colonel, he was called on to join a campaign against Maj. Patrick Ferguson, a British officer sent by Gen. Charles Cornwallis with about a thousand regulars and Loyalists to raid the back country of North Carolina and rally secret Loyalist sentiment there. Campbell marched some 400 Washington County men to a rendezvous with forces under Col. Isaac Shelby, Col. John Sevier, Maj. Joseph McDowell, and Maj. Joseph Winston. Of the 1800 men present, 900 were picked to seek out Ferguson. Campbell was chosen to lead the march, which found Ferguson drawn up in a defensive position atop an eminence known as King's Mountain in present-day York County, South Carolina, just south of the North Carolina border. On October 7 the militia attacked, Campbell being in the thick of the fight. The battle was a complete American victory; Ferguson was killed, nearly all of his men killed or captured, and Cornwallis's Carolina campaign finished. Campbell took part in the battle at Guilford Court House on March 15, 1781, where Gen. Nathanael Greene dealt a heavy blow to Cornwallis. After serving a brief term in the legislature Campbell was appointed brigadier general of militia; he joined the forces under Lafayette at Jamestown but a short time later was taken ill and died at Rocky Mills, Hanover County, Virginia, on August 22, 1781.

Canby, Edward Richard Sprigg (1817–1873), army officer. Born in Kentucky in August 1817, Canby grew up in Indiana and after graduating from West Point in 1839 was commissioned in the 2nd Infantry. From 1839 to 1842 he served in the Seminole War in Florida. After several years of garrison and recruitment duty he was promoted to first lieutenant in June 1846. Promoted to captain and assistant adjutant general the next year, he served in Gen. Winfield Scott's army in the Mexican War, seeing action at Veracruz, Cerro Gordo, Contreras, and Churubusco and winning brevets to major and lieutenant colonel. After the war he served as lieutenant colonel in the adjutant general's department, returning to the line of the army in March 1855 with appointment as major of the 10th Infantry. Canby was engaged in frontier duty for several years, including the Mormon expedition under Col. Albert S. Johnston in 1857–1858, and in May 1861, while posted at Fort Defiance, New Mexico, he was promoted to colonel in command of the 19th Infantry and, as acting brigadier general, of the Department of New Mexico with headquarters at Fort Craig. On February 21, 1862, he was forced from the field at Valverde by Gen. Henry H. Sibley leading a Confederate column across the Southwest toward California. He quickly adopted a harrying strategy, however, drawing Sib-

ley away from his supply lines, and on March 27 and 28, at Apache Canyon and Glorieta Pass, Canby's men, joined by Colorado volunteers under Maj. John M. Chivington, stopped Sibley's advance and the Confederate threat in the West. Appointed brigadier general of volunteers in that month, Canby was made assistant adjutant general in the War Department. Briefly in 1863 he held command of troops in New York City following the draft riots there. In May 1864 he was promoted to major general of volunteers in command of the Division of West Mississippi. He was badly wounded in a guerilla attack at the White River in Arkansas in November 1864 but otherwise saw little action until the early spring of 1865, when he undertook a compaign against Mobile, Alabama, culminating in its capture on April 12. In March he had been brevetted brigadier and major general in the regular army. He received the surrenders of Gen. Richard Taylor, May 4, and Gen. Edmund Kirby-Smith, May 26, who commanded the last Confederate armies in the field. After the war he served in various capacities in the South and in Washington, D.C., receiving regular rank of brigadier general in July 1866. In 1870 he took command of the Department of the Columbia on the Pacific coast. In the spring of 1873 he traveled to northern California to attempt to negotiate a settlement of the Modoc War. On April 11, 1873, while in conference, unarmed, with the Modoc representatives, Canby was murdered by Captain Jack, the Modoc leader.

Caniff, Milton Arthur (1907–   ), cartoonist. Born on February 28, 1907, in Hillsboro, Ohio, Caniff began newspaper cartoon work while still in high school and was on the art staff of the *Columbus Dispatch* while attending Ohio State University. After graduating in 1930 and choosing cartooning over acting as a career—he had appeared in small roles in a few movies during an earlier residence in California —he joined the Associated Press in New York and turned out two minor comic strips for two years. In 1934 he moved to the Chicago Tribune–New York Daily News Syndicate and began an innovative strip, *Terry and the Pirates,* which quickly attracted fans in the tens of thousands. An action-adventure story line set in the mysterious Orient was given strongly adult orientation in *Terry,* the depth of characterization and frank sensuality of the figures adding to their interest. Terry and dashing Pat Ryan, heroes straight from the movie tradition, faced a succession of bizarre villains, most notably the Dragon Lady, and encountered a series of alluring females of various sorts. When one of the feminine characters, a favorite named Raven Sherman, was allowed to die in an episode in 1941, Caniff and the syndicate were flooded with letters both of protest and of condolence. Rendered in a dramatic chiaroscuro style, with painstaking and thoroughly researched detail, and often reflecting current events, such as the Japanese invasion of China, the strip attained a level of sophisticated realism unprecedented in the field. It also inspired a radio program that was popular for many years. During World War II Caniff drew another strip, *Male Call*, for armed services publications, and illustrated an official servicemen's handbook on China for the War Department. In 1947 he joined the Publishers-Hall Syndicate, leaving *Terry* to others (the strip continued until 1973) and began *Steve Canyon*, a similar strip featuring an air force officer that also became popular. Caniff was the recipient of a great many honors and awards from, among others, the Boy Scouts, the Freedoms Foundation, the armed forces, and various servicemen's organizations.

Canonchet (?–1676), Indian leader. Born at a time and place unknown, Canonchet was the son of a chief of the Narragansett Indians and himself became "chief sachem" of the tribe. Soon after the outbreak of King Philip's War in 1675 the English colonists became suspicious of the Narragansetts' intentions, despite their having been at peace for 30 years. On July 15 Canonchet and other Narragansett leaders were forced to sign a treaty, renewed in October, promising all aid to the colonists in the fight with the Wampanoags and their allies. As the war widened, however, the Narragansetts were drawn more and more to King Philip's side. On December 19, 1675, more than 1000 colonial militia under Gov. Josiah Winslow attacked the Narragansett fortified village near South Kingston, Rhode Island, killing hundreds of warriors, women, and children in what was called the Great Swamp Fight. Canonchet and a few other survivors escaped and in March 1676 won partial revenge in killing some 40 militia under Capt. Michael Pierce near Providence. The power of the Narragansetts was broken, however, and Canonchet was captured on April 3 while attempting to make his way to the Connecticut valley. He refused to make peace and was taken to Stonington, Connecticut, a prisoner; given into the hands of Pequot and Mohican allies of the colonists, he was shot and beheaded.

Caperton, William Banks (1855–1941), naval officer. Born in Spring Hill, Tennessee, on June 30, 1855, Caperton graduated from the Naval Academy in 1875. Commissioned ensign in 1877, he made his first voyage on the *Hartford*, and in 1878 he served aboard the old *Constellation*. Various routine assignments on shore and at sea followed, and he advanced to lieutenant (junior grade) in October 1883 and to lieutenant in October 1889. In 1896 he attended the Naval War College. During the Spanish–American War he was executive officer of the *Marietta*, which accompanied the *Oregon*, Capt. Charles E. Clark, in the famous run from San Francisco to Key West. Promoted to lieutenant commander in March 1899

and commander in August 1904, he fulfilled assignments as ordnance inspector in 1899–1901, lighthouse inspector for the 15th Naval District (Mississippi River) in 1904–1907, secretary of the Lighthouse Board in 1909–1910, at the Naval War College in 1904 and 1910, and on the Naval Examining and Retiring Board in 1910–1912. His sea commands included the *Prairie*, 1901–1904, and the new *Maine* in 1908–1909. He became captain in July 1908. In 1912 he took command of the 2nd Naval District at Newport, Rhode Island, receiving promotion to rear admiral in February 1913. He was named commander of the Atlantic Reserve Fleet in November 1913 and of the cruiser squadron, Atlantic Fleet, in November 1914. Early in 1915, at the request of the State Department, Caperton was sent aboard the *Washington* to Haiti to look into the growing unrest there. On July 28 he landed bluejackets and marines to quell rioting in Port-au-Prince, preparing the way for the much larger intervention force (under Col. Littleton W. T. Waller) that followed. In May 1916 he repeated the feat at Santo Domingo, putting down the rebellion there. In July 1916 he was given command of the Pacific Fleet with the rank of admiral. During World War I his scope of operations included the east coast of South America and the South Atlantic generally, which with aid from British and French forces he kept clear of German aggression. In 1918 and 1919 he served also in a diplomatic role as U.S. representative at the inaugurations of presidents of Brazil and Uruguay; aboard the *Pittsburgh*, accompanied by a squadron of cruisers, he made a series of goodwill calls at South American republics. Caperton was relieved of command of the Pacific Fleet in April 1919, and he retired in the rank of admiral in June. He died in Newport, Rhode Island, on December 21, 1941.

Captain Jack (1837?–1873), Indian leader. Born about 1837 probably in northern California, Kintpuash, or Kientpoos, was a minor chief of the Modoc tribe of that region. From whites he acquired the nickname Captain Jack, partly in allusion to his fondness for military ornament. The Modocs had been placed on a reservation in southern Oregon with the Klamath Indians, traditionally unfriendly to the Modocs, and considerable unrest ensued. In 1872 Captain Jack, with perhaps 50 followers, escaped from the reservation and returned to the hereditary Modoc lands on the Lost River in northern California. An army detachment of some 400 men was sent to force them back to the reservation, and on November 29 a fight between them marked the beginning of the Modoc War. Captain Jack retreated to a natural fortress, the Lava Beds at the southern end of Tule Lake. Reinforced by about 30 more warriors, he held off a concerted army attack on January 17, 1873. Three subsequent engagements had the same result.

In April the commander of the Department of the Columbia, Col. Edward R. S. Canby, called for negotiations. At the meeting on April 11 Captain Jack and his warriors rose up suddenly and killed Canby and the Rev. Eleazar Thomas. As a result a combined army–civilian force of more than a thousand men under Col. Jefferson C. Davis drove the Modocs from the Lava Beds. Captain Jack was captured on June 1, court-martialed with five others for the murder of Canby and Thomas, and hanged with three of them on October 3, 1873, at Fort Klamath, Oregon.

Carlson, Evans Fordyce (1896–1947), army and marine officer and author. Born on February 26, 1896, in Sidney, New York, Carlson was the son of a Congregational minister and consequently spent his childhood in various towns in New England. By fifteen he had left home and school, and in 1912, at sixteen, he enlisted in the army. After three years of service in the Philippines and Hawaii he was discharged. He was recalled in 1916 for duty in the Mexican border disturbances. He was commissioned shortly after the United States entered World War I, and he rose quickly to captain, seeing overseas duty only briefly on the staff of Gen. John J. Pershing. Resigning in 1919, he worked for a time as a salesman, but in 1922, on discovering that he could reenlist in the army only at a lower rank, he entered the marine corps instead as a private. He was commissioned second lieutenant in 1923 and after various domestic assignments was sent to Shanghai, China, in 1927 as an intelligence and operations officer. That tour ended in 1929, and in 1930 he served with distinction in Nicaragua. After a second tour in Peking, China, in 1933–1935, he was promoted to captain and assigned to the military guard posted at Warm Springs, Georgia, President Franklin D. Roosevelt's retreat. He formed there a friendship with the President that led to a private correspondence when he returned to China in 1937 as an observer with Chinese armies fighting the Japanese. He became particularly interested in the Eighth Route Army, the principal Communist force in the north of China, commanded by Chu Teh, and made two long marches with it through the interior. His outspoken praise of the Communists' discipline, determination to oust the Japanese, and elemental democracy, contrasting sharply with the Nationalist regime of Chiang Kaishek, led Carlson into a dispute with his superiors that eventuated in his resignation in April 1939. For two years he traveled, in the United States and again in China; lectured on China, the Red Army, and Japan; and wrote *The Chinese Army*, 1940, and *Twin Stars in China*, 1940, along with periodical pieces. In April 1941 he was commissioned at his own request a major in the marine reserves, going on active duty the next month. Early in 1942 he was promoted to lieutenant colonel in command of the 2nd Marine Raider Battalion, a picked volunteer commando force that became known as Carlson's Raiders. Maj. James Roosevelt, the President's son, was executive officer of the battalion. Applying the lessons of the Chinese Eighth Route Army, Carlson organized the battalion on radically democratic principles, abolishing officers' mess and other privileges, issuing identical dress and equipment to all, and encouraging discussion of mission objectives and tactics both before and after execution. Carlson's Raiders went into action in August 1942 in an attack on Makin Island in the Gilbert chain, a successful raid that attracted considerable publicity. Late in that year they operated behind Japanese lines on Guadalcanal in another highly successful exploit. The Raiders' battle cry was "Gung Ho!"—a slogan actually derived from an abbreviated form of the Chinese name for an industrial cooperatives society but misconstrued by Carlson as meaning "work together." Carlson's methods inevitably aroused hostility, however, and early in 1943 his Raiders were merged with three other battalions into a raider regiment with Carlson second in command. Later he was invalided home for a time. He was an observer at the landings on Tarawa in November 1943 and at the assault on Saipan in June 1944, where he was badly wounded. He retired with rank of brigadier general in July 1946 to a home in Brightwood, Oregon. He continued active on behalf of U.S.–Chinese understanding, international peace, and the Progressive Party until his death in Portland, Oregon, on May 27, 1947.

Carmick, Daniel (1772–1816), marine officer. Born in Philadelphia in 1772, Carmick very likely went to sea at an early age. In May 1798 he was appointed a lieutenant of marines, and he commanded the marine detachment aboard the *Ganges*, Capt. Richard Dale, on a cruise in May–August of that year. On July 11 of that year an act establishing the marine corps was passed by Congress, and in August Carmick was appointed one of four captains under Commandant William W. Burrows. After a period of recruiting duty he took charge at Lancaster, Pennsylvania, of the French prisoners taken by Capt. Thomas Truxtun in the defeat of the *Insurgente*. In 1799 he took command of the marine detachment aboard Commodore Silas Talbot's flagship *Constitution* in the West Indies. On May 11, 1800, about 40 of his marines constituted half of a party, under Lt. Isaac Hull, that slipped into the harbor of Puerto Plata, Santo Domingo (Dominican Republic), aboard a merchant sloop and took by surprise the French privateer *Sandwich*. Carmick then took the marines ashore and spiked the guns of the fort. The entire exploit was one of the most celebrated of the quasi-war with France. In 1802 he sailed aboard Commodore Richard V. Morris's flagship *Chesapeake* as senior marine officer of the squadron sent to Tripoli;

he returned with that ship in 1803. Early in 1804 he established the first marine barracks at New Orleans, only recently transferred to U.S. ownership. Over the next several years marine detachments manned Fort Adams, Pointe Coupée, Fort St. John, Louisiana, and the new navy yard in New Orleans, increasing from their original strength of 100 to 300 within 5 years. In March 1809 Carmick was promoted to major. Marines at New Orleans regularly served aboard coastal and river gunboats and helped preserve order during various disturbances in bordering Spanish areas, notably the revolt against Spain and annexation by the United States of West Florida in 1810. When New Orleans became a scene of action late in the war of 1812, Carmick dispatched marines to serve in Lt. Thomas ap Catesby Jones's flotilla on Lake Borgne and in other capacities with Commodore Daniel T. Patterson's naval command. When the British army under Gen. Edward Pakenham began the advance overland to New Orleans, the marines took part in the defense of the city. Carmick was severely wounded in a skirmish on December 28, 1814, and was thus not present at the final battle under Gen. Andrew Jackson, January 8, 1815, where his men earned the commendation of Jackson and Patterson. Carmick never fully recovered; he died on November 6, 1816 in New Orleans.

Carney, Robert Bostwick (1895–   ), naval officer. Born on March 26, 1895, in Vallejo, California, Carney graduated from the Naval Academy in 1916 and by the end of World War I in 1918 had served on the *New Hampshire,* the *Dixie,* and the *Fanning* and risen to the rank of lieutenant. Over the next ten years he had various routine assignments at sea and on shore, including a period in 1923–1925 as an instructor at the Naval Academy. He was promoted to lieutenant commander in 1927. During 1928–1930 he was on staff duty in Washington, D.C., and from 1933 to 1935 he had charge of the receiving station at Washington navy yard. His later sea commands included those of the *Buchanan,* 1935–1936, the *Reid,* 1936–1937, and the *Sirius,* 1937–1938. He advanced to commander in 1936. During 1938–1940 he served in the office of the secretary of the navy. From March 1941 to September 1942 Carney was chief of staff of the support force, Atlantic Fleet, concerned with convoy protection and antisubmarine warfare. Promoted to captain, he commanded the light cruiser *Denver* in the Southwest Pacific area until July 1943, taking part in actions in the Solomon Islands. He then became chief of staff, with rank of rear admiral, to Adm. William F. Halsey, commander of the South Pacific area. In June 1945 he became chief of staff of the Third Fleet, also under Halsey. He was named assistant chief of naval operations for logistics in February 1946 and in July of that year was made deputy chief with rank of vice admiral. In April

1950 he became commander of the Second Fleet; in September he was promoted to admiral and placed in command of U.S. naval forces in the eastern Atlantic and the Mediterranean. In June 1951 he was named commander in chief of North Atlantic Treaty Organization forces in the Mediterranean and NATO naval forces in southern Europe, becoming commander in chief of all NATO forces in southern Europe a year later. In August 1953 he was appointed chief of naval operations, and he held that post until his retirement in August 1955. He devoted himself thereafter to various business interests, serving as chairman of the board of the Bath (Maine) Iron Works, as a director of the Fairchild Corporation, and from 1960 as board chairman of the Bell Intercontinental Corporation.

Carr, Eugene Asa (1830–1910), army officer. Born in Concord, Erie County, New York, on March 20, 1830, Carr graduated from West Point in 1850 and was commissioned in the Mounted Riflemen (later the 3rd Cavalry). On duty on the western frontier, he saw action in skirmishes with Apache, Sioux, Kiowa, Comanche, and other tribes, as well as in the Mormon expedition and the Kansas border wars, advancing to first lieutenant in the 1st Cavalry in 1855 and captain in June 1858. On the outbreak of the Civil War he marched to Fort Leavenworth and then joined the command of Gen. Nathaniel Lyon in Missouri. He was brevetted lieutenant colonel for his actions at the battle of Wilson's Creek on August 9, 1861, and a week later he was appointed colonel of the 3rd Illinois Cavalry. He was soon acting brigadier general under Gen. John C. Frémont, and in February 1862 he took command of a division of the Army of the Southwest under Gen. Samuel R. Curtis. At the battle of Pea Ridge, Arkansas, on March 7–8, against Gen. Earl Van Dorn's forces, he was three times wounded and performed with such gallantry as to win the Medal of Honor (awarded in 1894). Shortly after the battle he was commissioned brigadier general of volunteers. He was engaged in Arkansas during the remainder of 1862 and in 1863 commanded a division during the Vicksburg campaign, where he received a brevet in regular rank to colonel. His division led the assault on the city on May 18 and four days later was the first to reach enemy works. After brief service at Corinth he was transferred in December 1863 to the Army of Arkansas, where he took part in numerous small actions. He joined Gen. Edward R. S. Canby for the campaign against Mobile, Alabama, in April 1865. By war's end he had been brevetted twice more, to major general. Reverting to permanent rank of major, he returned to the frontier and was engaged in Indian campaigns for many years: with the 5th Cavalry against Sioux and Cheyenne in Kansas and Wyoming 1868–1869; as lieutenant colonel (promoted in January 1873) in command of the Black Hills district from 1873; and as colonel of the 6th Cavalry from April 1879 against Apaches in Arizona and New Mexico. Promoted to brigadier general in July 1892, he retired in February 1893, one of the most able and experienced cavalry commanders produced on the frontier. Carr died in Washington, D.C., on December 2, 1910.

Carrington, Henry Beebee (1824–1912), army officer. Born on March 2, 1824, in Wallingford, Connecticut, Carrington graduated from Yale College in 1845 and for some years was a teacher, at Irving Institute in Tarrytown, New York, where he became a friend of Washington Irving, and at New Haven Collegiate Institute in Connecticut. While at the latter, he studied law at Yale Law School, and in 1848 he entered practice in Columbus, Ohio. An active Republican and associate of Salmon P. Chase, then governor of Ohio, Carrington took responsibility in 1857 for reorganizing the Ohio militia and was subsequently appointed adjutant general. Under his direction Ohio sent nine regiments of militia into the western part of Virginia (later West Virginia) immediately after President Abraham Lincoln's first call for troops in May 1861, and in that month he was appointed colonel of the 18th Infantry. After training duty in Ohio and recruitment in Indiana he was promoted to brigadier general of volunteers in November 1862. He continued mainly in recruitment duty and roused a storm of controversy by his harsh treatment, ultimately reversed by the Supreme Court, of groups sympathetic to the Confederacy, such as the "Sons of Liberty" in Indiana. In September 1865 he was mustered out of the volunteer service, and after duty on a military commission trying guerrillas in Louisville, Kentucky, he joined the 18th Infantry at Fort Kearny, Nebraska. In 1866 he was ordered to establish posts along the Bozeman Trail, known also as the Powder River Road, from Fort Laramie to the mining country of Montana. The road cut through vital hunting grounds in the foothills of the Big Horn Mountains reserved by treaty to the Sioux, Northern Cheyenne, and Arapaho. Carrington left Fort Laramie in June and marched to Fort Connor on the Powder River, relieving the garrison there; he enlarged the fort and renamed it Fort Reno. He proceeded north to the Piney Fork in the Big Horn foothills just south of the Montana–Wyoming border and built his headquarters, Fort Phil Kearny. A detachment was sent 90 miles farther northwest to the Big Horn river to establish Fort C. F. Smith. Throughout the summer his command was harassed by aroused Sioux under Red Cloud; they made more than 50 hostile demonstrations before Fort Phil Kearny alone. When a wood train from the fort was attacked on December 21, 1866, Carrington sent out a relief column under Capt. William J. Fetterman that, through a ruse, was wiped out to a man. Not long thereafter Carrington

was relieved of that command and transferred to Colorado, and in December 1870 he retired. From 1870 to 1873 he taught military science and tactics at Wabash College, Indiana, and thereafter he devoted himself largely to literary work. Among his books were *Battles of the American Revolution*, 1876, *Battle Maps and Charts of the American Revolution*, 1881, *The Six Nations* 1892, and *Washington the Soldier*, 1898. In 1889 he negotiated a treaty with the Flathead Indians and in 1891 was involved in moving Indians to reservations in western Montana. Carrington died on October 26, 1912.

Carson, Kit (1809–1868), trapper, guide, Indian agent, and army officer. Born on December 24, 1809, in Madison County, Kentucky, Christopher Carson spent his early childhood in Boone's Lick, on the Missouri frontier. His father died when he was nine, and he received no schooling. In 1825 his mother apprenticed him to a saddlemaker, but he ran away the next year to join an expedition to Santa Fe. There, over the next few years, he learned to trap for furs and fight Indians, and he established a home base in the region of Taos, New Mexico. He trapped in California and as far north as Montana, associating at various times with Thomas Fitzpatrick, Jim Bridger, and other famous mountain men. He was often employed as a hunter by Bent's Fort. He married a woman of the Arapaho tribe about 1836. On a steamboat from St. Louis in 1842 he met Lt. John C. Frémont, who subsequently engaged him as a guide on three expeditions in 1842, 1843–1844, and 1845–1846. He fought in several battles for the conquest of California, including San Pascual, December 6, 1846, whither he had guided Gen. Stephen W. Kearny's Army of the West and from which he managed to escape to San Diego for reinforcements; and Los Angeles, January 8–9. Later, bearing dispatches to Washington, D.C., he discovered that he was a national hero for his daring in the war. He returned to private life, farming in Taos, driving sheep to Sacramento, and serving as a guide and, from 1853, as U.S. agent to the Ute tribe. He was extremely effective in that position, even though he was illiterate; he dictated his government reports to other people. One of these scribes, an army surgeon, took down his autobiography but embellished it so much that Carson had to admit that it was more fictional than real. He resigned as an Indian agent when the Civil War began, raised the 1st New Mexican Volunteer Infantry, of which he was commissioned lieutenant colonel in July 1861 and colonel in September, and successfully battled Indian tribes which had terrorized settlers for years. He fought under Gen. Edward R. S. Canby at Valverde, February 21, 1862. But his final battle in Texas in 1864 was a defeat; 5000 Indians met his poorly armed group of 400 soldiers at Adobe Walls on November 25 and retreat was inevitable. Nevertheless, he was brevetted brigadier general of volunteers in March 1865, and in 1866 he was named commander of Fort Garland, Colorado; he was forced to resign the next year because of ill health. He attended a conference in Washington with the Utes, although his health continued to be poor, and made fruitless trips to New York and Boston, hoping to find medical relief. On May 23, 1868, he died at Fort Lyon, Colorado. A temperate, modest, and widely respected man, he created for himself an important place in American frontier legend.

Carter, Samuel Powhatan (1819–1891), naval and army officer. Born in Elizabethton, Tennessee, on August 6, 1819, Carter attended Washington College in Tennessee and Princeton. In February 1840 he entered the navy as a midshipman and after five years of sea duty in the Pacific and on the Great Lakes was transferred to the Naval Academy to graduate with the class of 1846. Over the next several years he served in the Mexican War aboard the *Ohio* at Veracruz, at the Naval Observatory, as assistant professor of mathematics at the Naval Academy from 1850 to 1853, in the Pacific and Brazil squadrons, and elsewhere, rising in April 1855 to the rank of lieutenant. He took part, aboard the *San Jacinto,* in the attack on the barrier forts in China in 1856, and from 1857 to 1860 he was on the staff of the Naval Academy. Early in 1861 a letter in which he stated that he would remain loyal to the Union should civil war break out came to the attention of Andrew Johnson, then governor of Tennessee, who arranged with the War Department to have Carter recruit and train militia in the eastern part of the state. In May 1862 he was commissioned brigadier general of volunteers. He led successful cavalry operations at Mill Springs (January 19, 1862) and at Cumberland Gap (June 1862) and conducted raids at Holston, Carter's Station, and Jonesville in December in support of Gen. William S. Rosecrans at Murfreesboro. In July 1863 he became commander of the cavalry division of the XXIII Corps. He campaigned in Tennessee throughout 1863. In 1865 he was in North Carolina and in March of that year was brevetted major general; for a time he commanded the XXIII Corps. In January 1866 he was mustered out of the volunteer service and returned to the navy, by which he had been promoted to the rank of commander during his army duty. He served again in the Pacific in command of the *Monocacy* and in October 1870 was promoted to captain. From that year to 1873 he was commandant of midshipmen at the Naval Academy. He then returned to line duty in European waters. From 1877 to 1880 he was a member of the Lighthouse Board. In November 1878 he became a commodore; he retired in August 1881, and in May 1882 he was made rear admiral, retired, thus becoming the only American ever to attain both the rank of rear admiral and that

of major general. Carter died in Washington, D.C. on May 26, 1891.

Carver, Jonathan (1710–1780), colonial army officer and explorer. Born in Weymouth, Massachusetts, on April 13, 1710, Carver was a sergeant in the British army at the siege of Fort William Henry in 1757. He then joined a provincial regiment, and in 1759 he was promoted to lieutenant; the next year he was made captain. In 1766 he was engaged by Maj. Robert Rogers and sent by him on a journey of exploration westward from Mackinac. He traveled west through the Great Lakes region, via Green Bay and the Fox and Wisconsin rivers, to the Mississippi and up the river to the region of the Sioux Indians at the Falls of St. Anthony. He remained during the winter of 1766–1767 in a Sioux camp on the Minnesota River. Returning to Mackinac, he met Capt. James Tute at the mouth of the Wisconsin River. Tute was in charge of a party sent by Rogers to seek a route to the Pacific Ocean. Carver joined the party as a draftsman and third in command; they traveled up the Mississippi and reached the shores of Lake Superior by the Chippewa and St. Croix rivers, then proceeded to the Grand Portage. They returned to Mackinac by the north shore of Lake Superior in 1768. Never paid for his services by Rogers, who had hired him without authorization, Carver attempted without success to publish his travel journal, then left for England in 1769 to seek payment and to have the manuscript published. But the project met with many delays, and he did not benefit when the journal was finally printed in London two years before his death. Called *Travels Through the Interior Parts of North America in the Years 1766, 1767, 1768,* it became popular at once; through many editions it remained the most widely read and enjoyed account of early American travel and adventure. Although the second part, dealing with Indian manners and customs, was traceable to French authors and brought charges of plagiarism, this detracted little from the book as a whole. Carver's name was also on a *New Universal Geography* that was published in 1779 and on a discourse on raising tobacco. He died in London on January 31, 1780.

Casey, Silas (1807–1882), army officer. Born in East Greenwich, Rhode Island, on July 12, 1807, Casey graduated from West Point in 1826 and was commissioned second lieutenant in the 2nd Infantry. For ten years he was on duty at various frontier posts, advancing to first lieutenant in June 1836, and during 1837–1842 he served with distinction in the Seminole War in Florida. He was promoted to captain in July 1839. He fought under Gen. Winfield Scott in the Mexican War, taking part in the battles of Contreras and Churubusco, August 19–20, 1847, for which he was brevetted major; Molino del Rey, September 8;

and Chapultepec, September 13, where he was severely wounded leading the storming party in the advance of Gen. John A. Quitman's division and was again brevetted, to lieutenant colonel. Casey then returned to frontier duty, chiefly in the Pacific northwest, becoming lieutenant colonel of the newly organized 9th Infantry in March 1855. During 1856–1857 he commanded the Puget Sound district, Washington Territory. In 1861, the year he was promoted to colonel, he published his two-volume *System of Infantry Tactics*, which was adopted by the army the following year and long remained a standard work in the field, known usually as "Casey's Tactics." In August 1861 he was appointed brigadier general of volunteers for Civil War service. After a period devoted to training and organizing he was given command of a division of Gen. Erasmus D. Keyes's IV Corps, Army of the Potomac, and led it through the Peninsular campaign in May–June 1862. On May 31 at Fair Oaks (Seven Pines) his gallantry won him a brevet in regular rank to brigadier general and appointment as major general of volunteers. In August 1862 he took command of a division engaged in the defense of Washington, D.C., where he remained for the rest of the war. From 1863 to 1865 he was president of the board of examination of candidates for officers of black troops. Brevetted regular major general in March 1865 for his services, he was mustered out of volunteer service in August. He returned to command of the 9th Infantry until his retirement in July 1868. Casey died in Brooklyn, New York, on January 22, 1882.

Casey, Thomas Lincoln (1831–1896), army officer and engineer. Born on May 10, 1831, at Madison Barracks, Sackett's Harbor, New York, Casey was the son of Lt. (later Brevet Major General) Silas Casey. He graduated from West Point in 1852 and was commissioned in the engineers. During 1852–1854 he was engaged in the rebuilding of Fort Delaware, on the Delaware River below Wilmington, and, after five years on the faculty at West Point, he was ordered to Washington Territory in 1859 to supervise construction of the first road between the Columbia River and Puget Sound. At the outbreak of the Civil War in 1861 Casey was attached briefly to the Department of Virginia and then ordered to construct coastal fortifications in Maine. The task presented huge engineering problems—high tides, near inaccessibility of needed materials, shortages of skilled labor—all of which he overcame in the building of Fort Scammel, Fort Gorges, and Fort Preble in Portland harbor, Fort Popham on the Kennebec, and Fort Knox on the Penobscot. He was advanced to captain in August 1861 and to major in October 1863, and for his services during the war he was brevetted lieutenant colonel and colonel in March 1865. During 1866–1867 he took a short leave of absence to work for a

manufacturer of heavy equipment in Portland, Maine, returning afterward to the post of chief army engineer for the Portland district. Called to Washington, D.C., in November 1867 as head of the division of fortifications in the office of the chief of the Corps of Engineers, he remained in that post for ten years. In March 1877 he became the superintending engineer for public buildings, grounds, and work in the capital, in which capacity he directed construction of the State, War and Navy Building, the Washington aqueduct, the White House conservatory, the Army Medical Museum, and other major works. In 1878 he took charge of the Washington Monument, abandoned unfinished 23 years before. Solving the problems inherent in its faulty design and foundation, he oversaw the growth of the monument from 173 feet to its full 555 feet, himself personally designing and setting on the pyramidion capstone on December 6, 1884. In addition to his duties in the capital Casey served also as president of the board of fortifications and public works for New York City in 1886–1888. In July 1888 he was promoted to brigadier general in command of the Corps of Engineers. Retired in May 1895, he continued to supervise the completion of the Library of Congress until his death in Washington on March 25, 1896.

Cassin, Stephen (1783–1857), naval officer. Born in Philadelphia on February 16, 1783, Cassin was the son of a prominent naval officer. He was appointed a midshipman in February 1800, served well in the Tripolitan War, and was advanced to lieutenant in February 1807. In 1812 he was ordered to Lake Champlain, where Lt. Thomas Macdonough was engaged in building a fleet to oppose a British advance down the lake from Canada. In the battle of Lake Champlain on September 11, 1814, Cassin, who was that day promoted to master commandant, commanded the sloop *Ticonderoga*, 17 guns, the third heaviest ship in the American fleet. His gallant performance in the battle—fighting off many assaults and boarding attempts while exposing himself to heavy fire—was credited by later naval historians with contributing greatly, perhaps decisively, to the victory that day. He was granted a gold medal by Congress in October 1814. He won further renown in 1822 while on pirate patrol aboard the sloop *Peacock*, 18, in West Indian waters; on September 28–30 alone he captured five pirate craft. The next year, commanding a small squadron off the northern coast of Cuba, he captured or destroyed several more. Cassin was promoted to captain in March 1825 and to commodore in 1830. He died in Georgetown, D.C., on August 29, 1857.

Castle, Vernon Blythe (1887–1918), dancer and aviator. Born in Norwich, England, on May 2, 1887, Vernon Blythe early intended to pursue a career in engineering but in 1906 came to the United States with his sister, who was an actress. Through her he won a small role in a 1907 Lew Fields production of *The Girl Behind the Counter*, in which he did a brief but fascinating dance routine that caught the audience's attention. Taking the name Castle, he was thereafter often engaged to choreograph dances for other shows. In 1911 he married Irene Foote (1893–1969), who had been born in New Rochelle, New York, on April 7, 1893. They began dancing together at private social functions but had no notable success until 1912, when they went to Paris and were a sensation in café performances. They then returned to New York and were in great demand in cafés and theaters. The Castles introduced a number of new dance steps that were taken up by the public, including the one-step, the turkey trot, and the Castle walk; and Mrs. Castle was also something of a trend-setter in fashion. In 1914 they published *Modern Dancing*. Having taken up flying in 1915, Vernon returned to England in February 1916 to enlist in the Royal Flying Corps. In air combat over France he distinguished himself on a number of occasions, shot down two German planes, and was awarded the Croix de Guerre. He was sent to Fort Worth, Texas, at the beginning of 1918 as a flying instructor and was killed there on February 15, 1918, in a collision of his plane with another aircraft after he had maneuvered to save the other pilot's life. Mrs. Castle, sometimes credited with starting the "bobbed hair" craze of the 1920s, retained her name through subsequent marriages and became known as a devoted protector of animals, founding the Orphans of the Storm shelter in Deerfield, Illinois, in 1928. She died in Eureka Springs, Arkansas, on January 25, 1969.

Caswell, Richard (1729–1789), public official and Revolutionary militia officer. Born in Cecil County, Maryland, on August 3, 1729, Caswell moved in his youth to Raleigh, North Carolina, and worked as a surveyor and lawyer. He held various local offices and from 1754 to 1771 was a member of the colonial assembly, serving as speaker from 1769. He commanded, in the rank of colonel, the right wing of the provincial militia under Gov. William Tryon at the battle of Alamance, May 16, 1771, the climax of Tryon's campaign against the rebellious Regulators. During 1774–1776 he was a delegate to the Continental Congress. Early in 1776 he returned to North Carolina to find the patriot cause at low ebb, with British and Loyalist forces ascendant throughout the state. Commanding in Col. James Moore's absence a body of minutemen, numbering finally about 1100, at Moore's Creek on February 27 he met and defeated a column of 1600 Loyalists and Highland regulars, under Gen. Donald Macdonald, who were en route from Cross Creek (now Fayetteville) to join Gen. Charles Cornwallis at Wilmington. Caswell's troops

suffered 2 casualties to the regulars' 50, and took some 900 prisoners. The battle was the first Whig victory in North Carolina and put the state firmly on the side of the Revolution. Caswell was commended by Congress for his success. In November the newly organized provincial congress of North Carolina elected him first governor of the independent state. He held that post until 1780, when he was appointed major general in command of the state militia. His popularity suffered somewhat following the disastrous defeat at Camden, South Carolina, where he had led the militia to join Gen. Horatio Gates's army. In 1782 he was appointed comptroller general of North Carolina, and he served a second time as governor in 1785–1787. He declined to be a delegate to the Constitutional Convention in 1787. In 1789 he was elected to the state senate, and he was stricken while presiding over that body in November; he died a few days later, probably on November 10, 1789, in Fayetteville, North Carolina.

Cates, Clifton Bledsoe (1893–1970), marine officer. Born in Tiptonville, Tennessee, on August 31, 1893, Cates graduated with a law degree from the University of Tennessee in 1916. In June 1917 he took a second lieutenant's commission in the marine corps reserve, and in January 1918 he went overseas with the 6th Marine Regiment, an element of the 2nd Infantry Division of the First Army. He distinguished himself in numerous engagements, including Château-Thierry, Soissons, the St. Mihiel salient, and the Meuse–Argonne offensive. After occupation duty he returned to the United States in September 1919 and served in various staff capacities, including aide to President Woodrow Wilson, until taking command of the marine detachment aboard the *California* in 1923. Between routine duty at various marine barracks (twice in Shanghai, 1929–1932 and 1937–1939) he completed courses at the Army Industrial College in 1932, the Marine Corps School in 1934, and the Army War College in 1939. On August 7, 1942, then a colonel, he commanded the 1st Regiment of the 1st Marine Division, under Gen. Alexander A. Vandegrift, in the landing on Guadalcanal, remaining there until December. During 1943–1944, as a brigadier general, he was commandant of the Marine Corps Schools, Quantico, Virginia. Promoted to major general, he took command in July 1944 of the 4th Marine Division and, leading it as a unit of Gen. Holland M. Smith's V Amphibious Corps, saw action on Saipan, Tinian, and (in February-March 1945) Iwo Jima. In June 1946 he became commander of the marine barracks at Quantico, and in January 1948 he was appointed commandant of the marine corps with the rank of general. During his term he fought off all threats of reduction in the corps's strength or autonomy under the program of unification of the armed services, and after the outbreak of the Korean War he fought equally hard for the retention of the marine air arm. At the end of his term in January 1952, unable to retire owing to a peculiarity of law, he reverted to rank of lieutenant general and again became commandant of the Marine Corps Schools. On his retirement in June 1954 he was restored to the rank of general. Cates died in Annapolis, Maryland, on June 4, 1970.

Chaffee, Adna Romanza (1842–1914), army officer. Born in Orwell, Ohio, on April 14, 1842, Chaffee set out in July 1861 to enlist in an Ohio volunteer regiment and, encountering a recruiting party from the regular 6th Cavalry en route, promptly joined that unit. He was promoted to sergeant within weeks and, after service in the Peninsular campaign and at Antietam, became a first sergeant in September 1862. In May 1863 his highly capable service came to the attention of Secretary of War Edwin M. Stanton, who ordered him commissioned a second lieutenant. Sent with his regiment to join the Army of the Potomac, he saw action at Gettysburg, where he was wounded and narrowly escaped capture, and took part in other major battles; he was advanced to first lieutenant in February 1865. In March 1867 he resigned his commission but within a week was persuaded to seek restoration to rank. Promoted to captain in October 1867, until 1888 he served mainly in the Southwest, fighting in numerous battles with the Indians. He was brevetted major for his part in the defeat of Comanches at Paint Creek, Texas, in March 1868 and promoted to regular major in July 1888. Transferred to the 9th Cavalry, he later served as an instructor at the Infantry and Cavalry School, Fort Leavenworth, Kansas, until June 1897, when he was appointed lieutenant colonel of the 3rd Cavalry. In May 1898 he was made brigadier general of volunteers in command of a brigade of Gen. Henry W. Lawton's 2nd Division of the army in Cuba, and after his performance in the taking of El Caney (July 1) in the Santiago campaign was promoted to major general of volunteers. Following a brief period in the United States he returned to Cuba late in 1898 as chief of staff of the military government under Gen. Leonard Wood, a post he held until 1900. He lost his volunteer rank in the reduction of the army but was reappointed brigadier general of volunteers in April 1899 (his regular rank was colonel from May 1899). He was again appointed major general of volunteers in July 1900 and placed in command of the U.S. contingent—some 2500 troops, including the 9th and 14th Infantry, 6th Cavalry, and other units—in the joint relief expedition sent to China to quell the Boxer Rebellion. It was American troops under Chaffee who finally captured the gates of Peking on August 14, 1900, and were the first into the city to relieve the besieged legations. After the successful completion of that mission, during which he won the admiration

not only of the troops and commanders sent by the other Western powers but also of the Chinese themselves, he was made a major general in the regular army in February 1901 and named military governor and commander of U.S. forces in the Philippines, where he remained until October 1902. Chaffee served as commander of the Department of the East in 1902–1903 and, with the rank of lieutenant general, was chief of staff of the army from January 1904 to January 1906; he retired the next month. Settling in Los Angeles, he lived there until his death on November 1, 1914.

Chaffee, Adna Romanza (1884–1941), army officer. Born on September 23, 1884, in Junction City, Kansas, Chaffee accompanied his father, Gen. Adna R. Chaffee, to China in 1900–1901 and then entered West Point, graduating in 1906 and receiving his commission in the cavalry. His horsemanship led to his selection for the Mounted Service School at Fort Riley, Kansas, from which he graduated in 1908, and he received further training at the cavalry school of the French army in 1911–1912. He was promoted to first lieutenant in 1912. He was for a time an instructor at Fort Riley and in 1914–1916 was in the Philippines with the 7th Cavalry. Promoted to captain in July 1916, he was assigned to the staff at West Point until 1917. During World War I he served with distinction with the American Expeditionary Force, seeing action on the St. Mihiel and Meuse–Argonne fronts with the 81st Division and on the staff of the III Corps and advancing to the rank of colonel (temporary). After the war he held numerous troop and staff assignments. He was promoted to major in July 1920 and graduated from the School of the Line, Fort Leavenworth, Kansas, in 1921 and from the Army War College in 1925. In 1927 he was assigned to the General Staff and there worked to promote the development of the mechanized armored striking force, a new kind of army offensive unit based on the tank and other mobile armor. His leadership in the movement for the adoption of such novel weaponry earned him the title of "father of the Armored Force." He advanced to lieutenant colonel in December 1929. In 1931, with the rank of colonel, he was given command of the 1st Cavalry, moving it in 1933 from Texas to Fort Knox, overseeing its mechanization, and with it conducting much pioneering experimental work in mechanized warfare. From 1934 to 1938 he was again on General Staff duty. In November 1938, promoted to brigadier general, he was stationed at Fort Knox in command of the 7th (mechanized) Cavalry Brigade. In July 1940 he at last won approval for the organization of the Armored Force, of which he was duly named chief. He was given temporary rank of major general in September and by the next month had organized two armored divisions. His rank of major general was made permanent in August 1941; he died in Boston less than three weeks later, on August 22, 1941.

Chaillé-Long, Charles (1842–1917), army officer and explorer. Born on July 2, 1842, in Princess Anne, Somerset County, Maryland, Chaillé-Long deserted his studies at Washington Academy in 1861 to enlist in the 1st Eastern Shore Maryland Volunteers. The next year he was promoted to captain in the 11th Maryland Volunteers, with which he served through the remainder of the Civil War. After the war, having acquired a taste for the military life, he sought a commission in the army of the Khedive Ismail I of Egypt, and in 1869 he was appointed lieutenant colonel on the Khedive's general staff. In February 1874 he became chief of staff to Gen. C. G. "Chinese" Gordon, governor of the Egyptian Sudan, who was then engaged in the suppression of the slave trade. In that year Chaillé-Long was sent on a diplomatic mission to Uganda, during which he conducted explorations in the upper Nile basin, discovering Lake Kyoga and filling in one of the last gaps in the map of the river's course. After successfully concluding a treaty with Mutesa, ruler of Uganda, Chaillé-Long returned to Egypt and in November was promoted to colonel and given the title of bey. After a second exploration of Nile tributaries in 1875, his health impaired, he retired from the Khedive's service in August 1877. Returning to the United States, he enrolled at Columbia University Law School, graduating in 1880. In 1882 he took up the practice of international law in Alexandria, Egypt, and for two months that year acted as U.S. consul while the regular officials were absent during the uprising in the city; hundreds of Europeans were given refuge in the consulate or on American ships in the harbor as, aided by sailors and marines, he maintained a semblance of security. He moved his practice to Paris later in 1882. In March 1887 he joined the consular service with appointment as U.S. consul general and secretary of legation to Korea. In 1889 he returned to the United States and in later years continued to serve in various diplomatic capacities. A prolific writer, he published *Naked Truths of Naked People*, an account of his Nile exploration, 1876, *L'Afrique Centrale*, 1877, *The Three Prophets*, 1884, *Les Sources du Nile*, 1891, and *My Life in Four Continents*, 1912. He died on March 24, 1917, in Virginia Beach, Virginia.

Chamberlain, Joshua Lawrence (1828–1914), educator, army officer, and public official. Born in Brewer, Maine, on September 8, 1828, Chamberlain graduated from Bowdoin College in 1852 and from Bangor Theological Seminary in 1855. In the latter year he joined the Bowdoin faculty as instructor in natural and revealed religion, and over the course of several years he taught also rhetoric and modern languages, becoming professor of the former in 1856 and

of the latter in 1861. In 1862 he accepted appointment as lieutenant colonel of the 20th Maine Infantry; he was promoted to colonel in May 1863 and commanded his regiment throughout the war. He saw action in 24 major engagements and was wounded 6 times. At Gettysburg on July 2, 1863, he performed with distinction in the holding of Little Round Top and the subsequent taking of Great Round Top, for which he was later (1888) awarded the Medal of Honor. On June 18, 1864, during the siege of Petersburg, he was wounded while leading a brigade and was promoted on the spot to brigadier general of volunteers by Gen. Ulysses S. Grant, Congress subsequently confirming the promotion. For a successful assault on Gen. Robert E. Lee's right at Quaker Road on March 29, 1865, in which he was wounded, he was brevetted major general of volunteers. At the conclusion of the campaign against Lee's army, Chamberlain was designated to receive the formal Confederate surrender of arms and colors on April 9, 1865. Mustered out in June 1866, he returned to Bowdoin and later in the year was elected governor of Maine, a post he held, through four reelections, until 1871. In 1871 he became president of Bowdoin, a post he held until 1883, serving also as professor of mental and moral philosophy in 1874–1879 and until 1885 as lecturer on political science and public law. During the riotous winter of 1878–1879, when Democratic-Greenback and Republican factions contested possession of the government, Chamberlain, as major general of the state militia, kept public order. From 1884 to 1889 he was interested in railroad and other undertakings in Florida. He was appointed U.S. surveyor of customs for the port of Portland, Maine, in 1900, and he remained in that post until his death on February 24, 1914.

Chapman, Leonard Fielding, Jr. (1913–   ), marine officer. Born on November 3, 1913, in Key West, Florida, Chapman graduated from the University of Florida in 1935 with a reserve commission in the army. He resigned, however, to take an active commission in the marine corps and after completing basic and field artillery training was promoted to first lieutenant in 1938. In 1940 he was assigned to command of the marine detachment aboard the *Astoria,* Pacific Fleet; he was promoted to captain in April 1941 and to major in May 1942. He became an artillery instructor in that year at the Quantico, Virginia, marine base and in May 1943 was promoted to lieutenant colonel. In mid-1944 he entered combat with the 1st Marine Division in the Pacific, serving on the staff of the 11th Artillery and then as commander of the 4th Battalion, seeing action at Peleliu in the southern Palau Islands in September-October 1944. Chapman was secretary of the general staff, Fleet Marine Force, Pacific, in 1945–1946 and then joined the headquarters staff in Washington, D.C. Graduating from Amphibious Warfare School at Quantico in 1950, he was in that year promoted to colonel. From 1952 to 1954 he commanded the 12th Regiment in Japan and from 1954 to 1956 the marine barracks at Yokosuka. From 1956 to 1958 he commanded the marine barracks in Washington, D.C., and on being promoted to brigadier general in July of the latter year he became commander of force troops, Fleet Marine Force, Atlantic, at Camp Lejeune, North Carolina. Transferred to duty as deputy assistant chief of staff at headquarters in September 1961, he was promoted to major general two months later. In January 1964 he advanced to lieutenant general and chief of staff of the corps; in July 1967 he was appointed assistant commandant, and in January 1968 he succeeded Gen. Wallace M. Greene as commandant of the marine corps with the rank of general. The first artillery officer to hold the post, Chapman was recognized as an expert in management techniques and military logistics and communications. He retired after the expiration of his term as commandant in January 1972. In 1973 he was appointed by President Richard M. Nixon commissioner of the Immigration and Naturalization Service, a post he held until retiring in May 1977 and one that became particularly sensitive when public concern over illegal immigration and its effect on employment opportunities flared during that period.

Chapman, Victor Emmanuel (1890–1916), army officer and airman. Born in New York City on April 17, 1890, Chapman was the son of John Jay Chapman, author and eccentric. He enjoyed a wealthy and cultured upbringing and graduated from Harvard in 1913. Traveling to Paris to enter the École des Beaux Arts, he was led by his impulsive, chivalrous, and somewhat daredevil nature to enlist in the French Foreign Legion in August 1914 for service against Germany. After a year in the trenches he transferred to the aviation corps, and in April 1916, his training completed, he joined the newly organized Escadrille Américaine No. 124 (later known as the Volunteer Escadrille No. 124 and from December 1916 as the Lafayette Escadrille), composed of American flyers enlisted in the French cause. A daring and eager pilot, he was assigned to the Verdun sector and quickly established a reputation for air combat. He rose to the rank of sergeant. On June 23, 1916, he rushed to the assistance of three comrades, including Raoul Lufbery, who were engaging five German planes. The three comrades escaped the battle, but Chapman was shot down over German territory, the first Lafayette Escadrille pilot killed in action.

Chase, William Curtis (1895–   ), army officer. Born in Providence, Rhode Island, on March 9, 1895, Chase graduated from Brown University in

1916, having already served three years in the Rhode Island national guard. Commissioned a second lieutenant in the cavalry in November 1916, he underwent training in Kansas and Texas and was assigned first to the 3rd and then to the 6th Cavalry. In March 1918 he was transferred to the 11th Machine Gun Battalion, an element of the 4th Infantry Division, with which he saw action in France in World War I. In 1919 he joined the 16th Cavalry in Texas, advancing to captain in September. From 1921 to 1925 he taught military science at Michigan Agricultural College (now Michigan State University). He graduated from Cavalry School, Fort Riley, Kansas, in 1926; from Infantry School, Fort Benning, Georgia, in 1927; and, after a time with the 14th Cavalry and promotion to major (December 1928), from the Command and General Staff School, Fort Leavenworth, Kansas, in 1931. After a tour in the Philippines, 1931–1934, he attended the Army War College, graduating in 1935, and was then assigned as an instructor at the Cavalry School. Promoted to lieutenant colonel in October 1938, he joined the faculty of the Command and General Staff School for a two-year period and from 1940 to 1942 was on the staff of the VIII Corps, Fort Sam Houston, Texas. From 1942 to 1943, with the rank of colonel, he commanded the 113th Cavalry, and in February of the latter year he took command of the 1st Cavalry Brigade, 1st Cavalry Division, advancing to the rank of brigadier general. In February 1944 the 1st Division made the first landing in the Admiralty Islands, capturing Momote airstrip; on October 20 it landed on Leyte in the Philippines as part of the X Corps, swept across the island, and jumped to Luzon on January 27, 1945. On February 3 a motorized column of the 1st Division, led by Chase, was the first American unit to enter Manila. Promoted to temporary major general and given command of the 38th Infantry Division later in February, Chase was engaged in the clearing of Manila, the Bataan peninsula and other areas for several months. He took command of the 1st Cavalry Division in July 1945. On September 8 he led his division as the first American troops to enter Tokyo. In February 1949 he returned to the United States as chief of staff of the Third Army, at Fort McPherson, Georgia, becoming deputy commander in December 1950, and in April 1951 he was named head of the American Military Assistance Advisory Group to the Chinese Nationalist government on Taiwan. After his retirement in July 1955 he continued to be an outspoken advocate of U.S. support for the Nationalist regime before Congress and in public.

Chauncey, Isaac (1772–1840), naval officer. Born in Black Rock, Fairfield County, Connecticut, on February 20, 1772, Chauncey entered the merchant service at an early age and by nineteen had his own command. In June 1799 he entered the navy with a commission (dating from September 1798) as first lieutenant of the frigate *President*, then still under construction. He made a cruise on the *President* under Commodore Thomas Truxtun in 1800. Retained in the reduction of the navy following the hostilities with France, he was acting captain of the frigate *Chesapeake* in 1802, later captain of the *New York*, and, promoted to master commandant in May 1804, he commanded the *John Adams* at the last three attacks on Tripoli by Commodore Edward Preble in August–September 1804. In April 1806 he was promoted to captain. After a leave of absence, during which he was again in the merchant service, he became commander of the New York navy yard. In September 1812, soon after the outbreak of war with Great Britain, Chauncey was appointed commander of naval forces on Lake Ontario and Lake Erie, making his headquarters at Sackett's Harbor, New York. He immediately set about building up a lake fleet; vessels were built in amazingly quick succession, and the complementary port facilities arose alongside. In November he made a brief cruise, pursuing the British lake fleet into Kingston (Ontario) harbor. In April 1813 he undertook a major cruise, commanding from the flagship *Madison* a fleet of 14 ships transporting Gen. Henry Dearborn's army, under command of Gen. Zebulon M. Pike, across to York (now Toronto), which was captured with support from naval guns on April 27. On May 26–27 Chauncey's fleet supported Dearborn in the capture of Fort George. On September 28, aboard his new flagship *General Pike*, he drove the British fleet under Adm. Yeo out of York bay, but the engagement was inconclusive. During the remainder of the war he occupied himself in occasionally transporting troops and otherwise fighting a war of maneuver with Yeo, his principal concern being the defense of Sackett's Harbor. He failed to operate against the British lines of communication, vulnerable as they were, and at critical times failed to support land forces, as during Gen. Jacob J. Brown's campaign in July 1814. In 1815 he took command of the ship of the line *Washington*, from which he commanded the Mediterranean Squadron in 1816–1818, during which time he negotiated a treaty with Algiers in conjunction with U.S. Consul William Shaler. During 1821–1824 he served on the naval Board of Commissioners, and from 1825 to 1832 he was commandant of the New York navy yard. In 1832 he was again appointed to the Board of Commissioners, in which post he remained until his death in Washington, D.C. on January 27, 1840.

Cheatham, Benjamin Franklin (1820–1886),

Confederate army officer. Born on October 20, 1820, in Nashville, Tennessee, Cheatham served in the Tennessee volunteers in the Mexican War, rising from captain to colonel of the 3rd Tennessee Regiment and seeing action at Monterrey and Cerro Gor-

do and in the Mexico City campaign. He joined the gold rush to California in 1849 but soon returned to Tennessee, becoming major general of the state militia. In May 1861 he was appointed brigadier general in the state volunteer forces and in July in the Confederate army. Commanding a division attached first to Gen. Leonidas Polk's corps and later to Gen. William J. Hardee's, he served through Gen. Braxton Bragg's campaign in Tennessee and Kentucky, taking part in the battles at Shiloh, Perryville, Murfreesboro (Stones River), where he was wounded, Chickamauga, and Chattanooga. He was promoted to major general in March 1862. Late in 1864 he commanded one of three corps making up Gen. John B. Hood's Army of Tennessee. Hood, having given up Atlanta to Gen. William T. Sherman, had waited until Sherman cut his own communications and moved off toward the sea; he then turned his sights north toward Nashville, protected only by a small force under Gen. John M. Schofield. Hood pushed Schofield back and on November 29 caught him in an exposed and very vulnerable position at Spring Hill, Tennessee. For some reason he failed to attack. Cheatham's was the corps in position to do so, but afterward Cheatham and Hood blamed each other for the failure, the two giving contradictory versions of what orders had been issued. The failure was followed by the disastrous battle at Franklin the next day. Cheatham subsequently fought at Nashville, December 15–16, and then joined Gen. Joseph E. Johnston's regrouped Army of Tennessee in North Carolina. At the end of the war he resumed farming in Tennessee; for four years he was superintendent of state prisons, and in October 1885 he was appointed postmaster of Nashville. Cheatham died in Nashville on September 4, 1886.

Chennault, Claire Lee (1890–1958),

army officer and airman. Born in Commerce, Texas, on September 6, 1890, Chennault worked his way through Louisiana State Normal College (now Northwestern State College) and became a school teacher in Texas. In 1917 he attended Officers' Training Camp at Fort Benjamin Harrison, Indiana, and in November was commissioned first lieutenant in the infantry reserve. He failed to get overseas duty but transferred to the aviation section of the Signal Corps and became a pilot and then a flying instructor. Discharged in April 1920, he took a regular army commission later in the year and resumed his flying career. He was stationed at various airfields over the next several years, including three years, 1923–1926, in Hawaii as commander of the 19th Pursuit Squadron, and during that time he began a deep and detailed study of pursuit maneuvers and tactics. Promoted to captain in 1929, he graduated from the Air Corps Tactical School, Langley Field, Virginia, in 1931 and remained there as an instructor, publishing in 1935 a long-used textbook *The Role of Defensive Pursuit.* From 1932 to 1936 he led the Air Corps Exhibition Group, known as "Three Men on a Flying Trapeze," with which he worked out details of formation flying. Promoted to temporary rank of major in 1936, Chennault was retired (for deafness) in 1937 at the rank of lieutenant colonel. Later in that year he was hired by Madame Chiang Kai-shek, wife of the Nationalist Chinese leader, to take over the training and organizing of air defenses against Japan. In 1940 he returned to the United States to recruit pilots and mechanics to fight for China; many were enticed out of U.S. armed forces, attracted by high pay and a taste for romantic adventure. In August 1941 Chennault began training his American Volunteer Group in K'un-ming, and on December 20 they flew their first mission. Although the A.V.G. flew only for seven months and never had more than 50 pilots on call at a time, it became the terror of the air over southern China and Burma. Chennault concentrated on pilot training, tactical drill, and a thorough understanding of Japanese methods and capabilities; and the resulting score for seven months' air combat was 299 Japanese airplanes shot down to 32 A.V.G. planes and 10 pilots lost in combat (9 more pilots died in accidents). The "Flying Tigers," as the A.V.G. became known from the decoration on their P-40s, were the most colorful and publicized air unit of the war. In April 1942 Chennault was recalled to active duty in the Army Air Forces as a colonel (he was a brigadier general in the Chinese service) and shortly afterward was promoted to brigadier general. On July 4 the work of the A.V.G. was absorbed by the 23rd Fighter Squadron, and Chennault became chief of Army Air Forces in China, organizing the China Air Task Force to carry on the war. In March 1943 he was promoted to major general in command of the Fourteenth Air Force. The Fourteenth fought a war of attrition and tactical support of American and Chinese ground forces, principally those under Gen. Joseph W. Stilwell, from bases throughout southern China. Following Stilwell's relief in October 1944, Chennault commanded the China theater for a week before turning it over to Gen. Albert C. Wedemeyer. He remained in command of the Fourteenth until August 1945; he retired from the army in October 1945. Critical of what he considered a failure of U.S. authorities to support Chiang's government, he rejoined the Nationalists in 1946 to organize the Chinese National Relief and Rehabilitation Air Transport (later the Civil Air Transport) service and to direct other aviation organizations on Taiwan. He returned to the United States in January 1958 for medical treatment and died in New Orleans on July 27, 1958.

Chivington, John Milton (1821–1894), clergyman and army officer. Born on January 27, 1821, in Warren County, Ohio, Chivington worked in his family's timber business and as a carpenter before becoming a preacher in the Methodist church in 1844. In 1848 he left Ohio to become an itinerant missionary among both white settlers and Indians on the frontier. In Kansas during the 1850s he was a prominent figure on the antislavery side of the disturbances known as the "Border Wars," gaining the sobriquet of "Fighting Parson." At the outbreak of the Civil War in 1861 he was commissioned major in the 1st Colorado Volunteers; promoted to colonel in 1862, he served under Col. Edward R. S. Canby in the campaign against Gen. Henry H. Sibley in New Mexico, particularly distinguishing himself at Apache Canyon on March 27, 1862. In 1863 Chivington was appointed commander of the military district of Colorado. In that post he was responsible for dealing with Indian disturbances, which had been on the increase during the war and the absence of regular federal troops. By late 1864 the Indians, Cheyenne and Arapaho under Black Kettle, had cut lines of communication between Denver and the Missouri River, the main supply line of the West. The approach of winter led Black Kettle to think of peace, however, and after contacting the federal commander at Fort Lyon he led his 700 followers into camp on Sand Creek, a tributary of the Arkansas in southeastern Colorado. Chivington, eager to settle the Indian problem once and for all and backed by Gov. John Evans, led a force of 900 to 1000 militia and volunteers to Fort Lyon. Late on November 28, 1864, they left the fort for Black Kettle's village, and at dawn on November 29 they attacked. Black Kettle, under the impression he had made peace with the Fort Lyon soldiers, raised an American flag and then a white one, but the Colorado militiamen raged through the camp for hours. Of the 700 Indians (500 of them women and children) upwards of 400 were killed, many brutally. The Sand Creek Massacre, or Chivington Massacre, immediately became a matter of violent controversy. Three separate hearings were held, and while Chivington was harshly criticized then and later no official action was taken. After the war he was for a time engaged in the express business in Nebraska; later he returned to Colorado, entered journalism, and held various public offices. He died in Denver on October 4, 1894.

Christian, William (1743?–1786), Revolutionary militia and army officer. Born about 1743 in Staunton, Virginia, Christian was by the age of twenty a captain of militia. About 1767 he took up the study of law under Patrick Henry, whose sister Anne he subsequently married. He served in the state assembly from 1773 to 1775 and in the state senate in 1776. He commanded a regiment of militia in Lord Dunmore's War against the Indians in 1774. In February 1776 he was appointed lieutenant colonel of the 1st Virginia Regiment in Continental service, advancing to colonel in March. In July he resigned his commission, however, to return to militia service for duty against marauding Overhill Cherokee Indians in western Virginia. With about 1700 militiamen from Virginia and North Carolina, Christian set out from Long Island in the Holston River (near the present site of Kingsport, Tennessee), where invading Indians had been repelled a year before, and pushed southwest to the French Broad River, laying waste Indian villages and crops and forcing a truce. He extracted an agreement that Indian representatives would appear at Long Island the next year to sign a permanent treaty. After rebuilding the fort at Long Island, naming it Fort Patrick Henry, Christian disbanded his men. In 1777 he was appointed one of three commissioners to meet the Indians at Long Island. By the treaty signed on July 20 the Cherokee ceded large areas of land in what are now Tennessee and Kentucky. After serving again in the Virginia senate in 1780–1783 Christian took up a grant of land on Bear Grass Creek, near Louisville, Kentucky, in 1785. On April 9, 1786, he was killed while leading a raid against Wabash Indians near the site of present-day Jeffersonville, Indiana.

Church, Benjamin (1639–1718), colonial militia officer. Born in 1639 in Plymouth Colony (Massachusetts), Church worked as a carpenter in various frontier settlements. He took part in several small skirmishes with Indians early in King Philip's War in 1675 and was captain in command of a company of Plymouth troops at the Great Swamp Fight near South Kingston, Rhode Island, on December 19, 1675, when the Narragansetts were scattered. Early in 1676 Gov. Josiah Winslow of Plymouth relinquished command of the colonial troops in the field to Church. He continued active against Philip through 1676, destroying Indian villages and crops, enlisting numbers of Indians on the colonial side, and capturing on August 1 members of Philip's family. Church finally tracked Philip to his refuge in a swamp near Mt. Hope, in what is now Bristol, Rhode Island, and on August 12 Philip was shot by one of Church's Indian scouts. That death effectively ended the war. Church later served in King William's War, 1689–1697; and in Queen Anne's War, by then a colonel, he led an expedition against Port Royal, Nova Scotia, in 1704. He retired from service in the militia later in that year. He died near Little Compton, Rhode Island, on January 17, 1718. His son Thomas Church published in 1716 *Entertaining Passages Relating to King Philip's War,* based on the elder Church's notes and recollections.

Clark, Charles Edgar (1843–1922), naval officer. Born in Bradford, Vermont, on August 10, 1843, Clark entered the Naval Academy in 1860 and graduated, under pressure of wartime, in 1863, having taken part in the transfer of the midshipmen's corps from Annapolis to Newport, Rhode Island, in 1861. Assigned to the gunboat *Ossipee* in Adm. David G. Farragut's West Gulf Blockading Squadron in 1863, he saw action at Mobile Bay on August 5, 1864. After the war he served in the Pacific Squadron aboard the *Vanderbilt* and the *Suwanee,* surviving the wreck of the latter near Vancouver Island in July 1868. Clark was promoted to lieutenant in February 1867, lieutenant commander in March 1868, and commander in November 1881. He later commanded the *Ranger,* engaged in survey work along the Pacific coast during 1883–1886; the *Mohican,* flagship of a squadron cruising the Bering Sea in 1893–1894; and, promoted to captain in June 1896, the *Monterey* in 1896–1898. Early in 1898 he was transferred to command of the new battleship *Oregon,* pride of the Pacific Squadron, and, in anticipation of war with Spain, was ordered to bring it from San Francisco to the Atlantic. Departing San Francisco on March 19, "Clark of the *Oregon,*" as he became known, undertook one of the most famous and most publicized runs in naval history. For 71 days the progress of the *Oregon* was a newspaper epic, a sign both of growing American pride in the "New Navy" and of anxiety over the Spanish fleet. (The voyage was to add considerable impetus to the movement for an isthmian canal a few years later.) Joining Adm. William T. Sampson's squadron at Key West on May 25, having rounded the Cape and completed the 15,000-mile voyage in battle-ready condition, the *Oregon* proceeded with it to blockade Santiago, Cuba. On July 3, as the Spanish fleet attempted to escape, the *Oregon* gave good account of herself, engaging all of the enemy ships as they appeared and running down the *Colón* and forcing it to beach. A few days later Clark was appointed chief of staff in a Flying Squadron assembled to sail for Spain, but the expedition did not materialize. In March 1899 Clark became commandant of League Island navy yard in Philadelphia; he was governor of the Naval Home there in 1901–1904, receiving promotion to rear admiral in June 1902, and after a year as president of the naval Examining and Retiring Board he retired from active service in August 1905. He died on October 2, 1922, in Long Beach, California.

Clark, George Rogers (1752–1818), frontier leader and Revolutionary militia officer. Born near Charlottesville, Virginia, on November 19, 1752, Clark was an elder brother of William Clark. He received little formal education but learned surveying from his grandfather and by the time of the Revolution was well known as an explorer in the western frontier region of Virginia, which is now Kentucky. His first military service came during Lord Dunmore's War against the Shawnee Indians in 1774, during which he served as a captain of Virginia militia. He then settled in the region that was to become Kentucky and became a prominent figure as well as a leader among those who favored maintaining their connection with Virginia against the setting up of a new colony, Transylvania. Soon after the Revolution broke out, he persuaded Gov. Patrick Henry and the Virginia legislature to provide for the protection of the western region and was made commander of frontier militia with the rank of major. A shipment of powder enabled the Kentuckians to suppress the Indian raids that Clark believed were instigated by the British. With the further approval of the legislature and a commission as lieutenant colonel, he recruited a force of about 175 men and set out in May 1778 to subdue the Indian allies of the British and to clear the Illinois territory of enemy forces. On July 4 he surprised and captured Kaskaskia; by August he had captured the outposts of Cahokia and Vincennes as well and had won the allegiance of the French settlers in the area. A force under Lt. Gov. Henry Hamilton from the principal western post of the British, Detroit, recaptured Vincennes in December but failed to maintain the initiative; after a daring and terrible midwinter forced march, Clark and his men retook the settlement on February 25, 1779, taking Hamilton prisoner. The failure of Virginia to send reinforcements or supplies made his planned march on Detroit an impossibility, and for the rest of 1779 he remained at Fort Nelson, which he had built near what is now Louisville. From 1780, when he was appointed brigadier general, to 1782 he conducted several successful campaigns against the Shawnee, destroying their villages at Piqua and Chillicothe, and defended Cahokia and St. Louis (then a Spanish settlement) against a British–Indian expedition. In January 1781, while seeking support for a Detroit expedition, he joined in the defense against Gen. Benedict Arnold's invasion of Virginia. The Detroit campaign never materialized for lack of support, but Clark had conquered and held the Old Northwest (the Illinois country), and this was reflected, though not explicitly stated, in the terms of the peace made by the treaty of Paris in 1783. He and his men had received no pay for their services, and he himself had advanced considerable sums of money to the cause; although a large tract of land was granted by Virginia to the "Illinois Regiment," Clark never received his due and found himself deeply in debt. He remained in the West as Indian commissioner and led his last military expedition against the Wabash tribes in 1786. In that year James Wilkinson, secretly a Spanish agent, successfully conducted an intrigue against Clark, who was discredited and relieved of his post. During the next several years he became involved in a number of abortive Western military and colonizing schemes initiated by the Spanish and French. He accepted commissions freely—in particular, a French major general's commission offered in 1793 in con-

nection with the schemes of French ambassador Edmond Charles Genêt—apparently reserving his ultimate loyalty to the idea of Western expansion. He took refuge in St. Louis for a time in 1798 rather than surrender his French commission. In 1799 he returned to Louisville, and there he lived, except for a few years spent in Indiana, until his death on February 13, 1818.

Clark, Mark Wayne (1896–   ), army officer. Born on May 1, 1896, at Madison Barracks, New York, the son of an army officer, Clark graduated from West Point in 1917 and was commissioned in the infantry. After a year of training with the 11th Infantry at Chickamauga Park, Georgia, during which period he advanced to temporary captain, he was ordered to France in April 1918. He saw combat in command of a battalion of the 11th, a unit of the 5th Infantry Division, until being wounded in June; thereafter he was on the staff of the First Army and, during the occupation period, that of the Third Army. Promoted to captain in November 1919, shortly after his return to the United States, Clark was stationed in rapid succession at Fort Leavenworth, Kansas; Fort Snelling, Minnesota; and Fort Crook, Nebraska, in 1919–1921. After three years with the General Staff he entered the Infantry School, Fort Benning, Georgia, graduating in 1925. In 1925–1928 he was at the Presidio, San Francisco, and after periods at Fort D. A. Russell, Wyoming, and as an instructor with the Indiana National Guard, during which he advanced to major in January 1933, he entered the Command and General Staff School, Fort Leavenworth, graduating in 1935. In 1935–1936 he was assigned to duty with the Civilian Conservation Corps in Omaha, Nebraska. He graduated from the Army War College in 1937, and after serving on the staff of the 3rd Infantry Division at Fort Lewis, Washington, he returned to the War College as an instructor in 1940. Promoted to lieutenant colonel in August, he was attached to the General Staff a short time later. He was promoted to temporary brigadier general in August 1941. During 1940–1942 he was deeply involved in the problems of organizing and training a rapidly expanding army; in this work he was associated closely with Gen. Lesley J. McNair, chief of General Headquarters (GHQ) and, from its formation in March 1942, of the Army Ground Forces. Clark was promoted to temporary major general in April 1942 and in May became chief of staff of Army Ground Forces. In July he was named commander of all U.S. ground forces in Europe. From his headquarters in England he oversaw the buildup and training of a large body of American troops there, organized as the II Corps. In October he relinquished command of II Corps to undertake a highly secret and hazardous mission. Traveling by submarine and then rubber boat, he landed on the coast of Algiers with a small staff and made his way to a rendezvous with French officers, from whom he secured information on Vichy French forces in North Africa. In November he was promoted to temporary lieutenant general and made deputy commander, under Gen. Dwight D. Eisenhower, of the Allied forces in North Africa. In January 1943, at Oujda, Morocco, he established a headquarters for the new Fifth Army and began planning for the invasion of Italy. The Fifth Army, composed of the VI Corps, Gen. John P. Lucas, and the British X Corps, was combined with the British Eighth Army, Gen. Sir Bernard L. Montgomery, forming the 15th Army Group under Gen. Sir Harold R. L. G. Alexander. Following Montgomery's crossing from Sicily to Reggio di Calabria, Italy, on September 3, 1943, Clark's Fifth Army was landed at Salerno on September 9 by Adm. H. Kent Hewitt's amphibious forces. Despite Italy's surrender before the Allied invasion, German resistance to the advance northward was extremely heavy. Several days were required simply to render the beachhead at Salerno secure. Naples was captured on October 1, and later in the month the defensive line of the Volturno River was reached. The advance through the mouains was halted some 90 miles south of Rome at the Germans' Winter Line, anchored on the heavily defended town of Cassino. On January 22, 1944, the VI Corps was embarked on naval amphibious craft and landed 60 miles behind the German line at Anzio. Still, little progress was made until May, when the Germans began to fall back slowly; the Anzio beachhead, bottled up, had failed to cut enemy communications. On June 4 Allied forces finally entered Rome. In August a new front developed on the Gothic Line across the northern Apennines. In December 1944 Clark moved up to command of the 15th Army Group, turning the Fifth Army over to Gen. Lucian K. Truscott, and in March 1945 he was promoted to temporary general. The spring offensive of 1945 was a rapid one: Bologna was taken on April 21, followed by Genoa, Brescia, Padua, Milan, and Venice; and on May 2 the German forces remaining in Italy surrendered in the first major capitulation of the war. Later in that month Clark moved forces into Austria and was named commander of U.S. forces in that country; in June, shortly before the deactivation of the 15th Army Group, he was appointed Allied High Commissioner for Austria. He held those posts until May 1947 and then returned to the United States, taking command of the Sixth Army at the Presidio, San Francisco, in June. From 1949 to 1952 he was commander of Army Field Forces at Fort Monroe, Virginia. In May 1952 Clark was named to succeed Gen. Matthew B. Ridgway as commander of U.S. forces and supreme commander of United Nations forces in Korea. He held that post through the long and frustrating period of negotiation that resulted finally in the armistice agreement signed on July 27, 1953. He

retired from the army in October of that year. Clark published two volumes of war memoirs, *Calculated Risk*, 1950, and *From the Danube to the Yalu*, 1954. From 1954 to 1960 he was president of The Citadel. After his retirement in 1960 he held the title of president emeritus of The Citadel.

Clark, William (1770–1838), army officer and explorer. Born in Caroline County, Virginia, on August 1, 1770, William was the younger brother of George Rogers Clark, the conqueror of the Old Northwest during the Revolution. In 1785 he moved west with his family and settled near Louisville; four years later he followed his brother into military service and participated in several militia campaigns, under Col. John Hardin, Gen. Charles Scott, and others, against hostile Indian tribes. In March 1792 he was commissioned a lieutenant in the regular army and served for four years under Gen. "Mad Anthony" Wayne, taking part on August 20, 1794, in the Battle of Fallen Timbers. Meriwether Lewis, his future partner in exploration, was for a time under his command. He resigned from the army in July 1796 and spent several years traveling and attending to his estate in Louisville and to the claims of his brother against Virginia. In 1803 he was invited by Capt. Lewis to share command of the government-sponsored expedition to the Far West in search of a land route to the Pacific, then being organized at the behest of President Thomas Jefferson. He quickly accepted both the invitation and a commission as second lieutenant (March 1804) and devoted the next three years to this project, which ended with the explorers' return to St. Louis in 1806. During the journey up the Missouri River, across the Continental Divide, and down the Columbia River to the sea, Clark, although nominally under the command of Lewis, shared equally in the responsibilities of leadership. He devoted particular care to mapmaking and to studying the natural history of the hitherto unexplored region. (For more detail, see **Lewis, Meriwether**) On his return he began to collect the records, both official and personal, of the expedition, laying the groundwork for Nicholas Biddle's editorial work and the publication of the complete journals in 1814. In February 1807, having resigned again from the army, Clark was appointed brigadier general of militia and superintendent of Indian affairs for the Louisiana Territory and established his headquarters in St. Louis. He was an incorporator, with Pierre and Auguste Chouteau, Manuel Lisa, Pierre Menard, Andrew Henry, and others of the St. Louis Missouri Fur Company in 1809. In July 1813 he became governor of the recently formed Missouri Territory, holding the post until September 1820, when the first elected officials of the state of Missouri took office. He led volunteers in several campaigns during the War of 1812 and in 1814 at Prairie du Chien established Fort

Shelby, the first U.S. outpost in what is now Wisconsin. For several years after the war he was primarily concerned with establishing treaties with various Indian tribes, often engaging the aid of Auguste Chouteau, and in 1825 he joined the governor of Michigan Territory, Lewis Cass, in the negotiations at Prairie du Chien that attempted to settle permanently all Indian territorial disputes. He took an important part in the suppression of the uprisings of the Winnebago in 1827 and of the Sauk, under the leadership of Black Hawk, in 1832 (the Black Hawk War). Clark was also surveyor general for Illinois, Missouri, and Arkansas during 1824–1825, and in 1828 he platted the site of Paducah, Kentucky. He died in St. Louis on September 1, 1838.

Clay, Lucius DuBignon (1897–   ), army officer, businessman, and diplomat. Born in Marietta, Georgia, on April 23, 1897, Clay graduated from West Point in 1918. He was immediately promoted to first lieutenant and temporary captain and was assigned to training duty at Camp Humphrey, Virginia. In 1920, after completing an engineering course at Camp Humphrey, he joined the faculty of Alabama Polytechnic Institute (now Auburn University) for a year, returning to Camp Humphrey in 1921 as engineering officer and instructor. From 1924 to 1928 he was an instructor at West Point. From 1930 to 1937 he fulfilled various river and harbor assignments in the Canal Zone, Pittsburgh, and Washington, D.C., receiving permanent rank of captain in June 1933. During 1937–1938 he was on the staff of Gen. Douglas MacArthur in the Philippines and was an adviser to the Philippine government. From 1938 to 1940 he was in charge of the Red River dam project in Texas, and in the latter year he undertook a nationwide program of airport improvement and systematization. Promoted to temporary brigadier general in March 1942, Clay was assigned to General Staff duty in Washington, D.C., with responsibilities in supply and matériel. In December 1942 he advanced to temporary major general. In November 1944 he was ordered to Europe to take command of the supply base in Normandy, where he greatly improved the processing of supplies from the port of Cherbourg to the front. In December 1944 he was named deputy director for war programs and general administration in the Office of War Mobilization and Reconversion, taking leave of absence from active duty while in that post. In April 1945, promoted to temporary lieutenant general, he was named deputy military governor of the American Zone of occupied Germany under Gen. Joseph T. McNarney, and in March 1947 he succeeded McNarney as military governor of the zone and commander of U.S. forces in occupied Germany and Europe, receiving temporary rank of general. In that post he was called upon to deal with the critical situation brought about by the Soviet-imposed blockade of Berlin from June 24, 1948. Clay oversaw the organization and maintenance of the massive airlift of food, fuel, and other supplies by which the city was kept alive and functioning. During that time he assisted in the drafting of the constitution for the Federal Republic of Germany. In May 1949 he returned to the United States and retired from the army, receiving permanent rank of general at that time. In 1950 he published *Decision in Germany* and *Germany and the Fight for Freedom.* In that year he became chairman of the board and chief executive officer of the Continental Can Company, a position he held until 1962. He was a frequent adviser at high government levels on German questions, and in September 1961 he was named personal representative of President John F. Kennedy, with rank of ambassador, for a mission to Berlin lasting until May 1962. Clay continued as a governmental adviser and in various business interests in later years, serving as board chairman of the Federal National Mortgage Association in 1970–1971. A son, Lucius D. Clay, Jr., rose to the rank of general in the air force.

Cleburne, Patrick Ronayne (1828–1864), Confederate army officer. Born on March 17, 1828, in County Cork, Ireland, Cleburne attended Trinity College, Dublin, for a time but, failing to pass the apothecaries' course, he enlisted in the 41st Regiment of Foot. After three years he obtained his release and emigrated to the United States, arriving in New Orleans in December 1849 and settling in Helena, Arkansas, in 1850. While working as a druggist's clerk, he studied law and in 1856 was admitted to the bar. In 1860, by which time he was a prominent figure in the region, he joined in the organization of the Yell Rifle company. He became captain of the company shortly after its seizure in March 1861 of the federal arsenal in Little Rock, a somewhat precipitate action planned largely by Cleburne. Appointed colonel of the 1st (later 15th) Infantry later in 1861, he was promoted to brigadier general in March 1862. At the battle of Pittsburg Landing (Shiloh), April 6–7, 1862, he commanded a brigade of Gen. William J. Hardee's corps and performed with distinction. He was wounded at Richmond, Kentucky, August 30, where he was serving under Gen. Edmund Kirby-Smith, and again at Perryville on October 8. In December 1862 he was advanced to major general. He earned a high reputation leading a division, generally under Hardee, of Gen. Braxton Bragg's Army of Tennessee at Murfreesboro (Stones River), December 31, 1862–January 3, 1863, Chickamauga, September 18–20, 1863, and Chattanooga, November 24–25, and was formally thanked by the Confederate congress for his actions in defending Ringgold Gap against repeated attacks by Gen. Joseph Hooker on November 27, 1863. During the winter he became one of the first Confederate military leaders to urge the use of free colored troops. In 1864 he fought under Gen. Joseph E. Johnston and Gen. John B. Hood in the Army of Tennessee, taking part in the defense of Atlanta. Known as "the Stonewall of the West," Cleburne died in the battle of Franklin, Tennessee, on November 30, 1864, after his men had carried two lines of Union works.

Clinton, George (1739–1812), Revolutionary army officer and public official. Born on July 26, 1739, in Little Britain, Ulster (later Orange) County, New York, Clinton was a brother of James Clinton. He went to sea briefly when he was eighteen, served as a lieutenant in Col. John Bradstreet's August 1758 expedition against Fort Frontenac in the French and Indian War, and about 1762 took up the practice of law. In 1768 he was elected to the New York provincial assembly where he served until 1775, when he was elected to the Continental Congress. In December of the same year he was appointed brigadier general of the state militia and sent to defend New York City and the Hudson River. His duties were nearly entirely garrison in nature; in March 1777 he was commissioned brigadier general in the Continental army. On October 6, 1777, he was forced to surrender Fort Montgomery to a British army under Sir Henry Clinton, who also captured nearby Fort Clinton, commanded by George Clinton's brother James. In June 1777 he was elected both governor and lieutenant governor of New York. He declined the latter office but remained New York's first state governor for 18 years. He had a profound distrust of centralized government and in letters and debate and as president of the state convention called to consider the question he strongly opposed New York's ratification of the Constitution in 1788. He was a follower of Thomas Jefferson and was instrumental in promoting Aaron Burr's rise to prominence. He retired from the governorship in 1795 but returned for another term in 1801. In 1804 he was elected vice-president under Jefferson and, after an unsuccessful bid for the presidential nomination in 1808, was reelected to the office for a second term under James Madison. In 1811, as president of the Senate, he cast the deciding vote against the rechartering of the First Bank of the United States. He died in Washington, D.C., on April 20, 1812.

Clinton, James (1733–1812), Revolutionary army officer. Born at the family seat of Little Britain, Ulster (now Orange) County, New York, on August 9, 1733, Clinton was an elder brother of George Clinton, later governor of New York. James early joined the Ulster militia and was a captain in Col. John Bradstreet's expedition against Fort Frontenac in July –August 1758. He had risen to lieutenant colonel by the outbreak of the Revolution, and in October 1775, while taking part in Gen. Richard Montgomery's

Quebec expedition, he was appointed colonel of the 3rd New York. After the expedition ended in failure he returned to New York early in 1776. In October of that year he was commissioned brigadier general in the Continental army and placed in command of Fort Clinton on the west bank of the Hudson below West Point. In October 1777 the upper Hudson fortifications were attacked by British troops under Gen. Sir Henry Clinton; James Clinton and his 600 men stoutly defended the fort against 3000 attackers but were at length forced to abandon it, Clinton himself being the last to escape and sustaining a severe bayonet wound in so doing. From November 1778 he was engaged in defending the New York frontier against Indian marauding, and the following year he cooperated with the expedition sent out under Gen. John Sullivan in the aftermath of the Wyoming and Cherry Valley massacres. By July he had collected some 1500 troops and all his supplies at the foot of Lake Otsego; he dammed the lake's outlet, let the water build up, and then broke the dam, releasing sufficient water to float his more than 200 heavily laden boats downstream to a rendezvous with Sullivan in Pennsylvania. Their combined forces decisively defeated the Indians under Joseph Brant and the Tories and British troops under Col. John Butler at Newtown, Pennsylvania, near present-day Elmira, New York, on August 29. The expedition devastated Indian crops and destroyed some 40 villages, effectively ending the menace to the frontier. In 1780 Clinton was given command of the Northern Department, headquartered in Albany, but in 1781 he led a brigade to join the army of Gen. George Washington in the siege of Yorktown. In 1785 Clinton served on the New York–Pennsylvania boundary commission, and in 1788 he was a member of the New York constitutional ratifying convention, casting his vote against ratification. He died at Little Britain, New York, on December 22, 1812. His son was DeWitt Clinton.

Cochise (1812?–1874), Indian leader. Born about 1812, probably in present-day Arizona, Cochise was a chief of the Chiricahua band of the Apaches. Under Spanish and Mexican rule the Apaches had been the particular victims of slave traders and scalp hunters and the Southwest was in constant turmoil. With the coming of U.S. authority in 1850 a brief period of relative peace began. In February 1861 the peace was broken when Cochise, falsely accused of having kidnaped a white child, appeared at an army post to deny the charge and was imprisoned. Escaping, he took hostages to exchange for other members of his band still held by the army; the exchange did not take place and both sides executed their hostages. Cochise joined his father-in-law, Mangas Coloradas (or Colorado), chief of the Mimbreño Apaches, in a long series of raids and skirmishes that soon threatened to drive the Americans from Arizona. In July

1862, with some 500 warriors, they held Apache Pass against Gen. James Carleton and 3000 California volunteers until forced out by artillery fire. Mangas Coloradas was later captured and killed in prison, leaving Cochise to lead Apache resistance. Gradually driven deeper and deeper into the hidden recesses of the Dragoon Mountains, he nonetheless maintained a reign of terror over white settlers until June 1871, when Col. George Crook assumed command of the army in Arizona. Using other Apaches as scouts, Crook tracked Cochise down and forced him to surrender in September. Early the next year the Chiricahua were ordered transferred to a Mescalero reservation near Tularosa, New Mexico; refusing to leave the ancestral lands that had been guaranteed them by the Americans, Cochise and a small band of followers again took to the mountains and resisted until midsummer. Later in that year a new treaty was negotiated by the Indian commissioner, Gen. Oliver O. Howard, and Cochise retired to the Chiricahua reservation in Arizona, where he died peacefully on June 9, 1874.

Cochran, Jacqueline (1910?-   ), aviator and business leader.

Born in Pensacola, Florida, about 1910, Miss Cochran grew up in poverty in a foster home. At eight she went to work in a cotton mill in Georgia; she later was trained as a beautician and pursued that career in Montgomery, Alabama, in Pensacola, and from about 1931 in New York City. She took her first flying lessons in 1932 and soon mastered the technical aspects of aviation and navigation, later studying privately with a navy pilot friend in San Diego. Meanwhile, in 1934, she had organized a cosmetics firm that grew and prospered under her management. In 1935 Miss Cochran became the first woman to enter the Bendix Transcontinental Air Race; in 1937 she came in third, and in 1938 she won the Bendix Trophy, flying a Seversky pursuit plane. In 1941 she piloted a bomber to England and there, as a flight captain in the British Air Transport Auxiliary, trained a group of woman pilots for war transport service. Upon her return to the United States she undertook a similar program for the Army Air Forces and in July 1943 was named director of the Women's Airforce Service Pilots—the WASPs—which supplied more than a thousand auxiliary pilots for the armed forces. At the end of the war she served for a time as a Pacific and European correspondent for *Liberty* magazine. In 1945 she became the first woman civilian to be awarded the Distinguished Service Medal and in 1948 was commissioned a lieutenant colonel in the air force reserve. Eager to make the transition to jet aircraft, she became the first woman to break the sound barrier in 1953, piloting an F-86, and that year set world speed records for 15-, 100- and 500-kilometer courses. She continued to break her old records and set new ones, including an altitude mark of 55,253 feet in 1961, and in 1964 she set the standing women's world speed record of 1429 miles per hour in an F-104G Super Star jet. In 1969 she was promoted to colonel in the reserve. In 1959 she became the first woman president of the Fédération Aéronautique Internationale, and she was also a member of many other aviation and service-connected organizations.

Cody, William Frederick (1846–1917), "Buffalo Bill," frontiersman and entertainer.

Born in Scott County, Iowa, on February 26, 1846, Cody had little education and went to work at the age of twelve. By the outbreak of the Civil War he had been by turns a horse wrangler, a mounted messenger for a freight company, an unsuccessful prospector, and a pony-express rider. The family had moved to Kansas some years before the war came; Cody rode with the anti-slavery guerrillas, the Jayhawkers, for a time before enlisting in 1863 as a scout with the 9th Kansas Cavalry. Later he was a scout with the Union army in operations in Tennessee and Missouri. Soon after the war he took a job as a hunter for a company that had contracted to supply meat for the construction crews of the Kansas Pacific Railroad, and during 1867–1868 he killed, by his own count, 4280 buffalo. For the next four years he was again with the army, serving as chief scout of the 5th Cavalry in various Indian campaigns. During this time, in 1869, he met the writer E. Z. C. Judson—"Ned Buntline"—who, seeing in him the makings of a popular hero, dubbed him "Buffalo Bill" and proceeded to feature him in a series of highly fictionalized and sensational dime novels. In 1872 Judson wrote a play, *Scouts of the Plains* (later *Scouts of the Prairies*), which opened in Chicago in December 1872 and later successfully toured Eastern cities with Cody, under his new name, and "Texas Jack" Omohundro, later replaced by "Wild Bill" Hickok, as its stars. In 1876 Cody returned briefly to the 5th Cavalry, then commanded by Col. Wesley Merritt, and in the fight at War Bonnet Creek (now Hat Creek, near Montrose, Nebraska) on July 17 of that year killed and scalped Yellow Hand, a Cheyenne leader, in a famous duel. He soon returned to the stage and until 1883 divided his time between show business and his Nebraska ranch. In 1883 he organized the highly successful "Buffalo Bill's Wild West Show" (originally the "Wild West, Rocky Mountain and Prairie Exhibition"), opening at Omaha on May 17, and over the next three decades he played to audiences in the East, in Great Britain, and in Continental Europe; the show featured Cody, the famed woman marksman Annie Oakley, and, briefly, Sitting Bull. The show had a particularly successful run in 1893 at the World's Columbian Exposition in Chicago. The show was merged with that of "Pawnee Bill" in 1908 and with the Sells-Floto circus in 1913. Cody himself last appeared in 1916. In the 1890s Cody settled on an extensive tract of land in the Bighorn Basin granted him by the state of Wyoming, and there the city of Cody was built. On January 10, 1917, he died suddenly in Denver; he was buried in a solid rock tomb at the top of nearby Lookout Mountain. His *Life of Hon. Wm. F. Cody, Known as Buffalo Bill,* which first appeared in 1879, went through many editions.

Collins, Joseph Lawton (1896–   ), army officer. Born in New Orleans on May 1, 1896, Collins graduated from West Point in 1917 and was commissioned second lieutenant in the 22nd Infantry. Promoted to captain in 1919, he was ordered to duty with U.S. troops in occupied Germany in May. From 1921 to 1925 he was an instructor at West Point. He graduated from the Infantry School, Fort Benning, Georgia, in 1925 and was an instructor there from 1927 to 1931; promoted to major in 1932, he graduated from the Command and General Staff School, Fort Leavenworth, Kansas, in 1933, and after a tour of duty in the Philippines he completed courses at the Army Industrial College in 1937 and the Army War College in 1938. He was an instructor at the latter until 1941, when he was named chief of staff of the VII Corps in Alabama. Immediately after the attack on Pearl Harbor he became chief of staff to the new commander of the Hawaiian Department, Gen. Delos C. Emmons. In February 1942 he was promoted to temporary brigadier general and in May was advanced to temporary major general and named commander of the 25th Infantry Division, which in December landed as a relief force on Guadalcanal. He distinguished himself there and in the campaign on New Georgia. In March 1944 he took command of the VII Corps in England. As part of Gen. Omar Bradley's First Army in the Normandy assault, the VII Corps spearheaded the breakout at St. Lô in July 1944. The VII Corps took part in the First Army's campaign across northern France and Belgium, into the Rhineland, and on to the Elbe River. Promoted to temporary lieutenant general in April 1945, Collins returned to the United States in August to duty as deputy commanding general and chief of staff, Army Ground Forces. From December 1945 to September 1947 he was director of information in the War Department; named deputy chief of staff in September 1947, he was promoted to permanent major general and temporary general in January 1948 and appointed vice chief of staff in November. In August 1949 Collins became chief of staff of the army, a post held until August 1953. From 1953 to 1956 he was the U.S. representative to the Military Committee and Standing Group of the North Atlantic Treaty Organization; during that period, in 1954–1955, he served also as special envoy, with rank of ambassador, to Vietnam. Retiring from the army in March 1956, he served for a year as vice chairman of the President's Committee for Hungarian Refugee Relief. From 1957

he engaged in private business, serving as vice chairman of the board of Pfizer International subsidiaries, and was active in various international educational organizations.

Collins, Michael (1930–   ), air force officer and astronaut. Born on October 31, 1930, in Rome, Italy, Collins was the son of an American army officer. He graduated from West Point in 1952 and took a commission in the air force, completing pilot training a year later. After duty at various bases in the United States and abroad he entered test pilot training at Edwards Air Force Base, California, in 1960, remaining there until 1963. In that year he was included among the third group of men selected for astronaut training. His first space flight was aboard *Gemini X* in a three-day earth orbit mission in July 1966 during which the feasibility of refueling in space was demonstrated and Collins twice performed extravehicular activities (EVA, or space walks). He was promoted to lieutenant colonel after the flight. He was removed from the crew of the moon-orbiting *Apollo VIII* mission in December 1968 for health reasons, but in July 1969 he was pilot of the command module *Columbia* on the historic *Apollo XI* mission on which Neil Armstrong and Edwin E. Aldrin became the first men to land on the moon. Shortly after the completion of that mission Collins, who had then attained the rank of colonel, resigned from the National Aeronautics and Space Administration. From January 1970 to February 1971 he served as assistant secretary of state for public affairs. In 1971 he became curator of the National Air and Space Museum of the Smithsonian Institution. In 1974 he published *Carrying the Fire: An Astronaut's Journeys.* The book, a description of his experiences in and reflections on space travel, was well received. Collins's numerous honors and awards included the Hubbard Medal and the Collier and Harmon trophies.

Collins, Napoleon (1814–1875), naval officer. Born in Pennsylvania on March 4, 1814, Collins was appointed midshipman in the navy in January 1834. He was promoted to lieutenant in November 1846, and in the Mexican War he served on the sloop *Decatur,* taking part in the actions at Tuxpan and Tabasco under Commodore Matthew C. Perry. After the outbreak of the Civil War he commanded the gunboat *Anacostia* in the Potomac Flotilla for a few months in 1861, taking part in the attack on Confederate batteries at Aquia Creek on May 31–June 1. In September 1861 he took command of the gunboat *Unadilla* of the South Atlantic Blockading Squadron under Flag-Officer Samuel F. DuPont and had a hand in the capture of Port Royal on November 7. In July 1862 Collins was promoted to commander and given command of the steamer *Octorara* of the West India Squadron. After a year of successful patrolling in waters around the Bahamas he took the steam sloop *Wachusett* in January 1864 to cruise off the South American coast. On October 5, 1864, while the *Wachusett* was in the harbor of Bahia, Brazil, the Confederate raider *Florida*, 37 prizes to her credit, entered the harbor from a long Atlantic cruise. Disregarding Brazilian neutrality, Collins made for the *Florida* early in the morning of October 7, while her captain and half her crew were ashore. After ramming the raider ineffectually he fired a few small arms volleys and called for her surrender, which was promptly given by the officers in command. He quickly made fast both ships and stood out to sea, ignoring threats from a Brazilian navy vessel nearby and some shots from a harbor fort. He brought the *Florida* to Hampton Roads where she collided with an army transport and sank just as Collins was preparing to return her to Brazil as a result of that nation's protest. Diplomatic form required that he be court-martialed for neutrality violation, and in April 1865 he was sentenced to dismissal; sentence was disapproved, however, by Secretary of the Navy Gideon Welles, and in July 1866 Collins was promoted to captain and given command of the steam sloop *Sacramento*, which was wrecked in the Bay of Bengal in June 1867. He was suspended from duty for nearly two years. He advanced to commodore in January 1871 and to rear admiral in command of the Pacific Squadron in August 1874. He died in Callao, Peru, on August 9, 1875.

Colt, Samuel (1814–1862), inventor and businessman. Born in Hartford, Connecticut, on July 19, 1814, Colt worked as a youth in his father's textile factory in Ware, Massachusetts, and attended school until he went to sea in 1830. While on a voyage to India, he conceived the idea for a repeating firearm that would utilize an automatically revolving set of chambers, each of which would be brought successively into alignment with a single barrel. He made a wooden model for such a revolving-breech pistol and soon after his return to the United States had in hand two working models, one of which exploded. In order to finance improved prototypes he toured for a time as "Dr. Coult," demonstrating "laughing gas" (nitrous oxide) and taking up collections. Finally, with good working models, he secured English and French patents in 1835 and a U.S. patent in 1836. In March of that year he founded the Patent Arms Manufacturing Company in Paterson, New Jersey, to manufacture his revolvers by the most efficient methods available: mass production of completely interchangeable parts, assembly-line procedure, and inspection of the final product by trained personnel. He also developed a breech-loading revolver rifle. Although popular with individuals, including Andrew Jackson and the soldiers under Lt. Col. William S. Harney who were able to use them effectively in the Seminole campaign of 1837 in Florida, the Colt revolvers—"six-shooters"—failed to interest the army and the company went out of business in 1842. For the next several years Colt worked on perfecting an underwater mine system for harbor defense; from that he turned to telegraphy and experimented with submarine cable (he laid a successful one from Coney Island and Fire Island to New York City in 1843). The outbreak of the Mexican War finally generated a demand for his revolver; many Westerners, particularly Texans and Texas Rangers, would use no other, and the army, impressed at last, ordered 1000 Colts. He hurriedly subcontracted much of the production to Eli Whitney's factory in Whitneyville, Connecticut, until he began manufacturing in his own factory in Hartford in 1848. Orders soon began to pour in from England, Europe, Australia, and elsewhere. Success and fortune secured, he continued to direct the Colt's Patent Fire-Arms Manufacturing Company, the largest private armory in the world, until his death in Hartford, Connecticut, on January 10, 1862. The revolver, the nineteenth century's major development in small-arms weaponry, played a crucial (and legendary) role in the settlement of the West as well as in warfare.

Conner, David (1792–1856), naval officer. Born in 1792 in Harrisburg, Pennsylvania, Conner was appointed a midshipman in the navy in January 1809. In August 1811 he entered sea duty on the sloop *Hornet*, 18 guns, under Master Commandant James Lawrence. He was captured in 1812 while captain of the prize crew on the privateer *Dolphin*, taken by the *Hornet* in July, but he was exchanged and returned to the *Hornet* in time to take part in the capture of the brig *Peacock* on February 24, 1813. Promoted to lieutenant in July 1813, he remained with the *Hornet* under Capt. James Biddle and was severely wounded in the capture of the sloop *Penguin*, 19, on January 22, 1815, the last engagement of men-of-war in the War of 1812. Conner was voted a medal by Congress for his part in the battle. In 1817–1818 he again served under Biddle aboard the *Ontario* on the mission to take possession of Oregon. Promoted to commander in March 1825 and to captain in March 1835, he held various commands at sea and ashore over the years. In December 1843 he took command of the Gulf Squadron, in which post he was responsible for the establishment of the blockade of Mexican ports in the Gulf in May 1846. Hampered by illness, he did not take as aggressive a course as was open to him; nonetheless he did accomplish, through his second in command, Commodore Matthew C. Perry, the capture of several Mexican ports, including Frontera, October 23, 1846, and Tampico, November 14, and the landing of Gen. Winfield Scott's army at Veracruz on March 9, 1847. The plan of the Veracruz campaign was developed by Conner and Scott jointly. On March 21, before the final attack on the city,

Conner was relieved by Perry. After a period of recuperation he was appointed commandant of the Philadelphia navy yard in October 1849. He held that post until June 1850. Put on the reserve list in 1855, he died in Philadelphia on March 20, 1856.

Conway, Thomas (1735–1800?), Revolutionary army officer. Born in Ireland on February 27, 1735, Conway grew up and was educated in France and there joined the army in 1749. In 1777, then a colonel, he sailed to America with a recommendation from Silas Deane, colonial agent in Paris, to offer his services to the Revolution and in May was appointed brigadier general. He saw action at Brandywine and Germantown and was later proposed for promotion to major general. Gen. George Washington, who held Conway in no high regard either personally or professionally, opposed the idea as unfair to American officers of greater competence and experience. When the promotion failed to materialize, Conway resigned; Congress, which was disturbed by Washington's defeats and some of whose members were already considering his replacement, refused to accept the resignation, promoted Conway to major general in December 1777, and appointed him inspector general. There followed a very confusing episode. Gen. Horatio Gates, buoyed by his victory at Saratoga, had ambitions to become commander in chief, and some New England members of Congress, generally jealous of Southern influence, backed him; some secret correspondence was exchanged on the subject and a letter from Conway to Gates, in which Washington was criticized, was intercepted by Gen. James Wilkinson of Gates's staff. Wilkinson passed along a somewhat dramatized version of Conway's comments to another officer and it came to Washington's attention. Washington wrote frankly to Conway and to Congress on the matter, and the whole notion of replacing him immediately dissolved. Whether or not an actual conspiracy was afoot, the affair became known as the Conway Cabal, taking its name from the least culpable but most exposed participant. Conway was subsequently placed third in command under the Marquis de Lafayette (who refused to have him as second) of a proposed Canadian expedition. He was later assigned to a less sensitive post; he again threatened to resign, and in April 1778 Congress accepted the offer, much to his chagrin. A few months later he was severely wounded in a duel with Gen. John Cadwalader that had arisen because of his criticisms of Washington and, on the point of death, he wrote the commander in chief a letter of full apology. He recovered, however, and returned to France. Again in the French army, he saw duty in Flanders and in India, and in 1787 Conway was appointed governor general of French India. In 1793, once again back in France, he was exiled as a royalist. He died about 1800.

Conyngham, Gustavus (1744?–1819), Revolutionary naval officer. Born about 1744 in County Donegal, Ireland, Conyngham came to America in 1763, settling in Philadelphia and entering the merchant service. In 1776 he found himself stranded in Holland when his ship, the *Charming Peggy,* about to carry military supplies to America, was impounded at the insistence of the British consul. In March 1777 he was given a commission in the Continental navy in Paris and put in command of the lugger *Surprise,* 10 guns. Sailing out of Dunkerque in May, he quickly took two prizes, but on his return the prizes were released and he was imprisoned by French authorities responding to British pressure. He sailed again in July, however, with a captain's commission and in command of the cutter *Revenge,* 14. Taking many prizes over the next several months, he became the terror of British shipping in the home waters of the North Sea, Irish Sea, and Atlantic. Early in 1778 he began operating out of Spanish ports, principally El Ferrol. British pressure was again applied, and Conyngham sailed at last for America by way of the West Indies, where he captured more prizes, bringing his total in 18 months to 60. Soon after his arrival in Philadelphia in February 1779 the *Revenge* was refitted as a privateer, and in April, cruising off New York, he was captured by the *Galatea.* Confined under very harsh conditions in Mill Prison, Plymouth, England, he managed to escape on his third attempt in November 1779. He made his way to Holland, and after a cruise on the *Alliance* of Commodore John Paul Jones's squadron he set out for the United States aboard the *Experiment* in March 1780. That ship was captured, and Conyngham was returned to Mill Prison. Exchanged in 1781, he returned to the United States after the end of the war and rejoined the merchant service. His efforts to reenter the navy and to secure compensation for his Revolutionary services were unavailing. He died in Philadelphia on November 27, 1819.

Cooke, Philip St. George (1809–1895), army officer. Born in Leesburg, Virginia, on June 13, 1809, Cooke graduated from West Point in 1827 and was commissioned in the 6th Infantry. He saw much duty on the frontier, taking part in the Black Hawk War, notably the battle of Bad Axe on August 2, 1832. In March 1833 he was promoted to first lieutenant in the 1st Dragoons (later the 1st Cavalry), organized in that year for action against mounted Indians. He advanced to captain in May 1835. Shortly after the beginning of the Mexican War in May 1846, Cooke and 12 men proceeded to Santa Fe in advance of Gen. Stephen W. Kearny's Army of the West and began negotiations for the abandonment of the territory by Mexican authorities. Among the reinforcements soon sent to Santa Fe was a motley group of 549 persons recruited among Mormon camps in Iowa. The number included old men, several families, and others unsuitable for military discipline; nonetheless, Cooke, with temporary rank of lieutenant colonel, managed to make the so-called Mormon Battalion into a presentable organization and in a march marked by considerable hardship led it by way of the Gila River to California, where at San Diego it was disbanded in January 1847. He was promoted to major of the 2nd Dragoons in February 1847 and brevetted lieutenant colonel a few days later; he was stationed for a time in Mexico City in 1848. After the war he continued in frontier duty, engaging Sioux and Apache, helping quell the Border Wars in Kansas in 1856–1857, taking part in the Mormon expedition of 1857–1858 under Col. Albert S. Johnston as commander of the cavalry, and advancing to lieutenant colonel in 1853 and colonel in command of the 2nd Dragoons in June 1858. His system of cavalry training, devised in 1859 and published in 1861 as *Cavalry Tactics*, was long in use. At the outbreak of the Civil War he remained loyal to the government despite family ties (his son-in-law was J. E. B. Stuart), and in November 1861 he was promoted to brigadier general. He commanded a cavalry brigade in Washington, D.C., and took part in the Peninsular campaign in May–June 1862 as commander of a division of reserve cavalry. He was engaged in court-martial duty for a year, commanded the Baton Rouge district until 1864, and from then until 1866 was general superintendent of recruiting. After the war he commanded the departments of the Platte, 1866–1867, the Cumberland, 1869–70, and the Lakes, 1870–73. He retired in October 1873. Cooke published an autobiography, *Scenes and Adventures in the Army*, 1857, and a history of *The Conquest of New Mexico and California*, 1878. He died on March 20, 1895, in Detroit.

Coontz, Robert Edward (1864–1935), naval officer. Born in Hannibal, Missouri, on June 11, 1864, Coontz graduated from the Naval Academy in 1885 and was commissioned ensign two years later. Among his assignments over the next several years was one of six years aboard the gunboat *Pinta* in Alaskan waters, where he became a qualified pilot. He was promoted to lieutenant (junior grade) in September 1896. During the Spanish–American War he served on the *Charleston,* which took possession of Guam unopposed on June 20, 1898; and he took part in the actions at Iloilo, Subic Bay, and elsewhere during the Philippine Insurrection. He advanced to lieutenant in March 1899, lieutenant commander in January 1905, and commander in January 1909. During 1908–1909 he was executive officer of the *Nebraska* in the world cruise of the battleship fleet under Adm. Charles S. Sperry. In 1910–1911 he was commandant of midshipmen at the Naval Academy. He was promoted to captain in July 1912 and during 1912–1913

was governor of Guam. From 1913 to 1915 he commanded the *Georgia,* and in the latter year he took command of the 13th Naval District at Puget Sound. Promoted to rear admiral in December 1917, he served briefly as acting chief of naval operations during Adm. William S. Benson's absence and in August 1918 became commander of the 7th Division, Atlantic Fleet, aboard the *Wyoming.* The *Wyoming* followed the transatlantic flight of the NC-4 (Lt. Cmdr. Albert C. Read) in July 1919. Shortly thereafter he was transferred to the Pacific Fleet as deputy commander, and in October 1919 he became chief of naval operations with the rank of admiral. During his four-year term he was concerned with maintaining naval strength and increasing efficiency in the face of pressure from many quarters for reduction. From August 1923 to October 1925 Coontz was commander in chief, U.S. Fleet, aboard the *Seattle.* From 1925 until his retirement in June 1928 he commanded the 5th Naval District, Norfolk, Virginia. He died in Bremerton, Washington, on January 26, 1935.

Cooper, Samuel (1798–1876), Confederate army officer. Born on June 12, 1798, in Hackensack, New Jersey, Cooper graduated from West Point in 1815 and was commissioned second lieutenant in the artillery. Promoted to first lieutenant in 1821, he served in various garrison posts and from 1828 to 1836 was aide-de-camp to Gen. Alexander Macomb, commanding general of the army, advancing to captain in June of the latter year. He was on staff duty in Washington, D.C., until 1841, becoming assistant adjutant general with rank of major in 1838, and then took part in the Seminole War in Florida, 1841–1842, as chief of staff to Col. William J. Worth. Again on staff duty in Washington from 1842 to 1852, he rose to lieutenant colonel in March 1847 and was made adjutant general of the army with rank of colonel in July 1852. In March 1861 he resigned his commission and offered his services to the Confederacy. In light of his great administrative experience, at a premium in the Confederacy, he was appointed adjutant general and inspector general of the Confederate army and in August was given the rank of general; he remained the senior officer of the army throughout the Civil War. He fled south from Richmond with President Jefferson Davis and the cabinet in April 1865 but surrendered peacefully a short time later. He later retired to an estate in Cameron, Virginia, where he died on December 3, 1876.

Corbin, Margaret (1751–1800), Revolutionary heroine. Born on November 12, 1751, in what is now Franklin County, then on the western Pennsylvania frontier, Margaret Cochran, having lost both of her parents in an Indian raid when she was five, grew up with relatives. She married John Corbin in 1772, and when he enlisted in the First Company of Pennsylvania Artillery for service in the Revolution she followed him east. On November 16, 1776, Corbin was manning a gun on a ridge near Fort Washington, New York, when he was killed during a Hessian advance. Observing from nearby, Margaret immediately leaped to the gun and continued to serve in her husband's stead until she was felled by grapeshot wounds. Upon the surrender of the American position she was not taken among the prisoners. She made her way to Philadelphia and there, completely disabled, came to the attention of the state's Executive Council, by which she was granted temporary relief in June 1779. The next month the Continental Congress approved the granting of a lifetime soldier's half-pay pension to her. She was thereafter included on military rolls and in April 1783 was formally mustered out of the Continental army. She lived in Westchester County, New York, until her death on January 16, 1800. The story of her battle service has sometimes been confused with that of Mary McCauley, "Moll Pitcher."

Cornstalk (1720?–1777), Indian leader. Born about 1720, perhaps in Pennsylvania, Cornstalk was a Shawnee Indian whose common English name was a translation of the Indian Keigh-tugh-qua. Nothing is known of him before 1759, when in the French and Indian War he led a raiding party into central Virginia. He led a similar raid in western Virginia in 1763, during Pontiac's War, and in October of the next year was held hostage by Col. Henry Bouquet at the Muskingum River in Ohio against the release of white captives and the signing of a treaty. Cornstalk remained at peace for ten years, during which tensions between Indians and encroaching settlers in the Ohio country nevertheless increased steadily, exacerbated by rivalry between Pennsylvanians and Virginians over possession of key points such as Fort Pitt. Incidents and skirmishes multiplied, notably the massacre of James Logan's family in April 1774, and finally he yielded to the Shawnees' desire for war. In October 1774, with Virginia's governor, Lord Dunmore, already taking the field with an army from Fort Dunmore (Fort Pitt, later Pittsburgh) in what came to be known as Lord Dunmore's War, Cornstalk led his Shawnees against a second colonial force, the militia of southwest Virginia, some 1100 men under Col. Andrew Lewis. On the morning of October 10 the Indians attacked the militia at Point Pleasant at the mouth of the Kanawha River in what is now West Virginia. The battle lasted all day, with casualties heavy on both sides, but in the end the Shawnees retired, their power broken. Peace was established a few days later by the Treaty of Camp Charlotte, signed by Cornstalk and Lord Dunmore at a point on the Pickaway Plains of the Scioto in Ohio. Cornstalk kept the peace and in 1777 made his way to Fort Randolph at Point Pleasant to warn that the Shaw-

nees were being stirred up by British agents. He was detained at the fort and murdered a short time later by soldiers rampaging after the killing of one of their comrades.

Corse, John Murray (1835–1893), army officer. Born in Pittsburgh on April 27, 1835, Corse grew up in Burlington, Iowa. He entered West Point in 1853 but left after two years to take up the study of law in Albany, New York. He entered practice in Iowa in 1860. In July 1861 he was appointed major of the 6th Iowa Infantry and was assigned to duty with Gen. John C. Frémont and then Gen. John Pope, serving on the latter's staff during the New Madrid and Island No. 10 operations. In May 1862 he was promoted to lieutenant colonel; joining his regiment in the field, he saw action at Corinth and, after promotion to colonel in March 1863, in the Vicksburg campaign. He distinguished himself in the capture of Jackson, Mississippi, and in August 1863 he was appointed brigadier general of volunteers. In the Chattanooga campaign he distinguished himself at Chickamauga, September 18–20, and was badly wounded at Missionary Ridge on November 25. After recuperating he joined the staff of Gen. William T. Sherman, and in July 1864 he again took the field in command of a division of Gen. Grenville M. Dodge's XVI Corps, Army of the Tennessee. Early in October, while Sherman was preparing to leave Atlanta on his march to the sea, Corse was ordered to Allatoona, Georgia, a major railroad and supply depot midway between Atlanta and Rome. Between the troops he brought with him and those already at Allatoona Pass, Corse had about 2000 men; a Confederate division under Gen. S. G. French, detached from Gen. John B. Hood's Army of Tennessee, threatened with more than twice that number. On October 5 French demanded surrender, which Corse refused defiantly. Through the day Union forces repelled numerous attacks on their fortifications, with heavy losses on both sides; Corse was badly wounded and for a short time incapacitated. A relief force was sent out at length by Sherman, and the messages of mutual reassurance exchanged between besieged and relievers by wigwag and heliograph later inspired the popular hymn "Hold the Fort" (Philip P. Bliss and Ira D. Sankey). Corse's spirit was epitomized in his message the next day: "I am short a cheekbone and one ear, but am able to whip all hell yet!" Brevetted major general of volunteers, he was thanked by Sherman in general orders; he subsequently took part in the march to the sea. He was mustered out of volunteer service in April 1866, declining a regular commission, and from 1867 to 1869 served as collector of internal revenue in Chicago. After a European tour and a period of railroad building he settled in Massachusetts, serving as postmaster of Boston in 1886–1889. He died in Winchester, Massachusetts, on April 27, 1893.

Cox, Jacob Dolson (1828–1900), army officer, public official, and educator.

Born on October 27, 1828, in Montreal, Cox was the son of American parents with whom he returned to New York City shortly thereafter. From 1842 to 1844 he studied in a law office, and two years later, having come under the influence of revivalist Charles G. Finney, he entered the preparatory department of Oberlin College, from which he graduated in 1851. He had married Finney's daughter Helen in 1849. From 1851 to 1853 he was superintendent of schools in Warren, Ohio, and then, winning admission to the bar, he began the practice of law there. He was active in the organization of the Republican party in the state and in 1859 was elected to the legislature. The following year he was appointed a brigadier general in the state militia, and in April 1861, upon recruiting a large number of men for Civil War service, he was commissioned brigadier general of volunteers. Cox saw action under Gen. George B. McClellan in the West Virginia campaign, was in command of the Kanawha valley region in the summer of 1862, and took part in the battles of South Mountain and Antietam (Sharpsburg), September 14 and 17, at the former succeeding to temporary command of the IX Corps on the death of Gen. Jesse L. Reno. In October 1862 he was promoted to major general of volunteers, but the promotion was rescinded the following April after the discovery that the quota for the grade had been exceeded. During most of 1863 he commanded the District of Ohio, and in 1864 he commanded a division of the XXIII Corps, Army of the Ohio, under Gen. John M. Schofield in the Atlanta campaign. He was again promoted to major general in December 1864. He took part in the battle of Nashville, December 15–16, and in March 1865 led an expedition into North Carolina to effect a junction with Gen. William T. Sherman's army. At the end of the war he resigned his commission. In 1866 he was elected governor of Ohio. Even though he had supported President Andrew Johnson's Reconstruction policies and had attempted to mediate the dispute between Johnson and the dominant Radical wing of the Republican party, he was chosen two years later chairman of the Republican national convention. Upon the election of Ulysses S. Grant as President, Cox was appointed secretary of the interior in March 1869; he served only until October 1870 but was effective in opposing patronage and in promoting a merit system. He returned to law practice in Cincinnati and in 1873 became president of the Toledo and Wabash and Western Railroad. He held that position until taking a seat in the House of Representatives in March 1877; he did not seek reelection in 1878, serving only until March 1879. After 1879 Cox took no further part in political affairs. In 1881 he became dean of the Cincinnati Law School, where he remained until 1897, serving also from 1885 to 1889 as president of the University of Cincinnati.

He declined a number of positions offered by business and government and during his later years acquired an international reputation as a microscopist. He also wrote several distinguished works on the Civil War, including *Atlanta*, 1882, and *The March to the Sea, Franklin, and Nashville*, 1882, both for the Campaigns of the Civil War series, and *Military Reminiscences of the Civil War*, published posthumously in 1900. Cox died in Magnolia, Massachusetts, on August 8, 1900. The painter Kenyon Cox was his son.

Craig, Malin (1875–1945), army officer.

Born in St. Joseph, Missouri, on August 5, 1875, Craig, the son of a cavalry officer, graduated from West Point in 1898 and after a brief time with an infantry regiment was assigned to the 4th Cavalry. He took part in the Santiago campaign in 1898, with the 6th Cavalry in the Peking Relief Expedition in 1900, and in the Philippine Insurrection, 1900–1904, where he was promoted to first lieutenant in February 1901 and served the last two years as aide-de-camp to Gen. J. Franklin Bell. During 1904–1905 he attended the Infantry and Cavalry School and the Staff College, Fort Leavenworth, Kansas, receiving promotion to captain in May 1904. He performed with distinction in relief work following the San Francisco earthquake of 1906, and, after a second tour in the Philippines, 1907–1909, he attended the Army War College in 1909–1910, remaining a year more as an instructor. Various routine assignments followed. Promoted to major in May 1917 and temporary lieutenant colonel in August, Craig went to France in September as chief of staff to Gen. Hunter Liggett of the 41st Division. In January 1918 he became chief of staff of the I Corps, again under Liggett, and held that post through the Aisne–Marne, St. Mihiel, and Meuse–Argonne operations. He was promoted to temporary colonel in February 1918 and to temporary brigadier general in June, and after a period as chief of staff of the Third Army in occupied Germany he reverted to major on his return to the United States in August 1919. He then served as director of the Army War College, 1919–1920. Promoted to colonel in June 1920 and brigadier general in April 1921, he was commandant of the Cavalry School, Fort Riley, Kansas, from September 1921 to June 1923, and commander of coast artillery in the Manila–Subic Bay area in 1923–1924. Promoted to major general in July 1924, he served as the army's chief of cavalry until April 1926, and as assistant chief of staff for organization and training until April 1927. After a few months as commander of the IV Corps area, Atlanta, Georgia, he was in command of the Panama Canal Division and Department in 1927–1930 and of the IX Corps area, San Francisco, from 1930 to 1935, serving also as commander of the Fourth Army in 1933–1935. After ten months as commandant of the Army War College he was appointed in October 1935 chief of staff of the army with the rank of general. During his term Craig took important steps to increase the size of the army, modernize its equipment, and improve training. He retired in August 1939 in the rank of general and for a time was associated with the Columbia Broadcasting System. In September 1941 he was recalled to active duty to serve as chairman of the Personnel Board in the War Department. He died in Washington, D.C., on July 25, 1945.

Craven, Thomas Tingey (1808–1887), naval officer. Born on December 20, 1808, in Washington, D.C., Craven, the eldest brother of Tunis A. M. Craven, inherited a naval tradition on both sides of his family. He entered the navy as a midshipman in May 1822, and from 1823 to 1828 he served on the *United States* and then the *Peacock* of the Pacific Squadron. Made passed midshipman in 1828, he served on the *Erie* of the West India Squadron until 1830, when, promoted to lieutenant, he was assigned to the *Boxer*, cruising in Brazilian and later East Indian waters. In 1835–1836 he was on the receiving ship at the New York navy yard and in 1836–1838 on the *John Adams*. During 1838–1839 he was first lieutenant on the *Vincennes*, flagship of Lt. Charles Wilkes's expedition to the South Seas. For several years in the 1840s he served in the Africa Squadron engaged in suppressing the slave trade; for a time he commanded the *Porpoise*. After duty in New York, on the *Ohio* of the Pacific Squadron, and on the *Independence* of the Mediterranean Squadron, he was appointed in July 1850 commandant of midshipmen at the Naval Academy, a post he held until June 1855. At the Academy he initiated the highly useful practice cruise. In December 1852 he was promoted to commander. During 1855–1858 he commanded the *Congress* in the Mediterranean, and from 1858 to 1860 he was again commandant of midshipmen. After a brief period of recruiting duty he was put in command of the Potomac Flotilla in June 1861, succeeding Commander James H. Ward, and promoted to captain. Early in 1862 he took command of the *Brooklyn*, one of the larger ships of the West Gulf Blockading Squadron. In the expedition under Flag-Officer David G. Farragut against New Orleans in April 1862, the *Brooklyn* sailed with the center division of the squadron and was very effective against Fort St. Philip. In June the *Brooklyn* helped cover the first running of the Vicksburg batteries. Promoted to commodore in 1863, Craven was ordered to Europe in command of the steam frigate *Niagara* to protect Union commerce from Confederate raiders. He captured the raider *Georgia* off the Portuguese coast in August 1864. In January 1865, accompanied by the sloop *Sacramento* under Capt. Henry Walke, from nearby La Coruña (Corunna), Spain, he attempted to blockade the ironclad raider *Stonewall*, Capt. Thomas

J. Page, at El Ferrol, Spain. Page sailed out to challenge in March, and Craven, both of whose vessels were unarmored and no match for the *Stonewall*, permitted him to escape. A court-martial presided over by Farragut suspended Craven from duty for two years, but Secretary of the Navy Gideon Welles overruled the court. In September 1866 Craven took command of the navy yard at Mare Island, California, receiving promotion to rear admiral in October. In August 1868 he became commander of the Pacific Squadron. He retired in December 1869, and for a year thereafter he served as port admiral at San Francisco. Craven died in Boston on August 23, 1887.

Craven, Tunis Augustus Macdonough (1813–1864), naval officer. Born in Portsmouth, New Hampshire, on January 11, 1813, Craven, a younger brother of Thomas T. Craven, was of a family with a long naval tradition. He was appointed a midshipman in February 1829 and promoted to passed midshipman in 1835 and to lieutenant in 1841. From 1835 he was engaged, with a few interruptions, in coast survey and hydrographic work, becoming an outstanding expert in those lines. During the Mexican War he served aboard the sloop *Dale* in the Pacific Squadron under Commodore James Biddle and Commodore William B. Shubrick. During 1857–1858 he led an expedition to survey a canal route through the Isthmus of Darien, and in 1859–1861 he commanded the *Mohawk* on patrol against slave traders in Cuban waters. Early in 1861 he took command of the steamer *Crusader*, which played a part in the saving of the Union stronghold at Key West. Promoted to commander in April 1861, he took command of the sloop *Tuscarora* in September and for more than a year patrolled European waters against Confederate cruisers and privateers; aided by the *Kearsarge* and *Ino*, he was able to blockade the *Sumter*, Capt. Raphael Semmes, at Gibraltar and force its abandonment in April 1862. In 1863 he took command of the ironclad *Tecumseh*. After a period with the James River Flotilla under Adm. Samuel P. Lee he was ordered to join Adm. David G. Farragut's West Gulf Blockading Squadron for the attack on Mobile. Craven arrived at Mobile Bay on the evening before the attack, and on the morning of August 5, 1864, the *Tecumseh* led the column of ironclads into the bay and fired the first shots at Fort Morgan. Less than an hour later the *Tecumseh* struck an underwater mine ("torpedo" in the terminology of the day) and began to sink rapidly. Craven and the ship's pilot, John Collins, reached the foot of the ladder leading to the top of the turret simultaneously; Craven drew back, saying "After you, pilot." Collins escaped, as had 14 others, but the brief delay was fatal to Craven.

Crazy Horse (1849?–1877), Indian leader. Born about 1849 into the Oglala Sioux tribe, Tashunca-

Uitco, or Crazy Horse, distinguished himself in battle while yet a youth. Using masterly decoy tactics, he fought in Red Cloud's War over the hated Powder River army road (the Bozeman Trail), playing a leading role in the Fetterman Massacre on December 21, 1866, and the Wagon Box fight of August 2, 1867, at Fort Phil Kearny. He refused to settle on the Sioux reservations established in 1868 by the Treaty of Fort Laramie. Instead he moved north with a band of 1200 Oglala and Cheyenne (his marriage to a Cheyenne woman had gained him an alliance with the tribe) and joined forces with Sitting Bull. He was the principal leader of the Sioux in the uprising of 1876 and 1877 which broke out, after the invasion of the sacred and treaty-reserved Black Hills country by the army and by gold prospectors, as a protest against the order by the War Department that all Sioux remain on reservations after January 31, 1876. Eight days after Crazy Horse led his warriors to victory over Gen. George Crook at the battle of the Rosebud, June 17, 1876, occurred the most famous battle of the war, fought at the Little Bighorn River in Montana on June 25. Crazy Horse and his warriors surrounded Col. George A. Custer and his command, assailing them from the north and west, while Gall, war chief of the Hunkpapa Sioux, attacked from the south and west. Custer was killed and his entire immediate command was destroyed. After the battle the Indians dispersed into bands that went separate ways. Crazy Horse led about 800 warriors back to Sioux territory, hoping to gather supplies, but was relentlessly pursued by forces under Col. Nelson A. Miles. An attack by Miles on his village at Wolf Mountain on January 7, 1877, was particularly devastating. He surrendered at the urging of Red Cloud on May 6, 1877, with about 1000 men, women and children, at the Red Cloud Agency, near Camp Robinson, Nebraska. Promised a limited amount of freedom, he was arrested in September on suspicion of agitating for war among the Oglala. He was said to have resisted his captors and was killed on September 5, 1877.

Cresap, Michael (1742–1775), Indian fighter and Revolutionary militia officer. Born on June 29, 1742, in what is now Allegany County, Maryland, Cresap was the son of a well known pioneer and frontier trader. He followed in the same line of work in the vicinity of Wheeling (now in West Virginia), settling there early in 1774. On April 30 of that year the tension long building between Indians and white settlers on the frontier erupted in the Yellow Creek Massacre, in which a party of whites led by Daniel Greathouse killed a number of Mingo Indians, including several members of the family of Logan. Cresap, the acknowledged leader of the loosely organized forces in the area, was absent; but having led in a skirmish with Indians only four days earlier, he came to be blamed by many, including Logan, for the

massacre. The events in that region, often known together as Cresap's War, led into the larger Lord Dunmore's War, in which Cresap served as a captain of Virginia militia, taking part under Col. Andrew Lewis in the battle of Point Pleasant on October 10. (It was shortly after the battle that Logan made his famous speech, thus unjustly immortalizing Cresap.) In July 1775 he led a company of Maryland riflemen from Frederick to Boston, the first southern troops to join Gen. George Washington's Continental army. He had been ill for some time, however, and soon thereafter was forced to relinquish his command. On his way home he died in New York City on October 18, 1775.

Crittenden, George Bibb (1812–1880), Confederate army officer. Born in Russellville, Kentucky, on March 20, 1812, Crittenden was the eldest son of John J. Crittenden, later senator and governor, and brother of Thomas Leonidas Crittenden, later a Union major general. He graduated from West Point in 1832, and after brief service in Black Hawk's War and frontier garrison duty in Arkansas he resigned his commission in April 1833. After a time spent in the study of law he made his way to Texas, where border skirmishing with Mexican forces had continued since the winning of independence in 1836. He joined a Texas expedition against the Mexican village of Mier in November 1842 and in battle in December was taken prisoner along with the entire expedition of 250, of whom every tenth man was executed; he was held in Mexico City until his release was won, mainly through the efforts of Secretary of State Daniel Webster. At the outbreak of the Mexican War in 1846 he again left Kentucky as captain of a volunteer company of mounted rifles. He was brevetted major for his actions at Contreras and Churubusco, August 19–20, 1847, was promoted regular major in April 1848, and remained in the army after the war. Engaged in frontier duty, he rose to lieutenant colonel in December 1856. In June 1861 he resigned and shortly thereafter was commissioned brigadier general in the Confederate army. A short time later he was advanced to major general. On January 19, 1862, at Mill Springs, Kentucky, on the Cumberland river, he attacked a Union force under Gen. George H. Thomas that, with large reinforcements quickly brought up, soundly defeated his 4000-odd troops and forced them to retreat across the river, abandoning artillery and baggage. The popular Gen. Felix K. Zollicoffer was killed in the attack. Crittenden was censured for his action and kept under arrest until November. He resigned his commission but served the rest of the war as a civilian volunteer on the staff of Gen. John S. Williams. After the war he lived in Frankfort, Kentucky, and was state librarian from 1867 to 1874. He died in Danville on November 27, 1880. He and his brother were unique in being major generals on opposite sides of the Civil War.

Crittenden, Thomas Leonidas (1819–1893),

army officer. Born in Russellville, Kentucky, on May 15, 1819, Crittenden was a son of John J. Crittenden, senator and later governor, and a younger brother of George B. Crittenden, later Confederate major general. He studied law under his father, was admitted to the Kentucky bar in 1840, and was elected commonwealth's attorney two years later. In 1846 he was commissioned a lieutenant colonel of Kentucky infantry and served as aide to Gen. Zachary Taylor, seeing action at Buena Vista, February 22–23, 1847. Later he served as colonel of the 3rd Kentucky. Mustered out in 1848, Crittenden was appointed in 1849 U.S. consul to Liverpool, England, by President Taylor. He returned to his law practice in Frankfort, Kentucky, in 1853, later moving to Louisville. In 1860 he was commissioned major general of militia under Gen. Simon B. Buckner, succeeding to command in September when Buckner joined the Confederacy. In October he was appointed brigadier general of volunteers in federal service. He commanded a division in Gen. Don Carlos Buell's Army of the Ohio at Shiloh, April 6–7, 1862, and for his actions there was advanced to major general. At Murfreesboro (Stones River), December 31–January 3, 1863, he commanded the left wing of Gen. William S. Rosecrans's Army of the Cumberland; and at Chickamauga, September 18–20, 1863, he commanded the XXI Corps, Army of the Cumberland. He was roughly handled at the latter engagement and was for a time suspended from command. In February 1864 he returned to the field with a division of the IX Corps, Army of the Potomac, in the Virginia campaign. He resigned his commission in December 1864. In January 1866 he was appointed treasurer of Kentucky, but he resigned the post in July to accept a commission as colonel of the 32nd Infantry. In March 1867 he was brevetted brigadier general in honor of his actions at Murfreesboro. He served at various frontier posts and then at Governors Island, New York, until his retirement in May 1881. He died in Annandale, Staten Island, New York, on October 23, 1893. He and his brother were only two of many to be separated by the Civil War, but they were the only pair to attain such high rank on either side.

Crockett, David (1786–1836), frontiersman and

public official. Born near the site of present-day Greeneville, Tennessee (then in the short-lived state of Franklin), on August 17, 1786, Davy Crockett grew up on the frontier and received virtually no formal education. By 1809 he was married and settled as a farmer in Lincoln County. He served as a scout under Andrew Jackson in the Creek War of 1813–1814 and afterward moved farther west into Tennes-

see. A poor farmer but an awesome hunter, he was for several years a local magistrate in Giles County and in 1821 was elected to the state legislature. He was elected again in 1823, from a district still farther west, as before building up an enthusiastic local following with his humorous and homely oratorical style. After an unsuccessful campaign in 1825, he was elected to the House of Representatives in 1827 and served two terms as a Democrat; defeated in 1831, he returned as a Whig for a final term in 1833. In 1834 he made a much celebrated tour of Northern cities in an effort to rouse support for the Whig party; the party's hope was to fashion from Crockett, with his colorful history as a "b'ar-hunter" (he claimed a count of 105 for the 1822 season) and largely illiterate frontiersman, an answer to the Democrats' Jackson. The determined opposition of the Jackson forces defeated his bid for reelection to the House in 1835. He then left Tennessee to join the war for independence in Texas. He arrived at the Alamo in February 1836, joining the handful of defenders under Col. William B. Travis, and died in the massacre there on March 6. The growth of Davy Crockett into a legendary figure began before his death, aided by his supposed autobiography, *A Narrative of the Life of David Crockett, of the State of Tennessee*, 1834, and by numerous Whig campaign pieces attributed to him. The mythmaking continued with the publication from 1835 to 1856 of a series of Crockett almanacs, containing numerous accounts, in the best frontier tall-tale tradition, of adventures in which he, Mike Fink, and other frontier heroes had supposedly been involved.

Croghan, George (1791–1849), army officer.

Born on November 15, 1791, near Louisville, Kentucky, Croghan was no relation of the famous Indian agent of the same name, but he was a nephew, through his mother, of George Rogers Clark and William Clark. He graduated from William and Mary College in 1810. He served as a volunteer aide-de-camp at the battle of Tippecanoe, November 7, 1811, and in reward was commissioned, at Gen. William Henry Harrison's recommendation, captain of the 17th Infantry in March 1812. He subsequently distinguished himself in the defense of Fort Meigs and became aide-de-camp to Harrison with rank of major from March 1813. A short time later he was placed in command of Fort Stephenson (on the site of present-day Fremont, Ohio) on the Sandusky. On August 1 and 2, 1813, Croghan and the 160 or so men under his command held off repeated attacks by a force of some 1200 British regulars and Indians, equipped with several light artillery pieces, under the command of Col. Henry Proctor. Gen. Harrison had ordered Croghan to withdraw if faced by such odds, but he chose instead to remain. The American defenders suffered one killed and seven wounded, while inflicting heavy losses on the British, who gave up on August 3. The defense of Fort Stephenson by the youthful Croghan—he was just 21—became a much celebrated victory in the dark days of the War of 1812. He was brevetted lieutenant colonel, and Congress presented him with a gold medal in 1835. He was promoted regular lieutenant colonel in February 1814, and in 1817 he resigned from the army. In 1824 he was postmaster of New Orleans. In December 1825 he was appointed inspector general of the army with the rank of colonel, a post he retained until his death. In 1846 he served in Mexico under Gen. Zachary Taylor and took part in the battle of Monterrey. Croghan died in New Orleans on January 8, 1849.

Cronkhite, Adelbert (1861–1937), army officer. Born on January 5, 1861, in Litchfield, New York, Cronkhite graduated from West Point in 1882 and was commissioned in the artillery. He was promoted to first lieutenant in January 1889. He served in the Sioux war of 1890–1891, in Cuba and Puerto Rico during the Spanish–American War, and in various staff capacities over the years. He advanced to captain in March 1899, major in November 1905, lieutenant colonel of coast artillery in January 1909, and colonel in August 1911. During 1904–1907 he was attached to the Quartermaster Corps, and in 1907–1911 to the inspector general department. During 1911–1914 he was in command of the coastal defenses in New York, and from 1914 to 1917 he commanded the coastal defenses in Panama. He was promoted to brigadier general early in 1917 and to temporary major general in August, and in September he took command of the 80th Infantry Division at Camp Lee, Virginia. After several months of training he led it overseas in June 1918. The 80th took part in the Somme offensive and the Meuse–Argonne operations as part of the First Army (Gen. John J. Pershing and later Gen. Hunter Liggett), and Cronkhite remained in command until November 1918. From January to April 1919 he commanded the VI Corps in occupied Germany. On his return to the United States he devoted himself single-mindedly to an investigation of the shooting death of his son, Maj. A. P. Cronkhite, during a training maneuver. He uncovered much evidence that the son's death was not accidental, but no convictions were ever obtained. His relentless pursuit of the case, however, led to considerable friction with his superiors, and at length, in February 1923, he was ordered retired early, under an obscure regulation, by President Harding. Cronkhite died in St. Petersburg, Florida, on June 15, 1937.

Crook, George (1829–1890), army officer. Born near Dayton, Ohio, on September 23, 1829, Crook graduated from West Point in 1852 and was commissioned in the infantry. He was assigned to explora-

tion and frontier defense duties in the Northwest, taking part in several Indian campaigns and rising to the rank of captain. He remained there until September 1861, when he was commissioned colonel of volunteers and placed in command of the 36th Ohio Infantry. He saw action in West Virginia early in 1862, receiving a brevet in regular rank to major in May, and, promoted to brigadier general of volunteers in August 1862, took part in the battles of South Mountain and Antietam (Sharpsburg), September 14 and 17, being brevetted lieutenant colonel after the latter. In 1863 he commanded a division of cavalry in Gen. William S. Rosecrans's Army of the Cumberland at Chickamauga, September 18–20, and in October pursued Confederate cavalry under Gen. Joseph Wheeler back into Tennessee, defeating him at Farmington, October 7, for which achievement he was brevetted colonel in the regular army. Early in 1864 he conducted successful operations against Confederate railroad traffic in West Virginia, and in September–October, under Gen. Philip H. Sheridan, saw action at Winchester, Fisher's Hill, and Cedar Creek in the Shenandoah campaign, winning promotion to major general of volunteers. In March 1865, under Sheridan, he led a cavalry division through the battles of the Petersburg campaign. After the war Crook's rank (brevet major general as of March 1865) reverted to lieutenant colonel, 23rd Infantry, and he was assigned to Boise, Idaho. There he succeeded in ending an Indian war of several years' duration. In 1871 he was sent to Arizona to pacify the Apaches, who, under Cochise and other leaders, were terrorizing the white settlements then encroaching upon the Indian country. His success in two years was such that he was promoted two grades, to brigadier general, in 1873. In 1875 he took command of the Department of the Platte and, following the discovery of gold in the Black Hills and the consequent invasion of Indian lands by whites, was again heavily engaged in Indian campaigning. He spent all of 1876 in the field against the Sioux and Cheyenne. In March he left Fort Fetterman on the North Platte to rendezvous with Gen. Alfred H. Terry at the Yellowstone. On June 17, at Rosebud Creek, he engaged some 1500 Sioux and Cheyenne under Crazy Horse and, though only slightly outnumbered, was forced to retire. In the aftermath of Col. George A. Custer's disaster eight days later, Crook marched for the Black Hills and on September 9 destroyed the Sioux village of American Horse at Slim Buttes. In 1882 he was once more sent to Arizona to put down an uprising of Chiricahua Apaches under Geronimo. He pursued the rebels to their stronghold deep in the Sierra Madre of Mexico and in May 1883 brought them back to the reservation. Geronimo and a small band escaped in 1885, and Crook again tracked them until he was relieved by Gen. Nelson A. Miles and returned to command of the Department of the Platte in 1886. In April 1888 he was promoted to major general and given command of the Division of the Missouri; he moved to his headquarters in Chicago and died there on March 21, 1890.

Crossfield, Albert Scott (1921–   ), test pilot.

Born in Berkeley, California, on October 2, 1921, Scott Crossfield learned to fly in his youth and after a year at the University of Washington, 1940–1941, and another with the Boeing Airplane Company he entered the navy in 1942 as a pilot instructor. He returned to the University of Washington in 1945, graduated in aeronautical engineering in 1949, and took an M.S. degree in 1950. He then joined the National Advisory Committee for Aeronautics (forerunner of the National Aeronautics and Space Administration) at the high speed flight research station at Edwards Air Force Base, California. Over the next five years he was project supervisor, test engineer, flight evaluator, and designer in addition to pilot for a great many experimental craft—those that became the F-86, F-100, and F-102 fighters, the Douglas D558-I and D558-II, and especially the X-series of rocket planes. In the D558-II he became in 1953 the first man to attain the speed of Mach 2 (twice the speed of sound). His work with the X-1, X-4, and X-5 led to the development of basic techniques, designs, and planning methods later used in the space program. Having contributed from the beginning to the conception of the X-15, intended to reach Mach 6 and a 50-mile altitude, he resigned from NACA in 1955 to join North American Aviation, prime contractor for the vehicle. The X-15 made its first flight in March 1959 attached to the wing of a B-52 mother ship. In June the first free flight was a success, and in September the first powered flight reached Mach 2.3. The pilot throughout the testing period, Crossfield eventually pushed the X-15 to Mach 3 and had mastered various in-flight emergencies by the time the plane was turned over to the air force in 1960. He later became director of testing for North American's Hound Dog, Apollo command module, Paraglider, and Saturn S-II booster missile projects. In 1966 he became technical director of the research engineering and test division. In 1967 he joined Eastern Air Lines as system director of flight research; he became vice-president in 1968 and in 1971 took responsibility for general transportation systems development. Crossfield was the recipient of numerous honors and awards in the field of aeronautics.

Crowder, Enoch Herbert (1859–1932), army

officer and diplomat. Born in Edinburg, Grundy County, Missouri, on April 11, 1859, Crowder graduated from West Point in 1881 and was commissioned second lieutenant in the 8th Cavalry. While posted at Fort Brown, Texas, he studied law and received a license to practice in 1884. From 1885 to 1889 he taught military science and tactics at the University of Missouri, taking a law degree there in 1886 and receiving promotion to first lieutenant in July of the same year. During 1889–1891 he saw frontier duty in the Dakotas and in the latter year was promoted to captain and made acting judge advocate of the Department of the Platte at Omaha, Nebraska. Promoted to major in January 1895 and appointed lieutenant colonel of volunteers in June 1898, he served as judge advocate on the staff of Gen. Wesley Merritt in the Philippines in 1898 and as military secretary to the island's military governors, Gen. Elwell S. Otis and Gen. Arthur MacArthur, until 1901. He served also on the civil supreme court and on various boards. From August 1899 to May 1901 he held a commission as lieutenant colonel of the 39th Infantry Volunteers, and in the latter month he was promoted to lieutenant colonel in the regular Judge Advocate Corps. He was promoted to brigadier general of volunteers in June 1901. After his return to the United States he took up duties in the judge advocate general's department; he was promoted to colonel in April 1903 and later in the year became chief of the 1st Division of the army's first General Staff. He was an observer in the Russo–Japanese War in 1904–1905; in Cuba from 1906 to 1909 he served on the staff of the provisional governor, supervised the election of 1908, and contributed significantly to the drafting of a body of organic law. He was a delegate to the Fourth Pan-American Conference in Buenos Aires in 1910. In February 1911 Crowder was promoted to brigadier general and appointed judge advocate general of the army, a post he held for 12 years. Under his direction the Articles of War and the *Manual for Courts-Martial* were thoroughly revised. Crowder was chiefly responsible for the drafting of the Selective Service Act passed in May 1917, and as provost marshal general he had responsibility for administering the system during World War I. He was promoted to major general in October 1917. In 1921 he went to Cuba as President Woodrow Wilson's personal representative to settle a dispute over elections. Upon his retirement from the army in February 1923 he was appointed U.S. ambassador to Cuba. He returned to the United States in 1927 and entered private law practice in Chicago. He died in Washington, D.C., on May 7, 1932.

Crozet, Claude (1790–1864), army officer, engi-

neer, and educator. Born in Villefranche, France, on January 1, 1790, Crozet was educated at the École Polytechnique in Paris and was commissioned in the artillery in 1807. He served in the Napoleonic Wars, rising to the rank of captain, and was held prisoner in Russia for two years after the Moscow campaign of 1812. He was again with Napoleon in the final campaign to 1815. In 1816 he accompanied Gen. Simon Bernard to the United States and, with further recommendation from Lafayette, was appointed assistant professor of engineering at West Point. He remained there for seven years, from March 1817 as professor and head of the department, during which he thoroughly reorganized the course of engineering instruction, laying it upon a professional basis. His *Treatise of Descriptive Geometry for the Use of the Cadets of the United States Military Academy*, 1821, was the first such text in America. In 1823 he resigned to become state engineer of Virginia, a post he held until 1832 and, after an interlude in Louisiana, again from 1839. He planned and saw constructed a great many roads and other improvements and in 1849–1858 directed the building of the first railroad over the Blue Ridge to the interior. At the organization of the Virginia Military Institute in 1839 he served on the board of visitors and was chosen president of the new school. He made it into a close copy of West Point, instituting the same high standards of instruction and the same emphasis on mathematical training. He left that post in 1845. In 1857 he served as chief assistant to Capt. Montgomery C. Meigs in the construction of the aqueduct over the Potomac into the District of Columbia. He became principal of the Richmond Academy in 1859 and remained there until his death in Richmond, Virginia, on January 29, 1864.

Crozier, William (1855–1942), army officer and inventor. Born on February 19, 1855, in Carrollton, Ohio, Crozier grew up in Kansas. He graduated from West Point in 1876 and was commissioned second lieutenant in the 4th Artillery. After three years of campaigning against Indians on the frontier he returned to West Point as assistant professor of mathematics and was promoted to first lieutenant in the Ordnance Corps in July 1881. In 1887 he was assigned to the office of the chief of ordnance, where he developed the interest in siege and coastal defense guns that led to his invention of a wire-wrapped gun of large caliber and, with Gen. A. R. Buffington, later chief of ordnance, of the Buffington-Crozier disappearing gun carriage, later adopted for coastal guns. Promoted to captain in June 1890, he served as inspector general of Atlantic and Gulf Coast defenses during the Spanish–American War and, with volunteer rank of major, as inspector general of volunteers for several months in 1898. He was a delegate to the International Peace Conference at The Hague in 1899. In 1900 he was in the field in the Philippine Insurrection and in the Peking Relief Expedition. After a few months as an instructor at West Point, in November 1901 he was appointed chief of ordnance with the rank of brigadier general; he retained that post until 1918, with a brief absence in 1912–1913 when he served as president of the Army War College. As chief of ordnance Crozier gave particular attention to the use of federal armories as testing grounds not only for new weapons but for new industrial tech-

niques; in his search for efficiency in manufacturing he even consulted Frederick W. Taylor, the pioneer in efficiency engineering. His work contributed greatly to the army's readiness for World War I. His rank as chief of ordnance was raised by statute to major general in October 1917. During the war Crozier was a member of the Supreme War Council; his opposite number in the British government, with whom he had a close working relationship, was Winston Churchill. In July 1918, promoted to major general of the line, he became commander of the Northeastern Department in Boston, and he retired in January 1919. He died in Washington, D.C., on November 10, 1942.

Curtis, Samuel Ryan (1805–1866), army officer and engineer. Born on February 3, 1805, near Champlain, New York, Curtis grew up in Licking County, Ohio. He graduated from West Point in 1831 and was commissioned in the 7th Infantry, but he resigned the next year and turned to civil engineering in Ohio. After a time employed on the National Road he became chief engineer of the Muskingum River improvements in 1837–1839. He then took up the study of law and from 1841 to 1846 practised in Wooster. An officer of the Ohio militia since 1833, he became colonel in 1843 and in 1846, at the outbreak of the Mexican War, was appointed state adjutant general. He saw active service in Mexico as colonel of the 3rd Ohio Infantry, was later on the staff of Gen. John E. Wool, and in 1847–1848 was military governor of Saltillo. After the war he was chief engineer of Des Moines River improvement at Keokuk, Iowa, in 1848–1849 and city engineer of St. Louis in 1850–1853. He returned to Keokuk in 1855 and the next year was elected mayor. Later in 1856 he was elected to Congress as a Republican, and he held his seat through two reelections. He resigned in August 1861 after receiving appointment as brigadier general of volunteers. He commanded in southwestern Missouri from December 1861 to February 1862 and the Army of the Southwest until August 1862. On March 7–8 he fought a heavy engagement with Gen. Earl Van Dorn and Gen. Sterling Price at Pea Ridge (Elkhorn), Arkansas, that for the time being effectively ended organized Confederate military efforts in the trans-Mississippi region. Curtis was thereupon promoted to major general of volunteers. In September he was given command of the Department of Missouri, a post he held until May 1863; from January 1864 to February 1865 he commanded the Department of Kansas, again engaging and, in conjunction with Gen. Alfred Pleasonton, defeating Price in the battle of Westport, near Kansas City, Missouri, October 21–23, 1864. The battle, sometimes called the "Gettysburg of the West," ended Price's third invasion of Missouri and Confederate operations in the state generally. From February to July 1865 he commanded the Department of the Northwest. Subsequently he served as commissioner to negotiate with Indian tribes on the Missouri River and, after being mustered out of volunteer service in April 1866, to examine and report on the Union Pacific Railroad. He died in Council Bluffs, Iowa, on December 26, 1866.

Curtiss, Glenn Hammond (1878–1930), aviator and inventor. Born on May 21, 1878, in Hammondsport, New York, Curtiss worked as a telegraph messenger boy and for a time for the Eastman Kodak Company in Rochester before returning home in 1895 and opening a bicycle shop. He became a highly successful bicycle racer and soon took up the motorcycle, establishing an engine and motorcycle plant in 1902. He continued to race and in 1907 set a land speed record of 67.4 miles per hour at Ormond Beach, Florida. At the same time he had developed an interest in aeronautics; he produced the engine for the dirigible *California Arrow* that won top prize for airships at the Louisiana Purchase Exposition in St. Louis in 1904 and the next year built Dirigible No. 1 for the army. In 1907 he became director of experimental work of the Aerial Experiment Association founded by Alexander Graham Bell. His first notable airplane, the *June Bug,* was built in 1908 and won the trophy offered by *Scientific American* magazine for the first public flight of more than a kilometer. In 1909 he won the trophy again for a 25-mile flight and, as the Aero Club of America's entrant, won the James Gordon Bennett Cup and the Prix de la Vitesse at the First International Aviation Meet in France. Later in the year he won the Tour de Brescia competition in Italy. In May 1910 he won his third *Scientific American* trophy and the $10,000 *New York World* prize for a flight from Albany to New York City, and in the same year another pilot in one of his biplanes made the first successful takeoff from a ship. By that time Curtiss had installed pontoon floats on the *June Bug,* renamed it the *Loon,* and experimented with takeoffs from and landings on water; at San Diego, California, in January 1911, he successfully demonstrated the first practical seaplane and was awarded the Collier Trophy. Later in that year, after protracted litigation with the Wright brothers, Curtiss and his associates at the Aerial Experiment Association were awarded a patent for their most important single contribution to aviation, the aileron. In 1912 he developed a flying boat type of seaplane. He built several seaplanes for the navy and for foreign governments and in 1914 produced a three-engined flying boat for an attempt to cross the Atlantic; the flight never took place because of the outbreak of World War I. During the war the Curtiss Aeroplane & Motor Company, organized in 1916 with Curtiss as president, produced more than 5000 JN-4 ("Jenny") biplanes for use in aviation training at army and navy flight schools, many of which Curtiss himself had estab-

lished. In 1919 the NC-4 flying boat, built for the navy, made the first transatlantic flight, piloted by Lt. Cmdr. Albert C. Read. In his later years Curtiss became interested in other ventures, including Florida real estate development, and experimented with automobiles and a streamlined automobile trailer. The Curtiss firm merged in 1929 with its former rivals to form the Curtiss–Wright Company. He died in Buffalo, New York, on July 23, 1930. Three years later Curtiss was awarded a posthumous Distinguished Flying Cross by the army for his contributions to aviation.

Cushing, William Barker (1842–1874), naval officer. Born on November 4, 1842, in Delafield, Wisconsin, Cushing moved with his family to Chicago, then to Gallipolis, Ohio, and finally in 1847 to Fredonia, New York. He worked to support his widowed mother and in 1856 was appointed a page in the House of Representatives. The following year he entered the Naval Academy, but his casual approach to academics and discipline, capped by a prank played on one of his professors, led to his forced resignation in March 1861. With the pressing need for sailors for Civil War service, however, he secured a place on the steam frigate *Minnesota* with the rank of acting master's mate. After he had twice successfully sailed captured prize ships into port he was enrolled again in the navy as acting midshipman in October 1861, receiving promotion to lieutenant the following July, before his twentieth birthday. In October 1862, serving as executive officer of the steamer *Commodore Perry,* he acted almost singlehandedly to save the ship from capture when it grounded in the Blackwater River near Franklin, Virginia. With his own command, the *Ellis,* he later captured several prizes and the town of Jacksonville, North Carolina, raided Confederate camps along the North Carolina coast, and when the *Ellis* grounded made a daring escape in an open boat from near-certain capture. A series of commands on the *Commodore Barney,* the *Shokokon,* and the *Monticello* followed, and Cushing continued to perform brilliant feats in blockade duty and in shore raids. On October 27, 1864, he and a volunteer crew took a steam launch armed with a bow torpedo up the Roanoke River to Plymouth, North Carolina. Under a hail of fire he rammed and sank the last Confederate ironclad, the *Albemarle,* which had of late sunk several Union ships, captured Plymouth, and played havoc with the blockade. His launch was blown up and he and one of his crew were the only ones to escape death or capture, swimming down the river to safety. The exploit brought him the thanks of Congress, promotion to lieutenant commander, and other honors. On January 15, 1865, at the climax of an expedition under Adm. David D. Porter and Gen. Alfred H. Terry, he led a heroic charge over the parapet in the capture of Fort Fisher at Wilmington,

North Carolina. (He had previously spent six hours under fire in a small boat, sounding the channel for the attack.) Between major adventures he had continued to take, seemingly routinely, one prize ship after another. Although on several occasions he was long under enemy fire, he received not a scratch through the entire war and many times was the only survivor of an encounter. Such fortune, together with his courage and daring, fostered among his men an almost superstitious trust in him, and prompted Secretary of the Navy Gideon Welles to refer to him as "*the* hero of the war." After the war he held various commands in the Pacific and Asiatic squadrons and in 1870 became ordnance officer of the Boston navy yard. In January 1872, at the age of twenty-nine, he was promoted to commander. In November 1873, in command of the *Wyoming*, he sailed on his own initiative to Santiago, Cuba, to stop the execution of sailors from the *Virginius*, an American-registered merchantman that had been caught carrying arms to Cuban rebels. The next year he was transferred to the navy yard in Washington, D.C. He died in Washington on December 17, 1874.

Cushman, Robert Everton, Jr. (1914–   ), marine officer. Born in St. Paul, Minnesota, on December 24, 1914, Cushman graduated from the Naval Academy in 1935 and was commissioned second lieutenant of marines. He advanced to first lieutenant in August 1938 and captain in March 1941, serving at various marine posts including that in Shanghai. In June 1941 he took command of the marine detachment aboard the battleship *Pennsylvania*, with which he was present at the Japanese attack on Pearl Harbor on December 7. By 1943 he had advanced to lieutenant colonel, and he led a battalion of the 9th Marines in action on Bougainville, Guam, and Iwo Jima. From 1945 to 1948 he was a senior student and then an instructor at the Marine Corps Schools, Quantico, Virginia, and after a year as head of the amphibious warfare branch of the office of naval research he joined the Central Intelligence Agency in 1949. He was promoted to colonel in 1950. From 1951 to 1953 he was attached to the plans division of the Eastern Atlantic and Mediterranean fleet, and in 1953 he joined the faculty of the Armed Forces Staff College, becoming director of plans and operations in 1954. In 1957, by then a brigadier general, he was named assistant for national security affairs to Vice-President Richard M. Nixon. He was promoted to major general in 1958. During 1961–1962 he commanded the 3rd Marine Division on Okinawa; from 1962 to 1964 he was assistant chief of staff of the marine corps; and from 1964 to 1967 he was commander of Camp Pendleton, California. In April 1967 he was named commander of the 3rd Marine Amphibious Force, occupying and operating in the I Corps area of northernmost South Vietnam; his force

of more than 160,000 men was the largest combat force ever commanded by a marine officer. In April 1969 he was appointed deputy director of the Central Intelligence Agency, and in January 1972 he became commandant of the marine corps with the rank of general, holding that post until his retirement in June 1975. He was succeeded as commandant of the marine corps by Gen. Louis H. Wilson.

Custer, George Armstrong (1839–1876), army officer. Born in New Rumley, Harrison County, Ohio, on December 5, 1839, Custer was appointed to West Point in 1857 and graduated last in his class four years later. His court-martial for a minor dereliction of duty was overlooked in the rush to build up the army rapidly, and, commissioned in the 2nd Cavalry, he joined his regiment on the morning of the first battle of Bull Run (Manassas), July 21. He quickly established a reputation for daring and brilliance in battle. He served as an aide to Gen. George B. McClellan during the Peninsula campaign, his temporary volunteer rank of captain lapsing, on McClellan's replacement, to first lieutenant. Subsequently he was on the staff of Gen. Alfred Pleasonton, at whose recommendation he was, in June 1863, at the age of twenty-three, made a brigadier general of volunteers. He led a brigade at Gettysburg, and for his actions there he was brevetted regular major. From 1864 to the end of the Civil War he served under Gen. Philip H. Sheridan, who had only the highest praise for the dashing Custer. He was brevetted lieutenant colonel for his actions at Yellow Tavern, May 11, 1864, colonel for Winchester, September 19, and major general of volunteers in October for Winchester and Fisher's Hill, September 22. In command of the 3rd Cavalry Division, he performed with particular distinction during the final battles around Richmond in April 1865, maintaining a constant pressure on Gen. Robert E. Lee and thus contributing to Lee's decision to surrender. He was brevetted brigadier general of regulars in March 1865 and major general in April. After a brief assignment in Texas he was chief of cavalry of the army from November 1865 until mustered out of volunteer service in March 1866. Although a hero of national stature, he was forced by the disbanding of the volunteer service and the reduction of the standing army to revert to his permanent rank of captain. In July of that year the 7th Cavalry was organized and Custer was appointed its lieutenant colonel; he remained, in the absence of a colonel (Col. Andrew J. Smith was assigned to other duty and resigned in May 1869) the regiment's acting commander until his death. The regiment was ordered west to Kansas to take part in what emerged as a rather thoroughly muddled campaign, under Gen. Winfield Scott Hancock, against the Indians of the middle Plains. Suspended from service for a year following a court-martial for absence from duty, Custer was recalled late in 1868 by Hancock's successor, Gen. Philip Sheridan, and was in command at the decisive action of the campaign, the total destruction of an encampment of Black Kettle's Cheyenne people at the Washita River on November 27, 1868. The 7th was dispersed to various posts in 1870; Custer remained in the West and resumed command when the regiment was reassembled in 1873, establishing himself at Fort Abraham Lincoln on the Missouri River opposite Bismarck, Dakota Territory. In 1874, the year in which he published *My Life on the Plains,* he led an exploring expedition of 1200 troops and scientists into the Indian reservation lands of the Black Hills. The discovery of gold in the area sparked a massive influx of prospectors and settlers and soon thereafter led to the resumption of skirmishing and, finally, full-scale warfare with the Cheyenne and the Sioux, to whom the Black Hills were reserved by the 1868 Fort Laramie treaty and sacred by tradition. A concentrated offensive against the Indians was mounted in May 1876 under the command of Gen. Alfred H. Terry. Approaching the Bighorn Mountains from the east, Terry divided his forces and sent a column under Custer to swing south and come up on the rear of the reported Indian encampment on the Little Bighorn River in present-day southern Montana. (Terry was to come in from the north, thus encircling the Indians.) Custer drew near the encampment on June 24, 1876, and with characteristic but fatal vainglory decided to ignore Terry's plan. (Controversy raged long afterward over the degree of discretion allowed in Terry's orders; Custer may well have acted within them.) Unaware or heedless of the strength of the Indian forces—several thousand warriors under the leadership of Sitting Bull, Crazy Horse, Gall, and other chiefs—"Long Hair" Custer divided his command into three units and launched a surprise attack on the morning of June 25. The battle lasted only a few hours. The central unit, 266 men and officers under Custer, was quickly surrounded on a hill and killed to the last man. The other two units, under Maj. Marcus A. Reno, who, having fallen back at a critical point in the attack, was afterwards blamed for the disaster by Custer's partisans, and Capt. Frederick W. Benteen, both of whom were inexplicably slow to follow orders and failed completely to attempt the relief of Custer's column, were able to retreat to defensive positions and were saved from destruction by the arrival of Terry with the main force. "Custer's Last Stand," as the battle soon became known, was the army's worst defeat in the western campaigns and remained the best known and most enduringly controversial engagement of the Indian wars. The Little Bighorn battlefield became a national cemetery in 1879.

D

Dade, Francis Langhorne (1793?–1835), army officer. Born in King George County, Virginia, about 1793, Dade entered the army in March 1813 as third lieutenant in the 12th Infantry. He advanced to first lieutenant in 1816, captain in 1818, and brevet major in 1828. In 1835 he was stationed at Fort Brooke, on Tampa Bay, Florida. There was considerable unrest among the Seminole Indians of the area, who were bound by treaty to move west to Arkansas by January of the next year. On December 28, 1835, Dade was in command of a column of 110 soldiers and 6 other officers sent to reinforce Fort King, about 120 miles to the northeast. A band of some 200 Indians attacked the column from ambush and killed all but two (or, in some sources, three or four) soldiers, who made their way back to Fort Brooke with the news. The "Dade Massacre," as it became known, together with the murder of Indian agent Wiley Thompson by Osceola near Fort King on the same day, marked the beginning of the Second Seminole War. Dade County, Florida, was named for Maj. Dade.

Dahlgren, John Adolphus Bernard (1809–1870), naval officer and inventor. Born in Philadelphia on November 13, 1809, Dahlgren received a sound classical education in private schools and at home. At fifteen he was refused enlistment by the navy, but after a short voyage in the merchant service he was appointed acting midshipman in February 1826 and assigned to the *Macedonian* under Capt. James Barron. Over the next several years he served in the Mediterranean Squadron, at the Philadelphia Naval Station, and, because of his proficiency in mathematics, from 1834 to 1837 as an assistant to Ferdinand R. Hassler of the Coast Survey. From March 1837, when he was promoted to lieutenant, until 1843 he was on leave of absence because of eyesight problems, but he then returned to active service and made an extended Mediterranean cruise on the *Cumberland*. He had already invented a type of percussion lock when he was assigned to the Washington navy yard as ordnance officer in 1847, and there he continued to experiment while promoting the establishment of a full-fledged ordnance department. He succeeded in securing laboratories, a foundry, a test range, and other facilities and began manufacturing cannon of a new type after his own design. A series of tests had shown him that the pressure inside a cannon was greatest at the breech and decreased toward the muzzle; accordingly, he cast cannon thicker at one end, curving smoothly inward to the other in a shape that gave the Dahlgren guns the nickname of "soda-water bottles." The smooth curve further improved the overall strength of the metal by regularizing the pattern of crystallization in cooling. Cast solid and bored smooth, 11-inch Dahlgrens were made in 1851 and installed in shore batteries, and, after skepticism that ships could support their great weight had been dispelled by a successful voyage of the armed sloop *Plymouth* in 1857, they were mounted on several ships, later including the ironclad *Monitor.* He also devised a "boat howitzer," a light, accurate piece adaptable to both naval and field use. He wrote a number of books on the design and uses of ordnance and in October 1855 was promoted to commander. At the outbreak of the Civil War his superior at the Washington navy yard, Franklin Buchanan, resigned because of his Confederate sympathies, and although command of the yard was restricted by law to captains, President Abraham Lincoln insisted upon Dahlgren's taking the position. A special act of Congress to make that possible was passed; and in July 1862, after being appointed also chief of the Bureau of Ordnance, he was at last promoted to captain. In February 1863 he was promoted to rear admiral, and in July of that year, having requested active duty, he succeeded Samuel F. Du Pont as commander of the South Atlantic Blockading Squadron. In combat, his services included the attempted reduction of the defensive batteries around Charleston, South Carolina—a nearly hopeless task that the navy finally abandoned in October—and in December 1864 aiding in the capture of Savannah, Georgia. After the war he returned to Washington, served from 1866 to 1868 as commander of the South Pacific Squadron, from 1868 to 1869 again as chief of the Bureau of Ordnance, and from August 1869 as commandant of the Washington navy yard. Dahlgren died in Washington on July 12, 1870.

Dale, Richard (1756–1826), naval officer. Born in Norfolk County, Virginia, on November 6, 1756, Dale went to sea at the age of twelve and rose to the rating of chief mate in the merchant service by 1775. The next year be became a lieutenant in the Virginia navy. The cruiser on which he was sailing was captured, and after a brief confinement on a prison ship he signed as mate on a Tory tender. In July 1776 his vessel was captured by the *Lexington* under Capt. John Barry and Dale immediately entered the Continental navy as a midshipman. He remained on the *Lexington* under succeeding captains and in September 1777, when it was taken by the British *Alert* in the English Channel, was imprisoned with the rest of the crew in Mill Prison in Plymouth. After an earlier unsuccessful attempt he escaped in 1779, made his way to France, and was taken on the *Bonhomme Richard* as first lieutenant to Capt. John Paul Jones. On September 23 of that year he took part in the famous battle with the frigate *Serapis,* commanding the gun deck and then, despite a serious wound, leading the boarding party. He remained with Jones on later cruises aboard the *Alliance* and the *Ariel.* In August 1781, serving as first lieutenant of the frigate *Trumbull,* Capt. Samuel Nicholson, he was again wounded in an engagement with the frigate *Iris.* After service on the privateer *Queen of France,* which for a time he commanded, he took leave from the navy in 1783 and commanded merchantmen in the East India and China trade until 1801, returning to active service twice for brief periods, in 1794–1795 as fourth-rated captain of the navy and in 1798–1799; the second term of service he curtailed after a dispute over rank with Capt. Thomas Truxtun. In 1801 he was recalled to command an observation squadron in the Mediterranean, where in May Tripoli had declared war on the United States. Commodore Dale, aboard his flagship *President,* arrived in July and instituted in August a blockade of Tripoli after making shows of force at other Barbary ports, notably Algiers and Tunis. In March 1802 he returned to the United States, turning command of the squadron over to Commodore Richard V. Morris, and in December 1802 resigned from the navy, in which he was then the third-ranking officer. He retired to Philadelphia and lived there quietly until his death on February 26, 1826.

Darragh, Lydia Barrington (1729–1789), Revolutionary heroine. Born in Dublin, Ireland, in 1729, Lydia Barrington married William Darragh, a teacher, in 1753; shortly thereafter they emigrated to America, settling in Philadelphia. She worked as a nurse and midwife with considerable skill and success. In a story first published in 1827 and later elaborated upon, she was credited with saving Gen. George Washington's army: During the British occupation of Philadelphia Gen. William Howe had his headquarters opposite the Darragh house. On the night of December 2, 1777, the adjutant general and other officers commandeered one of her rooms for a secret conference, and, listening at the keyhole, she learned of their plan to attack Washington at Whitemarsh, eight miles away, two nights later. On the morning of the day, December 4, she let it be known that she needed flour from the Frankford mill and obtained a pass to leave the city for that purpose. Once away, she made for Whitemarsh. Encountering Col. Thomas Craig, a friend, on the road, she told him

what she had learned and then, securing her flour, hurried home. The British march that night found the Continental army at arms and ready to repel, and Howe was forced to return to Philadelphia. Mrs. Darragh lived in Philadelphia until her death on December 28, 1789.

Dauser, Sue Sophia (1888–   ), nurse and naval officer. Born in Anaheim, California, on September 20, 1888, Miss Dauser attended Stanford University for two years, 1907–1909, and in 1911 entered the California Hospital School of Nursing, Los Angeles, graduating in 1914. In September 1917 she joined the naval reserve, going on active duty the next month. In July 1918 she entered the regular navy. After duty at Base Hospital No. 3 in Edinburgh, Scotland, during the final months of World War I, she served tours of duty at naval hospitals in Brooklyn and San Diego and aboard ship. In 1923 she sailed on the *Henderson* on President Warren G. Harding's Alaskan visit and attended him during his last illness. She later served on Guam, in the Philippines, and at San Diego, Puget Sound, and Mare Island and Long Beach, California. In 1939 she was named superintendent of the Navy Nurse Corps. Her task in that post was twofold: to organize and administer a greatly expanded Nurse Corps in preparation for and then throughout World War II, and to secure for navy nurses equitable rank and privileges. In July 1942 Congress provided for relative rank for nurses (title and uniform, but not the commission, pay, or other benefits of regular rank), and she became a lieutenant commander. Pay was made equivalent in December 1942. In December 1943 she was promoted to (relative) captain, equivalent to Florence A. Blanchfield's army colonelcy and the highest naval rank yet attained by a woman. In February 1944 temporary commissions were authorized for army and navy nurses. Capt. Dauser retired as superintendent of nurses in November 1945 and from the navy in April 1946. She lived afterward in retirement in La Mesa, California.

Davie, William Richardson (1756–1820), Revolutionary army officer. Born on June 20, 1756, in Egremont, Cumberland, England, Davie came with his father to America in 1763 and settled in the Waxhaw District of South Carolina. By the time he graduated from the College of New Jersey (now Princeton) in the autumn of 1776, he had already served a short time in the Continental army in the New York campaign. He began the study of law in Salisbury, North Carolina, but was soon involved in the war again. In April 1779 he was commissioned lieutenant of dragoons and he quickly rose to major. He joined Pulaski's Legion and fought with it at Stono Ferry on June 20, 1779, receiving there a serious wound. Early in 1780 he raised and, largely with his own money, equipped a cavalry troop, which operated for the most part in western North Carolina. On August 1, 1780, he defeated three companies of Tories and five days later joined Gen. Thomas Sumter in the successful Battle of Hanging Rock, near Lancaster, South Carolina. In September he was promoted to colonel. In the aftermath of Gen. Horatio Gates's disaster at Camden, Davie fought a brilliant rearguard action against Gen. Cornwallis at Charlotte on September 26. In January 1781, at the urgent request of Gen. Nathanael Greene, newly appointed commander of the southern army, he took on the arduous and frustrating job of commissary general. Though he was often criticized for his conduct of the post, he contributed greatly to the success of Greene's campaign through 1781. After the war he settled in Halifax, North Carolina, and began his law practice. He was in the legislature almost continuously from 1786 to 1798. In 1787 he was a delegate to the Constitutional Convention, although illness prevented him from signing the completed document, and he was a leading member of the ratifying convention in North Carolina. He was principally responsible for the chartering and foundation of the University of North Carolina in 1789; and he served on several North–South Carolina boundary commissions. Appointed major general of militia in 1794, Davie was elected governor in 1799. In the same year he was appointed a brigadier general in the United States Provisional Army in anticipation of war with France, and later he was sent to France as a peace commissioner. He negotiated a treaty with the Tuscarora Indians in 1802. After an unsuccessful bid for a seat in Congress in 1803, he retired to a plantation in Lancaster County, South Carolina, where he died on November 29, 1820.

Davis, Benjamin Oliver (1877–1970), army officer. Born on July 1, 1877, in Washington, D.C., Davis entered Howard University in 1897 and left the following year to serve as a first lieutenant in the 8th Infantry Volunteers in the Spanish–American War. Mustered out in 1899, he immediately reenlisted as a private in the 9th Cavalry of the regular army and during service in the Philippines rose rapidly through the ranks to a commission as second lieutenant in February 1901. In 1905, following a promotion to first lieutenant in March, he was detailed to Wilberforce University as professor of military science and tactics, remaining there for four years. During 1909–1912 he was military attaché in Monrovia, Liberia, and for the next three years was on garrison and border-patrol duty in the West, again with the 9th Cavalry; he returned to Wilberforce in 1915, in which year he was promoted to captain. Another tour of duty in the Philippines in 1917–1920, during which he advanced to lieutenant colonel, was followed by assignment as professor of military science

and tactics at Tuskegee Institute, where he remained until 1924. For the next 14 years he alternated between teaching at Tuskegee and Wilberforce, receiving promotion to colonel in 1930. In 1938 he was given his first independent command, that of the 369th New York National Guard infantry regiment. Two years later, in October 1940, he became the first black soldier to hold rank as a general officer in the U.S. army; his promotion to temporary brigadier general aroused a brief but intense controversy, both on account of his race and because, coming just a month before a presidential election, it was interpreted by some as politically motivated on the part of President Franklin D. Roosevelt. He commanded a brigade of the 2nd Cavalry Division at Fort Riley, Kansas, from January 1941 to his retirement in June 1941. He was immediately recalled to active duty and assigned to the office of the inspector general in Washington. During World War II he served in the European theater of operations as an adviser on race relations in the army. Returning to his post as assistant inspector general in November 1945, Davis retired from the army in 1948 after 50 years of service. He died in North Chicago, Illinois, on November 26, 1970.

Davis, Benjamin Oliver, Jr. (1912–   ), army and air force officer. Born in Washington, D.C. on December 18, 1912, Davis was the son of then Lt. Benjamin O. Davis, later the first black general. The younger Davis attended Western Reserve University in 1929 and the University of Chicago in 1930–1932 before entering West Point, from which he graduated in 1936, having endured, among other things, a first year of silent treatment. Commissioned in the infantry, he served as an instructor of military science at Tuskegee Institute from 1938 to 1941 and in the latter year was among the first group of blacks admitted to the Air Corps and pilot training. He had been promoted to first lieutenant in June 1939 and to captain in September 1940 and by late 1942, as temporary lieutenant colonel, he had organized the 99th Fighter Squadron, an all-black unit that he led with distinction flying tactical support missions over North Africa, Sicily, and Italy. In 1943 he organized and commanded the 332nd Fighter Group, which flew in Italy, Germany, and the Balkans and supported the landings in southern France in August 1944. In May of that year he was promoted to colonel. After the war he commanded Godman Field, Kentucky, in 1945–1946, the 477th Fighter-Bomber Group at Lockbourne Air Base, Ohio, in 1946–1949 (transferring to the air force in 1947), and after graduating from the Air War College in 1950 he was appointed chief of the fighter branch and deputy for operations at air force headquarters in Washington. During 1953–1954 he commanded the 51st Fighter-Interceptor Wing in Korea and, promoted to brigadier general in October 1954, then served in various other capacities in the Far East. From 1957 to 1959 he was chief of staff, Twelfth Air Force, in Germany. Promoted to major general in June 1959 (the first black officer to attain two-star rank), he served for two years as deputy chief of staff of air forces in Europe; from 1961 to 1965 he was again in Washington, and after receiving promotion to lieutenant general in the latter year he became chief of staff of U.S. forces and the United Nations Command in Korea. From 1968 until his retirement in 1970 he was deputy commander, U.S. Strike Command, at McDill Air Force Base, Florida. In February 1970 Davis was appointed director of public safety for the city of Cleveland and later in the same year he was named director of civil aviation security to head the force of special federal marshals, the "sky marshals," organized to combat aircraft hijacking. In July 1971 he was appointed assistant secretary of transportation. At his retirement in 1970 Davis had been the senior black officer in the armed forces.

Davis, Charles Henry (1807–1877), naval officer. Born in Boston on January 16, 1807, Davis attended Harvard for two years and in August 1823 was appointed midshipman in the navy. Over the next 15 years he served aboard the *United States* and the *Dolphin* in the South Pacific, the *Ontario* in the Mediterranean, and other vessels, advancing to lieutenant in March 1834 and in 1842 completing his studies and taking a degree from Harvard. From 1842 to 1856 he was engaged primarily in scientific work; he surveyed the waters around Nantucket, discovering several previously unknown shoals, published studies of tidal action, and was a major contributor to the establishment in 1849 of the *American Ephemeris and Nautical Almanac,* with which he remained associated until 1855. He was promoted to commander in June 1854. During 1856–1859 he commanded the *St. Mary's* in the Pacific Squadron, in which capacity he arranged for the surrender of William Walker and his filibuster followers in Nicaragua in May 1857 and transferred them safely to Panama. In 1859 he returned to work at the *Almanac* office. He was promoted to captain in November 1861, and through the early months of the Civil War he was one of the principal planners and organizers of naval operations, particularly of the blockade and of the expeditions against Hatteras Inlet in August 1861 and Port Royal in November, the latter of which he accompanied as Flag-Officer Samuel F. Du Pont's fleet captain. In May 1862 he joined the Upper Mississippi Flotilla as second in command to the disabled Flag-Officer Andrew H. Foote, whom he soon succeeded. On June 6, following the Confederates' abandonment of Fort Pillow, he moved downriver to Memphis and, reinforced by rams commanded by Col. Charles Ellet, sank or captured seven of the eight rams in the Confederate fleet. He then accepted the surrender of the city of Memphis. In July he was promoted to commodore and named chief of the Bureau of Navigation, although he remained on the river, with Adm. David G. Farragut at Vicksburg, until September. In February 1863 he was promoted to rear admiral. From 1865 to 1867 he was superintendent of the Naval Observatory. Following a final sea command, of the South Atlantic Squadron in 1867–1869, he returned to shore duty as commander of the Norfolk navy yard, 1870–1873, and again at the Naval Observatory from 1873. He died in Washington, D.C., on February 18, 1877. One of Davis's daughters married Brooks Adams; another, Henry Cabot Lodge.

Davis, Jefferson Columbus (1828–1879), army officer. Born in Clark County, Indiana, on March 2, 1828, Davis enlisted in an Indiana volunteer regiment for service in the Mexican War and for gallantry at Buena Vista, February 22–23, 1847, was commissioned second lieutenant of the 1st Artillery in June 1848. He remained in the army afterward, advancing to first lieutenant in 1852. He was in Fort Sumter at the time of its bombardment in April 1861. Promoted to captain in May, he raised and was appointed colonel of the 22nd Indiana Infantry Volunteers. He commanded a brigade in the Western department under Gen. John C. Frémont and then Gen. David Hunter, winning promotion to brigadier general of volunteers for his actions at the battle of Blackwater, near Milford, Missouri, in December 1861. He led a division under Gen. Samuel R. Curtis at Pea Ridge, March 7–8, 1862, and took part in the siege of Corinth, Mississippi, in May, after which he was attached to the Army of the Tennessee. On September 29, 1862, at the Galt House hotel in Louisville, he happened to encounter Gen. William Nelson, by whom he claimed to have earlier been treated with undue harshness. A quarrel broke out and Davis suddenly shot and killed Nelson. He was arrested but soon released, apparently through the influence of Gov. Oliver P. Morton of Indiana, a friend, and no trial was ever held. He was returned to duty and served with distinction at Murfreesboro (Stones River) and Chickamauga, and in 1864 he commanded the XIV Corps in Gen. William T. Sherman's march to the sea. He never received promotion to major general of volunteers, though he was given that rank by brevet in March 1865. In July 1866, mustered out of volunteer service, he became colonel of the 23rd Infantry. He served on the Pacific coast and in Alaska, and in April 1873 he took command in the Modoc War following the murder of Gen. Edwin R. S. Canby. Again, he failed to be promoted. He died in Chicago on November 30, 1879.

Davison, Gregory Caldwell (1871–1935), naval officer and inventor. Born on August 12, 1871, in Jefferson City, Missouri, Davison graduated from the Naval Academy in 1892 and after a cruise aboard the *San Francisco* was commissioned ensign in 1894. Subsequently he served on torpedo boats and then on the *Oneida* in Cuban waters during the Spanish–American War, and in 1900 he commanded various torpedo boats. He was promoted to lieutenant (junior grade) in March 1899 and lieutenant in July 1900. In 1901 he joined the *New York*. Ordered to overhaul the *New York*'s engines, he completed the task so efficiently that the ship was able to exceed the speed of its original trial runs. Also while on the *New York* he assisted Guglielmo Marconi in ship-to-shore radio experiments. During 1901–1902 Davison was attached to the Bureau of Ordnance, where he conceived the idea of using steam turbines in torpedoes. After a period commanding a torpedo boat and then the reserve torpedo boat fleet at Norfolk navy yard, he took the torpedo boat destroyer *Paul Jones* on a Pacific cruise in 1903–1905, twice winning the gunnery trophy with the aid of the "Davy Jones" gunsight of his own invention. During 1905–1907 he was on duty at the Naval Torpedo Station, Rhode Island, and there perfected the balanced turbine torpedo, overcoming defects in his earlier design. He was promoted to lieutenant commander in July 1906. He resigned from the navy in December 1907 and became a vice-president of the Electric Boat Company, builders of submarines and torpedoes, for which he invented a steam generator for torpedoes and a recoilless gun for aircraft. During World War I he served in addition as chief engineer and general manager of the General Ordnance Company, and there he devised the Y-gun for throwing depth charges, a device that was soon standard on all destroyers and submarine chasers. In 1922 he resigned from Electric Boat to enter the oil business in Kentucky and West Virginia. In 1933 he returned briefly to the ordnance business with the invention of the Davison all-purpose gun, a combination light mobile field and antiaircraft weapon. He died in Lyme, Connecticut, on May 7, 1935.

Dawes, William (1745–1799), Revolutionary patriot. Born in Boston on April 6, 1745, Dawes took up the trade of tanner and during the period of unrest that preceded the Revolution took part in various patriot activities. Early in 1775 he was one of two men chosen to spread the alarm should the British troops in Boston attempt a movement against the countryside. On the night of April 18 such a move was begun, and while Paul Revere took his lantern message in Charlestown and set off for Lexington, Dawes was sent by Dr. Joseph Warren over a different route to the same destination. He roused patriots in Roxbury and Cambridge and joined Revere at Parson Clarke's in Lexington, where Samuel Adams and John Hancock were in hiding. Having warned the two leaders, Revere and Dawes, joined by Dr. Samuel

Prescott, set out for Concord. They were stopped by a British patrol near Lincoln, some miles short of their goal; Revere was captured, Dawes turned back to Lexington, and Prescott escaped to carry on. Dawes later served in the Continental army in the siege of Boston and possibly at Bunker Hill. Later still he was a commissary to the army at Worcester. He died in Boston on February 25, 1799.

Dean, William Frishe (1899–   ), army officer. Born on August 1, 1899, in Carlyle, Illinois, Dean graduated from the University of California in 1922. He had joined the army reserve the year before, and in 1923 he was commissioned a second lieutenant of infantry in the regular army. He saw routine duty at various posts at home and overseas and graduated from the Command and General Staff School, Fort Leavenworth, Kansas, in 1936, from the Army Industrial College in 1939, and from the Army War College in 1940. Promoted to major in July 1940, lieutenant colonel in December 1941, colonel in August 1942, and brigadier general in December 1942, he served during the early part of World War II on staff duty in Washington, D.C. In mid-1944 he was appointed deputy commander of the 44th Infantry Division, an element of Gen. Alexander M. Patch's Seventh Army, and in January 1945, after three months of combat, he succeeded to full command. The 44th fought through the Vosges Mountains, captured Strasbourg, crossed the Rhine at Worms in March 1945, crossed the Danube in April, and ended the war occupying Austria. Dean was promoted to major general in March. From his return to the United States in July to mid-1947 he was on the staff of the Command and General Staff School. In October 1947 he was named military governor of South Korea. After the installation of constitutional government there in August 1948, he was placed in command of the 7th Infantry Division stationed in Japan, serving also as chief of staff, Eighth Army. In October 1949 he became commander of the 24th Infantry Division, which in June 1950 was hurriedly sent to Korea to meet the first North Korean attack on the South. At Taejon on July 20–21 he became involved in a rearguard action, stayed behind to organize the retreat, and performed with great valor against attacking armor. He became separated from the division and after several days wandering was taken prisoner. He was awarded the Medal of Honor in September 1950, but no word of him was heard until December 1951, when it was learned he was a captive. He was liberated in September 1953. In 1954 he was appointed deputy commander, Sixth Army, in San Francisco. In that year he published *General Dean's Story* (with W. L. Worden), an account of his ordeal in North Korea. He retired in October 1955 and lived afterwards in Berkeley, California, where he was prominent in civic affairs.

Dearborn, Henry (1751–1829), Revolutionary army officer and public official. Born on February 23, 1751, in Hampton, New Hampshire, Dearborn took up the study of medicine, beginning practice in 1772 in Nottingham Square, New Hampshire. He organized and commanded a militia company in preparation for war with England, and immediately upon hearing of the battle of Lexington marched his men to Cambridge, arriving in time to take part in the battle of Bunker Hill, June 17, 1775. He then volunteered to join Col. Benedict Arnold's Quebec expedition; he was captured in the attack on the city on December 31 and for more than a year was on parole awaiting exchange. Returning to active service in March 1777, he was promoted to major and saw action under Gen. Horatio Gates at Ticonderoga and Saratoga in the campaign against Gen. John Burgoyne. After wintering at Valley Forge he distinguished himself at the battle of Monmouth, June 27, 1778. In 1779 he accompanied Gen. John Sullivan's expedition against Butler's Rangers and the Indian allies of the British in Pennsylvania and western New York, and in 1781, with the rank of colonel, was on Gen. George Washington's staff at Yorktown. Upon being discharged from the army in June 1783 he settled in Kennebec County, Maine (then still a district of Massachusetts), becoming in 1787 brigadier general and in 1795 major general of militia, and in 1790 being appointed U.S. marshal for the district. Dearborn was elected to the House of Representatives in 1792 and served until 1797. In March 1801 President Thomas Jefferson appointed him secretary of war, in which post he ordered the establishment of a fortification at "Chikago" in 1803; this began the lasting association of his name with the city that was later built around the site of Fort Dearborn. He left the cabinet in March 1809 and was collector of the port of Boston until January 1812, when President James Madison named him senior major general of the army in command of the northern border in the War of 1812. Despite his announced intention to invade Canada, little beyond an amount of marching and countermarching was achieved during 1812, while the British won major victories at Detroit and Queenston. Finally, in April 1813, the invasion was begun in conjunction with the Lake Ontario fleet under Commodore Isaac Chauncey. York (now Toronto) was captured on April 27, with the loss of Gen. Zebulon M. Pike, and sacked. (Dearborn was ill and absent from the field.) Dearborn soon abandoned York to move against Fort George on the Niagara, taking it on May 27 but losing two field engagements with inferior forces. The American base at Sackett's Harbor had meanwhile been left nearly defenseless and was saved only by the remarkable exertions of Gen. Jacob J. Brown. Delay, miscalculation, and general ineptitude had marked Dearborn's command, and his failing health provided a useful

excuse for his relief in July 1813. He subsequently commanded in New York City. Before retiring in June 1815 he presided over the court-martial of Gen. William Hull, whose loss of Detroit to the British had been to a significant degree the result of Dearborn's failure to prepare adequate defenses. He was proposed as secretary of war by Madison in 1815, but a hail of criticism forced the withdrawal of his name. In 1822 President James Monroe appointed him minister to Portugal. After two years in that post Dearborn retired to Roxbury, Massachusetts (now part of Boston), where he died on June 6, 1829.

Decatur, Stephen (1779–1820), naval officer. Born on January 5, 1779, in Sinepuxent, Maryland, Decatur grew up in Philadelphia and, after a year of study at the University of Pennsylvania, entered a shipping firm in that city. In April 1798 he was commissioned a midshipman in the navy, and he made his first cruise on the *United States* under Commodore John Barry. He became acting lieutenant in 1799 and in May 1801 was made first lieutenant on the *Essex* in the squadron sent to Tripoli under Commodore Richard Dale. He was again in the Mediterranean in 1802–1803 aboard the *New York*, Capt. James Barron, and he returned a third time late in 1803 in command of the *Argus* and later of the *Enterprise*. On February 16, 1804, aboard a ketch (*Intrepid*, ex-*Mastico*) that he had captured, he led a daring raid into the harbor of Tripoli to burn an American frigate, the *Philadelphia*, that had been captured after running aground. He escaped with but one of his crew injured and in May was promoted to captain. Through 1804 and 1805 he took part in hostilities off Tripoli, performing with great dash and distinction; in 1805 he negotiated personally with the Bey of Tunis and returned to the United States with a Tunisian ambassador. For several years he held various commands in home waters, and he served on the court-martial that suspended Capt. Barron in 1808. Soon after the outbreak of the War of 1812 Decatur sailed in command of the *United States*; on October 25, 1812, he captured the British frigate *Macedonian* in one of the war's great naval victories. The following year he was appointed commodore of a squadron defending New York harbor. In January 1815 he ran the British blockade of the harbor in the *President*; pursued, he disabled the British warship *Endymion* before being forced to surrender to overwhelming numbers. In May 1815 he sailed for the Mediterranean, aboard the *Guerrière*, in command of a nine-ship squadron sent to deal with new outbreaks by the Barbary pirates (the "Algerine War"). He successfully ended corsair raids from Algiers, Tunis, and Tripoli, ended U.S. payment of tribute to the Barbary states, and secured reparations for damages to U.S. shipping. At a dinner given in his honor shortly after his triumphal return to the United States, he proposed his famous toast: "Our country! In her intercourse with foreign nations may she always be in the right; but our country, right or wrong." From November 1815 until he died he served on the newly created Board of Naval Commissioners. In 1820 he was accused by Capt. Barron of leading a conspiracy to block Barron's promotion; Barron challenged Decatur to a duel in which, on March 22, 1820, near Bladensburg, Maryland, Decatur was killed.

Decker, George Henry (1902–   ), army officer. Born in Catskill, New York, on February 16, 1902, Decker graduated from Lafayette College in 1924 and was commissioned second lieutenant of infantry in June of that year. He graduated from Infantry School, Fort Benning, Georgia, in 1932 and from Command and General Staff School, Fort Leavenworth, Kansas, in 1937, and over the years served at various posts in Hawaii, Washington, and the South. During the early years of World War II he served on staff duty in Washington, D.C., later becoming deputy chief of staff of the Third Army in Texas and then, in February 1943, of the Sixth Army, under Gen. Walter Krueger, in the Southwest Pacific theater. Promoted to colonel, he became chief of staff, Sixth Army, in May 1944. He advanced to temporary brigadier general in August 1944 and to temporary major general in June 1945, taking part in the Philippine campaign and later the occupation of Japan. In July 1946 he was appointed deputy commander and chief of staff of the Middle Pacific Army Forces, and in July 1948 he was named commander of the 5th Infantry Division, Fort Jackson, South Carolina. In March 1950 he returned to Washington, becoming chief of the budget division and in 1951 comptroller of the army. He was promoted to temporary lieutenant general in May of the latter year. From February 1955 to June 1956 he was commander of the VII Corps in Germany, and from June 1956, following his promotion in May to temporary rank of general, he was deputy commander, U.S. European Command. In July 1957 he was named commander of United Nations forces, United States forces, and the Eighth Army, all in South Korea. In August 1959 he was appointed vice chief of staff of the army, and in October 1960 he succeeded Gen. Lyman L. Lemnitzer as chief of staff. At the expiration of his term in October 1962 he retired from the army. From 1963 to 1969 he was president of the Manufacturing Chemists Association.

De Haven, Edwin Jesse (1816–1865), naval officer and explorer. Born in Philadelphia on May 7, 1816, De Haven was appointed a midshipman in the navy in October 1829. He served aboard various vessels in the West Indies and the Brazil Squadron, and at Callao in 1839 he was attached to the *Vincennes,* flagship of the South Seas exploring expedition under Lt. Charles Wilkes. In September 1841 he distinguished himself in rescuing a boat crew after the wreck of the *Peacock* off Cape Disappointment at the mouth of the Columbia River, and shortly thereafter he was promoted to lieutenant. Routine service followed the end of the Wilkes expedition in 1842. During the Mexican War he served on the *Mississippi,* which took part in the Veracruz campaign under Commodore David Conner and the various coastal actions under Commodore Matthew C. Perry. From 1848 to 1850 he served under Lt. Matthew F. Maury at the Naval Observatory. Early in 1850 he was chosen to command the Grinnell Arctic expedition, sponsored by New York merchant Henry Grinnell and manned by volunteer navy officers and men. De Haven sailed from New York in May 1850 in command of two small brigs, *Advance* and *Rescue,* with the principal purpose of searching for the English explorer Sir John Franklin, lost in the Arctic for five years. The expedition was 16 months in the Arctic, 9 of them frozen in pack ice. Grinnell Land, in the central region of Ellesmere Island, was discovered, but Franklin was not. De Haven and his party returned to New York in September 1851. He made a final voyage for the Coast Survey in 1853–1857 and, his health failing, he retired in 1862. He died in Philadelphia on May 1, 1865.

De Long, George Washington (1844–1881), naval officer and explorer. Born in New York City on August 22, 1844, De Long won appointment to the Naval Academy in 1857, but, deferring to his parents' wish, he took up the study of law instead. In 1861, however, he reapplied and was graduated in 1865. After a three-year cruise on the *Canandaigua* he was promoted to master commandant in March 1868, and a year later he advanced to lieutenant. He served on various ships of the European and South Atlantic squadrons over the next few years. In 1873 he was ordered to the *Juniata,* which was sent in that year to search in the North Atlantic for the missing steamer *Polaris.* While the *Juniata* was searching Baffin Bay, De Long was sent out in a steam launch to examine the ice pack on Melville Bay on the northeast coast of Greenland. From 1875 to 1878 he was executive officer of the school ship *St. Mary's* in New York harbor. His taste for Arctic exploration having been whetted, he began during that period to plan an expedition to the North Pole and interested James Gordon Bennett of the *New York Herald* in the project; Bennett bought the steamer *Pandora,* veteran of two Arctic voyages, rechristened her the *Jeanette,* and fitted her out for a try for the Pole. The *Jeanette* sailed from San Francisco on July 8, 1879, with De Long in command of 32 officers and men. He sailed through Bering Strait into the Chukchi Sea, but on September 5, near Herald Island, the *Jeanette* became frozen in pack ice, and she remained caught, drifting slowly northwest, for 21 months. On June 12, 1881, at 77° 15' N., 155° E., some 600 miles from where she was caught, the *Jeanette* was finally crushed and sank. De Long (who had been promoted to lieutenant commander in November 1879) salvaged most of his equipment and supplies and set out for the Siberian coast, alternately sledging and boating over broken pack ice. The party reached open water at the New Siberian islands in mid-August and then took to their boats to make their way to the Lena River delta, some 200 miles away. The boats became separated in a gale on September 12 and one was lost. De Long's boat finally struck the coast at one of the northern mouths of the Lena, in an uninhabited region. From September 17 to October 9 he led his party overland toward the south, but finally the burden of illness and exhaustion was too great. Two men were sent on to seek help while the others rested, one by one dying of starvation. De Long died on October 30, 1881. The bodies of the party were recovered in March 1882 by Chief Engineer George W. Melville, commander of the third boat, who had landed in an inhabited area to the east.

Denfeld, Louis Emil (1891–1972), naval officer. Born on April 13, 1891, in Westboro, Massachusetts, Denfeld graduated from the Naval Academy in 1912. He was promoted to lieutenant (junior grade) in June 1915 and to lieutenant and temporary lieutenant commander in June 1918. During World War I he was primarily engaged in escort duty aboard various destroyers in the North Atlantic. His first sea command was the *McCall* in 1919, and in 1923–1924 he gained supplementary experience in command of submarine *S-24*. Sea and shore duty alternated for several years; after a period as aide to the commander of Battle Force and then of the U.S. Fleet, and promotion to commander in March 1933, he commanded Destroyer Division 11 in 1935–1937 and then became aide to the chief of naval operations, Adm. William D. Leahy. Promoted to captain in July 1939, he served as commander of Destroyer Division 18, then of Destroyer Squadron 1, and during 1941 was on the staff of the commander of the Atlantic Fleet support force. In January 1942 he was named assistant chief of the Bureau of Navigation (later redesignated the Bureau of Personnel), receiving promotion to rear admiral in May 1942. During 1945 he commanded Battleship Division 9 in the Pacific. In September 1945 he was appointed chief of the Bureau of Personnel, with rank of vice admiral. In January 1947 Denfeld was promoted to admiral, and the next month he took command of the Pacific Fleet and all U.S. forces in the Pacific. He assumed the post of chief of naval operations from Adm. Chester W. Nimitz in December 1947, but his vigorous defense of naval independence and prerogatives during the process of unification of the armed forces led to his removal from the

office in October 1949, just after he had been reappointed for a second term. He retired in February 1950, and from that year until 1971 he served as a consultant to the Sun Oil Company. Denfeld died on March 28, 1972, in Westboro, Massachusetts.

De Seversky, Alexander Procofieff (1894–1974), aviator and aeronautical engineer. Born in Tbilisi (Tiflis), Russia, on June 7, 1894, De Seversky was originally named Alexander Nicolaievitch Procofieff-Seversky. He graduated from the Imperial Naval Academy in 1914 and later received aviation training. He was sent to the front soon after Russia entered World War I and became one of that nation's outstanding air aces, credited with 13 German planes downed despite a crash in 1915 that cost him a leg and forced him to learn to fly all over again with an artificial limb. In 1917 he left Russia on a mission to the United States just as the Russian Revolution broke out; en route he acquired a French passport and, through a transcription error, the form of his name that he adopted permanently. He remained in the United States and quickly found employment as a test pilot and consulting engineer for the U.S. Air Service. At the request of Gen. William Mitchell he devoted three years to the development of a gyroscopically stabilized bombsight for aircraft, a project he completed in 1922. In that year he founded the Seversky Aero Corporation, the first of a series of ventures into the rapidly growing aviation industry. Naturalized in 1927, De Seversky joined the Army Air Corps reserve in 1928 and rose to the rank of major while making important contributions to military aviation; he resigned his commission in 1933. In 1936 he developed an all-metal, cantilevered-wing training craft for the army and in 1938 built a turbo-supercharged air-cooled fighter plane that served as the prototype for the P-47. He set world speed marks in 1933 and 1935 with his amphibian aircraft and developed midair refueling apparatus and other improvements. Despite such successes and the development of other aircraft that set numerous speed records and captured no fewer than three Bendix trophies, De Seversky lacked business acumen and in 1939, eight years after founding the new company, was ousted from the presidency of the Seversky Aircraft Corporation, which then became the Republic Aircraft Corporation. He remained nonetheless a major figure in military aviation and in 1942 published the widely read and highly influential *Victory Through Air Power*. During World War II he continued to promote a strong air arm of the armed forces and afterward campaigned for the establishment of an independent air force. In recognition of his contributions to military aviation he was awarded in 1947 the War Department's Medal for Merit and the International Harmon Trophy, the latter presented by President Harry S. Truman. In 1948 he founded a new Seversky Aviation Corporation, of which he was thereafter president. De Seversky continued to promote the cause of aviation, working on defense against nuclear attack, and in later years also developed an interest in solving the problems of air pollution, inventing a new type of electrostatic precipitator and forming the Seversky Electronatom Corporation in 1952, serving as its president until 1968 and thereafter as chairman of the board. In 1970 he was elected to the Aviation Hall of Fame in Dayton, Ohio. He also published *Air Power, Key to Survival*, 1950, and *America: Too Young to Die*, 1961, was from 1957 a consultant to the air force chief of staff, and lectured regularly on air power. He died in New York City on August 24, 1974.

Devers, Jacob Loucks (1887–   ), army officer. Born in York, Pennsylvania, on September 8, 1887, Devers graduated from West Point in 1909 and was commissioned in the artillery. He was promoted to first lieutenant while on the faculty, 1912–1916, of West Point, to captain in May and temporary major in August 1917 while with the 9th Field Artillery in Hawaii, and to temporary lieutenant colonel and colonel in July and October 1918 while on the staff of the School of Fire (later the Field Artillery School) at Fort Sill, Oklahoma. During March–May 1919 he commanded the 1st Field Artillery. After a tour of occupation duty in Europe he reverted to captain in August 1919. He was again assigned to West Point from 1919 to 1924, receiving promotion to major in 1920, and in 1925 he graduated from the Command and General Staff School, Fort Leavenworth, Kansas. After three years at the Field Artillery School, a period of staff duty in the War Department, graduation from the Army War College in 1933, promotion to lieutenant colonel in 1934, and various field assignments, he was once again attached to the staff at West Point in 1936, receiving promotion to colonel in that year. During 1939–1940 he was chief of staff of the Panama Canal Department. He was promoted to brigadier general in May 1940 and to temporary major general in October, and during that year he aided in the selection of sites for U.S. bases acquired in the destroyer deal with Great Britain. From October 1940 to July 1941 he commanded the 9th Infantry Division at Fort Bragg, North Carolina; he then took command of the Armored Force, Fort Knox, Kentucky, advancing to temporary lieutenant general in September 1942. In May 1943 he was named commander of the European theater of operations, U.S. Army, and from January to October 1944 he was commander of army forces in North Africa and deputy supreme allied commander, Mediterranean theater. He then took command of the 6th Army Group, consisting of the Seventh Army under Gen. Alexander M. Patch, the French First Army, and other units. The Seventh had made on August 15 the landing in southern France

(Operation Dragoon) and then been absorbed by the 6th Army Group. As the 6th, Devers's forces moved north to the Vosges and then eastward through Alsace, through the Germans' Siegfried Line, over the Rhine and into Germany, linking up with Gen. Mark W. Clark's Allied forces in Austria and northern Italy. Devers was promoted to general in March 1945. In June he was named chief of Army Ground Forces, a title changed by reorganization to chief of Army Field Forces in March 1948. He retained the post until his retirement in September 1949. For a year thereafter he was associated with the American Automobile Association. During 1951 he was chief military adviser to the United Nations mission to India and Pakistan, an attempt to resolve the Kashmir dispute, and he took part in negotiations on the issue in 1952. From 1951 to 1959 he was associated with the Fairchild Engine and Airplane Corporation.

Dewey, George (1837–1917), naval officer. Born on December 26, 1837, in Montpelier, Vermont, Dewey prepared at Norwich University and graduated from the Naval Academy in 1858. He became a lieutenant in April 1861 and during the Civil War served aboard the side-wheeler *Mississippi*, Capt. Melancton Smith, under Adm. David G. Farragut in operations against New Orleans and on the Mississippi River. He was later on duty with the Atlantic blockade, and aboard the *Colorado*, Commodore Henry K. Thatcher, he took part in the attacks on Fort Fisher under Adm. David D. Porter in December 1864 and January 1865. After the war he held various routine commands at sea and ashore. He rose to commander in April 1872, captain in September 1884, and commodore in February 1896. As chief of the Bureau of Equipment, 1889, and president of the Board of Inspection and Survey, 1895, he became familiar with the modern battleships of the navy. Assigned to sea duty—command of the Asiatic Squadron—at his own request in November 1897, he received word of the outbreak of the Spanish–American War while in Hong Kong. He had had the foresight to arrange beforehand for supply facilities, full magazines, drills, and information on Philippine waters, particularly Manila Bay. With orders to capture or destroy Spanish vessels in Philippine waters, he entered Manila Bay with his squadron, consisting of four cruisers and two gunboats, on May 1, 1898. Mines and shore batteries proved no problem. The Spanish fleet was found at anchor at Cavite, and at 5:30 A.M. Dewey spoke to Capt. Charles V. Gridley of the flagship *Olympia* the long-remembered words "You may fire when you are ready, Gridley." The squadron steamed nearly three times through a flat elliptical course, bringing both broadsides alternately to bear. Rapid, accurate fire sank or destroyed all ten ships of the Spanish fleet before noon, while there was little damage to American vessels and only eight injuries to American seamen. By demonstrating the readiness of the navy and the superiority of her new ships, the victory earned for the United States the position of the major Pacific power. Dewey was promoted to rear admiral on May 10, 1898, and formally commended by Congress. For several months he was compelled to occupy the harbor and guard Manila without land forces and to deal diplomatically with naval observers of other nations. (He found it necessary to be particularly firm with the German admiral.) In August his fleet assisted in the occupation of Manila by land forces under Gen. Wesley Merritt, and in September 1899 he returned to the United States, where he was given a hero's welcome. In March 1899 he had been made admiral of the navy, a rank created especially for him and the highest ever held by an American naval officer. By special provision he was allowed to remain on active duty despite his age, and from 1900 he served as president of the General Board of the navy. He made himself very nearly absurd when for a brief time in 1900 he encouraged the notion that he might run for President; his announced belief that "the office . . . is not such a very difficult one to fill" effectively ended the idea. He published his autobiography in 1913 and died in Washington, D.C., on January 16, 1917.

De Witt, John Lesesne (1880–1962), army officer. Born on January 9, 1880, at Fort Sidney, Nebraska, De Witt left Princeton University after two years to serve in the Spanish–American War. He was commissioned a second lieutenant in the regular infantry in October 1898, promoted to first lieutenant a short time later, and from 1899 to 1902 was stationed in the Philippines, seeing action against the insurrectionists. After routine duty at home he was again in the Philippines in 1903–1905. He was promoted to captain and graduated from the Infantry and Cavalry School, Fort Leavenworth, Kansas, in 1907, and after a period of garrison duty with the 20th Infantry in Monterey, California, and service in 1909 on the army's Infantry Board, he was stationed for a third time in the Philippines. In 1911–1912 and again in 1914–1917 he was attached to the office of the quartermaster general in Washington, D.C. Promoted to major shortly after the entry of the United States into World War I, De Witt was an instructor at the Officers' Training Camp, Plattsburg, New York, in May–August of that year. In November he arrived in France as quartermaster of the 42nd Infantry Division. He was assigned to duty on the headquarters staff of the American Expeditionary Force in January 1918 and was assistant chief of staff for supply of the I Corps in February–July and of the First Army from August to January 1919. In 1919–1920 he was an instructor at the Army War College and from 1919 to 1924 was attached to the Supply and later the War Plans Division of the General Staff. He was promot-

ed to colonel in May 1921. In 1924–1926 he commanded the 1st Infantry at Fort Sam Houston, Texas; in 1926–1928 he was again with the Supply Division; and in 1928–1930 he was assistant commandant of the War College. From 1930 to 1934 he was quartermaster general of the army with statutory rank of major general. Promoted to permanent brigadier general in March 1934, De Witt commanded the 1st Brigade, 1st Division, in New York City in 1934–1935, the 23rd Brigade in the Philippines in 1935–1936, and, promoted to major general in December 1936, the Division of the Philippines in 1937. In July 1937 he became commandant of the Army War College. In December 1939, promoted to temporary lieutenant general, he was named commander of the Fourth Army and the IX Corps area, with headquarters in San Francisco. During 1940–1941 the Fourth Army was assigned to the army's field forces and took part in various training exercises, but immediately following the Japanese attack on Pearl Harbor on December 7, 1941, it became the constituent force of the Western Defense Command, which De Witt had also commanded from its activation in March 1941. As commander of a theater of war, De Witt possessed wide discretionary authority over civil affairs on the entire Pacific coast. His powers were enlarged vastly in January and February 1942, when, in response to public and official pressure including De Witt's own urgings, he was granted new and unprecedented authority: first, by orders of the U.S. attorney general, Francis Biddle, in January, to designate security zones in which the movement of certain persons—in practice, all those of Japanese ancestry—was regulated; and second, by two executive orders of President Franklin D. Roosevelt in February, to exclude those persons entirely and then to encourage their voluntary migration to relocation centers in nonsensitive areas far from the coast. In March the relocation program was made mandatory and placed under civil authority; eventually more than 110,000 persons of Japanese ancestry, two-thirds of them American citizens, were interned in camps, principally in the Southwest and Midwest. In September 1943 De Witt relinquished the Fourth Army to Gen. William H. Simpson and the Western Defense Command to Gen. Delos C. Emmons and became commandant of the Army and Navy Staff College in Washington, D.C. From November 1945 to April 1947 he was attached to the office of the chief of staff of the army; he retired in June 1947 in the rank of major general. In July 1954 he was promoted to general on the retired list. De Witt died in Washington, D.C., on June 20, 1962.

Dickinson, Philemon (1739–1809), Revolutionary militia officer and public official. Born on April 5, 1739, in Talbot County, Maryland, Dickinson was a younger brother of the statesman John Dickinson.

He graduated from the College of Philadelphia (now the University of Pennsylvania) in 1759, studied law with his brother, and took up an estate near Trenton, New Jersey. In July 1775 he was appointed colonel in the New Jersey militia and in October he was promoted to brigadier general. In 1776 he was a delegate to the provincial congress. In January 1777, in command of some 400 untrained recruits, he met and routed a large foraging party sent out by Gen. Charles Cornwallis near Somerset Court House, capturing a large quantity of stores. He was promoted to major general and commander of the militia in June, and in November he made an attack on Staten Island. During June 1778 he conducted harassing and delaying operations around Philadelphia as British forces under Gen. Henry Clinton withdrew toward New York, and he performed gallantly in the battle of Monmouth Court House on June 27. On July 4, 1778, Dickinson acted as second to Gen. John Cadwalader in the duel in which Gen. Thomas Conway was wounded. During 1778–1779 he was chief signal officer of the Middle Department, and he took part in Gen. Nathanael Greene's repulse of Clinton at Springfield, New Jersey, on June 23, 1780. In 1782 he was elected to Congress from Delaware and during 1783–1784 he was vice-president of the New Jersey state council. He was named in 1784, with Robert Morris and Philip Schuyler, to a commission to select a site for a federal capital. In November 1790 he entered the Senate to fill William Paterson's unexpired term, remaining in that body until March 1793. He lived thereafter at his estate near Trenton and died there on February 4, 1809.

Dickman, Joseph Theodore (1857–1927), army

officer. Born in Dayton, Ohio, on October 6, 1857, Dickman graduated from West Point in 1881 and was commissioned in the 3rd Cavalry. For several years he was on duty in the West, taking part in the campaign against Geronimo and patrolling on the Mexican border. He graduated from the Infantry and Cavalry School, Fort Leavenworth, Kansas, in 1883 and was promoted first lieutenant in January 1886. He was an instructor at the Cavalry and Light Artillery School, Fort Riley, in 1893–1894 and at Fort Leavenworth in 1895–1898, receiving promotion to captain in May 1898. During the Spanish–American War he was on the staff of Gen. Joseph Wheeler in the Santiago campaign. In 1899–1900 he was in action against the Philippine Insurrection, being appointed major of volunteers in July 1899 and promoted to lieutenant colonel of volunteers in September. During the latter part of the Peking Relief Expedition in 1900, he was chief of staff to Gen. Adna R. Chaffee. Mustered out of the volunteers in May 1901, he was at Fort Leavenworth again in 1902 and the next year was named to the first General Staff. He graduated from the Army War College in 1905, was promoted to major in

March 1906, lieutenant colonel in February 1912, and colonel in December 1914, and was commander of the 2nd Cavalry from 1915 to 1917. In May 1917 he was promoted to brigadier general and in August appointed temporary major general in command of the 85th Infantry Division at Camp Custer, Michigan. In November he took over the 3rd Infantry Division; he was sent to France in March 1918 and was followed by the division in April. The 3rd went into combat at Château-Thierry on May 31 and held the Marne crossings against numerous attacks, including the final great German offensive of the war on July 15–16 when, while French lines on either side fell back, the 3rd held fast. The 3rd, and in particular the 38th Regiment under Col. Ulysses G. McAlexander, became known as the "Rock of the Marne." From August to October 1918 Dickman commanded the IV Corps, taking part in the St. Mihiel offensive; in October–November he commanded the I Corps in the Meuse–Argonne offensive. In November he was placed in command of the newly formed Third Army and remained in occupied Germany until April 1919. Promoted to regular major general in January 1919, he commanded the Southern Department (redesignated the VIII Corps area in 1920) until his retirement in October 1921. Dickman wrote a number of service manuals and also *The Great Crusade*, 1927, an account of his war experiences. He died in Washington, D.C., on October 23, 1927.

Dix, John Adams (1798–1879), army officer and

public official. Born in Boscawen, New Hampshire, on July 24, 1798, Dix was well educated at home, at Phillips Exeter Academy, and for a year at the College of Montreal. Although only fourteen at the outbreak of the War of 1812, he secured, with his father's aid, an army commission and saw battle at Lundy's Lane, July 25, 1814. After the war he remained in the army, for some years serving as aide to Gen. Jacob J. Brown, and rose to the rank of major while studying law and winning admission to the bar in 1824. Resigning his commission in July 1828, he settled in Cooperstown, New York, and began his law practice, becoming at the same time active in Democratic politics. In 1830 he was appointed state adjutant general, a post that made him one of the clique called the "Albany regency." From 1833 to 1839 he was secretary of state of New York and, as ex officio superintendent of public schools, made several notable contributions to education. In 1841 he served in the legislature and then returned to law; he also published the *Northern Light*, a scientific and literary journal, from 1841 to 1843. In January 1845 he was elected to fill an unexpired term in the Senate, where he was a prominent figure in the antislavery wing of the Democratic party. He supported Martin Van Buren on the Free-Soil ticket in 1848 and was himself that party's unsuccessful candidate for governor. Upon leaving the Senate in March 1849 he returned to his law practice and during the next several years held positions in a number of railroad companies; during his career he was president of both the Union Pacific (1863–1868) and Erie (1872) railroads. Attempts to appoint him to high political offices, including a cabinet post, were defeated by Southern Democrats, but in May 1860, following a scandal in the office, he was named postmaster of New York City by President James Buchanan. The great esteem in which he was held by the Eastern business community was reflected in his appointment as secretary of the treasury in January 1861. His two months in that position were of great value to the Union; he inspired the confidence of bankers by his efficient organization and personal integrity and of the general public by a famous telegraph message he sent to a treasury officer in New Orleans: "If anyone attempts to haul down the American flag, shoot him on the spot." In March 1861 President Abraham Lincoln commissioned Dix a major general of volunteers. He commanded various rear-area military districts, the last of which was New York, 1863–1865; despite his advancing age he was an effective administrator. From 1866 to 1869 he served as minister to France and in 1872, although still a Democrat, was nominated for governor of New York by the Republicans. Elected by a large majority, he served until 1874, when he was defeated for reelection by Samuel J. Tilden. He then retired to New York City, where he died on April 21, 1879. Fort Dix, in New Jersey, is named for him.

Dixon, William (1850–1913), frontiersman and scout. Born on September 25, 1850, in Ohio County in what is now West Virginia (then a part of Virginia), Billy Dixon was left an orphan at twelve and after living a couple of years with an uncle in Missouri he made his way westward to the frontier. From 1865 to 1869 he was a mule driver for the government, and then he took up buffalo hunting. He was one of 28 hunters at the trading post of Adobe Walls, on the Canadian River in the Texas Panhandle (present Hutchinson County) when some 700 Comanche warriors under Quanah attacked on June 27, 1874, and after conspicuous service in driving off the Indians he bore the news to Fort Dodge. There Col. Nelson A. Miles, commander of the 5th Infantry, appointed him a scout. On September 12 Dixon and five other men were set upon by more than a hundred Comanche and Kiowa warriors; all were wounded, but largely through the efforts of Dixon, who carried one of his companions to refuge, five survived, fought off the Indians, and in November were awarded the Medal of Honor. He continued in service as a scout until 1883, when he homesteaded in the Adobe Walls vicinity. Over the next 20 years he held a variety of local offices, including postmaster. In 1906 he moved to a new homestead in Cimarron County, Oklahoma. He died on March 9, 1913; his reminiscences, *Life and Adventures of "Billy" Dixon,* appeared the following year.

Dodge, Grenville Mellen (1831–1916), army officer and engineer. Born in Danvers, Massachusetts, on April 12, 1831, Dodge took a degree in civil and military engineering from Norwich University in 1851. He traveled west to Illinois, where after a year of surveying in and around the town of Peru, he secured a position with the Illinois Central Railroad. In 1853 he directed a large portion of a survey across Iowa for the Mississippi & Missouri Railroad; he subsequently settled in Council Bluffs, Iowa, and for the next several years engaged in railroad construction and in business ventures throughout the state. In 1856 he organized a militia company, the Council Bluffs Guards, and five years later volunteered its services for the Civil War. Commissioned colonel of the 4th Iowa Volunteers, he served in Missouri under Gen. John C. Frémont and commanded a brigade and was wounded at Pea Ridge, Arkansas, March 7–8, 1862, following which he was promoted to brigadier general of volunteers. He took part in the Vicksburg campaign and won high praise for his work in bridge and railroad construction and reconstruction for the army. For his actions at Sugar Valley, May 9, 1864, and Resaca, Georgia, May 14–15, in the Atlanta campaign, he was promoted to major general of volunteers in June, and he commanded the XVI Corps under Gen. William T. Sherman for the duration of the campaign. After recovering from a serious wound he took command of the Department of Missouri in December 1864. Receiving his discharge in May 1866, he entered upon the major phase of his career upon becoming chief engineer of the Union Pacific Railroad. He was elected to Congress in the same year, but after a single term he declined further service in order to devote full time to the Union Pacific. Although some preliminary work on the line running west from Omaha had been done, the bulk of the huge task fell upon Dodge, and he completed it with success and remarkable speed, the last spike being driven at Promontory Point, Utah, on May 10, 1869. The following year he left the Union Pacific and in 1871 became chief engineer for the Texas & Pacific Railroad. He was associated for many years with that line and several others in the Southwest, supervising construction of many. His last accomplishment was the completion of a trunk line from Santa Clara, Cuba, to Santiago de Cuba in 1903. During his career Dodge oversaw the building of more than 10,000 miles of railroad, and his surveys covered many times that distance. He also headed the Dodge Commission appointed by President William McKinley in 1898 to investigate the army's conduct, particularly in the commissary department, during the Spanish–American War; many changes in army organization resulted from his 1900 report. He retired to Council Bluffs and died there on January 3, 1916.

Dodge, Henry (1782–1867), army officer and public official. Born on October 12, 1782, in Vincennes, Indiana, Dodge grew up principally in Ste. Genevieve, then part of Spanish Louisiana (now Missouri). He became district sheriff in 1805 and territorial marshal in 1813. Early in the War of 1812 he commanded a volunteer company of mounted riflemen; he was commissioned major of militia in April 1813 and by the end of 1814 had risen to major general. In 1827 he removed to Wisconsin (then part of Michigan Territory), settling in the vicinity of present-day Dodgeville. He saw action during the Winnebago War in that year, and at the outbreak of Black Hawk's War in April 1832 he was appointed colonel of Michigan militia. In June President Andrew Jackson appointed him major in the regular army in command of a battalion of mounted rangers, and on July 21 he engaged Black Hawk in the indecisive battle of Wisconsin Heights. In March 1833 the mounted rangers were replaced by the 1st Dragoons and Dodge was promoted to colonel in command of the regiment. He campaigned against the Pawnee on the Red River in 1834 and as far west as the Rocky Mountains in 1835. In May 1836 he was appointed by Jackson governor of the newly organized Wisconsin Territory (comprising what are now Wisconsin, Minnesota, Iowa and parts of Michigan and the Dakotas), resigning from the army in July. He served also as superintendent of Indian affairs for the region. He was removed as governor by President John Tyler in 1841, and from that year to 1845 he served two terms as territorial delegate to Congress. President James K. Polk reappointed him governor in 1845, and he retained the post until Wisconsin achieved statehood in 1848, whereupon he was elected to the Senate, serving until 1857. He died in Burlington, Iowa, on June 19, 1867.

Doniphan, Alexander William (1808–1887), army officer and public official. Born on July 9, 1808, near Maysville, Kentucky, Doniphan graduated from Augusta College, Augusta, Kentucky, in 1826 and took up the study of law, winning admission to the bar in 1828. In 1830 he moved to Missouri, settling first in Lexington and then in Liberty, and quickly rose to prominence in the law. He was elected to the legislature in 1836 and 1840 and took an active role in the state militia, advancing to brigadier general. In 1838, at the height of the persecution of Mormons settled in Missouri, a military campaign against them was ordered by Gov. Boggs through the militia commander, Gen. Lucas. After the court-martial of Joseph Smith and other Mormon leaders, Doniphan was ordered to carry out the sentence of execution; he

refused, declaring such an act cold-blooded murder, and vowed he would bring to justice anyone who carried out the execution. (No one did.) Early in 1846 he organized and was elected colonel of the 1st Missouri Mounted Volunteers for service in the Mexican War. The regiment joined Gen. Stephen W. Kearny's Army of the West at Fort Leavenworth and marched with it to Santa Fe, where Doniphan was left in command of the New Mexico Territory after Kearny's departure for California. He concluded a treaty with the Navajo Indians (a treaty soon broken) and in December, turning command of the territory over to Col. Sterling Price, began an expedition against Mexico. On December 25, 1846, at the junction of the Brazito and the Rio Grande, he met and was challenged by a much superior force of Mexican troops; he returned the challenge and in a half-hour fight routed the Mexicans, who had 63 killed to none for the Americans. On December 27 he took possession of El Paso. Early in February 1847 he set out for Chihuahua and on February 28, at the Sacramento River, he encountered some 4000 Mexicans in fortified positions. With a quarter of the force, he attacked furiously, stormed and carried the Mexican position, and captured all the artillery and supplies; the Mexicans had 300 killed to Doniphan's 1. On March 1 he occupied Chihuahua. After a 700-mile march to Saltillo, the war in northern Mexico having ended, he led his men on to New Orleans, where they were mustered out. The expedition had covered 3600 miles on land, 2000 on water, in 12 months, with no supply line, regular equipment, communications, or even military order. Doniphan resumed his law practice and in 1854 was again elected to the legislature. In February 1861 he was a delegate to the Peace Conference in Washington, D.C. He opposed secession and urged neutrality for Missouri at the state convention. For two weeks in June 1861 he was major general of the state militia, resigning for family reasons. He spent the Civil War mainly in St. Louis. In 1868 he moved to Richmond, Missouri, where he died on August 8, 1887.

Donovan, William Joseph (1883–1959), army officer and public official. Born on January 1, 1883, in Buffalo, New York, "Wild Bill" Donovan graduated from Columbia University in 1905 and remained to take a law degree two years later. He began practice in Buffalo and in 1912 also began a military career by organizing a cavalry troop for the New York National Guard. He saw service on the Mexican border with his troop in 1916 and by the outbreak of World War I held the rank of major. Serving with the 27th Division and later as lieutenant colonel and colonel of the 165th Infantry—the former "Fighting 69th" New York regiment—he was three times wounded, won numerous decorations, including the Medal of Honor for gallantry in leading his regiment against the Hindenburg Line at Landres-et-St. Georges, October 14–15, 1918, in the Meuse–Argonne offensive. He had by that time already acquired the nickname "Wild Bill." After a time as an unofficial U.S. military observer in Asia, he resumed his law practice in 1920; becoming active in Republican politics, he served as U.S. district attorney for western New York from 1922 to 1924, as assistant U.S. attorney general from 1924 to 1925, and as assistant to the attorney general from 1925 to 1929. During that time he was also a member of several international commissions, including the Rio Grande Compact Commission, of which he was chairman, in 1928, and the Colorado River Commission, also as chairman from 1929. In the latter year he declined President Herbert C. Hoover's offer of the governorship of the Philippines. He ran unsuccessfully against Herbert H. Lehman for governor of New York in 1932. From 1935 to 1941 Donovan made a number of trips as an unofficial observer for the U.S. government to Italy, Spain, England, and the Balkans. He then drew up, at the request of President Franklin D. Roosevelt, comprehensive plans for a military intelligence agency to operate throughout the world. Upon creation of the Office of Strategic Services (OSS) in June 1942 Donovan was named to direct its activities. Given the rank of brigadier general in April 1943 and promoted to major general in November 1944, he oversaw the wide-ranging operations of the OSS, which gathered intelligence and operated clandestinely behind the lines in every theater of World War II, until its dissolution in October 1945. After brief service as aide to Justice Robert H. Jackson, chief U.S. prosecutor at the Nuremberg trials of Nazi war criminals, he again returned to private practice. On appointment by President Dwight D. Eisenhower he was U.S. ambassador to Thailand from 1953 to 1954. Donovan died on February 8, 1959, in Washington, D.C.

Dooley, Thomas Anthony (1927–1961), physician and naval officer. Born in St. Louis on January 17, 1927, Dooley entered the University of Notre Dame in 1944 but left shortly afterward to enlist in the navy. After two years of service in the Medical Corps he returned to Notre Dame to prepare for medical school. He took his M.D. from the St. Louis University School of Medicine in 1953 and began his internship as a medical officer with rank of lieutenant (junior grade) in the naval reserve; he was stationed first at Camp Pendleton, California, and later in Japan. In 1954 he volunteered for service on a ship bearing refugees from North to South Vietnam. The only medical man available for 2000 passengers, he was deeply impressed by the immensity of the medical needs of the people of Southeast Asia. He was then sent to Haiphong to organize and manage camps where refugees could await transportation south; with only minimal facilities, his small medical

unit processed and cared for more than 600,000 people in less than a year. Transferred back to the United States in 1955, he described his experiences in Vietnam in *Deliver Us from Evil*, 1956. Resigning from the navy, he used his income from the book to organize a private medical mission to the village of Nam Tha in northern Laos. Sheer persistence and untiring labor enabled him to overcome the suspicions of the people and to begin attacking the problems of disease among a populace largely deprived of modern medical knowledge. In 1957 he returned briefly to the United States and, with Peter D. Comanduras, founded Medico, an international medical-aid mission sponsored by the International Rescue Committee and supported by voluntary contributions. He then returned to Asia, setting up seven hospitals in Cambodia, Laos, and Vietnam. Dooley wrote two more books, *The Edge of Tomorrow*, 1958, and *The Night They Burned the Mountain*, 1960, again using his royalties for medical work. His last years were troubled by a malignant cancer; he visited the United States in 1959 for treatment and then a fund-raising tour, and returned again in late 1960. Hospitalized on the second visit, he died in New York City on January 18, 1961.

Doolittle, James Harold (1896–   ), army officer and airman. Born on December 14, 1896, in Alameda, California, Doolittle grew up there and in Nome, Alaska. He was educated at Los Angeles Junior College and the University of California, and in October 1917 he enlisted in the army reserve. Assigned to the Signal Corps, he served as a flying instructor during World War I, was commissioned first lieutenant in the Air Service, regular army, in July 1920, and became deeply involved in the development of military aviation. On September 4, 1922, he made the first transcontinental flight in under 24 hours. In 1922 he was granted a degree, as of 1918, by the University of California and then sent by the army to the Massachusetts Institute of Technology for advanced engineering studies, taking a Sc.D. degree in 1925. Assigned to various test-facility stations, he spent five more years in diverse phases of aviation, winning a number of trophy races, demonstrating aircraft in South America, and in September 1929 making the first successful test of blind, instrument-controlled landing techniques with equipment developed in conjunction with the Guggenheim Fund for the Promotion of Aeronautics. In February 1930 he resigned his active commission, retaining the reserve rank of major, and became manager of the aviation department of the Shell Oil Company, where he helped develop aviation fuels. He continued to race, winning the Harmon trophy in 1930 and the Bendix in 1931 and setting a world speed record in 1932, and to serve on various government and military consultative boards during this period.

In July 1940, shortly before U.S. entry into World War II, he returned to active duty as a major with the Army Air Corps, and after a tour of industrial plants then converting to war production he joined AAC headquarters for an extended period of planning that bore spectacular results on April 18, 1942. From the deck of the carrier *Hornet*, referred to publicly by President Franklin D. Roosevelt as the mysterious "Shangri-La," Doolittle, then a lieutenant colonel, led a flight of 16 B-25 bombers on a daring raid over Japan, hitting targets in Tokyo, Yokohama, and other cities and scoring a huge victory for U.S. morale at a time when Japan's position in the Pacific seemed impregnable. Promoted to brigadier general the next day and later awarded the Medal of Honor for the Japan raid, he was then transferred to England, where he organized the Twelfth Air Force in September 1942 and, promoted to temporary major general in November, commanded it during the invasion of North Africa. In successive command of the Strategic Command of the Allies' Northwest Africa Air Force under Gen. Carl Spaatz, March–November 1943, the Fifteenth Air Force (strategic arm of the Allied Mediterranean Air Forces, based at Foggia, Italy) from November 1943 to January 1944, and the Eighth Air Force in England from January 1944 to September 1945, Doolittle directed intensive strategic bombing of Germany during 1944–1945. He received promotion to temporary lieutenant general in March 1944. In 1945, when air operations ended in the European theater, he moved with the Eighth Air Force to Okinawa in the Pacific. In May 1946 he returned to reserve status and rejoined Shell Oil as vice-president and director. He served on the National Advisory Committee for Aeronautics from 1948 to 1958, the last two years as chairman; the Air Force Science Advisory Board as chairman in 1955; and the President's Science Advisory Committee in 1957. Doolittle retired from both the air force and Shell Oil in 1959, but remained active in the aerospace industry. He continued to serve on a great many advisory boards and committees on aerospace, intelligence, and national security.

Doubleday, Abner (1819–1893), army officer and sports figure. Born in Ballston Spa, New York, on June 26, 1819, Doubleday attended schools in Auburn and in Cooperstown, where he became known as an organizer of team ball games. After a time spent working as a surveyor he entered West Point. Graduating in 1842, he was assigned to the 3rd Artillery and during the Mexican War served under Gen. Zachary Taylor at Monterrey and elsewhere. He was promoted to first lieutenant in March 1847 and captain in March 1855. During 1856–1858 he saw action against the Seminoles in Florida and later was stationed at various posts on the Atlantic coast, in 1860 being assigned to Charleston Harbor, where on April 12, 1861, he manned the first of Fort Sumter's guns to respond to the sudden South Carolina bombardment. In May he was promoted to major and for nearly a year served with an infantry regiment in the Shenandoah valley and then in the defenses around Washington, D.C. In February 1862 he was made a brigadier general of volunteers and during the year took part in the major battles in Maryland and northern Virginia: the second battle of Bull Run (Manassas), South Mountain, Antietam, and Fredericksburg. Promoted to major general of volunteers in November 1862, he commanded a division at Gettysburg and on the death of Gen. J. F. Reynolds on the first day, July 1, 1863, he succeeded to command of the I Corps, holding the field against heavy odds. Despite his performance he was returned to divisional command upon the appointment of a new corps commander; bitterly disappointed, he nonetheless continued to render valuable service through the second and third days of the battle, particularly in the repulse of Pickett's Charge. Doubleday was thereafter on duty in Washington, and in January 1866 reverted to the regular rank of lieutenant colonel, to which he had been promoted in September 1863. He advanced to colonel in September 1867 and after service in Texas and San Francisco retired from the army in December 1873. He settled in Mendham, New Jersey, and died there on January 26, 1893. During the late years of the nineteenth century, as baseball grew into a national sport and pastime, much interest in its origins developed; many who championed the notion of baseball as a native American game nominated Doubleday as its originator, citing his sports activities in Cooperstown and giving the year 1839 for his invention of the game. The story became widespread and in 1907 Albert G. Spalding, baseball player and sporting goods manufacturer, set up a committee of leading figures in professional baseball to research the history of the game. In its 1908 report the committee ratified the common theory, which subsequently became firmly implanted in American lore. Later investigations showed that a game very similar to baseball, and often called by that name, had been played in America, and even in England, much before Doubleday's time. A variant of the traditional English game of rounders, it had been known in the American colonies as town-ball and by other names and resembled modern baseball much more closely than did the "one-(two, three, or four) old-cat" game cited as baseball's ancestor by the Spalding committee; old cat, a bat-and-ball game, was apparently played when there were too few players for baseball. Doubleday's name remained nonetheless connected with baseball; in 1920 the village of Cooperstown dedicated Doubleday Field as the game's birthplace and in 1939, the supposed centennial of the game's invention, the National Baseball Hall of Fame was established there.

Doughty, John (1754–1826), army officer. Born in New York in 1754, Doughty served in the Continental army through the Revolution and continued in it afterward, advancing to the rank of captain of artillery by 1784. On June 2 of that year Congress ordered the Continental army disbanded except for the artillery company at West Point, commanded by Doughty, and the one at Fort Pitt, in all 80 men. On June 20, either by specific appointment by Gen. George Washington (retired) or simply by force of seniority, Gen. Henry Knox retiring on that day, he became the senior ranking officer of the army. He was superseded on August 12 by Josiah Harmar, just returned from France and commissioned lieutenant colonel. In 1785 Doughty built Fort Harmar at the junction of the Muskingum and the Ohio rivers, where three years later the town of Marietta was begun, and in 1789–1790 he built Fort Washington at Losantiville, renamed in the latter year Cincinnati. He was promoted to major in 1789 and to lieutenant colonel in 1798. He resigned from the army in May 1800 and died in Morristown, New Jersey, on September 16, 1826. Doughty was the lowest ranking officer ever to be senior in the army, and it is through his company at West Point that Battery D, 5th Field Artillery Battalion (1st Infantry Division), claims descent from Alexander Hamilton's Provincial Company of Artillery of New York, organized in March 1776, and thereby title as the oldest unit in the United States army.

Douglas, Donald Wills (1892–   ), engineer and industrialist. Born in Brooklyn on April 6, 1892, Douglas attended the Naval Academy for three years, 1909–1912, and then transferred to the Massachusetts Institute of Technology in order to study aeronautical engineering. On graduating in 1914 he became an assistant to Jerome C. Hunsaker of the MIT aerodynamics laboratory. In 1915 he was appointed chief engineer of the Glenn L. Martin aircraft company in Los Angeles. On leave from the company he served as chief civilian aeronautical engineer for the army Signal Corps in 1916–1917. In 1920, by that time a vice-president of the Martin firm, he formed with a partner the Davis–Douglas Company in Santa Monica, California. (The firm became the Douglas Company a year later.) By mid-1921 he had built and successfully demonstrated his streamlined "Cloudster" biplane and won a navy contract for three such craft adapted to torpedo bombing. In 1924 he completed an army contract for four DWC aircraft, subsequently designated Douglas–Liberty 400s, two of which in April–September made the first around-the-world flight in 175 days. In 1928 the company was reorganized as the Douglas Aircraft Company, with Douglas continuing as president, and in 1932 the Northrop Corporation was acquired. Aircraft designed and built at Douglas during its formative

years included the DC-1 (1932) which evolved in four years into the DC-3, one of the most functional and reliable aircraft ever built, later modified for military use as the workhorse C-47 Skytrain; the DC-4 (1938), later modified into the C-54 Skymaster; the A-20 Havoc light bomber, also made into a fighter as the P-70 (1939); the SBD (A-24) Dauntless navy dive bomber (1939); the B-19 heavy bomber (1941); the A-26 Invader attack bomber (1944); the C-74 Globemaster (1945); and the DC-6 (1948). Douglas remained president of the company until 1957, when he became chairman of the board and chief executive officer; in 1967, on the merger of Douglas Aircraft into the McDonnell Douglas Corporation, he was named honorary chairman of the board. He was the recipient of numerous honors for his contributions to aeronautical progress.

Downes, John (1784–1854), naval officer. Born in Canton, Massachusetts, on December 23, 1784, Downes entered the navy in September 1800 as acting midshipman and became midshipman two years later. He served aboard the frigate *New York* under Capt. James Barron in the Tripolitan War and in May 1803 took part in Lt. David Porter's boat raid on Tripolitan feluccas. He was promoted to lieutenant in March 1807. In 1809 he joined the frigate *Essex*, Capt. Porter, and was still with her when, in October 1812, she began one of the most remarkable cruises of the War of 1812. Sailing from Delaware, the *Essex* became the first American man-of-war to enter the Pacific Ocean, where in April Downes captured two prizes, one of which was fitted out as a cruiser with Downes in command. In June he captured the privateer *Hector*. A larger prize taken by Porter was recommissioned *Essex Junior*, 20 guns, and placed under Downes. In October Porter's squadron put in at Nuku Hiva in the Marquesas Islands to refit, and on November 27 Downes led a shore party of 35 sailors and marines, with native allies, against several thousand hostile islanders, suffering a broken leg in the battle. On March 28, 1814, the *Essex* and *Essex Junior* engaged the British frigate *Phoebe*, 53, and sloop *Cherub*, 28, off Valparaiso, and after the bloody fight and the surrender of the *Essex* Downes returned home with Porter and the other survivors on the disarmed *Essex Junior*. He had been promoted to master commandant in 1813, and in May 1815 he set sail for Algiers in command of the brig *Epervier*, 18, in Commodore Stephen Decatur's squadron. He played a leading role in the capture of the Algerian flagship *Mashuda*, 46, on June 17, 1815, and for a time was given command of Decatur's flagship, the *Guerrière*. Downes was promoted to captain in March 1817 and in 1818 he undertook a lengthy Pacific cruise in command of the frigate *Macedonian*. During more than two years in the Pacific the *Macedonian* rendered valuable services to American shipping and whaling vessels. During 1828–1830 Downes was in the Mediterranean aboard the *Java*, and early in 1832 he sailed from New York aboard the frigate *Potomac*, bound for Sumatra by way of Cape Town. On February 6, 1832, he reached the town of Quallah Battoo (Kualabatee), on the west coast of northern Sumatra, where the merchant ship *Friendship*, out of Salem, Massachusetts, had lately been attacked and plundered. Downes landed a force of 282 sailors and marines which captured 3 forts, burned the town, and killed 150 Malays; the *Potomac* reduced a fourth fort by gunfire. Having extracted a pledge of good behavior in the future, Downes made several more calls across the Pacific and returned to the United States in May 1834. He was thereafter on shore duty, commanding the Boston navy yard in 1835–1842 and again in 1849–1852. He died in Charlestown, Massachusetts, on August 11, 1854.

Du Coudray, Philippe Charles (1738–1777), engineer and Revolutionary army officer. Born on September 8, 1738, in Reims, France, Du Coudray, whose full given name was Philippe Charles Jean Baptiste Tronson, was educated as a mining engineer in the army. After distinguished service in the Corsican campaign of 1768–1769 he became adjutant general of artillery. In 1776 he offered his services to Benjamin Franklin and Silas Deane in Paris and was promised a commission as major general and command of the artillery in exchange for a certain quantity of supplies. His claim to command of the artillery and the engineers aroused considerable bitterness upon his arrival in America in June 1777, and several senior officers, including generals Henry Knox, John Sullivan, and Nathanael Greene, threatened to resign. At length he allowed his claim to lapse, and in August he accepted the post of inspector general of the Continental army with the rank of major general. He had charge of the defensive works on the Delaware River for a time thereafter. While rushing to take part in the battle on Brandywine Creek to the west, on September 11, 1777, he was thrown from his frightened horse while crossing the Schuylkill river by ferry and drowned.

Duffy, Francis Patrick (1871–1932), clergyman. Born on May 2, 1871, in Cobourg, Ontario, Duffy graduated from St. Michael's College, University of Toronto, in 1893. He took a master's degree from St. Francis Xavier College in New York City in 1894, and after two years at St. Joseph's Seminary in Troy, New York, he was ordained a priest of the Roman Catholic church in September 1896. In 1898 he received an S.T.B. degree from Catholic University, Washington, D.C., and then was appointed to the faculty of St. Joseph's Seminary in Yonkers, New York, where he remained until 1912. He was naturalized a U.S. citizen in 1902. In 1912 he established Our Saviour par-

ish in the Bronx. In 1915 Father Duffy, who had served as a chaplain at Montauk Point during the Spanish–American War, was appointed chaplain to the 69th Regiment, New York National Guard, the "Fighting 69th" of heavily Irish accent. Upon mobilization of the National Guard for World War I service, the 69th became the 165th Infantry Regiment of the 42nd ("Rainbow") Division. The 165th, under Col. Frank R. McCoy and then Col. William J. Donovan, saw heavy action in the Champagne–Marne, St. Mihiel, and Meuse–Argonne operations, and Father (Captain and later Major) Duffy served alongside the soldiers, caring for wounded, consoling, cheering. He was enormously popular with the men in his care and with other chaplains of the division, of whom he was the acknowledged head. "The way the Clergy of different churches got along in peace and harmony in this Division," he said, "would be a scandal to pious minds." His wartime services brought him many decorations, including the Distinguished Service Cross, the Distinguished Service Medal, and the Croix de Guerre, and on his return home he was a great popular hero in New York. *Father Duffy's Story* was published in 1920. He continued to serve as chaplain to the 165th, being promoted to lieutenant colonel in 1928. In 1921 he became pastor of Holy Cross parish in New York City, with which he remained until his death. In 1926 he became president of the Catholic Summer School of America (affiliated with Fordham University from 1928). He died in New York City on June 26, 1932; five years later a statue of him was placed in Times Square.

Du Pont, Henry Algernon (1838–1926), army officer, businessman, and public official. Born near Wilmington, Delaware, on July 30, 1838, Du Pont was a grandson of Éleuthère Irénée Du Pont, founder of the American Du Ponts, and a cousin of Samuel Francis Du Pont. He graduated at the head of his class from West Point in 1861, was commissioned in the engineers, and was promptly promoted to first lieutenant. The first three years of the Civil War he spent mainly in defensive and staff posts, but soon after his promotion to captain in March 1864 he became involved in active field service. He took part with the 5th Artillery in the battle of New Market, Virginia, May 15, 1864, skillfully covering the retreat of Gen. Franz Sigel, and shortly thereafter was appointed chief of artillery for the Department of West Virginia. He was in the battles of Piedmont, Lexington, and Lynchburg during June and in July was appointed chief of artillery of the Army of West Virginia under Gen. David Hunter. He was at Halltown, August 23; Berryville, September 3; Winchester, September 19; for his actions at Fisher's Hill, September 22, he was brevetted major; and for his part in the battle at Cedar Creek, October 19, he was brevetted lieutenant colonel and awarded the Medal of Honor (awarded in 1898). After the war he held various artillery and post commands in the East and in 1873–1874 served on a board of officers appointed to assimilate the tactics of the artillery, infantry, and cavalry arms. He resigned from the army in March 1875 and from 1878 associated himself with the family business. He was also president of the Wilmington and Northern Railroad from 1879 to 1899, and in the latter year became a vice-president of the reorganized and incorporated E. I. du Pont de Nemours Co. He retired from business in 1902. He had been elected to the Senate by the Delaware legislature in 1895, but the election was disputed and he at length was not seated. He was elected to an unexpired term in June 1906 and reelected in 1911, retaining his seat until March 1917. In later years he undertook considerable literary work, publishing, among other books, *The Campaign of 1864 in the Valley of Virginia*, 1925, and *Rear-Admiral Samuel Francis Du Pont, a Biography*, 1926. He died in Wilmington, Delaware, on December 31, 1926.

Du Pont, Samuel Francis (1830–1865), naval officer. Born on September 27, 1803, in Bergen Point, New Jersey, Du Pont, a grandson of Pierre Samuel du Pont de Nemours, moved with his family to Angelica, New York, and later to Delaware. In December 1815 he was offered by President James Madison his choice of appointments to West Point and as a midshipman; he chose the midshipman's berth out of enthusiasm for the navy's exploits in the War of 1812. His first sea duty, a Mediterranean cruise on the *Franklin*, was in 1817; for 30 years he served on a succession of ships in European and South American waters, rising to lieutenant in April 1826 and to commander in January 1843. In 1845 he sailed to the Pacific in command of the *Congress*, flagship of Commodore Robert F. Stockton. In July 1846, just returned to San Francisco from Hawaii, he took command of the sloop of war *Cyane*, aboard which he transported Maj. John C. Frémont's troops to San Diego, which was occupied by a landing party from the *Cyane* under Lt. Stephen C. Rowan, then continued south and entered the Gulf of California where, in a series of sea battles and daring landings, notably at Guaymas, Mazatlán, and San José, he cleared the waters and the coastal area entirely of Mexican forces. In the later operations he cooperated with Commodore William B. Shubrick. On his return to Norfolk, Virginia, in October 1848 he was commended officially. For several years he was on shore duty, aiding in organizing the work of the new Naval Academy, promoting the adoption of steam power by the navy, and serving on the Lighthouse Board. In 1855 he was a member of a board appointed to evaluate all officers of the navy; the board's report, finding 201 officers incompetent, was accepted by the Department of the Navy but aroused a storm of public

and congressional criticism, most of which fell on Du Pont personally. He was nonetheless promoted to captain in September of that year. Following a China cruise in command of the new frigate *Minnesota* in 1857–1859 he was named commandant of the navy yard in Philadelphia in 1860, and in June 1861 became senior member of the navy's Commission of Conference to plan sea operations and strategy for the Civil War. In September 1861 Du Pont became commander, or "flag-officer," of the South Atlantic Blockading Squadron and was assigned to carry out an attack on Port Royal, South Carolina. Despite widespread doubts about the possibility of capturing land fortifications from the sea, he managed the operation brilliantly. Port Royal and its two forts, Walker and Beauregard, were taken with minimal losses on November 7 (Du Pont himself, aboard flagship *Wabash*, led the column attacking the forts), providing the Blockading Squadron with an invaluable southern base. A large army force under Gen. Thomas W. Sherman was used principally for occupation duty after being landed from transports. He was rewarded with the thanks of Congress and in July 1862 with promotion to rear admiral. Further successes in coastal operations followed, and in February 1863 he was ordered to attempt the capture of Charleston, South Carolina, a haven for blockade runners and a much more heavily defended stronghold than Port Royal. Although he was provided with a number of ironclads and monitors for the mission, he was himself dubious as to their value in such an undertaking, and his doubts were reinforced by a series of trial attacks on Fort McAllister by Commander John L. Worden. Nonetheless he entered Charleston harbor with his flagship, the ironclad *New Ironsides*, seven monitors, and a gunboat on April 7, suffered severe damage from the batteries of Fort Sumter, and in two hours was forced out to sea. His offer to turn over his command was accepted; in July, just after the capture of the Confederate ironclad *Atlanta* by Capt. John Rodgers of his squadron, he was replaced by Adm. John A. B. Dahlgren. He retired to his home near Wilmington, Delaware, and took little part in naval affairs thereafter, although for some time he engaged in a dispute with Secretary of the Navy Gideon Welles over responsibility for the failure of the Charleston attack. Du Pont died in Philadelphia on June 23, 1865. In 1882 Du Pont Circle in Washington, D.C., was named for him, as was the fountain by sculptor Daniel Chester French unveiled there in 1921.

Duportail, Louis Lebèque (1743–1802), engineer and Revolutionary army officer. Born in 1743 in Pithiviers, France, Duportail was educated at the military school of Mézières and acquired a high reputation as a military engineer. He was engaged by Benjamin Franklin and Silas Deane for service in the

Revolution in 1776 and was commissioned colonel of engineers. In November 1777 he was advanced to brigadier general. In December of that year he helped select and fortify the site at Valley Forge for the Continental army's winter encampment. He took part in the battle of Monmouth, New Jersey, June 27, 1778. In October 1781 Duportail had charge of the engineering operations during the siege of Yorktown, a classic example of the 18th century tactic of approach by lines of parallel trenches. In November he was promoted to major general. He returned to France in 1782 and was made a field marshal in 1788. During that time he assisted in the reorganization of the army of the kingdom of Naples. He was appointed minister of war in November 1790, but with the fall from favor of his friend and patron Lafayette he was forced to resign in December 1791. He resigned from the army under threat in 1792 and in 1794 entered secret exile in America. In 1802 he sailed for France but died at sea.

Dye, William McEntyre (1831–1899), army officer. Born in Pennsylvania in February 1831, Dye won appointment to West Point from Mansfield, Ohio, where he lived with a guardian. Little else is known of his early years. Graduating in 1853, he served with the 8th Infantry in routine frontier and garrison duties until the Civil War, advancing to the rank of captain in May 1861. After a period of recruiting work he was appointed colonel of the 20th Iowa Volunteers in August 1862 and served with them in Missouri and Arkansas. At Vicksburg he won brevet rank of major in the regular army, and he was advanced to brevet lieutenant colonel for his performance in the Red River campaign under Gen. Nathaniel P. Banks in May 1864. At Mobile in September 1864 he was briefly in command of a brigade. After service as assistant provost marshal general of Kansas, Nebraska, Colorado, and Dakota, he was again brevetted to brigadier general of volunteers in March 1865 and to colonel of regulars in April. On being mustered out of volunteer service in July 1865 he reverted to his permanent rank of captain; in January 1866 he was promoted to major of the 4th Infantry. The peacetime army failed to satisfy him, however, and in September 1870 he was discharged at his own request. A period of farming in Marion, Iowa, followed, but in 1873 he eagerly accepted a commission in the army of Khedive Ismail Pasha of Egypt, and in 1875 he was assistant to Gen. Charles P. Stone, the chief of staff, in that army's expedition against Abyssinia. A wound sustained in that campaign together with a personal dispute with an Egyptian offi-

cer led to his resignation and return to the United States in June 1878. A record of his experiences appeared as *Moslem Egypt and Christian Abyssinia, or Military Service Under the Khedive* in 1880. Dye held the post of chief of police of Washington, D.C., for several years until 1888, when, at the suggestion of Gen. Philip Sheridan, he sought further military employment in Korea. As chief military adviser to the Korean government he attempted to organize and train an army along modern lines and to develop a body of military doctrine suitable to that nation. His success was limited by the feudal character of Korean society and, more importantly, by the interference in Korean affairs of Japan and China. After the outbreak of the Chinese–Japanese war in 1894 Dye's military role was essentially ended, but he was retained by King Kojong as a sort of bodyguard until 1896, when the king surrendered himself to Russian protection. Dye remained in Korea as supervisor of an experimental farm until May 1899, when he returned to the United States. He died in Muskegon, Michigan, on November 13, 1899.

Dyer, Alexander Brydie (1815–1874), army officer. Born on January 10, 1815, in Richmond, Virginia, Dyer graduated from West Point in 1837 and was commissioned in the artillery. He served in the second Seminole War in Florida in 1837–1838 and in the latter year was transferred to the Ordnance Corps. In 1846 he was appointed chief of ordnance, Army of the West, under Gen. Stephen W. Kearny, and he served through the New Mexico campaign, being wounded at Taos, February 4, 1847, and twice brevetted, to first lieutenant and to captain. He was promoted to captain in March 1853, and for several years he commanded the North Carolina arsenal. He remained loyal at the outbreak of the Civil War and in August 1861 was assigned to command of the National Armory, Springfield, Massachusetts. His energetic and efficient conduct of that post resulted in a rapid expansion of the armory and a huge increase in its output, up to a thousand rifles a day. He himself invented a cannon projectile that was accepted by the government, although he refused reward for it. Dyer was promoted to major in March 1863. In September 1864 he was named chief of ordnance of the army, with the rank of brigadier general. He conducted his office, in many ways perhaps the most important staff department, with great skill, and in March 1865 he was brevetted major general for his efforts. He continued after the war as chief of ordnance until his death in Washington, D.C., on May 20, 1874.

E

Eaker, Ira Clarence (1896–   ), army officer and airman. Born in Field Creek, Llano County, Texas, on April 13, 1896, Eaker graduated from Southeastern State Teachers College, Oklahoma, in 1917 and later in the year took a reserve commission in the infantry. In November he was transferred to the aviation section, Signal Corps, and ten months later was a rated pilot and first lieutenant. During 1919–1922, while stationed in the Philippines, he continued his studies at the University of the Philippines, advancing to captain in July 1920; and in 1922, while at Mitchel Field, New York, he took law courses at Columbia University. From 1924 to 1926 he was in the office of the chief of the Air Service, and during 1926–1927 he was one of the pilots in a Pan-American Flight goodwill tour. In January 1929, while detached from his station at Bolling Field, Washington, D.C., Eaker was one of the pilots (Maj. Carl Spaatz was another) who kept a Fokker monoplane, the *Question Mark*, aloft over Los Angeles for a record 150 hours. In 1932 he entered the University of Southern California, from which he took a journalism degree in 1933. Promoted to major in 1935, he graduated from the Air Corps Tactical School in 1936 and from the Command and General Staff School in 1937. In 1936 he made the first transcontinental flight purely on instruments, and in the same year he and Gen. Henry H. Arnold published *This Flying Game* (they later published *Winged Warfare*, 1941, and *Army Flyer*, 1942). In 1937 Eaker returned to duty in the office of the chief of the Air Corps, becoming temporary lieutenant colonel in December and permanent in August 1940. As temporary colonel in 1941 he took command of the 20th Pursuit Group at Mitchel Field. He was promoted to temporary brigadier general in January 1942, and in July of that year he was named to command of the 8th Bomber Command, based in England. On August 17, 1942, he led the first heavy-bomber (B-17) attack on continental Europe, a raid on Rouen, France. Promoted to temporary major general in September, he became commander of the Eighth Air Force in December. The Eighth carried on a sustained campaign of precision daylight bombing attacks against industrial and military targets across Europe. Eaker was promoted to temporary lieutenant general in September 1943, and in January 1944 he was named commander of the Mediterranean Allied Air Forces, in which post he planned the shuttle-bombing missions to Russia and led the first of them in June. From 1945 to his retirement in August 1947 he was deputy commander of the army air forces and chief of the air staff. From 1947 to 1957 he was a vice-president of the Hughes Tool Company; from 1957 to 1961 he was a vice-president of Douglas Aircraft; and from 1961 he was chairman of the advisory board of Hughes Aircraft Company. Eaker was one of the founding pioneers of modern concepts of strategic air power, and he was inducted into the Aviation Hall of Fame, Dayton, Ohio, in 1970.

Early, Jubal Anderson (1816–1894), Confederate army officer. Born in Franklin County, Virginia, on November 3, 1816, Early graduated from West Point in 1837, was commissioned in the 3rd Artillery, and was immediately sent to take part in the Seminole War in Florida. He resigned his commission the following year, shortly after his promotion to first lieutenant in July, and took up the study of law, winning admission to the bar in 1840. Aside from a term in the Virginia legislature in 1841–1842 his only public service before the Civil War was as a major of a Virginia militia regiment in the Mexican War, during which he saw little but garrison duty in northern Mexico. Early vigorously opposed Virginia's secession, but when war broke out he quickly offered his services and as colonel of the 24th Virginia Infantry took a creditable part in the first battle of Manassas (Bull Run), July 21, 1861. Promoted to brigadier general and in January 1863 to major general, he served with the Army of Northern Virginia throughout the campaigns of 1861–1863. In May 1864 he was promoted to lieutenant general and given a large and completely independent command, the II Corps, in the Shenandoah valley, where his assignment was to draw Union forces away from Richmond. Faced with little opposition, he swept down the valley gathering provisions and preparing for an attack on Washington itself. Union forces in the valley, under Gen. David Hunter, kept well ahead of him. Early crossed the Potomac and at the Monocacy River engaged and defeated a small force under Gen. Lew Wallace; this delayed him for two days, time enough for Gen. Ulysses S. Grant to dispatch two corps to defend Washington. On July 11 Early's advance troops entered the District of Columbia; within sight of the Capitol, in action viewed by President Abraham Lincoln, he skirmished about Fort Stevens for two days before retiring to the Shenandoah valley. There his forces ranged and raided freely (as far as Chambersburg, Pennsylvania, burned July 30) until the appearance of Gen. Philip H. Sheridan, by whom he was defeated at Winchester (Opequon Creek) and Fisher's Hill, September 19 and 22 and, after Sheridan's famous "20-mile ride," at Cedar Creek, October 19. Finally, on March 2, 1865, his forces were virtually destroyed by Sheridan at Waynesboro. Removed from command, Early set out for the West; following the Confederate surrender in April he continued on to Mexico, later sailing to Canada, where he published his *Memoir of the Last Year of the War for Independence in the Confederate States of America*, 1866. In 1867 he returned to Virginia and soon resumed his law practice in Lynchburg. His widespread unpopularity following Waynesboro gradually gave way to general admiration in the South, largely because he refused to the end of his life to be reconciled to the Confederate defeat. In later years he was for a time president of the Southern Historical Society and was briefly associated in the management of the Louisiana lottery with Gen. P. G. T. Beauregard. Early died in Lynchburg, Virginia, on March 2, 1894.

Eaton, William (1764–1811), army officer and diplomat. Born in Woodstock, Connecticut, on February 23, 1764, Eaton ran away from home in 1780 to join the Continental army in the last months of the Revolutionary War. Afterward he entered Dartmouth College and, supporting himself by teaching school, graduated finally in 1790. In March 1792, while teaching in Windsor, Vermont, he secured a captain's commission in the army and in the years following saw duty against the Indians in Ohio and in Georgia, and as a secret investigator of the Blount conspiracy in Tennessee in 1797. His performances, particularly in the last assignment, attracted the notice and then the patronage of Secretary of State Timothy Pickering, who in 1798 persuaded President John Adams to appoint Eaton U.S. consul in Tunis. There he renegotiated a treaty that had been rejected by the Senate. In May 1801 the neighboring state of Tripoli, under the rule of a usurper, declared war on the United States in an effort to extort larger tributes for the "protection" of Mediterranean shipping from the Barbary pirates. Eaton conceived the idea of helping the dethroned pasha, Hamet Karamanli, to regain control, and in 1803 he returned to the United States to win over President Thomas Jefferson to his plan. In 1804, with official approval, he sailed to Upper Egypt, located the exiled Karamanli, and with him and a handful of U.S. marines set out on a 500-mile trek across the Libyan Desert, gathering a motley army of Greeks, Arabs, and others along the way. In April 1805 he arrived at the city of Derna, which, with the aid of three U.S. warships under Capt. Isaac Hull, he occupied. Before he was able to march on Tripoli, however, he was ordered to abandon his plan

and leave the region while a treaty ending the Tripolitan War was negotiated with the usurper. Embittered, he returned to the United States. His last years were marked by almost constant public bickering over what he believed to have been a personal humiliation. In 1807–1808 he served a term in the Massachusetts legislature. Eaton died in Brimfield, Massachusetts, on June 1, 1811.

Eberle, Edward Walter (1864–1929), naval officer. Born on August 17, 1864, in Denton, Texas, Eberle grew up in Fort Smith, Arkansas. He graduated from the Naval Academy in 1885 and for nine years served in routine duties in the Atlantic, Pacific, and Asiatic stations and for a time in charting and survey work. In June 1896 he was promoted to lieutenant (junior grade) and assigned to the battleship *Oregon*, then still under construction in San Francisco, and he was aboard her during the famous run around Cape Horn to the Caribbean in 1898 and in the battle of Santiago. On the *Oregon* he went then to the Philippines and as acting chief of staff of the Asiatic Fleet took part in the suppression of the Philippine Insurrection. He was promoted to lieutenant in March 1899. From late 1899 to 1901 he was on the staff of the Naval Academy, where he wrote *Gun and Torpedo Drills*, the first such manual for modern weapons. After a year as gunnery officer of the *Indiana* he was from 1903 to 1905 flag lieutenant to the commander, Atlantic Fleet, in which post he aided in the first installations of radio equipment on naval vessels and drew up the first instructions and codes for its use. He advanced to lieutenant commander in November 1904. He attended the Naval War College in 1905, served on the *Louisiana* in 1907–1908 during the first leg of the great world cruise of the fleet, was commandant of the San Francisco Training Station in 1908–1910, receiving promotion to commander in December 1908, and commanded the *Wheeling* and the *Petrel* on a world cruise in 1910–1911. During 1911–1913 he commanded the Atlantic Torpedo Fleet and in that post he devised smokescreen, minelaying, minesweeping, and air antisubmarine tactics. He was promoted to captain in July 1912. In 1914 he commanded naval forces at Santo Domingo (Dominican Republic) and aided in the suppression of the revolt and the election of a new government. From 1915 to 1919 he was superintendent of the Naval Academy, his temporary promotion to rear admiral of February 1918 becoming permanent in July 1919. During 1919–1921 he commanded the 5th and then the 7th Battleship divisions, Atlantic Fleet; and in 1921, with the temporary rank of admiral, he undertook the reorganization of the Pacific Fleet into the Battle Fleet. During these years he led in incorporating aircraft into naval tactics. From July 1923 to November 1927 Eberle was chief of naval operations. He then served as chairman of the executive committee of the navy's

General Board until his retirement in August 1928. He died in Washington, D.C., on July 6, 1929.

Edmonds, Sarah Emma Evelyn (1841–1898),

soldier. Born in December 1841 in New Brunswick (probably in York County), Sarah Edmonson, or Edmondson, received scant education as a child, and sometime in the 1850s she ran away from home. For a time she was an itinerant seller of Bibles, dressing as a man and using the name Frank Thompson. She gradually made her way west and by 1861 was living in Flint, Michigan. Shortly after the outbreak of the Civil War she enlisted, as Frank Thompson, in a volunteer infantry company in Flint that became Company F, 2nd Michigan Infantry. Her disguise was a complete success for nearly a year. She took part in the battles of Blackburn's Ford and first Bull Run and in the Peninsular campaign of May-July 1862; and at Fredericksburg, December 13, 1862, she was an aide to Col. Orlando M. Poe. Twice or more she undertook intelligence missions behind Confederate lines "disguised" as a woman. She accompanied the 2nd Michigan to Kentucky early in 1863 and in April, for reasons that are now unclear, deserted. Taking the name Sarah Edmonds, she worked as a nurse for the United States Christian Commission. In 1865 she published a lurid and very popular fictional account of her experiences as *Nurse and Spy in the Union Army*. She married in 1867 and thereafter moved often—to Michigan, Illinois, Ohio, Louisiana, Kansas. In 1882, living then in Fort Scott, Kansas, she began securing affidavits from old army comrades in order to apply for a veteran's pension, and in July 1884 the pension was granted by Congress to "Sarah E. E. Seelye [her married name], alias Frank Thompson." She later moved to La Porte, Texas, where she died on September 5, 1898. A short time before, she had in Houston become the only woman to be mustered into the Grand Army of the Republic as a regular member.

Eichelberger, Robert Lawrence (1886–1961),

army officer. Born in Urbana, Ohio, on March 9, 1886, Eichelberger attended Ohio State University from 1903 to 1905 and then entered West Point, graduating in 1909. Commissioned in the infantry, he was promoted to first lieutenant in 1915 and to captain in 1917, serving at various posts, particularly in the South and Southwest. He was engaged in training and General Staff work early in World War I, but in August 1918, with temporary rank of major, he was appointed assistant chief of staff of the American Expeditionary Force in Siberia under Gen. William S. Graves. His exploits in Siberia brought him several decorations and advancement to temporary lieutenant colonel in 1919. In April 1920 he was sent to the Philippines and later in the year to Tientsin, China, receiving promotion to permanent major. From 1921

to 1924 he was attached to the military intelligence division of the General Staff, except for a period in 1922 when he was American liaison officer with the Chinese delegation to the Limitation of Armaments Conference in Washington, D.C. Eichelberger graduated from the Command and General Staff School in 1926 and remained at Fort Leavenworth, Kansas, as a staff officer for three more years; in 1930 he graduated from the Army War College. From 1931 to 1935 he was adjutant and secretary at West Point, advancing to lieutenant colonel in 1934, and from 1935 to 1938 he was secretary of the General Staff. In August 1938 he was promoted to colonel, and shortly thereafter he took command of the 30th Infantry at the Presidio, San Francisco. Promoted to temporary brigadier general in November 1940, he was named superintendent of West Point. In March 1942 he took command of the 77th Infantry Division, with temporary rank of major general. In June he briefly commanded the XI Corps and then took over the I Corps, advancing to temporary lieutenant general in October. The I Corps, after assembling in Australia, went into combat in September 1942 in the Papua peninsula of New Guinea and in January 1943 achieved one of the first major ground victories in the Southwest Pacific campaign in taking Buna. The New Guinea–New Britain operation continued through 1943 and into 1944. In September 1944 Eichelberger was named commander of the Eighth Army. The Eighth followed Gen. Walter Krueger's Sixth Army into Leyte, Philippines, in December 1944, moved onto Luzon in January 1945, and subsequently made amphibious assaults on Palawan, Zamboanga, the Sulu Archipelago, Cebu, Bohol, and Negros. In July the Eighth took responsibility for the entire Philippines. On August 30 Eichelberger arrived at Atsugi Airdrome to begin the occupation of Japan; he remained in command of the Eighth Army, which in January 1946 assumed responsibility for all ground forces in Japan, until his retirement in September 1948. In 1950 he published *Our Jungle Road to Tokyo*. He was promoted to the rank of general, retired, in July 1954, and he died on September 26, 1961, in Asheville, North Carolina.

Eisenhower, Dwight David (1890–1969), army

officer and thirty-fourth president of the United States. Born on October 14, 1890, in Denison, Texas, "Ike" Eisenhower moved with his family in the following year to Abilene, Kansas, where he grew up in modest circumstances. In 1911 he was appointed to West Point; after his graduation four years later he served at a succession of army installations around the world, rising slowly but steadily in rank and responsibility. During World War I he was engaged in training duties and rose to temporary rank of lieutenant colonel. He was promoted to major in 1920. During 1922–1924 he served in Panama. In 1926 he graduated at the top of his class from the Command and General Staff School, Fort Leavenworth, Kansas, and two years later he graduated from the Army War College. From 1933 to 1935 he was in the office of the chief of staff in Washington, D.C., and from 1935 to 1939 in the Philippines, receiving promotion to lieutenant colonel in 1936, and in both assignments serving under Gen. Douglas MacArthur. His performance as chief of staff of the Third Army during training maneuvers in 1941 brought him promotion to temporary brigadier general in September. Soon after the Japanese attack on Pearl Harbor in December 1941 brought the United States into World War II, he was called to the War Plans Division of the army's staff headquarters in Washington. Promoted to temporary major general in April 1942, he became in June 1942 commander of the U.S. forces in Europe and began the task, both arduous and delicate, of planning the Allies' invasion of the European continent. Promoted to temporary lieutenant general in July, he was named Allied commander in chief for the invasion of North Africa that began in November 1942, and the following year he planned and directed Allied invasions of Sicily and Italy. In North Africa his principal force was eventually organized as the II Corps under Gen. George S. Patton. The Sicily assault, beginning July 10, 1943, was made by Patton's Seventh Army and British Gen. Bernard Montgomery's Eighth, comprising together the 15th Army Group under Gen. Sir Harold R. L. G. Alexander. The Italian campaign commenced with Montgomery's landing on September 3, followed by Gen. Mark W. Clark's Fifth Army at Salerno on September 9. Eisenhower became a temporary full general in February 1943. In November 1943 he returned to England to resume personal supervision of the planning of the invasion of France, becoming supreme commander, Allied Expeditionary Force, the next month. (In August 1943 he was promoted to permanent brigadier and major general.) In that post he oversaw the D-Day landing on June 6, 1944, and the subsequent campaigns leading to the surrender of Germany nearly a year later. The ground forces under his command consisted principally of the Sixth Army Group (Gen. Jacob L. Devers), the 12th Army Group (Gen. Omar N. Bradley), and the 21st Army Group (Field Marshal Bernard Montgomery); in addition he had at his disposal the First Allied Airborne Army (Gen. Lewis H. Brereton), the Eighth and Ninth air forces, and other elements. He was promoted to the five-star rank of general of the army in December 1944, the temporary rank being made permanent in April 1946. Throughout the war Eisenhower's success as supreme commander rested on both his ability as a strategist and his capacity for harmonizing the often prickly personalities of his national commanders and the often diverging national goals of the Allies. After briefly commanding U.S. occupation forces in Germany he returned to the United States in November 1945 as army chief of staff. In February 1948 he retired to become president of Columbia University; he published in the same year *Crusade in Europe*, his best-selling war memoir. In December 1950 President Harry S. Truman recalled him to active duty as commander of the newly organized forces of the North Atlantic Treaty Organization (NATO) in Europe; he served in that post until mid-1952. Long mentioned by both parties as a potential political candidate, Eisenhower at length abandoned his habitual reticence and consented to be considered for the 1952 Republican presidential nomination. He won the nomination narrowly over Sen. Robert A. Taft and the election by an overwhelming margin, taking 442 electoral votes to Democrat Adlai E. Stevenson's 89. Determined to remain above partisanship, and a firm believer in the tradition of separation of powers, Eisenhower viewed the presidency as an office primarily of moral leadership and brought to it a concept of government that he termed, enigmatically, "dynamic conservatism." He was content to leave the practical day-to-day workings of government largely to the direction of his staff and cabinet. His first term was dominated by foreign affairs. Having already fulfilled a campaign promise by traveling personally to Korea, he oversaw the establishment of a truce there in mid-1953. At the same time he took bold initiatives in proposing a new plan for world disarmament and the creation of an international agency to develop peacetime uses for nuclear energy, but this "Atoms for Peace" plan failed to win sufficient world support to become effectual. The disarmament proposal led eventually to a summit conference between Eisenhower and Soviet Premier Nikita S. Khrushchev in 1955 in Geneva, at which Eisenhower made his startling "Open Skies" proposal, whereby the United States and the Soviet Union would permit aerial surveillance of each other's territories and military activities. This plan, too, proved too radical. As a counter to Soviet intransigence at the conference table and expansionist moves in many parts of the world, Eisenhower allowed his secretary of state, John Foster Dulles, to construct a network of alliances to meet further Communist expansion with the threat of "massive retaliation." Such hard-line Cold War diplomacy was made credible by vigorous responses to crises, including in 1957 the landing of U.S. troops in Lebanon under the terms of the recently promulgated "Eisenhower doctrine" of military aid to free-world nations. On the domestic front the president, buoyed by his vast popularity, strove to remain above political squabbles, although it was wished by many that he would respond with the force of his prestige to the increasingly violent and scurrilous attacks of Senator Joseph R. McCarthy. Soon after his reelection in 1956 —again over Stevenson, and by a margin even greater than that of 1952, 457 to 73—he was forced to deal with his first major domestic crisis, the violent reaction to the court-ordered racial integration of schools in Little Rock, Arkansas. Nationalizing the Arkansas National Guard and sending in additional troops, he restored order in the city and obtained the compliance of local officials with the law; his refusal to exceed his fundamental executive responsibility epitomized his conception of the presidency. That conception changed eventually, however; in 1959, emerging from a long period of illness and stripped by resignation or death of many of his original close advisers, he suddenly undertook an unprecedented campaign of vigorous leadership and personal diplomacy. For the first time he took the initiative with Congress on legislation in various fields and began wielding his veto power with a purpose. More important were his diplomatic moves: after initiating and hosting what proved to be a highly successful visit by Premier Khrushchev, Eisenhower embarked on an 11-nation goodwill tour that showed him to be one of the most widely known and respected figures on the world stage. The high hopes aroused in his last year in office were dashed in May 1960, when the downing of a U.S. U-2 reconnaissance airplane in Soviet territory, coupled with Eisenhower's attempt to dismiss the incident, resulted in the cancellation by Khrushchev of a planned summit conference. After unsuccessfully supporting his two-term vice-president, Richard M. Nixon, in the presidential election of 1960, Eisenhower retired in 1961 to private life. In 1963 he published *Mandate for Change*, a volume of memoirs. Deteriorating health limited his activities, and after a lengthy period of hospitalization he died in Washington, D.C., on March 28, 1969.

Ellet, Charles (1810–1862), engineer and army officer. Born in Bucks County, Pennsylvania, on January 1, 1810, Ellet—known always as Charles Ellet, Jr.—was from an early age inclined toward mathematics, and at seventeen he found a job with a surveying party, later taking a position with the Chesapeake & Ohio Canal. In 1830 he undertook engineering studies at the École Polytechnique in Paris. He became assistant engineer of the James River & Kanawha Canal in 1835 and chief engineer a year later; he remained in that post until 1839. In 1841–1842 he built over the Schuylkill river at Fairmount, Pennsylvania, the first wire suspension bridge in the United States. From 1842 to 1847 he was president of the Schuylkill Navigation Company, and then he returned to bridge building, designing the first one to be built over the Niagara River below the falls and building another over the Ohio at Wheeling that, on completion in 1849, was at 1010 feet the world's longest single-span bridge. In 1850 he undertook for the War Department studies of flood control and navigation improvement on the Mississippi, pub-

lishing several reports of his surveys and plans. During the 1850s he was engaged mainly in railroad work in Virginia, particularly as engineer of the Virginia Central in 1853–1857, for which he built the remarkable line across the Blue Ridge at Rock Fish Gap. During that period he also developed his idea for a new sort of naval vessel, the ram. He found considerable interest in the idea abroad, especially in Russia, but none at home until the sudden appearance on March 8, 1862, of the Confederate ironclad ram *Virginia* (ex-*Merrimack*), rebuilt along lines suggested in Ellet's earlier published papers. Secretary of War Edwin M. Stanton quickly commissioned Ellet a colonel of engineers, reporting directly to Stanton, and directed him to acquire and equip a fleet of rams for service on the Mississippi. He bought nine steam vessels at Pittsburgh and Cincinnati, fitted them out as armored rams, and took them down the Ohio to join the Mississippi Flotilla under Capt. Charles H. Davis. He passed Fort Pillow on June 5 and the next day was before Memphis. His own ram, *Queen of the West*, rammed and sank the Confederate *General Lovell* but was itself damaged. Four of the eight Confederate vessels defending Memphis were sunk in the fight and the rest forced to flee. Davis pursued, sinking one more and capturing two. Ellet took a bullet in the fight—he was the only Union casualty—and he died on June 21, 1862, as the *Queen of the West* landed at Cairo, Illinois.

Ellet, Charles Rivers (1843–1863), army officer. Born in Philadelphia on June 1, 1843, Ellet was the son of Charles Ellet, engineer and builder of the Mississippi River ram fleet. The younger Ellet was studying medicine in Georgetown, D.C., at the outbreak of the Civil War and was shortly appointed medical cadet. On June 1, 1862, his 19th birthday, he joined his father on the Mississippi and served through the running of Fort Pillow and the battle before Memphis on June 6. On that day Ellet's father sent him ashore with two companions to demand the surrender of the city. Uniformed Confederate forces had withdrawn, but an angry mob threatened them repeatedly. The target of bricks, shots, and other threats, Ellet marched through town, removed the Confederate flag from the post office, and raised the flag of the United States. Later he made a hazardous crossing on foot of the peninsula opposite Vicksburg to bring news of the fall of Memphis to Adm. David G. Farragut. In November 1862 Ellet was commissioned colonel and placed in command of the ram fleet, and over the next several months he ran the Vicksburg batteries three times. At dawn on February 2, 1863, Ellet on the *Queen of the West* again ran the batteries and steamed for the landing on the south of the city, where he rammed and set fire to the Confederate ram *Vicksburg*. He continued downriver and the next day captured three valuable Confederate supply ships near the mouth of the Red River. On February 14 he began an ascent of the Red, but, his pilot running the *Queen of the West* aground while under fire from a concealed shore battery, he abandoned the ship and escaped aboard the companion *De Soto.* Late in March he again ran Vicksburg in the *Switzerland* in order to reinforce Adm. Farragut's fleet in the blockade of the Red River and lower Mississippi. He continued to take part in the operations that led to the siege of Vicksburg until his health failed; he retired to an uncle's farm in Bunker Hill, Illinois, and died there on October 29, 1863.

Elliott, George Frank (1846–1931), marine officer. Born on November 30, 1846, in Alabama, Elliott grew up there and in New Hampshire. He entered West Point in 1868 but left two years later to take a second lieutenant's commission in the marine corps. He was promoted to first lieutenant in March 1878 and captain in June 1892. In 1894, while serving as fleet marine officer on Asiatic station aboard the *Baltimore,* he led a marine force on a remarkable night forced march to protect the American legation in Seoul, Korea, where the Chinese–Japanese war threatened to overrun neutral observers. In 1898 he saw action in Cuba during the Spanish–American War and distinguished himself at Guantanamo in June. Promoted to major in March 1899, he was ordered to the Philippines for service against the insurrectionists. He advanced to lieutenant colonel in September and on October 8 led a brigade in the victory at Novaleta. In March 1903 he was promoted to colonel, and in October of that year he became commandant of the marine corps with the rank of brigadier general. During December 1903–March 1904 he commanded the marine expeditionary force on the Isthmus of Panama following the Panamanian revolt against Colombia. Elliott was promoted to major general in May 1908, and he continued as commandant until his retirement in November 1910. He died in Washington, D.C., on November 4, 1931.

Elliott, Jesse Duncan (1782–1845), naval officer. Born on July 14, 1782, in Hagerstown, Maryland, Elliott was appointed a midshipman in the navy in April 1804. He made his first cruise on the *Essex* under Commodore James Barron and from 1805 to 1807 was in the Mediterranean in action against Tripoli. In June 1807 he was aboard the *Chesapeake* when Barron was forced to submit to search by the *Leopard.* Elliott was promoted to lieutenant in April 1810. Soon after the outbreak of the War of 1812 he was ordered to Lake Erie to begin purchase and construction of a lake fleet, and on October 8 he and Capt. Nathan Towson of the army captured two British brigs, the *Caledonia* and the *Detroit,* under the guns of Fort Erie, for which exploit Elliott was rewarded by Congress. He had begun construction of

the *Lawrence* and the *Niagara* for the Erie fleet when he was superseded by Commodore Oliver H. Perry in February 1813. He served for a time on Lake Ontario as captain of the *Madison,* Commodore Isaac Chauncey's flagship, receiving promotion to master commandant in July, and took part in the attack on York (Toronto) on July 24. In August he returned to the Erie fleet as Perry's second-in-command on the *Niagara.* In the great battle with the British fleet under Capt. Robert Barclay on September 10, 1813, Elliott captained the *Niagara* until Perry transferred to it from the battered *Lawrence;* he then took command of the sloops of the fleet and performed with distinction. In October he succeeded Perry as naval commander on Lake Erie. During 1815–1817 he commanded the sloop *Ontario* in the Algerine War. Promoted to captain in 1818, he served until 1822 on a commission appointed to select sites for navy yards, lighthouses, and coastal fortifications. He commanded the *Cyane* in the Brazil Squadron in 1825–1827, and from 1829 to 1832 he commanded the West India Squadron. From 1833 to 1835 he commanded the Boston navy yard and from 1835 to 1838 was commander of the Mediterranean Squadron aboard flagship *Constitution.* On his return from that assignment a number of charges, largely minor, were brought against him by junior officers. Elliott being somewhat unpopular politically, he was convicted of some of the charges and suspended from duty for four years. In October 1843 President John Tyler remitted the remaining penalty, and in December 1844 Elliott was appointed commander of the Philadelphia navy yard. He died there on December 10, 1845. From 1813 until even after his death a controversy raged in naval circles over his actions in the battle of Lake Erie, his detractors claiming that he hung back for more than two hours, allowing the *Lawrence* to bear the brunt of British gunfire and incur the great bulk of the American casualties for the day. Perry, of course, had made no such charge at the time, but by 1818 the dispute between their partisans drew them in. Elliott challenged Perry to a duel; Perry declined and preferred charges against Elliott (quashed by President James Monroe). James Fenimore Cooper was prominent among Elliott's defenders and when Perry's party attacked him he sued, as usual, for libel. Later historians, notably Adm. A. T. Mahan, have criticized Elliott.

Ellsberg, Edward (1891–   ), naval officer, engineer, and author. Born on November 21, 1891, in New Haven, Connecticut, Ellsberg grew up in Denver and after a year, 1909–1910, at the University of Colorado he entered the Naval Academy, graduating in 1914. He saw sea duty aboard the *Texas* during the occupation of Veracruz in 1914 and in 1916 returned to his studies, first at the Academy and then at the Massachusetts Institute of Technology. During

World War I he was engaged in refitting captured or impounded German liners as transports. Returning to MIT, he took a master's degree in 1920. While serving at the Boston navy yard he invented an improved distiller subsequently installed on a great many ships. In 1924 he was transferred to the New York navy yard and the next year was granted leave to overhaul the liner S.S. *Leviathan.* In 1926 he was given responsibility for salvaging the submarine *S-51,* sunk off Block Island; his success in that operation (carried out under the general supervision of Commander Ernest J. King) won him the navy's first peacetime Distinguished Service Medal. He invented the underwater cutting torch in that year and later retired from the navy in the rank of lieutenant commander, taking the post of chief engineer for the Tidewater Oil Company. In December 1927 he was recalled to reserve duty to salvage the *S-4,* sunk off Provincetown, Massachusetts. In that operation he devised what became the standard procedure for submarine salvage, and in 1929 he was promoted to commander by special act of Congress for the *S-51* and *S-4* operations. *On the Bottom,* a successful popular account of his salvage work, appeared in 1929, and was followed quickly by *Thirty Fathoms Deep,* 1930, *Pigboats* (later made into a motion picture as *Hell Below*), 1931, *Ocean Gold,* 1935, *Spanish Ingots,* 1936, *Hell on Ice,* 1938, *Captain Paul,* 1941, and others. He resigned from his post with the Tidewater company in 1935, continuing as a consultant for six years thereafter. In December 1941 he returned to active duty in the rank of captain and in February 1942 was ordered to supervise salvage work in the Red Sea area. At the port of Massaua (Mesewa), Eritrea, Ethiopia, he managed to raise in nine days a huge floating dry dock sunk by the retreating Italian navy. In November 1942 he was named chief salvage officer for the western Mediterranean region. In June 1944 he took part in the Normandy landings, engaging in the construction and emplacement of artificial harbors for the use of supply ships. In 1945 he was appointed supervisor of naval shipbuilding for the Cleveland area. Promoted to rear admiral in 1951, Ellsberg retired in 1955. Later books of his included *Under the Red Sea Sun,* 1946, *No Banners, No Bugles,* 1949, *Passport for Jennifer,* 1952, and *The Far Shore,* 1960. Ellsberg was in later years a noted lecturer on naval and world affairs.

Ellsworth, Elmer Ephraim (1837–1861), army officer. Born on April 11, 1837, in Malta, Saratoga County, New York, Ellsworth failed, through lack of educational opportunity and political influence, to secure an appointment to West Point. After a time spent working as a clerk in Troy, New York, he went to New York City and then, in 1855, to Chicago, where he became a law student. His abiding interest in things military led him to join a local volunteer company of cadets. He soon became captain of the company and instituted the dress drill and other practices of the French zouaves. The brilliant dress and the spirited precision drill brought the company considerable attention. Strict rules of deportment, including the prohibition of alcohol, tobacco, and profanity, complemented the military discipline he achieved with the company, known after a time as the National Guard Cadets and the U.S. Zouave Cadets of Chicago. Ellsworth was appointed a major in the Illinois militia (later promoted to colonel), and his cadets became the governor's official guards. In 1860 he and the company made an exhibition tour of eastern cities that aroused much interest. On their return Ellsworth entered the law office of Abraham Lincoln as a student. He accompanied Lincoln to Washington, D.C., after the election. At the outbreak of the Civil War he went to New York City, raised a regiment among volunteer firemen, and trained it in the zouave drill. The New York Fire Zouaves, as they were known, sailed for Washington in April 1861 and were quickly mustered into the volunteer service as the 11th New York Infantry, Ellsworth taking a colonel's commission. The regiment took part in the occupation of Alexandria, Virginia, on May 24, and on that day Ellsworth, seeing a Confederate flag flying from the roof of the Marshall House hotel, dashed up and tore it down. As he descended the stairs from the roof he was shot dead by the hotel's proprietor, one James W. Jackson, who was in turn shot and killed by one of Ellsworth's guards, Pvt. Francis E. Brownell. Brownell's act was the earliest of the Civil War to be rewarded with a Medal of Honor (awarded in 1877).

Elzey, Arnold (1816–1871), Confederate army officer. Born in Somerset County, Maryland, on December 18, 1816, Arnold Elzey Jones graduated from West Point in 1837 and thereupon dropped his surname. Commissioned in the artillery, he served in the second Seminole War in Florida in 1837–1838. He was stationed in Brownsville, Texas, when the Mexican War began and himself fired the first gun in the war. He was twice brevetted, for his actions at Contreras and Churubusco, August 19–20, 1847, and served through the capture of Mexico City. He was promoted to captain in February 1849. In April 1861 he surrendered the arsenal in Augusta, Georgia, to a superior Confederate force and after conveying his men to Washington he resigned from the army, taking a Confederate commission of colonel in command of the 1st Maryland Infantry. At Manassas (Bull Run) on July 21, 1861, he took command of a brigade from the wounded Gen. Edmund Kirby-Smith and led the charge that began the rout of the Union forces. For his actions he was promoted to brigadier general on the spot by Jefferson Davis. Attached to Gen. Thomas J. Jackson's forces, he served through the Shenandoah valley campaign and the

Seven Days' Battles in June 1862. At Cold Harbor, June 3, 1864, he was severely wounded. After his recovery he was promoted to major general and given command of the Department of Richmond. His "Local Defence Brigade," organized among government clerks and others, performed many valuable services. Before the end of the war he had returned to the field as chief of artillery of Gen. John B. Hood's Army of Tennessee. After the war he returned to Maryland and took up a farm in Anne Arundel County. He died in Baltimore on February 21, 1871.

Emmons, Delos Carleton (1888–1965), army and air force officer. Born on January 17, 1888, in Huntington, West Virginia, Emmons graduated from West Point in 1909 and was commissioned in the infantry. He served with the 30th Infantry in San Francisco, Alaska, New York, and on the Mexican border and in 1917 secured a transfer to the aviation section, Signal Corps, and promotion to captain. Various assignments followed: promoted to major in 1920, he commanded the 91st Observation Squadron, Rockwell Field, California, from 1925 to 1927, served in the office of the chief of the Air Corps 1927–1928 and in that of the assistant secretary of war 1928–1931. He graduated from the Air Corps Tactical School, Maxwell Field, Alabama, in 1932 and from the Command and General Staff School, Fort Leavenworth, Kansas, in 1934. In that year he was promoted to lieutenant colonel and put in command of the 18th Composite Wing in Hawaii, serving also as air officer of the Hawaiian Department. From 1936 to 1939, with temporary rank of brigadier general, he commanded the 1st Wing, March Field, California, advancing to permanent colonel in 1938; and in March 1939 he was promoted to temporary major general and named commanding officer of General Headquarters Air Force, succeeding Gen. Frank M. Andrews. In October 1940 he was promoted to temporary lieutenant general, and in June 1941 he took command of the Air Force Combat Command. In December 1941, ten days after the Japanese attack on Pearl Harbor, Emmons was named to replace Gen. Walter C. Short as commander of the Hawaiian Department. He remained in that post until May 1943, and in September he succeeded Gen. John L. De Witt as commander of the Western Defense Command, headquartered in San Francisco. In June 1944 he moved to command of the Alaskan Department, succeeding Gen. Simon B. Buckner, Jr., and remained there until June 1946. Upon the organization of the Armed Forces Staff College in Norfolk, Virginia, in August 1946, Emmons was appointed its first commandant; he became an air force officer in September 1947 on the separation of that branch from the army and remained at the college until his retirement in June 1948. He died on October 5, 1965, in San Francisco.

Emory, William Hemsley (1811–1887), army officer. Born in Queen Annes County, Maryland, on September 7, 1811, Emory graduated from West Point in 1831 and was commissioned in the artillery. After service principally in the South he resigned in 1836, but in 1838 he accepted a commission as first lieutenant of topographical engineers. During 1844–1846 he was engaged in the survey of the northeast boundary, and in the latter year he was appointed chief engineer of Gen. Stephen W. Kearny's Army of the West, with which he served in the California campaign, taking part in the battles of San Pasquale, San Gabriel, and Plains of Mesa, and in Mexico. He was brevetted captain and major during the war. From 1848 to 1853 he was engaged in surveying the California–Mexico border, and from 1854 to 1857 he served on the commission to survey the Gadsden Purchase. Promoted to captain in 1851 and major in 1855, he served from 1857 in Kansas, Utah, and Indian Territory (Oklahoma) and in 1861 led his troops to reinforce Fort Leavenworth, contributing to the Union hold on Missouri. In May 1861 he was appointed lieutenant colonel, 6th Artillery, and in March 1862 was appointed brigadier general of volunteers. He saw action in the Peninsular campaign, distinguishing himself particularly at Hanover Court House, May 27, 1862. In the spring of 1864 he commanded the XIX Corps in Gen. Nathaniel F. Banks's Red River campaign. Brevetted major general of volunteers in July 1864, he served under Gen. Philip H. Sheridan in the Shenandoah valley campaign in that year, distinguishing himself at Opequon Creek, September 19, and at Cedar Creek, October 19. In March 1865 he was brevetted brigadier and major general in the regular army, and in September he was promoted to major general of volunteers and placed in command of the Department of West Virginia. In January 1866 he was mustered out of volunteer service, and after commanding the District of the Republican in Washington Territory, 1869–1871, and the Department of the Gulf, 1871–1875, he retired in the rank of brigadier general in July 1876. Emory died in Washington, D.C., on December 1, 1887.

Empey, Arthur Guy (1883–1963), soldier, author, and film producer. Born in Ogden, Utah, on December 11, 1883, Empey graduated from high school in Brooklyn, New York, and for several years knocked about the world in search of experience. He served for six years in the cavalry and was at various times a member of the New York and New Jersey national guard. In 1915 he enlisted as a private in the British army and served for 18 months in France, receiving his discharge after being wounded in the battle of the Somme in July 1916. The next year he joined the United States army and served in the tank corps, advancing by 1918 to commissioned rank of captain. Empey wrote vividly of his experiences in the British army in *Over the Top;* published in June 1917, a very opportune moment, it caught the tide of idealistic enthusiasm that swept America in the months just following the declaration of war and sold some 350,000 copies before the year was out. With total sales of over half a million, it remained the best remembered American book of World War I. Empey organized and was president of Guy Empey Pictures, which produced several motion pictures including a version of *Over the Top,* starring and partly directed by himself, and others such as *Pack Up Your Troubles, A Millionaire for a Day,* and *Just Orphans.* Others among his many books were *First Call,* 1918, *The Coward,* 1918, *Tales from a Dugout,* 1918, *The Enemy Within,* 1918, *The Madonna of the Hills,* 1921, *Liquid Gold,* 1921, and *Helluva War,* 1927. He died in Wadsworth, Kansas, on February 22, 1963.

Ericsson, John (1803–1889), engineer and inventor. Born in Värmland County, Sweden, on July 31, 1803, Ericsson displayed from an early age a fascination with machinery. At thirteen he joined an engineering corps engaged in canal construction and received from his older companions instruction in mathematics, science, and drafting. He later served as a topographer with the Swedish army, rising to the rank of captain, until 1827, a year after he had gone to London on leave of absence. For 13 years he remained there, working as an independent engineer and laying the groundwork for his later achievements. He was particularly interested in developing mechanical sources of motive power; while he made many improvements in steam-engine design and construction, he sought to find a more direct and efficient means of utilizing heat energy and through his life constructed various sorts of "caloric" engines, none of which, however, successfully competed with steam. In 1829 he constructed a locomotive, the *Novelty,* for the competition that was won by George Stephenson's *Rocket.* He also devised deep-sea sounding apparatus, a self-acting gun lock, a file-cutting machine, and numerous other inventions. Later he turned to ship design and propulsion; hitting on the idea of placing the engines below the water-line for protection from shells, he began using a screw propeller instead of the paddlewheel. In 1837 his ship *Francis B. Ogden* was successfully tested, and he followed it with the *Novelty,* the first propeller-driven commercial vessel. Commissioned by Capt. Robert F. Stockton of the U.S. navy to build another such ship, he went to New York City in 1839. His new propulsion system was quickly adopted for a number of commercial steamers, and in 1844 the *Princeton* became the first warship to be so powered. In 1848 Ericsson became a U.S. citizen. In 1861 his proposal for a new type of warship was approved by a government board and in an almost incredibly short time the *Monitor* was built and launched early in 1862. On March 9 it met the Confederate ironclad *Virginia* (formerly the *Merrimack*) in a much-celebrated battle in Hampton Roads. The *Monitor* opened the age of modern warships; powered solely by steam and propeller-driven, constructed entirely of iron and heavily armored, and armed with heavy guns mounted in a revolving turret, it began a revolution in naval warfare. Ericsson was widely hailed for his achievement and continued to design and build ironclads throughout the Civil War. In 1878 he launched the *Destroyer,* a ship capable of firing underwater torpedoes from a 16-inch gun in its bow. While continuing to work on versions of his "caloric" engine, he also investigated other possible sources of power, particularly solar energy, and made improvements in ordnance. The great number, variety, and importance of his inventions marked him as one of the most creative and far-sighted engineers of his century. He died in New York City on March 8, 1889; the following year, at the request of the Swedish government, his body was returned to his native land.

Erskine, Robert (1735–1780), engineer and geographer. Born in Dunfermline, Scotland, on September 7, 1735, Erskine attended the University of Edinburgh intermittently between 1748 and 1752 and in the latter year made his way to London, where he subsequently began a hardware business. His partner deserted, leaving him a bankrupt, and he turned to civil engineering work. He was highly successful in that line, inventing numerous devices including a centrifugal hydraulic engine, and in January 1771 he was elected to the Royal Society. In 1770 he was engaged by a group of investors to manage the American Iron Company mine and forge in Ringwood, New Jersey. After an inspection tour of iron works in England and Wales he sailed for America, arriving in June 1771. While managing the firm he became a prominent figure in the district and became a sympathizer with the colonial cause. In 1775 he organized the employees of the works into a military company and was commissioned a captain of militia. The American Iron Company turned out the chevaux-de-frise used unsuccessfully on the Hudson at Fort Washington and the great chain stretched across from West Point, in addition to shot and other war materials. In July 1777, as a result of a meeting with Gen. George Washington, Erskine was commissioned geographer and surveyor general to the Continental army. For three years he surveyed and produced maps of the country that contributed materially to the army's success. While in the field he fell ill, and he died in Ringwood on October 2, 1780.

Evans, Robley Dunglison (1846–1912), naval officer. Born in Floyd Court House, Virginia, on August 18, 1846, Evans grew up from the age of ten in Washington, D.C. By means of a legal subterfuge he was appointed to the Naval Academy from Utah Territory at thirteen and in October 1863 was commissioned acting ensign. The spirit that later inspired his nickname, "Fighting Bob," was demonstrated first at Fort Fisher, North Carolina, on January 15, 1865, when, at the head of a company of marines landed from Adm. David D. Porter's squadron, he continued to fight after taking four bullet wounds; and second in his prevailing upon Congress for reinstatement after he was invalided out of the service. Over the three decades that followed the Civil War Evans made numerous and very diverse contributions to the navy, including the invention of a signal lamp, effective agitation for the construction of a steel navy, and highly successful commands at sea combining seamanship with practical diplomacy. His most notable services came while he was commanding the gunboat *Yorktown* in Chilean waters in November–December 1891, where his actions following the killing of American sailors off the *Baltimore*, Capt. Winfield S. Schley, by a mob in Valparaiso in October earned him his nickname; and in the Bering Sea sealing dispute in 1892, when he again displayed both firmness and tact while in command of a flotilla patrolling an internationally sensitive area. At the opening of the Spanish–American War in 1898 he was in command of the *Iowa,* which began the attack on the Spanish fleet at Santiago. Evans was advanced in rank to lieutenant in July 1866, lieutenant commander in March 1868, commander in July 1878, captain in June 1893, and rear admiral in February 1901. In 1902 he was named commander of the Asiatic Fleet, a post he held for two years, and from 1905 to 1907 he was commander of the Atlantic Fleet. In the latter year he was chosen to command the round-the-world cruise of the Battle Fleet ordered as a demonstration of American naval strength by President Theodore Roosevelt. Consisting of sixteen battleships, the fleet sailed from Hampton Roads, Virginia, on December 16. After calling at Rio de Janeiro and negotiating the Straits of Magellan the fleet made north. At Magdalena Bay, Baja California, Evans fell ill, and on reaching San Francisco on May 6, 1908, he was compelled to relinquish command. He retired officially in August. (The fleet completed its voyage under command of Adm. Charles S. Sperry.) Evans wrote *A Sailor's Log; Recollections of Forty Years of Naval Life,* 1901, and *An Admiral's Log; being Continued Recollections of Naval Life,* 1910. He died on January 3, 1912, in Washington, D.C.

Ewell, Richard Stoddert (1817–1872), Confederate army officer. Born on February 8, 1817, in Georgetown, D.C., Ewell was a grandson of Benjamin Stoddert, first secretary of the navy. He graduated from West Point in 1840, was commissioned in the dragoons, and was posted to frontier duty until the Mexican War, in which he served in Gen. Winfield Scott's army from Veracruz through Cerro Gordo, Contreras and Churubusco, where he was brevetted for gallantry, Molino del Rey, Chapultepec, and Mexico City. Promoted to captain in August 1849, he was again on frontier duty after the war and saw much action against the Apaches in New Mexico. In May 1861 he resigned to enter Confederate service. Commissioned colonel and promoted to brigadier general in June and major general in October, he commanded a division under Gen. Thomas J. Jackson in the Shenandoah valley campaign in 1862, defeating Gen. Nathaniel Banks at Winchester, May 25, and a much superior force under Gen. John C. Frémont at Cross Keys, June 8, and taking part in the Seven Days' Battles around Richmond in June–July. At Cedar Mountain, August 9, he took part in another defeat of Banks's corps of Gen. John Pope's Army of Virginia. At Groveton, during the second Manassas (Bull Run) engagements, August 29–30, he was severely wounded, losing a leg. In May 1863 he returned to the field with the rank of lieutenant general, commanding, at the dying Jackson's recommendation, the II Corps. He campaigned up the Shenandoah valley, winning victories at Brandy Station and Winchester, and entered Pennsylvania, reaching Carlisle by the end of June. Called to reinforce Gen. Ambrose P. Hill's forces at Gettysburg, he arrived on July 1 and occupied the town but failed to press on to Cemetery Hill. In support of Gen. James Longstreet's general assault on the Union lines, Ewell attacked and captured a portion of Culp's Hill on July 2; he remained in the line the next day. In May 1864 he fought Gen. Ulysses S. Grant to a standstill in the Wilderness, May 5–7, and held firm at the "Bloody Angle" at Spotsylvania, May 8–12. A few days later he was badly injured when his horse was shot under him. Placed in command of the Department of Henrico and subsequently of besieged Richmond, he was captured with his corps by Gen. Philip H. Sheridan and Gen. Horatio G. Wright at Sayler's Creek on April 6, 1865. After four months' imprisonment he settled near Spring Hill, Tennessee, where he died on January 25, 1872.

F

Fannin, James Walker (1804?–1836), Texas revolutionary officer. Born probably on January 1, 1804, and probably in Georgia, Fannin was adopted by his maternal grandfather, grew up near Marion, Georgia, and in 1819 entered West Point under the name James F. Walker. He left after two years and returned to Georgia, where he remained until 1834. In that year he moved to Texas and soon became prominent in the agitation for independence from Mexico. He took part in the battle at Gonzales, the first of the revolution, on October 2, 1835, and as a captain performed gallantly in the battle at Mission Concepción on October 28, early in the siege of San Antonio. During a period of great confusion and discord in the provisional government of Texas, with the legislative council, Gov. Smith, and Gen. Sam Houston all at odds, Fannin, having declined a post on Houston's staff, secured appointment in January as an agent of the council, with rank of colonel and virtually dictatorial powers, to organize an expedition to capture the Mexican port of Matamoros. As a first step in the plan, he collected some 500 volunteers at Goliad on the south bank of the San Antonio River. On March 13 they were still there, except for a force of about 100 that had been detached to an advance post. On that day Fannin received orders from Houston to pull back. He delayed his move for six days, fatally, as it turned out, for on the afternoon of March 19 he was overtaken by a column of Gen. Santa Anna's army under Gen. José Urrea and captured. Held prisoner at Goliad, Fannin and his men believed their surrender terms guaranteed their return to the United States. Santa Anna, however, ordered their execution, and on March 27, 1836, 330 of them were marched out and shot, 27 escaping and a number of others having been spared for various reasons. Fannin, by all accounts a brave and loyal soldier, was nonetheless an inept leader. The loss of his command in what became known as the Goliad Massacre, following upon that of the Alamo defenders three weeks before, left Houston's band the only military force remaining to the revolutionists.

Fanning, Nathaniel (1755–1805), privateer and naval officer. Born on May 31, 1755, in Stonington, Connecticut, Fanning entered the merchant service at an early age. Little is known of him before 1778, when he sailed as a privateer against British shipping. In that year he was captured and imprisoned in England. On being released he made his way to L'Ori-

ent, France, where John Paul Jones took him aboard the *Bonhomme Richard*. In the great battle with the *Serapis* on September 23, 1779, Fanning was captain of the maintop and he succeeded, together with Lt. Edward Stack of the French marines, in establishing complete American control aloft. From the tops, yards, and rigging the crew of the *Serapis* was kept under gun and grenade attack, and at length the upper gun deck was silenced altogether. A grenade thrown from a yardarm fell through a hatchway and exploded amidst a cache of powder and cartridges, further damaging the structure and morale of the *Serapis*. Fanning was highly praised by Jones after the fight. He sailed with Jones on the *Ariel* in 1780 and later returned to privateering under French commission. He was imprisoned again briefly in 1781, became a French citizen in 1782, and finally took a commission as lieutenant in the French navy. He resigned and returned to America in 1783. In December 1804 he accepted a lieutenant's commission in the United States navy, but while commanding the naval station at Charleston, South Carolina, he died on September 30, 1805. His *Narrative of the Adventures of an American Naval Officer* (later called *Memoirs of the Life of Captain Nathaniel Fanning*) appeared in 1806.

Farragut, David Glasgow (1801–1870), naval officer. Born near Knoxville, Tennessee, on July 5, 1801, Farragut, son of George Farragut, moved with his family to New Orleans in 1807. At the age of nine, following the death of his mother, he was adopted by Capt. David Porter, and in December 1810 he was appointed a midshipman in the navy. Apparently in honor of his foster father, he changed his first name from James to David about 1814. From 1811 through the end of the War of 1812 he served under Porter on the *Essex* and, at the age of twelve, was briefly in command of a captured prize ship. He was imprisoned briefly after the capture of the *Essex* by the *Phoebe* and the *Cherub* on March 28, 1814. For the next several years he served on various ships, principally in the Mediterranean, and for a time studied under the U.S. consul at Tunis. He devoted considerable energy to remedying his neglected education and became fluent in several languages. In 1823–1824 he was again with Porter in a campaign to suppress piracy in Caribbean waters. Farragut was promoted to lieutenant in 1825, to commander in September 1841 (receiving command of the sloop

Decatur of the Brazil Squadron the next year), and to captain in September 1855; progress was slow, for his duties at sea and ashore during this period, including the Mexican War, had been routine. During 1854–1858 he was in California, where he established the Mare Island navy yard. After the outbreak of the Civil War he was chosen, in December 1861, largely on the recommendation of Assistant Secretary Gustavus V. Fox and of his foster brother, Commander David Dixon Porter, to command the West Gulf Blockading Squadron. His orders were to capture New Orleans and gain control of the Mississippi. In April 1862, following his instructions, Farragut first attempted to reduce the defending Fort Jackson by mortar fire (Porter commanded the mortarboat flotilla). This soon proving fruitless, he decided to run past the fort in the dark. Despite heavy fire the two columns of the squadron, one under Farragut on his flagship *Hartford* and the other under Capt. Theodorus Bailey on the *Cayuga*, passed Fort Jackson and Fort St. Philip farther upstream, defeated the small Confederate river flotilla, and captured New Orleans on April 24. Within days the two forts likewise surrendered to the squadron's mortar flotilla under Porter, and Union troops under Gen. Benjamin F. Butler occupied the city. The capture of New Orleans was a tremendous victory for the Union and had far-reaching diplomatic as well as military importance. In July Farragut was the first officer to be promoted to the newly created rank of rear admiral. For the next two years he was engaged in the blockade of the Gulf Coast and in controlling traffic on the lower Mississippi and its tributaries, contributing materially to the capture of Vicksburg (whose batteries he first ran in June 1862) in July 1863 and to the establishment of Union control over the entire river. In 1864 he was given an assignment he had long sought, the capture of the defenses of Mobile Bay. The entrance to the bay was heavily mined except for a narrow channel under the guns of Fort Morgan. On August 5 Farragut began his approach; the ironclads *Tecumseh*, Capt. Tunis A. M. Craven, and *Brooklyn*, Capt. James Alden, led the squadron into the channel, and as they came abreast of Fort Morgan the *Tecumseh* struck a mine (or torpedo, as they were then called) and was destroyed. The *Brooklyn* stopped and then backed in the channel, and the column was thrown into confusion. Farragut, on the steam-powered *Hartford*, quickly swung out and headed his ship into the minefield, crying "Damn the torpedoes!" to a warning shouted from the *Brooklyn*. Although several mines were contacted by his ships none exploded, and soon the entire squadron was within the bay. The Confederate ironclad *Tennessee*, Adm. Franklin Buchanan, was captured, along with the rest of the defending flotilla, and by the end of August all the harbor defenses, including Fort Morgan, had surrendered. In December Farragut was appointed to the

newly created rank of vice admiral; however, his active service was virtually at an end, for his health was declining. In July 1866 the rank of admiral was created especially for him. During 1867–1868 he made a goodwill tour of Europe as commander of the Mediterranean Squadron. He died while visiting the naval yard at Portsmouth, New Hampshire, on August 14, 1870.

Farragut, George (1755–1817), naval and militia officer. Born on September 29, 1755, in Ciudadela, Minorca, while the island was a British possession, Farragut was of a family prominent in the Balearic Islands and the service of Spain since at least the 13th century. At the age of ten he went to sea. In 1775, having for some years been engaged in trade in Caribbean and Gulf waters, he threw in his lot with the rebelling American colonies, and after bringing a cargo of munitions to Charleston, South Carolina, in 1776 he took up privateering. In 1778 he was commissioned a first lieutenant in the South Carolina navy, in which he served until taken prisoner in the capture of Charleston in May 1780. On his release he sailed again briefly as a privateer and then attached himself as a volunteer to the southern army, serving with Col. Francis Marion and with Gen. Daniel Morgan at the battle of Cowpens, January 17, 1781. Subsequently he raised an artillery company in North Carolina and then fought against Gen. Charles Cornwallis at the head of a company of volunteer cavalry, receiving a captain's commission from North Carolina. Farragut returned to the merchant service after the Revolution, but in March 1792 he accepted appointment as major of militia in the district of Washington, Southwest Territory (now the state of Tennessee) from Gov. William Blount. He took part in the militia campaign under Gen. John Sevier against the Cherokees in 1793. In 1807 he was appointed a sailing master in the navy and assigned to command of a gunboat at New Orleans. In 1811 he was transferred to the Bay of Pascagoula. During 1813–1814 he accompanied his friend, Gen. Andrew Jackson, in the campaign against the Creeks. He was discharged from the navy in March 1814, but he returned to take part in the battle of New Orleans, January 8, 1815. He died at Point Plaquet, West Pascagoula, Mississippi, on June 4, 1817. His second son was David Glasgow Farragut.

Fechteler, William Morrow (1896–1967), naval officer. Born in San Rafael, California, on March 6, 1896, Fechteler graduated from the Naval Academy in 1916. He served on the battleship *Pennsylvania* in World War I and in subsequent years progressed through the regular alternation of sea and shore duties, advancing to the rank of captain and the post of operations officer of the destroyer command, Battle Force, U.S. Fleet, by the outbreak of World War II.

From early 1942 to mid-1943 he was with the Bureau of Naval Personnel, and from August 1943 to January 1944 he commanded the battleship *Indiana* in the Gilbert, New Hebrides, and Marshall islands campaigns. Promoted to rear admiral, he was then named commander of Amphibious Group 8, Seventh Fleet Amphibious Force, under Adm. Daniel E. Barbey. He led the group in operations around New Guinea in the spring of 1944 and, in Barbey's absence, commanded the VII Force in the assault on Biak Island, May 27, and Sansapor, New Guinea, July 30. In the Philippines campaign he was responsible for landings in southwestern Luzon in January 1945 and on Palawan in February. In April 1945 he returned to staff duty in Washington, D.C., and in January 1946 he was named commander of battleships and cruisers, Atlantic Fleet, with the rank of vice admiral. From February 1947 to January 1950 Fechteler was deputy chief of naval operations for personnel. In February 1950 he was promoted to admiral and made commander of the Atlantic Fleet, and in August 1951, while awaiting confirmation as commander of NATO naval forces in the North Atlantic, he was appointed chief of naval operations to succeed Adm. Forrest P. Sherman. After two years in that post he became commander in chief of North Atlantic Treaty Organization forces in southern Europe. He retired in July 1956. He was associated with the General Electric Company until his death on July 4, 1967, in Bethesda, Maryland.

Fetterman, William Judd (1833?–1866), army officer. Born about 1833 at or near Fort Trumbull, Connecticut, where his father was stationed, Fetterman entered the army in 1861, saw action at Murfreesboro, Jonesboro, and elsewhere in the Civil War, and was twice brevetted, to major and lieutenant colonel, for gallantry. Remaining in the army after the war, he was assigned as a captain to the 27th Infantry in September 1866 and ordered to Fort Phil Kearny, in what is now Wyoming. On the morning of December 21, 1866, a wood train that had been sent out from the fort was attacked by a band of Sioux and Cheyenne six miles away and signaled for relief. Fetterman claimed command of the relief column, and the fort commander, Col. Henry B. Carrington, aware of Fetterman's impetuous and somewhat vainglorious nature as well as of his ignorance of frontier warfare, granted it to him with reluctance, ordering him repeatedly not to venture beyond Lodge Trail Ridge, the crest of a line of hills. Captain Fetterman rode out with 80 men toward the wood train. The Indians retired except for a few who carefully kept in sight but out of range, slowly drawing the soldiers toward the ridge. The decoys had found the perfect victim in Fetterman, and, disregarding Carrington's order, he rode over the ridge and down the far side. From ambush the main Indian body, under

High Backbone, fell on the soldiers and killed them all. The Fetterman Massacre left Fort Phil Kearny in desperate straits and led directly to the relief of Carrington from command; among Indian victories over the army it ranks second only to the defeat of Col. George A. Custer ten years later.

Fiske, Bradley Allen (1854–1942), naval officer and inventor. Born on June 13, 1854, in Lyons, New York, Fiske grew up there and in Cleveland and Cincinnati, Ohio. He graduated from the Naval Academy in 1874 and was commissioned ensign the next year. While serving in a routine succession of sea and shore assignments, in the course of which he was promoted to lieutenant (junior grade) in March 1883 and lieutenant in January 1887, he exercised his considerable flair for invention, devising apparatus for detaching boats lowered at sea, an electric mechanism for turning gun turrets, an electric range finder, and a telescopic sight for naval guns. The last was developed while Fiske was on leave from the *Yorktown*, on which he served, under Commander Robley D. Evans, in the demonstration at Valparaiso, Chile, in 1891. Although Evans failed to see the value of the sight, it was standard equipment throughout the fleet by the outbreak of the Spanish–American War. In 1894 Fiske was aboard the *San Francisco* in the force sent to Rio de Janeiro to face down the rebelling Brazilian navy. Subsequent inventions included an electric ammunition hoist, a speed and direction indicator, and a stadimeter, for the use of which under hazardous conditions in Manila Bay at the beginning of the great battle of May 1, 1898, he was commended by Adm. George Dewey. He was promoted to lieutenant commander in March 1899. During the Philippine Insurrection he served aboard the *Monadnock* and the *Yorktown*. Advanced to commander in March 1903 and to captain in August 1907, he later commanded the *Minneapolis, Arkansas,* and *Tennessee,* and after serving for a year on the navy's General Board he was promoted to rear admiral in August 1911. Others among his more than 60 patents were those for an electric semaphore system, a submarine detection device, various forms of range finder, improvements in torpedo design, and in 1912 the mechanisms whereby an airplane could launch a submarine torpedo. He was also a pioneer in the use of electric communication aboard ship. In 1912–1913 he commanded various battleship divisions of the Atlantic Fleet, and in February 1913 he was appointed aide for operations to the secretary of the navy, a post that was the forerunner of that of chief of naval operations, established in 1915 after Fiske's resignation as aide and in large part on his recommendation. His resignation was the culmination of a series of disagreements with the secretary, Josephus Daniels. In June 1916 he retired from the navy, having been one of the handful of officers—among the others were Stephen B. Luce and William S. Sims—who were responsible for the transformation of the navy into a technologically modern, fully trained, battle-ready force. Fiske wrote a number of books, including *War Time in Manila*, 1913, *The Navy as a Fighting Machine*, 1916, the autobiographical *From Midshipman to Rear Admiral*, 1919, and *The Art of Fighting*, 1920. He died in New York City on April 6, 1942.

Fiske, John (1744–1797), naval officer. Born in Salem, Massachusetts, on April 11, 1744, Fiske went to sea in the merchant service at an early age and by 1765 had risen to ship captain. He was a member of the Salem committee of safety and correspondence in 1775 and in April of the following year was commissioned a captain in the newly created Massachusetts state navy. On July 8 he put to sea in command of the state's first commissioned vessel, the brigantine *Tyrannicide*, with which he took a number of prizes. During 1777–1778 he sailed the larger *Massachusetts* in European and West Indian waters and captured many more prizes. Returning then to Salem, he was a successful merchant thereafter. In 1792 he was appointed major general of militia. He died in Salem on September 28, 1797.

Fitch, Aubrey Wray (1883–   ), naval officer. Born on June 11, 1883, in St. Ignace, Michigan, Fitch graduated from the Naval Academy in 1906 and was commissioned ensign in 1908. He served in various capacities over the next decade, including staff posts at the Academy, advancing to lieutenant in 1913. During World War I he served on the *Wyoming*, attached to the British Grand Fleet. Promoted to lieutenant commander in 1919, he was a member of a naval mission to Brazil in 1922–1927, and after sundry other commands he entered flight training in 1929. After qualifying as an aviator in 1930, he commanded the carriers *Wright* and *Langley*, receiving promotion to captain in July 1931, and in 1932 he took command of the Norfolk Naval Air Station. In 1935 he joined the carrier *Saratoga* and in 1936 he took command of the carrier *Lexington*. After graduating from the Naval War College in 1938 he was commander of the Pensacola, Florida, naval air station for two years. Shortly after taking command of Patrol Wing 2 in 1940 he was promoted to rear admiral (July), and he was subsequently assigned to the *Saratoga* as commander of Carrier Division 1. During the first months of World War II he commanded various carrier task forces in the Pacific. In May 1942, aboard his flagship *Lexington*, he joined his forces with those of Adm. Frank J. Fletcher on the *Yorktown*, and together they fought the vital battle of the Coral Sea, May 7–8, in which the tide of Japanese advance was for the first time stopped. It was the first sea battle in which opposing vessels exchanged no gunfire, indeed never even sighted one another,

the entire burden of fighting being carried by aircraft. The *Lexington* was sunk, but her task force took an enemy carrier with her. In September 1942 Fitch was placed in command of all aircraft in the South Pacific Fleet, and the next year all navy, marine corps, army, and New Zealand air forces in the South Pacific area came under his command. He was promoted to temporary vice admiral in December 1943, rank dating from a year earlier. By August 1944, when he left for a new post, the air forces under his direction had led the advance of American ground forces from island to island, softening up Japanese defenses, keeping Japanese naval forces on the defensive, and shooting down more than 3000 enemy aircraft. After a year as deputy chief of naval operations for air he was appointed superintendent of the Naval Academy in August 1945. From January to June 1947 he was a special assistant to the secretary of the navy, and at the end of that assignment he retired in the rank of admiral. For a time thereafter he was associated with the General Tire and Rubber Company. He was among the least well known of the major commanders in World War II.

Fletcher, Frank Friday (1855–1928), naval officer. Born on November 23, 1855, in Oskaloosa, Iowa, Fletcher graduated from the Naval Academy in 1875 and after a first cruise on the *Tuscarora* was commissioned ensign in 1876. Routine assignments occupied the several years following, highlighted by a world cruise on the *Ticonderoga* under Commodore Robert W. Shufeldt in 1878. In 1887 he was assigned to the Bureau of Ordnance, and over the next six years he made numerous contributions to gun mechanisms and gunnery practice, notably the Fletcher breech mechanism that increased the speed of rapid-fire guns. In 1890 the navy adopted his suggestion of the use of range lights on all vessels. He developed the first doctrines for torpedo warfare while commanding the torpedo boat *Cushing* in 1893, and in 1896 he was assigned to the battleship *Maine* (he was absent when the *Maine* blew up in Havana harbor in February 1898). Alternate sea and shore duties followed, including ordnance work, command of the torpedo station at Newport, Rhode Island, and a year on the General Board of the navy. In 1910 he was appointed an aide to the secretary of the navy; he was promoted to rear admiral in October 1911 and until 1913 commanded divisions of the Atlantic Fleet. In February 1913 he was named commander of naval forces on the east coast of Mexico, during a period of high tension between the two nations particularly marked by the refusal of President Woodrow Wilson to recognize the government of Gen. Victoriano Huerta. On April 9, 1914, Mexican authorities at Tampico arrested a boat crew from the *Dolphin* and refused Adm. Henry T. Mayo's demand for a 21-gun salute to the flag accompanying an apology. After consultation with Congress, President Wilson ordered Fletcher on April 21 to seize the customhouse at Veracruz. Fletcher landed a regiment of marines under Col. Wendell C. Neville, reinforced by seamen to a total of 787 men. More seamen and marines were landed later in the day and on the next day as Mexican resistance proved quite stubborn, but by noon on April 22 the entire city had been occupied. Fletcher turned command of the city over to Gen. Frederick Funston on April 30. For his part in the Veracruz operation he was later awarded the Medal of Honor. In September 1914 he was named commander of the Atlantic Fleet, receiving promotion to admiral in March 1915. He returned to shore duty in June 1916 and during World War I served on the navy's General Board and on the War Industries Board. He retired in November 1919 and died in New York City on November 28, 1928.

Fletcher, Frank Jack (1885–1973), naval officer. Born on April 29, 1885, in Marshalltown, Iowa, Fletcher graduated from the Naval Academy in 1906 and was commissioned an ensign two years later. His first sea command was that of the destroyer *Dale* in the Asiatic Squadron in 1909–1912. In April 1914, during the occupation of Veracruz, Mexico, by U.S. forces, he won the Medal of Honor for his valorous rescue of refugees on the transport *Esperanza*. In 1914 –1915 he was flag lieutenant of the Atlantic Fleet. During World War I he commanded the destroyer *Benham* on submarine patrol. He saw action in the suppression of the Philippine uprising in 1924. Fletcher graduated from the Naval War College in 1930 and from the Army War College in 1931. From 1933 to 1936 he was an aide to the secretary of the navy, and in 1938–1939 he was on the staff of the Bureau of Personnel. Promoted to rear admiral in 1939, he was assigned to command of Cruiser Division 3, Atlantic Fleet. Late in 1941 he was given command of the carrier *Yorktown* and an attending task force of two cruisers and four destroyers in the Pacific. He took part, under Adm. William F. Halsey, in the raid on the Marshall and Gilbert islands in February 1942, the first U.S. naval offensive in the war against Japan. In March he took part in the naval attack on New Guinea. Shortly thereafter he was promoted to vice admiral in command of the combined *Yorktown–Lexington* task forces (the latter under Adm. Aubrey W. Fitch). On May 7–8 he and Fitch, who had tactical command of the battle, engaged a larger Japanese carrier force in the battle of the Coral Sea, the first sea battle fought entirely in the air. In that battle, often considered to mark the end of the defensive phase of the war in the Pacific, the American forces suffered heavily—especially with the loss of the *Lexington*—but succeeded in ending the threat of invasion at Port Moresby and Australia. After making repairs to the *Yorktown* at Pearl Harbor he steamed full speed for Midway Island, 5000 miles distant, and joined the carrier force under Adm. Raymond A. Spruance for the battle of Midway, June 3–6, where the *Yorktown* was damaged and then sunk. The sinking of four Japanese carriers, however, made the battle a turning point in the war. In August Fletcher commanded the expeditionary force sent against Guadalcanal (under overall command of Adm. Robert L. Ghormley, and escorting Adm. R. Kelly Turner's South Pacific Amphibious Force). In the heavy naval fighting that followed that landing, he commanded the carrier strike group, comprising the *Enterprise, Saratoga,* and *Wasp.* An engagement on August 24, the battle of the Eastern Solomons, left his forces badly damaged. In December 1943 he was placed in command of the naval forces of the North Pacific area, which post he held until 1945. Following the Japanese surrender he oversaw the occupation of northern Japan. After the war he served as chairman of the General Board until his retirement in May 1947. He died in Bethesda, Maryland, on April 25, 1973.

Floyd, John Buchanan (1806–1863), public official and Confederate army officer. Born in Blacksburg, Virginia, on June 1, 1806, Floyd graduated from South Carolina College (now the University of South Carolina) in 1829 and took up the study of law, entering practice in Wytheville, Virginia. In 1836 he moved to Arkansas, but in 1839 he returned to Virginia, settling in Abingdon. He was elected to the legislature in 1847 and 1848 and to the governorship in 1849, serving in the latter post until 1852. He was again elected to the legislature in 1855. In 1856 he campaigned for James Buchanan and was subsequently appointed secretary of war in President Buchanan's cabinet. He served capably until December 1860, when he resigned. His resignation apparently grew in about equal measures from certain allegations of fiscal irregularities concerning Indian trust funds, a matter in which he seems to have been imprudent but not culpable, and from disagreement with President Buchanan over steps to be taken regarding the situation of Maj. Robert Anderson's forces in Charleston harbor. After his resignation it was widely charged that he had seen to the wide dispersal of the army and the transfer of excessively large stocks of arms and ammunition to southern arsenals as secret preparation for civil war. He was examined by a committee of the House of Representatives and found innocent of any such intentions. Although he had consistently opposed secession, he followed his state and accepted a commission as brigadier general in the Confederate army. He served in western Virginia late in 1861, engaging Union forces at Carnifex Ferry on August 26 and September 10, and early in 1862 was ordered to Fort Donelson, Tennessee. The fort was put under siege early in February 1862 by Gen. Ulysses S. Grant, and the three Confederate generals present failed to agree on a plan of defense. Floyd, the senior, decided to save what troops he could and passed command of the fort to Gen. Gideon J. Pillow, who in turn passed it to Gen. Simon B. Buckner. Floyd and Pillow then both escaped with some troops, leaving Buckner to surrender to Grant on February 16. Confederate President Jefferson Davis summarily removed him from command. A short time later he was appointed major general of Virginia troops, but his health failed and he died near Abingdon on August 26, 1863.

Foote, Andrew Hull (1806–1863), naval officer. Born on September 12, 1806, in New Haven, Connecticut, Foote was the son of a prominent merchant shipper and public official; his name was originally Foot, and he himself added the "e" later in life. In 1822 he entered West Point but resigned after six months to accept appointment in December as a midshipman in the navy. For 20 years he served in the Caribbean, the Mediterranean, and the Pacific, as well as on shore duty at the Philadelphia navy yard, advancing to lieutenant in December 1831. In 1843, as first lieutenant of the *Cumberland* in the Mediterranean, he succeeded in organizing the sailors into a temperance society. His abolition of the traditional grog on the vessel was the beginning of a campaign that resulted eventually in the end of the rum ration for the entire navy in 1862. During 1849–1851 Foote commanded the *Perry* off the coast of Africa and was zealous in putting down the slave trade, a goal he made almost a crusade with subsequent public lectures and his book *Africa and the American Flag*, 1854. From 1851 to 1856 he was again on shore duty, serving with Commander Samuel F. Du Pont on the navy's Efficiency Board of 1855. In 1856, with the rank of commander, he took command of the sloop *Portsmouth* in the Far East. In November 1856, at the height of hostilities between China and Great Britain, he responded to Chinese shelling by attacking and destroying four barrier forts before Canton. In 1858 he returned to the United States to take command of the Brooklyn navy yard. In August 1861 Foote was put in charge of naval operations on the vitally important upper Mississippi and its tributaries. His first task was to build a fleet of gunboats and mortarboats; that done, in February 1862 his fleet provided valuable support to Gen. Ulysses S. Grant in taking Fort Henry and Fort Donelson on the Tennessee and Cumberland rivers. Later, in April, he aided Gen. John Pope in capturing the strategic Island No. 10, opening the way to Memphis and the lower Mississippi. The Confederate forces on the heavily fortified island actually surrendered to the navy just three days after Commander Henry Walke had run the *Carondelet* past their batteries and thus threatened their supply line. Wounds sustained at Fort Donelson finally forced Foote to relinquish command to Capt. Charles H. Davis in June 1862; he was nonetheless promoted to rear admiral the next month. After a period in charge of the Bureau of Equipment and Recruiting he was named in June 1863 to succeed Adm. Samuel F. Du Pont as commander of the South Atlantic Blockading Squadron; before he could assume the command, he died in New York City on June 26, 1863.

Forman, David (1745–1797), Revolutionary army officer. Born in Monmouth County, New Jersey, on November 3, 1745, Forman may have attended the College of New Jersey (now Princeton) for a time. In June 1776 he was appointed colonel of a militia regiment and sent to join Gen. George Washington's army in New York. By the end of the year he had been given command of a Continental regiment. Early in 1777 he was promoted to brigadier general of militia, and he commanded the New Jersey troops at the battle of Germantown, October 4, 1777. The following month, after bringing his troops back to New Jersey, he resigned his commission in a dispute with the legislature. In 1778 he was assigned by Washington to the staff of Gen. Charles Lee, but his advice was ignored and after Lee's disastrous performance at Monmouth, June 27, Forman testified against Lee at the latter's court-martial. Forman remained in New Jersey for the rest of the war, suppressing with great harshness and even brutality the activities of Loyalists in the state, among whom he became infamous as "Black David" and "Devil David." His cruelty at length elicited a forceful complaint from Sir Henry Clinton in New York and a warning from Washington. After the Revolution Forman served for a time as a judge for Monmouth County. He later moved to Maryland. While he was sailing back from New Orleans after a visit to some property near Natchez, his vessel was captured by a privateer, and he died on the way to the Bahamas on September 12, 1797.

Forrest, French (1796–1866), naval and Confederate naval officer. Born in St. Marys County, Maryland, on October 4, 1796, Forrest entered the navy as a midshipman in June 1811. He may have served under Commodore Oliver H. Perry on Lake Erie, and he was aboard the *Hornet* under Capt. James Lawrence in the victory over the *Peacock* on February 24, 1813. Routine duty followed the action of the War of 1812; he was promoted to lieutenant in March 1817, to commander in February 1837, and to captain in March 1844. The outstanding event of those years was his firm action in June 1840, while commanding the sloop *St. Louis* on the Pacific coast, in obtaining the release of some 60 Americans and British taken from Monterey, California, and held prisoner in San Blas, Mexico. In the Mexican War he commanded the

Cumberland and later the *Raritan,* Commodore David Conner's flagships. He commanded the landing party of marines and seamen that took part in the capture of Frontera and Tabasco, October 23–26, 1846. At Veracruz on March 9, 1847, he was in charge of the landing of the more than 10,000 men of Gen. Winfield Scott's army, an operation managed with great skill and expedition. In later years Forrest served as commander of the Washington navy yard, 1855–1856, and of the Brazil Squadron, 1856–1859. In April 1861 he resigned his commission to accept another as captain in the Virginia navy. In June he was similarly commissioned in the Confederate service. He commanded the Norfolk navy yard until May 1862, the Bureau of Orders and Detail until March 1863, and the James River Squadron until May 1864. He died in Georgetown, D.C., on November 22, 1866.

Forrest, Nathan Bedford (1821–1877), Confederate army officer. Born near Chapel Hill, Tennessee, on July 13, 1821, Forrest received no formal schooling but educated himself to a fair degree. Responsible for the support of his family from the age of sixteen, he worked his way up from farmhand to livestock dealer to trader in slaves in Memphis. He eventually accumulated the money to purchase land in northwestern Mississippi, where cotton planting earned him a moderate fortune. At the outbreak of the Civil War he enlisted as a private in the unit that later gained fame as the 7th Tennessee Cavalry, but four months later, having raised a cavalry battalion on his own, he was commissioned a lieutenant colonel. Early in 1862 he was in northwestern Tennessee and took part in the defense of Fort Donelson; he refused to surrender with the rest of the garrison on February 16 and instead escaped with the entire 1500-man mounted force. He was promptly promoted to colonel and, after distinguished service at Pittsburg Landing (Shiloh), April 6–7, where he was badly wounded, to brigadier general in July. During 1862–1863 he was attached to Gen. Braxton Bragg's command and executed a series of daring raids, harassing Union communications throughout Tennessee and Kentucky. In April 1863 he engaged in a five-day running battle that resulted in the capture of an entire Union cavalry brigade near Rome, Georgia. He played a prominent part at Chickamauga, September 18–20, and after a violent quarrel with Bragg following that battle was transferred to a new command in Mississippi. In December he was given the rank of major general. In early 1864 he led raids into Tennessee and on April 12 recaptured Fort Pillow on the Mississippi River; an alleged massacre of the largely Negro garrison there created a major controversy, but the evidence concerning how the men met their deaths remains unclear. Throughout 1864 Forrest displayed his tactical genius in raids in Mississippi, Tennessee, Alabama, and Georgia, gaining a remarkable victory over a

much superior force under Gen. Samuel D. Sturgis at Brices Cross Roads, Mississippi, June 10, and thoroughly exasperating Union leaders. In August he eluded a large Union force and made a daring raid on Memphis, and in September he captured a large post at Athens, Georgia. In November he took command of the cavalry of Gen. John B. Hood's Army of Tennessee and performed gallantly in the disastrous Nashville campaign, achieving particular distinction in valiant rearguard actions. Forrest was promoted to lieutenant general in February 1865. In April he was driven out of Selma, Alabama, by an overwhelming force under Gen. James H. Wilson, and on May 9, following news of Gen. Robert E. Lee's surrender at Appomattox, he too surrendered. Entirely unschooled in military arts, Forrest won the admiration of leaders on both sides by his instinctive grasp of strategy and tactics, his boundless courage, and his deep concern for his men. After the war he lived in Memphis and for several years was president of the Selma, Marion & Memphis Railroad. He was a leading organizer and the first and only Grand Wizard of the short-lived original Ku Klux Klan, which disbanded in 1869. Forrest died in Memphis on October 29, 1877.

Forrestal, James Vincent (1892–1949), public official. Born on February 15, 1892, in Matteawan, now part of Beacon, New York, Forrestal worked for a series of small newspapers in New York state before entering Dartmouth College in 1911. A year later he transferred to Princeton, from which he graduated in 1915. In 1916 he joined a Wall Street firm, later Dillon, Read and Company, as a bond salesman. He returned as head of the bond sales department after serving in World War I as a naval aviator, advancing to a partnership in the firm in 1923 and to its presidency in 1937. In 1940 President Franklin D. Roosevelt, who had been impressed by Forrestal's positive testimony before congressional committees on various New Deal proposals for regulating the securities market, appointed him a presidential administrative assistant. After only a few weeks in that post he was named in August 1940 to the newly created office of undersecretary of the navy. Charged with responsibility for procurement and production, Forrestal played a vital role in building up U.S. naval strength before and in the early phases of World War II. He was on several occasions acting secretary of the navy and in May 1944, on the death of Frank Knox, became secretary. Although he had originally opposed the unification of the armed services, he threw himself wholeheartedly into the immense task created by the signing of the National Security Act of 1947 by President Harry S. Truman, and in September 1947 he was confirmed as the first secretary of defense to head the new National Military Establishment (now the Department of Defense). He worked diligently to promote the merger of the Department of the Army, the Department of the Navy, and the new Department of the Air Force and to maintain a high level of preparedness in all three, but came under considerable criticism for his apparent inability to control what many believed to be insubordination on the part of the air force with respect to appropriations and combat strength. In addition he fell out with Truman over such issues as the military budget, control of atomic weapons, and the partition of Palestine. He resigned from the cabinet at Truman's request in March 1949 and a few days later entered the naval hospital in Bethesda, Maryland. Diagnosed as suffering from nervous exhaustion and depression, he was thought to be recovering when he jumped from a window to his death on May 22, 1949.

Forsyth, George Alexander (1837–1915), army

officer. Born on November 7, 1837, in Muncy, Pennsylvania, Forsyth enlisted as a private in the Chicago Dragoons in April 1861 and in September was appointed a first lieutenant in the 8th Illinois Cavalry. Through the war he served with the Army of West Virginia, the Army of the Potomac, and the Army of the Shenandoah. He advanced to captain in February 1862, major in September 1863, brevet colonel in October 1864 for gallantry at Opequon and Winchester, and brevet brigadier general for services in March 1865, and was wounded four times. In February 1866 he was mustered out of volunteer service and in July was appointed major of the 9th Cavalry. In 1867 he received brevets in regular rank to lieutenant colonel and colonel for actions in the Civil War, at Dinwiddie Court House and Five Forks (April 1, 1865). From 1866 he was continuously on frontier duty. In the summer of 1868 he was ordered by Gen. Philip H. Sheridan, commander of the Department of the Missouri, to recruit a party of "fifty first-class hardy frontiersmen" to scout the Indians of the Kansas-Nebraska-Colorado region. He took the field in August. On September 16 he made camp on the Arickaree Fork of the Republican River, near the present-day Wray, Colorado. At dawn the next day the scouts were attacked by nearly 1000 Cheyenne, Sioux, and Arapaho led by Roman Nose. Forsyth and his men retreated to a sandy island in the bed of the river and dug in. They stood off repeated charges by the Indians, in the first of which Roman Nose and Forsyth's second-in-command, Lt. Frederick H. Beecher, were killed and Forsyth was wounded in three places. The scouts' horses were killed, and but for them there was no food. Four more men died in subsequent skirmishes, and the siege was maintained for nine days before relief came, just in time, in the form of a company of black troopers of the 10th Cavalry from Fort Wallace, Kansas. The engagement became known as the battle of Beecher Island, honoring Lt. Beecher. Forsyth, brevetted brigadier general

for his conduct in that fight, was later transferred to the 4th Cavalry in the Southwest and took part in the Apache wars. From 1869 to 1873 he was military secretary to Sheridan and from 1878 to 1881 his aide-de-camp. Forsyth was promoted to lieutenant colonel in June 1881 and he retired in March 1890. In 1900 he published *Thrilling Days in Army Life* and *The Story of the Soldier*. He was promoted to colonel on the retired list in April 1904. He died in Rockport, Massachusetts, on September 12, 1915.

Forsyth, James William (1836–1906), army of-

ficer. Born in Ohio on August 26, 1836, Forsyth graduated from West Point in 1856 and was commissioned in the infantry. He served in Washington Territory for five years, receiving promotion to first lieutenant in March 1861. In October of that year he was advanced to captain and appointed colonel of the 64th Ohio Volunteer Regiment. In the spring of 1862 he was on the staff of Gen. George B. McClellan during the Peninsular campaign. He was later transferred to the Army of the Cumberland, under Gen. William S. Rosecrans, and for his actions at Chickamauga, September 18–20, 1863, he was brevetted major of regulars. In April 1864 he became chief of staff of Gen. Philip H. Sheridan's cavalry corps. For gallantry in Sheridan's campaign against Gen. Jubal A. Early in the Shenandoah valley in the autumn of 1864 he was brevetted brigadier general of volunteers. Following the battle with Gen. George E. Pickett at Five Forks, Virginia, on April 1, 1865, he was brevetted regular colonel, and a few days later he was brevetted regular brigadier general for his services in the war. Full rank of brigadier general of volunteers came in May. He returned to routine duty in the rank of major after the war, serving on staff duty in the Department of the Gulf in 1866–1867, as aide to Gen. Sheridan, then commander of the Division of the Missouri, in 1869–1873, and as military secretary of the division in 1873–1878. In June 1886 he was promoted to colonel and given command of the 7th Cavalry. In December 1890 he was ordered to the region of the Pine Ridge Agency in South Dakota, where a band of Teton Sioux led by Big Foot had taken up arms and fled the custody of the reservation. A shortage of food, the coming of winter, the enthusiasm of the "Ghost Dance" religion, and the killing of Sitting Bull on December 15 had all contributed to a situation in which soldiers and other whites were fearful and the Indians desperate. On December 28 Maj. Samuel M. Whitside, commanding a detachment of the 7th, found Big Foot's people at Wounded Knee Creek. The next day Forsyth ordered the Indians disarmed; there was some resistance, during which a rifle was accidentally discharged into the air. The tension was too much for the soldiers and they began a general fire, some of them being armed with Hotchkiss rapid-fire weapons. In the end some 200 Sioux—

men, women, and children—were dead, including Big Foot, many more perishing later from wounds and exposure as they were left on the field to face a blizzard that struck the next day. The casualties among the soldiers were 25 killed, 37 wounded. The Wounded Knee battle, or massacre as it came to be considered, was the last engagement of any size in the Indian wars. Forsyth was promoted to brigadier general in October 1894, and he retired in May 1897 with the rank of major general. He died in Columbus, Ohio, on October 24, 1906.

Foss, Joseph Jacob (1915–   ), marine officer and public official. Born on April 17, 1915, in Sioux Falls, South Dakota, Foss attended Sioux Falls College and Augustana College for a year each before entering the University of South Dakota, from which he graduated in 1940. Shortly after the entry of the United States into World War II he enlisted in the marines, took aviation training, and, commissioned a second lieutenant, was ordered to Fighting Squadron 121 of the 1st Marine Aircraft Wing in the Southwest Pacific. He proved an outstanding fighter pilot and rose quickly to captain. Between October 9 and November 19, 1942 (by then executive officer of the squadron), he led escort, reconnaissance, and bombing missions over Guadalcanal and surrounding waters and shot down 23 Japanese aircraft. Three more on January 15, 1943, brought his score to 26, second among marine pilots only to Maj. Gregory Boyington. On January 25 he led a mixed squadron of 12 F4F and P-38 fighters in driving off a much superior force of Japanese bombers; 4 of the bombers went down, and none of the others was able to reach its target. In May 1943 Foss was awarded the Medal of Honor for his exploits. Discharged as a major in 1945, he returned to Sioux Falls and organized with a partner the Joe Foss Flying Service. While building this and other business ventures, he helped organize the state Air National Guard in 1947, commanding the 175th Flight Squadron and holding the rank of colonel in the air force reserve. In 1953 he became a brigadier general in the reserve and in the Air National Guard. He also became active in politics, serving in the legislature from 1949 to 1953 and winning election as governor of South Dakota in 1954 and again in 1956. In 1960 he was named commissioner of the newly organized American Football League, and later he was an officer of KLM Royal Dutch Airlines; he had various other business interests as well.

Foster, John Gray (1823–1874), army officer. Born on May 27, 1823, in Whitefield, New Hampshire, Foster graduated from West Point in 1846 and was commissioned in the engineers. During the Mexican War he served in Gen. Winfield Scott's army from the siege of Veracruz on, receiving a severe wound at Molino del Rey, September 8, 1847, and

being twice brevetted, to first lieutenant and captain. Later he engaged in the building of Fort Carroll, Maryland, and other engineering duties and in 1855–1857 was on the faculty at West Point. Promoted to captain in July 1860, he was made engineer in charge of fortifications in Charleston harbor, where in April 1861 he was second-in-command to Maj. Robert Anderson during the siege of Fort Sumter. In October 1861 he was appointed brigadier general of volunteers, and in January 1862 he took part in Gen. Ambrose E. Burnside's capture of Roanoke and New Bern, North Carolina, receiving brevets to regular lieutenant colonel and then colonel. In July he was made commander of the Department of North Carolina and was promoted to major general of volunteers. In November 1863 he was sent to relieve Gen. Burnside as commander of the Department (and Army) of Ohio, actually assuming the post in December after the lifting of the siege of Knoxville. Injuries sustained in a fall from his horse forced him to give up the command to Gen. John M. Schofield in February 1864. He returned to active service in May as commander of the Department of the South, in which post he cooperated with Gen. William T. Sherman in the campaign against Savannah and Charleston. In March 1865 he was promoted to major of engineers and brevet major general in the regulars. He commanded the Department of Florida in 1865–1867, receiving promotion to lieutenant colonel in March of the latter year, and he was subsequently engaged in various river and harbor projects in New England. He died in Nashua, New Hampshire, on September 2, 1874.

Fox, Gustavus Vasa (1821–1883), naval officer and public official. Born in Saugus, Massachusetts, on June 13, 1821, Fox was commissioned a midshipman in the navy in January 1838 and for the next 18 years was on active naval service, winning promotion to lieutenant in 1852. After his resignation from the navy in July 1856 he became an agent for a textile company in Lawrence, Massachusetts. Early in 1861 he was recommended to Gen. Winfield Scott, commanding general of the army, as a naval consultant on the problem of Fort Sumter at Charleston harbor, whose surrender had been demanded by South Carolina. His plan for relieving the garrison was tabled by President James Buchanan, but soon after his inauguration President Abraham Lincoln requested Fox to submit a plan for reinforcing Sumter. In April Fox set out for the fort to study conditions and arrived on the 12th, just in time to witness the bombardment by South Carolina forces. Unequipped to aid in the fort's defense, he sailed into the harbor and evacuated Maj. Robert Anderson and his men, who had been allowed to depart by Gen. P. G. T. Beauregard. A few weeks later he was appointed chief clerk of the Navy Department, and in August the post of assistant secretary was created for him. Through the rest of the Civil War he proved an invaluable aid to Secretary Gideon Welles, promoting the construction and deployment of vessels of the *Monitor* class ("monitors") and otherwise employing his extensive knowledge of naval affairs in highly productive ways. It was Fox, for example, who suggested Capt. David G. Farragut as commander of the naval expedition against New Orleans in 1862. On his resignation in May 1866 he undertook, with an impressive naval escort that included the *Miantonomoh,* the first monitor to cross the Atlantic, a diplomatic mission to Russia. He devoted himself to private business interests thereafter and died in New York City on October 29, 1883.

Franklin, William Buel (1823–1903), army officer. Born in York, Pennsylvania, on February 27, 1823, Franklin graduated from West Point in 1843 and was commissioned in the topographical engineers. After sundry surveying assignments he served under Gen. John E. Wool in the Mexican War and won a brevet as first lieutenant at Buena Vista, February 22–23, 1847. That rank became permanent in March 1853, and he advanced to captain in July 1857. Assigned to Washington, D.C., he was in charge of construction of the Capitol dome and other public works. In May 1861 he was appointed colonel of the 12th Infantry and immediately afterward appointed brigadier general of volunteers. At Bull Run (Manassas), July 21, 1861, he commanded a brigade of recruits, one regiment of whom claimed their discharge on the very morning of battle. At the beginning of the Peninsular campaign in March 1862 he commanded a division, rising in May to command of the VI Corps. He was brevetted brigadier general of regulars in June and promoted to major general of volunteers in July. After taking part in the defense of Maryland, including action at South Mountain and Antietam, September 14 and 17, he was appointed commander of the Left Grand Division, comprising the I and VI corps, in Gen. Ambrose E. Burnside's reorganization of the Army of the Potomac in November 1862. Following the disaster at Fredericksburg, December 13, Burnside charged Franklin with disobedience and carried his point with the Congressional Joint Committee on the Conduct of the War, which censured Franklin. He was left inactive until July 1863. In August of that year he was placed in command of the XIX Corps in Louisiana. He took part in an expedition against Sabine Pass, Texas, preliminary to a contemplated invasion of that state, which was repulsed on September 8, and during the Red River campaign under Gen. Nathaniel P. Banks the following spring he was badly wounded at Sabine Cross Roads, April 8, 1864. On July 11 a train he was riding near Baltimore was captured by a detachment from Gen. Jubal A. Early's corps, but he escaped

a day later. He resigned his volunteer commission in November 1865 and his regular commission in March 1866. From 1866 to 1888 Franklin was vice-president and general manager of the Colt's Patent Fire-Arms Company in Hartford, Connecticut. He superintended the construction of the new state capitol there during 1872–1880, was state adjutant general in 1877–1878, a chief judge of engineering and architecture at the Centennial Exposition in Philadelphia in 1876, and U.S. commissioner general at the Paris Exposition of 1888. He died in Hartford on March 8, 1903.

Frémont, John Charles (1813–1890), army officer, explorer, and political leader. Born in Savannah, Georgia, on January 21, 1813, Frémont grew up in Charleston, South Carolina, and attended the College of Charleston from 1829 to 1831. He secured a patron in Joel R. Poinsett, a prominent South Carolina politician, and through his efforts was appointed teacher of mathematics aboard the warship *Natchez* on an extended South American cruise. In July 1838 Poinsett arranged Frémont's appointment as a second lieutenant in the army's Topographical Corps. He was a member of J. N. Nicollet's expedition to explore and map the plateau region between the upper Missouri and Mississippi rivers, and in 1841 led his own exploratory party along the Des Moines River. Upon his return he married Jessie Benton, daughter of Sen. Thomas Hart Benton. In 1842, with Benton's support, he was sent to explore the route of the Oregon Trail and the Wind River Range in order to aid emigration to Oregon; his report, prepared with his wife's help, was widely reprinted. In the next year he set out on a much more extensive expedition. Guided, as he had been the year before, by Kit Carson and also by Thomas Fitzpatrick, he and his party of fewer than 40 men crossed Wyoming and Idaho to Oregon, followed the Columbia River to Fort Vancouver, and turned southeast to Nevada. Then, in a move bordering on foolhardiness, he made a winter crossing of the Sierra Nevada westward into the Sacramento valley of California. He traveled south to Los Angeles, explored parts of Arizona and Utah, and finally returned east in 1844. The journey and the report of it that was subsequently published were sensations and made Frémont a popular hero. In January 1845 he was brevetted first lieutenant and captain for his achievement. While the nature of his sojourns in the West is still a matter of debate—he has been viewed variously as a true explorer, as a pathfinder, and as a government-sponsored mapmaker—there is no dispute over the practical significance of his work for settlement and establishment of lines of communication. In the spring of 1845, with war with Mexico appearing imminent, he was sent on a third expedition to California with secret orders instructing him, should he find war had begun when he arrived, to convert his party into a military force. Ordered by

Mexican authorities to leave shortly after his arrival at Sutter's Fort in December 1845, he refused and briefly raised the American flag over fortifications he built on Gavilan (or Hawk) Peak. After a northward feint toward Oregon, he turned back, possibly in receipt of secret orders, and by a show of force lent his support to the Bear Flag revolt at Sonoma. When news that war had formally been declared reached California in July 1846, Frémont was appointed major of the "California Battalion," composed of his own men and U.S. volunteers, by Commodore Robert F. Stockton. On August 13 the combined forces under Frémont and Stockton captured Los Angeles. The town was later retaken by Mexican forces in Frémont's absence, and he returned in time to join Gen. Stephen W. Kearny in its final capture in January 1847. Frémont himself accepted the Mexican surrender at Cahuenga on January 13. There ensued a conflict of authority over California, and Frémont found himself caught between the two feuding principals. After two months as governor upon appointment by Stockton, Frémont was arrested by Kearny, his superior in the army, for mutiny, disobedience, and conduct prejudicial to military order. He was found guilty of the last two charges by a courtmartial in January 1848, and although President James K. Polk suspended his sentence, he resigned from the army. During the next several years he devoted himself to developing his huge estates in California. The discovery of gold made him rich, and he served a brief period (September 1850–March 1851) as one of California's first senators. He also conducted a number of expeditions looking for suitable mountain passes for a Pacific railroad. In 1856 his wide popularity and his antislavery opinions won him the presidential nomination of the new Republican party. After defeat in November by James Buchanan, Democrat, by 174 electoral votes to 114, he returned to California. At the outbreak of the Civil War he resumed his army commission; with the rank of major general he commanded the Department of the West from headquarters in St. Louis from July 1861 until political enemies and his own recklessness—he refused to retract an order freeing slaves in Missouri, forcing President Abraham Lincoln to countermand it—combined to cause his removal in November 1861. In a subsequent command—known as the Army of the Mountain Department—in western Virginia from March 1862, he was ineffectual against Gen. Thomas J. Jackson, then conducting his brilliant Shenandoah valley campaign. He was checked by a much smaller force under Gen. Richard S. Ewell at Cross Keys on June 8 and in late June, when his corps was placed under the command of Gen. John Pope, whom he detested, he again resigned from the army. He was dissuaded from seeking the nomination for the presidency in 1864 and retired to private life. The loss of some of his California holdings was followed by the loss of most of his fortune in the bankruptcy of the Memphis & El Paso Railroad, of which he had become president with the hope of building the line west to San Diego. From 1878 to 1883 he served as territorial governor of Arizona, afterwards returning to California. Early in 1890 he was restored to rank as major general on the retired list, and his pension sustained him until his death on July 13, 1890, while on a visit to New York City. His *Memories of My Life* appeared in 1887.

Fry, James Barnet (1827–1894), army officer. Born in Carrollton, Illinois, on February 22, 1827, Fry graduated from West Point in 1847, was commissioned in the artillery, and joined Gen. Winfield Scott's army in Mexico City. After assignments in Oregon, Louisiana, and Texas, he returned to West Point in 1853, first as assistant to Capt. George H. Thomas, at the time an instructor, and then as adjutant of the academy at the appointment of the superintendent, Col. Robert E. Lee. In March 1861 he commanded an artillery battery in Washington, D.C., and in that month he was appointed an assistant adjutant general of the army with brevet rank of captain. During May–July he was on the staff of Gen. Irvin McDowell, and from November 1861 to November 1862 he was chief of staff of the Army of the Ohio under Gen. Don Carlos Buell, earning commendations for his performance at Shiloh and Perryville. In December 1862 he was promoted to lieutenant colonel, and in March 1863 he was appointed to the newly created post of provost marshal general with responsibility for overseeing the administration and enforcement of military recruitment and conscription. His concerns included desertion, state quotas, bounties, and other problems associated with conscription, particularly the draft riots in Boston and New York. Under his administration 1.1 million men were inducted into the Union army. In April 1864 he was raised to the rank of brigadier general, but on the dissolution of the bureau he headed in August 1866 he reverted to lieutenant colonel. Through James G. Blaine he became involved in a long and acrimonious dispute with Roscoe Conkling, the two representatives debating at length in the House over Fry's conduct of the bureau and the question of making it permanent. Over considerable opposition he was subsequently given brevets of major general of volunteers and colonel and brigadier general of regulars, as of March 1865, and he served as adjutant general in several military divisions before his retirement in July 1881. Fry wrote a number of books on military affairs, including *A Sketch of the Adjutant General's Department*, 1875, *Army Sacrifices*, 1879, *McDowell and Tyler in the Campaign of Bull Run, 1861*, 1884, *Operations of the Army under Buell*, 1884, *New York and the Conscription of 1863*, 1885, and *Military Miscellanies*, 1889. He died in Newport, Rhode Island, on July 11, 1894.

Fuller, Ben Hebard (1870–1937), marine officer. Born on February 27, 1870, in Big Rapids, Michigan, Fuller graduated from the Naval Academy in 1889 and two years later transferred to the marine corps as a second lieutenant. He was promoted to first lieutenant in March 1893. He served during the Spanish–American War aboard the *Columbia,* which patrolled the Atlantic coast and later transported troops to Puerto Rico. He advanced to captain in March 1899. During the Philippine Insurrection he took part in the battle of Novaleta, and in 1900 he served under Maj. William P. Biddle in the Peking Relief Expedition, seeing action at Tientsin, July 13. Assignments at the Naval Academy, in the Panama Canal Zone, and in Cuba followed, and he received promotions to major in December 1903 and lieutenant colonel in February 1911. He graduated from the Army War College in 1914 and in 1915–1916 was fleet marine officer, Atlantic Fleet. Promoted to colonel in August 1916, he graduated from the Navy War College in 1917. From September 1918 to December 1919, with temporary rank (from July 1918) of brigadier general, he commanded the 2nd Provisional Marine Brigade in Santo Domingo. During 1923–1924 he was commandant of the Marine Corps Schools, Quantico, Virginia; in the latter year, his rank of brigadier general having become permanent in February, he took command of the 1st Brigade in Haiti. He was appointed assistant to the commandant of the marine corps, Gen. Wendell C. Neville, in 1925 and in July 1930 was himself named commandant with the rank of major general. He remained in that post until his retirement in March 1934. Fuller died in Washington, D.C., on June 8, 1937.

Fulton, Robert (1765–1815), engineer, inventor, and artist. Born in Little Britain, Lancaster County, Pennsylvania, on November 14, 1765, Fulton grew up and attended school in nearby Lancaster. He early exhibited an interest in and a remarkable aptitude for things mechanical; he became an expert gunsmith and as early as 1779 had designed a small paddle-wheel boat. In 1782 he moved to Philadelphia and was financially successful, first as a jeweler's apprentice and later as a painter and miniaturist. In 1786 he went to England to study under the artist Benjamin West; within a few years his interest in painting gave way to his growing interest in engineering. Particularly fascinated by the promise of canal systems for inland transportation, he devised a method for raising and lowering canal boats to integrate them into a surface railroad system. He also secured patents for machines to saw marble, spin flax, and twist hemp rope. In 1796 he published *A Treatise on the Improvement of Canal Navigation.* He submitted a number of proposals for various engineering projects, complete with detailed plans and cost estimates, to the British government and some of them, notably an iron aque-

duct over the Dee, were later built. From 1797, when he moved to France, he devoted several years to developing a practical submarine; in 1800 his *Nautilus* was successfully demonstrated. Its naval potential was made clear in a demonstration five years later when, equipped with torpedoes (also of Fulton's invention), it sank a heavy brig. He was unable to secure research funds from either France or Great Britain, however, and dropped the submarine project in favor of the development of a practical steamboat. In partnership with Robert R. Livingston, then U.S. minister to France, he planned a steamboat for service on the Hudson River, for steam navigation of which Livingston owned a monopoly. An experimental steamboat was demonstrated on the Seine in August 1803. Returning to the United States at the end of 1806, Fulton completed "The Steamboat," as he called it, and made the first trial run on August 9, 1807. On August 17 the vessel made a New York-Albany round trip in 62 hours of steaming time (five days elapsed time). By autumn a commercial schedule was established. Lengthened from 133 to 149 feet and powered by two side paddle wheels, the boat was registered as "The New North River Steamboat of Clermont," but was generally known simply as the *Clermont.* For the remainder of his life, Fulton oversaw the construction of steamboats and the organization of regular freight and passenger lines. His *New Orleans* was in 1811 the first steamboat on the Mississippi. During the War of 1812 he obtained congressional authority to construct a steam-powered warship, virtually a huge mobile floating fort, for the defense of New York harbor; the *Fulton the First,* or *Demologus,* 156 feet long by 56 feet wide, with a paddle wheel mounted between twin hulls, and showing 30 32-pounder guns, was launched shortly before the end of the war. He died two months later, on February 24, 1815, in New York City.

Funston, Frederick (1865–1917), army officer. Born in New Carlisle, Ohio, on November 9, 1865, Funston early moved with his family to Iola, Kansas. A restless youth, he worked at various jobs, attended the University of Kansas for a little more than two years, and in the early 1890s found employment as a special agent for the Department of Agriculture, for which he took part in an expedition to Death Valley in 1891 and later made a canoe trip down 1500 perilous miles of the Yukon River. Soon after the outbreak of the Cuban insurrection against Spain in 1895 he offered his services to the Cuban cause and, although he had no qualifications for such a post, was commissioned a captain of artillery. He arrived in Cuba in mid-1896 and for 18 months served creditably in various guerrilla operations under Gen. Gómez, rising to the rank of lieutenant colonel. He returned to the United States in 1898 and upon the U.S. declaration of war against Spain a short time later was given in May command of the 20th Kansas Volunteer Regiment. Sent to the Philippines, he arrived too late to see action against the Spanish but was quickly thrown into the campaign against the Philippine independence forces led by Emilio Aguinaldo. He led several daring actions and particularly distinguished himself at the battle of Calumpit, April 27, 1899, winning a Medal of Honor (awarded February 1900) and promotion to brigadier general of volunteers, but by early 1901, denied a commission in the regular army, he was scheduled for mustering out along with the rest of the volunteers. Early in March 1901 he learned from captured letters the whereabouts of Aguinaldo's secret headquarters. Enlisting a number of pro-U.S. Filipinos disguised as rebel recruits, a defected rebel for a guide, and six U.S. soldiers who posed as prisoners, he led his small raiding party by boat to a beach in northern Luzon and then through thick jungle to the rebel headquarters at Palanan; on March 23 Aguinaldo was taken by surprise and placed under arrest. His feat was widely hailed, and Funston was promptly transferred to the regular army as a brigadier general. Later placed in command of the Department of California, he was in charge of the early phases of emergency military administration and rescue work following the San Francisco earthquake in 1906. He later commanded the Department of Luzon, Philippines, in 1911–1913, and the Hawaiian Department, 1913–1914. In April 1914 he commanded the army force that took over from the navy, under Adm. Frank F. Fletcher, and marines, under Col. John A. Lejeune, the occupation of Veracruz, Mexico, and served as military governor of the city until November. Promoted to major general in that month, he commanded troops on the Mexican border from February 1915. He was still in that post when, while Gen. John J. Pershing was pursuing Pancho Villa across the border, he died in San Antonio, Texas, on February 19, 1917. His *Memories of Two Wars: Cuban and Philippine Experiences* had appeared in 1911.

G

Gaillard, David Du Bose (1859–1913), army officer and engineer. Born in Fulton, Sumter County, South Carolina, on September 4, 1859, Gaillard graduated from West Point in 1884 and was commissioned in the engineers. He graduated from the Engineer School of Application, Willets Point (now Fort Totten), New York, in 1887, having served also as an instructor there, and in October of that year was promoted to first lieutenant. After four years of harbor work in Florida he was appointed in 1891 to the U.S.–Mexican border commission. Promoted to captain in October 1895, he was assigned in that year to the Washington, D.C., aqueduct project, and in 1896 he spent some months in the survey of the Portland Channel in Alaska. In June 1898 he was appointed colonel of volunteers commanding the 3rd Engineer Volunteers, which was sent to occupation duty in Cuba and did valuable sanitation work in Cienfuegos. Mustered out of volunteer service in May 1899, Gaillard was again in Washington, D.C., from 1899 to 1901, and he then had charge of river and harbor work on Lake Superior until 1903, when he was assigned to duty with the General Staff Corps. He was promoted to major in April 1904 and graduated from the Army War College in 1905. In 1906–1907 he was with the occupation forces in Cuba. In March 1907 he was appointed to the Isthmian Canal Commission and in April placed in charge, by Col. George W. Goethals, chief engineer of the Panama Canal project, of the department of dredging and excavation. In July 1908 he took charge of the central division of the canal, a 33-mile section across the Continental Divide. The nine-mile Culebra Cut in the center had been declared impossible by some engineers, and it proved a massive and harrowing task in actual fact. Material removed from the cut had to be moved 30 miles to construct Gatun Dam. Earthslides were a constant menace. By unflagging exertion Gaillard, who was promoted to lieutenant colonel in April 1909, managed to solve or overcome all problems. The strain broke him, however, and shortly before the completion of his work he died, on December 5, 1913, in Baltimore. The name of Culebra Cut was subsequently changed to Gaillard Cut by order of President Woodrow Wilson, and the army post there became Camp Gaillard.

Gaines, Edmund Pendleton (1777–1849), army officer. Born on March 20, 1777, in Culpeper County, Virginia, Gaines moved as a child with his family to North Carolina and then to what is now Tennessee. In 1797 he entered the army, becoming a second lieutenant in January 1799 and first lieutenant in April 1802. From 1801 to 1804 he was engaged in surveying work, and in the latter year he was appointed collector of the port of Mobile and commandant of Fort Stoddert. He was promoted to captain in 1807, and it was he who arrested Aaron Burr in that year. He took extended leave from the army in 1811, studied law, and began practice in Mississippi Territory, but he returned to active service in March 1812 as a major, quickly advancing to lieutenant colonel and in 1813 to colonel. His regiment covered the American retreat from the battle of Chrysler's Field, November 11, 1813, during the Montreal campaign. He was then appointed adjutant general and given command of Fort Erie. Promoted to brigadier general in March 1814, he successfully defended Fort Erie against a British siege in August–September of that year and was brevetted major general. In 1817 he was one of the commissioners appointed to treat with the Creek Indians and was in command of the southern district when hostilities with the Creeks and Seminoles broke out a short time later. In 1821 he became commander of the new Western Department. He took the field in 1831 to repel the first invasion of Illinois by Black Hawk. On the outbreak of the second Seminole War in 1835 he was ordered to border duty in western Louisiana, although the fighting in Florida was technically within his department and not that of Gen. Winfield Scott, who was given field command there. Gaines nonetheless mounted an expedition in disregard of his orders, bringing an army by sea to Tampa Bay and engaging the Seminoles inconclusively at the Withlacoochee River, where he was wounded. During the Texas revolution in 1836 he led a force from Louisiana across the Sabine River and held Nacogdoches for five months. On the outbreak of the Mexican War in 1845 Gaines recruited, without authorization, several thousand volunteers in Louisiana, Alabama, Mississippi, and Missouri, and continued to do so in defiance of contrary orders. He was removed from his post, court-martialed and acquitted, and subsequently placed in command of the Eastern Department. He died in New Orleans on June 6, 1849.

Gale, Anthony (1782–1843), marine officer. Born on September 17, 1782, in Dublin, Ireland, Gale emigrated to the United States at a date unknown. Little is known of his life. He obtained a commission in the marine corps and by 1819 had risen to the rank of major. Following the death of Lt. Col. Franklin Wharton, commandant of the corps, in September 1818, the marines were without a commandant for six months; Maj. Archibald Henderson was acting commandant during that period. Finally in March 1819 Gale was named commandant with the rank of lieutenant colonel. He held the post for 19 months, during which he failed to perform his duties effectively. Financial irregularities may have been involved in his removal in October 1820, by which time he had nonetheless been advanced to colonel. After his removal he retired to Lincoln County, Kentucky, where he died in 1843.

Gall (1840?–1894), Indian leader. Born about 1840 on the Moreau River in South Dakota, Gall was a Hunkpapa Sioux. His name was originally Pizi and he later acquired his sobriquet when, orphaned and hungry, he attempted to eat the gall of a game animal belonging to another. As he grew into manhood he became noted as a warrior and was informally adopted by Sitting Bull. He was prominent in the battles and skirmishes of Red Cloud's War that accompanied construction of the Powder River army road and the three forts associated with it along the old Bozeman Trail in 1866–1867, and he spoke out furiously against the treaty negotiated at Fort Laramie in April 1868, which, while conceding the Powder River region to the Indians, provided for tribal reservations for the various Plains tribes. Although he was assigned to the Sioux reservation in Dakota Territory, Gall refused to adopt the government's "civilizing" program of homestead farming and instead accompanied Sitting Bull to the great encampment in Montana on the Little Bighorn River in 1876. By that time he was acknowledged as Sitting Bull's chief lieutenant. When the cavalry force of Col. George A. Custer attacked the camp on June 25, Gall, as war chief, led the counterattack that drove back the troops under Maj. Marcus A. Reno and pinned them down in the hills; then, after joining Crazy Horse in surrounding and annihilating Custer's men, he returned to again attack Reno, who, however, was able to escape the next day on the approach of Gen. Alfred H. Terry's main force. Gall remained with Sitting Bull through the retreat northward into Canada, but in 1880 he returned and early the next year surrendered with 300 followers and was placed on the Standing Rock reservation. There he was befriended by James McLaughlin, the resident Indian agent, and gradually reconciled himself to white rule, working thereafter to persuade other Indians to surrender and in 1889 becoming a judge of the Court of Indian Offenses. In opposition to Sitting Bull, he took no part in the final Sioux uprising of 1890. Gall died on December 5, 1894, on Oak Creek, South Dakota.

Gallery, Daniel Vincent (1901–1977), naval officer. Born in Chicago on July 10, 1901, Gallery graduated from the Naval Academy in 1920, in which year he was also a member of the U.S. Olympic wrestling team. After service on various ships he took aviation training at Pensacola Naval Air Station, Florida, in 1926–1927 and was an instructor there in 1929–1932. After advanced training in aviation ordnance and engineering he joined Scouting Squadron 4 in 1935, becoming squadron commander the next year. During 1938–1941 he was chief of the aviation section of the Bureau of Ordnance, and in the latter year he was named naval attaché for air at the U.S. embassy in London. On the entry of the United States into World War II in December 1941 Gallery was put in command of the Fleet Air Base at Reykjavik, Iceland, from which naval aircraft were dispatched for convoy service and antisubmarine patrols. In August 1943, by then a captain, he took command of the small carrier *Guadalcanal* and of a task group of five destroyer escorts detailed to antisubmarine duty in the Atlantic. The group sank the U-515 on April 9, 1944, near the Azores. On June 4, 1944, off Cape Blanc on the northwestern coast of Africa, Gallery's task group encountered the U-505. The submarine was forced to the surface by depth charges, and gunfire then forced the crew to abandon ship. Then, as the submarine began to sink (the crew having opened the sea cocks), Gallery gave the order that he had been planning for some time—"Away boarders." A boarding party from the *Pillsbury* boarded and secured the U-505 in the navy's first capture of an enemy vessel on the high seas since the capture of the *Nautilus* by Capt. Lewis Warrington of the *Peacock* in 1815. The U-505 was towed to Bermuda, where it yielded valuable information on German torpedoes and codes. (It was later installed in the Museum of Science and Industry, Chicago.) In 1945 Gallery took command of the *Hancock* in the Pacific. Promoted to rear admiral in December of that year, he was assistant chief of naval operations in 1946–1951, commander of Carrier Division 6 in the Mediterranean in 1951–1952, and commander of the Atlantic Fleet Hunter-Killer (antisubmarine) force in 1952. From late 1952 to 1953 he was chief of naval air reserve training at Glenview Naval Air Station, Illinois, and from 1954 to 1956 he commanded the Ninth Naval District at Great Lakes. From December 1956 to July 1960 Gallery commanded the Caribbean Sea Frontier and the Tenth Naval District at San Juan, Puerto Rico; he retired in November 1960. He was the author of several books, including *Clear the Decks!*, the story of the capture of the U-505, 1951, *Twenty Million Tons Under the Sea*, 1956, *Eight Bells and All's Well*, an autobiography, 1965, and *Now Hear This!*, a collection of short stories, 1965. Gallery lived in Virginia until his death in Bethesda, Maryland, on January 16, 1977.

Gansevoort, Peter (1749–1812), Revolutionary army officer. Born in July 1749 in Albany, New York, Gansevoort was appointed major in the 2nd New York Regiment in June 1775 and in September–December of that year took part in the invasion of Canada under Gen. Richard Montgomery. In March 1776 he was promoted to lieutenant colonel, and in November, while commanding Fort George, he became colonel of the 3rd New York. In April 1777 he was placed in command of Fort Schuyler (formerly Fort Stanwix) in the Mohawk valley. On August 3 a force of some 1700 British regulars, Loyalists, and Indians, under the general command of Col. Barry St. Leger, appeared before the fort on their way to join Gen. John Burgoyne at Albany. Gansevoort refused a demand for surrender and on August 6 sent forth a sortie to attack St. Leger in conjunction with forces under Gen. Nicholas Herkimer. The battle of Oriskany scattered Herkimer's militia, but inflicted considerable losses on St. Leger as well. St. Leger maintained the siege for nearly two weeks more, but Gansevoort stoutly held out, and on August 22, hearing exaggerated rumors of a large army approaching under Gen. Benedict Arnold, the British retired back up the valley. After a brief period in command at Albany, Gansevoort remained in command of Fort Schuyler through most of 1778. In 1779 he took a distinguished part in the campaign under Gen. John Sullivan against the Indians of the New York–Pennsylvania frontier. In March 1781 he was appointed brigadier general of New York militia, and he remained active in New York throughout the remainder of the Revolution and afterwards. In 1793 he advanced to major general of militia, commanding the western portion of the state, and he later served as Indian agent and military agent for the northern department of the army. In February 1809 he was commissioned brigadier general in the regular army. Gansevoort died in Albany, New York, on July 2, 1812.

Garand, John Cantius (1888–1974), inventor. Born on January 1, 1888, in St. Rémi, Quebec, Garand grew up there and in rural Connecticut. He attended school until he was twelve and then went to work in a textile mill, where he gradually worked his way up to machinist. He later found a position in a tool factory in Providence, Rhode Island, and in his spare time indulged his enthusiasm for guns and target shooting. In 1917, prompted by the reported difficulty the army was experiencing in developing a light machine gun, he took up the problem and on submitting a design to the War Department was given a position in the U.S. Bureau of Standards to perfect it. His first model was built in 1919, too late for use in World War I, but in that year he was appointed a consulting engineer at the U.S. Armory in Springfield, Massachusetts, to work on a semiautomatic in-

fantry rifle. It took 15 years to produce an acceptable model incorporating Garand's basic mechanism, in which a portion of the expanding propellant gas drove a piston that in turn operated the bolt, automatically ejecting the spent shell, cocking the hammer, and reloading the chamber. Weight was the principal problem, but finally in 1934 Garand patented a rifle weighing just over nine pounds that was simply constructed and easy to maintain and fired a clip of eight .276-caliber rounds. Adopted by the army in 1936, modified to use .30-caliber ammunition, and designated the M-1, the Garand rifle was quickly put into mass production to replace the 30-year old Springfield repeater. The M-1 was highly praised by military commanders, particularly during World War II, when it was credited with giving the U.S. infantry a great advantage. The M-1 remained the basic shoulder weapon of U.S. forces until it was gradually replaced following the appearance of the lighter, fully automatic M-14 in 1957. Garand himself received no royalties from his work, assigning all his patents freely to the government; widely honored, he remained at the Springfield Armory as a consultant until his retirement in 1953. He died in Springfield on February 16, 1974.

Gardiner, Lion (1599–1663), colonial officer. Born in England in 1599, Gardiner was educated in civil and military engineering and by 1635 had served in the armies of England and of the Prince of Orange. In that year he was engaged by a group of prospective colonizers, organized under the doubtful authority of the so-called Warwick Patent, who were interested in the region that is now Connecticut. He was to have charge of the defenses of the proposed colony. Arriving in Boston in November 1635, he remained there long enough to build the fortifications on Fort Hill and then proceeded to the mouth of the Connecticut River and erected Fort Saybrook. In April 1636 his son David was the first European child born in the settlement. In the spring of 1637 Saybrook was attacked by a party of Pequot Indians, and Gardiner directed the defense. Reinforced by companies under Capt. John Underhill and Capt. John Mason, Gardiner took part in planning an expedition against the Pequots and, although Mason was in command of the expedition, is generally credited with directing the assault on and razing of the Pequot fort at Mystic, Connecticut, on May 26, 1637, when much of the tribe was exterminated. At the expiration of his contract with the Warwick patentees in 1640 he moved to Gardiner's Island (until then known as the Isle of Wight and called by the Indians Manchonat) in Long Island Sound, which he had purchased the year before from the Indians. His title was subsequently confirmed by Lord Stirling and Governor Nicoll. In 1653 he removed to Long Island, settling in what is now Easthampton, where he had bought a large tract.

He died there in 1663. Gardiner's Island was erected into a manor in 1683, David Gardiner becoming the first lord of the manor, and the island remained thereafter in the family.

Gates, Horatio (1727?–1806), Revolutionary army officer. Born probably in Maldon, England, about 1727, Gates entered the British army at an early age. He served in Nova Scotia in 1749–1750 and later in the middle and northern colonies during the French and Indian War; he took part and was wounded in Gen. Edward Braddock's defeat on July 9, 1755. In 1762, after taking part in Gen. Robert Monckton's conquest of Martinique, he returned to England, where he remained until 1772, retiring as a major from the army in May 1765. In August 1772, encouraged by his friend George Washington, he returned to America, settling in Virginia. In June 1775 he was commissioned brigadier general by Congress and made adjutant general of the Continental army. Promoted to major general in May of the next year, he was directed to take command of the troops retreating from the siege of Montreal, but he was subsequently made subordinate to Gen. Philip Schuyler, commander of the Northern Department, and he remained at Fort Ticonderoga until December 1776. Congress shuffled commanders for some time, but by August 1777 he had finally replaced Gen. Schuyler in command of the Northern Department. His task was to repel Gen. John Burgoyne's advance down the Hudson valley toward Albany. He entrenched his 6000 men (augmented by militia to nearly 17,000 by mid-October) on Bemis Heights, near Saratoga, New York, and defeated Burgoyne's attacks at Freeman's Farm on September 19 (when Col. Daniel Morgan's Virginia riflemen took a heavy toll) and October 7 (when Gen. Benedict Arnold distinguished himself). On October 17 Burgoyne surrendered his army to Gates. In November Gates was appointed by Congress president of the Board of War. During the next several months there developed the Conway Cabal, a flurry of letters and discussions that gave at least the appearance of an intrigue among a number of officers (notably Gen. Thomas Conway) and members of Congress to have Gates replace Washington as commander in chief. Whether Gates was actually implicated in any plot is not clear; he was at least, however, not unaware of or adverse to its purported aim. From April 1778 to June 1780 he resumed command, first in the North and then in the East; he saw little combat and his problems were largely those of supply. After a brief retirement to Virginia he was placed in command in the South, where Gen. Benjamin Lincoln's surrender of Charleston had left the patriot cause in desperate straits, in June 1780. His disastrous defeat at Camden, South Carolina, by Gen. Charles Cornwallis on August 16, owing largely to the pusillanimous behavior of the militia (the Continental regulars, under Gen. Johann Kalb, distinguished themselves), led Congress to call for an investigation; in the end no inquiry was held, but Gates was relieved of command by Gen. Nathanael Greene in December 1780 and, except for a brief period under Washington's command in 1782, his military service was over. He retired to his Virginia plantation in 1783. In 1790 he freed his slaves and moved to a farm on Manhattan Island, where he died on April 10, 1806.

Gatling, Richard Jordan (1818–1903), inventor. Born in Hertford County, North Carolina, on September 12, 1818, Gatling was educated in local schools and in his youth helped his father develop machines for sowing and thinning cotton. For a time he taught school and he later ran a store, continuing meanwhile to exercise his considerable mechanical ability and imagination. He perfected a practical screw propeller in 1839, but the invention was anticipated by just a few months by that of John Ericsson and he received no patent. In 1844 he moved to St. Louis to engage in the manufacture of his sowing machine, which he adapted also to rice and wheat; he later established branch plants in Ohio and Indiana. Following an attack of smallpox, during which he was unable to find medical assistance, he entered the Ohio Medical College in Cincinnati; although he completed the course in 1850 he never practiced, resting content to be able to care for himself and his family. He continued to develop agricultural implements, inventing a hemp-breaking machine and in 1857 a steam plow. Upon the outbreak of the Civil War he turned his attention to military hardware; he succeeded in 1862 in building and (in November) patenting a rapid-fire gun that qualified as the first practical machine gun. With further improvements, the gun consisted of ten barrels clustered around a central revolving shaft and an automatic feed and ejection mechanism; crank-driven and making use of newly developed brass cartridge shells, it could fire some 350 rounds per minute. The gun was approved by the War Department too late to be much used in the Civil War, though a few found their way to Gen. Benjamin F. Butler's Army of the James, but in 1866 it was officially adopted by the army, which ordered a hundred. In 1870 Gatling moved to Hartford, Connecticut, to supervise manufacture of the Gatling gun at the Colt Patent Fire Arms Manufacturing Company. He made several more improvements in the gun, which eventually attained a rate of fire of 1200 rounds per minute (3000 when motor-driven), and then sold his patent rights to the Colt firm. The Gatling gun was used in a few engagements with Indians in the West, but its first use in war did not come until the battle of Santiago in 1898, by which time it was well on the way to obsolescence (largely because of Hiram S. Maxim's work). In later years Gatling worked on a new method for casting cannon and built a motorized plow. He died in New York City on February 26, 1903.

Gavin, James Maurice (1907–), army officer, businessman, and diplomat. Born on March 22, 1907, in Brooklyn, New York, Gavin grew up in an adoptive family near Mount Carmel, Pennsylvania. He left school at fifteen, worked for a time at odd jobs, and enlisted in the army in April 1924. His success in self-education was such that he won appointment to West Point by competitive examination in 1925. On graduating in 1929 he was commissioned in the infantry. After taking flight training at Brooks Field, Texas, and serving with the 25th Infantry in Arizona, he attended Infantry School, Fort Benning, Georgia, and graduated in 1933. Various routine assignments followed, and he was promoted to first lieutenant in 1934 and captain in 1939. He was an instructor at West Point in 1940–1941, and after completing parachute training he was attached to the Provisional Parachute Group at Fort Benning. He was promoted to temporary major in October 1941 and temporary lieutenant colonel in February 1942. He completed Command and General Staff School, Fort Leavenworth, Kansas, in 1942 and in August of that year took command of the 505th Parachute Infantry Regiment, advancing to temporary colonel in September. On July 9, 1943, the 505th (then designated a Combat Team), an element of Gen. Matthew B. Ridgway's 82nd Airborne Division, dropped onto high ground behind the beaches to cover the landing of American troops at Gela, Sicily. In September the regiment reinforced the Salerno beachhead on the Italian mainland. Promoted to temporary brigadier general in that month, Gavin became deputy to Ridgway in February 1944. On June 6, 1944, the 82nd dropped into Normandy before the beach landings began and fought for 33 days without relief, cutting off German attempts to reinforce their coastal defense forces. Gavin succeeded as commander in August (he was the youngest division commander in the war) and on September 17 led a drop into the Netherlands, 50 miles behind enemy lines, to link up with the British Second Army (Operation Market, under Gen. Lewis H. Brereton's First Allied Airborne Army). Gavin was promoted to temporary major general in October. In December the 82nd played a major part in blunting the northern salient of the Battle of the Bulge. In February 1945 the division crossed the Siegfried Line, in April it crossed the Elbe, and on May 2 it received the surrender of the German Twenty-first Army. Gavin and the 82nd were on occupation duty until January 1946 and then at Fort Bragg, North Carolina. In March 1948 he became chief of staff, Fifth Army; in June 1951 he became chief of staff, allied forces in southern Europe. He was named commander of the VII Corps in Germany

in December 1952 and in February 1954 took up duties with the General Staff in Washington, D.C. Promoted to lieutenant general in March 1955, he was named deputy chief of staff and chief of research and development in October, a post he retained until retiring in January 1958. His *War and Peace in the Space Age,* 1958, presented his criticism of U.S. strategic planning and its downgrading of conventional armaments and the capacity to conduct limited war. Later in that year he became a vice-president of Arthur D. Little, Inc., a consulting firm; he became president in 1960 and chairman of the board in 1961. In February of that year he was appointed U.S. ambassador to France by President John F. Kennedy. He resigned in July 1962. During the Vietnam war he was an outspoken critic of U.S. military strategy.

Geary, John White (1819–1873), army officer and public official. Born in Westmoreland County, Pennsylvania, on December 30, 1819, Geary attended Jefferson College briefly and then engaged in various pursuits, from school teaching to surveying. He studied law and won admission to the bar, speculated successfully in Kentucky land, and became assistant superintendent and engineer of the Allegheny Portage Railroad. On the outbreak of the Mexican War he returned to Pennsylvania to activate the "American Highlanders" militia company of which he had long been a member and was chosen lieutenant colonel of the 2nd Pennsylvania Infantry. He was in the forefront of the attack on Chapultepec, September 13, 1847, and remained in the city as military commander until the end of the war, becoming colonel of the regiment. Early in 1849 he was appointed by President James K. Polk the first postmaster of San Francisco and postal agent for the entire Pacific Coast; he was succeeded by an appointee of President Zachary Taylor shortly afterward, but almost immediately he was elected alcalde of the city. He was subsequently appointed also to the bench as chief judicial officer of San Francisco under the military government of the state. On the reorganization of the city government the following year Geary was elected the first mayor. In 1852 he returned to Pennsylvania and remained there until July 1856, when he was appointed territorial governor of Kansas by President Franklin Pierce. He was able, through vigorous and evenhanded measures, to quiet temporarily the factional warring between proslavery and antislavery forces in Kansas, and his report that "Peace now reigns in Kansas" was widely publicized as part of James Buchanan's presidential campaign that year. Order broke down, however, early in 1857, and the situation became so confused and frustrating that he resigned in March. He again returned to Pennsylvania, where in April 1861 he became colonel of the 28th Pennsylvania, enlisted for Civil War service. He was wounded at Harpers Ferry, October 16, 1861, and shortly after his capture of Leesburg, Virginia, on March 8, 1862, he was promoted to brigadier general of volunteers. He was badly wounded at Cedar Mountain, August 9; at Chancellorsville, May 2–4, 1863, he commanded a division of the XII Corps under Gen. Henry W. Slocum and continued with it at Gettysburg, Lookout Mountain, and Missionary Ridge. In 1864 he commanded a division of Gen. Joseph Hooker's XX Corps in the Atlanta campaign. He served as military governor of Savannah from its capture in December 1864 until the end of the war. In March 1865 he was brevetted major general of volunteers. From 1867 to 1873 Geary was governor of Pennsylvania, promoting a somewhat erratic but generally progressive program of legislation. Shortly after completing his second term he died, on February 8, 1873, in Harrisburg, Pennsylvania.

Geiger, Roy Stanley (1885–1947), marine officer. Born on January 25, 1885, in Middleburg, Florida, Geiger attended Florida State Normal School for two years and in 1907 graduated from John B. Stetson University. After a brief time in law practice he enlisted in the marine corps in November 1907. He won a commission in February 1909, was promoted to first lieutenant in 1915 after service at sea and in Nicaragua, Panama, China, and elsewhere, and in 1917, with the rank of captain, became the fifth marine officer to complete pilot training. In July 1918, by then a major, he took command of a squadron of the 1st Marine Aviation Force in France and flew numerous bombing missions. He was stationed in Haiti in 1919–1921, commanded the 1st Aviation Group, 3rd Marine Brigade, at Quantico, Virginia, in 1921–1924, and graduated from the army's Command and General Staff School, Fort Leavenworth, Kansas, in 1925. On graduating from the Army War College in 1929 he became commander of Aircraft Squadrons, East Coast Expeditionary Force, at Quantico. From 1931 to 1935 he was officer in charge of marine corps aviation at corps headquarters in Washington, D.C., receiving promotion to lieutenant colonel in 1934. He commanded Marine Air Group One, 1st Marine Brigade, from 1935 to 1939. Graduating from the Naval War College in 1941, he was promoted to brigadier general and placed in command of the 1st Marine Aircraft Wing, Fleet Marine Force, in September. A year later he led the wing to Guadalcanal, where Henderson Field became headquarters of a highly successful air campaign against Japanese air and sea forces. During that campaign he was promoted to major general. From May to November 1943 he was in Washington as director of the division of aviation, and he then succeeded Gen. Alexander A. Vandegrift as commander of the I Marine Amphibious Corps on Bougainville. He led the corps, later redesignated the III, in the invasion of Guam in July 1944 and the capture of the southern Palau Islands in September–

October. In April 1945 he led the III 'Phib in the assault on Okinawa in conjunction with the army XXIV Corps under Gen. John R. Hodge, the two corps comprising the Tenth Army. On the death of Gen. Simon B. Buckner on June 18, 1945, Geiger succeeded to command of the Tenth Army until it was taken over by Gen. Joseph W. Stilwell five days later. He was the first marine officer to command a field army. Promoted to lieutenant general, he was named commander of Fleet Marine Force, Pacific, in July 1945. He was assigned to duty in Washington in November 1946, and before his scheduled retirement he fell ill and died in Bethesda, Maryland, on January 23, 1947. In July 1947 he was voted honorary rank of general by Congress.

Geronimo (1829–1909), Indian leader. Born in June 1829 near the site of present-day Clifton, Arizona, Geronimo was given the name Goyathlay (or Goyakla). He grew up in a period of bloody raiding led by various Chiricahua chiefs, notably Cochise, and after 1858, when his family was killed, he came to be a skillful and courageous leader in raids of revenge against the Mexicans, by whom he was dubbed Geronimo (Jerome). Other raids in Arizona and New Mexico led to his confinement on a reservation in southern Arizona; but when, in 1876, the Chiricahua were moved to another reservation already occupied by Western Apaches, serious trouble ensued. Geronimo and his band escaped to Mexico, and during the next ten years outbreaks of raiding against American settlers alternated with periodic confinements. The reign of terror in the Southwest finally prompted the recall of Gen. George Crook, who had managed the pacification of the region in 1875. Crook enlisted Apache scouts and pursued Geronimo and his followers into the fastnesses of the Sierra Madre Mountains, securing the surrender of portions of the band in 1883 and 1884. In May 1885 Geronimo fled with about 40 warriors and 90 women and children from the San Carlos reservation, and Crook again pursued. In March 1886 he agreed to surrender to Crook and to be taken to a Florida reservation. Two days later he again escaped. Crook was replaced by Gen. Nelson A. Miles who, with more than 5000 troops, required five months to recapture Geronimo and his small band, which by that time included only 35 warriors, in September 1886. (The army detachment that made the capture was led by Capt. Henry W. Lawton.) Placed under military confinement by order of President Grover Cleveland, Geronimo and his followers were sent to Florida, to Alabama, and finally in 1894 to Fort Sill, Oklahoma, where they were allowed to remain. Geronimo took up farming and eventually adopted Christianity; his personal appearance was a feature at the Louisiana Purchase Exposition in 1904 in St. Louis, and he appeared in Theodore Roosevelt's inaugural procession in 1905. His autobiography, *Geronimo's Story of His Life*, was dictated to S. M. Barrett and published in 1906. He died at Fort Sill on February 17, 1909.

Gerow, Leonard Townsend (1888–1972), army officer. Born in Petersburg, Virginia, on July 13, 1888, Gerow graduated from Virginia Military Institute in 1911 and was shortly thereafter commissioned a second lieutenant of infantry. For several years, except for taking part in the occupation of Veracruz, Mexico, in April 1914, he saw mainly routine duty in the Southwest, receiving promotion to first lieutenant in 1916 and captain in 1917. From April 1918 to October 1919 he was in France, with responsibility for Signal Corps purchasing and later for disposal of surplus matériel; during that period he advanced to temporary lieutenant colonel. During 1919–1921 he was commandant of the Signal Corps School, Fort Sam Houston, Texas, receiving promotion to permanent major in June 1920, and he was then assigned to staff duty in Washington, D.C. He graduated from Infantry School, Fort Benning, Georgia, in 1925, from Command and General Staff School, Fort Leavenworth, Kansas, in 1926, and after another tour of duty in Washington, from the Army War College in 1931. After service in the Philippines and Shanghai, China, Gerow was assigned to the War Plans Division of the War Department in 1935, receiving promotion to lieutenant colonel in August of that year. In September 1940 he advanced to colonel, in October to temporary brigadier general, and in December he became chief of the War Plans Division. In December 1941, shortly after the Pearl Harbor attack, he was named in addition assistant chief of staff. Promoted to major general (temporary) in February 1942, he relinquished the War Plans Division to Gen. Dwight D. Eisenhower and took command of the 29th Infantry Division, which moved from Fort George Meade, Maryland, to training sites in Great Britain in October 1942. In July 1943 Gerow moved up to command of the V Corps, which, as a major component of Gen. Omar N. Bradley's First Army, took Omaha Beach on the Normandy coast on June 6, 1944. Gerow's corps fought for the liberation of Paris (he was the first American general to reenter the city), through northern France and Belgium to the Rhineland. In January 1945 Gerow was promoted to temporary lieutenant general in command of the newly organized Fifteenth Army, which operated on the northern European coast, staging, training, and equipping incoming units destined for service in the 12th Army Group, and neutralizing the German-held ports of St. Nazaire and L'Orient, France, the latter of which did not surrender until May 17. In July 1945 Gerow was designated president of the Theater General Board, charged with analyzing the entire European war. In October he was transferred to the Command and General Staff College, of which he was

commandant until January 1948. He then commanded the Second Army at Fort George Meade until his retirement in July 1950. He died in Petersburg, Virginia, on October 12, 1972.

Ghormley, Robert Lee (1883–1958), naval officer. Born on October 15, 1883, in Portland, Oregon, Ghormley grew up there and in Moscow, Idaho. He graduated from the University of Idaho in 1902 and from the Naval Academy in 1906. During a series of routine assignments he was promoted to lieutenant in 1911 and saw action in the Nicaraguan campaign of 1912. From 1913 to 1916 he was on the Naval Academy staff. During World War I he served with the battleship force of the Atlantic Fleet and then in the office of the chief of naval operations. He commanded the *Sands* in 1920–1922, served on the *Oklahoma* in 1926–1928, and was assistant chief of staff of the Battle Force in 1930–1931 and of the U.S. Fleet in 1931–1932. He commanded the *Nevada* in 1935–1936. After graduating from the Naval War College in 1938 he was promoted to rear admiral and appointed director of the navy's War Plans Office; in 1939 he became assistant to the chief of naval operations, Adm. Harold R. Stark. From 1940 to 1942 he was in England as a special naval observer, receiving promotion to temporary vice admiral in 1941 and serving briefly in 1942 as commander of U.S. naval forces in European waters. In April 1942, his rank made permanent, he arrived in New Zealand as commander of the South Pacific Forces and area, and in that position, under the general command of Adm. Chester W. Nimitz, he had immediate responsibility for the planning and execution of the invasion of the Solomon Islands, beginning with the marine assaults on Guadalcanal and Tulagi on August 7, the first American ground offensive in the Pacific and the first amphibious operation by U.S. forces since the Spanish–American War. The expeditionary force was commanded by Adm. Frank J. Fletcher, the amphibious force by Adm. R. Kelly Turner, and the marine assault force by Gen. Alexander A. Vandegrift. The battle of the Solomons was extremely hard fought, notably off Cape Esperance on October 11–12, and Ghormley carried it on until relieved by Adm. William F. Halsey in mid-October. From early 1943 to 1944 he was commander of the Hawaiian Sea Frontier and the 14th Naval District. In November 1944 he joined the staff of Adm. Harold R. Stark in European waters, and in May 1945 he was made commander of U.S. naval forces in German waters, responsible for the demobilization of the German navy. Ghormley retired in June 1946 and died on June 21, 1958, in Bethesda, Maryland.

Gibbon, John (1827–1896), army officer. Born near Philadelphia on April 20, 1827, Gibbon grew up in Charlotte, North Carolina, from 1839 and on graduating from West Point in 1847 was commissioned in the artillery. He arrived in Mexico too late to see action, but in 1849 he took part in suppressing the Seminole disturbances in Florida. He was promoted to first lieutenant in 1850. During 1854–1859 he was an instructor at West Point, preparing during that time his *Artillerist's Manual*, which was officially adopted in 1859; in November of that year he was promoted to captain. At the outbreak of the Civil War he was on duty in Utah; by October 1861 he was chief of artillery in the division under Gen. Irvin McDowell. In May 1862 he was appointed brigadier general of volunteers, and he led his famed "Iron Brigade" at second Bull Run, August 29–30, South Mountain, September 14, and Antietam, September 17. At Fredericksburg, December 13, then commanding a division, he was severely wounded. At Gettysburg he commanded a division of the II Corps (twice briefly commanding the corps in Gen. Winfield S. Hancock's absence) and on the third day, July 3, 1863, bore the brunt of the Confederate assault on Cemetery Ridge known as Pickett's Charge, and particularly Gen. Lewis A. Armistead's push to the summit. A wound received in that action kept him from the field until 1864. After leading his division in the Wilderness battles and at Petersburg in May–June he was promoted to major general of volunteers. In January 1865 he took command of the XXIV Corps, Army of the James, which he led until the surrender of Gen. Robert E. Lee at Appomattox. In January 1866 he was mustered out of volunteer service and in July appointed colonel of the 36th Infantry. Transferred to the 7th Infantry in 1869, he was stationed at Fort Ellis, Montana Territory, when he was ordered in 1876 to march eastward and join columns under Gen. Alfred H. Terry and Gen. George Crook for a campaign against the Sioux. His regiment was the first to arrive at the Little Bighorn battlefield and rescue the survivors of Col. George A. Custer's command on June 27. The next year he took part in the Nez Percé War, attacking Chief Joseph's camp on the Big Hole River, Montana, on August 9. His troops were soon driven off with 69 casualties, including Gibbon. He was promoted to brigadier general in July 1885 and placed in command of the Department of the Columbia. In 1886 he took command of the Department of the Pacific at San Francisco. He retired in April 1891 and died in Baltimore on February 6, 1896.

Gibbs, William Francis (1886–1967), naval architect.

Born in Philadelphia on August 24, 1886, Gibbs attended Harvard University from 1906 to 1910 and graduated from Columbia University in 1912, also taking a law degree from the latter in 1913. For several years he traveled and studied naval architecture and marine engineering. During World War I he worked as a naval architect for the War Department, and in 1919 he was an advisor to the U.S.

delegation at the Versailles peace conference. After a period as chief of construction for the International Mercantile Marine Company (later renamed the United States Line) he joined his brother, Frederic H., in 1922 in forming Gibbs Brothers, Inc., naval architects, which became in 1929, with the addition of another partner, Gibbs & Cox, Inc., of which William Gibbs remained president until his death. The firm grew to be one of the largest and most innovative in the world. Among many other vessels, Gibbs designed the *Malolo*, completed in 1927, the *America* in 1937, and the great *United States*, completed in 1952, which broke all transatlantic records that year and set new ones that still stand, including a pace of more than 35 knots for a round-trip voyage. He also did a great deal of work for the armed forces and from 1933 led in introducing the use of high-pressure, high-temperature steam turbines in navy destroyers, a form of power plant later adopted for nearly all war vessels. He also contributed to the design of new battleships, cruisers, and other types. In 1940 he produced plans for a cargo ship capable of being built by mass-production methods. The design, originally for a British order, was quickly converted to one for the standardized EC-2 "Liberty" ship, 441 feet long and displacing 10,490 tons, which was turned out in vast numbers during World War II—the 2610 of them built represented nearly half the merchant ships launched by U.S. civilian and naval yards during the war. The Gibbs firm's other work brought their total share of wartime production to over 60 percent of all major ships, not counting battleships and submarines. The first "Liberty" ship, the *Patrick Henry*, was launched in September 1941, and at the peak of production one of Henry J. Kaiser's yards (which built most of the "Liberty" ships) set a record of five days from keel-laying to launch. The "Liberty" ships were noteworthy also in featuring all-welded construction. Gibbs served as controller of shipbuilding for the War Production Board in 1942–1943 and in 1943 as chairman of the combined shipbuilding committee of the Combined (British and U.S.) Chiefs of Staff and as an advisor to the Office of War Mobilization. Gibbs received a great many honors and awards for his work. He died in New York City on September 6, 1967.

Gibson, John (1740–1822), Revolutionary army officer and public official.

Born in Lancaster, Pennsylvania, on May 23, 1740, Gibson took part in 1758 in the expedition under British Gen. John Forbes against Fort Duquesne, and he stayed at the renamed Fort Pitt afterwards as an Indian trader. During Pontiac's War in 1763 he was taken prisoner by Indians and held for a year, during which he may have married a sister of the Mingo leader Logan. His release was secured by Col. Henry Bouquet in 1764. Gibson took part in the expedition against the Shawnee and others under Lord Dunmore in 1774 and was the interpreter and transcriber of Logan's famous speech, which he may have improved in the translation. In 1775 he was appointed an agent of Virginia in pressing claims to western lands, and he worked at the same time to assure peace on the Indian frontier. Later in the year he entered the Continental army and served in Gen. George Washington's army in New York and New Jersey. He was commissioned lieutenant colonel in 1776 and colonel in 1777, and he commanded Fort Laurens, Ohio, in 1779 and Fort Pitt in 1781–1782. After the Revolution he settled in Allegheny County, Pennsylvania, where he was a judge, and soon was appointed major general of militia. He was a member of the convention that drafted the state constitution of 1790. In 1800 he was appointed secretary of the newly formed Territory of Indiana, and he served as acting governor until the arrival of William Henry Harrison in January 1801. He continued as secretary until Indiana's admission to statehood in 1816, again serving as acting governor in 1812–1813 when Harrison took the field with the army. Gibson returned to Pennsylvania in 1816 and died in Pittsburgh on April 16, 1822.

Gilliss, James Melville (1811–1865), naval officer and astronomer. Born on September 6, 1811, in Georgetown, D.C., Gilliss entered the navy at the age of fifteen. He was advanced to passed midshipman in 1831. Between 1833 and 1835 he studied for short periods at the University of Virginia and in Paris on leaves of absence and in 1836 was assigned to the Depot of Charts and Instruments in Washington, succeeding Lt. Charles Wilkes as head of the establishment the next year. From 1838, in February of which year he was promoted to lieutenant, to 1842 he was chiefly engaged in making astronomical observations to correlate with and supplement those being made by Wilkes on his exploratory voyage in the Southern Hemisphere; he found time, however, also to make independent studies of magnetic and meteorological phenomena and, despite the crudity of the instruments at hand, to make corrections in more than a thousand star positions in the standard catalogues. It was largely at Gilliss's prompting that an appropriation was made by Congress in August 1842 for the enlargement of the navy's small and inadequate observatory, and he bore the principal responsibility for planning and equipping the new building, traveling to Europe for the purpose and passing the superintendency of the Depot of Charts and Instruments to Lt. Matthew F. Maury. At its opening in 1844 the impressive new Naval Observatory, the first in America designed solely for research, was given into the charge of Maury, much to Gilliss's disappointment. He continued his work, however, and in 1846 published the first volume of astronomical observations issued in the United States. In 1849

he headed an expedition that established a supplementary observatory in Santiago, Chile, and remained there for three years making observations of Mars and Venus and continuing his catalogue work on the stars of the Southern Hemisphere. He also made careful observations of earthquakes and other terrestrial phenomena. On his return he published a multivolume report on Chile. Although he was placed on the navy's reserve list in 1855 because of his 20 years' absence from qualifying sea duty, he was retained in his position at the observatory by special order of the secretary of the navy. He directed expeditions to South America in 1858 and to Washington Territory in 1860 to observe solar eclipses and in April 1861, on the resignation of Maury, became head of the Naval Observatory. Most of his work during four years in the post concerned organizing and preparing for publication the observatory's masses of raw observational data; he also arranged cooperative research ventures with other observatories. Gilliss died suddenly in Washington, D.C., on February 9, 1865.

Gillmore, Quincy Adams (1825–1888), army officer and engineer. Born on February 28, 1825, in Black River, Lorain County, Ohio, Gillmore won appointment to West Point largely by his proficiency in mathematics and on graduating in 1849 was commissioned in the engineers. For three years he was employed on fortification work at Hampton Roads, Virginia, and he was then assigned to the staff at West Point. In 1856 he was promoted to first lieutenant and placed in charge of the engineer district of New York City. Promoted to captain in August 1861, he was named chief engineer on the staff of Gen. Thomas W. Sherman for the army-navy expedition against Port Royal, South Carolina, in November. He commanded the troops besieging Fort Pulaski at Savannah, Georgia, in April 1862, and after the capture of the fort on April 11 he was brevetted lieutenant colonel. His successful use of rifled artillery against the walls of that fort—two months of preparation and thirty hours of precise bombardment were required—was a revolutionary advance in siege warfare. Shortly thereafter he was appointed brigadier general of volunteers and given commands in Kentucky and West Virginia, receiving brevet regular rank of colonel after a victory at Somerset, Kentucky, on March 30, 1863. In June 1863 he took command of the X Corps and also of the Department of the South, taking the rank of major general of volunteers in July. In that month he undertook, in cooperation with Adm. John A. B. Dahlgren, a sustained campaign in Charleston harbor that by November resulted in the capture of Morris Island and Fort Wagner and the virtual demolition of Fort Sumter. Early in 1864 the X Corps was moved to the James River and sent into action at Bermuda Hundred and Drewry's Bluff in

May. In July Gillmore was transferred to Washington, D.C. He sustained a severe injury during the pursuit of Gen. Jubal A. Early following the latter's raid on Washington. From February to November 1865 he again commanded the Department of the South; he was mustered out of volunteer service in December and reverted to his regular rank of captain of engineers (he had been brevetted brigadier and major general of regulars in March 1865 for his work in Charleston harbor). He served subsequently in various coastal and harbor assignments, receiving promotions to major in June 1868, lieutenant colonel in January 1874, and colonel in February 1883. In 1879 he was appointed president of the Mississippi River Commission, and in 1881 he was given charge of all Atlantic coastal defenses from New York harbor to St. Augustine, Florida. He was the author of numerous technical works on artillery, siegecraft, and masonry construction. Gillmore died in Brooklyn, New York, on April 7, 1888.

Girty, Simon (1741–1818), frontiersman. Born in 1741 near Harris' Ferry (now Harrisburg), Pennsylvania, Girty grew up largely uneducated and, owing to the death of both his father and stepfather at the hands of Indians and his own three years' captivity (1756–1759) among the Seneca, intimately familiar with the ways and languages of Indians. For many years he was an interpreter at Fort Pitt, and in 1774 he served with Simon Kenton as a scout in Lord Dunmore's War. He was an interpreter for the Continental Congress in 1776 and subsequently served in the Virginia militia, achieving the rank of lieutenant. In March 1778 he deserted with several companions and was soon engaged as an interpreter by British authorities in Detroit. He was active in arousing the Indians of the frontier against white settlers and took part in numerous raids and battles. He was a participant in the burning at the stake of Col. William Crawford of Pennsylvania, leader of an ill-fated expedition against the Indians of Ohio, on June 11, 1782. In August of that year he led an expedition into Kentucky, laid siege briefly to Bryan's Station, near Lexington, and fought a heavy engagement with Kentuckians, including Daniel Boone, at Blue Licks on August 19. He remained in the Ohio country after the Revolution, operating a trading post for a time, and continued to stir up resentment among the Indians of the region. He took part in the defeat of Gen. Arthur St. Clair near the present site of Fort Wayne, Indiana, on November 4, 1791; he was prominent in the attack on Fort Recovery at the same spot on June 30, 1794; and he was at the Battle of Fallen Timbers against Gen. Anthony Wayne on August 20, 1794. In 1796 he moved to Canada. He was forced to hide in a Mohawk village during the American invasion of Canada in 1813. Known sometimes as the "Great Renegade," although his role in Indian atrocities was often exaggerated at the time, Girty died near Amherstburg, Ontario, on February 18, 1818.

Gist, Christopher (1706?–1759), frontiersman. Born in Maryland, probably near Baltimore, about 1706, Gist led an obscure life until 1750, when, apparently well known as a woodsman and surveyor and at the time living on the Yadkin River in North Carolina, he was engaged by the Ohio Company of Virginia to explore its Western grant. He set out from Maryland, crossed southwestern Pennsylvania, passing the later site of Fort Duquesne (still later Pittsburgh) and entered the Ohio country, traveling down the Ohio River as far as the Miami River, to the west of modern Cincinnati; he then crossed the Ohio into Kentucky—18 years before Daniel Boone—explored nearly as far as present-day Louisville, and returned east in May 1751 with valuable journal descriptions and maps of the western country. During 1751–1752 he explored the region between the Monongahela and Little Kanawha rivers and in 1753 returned to establish a small settlement near present-day Brownsville, Pennsylvania. In November 1753, at Cumberland, Maryland, he joined Maj. George Washington as a guide, conducting him, with Governor Robert Dinwiddie's ultimatum, to the French at Fort Le Boeuf; Gist twice saved Washington's life on the perilous winter journey through hostile Indian country. He remained with Washington in 1754 through his second western expedition, his defeat of a French detachment near Fort Duquesne, and the building and subsequent surrender of Fort Necessity. Gist was again with Washington as a scout in Gen. Edward Braddock's campaign and his disastrous defeat at Fort Duquesne in 1755. In 1756 he journeyed into eastern Tennessee and for some time was an Indian agent there. Gist died either in Georgia or South Carolina sometime in 1759.

Gladwin, Henry (1729–1791), British officer in America. Born near Chesterfield, England, on November 19, 1729, Gladwin was commissioned a lieutenant of infantry in 1753. His regiment, the 48th, was ordered to America and in July 1755 took part in Gen. Edward Braddock's disastrous expedition to Fort Duquesne. In 1761 he was ordered to Fort Detroit, which he garrisoned with men of the 80th Regiment. On May 7, 1763, the Ottawa leader Pontiac attempted to capture the fort by a ruse, but Gladwin was forewarned and foiled the attempt. Pontiac's several hundred warriors then laid siege to Fort Detroit, and Gladwin's hundred or so defenders prepared to resist. A detachment under Capt. James Dalzel attempted to relieve the fort in July but was badly defeated in an attack on Pontiac's camp at Parent's Creek, thereafter known as Bloody Run, on July 31, 1763. The Indians lacked discipline for a tight siege, particularly during winter, and supplies were brought to the fort by riverboat. The siege was finally lifted after 15 months, in August 1764, by Col. John Bradstreet, and it became an epic of the frontier (notably in Francis Parkman's *History of the Conspiracy of Pontiac*). Gladwin was promoted to lieutenant colonel in September 1763. He returned to England in 1765, and, although he was listed thereafter as deputy adjutant general of British forces in America, he never returned, declining to serve against the Revolution. He was promoted to colonel in August 1777 and major general in November 1782 on the half-pay list, and he died at his family home near Chesterfield on June 22, 1791.

Gleaves, Albert (1858–1937), naval officer. Born in Nashville, Tennessee, on January 1, 1858, Gleaves graduated from the Naval Academy in 1877 and was commissioned an ensign in January 1881. For 20 years he served in a routine succession of assignments, receiving promotions to lieutenant (junior grade) in May 1887 and lieutenant in January 1893 and in 1897 assuming his first sea command aboard the torpedo boat *Cushing*. During the Spanish–American War the *Cushing* was responsible for patrolling the Havana–Key West cable. Promoted to lieutenant commander in May 1900, he commanded the *Dolphin* in 1901–1903 and the *Mayflower* in 1903–1904, both used as presidential yachts by President Theodore Roosevelt, with whom he formed a close friendship. Both were also used in survey work; in 1902 Gleaves charted the deepest spot recorded up to that time in the Atlantic, a spot in the Puerto Rico Trench 27,984 feet deep. From 1904 to 1908 he commanded the Naval Torpedo Station, Newport, Rhode Island, where he conceived the idea of the navy manufacturing its own torpedoes and oversaw construction of the first factory for that purpose. He advanced to commander in July 1905. Subsequent commands included those of the *St. Louis* in the Pacific, 1908–1909, and with the rank of captain from July 1909, the *North Dakota*, 1910–1911, during 1912–1914 the New York navy yard, and in 1914–1915 the battleship *Utah*. In July 1915 he was promoted to rear admiral in command of the Atlantic Fleet destroyer force. With an eye toward possible American involvement in World War I he methodically brought the destroyer force up to a high level of readiness. He also devised a revolutionary method of refueling at sea. In May 1917 he was named commander of convoy operations; reconditioning a large number of interned German liners, including the great *Leviathan*, he created a highly efficient convoy force, and on June 14 he took personal command, aboard his flagship *Seattle*, of the first troop convoy bound for France. Under his supervision the convoy force carried half of the American Expeditionary Force to Europe and all of it back, without the loss of a single life at sea. In December 1918 he was promoted to vice admiral. He commanded the cruiser and transport force until September 1919, when, promoted to admiral, he became commander of the Asiatic station aboard the *South Dakota*. In 1921 he took command of the Boston navy yard, and in January 1922 he retired. Gleaves was the author of many periodical pieces on naval affairs and several books, including *Captain James Lawrence, U.S.N.*, 1904, and *Life and Letters of Rear Admiral S. B. Luce*, 1925. He died in Haverford, Pennsylvania, on January 6, 1937.

Glenn, John Herschel, Jr. (1921–   ), marine officer and astronaut. Born on July 18, 1921, in Cambridge, Ohio, Glenn grew up in nearby New Concord. He entered Muskingum College in 1939 and in 1942 joined the naval aviation training program. Taking his commission in the marine corps in March 1943, he flew 59 missions in the Pacific theater during 1944–1945, winning two Distinguished Flying Crosses and ten Air Medals. After the war he served at various marine air stations in the United States and abroad and in 1952, by then a major, was sent to Korea, where he flew 90 missions and earned two more DFC's and eight Air Medals. Glenn completed test-pilot training in 1954 and was then attached to the Naval Air Test Center, Patuxent River, Maryland, and from 1956 to the Fighter Design Branch of the Navy Department's Bureau of Aeronautics in Washington, D.C. While engaged in test-pilot work, he made in an F8U-1 Crusader the first transcontinental nonstop supersonic flight in July 1957, for which feat he received his fifth DFC. In April 1959, shortly after being promoted to lieutenant colonel, he was one of seven men selected by the National Aeronautics and Space Administration for the first astronaut training program of Project Mercury. For nearly three years he trained rigorously with his six fellow astronauts while aiding in the design of the space capsule for the project. Finally, after two of his colleagues had ridden suborbital missions, he was chosen to make the first U.S. flight to orbit the earth; on February 20, 1962, he piloted his *Friendship 7* capsule through 3 orbits of the earth, traveling some 81,000 miles in just under 5 hours and reaching an altitude of more than 185 miles. After splashing down in the Atlantic and undergoing a two-day debriefing session, he returned to Cape Canaveral (Cape Kennedy), starting point of the flight, and was personally greeted by President John F. Kennedy; parades in New York City and Washington and an address to a joint session of Congress followed, firmly establishing Glenn as the popular hero of the day. He remained with the astronaut program until January 1964, when he resigned from NASA to enter an Ohio senatorial primary election; an accidental injury forced him out of the race. He was promoted to colonel later in 1964, and he retired from the marine corps in January 1965. In 1970 he was defeated in a second try for the Democratic senatorial nomination, but in November 1974 he was elected to the Senate from Ohio. There he established a reputation for conscientiousness and in 1976 was chosen to give a keynote address to the Democratic National Convention.

Glover, John (1732–1797), Revolutionary army officer. Born on November 5, 1732, in Salem, Massachusetts, Glover became a shoemaker and later a fisherman in Marblehead. He was a member of the Marblehead committee of correspondence in the early revolutionary agitation, and in April 1775, in light of his experience as captain of the town militia, he was charged with responsibility for the defense of Marblehead and shortly afterward was commissioned colonel of the 21st Massachusetts. In June he led the regiment to Cambridge to join Gen. George Washington's army. Glover was then put in charge of assembling and manning a fleet of transport vessels for the use of the Continental army. His regiment was mustered into the Continental service as the 14th Infantry and ordered to New York, where it conducted the evacuation of Long Island on August 29, 1776. Glover's men fought well in Harlem Heights during the withdrawal from Manhattan and again at Pell's Point, October 18, and at White Plains, October 28. On the night of December 25, 1776, Glover's regiment supervised the boat crossing of the Delaware River by Washington's forces and then led the advance into Trenton, New Jersey. In February 1777 Glover was promoted to brigadier general. He took part in the campaign against Gen. John Burgoyne in the Hudson valley in that year and in Gen. John Sullivan's unsuccessful attempt to capture Newport, Rhode Island, in August 1778. Later he commanded at Providence, and in October 1780, while stationed at West Point, he sat on the court-martial that sentenced Maj. John André, Benedict Arnold's British contact. During the last year of the war he served in garrison and recruiting duties in upper New York and Massachusetts. He returned to Marblehead afterwards and served in the constitutional ratifying convention in 1788 and in the Massachusetts General Court in 1788–1789. He died in Marblehead on January 30, 1797.

Glynn, James (1801–1871), naval officer. Born in Philadelphia on June 28, 1801, Glynn served as acting midshipman in Commodore Isaac Chauncey's Lake Ontario fleet in the War of 1812 and in March 1815 was appointed a midshipman. He was promoted to lieutenant in January 1825 and to commander in September 1841. During the Mexican War he served on the California coast. In 1848 he took command of the sloop *Preble* in the East India Squadron. Learning from the Dutch consul at Canton, China, that 14 (some sources claim as many as 18) American seamen were being held captive in Nagasaki, Japan, Glynn sailed in March 1849 for that port. Arriving on April 17, he ignored boats attempting to keep him outside the harbor and sailed to anchorage close in under the guns of the town. While a sizable force of soldiers was being assembled on the shore, he declined to be awed and likewise refused to treat with minor officials; in negotiation with appropriately high-ranking officers he demanded firmly the release of the sailors. His insistent diplomacy succeeded, and on April 26 the seamen were delivered to the *Preble.* This first successful negotiation with the reclusive Japanese led Glynn to draw up a proposal for a major attempt to open relations with that nation. The proposal finally was fulfilled in 1853 by the expedition to Japan under Commodore Matthew C. Perry. Glynn was promoted to captain in 1855 but placed on inactive status until 1858. During the first year of the Civil War he was on patrol duty in the Caribbean. He retired in January 1862 and in 1867 was promoted to commodore on the retired list. He died in New Haven, Connecticut, on May 13, 1871.

Goethals, George Washington (1858–1928), army officer and engineer. Born on June 29, 1858, in Brooklyn, New York, Goethals attended public schools and the College of the City of New York (CCNY). He had aspired originally to a medical career, but he transferred to West Point and graduated in 1880. Commissioned in the engineers, he spent two years at the Engineer School of Application, Willett's Point, New York, and, promoted to first lieutenant in June 1882, was then employed on several civil works projects, including improvements on the Ohio and Cumberland rivers and completion of work on the Muscle Shoals Canal on the Tennessee River. From 1885 to 1889 and again from 1898 to 1900 he taught engineering at West Point. He was promoted to captain in December 1891. Appointed lieutenant colonel of engineers in May 1898, he served through the Spanish–American War as chief engineer of the I Corps in Puerto Rico. Mustered out of volunteer service in December 1898, he was promoted to major in February 1900. From 1903 to 1907 he was attached to the General Staff, during which time he graduated from the Army War College in 1905. In March 1907, with the rank of lieutenant colonel, he was appointed by President Theodore Roosevelt chief engineer and chairman of the Isthmian Canal Commission with complete responsibility for the construction of the Panama Canal. In addition to the monumental engineering problems involved, he was charged with supervising 30,000 civilian employees of various nationalities and supplying them with food, shelter, medical care, and recreation. Vested with virtually dictatorial powers, Goethals managed to construct an efficient organization while fostering an esprit de corps among the workers. Prominent among his associates in the project were Col. William C. Gorgas, Lt. Col. David D. B. Gaillard, Lt. Col. Harry F.

Hodges, and Maj. William L. Sibert. In 1913 the canal, the greatest ever built, was completed and on August 15, 1914, nearly six months ahead of schedule, it was opened to the world, shortening the voyage between the Atlantic and the Pacific by thousands of miles. Goethals, who had been promoted to colonel in December 1909, was appointed by President Woodrow Wilson the first governor of the Canal Zone in 1914, and in March 1915, by special act of Congress, he was promoted to major general and voted the thanks of Congress. He retired from the army in November 1916 and resigned as governor in January 1917. He continued to work on both government and private engineering projects until he was recalled to active army duty in December 1917 as acting quartermaster general. He was later also made chief of several supply divisions for the General Staff and a member of the War Industries Board. Retiring again from active duty in March 1919, he headed his own engineering firm and was a consultant to many municipalities and particularly to the Port of New York Authority. He died in New York City on January 21, 1928.

Goldsborough, Louis Malesherbes (1805–1877), naval officer. Born in Washington, D.C., on February 18, 1805, Goldsborough was warranted a midshipman at the age of seven and actually entered service four years later. He made cruises in the Mediterranean and the Pacific and was promoted to lieutenant in January 1825. For two years he studied in Paris and in 1827 was assigned to the *Porpoise,* from which he led a volunteer boat expedition to recapture a British brig from Greek pirates. In 1830 he took charge of the newly established Depot of Charts and Instruments in Washington. Early in the second Seminole War (1835–1842) he led a volunteer company of cavalry. On returning to naval service he was promoted to commander in September 1841. He commanded the *Ohio* during the Mexican War and in April 1847 Commodore Matthew C. Perry's squadron in an attack on Tuxpan. During 1849–1850 he served as senior naval member of a commission exploring California. In 1853 he was appointed superintendent of the Naval Academy, where he remained for four years, receiving promotion in 1855 to captain. During 1859–1861 he was in command of the Brazil station. In September 1861 he was appointed flag-officer in command of the Atlantic Blockading Squadron, remaining with the North Atlantic Squadron when two commands were created a month later. In February 1862 he commanded an expedition to land some 12,000 troops under Gen. Ambrose E. Burnside on Roanoke Island, North Carolina. The landing was accomplished on February 7, and on that and the next two days the gunboat force under Commander Stephen C. Rowan destroyed a Confederate gunboat fleet under Flag-Officer William F. Lynch.

Goldsborough returned to Hampton Roads, Virginia, in March, after the battle of the *Monitor* and the *Virginia* (ex-*Merrimac*) there, and in April organized naval support for Gen. George B. McClellan's Peninsular campaign. He conceived as his principal responsibility the protection of McClellan's base on the peninsula and the sea lines to it, and to that end he devoted much of his effort to keeping the *Virginia* bottled up in the Elizabeth River. That he did, refusing McClellan's repeated requests that he leave Hampton Roads and split his forces to attack Yorktown from the water and also move up the James River. McClellan finally succeeded, through President Abraham Lincoln, in getting a flotilla under Commander John Rodgers sent up the James on May 7. The flotilla was halted at Drewry's Bluff on May 15. Meanwhile Norfolk navy yard had been captured, and the *Virginia,* left without a base, was destroyed by her captain, Flag-Officer Josiah Tattnall, on May 11. Goldsborough cooperated with McClellan in shifting the army's base to the James River and in covering the withdrawal from the peninsula in late June. In July he was promoted to rear admiral, but the separation of the James River flotilla from his command, coupled with public criticism of his actions, led him to request being relieved of his command in September 1862. He served in an administrative capacity in Washington until 1865, commanded the European Squadron from 1865 to 1867, and was then again in Washington until his retirement in 1873. Goldsborough died in Washington, D.C., on February 20, 1877.

Goodpaster, Andrew Jackson (1915–   ), army officer. Born on February 12, 1915, in Granite City, Illinois, Goodpaster attended McKendree College for two years before entering West Point. On graduating in 1939 he was commissioned in the engineers, and during World War II he saw action in North Africa and Italy, rising to command of a battalion of engineers attached to the Fifth Army. In mid-1944 he was ordered to duty with the General Staff in Washington, D.C., and from there he went to Princeton University, where he took a Ph.D. in political science in 1950. In that year he was assigned to represent the army on the Joint Advanced Study Committee of the Joint Chiefs of Staff. In December 1950 he accompanied Gen. Dwight D. Eisenhower to Europe, becoming assistant to Eisenhower's chief of staff, Gen. Alfred M. Gruenther, at Supreme Headquarters, Allied Powers in Europe (SHAPE), the military arm of the North Atlantic Treaty Organization. In 1954, by which time he had advanced to colonel, he was briefly district engineer in San Francisco and in October was named staff secretary and defense liaison to President Eisenhower. He held that post, advancing to brigadier general in 1957, until January 1961. After a few months as assistant commander of the 3rd Infantry Division in Germany he was promoted to major general in command of the 8th Division in October 1961. In November 1962 he was named special assistant to Gen. Maxwell D. Taylor, chairman of the Joint Chiefs of Staff, becoming chief assistant with the rank of lieutenant general in January 1964. Goodpaster became director of the joint staff of the Joint Chiefs in August 1966. In May 1967 he was appointed senior U.S. army representative on the United Nations Military Staff Committee, and from July of that year to June 1968 he was also commandant of the National War College. After serving on the U.S. delegation to the Vietnam peace talks in Paris in May–July 1968 he was named deputy to Gen. Creighton W. Abrams, U.S. commander in Vietnam, and promoted to general. In July 1969 he succeeded Gen. Lyman L. Lemnitzer as SHAPE commander in Europe, and he held the post until December 1974, when he passed it on to Gen. Alexander M. Haig. Retiring from active duty in that month, Goodpaster subsequently became a senior fellow at the Woodrow Wilson International Center for Scholars at the Smithsonian Institution. In 1976 he was appointed to the faculty of The Citadel in Charleston, South Carolina. In June 1977 he became the first officer ever called out of retirement to serve as superintendent of West Point. His appointment was seen as an attempt to restore the Academy quickly to normal in the wake of a cheating scandal involving more than 130 cadets and of a general debate over the traditional honor code.

Gordon, John Brown (1832–1904), Confederate army officer and public official. Born on February 6, 1832, in Upson County, Georgia, Gordon attended the University of Georgia for a time, leaving before the graduation of his class of 1853, and then studied law. He practised in Atlanta and later had coal mining interests in northwestern Georgia. On the outbreak of the Civil War he was elected captain of a volunteer company, the "Raccoon Roughs," which was absorbed into the Army of Northern Virginia. He had risen to colonel by April 1862, and he saw action at Seven Pines (Fair Oaks), May 31, 1862, and Malvern Hill, July 1, in the Peninsular campaign, and at Sharpsburg (Antietam), September 17, and in November 1862 was promoted to brigadier general. He was at Chancellorsville, May 2–4, 1863, and Gettysburg, July 1–3, 1863, and after Spotsylvania in May 1864 he was promoted to major general. He took part in Gen. Jubal A. Early's campaign in Maryland, the attack on Washington, D.C., and the Shenandoah valley campaign. He served through the siege of Petersburg and by the end of the war, at the age of thirty-three, was lieutenant general in command of a wing of Gen. Robert E. Lee's army. He led troops of the II Corps in the brief capture of Fort Stedman on March 25, 1865, was engaged at Sayler's Creek on

April 6, and after the capture of Gen. Richard S. Ewell there commanded what remained of the corps at Appomattox. Afterwards he resumed his law practice in Atlanta. He was defeated as the Democratic candidate for governor in 1868 but in 1873 was elected to the Senate. Reelected in 1879, he resigned in May 1880 to take a post with the Louisville & Nashville Railroad. He was elected governor in 1886, and after four years in that post he was returned to the Senate in March 1891. He retired from politics in 1897. He was elected commander in chief of the United Confederate Veterans annually from its organization in 1889 until his death, and in 1903 he published *Reminiscences of the Civil War.* Gordon died in Miami, Florida, on January 9, 1904.

Gorgas, Josiah (1818–1883), Confederate army officer. Born in Dauphin County, Pennsylvania, on July 1, 1818, Gorgas left school early to help support his family, but he nonetheless won appointment to West Point and graduated in 1841. Attached to the ordnance service, he spent six years at the Watervliet Arsenal, New York, except for a period in 1845 when he made an inspection tour of European arsenals. In 1847–1848 he served in the Mexican War, taking part in the siege of Veracruz and then commanding the ordnance depot there. Thereafter he served in arsenals in various places, rising to the rank of captain in 1855. In April 1861, influenced by his wife's Southern connections, he resigned his commission and entered the Confederate service as a major. Appointed chief of ordnance for the entire Confederate army, he immediately faced the seemingly impossible task of supplying it with arms and ammunition. Little federal ordnance had been captured and most of it was obsolete, and manufacturing facilities in the South were virtually nonexistent. While the army fought with the arms at hand and supplemented them with captured material, Gorgas quickly surveyed the available raw materials and began establishing mines, mills, factories, and foundries to produce bullets, powder, small arms, and cannon. Imports from Europe, run through the Union blockade, helped tide the army over until his necessarily rather crude and highly decentralized manufacturing and distribution system went into operation. Despite the heavy handicaps under which he was forced to work—political and financial problems were at times added to the physical difficulties—he succeeded in providing a steady flow of arms and ammunition throughout the war. He was promoted to brigadier general in November 1864. From the end of the war until 1869 he managed an iron works in Alabama, then joined the University of the South as headmaster of the junior department, later becoming professor of engineering and in 1872 vice-chancellor. In 1878 he was named president of the University of Alabama, but ill health forced him to resign a year later; he remained as librarian until his death in Tuscaloosa, Alabama, on May 15, 1883.

Gorgas, William Crawford (1854–1920), army officer and physician. Born on October 3, 1854, in Mobile, Alabama, Gorgas was the son of Josiah Gorgas. He received an irregular education during the years of civil war and Reconstruction but graduated from the University of the South in 1875. He wanted to follow a military career, but could not gain admission to West Point; instead, he entered Bellevue Medical College in New York City, graduated in 1879, served an internship at Bellevue Hospital, and was appointed in June 1880 an assistant surgeon, with rank of first lieutenant, in the army Medical Corps. He survived an attack of yellow fever while serving at Fort Brown, Texas, and, thereafter immune to the disease, was often stationed at posts where it was particularly prevalent. He advanced to captain in June 1885 and to major in July 1898 while serving in the Dakotas, Florida, and elsewhere. He became head of sanitation at Havana in 1898 after it was occupied by U.S. forces in the Spanish–American War. He succeeded in greatly improving sanitary conditions in the city, but not until Walter Reed, also working in Cuba, had demonstrated that yellow fever was transmitted by a species of mosquito was Gorgas able to make headway in eliminating the disease. He immediately began to scour Havana for the mosquito's breeding places and to destroy them. The city was quickly rid of mosquitoes and disease disappeared. For this work he won international fame and in March 1903 was made colonel and assistant surgeon general by a special act of Congress. In March 1904 he became chief sanitary officer for the Panama Canal Zone, one of the world's worst pestholes, where yellow fever and malaria had been the bane of French efforts to build a canal. Initiating measures against yellow fever, he had also to overcome the opposition of the Canal Commission, who thought the plans were extravagant. When an outbreak occurred in November 1904 sufficient funds were at last allotted, and efforts against the mosquito proceeded. By the end of 1905 yellow fever had been eliminated from the Canal Zone, and sanitary conditions generally had been vastly improved. Throughout his work he was strongly supported by President Theodore Roosevelt, who in March 1907 appointed him to the Isthmian Canal Commission. In January 1914 Gorgas was promoted to brigadier general and made surgeon general of the U.S. army. In March 1915 he was promoted to major general. During World War I he supervised the army medical service, retiring in December 1918. For the International Health Board (of the Rockefeller Foundation), of which he was made a director in 1919, he was asked to investigate the control of pneumonia among miners in South Africa, and he also fought yellow fever in South and Central America and in West Africa. He died en route to the last, in London, on July 3, 1920.

Granger, Gordon (1822–1876), army officer. Born in Joy, Wayne County, New York, on November 6, 1822, Granger graduated from West Point in 1845 and was commissioned in the infantry. In 1846 he was transferred to the Mounted Riflemen (later the 3rd Cavalry), and he served in Gen. Winfield Scott's army in the Mexican War, winning brevets as first lieutenant at Contreras and Churubusco, August 19–20, 1847, and as captain at Chapultepec, September 13. He saw mainly frontier duty thereafter, receiving promotions to first lieutenant in 1852 and captain in 1861. He fought with distinction under Gen. Nathaniel Lyon at Wilson's Creek, Missouri, on August 10, 1861, and the next month was appointed colonel of the 2nd Michigan Cavalry volunteer regiment. While serving in Gen. John Pope's Army of the Mississippi in the operations against New Madrid, Missouri, and Island No. 10, he was promoted to brigadier general of volunteers in March 1862. He commanded the cavalry in Gen. Henry W. Halleck's move against Corinth, Mississippi, in May. In September he was promoted to major general of volunteers in command of the Army of Kentucky. In 1863 he was transferred to command of the reserve corps in Gen. William S. Rosecrans's Army of the Cumberland. On the third day of the battle of Chickamauga, September 20, he rushed forward on his own initiative to the aid of Gen. George H. Thomas, whose corps was alone in the field against the massed Confederate forces. During the siege of Chattanooga and the battle of Missionary Ridge, November 25, 1863, Granger commanded the IV Corps. He later took part in the relief of Knoxville and commanded a division and then the XIII Corps in the capture, in conjunction with Adm. David G. Farragut, of Fort Gaines and Fort Morgan in Mobile Bay in August 1864. He received the surrender of Mobile in April 1865. These operations brought him brevets of brigadier and major general. He was mustered out of volunteer service in January 1866 and in July was appointed colonel of infantry. While commanding the District of New Mexico he died in Santa Fe on January 10, 1876.

Grant, Lewis Addison (1829–1918), army officer and public official. Born on January 17, 1829, in Winhall, Vermont, Grant taught school for several years before winning admission to the bar in 1855. He entered practice in Bellows Falls, Vermont. In August 1861 he was appointed major of the 5th Vermont Infantry, and in September he was promoted to lieutenant colonel. A year later he was promoted to colonel, and at Fredericksburg, December 13, 1862, he was wounded while temporarily in command of his brigade, the "Old Vermont." He took command of it permanently in February 1863, and for his actions at Salem Heights, Virginia, May 3, 1863, he won the Medal of Honor (awarded in 1893). He was promoted to brigadier general of volunteers in April 1864, and his performance at Cedar Creek, Virginia, on October 19, 1864, commanding a division of the VI Corps against five of Gen. Jubal A. Early's divisions earned him a brevet to major general of volunteers. The "Old Vermont" brigade led the VI Corps attack that finally broke the Confederate lines at Petersburg on April 2, 1865. Grant was again wounded in that action. He was mustered out in August 1865, and he declined a regular commission the following year. He engaged in law and business in Chicago, from 1867 in Des Moines, Iowa, and from 1884 in Minneapolis. From April 1890 to December 1893 he was assistant secretary of war. He died in Minneapolis on March 20, 1918.

Grant, Ulysses S. (1822–1885), army officer and eighteenth president of the United States. Born in Point Pleasant, Ohio, on April 27, 1822, Grant worked on the family farm and attended local schools and in 1839 was appointed to West Point. He had already decided to reverse his given names, Hiram Ulysses, when on his arrival at West Point he discovered that he was recorded as Ulysses S., most likely on his congressman's mistaken assumption that he bore his mother's maiden name, Simpson. He acquiesced in the change, although he later maintained that the middle initial did not stand for anything. He graduated in 1843, having distinguished himself in horsemanship and little else, and was assigned to the 4th Infantry. In 1845 his regiment joined the forces under Gen. Zachary Taylor in Texas. Although he was not in sympathy with the Mexican War, Grant served well at Palo Alto, Resaca de la Palma, Monterrey, and, under Gen. Winfield Scott, in the Veracruz–Mexico City campaign, being distinguished for bravery in the battles of Molino del Rey, September 8, 1847, and Chapultepec, September 13, for which he was brevetted first lieutenant and captain. He was promoted to first lieutenant later in September. From 1848 to 1854 he was stationed at posts in New York, Michigan, the Oregon Territory, and California, advancing to captain in August 1853; in July 1854, frustrated by lack of advancement, financial difficulties, and separation from his family, he resigned and rejoined his family in Missouri. For six years he farmed and undertook various business ventures without success, and in 1860 he moved to Galena, Illinois, to become a clerk in a leather-goods store operated by his father and brothers. Shortly after the outbreak of the Civil War the following year he aided in organizing a Galena militia company, and while waiting in vain for a reply from Washington to his application for an army commission he served as an aide to the state adjutant general. In June the gov-

ernor of Illinois appointed him colonel of the 21st Illinois Infantry Volunteers, and two months later, on post in Missouri, he was appointed brigadier general of volunteers. Placed in command of the District of Southeast Missouri, with headquarters in Cairo, Illinois, he saw little action, save for a brief and inconclusive engagement at Belmont, Missouri (November 7), until January 1862, when Gen. Henry W. Halleck approved his plan to move on forts Henry and Donelson in Tennessee. Aided by a flotilla of gunboats under Commodore Andrew H. Foote, Grant quickly forced the abandonment of Fort Henry, on the Tennessee River, on February 6 and then vigorously besieged Fort Donelson, on the Cumberland. On February 16 he informed the fort's commander, Gen. Simon B. Buckner, that "No terms except an unconditional and immediate surrender can be accepted. I propose to move immediately upon your works." Buckner and some 15,000 troops, hopelessly surrounded, gave up their arms. The victory, not only Grant's but also the Union's first great success, aroused public enthusiasm in the North and brought Grant promotion to major general of volunteers commanding the Army of the Tennessee. His popularity sagged in April, when he failed to anticipate and was slow to react to a powerful attack on his forces at Shiloh, near Pittsburg Landing, Tennessee, by Gen. Albert S. Johnston (killed on April 6, he was succeeded by Gen. P. G. T. Beauregard). The arrival of reinforcements under Gen. D. C. Buell and Gen. Lew Wallace enabled Grant to clear the field on the second day of battle, but Union casualties were extremely high and brought forth a storm of public protest. After several months of planning Grant set out in November to take Vicksburg, the last major Confederate stronghold on the Mississippi River. The campaign was slow to develop and was further delayed by a series of minor Confederate victories, but in April 1863, encouraged by the success of Adm. David D. Porter's fleet in running past the Vicksburg batteries, Grant boldly cast loose from his communications and supply lines and landed his 20,000 men south of the city. Vicksburg was soon isolated by Gen. William T. Sherman's defeat of Gen. Joseph E. Johnston's army at Jackson and under siege; on July 4 the garrison, 30,000 men commanded by Gen. John C. Pemberton, surrendered. The Mississippi was under complete Union control when nearby Port Hudson fell a few days later, and the Confederacy was cut in half. Grant was made a major general in the regular army and in October was placed in command of the Military Division of the Mississippi. In November he moved to bring the war in the West to a virtual conclusion. Relieving Gen. William S. Rosecrans, who had allowed himself to be trapped at Chattanooga by Gen. Braxton Bragg, he directed a carefully coordinated attack on Bragg's strong points on Lookout Mountain (by Gen. Joseph Hooker) and Missionary

Ridge (Sherman and Gen. George H. Thomas) and drove him from the field, November 24 and 25. In March 1864 he was promoted to lieutenant general and named commander of the Union armies. Making his headquarters with Gen. George G. Meade's Army of the Potomac, he brought his considerable strategic talents to bear on the unsolved problem of evolving an overall plan of war; his cardinal strengths—dogged determination, patience, and a clear understanding of the situation—proved the key. On May 4, 1864, he began the final campaign, sending Gen. William T. Sherman against Gen. Joseph E. Johnston and toward Atlanta and at the same time pitting the Army of the Potomac against Gen. Robert E. Lee's Army of Northern Virginia with the object of taking Richmond. The brutal, costly war of attrition that moved slowly through the Wilderness Campaign, May 5–7, and the battles of Spotsylvania, May 8–12, and Cold Harbor, June 1–3, took an enormous toll but had precisely the desired effect of wearing down Lee's resources. In June Lee entrenched at Petersburg, before Richmond, and settled in for the months-long siege of the Petersburg campaign. In what has been called the first example of modern warfare, Grant pitted the total resources of the Union against the Confederacy and made the outcome almost inevitable. Ignoring public protests against heavy casualties and the seemingly interminable siege—"I propose to fight it out on this line if it takes all summer," he had earlier said—he forced Lee to withdraw from his position to seek supplies. The Confederate line was broken on April 2, and Lee was forced to abandon both Richmond and Petersburg and strike out to the west. The desperate move ended a week later, on April 9, 1865, when, further flight cut off by Gen. Philip H. Sheridan's cavalry, Lee surrendered to Grant at Appomattox Courthouse, Grant offering magnificently generous terms. The war ended with Johnston's surrender to Sherman in North Carolina on April 26. Grant moved then to Washington, D.C., where he oversaw the demobilization of the army and the military administration of Reconstruction. In July 1866 he was appointed to the newly created rank of general of the army. He served as interim secretary of war for five months in 1867–1868 during the dispute over the Tenure of Office Act between Congress and President Andrew Johnson and became permanently estranged from Johnson over the issue. He had long been courted by Republicans as a potential presidential candidate, and the break with Johnson strengthened his position with the dominant Radical Republicans. Nominated in 1868, he was elected over Democrat Horatio Seymour by a small popular majority but a large electoral vote (214 to 80) and quickly demonstrated his complete lack of political sophistication by assembling an unwieldy cabinet of friends, former associates, and assorted others. Only the Department of State, under Hamilton Fish, was in fully capable hands; Fish oversaw negotiation of the Treaty of Washington (1871), laying the foundation for the amicable arbitration of U.S.–British disputes, including the *Alabama* claims, and he managed to blunt Grant's persistent efforts to secure the annexation of Santo Domingo as a naval base. The Crédit Mobilier scandal tarnished the Republicans' reelection campaign of 1872, requiring the replacement of Schuyler Colfax by Henry Wilson as vice-president, but Grant's popular majority in his defeat of Horace Greeley, Democrat and Liberal Republican, was nonetheless larger than before (Grant won 286 electoral votes; Greeley dying, various Democrats shared 63 votes). Soon, however, revelations of widespread corruption in the government, involving Grant's private secretary, Orville E. Babcock, in the Whisky Ring, the secretary of war in corruption in the conduct of Indian affairs, and other high officials, soured the tone of the administration. Grant, scrupulously honest himself, became the target of reformers and critics of every stripe. Outside the field of foreign policy, only the fiscal measures of his administration were particularly creditable; a notable achievement was the passage of the Specie Resumption Act of 1875 and other sound, hard-money bills. On retiring from office in March 1877 he made a world tour on which he was everywhere hailed as a hero and then returned to Galena. The old-guard faction of the Republican party, then known as the Stalwarts, pushed hard to nominate him again in 1880, but the two-term tradition defeated the attempt. In 1881 he moved to New York City, where, with characteristic credulity, he invested nearly all of his money in a banking firm that three years later was discovered to have defrauded him. To pay his debts he wrote an article on the battle of Shiloh for the *Century* magazine and then, with the encouragement of his friend Mark Twain, began preparing his memoirs. *The Personal Memoirs of U. S. Grant* were completed just a few days before his death on July 23, 1885, at his Adirondack retreat at Mount McGregor; the two volumes, published in 1885–1886 by Twain, restored the Grant family to solvency and were hailed as a major work of autobiography. In March 1885 Congress had created for him the rank of general of the army on the retired list.

Graves, William Sidney (1865–1940), army officer. Born in Mount Calm, Texas, on March 27, 1865, Graves graduated from West Point in 1889 and was commissioned in the infantry. He served with the 7th and 6th Infantries in the West until 1899, serving in 1898–1899 as acting judge advocate of the Department of the Columbia and receiving promotions to first lieutenant in November 1896 and captain in September 1899. He was then ordered to the Philippines for service against the insurrectionists until 1902. Routine garrison duty followed, interrupted by a second tour in the Philippines in 1904–1906 and relief work after the San Francisco earthquake in April–May 1906. In 1909 he was assigned to duty with the General Staff in Washington, D.C., serving as secretary in 1911–1912 and 1914–1918. He was promoted to major in March 1911, lieutenant colonel in July 1916, colonel in June 1917, and temporary brigadier general in February 1918. In July 1918 he was promoted to major general in command of the 8th Infantry Division, but in August he was relieved of that post to undertake a highly secret mission under the direct orders of Secretary of War Newton D. Baker. He traveled immediately to Vladivostok, Siberia, to take command of an American force of two infantry regiments and auxiliary units—some 10,000 men in all—whose purpose was to protect Allied military stores in depots along the Trans-Siberian Railway, to render whatever aid possible (practically none was) to a Czech army stranded in Siberia, and (although this aim was not explicitly stated) to discourage any Japanese ambitions to annex Russian territories during the confusion and civil fighting that had followed the Russian revolutions of 1917. Graves carried out his orders scrupulously, firmly resisting pressure from British, French, and some American diplomatic officials who wished him to take action against the Bolshevist faction. The American expeditionary force was withdrawn from Siberia in April 1920. Graves was briefly commander of Fort William McKinley, Philippines, and then commanded the 1st Infantry Brigade, 1920–1925; the 1st Division, 1925; VI Corps Area, Chicago, 1925–1926; and Panama Canal Division and Department, 1926–1928. He retired in 1928. In 1931 he published *America's Siberian Adventure.* He died in Shrewsbury, New Jersey, on February 27, 1940.

Greely, Adolphus Washington (1844–1935),

army officer and explorer. Born on March 27, 1844, in Newburyport, Massachusetts, Greely enlisted in the 19th Massachusetts Volunteers in 1861 and served throughout the Civil War, seeing action in several major battles, sustaining serious wounds on three occasions, and rising in rank from private to brevet major of volunteers (he was a first lieutenant of volunteers from April 1864). In March 1867 he entered the regular army as a second lieutenant in the 36th Infantry. He was promoted to first lieutenant of cavalry in May 1873, and served mainly in the West and in Washington, D.C. In 1881 he volunteered for a scientific expedition to the Arctic being planned by the army according to the recommendations of the 1879 International Polar Geographical Conference, which had designated 1882–1883 as the first International Polar Year. Placed in command of a 25-man party sent to establish a meteorological station, Greely sailed in July 1881 from Newfoundland aboard the *Proteus* and in August landed at Lady

Franklin Bay on the eastern shore of Ellesmere Island. There he established his base camp, Fort Conger, where detailed meteorological, oceanographic, and geophysical observations were carried out and from which exploratory expeditions set out for the interior, discovering Lake Hazen and, on the western coast, Greely Fjord, and in May 1882 reaching their farthest north, 83° 24′. Supply and relief ships sent out in 1882 and 1883 failed to reach Fort Conger, and in August 1883, by prearrangement, Greely and his men broke camp and made their way south by boat to Cape Sabine, beyond which they could not go. With dwindling provisions they wintered there, and by the time relief arrived in June 1884 (the *Thetis,* the *Bear,* and the *Alert,* all under Commander Winfield S. Schley) there were left only Greely and six others, one of whom died shortly thereafter. Although he was publicly much criticized at first, it eventually became clear that, given his explicit orders and sheer physical necessity, he had performed correctly and courageously throughout the ordeal. Promoted to captain in June 1886, he became by order of President Grover Cleveland brigadier general and chief of the signal service in March of the following year. In that post he was responsible over the next 20 years for the construction of tens of thousands of miles of telegraph lines and submarine cables in Puerto Rico, Cuba, the Philippines, Alaska, and elsewhere, and for the army's earliest adoption of wireless telegraphy; he was also head of the U.S. Weather Service until it was transferred to the Department of Agriculture in 1891. He was a delegate to the International Telegraph Congress in London and the International Wireless Telegraph Congress in Berlin in 1903. In February 1906 he was promoted to major general and placed in command of the Northern Division; later transferred to the Pacific Division, he oversaw army relief operations following the San Francisco earthquake in that year. Greely retired in March 1908. In addition to his work on the official and scientific reports of the Lady Franklin Bay Expedition he wrote several other books, including *Three Years of Arctic Service,* 1886; *American Weather,* 1888; *American Explorers,* 1894; *Handbook of Arctic Discoveries,* 1896; *True Tales of Arctic Heroism,* 1912; and *Reminiscences of Adventure and Service,* 1927. He was widely honored for his scientific work and in 1935 was belatedly awarded the Medal of Honor. Greely died later that year, on October 20, 1935, in Washington, D.C.

Greene, George Sears (1801–1899), army offi-

cer and engineer. Born in Apponaug, now part of Warwick, Rhode Island, on May 6, 1801, Greene graduated from West Point in 1823 and was commissioned in the artillery. He remained at West Point as an instructor for four years and then served at various posts in New England, advancing to first lieutenant in 1829, until resigning from the army in June 1836.

He turned then to civil engineering, engaging in railroad construction as far afield as Virginia and in 1856 becoming an engineer with the Croton water project in New York City; he designed and built the Croton reservoir in Central Park. In January 1862 he was appointed colonel of the 60th New York Regiment and in April was promoted to brigadier general of volunteers in command of a brigade of the 2nd Division, XII Corps, under Gen. Henry W. Slocum. For a time, during the battle of Antietam, September 17, 1862, he commanded the division. At Gettysburg, July 1–3, 1863, the XII Corps was positioned atop Culp's Hill on the first day of battle, anchoring the right of the Union line. The rest of the corps being withdrawn, Greene's brigade was compelled to hold the hill alone, against troops of Gen. Richard S. Ewell's corps attacking in much superior numbers, throughout the second day. Although some forward trenches were given up, the hill remained under Greene's control; for Greene to have failed would have meant near-certain disaster for Union forces. Two months later his brigade accompanied the XII Corps to Tennessee, and during the Chattanooga campaign, at Wauhatchie on October 28, 1863, he was severely wounded. He returned to the field in January 1865 and took part in Gen. William T. Sherman's campaign in the Carolinas. In March he was brevetted major general of volunteers for his services in the war. Mustered out in April 1866, he resumed his engineering practice in New York, becoming chief engineer and commissioner of the Croton aqueduct department in 1867. During 1871–1872 he was chief engineer of public works in Washington, D.C. He was a founder and from 1875 to 1877 first president of the American Society of Civil Engineers. Greene died in Morristown, New Jersey, on January 28, 1899. One of his sons, Samuel Dana Greene (1840–1884) was executive officer of the ironclad *Monitor* during the Civil War.

Greene, Nathanael (1742–1786), Revolutionary officer. Born on August 7, 1742, in Potowomut, a part of Warwick, Rhode Island, Greene spent the years before the outbreak of the Revolution helping to manage his father's iron foundry and served for a short time in the colonial legislature. Although raised a Quaker, he was expelled from the Society of Friends for his unseemly interest in military matters. In October 1774 he helped organize a company of militia that was kept from going to the scene of conflict in Massachusetts in April 1775 by Rhode Island's Loyalist governor. The legislature, however, authorized the raising of three regiments in May and appointed Greene brigadier general in command. Soon given a similar commission in the Continental army, he served through the siege of Boston, and after briefly commanding the army of occupation there early in 1776, he set out to aid in the defense

of New York City. He was promoted to major general in August. Greene urged Gen. George Washington to attempt to hold Fort Washington and Fort Lee even after the British occupation of Manhattan, but after the capture of the former on November 16 Greene evacuated the latter and joined Washington in New Jersey. During the next year he rendered valuable service at Trenton, where he commanded the left column, Brandywine, Germantown, and, in 1778, at Monmouth. In March 1778 he assumed, in addition to his field command, the office of quartermaster general and, in the light of congressional and state recalcitrance in matters of finance and supply, discharged his duties more than creditably until relinquishing the office to Col. Timothy Pickering in August 1780. He took part in August 1778 in the defense of Newport, Rhode Island. In September 1780, with Washington temporarily absent, Greene was in command of the entire army; it was during this period that Benedict Arnold's plottings came to light and Greene sat as president of the board that condemned Maj. André. In October Greene was sent to South Carolina to replace Gen. Horatio Gates as commander of the army in the South. He arranged an efficient and dependable supply system and soon had the army, demoralized earlier at Camden, again in fighting trim. Facing Gen. Charles Cornwallis, he shrewdly divided his army, sending a force under Gen. Daniel Morgan to the victory at Cowpens, January 17, 1781; he then regrouped and allowed the British a Pyrrhic victory at Guilford Courthouse, March 15. Greene continued to hound the British, who had another expensive win at Hobkirk's Hill, April 25. By this time the movements and battles forced by Greene had exhausted the British and induced Cornwallis to give up his plans for conquest in the South and to retire with the bulk of his army northward to Yorktown, Virginia. On September 8, after a prolonged rest, Greene's forces won a major victory at Eutaw Springs, South Carolina, and by December they had laid seige to the last British stronghold in the South, Charleston, upon which the regulars defeated in September had fallen back. Although the earlier surrender of Cornwallis at Yorktown had effectively ended the war, Greene found it necessary to maintain the siege for a full year before the British withdrawal was completed in December 1782. After the war Greene experienced financial difficulties resulting from the mismanagement of funds and supplies by subordinate officers and government contractors and from the reluctance of the government to reimburse him for his heavy personal expenditures in supporting his army. He retired to an estate near Savannah, Georgia, and died there on June 19, 1786.

Greene, Theodore Phinney (1809–1887), naval officer. Born on November 1, 1809, in Montreal, Greene later moved to Vermont and from there entered the navy in November 1826. He was promoted to passed midshipman in 1832, sailed on the *Vincennes* under Commander John H. Aulick on a cruise around the world in 1834–1836, and became a lieutenant in 1837. During the Mexican War he served on the *Congress*, Commodore Robert F. Stockton's flagship on the Pacific coast, and for several months from November 11, 1847, he commanded the force of some 730 seamen and marines occupying Mazatlán. In September 1855 he was promoted to commander. He was stationed at the Mare Island, California, navy yard in 1861–1862, and in July of the latter year was promoted to captain, taking over command of the *San Jacinto* from Capt. Charles Wilkes. In 1863 he was assigned to the East Gulf Blockading Squadron, and in 1864 he was its commander. In 1865 he took command of the *Richmond* in Adm. David G. Farragut's West Gulf Blockading Squadron, and in April of that year he helped cover the landing of troops at Mobile, Alabama. After the war he was at the Portsmouth, New Hampshire, navy yard. Promoted to commodore in July 1867, he commanded the *Powhatan* in the Pacific Squadron during that year, and from 1868 to 1870 he commanded the navy yard at Pensacola, Florida. Greene retired in 1871 and in March 1872 was made rear admiral on the retired list. He died in Jaffrey, New Hampshire, on August 30, 1887.

Greene, Wallace Martin, Jr. (1907–   ), marine officer. Born in Waterbury, Vermont, on December 27, 1907, Greene attended the University of Vermont for a year and then entered the Naval Academy, graduating in 1930 and taking a commission in the marine corps. After further training and a two-year cruise aboard the *Tennessee* he was promoted to first lieutenant in November 1934; various assignments followed, including service on Guam and in Shanghai, China, and he advanced to captain in September 1937. He completed a course at the Marine Corps Schools, Quantico, Virginia, in 1940 and the next year was briefly assistant naval attaché at the U.S. embassy in London. Promoted to major in December, he joined the 3rd Marine Brigade, which was sent to Samoa in the Pacific in April 1942. He advanced to lieutenant colonel in August; in December 1943 he was appointed assistant chief of staff of the 1st Tactical Group, 5th Amphibious Force (under Gen. Holland M. Smith), and in that post helped plan and then took part in the assaults on Kwajalein Island in January 1944 and Eniwetok in February. Later, as a staff officer with the 2nd Marine Division, he took part in the Saipan and Tinian campaigns in June–July 1944. Greene advanced to colonel in 1947; he was assistant chief of staff, Fleet Marine Force, Pacific, in 1948–1950; he was on the staff of the Marine Corps Schools in 1950–1952, and after graduating from the National War College in 1953 he served two years on the staff of the Joint Chiefs of Staff. In September 1955 he was promoted to brigadier general and named assistant commander of the 2nd Marine Division at Camp Lejeune, North Carolina. He was appointed commander of the Parris Island base early in 1957 and of Camp Lejeune a few months later. He became assistant chief of staff of the corps in January 1958, receiving promotion to major general in July, and deputy chief of staff in April 1959. In January 1960 he was promoted to lieutenant general and named chief of staff of the marine corps, and in January 1964 he became commandant of the corps with the rank of general. He held that post until his retirement in January 1968. He was succeeded as commandant of the marine corps by Gen. Leonard F. Chapman.

Gridley, Charles Vernon (1844–1898), naval officer. Born on November 24, 1844, in Logansport, Indiana, Gridley grew up mainly in Michigan. He graduated from the Naval Academy in 1863 and was assigned to the corvette *Oneida*, of Adm. David G. Farragut's squadron, with which he took part in the battle of Mobile Bay in August 1864. After the Civil War he served in the Pacific aboard the *Kearsarge*, on the Great Lakes, in the South Atlantic, as an instructor at the Naval Academy in 1875–1879, and on European station, receiving promotions to lieutenant in February 1867 and commander in March 1882. Over the next 15 years he continued to fill routine assignments, often ashore, including several years as lighthouse inspector. In March 1897 he was promoted to captain and in July was given command of the *Olympia*, flagship of Commodore George Dewey, commander of the Asiatic Squadron. His health failed while in that post, and he had already been declared medically unfit for further service when word of the declaration of war against Spain arrived in Hong Kong. He succeeded in retaining his command, however, and when the squadron steamed into Manila Bay on May 1, 1898, Dewey gave his famous command "You may fire when you are ready, Gridley." Gridley directed the squadron's fire throughout the battle. On May 25 he left Manila Bay for home, but he died en route, in Kobe, Japan, on June 5, 1898.

Gridley, Richard (1711–1796), colonial officer and engineer. Born in Boston on January 3, 1711, Gridley worked as a civil engineer and surveyor in Massachusetts and had studied military engineering when in 1745 he was commissioned an officer in the expedition sent under William Pepperrell against the French fortress at Louisbourg, Cape Breton Island. Gridley commanded the artillery during the siege. In 1746 he planned fortifications for Boston harbor, and in 1752–1754 he was on the Kennebec River building Fort Western (on the site of Augusta, Maine) and Fort Halifax (Winslow, Maine). In 1755 he was commissioned colonel of provincial troops and commanded the artillery in the expedition under Gen. (soon after Sir) William Johnson against Crown Point. He built the fortifications around Lake George, including Fort William Henry. He took part in the second siege of Louisbourg by Gen. Jeffrey Amherst in 1758, and the next year he commanded the provincial artillery in the Quebec campaign under Gen. James Wolfe and took part in the battle on the Plains of Abraham, September 13, 1759. For his services he was granted the Magdalen Islands in the Gulf of St. Lawrence, where he made his home for several years, lands in New Hampshire, and a pension. In April 1775 Gridley was appointed chief engineer of Massachusetts forces, and in May he was commissioned colonel of artillery and major general of provincial troops. He constructed the breastworks on Breed's Hill in Charlestown on the night of June 16, 1775, and was wounded in the battle (known as that of Bunker Hill) the next day. During September–November 1775 he held a colonel's commission in the Continental army; from June 1775 to August 1776 he was chief engineer of the Continental army, during which time, in March 1776, he built the fortifications on Dorchester Heights that helped force the British from Boston, and from January 1777 to December 1780 he was engineer general of the eastern department. Gridley died in Stoughton, Massachusetts, on June 21, 1796.

Grierson, Benjamin Henry (1826–1911), army officer. Born in Pittsburgh, Pennsylvania, on July 8, 1826, Grierson moved to Ohio in his youth and later to Illinois, where he taught music for a time and then entered business. He enlisted as a private at the outbreak of the Civil War and in October 1861 was appointed major in the 6th Illinois Cavalry. In April 1862 he was promoted to colonel. During 1862 he took part in numerous raids and skirmishes, mainly in Tennessee. In December the cavalry was reorganized and Grierson became commander of the 1st Brigade of cavalry. In April 1863 he led some 1700 men in a 600-mile, 16-day raid from La Grange, Tennessee, to Baton Rouge, Louisiana, during which public property, communications (particularly the Vicksburg & Meridian and the New Orleans & Jackson railroads), and other potential war matériel were destroyed. Serving also to distract Gen. John C. Pemberton, the raid contributed substantially to the success of Gen. Ulysses S. Grant's siege of Vicksburg, and for it Grierson was promoted to brigadier general of volunteers in June. Through the rest of the war he continued to raid in Tennessee and Mississippi, commanding a division in Gen. Andrew J. Smith's defeat of Gen. Nathan B. Forrest at Tupelo, Mississippi, on July 14, 1864. In February 1865 he was brevetted major general of volunteers for the 1863 raid. He was mustered out of volunteer service in April and in May raised to permanent major general on the volunteer rolls. In March 1867 he received brevets of brigadier and major general of regulars for services in 1863 and 1864. In July 1866 he was appointed colonel of the 10th Cavalry and ordered to duty on the frontier. He served at various posts, took part in numerous engagements with the Indians, and commanded at various times the departments of Texas and Arizona. In 1886 he was appointed commander of the District of New Mexico, and in April 1890 he was promoted to brigadier general. He retired later in that year and died at Omena, Michigan, on September 1, 1911.

Griffiths, John Willis (1809–1882), naval architect. Born in New York City on October 6, 1809, Griffiths was apprenticed to his father, a shipwright, and early learned the fundamentals of shipbuilding and design. By the age of nineteen he had already designed a major vessel, the frigate *Macedonia.* Working for the navy yard in Portsmouth, Virginia, and later for a New York shipbuilding firm, he began proposing numerous innovations in ship design, including the use of the ram on warships, and in 1836 published a remarkable series of articles in the *Portsmouth Advocate* outlining his ideas. In 1842 he delivered in New York City the first formal lectures on naval architecture ever given in America and opened a free school in shipbuilding. After several years devoted to refining his ideas and two years of actual construction he saw launched in 1845 his *Rainbow,* a vessel built for the China trade and the first of the famous "extreme" clippers, the fastest ships afloat. While Donald McKay was working with the same basic approach to clipper design, Griffiths took it farther, producing ships with an extremely narrow bow, high stern, and aft-displaced beam. Primarily a theoretician rather than a shipbuilder, he advocated pure functionalism of design, claiming that beauty would flow naturally from it. The *Sea Witch,* another extreme clipper, was launched in 1846. In 1848 he invented an iron keelson for strengthening wooden ships, and during the early 1850s he designed a number of steamships that proved to be the finest of their time, showing a model of one at the Crystal Palace exhibition in London in 1851. He was coeditor and part owner of the *Nautical Magazine and Naval Journal* from 1856 to 1858, when he was appointed a special naval constructor for the U.S. government; in that capacity he designed the *Pawnee,* a heavily armed gunboat that featured twin screws, a drop bilge, and a remarkably shallow draft. Later inventions of his included the bilge keel to prevent rolling (1863), triple screws (1866), an improved rivet (1880), and a timber-bending machine which he used in building the *New Era* in 1870 and the *Enterprise* in 1872. From 1879 Griffiths was editor of the *American Ship* in New York City. His published works included *A Treatise on Marine and Naval Architecture,* 1850; *The Ship-builder's Manual and Nautical Referee,*

1853; and *The Progressive Shipbuilder*, 1874–1875. Griffiths died in Brooklyn, New York, on March 30, 1882.

Groves, Leslie Richard (1896–1970), army officer. Born in Albany, New York, on August 17, 1896, Groves attended the University of Washington for a year and the Massachusetts Institute of Technology for two before entering West Point, from which he graduated in 1918. Commissioned in the engineers, he took courses at the Engineer School, Camp Humphreys (now Fort Belvoir), Virginia, in 1918–1920 and 1921, with time out for brief service in France in 1919. His assignments over the next decade included San Francisco, Hawaii, Delaware, and Nicaragua. In 1931 he was attached to the office of the chief of engineers in Washington, D.C. He was promoted to captain in October 1934, graduated from Command and General Staff School, Fort Leavenworth, Kansas, in 1936 and from the Army War College in 1939, and then was assigned to General Staff duty. Promoted to major and then temporary colonel in July and November 1940, he was assigned to the office of the quartermaster general and then to that of the chief of engineers, where his responsibility for oversight of army construction projects included supervision of the building of the Pentagon. In September 1942 he was placed in command of the Manhattan Engineer District, established a month earlier, with rank of temporary brigadier general. "Manhattan Engineer District" was the cover name for the atomic bomb project. Under Groves's direction basic atomic research, mainly at Columbia University and the University of Chicago, was funded and coordinated with the planning and construction of new research facilities and manufacturing plants, principally the Clinton Laboratory at Oak Ridge, Tennessee, the Hanford Engineer Works near Pasco, Washington, and the secluded Los Alamos installation in New Mexico. Much of the more than $2 billion expended by Groves came through blind or hidden appropriations; purchase and transport of materials, hiring of labor (the work force reached a peak of 125,000), and construction of plants had all to be carried on with the utmost care and secrecy. Not the least of his tasks was to deal successfully with large numbers of civilian scientists and technicians employed in the project. The work culminated in the first successful explosion of a nuclear-fission bomb at Alamogordo, New Mexico, on July 16, 1945. In the three years since the project was organized no major obstacles and no serious breach of security had occurred. Groves had been promoted to temporary major general in December 1944, and he continued as head of the atomic energy establishment created during wartime until January 1947. He was then named chief of the army's Special Weapons Project. He was promoted to lieutenant general (temporary) in January 1948,

and he retired a month later. From that year until 1961 he was a vice-president of the Sperry Rand Corporation. Groves published *Now It Can Be Told; The Story of the Manhattan Project*, in 1962. He died on July 13, 1970, in Washington, D.C.

Gruenther, Alfred Maximilian (1899–   ), army officer. Born on March 3, 1899, in Platte Center, Nebraska, Gruenther took his degree from West Point in 1917 and was commissioned in the field artillery a year later. For the next 23 years his career followed the normal pattern of assignments to various posts and alternate command and staff positions. He was promoted to captain in May 1935 and, after graduating from Command and General Staff School in 1937 and from the Army War College in 1939, to major in July 1940. Promoted in September 1941 to temporary lieutenant colonel, he was appointed in October deputy to Gen. Dwight D. Eisenhower, then chief of staff of the Third Army. In December he succeeded to chief of staff with temporary rank of colonel. In August 1942 he was named deputy chief of staff of the Allied Force headquarters in London, taking temporary rank of brigadier general. In January 1943 he became chief of staff of the Fifth Army on the creation of that unit under the command of Gen. Mark W. Clark, and the next month he was promoted to temporary major general, a rank made permanent in August 1944. He served as Clark's chief of staff throughout the Sicilian and Italian campaigns, remaining with him when he took command of the 15th Army Group in December 1944. After the end of the war Gruenther was Clark's deputy commander of U.S. forces in Austria. Early in 1946 he returned to Washington, D.C., to serve as a deputy commandant of the newly organized National War College. On the formal establishment of the Joint Chiefs of Staff in 1947, Gruenther was chosen its first director of joint staff; he served also as an adviser to the secretary of defense. In September 1949 he was appointed deputy chief of staff of the army for plans, receiving promotion to lieutenant general at that time, and in December 1950 he was chosen chief of staff, Supreme Headquarters Allied Powers in Europe, by Eisenhower, the supreme commander. Promoted to general in July 1951, he held the post until July 1953, when he succeeded Gen. Matthew B. Ridgway as supreme commander of SHAPE. He retired from the army in November 1956. Thereafter he had numerous business interests, serving as director of several large firms, and was a frequent advisor to governmental agencies on armed forces matters, disarmament, and foreign military aid. From 1957 to 1964 he was president of the American Red Cross. He was also a director of the Institute for Defense Analysis from 1964. Gruenther was in addition widely noted as an expert on contract bridge and was the author of books on the game.

Grumman, Leroy Randle (1895–   ), aircraft designer and industrialist. Born in Huntington, Long Island, on January 4, 1895, Grumman had been interested in aircraft for several years when he graduated from Cornell University in 1916. After a year in the engineering department of the New York Telephone Company he entered the navy, becoming a pilot and pilot instructor and advancing to lieutenant (junior grade) before his discharge in 1920. Until 1929 he worked as an engineer and manager for the Loening Aeronautical Engineering Corporation, and in that year, with two partners, he formed the Grumman Aircraft Engineering Corporation. At first the firm subsisted on repair work, but by 1931 it was selling retractable aircraft floats and arresting gear to the navy. Late in that year the navy accepted the first of Grumman's XFF-1 aircraft incorporating a revolutionary retractable landing gear, which allowed greatly increased speed and maneuverability in the air. In the mid-1930s the firm developed a small, agile transport craft for private use that was adopted by the navy as the J4F Widgeon (later transport craft from Grumman were also used in World War II: the Goose, designated by the army OA-9 and by the navy JRF, and the Duck, OA-12 and J2F-5). By 1941 the firm was producing numbers of the F4F Wildcat carrier-based fighter, and after Pearl Harbor production was put on a wartime pace with remarkable speed. Wildcats were also used by the British forces under the name Martlets. During the war the extremely fast and maneuverable F6F Hellcat was introduced, and the TBF Avenger torpedo bomber, originally put into production in 1939, was greatly modified and improved. Both became mainstays of the navy's war in the air. Grumman also perfected a folding wing that greatly increased the storage capacity of aircraft carriers. In 1946 Grumman relinquished the presidency of the firm to become chairman of the board, and in 1966 he retired as honorary chairman. Among his many honors were the Presidential Medal of Merit in 1945 and the Daniel Guggenheim medal in 1948. He was named to the National Aviation Hall of Fame in 1972 and to the International Aerospace Hll of Fame the following year.

Gunnison, John Williams (1812–1853), army officer. Born in Goshen, New Hampshire, on November 11, 1812, Gunnison graduated from West Point in 1837 and was commissioned in the artillery. After a year of service in Florida in the Seminole War he was transferred to the newly organized Corps of Topographical Engineers. During 1838–1839 he assisted in the removal of the Cherokee nation to Indian Territory and was then in Florida again for a year. From 1840 to 1849 he was engaged continuously in survey work, on the Savannah and St. Mary's rivers in Georgia, around Lake Michigan, and in the Northwest, receiving promotion to first lieutenant in May 1846. During 1849–1850 he was a member of an army survey party under Capt. Howard Stansbury in Utah, and he recorded some of his observations of that period in *The Mormons, or Latter-Day Saints, in the Valley of the Great Salt Lake,* 1852. Promoted to captain in March 1853, he was ordered to conduct a survey of a railroad route from the Mississippi to the Pacific by way of the Huerfano River of southern Colorado, Cochetopa Pass, and river routes into southern Utah. Gunnison's was the first railroad survey party sent out by the federal government. The party reached the Sevier River, near the dry Sevier Lake and present-day Deseret, Utah, in October. On the morning of October 26, 1853, they were attacked by a band of Pahvant Indians; Gunnison and seven others were killed and their bodies horribly mutilated. The massacre was an act of revenge by the Indians for the earlier killing of a warrior by some California-bound emigrants, but it was for some time blamed on Mormons, a reflection of prevailing prejudices at the time.

H

Haan, William George (1863–1924), army officer. Born in Crown Point, Indiana, on October 4, 1863, Haan graduated from West Point in 1889 and was commissioned in the artillery. He was promoted to first lieutenant in August 1896. During 1898–1901 he served as a captain of volunteers in Cuba and in the Philippines, fighting the Spanish and then the insurrectionists. He was promoted to regular captain in February 1901 and mustered out of volunteer service the next month. From 1903 to 1906 he was a member of the General Staff, and in the former year he undertook a mission to Panama for President Theodore Roosevelt. He was acting chief of staff of the Pacific Division during the army's relief work following the San Francisco earthquake in 1906. Over the next several years he held various coastal defense commands and staff positions, advancing to major in April 1907, lieutenant colonel of coast artillery in December 1911, and, after another tour on the General Staff in 1912–1914, colonel in July 1916. Four months after American entry into World War I in April 1917 he was promoted to temporary brigadier general and assigned to command of the 57th Field Artillery Brigade of the 32nd Infantry Division at Camp MacArthur, Texas. In December he was advanced to temporary major general in command of the division. The 32nd became in February 1918 the sixth American division sent to France. It went into the line with the French Sixth Army in July, helped hold the German offensive of that month in the second battle of the Marne, and in August earned the nickname "Les Terribles" in the capture of Juvigny. The division took part in the final Meuse–Argonne offensive. In November, after the armistice, Haan was moved up to command of the VII Corps for occupation duty. A few days later he was promoted to permanent brigadier general. In April 1919 he returned to the United States with the 32nd, and after its inactivation he was again assigned to the General Staff. In July 1920 he was promoted to major general and named director of the War Plans Division. He retired in March 1922 and was for a time associated with the *Milwaukee Journal.* He died in Washington, D.C., on October 26, 1924.

Haig, Alexander Meigs, Jr. (1924–   ), army officer. Born on December 2, 1924, in Bala-Cynwyd, Pennsylvania, Haig attended the University of Notre Dame for two years before entering West Point in 1944. He graduated in 1947, completed Ground Gen-

eral School, Fort Riley, Kansas, and Armored School, Fort Knox, Kentucky, in 1948 and, promoted to first lieutenant, was ordered to the 1st Cavalry Division in Japan. He served for a time on the staff of Gen. Douglas MacArthur and during 1950–1951 was aide-de-camp to Gen. Edward M. Almond, taking part with the X Corps in several operations in Korea, including the Inch'on landing, and receiving promotion to captain in December 1950. He was at Fort Knox in 1951–1953, on the staff at West Point in 1953–1955, and on that of the Naval Academy in 1955–1956. He was promoted to temporary major in May 1957, while serving a tour in Europe. He graduated from the Naval War College in 1960, took an M.A. in international relations from Georgetown University in 1961, and, promoted to temporary lieutenant colonel in February 1962, was on staff duty in the Pentagon until 1965, becoming assistant to the secretary of the army in 1964 and later in the year deputy special assistant to the secretary of defense. In 1966 he graduated from the Army War College and was ordered to Vietnam, where after a period of staff work he commanded a battalion and later a brigade of the 1st Infantry Division in the field. In 1967 he returned to West Point, advancing to colonel in July, and the next year he was named deputy commandant of cadets. In January 1969 Haig became military adviser to Henry A. Kissinger, President Richard M. Nixon's assistant for national security. Haig's power and responsibility increased in step with Kissinger's, and he was soon chairing National Security Council meetings in Kissinger's absence, mediating between the State and Defense departments, and handling all security and intelligence material for the President. Promoted to brigadier general in October 1969, he was appointed deputy assistant for national security to the President in June 1970, and in March 1972, after handling the advance arrangements for Nixon's visit to the People's Republic of China, he was promoted to major general. In September of that year he was nominated by Nixon for promotion directly to general and named vice-chief of staff of the army. He assumed the rank and the post in January 1973, but in May he retired from active duty to become chief of the White House staff. He retained that position until the end of the Nixon administration in August 1974, becoming progressively more visible and influential; it was speculated by some observers that in Nixon's isolation during his last days in office Haig was the effective executive power in the government.

In December 1974 he returned to active duty as commander, at the appointment of President Gerald R. Ford, of U.S. forces in Europe, succeeding Gen. Andrew J. Goodpaster as commanding general of North Atlantic Treaty Organization forces in Europe in December. He was appointed to a second tour in the NATO command in November 1976.

Hale, Nathan (1755–1776), Revolutionary army officer. Born on June 6, 1755, in Coventry, Connecticut, Hale graduated from Yale in 1773. He taught school from then until July 1775, when, war having broken out, he was commissioned a lieutenant in the Connecticut militia. He soon joined the Continental army, served at the siege of Boston, and on January 1, 1776, was promoted to captain. After March of that year he served in the defense of New York City. According to legend, in May 1776 Hale led a small band of men in seizing a provision sloop from under the guns of a British man-of-war. In September he volunteered to undertake a reconnaissance mission on Long Island, behind enemy lines. Disguised as a Dutch schoolmaster, he gathered the required intelligence and was returning to his regiment on Manhattan Island when he was captured by the British on September 21. Brought before Gen. Sir William Howe, he was ordered hanged the next day. On the gallows he made a brief speech, ending, again according to tradition, with the words, "I only regret that I have but one life to lose for my country." Since that time he has been revered as a martyr to American independence and as a model for American youth.

Hallaren, Mary Agnes (1907–   ), army officer. Born in Lowell, Massachusetts, on May 4, 1907, Mary Hallaren was educated at the state teachers college in Lowell. While teaching in Lexington, Massachusetts, she traveled extensively in Europe, the Near East, and South America. In July 1942 she entered the Officer Candidate School of the newly organized Women's Army Auxilliary Corps. In July 1943, with the rank of captain, she was named commander of the first battalion to go overseas (the WAAC was redesignated the Women's Army Corps in that month and became a component of the Army of the United States). She served as director of WAC personnel attached to the Eighth and Ninth Air Forces, and in March 1945, by which time she had advanced to lieutenant colonel, she was appointed director of all WAC personnel in the European theater. In June 1946 she became deputy director of the WAC, and in May 1947 she succeeded Col. Westray B. Boyce as director, taking the rank of colonel. With the enactment on June 12, 1948, of the Women's Armed Services Integration Act the WAC became a component of the Regular Army; in consequence, in December of that year, Col. Hallaren became the first woman to receive a commission in the Regular Army

(except for those in the Medical Corps, made part of the Regular Army in 1947). She continued as director of the WAC until her retirement in January 1953. She was succeeded in that post by Col. Irene O. Galloway.

Halleck, Henry Wager (1815–1872), army officer. Born in Westernville, in Oneida County, New York, on January 16, 1815, Halleck graduated from West Point in 1839 and was commissioned a second lieutenant of engineers. After a period of work on the fortification of New York harbor he made an inspection tour of European fortifications in 1844 and a short time later delivered a course of lectures at the Lowell Institute of Boston that was published in 1846 as *Elements of Military Art and Science,* long a popular text and reference work, particularly among volunteer officers in the Civil War. He was promoted to first lieutenant in 1845. On the outbreak of the Mexican War in 1846 he sailed to California, where he worked on fortifications, took part in several skirmishes, served as aide to Commodore John T. Shubrick, and won a brevet to captain in May 1847. Over the next eight years he served in various capacities, including that of secretary of state in the military government of California under Gen. Bennet Riley, and in September 1849 helped draft the state constitution. He was promoted to captain in July 1853. During the latter part of his service in California he studied law, and soon after his resignation from the army in August 1854 he began practice in San Francisco, forming the firm of Halleck, Peachy & Billings, which became one of the most prominent in the state. Halleck acquired extensive and diverse business interests, was president of the Pacific & Atlantic Railroad, and served as a major general of the California militia. His *International Law,* 1861, was widely admired and in a condensed version was used in many law schools, and he published several studies and translations in the field of mining law. In August 1861, on the recommendation of Gen. Winfield Scott, President Abraham Lincoln commissioned Halleck a major general in the regular army and in November appointed him to succeed Gen. John C. Frémont in command of the Department of Missouri (after March 1862, and the inclusion of Kansas and Ohio, called the Department of the Mississippi). From his headquarters in St. Louis he quickly instilled stern discipline and efficiency throughout the previously lax command and during the early months of 1862 enjoyed the reflected glory of the successes of his subordinate commanders: Ulysses S. Grant, Army of the Tennessee, at Fort Henry, Fort Donelson, and Shiloh; Samuel R. Curtis, Army of the Southwest, at Pea Ridge; John Pope, Army of the Mississippi, at Island No. 10; and Don Carlos Buell, whose Army of the Ohio came under Halleck's command in March, at Shiloh. In his one excursion into the field, at Corinth, Mississippi, in May 1862, he showed himself, however, to be an overly cautious and ineffective warrior. In July 1862 he was called to Washington, D.C., as general in chief of the armies and principal military adviser to the President. Again he demonstrated great administrative abilities in recruiting, training, and organizing vast numbers of troops—services direly needed at the time—but his grasp of military affairs in the field was poor and his advice to his generals was often useless or worse. In March 1864 Grant was placed in supreme command and Halleck was moved to the new office of chief of staff, an administrative post more suited to his talents and one that, although representing a technical demotion, he accepted with grace. During the last weeks of the war he commanded the Military District of the James. From August 1865 to March 1869 he commanded the Division of the Pacific and was then transferred to the Division of the South. He died in Louisville, Kentucky, on January 9, 1872.

Halsey, William Frederick, Jr. (1882–1959),

naval officer. Born on October 30, 1882, in Elizabeth, New Jersey, the son of a naval officer, Halsey graduated from the Naval Academy in 1904 and was commissioned an ensign two years later. He served on the *Kansas* in the world cruise of the Battle Fleet, 1907–1909, and in 1911–1913, by then a lieutenant, he commanded the destroyer *Flusser*. In 1915–1917 he was on the staff of the Naval Academy. During World War I he commanded the destroyers *Benham* and *Shaw* in the destroyer force based in Queenstown, Ireland. He continued to command various destroyers and destroyer divisions after the war until 1921, when he was attached to the office of naval intelligence. In October 1922 he was appointed naval attaché at the U.S. embassy in Berlin, later serving also at the embassies in Denmark, Sweden, and Norway until June 1924. He commanded the *Dale* in 1924–1925 and the *Osborne* in 1925–1926 and served on the *Wyoming* in 1926–1927. For three years he commanded the *Reina Mercedes,* station ship at the Naval Academy, and after other routine assignments and graduation from the Naval and Army War colleges he entered aviation training at Pensacola Naval Air Station, Florida, being designated a naval aviator in March 1935, at the age of fifty-two. From that year to 1937 he commanded the carrier *Saratoga,* and in 1937–1938 he was commander of the Pensacola station. In June 1938, promoted to rear admiral, he took command of Carrier Division 2, including his flagship *Yorktown* and the *Enterprise.* In 1939 he transferred to the command of Carrier Division 1; and in June 1940, promoted to vice admiral, he became commander of Aircraft, Battle Force, in the Pacific and also of Carrier Division 2 again. At the time of the Japanese attack on Pearl Harbor, December 7, 1941, he was at sea, returning from a mission to Wake

Island on the *Enterprise*. Limited to a strategy of hit-and-run while the Pacific Fleet was rebuilt, Halsey led a task force, including the *Enterprise* and the *Yorktown,* in the first U.S. offensive in the central Pacific, a raid on Kwajalein in the Marshall Islands on February 1, 1942. That was followed by raids in the Gilberts and on Wake later in February and on Marcus in March. Designated commander of Task Force 16 and of the carrier force, Pacific Fleet, in April, he and the *Enterprise* escorted the *Hornet,* Capt. Marc A. Mitscher, carrying Col. James H. Doolittle's volunteer B-25 raider squadron, to within 800 miles of the Japanese homeland in that month. In mid-October Halsey was named to succeed Adm. Robert L. Ghormley as commander of the South Pacific force and area, where U.S. naval forces were extremely hard pressed in supporting the ground campaign on Guadalcanal. A series of engagements culminating in the naval battle of Guadalcanal, November 12–15, turned the tide, blunting the final major Japanese attempt to maintain supremacy in the Solomons and breaking the "Tokyo Express" supply line. In that month Halsey was promoted to admiral. Offensive operations resumed in June 1943, with Halsey's South Pacific forces working up the chain of the Central Solomons in step with Gen. Douglas MacArthur's Southwest Pacific forces around New Guinea. New Georgia, Vella Lavella, and lesser islands were secured between August and October, and on November 1 Gen. Roy S. Geiger's I Marine Amphibious Corps was landed on Bougainville. Heavy naval air strikes were launched at the major Japanese base at Rabaul, New Britain, which was isolated and neutralized. In June 1944 Halsey was designated commander of the Third Fleet, a force comprising most of the strategic forces of Adm. Chester W. Nimitz's Pacific Fleet and largely identical with the Fifth Fleet, the designation used when command was switched to Adm. Raymond A. Spruance. In either case the principal strike force was Adm. Mitscher's Task Force 38, or 58. Under his motto "Hit hard, hit fast, hit often," Halsey launched raids and surprise strikes at various points in the western Pacific, and in one such raid in the Philippines in September he discovered the weakness of Japanese defenses there that allowed the planned Leyte assault to be moved up two months to October. Task Force 38 virtually ended Japanese air power in the Philippines and on Formosa to the north preparatory to the Leyte landings on October 17. During a wide-flung naval battle for control of Leyte Gulf and surrounding waters, October 24–26, Halsey dispatched, somewhat tardily, reinforcements to Adm. Thomas C. Kinkaid's Seventh Fleet, heavily engaged at Surigao Strait and Samar, while farther north he fought, through TF 38, a battle at Cape Engaño, October 25, sinking four Japanese carriers and a destroyer. During November–December the Third Fleet supported operations on

Leyte and Luzon and throughout the Philippine area, and during January 10–20, 1945, made a broad sweep of the South China Sea, destroying huge amounts of Japanese shipping. In May Halsey began preparing for operations against the Japanese homeland. Air strikes from TF 38 were launched against Tokyo beginning on July 10, and naval gunfire was used against other targets. The formal surrender of Japan took place aboard his flagship *Missouri* on September 2 (for the ceremony the *Missouri* became flagship for Fleet Admiral Chester W. Nimitz, and Halsey moved to the *Iowa*). In December 1945 he was promoted to the rank of fleet admiral, and he was on special duty in the office of the secretary of the navy until his retirement in April 1947. He sat subsequently on the boards of various corporations, notably that of the International Telephone & Telegraph Corporation. Halsey died at Fishers Island, New York, on August 16, 1959.

Hampton, Wade (1751?–1835), army officer and public official. Born in Halifax County, Virginia, probably in 1751, Hampton received little education and sometime during the winter of 1780–1781 joined the South Carolina militia forces under Gen. Thomas Sumter. He served, eventually as a colonel, through the rest of the war under Sumter and then under Gen. Nathanael Greene and distinguished himself at Eutaw Springs, September 8, 1781. He remained in South Carolina afterwards, serving in the legislature, opposing ratification of the federal Constitution in the convention called to consider it, and serving in Congress in 1795–1797 and 1803–1805. In October 1808 he accepted a colonel's commission in the army and in February 1809 was promoted to brigadier general. Later in that year he succeeded Gen. James Wilkinson in command at New Orleans, and during 1812–1813 he commanded the fortifications at Norfolk, Virginia. In March 1813 he was promoted to major general, and in July he was sent to command the Lake Champlain frontier with headquarters at Plattsburg, New York. Wilkinson, between whom and Hampton there was little but contempt and distrust, took command at Sackett's Harbor a short time later and the two were ordered to mount a two-pronged expedition against Montreal. Hampton, with about 4000 men, set out in October down the Chateaugay River, but on October 26 he met a British force under Gen. Sir George Prevost and hurriedly retired. He declined to offer any further assistance to Wilkinson, who had started down the St. Lawrence and who was destined also to fail. The Montreal campaign was one of the great fiascoes of the war, owing largely to suspicion and divided command. In April 1814 Hampton resigned. He devoted himself thereafter to the management of his large and growing land holdings in South Carolina and on the lower Mississippi, becoming reputedly the richest planter

in the South. He died in Columbia, South Carolina, on February 4, 1835.

Hampton, Wade (1818–1902), public official and Confederate army officer. Born in Charleston, South Carolina, on March 28, 1818, Hampton came of a wealthy planting family and was a grandson of Gen. Wade Hampton of the War of 1812. He graduated from South Carolina College (now the University of South Carolina) in 1836 and began assuming duties in connection with the family's vast plantation holdings, which he inherited on the death of his father in 1858. From 1852 to 1861 he served in the state legislature. When the question of secession arose he was opposed, as he considered the time inopportune; but when the Civil War began he raised "Hampton's Legion" and as its colonel saw action as early as the first battle of Manassas (Bull Run), July 21, 1861, receiving there the first of many wounds. Promoted to brigadier general in May 1862, he was wounded at Fair Oaks (Seven Pines), May 31, and in July was assigned to the cavalry of the Army of Northern Virginia, becoming in September Gen. J. E. B. Stuart's second in command. Hampton fought at Antietam, at Gettysburg, in the Wilderness, and in the Shenandoah valley and was particularly prominent at Trevilian Station, June 11–12, 1864. He was promoted to major general in August 1863 and in May 1864, on the death of Stuart, became commander of the cavalry corps. By that time he was reduced to largely defensive activities, which he nonetheless carried out with remarkable success in light of the shortages of mounts and supplies, fighting innumerable small battles and skirmishes and raiding Union arsenals and stores. He aided Gen. Robert E. Lee in the defense of Petersburg and early in 1865 joined Gen. Joseph E. Johnston in harrying the Union troops advancing through the Carolinas under Gen. William T. Sherman. He became a lieutenant general in February. After an abortive attempt to aid Jefferson Davis in escaping to Texas at the war's end he returned to South Carolina and set about supporting the moderate Reconstruction policies of President Andrew Johnson. While working for reconciliation, he opposed Radical rule and in 1876 led the Democratic party back to power in South Carolina as its successful candidate for governor. Reelected in 1878, he resigned in March 1879 to enter the Senate, where he remained until March 1891. From 1893 to 1897 he served as U.S. commissioner of Pacific railways. Hampton died in Columbia, South Carolina, on April 11, 1902.

Hancock, John (1737–1793), merchant and public official. Born in Braintree, Massachusetts, on January 12, 1737, Hancock was raised by a wealthy uncle in Boston. He graduated from Harvard in 1754, entered his uncle's mercantile business, and ten years later inherited it along with a large estate. His identification with the patriot cause dated from the Stamp Act of 1765, which, as a leading merchant, he both protested and evaded by smuggling. In 1769, soon after the British seized one of his ships, he was elected to the Massachusetts General Court, remaining a member until 1774. In 1770 he was made chairman of the Boston town committee formed as a result of the Boston Massacre. He was elected president of the first and second provincial congresses in 1774–1775 and in 1775 was forced to flee to Lexington and then to Philadelphia as one (with Samuel Adams) of the rebels specifically excepted from the pardon offered by Gen. Thomas Gage. From 1775 to 1780 Hancock was a delegate to the Continental Congress, serving as president for his first two years, and on July 4, 1776, he was the first to sign the Declaration of Independence. (His comment on the bold flourish with which he signed his name in large letters was "There, I guess King George will be able to read that.") Although wealthy and popular, he was a man of limited ability and was sorely disappointed when denied command of the Continental army, a position he had eagerly sought. In 1776, however, he was appointed major general of the Massachusetts militia, and in August 1778 he commanded the contingent of 5000 men from that state in Gen. John Sullivan's unsuccessful expedition against Newport, Rhode Island. In 1780 he served in the convention to frame the Massachusetts constitution and under it was elected the state's first governor; he served until 1785 and was then elected to Congress. He was again elected president of the Congress in November 1785, but owing to illness he resigned in May 1786 without having served. In 1787 he returned to the governorship and the next year presided over the Massachusetts convention for the ratification of the Constitution. Regularly reelected as governor, Hancock was in his ninth term when he died in Quincy, Massachusetts, on October 8, 1793.

Hancock, Joy Bright (1898–   ), naval officer. Born in Wildwood, New Jersey, on May 4, 1898, Joy Bright graduated from the Pierce School of Business Administration in Philadelphia in 1918 and promptly enlisted in the naval reserve. From 1919 she worked as a civilian for the navy at various stations and at the Department of the Navy in Washington, D.C. In 1924 she married Lt. Comdr. Lewis Hancock, a naval aviator who died in the crash of the dirigible *Shenandoah* the following year. In 1928 she took a civil pilot's license, and after a period of study at George Washington University and elsewhere she joined the navy's Bureau of Aeronautics. Her *Airplanes in Action* appeared in 1938. Shortly after the creation of the new women's naval reserve, the Women Accepted for Volunteer Emergency Service (WAVES), in July 1942 she joined, becoming a lieutenant in October,

lieutenant commander in November 1943, and commander in March 1945. In February 1946 she was named assistant director of the WAVES, and in July she became director with the rank of captain. The women's reserve passed out of existence in October 1948, but under provisions of the Women's Armed Services Integration Act of June 12, 1948, the navy was authorized to offer regular commissions to women. In October Capt. Hancock was among the first eight women so commissioned, taking rank of permanent lieutenant commander and temporary captain. She was appointed assistant chief for women of the Bureau of Personnel and continued as ex officio director of WAVES (the name, though unofficial, persisted) until her retirement in June 1953. She was succeeded in that post by Capt. Louise K. Wilde.

Hancock, Winfield Scott (1824–1886), army officer. Born on February 14, 1824, in Montgomery County, Pennsylvania, Hancock graduated from West Point in 1844 and was ordered to duty with the 6th Infantry in Texas. During the Mexican War he served under Gen. Winfield Scott, for whom he had been named, and saw considerable action, winning a brevet to first lieutenant for distinguished service at Contreras and Churubusco, August 19–20, 1847. From 1848 to 1861 he served in the Seminole War, in the suppression of the border disturbances in Kansas, and in the West, demonstrating in every assignment a gift for organization and command. He was promoted to captain in November 1855. In September 1861, on his arrival in the East after holding a vital military depot in Los Angeles, he was appointed a brigadier general of volunteers. He earned high praise for his part in the Peninsular campaign, succeeded to command of a division of Gen. Edwin V. Sumner's II Corps at Antietam, September 17, 1862, and in November 1862 was promoted to major general of volunteers. He distinguished himself at Fredericksburg, December 13, and in July 1863, by then commander (by virtue of his performance at Chancellorsville, May 2–4) of the II Corps of the Army of the Potomac, he was conspicuous in the battle of Gettysburg. He established defenses on Cemetery Ridge and absorbed Gen. Robert E. Lee's unsuccessful flanking attempt on July 2 and the next day the great assault on the Union center known as Pickett's Charge, in which he sustained a serious wound. In 1864 he led his corps through the fighting in the Wilderness, but he was often in Washington during the last months of the war. Rated as the most capable of the Union generals not exercising an independent command, Hancock had been promoted to the regular rank of brigadier general in August 1864 and in July 1866 became a major general. He commanded the defenses of Washington, D.C., from mid-1865 until taking command of the Department of the Missouri in August 1866. During 1866–1867 he was engaged in operations against the Indians, principally the Cheyenne, in Kansas, and was then transferred to command of the Department of Louisiana and Texas, where his refusal to usurp totally the functions of civil government roused the ire of Radical Republicans. He commanded the Division of the Atlantic in 1868–1869, the Department of Dakota from 1869 to 1872, and the Division of the Atlantic and the Department of the East from 1872 to 1886. His anti-Radical stand had led to interest in him on the part of the Democratic party as early as 1868, and in 1880 he was nominated for the presidency. Politically naive, he lost the election by a narrow popular margin (fewer than 10,000 votes, taking 155 electoral votes to 214) to Republican James A. Garfield and then returned to his military duties. Hancock died at his headquarters on Governors Island, New York, on February 9, 1886.

Hand, Edward (1744–1802), physician and Revolutionary army officer. Born in King's County, Ireland, on December 31, 1744, Hand studied medicine privately and for a time at Trinity College, Dublin, and was appointed a surgeon's mate in the 18th Royal Irish Regiment, which he accompanied to Philadelphia in 1767. He resigned his commission in 1774 and took up the practice of medicine in Lancaster, Pennsylvania. In 1775 he was appointed lieutenant colonel of the 2nd Pennsylvania, taking part in the siege of Boston. In March 1776 he was appointed colonel of Continental riflemen and saw action that year on Long Island and at White Plains, Trenton, and Princeton. He was promoted to brigadier general in April 1777 and sent to organize defenses on the Pennsylvania frontier. Early in 1778 he led the militia of Westmoreland County in the anticlimactic "Squaw Campaign," in which, prevented by bad weather from reaching their objective at Sandusky, Ohio, the troops routed two villages of Delawares, mostly women and children. Later in the year Hand succeeded Gen. John Stark in command at Albany, New York. In 1779 he took part in the expedition under Gen. John Sullivan against the Indians of New York and Pennsylvania. In August 1780 he was given command of a light infantry brigade, and in January 1781 he was appointed adjutant general of the Continental army, remaining in that post until November 1783. In the latter year he was brevetted major general. He returned to medicine after the war, served a term in Congress in 1784–1785 and one in the Pennsylvania legislature in 1785–1786, and was a member of the Pennsylvania constitutional convention in 1789–1790. In 1798, on George Washington's recommendation, he was appointed major general and adjutant general of the Provisional Army authorized for possible war with France. He died at his home near Lancaster, Pennsylvania, on September 3, 1802.

Handy, Thomas Troy (1892–   ), army officer. Born on March 11, 1892, in Spring City, Tennessee, Handy graduated from the Virginia Military Institute in 1914 and two years later was commissioned a second lieutenant in the field artillery. After training at various posts he was ordered to France with the 5th Field Artillery in August 1917 in the temporary rank of captain. He became a permanent captain in February 1918 and served during that year with the 42nd (Rainbow) Division until joining the 151st Field Artillery in August. In October he was promoted to temporary major. After occupation duty in Germany he was assigned to Fort Sill, Oklahoma, where he completed Artillery School in 1921. From 1921 to 1925 he was an instructor at VMI. He graduated from Command and General Staff School, Fort Leavenworth, Kansas, in 1927, and in 1928 became executive officer of the 3rd Field Artillery Brigade, advancing to permanent major in August. He was on staff duty in the Panama Canal Zone from 1929 to 1931, served as an instructor at Fort Sill until 1934, and after graduating from the Army War College in 1935 was a student and instructor at the Naval War College until 1936. From 1936 to 1940 he was attached to the General Staff in Washington, D.C., becoming lieutenant colonel in September 1938, and he returned there after a year as commander of the 78th Field Artillery Battalion at Fort Benning, Georgia. He was promoted to temporary colonel in October 1941 and temporary brigadier general in December. In June 1942 he succeeded Gen. Dwight D. Eisenhower as assistant chief of staff in charge of the Operations Division (formerly War Plans Division). He advanced to temporary major general in that month and temporary lieutenant general in September 1944; his permanent rank was brigadier general in September 1943 and major general in October 1944. In the latter month he was named deputy chief of staff of the army, and in March 1945 he was promoted to temporary general. In August 1945, as acting chief of staff in the absence of Gen. George C. Marshall, he transmitted the order for the use of the atomic bomb against Hiroshima and Nagasaki. In September 1947 Handy took command of the Fourth Army at Fort Sam Houston, Texas. In September 1949 he succeeded Gen. Lucius D. Clay as chief of the European Command, commanding all U.S. forces in Europe except those in Austria and Trieste. On the appointment of Gen. Matthew B. Ridgway as supreme commander, Allied Powers in Europe, in August 1952, Handy became deputy supreme commander. He held that office until 1953; he retired from the army in February 1954. Handy lived thereafter in Washington, D.C., and later in San Antonio, Texas.

Harbord, James Guthrie (1866–1947), army officer. Born near Bloomington, Illinois, on March 21, 1866, Harbord later moved with his family to Missouri and then to Kansas. He graduated from Kansas State Agricultural College (now Kansas State University) in Manhattan in 1886 and after a period of teaching school enlisted as a private in the army in 1889. In July 1891 he was commissioned a second lieutenant in the 5th Cavalry. He graduated from Infantry and Cavalry School, Fort Leavenworth, Kansas, in 1895, was promoted to first lieutenant in July 1898, and during the Spanish–American War was a major in a volunteer cavalry regiment. Promoted to captain in February 1901, he was ordered to the Philippines in 1902 and in August of the next year was appointed assistant commander of the Philippine Constabulary, with the acting rank of colonel. He held that post until January 1914 and in December of that year was promoted to major. He graduated from the Army War College shortly after the United States entered World War I in April 1917 and the next month was appointed chief of staff of the American Expeditionary Force under Gen. John J. Pershing, taking rank of lieutenant colonel and receiving promotion to temporary brigadier general in August. In May 1918 he took command of the 4th Marine Brigade, attached to Gen. Omar Bundy's 2nd Infantry Division, and led it in the battle of Belleau Wood, June 6–25. Late in that month Harbord was promoted to major general, and early in July he succeeded to command of the 2nd Division, which he led in the counteroffensive around Soissons. At the end of July he was placed by Pershing at the head of the Service of Supply (S.O.S.), a command of more than half a million military and civilian workers carrying on the whole business of war except combat. Harbord's administrative ability won high praise as he oversaw procurement, transportation, construction, communication, maintenance, entertainment, and other activities until May 1919. Later in that year he was head of the American Military Mission to Armenia, sent to investigate conditions in that area with an eye to a possible American mandate under the League of Nations. Promoted to permanent major general in September 1919, he resumed command of the 2nd Division at Camp Travis, Texas, on his return to the United States in November. In July 1921 he was named deputy to Pershing, then army chief of staff. He retired from the army in December 1922 and the next month became president of the Radio Corporation of America. He held that post until 1930, when he was elevated to chairman of the board; he retired from RCA in 1947 as honorary chairman. In 1932 he was proposed for the vice-presidential nomination at the Republican National Convention. Harbord was promoted to lieutenant general on the retired list in 1942. He died in Rye, New York, on August 20, 1947.

Hardee, William Joseph (1815–1873), Confederate army officer. Born in Camden County, Georgia,

on October 12, 1815, Hardee graduated from West Point in 1838 and was assigned to the 2nd Dragoons. He saw action against the Seminoles in Florida, was promoted to first lieutenant in December 1839, and in 1840 was sent to France to study cavalry tactics. He was promoted to captain in September 1844. In the Mexican War he took part in the capture of Monterrey under Gen. Zachary Taylor and then served through the Veracruz-to-Mexico City campaign under Gen. Winfield Scott, receiving brevets to major and lieutenant colonel for gallantry. Promoted to major in 1855, he was assigned to the 2nd Cavalry, whose other officers included Col. Albert S. Johnston, Lt. Col. Robert E. Lee, and Maj. George H. Thomas. In that year he published his *Rifle and Light Infantry Tactics,* commonly known as *Hardee's Tactics.* In 1856 he was promoted to lieutenant colonel and named commandant of cadets at West Point. In January 1861, while visiting his home state, he resigned his commission and accepted another as colonel in the Confederate army; in June he was promoted to brigadier general, and a short time later he advanced to major general. After organizing in Arkansas what became known as Hardee's Brigade he was transferred with it to Kentucky. At Pittsburg Landing (Shiloh), April 6–7, 1862, he commanded the III Corps (afterwards called Hardee's Corps) of the Army of Mississippi under Gen. Albert S. Johnston. He led it at Perryville, October 8, following which battle he was promoted to lieutenant general, and Murfreesboro, December 31–January 3, 1863. Commanding what amounted to one wing of Gen. Braxton Bragg's Army of Tennessee (Gen. John C. Breckinridge had the other), Hardee took part in the battle of Missionary Ridge, November 25, in the Chattanooga campaign. During 1864 he fought a delaying retreat across Georgia, impeding Gen. William T. Sherman's advance on Atlanta and thence to the sea. He was particularly prominent in the fighting at Peachtree Creek, July 22, where he defeated Gen. James B. McPherson, who was killed in the battle. He was named commander of the Department of South Carolina in September 1864. On December 20 he was forced to abandon Savannah, Georgia, to Sherman, and in February 1865 he left Charleston, South Carolina, as well, moving north to merge his corps with the Army of Tennessee under Gen. Joseph E. Johnston. He surrendered with Johnston on April 26, 1865. After the war he lived quietly in Alabama. He died in Wytheville, Virginia, on November 6, 1873.

Hardin, John (1753–1792), army officer. Born on October 1, 1753, in Fauquier County, Virginia, Hardin moved with his family to southwestern Pennsylvania about 1765. In 1774 he served in Lord Dunmore's War against the western Indians, and the following year he was commissioned a second lieutenant in the Continental army. With Col. Daniel

Morgan's regiment of riflemen he served with distinction in the Saratoga campaign, September–October 1777; his daring reconnaissance of the British lines just before the battle of Bemis Heights, October 7, contributed to the victory, although credit for the exploit was taken by Lt. Col. James Wilkinson. In December 1779 he resigned from the army and returned to the frontier. In 1786, a few months after he had moved to what is now Washington County, Kentucky, he took part, as lieutenant colonel of militia, in George Rogers Clark's expedition against the Wabash Indians. He led militia expeditions against the Shawnee in 1788 and 1789, and in 1790 he was a leader in Gen. Josiah Harmar's disastrous campaign against the Miami Indians. He was acquitted of responsibility for the defeats at the Maumee River in October. In May–June 1791 he took part in Gen. Charles Scott's expedition to the Wabash. In May 1792 he was sent by Gen. James Wilkinson to negotiate with the Miami Indians. Approaching the village near the site of present-day Shawnee, Ohio, under a flag of truce, he was set upon and killed. Hardin County, Kentucky, and Hardin County, Ohio, were named for him.

Harding, Seth (1734–1814), Revolutionary naval officer. Born in Eastham, Massachusetts, on April 17, 1734, Harding became a merchant sailor at an early age and by the time he moved to Norwich, Connecticut, in 1760 had been for some time in command of his own vessel. In 1771 he settled in Liverpool, Nova Scotia, but at the outbreak of the Revolution in 1775 he returned to Connecticut. Early in 1776 he was given command of the state brig *Defence,* with which in June, by a single brilliant action in Massachusetts Bay, he captured two armed British transports bearing munitions and several hundred men and officers of the 71st Highlanders. He took a third transport the next day. He subsequently commanded a new brigantine, also called the *Defence,* and in 1777 the *Oliver Cromwell,* with both of which he took several prizes. In September 1778, having been commissioned in the Continental navy, he took command of the *Confederacy,* 32 guns, with which he continued his successes against British shipping. In June 1779, in conjunction with the frigate *Boston,* 24, Capt. Samuel Tucker, he captured the privateer *Pole,* 24, the schooner *Patsey,* 6, and an unarmed merchantman. In October of that year he sailed for France bearing John Jay and the French minister, M. Gérard, but the *Confederacy* was damaged in a storm and forced to put into Martinique. After making repairs Harding resumed his raids on commerce in West Indian waters. On April 15, 1781, while convoying a French and American merchant fleet, he fell in with the British *Roebuck,* 44, and *Orpheus,* 32, and was compelled to surrender. Paroled early in 1782, he took the privateer *Diana* out of Norwich but was again captured and imprisoned

in Jamaica. On his release he was taken aboard the *Alliance* by Capt. John Barry; he took part in the engagement of March 10, 1783, the last of the Revolution, and shared with Barry the firing of the last gun. Harding returned to the merchant service after the Revolution and for some years struggled with poverty. For a time he traded among the Virgin Islands, where he acquired Danish citizenship. In 1786 he settled in New York City, age and old wounds ending his sea career. After several petitions he was granted half-pay as a naval captain by Congress in 1807. He died in Schoharie, New York, on November 20, 1814.

Harmar, Josiah (1753–1813), army officer. Born in Philadelphia on November 10, 1753, Harmar was appointed a captain in the 1st Pennsylvania at the outbreak of the Revolution. He became a major of the 3rd Pennsylvania in October 1776 and lieutenant colonel of the 6th Pennsylvania in June 1777. Until 1780 he served with his various regiments under Gen. George Washington; thereafter he saw action with the southern army under Gen. Henry Lee. He was given brevet rank of colonel in September 1783. On August 12, 1784, on his return from carrying the ratified treaty of peace to France, he was commissioned lieutenant colonel of infantry, and he became the senior officer in the army, succeeding Capt. John Doughty as commander of the 80-man force. Posted to the frontier as Indian agent for the Northwest Territory, he took part in the negotiation of the treaty of Fort McIntosh on the Ohio, signed in January 1785, by which much of what is now Ohio was ceded by the Indians. Since the virtual disbanding of the army in June 1784 Congress had relied upon state quotas of militia to meet the need for defense of the frontier, and Harmar had been charged with organizing the militiamen into the 1st American Regiment (now the 3rd Infantry, the oldest regiment in the Regular Army). In 1785 he undertook the task of clearing the Ohio country of Indians. Skirmishing was frequent in that year and for several years to come, but little progress resulted. In 1787 he was brevetted brigadier general. In late 1789 he established his garrison at Fort Washington, on the site of present-day Cincinnati. Under the pressure of increasing tension on the Indian frontier, Congress authorized an increase in the size of the Regular Army in April 1790, but Harmar had only 320 regulars among his 1453 men when, on September 30, 1790, he set out from Fort Washington for the Miami villages near the head of the Wabash River. A second column from Fort Vincennes under Maj. John Hamtramck turned back before reaching the villages. When Harmar arrived there he divided his forces and in three engagements on the Maumee River (near present Fort Wayne, Indiana), October 18 and 22, with Miamis under Little Turtle his militia scattered.

He withdrew to Fort Washington, and although he was generally criticized for his conduct of the expedition a court of inquiry in 1791 exonerated him, largely on the basis of the untrained condition of the militia. On March 4, 1791, Harmar was succeeded as senior officer by Arthur St. Clair, commissioned major general on that date. Harmar retired from service in January 1792. From 1793 to 1799 he was adjutant general of Pennsylvania. He died in Philadelphia on August 20, 1813.

Harmon, Ernest Nason (1894–   ), army officer. Born on February 26, 1894, in Lowell, Massachusetts, Harmon grew up there and in West Newbury, Vermont. He attended Norwich University for a year and then entered West Point, graduating in 1917 and receiving his commission in the cavalry. He was promoted to first lieutenant in May 1917 and to temporary captain in August, and after a period of training he went to France in March 1918, where he saw action in the St. Mihiel and Meuse–Argonne operations. He was promoted to permanent captain in August 1920, graduated from Cavalry School, Fort Riley, Kansas, in 1921, and until 1925 was an instructor at West Point. From 1927 to 1931 he taught military science and tactics at Norwich University; he graduated from Command and General Staff School, Fort Leavenworth, Kansas, in 1933, having been promoted to major in November 1932, and from the Army War College in 1934. From 1935 to 1939 he was attached to the General Staff. In July 1940 he was promoted to lieutenant colonel and named assistant chief of staff of the I Armored Corps, Armored Force, newly organized under Gen. Adna R. Chaffee at Fort Knox, Kentucky. In November 1941, by then a temporary brigadier general, he became chief of staff of Armored Force headquarters. In July 1942 Harmon took command of the 2nd Armored Division, receiving promotion to temporary major general the next month. He led a portion of the division in the landing in French Morocco in November 1942 and the campaign into Tunisia. In April 1943 he took command of the 1st Armored Division, assigned to Gen. John P. Lucas's VI Corps, which on September 9 took part in the landing of Gen. Mark W. Clark's Fifth Army at Salerno and Paestum, Italy. The 1st later moved to the VI Corps's beachhead at Anzio in January 1944 and in May led the breakout. It was the first division to cross the Tiber River, and in driving to and beyond Rome in June it covered 200 miles in 5 days. In July Harmon was transferred to command of the XIII Corps, Camp Bowie, Texas, but in September he returned to the field as commander of the 2nd Armored Division, then in Belgium. The 2nd, assigned by turns to Gen. Courtney H. Hodges's First Army and Gen. William H. Simpson's Ninth, broke the Siegfried Line in October and in January 1945 pushed through the Ardennes Forest to reduce the German

Bulge. At the end of January Harmon moved up to command the XXII Corps, with which he remained until its inactivation in January 1946. From April 1945 he had responsibility for control of the northern part of Rhine province. Briefly at the end of 1945 he commanded the Third Army occupying Czechoslovakia. In February 1946 he took command of the VI Corps in Germany, which he developed into a military police force known as the U.S. Constabulary (officially so designated in May 1946). He continued to command the Constabulary, which was responsible for the entire U.S. zone of occupation, until becoming deputy commander, Army Ground Forces, in early 1947. He retired in March 1948. In 1950 Harmon was named president of Norwich University, and he remained there until retiring in 1965. He lived thereafter in retirement in Florida, publishing in 1970 a volume of memoirs under the title *Combat Commander.*

Harmon, Millard Fillmore (1888–1945), army officer. Born in San Francisco on January 19, 1888, Harmon graduated from West Point in 1912 and was commissioned in the infantry. While in the Philippines in 1915 he tranferred into the aviation section of the Signal Corps; he attended aviation school the next year, was promoted to first lieutenant, and in 1916–1917 was attached as a pilot to the punitive expedition sent into Mexico under Gen. John J. Pershing. Promoted to captain in 1917, he served in staff positions and as a pilot with the French Group de Combat No. 13 during World War I. During 1918 he advanced to temporary major and lieutenant colonel. Various assignments followed the war: He graduated from Command and General Staff School, Fort Leavenworth, Kansas, in 1923, taught military science at the University of Washington for a year, graduated from the Army War College in 1925, and then was attached to the General Staff. After three years as commandant of the Air Corps Primary Flying School, March Field, California, he became an instructor at the Command and General Staff School in 1930. From 1933 to 1936 he commanded the 20th Pursuit Group, Barksdale Field, Louisiana, and in 1936–1938 he was at Luke Field, Hawaii. After two years as assistant commandant of the Air Corps Tactical School, Maxwell Field, Alabama, he was promoted to temporary brigadier general in October 1940 and briefly put in command of the 7th Pursuit Wing. Early in 1941 he was adviser on air matters to the consultation mission to Great Britain under W. Averell Harriman. Transferred to command of the Interception Command, Fourth Air Force, in April 1941, he was promoted to temporary major general in July and in August given command of the Second Air Force, then headquartered at McChord Field, Washington. In January 1942 Harmon was named chief of the Air Staff, Army Air Forces, and in June he took field command of the army ground and air forces in the South Pacific area, under the overall command of Adm. Robert L. Ghormley and later of Adm. William F. Halsey. In February 1943 he was promoted to lieutenant general. In August 1944 he became commander of all Army Air Forces in Pacific Ocean areas, under Adm. Chester W. Nimitz, and deputy commander of the strategic Twentieth Air Force. Late in February 1945 he left Hickam Field, Hawaii, aboard a C-87 transport that disappeared over the Pacific; he was listed missing on March 3.

Harney, William Selby (1800–1889), army officer. Born in Haysboro, near Nashville, Tennessee, on August 22, 1800, Harney was commissioned in the 1st Infantry in February 1818. Over the next two decades he took part in numerous actions, often against the Florida Indians, and he rose rapidly in rank to first lieutenant in January 1819, captain in May 1825, major in May 1833, lieutenant colonel in August 1836 and colonel of the 2nd Dragoons in June 1846. He took part in the Black Hawk War in 1832 and was brevetted colonel in December 1840 for gallantry in a Florida campaign. Early in the Mexican War Harney, the ranking cavalry officer in the army, clashed with Gen. Winfield Scott, commanding general in the field; they had long been antagonists, and Harney's refusal to relinquish command of the cavalry to a junior (Maj. Edwin V. Sumner) at Scott's order led to his court-martial. He was convicted of insubordination but not punished, while Scott was reprimanded. In the field Harney proved a brilliant leader, and at Cerro Gordo on April 18, 1847, he led a daring charge up El Telégrafo, a hill from which Gen. Santa Anna's artillery commanded the surrounding ground; for that act he was brevetted brigadier general. After the war he was assigned to frontier duty. In 1855 he was ordered to lead a punitive expedition against the Sioux and other Indians who had committed a number of massacres. He rode out of Fort Leavenworth, Kansas, in August at the head of 1200 men and on September 3 found a band of Brulé Sioux, under Little Thunder, at Ash Hollow in the Sand Hills region of Nebraska; 136 Indians were killed, virtually exterminating the band. The column proceeded on to the Missouri River, wintered at Fort Pierre (opposite the site of present-day Pierre, North Dakota), and the next spring built Fort Randall. In June 1858 Harney was promoted to brigadier general and given command of the Department of Oregon. The following year he took possession of San Juan Island, claimed by Great Britain, and in the ensuing diplomatic dispute he was recalled. He subsequently commanded the Department of the West in St. Louis. In April 1861 he was detained by Confederate authorities while on his way to Washington, D.C., and taken to Richmond, where Robert E. Lee, among others, sought unsuccessfully to win him to their

side. In May, back in St. Louis, he reached an agreement with Gen. Sterling Price of the Missouri militia not to move against his forces so long as they remained loyal, at least in deed. He was then removed from command on suspicion of harboring Confederate sympathies, being succeeded by Gen. Nathaniel Lyon. He remained inactive until his retirement in August 1863. In March 1865 he was brevetted major general for his long service. Harney died in Orlando, Florida, on May 9, 1889.

Harris, John (1795?–1864), marine officer. Born about 1795, Harris was commissioned a second lieutenant of marines in April 1814. For 45 years he saw largely routine service on board various naval vessels and at shore stations. During 1836–1837, by then a captain, he commanded a detachment of mounted marines in the field force in Florida under Col. Archibald Henderson. Late in the Mexican War, in September 1847, he led a battalion of marines to Mexico City but arrived too late to see action. Subsequently he commanded the marine barracks at Philadelphia and New York, receiving promotion to lieutenant colonel in December 1855, until he was appointed in January 1859 to succeed Henderson as commandant of the corps with the rank of colonel. Harris oversaw the deployment of marines through the first three years of the Civil War, in which they continued their traditional distinguished service aboard the navy's fighting ships but saw little action ashore. Harris died in Washington, D.C., on May 2, 1864.

Harrison, William Henry (1773–1841), army officer and ninth president of the United States. Born at Berkeley, his family's plantation in Charles City County, Virginia, on February 9, 1773, Harrison was the son of a wealthy and politically prominent father. He studied for three years at Hampden-Sydney College and then, in 1790, moved to Philadelphia, where he attended the College of Physicians and Surgeons and worked under Dr. Benjamin Rush. In August 1791 he joined the army as an ensign in the infantry and was sent to the Northwest Territory; there, as aide-de-camp to Gen. Anthony Wayne, he campaigned against the Indians and fought in the decisive battle of Fallen Timbers on August 20, 1794. Promoted to captain in May 1797, he commanded Fort Washington (on the site of Cincinnati) until June 1798, when he resigned from the army and was appointed secretary of the Northwest Territory. The following year he was sent by the Territory to the House of Representatives. In May 1800 he was appointed governor of Indiana Territory, a position he held until 1812. He negotiated a number of land-cession treaties with the Indians, including the 1809 Treaty of Fort Wayne, by which the Delaware, the Miami, the Potawatomi, and several other tribes ceded more than 2.5 million acres on the upper Wabash

River. Following the conclusion of the treaty growing dissatisfaction among the tribes led them to form a confederacy under the Shawnee chief Tecumseh and his brother Tenskwatawa, known as the Prophet, with the aim of ending encroachment by whites. Harrison led about 1000 militiamen, volunteers, and a regiment of regulars in a successful military campaign against an Indian encampment at the Tippecanoe River in November 1811. Although the battle on November 7 was actually inconclusive, Harrison won an immediate military reputation. His plans for a further Indian campaign were interrupted by the outbreak of the War of 1812. He maneuvered for some time to obtain a high command, and on the fall of Detroit he accepted appointment in August 1812 as major general of Kentucky militia. He overbore Gen. James Winchester at Cincinnati, taking the latter's army to relieve Fort Wayne, and in September received word that he had been appointed brigadier general in command of the Army of the Northwest. He was promoted to major general in March 1813. After Winchester's disastrous defeat at the Raisin River on January 22, Harrison built Fort Meigs and Fort Stephenson and awaited a propitious moment to move. Harrison's forces reoccupied Detroit in September 1813, following Commodore Oliver H. Perry's victory on Lake Erie. He then moved his army on Perry's ships across the lake to take Fort Malden and on October 5 launched a heavy mounted attack against Gen. Henry Proctor's regulars and Tecumseh's warriors at the Thames River. The battle was a complete victory (Tecumseh was killed) and largely ended the war in the West. Harrison resigned from the army in May 1814 and in the same year oversaw the negotiations for a final peace treaty with the Indians. Settling at North Bend, Ohio, he served in the House again from October 1816 to March 1819, in the Ohio legislature from 1819 to 1821, and in the Senate from March 1825 to May 1828. He was then appointed U.S. minister to Colombia, and in his service there from February to September 1829 he provoked considerable controversy by his connection with revolutionaries in that country. For the next several years he remained largely out of the public eye, but in 1835, on the strength of his military record, his lack of political commitment, and his availability, he was chosen by dissident Whigs to head a presidential ticket against Martin Van Buren in the next year's election. Although he lost, 73 electoral votes to 170, with other Whig candidates receiving 40, plans were immediately laid for 1840. In that year he won the regular Whig nomination and John Tyler was named his running mate in a move to placate Southerners offended by the party's refusal to nominate the too-outspoken Henry Clay. The Whig campaign of 1840 largely forsook policy for ballyhoo, employing campaign songs, raucous torchlight parades, the "log cabin and hard cider" symbols of his frontier days (symbols that were originally introduced by the Democrats and intended disparagingly, but which were gleefully adopted by the Whigs) and the slogan "Tippecanoe and Tyler Too!" The Whig ticket was overwhelmingly elected, 234 to 60. Left in a state of exhaustion by the campaign and by the importunities of the hordes of office seekers who immediately appeared, Harrison contracted pneumonia and died in Washington, D.C., on April 4, 1841, one month after his inauguration; he was the first president to die in office.

Hart, Thomas Charles (1877–1971), naval officer. Born on June 12, 1877, in Davison, Michigan, Hart graduated from the Naval Academy in 1897, and after serving aboard the *Massachusetts* in Cuban waters during the Spanish–American War he was commissioned an ensign in 1899. Routine duty followed until World War I, when he commanded a force of seven submarines based in Berehaven, Ireland. Promoted to captain in April 1918, he was on staff duty in Washington, D.C., in 1919–1920, and after commanding the *Beaver* and then the Asiatic Submarine Flotilla he attended the Naval War College, graduating in 1923, and the Army War College, graduating in 1924. He commanded the *Mississippi* in 1925–1927, the Torpedo Station at Newport, Rhode Island, until 1929, and, promoted to rear admiral in September of that year, the submarines in the Atlantic and Pacific fleets in 1929–1931. From 1931 to 1934 he was superintendent of the Naval Academy. He commanded the cruiser division, Scouting Force, from 1934 to 1936, and was then a member of the General Board until July 1939, when he was named commander of the small Asiatic Fleet with the rank of admiral. In that post he took steps to prepare for joint naval action with British, Dutch and other allied powers should war break out, and he also went to great lengths to maintain American presence and prestige in potential trouble spots. On December 25, 1941, he abandoned his headquarters at Cavite on Manila Bay in the Philippines and escaped by submarine to the Dutch East Indies. During January and February 1942 Hart was commander of all Allied naval forces in the Far East, operating under Gen. Sir Archibald P. Wavell, supreme commander of ABDA-COM (American-British-Dutch-Australian Command), from operational headquarters at Soerabaja, Java. The forces at his command were pitifully small after the havoc of the first Japanese offensives, and shortly after he was relieved of command by Admiral C. E. L. Helfrich of the Royal Netherlands Navy the Allied navy was defeated in the battle of the Java Sea in late February. Hart was retired in the rank of admiral (already a year past the statutory age) in June 1942 but immediately recalled to serve on the General Board. In February 1945 he returned to inactive status to accept appointment to fill an unexpired term in the

Senate from Connecticut, and he remained in the seat until December 1946. He died on July 4, 1971, in Sharon, Connecticut.

Hartsuff, George Lucas (1830–1874), army officer. Born on May 28, 1830, in Tyre, Seneca County, New York, Hartsuff grew up from the age of twelve in Michigan. He graduated from West Point in 1852 and was commissioned in the artillery. He saw action against Indians in Texas, where he was promoted to first lieutenant, and in Florida, where he was severely wounded in an engagement with Seminoles under Billy Bowlegs. From 1856 to 1859 he was an instructor at West Point and was then ordered to Fort Mackinac, Michigan. In March 1861 he was named assistant adjutant general with the rank of captain and was sent to Fort Pickens, Florida, in the defense of which he served until July. After several months as chief of staff to Gen. William S. Rosecrans in the Department of Western Virginia and a brief period in the War Department Hartsuff was appointed brigadier general of volunteers in April 1862. Through that year he fought at Cedar Mountain, August 9, Second Bull Run (Manassas), August 29–30, South Mountain, September 14, and Antietam (Sharpsburg), September 17, where he was wounded. In November he was promoted to major general of volunteers. For several months he worked at revisions of the articles of war and military code, and in April 1863 he returned to the field in command of the XXIII Corps in Kentucky and Tennessee. From November 1863 to July 1864 he was again inactive. He returned to the field in March 1865, when he took command of a portion of the siege line before Petersburg. He was subsequently in command of all the works at Petersburg. At the end of the war he was mustered out of volunteer service and reverted to regular rank of lieutenant colonel (he had been promoted to major in July 1862, lieutenant colonel in June 1864, and brevetted brigadier and major general in March 1865). In 1867 he was appointed adjutant general of the Fifth Military Division, comprising Texas and Louisiana. From 1869 until his retirement in June 1871 he was adjutant general of the Division of Missouri. By act of Congress he was retired as a major general. Hartsuff died in New York City on May 16, 1874.

Harwood, Andrew Allen (1802–1884), naval officer. Born in 1802 in Settle, Bucks County, Pennsylvania, Harwood was appointed a midshipman in the navy in January 1818. From 1819 to 1821 he sailed on the sloop *Hornet*, Capt. George C. Read, on patrol against the slave trade on the African coast. He was later engaged in the suppression of piracy in West Indian waters. He was promoted to lieutenant in March 1827 and fulfilled a wide variety of assignments at sea and in diplomatic missions. From 1843 to 1852 he was assistant inspector of ordnance, re-

ceiving promotion to commander in October 1848. He commanded the frigate *Cumberland* in the Mediterranean during 1853–1855 and in September of the latter year was promoted to captain. He was inspector of ordnance, 1858–1861, and was then named chief of the Bureau of Ordnance and Hydrography. In July 1862 he was promoted to commodore and put in command of the Washington navy yard and the Potomac Flotilla. He continued in those posts until January 1864, when he relinquished them to his executive officer, Commander Foxhall A. Parker. He retired from active service in that year but served as secretary of the Lighthouse Board and member of the Examining Board until February 1869, when he was made a rear admiral on the retired list. He published in 1867 *Law and Practice of United States Navy Courts-Martial,* and he was also author of a work on summary courts-martial. Harwood died in Marion, Massachusetts, on August 28, 1884.

Hatch, John Porter (1822–1901), army officer. Born in Oswego, New York, on January 9, 1822, Hatch graduated from West Point in 1845 and was commissioned in the infantry. At the beginning of the Mexican War he fought under Gen. Zachary Taylor at Palo Alto, May 8, 1846, and Resaca de la Palma, May 9, and was then transferred to the Mounted Rifles for service under Gen. Winfield Scott. At Contreras and Churubusco, August 19–20, 1847, he won a brevet to first lieutenant and at Chapultepec, September 13, another to captain. After the war he served on the frontier, from Washington to New Mexico, taking part in numerous Indian engagements and receiving promotion to captain in October 1860. In September 1861 he was appointed brigadier general of volunteers in command of a cavalry brigade. He executed a series of daring reconnaissance raids on the Rapidan and Rappahannock rivers and during March–August 1862 commanded the cavalry of the V Corps under Gen. Nathaniel P. Banks in the Shenandoah valley. He was then assigned to the infantry and for a week was in command of a division of Gen. Joseph Hooker's I Corps until he was severely wounded at South Mountain, Maryland, on September 14. For his gallantry there he was brevetted major general of volunteers and lieutenant colonel of regulars and awarded the Medal of Honor. He did not return to the field until October 1863, after which time he commanded various departments in the South. He was in charge of operations on John's Island, South Carolina, in July 1864 and at Honey Hill in November and cooperated closely with Gen. William T. Sherman in the Georgia–Carolinas campaign. At the end of the war, by which time he had been brevetted colonel and brigadier general of regulars, he was in command of the District of Charleston. He reverted to major on being mustered out of volunteer service and for twenty years thereafter was again on the frontier. He was promoted to lieutenant colonel in 1873 and colonel of the 2nd Cavalry in June 1881. He retired in January 1886 and died in New York City on April 12, 1901.

Hayes, Ira Hamilton (1922–1955), marine. Born in 1922 on a Pima Indian reservation in Arizona, Hayes enlisted in the marines early in World War II and served in the Pacific. He took part in the campaign on Iwo Jima and on February 23, 1945, happened to be one of six marines who raised an American flag—a battle ensign from an LST landing craft—atop Mount Suribachi. A photograph of the raising taken by Associated Press photographer Joe Rosenthal quickly became one of the most famous and widely reproduced images of the war. Three of the six men died on Iwo Jima, and the three remaining, Hayes among them, were received as heroes at home. Rosenthal's photograph, reproduced on a U.S. postage stamp in 1945 and in a 75-foot monument by Felix de Weldon unveiled in Arlington, Virginia, in November 1954, kept the three survivors of the event in the public eye. Hayes, who was shy and unsophisticated, reacted with growing confusion to celebrity. He became an alcoholic and was arrested numerous times for drunkenness. For that reason as well as for his being an Indian, he was unable to hold a steady job. He had been working for a time as a cotton picker when he was found dead of alcohol and exposure on January 24, 1955, on the Sacaton Indian Reservation, Arizona. After lying in state in the capitol in Phoenix, he was buried at Arlington National Cemetery, Virginia. His story was later the subject of a motion picture.

Hays, John Coffee (1817–1883), frontiersman and Texas army officer. Born in Wilson County, Tennessee, on January 28, 1817, Hays became a surveyor in his youth and after several years in Mississippi moved to Texas, arriving in 1836 shortly after the battle of San Jacinto. After four years of scout service with the Texas army in the border regions he was appointed a captain of the Texas Rangers, which was then a somewhat irregular collection of partisan bands only occasionally supported by the Texas government. Jack Hays's detachment, more disciplined and notably more effective than most, traced its success to the respect commanded by its leader; his calm assurance, democratic leadership, and martial skills soon came to be the ideal of the Rangers and remained so throughout their subsequent history. Hays was reputedly the first to introduce Samuel Colt's new revolving pistol—the "six-shooter"—to the West and to prove its value in a number of engagements with Comanche marauders. (In August 1840 he took part in the battle of Plum Creek, which broke the power of the Comanches in the region around San Antonio.) His Rangers became a power-

ful light cavalry force, able to hold their own against superior numbers and admired by both the Indians and the Mexican border garrisons. He served in the army through the Mexican War, for the most part as colonel of a volunteer Texas cavalry regiment attached to the command of Gen. Zachary Taylor, and he proved an invaluable asset to Taylor as a scout, advance-force commander, guerrilla fighter, and utterly fearless leader in battle, winning particular distinction at Monterrey, September 20–24, 1846. Hays later served under Gen. Winfield Scott in the Mexico City campaign. Discharged in 1848, he made his way to California the next year and from 1850 to 1853 was sheriff of San Francisco County. After a term as state surveyor general by appointment of President Franklin Pierce, he left public service and devoted himself to extensive business and real-estate interests. Hays died at his home near Piedmont, California, on April 28, 1883.

Hazelwood, John (1726?–1800), Revolutionary naval officer. Born about 1726 in England, Hazelwood went to sea at an early age and by 1753, having settled in Pennsylvania, was a prominent merchant captain out of Philadelphia. In July 1775 he was consulted by the Pennsylvania committee of safety in the matter of naval defenses. In December he was placed in command of a fleet of fire rafts with the rank of captain. During 1776 he was engaged in constructing defensive river works in Pennsylvania and New York. Early in 1777 he was advanced to commodore, and in September he was named commander of the state navy. On the capture of Philadelphia by the British in that month, Gen. William Howe determined to open a supply line to the city on the Delaware River. The river was then under the control of Hazelwood's combined Pennsylvania–Continental fleet, consisting of the flagship *Montgomery*, two floating batteries, a variety of sloops and schooners, thirteen galleys, and numerous smaller craft, supported by shore fortifications under Gen. James M. Varnum. On October 22 a British fleet attempted to force its way past Fort Mercer at Red Bank, New Jersey, and was repulsed; the next day it attacked Fort Mifflin, opposite Mercer on Fort Island, and was again driven off by the shore batteries and Hazelwood's fleet, losing the 64-gun *Augusta* and the *Merlin*, 18. For this success Hazelwood was voted a sword by Congress. When the British, with overwhelming force, did open the river to Philadelphia in November, Hazelwood retired up the Delaware, salvaging some of his fleet, and he continued to harass the British below. In 1778 the Pennsylvania fleet was dissolved. Hazelwood was later active in raising money and securing supplies for the Continental army. After the Revolution he was again in the merchant service. He died in Philadelphia on March 1, 1800.

Hazen, William Babcock (1830–1887), army

officer. Born in West Hartford, Vermont, on September 27, 1830, Hazen moved with his family to Hiram, Ohio, in 1833. He graduated from West Point in 1855 and was commissioned in the infantry. He served on the frontier, in Oregon and Texas, until 1859, when he was severely wounded in a fight with Comanches. Sent to West Point as an instructor in February 1861, he was promoted to first lieutenant in April and captain in May, following the outbreak of the Civil War, and in October was appointed colonel of the 41st Ohio Volunteers. He took command of a brigade of the Army of the Ohio in January 1862 and led it at Shiloh, April 6–7, Corinth, May 30, and Stones River (Murfreesboro), December 31–January 3, 1863. He was promoted to brigadier general of volunteers in November 1862. He served throughout the campaigns in Mississippi and Georgia, distinguished himself at Missionary Ridge, November 25, 1863, and in Gen. William T. Sherman's march to the sea he commanded a division of the XV Corps under Gen. John A. Logan. For his capture of Fort McAllister on December 13, 1864, in the siege of Savannah, he was promoted to major general of volunteers. By March 1865 he had received brevets in regular rank to major general. From May to August 1865 he commanded the XV Corps. On being mustered out of volunteer service in 1866 he was appointed colonel of the 38th Infantry, later transferring to the 6th. He was on frontier duty thereafter, except for a period in 1870 when he was a military observer in Europe, and he attracted notice in the later 1870s with his outspoken criticism of army contracting practices. In December 1880 he was appointed chief signal officer of the army with the rank of brigadier general. At that time the Weather Bureau was a part of the Signal Corps, and it was therefore under Hazen's authority that the Lady Franklin Bay meteorological expedition under army Lt. Adolphus W. Greely set out in 1881. The failure of relief vessels to reach Greely's party in 1882 and 1883 weighed upon him, and he urged that another be sent in September 1883. Secretary of War Robert T. Lincoln vetoed the idea, and when relief finally got through in 1884 to discover 18 of Greely's 25 men dead, the dispute between Hazen and Lincoln grew heated and public. Hazen was court-martialed and reprimanded for publicly criticizing Lincoln. He died in Washington, D.C., on January 16, 1887.

Heath, William (1737–1814), Revolutionary

army officer. Born in Roxbury, Massachusetts, on March 2, 1737, Heath became a prominent farmer in the town and in 1761 represented it in the General Court. Four years later he joined the Ancient and Honorable Artillery Company of Boston, of which he became captain in 1770, and in the tense years preceding the Revolution he was an outspoken advocate of military readiness. He was again in the Gen-

eral Court in 1771–1774 and afterwards sat in the successor provincial congress in 1774–1775. In February 1775 he was appointed brigadier general of provincial militia. Heath was largely responsible for training and organizing the Massachusetts troops, and following the battle of Bunker Hill, June 17, 1775, he was promoted to major general. Two days later, when the Massachusetts forces were absorbed into the Continental army, he was commissioned brigadier general. After commanding in Roxbury for a time he joined Gen. George Washington's main army in New York in the spring of 1776 and served through that campaign, being promoted to major general in August. His failure in January 1777 to carry out an assignment from Washington ended his field service. He commanded the Eastern Department for two years, which entailed guarding the prisoners of war from the surrender of Gen. John Burgoyne at Saratoga. In June 1779 he was placed in command in the lower Hudson valley, and he remained there until the end of the war, except for a brief time in 1780 when he helped prepare for the arrival of the Comte de Rochambeau's army in Rhode Island. He returned to farming after the war, served in the constitutional ratifying convention in 1788 and in the state senate in 1791–1792, and in 1798 published a volume of memoirs. At his death in Roxbury on January 24, 1814, Heath was the last surviving Revolutionary major general.

Heintzelman, Samuel Peter (1805–1880), army

officer. Born in Manheim, Pennsylvania, on September 30, 1805, Heintzelman graduated from West Point in 1826 and was commissioned in the infantry. He served in the West, in the Seminole War in Florida, and in a survey of the Tennessee River over the next 20 years, becoming a captain in November 1838. During the Mexican War he served under Gen. Winfield Scott in the Mexico City campaign and was brevetted major for gallant conduct. After a period at Fort Hamilton, New York, he was ordered to California, where he engaged in numerous Indian fights. In November 1850 he established at the confluence of the Gila and Colorado rivers, in what is now Arizona, Camp Independence, known from 1852 as Fort Yuma. He was promoted to major in 1855. At the outbreak of the Civil War he was called to Washington, D.C., and in May 1861 appointed brigadier general of volunteers. He opened Union military operations near the capital, capturing Alexandria, Virginia, on May 24 and distinguishing himself in leading a division at Bull Run (Manassas), July 21, where he was badly wounded. In the organization of the Army of the Potomac later in 1861 Heintzelman was given command of the III Corps. In the Peninsular campaign of 1862 he initiated the siege of Yorktown in April, occupied it on May 4, and the next day fought a major but inconclusive battle with Gen.

James B. Longstreet's forces at Williamsburg. On May 31, with the Army of the Potomac divided by the rain-swollen Chickahominy River, he was the senior Union officer south of the river, where Gen. Joseph E. Johnston attempted to direct a major attack. The resulting battle of Fair Oaks (Seven Pines) was again a draw. At the conclusion of the Seven Days' Battles, June 26–July 2, he was promoted to major general of volunteers. After the withdrawal from the Peninsula he led his corps in support of Gen. John Pope at second Bull Run, August 29–30. Heintzelman was then assigned to the defense of Washington, where he remained, commanding the XXII Corps, for more than a year, until October 1863. During much of 1864 he commanded the Northern Department with headquarters in Columbus, Ohio. From October 1864 he served mainly in courts-martial duty. In August 1865 he was mustered out of volunteer service and appointed colonel of the 17th Infantry, which was soon afterward ordered from New York to Texas. He retired in February 1869 and in April of that year was made major general on the retired list by act of Congress. He died in Washington, D.C., on May 1, 1880.

Henderson, Archibald (1783–1859), marine officer. Born in Dumfries, Fairfax County, Virginia, on January 21, 1783, Henderson was appointed a second lieutenant of marines in June 1806. He advanced to first lieutenant in March 1807 and, after brief service aboard the *Wasp* and the *Constitution* and while commanding the marines attached to the coastal gunboat flotilla at Charleston, South Carolina, to captain in April 1811. During the War of 1812 he served on the *Constitution* under Commodore William Bainbridge and later Capt. Charles Stewart, taking part in the actions against the *Java*, the *Cyane*, and the *Levant*. He was promoted to brevet major in 1814. He subsequently commanded the marine barracks at Boston and at Portsmouth, New Hampshire. In 1818 he was ordered to Washington, D.C., and he was acting commandant of the corps from the death of Lt. Col. Franklin Wharton in September 1818 until the appointment of Lt. Col. Anthony Gale in March 1819. On Gale's dismissal in October 1820 Henderson, then stationed at New Orleans, was appointed lieutenant colonel commandant. In July 1834 he was promoted to colonel. In 1836 he volunteered the marine corps and himself for service in the Indian wars in the South; before leaving he tacked a sign to his office door reading "Have gone to Florida to fight Indians. Will be back when the war is over." Sailing to Charleston, South Carolina, and Augusta, Georgia, in June, units of the corps marched to Columbus, Georgia, and established a base on the Chattahoochee River, where navy boats from Pensacola, Florida, supported them. Henderson's regiment of marines fought under Gen. Winfield Scott against the

Creeks and later supported Gen. Thomas S. Jesup against the Seminoles in Florida. For gallantry in a fight on the Hatcheluskee River in January 1837 he was brevetted brigadier general and given command of a brigade that included two regiments of regular army troops and a Georgia militia regiment in addition to the marines. Henderson returned to Washington, D.C., in May 1837; units of marines continued to operate in Florida into 1838. Henderson remained colonel commandant of the corps until his death in Washington, D.C., on January 6, 1859.

Herkimer, Nicholas (1728–1777), Revolutionary militia officer. Born in 1728 near present-day Herkimer, New York, Herkimer served as a lieutenant of militia in the French and Indian War and in 1758 won distinction in the defense of Fort Herkimer. He later moved to the vicinity of Canajoharie, New York, and in 1775 was made colonel of the Tryon County militia. He served also as chairman of the county committee of safety. In 1776 he was promoted to brigadier general of militia, his responsibility at that time being primarily to suppress both Indian depredations and a degree of Tory agitation that approached civil war. In July 1777 he called out the militia, and from the rendezvous at Fort Dayton (formerly Herkimer) on August 4 he marched with about 800 men to the relief of Fort Stanwix in the Mohawk valley, then besieged by Col. Barry St. Leger with 700 British regulars and 1000 Indians and Tories. On August 5 Herkimer sent messengers forward to the fort to arrange with the garrison commander, Col. Peter Gansevoort, for a sortie from the fort to coincide with the arrival of the militia. The plan failed owing to a delay in the march. On August 6 Herkimer allowed his caution to be overruled by impetuous junior officers and ordered an advance on the fort. The militia's approach had been detected, and while passing through a ravine near Oriskany Creek, they were ambushed by an Indian and Tory detachment. After the initial confusion the militiamen, accustomed to Indian-style fighting, settled into a bloody day-long musket battle in the woods. Herkimer was badly wounded in the leg, the shot also killing his horse, early in the battle, but he refused to retire; he had himself placed at the foot of a tree and, lighting his pipe, calmly directed the battle from there. The long expected sortie from the fort finally turned the tide. The Americans fell back from the Oriskany battlefield leaving nearly a third of their number dead, and, although they were too weakened to lift the siege, they had sharply reduced St. Leger's ability to continue it much longer; it ended two weeks later at word of Gen. Benedict Arnold's approach. Before that event Herkimer was dead. His wound necessitated the amputation of his leg, and as a result of an unskillful operation he died on August 16, 1777, at his home near Canajoharie, New York.

Herron, Francis Jay (1837–1902), army officer. Born in Pittsburgh on February 17, 1837, Herron attended the Western University of Pennsylvania (now the University of Pittsburgh) for a time, leaving in 1853. Two years later he moved to Dubuque, Iowa, and entered the banking business. In 1859 he helped organize and became captain of an independent militia company that in April 1861 was absorbed into the 1st Iowa Regiment. With that regiment Herron took part in the battle of Wilson's Creek, Missouri, on August 10, 1861, in which the Union commander, Gen. Nathaniel Lyon, was killed. In September Herron was appointed lieutenant colonel of the 9th Iowa, which took part in the Arkansas campaign under Gen. Samuel R. Curtis. At Pea Ridge (Elkhorn), March 7–8, 1862, Herron distinguished himself in desperate hand-to-hand fighting and was wounded and captured. After his exchange he was promoted to brigadier general of volunteers, and for his actions in that battle he was awarded the Medal of Honor in 1893. On December 7, 1862, he again distinguished himself in saving the battle of Prairie Grove, Arkansas (also known as the battle of Fayetteville or Illinois Creek), and was promoted to major general of volunteers, at twenty-five the youngest man to win that rank in the Civil War. In March 1863 he succeeded Gen. John M. Schofield in command of the Army of the Frontier, soon absorbed into the Army of the Tennessee. He commanded the left division of Gen. Ulysses S. Grant's army at Vicksburg in June–July 1863 and subsequently led an expedition, including gunboats under Commander John G. Walker, up the Yazoo River, culminating on July 13 in the capture of Yazoo City, Mississippi. Later he commanded the XIII Corps on the Texas frontier, where he provided secret aid to President Benito Juárez of Mexico. In February 1865 he took command of the northern district of Louisiana. He settled in New Orleans after the war, serving as U.S. marshal in 1867–1869 and as Louisiana secretary of state in 1871–1872, but his business activities and political involvements were generally failures. He moved to New York City in 1877 and remained there until his death on January 8, 1902.

Hershey, Lewis Blaine (1893–1977), army officer. Born on September 12, 1893, near Angola, Indiana, Hershey became a school teacher in 1910 after a year at Tri-State College and in part-time study earned degrees from there in 1912 and 1914. He joined the Indiana National Guard in 1911, and in 1917, while pursuing studies at Indiana University, he was called to active duty. He saw brief service in France, with the rank of captain, before the end of World War I. In July 1920 he secured a commission as captain in the field artillery branch, Regular Army. From 1923 to 1927 he taught military science at Ohio State University; he graduated from Command and General Staff School, Fort Leavenworth, in 1932 and from the Army War College in 1934, and he studied at the University of Hawaii while stationed at Fort Shafter in 1934–1936, during which time he was promoted to major. From 1936 to 1940, while attached to the General Staff, he was secretary and executive officer of the Joint Army and Navy Selective Service Committee, which was charged with drawing up comprehensive plans and making other preparations for a system of national conscription. He advanced to lieutenant colonel in August 1940. In October 1940, promoted to temporary brigadier general, he was assigned to the staff of the newly created Selective Service System (activated September 16, 1940), and in December he was named deputy director. In July 1941 he became director of Selective Service, a post he held—except for the time between his retirement in December 1946 and recall in January 1947, and for the few months between the expiration of the 1940 law in March 1947 and enactment of the first peacetime draft in June 1948—until February 1970. During the latter interim he headed the Office of Selective Service Records. He was promoted to major general in April 1942, lieutenant general in June 1956, and general in November 1969. He oversaw the conscription of men for service in World War II, in Korea, and in Vietnam, administering the operation of nearly 4,000 local draft boards and the registration and examination of tens of millions of young men. He was relieved as director of Selective Service in February 1970 and retired from duty—he was the oldest man on active status—in March 1973. Hershey died on May 20, 1977, while visiting Angola, Indiana.

Hess, Dean Elmer (1917–   ), air force officer. Born in 1917 in Marietta, Ohio, Hess learned to fly while attending Marietta College, and on graduating in 1941 he was ordained a minister in the Christian Church. On the outbreak of World War II he enlisted in the army, taking a regular commission in the Air Corps instead of a chaplain's commission. After completing flight training and serving as an instructor he was assigned in October 1944 to the 511th Fighter Squadron, Ninth Air Force, in Europe. Before the end of the war he flew more than 60 missions in P-47 Thunderbolt fighters and advanced to major. He took up graduate studies after the war at Ohio University and then Ohio State, but in 1948 he was recalled to active duty with the air force. In 1950 he was assigned to staff duty with the Far East Air Force in Japan, and at the outbreak of the Korean War in June 1951 he was ordered to South Korea as a combat pilot and instructor. He flew 250 missions in F-51 Mustang fighters while training a large number of pilots for the Republic of Korea Air Force and was promoted to lieutenant colonel. From the first he took a deep interest in the large numbers of refugees, especially children, created by the war, and he undertook informally to secure food and shelter for orphans in Seoul. When the fall of that city threatened, he prevailed upon the commander of the Fifth Air Force, Gen. Earle E. Partridge, to allow a number of C-54 transports to be used to evacuate several hundred orphans to Cheju Island, where Hess established the Fifth Air Force Orphanage. Contributions from servicemen and from individuals and groups in the United States supported the orphanage, and on his return home in 1952 Hess was active in raising money. In 1956 he published *Battle Hymn*, an autobiography that was well received and was subsequently made into a motion picture.

Hewitt, Henry Kent (1887–1972), naval officer. Born on February 11, 1887, in Hackensack, New Jersey, Hewitt graduated from the Naval Academy in 1906 and was commissioned an ensign in 1908. After service aboard several ships he returned to the Academy as an instructor in 1913–1916, and in World War I he commanded destroyers, first the *Cummings* and later the *Ludlow*, on convoy and submarine patrol duty. He was again at the Naval Academy from 1918 to 1921, aboard the *Pennsylvania* in 1921–1923, on staff duty at the Navy Department until 1926, and on the staff of Battle Fleet until 1928. He graduated from the Naval War College in 1929, served on the staff there until 1931, and in 1932, promoted to captain, was named force operations officer of the Battle Force. After three more years at the Academy he took command of the *Indianapolis* in 1936. Various shore assignments followed, and in July–October 1940 he commanded a squadron in the Canal Zone. He then assumed command of Cruiser Division 8 and in December 1940 was promoted to rear admiral. In April 1942 he was placed in command of the Amphibious Force, Atlantic Fleet, and in that post was responsible for accomplishing the amphibious landings in Morocco beginning on November 7, 1942. The Western Task Force, Army, consisting mainly of the I Armored Corps under Gen. George S. Patton, was put ashore at Mehedia, Fedhala, and Safi on the Moroccan coast. The assault entailed fighting the French naval forces at Casablanca, including the destroyer *Jean Bart*. Hewitt was promoted to vice admiral in that month and named commander of U.S. naval forces in northwest African waters (Eighth Fleet) in February 1943. He subsequently planned and directed the Western Naval Task Force in the American wing (Patton's Seventh Army) of the landings at Gela, Licata, and Scoglitti, Sicily, on July 10, 1943, and the Allied assault (Gen. Mark W. Clark's Fifth Army) at Paestum and Salerno, Italy, on September 9. He was in command of the Allied naval forces that landed Gen. Alexander M. Patch's Seventh Army on the beaches at St. Tropez and St. Raphaël in southern France on August 15, 1944, an operation involving 400,000 men and nearly 1000 ships

and small craft. Promoted to admiral in April 1945, he commanded the Twelfth Fleet from August 1945 to September 1946 and was then the U.S. naval representative on the United Nations Military Staff Committee until his retirement in March 1949. He died on September 15, 1972, in Middlebury, Vermont.

Heywood, Charles (1839–1915), marine officer. Born on October 3, 1839, in Waterville, Maine, Heywood was commissioned a second lieutenant in the marine corps in April 1858. He saw sea duty aboard the *Niagara* in a cruise to Africa, the *St. Louis* patrolling in Central American waters, and, from 1860, the *Cumberland*, then in the Gulf of Mexico. At the beginning of the Civil War, as commander of the marine force aboard the *Cumberland*, he took part in the destruction of the Norfolk navy yard, April 20, 1861. Promoted to first lieutenant in May and to captain in November, he took part in the attack on Hatteras Inlet by a naval expedition under Flag-Officer Silas H. Stringham on August 28, 1861, and the capture of Fort Hatteras and Fort Clark the next day. He had charge of the after-deck guns on the *Cumberland*, then under temporary command of Lt. George U. Morris, during the battle with the ironclad *Virginia* (ex-*Merrimac*) on March 8, 1862, and fired the last shot before the *Cumberland* went down. Brevetted major for his conduct in that engagement, he was later transferred to the frigate *Sabine* and in November 1863 to the *Hartford*, flagship of Adm. David G. Farragut's West Gulf Blockading Squadron, taking command of the marines of the squadron. He was brevetted lieutenant colonel for his part in the battle of Mobile Bay, August 5, 1864, in which he led the boarding of the Confederate flagship *Tennessee*, and the subsequent capture of Fort Gaines, Fort Morgan and Fort Powell, the last of which he garrisoned with marines. Heywood was again with Farragut in 1867–1868 as fleet marine officer aboard the flagship *Franklin* of the European Squadron. Promoted to major in November 1876, he commanded the marine barracks in Washington, D.C., from that year until 1880, that at Mare Island, California until 1883, and that in New York City in 1883–1885. He led a marine force to Panama during the revolution of 1885, taking part in the landing under Commander Bowman H. McCalla. In March 1888 he was promoted to lieutenant colonel and again put in command of the Washington barracks, and in January 1891 he was made colonel commandant of the marine corps. He continued as commandant as the statutory rank for that post was raised to brigadier general in March 1899 and to major general in July 1902. Under his leadership the size of the corps was more than tripled, and it rendered signal service in the Spanish–American War and the Peking Relief Expedition. Heywood retired in October 1903 and died in Washington, D.C., on February 26, 1915.

Hill, Ambrose Powell (1825–1865), Confeder-
ate army officer. Born on November 9, 1825, in Culpeper, Virginia, Hill graduated from West Point in
1847, was commissioned in the artillery, and went
immediately into service in the Mexican War. He was
later stationed at Fort McHenry, in Florida, and in
Texas, and he saw action in Florida against the Seminole Indians between 1849 and 1855. From 1855 until
1860 he was attached to the U.S. Coast Survey in
Washington, D.C. Hill, then a captain, resigned his
commission in March 1861 with the beginning of the
Civil War and was appointed a colonel in Confederate service and given command of the 13th Virginia,
which was in reserve at the first battle of Manassas
(Bull Run). He was promoted to brigadier general in
February 1862 and, while performing well at Williamsburg, May 5, and Fair Oaks (Seven Pines), May
31, in the Peninsular campaign, was made major general. He instituted an effective system of command
and discipline and developed his division into one of
the best in the Confederate army; for the speed with
which it marched it was dubbed the "Light Division." He was in the thick of the Seven Days' Battles
in June–July 1862, absorbing heavy casualties at Mechanicsville, June 26, Gaines' Mill, June 27, and Frayser's Farm, June 30, in order to keep up the pressure
on the Union army. Sent to northern Virginia, Hill
gave invaluable support to Gen. Thomas J. Jackson at
Cedar Mountain, August 9, and the second battle of
Manassas at the end of August, and aided in the
capture of Harpers Ferry in September. His timely
arrival at Sharpsburg (Antietam) on September 17
after a forced march from Harpers Ferry helped prevent the battle from becoming a decisive Union victory. Following the death of Jackson after the battle
of Chancellorsville, May 2–4, 1863, where Hill too
was wounded, he was promoted to lieutenant general
in command of the III Corps of Gen. Robert E. Lee's
Army of Northern Virginia. On July 1, 1863, for a
time in command of all Confederate troops in the
locality, he encountered a Union force at Gettysburg,
Pennsylvania, and launched an immediate attack
that, while resulting in heavy casualties, was successful in driving the Union I Corps, Gen. George G.
Meade, and XI Corps, Gen. Oliver O. Howard, out of
Gettysburg and onto the heights south of the town.
In the next two days of fighting, however, he was
unable to make further gains. Hill's corps led Lee's
advance over the Rapidan and toward Washington in
October 1863 until repulsed by Gen. Gouverneur K.
Warren at Bristoe Station on October 14. Hill took a
prominent part in the battles of the Wilderness campaign and Spotsylvania Court House in May 1864
and was entrenched before Petersburg when he was
killed by Union fire on April 2, 1865.

Hill, Daniel Harvey (1821–1889), Confederate
army officer. Born in York District, South Carolina,
on July 12, 1821, Hill graduated from West Point in
1842 and was commissioned in the artillery. For five
years he was on garrison duty, but in the Mexican
War he distinguished himself, taking part in virtually
every major battle and winning brevets to captain at
Contreras and Churubusco, August 19–20, 1847, and
to major at Chapultepec, September 13. Early in 1849
he resigned his commission and was appointed
professor of mathematics at Washington College
(now Washington and Lee University) in Lexington,
Virginia. In 1854 he joined the faculty of Davidson
College in Davidson, North Carolina, and in 1859 he
was named superintendent of the North Carolina
Military Institute in Charlotte. Soon after the outbreak of the Civil War he was appointed colonel of
the 1st North Carolina Regiment, and he took part in
the battle at Big Bethel, Virginia, on June 10, 1861,
the first notable army engagement of the war. Promoted to brigadier general in September and to major
general in March 1862, he was conspicuous in the
defense against Gen. George B. McClellan's Peninsular campaign. At Seven Pines (Fair Oaks) on May 31
his division defeated Gen. Silas Casey's troops and,
with reinforcements, repulsed an attack by Gen.
Erasmus D. Keyes's IV Corps. During Gen. Robert E.
Lee's invasion of Maryland in September 1862 a copy
of Lee's order to Hill transferring him from Gen.
Thomas J. Jackson's corps to Gen. James B. Longstreet's went astray, was found by a Union soldier,
and was passed to McClellan, revealing many of
Lee's tactical arrangements. At South Mountain on
September 14 Hill, with 5000 men, held the passes
against McClellan's 80,000 for four hours, allowing
Lee to pull back and regroup; he was heavily engaged
at Sharpsburg (Antietam), which followed quickly
on September 17, and at Fredericksburg on December
13. In 1863 he commanded the defenses of Richmond
during Lee's invasion of Pennsylvania, and in July he
was promoted to lieutenant general. Put in command
of a corps of Gen. Braxton Bragg's Army of Tennessee, he took part in the battle of Chickamauga, September 18–20. He was prominent in the agitation to
have Bragg removed from command after that battle
and in consequence was himself relieved and had his
appointment as lieutenant general held up by
Confederate President Jefferson Davis. He returned
to the field in time to command a division in Gen.
Stephen D. Lee's corps in the battle at Bentonville,
North Carolina, on March 19–21, 1865, between Gen.
Joseph E. Johnston and Gen. William T. Sherman.
After the war he settled in Charlotte, North Carolina,
where he founded a magazine, The Land We Love, in
1866 and a weekly newspaper, The Southern Home, in
1869. From 1877 to 1884 he was president of the
University of Arkansas. In 1885 he became president
of the Middle Georgia Military and Agricultural College (now Georgia Military College) in Milledgeville,
and he retained that post until shortly before his

death in Charlotte, North Carolina, on September 24, 1889.

Hillenkoetter, Roscoe Henry (1897–   ), naval officer. Born on May 8, 1897, in St. Louis, Hillenkoetter graduated from the Naval Academy in 1919. For nearly three decades he alternated sea duty, from submarines to battleships, with shore assignments, including a term as an instructor at the Academy, 1929–1931, the post of naval attaché in Paris, 1933–1935, and diplomatic and intelligence work in Madrid, Lisbon, and Vichy, France. Attached to the battleship *West Virginia* in 1941, he was wounded in the Japanese attack on Pearl Harbor on December 7; he subsequently served aboard the *Maryland* in the Pacific, receiving promotion to captain in June 1942. In September he was named chief intelligence officer on the staff of Adm. Chester W. Nimitz, commander in chief of the Pacific Ocean Areas. From March 1943 to February 1944 he commanded the *Dixie* in the Solomons–New Hebrides campaigns. He was then assigned to staff duty in Washington, D.C. After the war he commanded the *Missouri* until being named naval attaché in Paris in May 1946. He was promoted to rear admiral in November 1946. In April 1947 he returned to Washington and in May was appointed first director of the newly created Central Intelligence Agency by President Harry Truman. He held that post until September 1950, when (succeeded by Gen. Walter B. Smith) he was given command of the 7th Task Force in Formosan waters. In 1952 he became commander of the Third Naval District. Hillenkoetter was promoted to vice admiral in April 1956, and he retired in May 1957. Thereafter he engaged in various business pursuits. He was named in 1957 a vice-president and in 1958 chief executive officer of the American Banner Lines, and from 1962 he was vice-chairman and vice-president of the Hegeman-Harris Company.

Hines, John Leonard (1868–1968), army officer. Born on May 21, 1868, in White Sulphur Springs, West Virginia, Hines graduated from West Point in 1891 and was commissioned in the infantry. He was stationed for several years at Fort Omaha, Nebraska, and, promoted to first lieutenant in April 1898, served with the Quartermaster Corps in Cuba during the Spanish–American War. He advanced to captain in December 1900. He saw action in the Philippine Insurrection in 1900–1901 and was there again in 1903–1905. For several years he was on quartermaster and adjutant duty at various posts, advancing to major in May 1912. In 1916 he was appointed adjutant to Gen. John J. Pershing for the Mexican Punitive Expedition. In May 1917 he became assistant adjutant general of the American Expeditionary Force in France, receiving temporary rank of colonel in August. In November the rank became permanent as he

took command of the 16th Infantry. In April 1918 he was promoted to temporary brigadier general, taking command the next month of a brigade of the 1st Division under Gen. Robert L. Bullard. Promoted to temporary major general in August, he commanded the 4th Division in the St. Mihiel and Meuse–Argonne offensives until October, when he succeeded Bullard as commander of the III Corps, with which he remained until its inactivation in July 1919. He was the only American commander in World War I to lead a regiment, brigade, division, and corps in combat. In November 1918 he was promoted to permanent brigadier general. Hines commanded successively the 4th Division, November 1919 to September 1920, the 5th Division, September 1920 to July 1921, and, promoted to major general in March 1921, the VIII Corps area, October 1921 to December 1922. For two months thereafter he served as deputy chief of staff. He became chief of staff of the army in September 1924, remaining in that post until November 1926. From October 1930 until his retirement in May 1932 he was commander of the Department of the Philippines. In June 1940 he was advanced to the rank of general on the retired list. Hines died at the age of one hundred, on October 13, 1968, in Washington, D.C.

Hitchcock, Ethan Allen (1798–1870), army officer. Born in Vergennes, Vermont, on May 18, 1798, Hitchcock graduated from West Point in 1817 and was commissioned in the infantry. He was promoted to first lieutenant in 1818 and to captain in December 1824. From the latter year until 1827 he was an instructor at West Point and from 1829 to 1833 was commandant of cadets there. After three years at Fort Crawford, Wisconsin Territory, he was attached to the staff of Gen. Edmund P. Gaines in 1836 as acting inspector general, serving in the Seminole War in Florida and afterward testifying in Gaines's behalf at the court of inquiry investigating the latter's dispute with Gen. Winfield Scott. From 1837 to 1840 Hitchcock was stationed in the Northwest, receiving promotion to major in 1838. In 1841 he conducted an investigation of alleged fraud in the War Department's handling of Cherokee funds. He then returned to Florida with the 3rd Infantry, of which he became lieutenant colonel in January 1842. Later transferred to St. Louis and then to Louisiana, the 3rd, a crack regiment under Hitchcock's training, was part of Gen. Zachary Taylor's army in the early stages of the Mexican War. Hitchcock became inspector general on Scott's staff later and was brevetted colonel for gallantry at Contreras and Churubusco, August 19–20, 1847, and brigadier general for Molino del Rey, September 8. In 1851 he was promoted to colonel of the 2nd Infantry and named commander of the Division of the Pacific. In 1854 he ordered the seizure of a supply ship destined for William Walker's filibustering forces in Mexico, an act that effectively ended Walker's expedition and led to friction between Hitchcock and Secretary of War Jefferson Davis. That friction eventuated in Hitchcock's resignation from the army in October 1855. He lived in St. Louis until the beginning of the Civil War, when he offered his services and was appointed major general of volunteers. He served on the commission overseeing exchanges of prisoners, on the commission revising the military code, and as an adviser to President Abraham Lincoln; for a time in 1862 Hitchcock and the heads of the War Department bureaus constituted a board advising Lincoln and Secretary of War Edwin M. Stanton on the conduct of the war. He was mustered out in October 1867. After the war he lived in Charleston, South Carolina, until shortly before his death in Hancock, Georgia, on August 5, 1870. Among Hitchcock's many published writings were *The Doctrines of Spinoza and Swedenborg Identified*, 1846, *Christ the Spirit*, 1851, *Remarks upon Alchemy and the Alchemists*, 1857, volumes of commentary on Shakespeare, Spenser, Dante, and others. *Fifty Years in Camp and Field*, an autobiography, was published posthumously in 1909, and in 1930 *A Traveler in Indian Territory*, edited from his notes, appeared.

Hitchcock, Thomas, Jr. (1900–1944), polo player and airman. Born on February 11, 1900, in Aiken, South Carolina, Hitchcock was the son of a 10-goal polo player and early took up the game himself. By the age of sixteen he was a member of the Meadow Brook Club team of Long Island, then the leading team in the country. In 1917 he left St. Paul's School to enlist in the army aviation corps for service in World War I; rejected because of his age, he sailed to France, joined the French aviation service, and was assigned to the famed Lafayette Escadrille. He shot down several German aircraft in combat and in March 1918 was captured when his plane was forced down behind enemy lines. He escaped a few months later and rejoined his squadron, which had been transferred to the U.S. army as the 103rd Pursuit Squadron. After the war he resumed his polo playing and his position on the Meadow Brook team. (On graduating from Harvard in 1922 he entered banking, becoming in 1932 a partner in Lehman Brothers.) In 1922 he achieved the 10-goal rating, the highest possible handicap, and retained it for 13 consecutive years; in 1935 he dropped to a 9-goal rating, although he was still the top-ranked American player, and from 1936 to 1940 was again a 10-goal man. He captained the U.S. team in victories over Great Britain in Westchester Cup competition in 1921, 1924, 1927, 1930, and 1939, compiling a remarkable record by losing no games to the British team. He also led the U.S. team against Argentina for the Copa de las Americas in 1928. In dominating the game for nearly 20 years, Hitchcock earned the generally acknowl-

edged title of greatest American player of all time; many thought him the game's greatest player. He retired from international competition after the 1939 Westchester Cup match. In 1942 he obtained a commission as lieutenant colonel in the Army Air Corps; sent to England as an air attaché, he secured, despite his age, appointment as commander of a P-51 fighter group. He died in a plane crash in Salisbury, England, on April 19, 1944.

Hobby, Oveta Culp (1905–   ), public official, publisher, and army officer. Born on January 19, 1905, in Killeen, Texas, Oveta Culp was educated privately and for a time attended Mary Hardin-Baylor College and the University of Texas Law School. In 1925 she was appointed parliamentarian of the Texas House of Representatives, a post she held until her marriage in 1931 to William Pettus Hobby, publisher of the *Houston Post* and a former governor of Texas. She immediately went to work for the *Post*, rising to executive vice-president by 1938, and introduced a number of features of interest to women; she was often in effective charge of the newspaper. In 1937 she published a handbook on parliamentary law titled *Mr. Chairman*, and in 1939 and 1941 she again served briefly in her former post in the Texas House. In July 1941 she was appointed chief of the women's division of the Bureau of Public Relations in the War Department. She subsequently helped develop plans for a women's auxiliary branch for the army and on creation of the Women's Auxiliary Army Corps on May 14, 1942, she was appointed director with relative rank of major, later raised to colonel. She directed the WAAC (the name of which was changed to Women's Army Corps, WAC, on July 1, 1943, when it became a regular component of the army) throughout World War II, until July 1945; WAC strength reached at its peak approximately 100,000. After the war she returned to the *Post*, becoming coeditor and publisher. She also had numerous other interests, working as a director of KPRC radio and television broadcasting in Houston, serving as a consultant to the Hoover Commission investigating governmental efficiency, and becoming active in national Republican politics. She was active in the election of Dwight D. Eisenhower to the presidency and in January 1953 was named director of the Federal Security Administration. In March the FSA was elevated to Cabinet status as the Department of Health, Education, and Welfare, and Mrs. Hobby, as the first secretary of HEW, became in April the second woman to serve in the Cabinet. She retained the post until resigning in July 1955. In that year she became president and editor of the *Post*; she became chairman of the board of the *Post* in 1965 and of Channel Two TV Company in 1970. She was a director of the Corporation for Public Broadcasting from 1968 and of a number of business corporations. She remained prominent in

Republican politics and served on a great many advisory boards and commissions.

Hobson, Richmond Pearson (1870–1937),

naval officer and public official. Born in Greensboro, Alabama, on August 17, 1870, Hobson attended Southern University (later merged into Birmingham-Southern College) in 1882–1885 and in 1889 graduated from the Naval Academy. In 1893 he took a degree from the École d'Application du Génie Maritime in Paris. For several years he served at various navy yards, in the Navy Department, and at sea as a naval constructor, and in 1897–1898 he conducted a postgraduate course at the Academy in naval construction. Promoted to lieutenant, he was assigned early in 1898 to the *New York,* which in May became Adm. William T. Sampson's flagship in the Spanish–American War campaign in Cuban waters. On June 3, 1898, he led seven volunteers in manning the specially prepared collier *Merrimac* into the narrow channel leading to Santiago harbor, the plan being to sink the vessel at the narrowest point and thus bottle up Admiral Cervera's fleet in the harbor. The collier quickly came under fire from shore batteries, and a lucky shot carried away the steering gear. With the *Merrimac* adrift in the current, Hobson attempted to sink her in place by exploding the electric torpedoes he had placed in the hull, but several failed and when the vessel finally sank it was in a harmless spot. Hobson and his men were rescued by Cervera and held prisoner for three days in Morro Castle. On his return to the United States Hobson found that his exploit, despite failure, had made him one of the popular heroes of the war. Subsequent routine assignments salvaging and rebuilding Spanish vessels in Cuba, Hong Kong, and the Philippines were anticlimactic, and in February 1903 he resigned from the navy. In 1906 he was elected to Congress from Alabama, and he served four terms, from March 1907 to March 1915, during which his most notable service was in cooperating with Adm. Bradley A. Fiske in supporting the creation of the office of chief of naval operations (established March 3, 1915). Hobson devoted much time to various public causes, notably for the prohibition of alcoholic beverages and of narcotics and for peace and naval supremacy. He founded numerous national and international societies for the furtherance of the first two, and he wrote such books as *America Must Be Mistress of the Seas,* 1902, *Diplomacy and the Fleet,* 1908, *Arbitration and Armaments,* 1908, *The Great Destroyer,* 1911, *Our Country's Destiny,* 1913, *Alcohol and the Human Race for Truth Inoculation of Society,* 1919, *Narcotic Peril,* 1925, and *The Modern Pirates—Exterminate Them,* 1931. In 1933 he was awarded the Medal of Honor for his *Merrimac* exploit, and in 1934 he was promoted by act of Congress to rear admiral on the retired list. Hobson died in New York City on March 16, 1937.

Hodge, John Reed (1893–1963), army officer.

Born on June 12, 1893, in Golconda, Illinois, Hodge attended Southern Illinois Teachers College (now Southern Illinois University) and the University of Illinois before entering a reserve officers training program at Fort Sheridan, Illinois, in 1917. By the end of that year he held a regular commission as second lieutenant of infantry. During 1918–1919 he served in France and Luxembourg, and in July 1920 his temporary rank of captain became permanent. He taught military science at the Mississippi Agricultural and Mechanical College (now Mississippi State University) from 1921 to 1925, graduated from Infantry School, Fort Benning, Georgia, in 1926, and served in Hawaii until 1929. He completed the course at the Command and General Staff School, Fort Leavenworth, Kansas, in 1934, that at the Army War College in 1935, in August of which year he was promoted to major, and that at the Air Corps Tactical School, Maxwell Field, Alabama, in 1936. Attached to the General Staff in 1936, he was promoted to lieutenant colonel in 1940 and in early 1941 assigned to the staff of the newly formed VII Corps, of which he became chief of staff, with temporary rank of colonel, in December 1941. In June 1942 he was promoted to temporary brigadier general and named assistant commander of the 25th Infantry Division, which at the end of the year reinforced the 1st Marine Division under Gen. Alexander A. Vandegrift on Guadalcanal. In April 1943 Hodge advanced to temporary major general, and in May he took command of the Americal Division, then on defense and training duty in the Fiji Islands. He was detached from the Americal temporarily to reorganize the campaign on New Georgia, but in December 1943 he led the Americal onto Bougainville. In April 1944 he was transferred to the Central Pacific area and command of the XXIV Corps, a component of Gen. Walter Krueger's Sixth Army, which on October 20 opened the Philippines campaign with a landing at Dulag, Leyte. (The corps was put ashore by Adm. Theodore S. Wilkinson's Southern Attack Force, Seventh Fleet.) Leyte was cleared of Japanese forces by Christmas. The following spring the XXIV Corps, forming with Gen. Roy Geiger's Marine III Amphibious Corps (III Phib) the Tenth Army under Gen. Simon B. Buckner, Jr., took part in the assault on Okinawa on April 1. In June, at the end of a desperately fought campaign, Hodge was promoted to lieutenant general (temporary). In September 1945, still commanding XXIV Corps, he became commander of the American forces occupying Korea, with responsibility for establishing military government and overseeing the transition to civil government. He remained in Korea until the establishment of the republic in August 1948 and in November took command of the V Corps at Fort Bragg, North Carolina. In June 1950 he became commander of the Third Army at Fort McPherson,

Georgia, and in May 1952 he was named chief of army field forces with the rank of general from July. Hodge retired in June 1953 and died on November 12, 1963, in Washington, D.C.

Hodges, Courtney Hicks (1887–1966), army officer. Born in Perry, Georgia, on January 5, 1887, Hodges attended West Point in 1904–1905, and following his failure there he enlisted as a private in the army in 1906. In November 1909 he was commissioned a second lieutenant of infantry. He saw service at various posts at home and in the Philippines, took part in the Mexican Punitive Expedition in 1916–1917, and in World War I served as a major with the 6th Infantry, taking part in the St. Mihiel and Meuse–Argonne offensives. Following occupation duty in Germany and four years on the staff at West Point, 1920–1924, he attended the Command and General Staff School, Fort Leavenworth, Kansas, graduating in 1925. He was an instructor at the Infantry School, Fort Benning, Georgia, for a year and at the Air Corps Tactical School, Langley Field, Virginia, for three, and from 1929 to 1933 he was a member of the Infantry Board at Fort Benning. After graduating from the Army War College in 1934 he served in Vancouver, Washington, for two years and in the Philippines for two more; in 1938 he was named assistant commandant of the Infantry School, and in October 1940, six months after being promoted to brigadier general, he became commandant. He was succeeded in March 1941 by Gen. Omar N. Bradley. In May 1941 he was promoted to major general and named chief of infantry; he held that post until it was discontinued in the reorganization of March 9, 1942. After organizing the Training and School Command at Birmingham, Alabama, he took command of the X Corps in May 1942. In February 1943, promoted to lieutenant general, he was named commander of the Southern Defense Command, which included command of the Third Army, at Fort Sam Houston, Texas. After taking the Third Army to England in January 1944 he became deputy to Gen. Bradley, then commander of the First Army. In August, after the Normandy invasion and the securing of the beachhead, Hodges succeeded to command of the First Army, which, with Gen. George S. Patton's Third Army and later Gen. William H. Simpson's Ninth Army, constituted Bradley's 12th Army Group. Elements of the First Army were the first American troops to enter Paris and, after the campaign across northern France and through the Ardennes Forest, the first to cross the Siegfried Line into Germany in September 1944. After the bitter fighting in the Hürtgen Forest from November to February, elements of the First reached the Rhine in March and captured the Remagen Bridge intact. In April 1945 First Army made the first contact with Russian forces at Torgau; in the same month Hodges was promoted

to general (temporary). After the German surrender Hodges prepared to take the army to the Pacific theater, but the surrender of Japan in September ended that plan. He continued to command the First Army at Fort Bragg, North Carolina, and then Governors Island, New York, until his retirement in March 1949. He died on January 16, 1966, in San Antonio, Texas.

Hodges, Harry Foote (1860–1929), army officer and engineer. Born in Boston on February 25, 1860, Hodges graduated from West Point in 1881 and was commissioned in the engineers. After a period as assistant to Col. Orlando M. Poe at Sault Ste. Marie, Michigan, during which he was promoted to first lieutenant in February 1883, he taught engineering at West Point from 1888 to 1892. He was promoted to captain in May 1893 and was engaged in river and harbor work until June 1898, after the outbreak of the Spanish–American War, when he was appointed lieutenant colonel of the 1st Volunteer Engineers. During the war he was engaged principally in engineering work in Puerto Rico. In January 1899 he became colonel of the regiment, and a few days later he was mustered out of volunteer service. Thereafter he was chief engineer on the upper Ohio River, 1899–1901, chief engineer of the Department of Cuba, 1901–1902, receiving promotion to major in May 1901, and on the staff of the chief of engineers in Washington, D.C., until 1907. In that year he was named general purchasing officer for the Isthmian Canal Commission, becoming lieutenant colonel in August, and the next year he was appointed a member of the Commission and assistant chief engineer under Col. George W. Goethals. He was promoted to colonel in July 1911. During 1914–1915 he was engineer of maintenance of the completed Panama Canal. Promoted to brigadier general in March 1915, he commanded the North and then the Middle Atlantic Coast Artillery District until August 1917, when he was promoted to temporary major general in command of the 76th Infantry Division. Early in 1918 he was in France as an observer, and he commanded the 76th in combat from its arrival in August until the end of the war in November. From January to July 1919 he commanded the 20th Division at Camp Sevier, South Carolina, and Camp Travis, Texas; he then took command of the North Pacific and 3rd Coast Artillery District. He was promoted to permanent major general in December 1921 and retired a day later. Hodges died in Lake Forest, Illinois, on September 24, 1929.

Holcomb, Thomas (1879–1965), marine officer. Born on August 5, 1879, in New Castle, Delaware, Holcomb received a commission as second lieutenant of marines in 1900. During service in the Philippines, China, and various marine posts in the United States he advanced in rank, reaching major by 1917, at which time he was an aide to the commandant of the corps. Securing a combat assignment, he accompanied the 6th Marine Regiment to France, where it was attached to the army's 2nd Infantry Division, and commanded a battalion at Château-Thierry, Soissons and elsewhere; promoted to temporary lieutenant colonel and second in command of the regiment, he also saw action in the St. Mihiel and Meuse–Argonne offensives. After occupation duty in France he resumed routine service at home and in Cuba. He became permanent lieutenant colonel in 1920, graduated from the army's Command and General Staff School, Fort Leavenworth, Kansas, in 1925, and in 1928, while commanding the marine guard at the American legation in China, was promoted to colonel. He graduated from the Navy War College in 1931 and from the Army War College in 1932 and for three years thereafter was on naval staff duty in Washington, D.C., during which time, in 1935, he was promoted to brigadier general. After a year as commandant of the Marine Corps Schools, Quantico, Virginia, he was promoted to major general and commandant of the corps in November 1936. He was appointed to a second term as commandant in 1940 and in January 1942 was promoted to lieutenant general, the first marine to wear three stars. Overseeing the vast expansion of the corps for World War II, he continued as commandant until his retirement, with rank of general, on December 31, 1943. From January to April 1944 he returned to active duty with the Navy Department, and in April he was appointed U.S. ambassador to the Union of South Africa. He remained in that post until May 1948. Holcomb died on May 24, 1965, in New Castle, Delaware.

Holland, John Philip (1840–1914), inventor. Born on February 29, 1840, in Liscannor, County Clare, Ireland, Holland was educated in Limerick and from 1858 worked as a schoolteacher in various towns. He had long been interested in ships and by 1870 had read the literature on early experiments with submarine boats and had drawn plans for one of his own. In 1873 he emigrated to the United States and the next year settled and resumed teaching in Paterson, New Jersey. His submarine plans were rejected by the navy in 1875, but the Fenian Society of expatriate Irish nationalists, who saw in the submarine a potent weapon for Irish independence from Great Britain, supplied capital for construction of a model. Preliminary success in tests in the Passaic River in 1877 brought funds for building the full-scale *Fenian Ram,* which Holland tested successfully in New York harbor in 1881–1883. It was 31 feet long, carried a crew of 3, and featured an internal-combustion engine and advanced control and balance mechanisms. From 1879, when he gave up teaching, Holland devoted all his time to improving the submarine and on several occasions after the success of the *Feni-*

an Ram managed to arouse the technical, but not financial, interest of the navy. Lt. William W. Kimball of the Bureau of Ordnance was his staunch supporter within the navy. In 1895 his J. P. Holland Torpedo Boat Company was at last awarded a navy contract to build a submarine. The resulting *Plunger* was built in Baltimore under the supervision of Adm. George W. Melville of the Bureau of Steam Engineering and largely without Holland's advice, and it was as a consequence thoroughly unsatisfactory. With what money he had left Holland built and in 1898 launched his tenth model, the *Holland,* incorporating for the first time a combination of internal-combustion power for propulsion on the surface with electric power from storage batteries for running submerged and, as in the *Fenian Ram,* rudder planes that enabled the craft to dive rather than passively sink to a desired depth. Fitted also with a torpedo tube and a dynamite gun in the bow, the 53-foot *Holland* was capable of speeds of 8 knots on the surface and 5½ knots submerged. It was tested rigorously and in April 1900 was finally accepted as the navy's first submarine. Holland subsequently built several more submarines for the navy and filled orders from Great Britain, Russia, and Japan as well. He was later troubled by difficulties with the financiers who controlled his company (by then the Holland Submarine Boat Company, later the Electric Boat Company) and in his last years abandoned submarines to carry on experiments in aviation. Holland died in Newark, New Jersey, on August 12, 1914.

Hollins, George Nichols (1799–1878), Confederate naval officer. Born in Baltimore on September 20, 1799, Hollins entered the navy in 1814 as a midshipman. After brief service on the *Erie,* blockaded in Chesapeake Bay, he was assigned to the *President* under Capt. Stephen Decatur and was captured with him in January 1815. He was again with Decatur in the Algerine War later in that year. He was promoted to lieutenant in January 1825 and commander in September 1845, and his sea commands over the years included the *Peacock,* the *Savannah,* and the *Cyane.* In 1853, aboard the *Cyane,* he appeared opportunely at Greytown on the coast of Nicaragua, where resident Americans were under threat and much of their property had been damaged. The disturbances resumed after his departure, and in 1854 he was sent back. He issued an ultimatum on July 12, demanding reparations and guarantees of security for American lives and property and, receiving no satisfactory answer, proceeded on the next day to shell and destroy the town (with no loss of life, ample warning having been given). In September 1855 he was promoted to captain. Hollins tendered his resignation in May 1861 and was forced to elude authorities when he was ordered arrested instead; he was recorded as dismissed in June. Commissioned captain in the

Confederate States navy that month, he promptly managed the capture of a merchant steamer, which he refitted and used to capture several prizes in and around Chesapeake Bay. In July he was given command of the Confederate naval forces at New Orleans and on October 12, 1861, his "Mosquito Fleet," comprising the ironclad ram *Manassas* (converted from a tugboat) and six other tiny vessels, attacked a Federal squadron in the mouth of the Mississippi. The *Manassas* inflicted severe damage on the Federal flagship *Richmond* and forced it and another ship aground. By February 1862, when he was appointed flag-captain and given command of naval forces on the upper Mississippi, he had assembled by various means a sizable fleet of river craft. During the early months of 1862 he was busy attempting to maintain Confederate control of the upper river, fighting the Federal flotilla building strength there under Flag-Officer Andrew H. Foote, and maintaining supply lines to Fort Pillow, Island No. 10, and other strongholds. The fall of New Orleans to Capt. David G. Farragut in April ended Confederate naval power on the river and Hollins's active career. For the duration of the war he was in Richmond, and afterward he returned to Baltimore, where he worked for the city court until his death on January 18, 1878.

Holloway, James Lemuel III (1922–),

naval officer. Born on February 23, 1922, in Charleston, South Carolina, Holloway was the son of a distinguished naval officer. He graduated from the Naval Academy in 1942 (with the accelerated class of 1943), and after brief service in the Atlantic he was assigned to the destroyer *Bennion,* on which he took part in naval actions around Saipan, Tinian, the Palaus, and the Philippines, seeing action particularly in the battle of Leyte Gulf, October 24–26, 1944. After the war he entered flight training and was designated a naval aviator in January 1946. After assignments aboard the carrier *Kearsarge* and as an aviation instructor at the Pensacola Naval Air Station, Florida, he served two tours of duty in Korean waters, with Air Task Group 1 aboard the *Valley Forge* and later as executive officer of Fighter Squadron 52 aboard the *Boxer.* For several years thereafter he was assigned to routine shore duty. In August 1958, by then a commander, he took command of Attack Squadron 83 aboard the *Essex.* The *Essex* took part with the Sixth Fleet in supporting the landing of marines in Lebanon in that summer and then joined the Seventh Fleet in the Formosa Strait during the Quemoy–Matsu crisis in October. In January 1959 Holloway was attached to the office of the deputy chief of naval operations for air, and in 1962 he graduated from the National War College. In July of the latter year, then a captain, he took command of the seaplane tender *Salisbury Sound* in the Seventh Fleet. In July 1965, after a year of instruction under Adm.

Hyman G. Rickover, he took command of the *Enterprise,* the navy's first nuclear powered carrier. He remained with that vessel through two combat tours in Vietnamese waters, receiving promotion to rear admiral in May 1966. In July 1967 he returned to staff duty in Washington, D.C., where, as director of the strike warfare division, he helped develop the multipurpose carrier concept. In August 1970 he took command of Carrier Division 6; aboard the *Saratoga* he directed naval operations by a task force of the Sixth Fleet in the eastern Mediterranean during the Lebanese crisis of that year. Holloway was named deputy commander and chief of staff of the Atlantic Fleet with the rank of vice admiral in February 1971, and in May 1972 he became commander of the Seventh Fleet. He was appointed vice chief of naval operations with the rank of admiral in September 1973, and in July 1974 he succeeded Adm. Elmo R. Zumwalt as chief of naval operations. A highly decorated officer, Holloway brought to that post an unusual breadth of experience and at least one unique qualification in having commanded the first nuclear powered naval vessel ever to enter combat (*Enterprise*, as of December 1965).

Holmes, Theophilus Hunter (1804–1880),

Confederate army officer. Born in Sampson County, North Carolina, on November 13, 1804, Holmes graduated from West Point in 1829 and was commissioned in the infantry. He served on the Louisiana and Indian Territory frontier, against the Seminoles in Florida in 1839–1842, and in Texas, receiving promotion to first lieutenant in March 1835 and captain in December 1838. During the Mexican War he served with Gen. Zachary Taylor and was brevetted major for gallantry at Monterrey, September 20–24, 1846. Afterwards he was again engaged mainly in frontier duty. He was promoted to major in March 1855 and from 1859 to 1861 was superintendent of the general recruiting service at Governors Island, New York. In April 1861 he resigned, and after assisting in the organization of the North Carolina militia he was commissioned brigadier general in the Confederate army in June by his close friend, Jefferson Davis. He commanded a reserve brigade at Manassas (Bull Run), and after his promotion to major general in October 1861 he returned to North Carolina to recruit and train a division. He was with the Army of Northern Virginia in mid-1862, but his lackluster performance at Frayser's Farm and Malvern Hill on June 30–July 1 virtually ended his field service. He was subsequently given command of the Trans-Mississippi, succeeding Gen. Earl Van Dorn, and in October he was promoted to lieutenant general. Insecure in command, he managed in February 1863 to get himself subordinated to Gen. Edmund Kirby-Smith. On July 3, 1863, he led an attack on Union forces under Gen. Benjamin M. Prentiss at

Helena, Arkansas, which was repulsed with heavy losses. In April 1864 he was transferred back to North Carolina, where he commanded the reserves until the end of the war. He died at his home near Fayetteville, North Carolina, on June 21, 1880.

Hood, John Bell (1831–1879), Confederate army officer. Born in Owingsville, Kentucky, on June 1, 1831, Hood graduated from West Point in 1853 and for eight years served at posts in New York and California and then in Texas in the 2nd Cavalry, under Col. Albert S. Johnston and Lt. Col. Robert E. Lee. He resigned from the army in April 1861 and accepted a Confederate commission; he rose quickly through the ranks and by March 1862 was a brigadier general in command of the "Texas Brigade." He established a reputation as a "fighting general" at Gaines' Mill, June 27, the second battle of Manassas (Bull Run) August 29–30, and Sharpsburg (Antietam), September 17, and in October 1862 was promoted to major general. Attached to Gen. James Longstreet's corps, his division was at Gettysburg, July 1–3, 1863, and on the second day of the battle he was seriously wounded. In September he accompanied Longstreet to Tennessee to reinforce Gen. Braxton Bragg and was prominent on the field at Chickamauga, September 18–20, where he sustained a wound that necessitated the amputation of a leg. Promoted to lieutenant general in February 1864, he was sent to assist Gen. Joseph E. Johnston in opposing Gen. William T. Sherman's advance through Georgia. Johnston's continual retreat in the face of Sherman's overwhelming superiority in numbers was a succession of unavoidable but depressing defeats, and in July he was removed, Hood then succeeding to command of the Army of Tennessee with the temporary rank of general. Faced with an impossible task, Hood, too, slowly gave way before Sherman; two attempted counterattacks, at Peachtree Creek on July 20–22 and at Ezra Church on July 28, failed, and he found himself besieged in Atlanta. After five weeks he was forced to abandon the city on September 1 before being completely encircled. He attempted to resume the offensive by circling rapidly west and north to strike behind Sherman's lines. He wasted an opportunity to strike the unprepared Gen. John M. Schofield at Spring Hill, Tennessee, on November 29, and at Franklin on November 30 and at Nashville on December 15–16 he was repulsed with heavy losses first by Schofield and then by Gen. George H. Thomas, both detached from Sherman's army. After Nashville the Army of Tennessee hardly existed as a combat force. At his own request he was relieved of his command in January 1865. Sent west on a recruiting mission, Hood heard of the Confederate surrender at Appomattox in April and himself surrendered in Natchez, Mississippi, in May. Afterward he established himself in a mercantile business in New Or-

leans; his last years were passed there in poverty and he died on August 30, 1879.

Hood, Washington (1808–1840), army officer and topographer. Born in Philadelphia on February 2, 1808, Hood graduated from West Point in 1827 and was commissioned in the infantry. After two years of garrison duty at Jefferson Barracks, Missouri, he took up engineering work and in 1831 became a topographical engineer. Among his assignments were a survey of Indian reservation boundaries in the region west of the Mississippi and an 1835 survey, made with Lt. Robert E. Lee, of the Ohio–Michigan boundary, the dispute over which had come almost to civil war. Promoted to first lieutenant in 1835, he resigned from the army in 1836 to practice engineering privately, but after a year in Cuba he reentered the topographical engineers as a captain in July 1838. Subsequent tasks assigned him included the making of maps of the region of the Seminole War in Florida, of the territory of the headwaters of the Missouri River, of proposed systems of defense in the Northwest, and, most importantly, of the territory of Oregon, "exhibiting the various trading depots or forts occupied by the British Hudson Bay Company." That map, compiled in 1838, played a large role in the movement for occupation of Oregon. In 1839 Hood was ordered west again to compile a map of the country beyond the Mississippi that was to serve as the basis for Indian land grants. He exposed numerous errors in previous surveys, but his health failed in the course of the work and, while returning to the East, he died on July 17, 1840, in Bedford Springs, Pennsylvania.

Hooker, Joseph (1814–1879), army officer. Born on November 13, 1814, in Hadley, Massachusetts, Hooker graduated from West Point in 1837 and was assigned to the artillery. He saw action in the Seminole War, advancing to first lieutenant in November 1838, served for a time as adjutant at West Point, and, although a staff officer, was three times brevetted for his conduct during the Mexican War, in which he served under both Gen. Zachary Taylor and Gen. Winfield Scott and from which he emerged as a brevet lieutenant colonel. He was promoted to regular captain in March 1847. In the reduction of the army that followed the war opportunities narrowed, and Hooker, assigned to the Division of the Pacific from 1849 to 1851, took leave of absence in the latter year and resigned in February 1853. For several years he operated a large farm near Sonoma, California, later serving in 1858–1859 as superintendent of military roads in Oregon and in 1859–1861 as a colonel in the California militia. In 1861 he sought a Union commission and in May was appointed brigadier general of volunteers. For several months he commanded a division in the defense of Washington, D.C. He first came to prominence in the Peninsular campaign, serving through the siege of Yorktown, April 5–May 4, 1862, and bearing with his division (attached to Gen. Samuel P. Heintzelman's III Corps) the full force of the Confederate rearguard attack at Williamsburg, May 5, for which action he was promoted to major general of volunteers. After the Peninsular campaign Hooker was sent to reinforce Gen. John Pope's Army of Virginia before Washington, and he took part in the second battle of Bull Run (Manassas), August 29–30. Placed in command of the I Corps of the Army of the Potomac early in September, he was on the field at South Mountain, September 14, and at Antietam (Sharpsburg), September 17, where he was wounded; his vigorous execution of battle plans, which had already earned him the nickname "Fighting Joe," now brought him appointment as brigadier general in the regular army. At Fredericksburg, December 13, Hooker commanded the Center Grand Division (III and V Corps). He had opposed the plan of battle beforehand, and after it came to disaster and the Union commander, Gen. Ambrose E. Burnside, was relieved, President Abraham Lincoln, despite serious reservations caused by Hooker's penchant for expressing insubordinate opinions, appointed Hooker to command the Army of the Potomac. He instituted an effective reorganization of his command, abolishing Burnside's grand divisions, concentrating the scattered cavalry into a single corps as an independent combat arm, and introducing distinctive corps and division insignia. In spite of excellent planning and a huge superiority in numbers he failed to achieve the expected defeat of Gen. Robert E. Lee's forces at Chancellorsville, May 2–4, 1863, remaining in a defensive position while Lee stole the initiative, outmaneuvered him, and struck north into Pennsylvania. Hooker foresaw that the climactic battle would likely be at Gettysburg, but just days before it began he concluded that he no longer commanded the confidence of the government and was at his own request replaced by Gen. George G. Meade. In September he assumed command of the XI and XII Corps (later consolidated as the XX Corps), which were bound for the Department of the Cumberland to reinforce Gen. William S. Rosecrans at Chattanooga. His success in the Battle Above the Clouds at Lookout Mountain, Tennessee, November 24, 1863, won him a brevet to regular major general. When Gen. Ulysses S. Grant, who had replaced Rosecrans, was in turn succeeded by Gen. William T. Sherman, Hooker's corps became part of the vast army invading Georgia in 1864. During the Atlanta campaign Sherman showed his distrust of Hooker by passing over him to appoint Gen. Oliver O. Howard to the command of the Army of the Tennessee, and Hooker promptly requested and was granted relief from duty. From then until 1865 he commanded the Northern Department, from 1865 to 1866 the Department of the East, and from 1866 until his retirement as major general in October 1868 the Department of the Lakes. Hooker died in Garden City, New York, on October 31, 1879.

Hopkins, Esek (1718–1802), Revolutionary naval officer. Born in what is now Scituate, Rhode Island, on April 26, 1718, Hopkins went to sea at the age of twenty and, by dint of ability and his marriage three years later into a wealthy merchant family, rose quickly to command of a large merchant fleet. During the French and Indian War he engaged in some highly profitable privateering and became a figure of considerable consequence in Rhode Island, serving at various times in the colonial legislature. He retired to his farm in North Providence in 1772, but in October 1775 he was appointed brigadier general in command of the colony's military forces and charged with preparing defenses. Two months later, in December, the Continental Congress decided to organize a naval fleet and, partly through the influence of Hopkins's elder brother Stephen (formerly governor of Rhode Island), who was chairman of the naval committee, he was named commodore of the fleet on December 22. Early in 1776 he joined the new navy of eight small converted merchant ships (refitted by Joshua Humphreys) in Philadelphia and was ordered to sail to Chesapeake Bay and attack the British fleet there. After some delay Hopkins set forth on February 17 with the ships *Alfred*, Capt. Dudley Saltonstall, and *Columbus*, Capt. Abraham Whipple, the brigs *Andrew Doria*, Capt. Nicholas Biddle, and *Cabot*, Capt. John B. Hopkins (Esek's son), and four smaller vessels, two of which later became separated in a gale. Choosing to view his orders as discretionary, he avoided the strong British force in the Chesapeake and sailed to the Bahamas, where on March 3 a landing force of marines under Capt. Samuel Nicholas attacked the British post on New Providence and captured much valuable war matériel. On his return with the fleet, the *Columbus* captured the British schooner *Hawk* on April 4 off Block Island, and the *Alfred* took the brig *Bolton* the next day. Also on April 5 several of the fleet, led by the *Cabot*, fought an inconclusive battle with the British ship *Glasgow*. Later in the year a congressional investigation of Hopkins's conduct resulted from growing dissatisfaction with his lack of accomplishment, his disobedience of orders, and the long idleness of the fleet following the Bahamas venture. Despite a spirited defense by John Adams he was formally censured in October. Problems of recruitment and increasing hostility toward him on the part of his officers served to keep the fleet idle in Narragansett Bay, where in December it was finally bottled up by British ships. Formal charges were brought against Hopkins before Congress in March 1777; he was suspended from command at that time and dismissed from the naval service in January 1778. Hopkins remained an influential figure in Rhode Island, serving in the legislature from 1777 to 1786 and as a trustee of Rhode Island College (now Brown University) from 1782. He died in Providence, Rhode Island, on February 26, 1802.

Hopkins, John Burroughs (1742–1796), Revolutionary naval officer. Born on August 25, 1742, in Providence, Rhode Island, Hopkins was the eldest son of Esek Hopkins. He went to sea at an early age and in the years preceding the Revolution sided firmly with the colonial cause. In 1772 he took part with Abraham Whipple in the capture and burning of the armed British customs schooner *Gaspé* in Narragansett Bay. On December 22, 1775, the day his father was named by the Continental Congress commander in chief of the Continental navy, the younger Hopkins was commissioned captain of the brig *Cabot*, 14 guns. He took part in the capture of New Providence Island in the Bahamas on March 3, 1776, and on the return voyage was leading the fleet when, off Block Island on April 5, the British *Glasgow*, 20, was encountered. Two broadsides disabled the *Cabot* and Hopkins was severely wounded. In 1777 he was given command of the frigate *Warren*, 32, then blockaded in the Providence River. He escaped the blockade in March 1778 and took two prizes before putting into Boston harbor. In March 1779 he sailed from Boston in command of a squadron including the *Warren*, the *Queen of France*, 28, and the *Ranger*, 18. Off Cape Henry, Virginia, they captured the privateer *Hibernia*, 10, and then set off in pursuit of a convoy of nine vessels, of which they took seven, including the *Jason*, 20, and the *Mariah*, 16, both of which were subsequently converted to American privateers, as was the *Hibernia*. Considerable quantities of provisions and military stores, along with a number of British officers, were also captured. Hopkins was later suspended from duty for not having strictly followed the instructions of the marine committee of Congress, and the *Warren* was given to Capt. Dudley Saltonstall. In 1780 Hopkins was captured while commanding the Massachusetts privateer *Tracy*, and in 1781 he sailed again in command of the sloop *Success*, a Rhode Island privateer. His later life was entirely obscure; he died on December 5, 1796.

Hopkins, Juliet Ann Opie (1818–1890), administrator. Born on May 7, 1818, on a plantation in Jefferson County, Virginia, Juliet Opie was educated privately. In 1837 she married A. G. Gordon, a navy lieutenant who died in 1849; in 1854 she married Arthur F. Hopkins, a justice of the Alabama supreme court. She lived thereafter in Mobile, Alabama. At the outbreak of the Civil War she volunteered her services to the state and was sent to Richmond, Vir-

ginia, where she superintended the Alabama section of the Chimborazo Hospital. In November 1861 the Alabama legislature appointed Judge Hopkins state hospital agent, apparently with the understanding from the beginning that he was to have the title while Mrs. Hopkins had the actual job. Certainly it was she who proved a resourceful and effective administrator in overseeing the establishment, staffing, supply, and management of base and field hospitals. The high quality of medical care and the superior conditions in hospitals under her direction became widely known throughout the Confederacy and won public praise from such as Gen. Joseph E. Johnston. She several times went into the field to help with the wounded and at Seven Pines (Fair Oaks) May 31, 1862, was herself wounded and left with a permanent limp. When the state hospitals were merged into the Confederate Medical Department in 1863, her work was largely ended. Among the honors tendered Mrs. Hopkins was the use of her likeness on the Alabama 25-cent and 50-dollar bills. After the war she moved to New York City; she died while visiting Washington, D.C., on March 9, 1890, and was buried with military honors in Arlington National Cemetery.

Horton, Mildred Helen McAfee (1900–   ), educator and naval officer. Born on May 12, 1900, in Parkville, Missouri, Mildred McAfee was the daughter of a noted Presbyterian clergyman and granddaughter of the founder of Park College. She graduated from Vassar College in 1920, taught school for a year in Godfrey, Illinois, and for another year in Chicago, and in 1922–1923 was director of girls' work in a Chicago church. During 1923–1926 she was on the faculty of Tusculum College, Greeneville, Tennessee, and in 1927 she was named dean of women and professor of sociology at Centre College, Danville, Kentucky. She received an M.A. degree from the University of Chicago in 1928. From 1932 to 1934 she worked as executive secretary of the Vassar alumnae association, and in the latter year she was named dean of college women at Oberlin College. In 1936 she was chosen the seventh president of Wellesley College. She served, immediately after the entry of the United States into World War II, on a committee planning a women's naval reserve program. The committee's work led to the establishment on July 30, 1942, of the WAVES (Women Accepted for Volunteer Emergency Service), of which Miss McAfee became director, with relative rank of lieutenant commander, on August 3. The WAVES were from the start fully a part of the naval reserve (unlike the army's women's reserve, until July 1943 an auxiliary corps) and by September 1945 reached a peak strength of 86,000 officers and enlisted women. An estimated 50,000 navy men were released to service afloat or abroad by the work of the WAVES. Commander McAfee's rank was raised to captain in 1944, and she resigned from service in February 1946, returning to Wellesley. She had married the Rev. Douglas Horton in August 1945. She continued as president of Wellesley until 1949. From 1950 to 1953 she was president of the National Social Welfare Assembly; in 1959–1961 she was president of the American Board of Commissioners for Foreign Missions; in 1962 she was a delegate to the United Nations Educational, Scientific, and Cultural Organization (UNESCO); and in 1963–1964 she served as cochairman of the National Women's Commission on Civil Rights. Mrs. Horton, who lived in later years in New Hampshire, was also a director of a number of business corporations.

Houston, Samuel (1793–1863), army officer and public official. Born on March 2, 1793, near Lexington, Virginia, Houston grew up there and, after his father's death, in the frontier region of Tennessee. He received little schooling and at the age of fifteen, rather than take a clerkship in a local store, he moved into the woods and for three years lived among the Cherokee Indians. He served in the War of 1812 under Andrew Jackson and took part in the battle of Horseshoe Bend, March 28, 1814, against the Creek Indians. Remaining in the army after the war, he became an Indian agent and helped oversee the removal of the Cherokee from Tennessee to Arkansas. In May 1818, shortly after being promoted to first lieutenant, he resigned and took up the study of law. Admitted to the bar the same year, he practised in Nashville and in 1821 was chosen major general of the Tennessee militia. He was soon led into politics and in March 1823 entered the House of Representatives, remaining there for two terms. In 1827 he was elected governor; soon after he won reelection in 1829, however, his wife of three months deserted him, and in April he resigned and fled west to live again among the Cherokee. Houston was formally adopted into the Cherokee nation in October 1829 and for a few years operated a trading post in their territory. He made several trips to Washington, D.C., to plead for equitable treatment of the Indians and in 1832 was sent by President Andrew Jackson to negotiate with several tribes in Texas. He was caught up in the growing agitation for Texas independence and in April 1833 attended the San Felipe convention that drew up a petition to the Mexican government requesting statehood and wrote a constitution. By 1835 he had settled permanently in Texas and in November was appointed commander of the small army then being organized. He was a member of the Texas convention that declared independence on March 2, 1836. In April 1836, following the fall of the Alamo and the massacre of Col. James W. Fannin's men at Goliad, he engaged the Mexican army under Gen. Santa Anna and, although outnumbered by more than two to one, dealt it a smashing defeat at

San Jacinto, April 21, capturing Santa Anna. In September 1836 Houston was elected president of the Republic of Texas and served until 1838. From 1838 to 1840 he was in the Texas legislature and from 1841 to 1844 was again president. In this second term as president he succeeded in restoring to soundness the finances of the Republic, which had been suffering from the extravagances of his predecessor, Mirabeau B. Lamar, while holding off Mexican attempts to recapture Texan territory. In December 1845, with the admission of Texas to the Union, he was elected to the Senate, where he remained from March 1846 to March 1859. He spoke and voted always as a Union Democrat rather than as a Southerner, and he strongly opposed the Kansas–Nebraska Bill of 1854. In 1859, his pro-Union stand having become unpopular, he was defeated for the Senate but was again elected governor. He vigorously opposed secession but finally acquiesced; refusing to swear allegiance to the Confederacy, however, he was deposed in March 1861. He retired to Huntsville, Texas, where he died on July 26, 1863.

Hovgaard, William (1857–1950), naval architect. Born in Aarhus, Denmark, on November 28, 1857, Hovgaard graduated from the Danish Royal Naval Academy in 1879 and the next year was promoted to first lieutenant. During 1883–1886 he studied naval architecture at the British Royal Naval College in Greenwich, where one of his classmates was Lt. David W. Taylor of the United States navy. From 1886 to 1894 he was assigned to the Royal Navy Yard, Copenhagen; from 1895 to 1897 he was general manager of a civil shipyard and in the latter year he returned to active duty at the Royal Navy Yard, receiving promotion to commander. In 1901, while visiting the United States to study submarine design, he was prevailed upon by Taylor, by then a captain and the chief naval constructor, and others to accept a professorship at the Massachusetts Institute of Technology and organize a new program of study for naval constructors. He finally resigned his commission in the Royal Navy in 1905, and he became an American citizen in 1919. Hovgaard remained at MIT until his retirement in 1933, and through his classes and his textbooks—*Structural Design of Warships*, 1915 (rev. ed. 1940), *General Design of Warships*, 1920, and *Modern History of Warships*, 1920, all standard works—influenced entire generations of naval architects and constructors. He was a consultant to the navy's Bureau of Construction and Repair from 1909 to 1926 and worked with it actively during World War I in the inspection and maintenance of troop transports. During the 1920s he was involved in the design and construction of airships for the navy and the army and in 1935–1938 was a consultant to the Bureau of Yards and Docks. Others among his published works were *Submarine Boats*, 1887, *The Voy-*

ages of the Norsemen to America, 1914, and *The United World,* 1944. Hovgaard died in Morristown, New Jersey, on January 5, 1950.

Howard, John Eager (1752–1827), Revolutionary army officer and public official. Born in Baltimore County, Maryland, on June 4, 1752, Howard, well educated and the son of a wealthy planter, enlisted in the Maryland militia at the beginning of the Revolution and was commissioned a captain. He served in Gen. Hugh Mercer's "Flying Camp" militia brigade and with it took part in the battle of White Plains, October 28, 1776. In February 1777 he became major of the 4th Maryland, with which he saw action at Germantown, October 4. As lieutenant colonel of the 5th Maryland (from March 1778) he took part in the battle of Monmouth Court House, June 27, 1778, and, transferred to the 2nd Maryland in October 1779 and sent south to Gen. Horatio Gates's army, he was in the disaster at Camden, South Carolina, August 16, 1780. He was with Gen. Daniel Morgan's forces at the Cowpens, January 17, 1781, and distinguished himself in that battle, leading a bayonet charge on the British center that broke their line. He was voted the thanks of Congress and a medal for his actions. He subsequently took part in the battles at Guilford Court House, March 15; Hobkirk's Hill, April 15, where he succeeded to command of the 2nd Maryland; and Eutaw Springs, September 8, 1781, where he again distinguished himself and was badly wounded. After the war he returned to Maryland. He was elected governor in 1788 and reelected twice, holding the post until 1791, and from 1796 to 1803 sat in the Senate. In 1795 he declined the office of secretary of war. In 1798 he was appointed by George Washington (then holding rank of lieutenant general) a brigadier general in the Provisional Army for the expected war with France. In 1814, having already organized a volunteer corps of veterans, he prepared to take the field to defend Baltimore following the British occupation of Washington, D.C. In 1816 he was the Federalist candidate for vice-president, running with Rufus King. Howard died in Baltimore on October 12, 1827.

Howard, Oliver Otis (1830–1909), army officer. Born in Leeds, Maine, on November 8, 1830, Howard graduated from Bowdoin College in 1850 and entered West Point, from which he graduated four years later. After serving as an ordnance officer at various posts he returned to West Point in 1855 as an instructor in mathematics and remained there until June 1861, when he resigned his commission to become colonel of the 3rd Maine Regiment. He rose quickly to brigadier general of volunteers in September and saw action at the first battle of Bull Run (Manassas), July 21; in the Peninsular campaign, during which, at Fair Oaks (Seven Pines), May 31, 1862, he lost his

right arm; at South Mountain and Antietam, September 14 and 17; and at Fredericksburg, December 13, where he commanded a division of the II Corps. Promoted to major general of volunteers in November 1862, he took command of the XI Corps early in 1863. He committed blunders at Chancellorsville, May 2–4, where his corps was routed by Gen. Thomas J. Jackson, and on the first day of fighting at Gettysburg, July 1, where his subsequent performance nonetheless won the thanks of Congress. In the fall of 1863 his corps was transferred to Tennessee, where he took part in the Chattanooga campaign, and in 1864 he commanded the IV Corps, Army of the Cumberland, in Gen. William T. Sherman's campaign in Georgia, in July winning promotion (over Gen. Joseph Hooker) to command of the Army of the Tennessee. He retained that command through the campaign in the Carolinas. He was awarded the regular rank of brigadier general in December and in March 1865 a brevet to major general. In May 1865 he was appointed by President Andrew Johnson commissioner of the Bureau of Refugees, Freedmen and Abandoned Lands—known generally as the Freedmen's Bureau—and to the immense task he brought honesty, enthusiasm, deeply felt religious and humanitarian convictions, and virtually no administrative abilities; the result was rampant corruption in the Bureau, which he stoutly refused to recognize. Under his administration, however, a number of schools and other institutions were established, including in 1867 Howard University in Washington, D.C., named in his honor. He continued with the Freedmen's Bureau until it expired in June 1872 and was president of Howard University from 1869 to 1873. In 1872 he was sent by President Ulysses S. Grant to the Arizona country to negotiate with Cochise, whom he persuaded to accept reservation life for his Chiricahua Apaches. In 1874, having returned to active military duty, he was made commander of the Department of the Columbia; in that post he fought in 1877 the war with the Nez Percé under Chief Joseph. After defeats by the Indians at White Bird Canyon, June 17, and Clearwater River, July 11, Howard was joined by reinforcements under Gen. John Gibbon, Gen. Nelson A. Miles, and others, and the war ended with Joseph's surrender in October. In 1878 he conducted a campaign against the Bannock Indians. From January 1881 to September 1882 Howard was superintendent of West Point, from 1882 to 1886 commander of the Department of the Platte, and commander of the Division of the East from March 1886, when he was promoted to major general, until November 1894, when he retired from active service. In 1893 he was awarded the Medal of Honor for his action at Fair Oaks 31 years earlier. In 1895 he founded Lincoln Memorial University at Harrogate, Tennessee. Passing his last years in Burlington, Vermont, Howard wrote a number of books on military history and other topics including *Nez Percé Joseph*, 1881; *Fighting for Humanity*, 1898; *My Life and Experiences Among Our Hostile Indians*, 1907; and an *Autobiography*, 1907. He died in Burlington on October 26, 1909.

Howe, Robert (1732–1786), Revolutionary army officer. Born in 1732 in Bladen (now Brunswick) County, North Carolina, Howe, son of a well-to-do planter, was educated in England and himself became a wealthy planter. In 1764 he was chosen for a seat in the colonial assembly, to which he was six times returned, and in 1766 he was appointed captain of militia in command of Fort Johnston, near Wilmington. In 1768 he served as a colonel of artillery in Gov. William Tryon's expedition against the Regulators. As the Revolution approached, however, he broke his ties with the governor, serving in the provincial congress called at New Bern in 1774 and in August 1775 receiving appointment as colonel of the 2nd North Carolina Regiment from the revolutionary provincial government. Sent to Virginia, he assisted Col. William Woodford in driving out Lord Dunmore, the royal governor, in December, and in March 1776 he was commissioned a brigadier general in the Continental army. Soon after he was sent to South Carolina, an expedition was mounted by Gen. Charles Cornwallis to destroy Howe's plantation in Brunswick County. Howe soon became commander of the Southern Department, receiving promotion in October 1777 to major general. In the spring of 1778 he led an unsuccessful expedition against St. Augustine, Florida, and in December of that year, after being replaced as commander of the Southern army by Gen. Benjamin Lincoln and ordered to Savannah, Georgia, he lost that city to the British. A court-martial acquitted him of blame for the loss. Ordered north, he took part in Gen. Anthony Wayne's capture of Stony Point and Verplanck's Point on the Hudson, July 16, 1779, and subsequently commanded at West Point and in the Hudson Highlands. In January 1781 he was sent by Gen. George Washington to deal with the mutiny of three New Jersey regiments at Ringwood; his vigorous action quickly quelled the mutiny and his execution of three ringleaders discouraged repetitions. A mutiny of Pennsylvania troops in Philadelphia in June 1783 broke up at the mere news of Howe's approach. After the war Howe again settled in North Carolina and in 1786 was elected to the legislature, but before he was able to take his seat he died in Bladen County on December 14, 1786.

Howell, John Adams (1840–1918), naval officer and inventor. Born in Bath, New York, on March 16, 1840, Howell graduated from the Naval Academy in 1858 and after sea duty in the Mediterranean Squadron was promoted to lieutenant in April 1861. He served on various ships during the Civil War, including the *Ossipee* of the West Gulf Blockading Squadron in the battle of Mobile Bay, August 5, 1864. In March 1865 he was promoted to lieutenant commander. From 1867 to 1871 he taught astronomy and navigation at the Naval Academy, and, after a period of survey work in conjunction with the U.S. Coast and Geodetic Survey, during which, in March 1872, he was promoted to commander, he returned to the Academy in 1874. During 1879–1881 he commanded the *Adams* in the Pacific and was then assigned to the Bureau of Ordnance in Washington. He was promoted to captain in March 1884. During 1888–1890 he commanded the steel cruiser *Atlanta* in the European Squadron. In 1893 he was given command of the Washington, D.C., navy yard, becoming also president of the Examining and Retiring Board; promoted to commodore in May 1895, he was later that year given command of the League Island navy yard near Philadelphia. From the 1870s he took a great interest in torpedoes, especially in the use of gyroscopes for guidance, and after much experimenting he patented in 1885 the Howell torpedo, which was both driven and guided by a heavy flywheel. Over the years he also developed and patented several forms of torpedo launchers, explosive shells, a superior form of disappearing gun carriage, and an amphibious lifeboat. At the outbreak of the Spanish–American War in 1898 he was in command of the Mediterranean Squadron, but he returned to home waters aboard his flagship *San Francisco* to command the Northern Patrol Squadron, responsible for patrolling the coast from Maine to the Delaware Capes. In August 1898 he was promoted to rear admiral. Later in the year he was named president of the Examining and Retiring Board again, and he remained in that assignment until his own retirement in March 1902. He died in Warrenton, Virginia, on January 10, 1918.

Howze, Robert Lee (1864–1926), army officer. Born in Overton, Texas, on August 22, 1864, Howze graduated from West Point in 1888 and was commissioned in the cavalry. He served with the 6th Cavalry on the frontier and took part in the campaign against the Brulé Sioux in 1890–1891, winning the Medal of Honor for his actions in the battle at White River, South Dakota, on January 1, 1891, following the Wounded Knee massacre. He was promoted to first lieutenant in January 1896. In June 1898 he went with the 6th Cavalry to Cuba and, as captain and assistant adjutant general of volunteers, took part in the Santiago campaign. In July 1899 he was appointed lieutenant colonel in command of the 34th Volunteer Infantry organized for service in the Philippine Insurrection, where he distinguished himself in leading the rescue of 28 Americans held prisoner in northern Luzon. He advanced to captain of regulars in February 1901. Mustered out of volunteer service in April, in June 1901 he was reappointed brigadier general of volunteers and again mustered out a few days later.

In October 1901 he was sent to Puerto Rico as major of the Puerto Rico Provisional Infantry Regiment, a post he held until June 1904. With the temporary rank of lieutenant colonel, he served as commandant of cadets at West Point during 1905–1909 and then returned to command the Puerto Rico regiment and the District of Puerto Rico until August 1912. During that time he became a permanent major in November 1911. In 1916 he again distinguished himself in the Mexican Punitive Expedition. He was promoted to permanent lieutenant colonel in July of that year and attached to the General Staff in September. He was promoted to colonel in May 1917 and in June named chief of staff of the Northeastern Department. In December 1917 he was promoted to temporary brigadier general in command of the 2nd Cavalry Brigade at Fort Bliss, Texas. In August 1918 he was advanced to major general (temporary) in command of the 38th Infantry Division, which he led to France in October and into the Meuse–Argonne offensive. In November he took command of the 3rd "Rock of the Marne" Division and remained with it in occupation duty until August 1919. He then took command of the District of El Paso and on receiving promotion to brigadier general in July 1920 became commander of the 1st Cavalry Division; he advanced to major general in December 1922. In July 1925 he was transferred to command of the V Corps area, headquartered in Columbus, Ohio. In that year he presided over the court-martial of Col. William Mitchell. Howze died in Columbus on September 19, 1926.

Huger, Isaac (1743–1797), Revolutionary army officer. Born on a plantation in South Carolina on March 19, 1743, Huger served in the militia against the Cherokee Indians in 1760. Early in 1775 he was a member of the provincial congress, and in June of that year he was appointed lieutenant colonel of the 1st South Carolina Regiment. In September 1776 he was commissioned colonel of the 5th Continental Regiment. With the inferior forces at his disposal he made a good showing against British forces invading Georgia under Gen. Augustine Prevost and Gen. Archibald Campbell and in January 1779 was promoted to brigadier general. He was badly wounded while commanding the American left wing in the unsuccessful attack at Stono Ferry, South Carolina, on June 20, 1779, and on October 9 he commanded the South Carolina and Georgia militia in Gen. Benjamin Lincoln's unsuccessful attack on Savannah, Georgia. During the British siege of Charleston, South Carolina, he conducted mounted raiding operations against the enemy's lines of communication, but on April 14, 1780, he was defeated at Monk's Corner by Col. Banastre Tarleton. Joining his forces with the main southern army under Gen. Nathanael Greene, he commanded the Virginians at Guilford Court House, March 15, 1781, and the right wing at Hob-

kirk's Hill, April 15. He had been elected again to the provincial congress in 1778 but had not taken the seat; he was elected to the state assembly in 1782. In 1783 he was elected vice-president of the South Carolina branch of the Society of the Cincinnati. Huger died in Charleston, South Carolina, on October 17, 1797.

Hughes, Charles Frederick (1866–1934), naval officer. Born in Bath, Maine, on October 14, 1866, Hughes graduated from the Naval Academy in 1888 and was commissioned an ensign two years later. He served on routine sea duty until 1898, when he was aboard the monitor *Monterey,* which sailed from San Francisco to join Capt. George Dewey's Asiatic Squadron just before the bombardment of Manila. Promoted to lieutenant (junior grade) in April of that year and to lieutenant in March 1899, Hughes subsequently served on the *Massachusetts* in 1900–1904; with the Bureau of Equipment, 1904–1906, advancing to lieutenant commander in July 1905; and on the *Washington,* which accompanied President Theodore Roosevelt on his visit to Panama in 1906. He was with the Board of Inspection and Survey in 1909–1911, during which time he was promoted to commander in January 1910, and in 1911–1912 he commanded the cruiser *Birmingham,* with which he originated the North Atlantic ice patrol. After a mission with the *Des Moines* to Veracruz, Mexico, during the Diaz revolt in 1912 he was appointed chief of staff to the commander of the Atlantic Fleet in 1913. Promoted to captain in July 1914, he served on the General Board until October 1916, when he took command of the *New York,* which on American entry into World War I became the flagship of Adm. Hugh Rodman's 6th Battle Squadron of the British Grand Fleet. During the war, at Scapa Flow, the *New York* rammed a German submarine and, while probably sinking it, was itself damaged; in that condition it eluded, under Hughes's seamanship, three torpedoes fired from another submarine. In October 1918 he was promoted to temporary rear admiral (made permanent in 1921) and put in command of the Philadelphia navy yard and the 4th Naval District. During 1920–1923 he commanded various divisions of the Atlantic, Pacific, and Battle fleets, and on graduating from the Naval War College in July 1924 he was named director of fleet training. That post made him responsible for the sinking of the *Washington* under the terms of the 1922 Limitation of Arms Treaty. In October 1925 he became commander in chief of Battle Fleet, with the rank of admiral, aboard flagship *California,* and in September 1926 he was named commander of the U.S. Fleet. In November 1927 he was appointed chief of naval operations. He held that office until September 1930, and he retired in November of that year. Hughes died in Chevy Chase, Maryland, on May 28, 1934.

Hull, Isaac (1773–1843), naval officer. Born in Derby, Connecticut, on March 9, 1773, Hull grew up in Newton, Massachusetts, in the home of his uncle William Hull, later a general in the War of 1812. He went to sea as a cabin boy at fourteen and within six years was master of an oceangoing merchantman. In March 1798 he was given a commission in the navy and assigned to the frigate *Constitution,* under Capt. Samuel Nicholson and later Commodore Silas Talbot. During the undeclared naval war with France he distinguished himself by sailing a sloop into the harbor of Puerto Plata, Santo Domingo (now the Dominican Republic) and, aided by Capt. Daniel Carmick's marines, cutting out the French privateer *Sandwich.* (The exploit was later judged illegal, and the prize was returned.) Ranked second on the lieutenants' list at the end of the war, he was given command of the brig *Argus* in 1803 and assigned to Commodore Edward Preble's squadron for service in the Tripolitan War. Promoted to commander in May 1804, he provided the naval support for Gen. William Eaton's capture of Derna the next year. Hull's promotion to captain in April 1806 was followed by four years of shore duty, but in 1810 he returned to sea in command of the *Constitution.* After a mission to Europe bearing Joel Barlow, U.S. minister to France, and a payment on Dutch loans, he returned to the United States in time to refit his ship before the outbreak of the War of 1812. In July 1812, while en route to New York harbor, he encountered five British warships off Egg Harbor, New Jersey, and with brilliant seamanship confounded them, despite the dead-calm sea, by escaping after a three-day chase. Putting out in August from Boston, where he had taken refuge, he met the British frigate *Guerrière* off Barnegat Bay, New Jersey, on August 19 and, after holding his fire to gain position, so disabled the enemy vessel in a half-hour battle that it could not be brought to port. This first major naval victory of the war rallied the country, destroyed the myth of British naval invincibility, and earned for the *Constitution* the nickname "Old Ironsides." Requesting relief from his command, Hull was briefly commandant of the Boston navy yard, then transferred to the yard in Portsmouth, New Hampshire; in 1815, after sitting briefly on the newly formed Board of Naval Commissioners, he again took charge of the Boston yard. He returned to sea duty in January 1824, sailing the *United States* to take command of the Pacific Squadron. After a leave of absence following his return to the United States in 1827 he became in 1829 commander of the Washington, D.C., navy yard, holding the post until 1835. In 1838 he was appointed commander of the Mediterranean Squadron; on his return from that post in July 1841 he took an extended leave and the next year settled in Philadelphia. Hull died there on February 13, 1843, his last words being "I strike my flag."

Hull, William (1753–1825), army officer. Born in Derby, Connecticut, on June 24, 1753, Hull graduated from Yale in 1772 and, after studying at the Litchfield Law School, was admitted to the bar in 1775. Commissioned a captain in his town militia in July of that year, he served through the Revolution, seeing action at Boston, White Plains, Trenton (after which he was appointed major in the 8th Massachusetts), Princeton, Saratoga, Monmouth, and elsewhere, rising to the rank of lieutenant colonel by 1779, and winning the praise of Gen. George Washington. After the war he established a law practice in Newton, Massachusetts, and became active in local civic and political affairs and also, as a major general of militia, helped to suppress Shays's Rebellion. A prominent Jeffersonian, he was appointed governor of the newly created Michigan Territory in March 1805. In the spring of 1812 he was commissioned brigadier general and given command of the army in the northwest, a force of some 2000 men, in anticipation of war with England. He helped devise a disastrous strategy of complete reliance on his land forces to hold the Great Lakes region and even to capture large portions of Canada; this course seriously retarded the development of a U.S. naval presence on the lakes, although Hull himself had earlier pointed out the dependence of Detroit upon water lines of supply. Upon launching his men in their assigned invasion of Canada from Detroit in July 1812 he pursued an extremely cautious and time-consuming policy that, combined with Gen. Henry Dearborn's failure to advance on Niagara, enabled the British to reinforce their positions in the West. He failed to move on Fort Malden, vulnerable even after reinforcements came, and became more timid on learning of the loss of Fort Michilimackinac on July 17. He had already begun to withdraw from Canada when the appearance of British troops under Gen. Isaac Brock forced him back to Detroit. Fearing both the British and warring Indians, he surrendered the post without a fight on August 16. (He had earlier sent to Fort Dearborn for reinforcements; the column that left the fort was massacred and the fort itself taken on August 15, completing the destruction of American power in the West.) Promptly court-martialed, he was convicted of cowardice and neglect of duty, but in recognition of his Revolutionary service President James Madison stayed his death sentence. Hull returned to Newton, Massachusetts, and died there on November 29, 1825.

Hume, Edgar Erskine (1889–1952), army officer and physician. Born on December 26, 1889, in Frankfort, Kentucky, Hume graduated from Centre College in 1908, took a master's degree there a year later, and then entered the Johns Hopkins University medical school, from which he graduated in 1913. He pursued advanced studies at the University of Munich in 1914 and the University of Rome in 1915 and in the latter year became medical director of the American relief operations organized in the aftermath of the great earthquake of January 1915. In 1916 he received a reserve Medical Corps commission in the army and in January 1917 a regular commission as first lieutenant. Following brief assignments to the disciplinary barracks at Fort Leavenworth, Kansas, and to the office of the surgeon general, during the latter of which he was promoted to captain, major, and temporary lieutenant colonel, he was ordered to Europe in June 1918 to command Base Hospital 102, attached first to the Italian army and then to the British. During 1919 –1920 he was chief medical officer and subsequently American Red Cross commissioner in Serbia, where he dealt with great success with a typhus epidemic. From 1920 to 1922 he was in charge of the I Corps Area Laboratory in Boston, and during that time he studied public health and tropical medicine at Harvard and the Massachusetts Institute of Technology. During 1922–1926 he was assistant librarian of the Army Medical Library, editing its *Index Catalogue*, and in 1926–1930 he was medical inspector at Fort Benning, Georgia, where in 1928 he completed the Infantry School course. After two more years in Boston with the Massachusetts and New Hampshire National Guard he returned to the Army Medical Library as librarian, 1932–1936. Promoted to lieutenant colonel in January 1937 and temporary colonel in June 1941, he was on the staff of the Medical Field Service School, Carlisle Barracks, Pennsylvania, until 1942, when he was given command of the Winter Army General Hospital in Topeka, Kansas. In 1943 he became chief health officer with the Allied Military Government corps attached to Gen. George S. Patton's Seventh Army in Sicily. He was subsequently named chief of the AMG in Gen. Mark W. Clark's Fifth Army in Italy, and he was responsible for the reestablishment of civil government in Naples, Rome, and Florence as those cities were captured, bringing order out of what was often complete chaos in food and water supplies, sanitation, transportation, police and administrative operations, and political reorganization. Hume was promoted to temporary brigadier general in January 1944. He remained in Italy until 1945 and from then until 1947 was chief of military government in the American Zone in Austria. During 1947–1949 he was chief of the reorientation branch in the Department of the Army, becoming permanent brigadier general in April 1948. Promoted to major general in 1949, he was named chief surgeon, Far East Command, and in 1950 chief surgeon of United Nations forces in Korea. He retired in December 1951. Among Hume's many books were *Lafayette in Kentucky*, 1937, *The Papers of the Society of the Cincinnati, 1783–1824*, 1938, *Medical Work of the Knights Hospitallers of St. John of Jerusalem*, 1940, *General Washington's Correspondence Concerning the Society of the Cincinnati*, 1941, and *Victories of Army Medicine*, 1943. He also published hundreds of papers and articles. Hume, perhaps the most decorated medical officer in the history of the U.S. army, died on January 24, 1952, in Washington, D.C.

Humphreys, Andrew Atkinson (1810–1883), army officer and engineer. Born in Philadelphia on November 2, 1810, Humphreys was a grandson of Joshua Humphreys, shipbuilder. He graduated from West Point in 1831 and was commissioned in the artillery. He served at various posts and in the Seminole War in Florida in 1836, but at the end of that year he resigned his commission to become a civil engineer. He was employed in that capacity by the Topographical Bureau and put to work planning fortifications and lighthouses for Delaware Bay, and when the Bureau was elevated into the Corps of Topographical Engineers in July 1838 Humphreys was appointed a first lieutenant. From 1844 to 1850 he was on detached duty with the Coast Survey, receiving promotion to captain in May 1848. In 1850 he began a comprehensive survey of the Mississippi River delta, but illness forced suspension of the work the following year. After a tour of Europe, inspecting river and harbor works, he returned to the United States in 1854 and undertook an analysis of the results of survey parties sent west in 1853, in his report of 1855 identifying five possible routes for a transcontinental railroad (including those surveyed in detail by Lt. John W. Gunnison, Lt. John Pope, Gov. Isaac I. Stevens, and Lt. Amiel W. Whipple). He resumed the Mississippi project in 1857 with the assistance of Lt. Henry L. Abbot, and their report, published in 1861 as *Report upon the Physics and Hydraulics of the Mississippi River*, was a major contribution to the field. Promoted to major in August 1861, he was later attached to the staff of Gen. George B. McClellan. Appointed brigadier general of volunteers in April 1862, he was chief topographical engineer of the Army of the Potomac in the Peninsular campaign. In September 1862 he took command of a division of Gen. Fitz-John Porter's V Corps, and he led it in the battles of Antietam, September 17; Fredericksburg, where he won a brevet in regular rank to colonel, December 13; and Chancellorsville, May 2–4, 1863. Transferred to command of a division in Gen. Daniel Sickles's III Corps, he was engaged at Gettysburg, July 1–3, where he won brevet regular rank of brigadier general. After that battle he was promoted to major general of volunteers and named chief of staff of the Army of the Potomac by Gen. George G. Meade. In November 1864 he took command of the II Corps at Petersburg. For gallantry at Sayler's Creek, April 6, 1865, he was brevetted major general of regulars. After periods in command of the District of Pennsylvania and, from December 1865 to August 1866, in charge of the levee system on the Mississippi, he was mustered out of volunteer service and appointed chief of the Corps of Engineers with the rank of brigadier general. He held that post until his retirement in June 1879. In addition to professional writings he published *From Gettysburg to the Rapidan*, 1883, and *The Virginia Campaign of '64 and '65*, 1885. Humphreys died in Washington, D.C., on December 27, 1883.

Humphreys, Joshua (1751–1838), shipbuilder.

Born in Delaware County, Pennsylvania, on June 17, 1751, Humphreys was apprenticed to a Philadelphia ship carpenter at the age of fourteen. Rising quickly to charge of the shipyard where he was employed in 1771, he then opened his own yard and by the age of twenty-five was the foremost marine architect in America. He was called upon by Congress in November 1775 to refit eight small merchant vessels as a naval fleet for Revolutionary War service under the command of Esek Hopkins. During the war, and particularly afterward, during the organization of the United States, he devoted much thought to the problem of American naval inferiority. When Congress provided for the creation of a navy on March 27, 1794, Humphreys submitted his ideas on ship design to Secretary of War Henry Knox and in June of that year was appointed naval constructor to the government and directed to prepare detailed models for the six frigates authorized by Congress. His plans accepted, Humphreys proceeded with actual construction, himself supervising the building of the *United States* in Philadelphia, while the *Constitution* (later famed as "Old Ironsides"), *Chesapeake*, *Constellation*, *President*, and *Congress* were built elsewhere, all of them, except for some modifications on the *Chesapeake*, to his specifications. The *United States*, launched May 10, 1797, was the navy's first capital ship at sea. These first ships of the line of the U.S. navy incorporated numerous design innovations; longer, broader, and lower in the water than European warships, carrying comparable armament, they presented a more difficult target and were faster and more maneuverable, while the concentration of guns on one deck made for more efficient fire control. The six made the navy, despite its smallness, a more than adequate force, and among them they accounted for some of the most celebrated battles in U.S. naval annals. Humphreys completed his work as naval constructor in October 1801; in 1806 he was commissioned to build a major naval yard in Philadelphia. While he rejected numerous offers of employment from foreign nations, his design ideas came to be widely adopted by other navies of the world. He died on January 12, 1838, in Haverford, Pennsylvania.

Hunley, Horace Lawson (1823–1863), inventor

and Confederate army officer. Born on December 29, 1823, in Sumner County, Tennessee, Hunley grew up in New Orleans. In 1849 he received a law degree from the University of Louisiana (now Tulane) and was admitted to the bar. In 1857 he was appointed a clerk of the New Orleans customhouse, and by 1860 he had risen to the post of special collector of the port. In June 1861 he undertook a mission to the Confederate War Department, sailing the schooner *W. R. King*, recommissioned as the *Adela*, in Gulf and Caribbean waters in search of a munitions vessel, the *Windsor Forest*, in order to warn it of the federal blockade. At some time Hunley conceived the notion of building a submarine vessel for the protection of New Orleans. A prototype, the *Pioneer*, was tested successfully in Lake Pontchartrain in February 1862 but was scuttled in April when Federal forces under Flag-Officer David G. Farragut and Gen. Benjamin F. Butler approached the city. Hunley continued his experiments in Mobile, Alabama. His second submarine, the *American Diver*, took numerous lives in unsuccessful tests before it was abandoned. By mid-1863 he had designed and, at considerable cost to himself, built a third, commissioned as the CSS *H. L. Hunley* in his honor. Constructed from an old iron boiler, the *Hunley* was some 40 feet long and was driven by a propeller cranked by eight of the nine men comprising the crew. With control fins and ballast the *Hunley* was a genuine submersible, unlike the better known semisubmersible torpedo boats called, after the prototype, *Davids*. The vessel was tested successfully in Mobile Bay and then shipped by rail to Charleston, South Carolina, where it was hoped it would be effective against the federal blockade. Untrained crews and timid commanders kept the *Hunley* from being used effectively, and at least two crews were lost because of faulty handling. Finally in September Capt. Hunley prevailed upon Gen. P. G. T. Beauregard to allow him to come to Charleston and take over operation of the submarine. On October 15, 1863, after several successful test dives, Hunley and his men set out to attack the federal squadron; the vessel went down but failed to surface, and all aboard were drowned. Raised in November, the *Hunley* at last achieved her inventor's dream on February 17, 1864, when, under command of Lt. George E. Dixon, she sank the new federal sloop *Housatonic*. The explosion of her spar torpedo carried the submarine and its crew down as well. It was the first successful engagement of a surface vessel by a submarine and the last until World War I.

Hunsaker, Jerome Clarke (1886–   ),

aeronautical engineer. Born in Creston, Iowa, on August 26, 1886, Hunsaker graduated from the Naval Academy in 1908 and was posted to the navy's Construction Corps. He was sent to the Massachusetts Institute of Technology (MIT) in 1912 for graduate study in engineering and was awarded an M.S. degree and given an instructorship there. During 1913–1914 he studied abroad, at the National Physical Laboratories in London and at the Eiffel Observatory in Paris. He returned to MIT in 1914 and there organized the nation's first college course in aeronautics and aircraft design. Awarded a D.Sc. degree in 1916, he gave up academic work that year to take charge of the aircraft division of the navy's Bureau of Construction and Repair. In that post he greatly advanced the science of aircraft design and pushed the navy to the forefront in the development of air power. Hunsaker designed the NC-4 flying boat that, built by Glenn H. Curtiss, became in May 1919 the first heavier-than-air craft to cross the Atlantic Ocean. For that and other achievements he was awarded the Navy Cross in 1920. He also designed the huge airship *Shenandoah*, built in 1923 and in service until it crashed in a storm in September 1925. In 1923, by then a commander in the Construction Corps, Hunsaker was named assistant naval attaché at the U.S. embassy in London, and he filled similar posts in Paris, Berlin, and Rome before retiring from the navy in 1926. From 1926 to 1928 he was with the Bell Telephone Laboratories, working on problems of radio communication for aircraft, and from 1928 to 1933 he was with the Goodyear-Zeppelin Corporation. In 1933 he returned to MIT to head the department of mechanical engineering, later becoming chairman also of the department of aeronautical engineering, posts he held until his retirement in 1951. He continued to serve as an adviser to the navy and to the government on aviation matters and from 1941 to 1956 was chairman of the National Advisory Committee for Aeronautics. Among his many awards and honors were the Daniel Guggenheim medal, 1933, the Franklin medal, 1942, and the Langley medal, 1955.

Hunter, David (1802–1886), army officer. Born on July 21, 1802, in Washington, D.C., Hunter graduated from West Point in 1822 and was commissioned in the infantry. He served mainly on the frontier, was promoted to first lieutenant in 1828 and to captain in the 1st Dragoons in 1833, and in 1836 resigned from the army to enter business in Chicago. Six years later he returned to the army as a paymaster with the rank of major. He served under Gen. John E. Wool in the Mexican War and later served at various posts in the Middle West and on the frontier. In February 1861 he accompanied President-elect Abraham Lincoln part of the way from Springfield, Illinois, to Washington, until an injury disabled him. In May he was appointed colonel of the 6th Cavalry and then brigadier general of volunteers in command of the 2nd Division of the army under Gen. Irvin McDowell. At Bull Run (Manassas), July 21, Hunter's division led the main attack on the Henry House plateau, and Hunter was badly wounded. Promoted to major general of volunteers in August, he was ordered to Missouri, where he

first served under Gen. John C. Frémont and then in November relieved him as commander of the Western Department. Shortly thereafter he moved his command to Kansas, whence he dispatched troops to reinforce Gen. Ulysses S. Grant in the Fort Henry-Fort Donelson campaign and Gen. Edward R. S. Canby in New Mexico. In March 1862 he took command of the Department of the South, encompassing South Carolina, Georgia, and Florida, with headquarters at Port Royal, South Carolina. On April 11 Fort Pulaski, Georgia, fell to troops and artillery under Capt. Quincy A. Gillmore of Hunter's command. On May 9 Hunter issued a proclamation declaring free all slaves in the department, but Lincoln annulled the order ten days later. Later Hunter organized the 1st South Carolina Regiment of former slaves, an act that, upheld by Congress, led to his being declared in August 1862 a felon under sentence of execution in the Confederacy. He was president of the court-martial that tried Gen. Fitz-John Porter in September 1862 and in June 1863 was effectively relieved of command of the Southern Department. In May 1864 he was recalled from court-martial and inspection duties to command the Department and Army of West Virginia. He undertook a campaign up the Shenandoah valley, winning a battle at Piedmont on June 5, but on meeting Gen. Jubal A. Early's corps at Lynchburg he retired back down the valley and into West Virginia; he failed to stop Early's drive toward Washington, D.C. In August he relinquished his command to Gen. Philip H. Sheridan and was thereafter again on court-martial duty, being brevetted brigadier general and major general of regulars in March 1865 for his services in the war. In April 1865 he accompanied Lincoln's body back to Springfield and then presided over the military commission that tried the conspirators in the assassination. In July 1866 he retired as a colonel; he died in Washington, D.C., on February 2, 1886.

Hurlbut, Stephen Augustus (1815–1882), army officer and public official. Born in Charleston, South Carolina, on November 29, 1815, Hurlbut took up the study of law and in 1837 was admitted to the bar. He served in the militia in the Seminole War in Florida and in 1845 moved to Belvidere, Illinois. He was a member of the state constitutional convention in 1847 and, as a Whig, of the legislature in 1858–1859 and 1860–1861. In May 1861 he was appointed brigadier general of volunteers. He served in northern Missouri for a time, was put in command of Fort Donelson after its capture by Gen. Ulysses S. Grant on February 16, 1862, and commanded the 4th Division at Shiloh (Pittsburg Landing) on April 6–7. Promoted to major general of volunteers in September, he took part in the battle of Corinth, Mississippi, on October 3, under Gen. William S. Rosecrans, and two days later attacked the retreating forces of Gen. Earl

Van Dorn at the Hatchie River; during the battle he was temporarily superseded in command by Gen. Edward O. C. Ord. In December he was given command of the XVI Corps. During the Vicksburg campaign in 1863 he was responsible for the defense of Grant's base at Memphis. In February 1864 he took part in Gen. William T. Sherman's expedition against Meridian, Mississippi. In August 1864 he was appointed commander of the Department of the Gulf, where he created some friction with loyal Louisiana authorities and may have been involved in corrupt dealings. Mustered out of service in June 1865, he returned to Illinois. He was an organizer and was elected first national commander of the Grand Army of the Republic at Indianapolis in November 1866, was elected as a Republican to the Illinois legislature in 1867, and from 1869 to 1872 was U.S. minister to Colombia. Elected to Congress in 1872, he held his seat until March 1877. In 1881 he was appointed minister to Peru; he died in Lima on March 27, 1882.

Hutchins, Thomas (1730–1789), surveyor and geographer. Born in 1730 in Monmouth County, New Jersey, Hutchins was orphaned in his youth. He grew up in the frontier region of Pennsylvania, serving in the colonial militia during the French and Indian War and then entering the 60th Royal Americans of the regular British army. An accomplished surveyor and military engineer, he planned posts and fortifications at Fort Pitt (the present-day Pittsburgh) and at Pensacola, Florida, and he published several topographical and historical works on the Middle Atlantic and Gulf regions. He was in London when the Revolution began and, on declining to serve against his countrymen, was briefly imprisoned in 1779. Released the following year, he resigned his captain's commission and made his way back to America by way of France, where he secured a recommendation from Benjamin Franklin. Soon after landing in Charleston, South Carolina, he joined the staff of Gen. Nathanael Greene; in May 1781 he was named by Congress geographer of the army in the South and in July became geographer of the United States. He retained the title after the end of the war, and he was employed also by various states for official surveying work, including running the western portion of the Pennsylvania–Virginia boundary in 1783. With the passage of the Ordinance of 1785 Hutchins became responsible for beginning the immense task of surveying and platting the public lands of what soon became known as the Northwest Territory. Beginning at the intersection of the Ohio River with the Pennsylvania border, he ran the Geographer's Line due west along 40°38'2" N latitude in six-mile lengths; for the first four of those lengths and a part of the fifth he completed laying out the six-mile-square townships south of the line that, with the two lengths later surveyed by his successors, formed the Seven Ranges, the basis for the land survey of nearly all the country lying to the west of the original 13 states. He made three expeditions west—in 1785, 1786–1787, and 1788–1789—in the course of the work, pausing in 1787 to run the New York–Massachusetts boundary. On the third trip to the scene of the survey he fell ill and died in Pittsburgh on April 28, 1789.

I

Imboden, John Daniel (1823–1895), Confederate army officer. Born near Staunton, Virginia, on February 16, 1823, Imboden attended Washington College (now Washington and Lee University) during 1841–1842 and later took up the study of law. He entered practice in Staunton, served two terms in the legislature, and became active in the militia as organizer of the Staunton Artillery. Commissioned colonel at the beginning of the Civil War, he was conspicuous at Manassas (Bull Run) on July 21, 1861, coming to the support, along with Gen. Barnard E. Bee's brigade, of the forces defending Stone Bridge. In 1862, commanding the 1st Partisan Rangers, he was with Gen. Thomas J. Jackson in the Shenandoah valley, taking part in the battles of Cross Keys, June 8, and Port Republic, June 9, and he led the Staunton Artillery in the capture of Harpers Ferry on September 15. Promoted to brigadier general early in 1863, Imboden undertook on April 20 a raid into West Virginia at Beverly with over 3300 men, sending a second force of 2200 cavalry under Gen. William E. Jones against Moorefield to the north. Railroads, most importantly the Baltimore & Ohio, were cut and bridges burned, vast stores destroyed or taken, and livestock much needed for the Army of Northern Virginia captured. After the two forces joined at Weston, they laid waste the petroleum fields in the Kanawha valley. By May 14 the Imboden Raid was over, and he rejoined the main army under Gen. Robert E. Lee for the invasion of Pennsylvania. Screening the army's left on the march northward, he arrived at Gettysburg on the final day of the battle, July 3, and covered the Confederate retreat. During the Bristoe campaign in October 1863, while the main army moved toward Washington, D.C., Imboden captured the federal garrison at Charleston, West Virginia. In 1864 he was again in the Shenandoah valley, and on May 15 he and Gen. John C. Breckinridge defeated Gen. Franz Sigel at New Market. He continued operating in the valley under Gen. Jubal A. Early until his health failed late in 1864, and he was thereafter on prison duty at Aiken, South Carolina. After the war he resumed the practice of law, first in Richmond and then in Washington County, Virginia. He was much involved in the development of the coal and iron resources of the state. Imboden died in Damascus, Virginia, on August 15, 1895.

Ingersoll, Royal Eason (1883–1976), naval officer. Born on June 20, 1883, in Washington, D.C.,

Ingersoll was the son of a distinguished naval officer. He graduated from the Naval Academy in 1905, and after cruises on the *Missouri* and other vessels he was commissioned an ensign in 1907. In 1907–1909 he served on the *Connecticut* in the world cruise of the Battle Fleet under Adm. Charles S. Sperry. During 1911–1913 he was an instructor at the Academy. Between 1913 and 1916 he served on the *Sarasota* and later the *Cincinnati* of the Asiatic Squadron, while on the former serving also as aide and then flag secretary to the squadron commander. During 1916–1918 he was attached to the communications section of the office of the chief of naval operations, and in 1918–1919 he was communications officer for the U.S. delegation to the Versailles peace conference. After service on the *Connecticut* and the *Arizona* in 1919–1921, he was assigned to naval intelligence in 1921–1924, concentrating on Japanese affairs. During 1924–1926 he commanded the survey ship *Nokomis* in Cuban waters. On graduating from the Naval War College in 1927 he was promoted to captain, and after another year at the college as a staff member he became assistant chief of staff to Adm. William V. Pratt, commander of the Battle Fleet, in 1928; he became Pratt's chief of staff in 1929 when Pratt moved up to command of the U.S. Fleet. He was again in the office of the chief of naval operations in 1930–1933. Ingersoll commanded the *Augusta* in 1933 and the *San Francisco* in 1934–1935, and in 1935 he returned to staff duty in Washington, D.C., as chief of the War Plans Division. Promoted to rear admiral in 1938, he was again on sea duty in 1938–1940 as commander of Cruiser Division 6 of the Pacific Fleet. In 1940 he was named assistant to Adm. Harold R. Stark, chief of naval operations. Shortly after the entry of the United States into World War II, in January 1942, Ingersoll was promoted to vice admiral and appointed commander of the Atlantic Fleet, succeeding Adm. Ernest J. King; he advanced to admiral in July 1942. The responsibilities of the Atlantic Fleet were primarily convoy protection, antisubmarine patrol by surface (until the organization of the Tenth Fleet, under Adm. King, in May 1943) and air, and the naval defense of the Western Hemisphere. Operating out of bases ranging from Iceland to South America, the fleet also carried on much of the training work of the navy; and the North Africa landings of November 1942, commanded by Adm. H. Kent Hewitt, were carried out under Ingersoll's general authority. In November 1944 he relinquished command of the Atlantic Fleet to Adm. Jonas H. Ingram and became commander of the Western Sea Frontier, being appointed at the same time deputy chief of naval operations and deputy commander of the U.S. Fleet, both posts under Adm. King. Ingersoll retained those positions until his retirement in August 1946. He died in Bethesda, Maryland, on May 20, 1976.

Ingraham, Duncan Nathaniel (1802–1891), Confederate naval officer. Born in Charleston, South Carolina, on December 6, 1802, Ingraham was of a line of seamen, his father having been aboard the *Bonhomme Richard* in the fight with the *Serapis*. He was appointed a midshipman in the navy at the age of nine and during the War of 1812 served on the *Congress* and later on the *Madison* in Commodore Isaac Chauncey's Lake Ontario fleet. He was promoted to lieutenant in 1825 and to commander in May 1838. During the Mexican War he took part in the blockade of Veracruz and was flag captain to Commodore David Conner aboard the *Union* in the capture of Tampico, November 14, 1846. From 1850 to 1852 he commanded the Philadelphia navy yard, and in the latter year he took command of the sloop *St. Louis* of the Mediterranean Squadron. In June 1853, on arriving in the harbor of Smyrna, Turkey, he learned that the Austrian brig *Hussar* was holding prisoner one Martin Koszta, a Hungarian exile who had fled to New York in 1851 after the Kossuth uprising and had claimed American citizenship. He had failed to remain in the United States for the required length of time before going to Turkey on business, however, and Ingraham secured advice from the resident American chargé d'affaires before taking steps. On July 2, having received the opinion that Koszta deserved the protection of a citizen, Ingraham cleared the *St. Louis* for action and demanded the release of Koszta by evening. Although the *Hussar* and its supporting vessels were more than a match for the American ship, Ingraham's boldness carried the day, and Koszta was released to the custody of the French consul pending a final diplomatic solution (he was ultimately released to American custody). On his arrival in the United States Ingraham was given a hero's welcome and a medal from Congress. He was promoted to captain in September 1855. He was chief of the Bureau of Ordnance from 1856 to 1860, and in January 1861, on the secession of South Carolina, he curtailed a cruise in command of the *Richmond*, resigned, and in March took a commission as commodore in the Confederate States navy. He was chief of ordnance in Richmond until November 1861, and then was transferred to Charleston, South Carolina, as commander of the naval forces based there. He oversaw construction of two ironclads, the *Palmetto State* and the *Chicora*, and on January 31, 1863, he led them from aboard the former in an attack

on the federal blockading force of ten vessels. The *Palmetto State* rammed the *Mercedita* and forced it to surrender, and both Confederate vessels attacked the *Keystone State*, inflicting heavy damage. The blockade force retired, towing the damaged vessels, but later resumed the blockade when the rams returned to the harbor. Ingraham was relieved of command of the flotilla by Commodore John R. Tucker in March 1863 but remained in command of the Charleston station until the end of the war. He died in Charleston on October 16, 1891.

Ingraham, Prentiss (1843–1904), soldier of fortune and author. Born in Adams County, Mississippi, on December 22, 1843, Ingraham was the son of clergyman and writer Joseph H. Ingraham. He attended Jefferson College, in Mississippi, and Mobile Medical College. He left school in 1861 to enlist in the Confederate army. During his varied service to the Confederacy he was twice wounded, first in the siege of Port Hudson, June–July 1863, and then at Franklin, Tennessee, November 30, 1864. He eventually became a commander of scouts in Texas and, apparently, acquired a taste for war and adventure. After the Civil War ended, he traveled to Mexico to fight under Benito Juarez and later took part in the Austro-Prussian War and performed martial exploits in Crete, in Africa, and in the Cuban revolution beginning in 1868, in which he held the ranks of naval captain and cavalry colonel. His Cuban exploit ended with his escape from a Spanish prison in which he was being held under sentence of death as a filibuster. In 1870 he settled in London and began mining his experiences and his vivid imagination for material for a veritable flood of sensational novels of romance and adventure. More prolific even than his father, he produced nearly 700 novels, most of them for Erastus F. Beadle's Dime Library and Half Dime Library. Living later in New York City and Chicago, he became a close friend of Buffalo Bill Cody, about whom he wrote more than 200 of his books. Among his titles were *The Beautiful Rivals, or Life at Long Branch*, 1884; *Buck Taylor, King of the Cowboys, or Raiders and Rangers*, 1887, about one of the stars of Buffalo Bill's Wild West Show; *Darkie Dan*, 1888; *Cadet Carey of West Point*, 1890; *Red Rovers on Blue Waters*, 1890; *An American Monte Cristo*, 1891; *The Wandering Jew of the Sea*, 1891; *Trailing with Buffalo Bill*, 1899; *Land of Legendary Lore*, 1899; and *The Girl Rough Riders*, 1903. These and others virtually poured from his pen, along with a number of successful plays and countless short stories and poems. "Colonel" Ingraham, as he often styled himself, died at the Beauvoir Confederate Home in Beauvoir, Mississippi, on August 16, 1904.

Ingram, Jonas Howard (1886–1952), naval officer and football official. Born on October 15, 1886, in

Jeffersonville, Indiana, Ingram graduated from the Naval Academy, where he was an outstanding football player, in 1907 and was commissioned an ensign in 1909. During 1909–1912 he alternated sea duty with coaching the Academy football team. Promoted to lieutenant (junior grade), he served on the *Arkansas* in 1912–1915, and, as turret officer of that ship at the occupation of Veracruz, Mexico, in April 1914, won the Medal of Honor. From 1915 to 1917 he was head football coach at the Academy. In April 1917 he was appointed aide and flag lieutenant to Adm. Hugh Rodman, commander of the 6th Battle Squadron attached to the British Grand Fleet. When Rodman became commander of the Pacific Fleet in 1919 Ingram accompanied him and remained on his staff until 1921, when he was named chief of staff of the 4th Naval District at Great Lakes, Illinois. Promoted to commander in 1924, he commanded the *Stoddert* for two years and then returned to the Naval Academy as director of football, later becoming director of athletics. In 1930 he was assigned to the *Pennsylvania*. In 1933 he was named director of public relations for the navy and aide to the secretary of the navy. After a year, 1936–1937, as commander of Destroyer Squadron 6, Battle Fleet, and two years as captain of the New York navy yard, he entered the Naval War College, graduating in 1940. He then commanded the *Tennessee* on convoy duty until January 1941, when he was promoted to rear admiral and went aboard the *Memphis* as commander of the cruiser division, Atlantic Fleet. From April 1941 he patrolled the South Atlantic and the Brazilian coast, securing naval bases there and an air base on Ascension Island from which to carry out submarine operations. He was promoted to vice admiral in February 1942, and in September his command, which had been known as Task Force 3, was designated South Atlantic Force, comprising all U.S. naval and army forces and all British, Free French, and Brazilian naval and air force units in the region. In November 1944 he succeeded Adm. Royal E. Ingersoll in command of the Atlantic Fleet with the rank of admiral, and he remained in that post until his retirement in April 1947. From then until 1949 he was commissioner and president of the short-lived All America Football Conference (absorbed by the National Football League in 1950). In 1949 he became a vice-president of the Reynolds Metals Company. Ingram died on September 10, 1952, in San Diego, California.

Irvine, William (1741–1804), Revolutionary army officer and public official. Born on November 3, 1741, in Enniskillen, County Fermanagh, Ireland, Irvine was educated at Trinity College, Dublin, and after studying medicine served as a surgeon aboard a British man-of-war in the latter part of the Seven Years' War. In 1763 he left the service and emigrated to America, settling the next year in Carlisle, Penn-

sylvania. An early adherent of the colonial cause, he was a member of the provincial convention of July 1774 that called for a general congress, and in January 1776 he was appointed colonel of the 6th Pennsylvania Regiment. The 6th was sent to reinforce Gen. Benedict Arnold at Quebec, but at the battle of Three Rivers, June 8, 1776, Irvine was taken prisoner. Exchanged in May 1778, he reached the army in time to take part in the battle of Monmouth Court House, June 27, and in the aftermath he was a member of the court-martial that tried and suspended Gen. Charles Lee. In May 1779 he was promoted to brigadier general in the Continental army and given command of the 2nd Pennsylvania Brigade. He took part in the expedition of Gen. William Alexander (Lord Stirling) to Staten Island in January 1780 and in Gen. Anthony Wayne's attack at Bull's Ferry on the Hudson River in July. Late in 1781 he was ordered to Fort Pitt to take over the defense of the northwestern frontier. He remained there, struggling with raw, poorly supplied troops and Indian raids, until October 1783. After the war Irvine was given a considerable land grant and in 1785 put in charge of distributing lands granted to Revolutionary veterans. At that time he suggested the acquisition by Pennsylvania of a tract in the northwest known as the Triangle, which would give the state an outlet on Lake Erie; the tract was eventually bought by the United States (from rival claimants New York, Connecticut, and Massachusetts) and sold to Pennsylvania in 1792. In 1786 he was elected to the Continental Congress, in 1790 he was a member of the state constitutional convention, and in 1793 he was elected to the 3rd Congress. In 1794 he was dispatched to western Pennsylvania to negotiate with the leaders of the Whisky Rebellion, and on the failure of that mission he commanded the militia force sent to put down the rebellion. In 1795 he helped found the city of Erie in the Triangle. He was chosen president of the state branch of the Society of the Cincinnati in 1801, and he held the post until his death in Philadelphia on July 29, 1804.

Isherwood, Benjamin Franklin (1822–1915), engineer and naval officer. Born in New York City on October 6, 1822, Isherwood attended Albany Academy for several years and in 1836 went to work for the Utica & Schenectady Railroad. Later he studied civil engineering with his stepfather and then under a district engineer of the Erie Railroad. After a period engaged in the construction of lighthouses he was appointed a first assistant engineer in the newly established Engineer Corps of the navy in May 1844. He was stationed at the Pensacola navy yard for a year and then assigned to the *General Taylor* in 1846. During the Mexican War he served aboard John Ericsson's *Princeton,* the navy's first screw-propeller vessel, and then on the schooner *Spitfire,* which took part in the capture of Frontera, Tabasco, and Tampico and the bombardment of Veracruz. Promoted to chief engineer in October 1848, Isherwood was on special duty with the Navy Department in Washington, D.C., in 1852–1853 and during 1854–1858 was chief engineer of the *San Jacinto* of the East India Squadron. He was again in the Navy Department in 1859–1860, and in the former year the first fruits of his observations, experiments, and practical experience in the design and operation of steam power plants appeared under the title *Engineering Precedents*. In 1863 and 1865 he published the two volumes of *Experimental Researches in Steam Engineering*, a fundamental and even revolutionary contribution to the science of practical design and construction of steam engines. In 1861 he was appointed engineer in chief of the navy, becoming in 1862 chief of the newly established Bureau of Steam Engineering. Under his direction the steam navy grew during the Civil War from 12 frigates and sloops and various odd vessels—28 in all—to over 600. His most famous design was that of the fast, powerful *Wampanoag*-class sloops, called by him "commerce-destroyers," which were a great success in blockade work. During 1869–1870 he was at Mare Island navy yard, California, and he was employed in various special duties—experimentation, inspection of foreign naval work, and service on numerous navy boards—until his retirement in June 1884 as chief engineer with the relative rank of commodore. He was advanced to the relative rank of rear admiral before his death in New York City on June 19, 1915.

Izard, George (1776–1828), army officer and public official. Born on October 21, 1776, in Richmond (now a borough of London), England, Izard was the son of Ralph Izard, a South Carolina planter and later diplomat and member of Congress. The father returned to America in 1780, but the son and his mother remained in France until 1783. He was educated in Charleston and Philadelphia and later studied for five years in Europe. While attending the engineering school of the French army, in June 1794, he was given a commission of second lieutenant in the United States army, and after his return to Charleston in 1797 he was put in command of the harbor fortifications. In July 1799 he was promoted to captain and a few months later placed on the staff of Alexander Hamilton, senior major general of the Provisional Army authorized in anticipation of war with France. He resigned his commission in 1803 but in March 1812 accepted appointment as colonel of the 2nd Artillery. He was promoted to brigadier general in February 1813, and that fall he took part in the ill fated expedition toward Montreal under Gen. Wade Hampton, leading a brigade in the battle on the Chateaugay River on October 26. In the expansion of the army in January 1814 he became major general, and in May 1814 he succeeded Hampton as commander of the Lake Champlain frontier at Plattsburg, New York. In August he was ordered to Sackett's Harbor, leaving Plattsburg open to attack by British troops under Gen. Sir George Prevost and defended only by militia and the Lake Champlain fleet under Commodore Thomas Macdonough. He joined his 4000 men with the troops under Gen. Jacob J. Brown on the Canadian side of the Niagara River after an arduous march of 400 miles. Rather than storm the strong British entrenchments behind the Chippewa River, Izard chose to withdraw to the American side, destroying Fort Erie behind him. His caution was seized upon by John Armstrong, the disgraced secretary of war, who raised a storm of public criticism, and as a result Izard resigned his commission in January 1815. In March 1825 he was appointed governor of Arkansas Territory by President James Monroe. He was an effective governor and was particularly successful in dealing with the Indians of the territory. He died in Little Rock, Arkansas, on November 22, 1828.

J

Jackson, Andrew (1767–1845), army officer and seventh president of the United States. Born on March 15, 1767 to Irish immigrant parents in the Waxhaw settlement on the Carolina frontier—probably in what is now South Carolina—Jackson received little formal schooling. The back-country warfare during the Revolution, in which he took part, left him without a family at fourteen. In 1784 he began the study of law in Salisbury, North Carolina, was admitted to the bar in 1787, and the next year traveled across the Appalachians to the region that was to become Tennessee. He soon gained appointment as prosecuting attorney for the district, then part of North Carolina, and, with the collection of debts as his principal duty in that unsettled area, he became allied with the comparatively wealthy class. In 1791 he married Mrs. Rachel Overton Robards, whose first, unhappy marriage they both mistakenly believed had been dissolved. A divorce on grounds of desertion and adultery was won by her first husband in 1793, whereupon she and Jackson were quietly remarried; the episode was a source of gossip and innuendo throughout Jackson's career. He engaged in land speculation, trade, and planting and in 1795 established his home at The Hermitage, a plantation near Nashville. The following year he helped draft the constitution of the new state of Tennessee and with the aid of his political patron, William Blount, was immediately elected to its one seat in the House of Representatives. In March 1797 he was elected to the Senate but was forced by financial reverses at home to resign a year later; he was soon appointed to the state superior court and he served there until July 1804, when he resigned, again for financial reasons. In 1802 he had been elected major general of the state militia, and from 1804 to 1812 this post was his only connection with public life. In 1812, with the outbreak of war with England, it ceased to be a largely honorary position. His offer of service to the federal government was not taken up, but at the instance of the governor he took the field late in 1813 in command of a militia force to subdue the Creek Indians (Upper Creeks, or "Red Sticks"), allies of the British, who under Red Eagle had in August 1813 perpetrated a massacre at Fort Mims in Mississippi. He campaigned through great difficulties for five months. With about 2000 men he won a victory at Talladega (now in Alabama) on November 8, 1813, and then utterly defeated the Indians at the battle of Horseshoe Bend (Tohopeka), March 27, 1814, and by

the Treaty of Fort Jackson in August 1814 obtained from them a vast region in the Mississippi Territory. Commissioned in April a brigadier general and in May a major general in the regular army, he moved his army south to Mobile. From there he proceeded to Pensacola, Florida, capturing it in November, and then hurried to New Orleans where, aided by a naval force under Commodore Daniel T. Patterson, he repulsed an attempted British invasion by a large force of veteran regulars under Gen. Sir Edward Pakenham (who was killed in the battle) on January 8, 1815. News of his victory reached Washington shortly ahead of news that the war had been ended before the battle by the signing of the Treaty of Ghent. Jackson—nicknamed "Old Hickory"—was by then a national figure and already was considered by many a potential president. He retained the major general's commission and was made commander of the Southern District. In 1818 he was sent to put down the latest in a series of outbreaks (the Seminole War) by the Seminole Indians and in doing so invaded Spanish Florida. In capturing Spanish territory, including Pensacola on May 24, and in executing two British subjects, Alexander Arbuthnot and Robert Armbrister, for stirring up further Indian troubles, he raised a diplomatic and political storm in which John Quincy Adams, the secretary of state, was his staunchest supporter. By virtue of his frontier origins, his philosophy of expansionism, his exploits against the Indians and the British, and his obvious independence, Jackson was by now the hero of the West and South and, by association at least, was the representative of the growing democratic spirit in those sections. Although for a time he disavowed presidential aspirations, friends and supporters began preparing for the campaign of 1824. After a brief period as territorial governor of Florida in March–July 1821 he retired to The Hermitage until he was elected to the Senate in March 1823. At the end of the electoral balloting in the next year's presidential election he led by 99 votes to Adams's 84, the stricken William H. Crawford's 41, and Henry Clay's 37; the contest went to the House for decision and Adams was chosen. When Clay, who had controlled the deciding votes, became secretary of state in Adams's cabinet the Jackson group raised the cry of "corrupt bargain." Organizing and campaigning began immediately for 1828, however, (Jackson resigned his Senate seat in October 1825), and that year Jackson defeated Adams decisively, 178 to 83. Almost from the beginning his administration was beset by controversy. Objections to his application of the spoils system were followed closely by the social ostracism of Peggy O'Neale Eaton, the wife of the secretary of war, who had Jackson's social backing, by other cabinet wives, an affair which began the split between Jackson and Vice-President John C. Calhoun. Other problems followed from a continuing rivalry between officials of the executive branch and Jackson's personal advisers, who formed the "kitchen cabinet." The protective Tariff of 1828—the "Tariff of Abominations"—became a crucial issue in the growing area of disagreement between the North and the South, and Jackson and Calhoun had adopted clear and completely opposed positions by 1830. In 1832 South Carolina, with Calhoun's support, nullified the tariffs of 1828 and 1832. Jackson immediately and vehemently denounced the move and in March 1833 secured from Congress both the authority—the Force Bill—to use federal troops to insure the state's compliance with federal law and a reduction of the objectionable rates. South Carolina then withdrew its earlier nullification proclamation but saved face by nullifying the Force Bill. The clash over the states'-rights issue was thus postponed. Meanwhile Jackson had been reelected over Henry Clay—Calhoun having been replaced by Martin Van Buren—by 219 electoral votes to 49, following a campaign based primarily on the issue of the Second Bank of the United States. Jackson had vetoed a bill rechartering the bank in July 1832 and thereby reinforced his popularity; he was vindicated in the election and thereafter continued his campaign against the bank by withdrawing from it all deposits of federal money. By the time the bank's charter expired in 1836 the government's money had been distributed among several state banks; this action, combined with the policy begun the same year of accepting only gold or silver in payment for public land, led directly to a financial panic in 1837, after Jackson had been succeeded as president by Van Buren. When Jackson left office in March 1837, the large but disorganized movement of voters, largely Westerners and Southerners, that had originally elected him had been transformed into the Democratic party. Despite the fact that he had often had little sympathy for the movement and had in fact often allied himself with opposing interests, his name became firmly attached to it. He was in many ways more the accepted symbol than the living representative of "Jacksonian democracy." His rise from humble frontier origins to national eminence, his success in dealing with the established political powers, and his concept of a vigorous president all appealed to the restless, optimistic young nation. His policies were those of the democratic frontier: monetary inflation; expansionism—he attempted but failed to arrange for the annexation of Texas after its revolution; Indi-

an removal—he refused to move to enforce a Supreme Court ruling in 1832 that voided a Georgia attempt to annex Cherokee land and thus set the stage for the Indians' relocation across the Mississippi; and energetic nationalism. Even more popular on leaving the presidency than he had been on entering it, he retired to his home and remained there in declining health until his death on June 8, 1845 at The Hermitage, where he was buried.

Jackson, Thomas Jonathan (1824–1863), "Stonewall," Confederate army officer. Born on January 21, 1824, in Clarksburg, Virginia (now West Virginia), Jackson was orphaned early in life and was brought up by relatives. Despite limited schooling he received an appointment to West Point in 1842 and graduated four years later. Commissioned a second lieutenant of artillery, he was immediately sent to join Gen. Winfield Scott's army in Mexico, where he distinguished himself at the battles of Veracruz, Cerro Gordo, and Chapultepec and rose to brevet major. For three years he served at various posts, but in 1851 he accepted an appointment as a professor at the Virginia Military Institute, and in February 1852 he resigned his commission. He lived quietly for the next ten years in Lexington, Virginia. With the outbreak of the Civil War in April 1861 he was ordered to move his cadet corps to Richmond. He was commissioned a colonel in the Confederate army and in June was promoted to brigadier general and assigned to duty under Gen. Joseph E. Johnston. In July he was ordered to the field at the first battle of Manassas (Bull Run), and there his stout resistance to the Union advance at the Henry House earned him the nickname "Stonewall" from Gen. Barnard E. Bee. In October Jackson was promoted to major general and a month later assumed command of the forces in the Shenandoah valley. There, early in 1862, he began his famous Valley campaign, in which, by rapid movements of his forces, he tied up much greater numbers of Union troops, prevented reinforcements from being sent to join Gen. George B. McClellan's Peninsula campaign against Richmond, and threatened Washington. After suffering heavy losses in an attack on Gen. James Shields at Kernstown, March 23, he defeated Gen. Nathaniel P. Banks at Front Royal, May 23, and Winchester, May 24–25, and then maneuvered between two superior forces, sending a division under Gen. Richard S. Ewell to defeat Gen. John C. Frémont at Cross Keys, June 8, and himself disposing of Gen. Shields at Port Republic, June 9. Gen. Irvin McDowell's move into Virginia from the north was pulled back to Washington as a result of Jackson's success in clearing the valley of federal forces. By this time Jackson was working closely with Gen. Robert E. Lee, and the two formed an apparently invincible team. In June Jackson's forces hurried by train to Richmond to help expel McClellan from Virginia. In the Seven Days' Battles he fought to exhaustion, and, after failing to pursue the enemy through White Oak Swamp, he retired from the line before the battle of Malvern Hill on July 1. In August Jackson and his famed "foot-cavalry" executed an encircling movement to the north and on August 27 destroyed Gen. John Pope's base at Manassas Junction. Jackson held his position at Groveton, August 28–29, and at the second battle of Manassas (Bull Run), August 29–30, rejoined Lee and again drove the Union forces back to the Potomac. He took conspicuous part in the invasion of Maryland in September, particularly during the action at Sharpsburg (Antietam), September 17. In October he was made a lieutenant general and placed in command of one of Lee's two corps, and on December 13 he helped repulse Gen. Ambrose E. Burnside at Fredericksburg. In early May 1863 Jackson performed his last great service. Outnumbered by more than two to one, Lee's forces were threatened at Chancellorsville by Gen. Joseph Hooker. Jackson was sent in another encircling movement and on May 2 took the enemy completely by surprise, rolling up Gen. Oliver O. Howard's XI Corps on Hooker's right flank and forcing the Army of the Potomac to retreat. In the confusion of this twilight attack, however, Jackson was caught in the rifle fire of his own men. Lee wrote to him two days later: "You are better off than I am, for while you have lost your *left,* I have lost my *right* arm." A stern and respected leader of men and a master tactician, Jackson had been indeed Lee's right arm, and he was, in fact, lost to Lee and the South. He contracted pneumonia in his weakened state and died on May 10, 1863, at Guinea Station (now Guinea), south of Fredericksburg, Virginia.

Jadwin, Edgar (1865–1931), army officer and engineer. Born in Honesdale, Pennsylvania, on August 7, 1865, Jadwin attended Lafayette College for two years before entering West Point, from which he graduated in 1890. He was commissioned in the engineers, and after two years in construction work on Ellis Island in New York harbor, he was sent to the Engineer School of Application, Willet's Point (now Fort Totten), New York, graduating in 1893. After various other assignments and promotion to first lieutenant in May 1895, he was attached to the office of the chief of engineers in 1897. In June 1898 he was appointed major of the 3rd Engineer Volunteers, of which he became lieutenant colonel in September, and saw duty in Matanzas, Cuba. After the Spanish–American War he served in routine assignments in New York and California and during 1903–1907 had charge of the construction of a sea wall and ship channel in Galveston, Texas. He was promoted to captain in January 1900 and to major in September 1906. In 1907 he was appointed division engineer of the Chagres Division of the Panama Canal construc-

tion project, and in 1908 he was moved to the Atlantic Division; in his four years with the canal he built the Gatun Dam and spillway and the Colón breakwater. In 1911 he was briefly in command of the Tennessee engineer district and was then ordered to duty in the office of the chief of engineers. Jadwin was promoted to lieutenant colonel in October 1913. After a year in charge of the Pittsburgh district and of upper Ohio River work he organized in 1917 the 15th Engineers (Railway) for service in World War I, receiving promotion to temporary colonel in July and in that month leading the regiment to France (en route it became the first American regiment to pass through England under arms). He served as chief engineer of advanced lines of communication until February 1918, as director of light railways and roads until March, and thereafter as director of construction and forestry, Service of Supply; he was promoted to temporary brigadier general in December 1917. In all Jadwin oversaw the construction of nearly 1000 miles of railroad, nearly 10,000 miles of roads, and huge numbers of barracks, hospitals, supply and storage areas, and veterinary compounds, along with water supply, sewage, and refrigeration facilities. In 1919 he served on missions to Poland and the Ukraine and then, promoted to permanent colonel in September of that year, was sent in 1920 to Fort Sam Houston, Texas, as VIII Corps area engineer. From 1922 to 1924 he was Southeast District engineer in Charleston, South Carolina. In June 1924 he was promoted to brigadier general and named assistant chief of engineers. He became chief of engineers with the rank of major general in June 1926, and he retained that post until his retirement in August 1929 in the rank of lieutenant general, the first chief of engineers to attain that grade. He served as chairman, 1924–1929, of a joint Canadian-American board for the development of navigation in the St. Lawrence River, and following the Mississippi River flood of 1927 developed the comprehensive Jadwin Plan for flood control, which was subsequently adopted. He served in several advisory capacities after retirement and in 1930, after declining appointment as chairman of the new Federal Power Commission, accepted the chairmanship of the Interoceanic Canal Board, created to investigate the need for a Nicaraguan canal. While engaged in that work Jadwin died in the Panama Canal Zone on March 2, 1931.

James, Daniel, Jr. (1920–   ), air force officer. Born on February 11, 1920, in Pensacola, Florida, James learned to fly while attending Tuskegee Institute, and after graduation in 1942 he continued in civilian flight training until receiving appointment as a cadet in the Army Air Corps in January 1943. He was commissioned in July and through the remainder of World War II trained pilots for the all-black 99th Pursuit Squadron and worked in other assignments.

He was subsequently stationed in Ohio and in the Philippines. During the Korean War he flew 101 missions in fighters. From 1953 to 1956 he commanded the 437th and then the 60th Fighter Interception Squadron at Otis Air Force Base, Massachusetts, receiving promotion to major in that period; and on graduating from the Air Command and Staff College, Maxwell Air Force Base, Alabama, in 1957 he was assigned to staff duty in Washington, D.C. From 1960 to 1964 he was stationed in England, from 1964 to 1966 in Arizona, and from 1966 to 1967 in Vietnam, where he flew 78 combat missions. By then a colonel, he was vice commander of the 33rd Tactical Fighter Wing, Eglin Air Force Base, Florida, in 1967–1969 and then, promoted to brigadier general, was named base commander of Wheelus Air Force Base, Libya. In March 1970 James became deputy assistant secretary of defense for public affairs, and in that post he advanced to major general. In September 1974, with the rank of lieutenant general, he became vice commander of the Military Airlift Command at Scott Air Force Base, Illinois. In September 1975 he became the first black officer to attain four-star rank in any service. He was at that time named commander of the North American Air Defense Command (NORAD), with responsibility for all aspects of the air defense of the United States and Canada. James was also a much sought-after public speaker and devoted considerable time to addressing youth groups, particularly minority students.

Jasper, William (1750?–1779), Revolutionary soldier. Born about 1750, probably near Georgetown, South Carolina, Jasper enlisted in a company of the 2nd South Carolina Infantry under Col. William Moultrie in July 1775. He was appointed sergeant in the company and in September went with it to Fort Johnson, which commanded from James Island the harbor of Charleston (then styled Charles Town). In the spring of 1776 the 2nd took up a new post in Fort Sullivan, on nearby Sullivan Island; the fort was an incomplete structure of palmetto logs and sand. During the bombardment of the fort on June 28, 1776, the staff of Col. Moultrie's blue flag was shot away, the flag falling into a ditch outside the walls. Braving a galling fire from the British fleet only 400 yards off, Jasper leaped over the wall, tied the flag to a stick, and planted it on the parapet of the fort facing the fleet. For that act he was rewarded by Gov. John Rutledge and offered a lieutenant's commission, which he declined because he believed himself insufficiently educated. He was thereafter a roving scout in South Carolina and Georgia, later serving under Gen. Francis Marion and Gen. Benjamin Lincoln and performing several exploits that were in later years favorite material for legendizers. He was with Lincoln in the unsuccessful assault on British-held Savannah in September–October 1779, and on Octo-

ber 9 he was killed while planting the colors of the 2nd South Carolina on the parapet of the Spring Hill redoubt.

Jesup, Thomas Sidney (1788–1860), army officer. Born in Berkeley County, Virginia (now West Virginia), on December 16, 1788, Jesup entered the army as a second lieutenant in the infantry in May 1808. He was promoted to first lieutenant in December 1809, to captain in January 1813, and to major in April 1813. Early in the War of 1812 he was on the staff of Gen. William Hull. In 1814, commanding the 25th Infantry in Gen. Winfield Scott's brigade, he distinguished himself at Chippewa, July 5, winning a brevet to lieutenant colonel, and again at Lundy's Lane, July 25, for which he was brevetted colonel. He was promoted to lieutenant colonel in April 1817 and to colonel in March 1818. From March to May 1818 he was temporarily adjutant general of the army, and in the latter month he was appointed quartermaster general with the rank of brigadier general. He was an able and effective administrator and is generally considered the father of the modern Quartermaster Corps. He held the post for 42 years, a span far exceeding the service of any other officer as head of a department or corps. He was brevetted major general in May 1828 for his first ten years' service. In May 1836 he was given a field command in operations against the Creek Indians, and in December of that year he was given command of the army in Florida, then engaged in the second Seminole War. He managed to win several skirmishes and battles, though none was decisive; and in frustration he called for a council, under a flag of truce, with the Seminole leader, Osceola. When Osceola appeared Jesup made him prisoner, an act that failed to end the war and outraged public and congressional opinion. Jesup was wounded in a skirmish in January 1838 and in May of that year was relieved of command (he was succeeded by Gen. Zachary Taylor). He continued in his duties as quartermaster general, with notable success in the Mexican War, until his death in Washington, D.C., on June 10, 1860.

Johnson, Clarence Leonard (1910–), aeronautical engineer. Born on February 27, 1910, in Ishpeming, Michigan, Johnson grew up there and in Flint. He was educated at Flint Junior College and the University of Michigan, graduating from the latter in 1932 and earning a master's degree in aeronautical engineering the next year. In 1933 he joined the staff of Lockheed Aircraft in Burbank, California, and five years later was named chief research engineer. His speed and accuracy in design, together with his acute problem-solving insight and ability to put together design teams of great productivity, made Johnson one of the most prolific and successful creators of aircraft in the world. His first complete design was that of the P-38 Lightning, a one-seater (later modified to a two-seater) interceptor and fighter-bomber that featured unorthodox twin-tail booms; it was used with great effectiveness in every theater of World War II. In 1943 he designed the P-80, subsequently redesignated the F-80 Shooting Star, the air force's first tactical jet fighter and a plane that was produced in greater numbers than any previous military aircraft because of the demand for it in the Korean War. The same year saw the maiden flight of the Constellation, a transport that saw some war service as the C-69 but became the world's leading commercial liner beginning in 1946, setting a great many commercial speed records. The distinctive triple-tailed Constellation was surpassed in 1950 by the Superconstellation, also a Johnson design. He was named chief engineer of Lockheed in 1952, vice-president for research and development in 1956, and vice-president for advanced development in 1958. In 1956 his F-104 Starfighter was unveiled, a Mach-2 fighter with remarkably small wings and great maneuverability. In the same year, but under top security, his U-2 high-altitude reconnaissance plane went into service and remained a secret and invaluable tool of military intelligence until one was shot down inside the U.S.S.R. in May 1960. Johnson subsequently improved upon the U-2 with the A-11 (navy YF-12A) and the SR-71, the latter of which, put into production in 1964, could fly at Mach 3 and 100,000 feet. Virtually every one of Johnson's 40 or more designs represented major breakthroughs in aeronautical science and practice, and he was widely honored for his achievements, receiving the Medal of Freedom from President Lyndon B. Johnson in 1964 as well as the Wright Brothers Medal, 1941, the Collier Trophy, 1959 and 1964, the National Medal of Science, 1966, and many others. He retired from Lockheed in January 1975. On the same day he was inducted into the Aviation Hall of Fame at Dayton, Ohio.

Johnson, Harold Keith (1912–   ), army officer. Born on February 22, 1912, in Bowesmont, North Dakota, Johnson graduated from West Point in 1933 and was commissioned in the infantry. While serving in routine assignments he was promoted to first lieutenant in June 1936, and he graduated from the Infantry School, Fort Benning, Georgia, in 1938. In 1940 he was sent to join the 57th Infantry, the "Philippine Scouts," in Manila, Philippines, becoming a captain in September of that year, and soon after the outbreak of World War II the 57th took up positions on the Bataan Peninsula. By the fall of Bataan in April 1942 Johnson had advanced to lieutenant colonel commanding a battalion of the 57th. He survived the terrible "Bataan death march" and prisoner-of-war camps in the Philippines, in Japan, and finally in Korea before being liberated in September 1945. On

his return to the United States he entered the Command and General Staff College, Fort Leavenworth, Kansas, graduating in 1947, and in 1950 completed the course at the Armed Forces Staff College, Norfolk, Virginia. In the latter year he was sent to Korea in command of the 1st Provisional Infantry Battalion and saw almost constant combat, becoming assistant chief of staff of the I Corps in February 1951 and receiving promotion to colonel. He returned to the United States late in 1951, graduated from the Army War College in 1953, and in January 1956, after three years of General Staff duty, was promoted to brigadier general and named assistant commander of the 8th Infantry Division at Fort Carson, Colorado, and later in Germany. In September 1957 he became chief of staff of the Seventh Army. In April 1959 he became assistant chief of staff, U.S. Army in Europe, and late in that year he was named chief of staff of the Central Army Group, North Atlantic Treaty Organization forces in Europe, with the rank of major general. In August 1960 he was appointed commandant of the Command and General Staff College. He returned to General Staff duty early in 1963, becoming deputy chief of staff with the rank of lieutenant general in July and serving also as deputy chief of staff of the Joint Chiefs of Staff. A year later he succeeded Gen. Earle G. Wheeler as chief of staff of the army with the rank of general, and he held the post during the period of rapidly increasing involvement of U.S. combat forces in Vietnam. Johnson relinquished the post to Gen. William C. Westmoreland and retired from the army in July 1968. In 1969 he was chosen president of the Herbert Hoover Presidential Library Association; he was also a director of various defense-related business corporations.

Johnson, Hugh Samuel (1882–1942), army officer, public official, and journalist. Born in Fort Scott, Kansas, on August 5, 1882, Johnson grew up from 1893 in Oklahoma Territory. He graduated from West Point in 1903 and was commissioned a second lieutenant of cavalry. In 1906 he was acting quartermaster of army relief work in the wake of the San Francisco earthquake. After years of routine service, during which he published two books of boys' adventure stories, he was sent by the army to the University of California, where he earned a B.A. in 1915 and a doctor of jurisprudence degree the next year. In 1916, promoted to captain in July, he was a member of Gen. John J. Pershing's Mexican Punitive Expedition but was soon transferred to Washington, where, as deputy provost marshal general (with the rank of major from May 1917) under Gen. Enoch H. Crowder, he helped devise and direct the conscription program during World War I. He also served on the War Industries Board with Bernard Baruch and headed the Purchase, Storage, and Traffic Division of the General Staff. He rose rapidly in rank to temporary lieutenant colonel in August 1917, to temporary colonel in January 1918, and in April 1918 to temporary brigadier general (at 35 the youngest since the Civil War), but he was unsuccessful in obtaining a combat command. He resigned from the service in February 1919 and entered business. Among his activities was serving as an industrial and economic adviser to Baruch, who brought him to the notice of Gov. Franklin D. Roosevelt of New York. Soon after attaining the presidency Roosevelt appointed him director of the National Recovery Administration (NRA) in June 1933. Johnson became, with his gruff and forcefully direct manner, a most colorful character in government and a particular favorite of the press, but he was not a good administrator, and he resigned from the NRA in October 1934. His experiences were recounted, pithily, in *The Blue Eagle from Egg to Earth*, 1935. In that year, after a widely noted attack on Father Charles E. Coughlin and Sen. Huey P. Long in a dinner speech, he was immediately signed to write a daily newspaper column for the Scripps-Howard syndicate. He accepted the job of director of the New York City branch of the Works Progress Administration (WPA) shortly thereafter, but he was unhappy with both the philosophy and the technicalities of the WPA, and he resigned after three months. He turned against Roosevelt after the "courtpacking" incident of 1937 and continued in his column for the rest of his life to excoriate Roosevelt and the New Deal, charging that the United States was unprepared for war and urging national rearmament. In 1940 he violently opposed Roosevelt's attempt to win a third term in the White House, while he painted alarming pictures of the threat of a Fascist invasion of the United States. Johnson was also a popular lecturer and radio commentator. He died in Washington, D.C., on April 15, 1942.

Johnson, James (1774–1826), militia officer. Born on January 1, 1774, in Orange County, Virginia, Johnson moved with his family to Pennsylvania and then to Kentucky, settling at Bryan Station, near Lexington, in 1780. Johnson's brother Richard Mentor was born in that year. In 1782 Bryan Station was the scene of an Indian attack, one of the leaders of which was Simon Girty, the "great renegade." In 1813 James Johnson was lieutenant colonel of his brother's regiment of mounted riflemen serving under Gen. William Henry Harrison, and at the battle of the Thames, October 5, 1813, against some 900 British regulars and about 2000 Indians under Tecumseh, he led the mounted assault on the regulars. Advancing slowly into two deadly volleys from the British, he allowed them to empty their muskets and then charged through their line, completely routing them. Johnson returned to private life in Kentucky. His business ventures, including a contract in 1819–1820 to supply troops posted on the Missouri and Mississippi rivers,

were generally failures. He was elected to Congress in 1824, but before the expiration of his term he died on August 13, 1826, in Great Crossings, Scott County, Kentucky.

Johnson, Richard Mentor (1780–1850), militia officer and vice-president of the United States. Born in Beargrass, an early settlement on the site of present-day Louisville, Kentucky, in 1780, Johnson grew up at Bryan Station, near Lexington. He received little formal education, but he studied law under professors at Transylvania University and was admitted to the bar in 1802. In 1804 he was elected to the state legislature and served there until 1807, when he entered the House of Representatives, to which he was reelected as a Democrat five successive times, serving from March 1807 to March 1819. With the outbreak of the War of 1812 he became colonel of a Kentucky regiment of mounted riflemen; serving under Gen. William Henry Harrison, he performed gallantly at the battle of the Thames, October 5, 1813. At his suggestion the mounted troops divided, one column under his brother, Lt. Col. James Johnson, attacking the British regulars and the other, led by himself, charging the Indians. He was seriously wounded and in the battle reputedly killed Tecumseh. He returned to his seat in the House as soon as he recovered and in 1818 was honored by a congressional resolution and the presentation of a ceremonial sword. The following year he was elected to the Kentucky legislature and subsequently by that body to the Senate, where he took in December 1819 the seat vacated by John J. Crittenden; he remained in the Senate until March 1829. He was a leading advocate of the abolition of imprisonment for debt, and he kept up a campaign to that end until the Senate approved his bill in 1832. He also added to his national reputation by his authorship in 1829 of a committee report on religious freedom occasioned by a heated public controversy over the propriety of operating post offices on Sunday. He was defeated for reelection in 1829 but was promptly elected to the House of Representatives, where he remained four terms, March 1829–March 1837. He was a thoroughly regular Democrat and an even more regular supporter of President Andrew Jackson; he was a close and trusted assistant to the President and in 1836 was handpicked by him to be Martin Van Buren's running mate. His selection for the vice-presidential nomination was ratified by the party, but in the election none of the four candidates for vice-president received a majority of the electoral vote. In the only such occasion in U.S. history, Johnson was chosen for the post by the Senate in February 1837. His four-year term was uneventful, but he became estranged from party leaders and in 1840 the party refused to make a nomination for vice-president. He returned to Kentucky, served again for a time in the legislature, 1841–1842, and died in Frankfort on November 19, 1850.

Johnson, Sir William (1715–1774), colonial army officer and public official.

Born in County Meath, Ireland, in 1715, Johnson had come to America by early 1738, in which year he was managing an estate in the Mohawk valley of New York that belonged to his uncle, Sir Peter Warren. In 1739 he purchased a tract of land of his own, the first in a series of acquisitions that continued throughout his life and finally resulted in his possessing one of the largest landed estates in the colonies. He set about developing his properties with great energy, engaged successfully in the fur trade, and made it his business to cultivate the friendship of the Indians of the Six Nations, particularly the Mohawks, who were his neighbors. In 1745 he was able to restrain the Six Nations from allying with the French in King George's War; in consequence he was appointed colonel of the Six Nations and given responsibility for their affairs by Gov. George Clinton in 1746. His affairs prospered in the later 1740s, and he was appointed a member of the Council of New York in 1750, a post he held for the rest of his life. In spite of the protests of the Indians, he resigned as manager of the affairs of the Six Nations following a dispute with the New York assembly, but he continued as an unofficial adviser both to the tribes and to the colonial government. He was persuaded to take up duties with the Indians again by Gen. Edward Braddock in 1755, a year that saw the resumption of the French and Indian Wars, and he was at the same time commissioned a major general and placed in command of the British force sent against Crown Point. At Lake George, on September 8, 1755, he was attacked by a force of French and Indians under Baron Ludwig August Dieskau. Johnson soundly defeated the force led by Dieskau in what came to be called the Battle of Bloody Pond, but he failed to capture Crown Point. His victory over Dieskau secured the northern border, however, and made him a hero. George II made him a baronet in November 1755, and the next year he was named sole agent and superintendent of the affairs of the Six Nations (a superintendent also being appointed for the tribes south of the Ohio River). He devoted himself in the years that followed to protecting the northern frontiers; he was in charge of the force that finally took Niagara on July 25, 1759, and he joined Gen. Jeffrey Amherst in his successful attack on Montreal the next year. The fall of French Canada brought a vast new territory and many tribes under his jurisdiction, and even with the able assistance of his deputy, George Croghan, he was often overwhelmed by the difficulty of his task. A remarkable accomplishment was his journey to Detroit in 1761, where in September he held council with Indian leaders, allayed their resentments, and managed to forestall the outbreak of hostilities. After the conclusion of Pontiac's War he met at Oswego, New York, in July 1766 with Pontiac and other leaders and settled the peace in the Northwest. He favored a centralized and independent Indian department as well as centralized control of the fur trade, and he attempted to restrain settlement by whites in Indian hunting grounds and even advocated the drawing of an Indian boundary beyond which whites were not to pass, although he found an attempt to do so in the Proclamation of 1763 unworkable. In 1768 he negotiated the treaty of Fort Stanwix, signed November 5, which pushed the settlement line west to the Tennessee River. His many friendly negotiations with Indian leaders resulted in vast increases in his own estates, but he nevertheless respected the Indians and worked for a resolution of differences advantageous to both sides. He supported education for Indians and missionary activities among them, and he never ceased to be held by the Indians themselves in high esteem, in part because of the genuine interest manifested in his command of their language and adoption of their clothing and customs. After the death of his first wife he took an Indian woman named Caroline, who was the niece of a Mohawk chief, as his housekeeper and by her had three children; she was succeeded by Molly Brant, sister of Joseph Brant, by whom he had eight children. When Lord Dunmore's War broke out in Virginia in 1774, he was called upon again to try to keep the Six Nations from becoming involved. On July 11, 1774, at his home, Johnson Hall, shortly after giving a long speech to the Indians in reply to their complaints about white encroachments and the Indian trade, he was taken ill and died.

Johnston, Albert Sidney (1803–1862), Confederate army officer.

Born in Washington, Kentucky, on February 2, 1803, Johnston was appointed to West Point in 1822 and on graduating four years later was commissioned in the infantry. After a series of posts —including service as a regimental adjutant in the Black Hawk War—he resigned his commission in April 1834 because of the illness of his wife. After her death the next year he tried farming near St. Louis but soon gave it up and went to Texas, where he enlisted as a private in the Texas army. His progress upward was swift. Within a year he had been appointed adjutant general and, as senior brigadier general, he assumed command of the army in January 1837. His rapid rise aroused the jealousy of a rival who challenged him to a duel in which he was seriously wounded. He was well again by the end of 1838, when he was appointed secretary of war of the Republic of Texas. He fell out with Gen. Sam Houston, however, and resigned in March 1840, taking up farming at China Grove, in Brazoria County, where he suffered financial difficulties. Upon the outbreak of the Mexican War he offered his services and was commissioned colonel of the 1st Texas Rifle volunteers. He later resumed farming until December 1849, when he was commissioned paymaster and major in the U.S. army. In 1855 he assumed command of the 2nd Cavalry, whose lieutenant colonel was Robert E. Lee and whose majors were George H. Thomas and William J. Hardee. He was appointed commander of the Department of Texas in April 1856, and in 1857–1858, with the rank of brevet brigadier general, he conducted a successful and bloodless campaign against the Mormons in Utah. He commanded, in addition to the 2nd Cavalry, the 5th and 10th Infantry regiments and two artillery battalions in the expedition. After a winter of hardships at Fort Bridger the expedition entered Salt Lake City unopposed in June 1858 and established federal authority. Johnston sailed to San Francisco at the end of 1860 to take command of the Department of the Pacific, but when Texas seceded from the Union in April 1861 he resigned his commission, although he continued to serve until relieved formally by Gen. Edwin V. Sumner. Offered the position of second in command of the Union army under Gen. Winfield Scott, he refused and returned to the South. Jefferson Davis appointed him the second-ranking general in the Confederate army (after Samuel Cooper) in September 1861 and placed him in command of the Western Department. He set about creating an army in Kentucky to defend the Confederacy's vulnerable flank there, but he was hindered by his inability to obtain enough troops or supplies. At the hands of Gen. Ulysses S. Grant and other Union commanders he suffered a series of reverses in engagements—notably Fort Henry and Fort Donelson, both lost to Grant in February—in which his men were usually heavily outnumbered. In March his army, now designated the Army of Mississippi and reinforced by troops from several states, concentrated at Corinth, Mississippi. The army's three line and one reserve corps were commanded by Gen. Leonidas Polk, Gen. Braxton Bragg, Gen. Hardee, and Gen. John C. Breckinridge. Johnston gained a celebrated victory over Grant at the battle of Pittsburg Landing (Shiloh), Tennessee, where, on April 6, 1862, he struck a surprise blow at a strong Union position and rolled back Grant's men until they broke in rout and withdrew to the Tennessee River. He was mortally wounded, however, and died that day on the field. Bereft of his leadership and facing freshly reinforced Union troops, the Confederate forces were compelled to retire on the second day of the battle.

Johnston, Joseph Eggleston (1807–1891), Confederate army officer. Born near Farmville, Virginia, on February 3, 1807, Johnston graduated from West Point in 1829. For eight years he served as an artillery officer, seeing action in the Seminole War

and being promoted to first lieutenant in July 1836. He resigned in May 1837 to become a civil engineer. A year later renewed Indian troubles in Florida brought him back into the army as a lieutenant in the Corps of Topographical Engineers. Promoted to captain in September 1846, he performed with distinction under Gen. Winfield Scott during the Mexican War, receiving brevet rank of colonel following the battle of Cerro Gordo, April 18, 1847. Returning to duty with the topographical engineers, he served in Texas and in the Mormon expedition of 1857–1858 under Col. Albert S. Johnston, and in June 1860 he was appointed quartermaster general of the army with the rank of brigadier general. He resigned his commission when Virginia seceded from the Union in April 1861 and offered his services to his native state. He was named brigadier general of the Confederate army in May and placed in command of the Army of the Shenandoah. In July 1861, using his cavalry under Col. J. E. B. Stuart as a screen, he adroitly evaded the Union force that was intended to tie him down at Harpers Ferry and reinforced the beleaguered Gen. P. G. T. Beauregard at Manassas, his lead brigade under Gen. Thomas J. Jackson arriving on July 20. The next day his forces distinguished themselves in the first battle of Manassas (Bull Run). He was the ranking officer at this first major Confederate victory (although he yielded tactical command to Beauregard), and he was subsequently promoted to general and placed in command of the Army of Northern Virginia. The next spring he was charged with opposing Gen. George B. McClellan's drive on Richmond in the Peninsular campaign. Johnston withdrew from the peninsula toward Richmond, leaving Gen. James Longstreet to fight a rearguard action at Williamsburg, May 5, and then making a poorly coordinated attack on McClellan's divided army at Fair Oaks (Seven Pines), May 31, during which he was badly wounded. He passed command of the army to Gen. Robert E. Lee. Upon his recovery in November 1862 he was placed in command of the Department of the West, consisting of the armies of Gen. Braxton Bragg, Gen. John C. Pemberton, and, nominally, Gen. Edmund Kirby-Smith. In May 1863 he took personal command as Gen. Ulysses S. Grant threatened Pemberton at Vicksburg. From his base in Jackson, Mississippi, he was unable to reach Vicksburg, and his evacuation order to Pemberton there was countermanded by Jefferson Davis. Driven out of Jackson by Gen. William T. Sherman on May 14, he could only watch as Vicksburg surrendered in July. In December he took command of the Army of Tennessee from Gen. Braxton Bragg. His force, too weak to move northward, entrenched itself near Dalton, Georgia, awaiting attack by Gen. William T. Sherman's forces from the north. Sherman preferred to maneuver, and Johnston, outnumbered and outflanked, found himself forced to retreat slowly toward Atlanta. Only one battle stood out from the constant maneuvering and skirmishing, and in that, at Kennesaw Mountain, June 27, 1864, Johnston was victorious for the moment. In July, with his back to Atlanta, he was replaced in command by Gen. John B. Hood. In February 1865 Gen. Robert E. Lee restored him to command of the Army of Tennessee, now broken and scattered, and all troops in Florida, Georgia, and South Carolina, with orders to oppose Sherman's march northward through the Carolinas. In that hopeless campaign his forces were outnumbered four to one. After two months of maneuvers and minor engagements he was forced to surrender to Sherman on April 26 at Durham Station, North Carolina. In the years following the war he engaged in the insurance business in Savannah, Georgia, and in 1878 was elected to a term in the House of Representatives from Richmond, Virginia. He remained in Washington, D.C., thereafter and in 1885 was appointed U.S. railroad commissioner by President Grover Cleveland. Johnston died on March 21, 1891, in Washington, D.C.

Jones, Catesby ap Roger (1821–1877), Confederate naval officer. Born in Fairfield, Virginia, on April 15, 1821, Jones was the son of Col. Roger Jones, adjutant general of the army from 1825 to 1852. The younger Jones entered the navy as a midshipman in June 1836 and saw his first sea duty aboard the *Macedonian* under his uncle, Capt. Thomas ap Catesby Jones. He served some years in the Pacific Squadron, for a time as aide to Commodore George C. Read, and during 1842–1843 he was in the Depot of Charts and Instruments in Washington, D.C. Subsequent sea duty took him around the world in 1843–1845, and during the Mexican War he was aboard the *Ohio* in the Pacific, seeing little action. He was promoted to lieutenant in May 1849. From 1853 to 1856 he worked under Lt. John A. B. Dahlgren at the Washington navy yard, perfecting the Dahlgren gun, and thereafter he served as ordnance officer on various ships until 1860. In April 1861, following the secession of Virginia, Jones was appointed captain in the Virginia navy, and in June he was commissioned lieutenant in the Confederate States navy. In November he was ordered to the new ironclad *Virginia* (ex-*Merrimac*) to assist in fitting her out, and when the vessel entered active service the following spring he was executive officer. In the attack on the *Cumberland* in the Hampton Roads, Virginia, on March 8, 1862, the *Virginia's* captain, Franklin Buchanan, was injured, as was the second-in-command, and Jones succeeded to command. That night the *Monitor* appeared in Hampton Roads, and early the next morning the two vessels began an epic sea battle. The *Virginia* was in damaged condition, two of its ten large guns out of commission, its iron ram gone, and many armor plates loosened from the previous

day's fighting; it was, moreover, larger, heavier, and slower than the *Monitor*. Lt. John L. Worden, commanding the *Monitor*, made good use of his advantages in the narrow channel, running often into shallow water where the *Virginia* could not follow. Neither vessel's guns were of particular effect, the *Virginia's* superiority in armament being balanced by the *Monitor's* presenting a much more difficult target, until a shot from *Virginia* struck the *Monitor's* pilothouse and temporarily blinded Worden. The *Monitor* drew off and the *Virginia* made its way back to the shelter of Norfolk. The fight, mostly at close quarters, had lasted nearly four hours. Three weeks later Jones was relieved by Capt. Josiah Tattnall and resumed the post of executive officer; he was the last man to leave the *Virginia* when she was burned at Norfolk on May 11. He later commanded the *Chattahoochee* and the naval station at Charlotte, North Carolina. Promoted to commander in April 1863, Jones was given command of the gun foundry and ordnance works at Selma, Alabama, in May, remaining in that post through the remainder of the war. He lived afterwards in Selma; he was shot and killed in an altercation with a neighbor on June 20, 1877.

Jones, David C. (1921–   ), air force officer. Born on July 9, 1921, in Aberdeen, South Dakota, Jones attended the University of North Dakota and then Minot State College from 1939 until shortly after the entry of the United States into World War II. He then enlisted in the army and in April 1942 entered aviation training at Roswell Field, New Mexico. In February 1943 he was designated a pilot and commissioned a second lieutenant. He was an aviation instructor at various Army Air Forces training schools until the end of the war, advancing to first lieutenant in February 1944. From August 1945 to May 1948 he was stationed in Japan, receiving promotion to captain in April 1946. During 1949 he attended various air force technical schools. From January 1950 to May 1953 he was attached to the 19th Bombardment Squadron, with which he flew a large number of combat missions over North Korea; promoted to major in February 1951, he rose to command of the squadron before returning to the United States. During 1953–1954 he commanded the 22nd Air Refueling Squadron and then the 33rd Bombardment Squadron at March Air Force Base, California, advancing to lieutenant colonel in June 1953. From January 1955 to July 1957 he was aide to Gen. Curtis E. LeMay, commander of the Strategic Air Command. Promoted to colonel in April 1957, Jones was attached to the 93rd Bombardment Wing at Castle Air Force Base, California, in 1957–1959, and after graduating from the National War College in 1960 he was assigned to duty at air force headquarters in Washington, D.C., until 1964. After a few months as commander of the 33rd Tactical Fighter Wing at

Eglin Air Force Base, Florida, Jones was named inspector general at the headquarters of the United States Air Forces in Europe (USAFE) in Wiesbaden, Germany, in October 1965, receiving promotion to brigadier general (temporary) in December. During January–June 1967 he was temporarily chief of staff of USAFE, and from June 1967 to January 1969 he was deputy chief of staff, USAFE, advancing to temporary major general in November 1967. In February 1969 he was named deputy chief of staff of the Seventh Air Force, under Gen. George S. Brown, based in South Vietnam, and in June–July of that year he was vice commander of the Seventh. In August 1969, promoted to temporary lieutenant general, he became commander of the Second Air Force at Barksdale Air Force Base, Louisiana. In April 1971 he returned to USAFE as vice commander, becoming commander with the rank of temporary general in September of that year. On the elevation of Gen. Brown to the chairmanship of the Joint Chiefs of Staff in July 1974, Jones was appointed to succeed him as chief of staff of the air force by President Richard M. Nixon. A much decorated officer, Jones brought to that post a highly varied experience, although he was little known outside military circles.

Jones, Jacob (1768–1850), naval officer. Born near Smyrna, Delaware, in March 1768, Jones was orphaned and reared by his stepmother. He studied medicine privately and for a time at the University of Pennsylvania and began practice in his home county, later abandoning it to become clerk of the state supreme court. In April 1799, aged thirty-one, he entered the navy as a midshipman. He served on the *United States* under Capt. John Barry, was promoted to lieutenant in February 1801, and was aboard the *Philadelphia*, Capt. William Bainbridge, when she grounded in Tripoli harbor on October 31, 1803. He returned to duty after 20 months in prison in Tripoli. He was promoted to commander in April 1810. In October 1812 he sailed from Philadelphia in command of the sloop *Wasp*, 18 guns, and on the 18th he fell in with the British brig *Frolic*, 22, convoying five merchantmen. The two ships engaged and in a furious 45-minute battle in a heavy sea inflicted considerable damage on each other. A boarding party led by an impulsive seaman, Jack Lang, and Lt. James Biddle found the deck of the *Frolic* nearly deserted, fewer than 20 of the 110 crewmen remaining uninjured. Later in the day the British ship of the line *Poictiers*, 74, appeared and captured both vessels. After a brief imprisonment in Bermuda, Jones was promoted to captain in March 1813 and put in command of the *Macedonian*, recently captured by Commodore Stephen Decatur and at the time blockaded in New York harbor. During much of 1814 he commanded the *Mohawk* on Lake Ontario. In 1815 he returned to the *Macedonian* and took part under Decatur in the Alge-

rine War. Jones later commanded the Mediterranean Squadron, 1821–1823, the Pacific Squadron, 1826–1829, and the Baltimore naval station, 1829–1839. He was port captain in New York harbor, 1842–1845, and then governor of the Philadelphia Naval Asylum until his death there on August 3, 1850.

Jones, John Paul (1747–1792), sea captain and Revolutionary naval officer. Born in Kirkcudbrightshire, Scotland, on July 6, 1747, John Paul (who later changed his name) received little schooling and at the age of twelve was apprenticed to a merchant shipper. He sailed as a cabin boy to Fredericksburg, Virginia, and there visited his elder brother, a tailor. In 1766 his apprenticeship ended when his master's business failed, and for two years he shipped in the slave trade. By 1769 he had his own command, the merchant ship *John*. The following year he flogged the ship's carpenter, who then shipped on another vessel and soon died, and in Scotland Paul was arrested for murder. He was cleared, but in December 1773, again commanding a ship in the West Indian trade, he killed the leader of a mutiny. Advised to flee, he returned to Fredericksburg and added "Jones" to his name. With the outbreak of hostilities between Great Britain and the American colonies he traveled to Philadelphia and in December 1775 was commissioned senior lieutenant of the Continental navy. Assigned to the *Alfred*, Capt. Dudley Saltonstall, the first naval vessel on which the Grand Union flag was flown, he sailed with the small fleet under the command of Commodore Esek Hopkins to the Bahamas early in 1776; his knowledge of the islands aided greatly in the capture of a large quantity of war matériel at New Providence on March 3, and after distinguishing himself in the fight with the *Glasgow* in April he was given command of the sloop *Providence*. He was commissioned a captain in August 1776 and in a six-week cruise captured eight vessels and destroyed eight more. In November he took over the *Alfred* and returned from another highly successful cruise in Nova Scotian waters in December. He found himself barred from promotion, largely because of intraservice politics; he was promised command of a frigate, however, and in November 1777 he sailed the *Ranger* to France to receive the frigate *Indien* from its French builders, only to have politics interfere again when the *Indien* was sold to France to prevent its being seized by British authorities. From February to May 1778 he sailed the *Ranger* around the British Isles, made two shore raids, and captured the sloop *Drake* on April 24, the first enemy warship to surrender to an American vessel. He saw no further action until August 1779, when he set sail from L'Orient, France, aboard a refitted merchant ship of 42 guns that he renamed *Bonhomme Richard* in honor of Benjamin Franklin, creator of Poor Richard. He was accompanied by the frigate *Alliance*, 32, and two

French ships, the *Pallas,* 32, and the *Vengeance,* 12. Again he sailed around the British Isles, capturing a number of prizes. On September 23, off Flamborough Head, England, he came upon the Baltic trading fleet and its naval escorts, *Countess of Scarborough,* 20, and *Serapis,* 50. Jones engaged the *Serapis,* although he was heavily outgunned and outmanned. He maneuvered in close, lashed the vessels together, and in three and a half hours of one of the fiercest and bloodiest naval battles on record simply wore down the enemy with his blank refusal to give up (it was in this battle that he is supposed to have replied to a suggestion that he surrender: "I have not yet begun to fight!"). During the fight the *Alliance,* commanded by a disgruntled French captain, circled and fired indiscriminately, damaging both ships. The *Pallas,* meanwhile, engaged and captured the *Countess of Scarborough.* At length the *Serapis* surrendered, and Jones transferred his crew to the British ship, the heavily damaged *Bonhomme Richard* sinking two days later. On the arrival of the squadron at Texel Island off the Netherlands north coast Jones transferred to the *Alliance.* From December 1779 to April 1780 he cruised aboard the *Alliance;* he then returned to Paris, where he was lionized. Louis XVI presented him with a sword and made him, with the permission of Congress, a chevalier of France. In December he borrowed the French ship *Ariel* and returned to the United States. Congress voted him thanks in April 1781 and in June appointed him to command of the huge 74-gun *America,* then being built at Portsmouth, New Hampshire. Delays in construction were followed by the decision to give the ship to the French government instead, and Jones's services to the Revolution were over. In 1783 he was sent to France to negotiate payment for captured U.S. prize ships held by France, and in 1788 he performed a similar service in Denmark. On his last visit to the United States, in 1787, Congress honored him with the only gold medal given to a Continental naval officer. In 1788 he accepted a commission from Empress Catherine as a rear admiral in the Russian navy; his services were valuable in the war against Turkey, but he was the victim of intrigues and was dismissed in 1789. He retired to Paris and remained there in declining health until his death on July 18, 1792. His unmarked grave lay undiscovered for more than a century, but in 1905 what were believed to be his remains were returned to the United States under escort of U.S. naval vessels and placed in a crypt in the chapel of the U.S. Naval Academy in Annapolis, Maryland.

Jones, Thomas ap Catesby (1790–1858), naval officer. Born in Westmoreland County, Virginia, on April 24, 1790, Jones was appointed a midshipman in the navy in November 1805. He served under various captains in Atlantic and Gulf waters over the next several years, becoming a lieutenant in May 1812 and distinguishing himself in an attack under Commodore Daniel T. Patterson on Jean Laffite's pirate stronghold of Barataria in the Mississippi delta region in September 1814. Three months later, under the general direction of Patterson, he commanded a flotilla of five gunboats supplemented by the schooner *Sea Horse* and the tender *Alligator* at the entrance to Lake Borgne, the route of advance of British Adm. Sir Alexander Cochrane's fleet transporting Gen. Edward Pakenham's army to New Orleans. On December 14 the British appeared on the lake, nearly a thousand men in 47 boats. Jones's flotilla fought gallantly for two hours before being overwhelmed. After recovering from a wound sustained in the fight he served in the Mediterranean Squadron for three years and at the Washington navy yard for five, becoming master commandant in March 1820. In 1825 he was given command of the Pacific Squadron. In August 1826 his flagship, *Peacock,* became the first American man-of-war to call at Tahiti, where he established relations with King Pomare III; and in October he drew up a treaty with King Kamehameha III of the Sandwich (now Hawaiian) Islands, the first ever signed by that nation. Promoted to captain in March 1829, Jones was on ordnance duty from 1831 to 1836, and from June 1836 until his health failed in December 1837 he commanded the South Seas Surveying and Exploring Expedition (then in the preparation stage; it went to sea in 1838 under Lt. Charles Wilkes). He returned to active service in 1842, again in command of the Pacific Squadron. War with Mexico was in the air, and Jones, at sea off Callao, was led by the behavior of a British warship to believe it had broken out; he immediately sailed north to California, and on October 19, 1842, took possession of the town of Monterey. Informed of his error, he withdrew, and to conciliate the Mexican government he was relieved of command. He returned to command of the Pacific Squadron in 1844 and remained there through the Mexican War. In 1850 he was court-martialed and suspended from duty for five years for misuse of certain funds; sentence was remitted in 1853 by President Millard Fillmore, but Jones saw no further active service. He died in Sharon, Fairfax County, Virginia, on May 30, 1858.

Jordan, Thomas (1819–1895), Confederate army officer, adventurer, and journalist. Born in Luray, Virginia, on September 30, 1819, Jordan graduated from West Point in 1840 and was commissioned in the 3rd Infantry. He saw action in the Seminole War in Florida and was on frontier duty at the outbreak of the Mexican War. He took part in the battles of Palo Alto and Resaca de la Palma, May 8–9, 1846, and in June was promoted to first lieutenant. He advanced to captain in March 1847 and served as quartermaster under Gen. Winfield Scott, in 1848 supervising the embarkation of the army at Veracruz. He was again in Florida in 1848–1850 and then on duty in the West and Northwest. In May 1861 he resigned to accept a commission of lieutenant colonel of Virginia troops. He was adjutant general of the Confederate army at Manassas (Bull Run), July 21, and in February 1862 he was appointed chief of staff to Gen. P. G. T. Beauregard. For gallantry at Pittsburg Landing (Shiloh), April 6–7, 1862, he was promoted to brigadier general. After a brief period on the staff of Gen. Braxton Bragg he was again Beauregard's chief of staff until the end of the war. In October 1865 he published in *Harper's Magazine* an article critical of Jefferson Davis that won widespread attention, and in 1866 he edited the *Memphis Appeal*. With J. B. Pryor he wrote *The Campaigns of Lieutenant-General N. B. Forrest*, 1868. Soon after the declaration of revolt in Cuba (October 1868) Jordan secured appointment as chief of staff of the rebel army. He organized and drilled the army, and soon after landing with 300 men at Mayarí and making his way to the interior he was, in December 1869, made commander. In January 1870 he defeated a larger Spanish force at Guáimaro. The next month, the rebels being disorganized, supplies being exhausted, and a price having been placed on his head, he resigned. Later in the year he founded in New York City the weekly *Financial and Mining Record*, which he continued to edit until 1892. He died on November 27, 1895, in New York City.

Joseph (1840?–1904), Indian leader. Born about 1840, probably in Oregon's Wallowa valley, which had been long inhabited by the Nez Percé, Joseph was given the name Hinmatonyalatkit, meaning "thunder coming up over the land from the water." His father, also known as Joseph, was leader of one of the major Nez Percé bands; in 1863, the year gold was discovered on their lands, this band refused to participate in a renegotiation of the land-cession treaty of 1855. Other bands did renegotiate, however, and government authorities held the new treaty ceding the disputed lands to be binding on all Nez Percé. Upon the death of his father in 1873, Joseph succeeded him as leader of the resisting Nez Percé and, as Chief Joseph, continued his father's policies of passive noncompliance with the 1863 treaty. After years of delay the government finally took action in 1877; through Gen. Oliver O. Howard, commander of the army Department of the Columbia, an ultimatum was issued, ordering Joseph and his people to leave the lands coveted by the whites or be removed forcibly. Joseph was troubled, but decided to leave: "I would give up everything rather than have the blood of my people on my hands. . . . I love that land more than all the world. A man who would not love his father's grave is worse than a wild animal." In his absence, however, Nez Percé braves killed several whites in June 1877; on hearing of this Howard dis-

patched troops to capture the band. In the ensuing battle of White Bird Canyon, June 17, the soldiers were nearly annihilated by the Nez Percé, led by chiefs other than Joseph. During this and 18 subsequent conflicts he guided his warriors' decisions, counseled his people, and cared for the women, children, aged, and wounded. The army assumed that he was the war chief or battle leader, however, and his reputation grew to legendary proportions. The band defeated Col. John Gibbon at Big Hole River, Montana, on August 9 and Col. Samuel D. Sturgis at Canyon Creek on September 13. After two days' fighting near Kamiah, Idaho, Howard and 600 soldiers finally succeeded in weakening the tribe's fighting power. Joseph, rather than surrender, executed a masterly retreat. Heading for the Canadian border and the nation of Sitting Bull, he led 750 people through four states, twice over the Rockies, across what is now Yellowstone National Park, and across the Missouri River, a distance of more than 1500 miles. They outfought pursuing troops and were in Montana, within 30 miles of the Canadian border, when fresh troops from Fort Keogh under Col. Nelson A. Miles surrounded them, on October 5, 1877. Joseph surrendered with dignity: "I am tired of fighting. Our chiefs are killed. . . . It is cold and we have no blankets. The little children are freezing to death. My people, some of them, have run away to the hills, and have no blankets, no food; no one knows where they are—perhaps freezing to death. I want to have time to look for my children and see how many of them I can find. Maybe I shall find them among the dead. Hear me, my chiefs! I am tired; my heart is sick and sad. From where the sun now stands I will fight no more forever." He devoted himself thereafter to the tribe's welfare. He and his band were sent to Indian Territory (Oklahoma), and in 1885 they were moved to the Colville Reservation in Washington. There Chief Joseph died, on September 21, 1904.

Jouett, James Edward (1826–1902), naval officer. Born near Lexington, Kentucky, on February 7, 1826, Jouett was appointed a midshipman in the navy in September 1841. He served on the *Independence*, 1841–1843, and on the *Decatur* in action against the slave trade, 1843–1845. During the Mexican War he was among the sailors and marines landed at Point Isabel, Texas, on May 8, 1846, to protect Gen. Zachary Taylor's base during the battle of Palo Alto. He was aboard the *St. Lawrence* in northern European waters in 1848–1850, and in the Pacific on the *Lexington*, 1851–1852, and the *St. Mary's*, 1853–1857, becoming a lieutenant in September 1855. He later served on the Great Lakes, in the Brazil Squadron, and in the Gulf. At the outbreak of the Civil War he was captured at Pensacola, Florida, but soon released and assigned to the West Gulf Blockading

Squadron before Galveston, Texas. On the night of November 7–8, 1861, he led a boat party of sailors and marines from the *Santee* past the guns of Fort Bolivar and Fort Point into Galveston Bay; there, after hand-to-hand fighting in which he was badly wounded, he captured and burned the armed schooner *Royal Yacht* and escaped back to the *Santee* with 12 prisoners. For that exploit he was given command of the steamer *Montgomery* in December. Promoted to lieutenant commander in July 1862, he later took command of the steamer *R. R. Cuyler* before Mobile. In September 1863 he took command of the fast side-wheeler gunboat *Metacomet*. In Adm. David G. Farragut's attack on Mobile Bay, August 5, 1864, the *Metacomet* was lashed to Farragut's flagship *Hartford*. Once past the forts the *Metacomet* went after Confederate gunboats, chasing off two and capturing the *Selma*. Jouett was promoted to commander in July 1866, captain in January 1874, and commodore in January 1883 and served in various routine duties until 1884, when he became commander of the North Atlantic Squadron. In the spring of 1885 he commanded a force of 8 ships and more than 2600 men sent to the Isthmus of Panama to quell a revolt and restore transit across the isthmus. Vigorous action, particularly by a landing force under Commander Bowman H. McCalla, ended the revolt in May. Jouett was promoted to rear admiral in February 1886 and served as president of the Board of Inspection and Survey until his retirement in February 1890. He died on September 30, 1902, in Sandy Spring, Maryland.

Joy, Charles Turner (1895–1956), naval officer. Born on February 17, 1895, in St. Louis, Missouri, Joy graduated from the Naval Academy in 1916. He served aboard the *Pennsylvania* through World War I until December 1920, when, by then a lieutenant, he undertook advanced studies in ordnance engineering, taking a master's degree from the University of Michigan in 1922. From 1923 to 1925 he was on the staff of the Yangtze Patrol in China. During 1926–1928 he was in the aviation ordnance section of the Bureau of Ordnance, receiving promotion to lieutenant commander in June 1927, and in 1928–1931 he was aboard the *California*. After two years at the Naval Mine Depot, Yorktown, Virginia, he took command of the *Litchfield* in May 1933. During 1935–1937 he was on the staff of the commander of destroyers, Battle Force, advancing to commander in July 1936, and he then spent three years on the staff of the Naval Academy. He was on the staff of the commander, Scouting Force, in the Pacific at the outbreak of World War II, and, promoted to captain in January 1942, he was with the reorganized Task Force 11 in operations at Rabaul, New Guinea, and Bougainville in February–March 1942. In September 1942 he took command of the heavy cruiser *Louisville* and saw action in the Aleutians and the Solomons. From August 1943 to April 1944 Joy headed the Pacific plans division in U.S. Fleet headquarters and then, promoted to rear admiral, returned to sea as commander of Cruiser Division 6, taking part in the assault on Saipan, June 14–15, 1944; the first battle of the Philippine Sea, June 19–20; the occupation of Guam, July–August; carrier operations around the Philippines, Okinawa, Iwo Jima, Formosa, and elsewhere, September–October; the Leyte landings, October 17–20; the second battle of the Philippine Sea, October 24–26; the Lingayen Gulf landings, January 19–20, 1945; the Iwo Jima assault, February 1–27; and other actions. In June 1945 he took command of Amphibious Group 2, training in California for an assault on Japan. From September 1945 to January 1946 he commanded the Yangtze Patrol, and he then commanded Task Force 74 in Hong Kong until April 1946. In June of that year he became commander of the Naval Proving Grounds, Dahlgren, Virginia. In August 1949 he was promoted to vice admiral in command of U.S. Naval Forces, Far East, and on the outbreak of the Korean War in June 1950 he became commander of United Nations naval forces. In that capacity he was responsible for establishing the naval blockade of North Korea and for organizing and directing the hazardous amphibious landing (carried out by Adm. Arthur D. Struble) of Gen. Edward M. Almond's X Corps on September 15 at Inch'on, where extreme tides in a narrow channel posed huge problems. In July 1951 Joy was appointed senior UN delegate to the armistice negotiations, a task he kept at under the most frustrating circumstances until May 1952. He served as superintendent of the Naval Academy from August 1952 until his retirement from the navy with the rank of admiral in July 1954. In 1955 he published *How Communists Negotiate*. He died in San Diego on June 6, 1956.

K

Kalb, Johann (1721–1780), soldier of fortune. Born in Hüttendorf, Germany, on June 29, 1721, Kalb was of peasant birth, but by the time he was twenty-two and serving as a lieutenant in a German infantry regiment in French service he was styling himself Jean de Kalb; he was later often called "Baron de Kalb." Unremittingly ambitious for glory, he served with distinction in the War of the Austrian Succession and the Seven Years' War, advancing to captain in 1747 amd to major in 1756. In 1764 his marriage to an heiress gave him an independence he had theretofore lacked. He went to America on a secret mission for the French government in 1768, remained for four months, and had to return to France when his dispatches were intercepted. He was made a brigadier general in November 1776, but by that time he had already secured in Paris a promise from Silas Deane of a major general's commission in the Continental army. He arrived in America with his young friend, the Marquis de Lafayette, in July 1777 and was bitterly disappointed when Lafayette was made a major general and he himself was left without a command. In September, on the point of returning to France, he also was made a major general. He spent the winter of 1777–1778 with Gen. George Washington at Valley Forge and was Lafayette's second-in-command in the abortive invasion of Canada in the spring of 1778. Kalb remained with the northern army until 1780, although he had no opportunity to distinguish himself. In April of that year he was ordered to South Carolina; arriving too late to relieve Gen. Benjamin Lincoln, then besieged in Charleston, in July he joined with the army of the newly appointed commander of the Southern Department, Gen. Horatio Gates. Gates determined, against Kalb's advice, to attack the British post at Camden, South Carolina. Gen. Charles Cornwallis pursued with a large force and found the American army outside the town on August 15. In the battle the next day Kalb commanded the right wing, the Continental regulars; the rest of Gates's army was raw militia, and at the first British advance they broke and fled, Gates leading. Kalb and his men fought valiantly but hopelessly. He was wounded several times and after leading a final charge was taken prisoner. He died three days later, August 19, 1780, at Camden, South Carolina.

Kane, Elisha Kent (1820–1857) physician, naval officer, and Arctic explorer. Born in Philadelphia on February 3, 1820, Kane entered the University of Virginia in 1838 with the intention of becoming an engineer, but an attack of rheumatic fever left his heart permanently damaged and he transferred to the University of Pennsylvania, from which he received a medical degree in 1842. Determined not to be hindered by ill health in his search for experience and adventure, he joined the navy as a surgeon in July 1843, visited India, China, and Ceylon, traveled in the Philippine Islands (where he descended into a volcanic crater), and served as a surgeon in Africa, where he contracted a lingering fever that further weakened his health. He returned to the United States in time to serve with distinction in the Mexican War. In 1850, assigned to the U.S. Coast Survey, he joined the first Grinnell expedition under Lt. Edwin J. De Haven of the navy, organized to seek traces of Sir John Franklin, the British Arctic explorer who had disappeared in the Lancaster Sound region in 1845 while searching for the Northwest Passage. The two ships provided to the navy by Henry Grinnell did not find Franklin or his party, but Kane had seen and learned enough so that his book *The U.S. Grinnell Expedition in Search of Sir John Franklin*, 1853, became a best seller; it was reissued in 1915 as *Adrift in the Arctic Ice Pack*. Kane set to work with characteristic energy and enthusiasm to organize a second expedition, which departed under his command from New York harbor, in the brig *Advance*, in May 1853. Kane and his men passed through Smith Sound into previously unknown waters that are now named Kane Basin, spent the ensuing winter on the west coast of Greenland, where they suffered greatly from severe hardships, and the next summer explored by sled, reaching farther north than any previous expedition, passing 80°N, and finding what is now Kennedy Channel, connecting the Kane and Hall basins. The party's careful observation and recording of scientific data laid the foundation for subsequent rigorous Arctic studies. The *Advance* was frozen in for still another winter and was finally abandoned by Kane and the surviving members of his party, all of them racked by disease and hunger, in May 1855. Traveling 1200 miles through open water and broken ice, they finally arrived in August 1855 at Sanderson's Hope, near Upernavik, Greenland, after 83 terrible days, having accomplished one of the great feats in the annals of Arctic exploration. Kane's *Arctic Explorations: The Second Grinnell Expedition in Search of Sir John Franklin, in the Years 1853, '54, '55,* published in two volumes in 1856, became one of the country's most widely read books of the nineteenth century. By this time Kane's health was ruined; but he continued to travel, going first to England and then to Havana, where he died on February 16, 1857. A national hero, he was mourned widely, his body lying in state in New Orleans, then in Louisville, Kentucky, Columbus, Ohio, and Baltimore, and finally in Independence Hall in Philadelphia. He had been a close friend of spiritualist Margaret Fox, and in 1866 she published a crudely edited book, *The Love Life of Dr. Kane,* printing what purported to be their correspondence and containing the claim that they had shared a common-law marriage.

Kármán, Theodore von (1881–1963), aeronautical engineer and physicist. Born in Budapest on May 11, 1881, von Kármán graduated from the Budapest Royal Technical University in 1902. He taught for a year at the university and for two years held a position in mechanical engineering before enrolling at the University of Göttingen in 1906 to work for his doctorate. He received his Ph.D. degree two years later and remained at the university as a faculty member until 1912. At that time he was offered the directorship of the new Aeronautical Institute at the University of Aachen. Except for military service in the Austrian air force during World War I, he remained at Aachen until coming to the United States in 1930 to teach at the California Institute of Technology (Caltech) and to serve as head of the Guggenheim Aeronautical (from 1942 the Jet Propulsion) Laboratory there. Von Kármán became a U.S. citizen in 1936. He became professor emeritus at Caltech in 1949 and in 1951 helped found and was chosen chairman of the advisory group for aeronautical research and development for the North Atlantic Treaty Organization (NATO), a post he retained for the rest of his life. During the years he held teaching and research posts in Germany and the United States, von Kármán also served as engineering consultant to several airplane-manufacturing corporations in Europe, Japan, and the United States. He was one of the leading theoreticians of aerodynamics in the twentieth century, a leader in the transformation of the field from an empirical to a rigorously mathematical one, and his research made possible the development of supersonic aircraft and of guided missiles. Among his special interests were subsonic, supersonic, and viscous flow, effects of vibration, and strength of materials. In 1935, at the Fifth Volta Congress in Italy, he announced his theory of air resistance to bodies moving with supersonic speed, leading to the concept known as the Kármán vortex trail. During World War II he cooperated with the air force on its first jet-propulsion program and began research on the Bell X-1 plane, the first aircraft to break the sound barrier. He also developed a supersonic wind tunnel at Caltech to aid in ballistic-missile research.

In 1942 he formed the Aerojet Engineering Corporation, to manufacture solid- and liquid-fuel rockets, particularly the jet-assisted takeoff (JATO) units he had helped develop. The firm became, under the later name of Aerojet-General, one of the leading manufacturers of rockets and missiles. In 1944 he became chairman of the scientific advisory board for the air force, a post he held until 1955 when the General Dynamics Corporation hired him as a consultant on guided missiles and nuclear research. He was the author of many books and articles in the fields of aeronautical engineering and physics, including *Aerodynamics,* 1954. He died in Aachen, Germany on May 7, 1963.

Kean, Jefferson Randolph (1860–1950), army officer and physician. Born in Lynchburg, Virginia, on June 27, 1860, Kean graduated with a medical degree from the University of Virginia in 1883 and after a year of further study at the New York Polyclinic Hospital and Medical College was commissioned a first lieutenant and assistant surgeon in the army medical department in December 1884. He was subsequently stationed at Fort Sill, Indian Territory (now Oklahoma), and Fort Robinson, Nebraska, receiving promotion to captain in December 1889, and during the winter of 1890–1891 took part with the 9th Cavalry in the Wounded Knee campaign against the Sioux. He later served in Florida and Boston. In June 1898, shortly after the outbreak of the Spanish-American War, he was appointed major of volunteers, going to Cuba with occupation forces in December 1898 and the following February becoming chief surgeon of the VII Corps with the rank of lieutenant colonel of volunteers. After recovering from a bout of yellow fever he served on Maj. Walter Reed's Yellow Fever Board. Promoted to major and surgeon of regulars in February 1901, Kean was superintendent of the Cuban Department of Charities in Gen. Leonard Wood's government. From 1902 to 1906 he was attached to the office of the surgeon general, and from 1906 to 1909 he was again in Cuba as adviser to the Department of Sanitation in the provisional government. He was author of the law by which the Medical Reserve Corps was created in 1908 (eight years before the army's regular reserve program was instituted). He advanced to lieutenant colonel in January 1909. During a second period with the surgeon general's office, 1909–1913, he inaugurated a system of field medical supply depots. Promoted to colonel in April 1914, Kean was assigned in January 1916 to the American National Red Cross as organizer and director general of the department of military relief. In that capacity he organized 32 base hospital units, along with numbers of ambulance companies and forward field hospitals; these, supplied by the depot system created earlier, rendered the medical service fully prepared for World War I.

In July 1917 he was sent to France to organize Field Service and Red Cross volunteer ambulance companies serving with the French army into the U.S. Ambulance Service, and in February 1918 he was named deputy chief surgeon of the American Expeditionary Force. In June 1918 he was promoted to temporary brigadier general. After the war he served as I Corps area surgeon in Boston until his retirement in June 1924. An avid student of the life and work of Thomas Jefferson (and, through his mother, a descendant), he organized the Monticello Association in 1913 and served on the commissions for the construction of a National Expansion Memorial in St. Louis (1934) and for the creation of the Jefferson Memorial in Washington, D.C. (1938). He died in Washington, D.C., on September 4, 1950.

Kearny, Lawrence (1789–1868), naval officer. Born on November 30, 1789, in Perth Amboy, New Jersey, Kearny was a cousin of Stephen W. Kearny; his mother was a half-sister of James Lawrence. He was appointed midshipman in the navy in July 1807 and saw duty on various vessels, receiving promotion to lieutenant in March 1813 and having his first command on the schooner *Caroline.* He commanded the *Enterprise* on pirate patrol in the Caribbean in 1821–1823, early in 1821 breaking up the pirate stronghold of Jean Laffite at Galveston. After being promoted to master commandant in March 1825 he was sent to the eastern Mediterranean in command of the *Warren* to protect American shipping from Greek pirates, in which task he was highly successful, earning the thanks of the British Parliament. On his return to the United States he was promoted to captain in December 1832 and given command of the *Potomac.* Named commander of the East India Squadron in 1840, he sailed from Boston aboard flagship *Constellation* and arrived at Macao in March 1842, just as the British–Chinese Opium War was ending. The Chinese being particularly accommodating to American interests, Kearny succeeded in securing indemnity for American property lost in the war and at the same time took steps to end the participation of Americans in the opium trade. He formed good relations with Chinese officials right up to the viceroy, and on learning of the Treaty of Nanking in August 1842, whereby five Chinese ports were opened to British commerce, he urged the granting of most-favored-nation status to the United States, dispatching reports by three separate routes to Washington. Kearny sailed for home in July 1843, but the diplomatic initiatives he had taken bore further fruit in August, when China declared the five ports open to the commerce of all nations—a forerunner of the later "Open Door" policy—and in July 1844, when Caleb Cushing negotiated the first U.S.-Chinese treaty. On his way home Kearny called at the Sandwich (Hawaiian) Islands and, on learning that King Kamehameha III had ceded sovereignty

over the islands to a British admiral, Lord George Paulet, he lodged a strong protest; the cession was soon thereafter revoked. Kearny's later years were spent in routine duty, including command of the Norfolk navy yard in 1847 and of the New York navy yard in 1857. He was mayor of Perth Amboy in 1848–1849. He retired in November 1861 and was promoted by Congress to commodore on the retired list in April 1867. He died in Perth Amboy on November 29, 1868.

Kearny, Philip (1814–1862), army officer. Born in New York City on June 1, 1814, Kearny early determined upon a military career. Family pressure sent him to Columbia College, from which he graduated with a law degree in 1833; but in March 1837, soon after the death of his grandfather and guardian and his inheriting of a substantial fortune, he secured a commission as second lieutenant of cavalry and was attached to the 1st Dragoons, on duty on the western frontier under the command of his uncle, Col. Stephen W. Kearny. In 1839 he was sent to France to study cavalry tactics and training, serving with the French cavalry in Algeria in 1840 and preparing a manual for the U.S. army on his return. After further service on the frontier and as aide to Gen. Alexander Macomb and to Gen. Winfield Scott, successive commanding generals of the army, he resigned his commission early in 1846, only to return to duty a month later for service in the Mexican War. Recruiting and equipping his own cavalry company and receiving promotion to captain in December 1846, he performed with distinction in Gen. Scott's army, losing an arm at Churubusco, August 20, 1847, and being brevetted major. He remained in the army until October 1851, when he retired for several years to his New Jersey estate. The prospect of adventure and glory lured him to France in 1859, where he served with the Imperial Guard of Napoleon III in Italy and became the first American to earn the cross of the French Legion of Honor. On the outbreak of the Civil War he returned to the United States and in May 1861 was appointed a brigadier general of New Jersey volunteers. In command of a division of Gen. Samuel P. Heintzelman's III Corps during the Peninsular campaign he played a conspicuous role at the battles of Williamsburg, May 5, and Fair Oaks (Seven Pines), May 31, and in July was promoted to major general of volunteers. His fearlessness and dash made him a highly popular as well as valuable commander; his leadership in a dozen cavalry engagements won the respect of his superiors and the enemy alike. While on a reconnoitering mission near Chantilly, Virginia, Kearny unwittingly crossed Confederate lines and was killed on September 1, 1862.

Kearny, Stephen Watts (1794–1848), army officer. Born in Newark, New Jersey, on August 30,

1794, Kearny entered Columbia College in 1811 but left a year later to serve in the War of 1812, taking a commission as first lieutenant in the 13th Infantry in March 1812. He was wounded and captured at Queenston Heights, October 13, 1812, and promoted to captain in April 1813. After the war he served at various posts on the western frontier and fought in numerous Indian wars and skirmishes during the subsequent decades, serving with Col. Henry Atkinson and aiding in the establishment of several army outposts. He was promoted to major in May 1829, to lieutenant colonel in March 1833, and to colonel of the 1st Dragoons in July 1836. In 1842 he became commander of the Third Military Department, comprising most of the Great Plains region. In May 1846 he was named commander of the Army of the West and shortly thereafter given the rank of brigadier general. The Mexican War having broken out, he marched from Fort Leavenworth by way of Bent's Fort and entered Santa Fe, New Mexico, with some 1700 troops on August 18, 1846. For the next month he was military governor of the territory, organizing in short order a civil government. He set out with just over 100 men for California (leaving New Mexico to the command of Col. Alexander W. Doniphan) on September 25 and, after heavy losses at San Pasqual on December 6, joined with forces already sent there by Commodore Robert F. Stockton and took San Diego, December 10, and San Gabriel and Los Angeles, January 8–9, 1847. The defeated Californians, however, surrendered (on January 13) not to Kearny or Stockton but to Lt. Col. John C. Frémont, a fact that fed a bitter quarrel that had already begun between Kearny and Stockton as to who was to exercise final authority. (Stockton had earlier proclaimed himself governor, and Kearny had tactfully acquiesced.) Kearny's authority was supported by Washington, and he removed Frémont, who had been appointed governor by Stockton, from his command and arrested him; a court-martial later convicted Frémont of insubordination and conduct prejudicial to military order, whereupon he resigned from the army. After completing the pacification of California as military governor until August 1847 and waiting for a time at Fort Leavenworth, Kansas, Kearny proceeded to Mexico, where for a short period in 1848 he was governor general of Veracruz and later of Mexico City. In September 1848 he was promoted to major general despite the heated opposition of Sen. Thomas Hart Benton, Frémont's father-in-law, but while at Veracruz he had contracted a tropical disease from which he died in St. Louis, Missouri, on October 31, 1848.

Kelley, Benjamin Franklin (1807–1891), army officer. Born on April 10, 1807, in New Hampton, New Hampshire, Kelley moved to Wheeling, Virginia (now West Virginia) in 1826 and engaged in mercantile pursuits until 1851, when he became a freight agent for the Baltimore & Ohio Railroad. In May 1861, having had some militia experience, he raised a regiment that was mustered into federal service as the 1st Virginia Volunteers, the first loyal regiment from below the Mason-Dixon line. Kelley was appointed colonel and then brigadier general of volunteers, and on May 27 he marched on Grafton, then occupied by about 1000 Confederates under Gen. George A. Porterfield. Porterfield withdrew and Kelley pursued until June 3, when a skirmish occurred at Philippi, probably the first field engagement of the Civil War. Kelley was seriously wounded. He returned to active service in August and after his capture of Romney on October 26 was appointed commander of the Department of Harpers Ferry and Cumberland. In January 1862 he was relieved at his own request because of wounds. He returned to action in the summer of 1862, served under Gen. John C. Frémont, and remained active in the West Virginia–Virginia border area, becoming commander of the Department of West Virginia in July 1863. In November 1863 he destroyed the camp of Gen. John D. Imboden at Morefield, Virginia. In August 1864 he distinguished himself in battles at Cumberland, Maryland, and New Creek and Morefield, Virginia with Gen. John McCausland, who was retreating from the burning of Chambersburg, Pennsylvania. He was brevetted major general of volunteers for his services in March 1865. After the war he was a collector of internal revenue in West Virginia and in 1876 was appointed superintendent of the Hot Springs Reservation in Arkansas. In 1883 he was appointed federal examiner of pensions. Kelley died on July 17, 1891, in Oakland, Maryland.

Kelly, Luther Sage (1849–1928), army officer and scout. Born on July 27, 1849, in Geneva, New York, Kelly dissembled his age and enlisted as a private in the 10th Infantry in March 1865. Unbeknownst to him at the time, the 10th was Regular Army, not Civil War volunteer, and after the war ended he was ordered west. He was discharged at Fort Ransom, Dakota Territory, in 1868 and immediately set about becoming one of the greatest hunters, trappers, and scouts in the West. In 1870 he performed one of the exploits that earned him fame in volunteering to carry army dispatches from Fort Buford, Montana, 50 miles through Sioux country to Fort Stevenson; on the return leg he was ambushed by two Sioux warriors, one of whom lived to warn his fellows never to ambush Kelly. He was a guide to various expeditions, his knowledge of the trails of the Wyoming and Montana country being unmatched—hence his nickname "Yellowstone"—and during the Sioux campaigns of 1876–1878 he was chief scout to Col. Nelson A. Miles. In later years he worked as a clerk for the War Department. In 1898 he was guide to an exploring expedition to Alaska under Capt. E. F. Glenn, and the next year he guided a similar expedition sponsored by Edward H. Harriman, the railroad magnate. In 1900 he was appointed captain in the 40th Volunteer Infantry for service in the Philippine insurrection. He served there until 1904, for a time in 1903 as governor of Surigao Province, and distinguished himself on more than one occasion. From 1904 to 1908 he was Indian agent at the San Carlos Reservation, Arizona Territory, and later he supervised a gold mine in Nevada. In 1915 he moved to California and settled on a ranch near Paradise. His autobiography, *"Yellowstone Kelly": The Memoirs of Luther S. Kelly*, appeared in 1926. He died on his ranch on December 17, 1928.

Kemble, Gouverneur (1786–1875), manufacturer. Born in New York City on January 25, 1786, Kemble graduated from Columbia College in 1803 and devoted the next few years to literary pursuits. He was a close friend of Washington Irving and a member of Irving's coterie, which often assembled at the Kemble home in Passaic, New Jersey, dubbed "Cockloft" in Irving's *Salmagundi* papers. Kemble's interest in business emerged when, while serving as U.S. consul in Cadiz during the War of 1812, he studied Spanish methods of casting cannon. Returning to the United States after notable service securing supplies for the U.S. navy in the Algerine War, he "turned Vulcan and began forging thunderbolts," as Irving expressed it, at the West Point Foundry, which he established in 1818 at Cold Spring, New York, across the Hudson River from West Point. He produced the best cannon cast in America up to his time, continuously improving them and becoming the chief supplier of the Union armies during the Civil War. Beginning by manufacturing Col. George Bomford's smoothbore, low-trajectory "Columbiads," the West Point Foundry later turned to producing Dahlgren cannon, named after their inventor, John A. B. Dahlgren. The Dahlgren smoothbores were followed by the giant Parrott rifles developed by Robert Parker Parrott, who had become Kemble's successor at the foundry and his brother-in-law in 1839. All told, the foundry produced more than 3000 cannon and 1.6 million projectiles. Kemble served in the House of Representatives from 1837 to 1841 and was a delegate to Democratic national conventions in 1844 and 1860, but in his later years he devoted himself mainly to hospitality, holding open house for the professors and principal officers of the U.S. Military Academy at West Point every Saturday evening until the end of his life. He died at Cold Spring, New York, on September 16, 1875.

Kempff, Louis (1841–1920), naval officer. Born near Belleville, Illinois, on October 11, 1841, Kempff was appointed to the Naval Academy in 1857 and entered active service in April 1861 before graduating. He served in the blockade of Charleston and took part in the attack on Port Royal, South Carolina, in November 1861, and the recapture of Norfolk, Virginia, in May 1862. Commissioned midshipman in 1862 and promoted to lieutenant in August of the same year, he served aboard the *Sonoma* in the Sabine River in June–July 1863, on the *Connecticut* into 1864, and on the *Suwanee* of the Pacific Squadron in 1865–1867. He was promoted to lieutenant commander in July 1866, commander in March 1876, and captain in May 1891, serving during those years on various ships in the Pacific, taking part in the *Mohican* eclipse expedition to Siberia in 1869, and fulfilling shore assignments at Mare Island, California. He commanded the *Alert* in 1881–1882, the *Adams* in 1885–1888, and the *Monterey* in 1893–1895. After attending the Naval War College in 1895 he served briefly on the Examining and Retiring Board, commanded the receiving ship *Independence* in 1896–1899, and, promoted to rear admiral in March 1899, commanded the Mare Island station until becoming second-in-command of the Asiatic Fleet early in 1900. When the Boxer rebellion in China threatened American interests he was sent there as senior U.S. naval commander. In May 1900 he arrived off Taku, China, aboard the *Newark*. A force of marines and sailors was dispatched to Peking to help guard the U.S. legation as the uprising grew more heated, and early in June Capt. Bowman H. McCalla of the *Newark* led a second force to Tientsin. When the Allied fleet at Taku demanded the surrender of the forts guarding the town and the entrance to the Pei Ho River, and then bombarded them into surrender on June 17, Kempff declined to participate in an action he conceived to be contrary to U.S. policy and prejudicial to U.S.–Chinese relations. He was later honored for his decision. He took part in subsequent Allied actions, once the United States had formally entered into the affair. After his return home he commanded the Pacific Naval District until his retirement in October 1903. He died in Santa Barbara, California, on July 29, 1920.

Kenney, George Churchill (1889–1977), army and air force officer. Born on August 6, 1889, in Yarmouth, Nova Scotia (to visiting U.S. parents), Kenney attended the Massachusetts Institute of Technology from 1907 to 1911 and then worked as a railroad surveyor and engineer until 1917, when he enlisted in the army reserve. He was assigned to the Signal Corps aviation section, trained as a pilot, and shipped to France as a first lieutenant in November 1917. In February 1918 he joined the 91st Aero Squadron; he shot down two German planes before the armistice and remained in Europe until June 1919. Promoted to captain, he served at various airfields and graduated from the Air Service Engineering

School, McCook Field, Ohio, in 1921; the Air Corps Tactical School, Langley Field, Virginia, in 1926; the Command and General Staff School, Fort Leavenworth, Kansas, in 1927; and the Army War College in 1933. By then a major, he was attached to the office of the chief of the Air Corps for two years; subsequently he was in a staff position at Langley Field, an instructor at the Infantry School, Fort Benning, Georgia, and from 1938 to 1940, with the rank of colonel, commander of the 97th Observation Squadron at Mitchel Field, New York. Early in 1941, promoted to brigadier general, he became commander of the Air Corps Experimental Depot, Wright Field, Ohio. In April 1942, with the rank of temporary major general, he was named commander of the Fourth Air Force at March Field, California, where he remained until July. In September, with the rank of temporary lieutenant general, he became commander of the Fifth Air Force, the new designation of the Far East Air Force, formerly based in the Philippines, and of all Allied air forces in the Southwest Pacific area. His command, Gen. Douglas MacArthur's air arm, took part in campaigns in the Netherlands East Indies, the battle of the Coral Sea, the landings in New Guinea and the Palaus, and major air offensives in the Bismarck Sea, the Celebes, the Philippines and elsewhere. In June 1944 he relinquished command of the Fifth Air Force, remaining commander of the Southwest Pacific Allied air forces until March 1945, when he became commander of all Allied air forces in the Pacific with the rank of general. In 1946 he served for a time as senior U.S. representative on the military staff committee of the United Nations. Later in the year he was named commander of the Strategic Air Command at Andrews Field, Maryland. In September 1947 he became an officer of the newly independent air force. In June 1948 he was appointed commandant of the Air University, Maxwell Air Force Base, Alabama, in which post he remained until his retirement in August 1951. Kenney was the author of *General Kenney Reports*, 1948, *The MacArthur I Know*, 1951, *The Saga of Pappy Gunn*, 1959, and *Dick Bong, Ace of Aces*, 1960. He died near Miami, Florida, on August 9, 1977.

Kent, Jacob Ford (1835–1918), army officer. Born in Philadelphia on September 14, 1835, Kent graduated from West Point in 1861 and was commissioned in the infantry. He served throughout the Civil War, from January 1863 to August 1865 as lieutenant colonel and assistant inspector general of volunteers. During that time he attained the rank of captain of regulars in January 1864 and received brevets to major, lieutenant colonel, and colonel for gallantry at Marye's Heights, Virginia, May 23, 1863; at Spotsylvania, May 12, 1864; and before Richmond in October 1864. For a time after the war he was an instructor at West Point. From 1869 to 1898 he was

engaged in garrison and frontier duty, advancing to major in July 1885, to lieutenant colonel in January 1891, and to colonel in command of the 24th Infantry Regiment in April 1895. In May 1898, after the declaration of war on Spain, he was appointed brigadier general of volunteers and placed in command of the 1st Infantry Division of Gen. William R. Shafter's V Corps, which landed in Cuba late in June. On July 1 his division formed the left of the American line of assault on the heights before Santiago. San Juan Hill, in the center, was carried by Kent's division and a division of dismounted cavalry under Gen. Joseph Wheeler, while at the extreme right the separate Kettle Hill was taken by other cavalry regiments—the 9th, the 10th, and the 1st Volunteers (the "Rough Riders") under Lt. Col. Theodore Roosevelt. (Ironically, although the battle is remembered as that of San Juan Hill, only Roosevelt, who was not on San Juan Hill, is remembered in connection with it.) Later in July Kent was promoted to major general of volunteers. He subsequently saw brief service in the Philippines. He was promoted to brigadier general of regulars in October 1898 and retired later in the same month. He lived thereafter in Troy, New York, until his death on December 22, 1918.

Kenton, Simon (1755–1836), frontiersman and scout. Born on April 3, 1755, in Fauquier County, Virginia, Kenton received no schooling and at sixteen, believing he had killed a rival in a fight, he fled west into the Kentucky country. He took the name Simon Butler for a time and ranged throughout the region, becoming a hunter and woodsman of note. In 1774 he served as a scout in Lord Dunmore's War. The next year he settled briefly in Boonesborough; he was often a companion of Daniel Boone in skirmishes with Indians and on one occasion saved his life. In 1778 Kenton scouted for Col. George Rogers Clark, taking part in the capture of Kaskaskia. Later in that year, while scouting on the Little Miami River, he was captured by Indians and saved from death only by the intervention of the renegade Simon Girty. He was held in Detroit until he escaped in 1779. He was again with Clark in 1780 and 1782. Soon thereafter, learning that his boyhood enemy was still living, he returned to Virginia and brought his father's family out to Kentucky, settling in Maysville in 1784 or 1785. He served as major of a battalion of Kentucky volunteers in Gen. Anthony Wayne's campaign against the Indians in 1793–1794. In 1798 he moved to Ohio, living near Springfield for a time and later in Urbana. He was appointed brigadier general of militia in 1805 and took part, with Gov. Isaac Shelby's Kentucky volunteers, in the battle of the Thames, October 5, 1813. From about 1820 he lived in Logan County, Ohio. His later years were beset by poverty, as his titles to Ohio and Kentucky lands proved defective, and in 1824 he appealed for relief to the Kentucky legislature. Some of his land was restored, and he was granted a small pension by Congress. Generally considered second in importance only to Daniel Boone among pioneers of the trans-Allegheny, Kenton died in Logan County, Ohio, on April 29, 1836.

Keyes, Erasmus Darwin (1810–1895), army officer. Born on May 29, 1810, in Brimfield, Massachusetts, Keyes grew up there and in Kennebec County, Maine. He graduated from West Point in 1832, was commissioned in the artillery, and was stationed at Fort Monroe, Virginia. He was at Charleston, South Carolina, during the nullification crisis of 1832–1833. From 1837 to 1841, except for an interruption in 1838, he was aide-de-camp to Gen. Winfield Scott. Promoted to captain in November 1841, he was on garrison duty in the South from 1842 to 1844, and served as an instructor at West Point from 1844 to 1848. From 1851 to 1860 he was for the most part in the Northwest, taking part in campaigns against the Indians in Washington Territory in 1855 and 1858 and advancing to major in October of the latter year. In January 1860 he was appointed military secretary to Gen. Scott with the rank of lieutenant colonel, and he retained that post until May 1861, when he was promoted to colonel of the 11th Infantry and then appointed brigadier general of volunteers. In April he joined Capt. Montgomery C. Meigs aboard Lt. David D. Porter's *Powhatan* in an expedition to relieve Fort Pickens, Florida. He led a brigade of Gen. Irvin McDowell's army at Bull Run (Manassas), July 21, 1861, and in the Peninsular campaign in the spring of 1862 commanded the IV Corps in Gen. George B. McClellan's Army of the Potomac. He was promoted to major general of volunteers during the campaign, in May, and for his actions at Fair Oaks (Seven Pines), May 31, was brevetted brigadier general of regulars. The IV Corps remained on the Yorktown peninsula after McClellan's campaign ended, and in 1863 Keyes organized several raids against Confederate points, including White House, January 7, and West Point, May 7. He came into conflict with Gen. John A. Dix, commander of the Department of Maryland, however, and in July 1863 relinquished field command to serve on a retiring board. He resigned his commission in May 1864 and traveled to California, settling in San Francisco. He served as president of the Maxwell Gold Mining Company from 1867 to 1869, as vice-president of the California Vine-Culture Society in 1868–1872, and in other positions. In 1884 he published *Fifty Years' Observation of Men and Events*. He also traveled extensively and died while visiting Nice, France, on October 14, 1895.

Kilmer, Joyce (1886–1918), poet, author, and soldier. Born in New Brunswick, New Jersey, on December 6, 1886, Alfred Joyce Kilmer attended Rutgers College for two years and graduated from Columbia College in 1908. After a year spent teaching Latin in a New Jersey high school he moved to New York City to seek a literary career. He worked for a dictionary publisher and wrote for magazines and in 1913 obtained a position with the *New York Times* book review. He was poetry editor of the *Literary Digest* and of *Current Literature*, wrote introductions to books, and lectured widely on current literary subjects. His first book of poems, *Summer of Love*, appeared in 1911; *Trees and Other Poems* was published in 1914, the title poem, which achieved worldwide fame, having appeared in *Poetry* magazine in August 1913. He enlisted in the army when the United States joined the Allies in World War I and sailed for France with the 165th Infantry (New York's 69th National Guard) in October 1917. At the end of July 1918 his regiment attacked on the front along the Ourcq River in the Aisne, and on July 30 Kilmer was found among the dead. Although he was only a sergeant in rank, he was buried with the officers at the spot, was mentioned in dispatches, and was awarded the Croix de Guerre by the French army. Among his other books were *Main Street and Other Poems*, 1917; *The Circus, and Other Essays*, 1916; and *Literature in the Making*, 1917, a series of interviews with writers. His unfinished history of the 165th was appended to *Father Duffy's Story* by Chaplain Francis P. Duffy.

Kilpatrick, Hugh Judson (1836–1881), army officer and diplomat. Born near Deckertown, New Jersey, on January 14, 1836, Kilpatrick graduated from West Point in 1861 and was commissioned in the artillery. He soon obtained appointment as captain in the 5th New York Volunteers and, ordered to Fort Monroe, Virginia, took part with that regiment in the battle of Big Bethel, June 10, where he was badly wounded. Appointed lieutenant colonel of the 2nd New York Cavalry for gallantry there, he was thereafter almost constantly in the field. He took part in cavalry operations on the Rappahannock and in northern Virginia in 1862, including the battles at Thoroughfare Gap, August 28, and second Bull Run (Manassas), August 29–30. In April–May 1863 he took part in Gen. George Stoneman's raid toward Richmond; on June 9 he was in command of a brigade under Gen. Alfred Pleasonton at Brandy Station (Beverly Ford); promoted four days later to brigadier general of volunteers, he won a brevet in regular rank to major at Aldie a few days later and took part in all operations leading up to Gettysburg, where he was also on the field, July 1–3. On February 28–March 1, 1864, he led a cavalry raid on Richmond for the purpose of taking the infamous Libby Prison and releasing federal prisoners; the raid was repulsed with heavy losses. In May he took command of the 3rd Cavalry Division in Gen. George H. Thomas's Army of the Cumberland and served through the Atlanta campaign. He was badly wounded at Resaca, Georgia, on May 13, winning a brevet to regular colonel; and after his recovery he led a cavalry raid around Atlanta, August 18–22. He performed with distinction in command of the cavalry in the Carolinas campaign, taking conspicuous part in the capture of Fayetteville, North Carolina, on March 11, 1865, and shortly thereafter receiving brevets to brigadier and major general. In June he was promoted to major general of volunteers. Later in 1865 he was appointed U.S. minister to Chile. He was recalled in 1868. He campaigned for Horace Greeley, Liberal Republican, in 1872, ran unsuccessfully for Congress in 1880, and in 1881 was again named minister to Chile. He died there on December 2, 1881.

Kimball, William Wirt (1848–1930), naval officer.

Born in Paris, Maine, on January 9, 1848, Kimball graduated from the Naval Academy in 1869 and the next year was commissioned an ensign. He was in the first class to study at the Naval Torpedo Station, Newport, Rhode Island, in 1870–1871, and after duty aboard the *Shawmut* he was promoted to lieutenant in 1874 and assigned as torpedo officer to the *Intrepid*, one of the navy's first two torpedo boats. During 1875–1879 he held a similar post on the other torpedo boat, *Alert*, in Asian waters. During 1879–1882 he was engaged in ordnance work, concerning himself in particular with machine gun and magazine development. He took part in the occupation of the Isthmus of Panama in April 1885, constructing armed railroad cars for the reopening and protection of rail transit. From 1886 to 1890 he was again on ordnance duty, and from that period dated his long and fruitful association with John P. Holland, whose ideas of submarine design Kimball championed within the navy. In 1894 he was executive officer of the *Detroit* in the squadron assembled under Adm. Andrew Benham to reopen Rio de Janeiro, closed by the rebel Brazilian navy, to American shipping. Kimball was head of naval intelligence from 1894 to 1897, when, promoted to lieutenant commander, he organized and commanded the Atlantic Torpedo Boat Flotilla, the first such flotilla, remaining with it through the Spanish–American War. He advanced to commander in 1899. Later he commanded the *Alert* in 1901–1903, and, promoted to captain in 1905, the *New Jersey* in 1905–1907. From 1907 to 1909 he served on the boards of Construction, Examination, and Retirement, and in 1908 he was promoted to rear admiral. In December 1909 he was given command of the Nicaragua Expeditionary Squadron, a post he held until April 1910 notwithstanding his mandatory retirement for age in January 1910. He was relieved from active service in June. During World War I he returned to duty as president of the Board of Examination and head of the historical section of the office of operations. He died in Paris, Maine, on January 26, 1930.

Kimmel, Husband Edward (1882–1968), naval officer.

Born on February 26, 1882, in Henderson, Kentucky, Kimmel graduated from the Naval Academy in 1904. Over the next decade he served on the *Kentucky*, on the *Virginia* during the Cuban pacification in 1906, on the *Georgia* in the Battle Fleet's world cruise in 1907–1909, and on other ships. In April 1914, while serving on the staff of the Pacific Fleet commander, he was wounded in the occupation of Veracruz, Mexico. In 1915 he was briefly an aide to the assistant secretary of the navy, Franklin D. Roosevelt. During World War I he taught new gunnery techniques to the British Grand Fleet and then served as squadron gunnery officer with the American 6th Battle Squadron attached to the fleet. During 1920–1923 Kimmel was assigned to the Naval Gun Factory in Washington, D.C.; and during 1923–1925 he was in the Far East, as captain of the Cavite navy yard, Philippines, and then as commander of Destroyer Squadron 12. After three years in the office of the chief of naval operations he commanded the *New York* in 1933–1934 and was then chief of staff to the commander of battleships, Battle Force. Promoted to rear admiral in 1937, he was on staff duty in Washington until June 1939, when, after a South American goodwill cruise commanding Cruiser Division 7, he became commander of cruisers, Battle Force, Pacific Fleet. In February 1941 he was advanced over several seniors to the post of commander in chief, U.S. Fleet, with the rank of admiral. He was also commander of the Pacific Flet, flagship *Pennsylvania.* (The reorganized U.S. Fleet also included the Asiatic Fleet under Adm. Thomas C. Hart and the Atlantic Fleet under Adm. Ernest J. King.) Kimmel was thus the highest ranking naval officer afloat. He was also senior officer present at Pearl Harbor when the Japanese attacked on December 7, 1941, catching the entire military and naval establishment unprepared and inflicting severe damage on all installations, especially the Pacific Fleet elements in port. Ten days later Kimmel was suspended from command pending investigation. Controversy was immediate, heated, and long-lived over what sort of warnings (if any) of Japanese intentions had been sent from Washington to Kimmel and to Gen. Walter C. Short, army commander of the Hawaiian Department, and why security arrangements were so loose as to permit complete surprise. A presidential board of inquiry headed by Supreme Court Justice Owen J. Roberts reported early in 1942 that Kimmel and Short had both been guilty of dereliction of duty. (Kimmel retired in March, reverting to the rank of rear admiral, pending court-martial or other disposition.) A naval court of inquiry in 1944 found, on the other hand, no blame or mistakes in judgment. A congressional investigation in 1945–1946 found errors in judgment but no dereliction of duty. No court-martial was ever held. Kimmel was employed thereafter by a marine engineering firm. In 1955 he published *Admiral Kimmel's Story*, presenting his side of the affair. He died in Groton, Connecticut, on May 14, 1968.

King, Ernest Joseph (1878–1956), naval officer. Born in Lorain, Ohio, on November 23, 1878, King graduated from the Naval Academy in 1901, having seen some action already aboard the *San Francisco* in the Spanish–American War. Commissioned ensign in 1903, he served over the next decade on the *Cincinnati*, on the *Alabama*, as an instructor at the Academy in 1906–1909, on staff duty, and on the *New Hampshire*. In command of the *Terry* he took part in the occupation of Veracruz in April 1914, and in 1916 he joined the staff of Adm. Henry T. Mayo, commander of the Atlantic Fleet, remaining in that post through World War I. He took command of Submarine Division 11 in 1922, Submarine Division 3 in 1923, and the New London, Connecticut, submarine base in 1923. In 1928, at the age of 49, he took aviation training and the next year became assistant chief of the Bureau of Aeronautics. In 1930 he took command of the aircraft carrier *Lexington*, and after graduating from the Naval War College he was named chief of the Bureau of Aeronautics by President Franklin D. Roosevelt in 1933. It was customary to name an admiral to the post, but Roosevelt, finding that no admiral could fly a plane, chose King, who was promoted to rear admiral in November 1933. Made vice admiral and commander of the five-carrier Aircraft Battle Force in 1938, he served on the General Board in 1939–1940 and in February 1941 was appointed chief of the Atlantic Fleet. A few days after Pearl Harbor he succeeded Adm. Husband E. Kimmel as commander in chief of the U.S. Fleet with the rank of admiral. By executive order of the President in March 1942 he became the first man to combine this post with the position of chief of naval operations; in his dual capacity he commanded the greatest aggregation of fighting ships, planes, and men in the history of naval warfare. In the Atlantic, under Adm. Royal E. Ingersoll and later Adm. Jonas H. Ingram, the navy's role consisted primarily of convoy protection, antisubmarine patrol, and amphibious operations. In the Pacific the war with Japan was more nearly a naval one, with fleet action on sea and in the air a dominant element of strategy. Amphibious support was also a major task in the island campaigns. The principal Pacific naval units were the Third Fleet under Adm. William F. Halsey, the Fifth under Adm. Raymond A. Spruance, and the Seventh under Adm. Thomas C. Kinkaid. By 1945 the navy had grown to 4 million men and over 92,000 ships and other craft. In June 1944 King observed personally the beachhead at Normandy. In December 1944 he was given temporary five-star rank of fleet admiral, made permanent in April 1946. In addition to his heavy responsibilities for the conduct of a naval war around the globe, King was also President Roosevelt's chief naval adviser and in that capacity was involved in high-level diplomacy at conferences of Allied leaders at Casablanca, Teheran, Cairo, and Yalta. The post of commander in chief of the U.S. Fleet was abolished in October 1945, and after relinquishing the post of chief of naval operations to Adm. Chester W. Nimitz in December, King went on inactive status—a five-star admiral need not retire—but returned to limited duty in 1950, after an extended illness, as an adviser to the secretary of the navy, the Department of Defense, and the President. He died on June 25, 1956, at Portsmouth, New Hampshire.

Kinkaid, Thomas Cassin (1888–1972), naval officer. Born on April 3, 1888, in Hanover, New Hampshire, Kinkaid graduated from the Naval Academy in 1908 and after a cruise on the *Nebraska* was commissioned an ensign in 1910. From 1911 to 1913 he was aboard the *Minnesota*, and he was then assigned to advanced studies in ordnance, except for a brief cruise in Mexican waters in 1914, until 1916. Promoted to lieutenant (junior grade), he served on the *Pennsylvania* for a year, was attached to the British admiralty in 1917, and in 1918–1919 was on the *Arizona*. After three years in the Bureau of Ordnance he was promoted to lieutenant commander in 1922 and placed on the staff of Adm. Mark L. Bristol in the eastern Mediterranean. In 1924 he had his first command on the *Isherwood*. Various duties followed: he was promoted to commander in 1926, graduated from the Naval War College in 1930, and was appointed technical adviser to the American delegation to the Geneva Disarmament Conference in 1932. He served on the *Colorado* in 1933–1934 and in the Bureau of Navigation in 1934–1937, and, promoted to captain, he commanded the *Indianapolis* in 1937–1938. In November 1938 he was appointed naval attaché and naval attaché for air in Rome; he became also naval attaché for Belgrade, Yugoslavia, in April 1939, and retained both posts until March 1941. Promoted to temporary rear admiral in November 1941 (made permanent in April 1942), he took command of the carrier *Enterprise* following Pearl Harbor and went immediately into action, taking part, under the general command of Adm. William F. Halsey, in the raids on the Gilbert and Marshall islands as well as actions at Bougainville, Wake, and Marcus islands in February 1942; in the battle of the Coral Sea, May 7–8, under Adm. Chester W. Nimitz; in the battle of Midway, June 3–6; in the battle of the Eastern Solomons as part of Adm. Frank J. Fletcher's carrier strike group, August 24; in the battle of Santa Cruz, October 26–27; and in subsequent action in the Solomons in November, commanding a task group centered on the *Enterprise*. In January 1943 Kinkaid became commander of naval forces in the North Pacific area, directing the battle for the Aleutians. He was promoted to vice admiral in June 1943 and in November named commander of the Seventh Fleet and Allied naval forces of the Southwest Pacific area. As Gen. Douglas MacArthur's naval commander he had charge of the naval, naval air, and (through Adm. Daniel E. Barbey's VII Amphibious Force) amphibious phases of the New Guinea operations and the invasion of the Philippines, beginning with the assault on Leyte, October 17, 1944. During October 24–26, still protecting the beachhead of Gen. Walter Krueger's Sixth Army, Kinkaid's forces, aided by others from Halsey (mainly parts of Adm. Marc A. Mitscher's Task Force 38), fought the battle of Leyte Gulf, or the second battle of the Philippine Sea, inflicting extremely heavy losses on the Japanese in what was, in terms of vessels (nearly 300) and men (nearly 200,000) involved, the greatest naval battle in history. He continued to support MacArthur until September 1945, advancing to admiral in April of that year. In September he landed Gen. John R. Hodge's XXIV Corps in Korea and jointly with Hodge accepted the surrender of Seoul. He oversaw the Allied occupation of other northern areas and the transportation of Chinese Nationalist armies to occupation points until relinquishing command of the Seventh Fleet in November 1945. In January 1946 he was named commander of the Eastern Sea Frontier and the Atlantic Reserve force. He retired from active service in April 1950. Kinkaid died in Washington, D.C., on November 17, 1972.

Kirby-Smith, Edmund (1824–1893), Confederate army officer and educator. Born in St. Augustine, Florida, on May 16, 1824, Kirby-Smith's surname was originally Smith, and the hyphenated form including his middle (and mother's maiden) name evolved much later. He graduated from West Point in 1845, was commissioned in the infantry, and took part in nearly all the major battles of the Mexican War from Palo Alto, May 8, 1846, to Mexico City, September 13–14, 1847, receiving brevets of first lieutenant at Cerro Gordo, April 18, 1847, and captain at Contreras, August 19–20. After a period at Jefferson Barracks, Missouri, he was an instructor at West Point from 1849 to 1852 and then returned to frontier duty. He was promoted to captain in 1855. He served with the 2nd Cavalry, under Col. Albert S. Johnston, in the Southwest, taking part in numerous Indian campaigns and receiving promotion to major in December 1860, until he resigned in March 1861 to accept a commission as colonel of cavalry in the Confederate army. As chief of staff to Gen. Joseph E. Johnston he helped organize the Army of the Shenandoah and in June, promoted to brigadier general, took command of the 4th Brigade. He distinguished himself and was badly wounded at Manassas (Bull Run), July 21, and in October was promoted to major general in command of a division of Gen. P.G.T.

Beauregard's army in the western theater. Early in 1862 he took command of the Department of East Tennessee (including Kentucky, northern Georgia, and western North Carolina). In the summer of 1862 he moved into eastern Tennessee and then Kentucky, capturing Richmond on August 30 and occupying Lexington, clearing the entire Cumberland Gap area of federal forces and creating a threat to Cincinnati. Support from Gen. Braxton Bragg failed to appear, however, and he was compelled to withdraw. He took part in the battles of Perryville, October 8, and Stones River (Murfreesboro), December 31–January 3, 1863. In October he had been promoted to lieutenant general, and in February 1863 he was given command of the Trans-Mississippi Department, comprising Arkansas, Louisiana, Texas, and Indian Territory. The cutting of the last link with the East in the fall of Vicksburg on July 4 merely underlined his position as the supreme authority, both military and civil, in the region. By running the blockade of Galveston he maintained trade with Europe and managed to send food and supplies to the East. Importing machinery in return for cotton, he established ammunition and arms factories, salt works, and other enterprises. He was promoted to general in February 1864. In April of that year he repulsed Gen. Nathaniel P. Banks's Red River campaign, sending Gen. Richard Taylor to defeat Banks at Sabine Cross Roads (Mansfield, Louisiana) on April 8 and pursuing him back to the Mississippi. Kirby-Smith remained in command of the department until May 26, 1865, when he surrendered to Gen. Edward R. S. Canby, the last Confederate commander to lay down arms. He traveled to Mexico and to Cuba but returned late in 1865 to the United States. He was president of the Atlantic and Pacific Telegraph Company, 1866–1868, of the Western Military Academy, 1868–1870, and of the University of Nashville, 1870–1875. He was professor of mathematics at the University of the South from 1875 until his death in Sewanee, Tennessee, on March 28, 1893. At his death he was the last surviving full general of the Civil War.

Kirk, Alan Goodrich (1888–1963), naval officer and diplomat. Born on October 30, 1888, in Philadelphia, Kirk graduated from the Naval Academy in 1909 and was commissioned an ensign two years later. He served aboard the *Wilmington* in Chinese waters during the revolution of 1911 under Sun Yat-sen, on the *Utah* in 1914–1916, and during World War I at the Naval Proving Ground, Dahlgren, Virginia, where he tested such new weapons as heavy railway guns and depth charges. Promoted to temporary lieutenant commander in February 1918, he later served aboard the *Connecticut*, the *Arizona*, and in 1920–1921 the presidential yacht *Mayflower*, with additional duty as White House naval aide. During 1922–

1924 he was on staff duty in Washington, D.C., during 1924–1926 aboard the *Maryland,* and during 1926–1928 on the staff of the commander of the Scouting Force. After graduation from the Naval War College in 1929 and two years as an instructor there he had his first command on the destroyer *Schenk.* He served aboard the *West Virginia* for a year and in the office of the chief of naval operations for three, 1933–1936; in 1937 he joined the staff of the commander of the Battle Force and, promoted to captain in 1938, moved up to the staff of the commander of the U.S. Fleet. In 1939 he was appointed naval attaché and naval attaché for air in London, where he established valuable diplomatic contacts and helped organize Anglo-American cooperation in the early phases of World War II. In March 1941 he returned to Washington as head of naval intelligence. In October he took command of a division of destroyer escorts in the Atlantic Fleet, receiving promotion to rear admiral in November, but in March 1942 he returned to London as naval attaché and chief of staff to Adm. Harold R. Stark, commander of U.S. naval forces in Europe. In February 1943 Kirk was named commander of the Amphibious Force, Atlantic Fleet, succeeding Adm. Henry K. Hewitt. He commanded, under Hewitt's Western Task Force, the landing of Gen. George S. Patton's Seventh Army on Sicily on July 10, 1943, a hazardous operation carried out under constant air and land bombardment. He had personal command of the "Cent Force," which landed Gen. Omar N. Bradley and his II Corps staff near Scoglitti. In the planning and carrying out of the Allied invasion of Europe, Kirk commanded the U.S. naval task forces operating on the American wing; on June 6, 1944, he directed from his flagship *Augusta* the landing of Gen. Omar N. Bradley's First Army on Utah and Omaha beaches in Normandy, providing fire and logistical support for the operation. In the twelve days beginning with the assault, the Western Task Force landed more than 314,000 troops, 41,000 vehicles, and over 115,000 tons of supplies. Later in the month naval forces under his command joined in the capture of the important port of Cherbourg. In October 1944 he was named commander of U.S. naval forces in France, in which capacity he directed naval support operations in the interior, including the crossing of the Rhine River. After the war he served on the navy's General Board, receiving promotion to vice admiral in May 1945 and retiring with the rank of admiral in February 1946, upon his nomination as ambassador to Belgium and minister to Luxembourg. He held those posts until April 1949, when he became ambassador to the U.S.S.R., a difficult post made more so by the Korean War. He held the post until October 1951, and on his return to the United States in February 1952 he was elected chairman of the American Committee for the Liberation of the Peoples of Russia and helped establish Radio Libera-

tion in Europe. He served also as head of the National Security Council's Psychological Strategy Board in 1952–1953, and in various other formal and informal intelligence capacities. In 1961 he was President John F. Kennedy's personal envoy during the Congo crisis. In May 1962 he was appointed ambassador to the Republic of China (Taiwan), but ill health forced his resignation in April 1963. Kirk died in New York City on October 15, 1963.

Knight, Austin Melvin (1854–1927), naval officer. Born in Ware, Massachusetts, on December 16, 1854, Knight graduated from the Naval Academy in 1873, was commissioned an ensign in 1874, and after three years on various ships in the Pacific he returned to the Academy as an instructor. In 1878 he went aboard the *Quinnebaug* in the Mediterranean Squadron and in 1880 transferred to the *Galena,* at sea in the Mediterranean and later in the South Atlantic. Promoted to lieutenant (junior grade) in March 1883, he was assigned that year to the ordnance experimental station at Annapolis, Maryland; in December 1885 he was promoted to lieutenant and given command of the station. From 1889 to 1892 he served aboard the *Chicago,* flagship of the "White Fleet" of new steel cruisers. He was again an instructor at the Academy in 1892–1895 and then served at sea for two years in the South Atlantic Squadron. During the Spanish–American War he was aboard the monitor *Puritan* on blockade duty in Cuban waters and subsequently in the Puerto Rico campaign. From 1898 to 1901 he was head of the department of seamanship at the Academy, advancing to lieutenant commander in March 1899. In 1901 he published *Modern Seamanship,* an internationally used text. In that year he attended the Naval War College, and in 1901–1903 he commanded the survey ship *Yankton,* being promoted to commander in June 1902. After a cruise off China in command of the *Castine,* 1903–1904, he was for three years president of a board on naval ordnance and of a joint army-navy board on smokeless powder. Promoted to captain in July 1907, Knight commanded the cruiser *Washington* in the Pacific for two years. In January 1911 he advanced to rear admiral, and in 1912, while serving as commander of the Reserve Fleet, he was sent to the eastern Mediterranean in command of a squadron to protect American interests during the Balkan war. From December 1913 to February 1917 he was president of the Naval War College, which was greatly enlarged and modernized during that period, and commander of the 2nd Naval District. Knight was named commander of the Asiatic Fleet in April 1917 with the rank of admiral. From his flagship *Brooklyn* he was in charge of the early phases of American operations at Vladivostok and in Siberia, later relinquishing that responsibility to Gen. William S. Graves, and in 1918 he visited the region again to report on conditions to President Woodrow

Wilson. He was placed on the retired list in December 1918, although he continued in service as president of a board of award until February 1919. Knight died in Washington, D.C., on February 26, 1927.

Knowlton, Thomas (1740–1776), Revolutionary army officer. Born in November 1740 in West Boxford, Massachusetts, Knowlton grew up there and in Ashford, Connecticut. In 1755 he enlisted in the British colonial forces for service in the French and Indian War, reaching the rank of lieutenant, and in 1762 he took part in the expedition to Cuba and the capture of Havana on August 12. In April 1775, on hearing of the battle at Lexington, he marched as captain of a company of Ashford militia to Lexington and thence to Boston. At the battle of Bunker Hill, June 17, his company held an advanced line on the left at the foot of the hill (actually Breed's Hill); throughout the battle he prevented the British from flanking the American fortifications, and at the end he covered the American withdrawal. In January 1776 he was commissioned major in the 20th Continental Infantry. On the night of January 8 he led a daring raid into Charlestown, burning part of the British headquarters and taking prisoners. Promoted to lieutenant colonel in August 1776, he took part in the battle of Long Island, August 22–29, and shortly thereafter organized a corps of rangers numbering about 120 picked volunteers. On September 16 Gen. George Washington sent Knowlton and his rangers to scout the British position on Harlem (Morningside) Heights and then ordered him to encircle, attack from the rear, and capture an advanced detachment. During the movement he attacked too soon, on the flank instead of at the rear; the British detachment withdrew to the Heights, and in the skirmish Knowlton was killed.

Knox, Henry (1750–1806), Revolutionary army officer. Born in Boston on July 25, 1750, Knox became the sole support of his mother at the age of twelve, when his father died, and he left school to go to work for a bookseller. When he was twenty-one he established his own bookshop in Boston; the business throve, but he gave it up for a military career when the Revolutionary War broke out. He had joined the Boston Grenadier Corps in 1772, and he became an avid student of tactics, particularly of artillery. Commissioned a colonel and given command of the Continental artillery in November 1775, he overcame enormous difficulties in conveying 55 artillery pieces, captured by Ethan Allen at Fort Ticonderoga, 300 miles over the rugged Berkshire Hills in dead of winter to Boston, where they were used to take the city. With the new artillery commanding the city from Dorchester Heights, the British evacuated Boston in March 1776. Knox remained throughout the war a trusted adviser to Gen. George Washington,

with whom he had formed a close friendship; indeed, he was probably closer to Washington during the years of the war than any other man and was present at almost every important engagement in the northern campaigns as well as at Yorktown. He participated in the fighting around New York City in 1776, and when Washington crossed the Delaware River on Christmas night of that year to march on Trenton, New Jersey, it was Knox who organized the movements of the troops, his stentorian voice carrying over the gale as he relayed the orders of his chief. He was promoted to brigadier general after the battle of Trenton. He was with Washington at the winter quarters at Valley Forge during 1777–1778, and rendered a good account of himself at Monmouth, June 27, 1778. In 1779 he was the founder of a military academy in Morristown, Pennsylvania, that was the progenitor of West Point. After sitting on the court-martial that tried British Maj. John André as a spy in 1780, he was promoted to major general on November 15, 1781, shortly after the siege of Yorktown, where he had directed the artillery to good effect, "the resources of his genius," as Washington said, supplying "the deficit of means." He was the youngest major general in the Continental army. The chief organizer of the Society of the Cincinnati in May 1783 and its secretary for many years, he was the first to shake Washington's hand in Fraunces Tavern in New York City on December 4, 1783, when Washington bade farewell to his officers. From August 1782 he commanded the fort at West Point, and from Washington's resignation on December 23, 1783, until his own on June 20, 1784, he was the senior officer of the army. Afterward Knox returned to Boston to reenter business. He was elected secretary of war by Congress, operating under the Articles of Confederation, on March 8, 1785; he was retained in the post by President Washington in the new government organized in 1789 under the Constitution. His career in the cabinet was darkened by disputes with Alexander Hamilton, and he resigned on December 28, 1794, to return to private life, after having helped lay the groundwork for the reestablishment of the U.S. navy. In 1798 he was appointed a major general in the Provisional Army in anticipation of war with France. He lived during his last years on a large estate near Thomaston, Maine (then a district of Massachusetts), where he died suddenly on October 25, 1806, as a consequence of having swallowed a chicken bone.

Kościuszko, Tadeusz (1746–1817), Revolutionary army officer and Polish hero. Born on February 4, 1746, in Mereczowszczyzna, Belorussia (then under the control of the union of Poland and Lithuania, and now part of the Soviet Union), Tadeusz Andrzej Bonawentura Kościuszko graduated from the Royal School at Warsaw in 1769, was commissioned a captain in the Polish army, and studied engineering at

Mézières, France. Later, after returning to Poland in 1774 and escaping an unlucky love affair, he studied painting in Paris. News of the American Revolution stirred him to apply to Benjamin Franklin for a recommendation to the Continental Congress. Arriving in Philadelphia in August 1776, he was commissioned a colonel of engineers in the Continental army on October 18 of that year. He distinguished himself at Ticonderoga the following spring, made an important contribution to Gen. Horatio Gates's brilliant victory over Gen. John Burgoyne at Saratoga, on September 17, 1777, and the next year was placed in charge of building the fortifications at West Point. From 1780 to the end of the war he served meritoriously as chief engineer of the southern army under Gen. Nathanael Greene in the Carolina campaign, performing as both an engineer and a cavalry officer. In October 1783 he received the thanks of Congress and permanent American citizenship and was made a brigadier general. Finding himself once again with no duties to perform, he left New York City for Paris in July 1784 and thence went to Poland, where he languished in rural retirement. He reemerged as major general of the Polish army in 1789 and led pathetically inadequate forces against the Russians in the spring of 1792. Upon the defeat of the Poles and the second partition of his country in 1793 he retired to France, but he returned to Poland in 1794 to lead an uprising in that year. He was chosen dictator and instituted liberal reforms, but he was defeated by a vastly superior Russian force at Maciejowice in October 1794 and taken prisoner. Released by Czar Paul I in November 1796 on his promise that he would not take up arms against Russia, he revisited the United States in 1797. Congress appropriated more than $18,000 in pay that was due him and made him a grant of 500 acres of land in Ohio. The money he used to buy slaves and set them free. He returned to France in 1798 to live in retirement near Fontainebleau, refusing in 1806 to aid Napoleon in his invasion of Russia because of his previous promise to the czar. He moved to Switzerland in 1816 and died in Solothurn on October 15, 1817. His remains were carried to Kraków (Cracow) and interred in the cathedral, while the people of Poland mourned him as a national hero. He had freed the serfs on his Polish estate earlier the same year, and his will directed that the funds derived from the sale of his Ohio lands be used to free as many slaves as possible. The money was employed to found the Colored School at Newark, New Jersey, one of the first educational institutions for black students to be established in the United States.

Krueger, Walter (1881–1967), army officer. Born on January 26, 1881, in Flatow, West Prussia (now Zlotow, Poland), Krueger came with his family at the age of eight to the United States. In 1898 he enlisted for volunteer service in the Spanish–American War, and in 1899, having served in Cuba, he enlisted as a private in the regulars. While serving in the Philippines with the infantry he advanced to the rank of sergeant and in June 1901 was commissioned a second lieutenant in the 30th Infantry. He returned to the United States in 1903, graduated from the Infantry and Cavalry School, Fort Leavenworth, Kansas, in 1906 and the Staff College there in 1907, and after a second tour in the Philippines was assigned to various routine duties. He took part in the Mexican Punitive Expedition under Gen. John J. Pershing in 1916. He went to France in February 1918 and served as assistant chief of staff of the 26th Division and later of the 84th Division, as chief of staff of the Tank Corps, and then as assistant chief of staff of the VI and IV Corps in occupation duty, advancing to the rank of temporary colonel. After periods at the Infantry School, Fort Benning, Georgia, and in command of the 55th Infantry at Camp Funston, Kansas, he attended the Army War College, graduating in 1921 and remaining for a year as an instructor. From 1922 to 1925 he was in the War Plans Division of the General Staff; he graduated from the Naval War College in 1926 and from 1928 to 1932 taught there. He commanded the 6th Infantry at Jefferson Barracks, Missouri, for two years and then returned to the War Plans Division, becoming chief of the division in May 1936 and receiving promotion to temporary brigadier general in October. In June 1938 he went to Fort George Meade, Maryland, as commander of the 16th Infantry Brigade; promoted to temporary major general in February 1939, he then commanded the 2nd Division at Fort Sam Houston, Texas, rising in October 1940 to command of the VIII Corps. In May 1941 Krueger was promoted to temporary lieutenant general in command of the Third Army and the Southern Defense Command. A month after activation of the Sixth Army in January 1943 Krueger took command, making his headquarters in Australia. He remained in command of the Sixth Army, which included, in various combinations at different times, the I, X, XIV, and XXIV Corps, throughout its combat period. Operations of the Sixth included those on Kiriwina and Woodlark islands, July 1943; New Britain, December 1943–February 1944; the Admiralty Islands, February–May 1944; Biak Island, May–August 1944; New Guinea, July–August 1944; Morotai, September–October 1944; Leyte and Mindoro, Philippines, October–December 1944; and Luzon, January–June 1945. In September 1945 the Sixth Army took up occupation duty on Honshu, Japan; in January 1946 it was inactivated. Krueger, who had been promoted to temporary general in March 1945, reverted to lieutenant general in January 1946 but was retired as a general in July 1946. Noted not only as an expert on discipline and training but also as a historian and scholar of military affairs, Krueger published translations of several classic German texts and in 1953 published *From Down Under to Nippon: the Story of the Sixth Army in World War II.* He died in Valley Forge, Pennsylvania, on August 20, 1967.

L

Lafayette, Marquis de (1757–1834), Revolutionary army officer and French statesman. Born on September 6, 1757, at Chavaniac in Auvergne of an aristocratic French family, Marie Joseph Paul Yves Roch Gilbert du Motier, the Marquis de Lafayette, lost his father, killed fighting the British at Minden, when he was two. Upon the death of his mother and grandfather in 1770 he inherited the family fortune. His formal schooling, begun when he was eleven, ended when he was fifteen. He enlisted in a company of musketeers in 1771 and two years later transferred to a regiment of dragoons. Bent on the glory of a military career, he acquired a captaincy of dragoons in 1774, but, dissatisfied with the court life at Versailles and with his imagination fired by an account of the American Revolution, in December 1776 he arranged through Silas Deane in Paris for a commission as major general in the Continental army. He left for America in April 1777 despite opposition from king and family, sailing with his recently acquired friend, Johann Kalb, who had also been promised a commission. They arrived in Philadelphia in July and met with the Continental Congress. The young marquis agreed to serve without pay and without a specific command and was commissioned a major general. In August he conferred with Gen. George Washington in a meeting that proved to be the beginning of a long and warm friendship. Whatever reservations the army or Congress might have had about the youthful foreign adventurer were erased at the battle of Brandywine, September 11, 1777, where he fought well and was wounded. Recovering in a month's time, he rejoined Washington and again distinguished himself in a skirmish with German mercenaries. In December he was given his own command, a division of Virginians, and after spending the winter with Washington at Valley Forge he was appointed to lead an expedition into Canada. The invasion proved abortive owing both to lack of supplies and, as Lafayette thought, to the Conway Cabal; but on May 18, 1778, his skillful retreat from a larger force under Gen. Sir Henry Clinton at Barren Hill was highly praised, and a month later at the battle of Monmouth, June 28, his participation as a division commander stood out in the defeat. (He was originally to have led the attack in that battle, but Gen. Charles Lee had asserted his seniority and claimed the honor.) In the succeeding months Lafayette played an increasingly important role both in the field and as an instrument of the growing alliance

with France, which by May had become a reality. A French fleet under Count d'Estaing reached Rhode Island in July 1778, and Lafayette served as liaison during and after Gen. John Sullivan's unsuccessful attack on Newport. In early January 1779 he went to France a popular hero, staying there for some time in order to obtain substantial French help for the American cause and receiving promotion to colonel in the French army while there. In April 1780 he returned to the United States with news of the forthcoming dispatch of a French expeditionary force under Count de Rochambeau and was restored to command of the Virginia light troops. Late in the year he sat on the court-martial of Maj. John André. In March 1781 he participated in the unsuccessful attempt to capture Benedict Arnold at Hampton Roads, Virginia, and beginning in April he held a major command in the campaign in Virginia against Gen. Charles Cornwallis. He skillfully retreated from Cornwallis's northward march until reinforced by Gen. Anthony Wayne, and then slowly forced the British back toward the Yorktown Peninsula. The arrival of Washington and Rochambeau closed the circle, and Cornwallis, hemmed in on the south by Lafayette and cut off from his own navy by the French West Indies fleet barring the entrance to Chesapeake Bay, finally capitulated at Yorktown on October 19, 1781, virtually bringing the Revolution to a close. Lafayette's spirited generalship and his role in securing French assistance had played a large part in the American victory. He returned to France in 1782 "the hero of two worlds," universally hailed as "America's Marquis," and was promoted to major general. His reception by his friends in the United States during a six-month visit in 1784 was equally warm; he was made a citizen of several states, and he departed again filled with enthusiasm for republicanism and ready to launch a new career in his native land. In 1787 he was chosen to the first assembly of notables and early in 1789 sat in the estates-general. There he presented the first draft of the Declaration of the Rights of Man and the Citizen, drafted with the aid of his friend Thomas Jefferson, then U.S. minister in France. He played a prominent part in the French Revolution and shortly after the capture of the Bastille in 1789 was placed in command of the new Paris militia. By 1790 he and the king were the two most powerful figures in France. In 1791, soon after the adoption of the new constitution, he resigned his command, but in December he reentered public service and accepted the rank of lieutenant general for the impending war with Austria. For five years, 1792–1797, after his suspension by the antimonarchical Assembly and his attempted flight to America, he was a captive of the Prussians and Austrians. Returning to France in 1799, he was not active in public life again until 1815, when he briefly entered the Chamber of Deputies and played a leading role in securing Napoleon's abdication. He was again a deputy in 1818–1824. In 1824, at the invitation of President James Monroe, he made a triumphant return to the United States. Touring for more than a year, he became the idol of a new generation of Americans, "the doyen," as Thomas Jefferson put it, "of the soldiers of liberty of the world." Congress voted him land and money, a timely act for he had lost most of his fortune in the turmoils in France. On returning to France, once again to an enthusiastic reception, he reentered politics. In 1827 he was again seated in the Chamber of Deputies and during the revolution of July 1830 again took command of the national guard. At first supporting Louis Philippe but later attacking him for unkept promises, Lafayette continued to espouse liberal causes in the Chamber of Deputies until his death in Paris on May 20, 1834.

Laffite, Jean (1780?–1825?), privateer. Little is known of Laffite's origins; he was probably born in France about 1780 and doubtless spent his youth at sea. In 1809 he and his brother Pierre ran a blacksmith shop in New Orleans that served as a front for smuggled goods. He soon became chief of the band of smugglers and established his headquarters on the islands of Barataria Bay. Between 1810 and 1814 he operated perhaps a dozen ships under privateering commission from the Republic of Cartagena (in present-day Colombia), preying on Spanish vessels in the Gulf of Mexico and selling the booty in Louisiana. When the British courted his assistance during the War of 1812, offering him a captaincy in the navy and substantial monetary reward, Laffite feigned interest and then warned Louisiana officials about what he had discovered about English plans to attack New Orleans. The Americans responded by raiding Laffite's colony on Barataria Bay in September 1814, the raid being led by Commander Daniel T. Patterson, and bringing his ships to New Orleans. Laffite was finally able to convince Gen. Andrew Jackson of his loyalty, and he and his men did valiant service manning the artillery during the battle of New Orleans, January 8, 1815. In February President James Madison honored a promise made by Jackson and granted pardons to Laffite and the men from his Barataria colony. In 1817 he and nearly a thousand of his followers went to the island that was later to become the site of Galveston, Texas, founded the settlement of Campeche, and reverted to privateering

against the Spanish. Laffite continued to respect American shipping but eventually some of the Campeche pirates escaped his control, and in 1819 several were hanged in New Orleans for piracy. In 1821, following the capture and scuttling of an American merchantman by some of Laffite's men, the navy dispatched the *Enterprise* under Lt. Lawrence Kearny to disperse the Galveston colony. Laffite himself picked a crew and sailed away in his favorite ship, the *Pride*. Until about 1825 there were stories of his activities on the Spanish Main, but, although nothing is known of the place or manner of his death, it seems to have occurred about then. After that, stories of his exploits were only legendary.

Lahm, Frank Purdy (1877–1963), army officer and airman. Born on November 17, 1877, in Mansfield, Ohio, the son of a pioneer balloon enthusiast, Lahm graduated from West Point in 1901 and was commissioned in the cavalry. After a tour of duty in the Philippines he was an instructor at West Point from 1903 to 1906. In October 1906, in one of his father's balloons, he won the first James Gordon Bennett International Aeronautical Cup, traveling 402 miles from Paris to a point in Yorkshire, England, in 23 hours. After study at the French army cavalry school at Saumur he was transferred in 1907 to the Signal Corps, for which he surveyed European progress in aeronautics. On September 9, 1908, he became the first army officer to ride as passenger in a Wright aircraft in trials at Fort Myer, Virginia (a week later the plane crashed, injuring Orville Wright and killing Lt. Thomas E. Selfridge), and on October 26, 1909, Lahm and Lt. F. E. Humphreys of the engineers became the first two certified army pilots after instruction by Wilbur Wright. He returned to the cavalry for a time since money for army aviation was lacking, but in 1912, while in the Philippines, he organized a flying school in Manila. Promoted to captain in April 1916, he was appointed secretary of the Signal Corps Aviation School at San Diego, California. In 1917, after a short period in command of the balloon school at Fort Omaha, Nebraska, he was ordered to France. After inspecting English and French balloon services he organized the lighter-than-air service of the American Expeditionary Force. He served successively on the staff of the chief of the Air Service, the Zone of Advance Air Service, and First Army Air Service, and in October 1918 organized and commanded the Second Army Air Service. During 1919–1920 he was a special student in the Army War College and then was named assistant to Gen. Charles T. Menoher, chief of the Air Service, receiving promotion to lieutenant colonel in July 1920. From 1924 to 1926 he was air officer of the IX Corps area at San Francisco. On the reorganization of the Air Service as the Army Air Corps in July 1926 he was named assistant to the chief (Gen. Mason M.

Patrick until December 1927, then Gen. James E. Fechet), with the temporary rank of brigadier general and with the task of organizing the Air Corps Training Center at Duncan (later Randolph) Field, Texas. In 1930 he reverted to lieutenant colonel and returned to his former post in San Francisco. Promoted to colonel in October 1931, he was appointed military attaché for air to France and Spain in that year; in 1933 he was attaché for France only, and in 1934 he became attaché for Belgium also. In 1935 he returned to the United States as air officer of the II Corps area in New York City with the rank of brigadier general. Promoted to major general in 1941, he served as commander of Randolph Field in October–November of that year; he then retired from the army. Lahm died in Sandusky, Ohio, on July 7, 1963.

Lake, Simon (1866–1945), engineer and inventor. Born in Pleasantville, New Jersey, on September 4, 1866, Lake included in his scanty schooling a short period of instruction at the Franklin Institute in Philadelphia. At twenty-three he began manufacturing in Baltimore several machines useful in ship construction and design. Shortly thereafter he began experimenting with designs for underwater vessels. His design for an 85-foot double-hulled submersible in 1893 lost in a government competition to John P. Holland's original *Plunger* design, and Lake decided to build a boat himself. His first experimental submersible, *Argonaut Jr.*, was completed in 1894, and in 1897, almost simultaneously with Holland's *Plunger* and from the same Columbian Iron Works yard in Baltimore, he launched the gasoline-engine-powered *Argonaut,* which in November 1898 traveled under its own power from Norfolk, Virginia, to New York City, becoming the first submarine to operate successfully in the open sea. Lake established the Lake Torpedo Boat Company at Bridgeport, Connecticut, in 1900 and two years later launched the *Protector,* a double-hulled submarine featuring fore-and-aft hydroplanes that enabled it to submerge on an even keel (a feature characteristic of Lake's designs from the first). He spent several years as a consultant to the Russians, who in 1906 bought *Protector* and were interested in submarines for clearing ice-bound ports, to the British, and to the Germans, who later pirated his designs and used one of his models when constructing their U-boats. His first submarine to be bougt by the U.S. navy was the *Seal* in 1911, and it was followed by 28 more of the same class. The shrinking of the navy in the 1920s led eventually to the sale of the firm. Lake was much interested in peaceful uses of the submarine, and in 1932 he designed another submersible for use in underwater salvage operations. In his later years he devoted much of his time to looking for sunken gold in New York harbor. He died on June 23, 1945, in Bridgeport, Connecticut.

Lamar, Mirabeau Buonaparte (1798–1859), Texas army officer and public official. Born on August 16, 1798, in Louisville, Georgia, Lamar first planned a career as a merchant but in 1823 accepted a position as secretary to Gov. George M. Troup of Georgia. Three years later he became the editor of the *Columbus* (Georgia) *Enquirer.* In 1833 he made an unsuccessful bid for a seat in the House of Representatives. He visited Texas in 1835 and the following year returned to serve as commander of the Texas cavalry, under Sam Houston, at the battle of San Jacinto, April 21. His bravery in the field earned him a place as secretary of war in the provisional government headed by D. G. Burnet and brought about his election as vice-president of Texas in October 1836. In December 1838, succeeding Houston, he became the second president of the Republic of Texas. During his three-year term he founded a new capital at Austin in 1840 and promoted measures to assure continued Texas independence and to extend the sovereignty of the Republic west to the Rio Grande (taking in much of New Mexico), goals that he felt required the expulsion of the Comanche and Cherokee Indians. Under his administration relations were established with England and France and a navy was formed, eventually comprising seven warships under the command of Commodore Edwin W. Moore. When he left office in 1841, on the other hand, the economy of Texas was in perilous condition. His sympathy with the Southern position on slavery led him, after 1844, to support statehood for Texas. After the admission of Texas as a state in 1845 and after the Mexican War, in which Lamar participated, he retired to his plantation at Richmond, Texas. A brief term as U.S. minister to Nicaragua and Costa Rica in 1857–1859 and the appearance of a book of poems, *Verse Memorials,* 1857, followed. He died in Richmond, Texas, on December 19, 1859.

Lane, James Henry (1814–1866), army officer and public official. Born in Lawrenceburg, Indiana, on June 22, 1814, Lane grew up on the frontier and studied law with his father before being admitted to the bar in 1840. Exemplary service in command of the 3rd and later the 5th Indiana Volunteer regiments and briefly of a brigade at Buena Vista in the Mexican War opened a political future that began notably with a term as lieutenant governor of Indiana, 1849–1853, followed by a term in the House of Representatives, March 1853–March 1855. In 1855 he emigrated to Kansas Territory, which, after the Kansas–Nebraska Act of 1854 that repealed the Missouri Compromise of 1820, became a bloody jousting ground for proslavery and antislavery forces until it was finally admitted to the Union as a free state on the eve of the Civil War. Throughout the period of the Border War, Lane was prominent among the Free-State forces, organizing a militia to defend Lawrence against the

"Border Ruffians" from Missouri in the "Wakarusa War" of December 1855, and, as a senator-elect under the Topeka constitution, journeying to Washington the following spring to advance the Free-Soil movement and to secure the admission of Kansas to the Union as a free state. In that effort he failed, Senator Stephen A. Douglas taking the lead in persuading the Senate to refuse to recognize Lane's credentials. In August 1856 he made his way back to the territory with an "army" of irregulars he had collected during a tour of the Old Northwest and began ravaging proslavery settlements. Hostilities subsided late in 1856 after intervention by federal troops and, when proslavery forces later lost control of the legislature, the Free-State party never thereafter relinquished its dominance. Late in 1857 the legislature appointed him major general of militia. Kansas became a state in January 1861, and Lane was sent by the legislature to the Senate as a Republican in April. In Washington he gained the favor of President Abraham Lincoln, who commissioned him brigadier general of volunteers in June 1861. In September–October 1861 his volunteer brigade operated against Gen. Sterling Price in Missouri. In July 1862 he became the Kansas recruiting commissioner and was instrumental in organizing a brigade of black troops for the Union forces. In 1864 he was for a time an aide to Gen. Samuel R. Curtis, commander of the Department of Kansas. He was not without enemies in Kansas, but an attempt to thwart his reelection to the Senate in 1865 failed as Lane's effective stump oratory secured a friendly state legislature. He finally lost favor at home by adhering to Lincoln's conservative Reconstruction policy, and after being implicated in a scandal over Indian contracts he became sufficiently depressed to commit suicide. He died on July 11, 1866, near Fort Leavenworth, Kansas.

Lardner, James Lawrence (1802–1881), naval officer. Born in Philadelphia on November 20, 1802, Lardner was a merchant seaman for a short time before entering the navy as a midshipman in May 1820. He served aboard the *Dolphin* and the *Franklin* in the Pacific Squadron under Commodore Charles Stewart; on the *Brandywine,* which in 1825 carried the Marquis de Lafayette back to France after his American tour; and, having been promoted to lieutenant in May 1828, on the *Vincennes* in a world cruise in 1829–1830. Subsequently he was on the *Delaware* in the Mediterranean, 1833–1834, and the *Independence,* 1837–1838. In 1845 he took command of the receiving ship at Philadelphia, remaining there until 1848 and seeing no action in the Mexican War. Promoted to commander in May 1851, he commanded the *Porpoise* in African waters in 1850–1853 and in 1855 became fleet captain of the West India Squadron. In May 1861 he was promoted to captain, and in September of that year he took command of the steam

frigate *Susquehanna,* on which he took part in the attack on Port Royal, South Carolina, on November 7 by Flag-Officer Samuel F. Du Pont. In June 1862 Lardner was placed in command of the East Gulf Blockading Squadron, and in July he was promoted to commodore. Ill health forced him to relinquish his command in November, but in June 1863 he returned to active duty as commander of the West India Squadron, succeeding Charles Wilkes. The squadron was responsible for protection of commerce and blockade but saw virtually no action. In November 1864 Lardner retired, and in July 1866 he was made rear admiral on the retired list. He was governor of the Philadelphia Naval Asylum from 1869 to 1872. He died in Philadelphia on April 12, 1881.

Lawrence, James (1781–1813), naval officer. Born in Burlington, New Jersey, on October 1, 1781, Lawrence decided against a career in the law to become a midshipman in the navy in September 1798. He served on various ships and in April 1802 was promoted to lieutenant. In 1803 he sailed for Tripoli on the *Enterprise* and served on her under Lt. Stephen Decatur, taking part as second-in-command in the daring raid into Tripoli harbor to burn the captured *Philadelphia* in February 1804. He remained in Tripolitan waters until 1808. Subsequently he served aboard the *Constitution* and other vessels, receiving promotion to master commandant in December 1811. As commander of the *Hornet* in Commodore John Rodgers's squadron early in the War of 1812, his most notable encounter occurred off the coast of South America near present-day Georgetown, Guyana, on February 24, 1813, when the *Peacock,* a brig having slightly less firepower than the *Hornet,* succumbed to Lawrence's superior tactics in a short but hot exchange that sent her to the bottom. Lawrence was promoted to captain in March, even before news of his victory over the *Peacock* reached home. On June 1, 1813, he went to sea again as commander of the *Chesapeake.* In what was later claimed to be a pointless sea fight—he was under orders to seek out British transports and storeships bound for Canada—he took on the frigate *Shannon* outside Boston harbor. Although the ships were about evenly matched in guns, the *Chesapeake* had the reputation of a poor sailer and had a poorly trained crew under a new captain. The fight was very brief, and Lawrence was mortally wounded during it. But even though he was decisively beaten and his ship captured, Lawrence died a hero on shipboard, on June 4, 1813, and his famous appeal, "Don't give up the ship," spoken as he was being carried below, is cherished by the U.S. navy and has served to rally succeeding generations of its fighting men.

Lawton, Henry Ware (1843–1899), army officer. Born in Manhattan, near Toledo, Ohio, on March

17, 1843, Lawton grew up from 1847 in Fort Wayne, Indiana. He left Fort Wayne Methodist Episcopal College at the outbreak of the Civil War in 1861 to enlist in the 9th Indiana. After service in West Virginia he was commissioned first lieutenant of the newly organized 30th Indiana in August 1861. He saw action at Shiloh, April 6–7, 1862, and a month later was promoted to captain; with the Army of the Cumberland he took part in the battles of Murfreesboro (Stones River), December 31–January 3, 1863, and Chickamauga, September 18–20, 1863, among many others; and on August 3, 1864, he won a Medal of Honor in a skirmish before Atlanta. In November 1864 he was promoted to lieutenant colonel; he was brevetted colonel in March 1865 and mustered out of service in November. Lawton then took up the study of law at Harvard, but in May 1867 he accepted a commission of second lieutenant of the 41st Infantry (Colored), receiving promotion to first lieutenant in July. In 1869 the 41st was absorbed into the new 24th. In January 1871 he was transferred to the 4th Cavalry, with which he served under Col. Ranald S. MacKenzie in Indian campaigns in Texas and Indian Territory, receiving promotion to captain in March 1879. He was later posted in Arizona, and in 1886, under the overall command of Gen. Nelson A. Miles, he led a column more than 1300 miles through the Sierra Madre Mountains in pursuit of Geronimo, whom he captured in September. In September 1888 he was promoted to major in the inspector general's department; he advanced to lieutenant colonel in February 1889 and to colonel in July 1898. In May 1898 he was appointed brigadier general of volunteers for service in the Spanish–American War. In command of the 2nd Division of Gen. William R. Shafter's V Corps in Cuba, he led the advance from the beachhead at Daiquiri on June 22, occupied Siboney on June 23, and in the general offensive against Santiago on July 1 captured the fortified village of El Caney. On July 8 he was promoted to major general of volunteers, and he served as military governor of the city and province of Santiago until October. He then took command of the IV Corps at Huntsville, Alabama. In January 1899 he was sent to the Philippines, where in March he took command of the 1st Division of Gen. Elwell S. Otis's VIII Corps. Operating north of Manila, he captured Santa Cruz on April 10 and San Isidro on May 15, in June he pushed insurgents back from Cavite south of Manila, and in October he held the right of the general advance into northern Luzon. In December he turned his division over to Gen. Loyd Wheaton and returned to Manila to lead an expedition to the east. On December 19, 1899, while attacking San Mateo, he was shot and killed.

Lea, Homer (1876–1912), soldier. Born in Denver on November 17, 1876, Lea was educated at Occiden-

tal College and at Stanford University, which he attended from 1897 to 1899 ostensibly to study law; but his obsession as a student was with military history, and he often predicted that he would become one of the great military commanders of history. These boasts were scoffed at by his friends and schoolmates, since he was a frail hunchback who was rebuffed when he tried to enlist in the U.S. army. He left Stanford in 1899 to go to China, arriving in time to join in the cooperative expedition mounted by the United States and several European powers for the relief of Peking during the Boxer Rebellion. He experienced many adventures and narrowly escaped death a number of times as he gained the esteem of the Chinese for his courage and military knowledge. Within a few months of his arrival in China he had met and become associated with the reformer K'ang Yu-wei, the leader of a movement attempting to restore Kuang Hsü to the throne of China. Lea was soon made a general and put in command of a group of volunteers in this effort. The plot being discovered, he fled to Hong Kong in 1900 and there met Sun Yat-sen, with whom he later went to Japan, becoming, incredibly, Sun's chief of staff before he had reached the age of twenty-five. He returned to the United States in 1901 but in 1904 was back in China with Sun Yat-sen, receiving the rank of lieutenant general. He continued to serve as Sun's confidential adviser even after his return to California during his last years, and early in 1912 he was offered the post of chief of staff of the revolutionary army, a post he declined because of ill health. He is probably best known for his authorship of two books, the first, *The Vermillion Pencil*, 1908, being a novel of the Manchu regime, and the second, *The Valor of Ignorance*, 1909, containing astute predictions of the course of military history of the twentieth century, particularly with regard to war between an aggressive Japan and the United States that would begin with a Japanese attack on Hawaii. His last book, *The Day of the Saxon*, 1912, predicted Japanese attacks on the British empire in the Far East. He died on November 1, 1912, near Los Angeles. He is remembered as one of the most brilliant, as well as one of the most enigmatic, figures in U.S. military history.

Leahy, William Daniel (1875–1959), naval officer and public official. Born on May 6, 1875, in Hampton, Iowa, Leahy graduated from the U.S. Naval Academy in 1897. His first sea duty was aboard the *Oregon*, Capt. Charles E. Clark, during its famous dash around the Horn and in the Spanish–American War. He subsequently saw service in the Philippine Insurrection and the Boxer Rebellion in China. After two years on the faculty of the Naval Academy he served in 1909–1912 on the *California* and in the latter year was chief of staff of the U.S. occupation forces in Nicaragua. Promoted to commander in 1915, he commanded the *Dolphin* during operations in Mexico, Santo Domingo (Dominican Republic), and Haiti in 1916. In World War I he commanded the *Nevada* and later a troop ship, receiving promotion to temporary captain in July 1918 (he became permanent in that grade in June 1921). It was during World War I that he became a close friend of the assistant secretary of the navy, Franklin D. Roosevelt. Posts in command of various ships and squadrons followed, and in 1927 he was named chief of the Bureau of Ordnance with temporary rank of rear admiral; he was promoted to permanent rear admiral in April 1930 and remained with that bureau until 1931, when he became commander of destroyers, Scouting Force. During 1933–1935 he headed the Bureau of Navigation, and in March 1935 he was promoted to vice admiral in command of battleships, Battle Force. In April 1936 he advanced to command of Battle Force, with the rank of admiral, and in January 1937 he became chief of naval operations. On his retirement in July 1939 he was appointed governor of Puerto Rico by Roosevelt, a post he held until November 1940. Throughout World War II, President Roosevelt was to rely heavily on his administrative ability and military advice. Between December 1940 and April 1942 he served as U.S. ambassador to the Vichy government in France; he was then recalled to fill the newly created position of chief of staff to Roosevelt. In that post he was the principal liaison between the President and the armed forces, and he presided over the then informally constituted Joint Chiefs of Staff. He also took part in virtually all the top-level Allied conferences. He remained at the President's side throughout the war and, after Roosevelt's death in April 1945, continued in the same position under President Harry S. Truman until March 1949, when he retired for a second time, with the rank, held since December 1944, of admiral of the fleet, being the first naval officer to achieve five-star rank since Adm. George Dewey in 1899. His war memoirs, *I Was There*, appeared in 1950. Leahy died on July 20, 1959, in Bethesda, Maryland.

Leavenworth, Henry (1783–1834), army officer. Born on December 10, 1783, in New Haven, Connecticut, Leavenworth grew up in Vermont and in Delhi, New York, where he was admitted to the bar in 1804. He began his military career as a captain in the infantry at the beginning of the War of 1812 and in August 1813 was promoted to major. He distinguished himself at the brief but hard fought battle of Chippewa, July 5, 1814, which restored waning American military prestige, and was promoted to the brevet rank of lieutenant colonel. Later that month, after the battle of Lundy's Lane at Niagara on July 25, he was made a brevet colonel. After the war, taking a leave of absence, he served a term in the New York state legislature, but in February 1818 he returned to active duty as lieutenant colonel of the 5th Infantry under Col. Josiah Snelling. The next 16 years were spent in service on the frontier, at first in the Old Northwest and later in the Southwest. In 1819 he established Fort Snelling (originally Fort St. Anthony) in what is now Minnesota; in 1821 he was named commandant at Fort Atkinson, built two years earlier opposite Council Bluffs, in what later became Nebraska, and in 1823 he led a punitive expedition against the Arikara Indians following their attack on a fur trapping party led by William H. Ashley. He was brevetted brigadier general in July 1824 and in December of that year promoted to colonel of the 3rd Infantry. He served at Green Bay, Wisconsin, before going in 1826 to Jefferson Barracks, near St. Louis, of which he became commander in 1829. Early in 1834 he was named commander of the entire southwestern frontier, as he was considered the man most likely to achieve a stable peace with the Indians, and in June of that year he rode out of Fort Gibson at the head of the newly organized 1st Dragoons to make a show of force at the Comanche and Pawnee villages up the Arkansas River. Much of the regiment fell ill, including Leavenworth, who died on July 21, 1834, at Camp Smith, near the junction of the Washita and Red rivers. A cantonment (later fort) that he had built in the summer of 1827 in present-day Kansas bears his name, as does the city later established nearby. He was reburied at Fort Leavenworth in 1902.

Ledyard, William (1738–1781), Revolutionary militia officer. Born in Groton, Connecticut, on December 6, 1738, Ledyard was an uncle of the explorer John Ledyard. Little is known of his early life. He was active in the patriot cause before the Revolution and in 1776 was appointed captain of artillery in the Connecticut militia. He had risen to colonel by 1781. On September 6 of that year New London, Connecticut, was attacked and captured by a British force commanded by Gen. Benedict Arnold. Ledyard, with 157 men, held Fort Griswold at Groton, across the Thames River from New London, and a force of some 800 British infantry and New Jersey Loyalist troops under Col. Eyre was sent to attack him. In a desperate defense Ledyard's men killed or wounded a fourth of the attackers, including Eyre and his second-in-command, but were eventually compelled to surrender. When the British entered the fort, Ledyard offered his sword to Maj. Bromfield, the Loyalist commander. He was immediately set upon and killed, apparently with his own sword and, in the generally accepted story, by Bromfield. A general massacre of the fort's defenders ensued, with 85 killed outright and many more wounded.

Lee, Charles (1731–1782), Revolutionary army officer. Born at Dernhall, Cheshire, England, in 1731, Lee early decided on a military career. At twenty he was commissioned a lieutenant in the 44th Regiment and during the French and Indian War participated in several battles in North America. His regiment was part of Gen. Edward Braddock's force at the British defeat at Fort Dusquesne, Pennsylvania, July 9, 1755. Lee became a captain in June 1756 and was wounded in July 1758 during the ill fated attack on Fort Ticonderoga by Gen. James Abercrombie. He also took part in the capture of Fort Niagara by Gen. Sir William Johnson in July 1759 and was with Gen. Jeffrey Amherst at Montreal in September 1760. Returning to England, he was promoted to major in August 1761 and within another year to lieutenant colonel. He fought in Portugal with much distinction under Gen. John Burgoyne in 1762, but the following year his regiment was disbanded and he was retired as a major on half-pay. Between 1765 and 1770 he twice went to Poland. During the civil war there in 1769–1770 his friendship with the king brought him a general's commission, and he participated in the campaign against the Turks. Illness forced him to retire and he returned to England. In 1773 he came back to America and acquired land in Virginia. When the Revolution broke out, Lee resigned from the British army (he had in May 1772 been promoted to lieutenant colonel at half-pay) and sided with the colonies. His apparent usefulness and his not inconsiderable ability to promote his talents led to his appointment in June 1775 as major general in the Continental army. Second only to Artemas Ward, he became the ranking major general after Ward's retirement in March 1776. His record of service, however, did not live up to expectations and is still surrounded by controversy. After a period engaged in arranging the defenses of the Southern Department he was called to join the Northern army in the autumn of 1776. His dislike of Gen. George Washington made him slow to obey orders, and his belief that the Americans could not stand up to the British regulars in head-on combat more than once put him at odds with his commander in chief. This belief led him to refuse to join his division at Philipsburg, New York, to the main army in Washington's retreat from White Plains in October 1776 and resulted in his being captured in December by a small party of British dragoons. He was imprisoned in New York City until April 1778, when he was exchanged. He rejoined the army just before the battle of Monmouth, June 27, 1778. He was at first unwilling to lead the attack but claimed command from Gen. Lafayette when he learned it was to be a major operation. At the height of the attack he suddenly ordered a retreat, leaving Gen. Anthony Wayne's vanguard unsupported. Washington quickly rode up, relieved Lee harshly, and reformed the American lines; had Washington not intervened, the Continental troops might well have lost the day. A subsequent court-martial suspended Lee from command for 12 months. He passed the time by addressing letters abusive of Washington and other leaders to Congress, one of which resulted in his being challenged and wounded in a duel by John Laurens. In January 1780 Lee was dismissed from the service after writing an insulting letter to Congress. He died in Philadelphia on October 2, 1782. The discovery in 1858, among the papers of a companion of the British Gen. Sir William Howe, of a document in Lee's hand outlining a plan for defeating the colonies, led to serious questions about whether his conduct at Monmouth had been treasonable. The document had apparently been prepared by Lee while he was confined by the British in New York City, although it is not clear to what use, if any, it was put.

Lee, Ezra (1749–1821), Revolutionary soldier. Born in 1749 in Lyme, Connecticut, Lee was a sergeant in the Continental army when, in August 1776, he was selected by Gen. Samuel H. Parsons from among several volunteers to man David Bushnell's *American Turtle* submarine. Somehow he mastered the difficult machine—he had to operate two sets of paddles by crank for locomotion, a rudder, a foot-operated sea cock and twin hand pumps for admitting and expelling water in order to submerge and rise, and a complicated mechanism for boring into a ship's hull, attaching the torpedo carried atop the *Turtle,* releasing the torpedo and tripping the timed detonation apparatus, all the while reading a compass and depth gauge lit by foxfire, subsisting on what little air there was (two air tubes were usable only when not submerged), and hoping the tar-covered vessel would not spring many leaks. One night in August Lee entered the *Turtle* near the Battery in lower Manhattan and set out for the British fleet anchored just north of Staten Island, his target Adm. Lord Richard Howe's flagship *Eagle,* 64 guns. The unexpectedly swift current in the harbor carried him past the fleet, and only mighty exertions brought him back. On reaching the *Eagle* he was foiled by its copper sheathing, proof against his auger. Exhausted, he rode the reversed tide up the Hudson, releasing his torpedo toward a pursuing barge manned by British marines; they turned away, the torpedo blew up just past Governors Island, and Lee came safely ashore after several hours in the *Turtle.* A second attempt on a frigate in the Hudson a few days later also failed. Congratulated nonetheless by Gen. George Washington, Lee later took part in the battles of Trenton, December 26, 1776, and Brandywine, September 11, 1777. In 1777 Lee piloted the *Turtle* again in Black Point Bay, near New London, Connecticut, going after the frigate *Cerberus.* He got the torpedo attached, but a crewman on a prize schooner alongside spotted the line and hauled it in. It exploded, destroying the schooner and killing three sailors. Lee, who also at various times served Washington in a secret capacity, later took part in the battle of Monmouth, June 27,

1778. After the war he lived in Lyme, Connecticut, until his death on October 29, 1821.

Lee, Fitzhugh (1835–1905), army officer and Confederate army officer. Born at Clermont, his family's estate in Fairfax County, Virginia, on November 19, 1835, Lee was the grandson of Henry "Light-Horse Harry" Lee and the nephew of Robert E. Lee. He graduated from West Point in 1856, was commissioned in the cavalry, and after two years as an instructor at Carlisle Barracks, Pennsylvania, was ordered to duty with the 2nd Cavalry, under Col. Albert S. Johnston, in Texas. He took part in various Indian campaigns until he was assigned to the faculty of West Point in 1860. Upon the outbreak of the Civil War he joined the Confederate army, following the example of his uncle. He was a first lieutenant on the staff of Gen. Joseph E. Johnston at the first battle of Manassas (Bull Run), July 21, 1861, and in August was commissioned lieutenant colonel of the 1st Virginia Cavalry. He saw action in the Peninsular campaign in April–June 1862; at Sharpsburg (Antietam), September 17; and Chancellorsville, May 2–4, 1863, where his cavalry screened Gen. Thomas J. Jackson's flanking march and discovered the unsupported position of Gen. Oliver O. Howard's XI Corps. Throughout he was of invaluable service in reconnaissance for the Army of Northern Virginia. He commanded cavalry brigades and divisions under J. E. B. Stuart, Wade Hampton, and Robert E. Lee, and was promoted to brigadier general in July 1862 and to major general in September 1863. On March 17, 1863, he fought a superior force under Gen. William W. Averell at Kelly's Ford, Virginia, in a brilliant and celebrated cavalry action. In 1864 he was of great service at Spotsylvania Court House, May 8–12, and later in the year he was with Gen. Jubal A. Early in the Shenandoah valley and was severely wounded at Winchester, September 19. In March 1865 he became senior cavalry officer in the Army of Northern Virginia. He led the last charge of the Confederates at Farmville, Virginia, on April 9, 1865, the same day that his uncle Robert surrendered the Army of Northern Virginia to Gen. Ulysses S. Grant at Appomattox. He surrendered two days later. After the end of the war he took up farming in Stafford County, Virginia. Over the next several years he made many attempts to reconcile the South to the consequences of defeat, and when the Democratic party was returned to power in the South he entered politics, being elected governor of Virginia in 1885 and serving until 1890. Appointed by President Grover Cleveland consul general in Havana in 1896, he was retained in the post by President William McKinley and found himself at the center of a storm of intrigue and revolution. Remaining in Havana as consul general until the sinking of the *Maine* and the subsequent U.S. declaration of war on Spain in April 1898,

he thereupon took in May a commission as major general of volunteers, one of three former Confederate generals to hold that rank during the Spanish–American War. He commanded the VII Corps, intended but never required for combat in Cuba, and in January 1899 was made military governor of Havana and of Pinar del Río Province. In March 1899, under a new volunteer service act, he became brigadier general of volunteers, and he later commanded the Department of the Missouri for a time. He retired from the army in March 1901 and died in Washington on April 28, 1905. His biography of Gen. Robert E. Lee had appeared in 1894, and he also wrote *Cuba's Struggle Against Spain*, 1899.

Lee, Henry (1756–1818), "Light-Horse Harry," Revolutionary army officer and public official. Born at Leesylvania, his family's estate in Prince William County, Virginia, on January 29, 1756, Lee graduated from the College of New Jersey (now Princeton) in 1773. His plans for a career in the law were abandoned with the outbreak of the Revolution. In 1776 he became a captain in the Virginia cavalry, which joined Gen. George Washington's army in April 1777, and in January 1778 he was made a major and given a command consisting of three troops of cavalry and three companies of infantry that soon was called "Lee's Legion." "Light-Horse Harry," as he came to be known, and his Legion won one of the most dramatic victories of the war in storming and capturing the fort at Paulus Hook, New Jersey (now Jersey City), on August 19, 1779. His reputation as a brilliant cavalry officer was enhanced in the Southern theater after he was sent to aid Gen. Nathanael Greene in the Carolina campaign; promoted to lieutenant colonel, he joined Greene late in 1780. On February 25, 1781, he wiped out a Loyalist cavalry detachment at Haw River, North Carolina. He performed with distinction at Guilford Court House, March 15; Augusta, Georgia, which he captured on June 5; and Eutaw Springs, September 8. He was present in October at the victorious siege of Yorktown that essentially ended the Revolution. A hero at war's end and a comrade and confidant of Washington, he soon became active in Virginia politics. He served concurrently from 1785 to 1788 in the state legislature and in the Continental Congress, and he voted for ratification of the new federal Constitution in 1788. He later served three terms, from 1792 to 1795, as governor of Virginia. In 1794 he was appointed major general in command of a portion of the militia called out as the "Army of the Constitution" to suppress the Whisky Rebellion in western Pennsylvania. After one term in the House of Representatives, 1799–1801, he retired from politics. At the death of Washington he wrote a congressional resolution containing the words he spoke in an address in Philadelphia a short time later, perhaps the most famous eulogy in American history: "First in war, first in peace, and first in the hearts of his countrymen." After 1800 he became involved in land speculation that ruined him financially. In 1808–1809 he was confined to debtors' prison, where he wrote *Memoirs of the War in the Southern Department*, 1812. In July 1812 he was injured in a Baltimore riot while defending the editor of a Federalist antiwar newspaper. His health deteriorated after that, and during his last years he left his family in Virginia and lived in the West Indies, hoping for a recovery. He died at Cumberland Island, Georgia, on March 25, 1818, while attempting to return home before expiring. He was the father, by his second wife, of Robert E. Lee.

Lee, John Clifford Hodges (1887–1958), army officer. Born on August 1, 1887, in Junction City, Kansas, Lee graduated from West Point in 1909 and was commissioned in the engineers. He served a year in Panama and was later at various other posts, receiving promotion to first lieutenant in February 1912. He took part in military surveys of Guam in 1913 and of Luzon, Philippines, in 1914. Subsequently he worked on Ohio River improvement projects. Promoted to captain in June 1916, he was aide to Gen. Leonard Wood in 1917–1918, and, advancing to temporary major in August 1917 and to temporary lieutenant colonel in February 1918, he went to France in the latter month. He was assigned to the staff of the 89th Division and served with it through the St. Mihiel and Meuse–Argonne operations and until June 1919 on occupation duty in Germany. Having reached the rank of temporary colonel in July 1918, he reverted to permanent major in March 1920 and from 1921 to 1923 was again in the Philippines. He was attached to the office of the chief of engineers in 1923–1926 and from 1926 to 1931 was district engineer at Vicksburg, Mississippi, engaged in navigation improvement and flood control on the Mississippi, Red, Ouachita, and Yazoo rivers. Lee graduated from the Army War College in 1932, taught briefly at the Army Industrial College, received promotion to lieutenant colonel in December 1933, and in 1934 was appointed district engineer in Philadelphia. In 1938 he became division engineer of the North Pacific Division at Portland, Oregon, advancing to colonel in June. In October 1940 he was promoted to temporary brigadier general in command of the embarkation port at Fort Mason, California. From November 1941 to May 1942 he commanded the 2nd Infantry Division at Fort Sam Houston, Texas, receiving promotion to temporary major general in February 1942. In May 1942 he was sent to England, where in July he became chief of the Services of Supply, European Theater of Operations (E.T.O.). In January 1944 he was given the additional responsibility of deputy commander of U.S. forces, E.T.O., a post tantamount to command since the commander, Gen. Dwight D.

Eisenhower, was preoccupied as supreme Allied commander. In February 1944 Lee was promoted to temporary lieutenant general. As chief of Services of Supply (redesignated Communications Zone, E.T.O., in June 1944) he planned and directed the establishment of bases and supply depots in Britain in preparation for the European campaign and oversaw the acquisition, transportation, and distribution of all supplies to American forces in that campaign, a task of gargantuan proportions and infinite complexity. In December 1945 Lee was named commander of U.S. army forces in the Mediterranean Theater of Operations with responsibility for military government and later for the disposition of supplies and facilities and the redeployment of forces. He relinquished the post in September 1947 and retired in December, reverting to his permanent rank of major general on the retired list. Lee died on August 30, 1958, in York, Pennsylvania.

Lee, Robert Edward (1807–1870), Confederate army officer. Born at Stratford, his family's estate in Westmoreland County, Virginia, on January 19, 1807, Lee was the son of Henry "Light-Horse Harry" Lee, famed Revolutionary War cavalry officer, and a member of a family long distinguished in public and military service. He grew up and was schooled in Alexandria and in 1825 won appointment to West Point. He graduated second in his class four years later and until 1846 was with the army engineers, acquiring a reputation as a highly competent engineer in work on Mississippi River flood control and Atlantic coastal defenses. He advanced to first lieutenant in 1836 and captain in 1838. In 1846 he was ordered to Texas, where he served under Gen. John E. Wool early in the Mexican War, and the next year he joined the command of Gen. Winfield Scott in Mexico; he distinguished himself at Veracruz, Cerro Gordo, (where his reconnaissance of the strong Mexican position was the basis of Scott's tactics), Churubusco, and Chapultepec, and when the Mexican War ended in 1848, Lee had risen to brevet colonel. For four years he was again with the engineers and then in September 1852 was appointed superintendent at West Point. In March 1855 he was appointed lieutenant colonel of the 2nd Cavalry, then stationed at Jefferson Barracks, Missouri, under Col. Albert S. Johnston; he later moved with the 2nd to Texas. He found himself spending much of his time on court-martial duties and this, combined with his father-in-law's death in the autumn of 1857 and his wife's chronic illness, led him to consider resigning from the army. He was on leave at his estate, Arlington House, on the Potomac opposite Washington, when, in October 1859, he was ordered to Harpers Ferry to dislodge John Brown and his raiders from the federal arsenal there. With a detachment of marines he put a quick and virtually bloodless end to the affair. He then rejoined his regiment in Texas, and from February 1860 to February 1861 was commander of the Department of Texas. As sectional strife gave way to secession, Lee maintained a devotion to the Union and an antipathy to slavery, but when his own state of Virginia began to talk of breaking away he wavered. Promoted to colonel of the 1st Cavalry in March 1861, in April he declined an offer of the field command of all federal forces because he would not fight his own people. He resigned his commission on April 20, on learning of Virginia's secession, and retired to his home, hoping to keep clear of hostilities. Within three days, however, he had accepted appointment as commander of Virginia's forces, with the rank of major general. For several months he was concerned solely with preparing defenses for the anticipated invasion of Virginia and in serving informally as military adviser to Confederate President Jefferson Davis. In August 1861 he took the rank of general in the Confederate States army, dating from June, but he did not assume field command until the campaign in which western Virginia, soon to be admitted to the Union as West Virginia, was lost by the Confederacy. His prestige shaken by that failure, he was nonetheless retained by President Davis and sent to fortify the southern Atlantic coastal region. In March 1862 he became official military adviser to Davis and, despite his lack of direct authority, managed to work through and around Davis and the Confederate field commander, Gen. Joseph E. Johnston, to send Gen. Thomas J. Jackson on his spectacular Valley campaign. When Johnston was incapacitated by a wound at Fair Oaks (Seven Pines) in the Peninsula campaign, Lee assumed command of the Army of Northern Virginia on June 1, 1862. Already a masterly strategist, he soon gained, under the pressure of dealing with often incompetent or recalcitrant subordinates, considerable tactical skill as well. In the Seven Days' Battles—Mechanicsville, Gaines' Mill, Savage Station, Frayser's Farm, White Oak Swamp, Malvern Hill—June 26–July 2, he and his much smaller army forced Gen. George B. McClellan to retreat from his position threatening Richmond, ending the Peninsula campaign. Lee then, in a brilliantly conceived and executed maneuver, and relying on Jackson as his most able lieutenant, defeated Gen. John Pope at the second battle of Manassas (Bull Run), August 29–30. The complete destruction of Pope failed to be achieved largely through the dilatory stubbornness of Lee's other lieutenant, Gen. James Longstreet. An attempt to carry the war to the North by invading Maryland was stymied by the interception of Lee's general orders by the Union forces and by his subsequent near-defeat by McClellan at Sharpsburg (Antietam), September 17. Three months later, on December 13, 1862, he dealt heavy casualties to the Union army in repulsing Gen. Ambrose E. Burnside's attack with much superior numbers at Fredericksburg. After a long hard winter, action resumed in May 1863 when Gen. Joseph Hooker, Burnside's successor at the head of the Army of the Potomac, attempted to move south to Richmond; Lee's daring strategy (and Hooker's timidity) gave the Confederate army a major victory at Chancellorsville, May 2–4, but cost the invaluable Jackson. He struck north again, this time into Pennsylvania, in the summer of 1863. The lack of cooperation from various subordinates (Gen. J. E. B. Stuart, his cavalry out of position; Gen. Richard S. Ewell; and the ever-slow Longstreet) in the fighting of July 1–3 culminated in disastrous defeat at Gettysburg, the greatest battle, and the turning point, of the war. There was little significant action in Virginia after Gettysburg until May 1864, when Gen. Ulysses S. Grant, the new Union commander, set out for Richmond with a force outnumbering Lee's nearly two to one. Faced at last with an opponent who would not retreat, Lee found that the chronic shortages of men and equipment that he had so far overcome now became decisive. Limited to a defensive role in the Wilderness campaign, Lee slowly retreated through Spotsylvania and Cold Harbor, May 8–12 and June 1–3, sending Grant's casualty list up to 50,000 in a month. Finally and hopelessly entrenched at Petersburg, Lee could only watch as Grant developed his siege lines during the winter of 1864–1865. In February 1865 he was named general-in-chief of all the armies of the failing Confederacy, but the action had little practical consequence. With retreat impossible, Lee saw the coming end of the bloody Petersburg campaign after his defeat at Five Forks on April 1; he began to abandon his lines the next day. In rapid succession Petersburg also fell, Richmond was taken, and Lee, cut off in his dash westward by Gen. Philip H. Sheridan's cavalry, surrendered to Grant at Appomattox Courthouse on April 9, 1865. Lee was released immediately on parole; in September he accepted appointment as president of Washington College in Lexington, Virginia, and he held that post until his death. He counseled acceptance of the defeat and hard work to restore the Union; his own application for amnesty and pardon in June 1865 remained unanswered. His former home at Arlington had been seized for taxes in 1863 and made into a military cemetery in 1864. Lee died on October 12, 1870, in Lexington, Virginia, and subsequently the college changed its name to Washington and Lee University. As a military leader Lee commanded the respect of his colleagues, friend, foe, and foreign observer alike. His weakness, if he had one, was a tendency to trust too much in subordinates. From even his enemies he won admiration for his valor and true gallantry, and the quiet dignity of his demeanor at Appomattox placed him firmly in the affections of his fellow Southerners and eventually of all Americans. Lee was restored to citizenship by act of Congress in 1975.

Lee, Samuel Phillips (1812–1897), naval officer.

Born in Fairfax County, Virginia, on February 13, 1812, Lee was a grandson of Sen. Richard Henry Lee. He entered the navy as a midshipman in November 1825, served on the *Hornet* in the West Indies, on the *Delaware* and the *Java* in the Mediterranean between 1827 and 1830, and on the *Brandywine* and the *Vincennes* in the Pacific. He was promoted to lieutenant in February 1837. During the Mexican War he commanded the survey brig *Washington* and took part in the capture of Tabasco by Commodore Matthew C. Perry on June 15, 1847. In 1851 he undertook an extensive sounding cruise in the Atlantic on the *Dolphin*. Promoted to commander in September 1855, he took command of the *Vandalia* in 1860 and was at the Cape of Good Hope when he learned of the outbreak of the Civil War. He returned immediately to home waters and was assigned to blockade duty at Charleston, South Carolina. In 1862 he was transferred to the West Gulf Blockading Squadron, and in April he commanded the corvette *Oneida* in the attacks under Flag-Officer David G. Farragut on Fort Jackson and Fort St. Philip and the capture of New Orleans. In the fight with the Confederate river fleet the *Oneida* saved a sister ship, the *Varuna*, and captured the Confederate steamer *Governor Moore*. Lee later commanded the *Oneida* in running past Vicksburg. Promoted to captain in July 1862, he was appointed acting rear admiral in September and sent to succeed Adm. Louis M. Goldsborough in command of the North Atlantic Blockading Squadron. In addition to blockade work, in which more than fifty blockade runners were captured or destroyed, Lee's squadron supported a great many army operations on shore, including Gen. Benjamin F. Butler's army at Bermuda Hundred and movements on the James River. In October 1864 he was succeeded by Adm. David D. Porter and placed in command of the Mississippi Squadron, which provided valuable support on the Cumberland and Tennessee rivers to Gen. George H. Thomas in his campaign against Gen. John B. Hood. He was also responsible for maintaining the isolation of the Confederate forces west of the Mississippi. Lee was chief of the Signal Service after the war, was promoted to commodore in July 1866, and served then as president of the Board of Examination. He became a rear admiral in April 1870, commanded the North Atlantic Squadron from then until 1872, and retired in February 1873. He died at Silver Spring, Maryland, on June 5, 1897.

Lee, Stephen Dill (1833–1908), Confederate

army officer. Born in Charleston, South Carolina, on September 22, 1833, Lee graduated from West Point in 1854 and was commissioned in the artillery. He served in Texas, Florida, Kansas, and Dakota, was promoted to first lieutenant in 1856, and was regimental quartermaster at the time of his resignation in February 1861. He was promptly commissioned captain of South Carolina volunteers, and, as aide to Gen. P. G. T. Beauregard, he took part in the negotiations with Maj. Robert Anderson of Fort Sumter before and after the bombardment of the fort in April. He was then commissioned in the Confederate army, and after several months in Charleston he finally secured a field post, receiving promotion to major in November. During 1862 he took part in the battles of Seven Pines (Fair Oaks), May 31, Savage Station, June 29, and Malvern Hill, July 1, against Gen. George B. McClellan on the Peninsula. During the summer he was for some weeks in command of the 4th Virginia Cavalry, receiving promotions to lieutenant colonel and colonel. He distinguished himself particularly at the second battle of Manassas (Bull Run), August 29–30, and at Sharpsburg (Antietam), September 17, and in November was promoted to brigadier general. Ordered to Vicksburg, he commanded the defense of the city in numerous engagements, notably Chickasaw Bluffs, where Gen. William T. Sherman's attack was repulsed on December 29, and Champion's Hill, May 16, 1863, but was superseded in command by Gen. John C. Pemberton before the fall of Vicksburg on July 4. After being exchanged he was promoted to major general in August. He was placed in command of the cavalry in Mississippi and in February 1864 of all cavalry west of Alabama. With a relatively tiny force he harassed Gen. Sherman's army as it moved toward Meridian, Mississippi, but was unable to engage him. He was promoted to lieutenant general in June 1864, at thirty the youngest officer of that rank in the Confederacy. Of the forces under his command, only that led by Gen. Nathan B. Forrest fought a major battle, against superior numbers under Gen. Andrew J. Smith, at Tupelo, Mississippi, on July 14. A short time later Lee took command of the infantry corps of the Army of Tennessee under Gen. John B. Hood and took part in the battle at Ezra Church, Georgia, on July 28, in operations around Atlanta, and in the battle of Nashville, December 15–16, where following the general rout of the Army of Tennessee, Lee's corps was the only one still organized. He was badly wounded in the fight but refused to relinquish command until a proper rearguard was organized. He returned to his corps in North Carolina and on April 26, 1865, surrendered along with Gen. Joseph E. Johnston. After the war he settled in Columbus, Mississippi, as a planter. He was elected to the legislature in 1878 and in 1880 was appointed first president of the newly organized Mississippi Agricultural and Mechanical College (now Mississippi State University), a post he held until 1899, when he was appointed by President William McKinley commissioner of Vicksburg National Park. He was a member of the Mississippi constitutional convention in 1890. In 1904 he was elected commander in chief of the United Confederate Veterans, which post he still held at his death in Vicksburg, Mississippi, on May 28, 1908.

Lejeune, John Archer (1867–1942), marine offi-

cer. Born in Pointe Coupee Parish, Louisiana, on January 10, 1867, the son of an impoverished plantation owner, Lejeune attended Louisiana State University in 1881–1884 and then entered the Naval Academy. He graduated in 1888, and after two years of sea duty, during which he served on the *Vandalia* and in March 1889 was shipwrecked in a hurricane at Apia, Samoa, he applied for transfer to the marine corps, a request that was at first denied because of his high academic standing but that he carried to the secretary of the navy and won in July 1890. Promoted to first lieutenant in February 1892, he commanded the marine detachment aboard the *Cincinnati* in the Spanish –American War, took part in the occupation of Puerto Rico, and received promotion to captain in March 1899. Promoted to major in March 1903, he was given command of a marine battalion attached to the Atlantic Fleet, and in November of that year the battalion was sent, aboard the *Dixie,* to the Isthmus of Panama, nominally to help maintain right of transit but actually to assure the success of the Panamanian revolt against Colombia. In 1905 Lejeune became commander of the marine barracks in Washington, D.C. During 1907–1909 he was mainly in the Philippines. Promoted to lieutenant colonel in 1909, he was the first marine officer admitted to the Army War College, from which he graduated in 1910. Various assignments followed at the Brooklyn navy yard, in Cuba and Panama, and elsewhere, and on being promoted to colonel in February 1914 he took command of the Advance Base Brigade at New Orleans and Pensacola. In April 1914 he led the brigade in occupying Veracruz, Mexico. The brigade, subsequently commanded by Col. Littleton W. T. Waller, remained in the city, along with an army occupation force under Gen. Frederick Funston, until December, during which period Lejeune directed the corps's first field aviation operations and organized its first motorized unit. From 1915 to 1917 he was assistant to the commandant of the corps, Gen. George Barnett, receiving promotion to brigadier general in August 1916. In September 1917 he became commander of the marine barracks at Quantico, Virginia. After considerable effort he secured assignment to France, arriving in June 1918 and soon taking command of the 4th Marine Brigade, the only marine brigade in the American Expeditionary Force. In July he was promoted to major general, and by the end of the month he had succeeded Gen. Omar Bundy in command of the 2nd Infantry Division, of which the 4th Brigade was a part, becoming the first marine officer ever to command an army division. He led the 2nd, generally thought to be the best division in the A.E.F., in the St. Mihiel offensive, in the battle of Blanc Mont

Ridge, October 3, which was hailed as one of the great achievements of the war by Marshal Pétain, and in the Meuse–Argonne operations. After returning from occupation duty in Germany with the 2nd in August 1919 Lejeune resumed command at Quantico until June 1920, when he became commandant of the marine corps. Under his leadership the corps underwent a rapid transition; professional standards were raised by various means, including the establishment of the Marine Corps Schools at Quantico, and the tactical doctrine and techniques of amphibious warfare were adopted beginning in 1921, in what proved to be prophetic anticipation of World War II requirements. On his retirement in March 1929 Lejeune was chosen superintendent of the Virginia Military Institute, the first marine officer ever selected for the post. In 1930 he published *Reminiscences of a Marine.* He retired from VMI in 1937. Lejeune died in Baltimore on November 20, 1942. Camp Lejeune, North Carolina, was named in his honor.

LeMay, Curtis Emerson (1906–   ), army and

air force officer. Born in Columbus, Ohio, on November 15, 1906, LeMay attended Ohio State University after trying unsuccessfully for an appointment to West Point. Although he did not complete the requirements for an engineering degree until 1932, he received a second lieutenant's commission upon completing the Reserve Officers Training Corps (ROTC) program and went on active duty in the army in 1928. In September of that year he became a cadet in the Army Air Corps flying school at March Field, California, and he received a regular commission as second lieutenant in January 1930. Promoted to first lieutenant in June 1935 and to captain in January 1940, LeMay gained a reputation as an outstanding pilot and navigator in assignments to various bombardment squadrons. He advanced to major in March 1941, lieutenant colonel in January 1942, and colonel in March 1942, and the next month he took command of the 305th Bombardment Group at Muroc, California, leading it later in the year to join Gen. Ira C. Eaker's Eighth Air Force in England. Highly decorated for his combat service in the 305th's B-17 bombers, he was made a temporary brigadier general in September 1943 and advanced to temporary major general six months later. In August 1944 he was named commander of the operating force (the 20th and later 21st Bomber commands) of the Twentieth Air Force in the China-Burma-India theater. The Twentieth, under the command of the Joint Chiefs of Staff through Gen. Henry H. Arnold, was the first strategic air force, and for the rest of World War II its mission was to bomb the Japanese homeland. In July 1945 LeMay was commander of the Twentieth, and he then became chief of staff of Gen. Carl Spaatz's Strategic Air Forces, planning the atomic bomb missions. After a period of staff duty in Washington, D.C., he was promoted to temporary lieutenant general in October 1947 (the air force having just become an independent service) and named commander of the air forces in Europe. In that capacity he directed the airlift of supplies to Berlin, under blockade by Soviet forces in Germany, in 1948. His reputation made him a logical choice, in October 1948, for chief of the Strategic Air Command (SAC), the planes of which, prior to the development of guided missiles, were the only carriers for the atomic weapons that were rapidly accumulating during the Cold War period. Under his command SAC developed a policy of constant alert, with aircraft aloft at all times and ready to respond to the threat of attack. He was promoted to temporary general in October 1951. In 1957 he became vice chief of staff of the air force, and in June 1961 he became chief of staff, holding that post until his retirement in February 1965. Partly as a result of his strong support of the U.S. military role in the Vietnam war, in 1968 he was a more or less reluctant vice-presidential candidate on the American Independent party ticket headed by Alabama's Gov. George C. Wallace. After their defeat in the November election LeMay again retired to private life and the chairmanship of the board of an electronics firm.

Lemnitzer, Lyman L. (1899–   ), army officer. Born on August 29, 1899, in Honesdale, Pennsylvania, Lemnitzer graduated from West Point in 1920 and was commissioned in the coast artillery. After graduating from the Coast Artillery School, Fort Monroe, Virginia, in 1921 he served in Rhode Island and the Philippines. He was an instructor at West Point from 1926 to 1930 and again, after a second tour of the Philippines and other assignments, in 1934–1935. After graduating from Command and General Staff School, Fort Leavenworth, Kansas, in 1936 he was an instructor at the Coast Artillery School until 1939. In 1940, on graduating from the Army War College, he was assigned to staff duty with coast artillery units in the South. In May 1941, by then a colonel, he joined the General Staff in Washington, D.C., serving in the War Plans Division and on the Army Ground Forces staff. In June 1942 he was promoted to brigadier general in command of the 34th Antiaircraft Brigade, but he soon received appointment as assistant chief of staff of Allied Force Headquarters, under Gen. Dwight D. Eisenhower, in London. After aiding in the planning of the North African invasion, he resumed command of the 34th in February 1943 and led it in the opening phase of Gen. George S. Patton's Sicilian campaign. In late July 1943 he became deputy chief of staff of the Allied 15th Army Group (American Seventh, British Eighth) under Gen. Sir Harold R. L. G. Alexander. Promoted to major general in November 1944, he remained with Sir Harold when the latter became, in

December 1944, field marshal and supreme Allied commander of the Mediterranean Theater. From November 1945 to August 1947 Lemnitzer was the army member of the Strategic Survey Committee of the Joint Chiefs of Staff, and he was then deputy commandant of the National War College until October 1949. After a year as director of the Office of Military Assistance in the Department of Defense he underwent parachute training—at the age of fifty-one—and was given command in December 1950 of the 11th Airborne Division at Fort Campbell, Kentucky. In November 1951 he was ordered to Korea to command the 7th Infantry Division. Promoted to lieutenant general in August 1952, Lemnitzer was named deputy chief of staff of the army for plans and research. In March 1955 he was appointed commander of U.S. army forces in the Far East and of the Eighth Army, with the rank of general, and in June he became commander of the Far East Command and of the United Nations Command and governor of the Ryukyu Islands. In July 1957 he returned to the United States as vice chief of staff of the army, and he succeeded Gen. Maxwell D. Taylor as chief of staff in July 1959. He held the post through September 1960, when he was appointed chairman of the Joint Chiefs of Staff. In November 1962 he became commander of U.S. forces in Europe, and in January 1963 he succeeded to supreme Allied command. Lemnitzer retired in July 1969. In 1975 he was appointed by President Gerald R. Ford to a blue-ribbon panel investigating domestic activities of the Central Intelligence Agency.

Letterman, Jonathan (1824–1872), physician and army officer. Born in Canonsburg, Pennsylvania, on December 11, 1824, Letterman graduated from Jefferson College in 1845 and from Jefferson Medical College, Philadelphia, in 1849. In June of that year he was appointed assistant surgeon in the army Medical Department. He served in Florida, in campaigns against the Seminole Indians, until 1853; and after a year at Fort Ripley, Minnesota, he was ordered to Fort Defiance, New Mexico Territory, where he saw action against the Apaches. In 1859 he was transferred to Fort Monroe, Virginia, and in 1860–1861 he was engaged in the Ute campaign in California. Late in 1861 he returned to the East and was assigned to duty with the Army of the Potomac. Named medical director of the Department of West Virginia in May 1862, he was the next month appointed medical director of the Army of the Potomac with the rank of major and surgeon. In that post he completely reorganized the medical service, devising a system of forward first-aid stations at the regimental level, mobile field hospitals behind divisions, and base hospitals, all linked by a proficient ambulance corps under the control of the medical rather than the quartermaster department, and arranging an efficient system of medical supply. The battle of Fredericksburg, December 13, 1862, in which the Army of the Potomac suffered 12,000 casualties, proved the efficacy of Letterman's administration. His system was subsequently adopted by other Union armies in the field and was established officially by act of Congress in March 1864. After a period as inspector of hospitals in the Department of the Susquehannah, Letterman resigned from the army in December 1864 and moved to San Francisco. His *Medical Recollections of the Army of the Potomac* appeared in 1866. Letterman died in San Francisco on March 15, 1872. On November 13, 1911, the army hospital at the Presidio in San Francisco was named Letterman General Hospital in honor of the man who revolutionized the care of battle casualties.

Levy, Uriah Phillips (1792–1862), naval officer. Born in Philadelphia on April 22, 1792, Levy went to sea against his family's wishes when he was ten, serving as a cabin boy on several coastal vessels. Before he was twenty he was master of the schooner *George Washington,* of which he was also part owner. The ship was lost in the course of a mutiny in January 1812, and in October of that year he applied for a commission in the navy. Commissioned a sailing master, he was aboard the *Argus* as acting lieutenant under Capt. William H. Allen in 1813 and was given command of a prize; when the British later retook it, he spent 16 months as a prisoner of war. He was promoted to lieutenant in March 1817. His service was marked by frequent bitter altercations: he was court-martialed six times, cashiered twice from the service (in 1819 and 1842) and then reinstated, and involved in at least one duel, which resulted in the death of his opponent. Most of these conflicts were brought about by the contempt in which he was held by many of his associates in the navy—for not only had he risen to command from the ranks, but he was also a Jew, one of the very few Jewish officers in the service. He was promoted to captain in March 1844 but for the next decade, despite frequent petitions, was unable to obtain a command; in 1855, as a consequence, he was dropped from the captains' list. A successful appeal before a congressional board of inquiry in 1857 restored him to rank and resulted in his being given command of a ship; he was shortly promoted to commodore and in 1860 was commander of the Mediterranean Squadron. He retired at the onset of the Civil War but, an ardent patriot, offered his personal fortune to President Abraham Lincoln for the defense of the Union. Before his death in New York City on March 22, 1862, he had, because of his intense admiration for Thomas Jefferson, purchased Monticello, Jefferson's home near Charlottesville, Virginia. The property had fallen into disrepair, and Levy evidently hoped to restore it and offer it to the nation as a public shrine. He willed Monticello to the

United States at his death, but litigation among his heirs kept the estate in private hands until 1923, when it was bought by subscription and opened to the public after restoration had been completed.

Lewis, Andrew (1720–1781), colonial militia and Revolutionary army officer. Born in 1720 in County Donegal, Ireland, Lewis came to America with his family in 1732 and settled near Staunton, Virginia. As a young man he moved to Salem, Virginia, and became active in the militia of Augusta County. In 1754 he was a major under Col. George Washington in the expedition to Fort Duquesne and the surrender of Fort Necessity. In 1758 he was taken prisoner during another expedition against Fort Duquesne under British Gen. John Forbes. In 1768 he represented Virginia at the negotiation of the Treaty of Fort Stanwix. In the spring of 1774 he was appointed brigadier general of militia, and in June he took command of the assembled militia of southwest Virginia, called out by the governor, Lord Dunmore, to suppress the Indians, mainly Shawnee under Cornstalk, who were harassing the frontier. He marched with about 1100 men from Camp Union (on the site of present-day Lewisburg, West Virginia) to Point Pleasant at the mouth of the Kanawha River. Dunmore was to march south from Fort Dunmore (Fort Pitt) and join Lewis, but before he arrived the Shawnee under Cornstalk attacked on October 10. The attack was sustained all day and the fighting was hard and at times desperate; casualties were heavy on both sides, the Virginians losing about 50 killed and 100 wounded. The Shawnee fled at sunset; later they met Dunmore at Camp Charlotte on the Pickaway Plains of Ohio and accepted a treaty that established the peace on the frontier. Lord Dunmore's War, and particularly the battle of Point Pleasant, not only kept the frontier peaceful during the early years of the Revolution, it also helped train and proved the mettle of colonial soldiers. Lewis and his men soon returned home. In 1775 he served in the various Virginia revolutionary conventions, and in March 1776 he was commissioned brigadier general in the Continental army, although Washington had recommended him for major general. He took command of forces at Williamsburg, Virginia, and in July he drove Lord Dunmore from his refuge on Gwynn's Island. Lewis resigned his commission in April 1777. He was a member of the executive council of Virginia until his death in Bedford County on September 26, 1781.

Lewis, Isaac Newton (1858–1931), army officer and inventor. Born in New Salem, Pennsylvania, on October 12, 1858, Lewis graduated from West Point in 1884 and was commissioned in the artillery. Two years later he graduated from Torpedo School, and over the next several years he invented a series of devices by which the work of the artillerist was made into a precise art, including the first successful range and position finder for artillery, a time-interval clock-and-bell signal system, and quick-reading mechanical verniers. He was promoted to first lieutenant in June 1891. From 1894 to 1898 he was on the Board of Regulation of coast artillery fire, and from 1898 to 1902 he was recorder of the Board of Ordnance and Fortification, advancing to captain in April 1900. During an inspection tour of European ordnance plants in 1900 he made observations that, on his return, led immediately to a complete rearmament of the army's field artillery with modern guns and ordnance and to the abandonment of the unwieldy system of mixed field and fortress artillery regiments in favor of the modern corps organization. From 1904 to 1911 he was commander of Fort Monroe, Virginia, and of the Artillery District of the Chesapeake and acting commandant of the Coast Artillery School there. Lewis was promoted to major in January 1907, to lieutenant colonel in March 1911, and to colonel in August 1913 and was retired for disability the next month. He moved to Liège, Belgium, and built a factory to manufacture a machine gun of his own invention, moving his operation to England on the outbreak of the war the next year and becoming associated with the Birmingham Small Arms Company. The Lewis gun was adopted and used in great numbers by the armies of Great Britain, France, and Belgium. The U.S. War Department tested and rejected the Lewis gun in 1916, but after considerable controversy, new tests, and certain modifications to the gun it was accepted and used in both infantry weapon and aircraft versions. After the war Lewis had branch firms in Belgium, Paris, London, and Cleveland. Among his non-military inventions were an electric car-lighting system and a windmill electric lighting system. He died in Hoboken, New Jersey, on November 9, 1931.

Lewis, Meriwether (1774–1809), army officer, explorer, and public official. Born in Albemarle County, Virginia, on August 18, 1774, Lewis grew up there and in Georgia, where his family moved when he was ten. He returned alone to Virginia three years later to be educated by private tutors and was still there when, as a member of the local militia, he was sent to take part in the suppression of the Whisky Rebellion in 1794. A year later he took a commission as ensign in the 2nd Legion of the regular army and served for several years, including a brief period under the command of his future companion in exploration, Lt. William Clark. Lewis was promoted to lieutenant in 1799 and captain in 1800. In 1801 President Thomas Jefferson offered him the position of private secretary and he immediately accepted; for two years thereafter he lived in the executive mansion in Washington, D.C., while Jefferson laid plans for an exploring journey to seek a land route across the continent and prepared Lewis to lead it. He was sent to Philadelphia to learn mapmaking and other needed scientific skills. Finally, in 1803, with a $2500 appropriation from Congress and detailed instructions from Jefferson, Lewis set out for Illinois to recruit and train an exploring party. At his request, a share of the command had been offered to William Clark, and the names of the two men were thenceforth linked. Training and equipping about 40 men occupied the winter and early spring of 1803–1804; on May 14, 1804, they set out "under a jentle brease up the Missourie" in three well stocked boats and by November had reached the villages of the Mandan, where they built Fort Mandan and wintered near what is now Bismarck, North Dakota. The next April, 16 men were sent back to St. Louis to report on the expedition's progress, and the rest, having built canoes, continued up the Missouri to the three forks, which they named the Jefferson, the Madison, and the Gallatin rivers. They followed the Jefferson to its source and then continued on foot. They were accompanied now by a French-Canadian, Toussaint Charbonneau, and his Shoshone wife, Sacagawea, whom they had engaged as interpreters and guides. Procuring horses from the Shoshone, they crossed the Continental Divide and then made their way by canoe down the Clearwater, Snake, and Columbia rivers, reaching the mouth of the Columbia on the Pacific Coast on November 15, 1805. They built Fort Clatsop, in which they wintered, near present-day Astoria, Oregon, and in March 1806 began the return journey. Just beyond the Great Falls of the Missouri the party split, Lewis exploring northward along the Marias River and Clark striking south to the Yellowstone. They reunited the parties at the Missouri–Yellowstone confluence and continued eastward. Their arrival in St. Louis on September 23, 1806, was cause for national celebration, not the least because in their overlong absence they had been given up as lost. The maps, notes, and mineral and botanical specimens they brought back were invaluable to scientists, and their journey to the West had greatly reinforced U.S. claims to the Oregon country. Among the remarkable accomplishments of the entire project was the fact that in more than two years of exploring unknown territory, traveling 4000 miles and dealing with sometimes hostile Indians, only one man had died. In November Lewis resigned from the army and was appointed governor of the Louisiana Territory by Jefferson; for nearly two years he carried out his duties with great skill from headquarters in St. Louis. In 1809, finding that some of his drafts on the government had not been honored, he set out for Washington to clear up the matter; he was near Nashville, Tennessee, when, under mysterious circumstances, he died on October 11, 1809. The journals of the Lewis and Clark expedition were finally published in 1814 under the editorship of Nicholas Biddle.

Lewis, Morgan (1754–1844), army officer and public official. Born in New York City on October 16, 1754, Lewis graduated from the College of New Jersey (now Princeton) in 1773 and took up the study of law. In 1775 he was elected a captain in a New York regiment serving in Boston, and when the regiment was mustered into the Continental army as the 2nd New York he was commissioned a major. In June 1776 he became deputy quartermaster general of the New York Department, and in 1777, with the rank of colonel, he was chief of staff and aide to Gen. Horatio Gates during the Saratoga campaign. He commanded in one or two minor engagements in New York in 1778. After the Revolution he resumed his legal studies, won admission to the bar, and in 1789 and 1792 was elected to the legislature. An alliance by marriage with the Livingston clan assured his success in New York politics. In 1791 he was elected attorney general and late in 1792 he was chosen a justice of the state supreme court; in 1801 he became chief justice. In 1804 Lewis was elected, as a Democratic–Republican, governor of New York, defeating Aaron Burr decisively. A falling out with party leader DeWitt Clinton limited his effectiveness, however, and in 1807 he retired to private life. In 1812 he secured election to the legislature, and later in the year, after war with England had broken out, he declined President James Madison's offer of the post of secretary of war in favor of appointment as quartermaster general of the army with the rank of brigadier general. In March 1813 he was promoted to major general and given a command on the Niagara frontier, but his age and the general confusion in the conduct of the war kept him from more than minor action in the field. In 1814 he was transferred to command of the region about New York City. During the war he advanced large sums of his own money for the discharge of American prisoners in Canada. Lewis retired afterwards to his private interests, which were large. He was president-general of the Society of the Cincinnati from 1839 until his death on April 7, 1844, in New York City.

Lieber, Francis (1800–1872), editor and political scientist. Born in Berlin on March 18, 1800, Lieber studied at the universities of Jena, Halle, and Dresden, interrupting his studies in 1815 to serve in the last campaign of the Napoleonic Wars at Waterloo, and was awarded a Ph.D. from Jena in 1820. In 1819 he had been imprisoned briefly for harboring too-liberal political views. In 1822 he joined the large number of liberal young Germans who enlisted in the Greek war of liberation from Turkish rule; he found the experience disillusioning and soon went to Rome, where he met and was profoundly influenced by the German diplomat-historian B. G. Niebuhr. In 1823 he returned to Berlin and continued studying mathematics until he was imprisoned again in 1824 for his liberal views. In 1826 he went to England; was em-

ployed for a time as a tutor, and the next year emigrated to the United States. He soon embarked upon his first major scholarly enterprise, founding and editing the *Encyclopaedia Americana*, which appeared in 13 volumes from 1829 to 1833. In 1834 he moved from Boston to Philadelphia, where among other activities he drafted the constitution of Girard College. In 1835 he accepted a professorship of history and political economy at South Carolina College (now the University of South Carolina), where he remained for 21 years. During this time he established a reputation as the nation's leading political theorist and was the first American thinker to construct a rigorous and systematic philosophy of political science. His major writings, *Manual of Political Ethics*, 2 volumes, 1838–1839, *Legal and Political Hermeneutics*, 1839, and *On Civil Liberty and Self-Government*, 2 volumes, 1853, were widely read and highly praised. Lieber was a strong advocate of nationalism, although he opposed the centralization of political power. Among his many shrewd insights into the political functioning of a modern state was his crediting of the vast complex of voluntary and nonpolitical associations in society with the maintenance of civil liberty. In 1857 he was invited to occupy the chair of history and political science at Columbia, and he retained this post until transferring to the Columbia Law School in 1865, where he remained for the rest of his life. During the Civil War he devised for the War Department *Instructions for the Government of the Armies of the United States in the Field;* this work, the first such code of military law and procedure in the world, was adopted as General Orders No. 100 in 1863. It was later adopted by the armed forces of several nations and was also embodied in international law in the Hague Conventions of 1899 and 1907. Lieber died in New York City on October 2, 1872.

Liggett, Hunter (1857–1935), army officer. Born on March 21, 1857, in Reading, Pennsylvania, Liggett graduated from West Point in 1879 and was commissioned in the infantry. For nearly twenty years he served in routine duty in Montana Territory, Dakota Territory, Texas, Florida, and Georgia, advancing to first lieutenant in June 1884 and captain in June 1897. In June 1898 he was appointed major and assistant adjutant general of volunteers for service in Cuba, and the following year, as major of the 31st Infantry Volunteers, he was ordered to the Philippines. Mustered out of volunteer service in June 1901, he was promoted to major of regulars in May 1902 and lieutenant colonel in June 1909. In 1910, on graduating from the Army War College, he became director of the college, receiving promotion to colonel in March 1912. In February 1913 he was promoted to brigadier general and later in the year he became president of the War College. The next year he took command of the 4th Brigade, 2nd Division, at Texas City, Texas, and in 1915 he returned to the Philippines as commander of the Provisional Infantry Brigade and of Fort William McKinley. From April 1916 to April 1917 he was commander of the Department of the Philippines, receiving promotion to major general in March 1917, and he was then named commander of the Western Department at San Francisco. In September 1917 Liggett was assigned to command of the 41st Infantry Division, and the next month he sailed for France. In January 1918 he moved up to command of the I Corps, then attached to the French Sixth Army. In the summer the I Corps took up defensive positions around and west of Château-Thierry. It absorbed much of the German offensive of July 15–18, the Champagne–Marne operation, and then began the Allied advance known as the second battle of the Marne that continued into August. In that month the I Corps became a part of the U.S. First Army under Gen. John J. Pershing. In September the I Corps, together with Gen. Joseph T. Dickman's IV Corps, attacked from the right on the south flank of the St. Mihiel salient, pushing it back and on the 16th, after only four days, closing it altogether. In the Meuse–Argonne offensive begun on September 26 the I Corps fought through the dense and treacherous Argonne Forest. On October 16 Liggett was moved up to command of the First Army with the temporary rank of lieutenant general. By the end of October the First Army was advancing all along a 90-mile front, and on November 5 elements reached the Meuse River. The pursuit of the Germans across the river continued until the armistice six days later. Liggett remained in command of the First Army in occupied Germany until its inactivation in April 1919, moving to command of the Third Army, also in occupation duty, until July. On his return to the United States he took command of the IX Corps area at San Francisco, reverting to major general. He retired in March 1921 and in June 1930 was promoted to lieutenant general on the retired list by act of Congress. Liggett died in San Francisco on December 30, 1935.

Lincoln, Benjamin (1733–1810), Revolutionary army officer and public official. Born in Hingham, Massachusetts, on January 24, 1733, Lincoln was educated in the common schools there before taking up farming. He was not prominent in Massachusetts politics until shortly before the Revolution; he then served in the legislature in 1772–1773 and in the provincial congress in 1774–1775. Having been a member of the Massachusetts militia since 1755, he was, when the Revolutionary War broke out, a brigadier general. In May 1776 he was promoted to major general. In August he took command of the Massachusetts troops engaged in the siege of Boston, and later he commanded the militia troops at New York. His performance in that duty impressed Gen. George Washington, and on his recommendation Lincoln was commissioned major general in the Continental service in February 1777. At Saratoga in September 1777, under Gen. Horatio Gates, he commanded the American works on Bemis Heights and contributed signally to the defeat of Gen. John Burgoyne; he was wounded in the campaign and forced to remain inactive for about ten months. After his recovery he was placed in command of the Continental army in the Southern Department in September 1778. He did not fare as well in the unfamiliar terrain of the South. While he was away from Charleston, South Carolina, early in 1779, the city was attacked by Gen. Augustine Prevost, and Lincoln returned barely in time to relieve it in May. In September he laid siege to Savannah, Georgia, supported by the French fleet under the Count d'Estaing, but the repulse of a major attack on the city on October 9 (in which Gen. Kazimierz Pulaski was mortally wounded leading an assault) forced him to abandon the campaign ten days later. In March 1780 Sir Henry Clinton launched a joint army-navy attack on Charleston, and Lincoln, instead of withdrawing to the hill country, allowed himself to be shut up in the town. Charleston finally fell on May 12, 1780, and Lincoln was made a prisoner. He was exchanged in time, however, to take part in the final campaign of the Revolution, ending with Gen. Charles Cornwallis's surrender at Yorktown, where on October 19, 1781, as Washington's deputy, he accepted the ceremonial sword. In that month the Continental Congress appointed him secretary of war. He resigned the post in October 1783 and returned to private life. In 1787 he took part in suppressing Shays's Rebellion in Massachusetts, and in 1788 he ran successfully for lieutenant governor of his native state. He was a member of the Massachusetts convention called to consider the proposed federal Constitution in 1788 and worked hard for ratification. In his later years he received a federal appointment as collector of the port of Boston, in which post he served from 1789 to 1809. He was also, in 1789 and again in 1793, appointed to treat on behalf of the federal government with various Indian tribes. He retired a year before his death at Hingham, Massachusetts, on May 9, 1810.

Lindbergh, Charles Augustus (1902–1974), aviator. Born in Detroit on February 4, 1902, Lindbergh, son of a Minnesota congressman, grew up mainly in Little Falls, Minnesota, and Washington, D.C. He entered the University of Wisconsin in 1920 but left in 1922 to enroll in a flying school in Lincoln, Nebraska. In 1923 he bought a World War I surplus Curtiss "Jenny" and made his first solo flight, subsequently making barnstorming trips through the Southern and Midwestern states. He entered the army flying school at Brooks Field, Texas, in March 1924, completed his training in a year, and was commissioned a second lieutenant in the Air Service. In

1926 he became an airmail pilot on the St. Louis–Chicago route. Drawn by a $25,000 prize offered several years before by Raymond Orteig for the first nonstop flight from New York to Paris, in 1927, with several St. Louis businessmen as his backers, he purchased a Ryan monoplane with a single radial air-cooled engine, which he christened *The Spirit of St. Louis.* On May 10 he flew the plane from the factory in San Diego to Long Island, New York, making one stop in St. Louis and setting a transcontinental record of 21 hours and 20 minutes. After being delayed by bad weather, he took off on May 20 from Long Island's Roosevelt Field, crossed the Atlantic by dead reckoning, and 33½ hours later arrived at Le Bourget airfield near Paris, having flown 3600 miles. He was met by a tumultuous crowd which was only with difficulty restrained from wrecking the *Spirit* for souvenirs. After a reception given by the French government he returned to the United States to be greeted with New York City's greatest ticker-tape parade. Dubbed "Lucky Lindy" and the "Lone Eagle," he was received as the supreme hero of the adulatory decade of the 1920s and was voted the Medal of Honor by Congress and promoted to colonel in the Air Service reserve by President Calvin Coolidge. In December he arrived at Mexico City from Washington after a 27-hour 10-minute flight, and at a reception held there in his honor he met Anne Spencer Morrow, daughter of U.S. ambassador Dwight W. Morrow. They were married in May 1929, and during the first years of their marriage they made numerous flights together to various parts of the world. In 1932 their two-year-old son was kidnapped and later found murdered; the publicity attendant upon the search for the child and, later, for his kidnapper made it the most sensational crime of the 1930s. A carpenter, Bruno Richard Hauptmann, was convicted of the crime and executed in 1936. From 1935 until 1939 the family lived in Europe, during which time Lindbergh was able to survey German air power and make significant reports to the U.S. government. In 1936 he worked with Dr. Alexis Carrel in experiments that led the latter to develop an artificial heart. In the United States during 1940–1941 Lindbergh was a leading member of the isolationist America First Committee and made speeches across the nation urging that the United States remain out of the European war. For these activities, and with the memory of his having accepted in 1938 a decoration from the German government, he was publicly criticized by President Franklin D. Roosevelt, and in April 1941 he resigned his colonel's commission in the Army Air Corps. After the United States entered the war he promptly offered his services and was employed in a civilian capacity as consultant to the Ford Motor Company and the United Aircraft Company, for which he accompanied 50 combat missions in the Pacific theater. After the war he went to Germany

with a naval commission to survey the development of German jet aircraft, rockets, and guided missiles. He then settled in Darien, Connecticut. He was named brigadier general in the air force reserve by President Dwight D. Eisenhower in April 1954 and was a consultant to the Department of Defense and a director of (until 1972) and consultant to (until 1974) Pan American World Airways. For his story of the flight to Paris, *The Spirit of St. Louis,* 1953, he won a Pulitzer Prize. He also wrote the autobiographical *We* in 1927, and *Of Flight and Life,* 1948. In later years Lindbergh became known as an active and effective proponent of conservation, notably in the campaigns to save the blue and humpback whales. About 1968 he began tentatively to break out of his long self-imposed public silence, speaking on behalf of various ecological programs. His wife was a writer of note, her books including *Listen, the Wind,* 1938; *Gift from the Sea,* 1955; and *Bring Me a Unicorn,* 1972. He died at his home in Kipahulu, Maui, Hawaii, on August 26, 1974.

Little, George (1754–1809), naval officer. Born in Marshfield, Massachusetts, on April 15, 1754, Little entered the Massachusetts navy early in the Revolution. The earliest record of his service notes his release from a British prison ship in March 1778. In July 1779 he was first officer aboard the state brigantine *Hazard* in the expedition under Commodore Dudley Saltonstall to recapture Castine on Penobscot Bay. The expedition ended in complete disaster in August. He was first officer of the state ship *Protector* in the capture of the British privateer *Admiral Duff* on June 9, 1780, and was captured with the *Protector* in 1781 and held in Mill Prison at Plymouth, England. By bribing a sentry he made an escape to France, where Benjamin Franklin helped him to return to America. In 1782 he was made captain of the sloop *Winthrop,* and with her he succeeded in capturing nearly the entire British force at Penobscot. He left the service in June 1783 and returned to his farm in Marshfield. In March 1799 he was commissioned captain in the United States navy, then readying for possible war with France. Placed in command of the frigate *Boston,* 28 guns, he sailed in July for the West Indies to patrol against French privateers. For his capture of a Danish brig, *Flying Fish,* in December he was later held liable, although he believed at the time that his orders covered such an act. In 1800 he took the French privateer *Deux Anges,* 20, and on October 12 he engaged the French naval corvette *Berceau,* 24, and in a heated fight took her. Little returned to Boston in November 1800 and was discharged from the navy in October 1801. He died in Weymouth, Massachusetts, on July 22, 1809.

Little Crow (1803?–1863), Indian leader. Born about 1803 in a village of the Mdewakanton clan of the Eastern Sioux near the site of present-day St. Paul, Minnesota, Little Crow was probably the fifth of his line to bear that name. He was by all accounts intemperate and untrustworthy both as a chief and as an ally or enemy to whites. He was a signer of the treaty at Mendota, Minnesota Territory, on August 5, 1851, whereby the Eastern Sioux ceded lands east of the Red and Big Sioux rivers in Minnesota and Iowa; other Sioux had ceded the same lands two weeks earlier at Traverse des Sioux. The treaty proved increasingly an irritant to the Indians, however, and the failure of stipulated payments, together with the poor hunting on lands remaining to them, led to a sudden outbreak of violence in August 1862. On August 18 Little Crow led a band of warriors off the Redwood Agency reservation. At Redwood Ferry a detachment of 24 soldiers from Fort Ridgely on the upper Minnesota River was ambushed and wiped out, and the next day the fort itself was put under siege. The attack there ceased on the 24th, but marauding continued throughout the territory. On August 24 a major attack was made on New Ulm, with many casualties on both sides. The former governor, Henry H. Sibley, raised a volunteer force at Fort Snelling and set out in pursuit of Little Crow. A volunteer detachment on burial duty was attacked at Birch Coulee on September 2 and took 60 casualties before Col. Sibley arrived in relief. The Sioux were decisively beaten by Sibley at Wood Lake on September 23. The uprising cost in all nearly 500 lives among soldiers and settlers and probably as many more among the Sioux. Thirty-eight Sioux were executed at Mankato in December. Little Crow escaped to the west after Wood Lake. The next year he made his way back into Minnesota Territory, and on July 3, 1863, he was shot and killed by a farmer near Hutchinson.

Little Turtle (1752?–1812), Indian leader. Born about 1752 in a village of the Miami Indians near present-day Fort Wayne, Indiana, Little Turtle was the son of a chief. In 1780 he led in the defeat of a body of French irregulars under Col. Mottin de la Balme after they had attacked the village. As an enemy of whites generally, he led the Miami in the defeats of Gen. Josiah Harmar in October 1790 and Gen. Arthur St. Clair in November 1791. When Gen. Anthony Wayne marched into Indian country in 1793 Little Turtle urged accommodation, believing that another victory over the army was not to be had. He took part in the attack on Fort Recovery, at the site of St. Clair's defeat, on June 30, 1794, but his caution led to charges of cowardice among his optimistic fellow chiefs and he was not in command of the Indians in the great defeat at Fallen Timbers on August 20. As the acknowledged chief of the Miami, however, he signed the Treaty of Greenville on August 3, 1795, and he later worked on behalf of Gov.

William Henry Harrison to win Indian support of subsequent land cessions, receiving a government annuity for his services. He made in later years several visits to the cities of the East and became one of the best known and most popular Indian figures of the day, although his prestige among Indians correspondingly declined. He lived most of the time in a home built for him by the government in the Miami village on the Eel River near Fort Wayne, Indiana. He died in Fort Wayne on July 14, 1812.

Logan, James (1725?–1780), Indian leader. Born about 1725 in the Delaware Indian village of Shamokin (subsequently Sunbury, Pennsylvania), Logan, whose Indian name was Tah-gah-jute, was the son of a Cayuga woman and of Chief Shikellamy, believed to have been a Frenchman raised by the Oneida Indians. Sometimes confused with his elder brother John Shikellamy, who also became a chief and succeeded his father as Iroquois representative at Shamokin, Logan, who never became a chief, was supposedly named for the Quaker James Logan, member of the council and chief justice of Pennsylvania, who for years had traded with the Indians and who numbered the elder Chief Shikellamy among his friends. Logan himself was an outspoken friend of the whites, both in Pennsylvania and later, until the events of 1774, in Ohio, where he was prominent among the Mingo bands. Logan's friendship turned to bitter hatred after his Shawnee wife and some other relatives were killed at the Yellow Creek (or Baker's Cabin) massacre of April 30, 1774, that precipitated Lord Dunmore's War. Although he always accused Capt. Michael Cresap, a leader of frontier militia, of his family's slaughter, it later appeared to have been committed by other whites. Logan spent the rest of his life seeking vengeance. At the war's end in November 1774, although he reputedly had scalped some 30 white men, which might have seemed ample revenge, he refused to attend the peace-treaty meeting at Camp Charlotte. His refusal was conveyed and translated at the conference by John Gibson (who may have been Logan's brother-in-law) in the form of a short oration, the eloquence of which caused it to be reprinted in many colonial newspapers, and even in European journals, at the time. Although its authenticity has been challenged, the statement became a permanent part of American Indian lore after Thomas Jefferson made use of it in Query VI of *Notes on the State of Virginia* as evidence against the allegedly degrading effects of living in the New World. "I appeal to any white man to say, if ever he entered Logan's cabin hungry, and he gave him not meat; if ever he came cold and naked, and he clothed him not," he is reputed to have said; "During the course of the last long and bloody war, Logan remained idle in his cabin, an advocate for peace. [But] Colonel Cresap, the last spring, in cold blood and unprovoked, murdered all the relations of Logan, not even sparing my woman and children. There runs not a drop of my blood in the veins of any living creature. This called on me for revenge. I have sought it; I have killed many; I have glutted my vengeance. For my country, I rejoice at the beams of peace. But do not harbor a thought that this is the joy of fear. Logan never felt fear. He will not turn on his heel to save his life. Who is there to mourn for Logan? Not one!" Logan continued to ravage white settlements until his death in 1780. He died at the hands of a relative near Lake Erie while aiding the British at Detroit during the Revolution.

Logan, John Alexander (1826–1886), army officer and public official. Born on February 9, 1826, near what is now Murphysboro, Illinois, Logan had scant schooling. He received some instruction in law before taking part in the Mexican War as a second lieutenant in the 1st Illinois Infantry Volunteers. He held local offices after he graduated from the law department of Louisville University and began to practice law in his native town in 1851. He served in the legislature in 1852, 1853, 1856, and 1857, was district attorney in 1853–1857, and was elected to the House of Representatives as a Democrat in 1858 and again in 1860. He had an excellent combat record in the Civil War. He rushed into action as a private soldier in a Michigan regiment at the first battle of Bull Run, July 21, 1861, while still a member of Congress, and then returned to Illinois, where, organizing the 31st Illinois Regiment, he was made in September its colonel. He served under Gen. Ulysses S. Grant, distinguishing himself at Belmont, Missouri, November 7, and taking part in the capture of Fort Henry, February 6, 1862, and Fort Donelson, February 16. In March he was promoted to brigadier general of volunteers. In the Vicksburg campaign in 1863 he commanded a division of Gen. James B. McPherson's XVII Corps and, promoted to major general of volunteers, in November he was given the XV Corps, Army of the Tennessee. In the Atlanta campaign in 1864 he succeeded to command of the army on the death of McPherson on July 22. However, Gen. William T. Sherman, while acknowledging his courage in combat, claimed that he neglected logistics and shortly thereafter had him returned to his corps command, giving the Army of the Tennessee to Gen. O. O. Howard. Declining to remain in the regular army after the war, Logan resumed his political career, serving in the House of Representatives in 1867–1871 and, after that, except for an interval in 1877–1878, in the Senate until his death. A Radical Republican after the war, he was one of the managers of President Andrew Johnson's impeachment trial. He was instrumental in the formation of the Grand Army of the Republic (GAR) and served as its national commander in chief from 1868 to 1874; GAR support

contributed to his selection as the vice-presidential candidate on the ticket with James G. Blaine in 1884. It was as commander of the GAR that he instituted in 1868 the observance of May 30 as Decoration Day (later called Memorial Day). He died in Washington, D.C., on December 26, 1886.

Long, Stephen Harriman (1784–1864), army officer and explorer. Born in Hopkinton, New Hampshire, on December 30, 1784, Long graduated from Dartmouth College in 1809 and after teaching for a time he entered the army in December 1814 as a second lieutenant of engineers. He was an instructor at West Point for two years and in April 1816 was transferred to the topographical engineers with brevet rank of major. He made his first journey west in 1817, when he explored the portages of the Fox and Wisconsin rivers, had a look at the upper Mississippi, and established Fort Smith at the confluence of the Arkansas and Poteau rivers in what is now the state of Arkansas. In July 1819 he accompanied the ill conceived expedition bound from St. Louis for the Rocky Mountains under Col. Henry Atkinson. Soon after the establishment of Fort Atkinson at Council Bluffs he returned east for the winter, but in the spring of 1820 he was back at Fort Atkinson. The larger expedition had by then been abandoned, but in June Long set out with 19 men to explore westward. He ascended the Platte and the South Platte to the Rockies, where Long's Peak was discovered and named and Pike's Peak was first scaled by one of the party (Dr. Edwin James, on July 14). Long then turned south and divided his party, sending one group down the Arkansas and leading the other to what he hoped was the Red but was actually the Canadian. In September he reached Fort Smith. His description of the country traversed lent authority to the general misapprehension that the region was barren, and he labeled it the "Great American Desert" on the official map. In 1823 Long explored the source of the Minnesota River (then known as the St. Peter's) and the U.S.–Canadian border region around the Great Lakes. He was promoted to brevet lieutenant colonel in 1826. In 1827 he was detached to the Baltimore & Ohio Railroad to survey the route, during which work he contributed to the adaptation of wooden bridge design to railroad use and worked out a series of tables for computing curves and grades, publishing them in his pioneering *Rail Road Manual,* 1829. He left the B & O in 1830. During 1834–1837 he surveyed railroad routes in Georgia and Tennessee and from 1837 to 1840 was chief engineer of the Atlantic & Great Western Railroad. He was promoted in 1838 to regular major on the organization of the topographical engineers as a separate corps. After 1840 he was a consulting engineer to several railroads in addition to his army duties. In 1856 he was put in command of navigation improvement work on the

Mississippi, and in 1861 he was called to Washington, D.C., to serve as chief of the Corps of Topographical Engineers with the rank of colonel. The corps merged into the Corps of Engineers in March 1863, and in June of that year Long retired. He died in Alton, Illinois, on September 4, 1864.

Longstreet, James (1821–1904), Confederate army officer. Born on January 8, 1821, in Edgefield District, South Carolina, Longstreet graduated from West Point in 1842 and was commissioned in the infantry. He saw mainly garrison duty on the Louisiana and Texas frontiers until the outbreak of the Mexican War. He was promoted to first lieutenant in February 1847. In the war he served under both Gen. Zachary Taylor and Gen. Winfield Scott, was brevetted captain at Churubusco, August 20, 1847, and major at Molino del Rey, September 8, and was severely wounded at Chapultepec, September 13. Longstreet advanced to captain in December 1852 and to major in July 1858 while serving in various routine assignments. On the outbreak of the Civil War he resigned, and in June 1861 he was commissioned a brigadier general in the Confederate army. On July 18 at Blackburn's Ford on Bull Run Creek he repulsed the leading division of Gen. Irvin McDowell's advancing army, and he distinguished himself in the battle of Manassas (Bull Run) three days later, at the end of which he led the pursuit of the Union army back to Washington, D.C. Promoted to major general in October, he commanded a division under Gen. Joseph E. Johnston on the Yorktown Peninsula in the spring of 1862 and on May 5 fought an effective rearguard action against troops of the III Corps (Gen. Samuel P. Heintzelman) of Gen. George B. McClellan's advancing Army of the Potomac at Williamsburg. At Seven Pines (Fair Oaks), May 31, he failed to carry out his instructions in a timely fashion, but he performed ably during the Seven Days' Battles, June 26–July 2, under Gen. Robert E. Lee, being particularly heavily engaged at Mechanicsville, June 26, and Frayser's Farm, June 30. In August, in command of more than half of Lee's infantry (five of nine divisions) he moved northward to join Gen. Thomas J. Jackson. On August 29 he arrived at Manassas, and the next day the reunited army defeated Gen. John Pope's Army of Virginia in the second battle of Manassas (Bull Run). In the invasion of Maryland that followed immediately (and which the cautious Longstreet opposed) he was engaged at South Mountain, September 14, and absorbed heavy attacks by Gen. Ambrose E. Burnside on the Confederate right at Sharpsburg (Antietam), September 17. In October he was promoted to lieutenant general, and his command was designated the I Corps, Army of Northern Virginia. At Fredericksburg, December 13, his divisions held Marye's Heights against a costly attack by Gen. Edwin V. Sumner and Gen. Joseph Hooker. In February

1863 he was dispatched by Lee to conduct defensive and foraging operations in the region around Petersburg and southward; his slowness, together with his fruitless siege of a Union garrison at Suffolk, Virginia, in April, resulted in his being absent with two full divisions from the battle of Chancellorsville in May. With the death of Jackson following that battle Longstreet became Lee's senior lieutenant, but by that time his deficiencies as a general had begun to affect his usefulness. A fierce fighter and a capable enough tactician, he had little grasp of strategy and little trust in any judgment but his own; in consequence, his response to battlefield orders, seldom quick, became dilatory and sometimes almost insubordinate when he disagreed with them. He disagreed emphatically with Lee's orders at Gettysburg. On the second day of battle, July 2, he delayed executing Lee's orders for a major attack on the Union left until Gen. George G. Meade and his corps commanders on that wing (principally Gen. Winfield S. Hancock, II Corps, and Gen. Daniel E. Sickles, III Corps) had established their lines and occupied the strategic Little Round Top. The attack that afternoon succeeded only in pushing Sickles out of the Peach Orchard and back onto Cemetery Ridge. Longstreet was almost in despair over Lee's plan for another major attack the next day, and he objected strenuously enough to keep his corps out of it except for the division under Gen. George E. Pickett. In September he was ordered to take his corps by rail to reinforce Gen. Braxton Bragg's Army of Tennessee at Chattanooga. He arrived on the field at Chickamauga on September 19, narrowly avoided capture, and commanded one wing (Gen. Leonidas Polk had the other) in the major attack the next day. He was quick to capitalize on Gen. William S. Rosecrans' mistaken order, which weakened the Union position, and swept forward; his corps carried all before it except the troops under Gen. George H. Thomas, who became the "Rock of Chickamauga" in resisting Longstreet's advance. In November Bragg sent him to attack Gen. Burnside at Knoxville. He arrived too late to catch Burnside in the open and instead laid siege to Knoxville. In his absence Bragg suffered defeat at Chattanooga, and at the end of November Longstreet withdrew into winter quarters in Virginia. In April 1864 he rejoined his corps to the Army of Northern Virginia. In the Wilderness campaign he arrived on the field on the second day of battle, May 6, rallied the beleaguered troops of Gen. Ambrose P. Hill's corps, and mounted a furious counterattack in which he was wounded by his own men. He relinquished command of the I Corps to Gen. Richard H. Anderson until his recovery in October. He then commanded it through the final campaign around Richmond and Petersburg and surrendered with Lee on April 9, 1865. After the war he settled in New Orleans, joined the Republican Party—an action that made him unpopular in the South—and from 1869 held a series of political jobs. He was appointed surveyor of customs at New Orleans by President Ulysses S. Grant in 1869, postmaster there by Grant in 1873, U.S. minister to Turkey by President Rutherford B. Hayes in 1880, and U.S. marshal for Georgia by President James A. Garfield in 1881, holding the last post for three years. In 1898 he was appointed U.S. railroad commissioner by President William McKinley. In 1896 he published his war memoirs, *From Manassas to Appomattox*. Longstreet died in Gainesville, Georgia, his home since 1875, on January 2, 1904.

Loring, William Wing (1818–1886), Confederate army officer. Born on December 4, 1818, in Wilmington, North Carolina, Loring grew up in Florida and at fourteen volunteered for service in the Florida militia against the Seminole Indians. In June 1837 he was commissioned a second lieutenant. Later he studied law at Georgetown (D.C.) College (now University) and shortly after being admitted to the bar in 1842 he was elected to the Florida legislature. In May 1846 he was appointed captain in the army's regiment of Mounted Rifles, advancing to major in February 1847; and he served under Gen. Winfield Scott in Mexico from Veracruz to Mexico City, distinguishing himself in command of the regiment at Contreras, August 19–20, 1847, and at Chapultepec, September 13, where he lost his left arm, and winning brevets of lieutenant colonel and colonel. Promoted to lieutenant colonel in March 1848, he led the regiment to the Pacific Coast in 1849 and took command of the Department of Oregon. In 1851 the regiment was transferred to Texas, where it saw considerable action against Indians. Loring was promoted to colonel in December 1856. In 1857–1858 he served under Col. Albert S. Johnston in the Mormon campaign, and after a year of travel in Europe and the Near East he resumed active service as commander of the Department of New Mexico in 1860–1861. In May 1861 he resigned his commission and was appointed brigadier general in the Confederate army, taking command of forces in West Virginia. He served under Gen. Thomas J. Jackson in the Shenandoah valley campaign, receiving promotion to major general in February 1862 and command of the Army of Southwestern Virginia. Later in the year he was ordered to the western theater. He commanded a division under Gen. John C. Pemberton at Vicksburg in 1863 and in June 1864 succeeded Gen. Leonidas Polk as commander of Polk's Corps, Army of Mississippi, in the Atlanta campaign. He led a division of Gen. Alexander P. Stewart's corps, Army of Tennessee, at Franklin, November 30, 1864, and at Nashville, December 15–16, serving as Gen. John B. Hood's second-in-command in those battles, and was with Gen. Joseph E. Johnston in the Carolina

campaign until his surrender in April 1865. For a time thereafter he engaged in banking in New York City, but in 1869 he accepted a commission of brigadier general in the army of Khedive Ismail I (Ismail Pasha) of Egypt. He served first as inspector general of the army and in 1870 was given command of the defenses of Alexandria and the coast. During 1875–1876 he took part in the expedition against Abyssinia, winning promotion to general of division and the title of pasha. In 1879 he was mustered out of Egyptian service. He lived for a time in Florida and then settled in New York City. In 1884 he published *A Confederate Soldier in Egypt*. Loring died in New York City on December 30, 1886.

Lovell, James Arthur, Jr. (1928–   ), naval officer and astronaut. Born on March 25, 1928, in Cleveland, Ohio, Lovell grew up there and in Milwaukee, Wisconsin. He attended the University of Wisconsin for two years, 1946–1948, and then transferred to the Naval Academy, graduating in 1952. Having already taken flight training at Pensacola Naval Air Station, Florida, he then took test pilot training, served in that capacity at the Navy Air Test Center, Patuxent River, Maryland, and later as a flight instructor. In 1962 he was among the second group of pilots chosen for astronaut training by the National Aeronautics and Space Administration (NASA). His first space mission was with *Gemini 7*, a 14-day orbital flight with Col. Frank Borman in December 1965 that included a rendezvous and docking, the first in the U.S. space program, with *Gemini 6*, manned by Walter M. Schirra and L. Gordon Cooper. Lovell was promoted to captain after that flight. In November 1966 Lovell and Maj. Edwin E. Aldrin made the last of the *Gemini* flights, *Gemini 12*, a four-day mission. On December 21, 1968, Lovell, Borman, and William A. Anders lifted off from Cape Kennedy aboard *Apollo VIII*, the first moon-orbital mission. Lovell, navigator of the mission, emerged from it after splashdown in the Pacific on December 27 as the astronaut with the most time logged in space—more than 570 hours. In 1969 he was named director of the President's Council on Physical Fitness. On April 11, 1970, Lovell again entered space as commander of the *Apollo XIII* mission, accompanied by Fred W. Haise, Jr., and John L. Swigert, Jr. On April 13, 56 hours into the mission, an explosion occurred in a liquid oxygen tank that caused some damage to the spacecraft but more importantly threatened the supply of electrical power and breathing oxygen. News of the event and of the difficult task of pinpointing what had happened and how much danger the astronauts were in electrified a listening world. The three crewmen moved into the lunar landing craft "Aquarius," using it as a lifeboat in order to shut down and preserve the power and oxygen reserve of the command module "Odyssey."

The orbit was changed from lunar-landing to circle-and-return. Long, tense hours passed as *Apollo XIII* rounded the moon and coasted back to splashdown on April 17, the astronauts having jettisoned "Aquarius" by then and powered up "Odyssey." With 715 hours in space after that flight, Lovell remained with NASA until March 1973, when he retired. Thereafter he pursued business interests in Houston, Texas. Among his numerous honors and awards was the 1969 Collier Trophy.

Lovell, Joseph (1788–1836), physician and army officer. Born in Boston on December 22, 1788, Lovell graduated from Harvard in 1807 and remained there to study medicine, graduating from Harvard Medical School in 1811 with the first class to receive the newly instituted degree of M.D. In May 1812 he entered the army as surgeon of the 9th Infantry posted on the Niagara frontier. He attracted much attention with his work at hospitals in Burlington, Vermont, and Williamsville, New York, the latter of which he established after being appointed a hospital surgeon in June 1814. His administrative ability and imaginative approach to his work as chief medical officer of the Northern Department led to his being chosen surgeon general of the army on the creation of the Medical Department in April 1818. (Previously there had been a surgeon general or chief physician, but no organization except in wartime.) One of Lovell's major innovations was to require of all medical officers quarterly reports of daily weather conditions along with their strictly medical and administrative reports. These constitute the oldest such reports in existence and, in addition to being the forerunner of the work of the later Weather Bureau, are of great historical and meteorological value. Lovell also championed the campaign against alcohol, particularly the rum ration of the army and navy, and supported the anatomical investigations of William Beaumont. The army Medical Department became, under his guidance, an efficient and generally esteemed operation. Lovell died in Washington, D.C., on October 17, 1836.

Lovell, Mansfield (1822–1884), Confederate army officer and engineer. Born in Washington, D.C., on October 20, 1822, Lovell was a son of Joseph Lovell, surgeon general of the army. He graduated from West Point in 1842 and was commissioned in the artillery. With the 4th Artillery he joined Gen. Zachary Taylor's forces in Texas in 1845 and after the outbreak of the Mexican War served in Taylor's campaign, being wounded at Monterrey in September 1846. Subsequently he served for a time as aide to Gen. John A. Quitman. He was promoted to first lieutenant in February 1847, and in that year he served in Gen. Winfield Scott's army, receiving a brevet as captain for gallantry at Chapultepec, September 13, where he was again wounded. After seven years of routine garrison duty Lovell resigned from the army in 1854 and entered the employ of Cooper & Hewitt's Iron Works in Trenton, New Jersey. In 1858 he was appointed superintendent of street improvements and a little later deputy street commissioner of New York City. In September 1861 he left New York to join the Confederacy, and in October he was commissioned major general and placed in command of New Orleans. The garrison there was small and composed of short-term volunteers poorly armed, the city had little artillery, and he had no river fleet of his own. Lovell could do little to resist the federal fleet under Flag-Officer David G. Farragut that attacked in April 1862. Fort Jackson and Fort St. Philip held the fleet off from April 18 to April 23, but once they were passed the city came under naval guns, while Gen. Benjamin F. Butler's army approached by land. Lovell abandoned the city and joined his forces to those of Gen. P. G. T. Beauregard upriver. Although his actions were approved by Gen. Robert E. Lee, considerable criticism followed him. He was commander of the I Corps and second-in-command to Gen. Earl Van Dorn at Corinth, Mississippi, on October 3, and two days later he was highly effective in covering the retreat from Coffeeville. In December, as a result of growing criticism of the evacuation of New Orleans, he was removed from field command. A court of inquiry requested by Lovell exonerated him in November 1863, but to little avail. For a time in 1864 he served as a volunteer on the staff of Gen. Joseph E. Johnston. After the war he lived for a time in New York City and then ventured into rice planting near Savannah, Georgia, an enterprise wiped out by flood in 1869. He then returned to New York and worked as a civil engineer. Lovell died in New York City on June 1, 1884.

Lovewell, John (1691–1725), Indian fighter. Born on October 14, 1691, in a part of Dunstable, Massachusetts, that is now in Nashua, New Hampshire, Lovewell became a farmer of sizable holdings and was reputed something of an adventurer. In December 1724, Massachusetts having placed a £100 bounty on Indian scalps, he raised a party of 30 men that killed an Indian man and captured a boy. In February 1725, leading a second party of 87 up the Merrimac past Lake Winnepesaukee, he discovered 10 Indians asleep and took 10 scalps. In the spring he organized 34 men into a third such expedition, which by early May had ranged as far as Ossipee Lake in what is now Maine. On May 9, the chaplain in the party having just scalped an Indian, they crossed the Saco River toward the Pequawket (or Pigwacket) village (on the site of present-day Fryeburg) and were suddenly ambushed by about 80 Indians. Lovewell and 11 others were killed immediately; the rest took up positions behind some fallen logs and held off the attack which lasted through the day. In the evening one of the party managed to shoot the Indians' medicine man, and the rest then withdrew. Eventually 18 survivors of what came to be known in legend and ballad as "Lovewell's Fight" reached home. In the principal contemporary written account the date of the fight was changed to May 8, apparently to protect the chaplain from censure for scalping on the Sabbath.

Lowe, Thaddeus Sobieski Coulincourt (1832 –1913), aeronaut and inventor. Born at Jefferson Mills (later Riverton), New Hampshire, on August 20, 1832, Lowe early became interested in the use of the free balloon for meteorological purposes. In order to test his conjectures about the direction and intensity of currents in the upper atmosphere, he made his first balloon ascent in 1858. In April 1861, two years after John Wise's spectacular flight from St. Louis to Henderson, New York (800 miles in 20 hours), Lowe made a balloon flight from Cincinnati, Ohio, to Pea Ridge, South Carolina, in record time, and although his interests were purely meteorological he became a prisoner of the Confederacy until his innocent intentions were proved. Lowe later offered his services to the Union army. Made chief of the aeronautic section of the army in June 1861, he performed valuable service as a balloonist-observer during the war, making the first airborne use of both the recently invented telegraph (a message to President Abraham Lincoln, June 18) and the camera, also just coming into widespread use. A total of five Lowe balloons were used during the war, principally at the first battle of Bull Run, in the Peninsula campaign, and at Chancellorsville. In September 1861 Lowe, in a captive balloon, directed artillery fire from Fort Corcoran, in the District of Columbia. The air service was discontinued in June 1863. Lowe turned his ingenuity to other areas after the war. His ice-making machine invented in 1865 was incorporated into the design of a refrigerated boat, but a business venture in transporting perishable foods failed. His work on the design of regenerative metallurgical furnaces (1869–1872) resulted in a practical alternative for producing fuel gas. His New Lowe Coke Oven (1897) led to a notable improvement in the manufacture of high-grade coke. In the early 1890s he achieved some celebrity by constructing an inclined railway up a peak in the San Gabriel Mountains in Southern California. The peak, at whose summit he established an observatory, is near Mt. Wilson and is named in his honor. In 1907 he published *Navigating the Air.* He died in Pasadena, California, on January 16, 1913.

Lucas, John Porter (1890–1949), army officer. Born on January 14, 1890, in Kearneysville, West Virginia, Lucas graduated from West Point in 1911 and was commissioned in the cavalry. After three years in

the Philippines he was assigned in 1914 to the 13th Cavalry at Columbus, New Mexico. He was there when Pancho Villa raided the town on March 9, 1916, and took part in driving the bandits out; subsequently he participated in the Mexican Punitive Expedition mounted under Gen. John J. Pershing. Early in 1918 he was promoted to temporary major and attached to the Signal Corps, and by May, when he sailed for France, he had advanced to temporary lieutenant colonel. In June he was wounded in action at Amiens and invalided home. During 1919–1920 he taught military science at the University of Michigan, and in 1920–1921 and 1922–1923 he was a student at the Field Artillery School, Fort Sill, Oklahoma. He graduated from the Command and General Staff School, Fort Leavenworth, Kansas, in 1924, and from 1924 to 1929 he taught military science at the Colorado Agricultural College (now Colorado State University), taking an M.S. degree himself in 1927. After two years at Fort Bliss, Texas, he attended the Army War College and on graduating in 1932 was assigned to General Staff duty. In 1936, by then a colonel, he took command of the 4th Field Artillery at Fort Bragg, North Carolina, and after serving on the Field Artillery Board in 1937–1940 he was placed in command of the 1st Field Artillery at Fort Sill. Promoted to temporary brigadier general, he was briefly in command of the 2nd Infantry Division at Fort Sam Houston, Texas, and, advanced to temporary major general in August 1941, he took command of the 3rd Division at Fort Lewis, Washington, in September. From April 1942 to May 1943 he commanded the III Corps at Fort McPherson, Georgia, and he was then sent to England to join the staff of Gen. Dwight D. Eisenhower. He served in a staff capacity in the North African and the Sicilian campaigns, and in September 1943 he took command of the VI Corps in Gen. Mark W. Clark's Fifth Army in Italy. When the Fifth Army's advance bogged down at the Winter (or Gustav) Line anchored on Cassino, Lucas and the VI Corps were embarked to land behind the German line at Anzio. The Anzio landing on January 22, 1944, established only a precarious beachhead, however, and failed to aid the campaign against Cassino. In February Lucas relinquished command of the corps to Gen. Lucian K. Truscott, and in March he joined Fourth Army headquarters at Fort Sam Houston, becoming commander in April. His rank of major general became permanent in August 1944. From June 1946 to January 1948 he was chief of the U.S. military advisory group in Nationalist China. Lucas was deputy commander, Fifth Army, in Chicago from April 1948 until his death on December 24, 1949, at Great Lakes Naval Base, Illinois.

Luce, Stephen Bleecker (1827–1917), naval officer. Born in Albany, New York, on March 25, 1827, Luce lived from the age of eight in Washington, D.C., and in October 1841, at the age of fourteen, he was appointed a midshipman in the navy. Over the next several years he served on the *North Carolina* and the *Congress,* cruised around the world in 1845–1846, and served on the Pacific Coast in the Mexican War aboard the *Columbus* under Commodore James Biddle. In 1848–1849 he studied at the Naval Academy. From 1849 to 1852 he was in the Pacific aboard the *Vandalia* as a passed midshipman, and in September 1855 he was promoted to lieutenant. From 1858 to 1860 he was on the *Jamestown,* and in March 1860 he was named assistant to the commandant of the Naval Academy. A year later he was ordered to the *Wabash,* and he took part with it in the operations against Hatteras Inlet under Flag-Officer Silas H. Stringham, August 27–29, 1861, and Port Royal under Flag-Officer Samuel F. Du Pont (whose flagship was the *Wabash*), November 7. In 1862 he was recalled to the Academy (which had been moved to Newport, Rhode Island) as head of the department of seamanship, being promoted to lieutenant commander in July. The following year his textbook, *Seamanship,* was published in the first of many editions, and it soon became the standard work in the field. In October 1863 he returned to sea duty in command of the monitor *Nantucket* in the North Atlantic Squadron; he later commanded the *Sonoma* and the *Canandaigua.* In January 1865 he took command of the *Pontiac* and the following month cooperated with Gen. William T. Sherman in the capture of Charleston, South Carolina. After the war he returned to the Academy as commandant of midshipmen, receiving promotion to commander in July 1866. From 1869 to 1872 he was at sea with the European Squadron. Promoted to captain in December 1872, he was on shore duty until 1875 and then for two years commanded the *Hartford.* From 1877 to 1881 he commanded the training ship *Minnesota,* and, promoted to commodore in November 1881, he was in command of all apprentice ships from then until 1884. Luce had long been interested in improving the training of seamen and naval officers—he was responsible for reviving the apprenticeship system in teaching basic seamanship—and he believed particularly that advanced training in tactics, strategy, and other requisites of high command was vital to the continued value of the navy. His talks and papers on the subject resulted finally in the establishment in October 1884 of the Naval War College at Newport. Luce was appointed first president of the college, and not the least among his contributions to its lasting importance was his appointment of Capt. Alfred T. Mahan to the faculty. Promoted to rear admiral in October 1885, Luce returned to sea in June 1886 as commander of the North Atlantic Squadron. He retired in March 1889. He later contributed to and helped edit various reference works and published a volume of navy songs. From 1901 to 1910 he was on special duty at the Naval War College. Luce died in Newport, Rhode Island, on July 28, 1917.

Ludington, Sybil (1761–1839), Revolutionary heroine. Born on April 5, 1761, in Fredericksburg (now Ludingtonville), New York, Sybil Ludington was the daughter of Henry Ludington, a noted New York militia officer and later an aide to Gen. George Washington. On April 26, 1777, a messenger reached the Ludington house with news of Gov. William Tryon's attack on Danbury, Connecticut, some 15 miles to the southeast, where the munitions and stores for the militia of the entire region were stored. Col. Ludington began immediately to organize the local militia. The messenger and his horse being exhausted, Sybil volunteered to bear the order for muster and to rouse the countryside. Through the night the sixteen-year-old girl rode her horse nearly 40 miles on unfamiliar roads around Putnam County, spreading the alarm. She ranged south to Mahopac and north to Stormville before returning home. In October 1784 Sybil married Edward Ogden, a lawyer, and she lived in Unadilla, New York, until her death on February 26, 1839.

Ludlow, William (1843–1901), army officer and engineer. Born in Islip, Long Island, New York, on November 27, 1843, Ludlow attended the University of the City of New York (now New York University) for a time before entering West Point, from which he graduated in 1864. Commissioned in the engineers, he was immediately appointed chief engineer of the XX Corps (Gen. Joseph Hooker and later Gen. Alpheus S. Williams) in the Georgia campaign. He was brevetted captain for gallantry at Peach Tree Creek, July 20, and major in December for service in the campaign. He was assistant engineer on the staff of Gen. William T. Sherman in the march to the sea and the Carolina campaign, and in March 1865, less than a year out of the Academy, he was brevetted lieutenant colonel for services. After the war he was stationed at Jefferson Barracks, Missouri. Promoted to captain in March 1867, he was assistant to the chief of engineers until November 1872, when he was appointed chief engineer, Department of Dakota. He made several valuable surveys of the Yellowstone and Black Hills regions while in that post. From 1876 to 1882 he was engaged in river and harbor work in Philadelphia, receiving promotion to major in June 1882; and from 1883 to 1886, by permission of Congress, he was chief engineer of the Philadelphia water department. During 1886–1888 he was engineer commissioner of Washington, D.C. From 1888 to 1893 he was primarily engaged in river, harbor, and lighthouse work on the Great Lakes, and from 1893 to 1896 he was military attaché at the U.S. embassy in London. While serving in April–November 1895 as chairman of the Nicaragua Canal Commission, he was promoted in August to lieutenant colonel. In February 1897 he was given charge of river and harbor work in New York City. In May 1898 Ludlow was appointed brigadier general of volunteers and chief engineer of the armies in the field. He landed in Cuba with the V Corps under Gen. William R. Shafter and commanded a brigade of Gen. Henry W. Lawton's 2nd Division at El Caney, July 1. In September he was promoted to major general of volunteers, and in December he was appointed military governor of the city and Department of Havana, remaining in that post until April 1900 and contributing much to the rebuilding of the city. While at Havana he was promoted in January 1900 to brigadier general of regulars. Early in 1900 he was named to head a board of officers, known thereafter as the Ludlow Board, which studied and recommended to Secretary of War Elihu Root the creation of an Army War College. A War College Board was established by Root in November 1901, and the College itself, along with the germinal General Staff, developed out it in 1902–1903. In May 1901 Ludlow was ordered to the Philippines to command the Department of Visayas, but he soon returned to the United States on sick leave. He died on August 30, 1901, in Convent, New Jersey.

Ludwick, Christopher (1720–1801), Revolutionary patriot and philanthropist. Born on October 17, 1720, in Giessen, Germany, Ludwick followed his father into the baker's trade. His adventurous early years included military service (1737–1741), including action against the Turks, more than three years as a baker in India, and seven years at sea as a common sailor. Quitting the sea in 1753, he settled in 1754 in Philadelphia, where, with equipment bought in London, he opened a bakery shop. During the next 20 years he married, his business prospered, and he became a respected landowner and member of the community. A champion and financial supporter of the Revolution, he achieved distinction upon volunteering in 1776 for a dangerous mission to a camp of German troops on Staten Island; disguised as a deserter, he induced hundreds of the mercenaries to join the patriot cause. In May 1777 Congress appointed him superintendent of bakers and director of baking for the Continental army. Admired for his honesty by Gen. George Washington, he was known as the Baker General and remained a popular figure in the army throughout the conflict. After the war he found himself in financial difficulties, most of his possessions having been plundered by the British. Although he never reestablished his prewar prosperity, he nevertheless was generous with his remaining fortune. A regular contributor to churches and charities, he left what remained of his estate for the support of free schools for the poor. He died in Philadelphia on June 17, 1801.

Lufbery, Raoul Gervais Victor (1885–1918), army officer and airman. Born on March 21, 1885, in Clermont, France, Lufbery was the son of an American father and a French mother. He remained in France when his father returned to the United States and grew up an adventurous and roving youth. He lived and worked at various times in Turkey, Germany, Connecticut (where he had gone seeking his father), Cuba, New Orleans, San Francisco (where he enlisted in the army for a tour in the Philippines), Japan, and India. At the outbreak of World War I in 1914 he was back in France and enlisted in the Foreign Legion. He quickly transferred to the aviation service, completed training and a brief assignment to a bombardment squadron, and in May 1916 joined the Escadrille Américaine No. 124, which in December became the Lafayette Escadrille. He was soon acknowledged the best pilot in that remarkable group, calm, methodical, and deadly. He had risen to command of the squadron and was credited with 17 victories against German airplanes when the Escadrille was taken into the U.S. army's Signal Corps aviation section in February 1918 as the 103rd Pursuit Squadron. Lufbery received a commission as major in the U.S. army and was assigned to command the 94th Aero Pursuit Squadron, the famed "Hat in the Ring" group that included, among others, Capt. Edward V. Rickenbacker. The 94th was out of combat for several weeks owing to a lack of guns. On May 19, patrolling near Nancy in the Toul sector, Lufbery engaged a German Albatross machine; an incendiary bullet set fire to his Spad and he jumped to his death from an altitude of 2000 feet. His official score of 17 victories ranked him third, after Rickenbacker and Lt. Frank Luke, among American aces. He actually shot down at least 23 more airplanes, not officially counted under the scoring rules of the time because the actions occurred behind German lines.

Luke, Frank, Jr. (1897–1918), army officer and airman. Born on May 19, 1897, in Phoenix, Arizona, Luke enlisted in the army immediately upon graduating from high school in 1917, was assigned to the Signal Corps aviation section, and entered flight training in Austin, Texas. Throughout his period of instruction he demonstrated outstanding ability in handling both airplanes and their guns. He was ordered to France in March 1918, and on completing advanced combat training he joined the 27th Aero Pursuit Squadron with the rank of second lieutenant in late July. He established an amazing record of 18 victories in the air (4 airplanes, 14 balloons) in just 6 weeks. (Many other craft shot down behind German lines were not counted under the scoring rules of the day.) A daring, almost reckless flier, he devised several novel tactics against German observation balloons, particularly dangerous targets because of their ever-present air cover in the form of Fokker fighters.

On September 29, 1918, he went out on a solo patrol over the Toul sector. He destroyed three balloons and then came under attack by six Fokkers, two of which he shot down—all in the space of twelve minutes, a feat unequaled in the war—before being shot down himself. On the way down he strafed a German infantry patrol. Landing his severely damaged airplane near Murvaux, he fought off German soldiers attempting to capture him until he died of wounds. He was awarded the Medal of Honor posthumously for his actions that day. Luke was the second-ranking American ace of the war, following Capt. Edward V. Rickenbacker.

Lynch, William Francis (1801–1865), naval officer, Confederate naval officer, and explorer. Born in Norfolk, Virginia, on April 1, 1801, Lynch was appointed a midshipman in the navy in January 1819. He made his first cruise on the *Congress* in 1819–1821, a circle of the world that included calls at Canton and Manila (the first visit of a U.S. naval vessel to the Philippines). Subsequently he served on the *Shark*, Capt. Matthew C. Perry, engaged in suppressing the slave trade off the African coast, and then in pirate patrol under Commodore David Porter of the West India Squadron. He was promoted to lieutenant in May 1828. During the Mexican War he served in the Gulf of Mexico. In 1847 he secured government backing for a proposed exploring expedition in the Levant. He sailed from New York in November aboard the storeship *Supply*, called at Constantinople for permission from the government of Sultan Abdul-Medjid I, and landed early in April 1848 at Acre. From there he and his party of 14 men hauled 2 metal boats overland to the Sea of Galilee, whence they boated down the Jordan River to the Dead Sea. Returning overland through Palestine to the Mediterranean, the party embarked and arrived back in New York in December 1848. The valuable scientific observations and other results of the expedition were published in the popular *Narrative of the United States Expedition to the River Jordan and the Dead Sea*, 1849, and the *Official Report*, 1852. Lynch also published *Naval Life; or, Observations Afloat and on Shore*, 1851. He was promoted to commander in September 1849 and to captain in April 1856. A plan for an exploration of the West African coast, proposed in the early 1850s, failed to win the necessary support. On the outbreak of the Civil War he resigned his commission and was appointed a captain in the Virginia navy and later, in June, in the Confederate States navy. He commanded the batteries at Aquia Creek on the Potomac during the May 31–June 1 bombardment by the Potomac Flotilla under Commander James H. Ward and thereafter commanded the defense of the North Carolina coast. On February 7–8 he commanded a squadron of seven gunboats in Albemarle Sound that tried vainly to fend off Flag-

Officer Louis M. Goldsborough's much superior squadron bearing Gen. Ambrose E. Burnside's troops to land on Roanoke Island. Beaten, he withdrew to Elizabeth City, where on February 9 he was attacked by a gunboat squadron under Commander Stephen C. Rowan. He lost two of his five gunboats and a schooner. From March to October 1862 Lynch commanded naval forces at Vicksburg on the Mississippi and then returned to North Carolina. In May 1864, aboard the *Raleigh*, he temporarily broke the blockade of Wilmington. During the attack on Fort Fisher by Adm. David D. Porter in January 1865 Lynch commanded defenses at Smithville on Smith Island opposite the fort. Lynch died in Baltimore on October 17, 1865.

Lyon, Nathaniel (1818–1861), army officer. Born in Ashford, Connecticut, on July 14, 1818, Lyon graduated from West Point in 1841 and was commissioned in the infantry. Until May 1842 he was in Florida in action against the Seminoles; from then until 1846 he was stationed at Sackett's Harbor, New York. In the Mexican War he served in Gen. Winfield Scott's army from Veracruz to Mexico City. Having been promoted to first lieutenant in February 1847, he was brevetted captain for gallantry at Contreras and Churubusco, August 19–20. After the war he was ordered to California, where he campaigned against the Indians. He was promoted to captain in June 1851. In 1854 he was ordered to Fort Riley, Kansas, and for the next seven years he was on duty in Kansas, Nebraska, and Iowa, taking part in some Indian campaigns, including the one under Col. William S. Harney in 1855. In February 1861 he was assigned to command of the federal arsenal in St. Louis, where he became active in promoting the Union cause, raising a volunteer pro-Union force called the Home Guards. With them, and on his own initiative but with the strong support of Congressman Francis P. Blair, Jr., he captured on May 10 Camp Jackson, a Missouri militia training camp near St. Louis established by Confederate sympathizers. A few days' later he was appointed brigadier general of volunteers and named to succeed (then General) Harney in command of the Department of the West. Shortly thereafter he led an expedition to Potosi to seize lead mines for the Union. He refused the demand of Gov. Claiborne F. Jackson that the Home Guards be disbanded, and when Jackson called for a militia on the other side Lyon moved on Jefferson City, the state capital, taking it on June 15 and defeating the State Guard at Boonville on June 17. Sending Col. Franz Sigel ahead, he pursued the militia forces to Springfield, which he occupied on July 13. On August 2 he defeated a State Guard force at Dug Springs. On the approach of a Confederate army under Gen. Ben McCulloch he chose to attack at Wilson's Creek on August 10, although his 5400 troops faced a combined force of nearly 11,000 Confederates and State Guards under McCulloch and Gen. Stirling Price. He sent Sigel to attack the right and himself attacked the left; Sigel's defeat exposed Lyon to the full enemy force and at the height of the battle he was killed. His army then retreated toward Rolla. Despite the defeat Lyon's actions had saved Missouri for the Union and had created one of the North's first heroes of the Civil War.

M

McAlexander, Ulysses Grant (1864–1936),
army officer. Born on August 30, 1864, in Dundas,
Minnesota, McAlexander grew up there and in Kansas. He graduated from West Point in 1887, was commissioned in the infantry, and embarked upon a career entirely unremarkable until nearly at an end. He
served several periods as an instructor in military
science and tactics, from 1891 to 1895 at Iowa Wesleyan College and in 1907–1911 and 1915–1916 at
Oregon State College. During the Spanish–American
War, with the rank of captain of volunteers from
May 1898, he took part in the Santiago campaign,
and in 1900–1902, 1905–1906, and 1912–1915 he was
in the Philippines. In 1906–1907 he was assigned to
General Staff duty. He was promoted to captain in
March 1899, major in January 1911, lieutenant colonel in July 1916, and colonel in May 1917. In June
1917, after a year as instructor and inspector with the
Oregon National Guard, he was ordered to France.
From July to December he commanded the 18th Infantry Regiment, and he served then on the inspector
general's staff until May 1918. Given command of
the 38th Infantry Regiment in Gen. Joseph T. Dickman's 3rd Infantry Division, he was assigned to a
portion of the Marne River front near Moulins,
where the great German offensive of July 1918, the
second battle of the Marne, occurred. German forces
crossed the river early on July 15; all along the 50-
mile front they advanced up to 4 miles beyond the
Marne except at Moulins, where the 38th, bearing the
brunt of the initial attack and subsequently coming
under fire from both flanks as other regiments fell
back, held a wooded rise for 21 hours. That brilliant
and courageous action blunted the offensive, which
bogged down on the 16th and ended entirely on the
18th. McAlexander and the 38th were both dubbed
the "Rock of the Marne." In August he was promoted to temporary brigadier general and given command of a brigade of Gen. Henry T. Allen's 90th
Division, which he led in the St. Mihiel and Meuse–
Argonne operations and commanded in occupation
duty until June 1919. Promoted to permanent brigadier general in March 1921, he retired as a major
general in July 1924. McAlexander died in Portland,
Oregon, on September 18, 1936.

MacArthur, Arthur (1845–1912), army officer.
Born in Chicopee Falls, Massachusetts, on June 2,
1845, MacArthur moved with his family to Milwaukee as a boy and was educated there. In August

1862, aged seventeen, he secured appointment as first
lieutenant in the 24th Wisconsin Infantry. He distinguished himself at Murfreesboro (Stones River),
December 31–January 3, 1863, and won the Medal of
Honor (awarded in 1890) for seizing his regimental
colors at a critical moment during the battle of Missionary Ridge, November 25, 1863, and planting
them on the captured enemy works at the crest of the
ridge. MacArthur was promoted two grades to major
in January 1864 and led the regiment, part of Gen.
George H. Thomas's Army of the Cumberland, at
Resaca, Kenesaw Mountain, and Jonesboro in the Atlanta campaign, and at Franklin, Tennessee, November 30, 1864, where he was severely wounded in
hand-to-hand fighting. In March 1865 he was brevetted lieutenant colonel and colonel and in May he
was promoted to lieutenant colonel, receiving the affectionate nickname of "Boy Colonel of the West"
(he was not yet twenty). Mustered out of volunteer
service in June, he reentered the army in February
1866 as second lieutenant of the regular 17th Infantry, receiving promotions to first lieutenant on the
same day and to captain in July. For more than 20
years he served on the frontier, mainly in the Southwest. In July 1889 he became a major in the adjutant
general's department, and in May 1896 he advanced
to lieutenant colonel. In May 1898, shortly after the
outbreak of the Spanish–American War, he was
made a brigadier general of volunteers and assigned
to the Philippines; his brigade took part in the capture of Manila by Gen. Wesley Merritt's VIII Corps
shortly after. Cited again for gallantry, he was promoted to major general of volunteers in August and
placed in charge of the main body of U.S. troops
opposing the insurrectionary forces of Emilio Aguinaldo, successfully repelling an attack on Manila in
February 1899 and then leading the occupation and
pacification of Luzon, which culminated in the occupation of Dagupan in November. Promoted to brigadier general of regulars in January 1900, he succeeded
Gen. Elwell S. Otis as commander of the Division of
the Philippines and military governor in May and in
that position instituted many democratic reforms. He
was promoted to major general in February 1901 and
returned to the United States in July. A series of
departmental commands followed. During the Russo
–Japanese War of 1904–1905 he was a special observer with the Japanese army. In September 1906, while
in command of the Division of the Pacific, he received promotion to lieutenant general and became

the ranking officer of the army. He retired in June 1909 and died in Milwaukee on September 5, 1912. Douglas MacArthur was his son.

MacArthur, Douglas (1880–1964), army officer.

Born on an army post near Little Rock, Arkansas, on January 26, 1880, MacArthur was the son of Capt. Arthur MacArthur. He graduated from West Point first in the class of 1903; commissioned in the Corps of Engineers, he was sent to survey and study the Philippines. In 1906–1907 he was an aide to President Theodore Roosevelt. From 1908 to 1912 he was an instructor in various army schools, and during 1913–1915 and 1916–1917 was attached to the General Staff. He took part in the occupation of Veracruz in April 1914. Having been promoted to captain in February 1911 and major in December 1915, he helped organize the 42nd (Rainbow) Division on the entry of the United States into World War I and served as chief of staff to its commander, Gen. Charles T. Menoher. Promoted to temporary colonel in August 1917, he was ordered to France with the 42nd in October. He advanced to temporary brigadier general in June 1918 and in November took command of the division for a short time. After occupation duty he returned to the United States in April 1919 and in June was named superintendent of West Point. He was promoted to brigadier general in January 1920. He was again in the Philippines from June 1922 until January 1925, receiving at the latter date promotion to major general. He served in that year on the court-martial of Col. William Mitchell. From 1928 to 1930 MacArthur commanded the Department of the Philippines, and in November 1930 he became chief of staff of the army with temporary rank of general, a post he held until October 1935, a longer period than any of his predecessors. In this post he was called upon by President Herbert Hoover in the summer of 1932 to roust the "Bonus Army" of unemployed veterans from Washington in a much-criticized action that came to be known sarcastically as the "battle of Anacostia Flats." In 1932 MacArthur directed the reorganization of the army's tactical forces, merging the old corps areas into four armies, each with regional as well as field responsibility. In 1935, reverting to permanent rank of major general, he was sent to organize the defense forces of the Philippines in anticipation of the islands' independence; he was appointed field marshal of the Philippines in August 1936, and in 1937, rather than be transferred to other duties before his task was complete, he resigned from the U.S. army. He was still in the islands in command of the Philippine military establishment when, in response to increasing tension in the Far East, the Philippine army was merged with the U.S. forces still remaining there in July 1941. MacArthur was recalled to active duty, promoted to temporary lieutenant general, and placed in command of the combined U.S. Army Forces in the Far East (USAFFE). On the same day that Pearl Harbor was raided by Japanese aircraft—December 7, 1941—Japanese forces invaded the Philippines; overwhelmed, MacArthur declared Manila an open city and withdrew his forces to the Bataan peninsula at the entrance to Manila Bay and finally to the fortified island of Corregidor. In February 1942, two months before the garrison, then commanded by Gen. Jonathan M. Wainwright, finally surrendered, he was ordered to leave the Philippines for Australia. Awarded the Medal of Honor and appointed supreme commander of the Allied forces in the Southwest Pacific area in April, he began his counteroffensive in the fall of that year and oversaw the "island-hopping" strategy that led the Allied forces slowly through New Guinea and the smaller islands toward Japan. In that campaign his ground forces, army and marine, were supplemented by a naval force, later expanded into the Seventh Fleet, under Adm. Thomas C. Kinkaid, and an air force under Gen. George C. Kenney. He was also able to call on support from Adm. William F. Halsey's South Pacific (later Third) Fleet and Adm. Raymond A. Spruance's Central (Fifth) Fleet. In October 1944 he fulfilled his famous promise—"I shall return"—of more than two years earlier by landing in the Philippines; two months later he was promoted to the rank of general of the army. In April 1945 MacArthur was named commander of all army forces in the Pacific. The Philippines were finally secured in July 1945, and on September 2 of that year MacArthur, as supreme commander of Allied powers (from August), accepted the surrender of Japan aboard the battleship *Missouri*. Appointed commander of the Allied occupation forces in Japan, he spent the next six years overseeing the reorganization of the government and the economy of the nation. In January 1947 he was named commander of the army's Far East Command. When in June 1950 North Korea launched the invasion of South Korea that began the Korean War, MacArthur was ordered to provide assistance to South Korea. Following United Nations (UN) resolutions that provided for concerted military assistance to South Korea under unified command, on July 8 he was made supreme commander of UN forces in Korea. The suddenness of the initial attack, the weakness of the South Korean army, and delay in dispatching U.S. forces allowed the North Koreans to overrun almost the entire peninsula and to bottle up the UN forces, mainly Gen. Walton H. Walker's Eighth Army, in a small area around Pusan. Carrying his plan over the objections of the Joint Chiefs of Staff and others, MacArthur created the X Corps under Gen. Edward M. Almond to carry out a daring amphibious counterinvasion at Inch'on in September 1950. A few days later X Corps recaptured Seoul, the South Korean capital. The forces hemmed in at Pusan broke out and swept northward. By October they had reached the 38th parallel, the border between North and South Korea. Following President Harry S. Truman's instructions, which were only later ratified by the UN, MacArthur ordered the troops to cross the demarcation line and invade the North, and by late October some units of the UN forces had reached the Yalu River, the border of the People's Republic of China. Faced with conflicting intelligence reports concerning the massing of Chinese forces just north of the Yalu and the substantial numbers of Chinese troops already in Korea, MacArthur chose to discount the likelihood of Chinese intervention and to press on to the river in force. In late November, as the last advance was begun, the Chinese poured vast numbers of troops across the Yalu, driving the UN forces back south of the 38th parallel. MacArthur, convinced that the entry of China into the fighting meant a "new war," one that should be carried by airpower directly to the new enemy, publicly disagreed with U.S. policy on war aims. Ordered to refrain from public disputation by President Truman, he persisted in calling for action against China, and on April 11, 1951, he was relieved of his command by the President. (Gen. Matthew B. Ridgway was appointed in his place.) His return to the United States was that of a hero; immense crowds greeted him in city after city, and this, combined with a stirring address to a joint session of Congress—an address remembered for the line "Old soldiers never die; they just fade away"—made him seem a potential political figure. He retired to private life, however, retaining his five-star rank as general of the army and active status and becoming in 1959 the senior officer of the army. A volume of his *Reminiscences* appeared in 1964. He died in Washington, D.C., on April 5, 1964.

McArthur, William Pope (1814–1850), naval officer and explorer. Born in Ste. Genevieve, Missouri, on April 2, 1814, McArthur was appointed a midshipman in the navy in February 1832. He served in the South Pacific for several years, attended the naval school at Norfolk, Virginia, and in 1837–1838 commanded one of a squadron of naval vessels sent to assist army operations against the Seminole Indians in Florida. He was severely wounded in that campaign. In 1840 he was assigned to the brig *Consort*, which under auspices of the Coast Survey conducted a survey of the Gulf coast in 1840–1841. He was promoted to lieutenant in the latter year. In 1848 he was given command of a hydrographic party sent out by the Coast Survey to conduct the first survey of the Pacific coast. En route, he discovered a state of virtual anarchy in Panama, principally the result of an unregulated influx of Americans; he promptly organized a vigilance committee and restored order. Commandeering the emigrant ship *Humboldt*, he sailed to

the California coast, selected Mare Island as the site for a navy yard, and aboard the schooner *Ewing* continued the survey of the coast as far north as the mouth of the Columbia River. The survey, accomplished in the face of great difficulty, was later published by the Coast Survey as *Notices of the Western Coast of the United States*, 1851. While returning home McArthur fell ill and died at sea off Panama City on December 23, 1850.

McAuliffe, Anthony Clement (1898–1975), army officer. Born on July 2, 1898, in Washington, D.C., McAuliffe attended West Virginia University in 1916–1917 before entering West Point, from which he graduated in November 1918 (the course being accelerated in wartime). Commissioned a second lieutenant of field artillery, he graduated from Field Artillery School, Camp Zachary Taylor, Kentucky, in 1920 and subsequently completed tours of duty at several bases in the United States and in Hawaii. Promoted to captain in May 1935, he attended Command and General Staff School, Fort Leavenworth, Kansas, in 1936–1937 and became a major in June 1940 on graduating from the Army War College. He was promoted to temporary lieutenant colonel shortly before the Japanese attack on Pearl Harbor in December 1941 and to temporary colonel in February 1942. By August he was a temporary brigadier general commanding the artillery of the 101st Airborne Division. With the 101st he was among the first troops parachuted into Normandy in the Allied invasion of France in early June 1944, and immediately thereafter he was named deputy division commander under Gen. Maxwell D. Taylor. He distinguished himself at Carentan and in the airborne invasion of the Netherlands, the disastrous Operation Market-Garden under Field Marshal Bernard Montgomery, in September. His greatest moment came during the Battle of the Bulge, the German Ardennes counteroffensive of December 1944, when, temporarily in command of the 101st, he held the strategic Bastogne salient until elements from the Third Army of Gen. George S. Patton broke through to him from the south. His command was completely surrounded by the advancing German army when his response to the enemy's surrender demand—"Nuts!"—inspired his troops to a last-ditch stand that helped turn the tide in what proved to be the last major counteroffensive in the battle of Europe. In January 1945 he was promoted to temporary major general and given command of the 103rd Division, which he led from Alsace across Germany into Austria and to a junction with Gen. Mark W. Clark's Fifth Army at the Brenner Pass. During July–August he commanded the 79th Division in occupation duties. From September 1945 to June 1946 he was chief of the Airborne Center, Camp Mackall, North Carolina, and he later commanded Fort Bragg, North Carolina. During 1947–

1948 he was the army's deputy director of research and development, and in October 1949, after a tour of duty in Japan, he was made permanent major general in command of the Chemical Corps. Promoted to lieutenant general in July 1951, he became deputy chief of staff for operations in February 1953 and commander of the Seventh Army in Germany in September 1953. In March 1955 he became commander of U.S. army forces in Europe with the rank of general. McAuliffe retired in that rank in May 1956 and the next year was named a vice-president of the American Cyanamid Company. In 1959–1963 he was chairman of the New York State Civil Defense Commission. He died in Washington, D.C., on August 11, 1975.

McCalla, Bowman Hendry (1844–1910), naval officer. Born in Camden, New Jersey, on June 19, 1844, McCalla graduated from the Naval Academy in 1864. For a decade he served aboard vessels in the South Pacific, the South Atlantic, and European waters; and during 1874–1878 he was an instructor at the Academy. He advanced to lieutenant in March 1868 and lieutenant commander in March 1869. Promoted to commander in November 1884, he was sent in the spring of 1885 to Panama with a force of 750 seamen and marines to reinforce Commodore James E. Jouett of the Atlantic Squadron. McCalla led a landing party that quickly occupied Panama City and ended the revolt. During 1887–1890 he commanded the *Enterprise* in the European Squadron. In the latter year he was court-martialed for striking a mutinous seaman and sentenced to suspension from duty for three years, but he was recalled in 1891. In 1897 he took command of the cruiser *Marblehead,* and on the outbreak of the Spanish–American War in April 1898 he was put in command of a blockade division stationed off Havana and later at Cienfuegos. Under his general direction a boat party made a daring approach under heavy fire on May 11 to raise and cut the submarine telegraph cable leading to Cienfuegos. The *Marblehead* was attached briefly to Adm. Winfield S. Schley's "Flying Squadron" and then, early in June, was sent to Guantánamo Bay. On June 8 he landed a force of marines and sailors, who entrenched on what came to be called McCalla Hill, and he established and commanded a naval base there for the duration of the war. He was promoted to captain in August 1898. After periods in command of the *Vulcan* and at Norfolk navy yard, he was given command of the *Newark* in 1899 and sent to the Philippines, where in December he relieved a besieged army force at Vigan and then received at Aparri the surrender of the provinces of Cagayan and Isabella of northern Luzon. In May 1900 he carried Adm. Louis Kempff on the *Newark* to China, where the Boxer Rebellion had broken out. From a station off Taku, at the mouth of the Pei Ho River, a force of 48 ma-

rines and 3 sailors off the *Newark* was dispatched under command of Capt. John T. Myers to Peking to reinforce the legation guard there. On June 5 McCalla himself led another landing party to Tientsin, where, following the cutting of the railroad connection with Peking, he proposed a relief expedition to that city. Other allied detachments joined, constituting a force of 2078 men under the command of British Adm. Sir Edward Seymour. McCalla and his 112 sailors were the vanguard. The expedition failed to reach Peking, coming under heavy attack 25 miles short of the city and withdrawing to a captured fort, where it was besieged until relieved on June 25 by an international force, including U.S. marines under Maj. Littleton W. T. Waller, from Tientsin. McCalla was wounded three times during the expedition. On his return home in 1901 he commanded the *Kearsarge* for a time and then Mare Island navy yard. Promoted to rear admiral in October 1903, he retired in June 1906. He died in Santa Barbara, California, on May 6, 1910.

McCallum, Daniel Craig (1815–1878), engineer. Born in Johnston, Renfrewshire, Scotland, on January 21, 1815, McCallum emigrated with his parents to the United States and settled in Rochester, New York. He received an elementary education and through his own efforts became a carpenter, builder, architect, and engineer. In 1851 he invented and patented an inflexible arched truss bridge, a type of timber bridge that was widely used and earned him a considerable income. McCallum worked mainly in bridge construction until 1855, when he became general superintendent of the New York & Erie Railroad. He left that post after a year and in 1858–1859 was president of the McCallum Bridge Company, which built railroad bridges throughout the country and as far afield as Panama. In February 1862 he was appointed by Secretary of War Edwin M. Stanton military director and superintendent of military railroads. (An act of January 31, 1862, empowered him to operate and if necessary seize any lines and equipment required for the prosecution of the war.) He was given an army commission of colonel and the position of aide-de-camp to the commanding general, and, although he was formally within the Quartermaster Department, he reported directly to Stanton. During the course of the Civil War McCallum came to control more than 2100 miles of track and over 1000 pieces of rolling stock. A construction corps under his command grew to nearly 10,000 men. The movement of troops and the supply of armies in the field often depended critically upon his vigorous actions, and he distinguished himself particularly in maintaining supply and communication lines to Gen. William T. Sherman during the Atlanta campaign in 1864, when Confederate raids again and again attempted to disrupt rail service. McCallum was brevetted brigadier general in September 1864 and major general in

March 1865; he was mustered out of service in July 1866. A short time later he retired to private life. In 1870 he published *The Water-Mill and Other Poems.* He died in Brooklyn, New York, on December 27, 1878.

McCauley, Charles Stewart (1793–1869), naval officer. Born in Philadelphia on February 3, 1793, McCauley entered the navy as a midshipman in January 1809. During the War of 1812 he saw action in Chesapeake Bay and on Lake Ontario, advancing to acting lieutenant in September 1813 and permanent lieutenant in December 1814. After service in the Mediterranean Squadron he took leave of absence in 1822–1825 to command a merchant vessel. During 1826–1829 he was aboard the *Boston* in the Brazil Squadron. Promoted to master commandant in March 1831 and captain in December 1839, he continued to serve in various routine posts. His first sea command was the *Delaware* of the Brazil Squadron in 1841–1844, and he later commanded the Washington navy yard, 1846–1849, the Pacific Squadron, 1850–1853, and the Home Squadron, 1855. In July 1860 he was put in command of the navy yard at Norfolk, Virginia, a facility of great importance. On April 20, 1861, following the firing on Fort Sumter and the secession of Virginia, McCauley ordered the navy yard destroyed to prevent its falling into Confederate hands. The loss to federal strength was enormous— 11 ships, including the nearly completed steam frigate *Merrimack;* 3000 guns, 300 of them the latest model Dahlgrens; and great quantities of supplies of various sorts. Even worse, the burning of the yard was poorly managed, and Confederate forces entering on the heels of the departing federals were able to save the dry dock, much of the stores, and some 2000 guns; the *Merrimack,* having been scuttled first, burned only to the waterline, leaving a salvageable hull that was later to appear as the ironclad *Virginia.* The abandonment of Norfolk ended McCauley's career. In December 1861 he was placed on the retired list; in April 1867 he was promoted to commodore on the retired list. He died in Washington, D.C., on May 21, 1869.

McCauley, Mary Ludwig Hays (1754–1832), "Molly Pitcher," Revolutionary heroine. Born in Trenton, New Jersey, on October 13, 1754, Molly Ludwig lived on a small dairy farm until 1769, when her father arranged for her employment as a servant to William Irvine, a doctor in Carlisle, Pennsylvania. She was married shortly thereafter to John Hays who, during the Revolution, served in the 7th Pennsylvania Regiment, commanded by Irvine. Mrs. Hays, with many other soldiers' wives, was with the regiment at the battle of Monmouth, on June 28, 1778. The day was a hot one, and Molly assisted the artillerymen in the battle by bringing drinking water

in a pitcher, earning thereby the nickname "Molly Pitcher." After her husband collapsed from the heat, she took his place at his gun and served heroically for the remainder of the battle. After the war she led an uneventful life at Carlisle. Hays died in 1789 and Molly's second marriage, to John (or George) McCauley, brought her no respite from her work as a servant. During the last ten years of her life she received a pension of $40 a year that was authorized by an act of the Pennsylvania assembly in February 1822 in commemoration of her heroism at Monmouth. She died in Carlisle on January 22, 1832. Her story, sometimes confused with that of Margaret Corbin, was revived and her grave marked in 1876. In 1916 a state monument was raised to her memory.

McCausland, John (1836–1927), Confederate army officer. Born on September 13, 1836, in St. Louis, Missouri, McCausland graduated from Virginia Military Institute in 1857 and after a year of further study at the University of Virginia became a professor of mathematics at VMI. In April 1861, following the secession of Virginia, he was sent by Gen. Robert E. Lee (then commander of Virginia forces) to recruit volunteers in the Kanawha valley. He was commissioned colonel in command of the 36th Virginia Regiment and served under Gen. John B. Floyd in western Virginia and then under Gen. Albert S. Johnston in Kentucky. He escaped from Fort Donelson before its capture on February 16, 1862, and for the next two years commanded a brigade in western Virginia and West Virginia. In May 1864 he was promoted to brigadier general and given command of a cavalry brigade. Ordered to the Shenandoah valley, he opposed a superior cavalry force under Gen. David Hunter and managed to hold until the arrival of Gen. Jubal A. Early's corps, with which he took part in the pursuit of Hunter from Lynchburg, playing a conspicuous part in the battle of the Monocacy, July 9, and the raid on Washington, D.C. In retaliation for Hunter's wanton burning of crops and homes in his retreat northward, Early sent McCausland on a raid into Pennsylvania. He crossed the Potomac on July 29 and the next day occupied Chambersburg. Following his instructions, he demanded a ransom of $100,000 in gold or $500,000 in greenback currency. The sum could not be raised, and McCausland burned the town. He quickly withdrew to the Potomac and then to Cumberland, Maryland, where he was beaten by Gen. Benjamin F. Kelley on August 1. He crossed the Potomac the next day, pursued by Kelley, and on August 7 was routed at Moorfield, Virginia, by another pursuing force under Gen. William W. Averell. The remnants of his command made their way to the Shenandoah valley, reassembled, and rejoined Early. In 1865 McCausland and his brigade joined Lee at Petersburg and took part in the flight to Appomattox but refused to join in the surrender on April 9. They broke through Union lines but were captured a short time later. After the war McCausland spent two years abroad and then returned to settle in Mason County, West Virginia, where he died on January 22, 1927.

McCawley, Charles Grymes (1827–1891), marine officer.

Born in Philadelphia on January 29, 1827, McCawley was the son of a marine captain, and after a period in an uncle's business in New Orleans he entered the corps as a second lieutenant in March 1847. He served in Gen. John A. Quitman's division of Gen. Winfield Scott's army in Mexico, winning a brevet to first lieutenant at Chapultepec, September 13, 1847. Years of routine duty at sea and ashore followed, and he advanced to first lieutenant in January 1855 and captain in July 1861. On May 10, 1862, he commanded the 200-man marine detachment that reoccupied the Norfolk navy yard. In August he was ordered to the South Atlantic Blockading Squadron. He took part in the landings on Morris Island in Charleston harbor in July 1863 and in the capture of Fort Wagner and Fort Gregg, and on September 8 he led a marine boat force as part of a massive attack by Adm. John A. B. Dahlgren on Fort Sumter. He was brevetted major for his actions in that operation. He was promoted to major in June 1864, while stationed in Philadelphia, and to lieutenant colonel in December 1867. From 1865 to 1871 he commanded the marine barracks at the Boston navy yard. He took command of the marine barracks in Washington, D.C., in June 1871 and was also made superintendent of recruiting. In November 1876 he was appointed commandant of the marine corps with the rank of colonel; he held the post until his retirement in January 1891. During that period new marine barracks were established at Annapolis, Maryland, and League Island, near Philadelphia. In 1882 he inaugurated the policy of appointing new marine officers from among graduates of the Naval Academy. He died in Rosemont, Pennsylvania, on October 13, 1891.

McClellan, George Brinton (1826–1885), army officer.

Born in Philadelphia on December 3, 1826, McClellan graduated from West Point second in his class in 1846 and was commissioned in the engineers. He was assigned to Gen. Winfield Scott's army in the Mexican War and won brevets to first lieutenant at Contreras and Churubusco, August 19–20, 1847, and to captain at Chapultepec, September 13. From 1848 to 1851 he was an instructor in military engineering at West Point, and from 1851 he engaged in a number of army projects, including the construction of Fort Delaware, river and harbor work, and railroad surveys. In March 1855 he was appointed captain of cavalry, and the next year, in a report on a year-long study of European military methods and operations in the Crimea, he submitted a new design for cavalry

saddles that was adopted and retained for many years as the "McClellan saddle." In January 1857 he resigned his commission to become chief engineer for the Illinois Central Railroad; he became vice-president of the line the next year and in 1860 president of the Ohio and Mississippi Railroad. At the outbreak of the Civil War in April 1861 he was commissioned a major general of Ohio volunteers, and a month later, upon being commissioned major general in the regular army, he assumed command of the Department of the Ohio. In a campaign culminating in the battle of Rich Mountain, July 11, he secured for the Union the territory that later became West Virginia. In that month he went to Washington to take command of the Division of the Potomac, then in great confusion since the Union defeat at the first battle of Bull Run (Manassas); and by November, when he succeeded Winfield Scott as general in chief of the Union armies, he had effectively organized, equipped, and trained the troops, restored morale, and made the Army of the Potomac, so named in August, into a capable and eager fighting force. He hesitated, however, to undertake offensive operations, and his hesitation lasted so long that President Abraham Lincoln, losing patience, finally issued his General War Order No. 1 on January 27, 1862, decreeing a general Union advance. McClellan delayed execution of Lincoln's order while lobbying for his own plan for an approach to Richmond along the Yorktown Peninsula. After a march out of Washington to Manassas early in March, where it was discovered that Gen. Joseph E. Johnston's Confederate army had retired to Fredericksburg, McClellan commenced his own plan with a move by sea on March 11 to Fort Monroe on the peninsula. (He was relieved of the chief command of Union armies while in the field with the Army of the Potomac.) He was overly cautious, the more so because Gen. Irvin McDowell's corps of 30,000 men had been retained in Washington for defense; he consistently overestimated Confederate strength, and as the Peninsular campaign dragged on no decisive victories were won by either side. McClellan spent from April 5 to May 4 in a siege of lightly-held Yorktown. His III Corps, under Gen. Samuel P. Heintzelman, took Williamsburg on May 5, and he then slowly followed the retreating Johnston up the peninsula. He repelled an attack at Fair Oaks (Seven Pines) on May 31 but then faced a new opponent, Gen. Robert E. Lee, who called Gen. Thomas J. Jackson from the Shenandoah valley to assist him. Lee struck at Mechanicsville on June 26, opening the Seven Days' Battles. McClellan began to withdraw and then executed a complex and dangerous shift of his supply base from White House on the Pamunkey River to Harrison's Landing on the James, fighting Lee at Gaines' Mill, June 27, Savage Station, June 29, Frayser's Farm and White Oak Swamp, June 30, and finally driving him off at Malvern Hill, July

1. In August McClellan was ordered to reembark his army and return to Washington. After Lee's defeat of Gen. John Pope, who had taken much of McClellan's army, at the second battle of Bull Run, August 29–30, McClellan was asked once again to apply his great organizational talents in preparing for the defense of the capital. As Lee invaded Maryland early in September, McClellan moved to meet him, but even with the advantage of having come into possession of a copy of the Confederate general's orders, he moved too slowly. Instead of the overwhelming victory that was within reach—he had 90,000 men to Lee's 55,000—there came only the minor success at South Mountain, September 14, and the check at Antietam (Sharpsburg), September 17, after which McClellan failed to pursue the retreating Lee. In November 1862 he was finally removed from command of the Army of the Potomac. (He was succeeded by Gen. Ambrose E. Burnside.) He was thereafter on waiting orders. In 1864 the Democratic party nominated him for president on a peace platform; he had been and still was an advocate of vigorous prosecution of the war, but he nonetheless accepted the nomination and tried with little success to reconcile his views with the platform. The Democrats were soundly defeated in the election (McClellan and his running mate, George H. Pendleton, received 21 electoral votes to the Lincoln-Johnson ticket's 212), and McClellan resigned his commission in November and sailed to Europe for a three-year visit. Upon his return he served as chief engineer for New York City's Department of Docks and was from 1878 to 1881 governor of New Jersey. He died on October 29, 1885, in Orange, New Jersey. *McClellan's Own Story*, an autobiographical work, appeared two years later, in 1887.

McClernand, John Alexander (1812–1900),

public official and army officer. Born on May 30, 1812, near Hardinsburg, Kentucky, McClernand grew up in Illinois, where in 1832 he was admitted to the bar. He was a militia volunteer in the Black Hawk War of 1832, and three years later he founded and edited a Democratic newspaper in Shawneetown. He served in the Illinois legislature from 1836 to 1842 and in the latter year was elected to Congress. He served four terms, March 1843 to March 1851, and, having moved to Jacksonville, was again elected to an unexpired term in November 1858; he was reelected in 1860. He held the rank of colonel in the Illinois militia at the outbreak of the Civil War, and in October 1861 he resigned from Congress to accept a commission as brigadier general of volunteers. Recruiting a brigade, he led it under Gen. Ulysses S. Grant at Belmont, Missouri, November 7, 1861, and commanded a division in the operations against Fort Henry and Fort Donelson in February 1862. In March he was promoted to major general of volunteers in spite of a falling-out with Grant over credit for the capture of Fort Donelson. He commanded the Union center at Shiloh (Pittsburg Landing), April 6–7. Ever a politician, he carried on private correspondence with President Abraham Lincoln and others, promoting his own claims to command and often criticizing Grant and other rival generals. In October 1862 he received authorization to organize a major expedition toward Vicksburg, independent of Grant's command. Early in January 1863 he relieved Gen. William T. Sherman, who had failed in an earlier move against Vicksburg, and organized his forces as the Army of the Mississippi, comprising the XIII Corps and Sherman's XV Corps. On January 11 he captured Arkansas Post (Fort Hindman) in a joint operation with Adm. David D. Porter's Mississippi Squadron. Grant reorganized his Army of the Tennessee a short time later and took in McClernand and the XIII Corps. In the Vicksburg campaign McClernand took part in the battles at Port Gibson, May 1, and Champion's Hill, May 16, and was charged with tardiness by Grant after the latter. Following the repulse of the general attack on Vicksburg on May 22 McClernand issued a public statement critical of Grant and of the other two corps of Grant's army, and Grant promptly removed him from command (he was succeeded by Gen. Edward O. C. Ord). Ordered to Illinois, he used his popularity and political influence in an unsuccessful attempt to win a court of inquiry. He was finally restored to command of the XIII Corps in February 1864, but the corps was scattered over a wide region in Louisiana and Texas and he saw no action. He soon fell ill and returned to Illinois, resigning his commission in November 1864. From 1870 to 1873 he was circuit judge for the Sangamon district of Illinois, and in 1876 he was chairman of the Democratic National Convention. He died in Springfield, Illinois, on September 20, 1900.

McClure, George (1770?–1851), militia officer.

Born about 1770 near Londonderry, Ireland, McClure emigrated to the United States about 1791, first settling in Baltimore and later moving to Pennsylvania and about 1793 to Bath, Steuben County, New York. He became a merchant, engaged in various businesses, held local political offices, and by 1812 had become a brigadier general of militia. With the outbreak of war with England, he was called into active service. Late in the year he took part in Gen. Alexander Smyth's fruitless attempts to cross the Niagara River and invade Canada. Late in 1813 McClure returned to the Niagara frontier, establishing his headquarters at Fort George on the Canadian side of the river. The failure of the Montreal campaign under Gen. James Wilkinson in November released British forces to attend to the Niagara region, while the expiration of militia enlistments depleted McClure's forces. By December 10 he had only 100 men, while five times that number of British approached. He decided to abandon Fort George, but before crossing the river he ordered the nearby town of Newark burned, a pointless act made positively cruel by the harsh weather. The act outraged the British and was generally condemned at home as well; his excuse that he wished to deny winter quarters to the British was rendered null by his having failed to destroy his own abandoned barracks and tents. The retaliatory burning by the British of Youngstown, Lewiston and Manchester on December 19 and Black Rock and Buffalo on December 30 further lowered McClure's standing. He played no further part in the war. He was nonetheless elected sheriff of Steuben County in 1815 and served three terms in the legislature. He moved to Illinois about 1834 and died in Elgin on August 16, 1851.

McConnell, John Paul (1908–   ), air force officer. Born on February 7, 1908, in Booneville, Arkansas, McConnell graduated from Henderson Brown College (now Henderson State) in 1927 and the next year entered West Point, from which he graduated in 1932. In 1933 he completed courses in aviation at Randolph and Kelly fields, Texas, and for four years he was assigned to the 79th Pursuit Squadron at Barksdale Field, Louisiana, receiving promotion to first lieutenant in April 1935. During 1937–1939 he was stationed at Hickam Field, Hawaii, and from June 1939 to January 1942 he was assigned to staff and training duty at Maxwell Field, Alabama, and elsewhere, advancing to captain in September 1940 and to major in July 1941. Promoted to lieutenant colonel in January 1942, he was attached to the office of the chief of the Army Air Forces (AAF) for four months and then assigned to the AAF technical training center at Knollwood Field, North Carolina, where he was deputy chief of staff and later chief of staff, receiving promotion to colonel in December 1942. After a brief period as deputy chief of staff of the AAF Training Command at Fort Worth, Texas, McConnell was ordered in November 1943 to the Southeast Asian theater of operations, where he served as chief of staff of the China-Burma-India air force training command until February 1944, as senior staff officer and deputy commander of the 3rd Tactical Air Force based at Comilla, India, until September 1944, and, having been promoted to brigadier general in August, as senior staff officer of the Southeast Asia Air Command in Kandy, Ceylon, until June 1945. In April 1946, after a period as acting deputy chief of staff for intelligence of the Eastern Air Command in Chungking, China, he was named commander of the Air Division, Nanking Headquarters Command, and senior air adviser to the Chinese Nationalist government. In June 1947 he returned to staff duty in Washington, D.C. McConnell was appointed deputy commander and chief of staff of the 3rd Air Division and Third Air Force in England in July 1950 and in December was promoted to temporary major general. In May 1951 he took command of the 7th Air Division in England, holding that post until March 1953 and during February–May 1952 also commanding the Third Air Force. From April 1953 to November 1957 he was deputy director and later director of plans of the Strategic Air Command (SAC) at Offutt Air Force Base, Nebraska. He commanded the Second Air Force at Barksdale Air Force Base, Louisiana, until August 1961, advancing to temporary lieutenant general in June 1959, and then returned to SAC as vice commander. McConnell was named deputy commander of the U.S. European Command in France in September 1962 and promoted to temporary general a month later. In August 1964 he became vice chief of staff of the air force, and in February 1965 he succeeded Gen. Curtis E. LeMay as chief of staff. He held that post until his retirement in July 1969, when he was succeeded as chief of staff by Gen. John D. Ryan. Among his later activities was his service from August 1970 as executive consultant to the Civil Air Patrol.

McCook, Alexander McDowell (1831–1903), army officer. Born in Columbiana County, Ohio, on April 22, 1831, McCook graduated from West Point in 1852 and was commissioned in the infantry. He served for a time on the frontier, seeing action against the Utes and the Apaches, and from 1858 to 1861 he was an instructor at West Point. He was promoted to first lieutenant in December 1858. In April 1861 he was appointed colonel of the 1st Ohio Volunteers. (The Civil War made his family famous as "the fighting McCooks." Fourteen of them served in the Union army or navy, all but one as commissioned officers: Alexander's father, Daniel, and his seven other sons, and the five sons of Daniel's brother John.) He distinguished himself at Bull Run (Manassas), July 21, and in September was promoted to brigadier general of volunteers. While serving in Kentucky he rose by January 1862 to command of a division; he won brevets in regular rank to lieutenant colonel for his part in the capture of Nashville, March 3, 1862, and to colonel at Shiloh (Pittsburg Landing), April 6–7; and in July he was promoted to major general of volunteers, taking command of the I Corps in Gen. Don Carlos Buell's Army of the Ohio. At Perryville, October 8, he won a brevet to regular brigadier general (awarded March 1865). With the organization of the Army of the Cumberland under Gen. William S. Rosecrans he commanded the right wing (at Stones River, or Murfreesboro, December 31–January 3, 1863) and subsequently the XIV and then the XX Corps. He took part in the Tullahoma campaign against Gen. Braxton Bragg during the summer of 1863 and was at Chickamauga, September 18–20. Following that battle he was blamed by Rosecrans for the disastrous defeat and relieved of command, but a court of inquiry later exonerated him. He returned to duty with the defenses of Washington, D.C., and in October 1864 was named commander of the District of Eastern Arkansas. Brevetted regular major general in March 1865, McCook returned to regular duty after October as lieutenant colonel of the 26th Infantry. He again saw frontier duty, was acting inspector general of the army in 1874–1875, and was aide-de-camp to Gen. William T. Sherman in 1875–1881. Promoted to colonel of the 6th Cavalry in December 1880, he was commandant of the Infantry and Cavalry School, Fort Leavenworth, Kansas, in 1886–1890, receiving promotion to brigadier general in the latter year and to major general in November 1894. He retired in April 1895. In May 1896 he represented the United States at the coronation of Nicholas II of Russia, and during September 1898–February 1899 he served on a commission appointed by President William McKinley to investigate the conduct of the Spanish–American War. McCook died in Dayton, Ohio, on June 12, 1903.

McCook, Edward Moody (1833–1909),

public official and army officer. Born on June 15, 1833, in Steubenville, Ohio, McCook was a brother of four of the Civil War "fighting McCooks" and a cousin of eight others, including Alexander M. McCook. At sixteen he traveled to Minnesota and thence to Colorado, where he won admission to the bar. He served in the legislature of Kansas Territory (representing a Colorado district) in 1859 and on the admission of Kansas to statehood was prominent in the organization of Colorado Territory. At the outbreak of the Civil War he hurried to Washington, D.C., and in May 1861 was commissioned a second lieutenant of cavalry. He won brevets at Shiloh (Pittsburg Landing), April 6–7, 1862, Perryville, October 8, and Chickamauga, September 18–20, 1863, and another in cavalry operations in eastern Tennessee. Appointed to the volunteer service, he became colonel of the 2nd Indiana Volunteer Cavalry and in April 1864 was promoted to brigadier general of volunteers in command of the cavalry of the Army of the Cumberland under Gen. George H. Thomas. During the Atlanta campaign in mid-1864 he performed brilliantly, destroying Confederate supply lines and preventing the reinforcement of Gen. John B. Hood's army in the city. Of particular note was his raid around Atlanta to Lovejoy's Station, July 27–31. In March 1865 he was brevetted brigadier general of regulars and major general of volunteers. From April to June 1865 he was military governor of Florida. He was mustered out of the volunteer service in January 1866 and resigned from the regular army in May. From then until 1869 he was U.S. minister to Hawaii, and from 1869 to 1873 he was governor of Colorado Territory, where he effectively promoted development but was unpopular. He held the post again briefly in 1874–1875.

He devoted himself thereafter to his extensive business interests. McCook died in Chicago on September 9, 1909.

McCoy, Frank Ross (1874–1954),

army officer and diplomat. Born on October 29, 1874, in Lewistown, Pennsylvania, McCoy graduated from West Point in 1897 and was commissioned in the cavalry. On the outbreak of the Spanish–American War in 1898 he was ordered from Fort Meade, South Dakota, to the 10th Cavalry (Negro), with which he took part in the Santiago campaign in Cuba. In 1899–1902 he was again in Cuba, becoming aide-de-camp to Gen. Leonard Wood and in the latter year accompanying Wood to Washington, D.C., where he became also an aide to President Theodore Roosevelt. He was promoted to first lieutenant in February 1901 and to captain in August 1903. He traveled with Wood to the Philippines in 1903 and saw both staff and political duty and considerable field service, notably in leading an expedition in 1905 that ended the guerilla warfare carried on by Datu Ali, the Moro chief. On his return to the United States in 1906 he was appointed aide to Secretary of War William H. Taft, whom he accompanied on a pacification mission to Cuba late in that year. In 1907–1908 he was again aide-de-camp to Roosevelt. On graduating from the Army War College in 1908 he joined the 3rd Cavalry at Fort Wingate, New Mexico. While attached to the General Staff in 1911–1914 he undertook a secret mission to Colombia concerning possible canal routes. Early in 1915 he rejoined the 3rd Cavalry and on patrols of the troubled Mexican border engaged rebel bands at Cavazas Crossing and Ojo de Agua. Early in 1917 he was named military attaché in Mexico City with the rank of major; he was promoted to major in March of that year. Ordered to France in June, he was promoted to temporary lieutenant colonel late in 1917 and to temporary colonel in May 1918, commanding the 165th Infantry (New York's "Fighting 69th" National Guard regiment) of the 42nd Division. He led the regiment in the Champagne–Marne and Aisne–Marne operations. He was promoted to temporary brigadier general in August 1918 and put in command of a brigade of the 32nd Division under Gen. William G. Haan. After brief occupation duty he was appointed director of the Army Transport Service at Tours in November, and he later was named director general of transport. He was chief of staff of the military mission to Armenia under Gen. James G. Harbord in August 1919. After his return to the United States McCoy held various posts, receiving promotion to permanent colonel in 1920, and in 1921–1925 he was again with Gen. Wood, then governor-general of the Philippines. Promoted to brigadier general in December 1922, he commanded American relief efforts following the Japanese earthquake of September 1923. After a brief period in the Bureau of Insular Affairs in Washington, D.C., in 1925, he commanded a brigade of the 2nd Infantry Division at Fort Sam Houston, Texas, until 1927. During 1927–1928 he was in Nicaragua, supervising elections and maintaining public order. In 1928 he was a delegate to the Pan-American Conference, and the next year he was appointed to head a commission investigating the dispute between Paraguay and Bolivia. Promoted to major general in September 1929, from then to 1932 he commanded the IV Corps area at Atlanta, Georgia, and during 1932 he was the U.S. member of a League of Nations panel investigating Japanese actions in Manchuria. McCoy took command of the 1st Cavalry Division at Fort Bliss, Texas, in March 1933, moving in October to command of the VII Corps area at Omaha, Nebraska. He became commander of the Second Army and VI Corps area at Chicago in February 1935, and of the II Corps area, Governors Island, New York, in May 1936. He retired in October 1938. In February 1939 he was chosen president of the Foreign Policy Association, retaining the post until 1946. He returned to public service in December 1941 as a member of the commission under Supreme Court Justice Owen J. Roberts appointed to investigate the Pearl Harbor disaster. In 1942 he headed a military commission appointed to try Nazi spies and saboteurs, and in 1943 he was briefly on active duty as chairman of the Procurement Review Board. During 1945–1949 he was a member (and first chairman) of the Far Eastern Commission appointed by President Harry Truman to negotiate and oversee the terms of the Japanese occupation. McCoy died in Washington, D.C., on June 4, 1954.

McCulloch, Ben (1811–1862), Texas and Confederate army officer. Born on November 11, 1811, in Rutherford County, Tennessee, McCulloch moved with his family to Alabama in 1820 and to Dyersburg, Tennessee, in 1830. Shortly after the departure of his friend Davy Crockett for Texas, he followed, arriving in time to take part under Gen. Sam Houston in the revolution's final battle, at San Jacinto, April 21, 1836. After a visit home he returned to Texas and settled in Gonzales, where he worked as a surveyor. A highly popular figure, he was elected to the Texas congress in 1839, and he was involved in numerous fights with the Indians of the region, particularly in the battle at Plum Creek that ended the great Comanche raid of August 1840. At the outbreak of the Mexican War in 1846, having already been appointed major general in command of Texas militia west of the Colorado, he organized a ranger company that served under Gen. Zachary Taylor at Monterrey and Buena Vista and whose exploits were widely publicized; he held the rank of major of volunteers from July 1846. In 1849 he migrated to California, where he was for a time sheriff of Sacra-

mento. He returned to Texas in 1852, and in March 1853 he was appointed U.S. marshal for the eastern district. He resigned the post in 1859. In 1858 he was one of two commissioners sent (behind Col. Albert S. Johnston's military expedition) to negotiate with the rebellious Mormons in Utah. In February 1861 he received the surrender of the federal forces and stores at San Antonio from Gen. David E. Twiggs, commander of the Department of Texas. In May he was commissioned brigadier general in the Confederate army and given command of the Southwestern Division, comprising Arkansas and Indian Territory. In mid-1861 he marched with 11,000 men into Missouri and joined state forces there under Gen. Sterling Price. At Wilson's Creek on August 10 they were attacked by Gen. Nathaniel Lyon; McCulloch drove back a flanking move by Gen. Franz Sigel and then joined Price in defeating Lyon, who was killed. Early the next year, back in Arkansas, he commanded a corps under Gen. Earl Van Dorn. At Pea Ridge (Elkhorn Tavern), March 7, 1862, while reconnoitering Union forces under Gen. Samuel R. Curtis, he was killed by a sharpshooter.

McDonald, David Lamar (1906–   ), naval officer. Born on September 12, 1906, in Maysville, Georgia, McDonald graduated from the Naval Academy in 1928. Following two years of sea duty aboard the *Mississippi* and the *Colorado* he entered pilot training, receiving his wings and promotion to lieutenant (junior grade) in 1931. He was assigned to the carrier *Saratoga* for two and a half years and then to the *Detroit*. From 1935 to 1938 he was a flight instructor at Pensacola Naval Air Station, Florida, advancing to lieutenant in July 1936, and from 1938 to 1941 was with Patrol Squadron 42 in Seattle and later in Alaska. He was engaged mainly in training work early in World War II, receiving promotions to lieutenant commander in January and commander in September 1942. In April 1944 he became air officer on the carrier *Essex*, part of Adm. Marc A. Mitscher's Task Force 38 (58), and saw action in the battle of Leyte Gulf in October. Promoted to captain in March 1945, McDonald was assigned to the staff of the Pacific Air Command in June. During 1947–1950 he was with the Bureau of Aeronautics in Washington, D.C., and after graduating from the Naval War College in 1951 he took command of the carrier *Mindoro*. During 1952–1954 he was on the staff of the Pacific Fleet, and after a period in command of the carrier *Coral Sea* he was named in November 1955 director of the air warfare division, office of the chief of naval operations; he advanced to rear admiral in January 1956. From 1957 to 1960 he was on the staff of Gen. Lauris Norstad, supreme Allied commander in Europe. In October 1960 he he took command of Carrier Division 6 in the Mediterranean, and in July 1961 he moved up to command of the Sixth Fleet.

receiving promotion to vice admiral. In April 1963 he was appointed commander of U.S. naval forces in Europe with the rank of admiral, and in August of that year he became chief of naval operations, succeeding Adm. George W. Anderson, Jr. McDonald retired from the navy in August 1967. He was succeeded as chief of naval operations by Adm. Thomas H. Moorer.

Macdonough, Thomas (1783–1825), naval officer. Born on December 31, 1783, at The Trap (subsequently Macdonough), New Castle County, Delaware, Macdonough entered the navy in February 1800 as a midshipman. For creditable service aboard the *Philadelphia* under Capt. William Bainbridge during the Tripolitan War he was made second officer on a Moorish prize vessel, and he later served on the *Enterprise* under Lt. Stephen Decatur, whom he accompanied in the daring raid to burn the captured *Philadelphia*, February 16, 1804. Promoted to lieutenant in January 1807, he performed various routine duties, taking leave of absence in 1810 to engage in a private trading venture. The War of 1812 brought him back to active duty, and in October of that year he was placed in command of a small fleet on Lake Champlain with orders to keep the British lake fleet at bay. Both sides avoided a contest when they lacked the advantage, and no decisive battle was fought until September 1814. By that time Macdonough, holding the rank of master commandant since July 1813, had built up his fleet to 14 vessels with 86 guns, while the British had 2 more vessels and a 6-gun advantage. Having lost their entire squadron on Lake Erie to Commodore Oliver Hazard Perry in September of the previous year, the British needed a victory on Lake Champlain to insure the success of Gen. Sir George Prevost's planned invasion down the Hudson valley. Prevost faced Gen. Alexander Macomb's forces at Plattsburg, New York, and depended upon the fleet of Commodore George Downie to swing the balance. On September 11, 1814, Macdonough, from his flagship *Saratoga*, deployed his forces at Plattsburg Bay and in the ensuing battle there skillfully outmaneuvered and ultimately captured the British fleet in a brilliant victory that saved New York and Vermont from occupation by British troops. The victory earned him the thanks of Congress and a captaincy in November. After the war his career was uneventful. While in command of the Mediterranean Squadron he became ill, and before he could reach home he died at sea on the merchantman *Edwin* on November 10, 1825.

McDougal, David Stockton (1809–1882), naval officer. Born in Chillicothe, Ohio, on September 27, 1809, McDougal was appointed a midshipman in the navy in 1828. Over the next several decades he served aboard various vessels of the West India and Mediterranean squadrons, and in 1840–1843 he was attached to the Coast Survey. He was promoted to lieutenant in February 1841. During the Mexican War he served aboard the *Mississippi* at Veracruz. In 1855–1856 he was in command of the steamer *John Hancock* off the coast of Washington Territory. Promoted to commander in January 1857, he was given command of the sloop *Wyoming* soon after the outbreak of the Civil War and ordered to the Asiatic station to patrol against Confederate raiders. While at Yokohama, Japan, in the summer of 1863 he learned that, pursuant to a controversial decree of the emperor that violated the U.S.–Japanese treaty in barring foreigners from Japan, the American merchant ship *Pembroke* had been fired on by guns of the Choshu daimyo (baron) in Shimonoseki Strait. He immediately set out for Shimonoseki and on July 16 boldly attacked. Under heavy fire from land batteries he ran down and sank two of the armed vessels there, silenced the third, and then opened up on the batteries, inflicting heavy damage on them. In the one-hour action the *Wyoming*, although maneuvered with great skill, took 11 hits in her hull. Following an unsuccessful search in the East Indies for the Confederate raider *Alabama* McDougal returned home in 1864, having been promoted to captain in March. He commanded the Mare Island navy yard until 1868, the steamer *Powhatan* in 1868–1869, and the South Pacific Squadron in 1870–1872. In September 1873 he was placed on the retired list as a rear admiral; he died in San Francisco on August 7, 1882.

McDougall, Alexander (1732–1786), patriot and Revolutionary army officer. Born on Islay, one of the Inner Hebrides islands of Scotland, in July or August 1732, McDougall came to America with his parents in 1738 and settled in Fort Edward, New York, later moving to New York City. He evidently went to sea at an early age, for during the war with France in 1755–1763 he commanded two privateers, the *Tyger* and the *Barrington*. Later he was a merchant of considerable means. In December 1769 he published a broadside sharply critical of the New York assembly for supporting the quartering of British troops and was arrested and charged with libel. Refusing to give bail, he remained in prison until March 1771, a popular hero whose visitors in prison were so numerous as to require appointments. He continued prominent in the agitation preceding the Revolution, serving in New York's first two provincial congresses and on July 6, 1774, presiding over a mass meeting in City Hall Park at which Alexander Hamilton made his first public appearance. In May 1775 he helped organize a provisional government for the city, and in June he was chosen colonel of the first New York regiment. In August 1776 he was appointed brigadier general in the Continental army. He took part in the battle of White Plains, October

28, 1776, and in the New Jersey campaign, was at Germantown, October 4, 1777, and a few days after the last was promoted to major general. His principal service to the Revolution was as commander of the Hudson Highlands from 1778, with responsibility for keeping the river secure. He was in command of West Point in July–December 1779, in June–July 1780, in September–October 1780 following Gen. Benedict Arnold's treason, and in June 1781–January 1782. In 1781 he declined appointment as minister of marine. In addition he was a New York delegate to the Continental Congress in 1781–1782 and again in 1784–1785. He sat in the legislature in 1783–1786. He was an organizer and the first president of the Bank of New York. McDougall died in New York City on June 9, 1786.

McDowell, Irvin (1818–1885), army officer. Born in Columbus, Ohio, on October 15, 1818, McDowell attended school in France before entering West Point, from which he graduated in 1838. Commissioned in the artillery, he served on the Canadian border until 1841, when he became an instructor and staff officer at West Point, receiving promotion to first lieutenant in October 1842. In October 1845 he was named aide-de-camp to Gen. John E. Wool; he held that post through the Mexican War and at Buena Vista, February 22–23, 1847, won a brevet to captain. Three months later he became a captain in the adjutant general corps. Staff work occupied him from 1848 to 1861, and in March 1856 he was promoted to major. In May 1861 he was promoted three grades to brigadier general (in part through friendship with Gen. Winfield Scott and Salmon P. Chase, secretary of the treasury) and assigned to organizing the troops assembling in Washington under Gen. Joseph K. F. Mansfield. As the troops were moved over the Potomac to form a field army, McDowell became their commander. They soon numbered some 50,000 —a battalion of new regulars, some partly-trained 90-day militia, and the rest raw volunteers. Political pressure for a quick campaign forced McDowell to take the field in July to a public chorus of "On to Richmond!" He set out with five divisions on July 16 along the Warrenton Turnpike toward Manassas Junction. On the 18th he occupied Centreville and spent three valuable days in reorganizing and reconnaissance. Early on the 21st he sent a small force forward to Stone Bridge on Bull Run Creek to divert attention while he led his main force in a swing around to the right. His plan to flank and envelope the Confederate army of Gen. P. G. T. Beauregard— some 22,000 men—was an excellent one, but he developed it with painful slowness and caution. Thus, after crossing Bull Run near Sudler Springs and falling on the Confederate left on the plateau occupied by the Henry and Robinson houses, he moved so slowly that Beauregard was able to redeploy and hold

him. Meanwhile Gen. Joseph E. Johnston's 11,000-man army, having made a masterly march from the Shenandoah valley, arrived to tip the balance. McDowell's army began to fall back, and retreat soon turned to panic and rout. The disaster of the Union's "best planned and worst fought" battle of the war shocked the North, while it may have made Confederate leaders overconfident. In August McDowell was replaced by Gen. George B. McClellan, who reorganized the troops as the Army of the Potomac, and McDowell was given command of the I Corps in March 1862 with the rank of major general of volunteers. The I Corps was retained to defend Washington, D.C., during the Peninsular campaign; it was later made a separate Army of the Rappahannock, and in July it became the III Corps in Gen. John Pope's Army of Virginia. At the second battle of Bull Run, August 29–30, McDowell incurred much criticism and was relieved of command; although exonerated by a court of inquiry he saw no further field service. In July 1864 he was named commander of the Department of the Pacific and in July 1865 of the Department of California. He became commander of the Department of the East in July 1868 and, promoted to major general in November 1872, he commanded the Division of the South from then until June 1876. After six years in command of the Department of the Pacific he retired in October 1882. He died in San Francisco on May 4, 1885.

McDowell, Joseph (1756–1801), Revolutionary militia officer and public official. Born on February 15, 1756, in Winchester, Virginia, McDowell grew up there and in Burke County, North Carolina. In 1776 he became a member of a militia regiment commanded by his brother Charles, rising to major of the regiment during the years of backwoods skirmishing with Loyalists and Indians that followed. In 1780 the McDowell regiment joined with the forces commanded by Col. Isaac Shelby to oppose the Loyalist army—the "American Volunteers"—invading the Carolinas under Maj. Patrick Ferguson. For several months they were limited by inferior numbers to harassing Ferguson, and on hearing of the defeat of Gen. Horatio Gates at Camden in August they gave up even that limited tactic and dispersed. They reassembled in September, however, after Ferguson threatened to desolate the countryside. In Charles's absence Joseph McDowell was in command of the regiment when the combined militia forces under Col. William Campbell attacked Ferguson at King's Mountain on October 7 and completely defeated him. On January 17, 1781, he led 190 mounted riflemen as part of Col. William Washington's cavalry (all under Gen. Daniel Morgan) in the battle of Cowpens. In 1782 he commanded his regiment in a campaign led by Charles, then a brigadier general of militia, against the Cherokee. After the Revolution

Joseph sat in the North Carolina legislature in 1785–1788 and 1791–1795 and opposed ratification in the conventions called to consider the Constitution in 1788 and 1789. In 1797–1799 he was a member of Congress. He died in Burke County, North Carolina, on August 11, 1801.

McGiffin, Philo Norton (1860–1897), naval officer. Born in Washington, Pennsylvania, on December 13, 1860, McGiffin graduated from the Naval Academy in 1882. After two years aboard the *Hartford* in the Pacific Squadron he was certified a passed midshipman, but there being no vacancies in the body of commissioned officers, he along with several classmates was discharged with a year's pay. Early in 1885 he made his way to China, then engaged in a protracted struggle with France concerning sovereignty over northern Indochina, and secured a commission in the newly established Chinese navy from the viceroy, Li Hung-chang. Before the conclusion of the war later in the year he succeeded in capturing a French gunboat in battle. He then became a professor in the naval college at Tientsin, a post he retained for ten years. He served also as naval constructor and was sent to England to supervise construction of four ironclads for the Chinese navy. By 1894 the navy owed its organization and the training of most of its officers to McGiffin. Nonetheless Chinese naval forces were badly defeated in the Chinese–Japanese War of 1894. The closest approach to a Chinese victory at sea was in the battle of September 17, 1894, near the mouth of the Yalu River, where the battleships *Ting Yuen*, flagship, and *Chen Yuen* withstood heavy Japanese fire and forced the attackers to withdraw; the outcome was mainly the result of McGiffin's maneuvering of the *Chen Yuen*, of which he was nominally executive officer but effectively commander. He was seriously wounded in the battle and, resigning his positions in China, he settled in New York City. He suffered physically and mentally from the wounds and finally was taken to a hospital, where on February 11, 1897, he eluded his attendants, secured a pistol, and killed himself.

McGillivray, Alexander (1759?–1793), Indian leader. Born in what is now the state of Alabama in the late 1750s, McGillivray was the son of a Scottish merchant and, reputedly, a French-Creek princess (Sehoy Marchand) of the Wind Clan of the Upper Creeks (sometimes known as the Red Sticks). Little is known of his early life. He grew up among Indians and about the age of fourteen left his father's trading post for Charleston, South Carolina, and later Savannah, Georgia, where arrangements had been made for his education and introduction to white society. He reportedly received some training for business in a countinghouse and, on his own time, taught himself history. The father's pro-British sentiments at the

outbreak of the Revolution led to the confiscation of his property and his subsequent return to Scotland, while young McGillivray returned to his mother's tribe, among whom his education as well as his descent (which was traced through the female line among the Creeks) assured him a position of leadership. In 1778 he was given the rank of colonel by the British, for whom he exerted his influence as chief of the Creeks to promote attacks on the frontier settlements. After the Revolutionary War he devoted his efforts to forming a united Indian front against the westward push of the white Americans that threatened both the interests of his people and his own interests as a trader. After the British retired, he sought to exploit the aid of the Spanish who, having reacquired the Floridas by treaty in 1783, wanted to establish a trading empire in the old Southwest. In 1784 he concluded a treaty with Spain on behalf of the Creek confederacy that also provided him a monthly salary for his services in assuring a Spanish monopoly of Creek trade. Throughout 1785 and 1786 Creek warriors conducted a war of attrition against settlements in Georgia and along the Cumberland in an effort to restore the Indian line of 1773 and to discourage American traders. McGillivray met with some measure of success so long as he was supplied with Spanish arms and the Americans were preoccupied with their own national problems. Repeatedly courted by the Americans, he was finally induced by the new government to come to New York City to conclude a peace treaty, signed on August 7, 1790. The terms included a tribute of $1200 annually and the rank of brigadier general in the United States army for McGillivray and the loss of some disputed lands for the Indians. This treaty was subsequently repudiated by him in an agreement with Spain in 1792, which, although it provided for a stipend triple that paid by the Americans, was motivated as well by continuing Creek resentment toward the United States. He died at Pensacola on February 17, 1793, before concluding the terms of an alliance of all Southern Indians with Spain against the United States.

McGuire, Thomas B. Jr. (1920–1945), army officer and aviator. Born on August 1, 1920, in Ridgewood, New Jersey, McGuire grew up there and in Sebring, Florida. He graduated from Georgia Institute of Technology in 1941 and enlisted in the Army Air Corps, completing pilot training and receiving promotion to captain early in 1942. After service in the United States and Alaska he was ordered in March 1943 to the 49th Fighter Group of the Fifth Air Force, then operating in the Southwest Pacific area and in particular providing an air screen for Darwin and northern Australia. He subsequently transferred to the 475th Fighter Group, Thirteenth Air Force, and won promotion to major. He was already a leading ace with a record of 31 Japanese airplanes shot down when he volunteered on December 25, 1944, to lead a squadron of 15 P-38s on a bomber escort mission over Mabalacat Airdrome on Luzon, Philippines. He shot down 3 of the 20 Japanese Zero fighters that attacked the squadron. The next day, on a similar mission over Clark Field near Manila, he exposed himself in order to draw fire away from a crippled bomber and shot down three of the four fighters attacking it. Another score on the way home that day brought his total for the war to 38. On January 7, 1945, while leading a flight of four P-38s over Los Negros Island, he attempted a highly dangerous maneuver to aid a comrade who was losing an encounter with a Zero fighter and crashed. McGuire was awarded a posthumous Medal of Honor in March 1946 for his actions on December 25–26, 1944, and January 7, 1945. His score of 38 enemy aircraft shot down made him the second leading American fighter pilot of the war, following Maj. Richard I. Bong. McGuire Air Force Base, New Jersey, was named in his honor.

McIntosh, Lachlan (1725–1806), Revolutionary army officer. Born in Raits, Inverness-shire, Scotland, on March 17, 1725, McIntosh came to America with his family in 1736 and settled in Inverness (now Darien), Georgia. About 1748 he moved to Charleston, South Carolina, and found work as a clerk, but he returned to Georgia some years later. In July 1775 he was elected to the provincial congress in Savannah. In January 1776 he was appointed colonel of a battalion of Georgia militia later mustered into Continental service, and in September of that year he was commissioned brigadier general in the Continental army. A personal and political dispute with Button Gwinnett, president of Georgia, led to a duel between the two on May 16, 1777; Gwinnett died of his wounds three days later. McIntosh thereupon secured transfer to the Northern Department, and after wintering at Valley Forge he was named commander of the Western Department, with headquarters at Fort Pitt, in May 1778. He succeeded in subduing the Indians of the region, and he planned an expedition to Detroit—erecting Fort Laurens on the site of present-day Bolivar, Ohio, by way of preparation—but was unable to carry it out. In March 1779 he was relieved of the Western command and in May ordered to join the army in the South. He commanded two South Carolina regiments in the disastrous attack by Gen. Benjamin Lincoln on Savannah, October 9, 1779, and at the fall of Charleston on May 12, 1780, he was taken prisoner. While in prison his enemies at home intrigued against him, and for a time he was suspended from service. He was at length exonerated, however, and in September 1783 was brevetted major general. On his return to Georgia in 1783 he found that his property had been largely destroyed. In 1784 he was elected a delegate to the Continental Congress, but he seems not to have taken his seat. On several occasions he was appointed to negotiate boundary disputes and Indian treaties. McIntosh died in Savannah, Georgia, on February 20, 1806.

McIntosh, William (1775?–1825), Indian leader and army officer. Born about 1775 in what is now Carroll County, Georgia, McIntosh was the son of a British army officer and Indian agent and a Creek mother. He was well educated and grew up to become leader of the Lower Creeks, whom he led in alliance with the United States in the War of 1812, taking part in the battles of Autossee (or Auttose), November 29, 1813, and Horseshoe Bend, March 27, 1814, against the Upper Creeks (or Red Sticks), and earning the reward of a brigadier general's commission in the army. During 1817–1818 he served under Gen. Andrew Jackson in campaigns against the Seminoles in Florida. McIntosh remained friendly to whites through all the land-cession treaties and disputes of the succeeding years; he argued that, the loss of the land to the ever-greedy whites being inevitable, it was better to sell it sooner than to have it stolen later. In 1823 his (white) cousin George M. Troup, newly elected governor of Georgia, exerted pressure for yet more cessions, culminating in the Treaty of Indian Springs, signed by McIntosh on February 12, 1825, on behalf of the Lower Creeks. Already proscribed by the Cherokee, to whom he was tied by marriage, he became the target of an Upper Creek plot. On May 1, 1825, a party of 50 warriors surrounded his house on the Chattahoochee River in Carroll County, and in the ensuing fight he was killed.

McKean, William Wister (1800–1865), naval officer. Born on September 19, 1800, in Philadelphia, McKean was a grandson of Thomas McKean, signer of the Declaration of Independence and congressman. He entered the navy as a midshipman in November 1814 and saw his first sea duty aboard the *Java* under Capt. Oliver H. Perry. Over the next several decades he saw service in the West Indies, in the Mediterranean, and in southern waters. He advanced to lieutenant in 1825 and commander in 1841. In the Mexican War he commanded the *Dale* on the Pacific coast. Promoted to captain in 1855, he commanded the steam frigate *Niagara* in 1860–1861, in the former year conveying home the first Japanese diplomatic mission to the United States. On his arrival in Boston from Japan in April 1861 he fitted out for blockade duty and took up station off Charleston, South Carolina. In October 1861 he was put in command of the newly organized West Gulf Blockading Squadron, in which post he remained until relieved by Flag-Officer David G. Farragut in February 1862. He saw no further active service. McKean died near Binghamton, New York, on April 22, 1865.

Mackenzie, Alexander Slidell (1803–1848), naval officer and author.

Born in New York City on April 6, 1803, Alexander Slidell entered the navy as a midshipman in January 1815. After seven years of varied service he took leave of absence in 1822 to command a merchant vessel. On his return to active duty he was assigned to pirate patrol in the West Indies. Shortly after his promotion to lieutenant in January 1825 he again took leave and undertook the travels that he later described in *A Year in Spain*, 1829. Over the next several years, while serving on the *Brandywine*, the *Independence*, and other vessels, he produced *Popular Essays on Naval Subjects*, 1833, *The American in England*, 1835, and *Spain Revisited*, 1836. In 1838, at the request of a maternal uncle, he took the name Mackenzie. In 1838–1839 he commanded the *Dolphin* in Brazilian waters. His *Life of Commodore Oliver Hazard Perry* appeared in 1840 and his *Life of Paul Jones* in 1841. Promoted to commander in September 1841, he was given command of the steamer *Missouri*, from which in 1842 he transferred to the brig *Somers*, then used as a training ship for apprentices. In September 1842 he sailed for Africa with an apprentice crew. Evidences of unrest soon appeared, in time worsening to the point of mutiny. Mackenzie at length called a court of inquiry, which recommended execution for the three ringleaders, chief of whom was Acting Midshipman Philip Spencer, son of the secretary of war and a notorious scapegrace who apparently planned to turn pirate. On December 1, 1843, the three were hanged at the yardarm. The case, the last such ever to occur in the U.S. navy, became a celebrated one on the return of the *Somers*. A court of inquiry and a court-martial acquitted Mackenzie of blame, and all efforts of the elder Spencer and of the younger's friends failed to start any civil action. Mackenzie nonetheless retired for a time from active service. In 1846 he published a *Life of Stephen Decatur*. In that year he was sent by President James K. Polk on a mission to Mexico. In the Mexican War he was one of two naval officers to receive the surrender of Veracruz, March 27, 1847, and he commanded the artillery in the second attack on Tabasco, June 15. After a tour as commander of the steamer *Mississippi* in 1847–1848 he returned to his home in Tarrytown, New York, where he died on September 13, 1848.

Mackenzie, Ranald Slidell (1840–1889), army officer.

Born on July 27, 1840, in New York City, Mackenzie, son of Lt. Alexander S. Mackenzie of the navy, attended Williams College before entering West Point. He graduated first in his class in 1862, was commissioned in the engineers, and received his baptism of fire almost at once. A model officer, he distinguished himself at the second battle of Bull Run (Manassas), August 29–30, 1862, for which he was brevetted first lieutenant, at Fredericksburg, December 13, at Chancellorsville, May 2–4, 1863, where he was brevetted captain, and at Gettysburg, July 1–3, where he was brevetted major. He was promoted to captain in November 1863 and in June 1864 was brevetted lieutenant colonel for actions in the siege of Petersburg. In July he was appointed colonel of the 2nd Connecticut Heavy Artillery Volunteers. In October he was brevetted colonel for gallantry at Cedar Creek and, at the age of twenty-four, was promoted to brigadier general of volunteers. In the final siege of Petersburg he rose to command a division of cavalry, distinguishing himself at Five Forks, April 1, 1865. In March he had been brevetted major general of volunteers and brigadier general of regulars. Praised by Gen. Ulysses S. Grant "as the most promising young officer in the army," he remained in the service after the war as colonel of the 4th Cavalry. During the next two decades Mackenzie acquired a reputation as a master tactician in the field and as one of the most formidable Indian fighters in the Southwest. His success with the 4th Cavalry against the Cheyenne, Comanche, and Kiowa in West Texas in 1874–1875 (notably at Palo Duro Canyon, September 24, 1874), a campaign under the overall command of Col. Nelson A. Miles, opened the way to the pacification of the whole state and led to his appointment as commander of Fort Sill in the Indian Territory. In 1876 he served with Gen. Philip H. Sheridan in his campaign against the Sioux and Cheyenne Indians. Called "Bad Hand" (because of a Civil War wound) by the Indians, he routed the bands of Red Cloud and Red Leaf in Nebraska in October, and his victory over Dull Knife on November 25, 1876, at Crazy Woman Creek in the Bighorn Mountains was instrumental in the final defeat of Crazy Horse and the Sioux. He later took part in Indian-fighting expeditions into Colorado and Utah, 1879–1881, as well as Arizona and New Mexico. Mackenzie was promoted to brigadier general in October 1882. More of a fighter than an administrator, he was at his best in the field. He was forced by ill health to retire in March 1884, at the age of forty-three. He died on Staten Island, New York, on January 19, 1889.

McNair, Lesley James (1883–1944), army officer.

Born on May 25, 1883, in Verndale, Minnesota, McNair graduated from West Point in 1904 and was commissioned in the artillery. He was promoted to first lieutenant a year later and assigned to the ordnance department. He advanced to captain in May 1907 and from 1908 to 1912 was with the 4th Field Artillery at Fort D.A. Russell (later Fort F.E. Warren), Wyoming. After a course at the School of Fire, Fort Sill, Oklahoma, in 1912 he was sent as an observer of artillery techniques to France. He took part in the occupation of Veracruz in April 1914, and in 1916–1917 he was a member of the Mexican Punitive Expedition. In June 1917, promoted to major, he was ordered to France, where he served briefly with the 1st Division and then until 1919 on the staff of General Headquarters, American Expeditionary Forces; he advanced in temporary rank to lieutenant colonel, August 1917, colonel, June 1918, and brigadier general, October 1918. After graduating from the School of the Line he remained at Fort Leavenworth, Kansas, as an instructor until 1921. He was stationed in Hawaii until 1924 and was then professor of military science at Purdue University until 1928. Promoted to lieutenant colonel in that year, he entered the Army War College, and on graduating in 1929 he was named assistant commandant of the Field Artillery School, Fort Sill. Various assignments followed, including a period with the Civilian Conservation Corps in Louisiana. Promoted to colonel in May 1935 and to brigadier general in March 1937, he commanded the 2nd Field Artillery Brigade at Fort Sam Houston, Texas, from the latter date to April 1939, when he was named commandant of the Command and General Staff School at Fort Leavenworth. He held that post until October 1940, by which time he had already begun to take on the responsibility (under the nominal command of Gen. George C. Marshall, army chief of staff) of chief of the newly organized General Headquarters (GHQ), the command responsible for the training, organization, and mobilization of the entire army. He was promoted to major general in September 1940 and to lieutenant general (temporary) in June 1941. In March 1942 the army's command structure was reorganized, and McNair became commander of Army Ground Forces, successor to GHQ. He pioneered the simulation of battle conditions in training and insisted upon high standards of physical fitness and mental preparation in the millions of men trained under his leadership. In June 1944 he was ordered to England and named commander of the diversionary (and nonexistent) 1st Army Group. In July he went to the Normandy front to observe and on July 25, 1944, was killed in a foxhole near St. Lô by an American bomb that fell short. He was the highest ranking American officer ever killed in action. He was promoted to general posthumously in 1945, and in January 1948 the reservation in the District of Columbia on which the Army War College (now the National War College) stands, and where GHQ and Army Ground Forces had been headquartered, was renamed Fort Lesley J. McNair.

McNamara, Robert Strange (1916–)

McNamara, Robert Strange (1916–   ), businessman and public official. Born on June 9, 1916, in San Francisco, McNamara graduated from the University of California, Berkeley, in 1937 and took a degree in business administration from Harvard in 1939. In 1940 he joined the Harvard faculty. During World War II he conducted special courses for Army Air Force officers at Harvard and in 1943 was attached to Eighth Air Force headquarters in England. He was given a captain's commission in that year, and he advanced to lieutenant colonel by 1946. In that year he joined a team of management experts that, while working under contract to Ford Motor Company, became known as the "Whiz Kids." McNamara became controller at Ford in 1949 and four years later was named assistant general manager of the Ford division. He advanced to division general manager in 1955, vice-president of car and truck divisions in 1957, and president in November 1960, the first non-member of the Ford family to hold that position. Only a short time later, however, in January 1961 he became secretary of defense in the administration of President John F. Kennedy. With his background in statistical and management techniques he undertook an ambitious program of reorganization in the department, instituting careful budget procedures, notably the methodology of cost-benefit analysis, and attempted to develop a closely integrated and efficient armory of modern weapons systems among the three services. His success as a manager was not absolute, and the political unrest generated in the later 1960s by the Vietnam war was often focused on him. In November 1967 he announced his resignation, effective the following March, and he thereupon became president of the International Bank for Reconstruction and Development, known generally as the World Bank. In that post he worked to encourage economic growth and stability in underdeveloped nations and promoted such causes as population limitation and the agricultural "green revolution."

McNarney, Joseph Taggart (1893–1972)

McNarney, Joseph Taggart (1893–1972), army and air force officer. Born in Emporium, Pennsylvania, on August 28, 1893, McNarney graduated from West Point in 1915 and was commissioned in the infantry. In 1916 he was promoted to first lieutenant and sent to the Signal Corps Aviation School at San Diego, California, where he was also an instructor. In 1917 he completed pilot training, was promoted to captain and temporary major, and in August was ordered to France. There he saw varied service in staff positions and as commander at various times of the 1st Aero Squadron; of aeronautical schools attached to the I and II Corps; of observation groups of the I Corps (during the Château-Thierry operation), IV Corps (during St. Mihiel), and V Corps (during Meuse–Argonne); of the III Corps and VI Corps air service; and of the 2nd Army Observation Group, the last in February–April 1919. Promoted to temporary lieutenant colonel, he commanded Godman Field, Kentucky, and then the flying school at Gerstner Field, Louisiana, until 1920. Reverting to captain, he was promoted to major in July 1920. After graduating in 1921 he was until 1925 an instructor at the Air Service Field Officers School, Langley Field, Virginia, and in 1926 he graduated from the Command and General Staff School, Fort Leavenworth, Kansas. He was attached for a time to the General Staff and then entered the Army War College, graduating in 1930. After commanding the Primary Flying School and then the 7th Bombardment Group at March Field, California, he returned to the Army War College as an instructor in 1933–1935. For three years thereafter he was on the staff of GHQ Air Force, receiving promotion to permanent lieutenant colonel in June 1936. In March 1939 he joined the War Plans Division of the War Department. In May 1940, with temporary rank of colonel, he was appointed to the U.S.–Canadian Permanent Joint Defense Board. Promoted to temporary brigadier general in April 1941, he was in England as an observer in that year, and following the attack on Pearl Harbor he served on the investigating commission headed by Justice Owen J. Roberts. In March 1942, with temporary rank of major general, McNarney was named deputy chief of staff under Gen. George C. Marshall. In May he was promoted to temporary lieutenant general (he was made permanent major general in June 1944). In October 1944 he succeeded Gen. Jacob L. Devers as commander of U.S. army forces in North Africa and in November he was named deputy supreme Allied commander and commander of U.S. army forces in the Mediterranean theater. Promoted to general in March 1945, in October he became acting supreme commander of all Allied forces in that theater, but in November he succeeded Gen. George S. Patton as commander of U.S. forces in Europe, a post that included the job of military governor of the U.S. zone of occupation in Germany. After leaving that post in March 1947 he served for a time on the United Nations Military Staff Committee. Transferred into the newly independent air force in September 1947, he became commander of the Air Matériel Command at Wright-Patterson Air Force Base, Ohio; in September 1949 he was called to the Department of Defense to head its management committee. McNarney retired in February 1952. In that year he became president of Consolidated Vultee Aircraft Corporation, retaining that post when it became in 1954 the Convair division of General Dynamics Corporation, of which he was thereafter a senior vice-president until retiring in 1958. He died on February 1, 1972, in La Jolla, California.

Macomb, Alexander (1782–1841), army officer. Born in Detroit on April 3, 1782, Macomb grew up mainly in New York, where his father was a wealthy landowner. In 1799 he joined a company of militia in New York City and shortly thereafter, on the recommendation of Alexander Hamilton, was commissioned a cornet of light dragoons in the Provisional

Army. Discharged at the passing of the threat of war with France, he reentered the army as a second lieutenant of infantry in February 1801. During 1801–1802 he was secretary of a commission (whose members included Gen. James Wilkinson and Gen. Andrew Pickens) appointed to negotiate with the Indians of the Southeast. In October 1802 he was promoted to first lieutenant in the newly established Corps of Engineers and assigned to West Point, where he was one of the first two students to complete a course of formal training. Promoted to captain in 1805, he was given command of coastal defenses in Georgia and the Carolinas in 1807, remaining in that post until 1812 and advancing to major in February 1808 and lieutenant colonel in July 1810. During April–July 1812 he was adjutant general of the army. Promoted to colonel of artillery in July 1812, he raised the 3rd Artillery and commanded it at Sackett's Harbor, New York, in 1812–1813. He took part in Col. Winfield Scott's capture of Fort George on May 27, 1813, and in Gen. Wilkinson's fruitless march toward Montreal in November. Promoted to brigadier general in January 1814, he was stationed on the Lake Champlain frontier at Plattsburg, New York, under the command of Gen. George Izard. He was left in command when Izard marched for the Niagara front in August and had in Plattsburg about 3300 men, later reinforced by militia to 4500, of whom not all were fit for duty. Facing him was an army of some 11,000 veteran British regulars under Gen. Sir George Prevost, attempting to march down Burgoyne's route in the Revolution. Macomb was well dug in at Plattsburg, and supporting him was Commodore Thomas Macdonough's fleet in Lake Champlain. Prevost attacked on September 11, and Macomb held him off while Macdonough routed the British lake flotilla; Prevost then retired back into Canada. Macomb was brevetted major general for the victory. After the war he commanded military districts at New York and Detroit and in June 1821, with the rank of colonel, was named chief of engineers. On May 29, 1828, following the death of Gen. Jacob J. Brown, he was named commanding general of the army with the rank of major general. In 1835 he briefly took the field during the Seminole disturbances in Florida. He remained commander until his death in Washington, D.C., on June 25, 1841.

McPherson, James Birdseye (1828–1864), army officer. Born in Sandusky County, Ohio, on November 14, 1828, McPherson graduated from West Point in 1853 and was commissioned in the engineers. After a year as an instructor at West Point he was assigned to river and harbor work, in New York harbor until 1857 and then in California, where among other projects he built the fortifications on Alcatraz Island in San Francisco Bay. He was promoted to second lieutenant in December 1854 and first lieutenant in December 1858. He was ordered to Boston at the outbreak of the Civil War; promoted to captain in August 1861, in November he was chosen aide-de-camp by Gen. Henry W. Halleck and given the rank of lieutenant colonel. He was chief engineer of Gen. Ulysses S. Grant's expedition against Fort Henry and Fort Donelson in February 1862 and in May was appointed brigadier general of volunteers. He became military superintendent of railways in the West Tennessee district shortly thereafter. In October he was ordered to collect four scattered regiments and lead them to the relief of Gen. William S. Rosecrans, then besieged in Corinth, Mississippi, by Gen. Earl Van Dorn. He conducted the pursuit of Van Dorn so ably that he was promoted to major general of volunteers in command of a division of what became in November the XIII Corps. In January 1863 he advanced to command of the XVII Corps, which he led through the Vicksburg campaign; he was made commander of the Vicksburg district after the capture of that city on July 4. In August he was promoted to brigadier general of regulars. In March 1864 he succeeded Gen. William T. Sherman as commander of the Army of the Tennessee, and he served through Sherman's Atlanta campaign. He was conspicuous in the battle of Dalton, Georgia, May 8–12, and Resaca, May 13–16, and especially at Dallas, May 25–28, and Kennesaw Mountain, June 27. While riding, accompanied only by an orderly, to join his troops in the field during the final encirclement of Atlanta on July 22, 1864, he was caught by a Confederate counterattack and killed.

Maffitt, John Newland (1819–1886), Confederate naval officer. Born on February 22, 1819, aboard the ship bearing his immigrant parents from Ireland to America, Maffitt grew up in New York City and later in an uncle's home in Fayetteville, North Carolina. He entered the navy as a midshipman in February 1832 and for ten years served on the *St. Louis*, the *Constitution*, the *Macedonian*, and other vessels. In 1842 he was attached to the Coast Survey, with which he remained, making a highly creditable record, until 1858; he was promoted to lieutenant in June 1843. After three years of service mainly in Cuban waters he resigned in April 1861 and the next month was commissioned a lieutenant in the Confederate States navy. Until November he commanded the gunboat *Savannah* at Port Royal, and he then spent three months as engineer officer on the staff of Gen. Robert E. Lee. In January 1862 he took a cargo of cotton to England and there took possession of the steamer *Oreto*, the first of the Confederate cruisers clandestinely built in England to go into service on the high seas. After refitting her as a warship at Nassau and renaming her the *Florida*, Maffitt set out for Mobile by way of Cuba. Yellow fever decimated his crew, and incomplete equipment rendered his guns inoperable, but on September 4 he ran the blockade at Mobile in broad daylight and made harbor. In January 1863 he escaped through the blockade and began a six-month cruise up and down the Atlantic coasts of North and South America. He captured 22 prizes, 2 of which he refitted as tenders and sent against Union commerce as well; one of them, the *Clarence*, under Lt. Charles W. Read, in turn took 23 prizes. In August Maffitt put into Brest, France, for repairs and took leave of absence. He had been promoted to commander in April. He commanded Confederate transports until June 1864, when he took command of the ironclad *Albemarle* at Plymouth, North Carolina. In September he was transferred to the transport *Owl*, on which he tested and eluded the blockade from Wilmington, North Carolina, to Galveston, Texas, before finding a safe harbor. After the close of the Civil War he commanded for two years the British steamer *Widgeon*, then in the service of Brazil in a war with Paraguay, and in 1870 he briefly commanded the *Cuba* of the Cuban revolutionist forces. He lived thereafter in Wilmington, North Carolina, and was author of numerous articles on the exploits of the Confederate navy. Maffitt died in Wilmington on May 15, 1886.

Magruder, John Bankhead (1810–1871), Confederate army officer. Born in Winchester, Virginia, on August 15, 1810, Magruder graduated from West Point in 1830 and was commissioned in the infantry. He subsequently transferred to the artillery and over the next several years served at various posts in the West, at Fort McHenry, Baltimore, and in the Seminole War in Florida, receiving promotion to first lieutenant in 1836 and captain in 1846. In the Mexican War he commanded a battery under Gen. Gideon Pillow and won brevets to major at Cerro Gordo, April 18, 1847, and lieutenant colonel at Chapultepec, September 13. Afterwards he continued in routine duty; during a period at Newport, Rhode Island, he was a great social success. In March 1861 he resigned from the army and took a commission as colonel of infantry in the Confederate army. On June 10 his troops repulsed at Big Bethel, Virginia, an attempt by Gen. Benjamin F. Butler to break out of Fort Monroe, and in consequence of his victory in this first large-scale engagement of the Civil War Magruder was promoted to brigadier general; in October he advanced to major general. As commander of forces on the Yorktown Peninsula he was responsible for opposing Gen. George B. McClellan's Army of the Potomac from the outset of the Peninsular campaign in March 1862. With only about 12,000 men at his disposal, he conducted a brilliant and deceptive defense, awing McClellan into wasting a month in besieging Yorktown. During the Seven Days' Battles he took part in nearly all the actions, especially Savage Station, June 29, and Malvern Hill, July 1, but his slowness and imprecision in executing orders lost him the favor of Gen. Robert E. Lee. In October 1862 he was transferred to command of the District of Texas; New Mexico and Arizona were subsequently added to the territory under his command. On January 1, 1863, he captured Galveston, Texas, and the Union revenue cutter *Harriet Lane* and destroyed or drove off the rest of the blockade squadron. In March 1864 he dispatched troops to aid Gen. Richard Taylor in opposing Gen. Nathaniel P. Banks's Red River campaign. After the close of the war he fled to Mexico, where he served for a time as major general in the army of Emperor Maximilian. He subsequently returned to the United States and in 1869 settled in Houston, Texas, where he died on February 18, 1871.

Mahan, Alfred Thayer (1840–1914), naval officer and historian. Born on September 27, 1840, in West Point, New York, Mahan was the son of Dennis H. Mahan, professor at the Military Academy. After two years at Columbia College he entered the Naval Academy, from which he graduated in 1859. After a two-year cruise on the *Congress* in the Brazil Squadron he was promoted to lieutenant in August 1861. He took part in Flag-Officer Samuel F. Du Pont's expedition against Port Royal in November, saw blockade duty in the South Atlantic and West Gulf squadrons, and in 1864–1865 served on the staff of Adm. John A. B. Dahlgren. Twenty years of routine duty followed the Civil War. He was promoted to lieutenant commander in June 1865, to commander in November 1872, and to captain in September 1885. That year, in recognition of his abilities and his reputation for scholarship, he received a call from Adm. Stephen B. Luce to lecture on naval history and strategy at the newly organized Naval War College in Newport, Rhode Island. In June 1886 he succeeded Luce as the institution's president and held the post until 1889. The next year his lectures were published under the title *The Influence of Sea Power upon History, 1660–1783;* a thoroughgoing analysis of sea power in its broadest manifestations, the book broke new ground in the examination of international affairs and won immediate recognition abroad. In 1892 Mahan's second major work appeared, entitled *The Influence of Sea Power upon the French Revolution and Empire, 1793–1812,* and, like the first, it became a classic. Assiduously studied in translation, the two books greatly influenced the worldwide buildup of naval forces in the period before World War I. In 1892–1893 Mahan was again president of the Naval War College, and in 1893, on a cruise in European waters in command of the cruiser *Chicago,* he was publicly honored by the British government and awarded honorary degrees by both Oxford and Cambridge universities. He retired from the navy in November 1896 but was recalled to service on the naval strategy board during the Spanish–American

War. He was a member of the U.S. delegation to the peace conference at The Hague in 1899, and in 1902 was elected president of the American Historical Association. In June 1906 he was promoted to rear admiral on the retired list. Notable among Mahan's many other works were *The Life of Nelson,* 1897; *The Interest of America in Sea Power, Present and Future,* 1897; and *The Major Operations of the Navies in the War of American Independence,* 1913. He died in Washington, D.C., on December 1, 1914.

Mahan, Dennis Hart (1802–1871), engineer and educator. Born on April 2, 1802, in New York City, Mahan grew up in Norfolk, Virginia, and, attracted by the courses in drawing, entered West Point in 1820. His brilliance attracted the notice of the superintendent, Maj. Sylvanus Thayer, and he was appointed an acting instructor in mathematics while still a student. On graduating at the head of his class in 1824 he was commissioned in the engineers and given a regular appointment on the West Point faculty. During 1826–1830 he was in France, observing military works and pursuing advanced studies at the School of Application for Engineers and Artillery at Metz. He then returned to West Point, where he remained for the rest of his life, becoming professor of civil and military engineering in 1832 and dean of the faculty in 1838. To supply the lack of suitable textbooks he wrote *Complete Treatise on Field Fortification,* 1836; *Elementary Course of Civil Engineering,* 1837; and *Elementary Treatise on Advance-Guard, Out-Post, and Detachment Service of Troops,* 1847; all of which were for decades standard works in the field. Later texts of his included *Industrial Drawing,* 1852; *Descriptive Geometry as Applied to the Drawing of Fortification and Stereotomy,* 1864; and *An Elementary Course of Military Engineering,* 1866–1867. Mahan's rigorous instruction, combined with his broad view of the requirements of military education, pushed the program at West Point to a high level of excellence; aside from its military significance, it led among American schools of engineering in setting new standards of instruction and preparation. In his classes the principles and lessons of military practice and history were instilled in generations of cadets, and nearly all the great Civil War generals were his students. Recommended for retirement because of age by the West Point board of visitors in 1871, he became despondent and on September 16, 1871, threw himself off a Hudson riverboat and drowned near Stony Point, New York.

Manley, John (1734?–1793), Revolutionary naval officer. Born about 1734, probably in Boston, Manley (or Manly) became a merchant seaman, rising to command of vessels in the West Indian trade. In October 1775, while the small and ill supplied Continental army was encamped about Boston, Gen.

George Washington gave Manley an army commission of captain and placed him in command of the schooner *Lee*, one of a tiny fleet with which Washington hoped to capture supplies intended for the British army in Boston. In November Manley captured the ordnance ship *Nancy*, bringing to Washington several guns and a great store of powder and other material. Other prizes were taken in December, and in January 1776 Manley was appointed commodore of "Washington's Fleet," comprising six schooners and a brigantine. He continued to cruise successfully and in April 1776 was commissioned by Congress a captain in the Continental navy, later being placed second on the captain's list. In August he was given command of the frigate *Hancock*, 32 guns, then building at Boston. He sailed in May 1777 and on June 7 captured the *Fox*, 28, but soon afterward lost her to the *Flora*. On July 8 he encountered the *Rainbow*, 44, and the smaller *Victor;* deserted by the *Boston*, which had been accompanying him, Manley was forced to surrender to superior force. He was held on a British prison ship in New York harbor until March 1778. After his exchange, the Continental navy having no suitable ship for him, he turned to privateering, making cruises on the *Marlborough*, on the *Cumberland*, which he was forced to surrender to the *Pomona* in 1779, and, after his escape from prison on Barbados, on the *Jason*, which was also captured on his second cruise. After two years in Mill Prison, Plymouth, England, he returned to the navy and in September 1782 took command of the frigate *Hague*. While cruising near Martinique he was set upon by a British 74-gun ship of the line and three smaller vessels; he ran aground on a sandbar but nonetheless escaped, firing 13 guns in defiance. This engagement, which took place after the preliminary articles of peace had been signed, was apparently the last between commissioned ships in the Revolution, and in January 1783, on the return voyage to Boston, he captured the *Baille*, the last prize of value taken by a Continental vessel. Manley died in Boston on February 12, 1793.

Mansfield, Joseph King Fenno (1803–1862), army officer and engineer. Born in New Haven, Connecticut, on December 22, 1803, Mansfield graduated from West Point in 1822 and was commissioned in the engineers. For nearly a quarter of a century he was engaged mainly in coastal fortification work, most notably in the construction of Fort Pulaski at the mouth of the Savannah River, Georgia. He was promoted to first lieutenant in 1832 and to captain in July 1838. On the outbreak of the Mexican War in 1846 he was named chief engineer on the staff of Gen. Zachary Taylor. He built Fort Texas (later Fort Brown) opposite Matamoros and for his part in defending it in May was brevetted major. He performed valuable reconnaissance work before the battles of

Monterrey, September 20–24, and Buena Vista, February 22–23, 1847, and for that as well as his actions in combat he was brevetted lieutenant colonel and colonel. After the war he resumed routine engineering duties until May 1853, when he was appointed inspector general of the army with the rank of colonel. He remained in that post, which involved him in travel to the farthest-flung outposts of the army, until May 1861, when he was promoted to brigadier general in command of the Department of Washington, with responsibility for the defense of the federal capital. He directed the construction of fortifications all around the city, including extensive earthworks on Arlington Heights across the Potomac. When his department was absorbed into Gen. George B. McClellan's Department of the Potomac late in 1861, Mansfield was ordered to join the forces at Fort Monroe under Gen. John E. Wool. He participated in the occupation of Norfolk and Suffolk, Virginia, in May 1862, becoming military governor of the latter city. He was appointed major general of volunteers in July. In September he took command of the XII Corps, Army of the Potomac, and at the battle of Antietam (Sharpsburg), Maryland, September 17, 1862, was killed while making a reconnaissance.

March, Peyton Conway (1864–1955), army officer. Born on December 27, 1864, in Easton, Pennsylvania, March graduated from Lafayette College in 1884 and then entered West Point, taking a commission in the artillery upon graduation in 1888. For ten years he served at various posts in the East and in California, receiving promotion to first lieutenant in October 1894. Shortly after graduating from the Artillery School in 1898 he was made captain of a battery outfitted for the army by John Jacob Astor and was sent to the Philippines, where he took part in the capture of Manila. In 1899 he returned to the Philippines as major of the 33rd Volunteer Infantry and was the American commander at the Battle of the Clouds at Tilad Pass, Luzon, on December 2, following which he received the surrender of Gen. Venancio Concepción, chief of staff of the insurgent leader Emilio Aguinaldo. Promoted to lieutenant colonel of volunteers in June 1900, he served for a time as aide-de-camp to Gen. Arthur MacArthur and in 1900–1901 as governor of various districts. In June 1901 he was discharged from volunteer service. From 1903 to 1907 he was attached to the General Staff, serving during that period as an observer with the Japanese army in the Russo–Japanese War. Promoted to major in January 1907, he joined the 6th Field Artillery at Fort Riley, Kansas. From 1911 to 1916 he served several assignments in the adjutant general's department. In August 1916 he was promoted to colonel in command of the 8th Field Artillery on the Mexican border. In June 1917 he was promoted to brigadier general and ordered to France as commander of artillery in the American Expeditionary Forces. Appointed temporary major general in August and made permanent in that grade in September, he organized several field artillery training schools in France and devised the program of instruction. In March 1918 he was recalled to the United States as acting chief of staff of the army, nominally under Gen. Tasker H. Bliss (who was also U.S. representative on the allied Supreme War Council and who had effectively retired in January) and in May he formally succeeded Bliss as chief of staff, receiving the rank of general, the third U.S. army officer ever to hold that rank (after Gen. John J. Pershing and Bliss). In addition to greatly increasing the rate of conscription, training, and forwarding to France of troops for the A.E.F.—one and a quarter million men in his first six months—March more importantly instituted a far-reaching reorganization of the General Staff and of his own office, making the chief of staff in reality the supreme office it had until then been only on paper. Bureau chiefs were required to report through him, and he even asserted—though he wisely did not attempt to exercise—authority over Pershing. Operations of supply and related functions were streamlined with the assistance of Gen. George W. Goethals, acting quartermaster general. March continued as chief of staff until his retirement in the permanent rank of major general in June 1921. He was raised to general on the retired list in 1930. In 1932 he published *The Nation at War*. He died in Washington, D.C., on April 13, 1955.

Marcy, Randolph Barnes (1812–1887), army

officer. Born in Greenwich, Massachusetts, on April 9, 1812, Marcy graduated from West Point in 1832 and was commissioned in the infantry. Until 1845 he served mainly in Michigan and Wisconsin territories, receiving promotion to first lieutenant in June 1837, and he was then ordered to Texas. On the outbreak of the Mexican War in 1846 he took part in the battles of Palo Alto, May 8, and Resaca de la Palma, May 9, and a few days later was promoted to captain. A period of recruiting duty followed, but in 1847 he returned to the Southwest, where he remained for the next 12 years. In 1849 he escorted an emigrant caravan of 100 wagons from Fort Smith, Arkansas, to Santa Fe, and in 1852 he led an exploring party to the headwaters of the Red and Canadian rivers. He was briefly in Florida in 1857, seeing action against the Seminoles. Later in the year he served in the Mormon expedition under Col. Albert S. Johnston. As supplies and pack animals dwindled during the winter camp at Fort Bridger, Marcy set out in November in command of a 35-man party and made a remarkable midwinter march of nearly a thousand miles to Fort Massachusetts, New Mexico, returning to Fort Bridger in June 1858 with 1500 animals and reinforcements. Soon thereafter he was appointed acting inspector

general of the Department of Utah. Ordered early in 1859 to New York, he prepared a handbook titled *The Prairie Traveler* based on his extensive experience. In August 1859 he was promoted to major in the paymaster's department. In May 1861 he was appointed chief of staff to Gen. George B. McClellan, who was also his son-in-law. He served in that capacity in West Virginia, in the Peninsular campaign, and in Maryland, receiving promotion to colonel and inspector general in August 1861 and appointment as brigadier general of volunteers in September 1861. In March 1863 his volunteer commission expired. He served as inspector in various departments from then until 1878, receiving brevet rank of brigadier and major general in March 1865. In December 1878 he was appointed inspector general of the army with the rank of brigadier general, holding that post until his retirement in January 1881. In addition to his handbook he published *Thirty Years of Army Life on the Border*, 1866, and *Border Reminiscences*, 1872. Marcy died in West Orange, New Jersey, on November 22, 1887.

Marion, Francis (1732?–1795), "the Swamp

Fox," Revolutionary army officer. Born in Berkeley County, South Carolina, probably in 1732, Marion first saw military service against the Cherokee in 1759 and again in 1761. The first provincial congress, to which he was elected in 1775, elected him in June of that year a captain in the second of two regiments then being raised, and he served under Col. William Moultrie when the British were repulsed at Sullivans Island on June 28, 1776. The following September his regiment was mustered into the Continental army, and he was promoted to lieutenant colonel. He fought under Gen. Benjamin Lincoln at Savannah in the fall of 1779 but escaped capture when Charleston fell to the British in May 1780. After the disastrous defeat of Gen. Horatio Gates at Camden, August 16, 1780, he gathered around himself a band of intrepid guerrillas whom he trained to fight while living off the land. For the next few months Marion operated in the enemy's territory. The only Continental force worth mentioning in South Carolina, "Marion's brigade" harassed the British by cutting communications, successfully engaging Loyalist strongholds, and sometimes risking an attack on larger bodies of British regulars. At home in the supposedly impassable swamps, he surprised the enemy in swift attacks and then dispersed his men to avoid capture. Even the dreaded Col. Banastre Tarleton could not find Marion, saying: "As for this damned old fox, the devil himself could not catch him." The remark earned Marion, who was promoted to brigadier general of militia in 1781, the sobriquet "Swamp Fox." He made two unsuccessful attempts to capture Georgetown, but a third attempt, in concert with Gen. Nathanael Greene's forces, took the town in

April 1781. He was in command of the militia at the major victory at Eutaw Springs on September 8, 1781, for which he received the thanks of Congress. He continued to serve ably under Greene until the end of the war. After the war he served several terms in the South Carolina senate and from 1784 to 1790 was commander of Fort Johnson in Charleston harbor, a post that was essentially a sinecure in reward for his labors. He died at his plantation home in Berkeley County on February 27, 1795.

Marshall, George Catlett (1880–1959), army officer and public official. Born in Uniontown, Pennsylvania, on December 31, 1880, Marshall graduated from Virginia Military Institute in 1901 and in February 1902 received a commission as second lieutenant of infantry. After service in the Philippines and at Fort Reno, Oklahoma, he graduated from the Infantry and Cavalry School in 1907 and the Staff College in 1908, both at Fort Leavenworth, Kansas, remaining there as an instructor until 1910. He was promoted to first lieutenant in March 1907. During 1913–1916 he was again in the Philippines, the last year as aide to Gen. Hunter Liggett. Promoted to captain in July 1916, he was for a time aide to Gen. J. Franklin Bell. In July 1917 he was ordered to France as a staff officer with the 1st Infantry Division. He remained with the 1st, under Gen. William L. Sibert and then Gen. Robert L. Bullard, until July 1918; in August, with temporary rank of colonel, he was moved up to the staff of the First Army. He accomplished a brilliant piece of work in September 1918 in overseeing the rapid movement of some 500,000 troops and 2700 guns from the St. Mihiel operation to the Argonne front in preparation for the great Meuse–Argonne offensive. In October Marshall was named chief of operations for the First Army, and in November he became chief of staff of VIII Corps. From 1919 to 1924 he was an aide to Gen. John J. Pershing, army chief of staff. Having reverted to captain, he was promoted to major in July 1920 and to lieutenant colonel in 1923. In 1924–1927 he was with the 15th Infantry at Tientsin, China, and from 1927 to 1932 he was assistant commandant of the Infantry School, Fort Benning, Georgia. Promoted to colonel in 1933, he served as commander of the 8th Infantry at Fort Moultrie, South Carolina, as senior instructor with the Illinois national guard, and in other duties, becoming brigadier general in 1936. In July 1938 he was attached to the General Staff. He became deputy chief of staff in October, acting chief of staff with the rank of major general in July 1939, and chief of staff with the rank of general in September 1939. Almost immediately he began an enormous expansion of the army and a reorganization of the General Staff, and from December 1941 he had the major responsibility for organizing, training, supplying, and deploying U.S. troops in World War II. By his direction in March 1942 the army was reorganized into three major commands: Army Ground Forces, under Gen. Lesley J. McNair, Army Service Forces, under Gen. Brehon B. Somervell, and Army Air Forces, under Gen. Henry H. Arnold. During the war Marshall himself worked out of the War Plans Division (later Operations Division), headed successively by Gen. Dwight D. Eisenhower, Gen. Thomas T. Handy, and Gen. John E. Hull. He was also a principal adviser to President Franklin D. Roosevelt on strategy and attended the major Allied planning conferences from Casablanca to Potsdam. As senior member of the Allied Combined Chiefs of Staff he was the principal architect of the Allied strategy for fighting a two-front war, putting first priority on the defeat of Germany, dealing with Britain's desire for an early move in North Africa and the Soviet Union's urging of a second European front, and brilliantly managing both military and political aspects of a global effort of immense complexity. From December 1944 he held the five-star rank of general of the army. Soon after resigning as chief of staff in November 1945 Marshall was sent by President Harry S. Truman to attempt—unsuccessfully—a mediation of the Nationalist–Communist civil war in China. In January 1947 he was appointed secretary of state by Truman, resigning his army commission in February. In June of that year, in a speech at Harvard, he proposed the European Recovery Program, a massive program of aid to the devastated nations of Europe that was undertaken the following year and became known universally as the Marshall Plan. During the four years following congressional action in April 1948 the United States contributed more than $112 billion toward European recovery. In January 1949 he resigned from the cabinet but returned in September 1950 as secretary of defense, a post he held for a year during the early phase of the Korean War. He retired permanently from public service in September 1951. During 1949–1950 he served as president of the American Red Cross. In 1953 he was awarded the Nobel Peace Prize, primarily for his plan for European recovery. He died on October 16, 1959, in Washington, D.C.

Mason, John (1600?–1672), colonial militia officer. Born in England about 1600, Mason may have served in the army in one or more campaigns in the Low Countries before emigrating to Massachusetts about 1630. He was appointed captain of militia for Dorchester in 1633 and in 1635 was one of the founders of Windsor, Connecticut. When the long-standing friction between settlers and the Pequot Indians erupted into warfare late in 1636, Mason was at Saybrook Fort, then commanded by Capt. Lion Gardiner, where early in 1637 he was joined by a small Massachusetts force under Capt. John Underhill. In May he set out with 90 volunteers to pursue the Pequots. He marched first to the country of the friendly Narragansetts, many of whom joined him, and then to the Pequot stronghold on the Mystic River. In a surprise attack on May 26, Mason's men and Indian allies massacred the Pequots—men, women, and children—to the number of 600 or more; 7 escaped. The Pequot War was effectively ended. Mason joined in hunting down the few remaining fugitives and then returned to Saybrook. A short time later he was promoted to major, and he commanded the Connecticut militia nearly continuously until his death. He was a deputy in the General Court from 1637 to 1642 and a magistrate from 1642 to 1660. In 1660 he was a founder of Norwich, where he lived thereafter, and in 1660–1669 he served as deputy governor of Connecticut. He was assistant from 1669 until his death in Norwich on January 30, 1672. His history of the war, written after 1656, was printed by Increase Mather in 1677 in his *Relation of the Troubles that Have Hapned in New England.*

Mauldin, William Henry (1921–), cartoonist.

Born on October 29, 1921, in Mountain Park, New Mexico, Mauldin neglected to complete high school but studied at the Chicago Academy of Fine Arts in 1939. He joined the army in September 1940; at Fort Sill, Oklahoma, he became a staff cartoonist for the *45th Division News,* and, going overseas in 1943, he joined the Mediterranean staff of the army newspaper *Stars and Stripes,* covering the campaigns in Italy, France, and Germany. He developed two characters named Willie and Joe, whose progressively deteriorating appearance and disenchanted attitudes reflected those of many soldiers overseas. The cartoons, enormously popular with servicemen, were featured in 100 newspapers in the United States as well as in *Stars and Stripes.* They were collected in several volumes, including *Up Front,* 1945, and made Mauldin famous. He won a Pulitzer Prize in 1945 for a cartoon captioned "Fresh American troops, flushed with victory," which showed grimy soldiers plodding in mud through a storm. Mauldin was discharged in June 1945. His postwar depictions of Willie and Joe trying to adjust to civilian life (collected in *Back Home,* 1947) and a new series of cartoons mocking racists, overzealous patriots, and stereotyped liberals were distributed to as many as 180 newspapers by the United Features Syndicate. During 1950–1951 he worked in Hollywood as a technical consultant and an actor in the war film *Teresa* and as co-star with Audie Murphy in *The Red Badge of Courage,* both released in 1951. Also released that year was *Up Front,* a movie based on the Willie and Joe cartoons. *Bill Mauldin in Korea,* 1952, was published after he visited the Korean war zone. In 1956 he ran unsuccessfully as a Democrat for a seat in the House of Representatives from New York. Two years later he became editorial cartoonist for the *St. Louis Post-Dispatch,* his work for that paper being syndicated eventually to some 140 newspapers. In 1958 he won a second Pulitzer Prize for his cartooned impression of Soviet novelist Boris Pasternak's fate: "I won the Nobel Prize for Literature. What was your crime?" In 1962 he joined the *Chicago Sun-Times,* which distributed his editorial cartoons to more than 200 newspapers. He wrote and illustrated numerous articles for popular magazines and published other collections, including *Sort of a Saga,* 1949; *What's Got Your Back Up,* 1961; *I've Decided I Want My Seat Back,* 1965; and *The Brass Ring,* 1972.

Maury, Matthew Fontaine (1806–1873), naval

officer and oceanographer. Born near Fredericksburg, Virginia, on January 14, 1806, Maury grew up there and, from the age of five, on a farm near Franklin, Tennessee. In 1825 he entered the navy as a midshipman and in the following nine years made three lengthy cruises, the first of which, on the *Brandywine,* was the return voyage of Lafayette to France after his visit in 1825, and the second of which was a circumnavigation of the globe on the *Vincennes* in 1829–1830. In 1836 he published his first major work, *A New Theoretical and Practical Treatise on Navigation.* He was promoted to lieutenant in that year. Later, under various pseudonyms, he published a number of articles criticizing the administration of the navy and suggesting reforms. An accident in 1839 rendered him permanently lame and unfit for sea duty, but three years later he was appointed superintendent of the navy's Depot of Charts and Instruments. From 1844 he directed the new Naval Observatory (in 1854 the two agencies were combined into the U.S. Naval Observatory and Hydrographic Office, but they were again separate from 1866). He launched an intensive program of research into winds and currents and in 1847 published his *Wind and Current Chart of the North Atlantic;* this work, together with subsequently published sailing directions, proved highly valuable in reducing sailing times. The work was based on old merchant and naval logs, with supplemental data from the work of Commodore Cadwalader Ringgold and Commander John Rodgers of the North Pacific Surveying Expedition of 1853–1856. Growing worldwide interest in his work culminated in 1853 in an international conference in Brussels, where his system of collecting and recording oceanographic data was universally adopted. He represented the United States at the meeting and secured the adoption of a plan for international cooperation in the gathering and collating of such data. With new sources of information available, he revised his earlier work and compiled charts for other ocean areas. In 1855 he published *The Physical Geography of the Sea and Its Meteorology,* considered the first work of modern oceanography. He later encouraged the idea of an Atlantic telegraph cable, preparing charts of optimum locations, and was often consulted by Cyrus Field when the latter undertook the project. In 1855 a naval board that had been convened to review the officer list, perhaps motivated by envy, placed him on leave of absence. In 1858 President James Buchanan restored him to active service with the rank of commander, retroactive to 1855. In April 1861, shortly after the secession of Virginia from the Union, he resigned from the U.S. navy and was promptly commissioned a commander in the Confederate navy. Placed in charge of coast, harbor, and river defenses, he conducted experiments at Richmond, Virginia, with an electric torpedo, continuing the work in England, where he was sent in 1862 as a special agent of the Confederacy. His reputation gained him considerable influence there, and he secured a number of warships for the Confederate fleet, notably the *Georgia,* which sailed from Scotland in April 1863 and took numerous Union prizes. While returning home in 1865 he learned of the fall of the Confederacy and went instead to Mexico. He was appointed imperial commissioner of immigration by Emperor Maximilian and attempted unsuccessfully to establish a colony of Confederate exiles, to be named "Carlotta," in that country. From 1866 to 1868 he was again in England, but in the latter year he returned to the United States to become professor of meteorology at the Virginia Military Institute. Others of his books were *Physical Geography,* 1864; *The World We Live In,* 1868; and *Manual of Geography,* 1871. During his later years he was much honored. He died in Lexington, Virginia, on February 1, 1873.

Maus, Marion Perry (1850–1930), army officer. Born in Burnt Mills, Montgomery County, Maryland, on August 25, 1850, Maus graduated from West Point in 1874 and was commissioned in the infantry. He was ordered to Fort Randall, Dakota Territory, and over the next several years took part in a number of Indian campaigns, notably as commander of scouts under Col. Nelson A. Miles in the pursuit and capture of Chief Joseph and the Nez Percés in 1877. He was promoted to first lieutenant in September 1879. He was ordered to Texas in 1880 and to Arizona in 1882. In 1885, as commander of Apache scouts, he took part in an expedition into Mexico in pursuit of Geronimo, and for his conduct in the attack on the renegade Apache band and in a battle with Mexican troops on January 10–11, 1886, he won the Medal of Honor (awarded November 1894). Promoted to captain in November 1890, he saw action against the Sioux in 1890–1891, was ordered to Chicago during the labor disturbances of 1894, and was aide to Miles during the latter's inspection tour of Europe in 1897 and during the Spanish–American War in 1898. He was promoted to major in June 1899 and a month later made inspector general of the Department of

California and the Columbia. He advanced to lieutenant colonel in June 1902 and during 1902–1903 accompanied Miles on a world tour. In January 1904 he became colonel of the 20th Infantry, which he commanded in the Philippines until 1906, when he returned to California. He was temporarily in command of the Division of the Pacific during the absence of Gen. Frederick Funston and played an important role in maintaining order in San Francisco following the earthquake in April 1906. Promoted to brigadier general in June 1909, he commanded the Department of the Columbia until 1911, when he was given command of a brigade of the 2nd Division in San Antonio, Texas. At his retirement in August 1913 he was commander of a brigade of the 1st Division at Albany, New York. Maus died in New Windsor, Maryland, on February 9, 1930.

Maxey, Samuel Bell (1825–1895), Confederate army officer and public official. Born in Tompkinsville, Kentucky, on March 30, 1825, Maxey graduated from West Point in 1846 and was commissioned in the infantry. He served in Gen. Winfield Scott's army in the Mexican War and was brevetted first lieutenant for gallantry at Contreras and Churubusco, August 19–20, 1847. After a period of garrison duty at Jefferson Barracks, Missouri, he resigned from the army in 1849, took up the study of law, and entered practice in Albany, Kentucky, in 1850. He removed to Paris, Texas, in 1857. On the outbreak of the Civil War he organized the 9th Texas Infantry, at the head of which he joined Gen. Albert S. Johnston at Decatur, Alabama, in March 1862. Promoted to brigadier general, he subsequently served under Gen. Braxton Bragg, took part in the defense of Port Hudson early in 1863, and was under Gen. Joseph E. Johnston at Jackson, Mississippi, during the Vicksburg campaign. In December 1863 he was appointed to command of the Indian Territory. He was generally successful in retaining the support of the Indian tribes in the territory, continuing the work begun by Gen. Albert Pike, and he organized three brigades from among them, notably the Cherokee under Gen. Stand Watie. On April 18, 1864, he won a valuable victory at Poison Springs, turning back Gen. Frederick Steele, who was attempting to join forces with Gen. Nathaniel P. Banks on the Red River. For that success he was promoted to major general. After the war Maxey resumed his law practice in Texas. He entered the Senate in 1875, where he remained until defeated in his bid for a third term in 1887. He died in Eureka Springs, Arkansas, on August 16, 1895.

Maxim, Hiram Stevens (1840–1916), inventor. Born on February 5, 1840, near Sangerville, Maine, Maxim was a mechanically precocious child and learned several trades, including that of carriage maker, before he was twenty. During the Civil War he worked at various jobs in Canada and upstate New York, then settled down in the engineering firm of an uncle in Fitchburg, Massachusetts. His mechanical ingenuity led to a number of inventions; his first patent, granted in 1866, was for a hair-curling iron. In the 1870s he was in New York City, and his success with illuminating gas equipment led to a post as chief engineer of the United States Electric Light Company in 1878. His method of treating the filaments in the incandescent carbon lamp proved a major advance in the design of light bulbs, but Maxim never was able to profit from it. At the Paris Exposition in 1881 he was decorated for his design of a self-regulating electric generator. He subsequently opened a laboratory in London and shortly began working on a fully automatic machine gun, an idea that he first heard from his father; its success was to secure for him an international reputation. By June 1884 he had progressed to the point where he had a workable design, using the principle of short recoil for generating a complete cycle, including reloading, in a single barrel. The gun fired 660 rounds per minute, the cartridges being fed in on a belt, and subsequent improvement and the introduction of smokeless powder assured the success of the Maxim gun. The Maxim was manufactured by the Maxim Gun Company, organized in 1884; four years later the firm was merged with the makers of the Nordenfeldt, an earlier rapid-fire gun, and in 1896 with Vickers Sons as Vickers Sons and Maxim, which, on Maxim's retirement 15 years later, became Vickers, Ltd. His machine gun was quickly adopted by every major power including the United States. It was used with devastating effect during World War I and permanently changed modern warfare. Maxim became a British subject in 1900 and, following the successful use of the Maxim gun by the British army in Egypt in 1897–1899, was knighted by Queen Victoria in 1901. Although he was known primarily for his machine gun, Maxim obtained more than 250 patents in Britain and the United States during his career. Among his inventions were a smokeless powder similar to cordite and a delayed-action fuse for artillery shells. In the early 1890s he designed a steam-powered flying machine that was aerodynamically sound, but although he was near success by 1894 the combined weight of fuel and water made the craft impracticable. He retired in 1911 and died at Streatham, England, on November 24, 1916. The Maxim gun reached its full potential only after the development of suitable explosives, the chief credit for which is due his brother, Hudson Maxim. Hiram Maxim's son, Hiram Percy Maxim (1869–1936), was also an inventor of note, patenting the Maxim silencer for firearms and an automobile muffler.

Maxim, Hudson (1853–1927), inventor. Born on February 3, 1853, in Orneville, Piscataquis County,

Maine, Hudson at eighteen changed his given name Isaac. For a while he studied chemistry at Wesleyan Seminary in Kents Hill, Maine. About 1871 he was associated with his brother Hiram in New York City, but he achieved his first success in 1881 as the publisher (along with Alden Knowles) of a book on penmanship of which a half-million copies were sold. In the mid-1880s he joined his brother at his gun factory in England but returned to Massachusetts after the merger with Nordenfeldt as American representative of the company in 1888. He immediately began to experiment with high explosives and within a year had secured his first patent. He built a dynamite and powder plant in 1890 at Maxim, near Farmingdale, New Jersey. A conflict with Hiram led to their estrangement and the termination of his contract with Maxim-Nordenfeldt in 1891, but his success in perfecting an improved form of dynamite led to the establishment of his own Maxim Powder Company at Squankum, New Jersey, in 1893. During the next two years he devoted himself to improving smokeless explosive powder, first introduced by the French in 1885, whose progressive burning qualities were ideally suited to the requirements of a rapid-fire gun. The controlled rapid burning of Maxim's improved powder stabilized and extended the range of the gun's projectile, while providing a consistent gas pressure for activating the recoil apparatus of the gun. Obtaining patent protection by 1895, he was unable to interest his brother in purchasing his patent, and in 1897 he sold factory and patents to E. I. du Pont de Nemours & Company, remaining with them as consulting engineer. By 1900 he had perfected maximite, a powerful explosive of such stability that it remained undetonated even as the shell penetrated heavy armor; it could then be exploded by a delayed-action fuse, also of his design. A more stable version of his smokeless powder was marketed as stabillite, and his motorite came into extensive use as a torpedo propellant. An outspoken critic of pacifism and a proponent of preparedness, he published *Defenseless America* in 1915. During World War I Maxim served as chairman of the committee on ordnance and explosives of the U.S. Naval Consulting Board. He died at Lake Hopatcong, New Jersey, on May 6, 1927.

Maxwell, William (1733?–1796), Revolutionary army officer. Born in County Tyrone, Ireland, about 1733, Maxwell came with his family to America about 1747 and settled in Sussex (now Warren) County, New Jersey. In 1754 he entered the British colonial army and the following year took part in Gen. Edward Braddock's expedition to Fort Duquesne. He was in the unsuccessful expedition against Fort Ticonderoga in 1758 under Gen. James Abercrombie, and he may have taken part in Gen. James Wolfe's capture of Quebec in September 1759.

Later, with the rank of colonel, he was stationed at Mackinac, where he remained until 1774. Returning to New Jersey in that year, he became active in the patriot cause, and in May 1775 he was elected to the provincial congress. In November he was appointed colonel of the 2nd New Jersey Battalion, and in the spring of 1776 he joined the expedition of Gen. John Sullivan to reinforce the northern army invading Canada. He was with Gen. William Thompson in the defeat at Three Rivers, June 8, and in the subsequent retreat from Canada. In October he was commissioned brigadier general of the Continental army. He conducted raids and small operations in New Jersey until mid-1777, and on September 3 attacked at Cooch's Bridge a British and Hessian force attempting to advance on Philadelphia, forcing it to retire; it is claimed that this was the first battle fought under the new American banner, the Stars and Stripes. Maxwell later took part in the battles of Brandywine, September 11, and Germantown, October 4, and after wintering at Valley Forge was at Monmouth, June 28, 1778. He remained in New Jersey with his brigade until June 1779, when he joined Sullivan's expedition against the Indians in Pennsylvania and New York. He then returned to duty in New Jersey, resigning from the army in July 1780. In 1783 he served a term in the New Jersey legislature. Maxwell died in Lansdown, New Jersey, on November 4, 1796.

May, Charles Augustus (1817–1864), army officer. Born in Washington, D.C., on August 9, 1817, May graduated from West Point in 1836 and was commissioned in the dragoons. He was immediately sent with the 2nd Dragoons to Florida, where the second Seminole War was in progress, and in that campaign he succeeded in capturing Philip, a principal Seminole chief. By 1846 he had risen to captain and on the outbreak of the Mexican War was chief of cavalry in Gen. Zachary Taylor's army. At Palo Alto, May 8, he won a brevet to major. The next day, at Resaca de la Palma, he led a detachment of dragoons in a daring dash that overran a well emplaced Mexican battery and captured its commander, Gen. La Vega, opening the way for a general American advance; for that day's actions he was brevetted lieutenant colonel. He was again brevetted to colonel following the battle of Buena Vista, February 22–23, 1847. May remained in the army until 1860, when he resigned to become vice-president of the Eighth Avenue Railroad in New York City. He died in New York City on December 24, 1864.

May, Geraldine Pratt (1895–   ), air force officer. Born on April 21, 1895, in Albany, New York, Geraldine Pratt grew up there and in Tacoma, Washington. She graduated from the University of California, Berkeley, in 1920 and for a number of years was a social worker and then an officer of the Camp

Fire Girls organization in San Francisco and Sacramento. In 1928 she married Albert E. May and for several years thereafter lived in Tulsa, Oklahoma. In July 1942, having returned to California, Mrs. May enlisted in the Women's Army Auxiliary Corps. She was in the first class to graduate from WAAC officers training school in Des Moines, Iowa, and was commissioned a second lieutenant. After several months of recruiting duty she was transferred to work with the Army Air Corps and in March 1943 became WAAC staff director for the Air Transport Command, receiving promotions to captain in April and to major in November. Personnel under her command were assigned to 41 different bases from Hawaii to India and North Africa. In May 1945 she was promoted to lieutenant colonel, and in October 1946 she was assigned to duty with the General Staff. In January 1947 she was named WAC (the name was changed in July 1943) staff director with Army Ground Forces. The signing into law of the Women's Armed Services Integration Act on June 12, 1948, established the Women in the Air Force (WAF) as a regular component of the air force, and two days later May was appointed first director of the WAF with the rank of colonel. She remained in that post until resigning in June 1951. She was succeeded as WAF director by Col. Mary J. Shelley.

Mayo, Henry Thomas (1856–1937), naval officer. Born on December 8, 1856, in Burlington, Vermont, Mayo graduated from the Naval Academy in 1876. He was commissioned an ensign in 1879, after sea duty with the Asiatic Squadron, and assigned to work with the U.S. Coast and Geodetic Survey in Puget Sound. In 1882–1885 he was aboard the *Yantic*, taking part in the Greely Relief Expedition of 1883. Promoted to lieutenant (junior grade) in 1885 and lieutenant in 1890, he was again with the Survey in 1886–1889 and 1892–1895, and in 1895–1898 was navigator of the hydrographic survey ship *Bennington,* carrying out the first such survey of Pearl Harbor. Mayo advanced to lieutenant commander in 1899 and to commander in 1905. In 1907–1908 he commanded the *Albany* and then, promoted to captain, served a year as secretary to the Lighthouse Board. In 1909–1910 he commanded the armored cruiser *California* and in 1911–1913 the Mare Island navy yard, California. Made an aide to Secretary of the Navy Josephus Daniels in April 1913, he was promoted to rear admiral in June, and he took command in December of the 4th Division, Atlantic Fleet. On April 9, 1914, a boat's crew from his flagship *Dolphin* was arrested at the wharf in Tampico, Mexico, for no apparent reason, and forced on a humiliating march through the city. Mayo promptly demanded of local authorities a public apology, disciplinary action against the officials responsible for the affront, and a 21-gun salute to the American flag.

The third demand was refused, and President Woodrow Wilson, fully backing Mayo, ordered on April 21 the seizing of the customhouse at Veracruz by Adm. Frank F. Fletcher, an action that developed into the occupation of the entire city. In June 1915 Mayo was promoted to temporary vice admiral and named commander of battleship squadron, Atlantic Fleet. In June 1916 he became commander of the Atlantic Fleet with the rank of temporary admiral, a post that constituted command of all U.S. naval forces in Atlantic and European waters and that he held through World War I until June 1919. His command was redesignated the U.S. Fleet in January 1919 and at the end of his term as commander was divided into the separate Atlantic and Pacific fleet commands. He represented the United States at the Allied naval conference in London in September 1917 and later made inspection tours on the *Pennsylvania* as the highest ranking U.S. naval officer at sea in the war. In June 1919 he reverted to permanent rank of rear admiral and was assigned to duty with the General Board. He retired in December 1920. In 1924–1928 he served as governor of the Naval Home in Philadelphia. He was advanced to admiral on the retired list in June 1930. Mayo died in Portsmouth, New Hampshire, on February 23, 1937.

Meade, George Gordon (1815–1872), army officer. Born of American parents in Cadiz, Spain, on December 31, 1815, Meade graduated from West Point in 1835, was commissioned in the artillery, and was immediately ordered to Florida for service in the Seminole War. In 1836 he resigned from the army and for six years engaged in engineering work for the Alabama, Florida & Georgia Railroad and in surveying the boundaries of Texas and Maine. In May 1842 he reentered the army as a second lieutenant in the topographical engineers. He remained in that capacity with the Maine survey work for a year and then was transferred to Philadelphia to work on lighthouse construction. After service in the Mexican War, during which he served under Gen. Zachary Taylor and saw action at Palo Alto and Resaca de la Palma and was brevetted first lieutenant for gallantry at Monterrey, September 20–24, 1846, he again engaged in engineering and survey duties in Philadelphia, Florida, and the Great Lakes region. He was promoted to first lieutenant in August 1851 and to captain in May 1856. In August 1861, soon after the beginning of the Civil War, he was appointed brigadier general of volunteers in Pennsylvania. He took part in Gen. George B. McClellan's Peninsular campaign in 1862 and was seriously wounded at Frayser's Farm, June 30. He recovered sufficiently to command his brigade at the second battle of Bull Run (Manassas), August 29–30, and a month later, at Antietam (Sharpsburg), September 17, he temporarily took command of the I Corps when Gen. Joseph Hooker

was wounded. He was promoted to major general of volunteers in November, and following Fredericksburg, December 13, he was given command of the V Corps. Later for a few days Meade commanded the Center Grand Division of the Army of the Potomac, comprising the III and VI Corps, but under Gen. Hooker he reverted to command of the V Corps in February 1863. He led it at the disastrous battle of Chancellorsville, May 2–4. On June 28, 1863, President Abraham Lincoln named Meade to succeed Hooker as commander of the Army of the Potomac. He accepted reluctantly. Three days later his army made contact with Gen. Robert E. Lee's Army of Northern Virginia at Gettysburg, and Meade displayed great tactical skill in developing a strong defensive position along Cemetery Ridge from Culp's Hill south to Little Round Top, and in repulsing furious Confederate attacks on July 2 and 3. Afterward, like his predecessors, he failed to press his advantage; nevertheless, Gettysburg proved to be a decisive battle. Meade was made brigadier general in the regular army and in January 1864 was voted the thanks of Congress. He retained command of the Army of the Potomac, but when Gen. Ulysses S. Grant was placed in command of all Union forces in March 1864 and made his headquarters with the Army of the Potomac in the field, Meade's independence was greatly reduced. He gave complete loyalty to Grant, however, and in August 1864 was promoted to major general in the regular army. He was of great service to Grant through the difficult and costly campaigns of 1864–1865—the Wilderness, Spotsylvania, Cold Harbor, and the siege of Petersburg. After the war he commanded the Division of the Atlantic and from August 1866 the Department of the East. From January 1868 to March 1869 he was commander of the Third Military District, comprising Georgia, Alabama, and Florida, in the Department of the South, and he then returned to his earlier post with the Division of the Atlantic. Meade died in Philadelphia on November 6, 1872.

Meigs, Montgomery Cunningham (1816–1892), army officer and engineer. Born in Augusta, Georgia, on May 3, 1816, Meigs entered the University of Pennsylvania in 1831 and transferred to West Point a year later, graduating in 1836. He was commissioned in the artillery but soon afterward transferred to the engineers. For 16 years he was engaged in routine work, first in the construction of Fort Mifflin on the Delaware River, later with Lt. Robert E. Lee in Mississippi River improvement at St. Louis. Promoted to first lieutenant in 1838, he was subsequently engaged in work on Fort Delaware and the Delaware Breakwater, on Fort Wayne on the Detroit River, and on Fort Montgomery on the New York–Canada border. In November 1852 he was called to Washington, D.C., to take charge of the construction of the Washington Aqueduct, a tremendous engineering task that involved the construction of the longest masonry arch in the world over Cabin John Branch. Promoted to captain in 1853, he remained with the aqueduct project until 1860, in 1853–1859 also supervising the building of the wings and dome of the U.S. Capitol and overseeing various other public works in the District. A falling-out with Secretary of War John B. Floyd led to his being sent in September 1860 to work on the building of Fort Jefferson in the Dry Tortugas Islands off the Florida coast, but he returned to Washington a few months later. In April 1861, with Lt. Col. Erasmus D. Keyes, he planned and, with Lt. David D. Porter of the navy, carried out aboard the *Powhatan* a secret relief expedition to Fort Pickens, Florida, which had been held by Lt. Adam J. Slemmer's tiny force since January. In May he was appointed colonel of the 11th Infantry and the next day promoted to brigadier general and made quartermaster general of the army. Efficient, hard-driving, and scrupulously honest, Meigs molded a large and somewhat diffuse department into a great tool of war. The Quartermaster Department had responsibility for the procurement of food, clothing, and all other equipment except ordnance; for all transportation by pack animal, road, rail, river, or sea, and the forage and fuel required; for construction and maintenance of barracks, depots, hospitals, and other installations; for inspection; and for maintaining the records and correspondence of the General Staff. Meigs saw to the maintenance of Gen. Ulysses S. Grant's bases of supply at Fredericksburg, Belle Plain, and City Point. When Gen. William T. Sherman reached the sea at Savannah, Georgia, in December 1864 a seatrain of quartermaster supply vessels was waiting offshore, and Meigs kept Sherman supplied through various ports throughout the campaign in the Carolinas, even delivering locomotives and rolling stock. Brevetted major general in July 1864, Meigs organized and commanded a division of War Department employees a few days later when the capital was threatened by Gen. Jubal A. Early. He continued as quartermaster general after the war and in addition supervised plans for the new War Department and National Museum buildings. He retired from the army in February 1882 and was later architect of the Pension Office building. Meigs died in Washington, D.C., on January 2, 1892.

Melville, George Wallace (1841–1912), naval officer, engineer, and explorer. Born on January 10, 1841, in New York City, Melville early exhibited mechanical ability and was educated at the Brooklyn Polytechnic Institute. He joined the navy as a third assistant engineer in July 1861 and served throughout the Civil War on various vessels, including the *Wachusett* under Commander Napoleon Collins. He advanced to first assistant engineer in 1865. His career

progressed routinely until 1873, when he volunteered to go to the Arctic as chief engineer of the *Tigress* on a successful mission to rescue the survivors of the *Polaris*, which had set out for the North Pole under Charles F. Hall two years earlier. In 1879 he volunteered to accompany the Arctic expedition led by Lt. George W. De Long as chief engineer aboard the *Jeannette*. They sailed through the Bering Strait but were caught in the Arctic ice pack near Herald Island and drifted west for 22 months, keeping afloat largely through Melville's efforts. After the *Jeannette* was finally crushed and sank in June 1881 near the New Siberian Islands, Melville took charge of one of three small boats, only two of which made it to the delta of the Lena River in Siberia. Many of the crew, including De Long, perished. Melville, the sole surviving boat commander, then led a 500-mile expedition in the Arctic night along the Siberian shore to recover the bodies of De Long and his boat crew as well as the ship's records. His *In the Lena Delta*, 1884, was an account of the hardships suffered on the journey. Melville, promoted to chief engineer in 1881, returned to the Arctic once again in 1884 aboard the *Thetis* under Commander Winfield S. Schley, who rescued 7 of the 25 members of the A. W. Greely expedition of 1881. Melville's sustained bravery and technical skill received the recognition of Congress, and in August 1887 he was selected over other ranking officers to become chief of the Bureau of Steam Engineering with the rank of commodore. Under his direction the bureau led the way in the conversion of the navy to more modern equipment. He supervised the design of the machinery of 120 navy ships; three of them for which he was immediately responsible, the *San Francisco*, *Columbia*, and *Minneapolis*, were for a time the world's fastest warships. He introduced the water-tube boiler and the triple-screw system and significantly increased efficiency by setting the boilers vertically. He also made an important contribution to the administrative reforms that streamlined the entire navy as well as the naval engineering department, being particularly influential in the decision to integrate the engineer corps into the line of the navy in 1899. Melville was promoted to rear admiral in March 1899 and retired in January 1903. He died in Philadelphia on March 17, 1912.

Menoher, Charles Thomas (1862–1930), army officer. Born in Johnstown, Pennsylvania, on March 20, 1862, Menoher graduated from West Point in 1886 and was commissioned in the artillery. Promoted to first lieutenant in December 1892, he graduated from the Artillery School, Fort Monroe, Virginia, in 1894 and during the Spanish–American War served in Cuba. He subsequently served three tours of duty in the Philippines. He was promoted to captain in February 1901. During 1903–1907 he was a member of the original General Staff, also graduating from the Army War College in the latter year and receiving promotion to major in January, and he then returned to Cuba as provost marshal of the U.S. pacification forces stationed there. He advanced to lieutenant colonel in May 1911. In July 1916 he was promoted to colonel in command of the 5th Field Artillery. Promoted to temporary brigadier general in August 1917, he was given command of the School of Instruction for Field Artillery of the American Expeditionary Forces at Saumur, France, in September. In November he was promoted to temporary major general, and in December he took command of the 42nd (Rainbow) Division, which participated in action in the Lunéville and Baccarat sectors, and in the Champagne–Marne, St. Mihiel, and Meuse–Argonne operations. Early in November 1918 Menoher was promoted to permanent rank of brigadier general in recognition of his services. On November 10, the day before the Armistice, the 42nd reached the heights above Sedan, the most advanced position attained by U.S. troops, and on the same day Menoher was raised to command of the VI Corps (he was succeeded in the 42nd by Gen. Douglas MacArthur). In December he returned to the United States, and in January 1919 he was named director of the Air Service, which in June 1920 was reorganized by consolidation of the thitherto divided supply and operations functions of the fledgling air arm, separated from the Signal Corps, and made a part of the line of the army. Largely because of friction with his assistant, Col. William Mitchell, he was relieved of the post at his own request in October 1921 (to be succeeded by Gen. Mason M. Patrick). He had been promoted to major general in March 1921. During 1922–1924 he commanded the Hawaiian Division, in 1924–1925 the Department of Hawaii, and in 1925–1926 the IX Corps area at San Francisco. Menoher retired in March 1926 and died in Washington, D.C., on August 11, 1930.

Mercer, Hugh (1725?–1777), Revolutionary army officer. Born about 1725 (perhaps as early as 1720) in Aberdeenshire, Scotland, Mercer studied medicine at the University of Aberdeen, graduating in 1744. He became a surgeon's mate in the army of Prince Charles Edward, the Young Pretender, but soon after the battle of Culloden (April 16, 1746), in which he took part, he left Scotland for America, arriving at Philadelphia and settling near the site of present-day Mercersburg, Pennsylvania. He practised medicine for several years but in 1755 took a captain's commission in the Pennsylvania Regiment of the British provincial army and took part in Gen. Edward Braddock's disastrous expedition of that year. He took part in Col. John Armstrong's attack on the Delaware Indian village, Kittanning, in September 1756 and was a lieutenant colonel in the expedition under Gen. John Forbes against Fort Duquesne

in 1758. He was then placed in command of the new Fort Pitt, receiving promotion to colonel in April 1759. Some time later he left the army and settled in Fredericksburg, Virginia, where he resumed his medical practice. He was an ardent patriot in the period before the Revolution and in September 1775 was elected colonel in command of the minutemen of four counties. In January 1776 he took command of the 3rd Virginia Regiment, and in June he was commissioned brigadier general in the Continental army. Gen. George Washington put Mercer in command of the "Flying Camp," a mobile militia force intended as a reserve but also used during the remainder of 1776 to harry British forces and protect northern New Jersey. He rejoined the main American army during the retreat across New Jersey in the autumn and took part in (and may have suggested) the recrossing of the Delaware and the attack on Trenton on December 26. Mercer may also have suggested the stroke by which Washington escaped Gen. Charles Cornwallis early on January 3, leaving his campfires burning and marching silently around the British. As the Continental army neared Princeton, Mercer led his brigade in advance and attempted to seize a bridge over Stony Brook. He encountered a British force marching to reinforce Cornwallis, and in the ensuing fight, in which his brigade was forced back, he was felled by a blow to the head and bayoneted several times. After the battle he was carried to a nearby farmhouse, where he died on January 12, 1777.

Merriam, Henry Clay (1837–1912), army officer. Born in Houlton, Maine, on November 13, 1837, Merriam entered Colby College in 1860 and was granted a degree in 1864 despite having left in 1862 to accept a commission as captain in the 20th Maine Volunteers. At Antietam (Sharpsburg), September 17, 1862, he won a brevet to lieutenant colonel, and he was at Fredericksburg, December 13. Early in 1863 he was sent to Louisiana to organize a new black regiment, and as commander of the 80th Colored Infantry (formerly the 1st Louisiana Native Guard), the first regiment of black soldiers in the army, he distinguished himself in the assault on Port Hudson on May 27. Promoted to lieutenant colonel, he again led the 80th in an assault on Fort Blakely at Mobile, Alabama, on April 9, 1865, capturing the fort and 6000 prisoners and earning a Medal of Honor and brevet promotion to colonel. Merriam was mustered out of the army in October 1865 but reentered in July 1866 as major of the 38th Infantry. He took part in various Indian campaigns and in 1873 was given command of Fort McIntosh, Texas. On April 10, 1876, when revolutionary turmoil in Mexico spilled over the border, he fired upon Mexican federal troops, and in August he led a party across the border to rescue an American citizen held by revolutionists.

Promoted to lieutenant colonel of the 2nd Infantry in June 1876, he took part in the campaign against the Nez Percé under Chief Joseph the next year. He became colonel in command of the 7th Infantry in July 1885, also commanding Fort Laramie, Wyoming Territory, until 1889. In 1890–1891 he led the 7th in the final Sioux campaign and disarmed some 300 warriors following the murder of Sitting Bull. In June 1897 he was promoted to brigadier general in command of the Department of the Columbia. A few months later he organized a midwinter relief expedition to rescue stranded miners in Alaska. In May 1898 he was appointed major general of volunteers; he took command of the entire Pacific coastal region and Hawaii and was given the task of organizing, training, equipping, and forwarding the troops to be employed in the Philippines. In January 1899 he was transferred to command of the Department of Colorado, reverting to regular rank in February. He was responsible for using troops to suppress the labor riots in Coeur d'Alene, Idaho, in that year. Merriam retired in November 1901 and was advanced to major general on the retired list in February 1903. He died in Portland, Maine, on November 18, 1912.

Merrill, Frank Dow (1903–1955), army officer. Born on December 4, 1903, in Hopkinton, Massachusetts, Merrill enlisted in the army in June 1922, and after three years of service in Panama he was accepted by West Point. On graduating in 1929 he was commissioned in the cavalry, and between routine assignments over the next several years he attended the Ordnance School in Watertown, Massachusetts, 1931–1932, and the Cavalry School, Fort Riley, Kansas, 1934–1935, receiving promotion to first lieutenant in November 1934. He was an instructor at the Cavalry School until 1938, when he was assigned to the U.S. embassy in Tokyo. His study while there of Japanese language and thought and military organization were to prove extremely useful. Promoted to captain in June 1939 and to temporary major in October 1941, he was named intelligence officer on the staff of Gen. Douglas MacArthur in Manila in November 1941. He was on a mission in Rangoon, Burma, at the time of the Japanese attack on Pearl Harbor and was subsequently reassigned as aide to Gen. Joseph W. Stilwell. He remained with Stilwell in the retreat into India early in 1942 and, promoted to temporary lieutenant colonel in May, began planning for the recapture of Burma. He advanced to temporary colonel early in 1943, and in October of that year began training a regiment-sized volunteer force in jungle warfare techniques. He was promoted to temporary brigadier general in November. In February 1944 "Merrill's Marauders," as the unit was known, undertook their first field action as part of a coordinated U.S.-Chinese offensive in Burma, with the construction of the Ledo Road follow-

ing the advance. Marching out of Ledo in northeastern India and circling 100 miles around the Japanese stronghold of Maingkwan, Burma, the Marauders proceeded to cut supply lines, defeat Japanese forces in several scattered engagements (capturing part of a division), and make their way over seemingly impassable terrain to the main Japanese base at Myitkyina. There the Marauders infiltrated, captured the airfield in May, and joined with Stilwell's Chinese troops to take the town on August 4. Merrill, suffering from heart trouble and malaria, was twice hospitalized during the campaign and after the fall of Myitkyina was transferred to duty as head of the liaison group of the Allied Southwest Asia Command. The Marauders were disbanded a short time later. Promoted to temporary major general in September, he became chief of staff of the Tenth Army (under Gen. Simon B. Buckner, Jr., and later Stilwell) in December, retaining that post until the Tenth was inactivated in October 1945. In 1946–1947 he was chief of staff of the Sixth Army at San Francisco. In February 1947 he was named deputy chief of the U.S. Advisory Military Mission to the Philippines. Shortly after his retirement in July 1948 Merrill was appointed commissioner of public works and highways for the state of New Hampshire. He died in Fernandina Beach, Florida, on December 11, 1955.

Merritt, Wesley (1834–1910), army officer. Born on June 16, 1834, in New York City, Merritt grew up there and, from 1841, in Illinois. He graduated from West Point in 1860, was commissioned in the dragoons, and in May 1861, promoted to first lieutenant, was made aide to Gen. Philip St. G. Cooke. He advanced to captain in April 1862. After taking part in Gen. George Stoneman's cavalry raid toward Richmond in April–May 1863 he was appointed brigadier general of volunteers in June, and for actions while commanding the reserve cavalry at Gettysburg, July 1–3, he was brevetted major of regulars. Assigned to Gen. Philip H. Sheridan's cavalry, at Yellow Tavern, May 11, 1864, he won brevet promotion to lieutenant colonel of regulars; after Hawes's Shop, May 28, he was brevetted colonel of regulars; and following Winchester, September 19, he was brevetted major general of volunteers. In March 1865 he was further brevetted brigadier and major general of regulars and in April promoted to major general of volunteers. After the war he served mainly in the West, becoming lieutenant colonel of the 9th Cavalry in July 1866 and colonel of the 5th Cavalry in 1876. On July 17, 1876, he intercepted a band of Cheyenne attempting to flee from the Red Cloud Agency at War Bonnet Creek (now Hat Creek, near the site of present-day Montrose, Nebraska) and turned them back in a fight that began with the famous duel between Yellow Hand and scout William F. Cody. From September 1882 to July 1887 he was superintendent of West

Point, receiving promotion to brigadier general in April 1887. Thereafter, between 1887 and 1897, he commanded the Department of the Missouri, the Department of Dakota, and the Department of Missouri again, receiving promotion to major general in April 1895. In 1897 he was put in command of the Department of the East. On the outbreak of the Spanish–American War he was named in May 1898 to command the forces to be sent to the Philippines. He sailed from San Francisco in June, arrived at Cavite, Manila Bay, in July with some 15,000 troops constituting the VIII Corps, and immediately took charge of the siege of Manila. The Spanish commander, well aware of the hopelessness of his situation, was nonetheless required by his orders to make a token resistance. Consequently, on receiving a negative response to a formal demand for surrender, Merritt launched a careful assault on the city on August 13. The movement was complicated by the necessity of passing through the lines of Philippine insurgents under Emilio Aguinaldo, who would have preferred to storm Spanish positions and take the city themselves. With fire support from Adm. George Dewey's fleet in the bay, the VIII Corps managed to occupy Manila with only 122 casualties. Merritt remained as military governor for only two weeks before being ordered to Paris to assist in the negotiation of the peace treaty with Spain. In December he resumed command of the Department of the East. He retired in June 1900 and died at Natural Bridge, Virginia, on December 3, 1910.

Mervine, William (1791–1868), naval officer. Born in Philadelphia on March 14, 1791, Mervine entered the navy as a midshipman in January 1809. He served on Lake Erie and Lake Champlain in the War of 1812 and was promoted to lieutenant in February 1815. Over the next several decades he saw routine service in the West India and Mediterranean squadrons and on duty suppressing the slave trade in African waters; promoted to commander in June 1834, he commanded the *Natchez* in the West Indies in 1836–1837. He was promoted to captain in September 1841 and commanded the *Cyane* in 1845–1846 and the *Savannah,* flagship of Commodore John D. Sloat of the Pacific Squadron, in 1846–1847. On July 7, 1846, on orders from Sloat, he landed with a party of 250 sailors and marines and took possession of Monterey, California. In October he attempted to take Los Angeles in a similar manner but was forced to retire by stout Mexican resistance. Mervine commanded the Pacific Squadron in 1855–1857. He had been on waiting orders for some time when he was assigned in May 1861 to take command of the newly organized Gulf Blockading Squadron. From his flagship *Colorado* he established an effective blockade of ports from Key West to Galveston, but in September, in large part because of age, he was relieved and in

December he was placed on the retired list. He subsequently performed special duty in Washington, D.C., and Philadelphia, and for a time was president of the retiring board. He was raised on the retired list to commodore in July 1862 and rear admiral in July 1866. Mervine died in Utica, New York, on September 15, 1868.

Metacomet *see* Philip

Mifflin, Thomas (1744–1800), Revolutionary army officer and public official. Born on January 10, 1744, in Philadelphia, Mifflin attended Quaker schools and graduated from the College of Philadelphia (subsequently the University of Pennsylvania) at the age of sixteen. When he came of age he formed a partnership with his brother and soon was established as a prominent merchant in Philadelphia. His identification with the patriot cause dated from his opposition to the Stamp Act in 1765, and thereafter his political fortunes rode the rising tide of sentiment for independence. While in the Pennsylvania assembly, 1772–1775, he championed a colonial congress and was elected to the first and second Continental Congresses. In May 1775 he received a major's commission in the Continental army, and in June he became aide-de-camp to Gen. George Washington, but he saw limited front-line duty after his appointment as quartermaster general of the army in August 1775. He rose in rank steadily, becoming colonel in December, brigadier general in May 1776, and major general in February 1777; but he was unhappy with his role and proved increasingly lax in carrying out his responsibilities, eventually pleading ill health and resigning the post of quartermaster general in October 1777, although he continued to carry out, in his way, the functions of the office until the appointment of Gen. Nathanael Greene in March 1778. Mifflin's part in the cabal against Gen. George Washington that bears Thomas Conway's name was brief but central, hinging on his membership, from November 1777, on the Board of War. Like Gen. Horatio Gates, whom he successfully promoted as president of the Board of War, Mifflin doubtless expected his own advancement through the apparent plan to make Gates commander in chief. On the exposure of the plot he denied any connection with it. In April 1778 he left the Board of War to return to the army. Accused of embezzlement while serving as quartermaster general, he blamed his subordinates; his resignation from the army, offered in August 1778, was accepted the following February without investigation of his handling of funds. He remained influential in Pennsylvania politics and in 1782 was elected to Congress under the Articles of Confederation, serving as its president from November 1783 to June 1784. He was a member of the Constitutional Convention of 1787, speaker of the Pennsylvania general assembly in 1785–1788, president of the state supreme executive council in 1788–1790, chairman of the state constitutional convention in 1789–1790, and the overwhelming choice, over Arthur St. Clair, for governor under Pennsylvania's new constitution in 1790. He served three successive terms, until 1799, having in that time to deal with the Whisky Rebellion (1794). He became progressively irresponsible during his last term. Incurably extravagant, he was forced by his creditors to flee Philadelphia in 1799. He died a pauper at Lancaster, Pennsylvania, on January 20, 1800, and his funeral was paid for by the state.

Miles, Nelson Appleton (1839–1925), army officer. Born on August 8, 1839, near Westminster, Massachusetts, Miles was commissioned captain in the 22nd Massachusetts Regiment at the outbreak of the Civil War. His baptism of fire came while serving on Gen. Oliver O. Howard's staff at Fair Oaks (Seven Pines), May 31, 1862, after which his bravery earned him a promotion to lieutenant colonel. He was promoted to colonel after assuming command of his regiment in the midst of the battle of Antietam (Sharpsburg), September 17, 1862. He distinguished himself and was seriously wounded at Fredericksburg, December 13, 1862, and again at Chancellorsville, May 2–4, 1863. For his actions at the latter he won, as of March 1867, brevet to brigadier general and later, in 1892, the Medal of Honor. He was present at almost every major engagement of the Army of the Potomac; he was appointed brigadier general of volunteers in May 1864 and commanded a division in the final campaign at Petersburg. In October 1865, at the age of twenty-six, he was named major general of volunteers in command of the II Corps. As commandant at Fort Monroe, Virginia, after the Confederate surrender, he became custodian of Jefferson Davis, and for keeping Davis shackled in his cell he was the target of severe public criticism, even in the North. In July 1866 he was made a colonel in the regular army and, in March 1869, commander of the 5th Infantry. His subsequent service on the Western frontier was dedicated and courageous during recurring hostilities with the Indians. He achieved victories against the Cheyenne, Comanche, Kiowa, and Arapaho on the Staked Plains of Texas in 1874–1875, notably the victory of Col. Ranald S. Mackenzie at Palo Duro Canyon, September 24, 1874, and later was instrumental in driving the Sioux under Sitting Bull into Canada and pacifying those under Crazy Horse. He captured Chief Joseph in 1877 after the Nez Percés' incredible march toward sanctuary in Canada, and the following year he pacified the Bannocks under Chief Elk Horn near Yellowstone. Promoted to brigadier general in December 1880, Miles commanded the Department of the Columbia until 1885 and the Department of

the Missouri in 1885–1886, and in April 1886 he succeeded Gen. George Crook as commander of the Department of Arizona, where he succeeded in September in finally capturing the elusive Apache leader Geronimo. He commanded the Division of the Pacific at San Francisco in 1888–1890, receiving promotion to major general in April 1890. In the last uprising of the Sioux in South Dakota in late 1890, during which Sitting Bull was killed, Miles restored U.S. control over the Indians; but his reputation was permanently tarnished by the massacre of some 200 Sioux, including women and children, by Col. James W. Forsyth's men of the 7th Cavalry at Wounded Knee, South Dakota, on December 29, 1890. In 1894, while commanding the Department of the Missouri, he was responsible for federal troops employed in suppressing the Pullman strike disorders in Chicago. Miles was placed in command of the Department of the East, with headquarters at Governors Island, New York, in 1894, and on the retirement of Gen. John M. Schofield he became on October 5, 1895, the army's commander in chief. His role during the Spanish–American War was mostly administrative, although he did conduct an expedition to occupy Puerto Rico, landing on July 25, 1898, and campaigning until August 13. In February 1901 he was promoted to lieutenant general. Late in that year he was reprimanded for having commented publicly on Adm. George Dewey's report on charges against Adm. Winfield S. Schley. In 1902, on his return from an inspection tour of the Philippines, he aroused a controversy with his criticisms of the conduct of certain U.S. officers there. Miles retired from the army in August 1903. He spent his remaining years in Washington, D.C., where he died on May 15, 1925. He published two volumes of autobiography, *Personal Recollections and Observations of General Nelson A. Miles*, 1896, and *Serving the Republic*, 1911.

Miller, James (1776–1851), army officer and public official. Born on April 25, 1776, in Peterborough, New Hampshire, Miller became a lawyer and practiced until 1808, when, apparently having gained experience in the militia, he entered the army as major of the 4th Infantry. He was promoted to lieutenant colonel in 1810. Shortly after the outbreak of the War of 1812 he was stationed in the Northwest, and on August 9, 1812, he led 600 men of the 4th in the victorious battle at Maguaga, near the site of present-day Trenton, Michigan, against a larger mixed force of British regulars and Indians under Tecumseh. In spite of that victory Miller's attempt to restore communication to Gen. William Hull's army in Canada failed. He was brevetted colonel following Maguaga. He was present at the capture of Fort George by Gen. Henry Dearborn's army on May 27, 1813, and by the following year was colonel in command of the 21st Infantry. He distinguished himself at Chippewa, July 5, 1814, and became a national hero at Lundy's Lane, July 25. At the height of the battle, with the nearly equal opposing forces fighting fiercely in the dark, Miller was asked by Gen. Winfield Scott if he thought he could capture a certain British battery. Miller's reply, "I'll try, sir!" was to remain with him for the rest of his life and become thereafter one of the army's best known slogans. Miller mounted a charge, captured the battery, and thereby helped swing the tide of battle. He was brevetted brigadier general in reward. In 1819 he was appointed by President James Monroe the first governor of the Territory of Arkansas, created in March of that year. He arrived in the territory early in 1820 and oversaw the removal of the capital to Little Rock in October. Miller resigned the post in 1825. He served as collector of the port of Salem, Massachusetts, from 1825 to 1849. He died in Temple, New Hampshire, on July 7, 1851.

Milner, Moses Embree (1829–1876), "California Joe," scout. Born on May 8, 1829, near Stanford, Kentucky, Milner joined the migration to California when he was 20 and presumably acquired his nickname sometime thereafter. In the Civil War he served in Col. Hiram Berdan's 1st Sharpshooters with the Army of the Potomac. Later he made his way west again and served in various Indian campaigns, building a reputation as a skilled scout, a brave soldier, and a colorful frontiersman such as legends are built on. Loud, profane, not infrequently drunk, with an idiosyncratic approach to dress and a fondness for mules, California Joe became a notable character of the Plains. He began a long and close association with Lt. Col. George A. Custer in October 1868, when Custer took command of the 7th Cavalry. His tenure as chief of scouts for the 7th was, however, extremely brief, owing to the abandon with which he celebrated the appointment. After the massacre of Black Kettle's Cheyenne and Arapaho camp on the Washita River on November 27, California Joe and one companion crossed the hundred dangerous miles back to Camp Supply on the Canadian River with the news in 18 hours, winning the admiration of Gen. Philip H. Sheridan. In 1875 he was a guide to a party under Lt. Col. R. I. Dodge in the Black Hills. Discharged from the service in that year, he took up prospecting in the newly opened Black Hills goldfield. On hearing of Custer's death at Little Bighorn the next summer he hurried to Fort Robinson, Nebraska, and enlisted as a scout with the 5th Cavalry. On October 29, 1876, he was shot in the back by a civilian with whom he had quarreled.

Mitchel, Ormsby MacKnight (1809–1862), astronomer and army officer. Born in Morganfield, Kentucky, on July 28, 1809, Mitchel grew up in Lebanon, Ohio. He graduated from West Point in 1829,

was commissioned in the artillery, and was immediately appointed assistant professor of mathematics at the academy. In September 1832, after a few months' duty at Fort Marion, Florida, he resigned from the army. Settling in Cincinnati, he entered the practice of law, but in 1836 he accepted the post of professor of mathematics, philosophy, and astronomy at Cincinnati College (now the University of Cincinnati), where he remained until 1844. During 1836–1837 he was also chief engineer of the Little Miami Railroad. Mitchel's teaching of astronomy led him to offer public lectures on that topic; he proved to have a gift for dramatic exposition, and his lectures became extremely popular. By 1842 public enthusiasm had led to the founding of the Cincinnati Astronomical Society and a public fund was begun to build an observatory. Construction began late in 1843 and the Cincinnati Observatory was opened in 1845 with Mitchel as director. There he conducted research on double stars (he discovered the small companion of Antares) and invented a number of telescopic setting, measuring, and recording devices. The influence of his public lectures, which he delivered in several cities, had at the same time lent impetus to the founding of a number of other observatories elsewhere in the country, notably those of Harvard and the navy. During 1846–1848 he published the *Sidereal Messenger*, the first magazine of popular astronomy, and among his other published works were *The Planetary and Stellar Worlds*, 1848, *The Orbs of Heaven*, 1851, and *Popular Astronomy*, 1860. He was also chief engineer of the Ohio and Mississippi Railroad in 1848–1849 and 1852–1853. In 1859 he accepted the directorship of the Dudley Observatory in Albany, New York. In August 1861 he was appointed brigadier general of volunteers and put in command of the Department of the Ohio. He later came under the command of Gen. Don Carlos Buell and served with the Army of the Ohio in the field in Tennessee, northern Alabama, and Kentucky in 1861–1862. In the spring of 1862 he conducted a daring raid in advance of Buell, reaching and capturing Huntsville, Alabama, on April 11 and securing the Memphis and Charleston Railroad that far. In April he approved the plan of James J. Andrews to destroy the Western and Atlantic Railroad in Georgia. Promoted to major general of volunteers, he asked to be relieved of command in the summer, owing in part to friction with Buell. In September he was named commander of the Department of the South and the X Corps at Hilton Head, South Carolina. He had barely assumed the post when he fell ill and died on October 30, 1862, in Beaufort, South Carolina.

Mitchell, William (1879–1936), army officer and aviator. Born of American parents in Nice, France, on December 29, 1879, Billy Mitchell, as he was called throughout his life, grew up in Milwaukee. He was educated at Racine College and at Columbian (now George Washington) University; he left Columbian in 1898 before graduating to enlist as a private in the 1st Wisconsin Infantry for service in the Spanish–American War. He served in Cuba and the Philippines, advancing to first lieutenant of volunteers, and in 1901 was commissioned a first lieutenant in the regular army and attached to the Signal Corps. He served in various duties, was promoted to captain in 1903, attended the School of the Line and the Staff College, Fort Leavenworth, Kansas, in 1907–1909, and after duty on the Mexican border was attached in 1912 to the General Staff. In 1915 he was assigned to the aviation section of the Signal Corps; he learned to fly the following year, when he was also promoted to major, and began his twenty-years' advocacy of the use of military air power. He was already in Europe as an observer when the United States entered World War I, and as the war progressed he advanced rapidly in rank and responsibility as he proved a highly effective air commander. In June 1917 he was named air officer of the American Expeditionary Forces, with the rank of lieutenant colonel; by May 1918 he was a colonel and air officer of I Corps, a combat post more to his liking. He was the first American airman to fly over enemy lines, and throughout the war he was regularly in the air. In September 1918 he successfully attempted a mass bombing attack with nearly 1500 planes as part of the attack on the St. Mihiel salient, and on October 9, as commander of the combined air service of the army group engaged in the Meuse–Argonne offensive, he led a large bombing force in a behind-the-lines air strike. In that month he was promoted to temporary brigadier general. His plans for strategic bombing of the German homeland and for massive parachute invasions were cut short by the armistice, and he returned home to become in March 1919 assistant chief of the Air Service under Gen. Charles T. Menoher. He outspokenly advocated the creation of a separate air force and continued working on improvements in aircraft and their use. He claimed that the airplane had rendered the battleship obsolete and, over the vociferous protests of the Navy Department, carried his point in 1921 and 1923 by sinking several captured and overage battleships from the air. He was persistently critical of the low state of preparedness of the tiny Air Service and of the poor quality of its equipment; but his harrying of his superior (Gen. Mason M. Patrick after October 1921) and of upper military echelons won him only a transfer to the minor post of air officer of the VIII Corps area at San Antonio, Texas, and reversion to the rank of colonel in April 1925. He continued, however, to use the press to fight his case, and when, in September 1925, the navy's dirigible Shenandoah was lost in a storm, he made a statement to the press charging "incompetency, criminal negligence, and almost treasonable

administration of the national defense by the War and Navy Departments." He was, as he expected, immediately court-martialed and, after he had made the trial a platform for his views, was convicted in December of insubordination and sentenced to five years' suspension from rank and pay. On February 1, 1926, he resigned from the army and retired to a farm near Middleburg, Virginia. He continued to promote air power and to warn against the danger of being outstripped by other nations, particularly Japan. He hypothesized a possible attack by Japanese aircraft launched from great carrier ships and directed at the Hawaiian Islands. He died in New York City on February 19, 1936. Mitchell's plea for an independent air force was met to a degree in the creation of GHQ Air Force in March 1935. Subsequent events, including the Japanese air attack on Pearl Harbor in December 1941, proved the validity of many of his prophesies, and many of his ideas were adopted by the Army Air Forces in World War II. The utter decisiveness that he claimed for air power never materialized, however. In 1946 Congress authorized a special medal in his honor that was presented to his son two years later by Gen. Carl Spaatz, chief of staff of the newly established independent air force. Among Mitchell's published works were Our Air Force, the Keystone of National Defense, 1921; Winged Defense, 1925; and Skyways, a Book on Modern Aeronautics, 1930.

Mitscher, Marc Andrew (1887–1947), naval officer. Born on January 26, 1887, in Hillsboro, Wisconsin, Mitscher grew up in Oklahoma City and in Washington, D.C. He graduated from the Naval Academy in 1910 and for five years served aboard the Colorado, the South Dakota, the California, and other vessels, being commissioned ensign in 1912. In 1915, promoted to lieutenant (junior grade), he entered flight training at Pensacola Naval Air Station, Florida, earning his pilot's wings in June 1916, and during World War I he commanded naval air stations on Long Island and at Miami, Florida. In May 1919 he was, with Lt. Patrick N. L. Bellinger, pilot of the NC-1, one of three seaplanes that attempted to fly the Atlantic; he was forced down in a fog near the Azores, but the NC-4, under Lt. Cmdr. Albert C. Read, reached Lisbon. After a period aboard the Aroostook, Pacific Fleet flagship, he commanded in 1920–1921 the air detachment at the San Diego base, receiving promotion to lieutenant commander in 1921. From 1922 to 1925 he commanded the naval air station at Anacostia, D.C.; after periods on the Langley and the Saratoga, the latter the navy's first aircraft carrier, he was attached in 1930–1933 to the Bureau of Aeronautics. He was promoted to commander in October 1930. Various assignments followed, and in 1937 he was given command of the Wright, receiving promotion to captain in 1938. After a time in command of Patrol Wing 1 he was named assistant chief of the Bureau of Aeronautics in 1939. In October 1941 he commissioned and took command of the carrier *Hornet*, becoming rear admiral in December. In April 1942 the *Hornet* was base—referred to publicly as "Shangri-La"—for Col. James H. Doolittle's daring bombing raid on Tokyo. On June 3–6 the *Hornet* was in the battle of Midway, and in July Mitscher left it to take command of Patrol Wing 2. In April 1943 he became air commander on Guadalcanal, directing naval, army, marine, and New Zealand air forces in the battle for the Solomons. In January 1944 he returned to sea as commander of the fast carrier force, Central Pacific area, with which he took part in operations against the Marshall Islands, Truk, and Tinian and Saipan in the Marianas. In March he was promoted to vice admiral. His task force, numbered alternately 58 and 38, depending as it was assigned to Adm. Raymond A. Spruance's Fifth Fleet or Adm. William F. Halsey's Third Fleet, evolved into an enormously powerful weapon, self-supporting, very fast, and capable of launching an overwhelming air attack. In the battle of the Philippine Sea, June 19–21, Mitscher's forces shot down on the first day alone nearly 400 Japanese planes while losing 16 in action that came to be called the "Marianas turkey-shoot." In August–September Task Force 58 supported amphibious operations in the Bonins, on Palau, and on Mindanao in the Philippines and struck at the Ryukyu Islands. During October 24–26 he took part in the battle of Leyte Gulf, cooperating with Adm. Thomas C. Kinkaid's Seventh Fleet. From January to May 1945 Mitscher's forces took part in supporting operations against Iwo Jima and Okinawa and launched attacks on the Japanese homeland. In July he was named deputy chief of naval operations for air. In March 1946 he was promoted to admiral and given command of the Eighth Fleet, and in September he advanced to command of the Atlantic Fleet. Mitscher died in Norfolk, Virginia, on February 3, 1947.

Moffett, William Adger (1869–1933), naval officer. Born on October 31, 1869, in Charleston, South Carolina, Moffett graduated from the Naval Academy in 1890. He served on various vessels, including the *Charleston* in Commodore George Dewey's fleet at the battle of Manila in May 1898, and by 1905 had risen to lieutenant commander. Promoted to commander in 1911, he took command of the *Chester* in late 1913; he was aboard it in Adm. Henry T. Mayo's division when the Tampico incident occurred on April 9, 1914, and he took part in the occupation of Veracruz that followed on April 21–22, winning the Medal of Honor for his daring unguided night entry into the inner harbor to land a force of marines and seamen. From 1914 to 1918 he commanded the Great Lakes Naval Training Station and the 9th, 10th and 11th naval districts, receiving promotion to captain in

August 1916. During 1918–1921 he commanded the *Mississippi*, and in March 1921 he was appointed director of naval aviation, in July becoming chief of the new Bureau of Aeronautics with temporary rank of rear admiral (made permanent in 1923). Too old for pilot training, he had qualified in June 1921 as an aerial observer, and the creation of the Bureau of Aeronautics owed much to his influence. He organized the navy's aviation program, exerted his influence for expansion and experimentation, oversaw the selection of sites for and building of naval air stations, and accomplished the installation of aircraft launching catapults on all battleships and cruisers of the fleet. He was particularly enthusiastic about the use of dirigibles, both in naval operations and more generally, and secured for the navy the airships *Los Angeles*, *Akron*, and *Macon*. He was reappointed to head the Bureau in 1925 and again in 1929. Moffett died on April 4, 1933, in the crash of the *Akron* in a storm off the New Jersey coast.

Montgomery, Richard (1738–1775), Revolutionary army officer. Born in Swords, County Dublin, Ireland, on December 2, 1738, Montgomery, son of a member of Parliament, entered the British army in September 1756 as ensign in the 17th Regiment of Foot. The next year he went with the regiment to Nova Scotia and in July 1758 took part in Gen. Jeffrey Amherst's capture of the French fortress at Louisbourg, receiving about that time promotion to second lieutenant. He was again under Amherst in the Lake Champlain campaign of 1759, and in 1760 he was present at Gen. James Wolfe's capture of Montreal. He later served in the West Indian campaigns that resulted in the capture of Martinique and Havana, and in May 1762 he was promoted to captain. After two years in New York he returned in 1765 to England, where he became an intimate of such Parliamentary liberals as Edmund Burke and Charles James Fox. In April 1772 he sold his commission and early the next year arrived in New York, where he bought a farm. In May 1775, already recognized as a strong supporter of the colonial cause, he was elected to the first New York provincial congress, and in June he was commissioned a brigadier general in the Continental army, the second (and the only non-New Englander) among the eight men of that rank. Named as second-in-command of an expedition against Montreal to be led by Gen. Philip Schuyler, he succeeded to command when Schuyler fell ill. In September Montgomery set out from Fort Ticonderoga with about 2000 men, marching up Lake Champlain and the Richelieu River. On September 17 he commenced a siege of the heavily fortified St. Johns, held by some 650 British regulars. The capture of nearby Fort Chambly on October 18 yielded new supplies and ammunition, and St. Johns fell finally on November 2, Montgomery thus capturing the first British colors of the war, those of the 7th Fusiliers. He then marched on poorly defended Montreal, which was abandoned by Gov. Guy Carleton and occupied by the Americans on November 13. Through illness and battle his army had by that time dwindled to only some 300. At Point aux Trembles, on the St. Lawrence just above Quebec, he made a rendezvous on December 2 with Col. Benedict Arnold's force of fewer than 700 who had made their way up the enormously difficult Kennebec route. Together they invested the city of Quebec. With insufficient provisions for a winter siege, they decided to assault the city. Early in the morning of December 31, in a blinding snowstorm, they attacked; Montgomery was killed in the battle, Arnold was wounded, and Quebec easily repelled the discouraged Americans. Congress had promoted Montgomery to major general early in December.

Moore, Edwin Ward (1810–1865), Texas naval officer. Born in Alexandria, Virginia, in June 1810, Moore entered the navy as a midshipman in January 1825. He served on the *Hornet, Fairfield,* and other vessels in the West Indian and Mediterranean squadrons and in March 1835 was promoted to lieutenant. He resigned from the navy in July 1839 to accept command of the Texas navy, recently established by Mirabeau B. Lamar, president of the republic. He was not commissioned officially until July 1842, when he was given the rank of "post captain commanding," but he was generally addressed as "commodore." His fleet consisted of the flagship *Austin,* 22 guns, the steamer *Zavala,* 11 guns, and five smaller vessels. In 1840–1841 he cruised the Gulf of Mexico, and on the failure of James Treat's negotiations with Mexico for recognition of Texas independence and the Rio Grande border he began actions against Mexican commercial shipping. He formed a working alliance with authorities in the rebel state of Yucatán and captured the town of Tabasco, exacting a heavy ransom. During subsequent cruises he also charted the Texas coast. During 1842 he was ready to mount a blockade of Mexican ports, but the changing political climate stayed Samuel Houston, then president, from issuing the order. By early 1843 Houston had begun to arrange the disbanding of the navy and the sale of the ships, but in April Moore sailed from New Orleans and, in accordance with an agreement he had reached privately with the Yucatán rebels, attacked the Mexican blockading squadron at Yucatán on April 30 and again on May 16, inflicting heavy damage both times. Houston declared Moore guilty of disobedience and mutiny, but after putting his fleet in at Galveston Moore submitted to examination by the Texas legislature and to court-martial and was exonerated of all but a few minor charges. Later in the year he published *To the People of Texas,* a history and defense of his actions. Moore won a sizable claim

from the Texas legislature for pay and expenses, and in 1857, having lost a suit with fellow veterans of the Texas navy for reinstatement in the U.S. navy, he was awarded five years' pay by way of settlement. He passed his last years in New York City, where he died on October 5, 1865.

Moore, James (1737–1777), Revolutionary army officer. Born in 1737 in New Hanover County, North Carolina, Moore was of a family of North Carolina soldiers, judges, and governors. He was a captain of militia during the French and Indian War, 1755–1763, for a year commanding Fort Johnston at the mouth of the Cape Fear River. From 1764 to 1771 and again in 1773 he sat in the colonial assembly, and he was a leader of North Carolina opposition to the Stamp Act of 1765. He served as a colonel of militia under Gen. Hugh Waddell in the campaign against the Regulators culminating in the battle at Alamance, May 16, 1771. In August 1774 he was a delegate to the first revolutionary provincial congress, and in August 1775 he sat in the third. The next month he was elected colonel of the 1st North Carolina Regiment of Continental troops. On February 27, 1776, troops under his command fought a mixed force of Loyalists and Highlander troops at Moore's Creek Bridge, north of Wilmington, North Carolina. Some 1100 state troops overwhelmed 1600 Loyalists and Scots in a three-minute engagement, capturing a great amount of ordnance, supplies, and treasure into the bargain. Although Moore was absent from the actual battle, which has been called the "Lexington and Concord of the South"—Col. Richard Caswell was in command on the field—he was properly credited with the campaign leading up to it and in March was rewarded with appointment as brigadier general in the Continental army and command of all forces in North Carolina. He remained in Wilmington until November, when he was ordered to reinforce Charleston, South Carolina. Ordered in February 1777 to join Gen. George Washington's army, he fell ill while preparing to do so and died in Wilmington, North Carolina, in April (perhaps April 9) 1777.

Moorer, Thomas Hinman (1912–   ), naval officer. Born on February 9, 1912, in Mount Willing, Alabama, Moorer graduated from the Naval Academy in 1933. In July 1936, following service aboard the *Salt Lake City* and then the new *New Orleans,* he qualified as an aviator and was promoted to lieutenant (junior grade). He served aboard various aircraft carriers in the Pacific and was with Patrol Squadron 22 of Fleet Air Wing 10, Asiatic Fleet, at Pearl Harbor when the Japanese attacked on December 7, 1941. In February 1942 his PBY airplane was shot down in the Arafura Sea north of Australia; the ship that rescued him was subsequently torpedoed. In October 1942 he was promoted to lieutenant commander and sent to

Great Britain as an observer, and in March 1943 he was given command of Bombing Squadron 132, based at Key West, Florida, and operating across the central Atlantic. A year later he was assigned to the air staff of the Atlantic Fleet. During 1945–1946, by then a commander, he was in Japan as part of the Strategic Bombing Survey; and after a period at the Naval Aviation Ordnance Test Station, Chincoteague, Virginia, he returned to sea in 1948–1949 on the carrier *Midway*. He served in various capacities concerned with carrier and air operations and ordnance development until 1955, receiving promotion to captain in 1951 and graduating from the Naval War College in 1953. In 1955–1956 he was aide to the assistant secretary of the navy for air, and after a year in command of the *Salisbury Sound* he was promoted to rear admiral in July 1957 and attached to the naval staff in Washington, D.C., serving as assistant chief of naval operations from January 1958 to July 1959. Moorer then commanded Carrier Division 6 until November 1960, when he returned to staff duty. Promoted to vice admiral in October 1962, he was given command of the Seventh Fleet, where he remained until becoming commander of the Pacific Fleet, with the rank of admiral, in June 1964. In April 1965 he was named commander of the Atlantic Fleet, the Atlantic Command, and the Atlantic forces of the North Atlantic Treaty Organization. In August 1967 he became chief of naval operations, a post he held until July 1970, when he succeeded Gen. Earle G. Wheeler as chairman of the Joint Chiefs of Staff. Moorer retired in July 1974. He was succeeded as chairman of the Joint Chiefs by Gen. George S. Brown.

Moreell, Ben (1892–   ), engineer, naval officer, and businessman.

Born on September 14, 1892, in Salt Lake City, Utah, Moreell grew up in New York City and St. Louis. He graduated from Washington University with a civil engineering degree in 1913 and for four years worked as a construction engineer for the city of St. Louis. In June 1917 he secured a commission as lieutenant (junior grade) in the navy's Civil Engineer Corps. During World War I he was stationed in the Azores, and afterwards he served at naval yards and installations in Massachusetts, Haiti, Virginia, and Washington. In 1929 he published the well received *Standards of Design for Concrete*. Having reached the rank of lieutenant commander, he studied in 1932–1933 at the École Nationale des Ponts et Chaussées in Paris and then returned to a variety of assignments. In December 1937 he was promoted to rear admiral and made chief of the Bureau of Yards and Docks and also of the Civil Engineers Corps; he was reappointed to those posts in 1941. The outbreak of the war with Japan placed a great burden on Moreell's command, for the Pacific war was to a large extent a naval one, and bases, yards, and other sorts

of installations by the hundreds became a pressing necessity. Until World War II naval construction had generally been done by civilian contractors and their employees. The task of building advance bases in wartime, however, called for construction crews able to drop tools and take up weapons at a moment's notice, so in December 1941 he began organizing the Construction Battalions, known as the Seabees (the name was officially authorized in March 1942), whose motto "Can Do" exemplified their accomplishments. Manned largely by experienced civilian construction men and officered by engineers or other trained personnel, Seabee units were in the field by early 1942 building bases at Bora-Bora, Efate, and Tongatapu. They built navy and marine bases, barracks, roads, drydock facilities, airfields, and the great naval repair facilities at Espiritu Santo, Manus, and Guam. Seabee units especially distinguished themselves on Guadalcanal and Tarawa. Seabee units often were among the first waves of assault troops in amphibious operations. At its peak, the Seabee corps reached a strength of 250,000 men and officers. In February 1944 Moreell was promoted to vice admiral. He became chief of the Material Division in the Navy Department in November 1945, a job that involved him in negotiating a settlement to the national strike of oil refinery workers. In May 1946 he was appointed to operate coal mines seized by the federal government and to negotiate a new contract with the United Mine Workers. Promoted to temporary rank of admiral in June 1946—he was the first staff corps chief ever, and the first non-graduate of the Naval Academy since the Academy's founding, to achieve that rank—Moreell retired in September and in October became president of the Turner Construction Company in New York City. In 1947 he joined the Jones and Laughlin Steel Corporation, serving as president, 1947–1952, chief executive officer, 1947–1957, and chairman of the board, 1947–1958, and remaining a director until 1965. During 1953–1955 he was chairman of the task force on water resources and power of the Hoover Commission. Other books by Moreell included *Our Nation's Water Resources*, 1956, and *The Admiral's Log*, 2 v., 1958–1960. He was active as a visitor and adviser to the Naval Academy.

Morgan, Daniel (1736–1802), Revolutionary army officer.

Born in Hunterdon County, New Jersey, in 1736, Morgan moved to Virginia while still a youth. He served as a civilian wagoner with Gen. Edward Braddock's expedition in 1755, as a lieutenant in Pontiac's War in 1763–1764, and in Lord Dunmore's War in 1774. In June 1775, with the outbreak of the Revolution, he received a commission as a captain of Virginia riflemen. He joined the Continental army at Boston and was put in command of three companies of Col. Benedict Arnold's force sent to join Gen. Richard Montgomery in the invasion of

Canada in September. He took part in the assault on Quebec on December 31, 1775, and, assuming command after Arnold was wounded, he and his men penetrated well into the city before being forced to surrender. He was commissioned colonel shortly after his exchange by the British in November 1776. Placed in command of a corps of 500 sharpshooters, he joined Gen. Horatio Gates in September 1777 and took a leading part in the victorious Saratoga campaign against Gen. John Burgoyne, especially at the first battle of Bemis Heights (Freeman's Farm), September 19. He then rejoined Gen. George Washington for the campaign around Philadelphia, but, dissatisfied with his rank and not in the best of health, he resigned from the army in July 1779 and retired to Virginia. He returned to active service in September 1780 and again joined Gates, recently defeated at Camden, South Carolina. After Gen. Nathanael Greene succeeded Gates in command in the South, Morgan, having been promoted to brigadier general in October, was given command of a corps in North Carolina. He is chiefly remembered for his brilliant victory over Col. Banastre Tarleton on January 17, 1781. Retreating before the British advance from Charleston, he took a stand with his outnumbered force on a slight hill at the Cowpens, near the Broad River in South Carolina. Posting a skirmish line in front, Morgan instructed them to fire and fall back; a second line of militia under Col. Andrew Pickens fired twice and fell back; a third line of Continental regulars under Col. John E. Howard held the British advance while the militia reformed behind the hill; then the militia swept around on the left, reserve cavalry under Col. William Washington came in from the right, and Howard's regulars charged with bayonets. Tarleton lost, out of 1100 men, more than 200 killed and wounded and 600 captured in an utter rout; American losses were 72 killed or wounded. Morgan then escaped from the pursuing Gen. Charles Cornwallis into North Carolina, rejoining Greene in February. Beset by ill health, he again retired to Virginia. He briefly resumed service in Virginia in June–August 1781. Morgan retired to his estate and prospered after the war. In November 1794 he commanded the Virginia militia sent to suppress the Whisky Rebellion in western Pennsylvania. He served one term in the House of Representatives (1797–1799) as a Federalist and died in Winchester, Virginia, on July 6, 1802.

Morgan, John Hunt (1825–1864), Confederate army officer. Born in Huntsville, Alabama, on June 1, 1825, Morgan grew up near Lexington, Kentucky. He enlisted in the cavalry for service in the Mexican War in 1846, and in 1857 he organized a militia company known as the Lexington Rifles. He joined the Confederate army in September 1861 and shortly became a captain of cavalry. Early in 1862, under the

authority of Gen. Braxton Bragg, he began the dashing raids for which he became famous. Striking quickly and avoiding direct combat, he interrupted telegraph communications, destroyed railroad lines and equipment, and burned Union supplies, in addition to taking prisoners. He operated very effectively, mostly in Tennessee and his native Kentucky, throughout 1862 and early 1863, and in December 1862 was promoted to brigadier general following a particularly successful raid at Hartsville, Tennessee, where he took 1700 Federal prisoners. His best known and most daring exploit was conducted in July 1863. With more than 2000 men under his command he led an unauthorized raid into Indiana and eventually was pursued into Ohio, riding wildly through the suburbs of Cincinnati. Although penetrating farther north than any other Confederate force during the war, the raid inflicted relatively little damage and accomplished little, although indirectly it helped relieve pressure on Bragg in eastern Tennessee for a time. Most of his force surrendered on July 19 at Buffington Island on the Ohio River in Meigs County, and Morgan himself was captured with his remaining men at Salineville on July 26 and confined at the state prison in Columbus, Ohio. He escaped in November and early in 1864 assumed command of the Department of Southwestern Virginia. Morgan was soon raiding in Kentucky again, but some of his men now began pillaging nonmilitary establishments in eastern Kentucky. Unwilling, perhaps unable, to restore discipline and now suffering heavier losses than before, he began to be thought of less value to the Confederacy in this stage of the war. Under investigation and about to be relieved of his command, he decided to lead one more raid, aiming at Knoxville, Tennessee, but was surprised and killed by Federal troops at Greeneville on September 4, 1864.

Morison, Samuel Eliot (1887–1976), historian and naval officer. Born in Boston on July 9, 1887, Morison entered Harvard in 1904; he graduated in the class of 1908 and studied for a year in France before returning to Harvard for an M.A., 1909, and a Ph.D., 1913. He subsequently traveled to Europe again and taught briefly at the University of California before accepting a post on the Harvard faculty in 1915. In 1918 he enlisted in the army, serving as a private, and stayed in Paris after the armistice while attached to the Russian division of the American Commission to Negotiate Peace and as a delegate to the Baltic Commission of the Peace Conference. He returned to Harvard in 1919 and published his second book (his dissertation on Harrison Gray Otis, one of his ancestors, had appeared in 1913), *Maritime History of Massachusetts 1783–1860,* 1921, before going to Oxford University in 1922 as the first Harmsworth professor of American history. He returned to Harvard again as a full professor in 1925 and remained there, except for service during World War II, and from 1941 as Jonathan Trumbull professor of American history, until his retirement in 1955. His two-volume *Oxford History of the United States* appeared in 1927. Two of his more than 25 books won Pulitzer prizes: *Admiral of the Ocean Sea: A Life of Christopher Columbus*, 1942, and *John Paul Jones*, 1959. He was appointed historian of naval operations with the rank of lieutenant commander in May 1942, and before commencing his 15-volume *History of U.S. Naval Operations in World War II*, 1947–1962, he devoted three years, 1942–1945, to personally observing naval operations, primarily in the Pacific theater, taking notes during most of the major naval campaigns. He retired from the navy in 1951 with the rank of rear admiral. In addition to his five-volume tercentennial history of Harvard, 1929–1936, his other major works included the widely used textbook *Growth of the American Republic*, 1930 and several later revised editions, written with Henry Steele Commager; *Portuguese Voyages to America*, 1940; *The Intellectual Life of Colonial New England*, 1956; *The Story of ·Mount Desert Island*, 1960; *One Boy's Boston*, 1962, an account of his youth; and *Two-Ocean War*, 1963, a shorter history of naval operations in World War II. His *Oxford History of the American People*, 1965, became a standard work in the field. *The European Discovery of America: The Northern Voyages* appeared in 1971. It was the first of two volumes on the subject; the second, devoted to the southern (and more famous) voyages of such explorers as Columbus, was published in 1974. His research for these books involved not only poring over old manuscripts in libraries but also travel by airplane and boat and on foot through Canada, New England, and the Caribbean, activities that he pursued enthusiastically despite advancing years. Morison received many honorary degrees and awards and was a recipient of the Presidential Medal of Freedom in 1964, especially for his work on the history of World War II. He died in Boston on May 15, 1976.

Morris, Charles (1784–1856), naval officer. Born in Woodstock, Connecticut, on July 26, 1784, Morris entered the navy as a midshipman in July 1799. He saw some sea duty on the frigate *Congress* during the undeclared naval war with France and was retained in the reduction of the navy in June 1801. In August 1803 he went aboard the *Constitution*, bearing Commodore Edward Preble to take command of the squadron at Tripoli. He was selected to take part in Lt. Stephen Decatur's daring run into Tripoli harbor to burn the grounded *Philadelphia*; when the ketch *Intrepid* came up on the *Philadelphia* on the night of February 15, 1804, Morris was the first to board, followed closely by Decatur. He took part in the subsequent bombardment of Tripoli and other actions. He

was promoted to lieutenant in January 1807 while on the *Hornet* in the Mediterranean. Routine duty followed until the outbreak of the War of 1812, at which time Morris was first lieutenant under Capt. Isaac Hull on the *Constitution*. He was largely responsible for engineering the becalmed *Constitution*'s escape from a British squadron off New York, July 17–19, 1812, by means of "kedging," or carrying anchors ahead in boats and then hauling in on the lines; and in the victory over the *Guerrière* on August 19 he was severely wounded while heroically attempting to board the enemy. For that exploit he was promoted two grades to captain as of March 1813. Placed in command of the frigate *John Adams*, he escaped the blockade of Chesapeake Bay in January 1814 and on a cruise in the eastern Atlantic took ten prizes, but in September, after grounding on the Maine coast, he was pursued up the Penobscot by two British vessels and at Hampden, deserted by the militia on shore and under fire, he was forced to scuttle and burn his ship. In 1815–1817 he commanded the *Congress*, first in Decatur's squadron in the Algerine War and then in the Gulf of Mexico, where he had command of the squadron. From 1817 to 1823 he commanded the Portsmouth, New Hampshire, navy yard, except during a short cruise to Buenos Aires in 1819–1820. In 1823–1827 he served on the Board of Navy Commissioners, taking time in 1825 to command the *Brandywine* bearing the Marquis de Lafayette home after his American visit. Morris commanded the Boston navy yard in 1827–1832 and then resumed his post on the Board of Navy Commissioners until 1841. After three more years of sea duty in command of the Brazil and then the Mediterranean squadrons, he was appointed in 1844 to head the Bureau of Construction. In 1851 he became head of the Bureau of Ordnance and Hydrography, a post he kept until his death in Washington, D.C., on January 27, 1856. His *Autobiography* was published in 1880.

Morris, George Upham (1830–1875), naval officer. Born on June 3, 1830, in Massachusetts, Morris was the son of Capt. Charles Morris, then commanding the Boston navy yard. The younger Morris entered the navy as a midshipman in August 1846 and while serving in various duties was promoted to master commandant and lieutenant in September 1855. Early in 1862 he was attached to the sloop *Cumberland* of the North Atlantic Blockading Squadron. On March 8, at anchor in Hampton Roads off Newport News, Virginia, the *Cumberland* was chosen by Flag-Officer Franklin Buchanan, commanding the Confederate ironclad *Virginia*, as his first test target. Capt. William Radford being ashore, Morris was in command of the *Cumberland*. Buchanan was interested mainly in testing his armor and his ram, but he opened the fight with a raking pass across the *Cumberland*'s bow. The Union vessel, unable to maneuver to bring her guns to bear, suffered terribly, as many casualties being inflicted by flying debris as by shot or shell. Gun crews were heavily hit, and only after the *Virginia* had rammed and then swung broadside in the current did the *Cumberland*'s guns begin to tell. Midway through the fight Buchanan again took up raking position and demanded surrender, to which Morris replied "Never! We will sink with our colors flying." Another rake and another ramming left the *Cumberland* sinking. Buchanan withdrew, leaving those who were able to reach shore; 173 of a complement of 410 survived. The stout courage of Morris and the *Cumberland*'s crew was not in vain, for the damage inflicted on the *Virginia* had its result in the epic battle with the *Monitor* the next day. In May Morris commanded the gunboat *Port Royal* in the expedition under Commander John Rodgers up the James River. He was promoted to lieutenant commander in July 1862 and commander in July 1866. He retired from the navy in October 1874 and died in Jordan Alum Springs, Virginia, on August 15, 1875.

Morris, Richard Valentine (1768–1815), naval officer. Born on March 8, 1768, at Morrisania, the family estate in Westchester County, New York, Morris was a son of Lewis Morris, signer of the Declaration of Independence, and nephew of Gouverneur Morris, statesman. He had already become an experienced seaman when he entered the navy with a captain's commission in June 1798. After serving as captain of the *Adams,* he was appointed to succeed Commodore Richard Dale as commander of the squadron then engaged in an attempted blockade of Tripoli, and he arrived in mid-1802 with a reinforcing squadron of five ships headed by his flagship *Chesapeake*. The force was still too small to make the blockade effective, and Morris was compelled to deal with outbreaks of hostility on the parts of Morocco, Algiers, and Tunis as well. The capture or destruction of several Tripolitan vessels in actions led by Capt. John Rodgers and Lt. David Porter led Morris to lift the blockade, prematurely, in June 1803, in which month Morocco declared war over his refusal to grant certain concessions. Morris was recalled, relinquishing command to Rodgers. A court of inquiry found, not altogether justly, that he had been insufficiently diligent in maintaining American prestige in the Mediterranean, and in May 1804 he was dismissed from the navy. He retired to Morrisania and died there on May 13, 1815.

Mosby, John Singleton (1833–1916), Confederate army officer. Born in Edgemont, Powhatan County, Virginia, on December 6, 1833, Mosby entered the University of Virginia at fifteen. While there he shot and wounded a fellow student in a quarrel; a six-month jail sentence was annulled and a $1000 fine remitted by act of the legislature. He graduated in 1852, was admitted to the bar in 1855, and practised law in Bristol, Virginia, until the outbreak of the Civil War. Enlisting in the Confederate cavalry in 1861, he was present at the first battle of Manassas (Bull Run), July 21, and later was attached as a scout to Gen. J. E. B. Stuart's cavalry during its famous ride around Gen. George B. McClellan's army in June 1862 during the Peninsular campaign. Mosby is remembered for his activities as a ranger, which he began early in 1863. Operating initially with nine men in Union-occupied northern Virginia, he attacked isolated Union outposts and cut communications and supply lines. The band avoided capture by dispersing immediately after an attack and regrouping at a prearranged location. Mosby, given a lieutenant's commission in February, steadily attracted recruits who preferred the undisciplined life of his rangers to that of the regular army. Self-supplied, audacious, and resourceful, his men followed the practice (legitimate under the law applying to partisans) of dividing among themselves the property they captured. "Mosby's Rangers" made one of their most spectacular raids when, 29 strong, they slipped through Union lines at Fairfax Court House on March 9, 1863, and captured Gen. Edwin H. Stoughton and about a hundred of his men. Mosby was promoted to captain for this exploit, and not long after, for a raid in April on Chantilly, he advanced to major. By June 1863 his irregular forces were designated Company A, 43rd Battalion Partisan Rangers. Before Gettysburg he provided valuable scouting reports. Mosby was promoted to lieutenant colonel in February 1864. Impossible to hunt down systematically, the Rangers were declared outlaws (because they confiscated private property as well as Union supplies) by the Union forces. During 1864 several of them were captured and, on Gen. Ulysses S. Grant's orders, hanged without trial. Mosby retaliated by hanging an equal number of Union cavalrymen, whereupon the executions of Rangers ended. During the summer and autumn of 1864 Mosby's was virtually the only organized Confederate force in northern Virginia, and his operations in the Shenandoah valley kept Gen. Philip H. Sheridan too occupied to reinforce Grant at Petersburg. In December 1864, when he was promoted to colonel, his force numbered eight companies. He conducted his final raid on April 10, 1865, the day following Gen. Robert E. Lee's surrender at Appomattox. Eleven days later he disbanded his troops after a final review at Salem (now Marshall), Virginia. He returned, a popular hero, to law practice in Warrenton, Virginia, but soon made enemies in the South by entering politics as a Republican. An admirer of Grant, he supported him for the presidency in 1872. Similarly he supported Rutherford B. Hayes in 1876. He held minor political offices after that: he was U.S. consul at Hong Kong, 1878–1885, and assistant attorney in the Department of Justice, 1904–1910. He published two books on his war experiences, *Mosby's War Reminiscences*, 1887, and *Stuart's Cavalry in the Gettysburg Campaign*, 1908, about the forces for which he had performed valuable services. The phrase "the Solid South," which first gained currency in 1878, has been attributed to Mosby. He died in Washington, D.C., on May 30, 1916.

Moultrie, William (1730–1805), Revolutionary army officer and public official. Born in Charles Town (now Charleston), South Carolina, on December 4, 1730, Moultrie was already a prominent landowner at an early age and was first elected to the provincial assembly in 1752; he served in that body, except for short intervals, until 1771. After fighting against the Cherokees in 1761 as a militia commander with the rank of captain, he became strongly interested in military affairs. He championed the patriot cause in the provincial congress in 1775, and he was shortly afterward elected colonel of South Carolina's 2nd Regiment. In March 1776 he took command of Sullivan's Island in Charleston harbor and there built Fort Sullivan, a structure of sand and palmetto logs. The work was not yet complete when it came under attack on June 28, 1776, by a British naval squadron under Adm. Sir Peter Parker attempting to land an army under Sir Henry Clinton. The spongy palmetto logs easily absorbed bombardment, while Moultrie used his 31 guns and scarce ammunition with devastating accuracy. After more than ten hours the British retired, Parker's flagship *Bristol* a riddled near-wreck. The fort was subsequently renamed Fort Moultrie in his honor. For the victory, which delayed British plans to establish a foothold in the southern colonies for about two years, he received the thanks of Congress, and three months later, after his regiment was mustered into Continental service, he was made a brigadier general in the Continental army. He subsequently served under Gen. Benjamin Lincoln in Georgia, 1778–1779, and again delayed British success in South Carolina by dislodging them from Beaufort in February 1779. In May 1779 he delayed Gen. Augustine Prevost's march on Charleston until Lincoln could hurry from Georgia to defend the city. He surrendered after the successful British siege of Charleston, March 12–May 12, 1780, and remained a prisoner on parole until exchanged in February 1782. He was promoted to major general in October 1782, but by that time the war was all but ended. His war record made him even more prominent in South Carolina politics, and after serving as lieutenant governor in 1784 he became governor of the state, serving from 1785 to 1787 and again from 1794 to 1796; he served in the state senate between terms. He retired from public life after his second term as governor. Two volumes of his war memoirs appeared in 1802; he died in Charleston on September 27, 1805.

Mower, Joseph Anthony (1827–1870), army officer. Born in Woodstock, Vermont, on August 22, 1827, Mower attended Norwich University in 1843–1845 and then worked as a carpenter. At the outbreak of the Mexican War in 1846 he enlisted in the army as a private of engineers and served for two years. In June 1855 he secured a commission as second lieutenant of infantry, and he received promotions to first lieutenant in March 1857 and to captain in September 1861. In March 1862, under the command of Gen. John Pope, he was conspicuous in the capture of New Madrid, Missouri, and in May he was elected colonel of the 11th Missouri Volunteers. In the same month he was brevetted major of regulars for gallantry at Farmington, Mississippi, May 8–9. Serving in Gen. William S. Rosecran's Army of the Mississippi, he again distinguished himself at Iuka, Mississippi, September 19, winning a brevet to lieutenant colonel, and he played an important role in repulsing Gen. Earl Van Dorn's attack on Corinth, Mississippi, on October 3. He was promoted to brigadier general of volunteers in November. In May 1863 he was brevetted colonel of regulars for his part in the capture of Jackson, Mississippi, by Gen. William T. Sherman, May 14, and in the first assault on Vicksburg, May 18, he gained and held a foothold on the ramparts. In the spring of 1864 he commanded a division under Gen. Nathaniel P. Banks in the Red River campaign, distinguishing himself at Fort de Russy early in March. In August he was promoted to major general of volunteers, and soon thereafter he joined Sherman's Division of the Mississippi command in Atlanta. He commanded a division of the XVII Corps, Army of the Tennessee, in the march to the sea and later the XX Corps, Army of Georgia, in the Carolinas campaign. In March 1865 he was brevetted brigadier general of regulars for Fort de Russy and major general for actions at the Salkehatchie River in South Carolina. Mower's record of promotions, brevets, and official commendations was almost unmatched in the Civil War. Mustered out in February 1866, he was appointed colonel of the 39th Infantry in July. In March 1869 he was transferred to command of the 25th Infantry. He was in command of the Department of Louisiana at his death in New Orleans on January 6, 1870.

Muhlenberg, John Peter Gabriel (1746–1807), religious leader, Revolutionary army officer, and public official. Born in Trappe, Pennsylvania, on October 1, 1746, John Peter was the eldest child of Henry Melchior Mühlenberg, Lutheran leader, and a brother of Frederick Augustus Muhlenberg, congressman. He went with two of his brothers to study at the University of Halle, Germany, in 1763 but was back in Philadelphia by 1767 after a brief enlistment in the British 60th (Royal American) Regiment of Foot. He subsequently studied privately for the ministry and assisted his father before going to England for ordination (apparently as an Episcopalian) in early 1772. Later that year he became pastor of a Lutheran church in Woodstock, Virginia, where he soon gained favor in the pulpit and as an enthusiast for the Revolution. In 1774 he was elected to the House of Burgesses. His patriotic fervor eventually gained the upper hand over the cloth; organizing the 8th Virginia Regiment, composed mostly of Germans, he was made colonel in or before January 1776 and fought under Col. William Moultrie at the defeat of the British at Sullivan's Island, South Carolina, in June 1776. Commissioned brigadier general in the Continental army in February 1777, he took part in a number of battles including Brandywine and Germantown, at both of which he particularly distinguished himself, Monmouth Court House, and Stony Point. At Yorktown he commanded the 1st Brigade of light infantry. He was brevetted major general in September 1783. After the war he moved to Philadelphia. His war record now opened a political career that he was quick to pursue. Elected to the Supreme Executive Council of Pennsylvania in 1784, he became vice-president of the state under Benjamin Franklin, 1785–1788, exerted his considerable influence in favor of ratification of the Constitution, and along with his brother Frederick Augustus became a member of the House in the first U.S. Congress, convened in March 1789. He was elected to the 3rd Congress as a Democratic-Republican in 1793 and served a third term during 1799–1801. He worked harmoniously with the supporters of Thomas Jefferson, whom he supported for president in 1796 and in 1801, and in February 1801 he won a Senate seat. He resigned from the Senate almost immediately and returned to Philadelphia, where he became supervisor of revenue and then, after 1802, collector of the port of Philadelphia. He died at his home near the city on October 1, 1807.

Muir, Charles Henry (1860–1933), army officer. Born in Erie, Michigan, on July 18, 1860, Muir graduated from West Point in 1885 and was commissioned in the infantry. For several years he was stationed on the frontier, in Dakota and Wyoming territories, and he took part in the Sioux campaign of 1890–1891. He was promoted to first lieutenant in January 1892 and in 1895 graduated from the Infantry and Cavalry School, Fort Leavenworth, Kansas, remaining there as an instructor for three years. In the Spanish–American War he took part in the Santiago campaign, June–July 1898. In March 1899 he was promoted to captain and in August appointed major of the 38th Volunteer Infantry for service in the Philippines. There he saw considerable action and distinguished himself on January 19, 1900, when he and ten others attacked Rosario, Luzon, capturing a major headquarters and treasury of the insurrectionists and freeing 300 Spanish prisoners. In 1903 he was selected to serve on the original General Staff; during 1907–1910 he was again in the Philippines, receiving promotion to major of regulars in March 1908, and from 1911 to 1915 he was an instructor of National Guard troops at Springfield, Illinois. He advanced to lieutenant colonel in January 1914. In 1915 he was sent to Texas and then to the Canal Zone, where in July 1916 he received promotion to colonel of the 33rd Infantry. In August 1917 he was promoted to temporary brigadier general; he advanced to temporary major general in November and in December was given command of the 28th Infantry Division, which he preceded from Camp Hancock, Georgia, to France. He led the 28th through the German Marne offensive of July 1918, and in the Aisne–Marne and the Meuse–Argonne offensives. In October Muir succeeded Gen. Joseph T. Dickman as commander of the IV Corps, with which he remained in occupation duty until May 1919. He was made permanent brigadier general in January 1919. He returned briefly to command of the 28th until its inactivation at Camp Dix, New Jersey, and in July 1919 became commandant of the General Staff School, Fort Leavenworth. A year later he was given command of Camp Lewis, Washington. Promoted to major general in March 1921, he was named commander of the III Corps area at Baltimore in 1922 and remained in that post until his retirement in July 1924. Muir died in Baltimore on December 8, 1933.

Mullan, John (1830–1909), army officer and explorer. Born on July 31, 1830, in Norfolk, Virginia, Mullan graduated from West Point in 1852 and was commissioned in the topographical engineers. In 1853 he was attached to the party under Gov. Isaac I. Stevens surveying a railroad route from St. Paul, Minnesota, to the mouth of the Columbia River. During his two years in that task Mullan explored widely among the Bitterroot and Rocky mountains, gathering valuable information especially in his courageous winter journeys. In 1855 he was promoted to first lieutenant and ordered to duty in Florida, where he saw action against the Seminoles. In 1858 he was ordered back to the Northwest to direct construction of a military wagon road from Fort Benton, at the head of navigation of the Missouri River, to Walla Walla, Washington Territory, on the Columbia. A certain amount of Indian skirmishing preceded the start of work, and Mullan distinguished himself at Four Lakes, near Spokane, September 1, 1858. Mullan secured additional appropriations from Congress through his old friend Stevens, and on July 1, 1859, work began. The road slowly advanced from Walla Walla and reached Fort Benton in 1860; additional work in 1861 and 1862 greatly improved the road. The Mullan Trail was the only wagon trail through the Bitterroot range, covering 624 miles of rugged terrain. Loaded wagons could make the trip in

47 days. Although built as a military road, the trail was of great importance in opening the interior Northwest to miners and settlers, making the rich Montana goldfields accessible from both east and west. In 1863 Mullan resigned from the army. He failed as a rancher near Walla Walla and in ventures into contract mail carrying (Chico, California, to Ruby, Idaho) and the express business. In 1865 he published a popular *Miners' and Travelers' Guide to Oregon, Washington, Idaho, Montana, Wyoming and Colorado*. Settling in San Francisco, he entered the practice of law, continuing in it after moving to Washington, D.C., in 1878. Mullan died in Washington, D.C., on December 28, 1909.

Murphy, Audie (1924–1971), soldier and actor. Born on a farm near Kingston, Hunt County, Texas, on June 20, 1924, Murphy grew up in poverty. His father, a sharecropper, abandoned the large family during the Depression of the 1930s, and after his mother died he enlisted in the army in June 1942, just before his eighteenth birthday. During 30 months of combat service he rose from private to lieutenant, serving with the 3rd Infantry Division, attached first to the Fifth Army and later to the Seventh, in the campaigns in Tunisia, Sicily, Italy (including the Anzio beachhead), France (where he landed in the south in August 1944), and Germany. Wounded three times, he was repeatedly decorated for gallantry in action. On January 26, 1945, with his unit pinned down in the Colmar Pocket in eastern France, Murphy single-handedly held off a German force of six tanks and some 250 men, earning the Medal of Honor (his 24th decoration) for bravery. On his return to the United States he was celebrated as the most highly decorated hero of the war, with a total of 28. Overwhelmed by newspaper and magazine publicity, he was induced to embark on a Hollywood film career. His first film, *Beyond Glory*, was released in 1948. Although he was never much of an actor, his appearances in films were effectively promoted and he continued to make money, mostly in Westerns. His biggest success was *To Hell and Back*, 1955, a film version of his autobiography in which he played himself in the leading role. His films, which eventually numbered about 40, continued to appear in the 1960s, but his popularity faded. He turned to business ventures (he had reportedly earned more than $2 million as an actor) but without success; he declared bankruptcy in 1968. He died in a plane crash near Roanoke, Virginia, while en route to Atlanta, Georgia, on a business trip. The wreckage of the light plane, which was reported missing on May 28, was discovered on June 1, 1971.

Myer, Albert James (1829–1880), army officer. Born in Newburgh, New York, on September 20, 1829, Myer graduated from Hobart College in 1847

and from Buffalo Medical College in 1851. In September 1854 he was appointed an assistant surgeon in the army and shortly thereafter ordered to duty in Texas. Since writing his M.D. thesis on deaf-mute sign language he had been interested in various means of signaling, and he had learned telegraphy during college. While he was in Texas, Indian smoke signaling also attracted his study. He drew up a memorandum on the subject, devoting much attention to a system of his own devising in which a single signal flag, moved back and forth by the staff holder, could be used for visual communication over considerable distances. An army board considered his proposal in 1858 and the "wigwag" system was tested in various Indian campaigns. In June 1860 Myer was appointed chief signal officer of the army with the rank and pay of a major of cavalry. In early 1861 he field-tested wigwag signaling in New Mexico, where Col. Edward R. S. Canby was engaged in Indian warfare. After the outbreak of the Civil War he began a period of valuable service on the staffs of armies in the field. He was at Bull Run in July and shortly thereafter was made signal officer of the Army of the Potomac. He served on Gen. George B. McClellan's staff through the Peninsular campaign and was brevetted lieutenant colonel for gallantry at Hanover Court House, May 27, 1862, and colonel for Malvern Hill, July 1. Myer made considerable progress in adapting the portable telegraph to tactical field use, and it was to play a real role in the battle of Fredericksburg, December 13, 1862. In March 1863 a Signal Corps was established by act of Congress, and Myer was appointed chief with the rank of colonel. His activity in the building of several thousand miles of telegraph line to various frontier posts brought him into conflict with the Military Telegraph office. He was relieved of the post of chief signal officer in October 1863 and transferred to survey work on the Mississippi River, becoming in May 1864 signal officer of the Division of West Mississippi; in July his colonelcy was revoked. In March 1865 he was brevetted brigadier general for his services as chief signal officer and in recognition of the relief of an apparently doomed garrison at Allatoona, Georgia, on October 5, 1864, by the use of wigwag. In July 1866 the Signal Corps was established as a permanent department, and in November Myer was reappointed chief signal officer of the army with the rank of colonel. On his urging, Congress in February 1870 established the U.S. Weather Bureau as a branch of the Signal Corps, and Myer, drawing on the work and advice of such pioneers as Cleveland Abbe, developed and organized the system of observers and telegraphic reports to the central office that marked the nation's first modern weather service. He issued the Bureau's first weather bulletin on November 1, 1870. He was effective at international meteorological congresses in Vienna, 1873, and Rome, 1879, in the establishment of international cooperation in weather observations. He was promoted to brigadier general in June 1880, and he died in Buffalo, New York, on August 24, 1880.

Myers, John Twiggs (1871–1952), marine officer. Born on January 29, 1871, to American parents in Wiesbaden, Germany, Myers graduated from the Naval Academy in 1892 and in March 1895 was commissioned a second lieutenant of marines. He attended the Naval War College in 1896 and was stationed at the marine barracks at Mare Island, California, in 1896–1898. In May 1898 he joined the marine detachment on the *Charleston*. The *Charleston*, Capt. Henry Glass, was ordered to the Philippines and en route stopped at Guam, where on July 21 Myers commanded a shore party of marines and sailors that accompanied Capt. Glass in disarming the Spanish garrison and taking possession of the island. During the Philippine Insurrection Myers led landing expeditions from the *Baltimore* at Olongapo, September 23, 1899, and Bacoor, October 2, and in December commanded a marine force occupying a captured naval station on Subic Bay. In May 1900, by then a captain, he was transferred to the *Newark*, Capt. Bowman H. McCalla. Late in that month, in reply to an urgent request from the U.S. minister in Peking, a force of 48 marines and 3 sailors under Myers was dispatched from Taku, where the *Newark* was anchored, by Adm. Louis Kempff, senior American officer in the region. Myers and his men joined small British, German, Russian, French, Italian, and Japanese forces in the legation quarter of Peking and beginning on June 24 fought off numerous attacks by Boxer rebels. On July 3 he led a gallant sortie against a tower built by Boxers to overlook and command the American legation; in that action he suffered a serious spear wound, and he was later brevetted major for his part in it. Following the arrival of the Peking

Relief Expedition in August he was hospitalized until December 1902. Various assignments followed: he was aboard the *Brooklyn* in 1903–1905; in command of the marine barracks in Washington, D.C., briefly in 1906; in the Philippines in 1906–1907; aboard the *West Virginia* as fleet marine officer of the Asiatic Fleet in 1907–1909; and aboard the *Tennessee* as fleet marine officer, Pacific Fleet, for a month in 1909. After another period of hospitalization he attended the army's School of the Line at Fort Leavenworth, Kansas, in 1911 and graduated from the Army War College in 1912. While commander of the Washington, D.C., barracks in 1912–1913, he commanded battalions in expeditions to Santo Domingo in 1912 and to Cuba in 1913. After a year in command of the marine barracks in Honolulu he took command of a battalion of the 4th Marine Regiment, remaining with it at various posts in California and on sea duty until June 1916. In that month, by then a lieutenant colonel, he was appointed fleet marine officer, Atlantic, and he served in that post and also on the staff of Adm. Henry T. Mayo, Atlantic Fleet commander, until August 1918. He was subsequently stationed at Parris Island, South Carolina, and Quantico, Virginia, and in 1919–1921 at Pearl Harbor, Hawaii. Myers was adjutant and inspector of the Department of the Pacific in 1921–1924 and commanded the marine base at San Diego in 1924–1925 and the 1st Marine Brigade in Haiti in 1925–1928. Promoted to brigadier general in July 1929 while attached to the headquarters staff in Washington, he was named assistant to Gen. Wendell C. Neville, commandant of the corps, in April 1930, later serving in the same capacity under Gen. Ben H. Fuller, and he advanced to major general in October 1931. He commanded the marine Department of the Pacific from March 1933 until his retirement in February 1935. Myers was promoted to lieutenant general on the retired list in 1942, and he died in Coconut Grove, Florida, on April 17, 1952.

N

Nash, Francis (1742?–1777), Revolutionary army officer. Born about 1742 in Prince Edward County, Virginia, Nash moved as a young man to Orange County on the North Carolina frontier, settling in Childsburg (now Hillsborough). He became a merchant and lawyer, was elected justice of the peace in 1763, and sat in the colonial assembly in 1764, 1765, 1771, and 1773–1775. He served as a captain of militia under Gen. Hugh Waddell in the campaign against the Regulators, taking part in the battle of Alamance, May 16, 1771. In April and August 1775 he was a representative in the second and third provincial congresses, and in September he was elected lieutenant colonel of the 1st North Carolina Regiment under Col. James Moore. He was promoted to colonel in April 1776. From November 1776 to February 1777 he was engaged in the defense of Charleston, South Carolina, and in the latter month was appointed brigadier general in the Continental army. After some weeks of recruiting in North Carolina he marched north to join Gen. George Washington's army, succeeding to command of all North Carolina troops on the death of Moore in April. At the battle of Germantown, October 4, 1777, his troops were part of the reserve but in the confusion became involved in the fighting. Nash was mortally wounded, and he died three days later, on October 7, 1777, in Germantown, Pennsylvania.

Nelson, William (1824–1862), naval and army officer. Born near Maysville, Kentucky, on September 27, 1824, Nelson entered the navy as a midshipman in January 1840. In the Mexican War he commanded a battery at the siege of Veracruz in March 1847. He was promoted to master commandant in September 1854 and to lieutenant in April 1855. In 1858 he commanded the *Niagara* of the Mediterranean Squadron, on which he returned to Africa 271 captives liberated from the slaveship *Echo*. He was in Washington, D.C., at the outbreak of the Civil War, and in April 1861 he went, at the request of President Abraham Lincoln, to study conditions in Kentucky. There he began organizing a pro-Union militia, the Home Guards, separate from Gen. Simon B. Buckner's neutralist State Guards. Although he was promoted to lieutenant commander in July and placed in command of the gunboats on the Ohio, he left naval service in September to accept appointment as brigadier general of volunteers. He supervised recruiting in eastern Kentucky for some months and then took command of the 4th Division of Gen. Don Carlos Buell's Army of the Ohio. His was the first unit of that army to reach the battlefield at Shiloh on the evening of April 6, 1862, and check the advance of Confederates against Gen. Ulysses S. Grant's unprepared troops. Subsequently he took part in the occupation of Corinth, Mississippi, and in July he was promoted to major general of volunteers. He was soon afterward ordered back to Kentucky to organize troops and on August 30 was wounded in battle with a much superior force under Gen. Edmund Kirby-Smith at Richmond. A short time later he was put in command of the defense of Louisville. On September 29, 1862, at the Galt House Hotel in Louisville, he encountered Gen. Jefferson C. Davis, whom he had reprimanded a few days before; an altercation ensued, and Nelson was shot and killed by Davis.

Neville, Wendell Cushing (1870–1930), marine officer. Born on May 12, 1870, in Portsmouth, Virginia, Neville graduated from the Naval Academy in 1890. After two years of sea duty he was commissioned a second lieutenant of marines in July 1892 and ordered to duty in Washington, D.C. He was promoted to first lieutenant in February 1894. In the Spanish–American War he took part in the landing at Guantánamo Bay, Cuba, in June 1898 and the establishment of Camp McCalla there, receiving a brevet to captain for gallantry. Promoted to captain in March 1899, he led a company of the 4th Battalion under Maj. William P. Biddle in the Peking Relief Expedition during August–October 1900 and was then ordered to the Philippines, where he was military governor of Basilan Province in 1901–1902. He returned to the United States in 1903, was promoted to major in June 1904, and during 1905–1907 was fleet marine officer, Atlantic. When political unrest in Cuba called forth armed intervention by the United States, Neville commanded the marine battalion, part of Col. Littleton W. T. Waller's brigade, that took Havana on October 1, 1906. During 1909–1910 he commanded a battalion in Nicaragua, and, promoted to lieutenant colonel in February 1914, he commanded the 2nd Regiment in the capture of Veracruz, Mexico, in April 1914, winning the Medal of Honor. From 1915 to 1917 he was in command of the marine guard at the American legation in Peking, China, receiving promotion to colonel in August 1916. In December 1917 he was sent to France to command the 5th Marine Regiment. He led the 5th, a unit of the army 2nd Division (successively under Gen. Omar Bundy, Gen. James G. Harbord, and Gen. John A. Lejeune), in the Aisne–Marne action, at Château-Thierry, and at Belleau Wood. In July 1918 he moved up to command of the 4th Brigade, comprising the 5th and 6th Marine regiments, and was promoted to brigadier general. He saw further action at Soissons, in the St. Mihiel and Blanc Mont operations, and in the Meuse–Argonne offensive. After occupation duty he returned to the United States in 1919. Promoted to major general in December 1923, he was named commander of the Department of the Pacific. He was later commander of the Fleet Marine Force, U.S. Fleet, and in March 1927 he took command of the marine barracks at Quantico, Virginia. In March 1929 he succeeded Lejeune as commandant of the marine corps. Neville died near Annapolis, Maryland, on July 8, 1930.

Newcomb, Simon (1835–1909), astronomer and mathematician. Born on March 12, 1835, in Wallace, Nova Scotia, the son of an itinerant schoolteacher, Newcomb received little or no formal schooling. He early developed an avidity for study, however, and was particularly fascinated by mathematics. At the age of eighteen, after about two years as an apprentice to an herb doctor, he traveled to Maryland, where for several years he taught in country schools while spending his spare time in Washington, D.C., studying under the occasional guidance of Joseph Henry of the Smithsonian Institution. On Henry's recommendation he was taken into the office of the *American Ephemeris and Nautical Almanac* in Cambridge, Massachusetts, in January 1857. While working as a computer for the *Nautical Almanac* he enrolled in Harvard's Lawrence Scientific School and graduated in 1858. In September 1861 he was named professor of mathematics by the navy and assigned to the Naval Observatory in Washington. His principal work there was an extension of that done for the *Nautical Almanac;* he set about finding and correcting errors in published values for the positions and motions of various celestial objects, including a large number of reference stars, the moon, several planets, and the sun. His work on the orbits of Neptune and Uranus and on the solar parallax was particularly valuable and widely hailed. He negotiated the contract for the great 26-inch telescope at the observatory, built by Alvan Clark and Sons and completed in 1873, and over the years directed a number of observing expeditions, including one to the Cape of Good Hope for the Venus transit of 1882. In September 1877 he became senior mathematics professor in the navy, with the rank of captain, and superintendent of the *Nautical Almanac* office, where he commenced the monumental task of thoroughly revising the motion theories and position tables for all the major celestial reference objects. Assisted by George

W. Hill, he carried on the vastly complex computations required for the project; the resulting new tables came into standard use throughout the world, and some remain in use to this day. In 1879 he inaugurated a series of *Astronomical Papers Prepared for the Use of the American Ephemeris and Nautical Almanac,* in which the results of these researches were published. From 1874 to 1901 he served as editor of the *American Journal of Mathematics.* He also found time to lecture at various colleges and in 1884 was appointed professor of mathematics and astronomy at The Johns Hopkins University, remaining there until 1894. In 1896 he attended an international conference in Paris, held largely at his instigation, at which it was decided to adopt for worldwide use a common system of astronomical constants; the system was mainly of Newcomb's devising, and a similar conference in 1950 reaffirmed that decision. In 1897 he reached the compulsory retirement age for navy captains; he continued his work thereafter under grants from the Carnegie Institution of Washington. In 1899 he helped found and for the next six years was the first president of the American Astronomical Society; he was a member of the world's leading scientific societies, and to his many honors was added in 1906 promotion to the rank of rear admiral (retired). Among his books were *Popular Astronomy,* 1878; *The Stars,* 1901; *Astronomy for Everybody,* 1902; and *Compendium of Spherical Astronomy,* 1906. His autobiography, *Reminiscences of an Astronomer,* appeared in 1903. Newcomb died in Washington, D.C., on July 11, 1909.

Nicholas, Samuel (1744?–1790), Revolutionary marine officer. Born about 1744 in Philadelphia of a prosperous Quaker family, Nicholas was a socially prominent sportsman in his youth. He was later apparently an innkeeper and may have served a time in the merchant service. On November 10, 1775, the Continental Congress authorized the enlistment of two battalions of marines for service with the fledgling Continental fleet, and on November 28 Nicholas was commissioned captain, the first officer of marines to be commissioned. With subordinate officers he proceeded with enlistment, and by the end of December five companies had been organized. In February 1776 the marines sailed on the ships of the fleet under Commodore Esek Hopkins, leaving Philadelphia February 17 and arriving in the Bahamas on March 1; Nicholas sailed on the flagship *Alfred.* On March 3 Nicholas led a force of 234 marines and 50 sailors ashore at New Providence Island under cover of the guns of the *Providence* and the *Wasp.* Advancing rapidly inland, the marines took Fort Montagu and Fort Nassau with little difficulty, capturing a large quantity of military stores. Nicholas and the detachment aboard the *Alfred* also took part in the engagement with the *Glasgow* on the return voyage.

Once back in Philadelphia, Nicholas was engaged in recruiting and training for the rest of 1776, receiving promotion to major in June. In December he led three new companies, about 80 men, from Philadelphia to join Gen. George Washington's army in New Jersey and then took part in the battles of Trenton, December 26, and Princeton, January 3, 1777, at the latter helping to hold the bridge over Assunpink Creek. Nicholas saw no further combat, and thereafter the Continental marines became a largely unrelated collection of detachments assigned to vessels of the fleet, the land marines being absorbed into the army. His position as senior officer of marines carried few responsibilities, so during 1777 Nicholas served as a muster master and quartermaster with the army and also worked closely with Robert Morris, virtual director of Continental finances. He was often entrusted with conveying large sums of money and quantities of stores between Philadelphia and Boston. In August 1779 he returned briefly to service to recruit a new company of marines in Philadelphia. In August 1781 he requested and was denied sea duty on the new frigate *America.* He was effectively retired at that time. By the end of 1781 the marine force was reduced to those aboard two frigates. The last Continental marine commission expired in September 1783. Nicholas resumed his business and social activities in Philadelphia after the Revolution. He died there on August 27, 1790.

Nicholson, Samuel (1743–1811), Revolutionary

naval officer. Born in 1743 in Maryland, Nicholson went to sea at an early age. Shortly after the outbreak of the Revolution he was in Paris, where he received from the American commissioners in December 1776 a captain's commission in the Continental navy. A short time later he obtained the cutter *Dolphin* at Dover, England, fitted it out for war in France, and in May sailed in a squadron under Commodore Lambert Wickes. On a cruise in the Irish Sea and northward several prizes were taken. Early in 1778 he sailed the newly completed frigate *Deane,* 32 guns, to America. In May–June 1779 he was commodore of a squadron including the *Confederacy,* Capt. Seth Harding, and the *Boston,* Capt. Samuel Tucker, that sailed from the Delaware River for the West Indies and took numerous prizes. In July–August he was again at sea, in company with the *Boston,* and among their eight prizes were the sloop of war *Thorn,* 16, and the packet *Sandwich;* they returned to Boston with 250 prisoners. In 1780 Nicholson cruised the South Carolina coast, and in early 1781 he convoyed a number of merchantmen from the West Indies. On another West Indian cruise in 1782 he took several prizes, including the *Jackal,* 20, the last prize taken by a Continental navy vessel. He was relieved of command some time later and in 1783 was court-martialed and acquitted on an unknown charge. In June

1794 he was commissioned captain in the new United States navy (still a part of the War Department), ranking second to Capt. John Barry, and ordered to supervise the construction of the frigate *Constitution* at Boston. Built to a design by Joshua Humphreys, the *Constitution* was launched in October 1797 and put to sea in July 1798, joining Barry's squadron in the West Indies late in the year. The *Constitution* proved too large for operations against French privateers, and Nicholson returned with her to Boston in May 1799. He was thereafter employed in shore duty, becoming superintendent of the Charlestown, Massachusetts, navy yard. After Barry's death in 1803 he was the senior officer in the navy. Nicholson died in Charlestown on December 29, 1811.

Nimitz, Chester William (1885–1966), naval

officer. Born on February 24, 1885, in Fredericksburg, Texas, Nimitz graduated from the Naval Academy in 1905. He was commissioned an ensign in 1907 while serving a tour on the China station and later gained unusual experience as a submarine commander on the *Plunger* and other early submarines. In 1910 he became a lieutenant, and in 1912, while commanding the *Skipjack,* he also received command of the Atlantic Submarine Flotilla. He went to Germany and Belgium in 1913 to study advances in diesel engines; returning to the United States, he supervised the construction of the first diesel ship's engine for the navy. In 1916 he was promoted to lieutenant commander, and during World War I he was chief of staff to the commander of the submarine division, Atlantic Fleet. Various assignments followed, and in 1921 he was promoted to commander. After attending the Naval War College in 1922–1923, Nimitz was assigned to the staff of the commander in chief of the Battle Fleet and in 1925 to that of the commander of the U.S. fleet. From 1926 to 1929 he was at the University of California, where he organized the first training division for officers in the naval reserve. Promoted to captain in 1927, he commanded Submarine Division 20 from 1929 to 1931 and the *Augusta* in 1933–1935, and in 1935–1938 he was assistant chief of the Bureau of Navigation. He was promoted to rear admiral in 1938 and for a year commanded a cruiser division and then a battleship division. In June 1939 he was made chief of the Bureau of Navigation, and immediately after the Japanese attack on Pearl Harbor on December 7, 1941, he was named commander in chief of the Pacific Fleet with the rank of admiral, replacing Adm. Husband E. Kimmel. Early in 1942 he was established as commander of all land, sea, and air forces in the Pacific Ocean Areas (North and Central subareas coming under his direct command, while the South was under Adm. Robert L. Ghormley and later Adm. William F. Halsey); his responsibilities were coordinate with those of Gen. Douglas MacArthur, commanding the Southwest Pacific theater. Through such subordinates as Halsey, Marc A. Mitscher, Raymond A. Spruance, Thomas C. Kinkaid, and Richmond K. Turner, he directed the several campaigns among the islands and archipelagoes of the Pacific. Halsey moved up the chain of the Solomons in support of MacArthur, while Central Pacific forces took Tarawa and Makin in the Gilberts, November 1943; Kwajalein and Eniwetok in the Marshalls, January–February 1944; Saipan, Guam, and Tinian in the Marianas, June–July 1944; the Palaus, September 1944; the Philippines, October 1944; Iwo Jima, February 1945; and the Ryukyus, notably Okinawa, March–June 1945. During these advances were fought the epic sea battles of Midway, June 3–6, 1942; the Philippine Sea, June 19–21, 1944; and Leyte Gulf, October 24–26, 1944. In December 1944 Nimitz was promoted to the newly created rank of admiral of the fleet. On September 2, 1945, the surrender of Japan was received aboard his flagship (formerly Halsey's), the battleship *Missouri*. From December 1945 to his retirement in December 1947 he was chief of naval operations, and afterward he served as special assistant to the secretary of the navy. In 1949 he was chosen to supervise the United Nations plebiscite in Kashmir. He coedited with E. B. Potter *Sea Power, a Naval History*, 1960. Nimitz died near San Francisco on February 20, 1966.

Nixon, John (1727–1815), Revolutionary army officer. Born in Framingham, Massachusetts, on March 1, 1727, Nixon enlisted in the colonial militia in 1745 and served under Sir William Pepperrell in the expedition against Louisbourg. In 1755 he enlisted again in a company from Roxbury, later transferring to a Concord company and in September receiving promotion to captain. He took part in the expedition under Gen. (later Sir) William Johnson against Crown Point in 1755 and continued to serve in various campaigns until the end of the war in 1763. The outbreak of the Revolution found him again at arms. He commanded a company of minutemen at Lexington, April 19, 1775, and a regiment at the battle of Bunker Hill, June 17. In January 1776 he was commissioned colonel of the 4th Infantry, Continental army, and in August he was promoted to brigadier general. During the New York campaign he commanded the forces on Governors Island. In 1777 he served under Gen. Horatio Gates in the campaign against Gen. John Burgoyne's invasion, distinguishing himself at the battles of Bemis Heights (Freeman's Farm, or Stillwater), September 19 and October 7, and receiving an injury that, added to his Bunker Hill wound, seriously impaired his health. After a furlough of several months he returned briefly to duty, and in October 1778 he sat on the court-martial of Gen. Philip J. Schuyler. His health continued to deteriorate, however, and in September 1780 he resigned. Sometime between 1803 and 1806

he moved to Middlebury, Vermont, where he died on March 24, 1815.

Norden, Carl Lukas (1880–1965), engineer and inventor. Born on April 23, 1880, in Semarang, Java, of Dutch parents, Norden grew up there and in the Netherlands, Germany, and Switzerland. He graduated in 1904 from the Federal Institute of Technology in Zurich and then came to the United States. For seven years he worked as an engineer for various manufacturing concerns in New York City, and in 1911 he joined the Sperry Gyroscope Company, where he designed the first gyrostabilizing equipment for American ships. He left Sperry in 1915 to work as a private consulting engineer and received several contracts from the navy, for which he developed various flight instruments, a radio-controlled target airplane, a drone flying bomb, and the catapults and arresting gear for the first aircraft carriers, the *Lexington* and the *Saratoga*. In 1921 he received a navy contract to work on the problem of precision aerial bombing. After six years of work, from 1923 in partnership with Theodore H. Barth, he produced his first bombsight, a gyrostabilized optical device of considerable power. In 1928 the firm of Carl L. Norden, Inc., was organized with Barth as president and Norden as consultant, and they were joined by Capt. Frederick I. Entwistle of the navy for further development of the bombsight. By 1931 the bombsight had attained its final form as the Mark XV, a 90-pound device of some 2000 precision parts that combined an optical system, a gyrostabilizing system, and a computer. Using it, a bombardier needed only to enter bomb weight, altitude, and airspeed into the computer and line up the optical sight on the target; the bombsight, through an automatic pilot link, would then take control of the aircraft, make all corrections for drift and other perturbations, and release the bomb load at the proper instant. The Norden bombsight was one of the most highly guarded secrets of World War II, perhaps second only to the atomic bomb. It was used on all U.S. multiengine bombers, and an elaborate ritual evolved around it: constantly under heavy guard, it was delivered, covered, to each plane before a mission; and each bombardier was sworn to destroy it, if need be, to prevent its falling into enemy hands. The very existence of the sight, together with the conspicuous air of secrecy, was a potent propaganda weapon, but its real importance lay in making possible the new technique of high-altitude precision bombing used heavily by U.S. strategic forces over Germany. In 1944 Norden, who nominally earned a dollar for each bombsight sold to the government but who declined to collect, was awarded the Holley Medal of the American Society of Mechanical Engineers. After the war he retired from the firm and lived mainly in Europe. He died in Zürich, Switzerland, on June 14,

1965. The Norden company eventually became a division of United Aircraft.

Norstad, Lauris (1907–   ), army and air force officer. Born on March 24, 1907, in Minneapolis, Minnesota, Norstad grew up in Red Wing and graduated from West Point in 1930. He was commissioned in the cavalry but the next year transferred to the Air Corps. In 1933–1936 he commanded the 18th Pursuit Group in Hawaii, and after three years on the staff of the 9th Bombardment Group at Mitchel Field, New York, he entered the Air Corps Tactical School, Maxwell Field, Alabama, graduating in December 1939. In 1940 he was assigned to intelligence duty with GHQ Air Force at Langley Field, Virginia, and in August 1942, after a few months as an adviser to Gen. Henry H. Arnold, he was named assistant chief of staff of the Twelfth Air Force, which in October left Bolling Field, D.C., to take part in the North Africa campaign. In March 1943 Norstad was promoted to brigadier general and in December named director of operations, Mediterranean Allied Air Forces, under Gen. Ira C. Eaker. In August 1944 he returned to Washington, D.C., as chief of staff of the strategic Twentieth Air Force, under Arnold's direct command. Promoted to major general in June 1945, he had direct responsibility for planning the atomic bomb missions carried out in August against Japan. In June 1946 he was appointed director of the plans and operations division of the General Staff. In that post he played a central role in the army-navy negotiations that led to the National Security Act of 1947 and with Adm. Forrest P. Sherman helped draft the act. Under its terms Norstad transferred into the newly independent air force in September 1947, receiving promotion to lieutenant general and becoming acting vice chief of staff for operations. In October 1950 he was named commander of U.S. air forces in Europe at Wiesbaden, Germany, and in April 1951 he became in addition commander of Allied air forces in central Europe. Norstad was promoted to general in July 1952. A year later he became air deputy to Gen. Matthew B. Ridgway, supreme Allied commander in Europe, continuing in that post under Gen. Alfred M. Gruenther and in November 1956 succeeding Gruenther as commander of all North Atlantic Treaty Organization forces in Europe. He remained in that post until retiring in January 1963. Later in that year he was named president of the Owens-Corning Fiberglass Corporation; he was chief executive from 1967 to 1972 and chairman from 1967.

North, Frank Joshua (1840–1885), scout and frontier figure. Born in Ludlowville, Tompkins County, New York, on March 10, 1840, North grew up in Richland County, Ohio, and moved with his family to Nebraska Territory in 1856. There he came into close contact with the Pawnee Indians, learning

their language and also Indian sign language. In 1861 he became a clerk-interpreter at the Pawnee reservation on the Loup River in Nebraska. In 1864 he was appointed lieutenant of a force of Pawnee volunteers by Gen. Samuel R. Curtis, commander of the Department of Kansas, and in October he was commissioned captain of Nebraska volunteers. During 1865 he led a company of Pawnee scouts in campaigns against Red Cloud and his allies in the Powder and Tongue river countries. He was discharged early in 1866. The next year he was appointed major of cavalry. Authorized to organize and command a battalion of four companies of Pawnee scouts, he was charged with protecting the work gangs on the Union Pacific Railroad against attacks by hostile Indians, mostly Cheyenne. From then until 1877 he led this and other companies of Pawnees against their traditional enemies, the Cheyenne and the Sioux. Notable engagements were fought against the Cheyenne at Plum Creek, Nebraska, on August 17, 1867, and at Summit Springs, Colorado Territory, on July 11, 1869, the latter involving also a detachment of the 5th Cavalry under Maj. Eugene A. Carr. In August 1876 he was ordered to organize a new company of Pawnee scouts for service in Gen. George Crook's campaign against Crazy Horse and others. He guided Col. Ranald S. Mackenzie to Red Cloud and Red Leaf in Nebraska in October and in November led the attack of the 4th Cavalry on Dull Knife's band at Crazy Woman Creek. Mustered out in April 1877, North engaged for five years thereafter in ranching in Nebraska with William F. "Buffalo Bill" Cody. In 1882 he was elected to the Nebraska legislature. From the first show in May 1883 he was a feature of Buffalo Bill's Wild West Show, leading his Pawnees in exhibitions of Indian warfare. He was probably the best revolver shot of his time on the plains, having beaten "Wild Bill" Hickok and others in competition in 1873; and he was an extraordinary leader of Indians in warfare, only one of his men being killed and a handful wounded in six extensive campaigns. In many of his campaigns he was accompanied by his brother, Luther North. In 1884 while appearing in one of the Wild West shows in Hartford, Connecticut, he was severely injured. He died as a result of these injuries on March 14, 1885, in Columbus, Nebraska, his home for many years.

Northrop, John Knudsen (1895–   ), engineer and industrialist. Born on November 10, 1895, in Newark, New Jersey, Northrop and his family moved often in his childhood, settling finally in California. After graduating from high school in 1913 he worked as a draftsman and mechanic for various firms, including a small aircraft company, a forerunner of Lockheed. After service in the aviation section of the Signal Corps during World War I he resumed his former job. Late in 1923 he became a draftsman for the Douglas Aircraft Company and worked his way up to designer and engineer before leaving in January 1927 to form with one of his former employers and other partners the Lockheed Aircraft Company, for which he designed and built the high-wing monocoque Vega. In 1928 he left Lockheed to form the Avion Corporation, where he carried on advanced experiments with a "flying wing" craft of all-metal construction. Avion was bought by the United Aircraft and Transport Corporation in 1930, and early in 1932 Northrop, with backing from Douglas, formed the Northrop Corporation. There he developed several commercial aircraft, notably the Northrop Gamma and Delta, and for military use the A-17 attack plane and the BT-1 dive bomber. In 1937 the Northrop firm was absorbed by Douglas, and in 1939 Northrop formed Northrop Aircraft, Incorporated,

with himself as president and chief engineer and designer. He continued experimenting with the flying wing idea but put it aside to develop the N3-PB seaplane and the P-61 Black Widow, which quickly became the army's standard large all-weather fighter after its introduction in 1941. In 1946 he completed the B-35 Flying Wing bomber, a huge, long-range aircraft that had a limited operational life. Others of Northrop's designs were the F-89 Scorpion all-weather jet fighter, which went into air service in 1950, largely replacing the P-61; the C-125 Raider, used for assault and Arctic rescue work; and the B-49 jet bomber, later adapted to photoreconnaissance work as the YRB-49. In November 1952 he left the company and the following year set up as an independent consulting engineer. He lived privately thereafter in southern California.

O

O'Bannon, Presley Neville (1776–1850), marine officer. Born in 1776 in Fauquier County, Virginia, O'Bannon was commissioned a second lieutenant of marines in January 1801. He advanced to first lieutenant in October 1802. During the Tripolitan War he was ordered to service with the naval squadron in the Mediterranean. In 1804 he was in command of the marine detachment aboard the *Argus*, Capt. Isaac Hull, and in November of that year, after the *Argus* had conveyed William Eaton to Egypt, O'Bannon and seven marines went ashore to assist in Eaton's projected expedition against Derna, then a Tripolitan stronghold. He functioned as Eaton's second-in-command during the long, difficult trek across the desert in March–April 1805 and was highly conspicuous in the successful storming of Derna on April 27, particularly after Eaton was wounded. O'Bannon's marine detachment raised the first American flag ever to fly over foreign soil on that day, and their accomplishment was later immortalized in the reference to the "shores of Tripoli" in the "Marine's Hymn." O'Bannon was rewarded for his services by Hamet Karamanli, the restored pasha, and later by the state of Virginia. He retired in March 1807 and lived quietly thereafter in Kentucky until his death in Logan County on September 12, 1850.

O'Brien, Jeremiah (1744–1818), Revolutionary naval officer. Born in 1744 in Kittery, Maine (then still a part of Massachusetts), O'Brien moved in 1765 to Machias, where he engaged in lumbering with his father. On June 2, 1775, the British naval schooner *Margaretta*, 4 guns, sailed into Machias harbor convoying two sloops, *Unity* and *Polly*, to carry lumber to Boston for the use of the British army. A Liberty pole had earlier been erected in the town, and O'Brien, an ardent patriot, temporized with the British commander until June 11, when he led a party of about 40 volunteers armed with axes, pitchforks, and a few muskets in the capture of the *Unity*. The next day the *Margaretta* slipped away, but O'Brien and his men pursued in the *Unity*; they fired off her single gun and then rammed and boarded the *Margaretta*, taking the schooner in fierce hand-to-hand fighting. Although it was not carried out under any official sanction, this engagement is accounted the first naval battle of the Revolution. Under authority of the Machias committee of safety O'Brien fitted out the *Unity* with the guns from the *Margaretta*, renamed her the *Machias Liberty*, and made ready for sea. On July 14 the British naval schooner *Diligent* and armed tender *Tapnaquish* appeared off Machias, and O'Brien and the *Liberty*, accompanied by the *Falmouth Packet*, captured both without a fight. Three weeks later O'Brien led in repelling an attack on Machias by several vessels from Halifax. In August the *Machias Liberty* and the *Diligent* were commissioned by Massachusetts, becoming the first vessels of the commonwealth's navy. O'Brien cruised on the former until the autumn of 1776, taking several prizes. In 1777 he sailed in command of the privateer *Resolution*, and in 1780, while commanding the privateer *Hannibal*, he was captured by two British frigates off New York. He was held in a prison ship and then in Mill Prison, Plymouth, England, whence he escaped to France after a few months. He returned to America in 1781 and settled again in Machias. In 1811 he was appointed collector of the port of Machias. He died there on September 5, 1818.

O'Hara, Theodore (1820–1867), journalist, army officer, and poet. Born in Danville, Kentucky, on February 11, 1820, O'Hara graduated from St. Joseph's College in Bardstown, Kentucky, in 1839 and took up the study of law in a Frankfort office; John C. Breckinridge was a fellow student. He was admitted to the bar in 1842, but after three years of practice he took a clerkship in the Treasury Department in Washington, D.C. In June 1846 he secured a commission as captain and assistant quartermaster of volunteers for service in the Mexican War, and he saw action at Contreras and Churubusco, winning brevet promotion to major, and at Chapultepec. He was mustered out in October 1848. He returned to Washington and later to Frankfort, where he worked for a newspaper, the *Yeoman*. Late in 1849 he joined the Cuban filibuster Narciso López, becoming colonel of a regiment of Kentuckians whom he led ashore at Cárdenas on May 19, 1850. O'Hara was severely wounded and invalided home the same day. From 1852 to 1855 he was an editor of the *Louisville* (Kentucky) *Times*. From March 1855 to December 1856 he was again in the army as a captain in the 2nd Cavalry. He then became an editor of the *Mobile* (Alabama) *Register*. Even before the Civil War actually began he raised a company of dragoons in Mobile, and he later served as a colonel on the staffs of Gen. Albert S. Johnston and of his old friend Breckinridge. After the war he was a cotton merchant in Columbus, Georgia. He died near Guerryton, Barbour County, Alabama, on June 6, 1867. O'Hara is remembered for one of his small number of fugitive poems, "The Bivouac of the Dead," a dirge commemorating the reinterment in Frankfort in July 1847 of the Kentuckians killed at the battle of Buena Vista (February 22–23, 1847). The poem has remained a standard anthology piece.

O'Hare, Edward Henry (1914–1943), naval officer and aviator. Born in St. Louis, Missouri, on March 13, 1914, "Butch" O'Hare, as he was known, graduated from the Naval Academy in 1937 and subsequently completed aviation training at Pensacola Naval Air Station, Florida. Early in 1942, with the rank of lieutenant, he was attached to the carrier *Lexington.* On February 20 the *Lexington* and its carrier strike force under Adm. Wilson Brown were near Bougainville in the Solomon Islands headed for the Japanese base at Rabaul, when they came under heavy attack by Japanese bombers. A squadron of F4F Wildcats already in the air from the *Lexington* engaged the bombers. In attacking and chasing the first wave of bombers most of the squadron were maneuvered out of position, leaving the second wave opposed only by O'Hare and one comrade, whose guns jammed. O'Hare attacked the nine heavily armed bombers alone, shooting down five and damaging three others in a four-minute bravura display of courage and skill, and causing the survivors to dump their bombs harmlessly and run for safety. (In all, 16 of the 18 bombers were shot down.) Credited with having saved the *Lexington,* O'Hare became the navy's first ace of the war on that day. In April he was rewarded with the Medal of Honor and promotion to lieutenant commander. On November 20, 1943, following an attack on a Japanese formation somewhere in the Pacific, he was listed as missing; he is believed to have been shot down. His combat record was 12 enemy planes shot down. O'Hare International Airport in Chicago was later named in his honor.

Ord, Edward Otho Cresap (1818–1883), army officer. Born on October 18, 1818, in Cumberland, Maryland, of a family with a long military tradition, Ord grew up in Washington, D.C., and graduated from West Point in 1839. He was commissioned in the artillery and was promoted to first lieutenant in 1841 for gallantry in action against the Seminole Indians in Florida. From 1842 to 1846 he was on garrison duty in the East, and in 1847 he was sent by way of Cape Horn to California, where he assumed responsibility for maintaining law and order in Monterey. He was promoted to captain in September 1850. From 1850 to 1852 he was at Fort Independence, Massachusetts, from 1852 to 1855 he was again in California, working with the Coast Survey, and between 1855 and 1859 he took part in campaigns against various Indian tribes in Oregon and

Washington territories. While at the Artillery School at Fort Monroe, Virginia, in October 1859 he was ordered to join the detachment under Col. Robert. E. Lee sent to capture John Brown at Harpers Ferry. At the outbreak of the Civil War he was stationed at the Presidio, San Francisco. He was appointed brigadier general of volunteers in September 1861 and ordered east to command a brigade of the Army of the Potomac. In November he was promoted to major of regulars. Leading a foraging expedition on December 20, 1861, he was attacked by and defeated a Confederate force under Gen. J. E. B. Stuart at Dranesville, Virginia, for which action he was brevetted lieutenant colonel of regulars. In May 1862 he was promoted to major general of volunteers and transferred to the Department of the Mississippi. In August–September he commanded the left wing of the Army of the Tennessee under Gen. Ulysses S. Grant and won a brevet to colonel of regulars at Iuka, Mississippi, September 19. On October 5, following the battle of Corinth, he arrived on the field where Gen. Earl Van Dorn was attempting to cross the Hatchie River; he assumed command of a division from Gen. Stephen A. Hurlbut, launched a vigorous attack on Van Dorn's superior force, and drove him back, receiving a severe wound. He was brevetted brigadier general of regulars for that action. He returned to active duty in June 1863 as commander of the XIII Corps, Army of the Tennessee, taking part in the capture of Vicksburg and Jackson, Mississippi. From August to October he was with the Army of Western Louisiana, but illness then kept him inactive until March 1864, when he joined Gen. Franz Sigel and Gen. George Crook in the Shenandoah valley. In July he took command of the VIII Corps, later transferring to the XVIII Corps. During operations around Richmond he was again severely wounded in the assault on Fort Harrison on September 29. He returned to the field in January 1865 as commander of the Army of the James and the Department of North Carolina. Brevetted major general of regulars in March, he took part in the final operations at Petersburg and in the pursuit of Gen. Robert E. Lee to Appomattox. He then commanded the Department of the Ohio. He was promoted to lieutenant colonel of regulars in December 1865 and brigadier general in July 1866, and on being mustered out of volunteer service in September 1866 he was given command of the Department of Arkansas. He subsequently commanded the departments of California, the Platte, and Texas. He retired in December 1880 and the next month was promoted to major general on the retired list. Ord died in Havana, Cuba, on July 22, 1883.

Osceola (1804?–1838), Indian leader. Born probably among the Creek Indians on the Tallapoosa River in Georgia about 1804, Osceola was also known as Powell, suggesting that his father (or grandfather)

was English or Scottish; but according to another view he was of pure Indian stock. He moved to Florida Territory with his mother and is believed to have fought with the Indians against Gen. Andrew Jackson in the first of the Seminole wars in 1817–1818, while still in his teens. His opposition to efforts to remove the Seminoles westward under treaty is recorded as early as 1832, when he opposed the treaty of Paynes Landing. On April 22, 1835, when the Seminole chiefs silently refused to acknowledge the treaty, Osceola is said to have angrily thrust his knife through the document in protest. He was thereupon arrested and imprisoned, but he escaped by feigning a change of heart. He later led a band of young braves in the murder of a Seminole chief who had agreed to the arrangement. On December 28, 1835, Osceola and a band of warriors ambushed and killed the Indian agent Wiley Thompson outside Fort King, near present-day Ocala. On the same day a second band of Seminoles massacred an army column led by Maj. Francis L. Dade. These events precipitated the second Seminole War, in the course of which Osceola, although not a chief, established himself as probably the dominant military leader of the Seminoles. Hiding the women and children of the tribe deep in the Everglades, he harassed the troops sent to stop him for two years with brilliant guerrilla tactics, with the result that the officer in command, Gen. Thomas S. Jesup, was severely criticized for his ineffectiveness. Jesup, enraged, tricked Osceola and several of his followers into coming out of the Everglades into St. Augustine in October 1837 under a flag of truce; when the Indians entered the compound they were arrested and imprisoned despite public protests. Osceola was later removed to Fort Moultrie near Charleston, South Carolina, where he died, possibly from poison or mistreatment, on January 30, 1838. The Seminole War continued intermittently for several more years and resulted in the extermination of most of the tribe.

Otis, Elwell Stephen (1838–1909), army officer. Born in Frederick, Maryland, on March 25, 1838, Otis graduated from the University of Rochester in 1858 and from Harvard Law School in 1861. He entered practice in Rochester, but in September 1862 he took a captain's commission in the 140th New York Infantry. He took part in all the engagements of the V Corps, Army of the Potomac, receiving promotion to lieutenant colonel in December 1863 and succeeding to command of the regiment when the colonel was killed at Spotsylvania in May 1864. He was severely wounded in October while in action before Petersburg and in January 1865 was mustered out, receiving in March brevets of colonel and brigadier general of volunteers. In July 1866 he entered the regular army as lieutenant colonel of the 22nd Infantry. Until 1880 he saw duty in the northwestern plains, taking part in numerous Indian campaigns, including the Sioux campaign of 1876–1877. In February 1880 he was promoted to colonel of the 20th Infantry. In 1881 he was ordered to establish a school for young officers at Fort Leavenworth, Kansas; the School of Application for Infantry and Cavalry (later, after various reorganizations, called the Command and General Staff School) formally opened in November 1881, and Otis continued as commandant until June 1885. He was with the 20th at Fort Assiniboine, Montana, until 1890, when he was appointed chief of the recruiting service. Promoted to brigadier general in November 1893, he commanded the Department of the Columbia until April 1896 and then the Department of Colorado. In May 1898 he was appointed major general of volunteers, and in July he sailed from San Francisco to reinforce Gen. Wesley Merritt in the Philippines. In August he succeeded Merritt as commander of the VIII Corps and the Department of the Pacific and as military governor. He oversaw the relief of Spanish authorities and, beginning in February 1899, undertook offensive operations against Filipino insurgents throughout the islands. In May 1900 he was succeeded in command by Gen. Arthur MacArthur. He was brevetted major general of regulars for his services on his return to the United States and in June was promoted to that rank. He commanded the Department of the Lakes from October 1900 until his retirement in March 1902. Otis died in Rochester, New York, on October 21, 1909.

P

Page, Richard Lucian (1807–1901), Confederate naval and army officer. Born in Clarke County, Virginia, on December 20, 1807, Page was a nephew of Col. Henry "Light Horse Harry" Lee. He was appointed a midshipman in the navy in 1824, served that year on the *John Adams* in the West India Squadron and the next year on the *Brandywine,* conveying the Marquis de Lafayette home after his American tour, and in 1834 advanced to lieutenant. During 1845–1847 he was on the *Independence,* flagship of Commodore William B. Shubrick, and he commanded the *Perry* in 1852–1854. During 1854–1857 he was at the Norfolk, Virginia, navy yard, receiving promotion to commander in 1855, and in 1857–1859 he commanded the *Germantown.* On the secession of Virginia in April 1861 Page resigned from the navy and became an aide to the governor of Virginia, John Letcher. He oversaw construction of fortifications on the James River and on Nansemond and Pagan creeks. In June he was commissioned a commander in the Confederate States navy and assigned to the captured Norfolk navy yard as ordnance officer. He helped direct the removal of equipment and machinery from Norfolk to Charlotte, North Carolina, where, promoted to captain, he built and for two years commanded an ordnance and construction depot. In March 1864 he was commissioned a brigadier general of provisional forces and put in command of the outer defenses of Mobile, Alabama, principally Fort Morgan. On August 5, 1864, a massive Union attack was mounted at Mobile bay, with Adm. David G. Farragut approaching by sea and Gen. Gordon Granger by land. Page resisted heavy bombardment until August 23, when he was compelled to surrender. He was held prisoner until September 1865. He settled then in Norfolk, Virginia, where from 1875 to 1883 he was superintendent of public schools. He died in Blue Ridge Summit, Pennsylvania, on August 9, 1901.

Page, Thomas Jefferson (1808–1899), naval officer and explorer. Born in Matthews County, Virginia, on January 4, 1808, of a family long distinguished on both sides, Page was appointed a midshipman in the navy in October 1827. After a cruise in the West Indies on the *Erie* he was attached to the Coast Survey for several years. He was promoted to lieutenant in December 1839. He served on the *Columbus* in 1842–1844 and at the Naval Observatory in 1844–1848, and he commanded the *Dolphin*

in Asian waters in 1848–1851. At the conclusion of that cruise he proposed a plan for a surveying expedition to the China seas that was approved by the secretary of the navy. The plan was subsequently expanded, however, to take in the North Pacific and the Bering Sea, and the larger expedition was given into the command of Commodore Cadwalader Ringgold; Page declined the position of second-in-command. Instead he was given command of the steamer *Water-Witch* and dispatched in February 1853 to explore the Plata River and its tributaries in South America. Page carried out the assignment creditably, exploring over the next two years some 3600 miles of river and large areas ashore, but his task was greatly complicated by delicate and changeable diplomatic relations with the nations involved. In February 1855, while on the Paraná River, the *Water-Witch* was fired on from a Paraguayan fort; the vessel suffered considerable damage and one sailor was killed. On his return to the United States in May 1856 Page began agitating for a punitive expedition. Such an expedition of 19 ships was sent out in October 1858 under Commodore William B. Shubrick, with Page, who had advanced to commander in September 1855, as fleet captain and second-in-command. The show of force produced a satisfactory diplomatic settlement. At the conclusion of that mission Page resumed the exploration of the Paraná until December 1860. In 1859 he published *La Plata: The Argentine Confederation and Paraguay* on his survey work. He resigned his commission in April 1861, entered Confederate service, and for a year commanded the heavy batteries at Gloucester Point on the York River. He received a commission as commodore in 1862, and in March 1863 he was sent to England to receive and command an ironclad being built there. That vessel was seized by British authorities before launching, and he was subsequently on waiting orders in France and Italy. In December 1864 he received command of the ironclad *Stonewall* (formerly the *Sphynx,* built in France and sold to Denmark), and in January 1865 he sailed from Copenhagen. After stops in Spain and Portugal and a successful challenge of an attempted blockade of El Ferrol, Spain, by the federal ship *Niagara,* Commodore Thomas T. Craven, Page crossed the Atlantic to Havana, where, on hearing of Gen. Robert E. Lee's surrender, he turned the *Stonewall* over to Spanish authorities. Subsequently he lived in Argentina, in England, where he supervised the construction of four vessels for the Argentine navy, and from about 1880 in Florence, Italy. He died in Rome on October 26, 1899.

Palmer, James Shedden (1810–1867), naval officer.

Born on October 13, 1810, in New Jersey, Palmer was appointed a midshipman in the navy in January 1825. After more than a decade of routine service he was promoted to lieutenant in December 1836. In 1838 he was aboard the *Columbia* under Commodore George C. Read and took part in the burning of Meuke, Sumatra, in retaliation for outrages committed against American shipping. During the Mexican War he commanded the steamer *Flirt* on blockade duty. At the outbreak of the Civil War he was in command of the *Iroquois* in the Mediterranean. He steamed home to join the blockade of Savannah, Georgia, and in September 1861 was ordered to seek out the Confederate raider *Sumter* in the West Indies. He found the *Sumter*, under Commander Raphael Semmes, at Saint-Pierre, Martinique, but was unable to maintain a blockade because the harbor was 15 miles wide and had two entrances. The escape of the *Sumter* in November led to Palmer's being relieved of command, but a court of inquiry later exonerated him, and in May 1862 he resumed command of the *Iroquois* in Adm. David G. Farragut's West Gulf Blockading Squadron. He took possession of Baton Rouge and Natchez for Farragut on May 13, and on June 28 led the first running of the Vicksburg batteries. He performed with conspicuous gallantry in the latter action, was promoted to captain in July, and shortly afterward was transferred to command of Farragut's flagship, the *Hartford*. In February 1863 he was promoted to commodore. On the night of March 14 he led the running of Port Hudson; only the *Hartford* and the gunboat *Albatross* succeeded in passing the batteries. In January 1864 Palmer succeeded Farragut as commander of the forces on the Mississippi and in the autumn of the year became acting commander of the West Gulf Blockading Squadron. He commanded the gunboats of the squadron under Adm. Henry K. Thatcher in the final operations against Mobile, Alabama, in April 1865. In December 1865 he was named commander of the West India Squadron, and in July 1866 he was promoted to rear admiral. While engaged in relief work following an earthquake and tidal wave at St. Thomas, Virgin Islands, he contracted yellow fever and died on December 7, 1867.

Parker, Ely Samuel (1828–1895), Indian leader, army officer, and public official.

Born in 1828 on the Seneca Indian reservation near Pembroke, Genesee County, New York, Parker was the son of a Seneca chief. He received a common-school education and in 1852 became a sachem of the tribe with the name Do-ne-ho-ga-wa. He was a dedicated and effective representative of his tribe in numerous public and legal roles throughout his life. He studied law for a time, but after being refused admission to the bar he took up civil engineering at Rensselaer Polytechnic Institute. He held various government jobs and in 1857 was appointed superintendent of construction of government works at Galena, Illinois, where he formed a close friendship with Ulysses S. Grant. He was eager to serve in the Civil War, but after obtaining a release from his post in Galena in mid-1862 he was unable to secure a state or federal commission for many months. He was finally commissioned captain of engineers in May 1863 and attached to the XVII Corps. In September Grant placed Parker on his own staff and in August 1864 made him his military secretary with the rank of lieutenant colonel of volunteers. At Appomattox on April 9, 1865, Parker wrote out the engrossed copy of the surrender terms; he was subsequently promoted to brigadier general of volunteers as of that date. He continued as Grant's military secretary, receiving commissions of second and first lieutenant in the regular army in 1866 and on March 2, 1867, receiving brevets of captain, major, lieutenant colonel, colonel, and brigadier general for meritorious services. In April 1869 he resigned his commission to accept appointment by President Grant as commissioner of Indian affairs. He encountered considerable opposition in that post, both because he was an Indian and, more directly, because of his efforts to secure just treatment of Indians by the government; after enduring an impeachment trial on trumped-up charges of fraud he resigned in 1871. Thereafter he engaged in business in New York City. Parker died in Fairfield, Connecticut, on August 31, 1895.

Parker, Foxhall Alexander (1821–1879), naval officer.

Born in New York City on August 5, 1821, Parker was appointed a midshipman in the navy in March 1839. After service on the *Levant* of the West India Squadron in the Seminole War in Florida, he attended naval school in Philadelphia, being made passed midshipman in June 1843. He served on the *Michigan* on the Great Lakes in 1844–1845, with the Coast Survey in 1848, on the *St. Lawrence* in the Mediterranean in 1849–1850, and, promoted to lieutenant in September 1850, on the *Susquehannah* in the East India Squadron in 1851–1853. He was again with the Coast Survey in 1854–1855. For four years thereafter he was on the reserve list. After two years with the Pacific Squadron he was appointed executive officer of the Washington navy yard in 1861. He took part in naval activities on the Potomac, and following the battle of Bull Run, July 21, he moved promptly to occupy Fort Ellsworth at Alexandria, Virginia, and shore up the defenses of the capital. Promoted to commander in July 1862, he was assigned briefly to training duty with the Mississippi flotilla under Commodore Andrew H. Foote and in September took command of the gunboat *Mahaska*, operating on the Virginia coast. In June 1863 he took command of the *Wabash*, engaged under Adm. John A. B. Dahlgren in operations against Charleston, South Carolina, and for a few days in August he had charge of a battery erected on Morris Island to bombard Fort Sumter. In January 1864 Parker was placed in command of the Potomac Flotilla, a post held through the rest of the war. He found time to compile a number of naval textbooks, including *Squadron Tactics under Steam*, 1864 *The Naval Howitzer Ashore*, 1865, *The Naval Howitzer Afloat*, 1866; those, and the later *Fleet Tactics under Steam*, 1870, were all in use at various times at the Naval Academy. In July 1866 he was promoted to captain and assigned to the Bureau of Navigation. He was on duty at Hartford, Connecticut, and then at Boston to 1870; he was commander of the *Franklin* in the European Squadron in 1870–1871 and chief of staff of the North Atlantic Fleet in 1872, receiving promotion to commodore in November of that year. He drew up a code of signals for steam tactics in 1872 and during 1873–1876 was chief signal officer of the navy. From 1876 to 1878 he commanded the Boston navy yard, and in 1878 he was appointed superintendent of the Naval Academy. In that year he also served as president of the Naval Institute, which he had helped form five years earlier. Parker died in Annapolis, Maryland, on June 10, 1879.

Parker, John (1729–1775), Revolutionary patriot. Born in Lexington, Massachusetts, on July 13, 1729, Parker had his first experience of war during the French and Indian War, seeing action at Louisbourg and Quebec; it is probable that he later saw service as a member of Rogers' Rangers. In peacetime a farmer and mechanic, he was a captain of minutemen by 1775. On the night of April 18, 1775—a date immortalized by Henry Wadsworth Longfellow's poetic account of Paul Revere's ride—Parker placed a guard of his minutemen around the Rev. Jonas Clarke's house in Lexington, where John Hancock and Samuel Adams were hiding, to protect them from an approaching British column, several hundred strong, under Maj. John Pitcairn. His force numbered about 130 men, but when reports indicated that the British were not coming after all, he dismissed them. Early the next morning, April 19, it was evident that the British were indeed coming, and he tried to reassemble his men, but found only from 40 to 70 of them. The British appeared, and Parker is supposed to have declared: "Stand your ground. Don't fire unless fired upon. But if they mean to have a war, let it begin here." There is considerable doubt that he actually spoke the words, but they are engraved on a stone on the Lexington green and on the memories of students of American history. Pitcairn is similarly credited with the order "Disperse, ye rebels!" He evidently ordered his regulars to fire, although that is not en-

tirely certain; in any event, someone did fire and in the skirmish that followed eight Americans were killed. Parker then assembled the rest of his company of irregulars and marched to join other minutemen in Concord, later harassing the British as they retreated back to Boston. Soon afterward, however, he became very ill, and he died on September 17, 1775.

Parker, William Harwar (1826–1896), Confederate naval officer. Born in New York City on October 8, 1826, Parker was a younger brother of Foxhall A. Parker. He entered the navy as a midshipman in October 1841, made cruises in the Pacific and Brazil squadrons, served on Commodore David Conner's flagship *Potomac* at Veracruz and Tabasco in the Mexican War, and in 1847–1848 attended the Naval Academy. Later he served on the *Yorktown* and was an instructor at the Academy in 1853–1857, receiving promotion to lieutenant in 1855. While on the *Merrimac* in the Pacific in 1857–1860 he wrote *Instructions for Naval Light Artillery*, 1862. After another year as an instructor at the Academy he resigned from the navy in 1861 and was commissioned in the Confederate service. He commanded the *Beaufort* in Flag-Officer William F. Lynch's "mosquito fleet" of gunboats around Roanoke, Virginia, in February 1862 and was with the same vessel under Flag-Officer Franklin Buchanan at Hampton Roads on March 8. In the winter of 1862–1863 he commanded the ironclad ram *Palmetto State* at Charleston, South Carolina, making several attempts to break the blockade. Promoted to captain in 1863, he organized later in the year the Confederate Naval Academy, of which he was thereafter superintendent. The academy consisted essentially of the gunboat *Patrick Henry* on the James River and about 50 cadets. The course of instruction made use of his own *Questions on Practical Seamanship*, 1863, and *Elements of Seamanship*, 1864. In the operations of the James River Flotilla in 1864 Parker also commanded the ironclad *Richmond*. On the evacuation of Richmond, Virginia, on April 2, 1865, Parker and his cadets were entrusted with guarding the Confederate archives and treasury, which they protected for a month before surrendering. From 1865 to 1874 Parker was captain of a mail steamer on the Panama-San Francisco run. He was president of Maryland Agricultural College (now Maryland State College) from 1875 to 1883, and in 1886 he was appointed U.S. minister to Korea by President Grover Cleveland. His *Recollections of a Naval Officer, 1841–1865* appeared in 1883. Parker died in Washington, D.C., on December 30, 1896.

Parrott, Enoch Greenleafe (1815–1879), naval officer. Born in Portsmouth, New Hampshire, on November 27, 1815, Parrott was a cousin of Robert P. Parrott, inventor. He entered the navy as a midshipman in December 1831 and after a decade of service in the Brazil Squadron and with the Coast Survey was promoted to lieutenant in September 1841. In 1841–1843 he was on the *Saratoga* on the African coast. During the Mexican War he was on the *Congress*, flagship of Commodore Robert F. Stockton, commander of the Pacific Squadron, and thus took part in the California campaign under Stockton and Capt. John C. Frémont; later, under Commodore William B. Shubrick, the *Congress* took part in the occupation of Mazatlán and Guaymas, Mexico, in November 1847. In 1852–1853 Parrott was on the *St. Louis* under Commander Duncan N. Ingraham; later he was on the *St. Mary's* in the Pacific, and during 1857–1858 he was at the Naval Observatory. He took part in the evacuation and burning of Norfolk navy yard on April 20, 1861, and, promoted to commander in that month, he shortly thereafter took command of the brig *Perry*. On June 3 he captured the Confederate privateer *Savannah* off Charleston, South Carolina; the *Savannah*, which had taken one prize in its brief career, was the first such privateer taken in the war, and Parrott was officially commended for his achievement. Parrott commanded the steamer *Augusta* in the expedition under Flag-Officer Samuel F. Du Pont against Port Royal, South Carolina, in November 1861 and on blockade duty thereafter. In 1864 he commanded the ironclad *Canonicus* in the James River Squadron under Adm. Samuel P. Lee, and he commanded the monitor *Monadnock* in the attacks of December 24–25, 1864, and January 13–15, 1865, by Adm. David D. Porter on Fort Fisher, North Carolina. He was promoted to captain in July 1866 while commanding the receiving ship at Boston navy yard and to commodore in April 1870. He commanded the Mare Island navy yard in California in 1871–1872 and the Asiatic Squadron from 1872, receiving promotion to rear admiral in November 1873 and retiring in April 1874. Parrott died in New York City on May 10, 1879.

Parrott, Robert Parker (1804–1877), army officer, inventor, and manufacturer. Born in Lee, New Hampshire, on October 5, 1804, Parrott graduated from West Point in 1824 and was commissioned in the artillery. He spent the next five years at West Point as an instructor in natural philosophy and mathematics, after which he served at various army posts, receiving promotion to first lieutenant in August 1831. His career may be said to have begun in 1834, when he was assigned to ordnance duty. He was promoted to captain in January 1836 and, after brief staff service in the Creek campaign, sent to Washington, D.C., as assistant to the chief of the Bureau of Ordnance. He set himself to study the subject in all of its aspects, and when he was appointed inspector of ordnance at the West Point Foundry, at Cold Spring, New York, later in the year he soon came to the attention of Gouverneur Kemble,

president of the foundry, who prevailed upon him to resign his commission in October and take over management of the foundry. In 1839 he succeeded Kemble as lessee of the foundry. One of his first actions was to purchase 7000 acres of woodland in New York to provide a dependable source of charcoal, and he also bought an iron furnace to provide a supply of pig iron. For the next four decades he managed the entire enterprise while he continued his study of ordnance. He learned in 1849 of the secret production of a rifled cannon by the Krupp factory in Germany, and he immediately set to work to produce such a weapon. After more than ten years of experimentation he patented in October 1861 the design for the famous Parrott rifle, which was a cast-iron rifled cannon whose breech was strengthened by a wrought-iron hoop; the rifle was cheap and easy to produce and allowed for the use of a larger explosive charge than other guns could accommodate. The larger caliber Parrott guns were hollow-cast on the system devised by Capt. Thomas J. Rodman. In August 1861 Parrott had patented an explosive shell with a ring of brass around it that expanded when the weapon was fired, filling the groves inside the rifle and thus attaining significantly greater accuracy than was previously possible. These developments came just at the beginning of the Civil War, and Parrott offered his guns to the Union army at cost. Thousands of cannon of various calibers were made, and they were used in every important engagement of the war, from the first battle of Bull Run (Manassas) in July 1861 to the siege of Richmond near the war's end; they were accounted the most effective ordnance in the world at the time. After the war Parrott ceased the manufacture of guns at the West Point Foundry but continued to operate, with his brother Peter, his charcoal and pig-iron supply operations. He sold the business to his brother in 1877 and retired. He died in Cold Spring, New York, on December 24, 1877.

Parsons, Samuel Holden (1737–1789), Revolutionary army officer and public official. Born in Lyme, Connecticut, on May 14, 1737, Parsons graduated from Harvard in 1756. He studied law and in 1759 was admitted to the bar, establishing a practice in Lyme. From 1762 to 1774 he sat in the colonial assembly, where he was an early advocate of an intercolonial congress and of independence. In 1770 he was appointed a major of militia, and in May 1775 he became colonel of the 6th Connecticut Regiment, which he led in the capture by Col. Ethan Allen and Col. Benedict Arnold of Fort Ticonderoga on May 10. He then marched to Boston to join the main army. In August 1776 he was commissioned brigadier general in the Continental army, and he fought well through the campaigns on Long Island, on Manhattan, and in upstate New York. He was thereafter on continuous duty in the Hudson Highlands or on the Connecticut shore. On January 20, 1778, a brigade under his command broke ground for the construction of fortifications at West Point, chosen in a survey of the Highlands as the optimum site for a river-defense citadel. In July 1779 he attacked the British forces that had occupied and burned most of Norwalk, Connecticut, but to little effect. In December 1779 he succeeded Gen. Israel Putnam as commander of the Connecticut line, and he was promoted to major general in October 1780. In the latter year he sat on the court-martial of Maj. John André. It has been charged and denied that during the latter part of the war Parsons held treasonable correspondence with Sir Henry Clinton through a double-agent intermediary; most likely the treason was that of the agent, William Heron, and Parson's part was incaution. After being mustered out in July 1782 Parsons resumed his law practice and became interested in western lands. In September 1785 he was appointed by Congress a commissioner to extinguish Indian claims in the Ohio territory. He was active in the formation of the Ohio Company of Associates in 1786 and was its agent until being replaced by the more effective Rev. Manasseh Cutler. He nonetheless became a director of the company in March 1787. In October 1787 he was appointed the first judge of the Northwest Territory, and in April 1788 he made his way to the new settlement of Marietta (now in Ohio). In 1789 he journeyed to the Western Reserve, where he had been granted by Connecticut the 24,000 acre Salt Springs Tract along the Mahoning River. Returning from there, he overturned his canoe in the Big Beaver River and drowned on November 17, 1789.

Partridge, Alden (1785–1854), army officer and educator. Born in Norwich, Vermont, on February 12, 1785, Partridge attended Dartmouth College from 1802 to 1805, when he entered West Point. In October 1806, having completed what was then the very irregular course of instruction, he was commissioned a first lieutenant of engineers. He remained at West Point thereafter as an instructor. Promoted to captain in July 1810, he became professor of mathematics and subsequently of engineering in 1813. In January 1815 he became superintendent of the academy. As an administrator he was notably deficient; he was arbitrary in his enforcement of rules and regulations, he feuded with faculty and students alike, and in a relatively short time he brought the academy close to uselessness. He was succeeded by Maj. Sylvanus Thayer in the summer of 1817 while away on leave, and on his return he attempted to wrest control from Thayer until an order from Washington, D.C., called for his arrest. Convicted of insubordination and neglect of duty, he was to be cashiered from the service, but the sentence was remitted by President James Monroe. Partridge resigned from the army in April 1818. After a period engaged in the survey of the

northeastern border of the United States he returned to Norwich, Vermont, and established the American Literary, Scientific and Military Academy, which opened in September 1820 with 100 cadets. It was Partridge's belief that the War of 1812 had demonstrated, almost tragically, the woeful lack of military readiness in the nation; that a trained citizen-soldiery was far preferable to a large standing army; and that, moreover, West Point would never be capable of educating all the officers that a national army would require. Thus his academy offered military instruction along with a sound professional course in engineering that featured such novelties as college-level agricultural training and summer courses of practical application in the field. It was also Partridge's plan that similar academies would be seeded from his, and in fact, aided by graduates of Norwich, he later established short-lived academies in Portsmouth, Virginia (1839–1846), Bristol, Pennsylvania (1842–1845), Harrisburg, Pennsylvania (1845–1848), Wilmington, Delaware (1846–1848), Reading, Pennsylvania (1850–1854), Pembroke, New Hampshire (1850–1853), and Brandywine, Delaware (1853–1854). Although none lasted, Partridge may justly be credited with the impulse that led to the later appearance of elementary and secondary military academies across the country. The Norwich school moved to Middletown, Connecticut, in 1825 but returned in 1829, selling its property in Middletown to the Methodist Church, which established Wesleyan University on it. In 1834 Partridge's school was chartered by the state of Vermont as Norwich University. In 1843 Partridge relinquished the presidency of the school. In 1845 he evicted the school from the property on which it stood, which he owned, and opened a rival school that lasted only a year. In addition to his activities as an educator he served as state surveyor of Vermont in 1822–1823 and sat in the legislature in 1833, 1834, 1837, and 1839. Partridge died in Norwich, Vermont, on January 17, 1854. In 1867, following a disastrous fire, Norwich University removed to Northfield, Vermont.

Partridge, Earle Everard (1900–   ), army and air force officer. Born on July 7, 1900, in Winchendon, Massachusetts, Partridge enlisted in the army in 1918 and served in France with the 79th Division. On his return home in 1919 he entered Norwich University, but in June 1920 he reenlisted in the army and in that year secured admission to West Point. He graduated in 1924, was commissioned in the Air Service, and over the next several years saw routine duty at various posts. Promoted to captain in 1935, he graduated from Air Corps Tactical School, Maxwell Field, Alabama, in 1937 and from Command and General Staff School, Fort Leavenworth, Kansas, in 1938. In March 1942 he was promoted to temporary colonel and attached to the General Staff. In December he advanced to temporary brigadier general, and in January 1943 he was named commander of the New York Air Defense Wing. A few months later he was assigned to the staff of the Northwest African Air Force, and shortly thereafter he became chief of staff of the Fifteenth Air Force under Gen. James H. Doolittle. In January 1944 he became deputy commander, again under Doolittle, of the Eighth Air Force, advancing to temporary major general in May, and in June he succeeded Gen. Curtis E. LeMay as commander of the 3rd Bombardment Division. In the summer of 1945 he oversaw the transfer of the Eighth Air Force from Europe to Okinawa and during September–November was its commander. In January 1946 Partridge was named assistant chief of the air staff for operations. Passing into the independent air force, he was made permanent major general in June 1948 and in October became commander of the Fifth Air Force at Nagoya, Japan. On the outbreak of the Korean War in 1950 Partridge and the Fifth moved to Korea, where he remained the senior air officer until July 1951. Promoted to temporary lieutenant general in April 1951, he was given command of the Air Research and Development Command at Wright-Patterson Air Force Base, Ohio, in July. In June 1953 he was appointed deputy chief of staff of the air force, and in April 1954 he took command of the Far East Air Forces with the rank of general. A year later he was named to command the Continental Air Defense Command, which in 1957 became the North American Air Defense Command. He held that post until July 1959, when he retired. The next year he became a trustee of Aerospace Corporation, formed by the air force to oversee its missile and space programs.

Patch, Alexander McCarrell (1889–1945), army officer. Born on November 23, 1889, at Fort Huachuca, Arizona Territory, where his father was stationed, Patch grew up in Lebanon County, Pennsylvania. After a year, 1908–1909, at Lehigh University he entered West Point, graduating in 1913 and taking a commission in the infantry. With the 18th Infantry he served on the Mexican border in 1916, and in June 1917, by then a captain, he was sent to France with the 1st Division. For five months he commanded a machine gun battalion, and for six months thereafter he directed the Machine Gun School of the American Expeditionary Forces. Having reached the rank of temporary lieutenant colonel, he returned to the United States in June 1919. He taught military science at Staunton (Virginia) Military Academy from 1920 to 1924, graduated from Command and General Staff School, Fort Leavenworth, Kansas, in 1925, and was again at Staunton until 1928. During 1928–1931 he was commander of Fort Washington, Maryland, and after graduating from the Army War College in 1932 he returned once

more to Staunton. Promoted to lieutenant colonel in 1935, he was appointed to the Infantry Board in 1936, on which he helped develop and test the three-regiment "triangular" division concept. In August 1940 he was promoted to temporary colonel in command of the 47th Infantry, and in December, by then a temporary brigadier general, he was ordered to training duty at Fort Bragg, North Carolina. In January 1942 he was selected to organize the defense of New Caledonia, an island strategically situated in the sea approaches to Australia. The forces available consisted of stray and often untrained units originally destined for the Philippines or Australia, but by May Patch, who had become temporary major general in March, had organized the Americal (American-Caledonia) Division (the army's only unnumbered division). Elements of the Americal undertook the first offensive operation of the army's war in the Pacific on Guadalcanal on October 13, 1942, and in December Patch succeeded Gen. Alexander A. Vandegrift as commander of all U.S. forces on Guadalcanal and Tulagi. He organized his army and marine forces as the XIV Corps, and soon after conclusion of that campaign in February he returned to the United States, taking command in April of the IV Corps area at Fort Lewis, Washington. In March 1944 he again went overseas, taking command of the Seventh Army, then in Sicily (the Seventh moved in July to Naples). Early in August he was promoted to temporary lieutenant general. On August 15, 1944, the Seventh, augmented by five French divisions, landed on the beaches of St. Tropez and St. Raphaël on the French Riviera in Operation Dragoon. The Seventh advanced rapidly northward, liberating Marseilles, Toulon, and Lyons, covering more than 400 miles up the Rhône valley to the Vosges Mountains in 30 days, and on September 11 making contact with Gen. George S. Patton's Third Army north of Dijon. On September 15 the French divisions were organized as the French First Army, which with the U.S. Seventh formed the Allied 6th Army Group, under Gen. Jacob L. Devers. The Seventh subsequently advanced through the Vosges into Alsace and in November took Strasbourg; it was the first army to reach the Rhine. In December it covered long defensive lines while the Third Army counterattacked in the north in the Battle of the Bulge. It met a heavy German attack in January and closed the Colmar pocket in February. Turning north, the Seventh cooperated with the Third in occupying the Saar; it then crossed the Rhine and occupied Nuremberg and Munich, making contact at the Brenner Pass with Gen. Mark W. Clark's Fifth Army on May 4. In June Patch was recalled to the United States to command the Fourth Army at Fort Sam Houston, Texas; in October he was appointed to direct a study of the army's postwar strength and organization. He died in San Antonio, Texas, on November 21, 1945.

Pate, Randolph McCall (1898–1961), marine officer. Born February 11, 1898, in Port Royal, South Carolina, Pate served briefly as a private in the army in 1918 before entering the Virginia Military Institute. Soon after graduating in 1921 he took a commission in the marine corps. Over the next 20 years he saw service in Santo Domingo (Dominican Republic) in 1923–1924, in China in 1927–1929, and at other marine posts and barracks, advancing by 1941 to the rank of major. As a lieutenant colonel he served with the 1st Marine Division on Guadalcanal from August 1942, and he was later deputy chief of staff to Gen. Holland M. Smith during the campaigns on Iwo Jima and Okinawa. In January 1946 he joined the staff of the Marine Corps Schools, Quantico, Virginia, becoming chief of staff in July 1948 and advancing to brigadier general the next year. In July 1951 he joined the staff of the Joint Chiefs of Staff and later in the year returned to Quantico. In September 1952, with the rank of major general, he became commander of the 2nd Marine Division at Camp Lejeune, North Carolina. In June 1953 he took command of the 1st Division in Korea; his tour in that country included the final months of bitter fighting before the armistice. He returned to the United States in May 1954, becoming in July assistant commandant and chief of staff of the marine corps with the rank of lieutenant general. In January 1956 Pate was appointed commandant with the rank of general. One of his first actions in that post was to institute reforms in the marine training system, largely as a result of the drowning of six recruits during a night disciplinary march at the Parris Island, South Carolina, boot camp in April 1956. Later in his term some 6000 marines were sent to Lebanon in July–October 1958 to help maintain order. Pate retired in January 1960 and died on July 31, 1961 in Bethesda, Maryland.

Patrick, Mason Mathews (1863–1942). army officer and airman. Born in Lewisburg, West Virginia, on December 13, 1863, Patrick graduated from West Point in 1886 and was commissioned in the engineers. For three years he was at the Engineers School of Application at Willets Point (later Fort Totten), New York, graduating in 1889 and receiving promotion to first lieutenant in July. In that year he joined in the relief efforts following the disastrous flood at Johnstown, Pennsylvania, on May 31. From 1892 to 1895 he taught engineering at West Point. From 1897 to 1901 he was involved in Mississippi River improvement, advancing to captain in May 1898, and after two years in the office of the chief of engineers he returned to the West Point faculty in 1903–1906. He was promoted to major in April 1904. In 1907–1909 he was chief engineer of the Army of Cuban Pacification. From 1909 to 1912 he was engaged in river and harbor work in Virginia, becoming lieutenant colonel in June 1910, and in 1910–1912 he

was also a member of the board directing the raising of the *Maine* in Havana harbor. He was in river and harbor work in Michigan from 1912 to 1916. Promoted to colonel of the 1st Engineers Regiment in March 1916, he served on the Mexican border in that year and in 1917 was sent to France. In August he was promoted to temporary brigadier general, and in September he was named chief engineer of the lines of communication and director of construction and forestry of the American Expeditionary Force. In May 1918 he was appointed by Gen. John J. Pershing to command the combined Air Service of the A. E. F., until then an uncoordinated collection of often competing units attached to army and corps staffs. In June he was advanced to temporary major general. Patrick remained with the Air Service until July 1919, returning then to the United States and to various engineering duties, including assistant chief of engineers in 1920–1921. In October 1921 he was promoted to major general and appointed chief of the Air Service, and, the better to execute his responsibilities in that post, he learned to fly. Under his direction the Air Service established experimental facilities at Wright Field, Ohio, and a large training center at San Antonio, Texas; it made great progress in aircraft design and doctrine; and its pilots set innumerable speed, distance, and altitude records. During April–September 1924 a team of army pilots in Douglas-Liberty 400 bombers made the first round-the-world flight, covering 26,345 miles in 363 hours of flying over a span of 175 days and winning the Collier Trophy for the Air Service. In 1925 Patrick sat on the court-martial of his former assistant, Col. William Mitchell. As a result of urging by Mitchell and Patrick, among others, the Air Service was reorganized as the Air Corps in July 1926, receiving an additional degree of autonomy under an assistant secretary of war. Patrick, reappointed chief in October 1925, retired in December 1927. The following year he published *The United States in the Air.* From 1929 to 1933 he was public utilities commissioner for the District of Columbia. He died in Washington, D.C., on January 29, 1942.

Patterson, Daniel Todd (1786–1839), naval officer. Born on Long Island, New York, on March 6, 1786, Patterson (whose middle name is sometimes given as Tod) began his naval service in June 1799 as acting midshipman aboard the sloop *Delaware.* After a cruise to the West Indies he received his warrant as midshipman in August 1800, and he was retained in the reduction of the navy the next year. In 1802–1803 he was on the *Constellation* in the squadron at Tripoli under Commodore Richard V. Morris, and later in 1803 he returned to Tripoli on the *Philadelphia* under Capt. William Bainbridge. He was held captive after the grounding of the *Philadelphia* on October 31 until mid-1805. He was stationed at New Orleans in 1806–

1807, receiving promotion to lieutenant in the latter year, and was there again from 1808, commanding a gunboat squadron on the Mississippi in 1810–1811. He was promoted to master commandant in July 1813 and in December of that year became commander of the New Orleans station. On September 16, 1814, he led an attack on the pirate base at Barataria, where Jean Laffite had his headquarters. When the British fleet under Adm. Sir Alexander Cochrane entered the Gulf of Mexico, Gen. Andrew Jackson assumed him to be headed for Mobile, but Patterson believed New Orleans to be the goal and refused to follow Jackson in November. He sent a flotilla of gunboats under Lt. Thomas ap Catesby Jones to hold Lake Borgne, and on December 14 the flotilla fought a gallant delaying action against overwhelming numbers. On December 23 Patterson, on his flagship *Carolina*, led an attack on the British army under Gen. Edward Pakenham, camped on the levee at Villere's Plantation eight miles below New Orleans. The *Carolina* was destroyed four days later, but Patterson's slow retreat up the river allowed Jackson time to prepare a defense of the city. In the battle of January 8, 1815, Patterson commanded a land battery on the west bank. In February he was promoted to captain. From 1824 to 1828 he commanded the *Constitution* and was fleet captain of the Mediterranean Squadron under Commodore John Rodgers. He was a navy commissioner in 1828–1832 and from 1832 to 1836 commanded the Mediterranean Squadron. In 1836 he became commander of the Washington navy yard; he died in Washington, D.C., on August 25, 1839.

Patton, George Smith, Jr. (1885–1945), army officer. Born on November 11, 1885, in San Gabriel, California, Patton studied for a year at the Virginia Military Institute and then entered West Point, from which he graduated in 1909. Commissioned in the cavalry, he served at a number of army posts, quickly gaining a reputation for ability and driving energy. In 1912 he represented the United States in the military pentathlon events of the Olympic Games in Stockholm. Afterward he attended briefly the French cavalry school in Saumur. While an instructor at the Mounted Service School, Fort Riley, Kansas, he wrote the army manual on the saber. After taking part in Gen. John J. Pershing's expedition into Mexico in pursuit of Pancho Villa in 1916, following which he was promoted to captain, he was assigned to Pershing's staff at the head of the American Expeditionary Forces (AEF) and sent to France in May 1917. He received training in the use of tanks, then a new weapon, and established the AEF tank school at Langres. He then organized and, as temporary lieutenant colonel, commanded the 304th Tank Brigade at St. Mihiel and in the Meuse–Argonne offensive. After the war he returned to the United States, reverting from temporary colonel to captain and receiv-

ing promotion to major in 1919, and commanded the 304th at Fort Meade, Maryland, for a year. Over the next 20 years he served with the 3rd Cavalry at Fort Myer, Virginia, did two tours in Hawaii, was in the office of the chief of cavalry in 1928–1931, and graduated from Cavalry School, Fort Riley, in 1923, Command and General Staff School, Fort Leavenworth, Kansas, in 1924, and the Army War College in 1932. He was promoted to lieutenant colonel in 1934 and colonel in 1937. From December 1938 to July 1940 he commanded the 3rd Cavalry at Fort Myer. He then was assigned to the 2nd Armored Division at Fort Benning, Georgia, advancing to temporary brigadier general in October, and in April 1941 he became divisional commander with the rank of temporary major general. There and later at the army's Desert Training Center (which he commanded during April–August 1942) on the California–Arizona border he molded the 2nd, and from January 1942 the I Armored Corps, into a highly efficient force. He was sent at the head of the Western Task Force to take part in the North African campaign in November 1942. The amphibious assault in Morocco, conducted with naval forces under Adm. H. Kent Hewitt, began November 7, and after the overcoming of brief French resistance the country was occupied. In the aftermath of the disastrous American defeat at Kasserine Pass, Tunisia, Patton was moved in to command the II Corps in Tunisia in March 1943, becoming lieutenant general in April. He enjoyed remarkable success in restoring discipline and morale to the II Corps and in combatting the enemy. He was then transferred to command of the I Armored Corps (Reinforced), which in July was redesignated the Seventh Army; the Seventh, with the British Eighth, under Gen. Bernard L. Montgomery, formed the 15th Army Group, Gen. Sir Harold R. L. G. Alexander, for the invasion of Sicily. Landed at Licata, Gela, and Scoglitti on the south coast by Adm. Hewitt's Western Naval Task Force on July 10, the Seventh pushed north, its II Corps, under Gen. Omar N. Bradley, taking Palermo on July 22. Patton drove relentlessly and reached Messina on August 16, ahead of Montgomery. At the end of the Sicily campaign, in an incident later much publicized, he slapped a hospitalized soldier whom he suspected of malingering; he was sharply reprimanded by Gen. Dwight D. Eisenhower and widely criticized in the press, and his promotion to permanent major general was held up for several months. Early in 1944 Patton was ordered to England, where he took command of the Third Army in preparation for the campaign on the continent. The Third Army became operational on August 1 at St. Lô, France. He immediately sent out three columns, one attacking west through Brittany to Brest, one south to the Loire River, and one east to cooperate with Gen. Courtney H. Hodges's First Army in capturing thousands of Germans in the Argentan pocket. Patton then dashed eastward, reaching the Seine on August 21 and the Meuse a few days later. By then he had outrun his logistical support, however, and a lull ensued. In December, poised on the Saar, he executed one of the most remarkable pieces of staff work and field maneuver in military history by quickly turning the Third Army northward to shore up the Allied southern flank against the Germans' Ardennes offensive, known also as the Battle of the Bulge. The Third's 4th Armored Division, led by Col. Creighton W. Abrams's 37th Tank Battalion, relieved the beleaguered 101st Airborne, Gen. Anthony C. McAuliffe, at Bastogne on December 26. On March 22, 1945, the Third crossed the Rhine at Oppenheim and continued its relentless drive across Germany, joining the First again to encircle the Ruhr pocket, moving through Bavaria into Czechoslovakia and Austria, and finally halting at the Elbe on May 5. Patton was promoted in April to temporary general. One of the most colorful commanders the army has ever known, "Old Blood and Guts," as he was known, displayed great courage, daring, and ruthlessness throughout this final campaign of the war, wearing all the while his matched ivory-handled revolvers. His public criticisms of the postwar denazification program in occupied Germany, based on his apprehensions of Communist takeovers in Europe, led to his being transferred in October 1945 from command of the Third Army and the military governorship of Bavaria to the largely paper Fifteenth Army. In that post he was also president of the Theater General Board, organized to prepare formal studies of the European campaign. In November Patton succeeded Gen. Dwight D. Eisenhower as commander of U.S. forces in Europe; after two weeks he was in turn succeeded in that post by Gen. Joseph T. McNarney. Patton died in Heidelberg, Germany, on December 21, 1945, following a car accident. An autobiography, War as I Knew It, was published in 1947.

Paulding, Hiram (1797–1878), naval officer.

Born on December 11, 1797, on a farm in Westchester County, New York, Paulding was a son of one of the captors of Maj. John André during the Revolution. Appointed a midshipman in September 1811, he served on Lake Champlain in the War of 1812 and performed gallantly as acting lieutenant of the Ticonderoga at the battle of Lake Champlain (Plattsburg), September 11, 1814. He later served on the Constellation in the Algerine War and in April 1816 was promoted to lieutenant. Service on other vessels followed, and for a time he studied at Norwich Military Academy in Vermont, graduating in 1823. In that year he took part in Commodore David Porter's pirate patrol in the West Indies as lieutenant on the Sea Gull, the navy's second steam vessel and the first of any navy to see combat. The next year, on duty in the Pacific aboard the United States, he volunteered to

carry dispatches from the Peruvian port of Callao to Simon Bolivar's headquarters deep in the Andes, a 1500-mile trek through the mountains on horseback. In 1825 he volunteered for a cruise in the South Seas as first lieutenant under Capt. John Percival of the Dolphin, in pursuit of mutineers from the whaleship Globe. On a small island Paulding found and seized one of the mutineers and, using his captive's body as a shield, marched him away to one of his ship's boats through a crowd of angry islanders. He described this and other events in his Journal of a Cruise of the U.S. Schooner Dolphin, 1831, and published an account of his Andean adventure in Bolivar in His Camp, 1834. He cruised in the Mediterranean in 1830–1832 and 1834–1837 and was promoted to commander in February 1837 and to captain in February 1844, whereupon he took the Vincennes on a three-year cruise to China. He returned to be given command of the new frigate St. Lawrence and sailed her to Bremen, the first U.S. warship to visit that German port. While there he was consulted on the creation of a German navy, and for a year he carried four German midshipmen on the St. Lawrence. He was commander of the Washington, D.C., navy yard from 1851 to 1855 and during the next three years commanded the Home Squadron, operating mostly in the Caribbean. In December 1857 he took into custody William Walker and 150 filibusters at Greytown (San Juan del Norte), Nicaragua, and sent them home. Sentiment in the Northern states as well as in the Nicaraguan government generally approved this action, but President James Buchanan freed Walker, whose regime in Nicaragua had been recognized by the United States, and relieved Paulding of his command. Appointed head of the Bureau of Detail in March 1861, he had the unpleasant task of overseeing the evacuation and burning of the Norfolk, Virginia, navy yard on April 20. The job was incompletely done under the difficult circumstances of those early days of the Civil War; some 3000 cannon had to be left behind, the unfinished Merrimac was left in salvageable condition, and Paulding was severely criticized. He was one of the strongest advocates of John Ericsson's revolutionary design for the Monitor and was credited with helping to win its adoption. Later in the year he took command of the New York navy yard, in which position he oversaw the supplying and servicing of the Union's blockading fleet during the rest of the war. He was technically retired for age in December 1861 but was kept on special duty, receiving promotion to rear admiral on the retired list in July 1862. After the war he served as governor of the Naval Asylum at Philadelphia, 1866–1869, and as port admiral of Boston, 1869–1870. He died at his farm near Huntington, New York, on Long Island Sound, on October 20, 1878. At his death he was the senior officer on the naval list and the last surviving officer of the battle of Lake Champlain.

Peary, Robert Edwin (1856–1920), naval officer and explorer. Born in Cresson, Pennsylvania, on May 6, 1856, Peary graduated from Bowdoin College in 1877 and two years later joined the U.S. Coast and Geodetic Survey. In October 1881 he was commissioned a lieutenant in the navy's Civil Engineering Corps. From 1884 to 1888 his official duties involved the surveying of a proposed ship canal route through Nicaragua, but during a six-month leave in 1886 he began his real career with an exploratory journey to the interior of Greenland. From 1888 to 1891 he was engaged in various engineering duties. In 1891, while on an 18-month leave, he returned to Greenland, wintered there (his wife becoming the first non-native woman to endure an Arctic winter), and the following spring sledged northward, arriving at the northern shore on July 4 and thus gaining substantial evidence of the insularity of Greenland. The daring and difficult 1300-mile journey into the region later called Peary Land, during which valuable scientific observations were made, won Peary a considerable reputation that eased the problem of financing his subsequent explorations. He made more trips to Greenland in 1893–1895, 1896, and 1897, and transported three huge meteorites—one of 90 tons—from the ice fields to the United States. In 1898 he published a record of his Arctic experiences in *Northward over the "Great Ice"* and announced his intention of reaching the North Pole. Securing a five-year leave from the navy, he surveyed northern routes and passages from 1898 to 1902, failing, however, to reach the Pole, although he attained the latitude 84°17' N. For a year he was again on active duty with the Bureau of Yards and Docks, but in 1903 he obtained a three-year leave. In 1905–1906, with the icebreaking ship *Roosevelt,* built to his specifications and underwritten by the Peary Arctic Club, he steamed and sledged to within 175 miles of the Pole, reaching 87°6' N on April 21, 1906. After publishing *Nearest the Pole* in 1907 he set out in July 1908 on his final Arctic journey. In March 1909 he began the final leg from Cape Columbia, Ellesmere Island, with six sledge teams, each of which took a turn at breaking trail before falling back. At last only Peary's sledge remained. Accompanied by his personal aide, Matthew A. Henson, and four Eskimos, he reached the North Pole on April 6, 1909. Soundings taken there proved the Pole to be located in a vast frozen sea. On his return to the United States he learned that Dr. Frederick A. Cook, a surgeon who had been with him in 1891, had claimed to have reached the Pole a year earlier, and a long and unpleasant controversy ensued. Cook's claim was eventually shown to be spurious, and even at the time was taken seriously by few experts, being largely a matter of publicity and newspaper controversy. Therefore, after publishing *The North Pole* in 1910, Peary was voted the thanks of Congress and given the rank of rear admiral (re-

tired) in March 1911. In his later years he was much interested in aviation and during World War I organized the National Aerial Coast Patrol Commission and served as chairman of the National Committee on Coast Defense by Air. He died in Washington, D.C., on February 20, 1920.

Pegram, John (1832–1865), Confederate army officer. Born on January 24, 1832, in Petersburg, Virginia, Pegram graduated from West Point in 1854 and was commissioned in the 1st Dragoons. He served mainly on the frontier, receiving promotion to first lieutenant in February 1857 and taking part in the Mormon expedition of 1857–1858 under Col. Albert S. Johnston. He resigned from the army in May 1861 and shortly thereafter was commissioned lieutenant colonel in the Confederate army. On July 11, 1861, at the opening of a campaign to secure western Virginia to the Confederacy, Pegram commanded a force holding a position at Rich Mountain. He was flanked by Gen. William S. Rosecrans and forced to surrender. After being exchanged he was chief engineer on the staff of Gen. Braxton Bragg for a time and later chief of staff to Gen. Edmund Kirby-Smith. In November 1862 he was promoted to brigadier general, and he took part in the battle of Murfreesboro (Stones River), December 31–January 3, 1863. While leading a foraging expedition into eastern Kentucky he was sharply defeated at Somerset on March 30, 1863, by Gen. Quincy A. Gillmore. At Chickamauga, September 18–20, 1863, he commanded a division in Gen. Nathan B. Forrest's corps, and a short time later he was promoted to major general and given command of Gen. Jubal A. Early's old division in the II Corps of Gen. Richard S. Ewell. In 1864 he fought in the Wilderness and in the Shenandoah valley. Pegram was killed in the battle of Hatcher's Run (known also as Dabney's Mill, or Armstrong's Mill), during the long siege of Petersburg, on February 6, 1865.

Pelham, John (1838–1863), Confederate army officer. Born on a plantation in Benton (now Calhoun) County, Alabama, on September 14, 1838, Pelham was a descendant of Peter Pelham, painter and engraver. He resigned from West Point in April 1861, shortly before graduating, and took a commission as first lieutenant in the Confederate army. In November, at the suggestion of Gen. J. E. B. Stuart, he organized a battery of horse artillery, becoming its captain. Under Pelham the horse artillery shared with the rest of Stuart's cavalry great mobility and precision of execution, while wielding firepower not normally available to a mobile corps. After a brilliant performance in the Seven Days' Battles, June–July 1862, he was promoted to major in August. Known occasionally as "the boy major," Pelham performed valuable services at the second battle of Manassas

(Bull Run), August 29–30, at Sharpsburg (Antietam), September 17, and at Fredericksburg, December 13. His promotion to lieutenant colonel was pending when, while serving with Gen. Fitzhugh Lee's division, he was killed on March 17, 1863, at Kelly's Ford, Virginia, in a celebrated engagement with Gen. William W. Averell's division of Union cavalry, which may have been the first purely cavalry battle of the war. Pelham, already an admired officer, soon became a rather romantic hero and figured in such novels as John Esten Cooke's *Surry of Eagle's Nest,* 1894.

Pemberton, John Clifford (1814–1881), Confederate army officer. Born in Philadelphia on August 10, 1814, Pemberton graduated from West Point in 1837 and was commissioned in the artillery. He took part in the Seminole War in Florida in 1837–1839, and after two years of garrison duty on the Maine–New Brunswick border he was promoted to first lieutenant in March 1842. He served through the Mexican War as aide to Gen. William J. Worth and was brevetted captain at Monterrey, September 20–24, 1846, and major at Molino del Rey, September 8, 1847. Promoted to captain in September 1850, he served subsequently in Florida, in Kansas, in the Mormon expedition of 1857–1858, and in the Northwest. In April 1861 he resigned to accept a commission of lieutenant colonel in the Confederate army. In May he became a colonel in the provisional army of Virginia and in June brigadier general in the Confederate service. In February 1862 he was promoted to major general in command of the Department of South Carolina, Georgia, and Florida. At Charleston, South Carolina, he built Fort Wagner and other works that later proved invaluable in the defense of the city. In October 1862 he advanced to lieutenant general, and early the next year he took command of the department comprising Mississippi, Tennessee, and eastern Louisiana. By spring he was in Vicksburg, Mississippi, last Confederate stronghold on the Mississippi River, with about 30,000 men at his disposal. The city had superb natural defenses and had so far frustrated the attempts of Gen. Ulysses S. Grant to capture it. In April Grant undertook a bold stroke, sending most of his army overland to the south, then across the river and northward towards Vicksburg's vulnerable eastern approaches. Pemberton, confused by a diversionary movement by Gen. William T. Sherman and by Col. Benjamin H. Grierson's cavalry raid across the state, failed to perceive Grant's plan. He was further hampered by conflicting orders. President Jefferson Davis insisted that Vicksburg be held at all costs while the area commander, Gen. Joseph E. Johnston, seeing through the diversions, ordered Pemberton to move out and attack the numerically inferior army of Grant. Steering a middle course, Pemberton spread his forces thinly.

After Johnston had been driven out of Jackson, Mississippi, by Sherman and Gen. James B. McPherson, Pemberton responded tardily and was defeated by Grant at Champion's Hill, May 16, and Black River Bridge, May 17. He promptly withdrew into Vicksburg. He was able to repel assaults on May 18 and 22, but he had no means to withstand a long siege, and, his army starving, he capitulated finally on July 4, 1863. After being exchanged he resigned his commission, but he served through the remainder of the war as an ordnance inspector and as a colonel of artillery in the defense of Richmond. After the war he lived on a farm near Warrenton, Virginia, until 1876 and then returned to Philadelphia He died in Penllyn, Pennsylvania, on July 13, 1881.

Pender, William Dorsey (1834–1863), Confederate army officer. Born in Edgecombe County, North Carolina, on February 6, 1834, Pender graduated from West Point in 1854 and was commissioned in the artillery. A year later he transferred to the 1st Dragoons. He saw service on the frontier from Washington Territory to New Mexico Territory and took part in numerous Indian fights. He was promoted to first lieutenant in May 1858. In March 1861 he resigned from the army, and, after a brief period as a provisional captain on Confederate recruiting duty in Baltimore, he was appointed colonel of the 3rd North Carolina Volunteers in May; in August he transferred to the 6th North Carolina. He served under Gen. Joseph E. Johnston in the Peninsula campaign, and for his actions at Fair Oaks (Seven Pines), May 31, 1862, he was promoted three days later to brigadier general. Attached to Gen. Ambrose P. Hill's division, he fought in the Seven Days' Battles, June 26–July 2, and was under Gen. Thomas J. Jackson at the second battle of Manassas (Bull Run), August 29–30, Sharpsburg (Antietam), September 17, Fredericksburg, December 13, and Chancellorsville, May 2–4, 1863, being wounded several times. Late in May 1863 he was promoted, at the age of twenty-nine, to major general. He commanded a division of Hill's corps at Gettysburg and led in driving Gen. Oliver O. Howard's XI Corps off Seminary Ridge on July 1. In the next day's fighting Pender received a serious leg wound. (On the third day, July 3, two brigades of his division would take part in Pickett's Charge.) He was evacuated to Staunton, Virginia, where, following the amputation of his leg, he died on July 18, 1863.

Pendergrast, Garrett Jesse (1802–1862), naval officer. Born in Kentucky on December 5, 1802, Pendergrast entered the navy as a midshipman in January 1812. Twenty-two of the next 49 years he spent at sea, advancing to lieutenant in 1821, commander in 1841, and captain in 1855. He commanded the Home Squadron in 1860 and the West India Squadron in 1861. Shortly after the outbreak of the Civil War he was at the Norfolk navy yard in command of the sloop of war *Cumberland*. The Virginia authorities attempted to capture the several naval vessels in the yard by obstructing the channel. On discovering the ploy, Pendergrast threatened to fire on the city of Norfolk if the obstructions were not immediately raised. They were, and the ships in the yard made their exit to open waters. A short time later he was given command of the Philadelphia navy yard, receiving promotion to commodore in July 1862. He held that post until two days before his death in Philadelphia on November 7, 1862.

Pendleton, Joseph Henry (1860–1942), marine officer. Born on June 2, 1860, in Rochester, Pennsylvania, Pendleton graduated from the Naval Academy in 1882 and two years later was commissioned a second lieutenant of marines. His first sea duty was aboard the *Pensacola*. Promoted to first lieutenant in June 1891, he commanded the marine barracks at Sitka, Alaska, from 1891 to 1894. Later he was attached to the Naval Academy, and during the Spanish–American War he served on the *Yankee* out of Annapolis. He advanced to captain in March 1899 and while again commanding at Sitka, 1899–1904, received promotion to major in March 1903. In 1904 he was put in command of the 1st Marine Regiment in the Philippines. In 1906 he briefly commanded the marine barracks on Guam and then that at Puget Sound, Washington, where he remained until 1909, advancing to lieutenant colonel in January 1908. In 1909 he took command of the 1st Marine Brigade in the Philippines, becoming the next year commander of the 2nd Regiment and of the post at Olongapo and in May 1911 being promoted to colonel. In the summer of 1912 he was named commander of the marine barracks at Portsmouth, New Hampshire. Late in August he was ordered to take the 1st Provisional Regiment to Nicaragua, where revolution had interrupted railway transit of the isthmus. Landing on September 4 at Corinto, he pushed through to Grenada by September 22, absorbing into his regiment marines already on the scene under Maj. Smedley D. Butler. On October 4 the marines stormed a rebel-occupied strongpoint on Coyotepe Hill, and other rebel bands subsequently surrendered. In November Pendleton and most of the marines were withdrawn. After a few months in command of a regiment of the 2nd Provisional Brigade at Guantánamo, Cuba, he took command of the Puget Sound barracks in 1913. In 1914 he took command of the 4th Regiment at San Diego. In June 1916 he was ordered to take the 4th to Santo Domingo (Dominican Republic), where orderly government had largely disappeared. Landing at the city of Santo Domingo on June 18 and taking command of naval and marine forces already ashore, he made a remarkable march from Montecristi to Santiago, occupying the latter city on July 5 after several skir-

mishes and effectively ending the rebellion. Promoted to brigadier general in August, he was given several portfolios in the provisional military government of the island in November, receiving also command of the 2nd Provisional Marine Brigade in December. In April 1917 a national police force was established under his direct command. For six months in 1917–1918 he was acting military governor of the Dominican Republic. In November 1918 he returned to the United States to take command of the marine barracks at Parris Island, South Carolina. In October 1919 he was put in command of the 2nd Advance Base Force at San Diego, California, and in October 1921 he became commander of the 5th Marine Brigade there. Pendleton was promoted to major general in December 1923, and from March 1924 until his retirement in June of that year he commanded the San Diego base. He later settled in Coronado, California, of which he was mayor in 1928–1930, and he died there on February 4, 1942. The Camp Pendleton marine base in California was named for him.

Pendleton, William Nelson (1809–1883), clergyman and Confederate army officer. Born on December 26, 1809, in Richmond, Virginia, Pendleton was a collateral descendant of Edmund Pendleton, Revolutionary statesman. He graduated from West Point in 1830 and was commissioned in the artillery, but in 1833 he resigned to become professor of mathematics at Bristol College in Pennsylvania. From 1837 to 1839 he taught at Delaware College (now the University of Delaware). During that period he studied for the ministry and was ordained a priest of the Protestant Episcopal church in 1838. From 1839 to 1844 he was principal of Episcopal High School in Alexandria, Virginia; during 1844–1847 he operated a private school in Baltimore, from 1847 to 1853 he was a parish priest in Frederick, Maryland, and in the latter year he settled in a parish in Lexington, Virginia. In May 1861 he accepted election as captain of the Rockbridge Artillery company, and in July he was commissioned colonel in the Confederate army and made artillery officer on the staff of Gen. Joseph E. Johnston. Promoted to brigadier general in April 1862, he joined the staff of Gen. Robert E. Lee in June and served with the Army of Northern Virginia through the war to Appomattox, where he was one of the commissioners appointed by Lee to arrange the terms of surrender. In addition to his duties as artillery officer of the army he organized religious services for the troops whenever conditions permitted. At the end of the war he returned to his parish in Lexington, where he remained until his death on January 15, 1883.

Pepperrell, Sir William (1696–1759), colonial merchant, militia officer, and public official. Born in Kittery, Maine (then a part of Massachusetts), on

June 27, 1696, Pepperrell (or Pepperell) was the son of an Englishman who had come to America penniless about 1690 and prospered as a merchant in lumber and fish. Indifferently educated, the younger Pepperrell enlisted in the militia at sixteen and soon after joined his father's shipbuilding and mercantile business. By the time he was thirty-three he had acquired on his own account most of the present townships of Saco and Scarboro, Maine. In 1726 he was elected to the Massachusetts General Court; in the same year he became colonel in command of the Maine militia, and in 1727 he was named to the colony's council, on which he remained until his death, serving as acting governor in 1756. In 1730 his friend Jonathan Belcher, governor of Massachusetts and New Hampshire, removed all of the incumbent justices and appointed Pepperrell chief justice. Pepperrell thereupon hurriedly began to study law and in time became a capable judge. With the death of his father in 1734, he inherited a fortune that made him one of the richest and most powerful men in New England. Ten years later, when the War of the Austrian Succession—known in the colonies as King George's War—broke out between England and France, he was appointed commander of the land forces, numbering about 4000 men, in the Louisbourg expedition mounted by Gov. William Shirley. The siege of the French fortress on Cape Breton Island began on April 30, 1745, with support from a small fleet. Pepperrell knew little about siegecraft, but his ignorance served him just as well. He managed to seize the grand battery of 30 heavy cannon on May 3 and turn it against the fortress. When the defenders saw American troops moving unpredictably in what was described as a rather boisterous enterprise, they panicked and surrendered on June 15. As a reward Pepperrell was created a baronet in November 1746, the first native of the American colonies to be so honored. He also served in the last of the French and Indian wars, being promoted to major general in February 1755 and to lieutenant general four years later, but he died in the same year, on July 6, 1759, in Kittery. His holdings in lumber, fishing, and real estate had continued to grow, and upon his death he left everything to his grandson, who, however, was a Loyalist in the Revolution; he fled to England, whereupon all the Pepperrell properties were confiscated.

Percival, John (1779–1862), naval officer. Born in West Barnstable Massachusetts, on April 5, 1779, Percival went to sea in 1793 and made numerous voyages to the West Indies and Europe. In February 1797, while in Lisbon, he was impressed into the British navy; he served on H.M.S. Victory (later Lord Nelson's flagship) among other vessels, and in 1799, at Madeira, he escaped to an American naval vessel. He entered the U.S. navy in that year as master's

mate, served on the Delaware through the naval war with France, and was discharged a midshipman in July 1801. For eight years he served as mate and master in the merchant service, acquiring the nickname "Mad Jack" (or "Roaring Jack"), provoking a wealth of half-improbable stories of adventure (including that of his navigating a ship single-handedly from Africa to Brazil after the crew died of yellow fever), and building an apparently warranted reputation as an unsurpassed seaman. In 1809 he reentered the navy as a sailing master. On July 5, 1813, he commandeered a fishing smack, hid 32 volunteers below, and captured the British tender Eagle in New York harbor. He was later sailing master of the sloop Peacock, under Capt. Lewis Warrington, and for his skilled sailing in the capture of the Epervier in the Bahamas on April 29, 1814, was recommended for promotion to lieutenant. In 1821–1822 he was on the Porpoise, patrolling against pirates in the West Indies; in 1823–1824 he was on the United States, Commodore Isaac Hull's flagship in the Pacific; and in 1825–1826 he commanded the schooner Dolphin, sent by Hull to track down the mutineers of the whaler Globe. In January 1826 the Dolphin arrived in the Sandwich (Hawaiian) Islands, the first American warship to call there in more than a decade. During a four-month stay Percival made himself generally useful, salvaging a merchant ship that had run onto rocks, quelling a riot of seamen that nearly destroyed the headquarters of the islands' missionaries, and forming a diplomatic tie with King Kamehameha. Percival was promoted to commander in 1831. He commanded the Cyane in the Mediterranean in 1838–1839 and, promoted to captain in 1841, supervised repairs on the Constitution at Norfolk navy yard in 1841–1843, having underbid a civilian contractor for the job. In 1843–1846 he commanded the Constitution on a world cruise, during which he rescued the Imam of Muscat from pirates in the Indian Ocean and was given by that ruler a jeweled sword in thanks. Percival saw no more sea duty after 1846, and in 1855 he was placed on the reserve list. One of the most colorful and admired figures of the old navy, he was the inspiration for much of the popular Tales for the Marines, 1855, by "Harry Gringo" (Henry A. Wise). Percival died in Dorchester, Massachusetts, on September 17, 1862.

Perry, Matthew Calbraith (1794–1858), naval officer. Born on April 10, 1794, in South Kingstown, Rhode Island, Matthew was a younger brother of Oliver Hazard Perry. He entered the navy as a midshipman in January 1809 and saw his first service aboard the schooner Revenge, commanded by his brother. During the War of 1812 he served on the President under Commodore John Rodgers and the United States, becoming a lieutenant in February 1813. Subsequent assignments took him to the Medi-

terranean and Africa, to the West Indies to suppress piracy, and to Russia, where the czar offered him a post in his naval service. He was promoted to master commandant in March 1826. From 1833 to 1837 he was second officer of the New York navy yard. Perry took a deep interest in naval education; he successfully advocated an apprentice system for the training of seamen and later, in 1845, helped establish the course of instruction at the Naval Academy. He was likewise a strong proponent of modernization of the navy, and soon after his promotion to captain in February 1837 he was given command of the country's first steam warship, the *Fulton*, aboard which he organized the first corps of naval engineers. On the *Fulton* off Sandy Hook, a peninsula in New Jersey, he conducted during 1839–1840 the navy's first gunnery school. From June 1841, when he was promoted to commodore, to 1843 he was chief of the New York navy yard, where he supervised construction of the steamers *Missouri* and *Mississippi*. In 1843 he assumed command of the Africa Squadron, which was sent, pursuant to provisions of the Webster-Ashburton Treaty, to suppress the slave trade. At the outbreak of the Mexican War he was second-in-command to Commodore David Conner of the squadron on the east coast. In October 1846, on the steam frigate *Mississippi*, he led an expedition against Frontera and Tabasco, in November he captured Tampico, and in December he took Laguna. During the siege of Veracruz in March 1847 he succeeded Conner in command of the squadron. In April and again in June he led expeditions up the Tabasco River and with land forces of marines and sailors captured several forts, much ordnance and stores, and the town of Tabasco itself. After four years of shore duty in New York he sailed on the *Mississippi* in November 1852 on a delicate diplomatic mission to Japan, a nation then closed to virtually all Westerners. He assembled a squadron at Naha, Okinawa (then known as Great Luchu Island), in May 1853 and sailed for Japan, determined "to demand as a right, and not to solicit as a favor, those acts of courtesy which are due from one civilized country to another." He arrived in the bay of Edo (now Tokyo), the capital, in July 1853 and demanded, with considerable pomp, an interview with the highest possible official in order to deliver a letter from President Millard Fillmore, threatening to land a force if necessary. After much negotiation, during which he refused even to see lesser officials, the Japanese government acceded to his demand, producing two royal princes to receive the letter amid great pageantry. Perry soon left, promising to return to receive a reply. He returned in February 1854, distributed gifts, and accepted a treaty, signed at Yokohama on March 31, 1854, providing for hospitable treatment of shipwrecked sailors and for trading privileges at two Japanese ports. Perry returned to the United States in January 1855; the next year his report of his

mission was published in three volumes as *Narrative of the Expedition of an American Squadron to the China Seas and Japan*. He died in New York City on March 4, 1858.

Perry, Oliver Hazard (1785–1819), naval officer. Born in South Kingstown, Rhode Island, on August 23, 1785, Perry, older brother of Matthew C. Perry, entered the navy as a midshipman in April 1799. He served in the West Indies during the naval war with France and in the Mediterranean during the Tripolitan War, becoming a lieutenant in January 1807. From 1807 to 1809 he was engaged in building and commanding coastal gunboats to enforce the Embargo Act of 1807. In 1809–1811 he commanded the schooner *Revenge* on the southern Atlantic coast. In August 1812 he was promoted to master commandant. He was ordered to Presque Isle (now Erie), Pennsylvania, in February 1813 to direct the construction of a naval fleet—consisting of ten small ships—for service on Lake Erie. The work occupied most of the summer. In May Perry joined Commodore Isaac Chauncey on Lake Ontario briefly and participated in the capture of Fort George. In August the fleet at Erie was ready for action. He moved his base of operations to Put-in-Bay, north of Sandusky, Ohio, and awaited the appearance of the British fleet of six ships under Commodore Robert Barclay. Early on September 10 Perry sighted the enemy; the battle was joined shortly before noon, the main burden being borne by Perry's flagship, the *Lawrence*, which, despite the U.S. superiority in firepower, was virtually destroyed. Perry then transferred to the *Niagara*, commanded by Master Commandant Jesse D. Elliott, continued the fight, and soon forced the British to surrender. Lake Erie was securely under U.S. control, and the British supply line to forces at Detroit and in northern Ohio was cut. At the close of the battle Perry sent to Gen. William Henry Harrison his famous message: "We have met the enemy and they are ours." Shortly after the battle of Lake Erie he transported Harrison's army across Lake Erie and took part in the battle of the Thames, October 5, where he led a cavalry charge. President James Madison promptly ordered his promotion to captain, and in January 1814 he was voted a gold medal and the thanks of Congress and was everywhere received as a great hero. After the war he commanded the *Java* in 1816–1817 in the Mediterranean and in 1819 was given command of a squadron sent on a mission to Venezuela. He contracted yellow fever while on the Orinoco River and died aboard the schooner *Nonesuch* a few days later, on August 23, 1819. He was buried in Trinidad, but in 1826 his remains were reinterred in Newport, Rhode Island.

Pershing, John Joseph (1860–1948), army officer. Born on September 13, 1860, near Laclede, Missouri, Pershing worked on his father's farm and taught school during his youth. He graduated from the Kirksville Normal School (now Northeast Missouri State University) in 1880 and two years later entered West Point, from which he graduated as senior cadet captain in 1886. Commissioned in the 6th Cavalry, he participated in several Indian campaigns, including one against Geronimo and the final one against the Sioux in 1890–1891. He was an instructor in military tactics at the University of Nebraska from 1891 to 1895, receiving promotion to first lieutenant in October 1892, and there took a law degree in 1893. After further service in the West he was sent to West Point as an instructor in tactics, 1897–1898. In 1898 he served in Cuba during the Spanish–American War. In August he was appointed major of volunteers and a year later, having organized the Insular Bureau in the War Department to administer Puerto Rico and the Philippines, was sent to the Philippine Islands as adjutant general of Mindanao Department. In February 1901 he was mustered out of volunteer service and promoted to captain of regulars. He led his troops successfully against Moro insurgents there and made considerable progress toward pacifying them, for which he was congratulated by President Theodore Roosevelt. In 1903 he was ordered home for duty on the new General Staff. He graduated from the Army War College in 1905 and in 1905–1906 was military attaché in Tokyo and an observer in the Russo–Japanese War. In September 1906 he was promoted from captain to brigadier general—over the heads of 862 senior officers—by Roosevelt. After three further periods of service in the Philippines—where he finally put down the Moro rebels in 1913—and assignments as an observer in the Balkans and as commander of the 8th Brigade in San Francisco, he was sent to patrol the troubled Mexican border in 1915. The following March, after Francisco "Pancho" Villa's bloody raid on Columbus, New Mexico, Pershing led a large force—the Mexican Punitive Expedition—into Mexico in pursuit of Villa, but a year later the search ended without success, in large part owing to severe restrictions placed on American movements. Nonetheless the campaign provided opportunity to experiment with such novelties as airplanes, field radio, and motorized units and gave field experience to scores of officers. During the campaign, in September 1916, Pershing was promoted to major general. On leaving Mexico in February 1917 he succeeded Gen. Frederick Funston as commander of the Southern Department, and in May, following U.S. entry into World War I, he was named to command the American Expeditionary Forces (AEF) to be sent to France. He arrived there in June, ahead of his troops, and set about planning for their training, supply, and deployment. On October 6, 1917, he assumed the rank of general for the duration of the national emergency; he was the first U.S.

army officer ever to hold that rank. Determined, with the support of the U.S. government, to preserve the identity and integrity of the AEF, Pershing was constantly at loggerheads with the Allied high command and, except for the crises of the German offensives at Amiens, Lys, and Aisne in the early spring of 1918, adamantly refused to split his forces into replacement units for the French and British armies. In May the 1st Division (Gen. Robert L. Bullard) took the offensive at Cantigny, and in May–June the 2nd (Gen. Omar Bundy) and 3rd (Gen. Joseph T. Dickman) saw heavy fighting at Château-Thierry, Belleau Wood, and other spots. In June Pershing organized three corps headquarters, and in August he took command of the First Army, which on September 12 began a successful push against the St. Mihiel salient. The success of that operation confirmed for the Allied commander, Marshal Ferdinand Foch, the value of a separate American army. On September 26, following a remarkable performance by the First Army staff under Col. George C. Marshall, the American army led off the general Allied offensive on the Meuse River. During the slow advance through the Argonne Forest, Pershing created a Second Army under Gen. Bullard, relinquished command of the First to Gen. Hunter Liggett, and moved himself up to army group level on October 16. The Allies were still advancing when armistice was declared on November 11. After nearly a year overseeing the American occupation and directing the return of the AEF's nearly two million troops and its equipment, Pershing returned to the United States in September 1919, was greeted as a hero, and by special act of Congress was made general of the armies, a rank never held before (although it had been created by Congress in 1799 for George Washington). From July 1921 to September 1924 he was army chief of staff; after his retirement from that post he remained, according to the terms of his rank, nominally on active duty as the senior officer of the army. He maintained an office in the War Department that was later transferred to the Pentagon. In 1925 he was appointed by President Calvin Coolidge head of a plebiscitary commission with the task, ultimately a failure, of settling the Tacna–Arica border dispute between Chile and Peru. In 1931 he published his widely read memoirs, *My Experiences in the World War*, for which he won a Pulitzer Prize. From 1941 he made his permanent residence in a special wing of the army's Walter Reed Hospital in Washington, D.C., where he died on July 15, 1948.

Pettigrew, James Johnston (1828–1863), Confederate army officer. Born in Tyrrell County, North Carolina, on July 4, 1828, Pettigrew graduated from the University of North Carolina in 1847 and was appointed assistant professor in the Naval Observatory. He resigned the post a year later to study law, and in 1849 he was admitted to the bar. After an extended European tour, during which he was briefly secretary of the U.S. legation in Madrid, he commenced practice in Charleston, South Carolina, in 1852. He was elected to the legislature in 1856 and was a prominent opponent of the resumption of the slave trade. He traveled to Sardinia in 1858 to study Italian army methods. On his return to Charleston he organized and drilled the 1st Regiment of Rifles of Charleston. In December 1860 he led the regiment in occupying Castle Pinckney in the harbor, later taking up fortified positions on Morris Island as well. In May 1861 Pettigrew was elected colonel of the 12th North Carolina Regiment, and for some time he was employed in constructing batteries and otherwise attempting to close the Potomac River to federal traffic. He was promoted to brigadier general early in 1862 and commanded a brigade under Gen. Joseph E. Johnston through the Peninsula campaign, receiving a serious wound and being taken prisoner at Seven Pines (Fair Oaks), May 31. On his exchange he commanded defenses at Petersburg and then Richmond, commanding the latter at the time of Gen. George Stoneman's cavalry raid in April–May 1863. He was in the field at Gettysburg, whence he sent to Gen. Robert E. Lee on June 30 the first information on the presence of Union troops in that town. He succeeded to temporary command of the wounded Gen. Henry Heth's division of Gen. Ambrose P. Hill's III Corps after the first day of battle, July 1, and on the third day he led the division as part of the celebrated and tragic Pickett's Charge. Though wounded, he ably directed the rearguard during the retreat from Gettysburg. On the night of July 14, while covering the Confederate army's crossing of the Potomac at Falling Waters, West Virginia, he was mortally wounded in an attack by Union cavalry. Pettigrew died three days later, July 17, 1863, in Bunker Hill, West Virginia.

Philip (1639?–1676), Indian leader. Born about 1639 in the region of the Wampanoag Indians (parts of what are now Massachusetts and Rhode Island), Metacomet, who was called Philip by the English and who became known as King Philip, was the son of Massasoit, sachem, or chief, of the Wampanoags. When his older brother, Wamsutta, or Alexander, died in 1662, Philip succeeded him as sachem and promised to honor the peace treaty and generous land grants that their father had arranged with the *Mayflower* colonists. But conflict over interpretation of the land treaties created tension. The Indians were willing to let the settlers use the land, but, lacking any notion of "ownership," had not conceived of being barred from hunting and fishing on it, while the English had definite concepts of "boundary" and "trespass." Despite Philip's promise he was suspected as early as 1671 of planning revolt, and in that year

he was fined and his people were partially disarmed. In January 1675 an Indian informer called John Sassamon revealed Philip's plans for revolt and was murdered, purportedly by three Indians whom the colonists identified as the culprits and executed. Furious at this violation of their jurisdiction, the Indians began war before strategy was even decided upon. Philip's role as a war chief was not clear, but he is not now regarded as the principal leader that the colonists thought him to be; indeed, he may have tried unsuccessfully to restrain the younger braves from going to war. Called "King Philip's War," the fighting began around Narragansett Bay in June 1675, raged through the Plymouth and Massachusetts Bay colonies, and extended as far west as the Connecticut River. The Wampanoags were aided by the Narragansett (under Canonchet), Nipmuck, Sakonnet, and Pocasset tribes and were successful until the colonists began destroying their corn crops, capturing their women and children, and offering amnesty to those who would disavow Philip's rule. Twelve towns were completely destroyed and thousands of settlers killed (the massacre at Deerfield, Massachusetts, on September 18 is probably the best remembered). In the "Great Swamp Fight" of December 19, 1675, at Kingstown (now Kingston), Rhode Island, the Indians were overwhelmed by colonists led by Josiah Winslow and aided by Mohegans, and the tide turned as the alliance of tribes was shattered. Philip sought refuge in a swamp near Mt. Hope, in what is now Bristol, Rhode Island, but was found and killed on August 12, 1676, by an Indian scout under Capt. Benjamin Church. King Philip's War was extremely costly to the colonists, both in lives and money, but its successful conclusion effectively destroyed the tribal and intertribal structures of southern New England and ended resistance to further white settlement.

Philip, John Woodward (1840–1900), naval officer. Born in Kinderhook, New York, on August 26, 1840, Philip graduated from the Naval Academy in 1861 and immediately entered Civil War service. He served as executive officer, and occasionally acting captain, on a number of vessels in the Gulf and South Atlantic blockades, on the James River, and in the siege of Charleston, South Carolina, receiving promotion to lieutenant in July 1862. He served on the *Wachusett*, 1865–1867, and on the *Hartford*, 1867–1869, in Asian waters, advancing to lieutenant commander in 1868; on the *Richmond*, 1870–1872, in Europe; and again on the *Hartford*, 1872–1873. Promoted to commander in December 1874, he was on leave for two years thereafter, during which time he commanded a Pacific mail ship. Various routine assignments followed, and in 1877 he was chosen to command the six-year Woodruff scientific expedition around the world, consisting of the ships *Tus-*

carora and *Ranger.* During 1884–1890 he was on shore duty, as lighthouse inspector of the 12th Naval District and later as commander of the receiving ship at Mare Island navy yard, California. He was promoted to captain in March 1889. He commanded the Boston navy yard in 1894–1897 and in the latter year returned to sea in command of the battleship *Texas.* At the outbreak of the Spanish–American War in 1898 the *Texas* was part of Commodore Winfield S. Schley's "Flying Squadron," held at Hampton Roads for home defense. Later the squadron was dispatched to Cuba to reinforce Adm. William T. Sampson's main fleet. At the naval battle of Santiago, July 3, Philip narrowly averted collision with the *Brooklyn* at the outset, when the latter, shrouded in smoke, made an unexpected turn in a direction opposite that of the rest of the fleet. The *Texas* played a distinguished role in the battle. As she passed the burning *Vizcaya,* Philip spoke to his crew a line long afterward remembered: "Don't cheer, boys, the poor devils are dying." He was promoted to commodore in August 1898. In January 1899 he took command of the Brooklyn navy yard, advancing to rear admiral in March. He died in Brooklyn, New York, on June 30, 1900.

Phips, Sir William (1651–1695), colonial governor. Born near what is now Woolwich, Maine, then a part of Massachusetts, on February 2, 1651, Phips (or Phipps) was apprenticed to a ship's carpenter by his impecunious parents and practised his trade for many years in Boston. In the early 1680s he became interested in the possibility of finding sunken Spanish treasure ships, and he gained the backing of Charles II for one such venture in 1683. It failed, but another, financed by the Duke of Albemarle, succeeded when Phips found an enormously valuable sunken treasure off the coast of Haiti in 1686. For his feat he was knighted the next year and was also made provost marshal general of Boston by James II. In 1684 the old charter government of Massachusetts had been replaced by dominion rule, and Phips, in London in 1687, came into contact with Increase Mather and worked with him, after the ascension to the throne of William III, to reinstate the old system. Again in Boston in 1690, Phips was a close associate of the Mather faction and was chosen to command the expedition of Massachusetts troops against Nova Scotia in King William's War. He was triumphantly successful, receiving the surrender of the French at Port Royal (now Annapolis Royal) on May 11 and returning to Boston to find himself a hero. This was the high point of his career. In August he sailed with 2000 men and 30 ships for Quebec, an expedition undertaken in cooperation with other colonies and simultaneously with a march by New York troops on Montreal. In October he failed to take Quebec and returned to Boston. Although he was shortly afterward named the first royal governor of Massa-

chusetts at Mather's suggestion, the political situation deteriorated around him from the time he arrived in Boston with the new charter in May 1692 until his death three years later. The new charter proved unpopular, and he was never able to cope with popular displeasure. His first governmental action was perhaps his best: Arriving in the midst of the witchcraft persecutions at Salem, he appointed a special court to try all cases of alleged witchcraft. After some months during which many were executed, scores were jailed awaiting trial, and the frenzy worsened, Phips took the advice of Cotton Mather and ruled out the use of unsubstantiated "spectral" evidence; the cases were then promptly disposed of and the reign of terror ended. But he came into conflict with various religious groups, annoyed the merchants by adhering to a free-trade policy, failed to aid the customs officers in their efforts to collect taxes for the Crown, gave at least tacit support to pirates, and by his pompous nouveau-riche manners offended both rich and poor. In 1694 he was ordered to England, and he died in London on February 18, 1695.

Pickens, Andrew (1739–1817), Revolutionary militia officer. Born on September 19, 1739, in Paxton, Pennsylvania, Pickens moved with his family to Virginia and in 1752 to the Waxhaw district of South Carolina. In 1761 he took part in an expedition against the Cherokee Indians and two years later took up a farm on Long Cane Creek. At the outbreak of the Revolution in 1775 he was elected captain of a company of militia, and he served principally on the frontier for the first few years of the war. In 1778 he advanced to colonel. On February 14, 1779, Pickens commanded the 400 militiamen who defeated 700 Loyalists at Kettle Creek in Wilkes County, Georgia, stopping the British advance into the back country. He was later at the battle of Stono Ferry, June 20, 1779. From the fall of Charleston, South Carolina, in May 1780 until early 1781 the only organized patriot forces in the southern department were partisan bands under such leaders as Pickens, Francis Marion, and Thomas Sumter. At the battle of Cowpens, January 17, 1781, Pickens commanded the second skirmish line under Gen. Daniel Morgan and for his performance there was promoted to brigadier general of militia. He took part in the siege and capture of Augusta, Georgia, in April–June and was with Gen. Nathanael Greene at the siege of Ninety-Six in May–June and at the battle of Eutaw Springs, September 8. In 1782 he conducted an expedition against the Cherokees that gained a sizable strip of territory for the state of Georgia. He sat in the South Carolina legislature from 1783 to 1794, and he served a term in Congress in 1793–1795. From 1785 to 1801 he was regularly employed as a Congressional agent with the southern Indian tribes, and in 1795 he was appointed major general of militia. He was again in the legislature in 1801 and 1812. In later years he removed to Tomassee, near the site of present-day Pendleton, South Carolina, and he died there on August 11, 1817. Fort Pickens, completed in 1834 in the harbor of Pensacola, Florida, was named for him.

Pickering, Timothy (1745–1829), Revolutionary army officer, public official, and political leader. Born in Salem, Massachusetts, on July 17, 1745, Pickering graduated from Harvard in 1763 and was admitted to the bar in Salem five years later. He held numerous local offices and from 1766 was a member of the militia, advancing to colonel by 1775. In that year he published a manual of drill and discipline that was widely adopted by state militias and by the Continental army until replaced by Baron von Steuben's manual in 1779. Valuable services in the early phase of the Revolution led to his appointment by Gen. George Washington to the post of adjutant general in June 1777. He held that post until January 1778. He became a member of the Board of War in November 1777 and from August 1780 to July 1785 was quartermaster general. He was in the field with the army at Brandywine and Germantown, September 11 and October 4, 1777, and again at Yorktown in October 1781. In 1786 he moved to Pennsylvania and in 1787 to the Wyoming Valley, bringing with him a commission from the Pennsylvania government to organize the new Luzerne County and settle land-claim disputes with Connecticut settlers in the region. He spent three difficult but fruitful years there; he helped found the town of Wilkes-Barre and was elected to both the Constitutional ratifying convention of 1788 and the Pennsylvania constitutional convention of 1788–1789. In 1790 he applied to President Washington for the office of postmaster general; he received instead a commission to treat with the Seneca Indians. He was offered the postmastership in August 1791 and held it for four years while continuing as an Indian commissioner. In January 1795 he became secretary of war and later that year, following the resignation of Edmund Randolph in August, he took what was intended to be temporary charge of the State Department as well. He resigned his war portfolio in December 1795 but was retained as secretary of state by President John Adams. A Federalist of Alexander Hamilton's faction, he was eager for war with France and schemed constantly with Hamilton to defeat various of Adams's conciliatory policies. Pickering came at length into open conflict with Adams and was dismissed in May 1800. Moving back to Massachusetts, he remained an influential Federalist leader and was in the U.S. Senate from 1803 to 1811. There, and in the House of Representatives from 1813 to 1817, he opposed the policies of Thomas Jefferson and of James Madison, most particularly the Embargo Act of 1807 and the War of 1812. At various times, but particularly during the war, he seriously considered secession on the part of New England, and among the group of extreme Federalists sometimes known as the "Essex Junto" he conducted private discussions and even agitated to that end. After 1817 he devoted himself to farming, in which he was a noted experimenter and advocate of scientific practices and education. He died in Salem, Massachusetts, on January 29, 1829.

Pickett, George Edward (1825–1875), Confederate army officer. Born in Richmond, Virginia, on January 25, 1825, Pickett studied law as a youth, but in 1842 he entered West Point, from which he graduated in 1846. Commissioned in the infantry, he went immediately to serve in the Mexican War, seeing action under Gen. Winfield Scott from the siege of Veracruz to the surrender of Mexico City. He was brevetted first lieutenant for gallantry at Contreras and Churubusco, August 19–20, 1847. On September 13 he was first over the parapet at Chapultepec, where he tore down the enemy's flag and hoisted his regiment's in its stead. Garrison duty in Texas from 1849 to 1856, during which he was promoted to captain in March 1855, was followed by service in the Northwest. There he became involved in a dispute between U.S. settlers and British forces at San Juan Island. He remained in command of a force occupying the island from 1859 until 1861, when he returned to Richmond, resigned from the army in June, and was promptly commissioned a colonel in the Confederate infantry. Made a brigadier general in February 1862, he distinguished himself at Williamsburg, Fair Oaks (Seven Pines), and Gaines' Mill in the Peninsula campaign but was severely wounded in the last engagement and did not return to action for some time. Promoted to major general in October 1862, he commanded the center division at Fredericksburg, December 13. At Gettysburg his division, part of Gen. James Longstreet's corps, survived the first two days of battle relatively unscathed and waited for orders all through the morning of July 3, 1863. Gen. Robert E. Lee, having decided to assault the center of the Union line on Cemetery Ridge, designated Pickett's division for the task, attaching to it the division under Gen. James J. Pettigrew and two brigades from that of Gen. William D. Pender. The total was about 15,000 men. A Confederate artillery barrage against the Union position began shortly after noon, and about two o'clock in the afternoon Pickett was given the order to charge by Longstreet. The soldiers, moving with almost parade precision, descended into a valley between two ridges, advanced over half a mile of broken ground in the face of terrible musket and artillery fire, and ascended the other side toward the well entrenched Union position on Cemetery Ridge. A few men actually reached the lines of Gen. Winfield S. Hancock's II Corps and leaped the stone wall, notably Gen. Lewis A. Armistead, but elsewhere the assault was driven back. Barely a fourth of the troops returned from the charge. This repulse determined the battle. Pickett himself, who is said to have blamed Lee for the disaster, believed at the time that it meant the end of "our cause," as he wrote three days after the battle. He subsequently commanded the Department of Virginia and North Carolina. In January–February 1864 he made an unsuccessful attempt to recapture New Bern, North Carolina, but later in the spring he contributed to keeping Gen. Benjamin F. Butler's Army of the James bottled up in Bermuda Hundred, Virginia. Later he was transferred to the defenses of Petersburg. He took part in the attack on Gen. Philip H. Sheridan at Dinwiddie Court House on March 31, 1865, and then bore the brunt of the Union attack at Five Forks on April 1. He was present at Lee's surrender at Appomattox on April 9. After the war Pickett declined a brigadier general's commission offered by the khedive of Egypt and an appointment by President Ulysses S. Grant as marshal of Virginia and instead worked as the Virginia agent of the Washington Life Insurance Company of New York. He died in Norfolk, Virginia, on October 25, 1875, and was buried in Richmond. After his death his fame continued steadily to grow, and "Pickett's Charge" remained one of the most celebrated actions in U.S. military history.

Pike, Albert (1809–1891), lawyer, Confederate army officer, and Freemason. Born in Boston on December 29, 1809, Pike was brought up in Byfield and Newburyport, Massachusetts. He attended schools in Newburyport and in Framingham, but at the age of fifteen he apparently took over his own education, studying privately and writing poetry. In 1831 he left New England for the West. He made his way to Independence, Missouri, where he joined a party of traders and hunters under Charles Bent bound for Santa Fe, New Mexico, and ended up in 1833 in Arkansas, where he taught school. He wrote a series of articles for the Little Rock *Arkansas Advocate* that resulted in his being asked to join the staff. He soon purchased an interest in the paper and by 1835 was its sole owner. By that time he had begun to study law, and he was admitted to practice in 1837, the year he sold the *Advocate.* He was a capable lawyer, serving as reporter of the Arkansas supreme court and publishing in 1842 *The Arkansas Form Book,* a compilation of information for lawyers. He achieved a reputation as a poet as well, having received recognition for *Prose Sketches and Poems Written in the Western Country,* 1834, and especially "Hymns to the Gods," 1839. He served in the Mexican War as commander of a troop of mounted Arkansas volunteers; his criticisms of his commander led to a duel with another officer in which no one was hurt. During the period between the Mexican and Civil

wars he continued to practice law, becoming a figure of prominence in Arkansas and a supporter of slavery in the state. He was a Whig in a predominantly Democratic area and later promoted the Know-Nothing party. When the Civil War began he was appointed a commissioner to negotiate on behalf of the Confederacy with various Indian tribes. A short time later he was commissioned brigadier general in command of the Indian Territory. There he organized an Indian partisan force, nominally for defense, under Gen. Stand Watie. They took part in the battle of Pea Ridge (Elkhorn), Arkansas, on March 7–8, 1862, and got somewhat out of control; some atrocities were committed for which Pike was criticized. He in turn criticized his commander in an open letter to President Jefferson Davis that subjected him to much obloquy. During 1862 he was involved in a complicated series of moves that included his resignation from the army, an attempt to resume his command, his arrest for insubordination, and his final retirement in November for the rest of the war. Afterwards he once again took up the practice of law, from 1867 to 1868 in Memphis and thereafter in Washington, D.C. Meanwhile he had become a Freemason; in 1859 he had been elected Sovereign Grand Commander of the Supreme Grand Council, Southern Jurisdiction of the United States, of the Scottish Rite Masons. He held that position until his death. He spent years rewriting the rituals of the order and published *Morals and Dogma of the Ancient and Accepted Scottish Rite of Freemasonry* in 1872; revised editions appeared in 1878, 1881, and 1905. He wrote capably on legal subjects and also produced many poems that were highly regarded in their time but are now largely forgotten. They were published in book form in a few private printings, in *Nugae,* 1854, and posthumously in three volumes, *Gen. Albert Pike's Poems,* 1900, *Hymns to the Gods and Other Poems,* 1916, and *Lyrics and Love Songs,* 1916; only his Confederate version of "Dixie," written and published in May 1861, is read today. He died in Washington, D.C., on April 2, 1891.

Pike, Zebulon Montgomery (1779–1813), army officer and explorer. Born on January 5, 1779, in Lamberton, now part of Trenton, New Jersey, the son of an army officer, Pike attended school until entering his father's company of the 2nd Infantry as a cadet at the age of fifteen. He became a lieutenant in November 1799. He served mainly on the frontier and in August 1805 was sent by Gen. James Wilkinson, recently appointed governor of the Louisiana Territory, to lead a party of 20 men from St. Louis to the source of the Mississippi River and to assert the U.S. claim to the region. He returned in eight months, mistakenly reporting Leech Lake, in Minnesota, as the source of the Mississippi, but he had informed Indians in the region that they must accede to U.S.

rule and warned British officers and subjects that they were violating U.S. territorial rights by remaining there. While in Minnesota he purchased the site on which Fort Snelling was built 14 years later. In July 1806 he was sent by Wilkinson with 24 men to travel southwest from St. Louis to the Arkansas River country and gain information about the Spanish territories. Passing through Colorado, he attempted to scale the peak now named after him (which he called Grand Peak) but failed. From the region of the Arkansas River he struck south in January 1807, looking for the source of the Red River. Unknowingly he followed the Rio Grande into Spanish territory, building a log fort on the Conejos, a small tributary. The Spanish learned of his presence, and he was taken without resistance to Santa Fe by New Mexican troops. Questioned by authorities in Chihuahua, Mexico, he was released in April 1807 but deprived of his notes and maps. He reached U.S. territory at Natchitoches in July. His *Account of the Expeditions to the Sources of the Mississippi and Through the Western Parts of Louisiana*, three volumes, 1810, contained the first reliable maps of the southwestern region to appear in English, but it also reported that much of the high plains and Southwest appeared uninhabitable, fostering the legend of the Great American Desert. Upon his return from Mexico he was questioned concerning the possible connection of his mission with the conspiracy of Aaron Burr and Wilkinson to build an empire in the Southwest. He was cleared of all charges by Henry Dearborn, the secretary of war. He had been promoted to captain during the expedition, in August 1806. He advanced to major in May 1808, lieutenant colonel in December 1809, and colonel of the 15th Infantry in July 1812. Promoted to brigadier general in March 1813, he was chosen by Gen. Dearborn to lead the assault on York (now Toronto) on April 27. Landing from Commodore Isaac Chauncey's fleet, his forces carried the outer defenses of the town, but the explosion of a magazine killed 100 Americans. Pike was mortally wounded; he died later that day aboard Chauncey's flagship *Madison*.

Pillow, Gideon Johnson (1806–1878), Confederate army officer. Born in Williamson County, Tennessee, on June 8, 1806, Pillow graduated from the University of Nashville (a forerunner of George Peabody College for Teachers) in 1827. He studied law, entered practice in Columbia, Tennessee, and for a time had James K. Polk for a partner. He achieved a position of great influence in Democratic politics and played a large role in securing the presidential nomination for Polk in 1844. Polk reciprocated by appointing Pillow brigadier general of volunteers in July 1846. He was for a short time with Gen. Zachary Taylor in northern Mexico but soon was transferred to Gen. Winfield Scott's army. He took part in the

entire campaign from Veracruz to Mexico City, receiving wounds at Cerro Gordo and Chapultepec and in April 1847 being promoted to major general of volunteers. Pillow considered himself Polk's personal representative at the front and clashed increasingly with Scott. He claimed credit for the success at Contreras and when disputed by Scott apparently sent an anonymous letter presenting his case to the *New Orleans Daily Delta*, which published it in September 1847. Two courts of inquiry investigated the feud and exonerated both men of all charges. After the war Pillow resumed his law practice and his political involvements, contributing largely to the nomination of Franklin Pierce in 1852 and unsuccessfully seeking the vice-presidential nomination then and in 1856. He resisted the secession movement but in May 1861 accepted appointment as major general of Tennessee's provisional army. In July he was commissioned brigadier general in the Confederate army. He was under Gen. Leonidas Polk at the battle of Belmont, Missouri, November 7, and in February 1862 was second-in-command, under Gen. John B. Floyd, of Fort Donelson. When Floyd relinquished command to him, he in turn passed it to Gen. Simon B. Buckner, and with Floyd he escaped before Buckner was compelled to surrender the fort to Gen. Ulysses S. Grant. He was suspended from duty for several months thereafter and for the rest of the war held only minor posts and saw little action. After the war, ruined financially, he resumed law practice in Memphis, Tennessee; he died in Helena, Arkansas, on October 8, 1878.

Pleasonton, Alfred (1824–1897), army officer. Born in Washington, D.C., on June 7, 1824, Pleasonton graduated from West Point in 1844 and was commissioned in the 2nd Dragoons. He served in the Mexican War, winning a brevet to first lieutenant at Palo Alto and Resaca de la Palma, May 8–9, 1846. He was promoted to first lieutenant in September 1849, while serving on the frontier, and to captain in March 1855. He was on the staff of Col. William S. Harney from 1855, taking part in numerous Indian campaigns. In September 1861 he commanded his regiment, the 2nd Cavalry, in a march from Utah to Washington, D.C. He was promoted to major in February 1862, and after brilliant service in the Peninsula campaign he was appointed brigadier general of volunteers in July. He commanded a division of cavalry in the Maryland campaign, taking part in the battles at South Mountain, September 14, Antietam (Sharpsburg), where he was brevetted lieutenant colonel of regulars, September 17, and Fredericksburg, December 13. At Chancellorsville on May 2, 1863, he organized a cavalry and artillery defense that slowed Gen. Thomas J. Jackson's charge after his initial success over Gen. Oliver O. Howard's corps, enough to prevent an utter rout of the Army of the

Potomac. On June 9, while reconnoitering Gen. Robert E. Lee's movements, he surprised Gen. J. E. B. Stuart's Confederate cavalry at Brandy Station, Virginia, and fought to a draw, largely with saber, one of the war's few mounted battles. Later in the month he was promoted to major general of volunteers, and at Gettysburg, July 1–3, he was in command of all the cavalry of the Army of the Potomac and won a brevet to colonel of regulars. Early in 1864 Pleasonton was transferred to Missouri, where in October he met the third invasion of the state by Gen. Sterling Price. He successfully defended the capital, Jefferson City, on October 8 and then joined his 6500 men with Gen. Samuel R. Curtis's 15,000 in the battle of Westport, actually a series of engagements around Kansas City. Pleasonton defeated a Confederate division at the Big Blue River on October 23 and two days later routed the remainder of Price's army at the Marais des Cygnes River in Kansas. In March 1865 Pleasonton was brevetted brigadier and major general; but reversion to permanent rank after the war placed him under former subordinates, and he resigned from the army in January 1868. During 1869–1870 he was a collector of internal revenue in New York, and in December 1870 he became commissioner of internal revenue. He lost that post in 1871, and from 1872 to 1874 he was president of the Cincinnati & Terre Haute Railway. In October 1888 he was placed on the army retired list as a major. He died in Washington, D.C., on February 17, 1897.

Poe, Orlando Metcalfe (1832–1895), army officer and engineer. Born on March 7, 1832, in Navarre, Ohio, Poe graduated from West Point in 1856 and was commissioned in the topographical engineers. For five years he was engaged in survey work on the Great Lakes, receiving promotion to first lieutenant in July 1860. On the outbreak of the Civil War he aided in organizing Ohio volunteers and in May–June 1861 was chief topographical engineer of the Department of the Ohio. He joined the staff of Gen. George B. McClellan in time to take part in the battle of Rich Mountain, July 11, and in September he was appointed colonel of the 2nd Michigan Volunteers. He took part in the Peninsula campaign, the second battle of Bull Run (Manassas), and the Maryland campaign and in November 1862 was promoted to brigadier general of volunteers. After Fredericksburg, December 13, he commanded a division until the expiration of his volunteer commission in March 1863, whereupon he reverted to captain. He was then chief engineer of the XXIII Corps, Army of the Ohio, and was brevetted major for his work in building fortifications and directing the defense of Knoxville, Tennessee, during the siege by Gen. James Longstreet. In December 1863 he was assigned to duty with the Military Division of the Mississippi, and in April 1864 he was raised to chief engineer on the staff

of Gen. William T. Sherman. He served through the Atlanta campaign, the march to the sea, and the Carolinas campaign, earning brevets to lieutenant colonel in September, colonel in December, and brigadier general in March 1865. For five years after the war he was secretary engineer of the Lighthouse Board, receiving promotion to major in 1867, and in 1870 he became engineer of the Upper Lakes Lighthouse District, in which capacity he built the Spectacle Reef Lighthouse on Lake Huron in 1870–1873. In January 1873 he was appointed colonel and aide to Gen. Sherman, a post he held until Sherman's retirement in 1884. Poe was promoted to lieutenant colonel of engineers in 1882 and to colonel in 1888. From 1883 he was superintending engineer of river and harbor works from Lake Erie to Lake Superior. He died in Detroit on October 2, 1895.

Polk, Leonidas (1806–1864), clergyman and Confederate army officer. Born in Raleigh, North Carolina, on April 10, 1806, Polk, a cousin of James K. Polk, attended the University of North Carolina in 1821–1823, leaving to enter West Point. There in his last year he was converted by the new chaplain, Charles P. McIlvaine (afterward Episcopal bishop of Ohio). Polk graduated in June 1827 and was commissioned in the artillery but resigned his commission six months later to enter Virginia Theological Seminary. He was ordained in the Protestant Episcopal church in April 1830 and a year later advanced to the priesthood. After a time as assistant rector of a church in Richmond, Virginia, he traveled in Europe for his health during the early 1830s, and not until September 1838, when he was appointed missionary bishop of the Southwest—his thinly inhabited territory including Louisiana, Alabama, Mississippi, Arkansas, and part of Indian Territory—did he take up the religious duties that were to make him famous. He was chosen as first bishop of Louisiana in October 1841. In addition to his episcopal duties, involving endless hazardous travel in the backwoods, he devoted himself to the care of his rich wife's many slaves, establishing a large plantation and conducting a Sunday school for blacks. The plantation failed, however, whereupon Polk set himself another task, that of founding a great Episcopalian educational institution in his region that would train the white aristocracy in their responsibility for the gradual emancipation of the slaves. On October 9, 1860, Polk laid the cornerstone of the University of the South, at Sewanee, Tennessee, having in the previous four years gathered $500,000 in contributions and secured a grant of 9500 acres of land. Delayed by the Civil War, the University finally opened for classes in 1868. With the outbreak of the Civil War, Polk was offered a commission as major general in the Confederate army by his West Point classmate, President Jefferson Davis. He accepted after some hesitation in

June 1861 and served ably, despite his lack of military experience. He saw action mainly in the Mississippi River defenses, for a time under his West Point roommate, Gen. Albert S. Johnston. He defeated Gen. Ulysses S. Grant in a small engagement at Belmont, Missouri, on November 7, 1861 following Grant's attack on Gen. Gideon J. Pillow. He commanded the I Corps on the right flank at Pittsburg Landing (Shiloh) April 6–7, 1862, where he performed gallantly, and for his conduct as second-in-command to Gen. Braxton Bragg at Perryville, October 8, 1862, he was promoted to lieutenant general. He commanded the armies of Kentucky and Mississippi in the retreat from Kentucky. He later saw action at Murfreesboro and at Chickamauga, but his record there was somewhat clouded by disputes with Bragg. For a time in 1863 he had charge of paroled prisoners from Vicksburg, and in December 1863 he succeeded Gen. Joseph E. Johnston in command of the Department of Alabama, Mississippi, and East Louisiana. He died of wounds suffered at Pine Mountain near Marietta, Georgia, on June 14, 1864.

Pomeroy, Seth (1706–1777), colonial and Revolutionary army officer. Born in Northampton, Massachusetts, on May 20, 1706, Pomeroy followed the family trade of gunsmithing. He enrolled in the militia in 1743, was promoted to captain in 1744, and in 1745 took part, as a major, in the expedition under William Pepperrell against Louisbourg. In 1755 he was a lieutenant colonel under Gen. (later Sir) William Johnson in the Crown Point expedition, and it was Pomeroy who personally captured the French commander, Baron Dieskau, at Lake George, September 8. He succeeded Col. Ephraim Williams in command of the western Massachusetts regiment at that battle. In 1774–1775 he was a member of the provincial congress, and he was elected a general officer in October 1774 and brigadier general of militia in February 1775. He was effective in recruiting in western Massachusetts. In June he made his way to Cambridge, and on June 17 he took part as a private soldier in the battle of Bunker Hill, where his presence in the front line, once discovered, greatly encouraged other soldiers. On June 22, 1775, he was listed first and thereby senior among the first eight brigadier generals commissioned by the Continental Congress, but, there being some difficulty in the adjustment of certain matters of rank, he declined the commission. He returned home and continued an effective recruiter. While on his way to join the Continental army in New Jersey at the head of a militia force, he fell ill and died in Peekskill, New York, on February 19, 1777.

Pontiac (1720?–1769), Indian leader. Born about 1720 near the Maumee River in what is now northern Ohio, Pontiac was the son of an Ottawa father and an Ojibwa mother. By 1755 he was chief of the Ottawas. After the victory of the English in the French and Indian War, many tribes of the Old Northwest grew resentful of them, for, unlike the French before them, they cheated the Indians in trading, did not welcome them into their forts, and planted and settled on Indian lands. In 1762, by persuasion and force of prestige, Pontiac forged a loose confederation of nearly all of the tribes of the trans-Appalachian region with a plan for what came to be known as Pontiac's War. British forts along the frontier were to be attacked simultaneously and frontier settlements destroyed. On May 7, 1763, Pontiac himself led a surprise attack on the garrison of Detroit, which was under the command of Maj. Henry Gladwin. Gladwin was forewarned of Pontiac's plan to take the fort by a ruse, and the conflict settled quickly into a siege that lasted for more than a year, during which, on July 31, 1763, Pontiac heavily defeated a column of regulars and rangers attempting relief at Bloody Run. The siege, a porous one, was lifted by the arrival of Col. John Bradstreet in August 1764. In the initial weeks of the war nearly every other western fort had been ransacked, and settlements from Niagara to Virginia had been burned. Fort Pitt and Fort Ligonier were among the posts that successfully resisted, both being relieved by a force under Col. Henry Bouquet, who defeated the Indians in Ohio in 1764 and forced them to sue for peace. Pontiac himself and a small number of followers refused to consider surrender at that time, but by the following year Pontiac saw that there was no hope of raising a sufficient Indian force to meet the increasing strength of the British. After a preliminary truce arranged by George Croghan in 1765, Pontiac attended peace talks at Fort Ontario with Sir William Johnson in July 1766 and signed a treaty, to which he thereafter adhered. The figure of Pontiac as a symbol of Indian resistance became almost legendary in his own lifetime, yet his actual role in the war, other than at Detroit, and the scope of his influence became a subject of debate. There are various accounts of his death in 1769, but he was probably killed at Cahokia, Illinois, by another Indian who had been bribed by an English trader.

Poor, Enoch (1736–1780), Revolutionary army officer. Born in Andover, Massachusetts, on June 21, 1736, Poor was a cabinetmaker when he enlisted in the militia in 1755. About 1760 he settled in Exeter, New Hampshire, where he became a shipbuilder. In 1774–1775 he sat in the provincial congress, and in May 1775 he was appointed colonel of the 2nd New Hampshire Regiment. After seeing to the defenses of his state he joined the Continental army during the siege of Boston. Early in 1776 his regiment was part of a brigade under Gen. William Thompson sent to reinforce Col. Benedict Arnold's exhausted forces in Canada, and he took part in the retreat down the

Hudson valley. He led a group of field officers in opposing Gen. Philip Schuyler's order for a further withdrawal from Crown Point to Ticonderoga in July and appealed to Gen. George Washington, who sustained Schuyler as a point of discipline while clearly favoring Poor's assessment. In December 1776 Poor rejoined Washington's army and took part in the battles of Trenton, December 26, and Princeton, January 3, 1777. In February 1777 he was commissioned brigadier general in the Continental army. He took part in the campaign under Gen. Horatio Gates against Gen. John Burgoyne's invasion of New York in June–October 1777, performing with particular gallantry at the second battle of Bemis Heights, October 7. He then rejoined the main army at Valley Forge. He took part in the battle of Monmouth Court House, June 27, 1778, and in 1779 commanded a brigade in Gen. John Sullivan's expedition against the Indians and Loyalists of western New York and Pennsylvania, again distinguishing himself at Newtown, August 29. In August 1780 he was given command of a new brigade of light infantry organized under Gen. Lafayette, but he fell ill and died shortly thereafter, on September 8, 1780, in Paramus, New Jersey.

Popé (?–1690), Indian leader. It is not known when Popé was born, but he was of the Tewa, or San Juan, Pueblo. He seems to have first come to the attention of the Spanish authorities in Santa Fe, New Mexico, in 1675, when he led the resistance against the persecution—imprisonment, enslavement, and frequent execution—of medicine men by the Roman Catholic Church for practising their traditional religion. On his release from prison he hid at Taos Pueblo and began to plan a large-scale revolt, the success of which seemed assured because of constant quarreling between the religious and secular arms of the Spanish colonial government. In winning other Pueblos to his plan, Popé claimed the sanction of the traditional Pueblo gods. The rebellion was scheduled to break out on August 13, 1680, but Popé advanced the date to August 10 when he learned that the plot had been revealed to the Spaniards. On that day almost all the Pueblos rose up; nearly 500 Spaniards throughout the region were killed by the Indians. On August 14 a confrontation occurred between about 500 Indian warriors and 1000 remaining colonists at Santa Fe. The Spaniards refused to accept an ultimatum to leave but after a furious fight began to retreat southward on August 21, regrouping eventually at El Paso on the Rio Grande. Meanwhile the rebels were devastating all evidences of Spanish presence in the region from Taos to Isleta. For the next 12 years, as a result of the most successful Indian uprising ever to occur on the North American continent, Popé and his warriors held absolute sway over Santa Fe and its environs. Old ways of life were restored, and all evidences of the Spanish language and of Christianity were obliterated. But Popé himself was no less a tyrant than the Spaniards had been. A fearful drought struck New Mexico, and the Apaches and Utes raided the Pueblo settlements; by 1690, when Popé died, the Pueblo population had decreased from 29,000 to 9000. The Spanish reconquest was complete by 1692.

Pope, John (1822–1892), army officer. Born in Louisville, Kentucky, on March 16, 1822, Pope graduated from West Point in 1842 and was commissioned in the topographical engineers. After four years of survey work in Florida and the Northeast he joined Gen. Zachary Taylor's army in Mexico, winning brevets to first lieutenant at Monterrey, September 20–24, 1846, and to captain at Buena Vista, February 22–23, 1847. He led a surveying party in Minnesota in 1849–1850, demonstrating the navigability of the Red River of the North, and then was chief topographical engineer of the Department of New Mexico in 1851–1853. From 1853 to 1859 he explored in the West, for a time surveying a southern route for a Pacific railroad; he was promoted to first lieutenant in March 1853 and to captain in July 1856. He was on lighthouse duty at the outbreak of the Civil War and in May 1861 was appointed brigadier general of volunteers and assigned to Gen. John C. Frémont's forces in Missouri. His most notable victory in the campaign against Gen. Sterling Price was at Blackwater, near Warrensburg, on December 18, where he took 1300 prisoners and a large quantity of supplies. In March 1862 he took command of the newly organized Army of the Mississippi, about 25,-000 strong, and began operations against the Confederate stronghold on Island No. 10 in the Mississippi some 55 miles south of Cairo, Illinois. The island was defended by 58 guns and 12,000 soldiers. Pope, promoted to major general of volunteers late in March, laid siege to New Madrid, Missouri, on March 3 and took it on March 14; he then cut a channel from there bypassing the guns of the island. Gunboats of the Western River Squadron under Flag-Officer Andrew H. Foote ran past the island and ferried Pope's troops over the Mississippi on the south; shore defenses were soon neutralized and on April 7 Island No. 10 surrendered. That victory was the first step in opening the Mississippi. He then joined his forces with Gen. Ulysses S. Grant's Army of the Tennessee and Gen. Don Carlos Buell's Army of the Ohio, all under command of Gen. Henry W. Halleck, for the campaign against Corinth, Mississippi. In June he was called east to organize the scattered forces in the Shenandoah valley and on the Rappahannock into the Army of Virginia, a task he undertook with a series of bombastic proclamations. He was promoted to brigadier general of regulars in July. He had some 45,000 men to begin with, and the army slowly grew as Gen. George B. McClellan's forces on the Peninsula were gradually withdrawn and transferred to Pope. Gen. Robert E. Lee sent Gen. Thomas J. Jackson north with 24,000 men to watch Pope, and a preliminary battle was fought by Jackson and Gen. Nathaniel P. Banks at Cedar Mountain, Virginia, on August 9. Lee, having joined Jackson, sent him circling around west of Pope to the north, where on August 27 he destroyed Pope's supply base at Manassas Station. Pope, unable to find the now superior Confederate forces, walked into a trap on the old Bull Run (Manassas) battlefield on August 29. Reinforcement by Gen. Samuel P. Heintzelman's III Corps and Gen. Fitz-John Porter's V Corps from McClellan failed to help, for Gen. James Longstreet appeared from Thoroughfare Gap at the same time to reinforce Lee. Pope's attacks on August 30 were poorly coordinated, and he was forced to retire toward Washington, D.C. During the retreat a sharp, bloody engagement was fought with Jackson at Chantilly on September 1. On September 5 Pope was relieved of command and the Army of Virginia was dissolved, the troops returning to McClellan and the Army of the Potomac. He insisted that his defeat was the result of Porter's failure to execute his orders to flank Jackson; Porter was subsequently court-martialed and cashiered. Pope was sent to the Department of the Northwest, where he was successful in suppressing Indian unrest. In January 1865 he took command of the Division (from June the Department) of the Missouri, and in March he was brevetted major general of regulars for the Island No. 10 campaign. In 1867 he built Fort Hays, Kansas. He commanded the Third Military District (Georgia, Alabama, Florida) in 1867 –1868; the Department of the Lakes, 1868–1870; the Department of the Missouri, 1870–1883, receiving promotion to major general in October 1882; and the Department of California and Division of the Pacific, 1883–1886. He retired in March 1886 and died in Sandusky, Ohio, on September 23, 1892.

Porter, David (1780–1843), naval officer. Born in Boston on February 1, 1780, Porter went to sea with his father, a veteran of the Massachusetts navy in the Revolution, in 1796 and entered the navy as a midshipman in April 1798. He was on board the *Constellation* under Commodore Thomas Truxtun when she captured the French frigate *Insurgente* in February 1799. Promoted to lieutenant in October 1799, he served on various vessels. In the Tripolitan War he rose to command of the schooner *Enterprise*. He was captured with the unlucky *Philadelphia*, Capt. William Bainbridge, in October 1803 and imprisoned until 1805. Promoted to master commandant in April 1806 and to captain in July 1812, he commanded the naval station at New Orleans in 1808–1810 and the frigate *Essex*, 32 guns, from July 1811. In July 1812 he sailed from New York on a cruise during which he took nine prizes, including, on August 13, near Bermuda, the sloop of war *Alert*, 16, the first British naval vessel captured in the War of 1812. In October 1812 he sailed again from Philadelphia and early in 1813 rounded Cape Horn into the Pacific, making the *Essex* the first U.S. naval vessel to sail those waters. He managed to maintain the *Essex* for more than a year by capturing British whalers and using their supplies, ammunition, and money. During this voyage he took possession on November 19, 1813, of Nuku Hiva, one of the Marquesas Islands, renaming it Madison Island; but the United States never confirmed his action. He was forced to battle fierce Taipi (or Typee) natives to retain his base there. Early in 1814 he entered Valparaiso harbor, Chile, accompanied by the *Essex Junior*, a recommissioned prize under Lt. John Downes. There he was found by the *Phoebe* and the *Cherub*, British men-of-war that he had earlier learned had been dispatched to stop his raiding. After being blockaded in the harbor for six weeks he made a dash for open sea on March 28, but a squall carried away his main topmast and he was set upon by both enemy ships and captured, losing many men in the fight. Paroled later in the year, he returned home in time to participate in naval operations around Washington, D.C., before the end of the war. By that time he was relatively wealthy, having married well and having profited from his many prizes, and on being named to the Board of Navy Commissioners in 1815—in which capacity he was apparently the first to propose a naval mission to Japan—he bought a farm on the heights overlooking the White House. But his restless spirit was dissatisfied with shore duty, and he resigned from the board in 1823 to take command of the West India Squadron, with which for two years he fought to suppress pirates. Impetuous and short-tempered, he responded to what he considered discourteous treatment by Spanish authorities at Fajardo, Puerto Rico, by landing an armed force, seizing a fort, and demanding an apology. Spain did not formally protest, but the action provided an excuse for the Navy Department, where Porter was not popular, to move against him, and in 1825 he was court-martialed and sentenced to a six-month suspension from duty. Furious, he resigned from the navy in August 1826 and went to Mexico, where he had been offered a post as commander in chief of the Mexican navy. His three years in that post were a grave disappointment, and he returned to the United States in 1829 seeking appointment as U.S. minister to Mexico so that he could avenge himself on enemies there. He settled in 1830 for the post of consul general in Algiers, later becoming chargé d'affaires and in due course minister to Turkey in 1839. He died in Constantinople on March 3, 1843. David Glasgow Farragut, his adopted son, and his natural son, David Dixon Porter, were both highly distinguished naval officers.

Porter, David Dixon (1813–1891), naval officer. Born on June 8, 1813, in Chester, Pennsylvania, Porter was the son of Capt. David Porter. He received little formal education and at the age of ten made his first sea cruise with the West India Squadron commanded by his father. When the elder Porter became commander in chief of the Mexican navy in 1826, young Porter joined also, serving as a midshipman for three years. In 1829, having been imprisoned by Spanish authorities following the capture of his ship, he was released and in February was commissioned a midshipman in the U.S. navy. He served on the *Constellation* and the *United States* in the Mediterranean and from 1836 to 1841 was attached to the Coast Survey. Similar duties followed his promotion to lieutenant in February 1841. During the Mexican War he participated in the naval bombardment of Veracruz and the capture of Tabasco by Commodore Matthew C. Perry and for a time commanded the steam schooner *Spitfire*. After the war he returned to his earlier duties, but, dissatisfied with his failure to advance, he went on furlough in 1849 and commanded Panama mail steamers. He returned to active duty in 1855, made two voyages to the Mediterranean to obtain camels for the army's use in the Southwest, and from 1857 to 1860 was assigned to the Portsmouth, New Hampshire, navy yard. He was on the verge of resigning again when he was given command of the *Powhatan* on a relief mission (with Capt. Montgomery C. Meigs of the army) to Fort Pickens, Florida, in April 1861. Promoted to commander in August, as of April, he performed blockade duty along the Gulf Coast and made a cruise in the West Indies in pursuit of the Confederate raider *Sumter*. From November 1861 until April 1862 he helped plan a naval offensive against New Orleans; he recommended his foster brother, Commander David G. Farragut, for chief command, and was himself placed in charge of the flotilla of 20 mortar boats. The bombardment inflicted by Porter's command on Fort Jackson and Fort St. Philip for several days preceding the attack opened the mouth of the Mississippi and aided the taking of New Orleans by the full squadron on April 27. The next day he received the surrender of the forts on his flagship, the *Harriet Lane*. He took part in Farragut's operations around Vicksburg later in the year. In October Porter was made acting rear admiral in command of the Mississippi Squadron, succeeding Commodore Charles Henry Davis, and during 1863 he provided the necessary naval support for Union actions on the river at Arkansas Post, January 10–11, in support of Gen. John A. McClernand; Grand Gulf, in April; and most importantly at Vicksburg. After running past the Vicksburg batteries on April 16, Porter ferried Gen. Ulysses S. Grant's army across the river to Bruinsburg on April 30, launching it on its way to victory in July. For his actions in the Vicksburg campaign he was given the official thanks

of Congress and made permanent rear admiral in July 1863. In August his command was extended south to New Orleans. After further campaigns on the Western rivers, including the unsuccessful Red River campaign in conjunction with Gen. Nathaniel P. Banks, (from which his squadron escaped only through the inspired work of Col. Joseph Bailey) he was called in October 1864 to command the North Atlantic Blockading Squadron. He was in command of the naval forces at the reduction of Fort Fisher, defensive stronghold of Wilmington, North Carolina, launching naval attacks and landing troops under Gen. Benjamin F. Butler on December 24–25, 1864, and again with Gen. Alfred H. Terry, on January 13–15, 1865, and was again formally thanked by Congress. From August 1865 to March 1869 he was superintendent of the U.S. Naval Academy and there introduced many improvements in organization and training. In July 1866 he was promoted to vice admiral. During 1869–1870, as adviser to the secretary of the navy, Porter was in virtually complete command of the navy. In August 1870, upon the death of Farragut, he became admiral and the senior officer of the service. Despite his eminence he found himself powerless and frustrated in these last years; his duties were virtually limited to membership on the Board of Inspection. He died in Washington, D.C. on February 13, 1891.

Porter, Fitz-John (1822–1901), army officer. Born in Portsmouth, New Hampshire, on August 31, 1822, Porter was a nephew of Commodore David Porter and a cousin of Adm. David D. Porter. He graduated from West Point in 1845, was commissioned in the artillery, and served under Gen. Zachary Taylor and Gen. Winfield Scott in the Mexican War, receiving promotion to first lieutenant in May 1847 and brevets to captain and major at Molino del Rey and Chapultepec, September 8 and 13, 1847. From 1849 to 1855 he was an instructor at West Point, and in June 1856 he was appointed captain in the adjutant general's department and stationed at Fort Leavenworth, Kansas. During 1857–1858 he took part in the Mormon expedition under Col. Albert S. Johnston. In 1860–1861 he performed several special assignments, including inspecting and reorganizing the defenses in Charleston harbor, South Carolina, conducting federal troops out of Texas after the secession of that state, and organizing volunteer troops in Pennsylvania. In May 1861 he was appointed colonel of the 15th Infantry and three days later brigadier general of volunteers. In the Peninsula campaign of 1862 he commanded a brigade in Gen. Samuel P. Heintzelman's III Corps and then was given command of the V corps. In June he was left isolated north of the main army by the rain-swollen, impassable Chickahominy Creek, and on June 26 and June 27 he withstood furious attacks by twice his numbers at Mechanicsville and Gaines' Mill. After the latter battle he managed to cross over to join Gen. George B. McClellan and the rest of the Army of the Potomac. The V Corps led the army in the shift of base to the James River and occupied the commanding Malvern Hill, where another bloody battle was fought July 1. Porter was promoted to major general of volunteers in July. On being withdrawn from the Peninsula, his corps was reassigned to Gen. John Pope's Army of Virginia. On August 29 he was ordered to attack Gen. Thomas J. Jackson's right flank and cut him off from reinforcement by Gen. James Longstreet, who was approaching the Bull Run (Manassas) battlefield from Thoroughfare Gap. Porter failed to attack then, but the next day was heavily engaged to good account. After Pope's retreat to Washington he accused Porter of insubordination on August 29. Porter continued in command of the V Corps, taking part in the Maryland campaign and the battle of Antietam (Sharpsburg), September 17, until November, when he was relieved and formally charged with disobeying orders. His defense was that Pope's orders were vague and that Longstreet had already arrived and entered the line, making the ordered flank attack impossible. On January 21, 1863, he was found guilty by a court-martial, cashiered from the army, and "forever disqualified from holding any office of trust or profit under the government of the United States." He immediately began a campaign to exonerate himself, a task that took years to achieve. In 1879 a panel of general officers examined the case and found in his favor. In May 1882 President Chester A. Arthur remitted the disqualification portion of his sentence. By an act of Congress of July 1886 he was restored in August to rank of colonel of infantry, dating from May 1861, and placed on the retired list. From 1865 to 1871 he had engaged in mercantile business in New York City. In 1869 he declined the offer of command of the army of Khedive Ismail I of Egypt, a post that then went to Gen. Charles P. Stone. Later Porter was superintendent of construction of a state asylum at Morristown, New Jersey; commissioner of public works in New York City, 1875–1876; assistant receiver of the Central Railroad of New Jersey; New York City commissioner of police, 1884–1888, and of fire, 1888–1889; and cashier of the New York post office, 1893–1897. Porter died in Morristown, New Jersey, on May 21, 1901.

Porter, John Luke (1813–1893), naval architect. Born on September 19, 1813, in Portsmouth, Virginia, Porter entered his father's shipbuilding business in his youth and gradually took on responsibility for design and construction. For the navy he designed and built in 1843–1844 the steam-powered *Water-Witch,* later used by Lt. Thomas J. Page in his South American explorations, and he superintended construction in 1846–1847 of the *Alleghany,* and in 1859 of the steam sloops *Seminole* and *Pensacola.* During

the 1850s he tried unsuccessfully to interest the navy in his ideas on ironclad warships. In October 1859 he was appointed a naval constructor and assigned to the Pensacola navy yard. When that yard was captured by state authorities early in 1861, Porter was recalled to Washington, D.C., and sent then to the Norfolk navy yard, but on the secession of Virginia in April he resigned and offered his services to the Confederacy. He was not actually commissioned a naval constructor until June 1862, but well before that he had done signal service. In June 1861 he joined Lt. John M. Brooke and engineer William P. Williamson to discuss the construction of an ironclad. They developed a design based on using the intact hull of the federal steamer *Merrimack,* scuttled and partly burned at the evacuation of Norfolk navy yard. The design was approved in July, and Porter set about reconditioning the hull and constructing an armored deck shield, while Brooke prepared the inclined side armor and the guns and Williamson worked on the engines. The rechristened *Virginia* was ready for action by March 1862 and on March 9 it fought the epic battle with the *Monitor* in Hampton Roads. Porter remained at Norfolk until it was abandoned by the Confederates in May 1862 and then worked in Richmond as chief constructor, turning out plans and specifications for upwards of 40 ironclad or partly armored vessels, including the *Richmond,* the *Palmetto State,* terror of the Charleston blockade, the *Chicora,* the *Albemarle,* and others. After the war Porter worked for various shipyards at Norfolk and Berkeley, Virginia, and later superintended the Norfolk and Portsmouth ferries. He died in Portsmouth, Virginia, on December 14, 1893.

Pratt, Richard Henry (1840–1924), army officer and educator. Born in Rushford, New York, on December 6, 1840, Pratt grew up from 1846 in Logansport, Indiana. At the outbreak of the Civil War he enlisted in the 9th Indiana Infantry, and he later served in the 2nd Indiana Cavalry and the 11th Indiana Cavalry, becoming first lieutenant in April 1864 and captain in September 1864 and being mustered out in May 1865. After two years in the hardware business he reentered the army in March 1867 as second lieutenant in the 10th Cavalry, a black regiment; he was promoted to first lieutenant in July. He took part in several Indian wars on the frontier and in 1875 was detailed to escort a number of Indian prisoners to Fort Marion at St. Augustine, Florida. Over the next three years he was successful in an attempt to educate his prisoners, and in 1878 he was sent to organize an Indian branch of the Hampton Normal and Agricultural Institute in Virginia. That experiment proved less successful, and in 1879 he obtained permission to convert a portion of the Carlisle Barracks in Pennsylvania into an Indian school. The school opened in October 1879 with 82 Sioux children and was formally recognized by Congress in 1882. The course at Carlisle combined academic work, eventually extending through the first two years of high school, with vocational training in a broad range of fields and the unique "outing" system, which placed students in white homes and schools or jobs for a year to further their adjustment to white society. The school was the model for many reservation schools built later. The school grew steadily, and in his 25 years as superintendent Pratt had charge of some 5000 Indian children of more than 70 tribes. He was promoted to captain in February 1883, major in July 1898, lieutenant colonel in February 1901, and colonel in January 1903. He retired in February 1903 and in April 1904 was advanced to brigadier general on the retired list. He died in San Francisco on March 15, 1924. Carlisle Indian School in later years fielded a formidable football team, coached in 1899–1904 and 1906–1915 by Glenn S. "Pop" Warner and led in 1911–1912 by All-American Jim Thorpe. The school had an enrollment of about 1000 at its closing in 1918.

Pratt, William Veazie (1869–1957), naval officer. Born on February 28, 1869, in Belfast, Maine, Pratt graduated from the Naval Academy in 1889 and after cruises on the *Atlanta* and the *Chicago* of the "White Squadron" was commissioned an ensign in July 1891. He served on the *Petrel* until 1895, at the Academy in 1895–1897, and on many vessels thereafter, advancing to lieutenant (junior grade) in August 1898 and lieutenant in March 1899 while seeing duty in the Spanish–American War, the Philippine Insurrection, and the Peking Relief Expedition. He was again at the Academy in 1900–1902, 1905–1906, and 1906–1908, and on the *Kearsarge*, 1902–1905, the *Newark*, 1906, and the *St. Louis*, 1908–1910. He was promoted to lieutenant commander in July 1905 and commander in July 1910, and after attending the Naval War College in 1911–1913 and serving two years on the staff of the Atlantic Fleet Torpedo Flotilla while also commanding the *Birmingham* in 1913–1915, he became captain in September 1915. After a brief tour in the Canal Zone he attended the Army War College in 1916–1917 and then was attached for some months to the office of the chief of naval operations. From August 1917 to January 1919 he was assistant chief of naval operations under Adm. William S. Benson, and in December 1918 he accompanied President Woodrow Wilson to France and was an adviser at the Versailles peace conference. During 1919–1920 he commanded the *New York* and in 1920–1921 the Pacific Fleet destroyer force. Promoted to rear admiral in June 1921, he sat on the General Board until 1923, serving also in 1921–1922 as an adviser to the American delegation to the Washington Limitation of Armaments Conference. Pratt commanded Battleship Division 4, Battle Fleet,

in 1923–1925, and after a few months again on the General Board was president of the Naval War College from September 1925 to September 1927. He was then named commander of Battleship Divisions, Battle Fleet, with the rank of vice admiral. In June 1928 he advanced to command of Battle Fleet with the rank of admiral, and the next year he was named commander in chief of the U.S. Fleet. In September 1930 Pratt was appointed chief of naval operations, remaining in that post until his retirement in July 1933. From 1940 to 1946 Pratt conducted a column of naval and military commentary in *Newsweek* magazine, and he was returned to active duty during January–July 1941 to assist in developing antisubmarine doctrine. He died in Chelsea, Massachusetts, on November 25, 1957.

Preble, Edward (1761–1807), naval officer. Born in Falmouth, Massachusetts (now Portland, Maine) on August 15, 1761, Preble ran away to sea at sixteen, and after sailing on a privateer for a time he was appointed midshipman in the Massachusetts navy in 1779 and assigned to the frigate *Protector.* That vessel was captured in 1781, and Preble was briefly held on the British prison ship *Jersey.* In 1782 he was lieutenant under Capt. George Little on the *Winthrop,* distinguishing himself on a cruise that netted five prizes. From 1783 to 1798 he was in the merchant service. In February 1798 he was commissioned lieutenant in the reorganized U.S. navy and put in command of the revenue cutter *Pickering* in Commodore John Barry's West India Squadron. Promoted to captain in May 1799, he sailed from Newport, Rhode Island, in January 1800 in command of the new frigate *Essex*, convoying a fleet of 14 merchantmen to the East Indies. There he cruised for several months, recaptured a number of American vessels from French privateers, and then convoyed another merchant fleet home, arriving in New York in November. In May 1803 he sailed aboard the *Constitution* to take command of the squadron before Tripoli. In the two years since war had been declared by Tripoli, the naval commanders there, Commodore Richard Dale, Commodore Richard V. Morris, and briefly Commodore John Rodgers, all hampered by limited forces, had accomplished little. Preble's arrival with reinforcements marked a new phase of the conflict. He arrived at Gibraltar in September and was immediately obliged to make a show of force at Tangier, where he thus persuaded the restive sultan to renew his treaty of 1786 with the United States. Preble rendezvoused with the squadron and learned only then of the grounding of the *Philadelphia* and the captivity of Capt. William Bainbridge and his crew. He quickly tightened the blockade of Tripoli, established a secure supply base at Syracuse, and borrowed from King Ferdinand I of the Two Sicilies two mortar boats and six gunboats able to operate in the shallow harbor of Tripoli. In February 1804 the *Philadelphia* was burned in a daring exploit by Lt. Stephen Decatur. On August 3 Preble launched a general attack on Tripoli, bombarding the shore from close range and boarding and capturing three Tripolitan vessels. The only American killed in the battle was Lt. James Decatur, Stephen's brother. Similar attacks were made on August 7, 24, and 28 and September 3. On September 4 the ketch *Intrepid* was loaded with more than seven tons of powder and sailed under cover of darkness into the harbor; she blew up prematurely, killing Lt. Richard Somers and his entire crew. A week later Preble was superseded in command by Commodore Samuel Barron, arriving with more reinforcements, but the war was essentially won. Preble had created the first working tactical naval squadron and was greatly disappointed to lose the opportunity to complete his task and capture Tripoli. His health broke soon after his return to the United States, and he died in Portland, Massachusetts (now Maine) on August 25, 1807.

Prentiss, Benjamin Mayberry (1819–1901), army officer. Born in Belleville, Virginia, on November 23, 1819, Prentiss moved to Marion County, Missouri, with his family in 1836. He moved to Illinois five years later and became a manufacturer of cordage. In 1844–1845 he was a lieutenant of militia in the campaign against the Mormons, and in the Mexican War he was a captain in the 1st Illinois Volunteers. He later took up the practice of law and ran unsuccessfully for Congress as a Republican in 1860. He was a colonel of militia at the outbreak of the Civil War, and on April 24–25 his forces captured two river steamers carrying contraband munitions. A few days later he was appointed colonel of the 10th Illinois Volunteer Infantry in federal service, and in May he was promoted to brigadier general of volunteers. In August he was put in command of the north and central districts of Missouri. On December 28 he defeated a large Confederate force at Mount Zion in southern Missouri. In the spring of 1862 he was ordered to join Gen. Ulysses S. Grant at Pittsburg Landing, Tennessee, where on April 1 he took command of the hastily organized 6th Division, Army of the Tennessee. On the first day of the battle of Shiloh, April 6, he distinguished himself in holding a difficult position against heavy attack, but at length he was captured. Released in October, he was promoted to major general of volunteers in November and placed in command of the eastern district of Arkansas. On July 4, 1863, he was attacked at Helena, Arkansas, by a Confederate force under Gen. Theophilus H. Holmes and Gen. Sterling Price and repulsed it with heavy losses to the enemy. In October he resigned his commission and resumed his law practice in Quincy, Illinois. In 1878 he moved to Sullivan County, Missouri, later moving to Kirksville and in

1881 to Bethany. He was postmaster of Bethany, Missouri, from 1888 until his death there on February 8, 1901.

Prescott, Samuel (1751–?1777), physician and Revolutionary patriot. Born in Concord, Massachusetts, on August 19, 1751, Prescott followed his father and grandfather in the practice of medicine. Late on the night of April 18, 1775, he started home from Lexington, Massachusetts, where he had made a call, and overtook Paul Revere and William Dawes, who had just come to Lexington to warn Samuel Adams and John Hancock of the approach of a force of British soldiers from Boston and were on their way to Concord to rouse the minutemen there. The two related their mission to Prescott, and the three rode on together. After a few miles they encountered a British patrol; Dawes escaped back to Lexington, and after a struggle Revere and Prescott broke away in separate directions. Revere was captured in a wood minutes later. Prescott, familiar with the country, eluded capture and roused the minutemen of Lincoln and Concord, enabling them to hide away the military stores that were the British goal and to gather under the command of Maj. John Buttrick for the fateful fight of April 19. Prescott served at Fort Ticonderoga in 1776. He was later captured and imprisoned in Halifax, Nova Scotia, where he died, probably sometime in 1777.

Prescott, William (1726–1795), Revolutionary militia officer. Born in Groton, Massachusetts, on February 20, 1726, Prescott saw service in the militia during King George's War, 1744–1748, and the French and Indian War, taking part in 1755 in an expedition to Nova Scotia and attaining the rank of captain. Thereafter he retired to his farm in Pepperell, Massachusetts. Colonel of a body of minutemen from 1774, he led them to Concord on April 19, 1775, but arrived too late for the fighting. He marched on to Cambridge to join the growing provincial army. His chance for action came two months later. Ordered to fortify Bunker Hill in Charlestown, he left Cambridge on June 16 with about 1000 men, but upon his arrival decided to fortify Breed's Hill instead, since it commanded the entrance to Back Bay and the town of Boston opposite more effectively. Breastworks were constructed by Col. Richard Gridley. As soon as the British—some 2200 regulars under Gen. Sir William Howe—saw the Americans in position on the morning of June 17 they opened fire, training their muskets especially on Prescott himself, who walked up and down the battlements paying no attention to the hail of bullets, several of which pierced his clothing. It was a warm day, and he took off his uniform and replaced it with a jacket and a broadbrimmed hat, in which guise he was later depicted in a statue on Bunker Hill. His extraordinary coolness under fire inspired his men, and he is remembered as the major hero of the battle erroneously named for Bunker Hill, although he was not the senior officer present, being ranked by Gen. Israel Putnam and Gen. Joseph Warren. He served in the Continental army in the campaign around New York City in 1776 and in the Saratoga campaign in 1777, but his years were beginning to tell, and an old injury made sitting on a horse almost impossible. Retiring to his farm, he undertook various civic duties in the remaining years of his life, including three years in the legislature. He died at Pepperell, Massachusetts, on October 13, 1795. The historian William H. Prescott was his grandson.

Price, Sterling (1809–1867), public official and Confederate army officer. Born on September 20, 1809, in Prince Edward County, Virginia, Price attended Hampden-Sydney College in 1826–1827 and later studied law. He moved to Missouri in 1831, settling in Chariton County. He was a member of the legislature in 1836–1838 and 1840–1844, serving during the latter period as speaker of the house, and in 1844 he was elected to Congress. He resigned his seat in August 1846 to serve in the Mexican War. As colonel of the 2nd Missouri Mounted Volunteers he accompanied Gen. Stephen W. Kearny's Army of the West to New Mexico, where he was left in command after Kearny's departure for California and Col. Alexander W. Doniphan's for Chihuahua. He put down a revolt in New Mexico, was promoted to brigadier general of volunteers in July 1847, and was named military governor of Chihuahua. He won a victory over Mexican forces at Santa Cruz de Rosales on March 16, 1848. In 1852 he was elected, as a Democrat, governor of Missouri, and during his four years in that post much progress was made in settling the state and improving the public schools. He was elected president of a state convention held in February 1861 to consider secession and was influential in the convention's decision for neutrality. In May the prosecession governor, Claiborne F. Jackson, appointed Price major general in command of the state militia with the aim of keeping federal troops out of the state. The seizure by Capt. Nathaniel Lyon and his pro-Union Home Guards of Camp Jackson, near St. Louis, on May 10 pushed Price—and thousands of Missourians—into the Confederate camp. After a widely noted conference with Lyon and Congressman Francis P. Blair at the Planters' Hotel in St. Louis that underlined the divisive effect on the state of the Camp Jackson affair, Price took command of the newly organized State Guard in Jefferson City. He fell back before Lyon's advance until August 10, when, in conjunction with a regular Confederate force under Gen. Ben McCulloch, he fought a pitched battle with Lyon, who was outnumbered 11,000 to 5400, at Wilson's Creek, southwest of Springfield.

Lyon was killed in the battle. Price, now with only about 1500 men, pursued the retreating federals northward and on September 12 laid siege to Lexington, defended by 2640 Union troops. The town capitulated eight days later, and Price secured considerable amounts of supplies. The approach of a large Union force under Gen. John C. Frémont compelled him to fall back to Springfield, whence he was driven into Arkansas in February 1862 by Gen. Samuel R. Curtis. He placed himself under Gen. Earl Van Dorn, and on March 7–8 they met Curtis at Pea Ridge (Elkhorn) and were again forced to retire. He and his troops were mustered into Confederate service in April, he becoming a major general, and they accompanied Van Dorn to Mississippi, where they fought Gen. William S. Rosecrans at Iuka on September 19 and took part in the larger battle at Corinth, October 3. In 1863 Price was ordered back to the trans-Mississippi. On July 4 he and Gen. Theophilus H. Holmes lost heavily in attacking Gen. Benjamin M. Prentiss at Helena, Arkansas, and he lost again in a fight at Pine Bluff, October 25. Federal forces under Gen. Frederick Steele drove him out of Little Rock, but in the spring of 1864 he succeeded in preventing Steele from joining Gen. Nathaniel P. Banks's Red River campaign, harrying him on the march and with Gen. Edmund Kirby-Smith attacking him sharply at Jenkins Ferry, April 30. In September Price returned to Missouri with more than 12,000 men; he was repulsed at Pilot Knob, September 27, with heavy losses and gave up his plan to take St. Louis. He moved on Jefferson City but, unable to take it from Union forces under Gen. Alfred Pleasonton on October 8, passed around it toward Independence. On October 21–23 he fought a running battle in and around Westport and Kansas City with Gen. Samuel R. Curtis and Gen. Pleasonton. This "Gettysburg of the West," the largest battle of the war west of the Mississippi, practically destroyed Price's army. He retreated to Arkansas and thence to Texas. At the end of the war he moved to Mexico where he attempted to establish a colony of Confederate veterans, but with the fall of Emperor Maximilian in 1866 he returned to Missouri. He died in St. Louis on September 29, 1867.

Pulaski, Kazimierz (1747–1779), Revolutionary army officer. Born at Winiary, Mazovia, Poland, on March 4, 1747, Pulaski was the oldest son of Count Jozef Pulaski, Polish patriot and one of the organizers of the Confederation of Bar. Casimir (the common anglicized spelling) and his two brothers all took part in the military activities of the confederation, and Casimir's defense of Czestochowa against the Russians in 1770–1771 brought him fame throughout Europe. But the failure of his attempt to kidnap King Stanislaw II in November 1771, following which the Russians were joined by Austrian and Prussian forces in 1772, rendered further resistance useless, and Pulaski went into exile, first in Turkey, then in Paris. There, after four years of restless inactivity, he was introduced to Silas Deane and Benjamin Franklin, who together arranged for him to go to America to serve in the Revolution. Arriving in June 1777, he served in a volunteer capacity with Gen. George Washington at Brandywine, September 11, and a short time later was made a brigadier general by Congress and put in command of the Continental cavalry. After service at Germantown, October 4, he was with the army at Valley Forge during the winter of 1777–1778. Differences with Gen. Anthony Wayne, under whom he refused to serve, led to his resigning his command, but in March 1778 he was given permission to organize an independent mixed corps of cavalry and light infantry, the Pulaski Legion, with which he waged guerrilla warfare against the British. None of his efforts was especially fruitful, however; at Egg Harbor, New Jersey, his legion was heavily defeated on October 15. He was ready to return to Poland when, in February 1779, he was ordered to join Gen. Benjamin Lincoln and the Southern army in South Carolina. During May 8–13 he held the city of Charleston against a British force until Lincoln's army arrived to break the siege. He commanded the combined French and American cavalry in the siege of Savannah, Georgia. In the general assault on October 9 he gallantly charged the British lines at the head of his cavalry. He was mortally wounded and died two days later, on October 11, 1779, on board the warship *Wasp* in Savannah harbor.

Puller, Lewis Burwell (1898–1971), marine officer. Born on June 26, 1898, in West Point, Virginia, Puller attended Virginia Military Institute for a short time before enlisting in the marines in August 1918. He was given a reserve commission in June 1919, but in the reduction of the corps following World War I he was discharged and then reenlisted as a corporal. During 1919–1924 he served in the Haitian gendarmerie (organized by Col. Smedley D. Butler in 1915) as acting first lieutenant, and after his return to the United States in March 1924 he was commissioned a second lieutenant of marines. Over the next several years he was stationed at Philadelphia, at Quantico, Virginia, in Hawaii in 1926–1928, and in Nicaragua in 1928–1931. In 1926 he took aviation training at the Pensacola, Florida, naval air station. He graduated from the army's Infantry School, Fort Benning, Georgia, in 1932; served a second tour in Nicaragua in 1932–1933; was attached to the marine force at Peking, China, in 1933–1934; and commanded the marine detachment on the *Augusta* of the Asiatic Fleet in 1934–1936 and again 1939–1940. During 1936–1939 he was an instructor at the Basic School in Philadelphia. From May 1940 to August 1941 he was with the 4th Marine Regiment in Shanghai, China,

advancing during that time to major and battalion commander, and he was then attached to the 7th Marines at Camp Lejeune, North Carolina, where he was a pioneer in his emphasis on training for jungle warfare. In September 1942 the 7th reinforced Gen. Alexander A. Vandegrift's 1st Marine Division on Guadalcanal, and in the climactic battle for Henderson Field on October 24–25 Puller particularly distinguished himself; his battalion held off repeated attacks by a full Japanese regiment, the Japanese losing 20 men to every American killed. "Chesty" Puller, as he was known, was awarded his third Navy Cross for that action. Promoted to lieutenant colonel, he took part in the landing on Cape Gloucester, New Britain, on January 16, 1944, and won a fourth Navy Cross in the heavy fighting of that campaign. In February he took command of the 1st Marine Regiment. With the 1st Marine Division the regiment took part in the landing on Peleliu, September 15, 1944. In November Puller returned to the United States and was assigned to training duty at Camp Lejeune, receiving promotion to colonel a short time later. Subsequently he was director of the 8th Marine Reserve District at New Orleans and commander of the marine barracks at Pearl Harbor, and in August 1950 he resumed command of the 1st Marine Regiment at Camp Pendleton, California. Sent to Korea immediately thereafter, he led the 1st in the landing at Inch'on in September and in the bitter house-to-house fighting for control of Seoul. Promoted to brigadier general in January 1951, he was assistant commander of the 1st Marine Division under Gen. Oliver P. Smith for a short time. In May he returned to Camp Pendleton to command the 3rd Marine Brigade, later redesignated the 3rd Division. Puller advanced to major general in September 1953. He was again at Camp Lejeune, as commander of the 2nd Division and later as deputy camp commander, from July 1954 until his retirement for disability in November 1955 with the rank of lieutenant general. "Chesty" Puller, the most decorated marine in the corps, was also perhaps its most colorful figure. Openly and imaginatively profane, he was quick to speak his mind publicly, and shortly after his return from Korea he created outrage among army, navy, and air force circles by his disparaging comments on their training programs. He died in Hampton, Virginia, on October 11, 1971.

Putnam, Israel (1718–1790), colonial and Revolutionary army officer. Born in Salem Village (now in Danvers), Massachusetts, on January 7, 1718, Putnam received little if any formal education as a youth. He early gained a great reputation for self-reliance and bravery. It was said, for example, that he once tracked a wolf right into its den and shot it. Moving to what is now Brooklyn, Connecticut, about 1740, he soon became a prosperous farmer there. He volunteered for military service at the outbreak of the

French and Indian War, was a captain under Gen. (later Sir) William Johnson at Crown Point, September 8, 1755, and subsequently became one of Maj. Robert Rogers's Rangers. He served under Gen. James Abercrombie at Ticonderoga in 1758, becoming an aide to the commander during the retreat. In the same year he was captured by Indians and was about to be burned alive—he was tied to a tree and the pyre was already built—when a French officer prevailed upon the Indians to release him. He was promoted to major in 1758 and to lieutenant colonel the next year. In 1759 he was with Gen. Jeffrey Amherst in the expedition against Montreal. In 1762 he joined an expedition to capture Havana, but his ship was wrecked off the Cuban coast. He was one of a handful who survived the wreck and the subsequent struggle to return to the mainland. After serving with the Connecticut forces in Col. John Bradstreet's army that relieved Detroit during Pontiac's War in 1764, he settled down on his farm. In 1766 and 1767 he served in the Connecticut legislature. In 1773 he joined an expedition (which included his cousin Rufus Putnam) sent to inspect land grants in West Florida and on the Mississippi River. In April 1775, as lieutenant colonel (since October 1774) of the 11th Regiment of Connecticut militia, he was called into action by news of Lexington and Concord, and, so the story goes, hastened from his plow to the battlefield without even changing his clothes. Named a brigadier general of Connecticut forces soon after his arrival in Cambridge, Massachusetts, and major general of the Continental army on June 15, he was one of the heroes of the battle of Bunker Hill, June 17, 1775, where he seems to have been the ranking officer present but apparently did not exercise command over Col. William Prescott and Col. John Stark. He did, however, issue the famous order of the day: "Men, you are all marksmen—don't one of you fire until you see the white of their eyes." But he was less capable as a general officer than he had been as a ranger and scout and regimental commander, and his record during the Revolution was on the whole not one of success. In August 1776 he was placed over Gen. John Sullivan in command of New York City. Hardly had he arrived than the British attacked Long Island, August 27. After the evacuation of New York he commanded in Philadelphia. He was dilatory in responding to Gen. George Washington's orders in the campaign around Princeton in January 1777 and again disobeyed his commander while stationed in the Hudson Highlands in May of that year. The loss of forts Montgomery and Clinton to the British led to a court of inquiry in October 1777 which exonerated Putnam. During 1778–1779 he was engaged in recruiting duty in Connecticut and filled other noncombat roles. Putnam's military service was brought to an end by a paralytic stroke in December 1779. He nevertheless retained his reputation for military bravery. He died in Pomfret, Connecticut, on May 29, 1790.

Putnam, Rufus (1738–1824), Revolutionary army officer and pioneer. Born in Sutton, Massachusetts, on April 9, 1738, Putnam, a cousin of Israel Putnam, received scant formal education and at sixteen was apprenticed to a millwright. In 1757 he enlisted for service in the French and Indian War and remained in the army until 1760, seeing action around Lake Champlain. He took up farming near New Braintree, Massachusetts, in 1761 and moved to Brookfield four years later. In addition to farming he worked occasionally as a surveyor and as a millwright. In 1773 he was, along with his cousin Israel, a member of a committee sent to inspect lands in Florida and along the Mississippi River granted by the Crown to veterans of the French and Indian War. Shortly after the battles of Lexington and Concord in 1775 he entered the Continental army as a lieutenant colonel, and during the first winter of the Revolution he constructed defensive works in Roxbury and on Dorchester Heights. From March 1776 he was engaged in the construction of fortifications around New York City, and in August he was appointed by Congress chief engineer of the army with the rank of colonel. Unable to win provision for a separate corps of engineers, however, he resigned in December and was promptly commissioned colonel of the 5th Massachusetts Regiment, with which he served with distinction under Gen. Horatio Gates in the Saratoga campaign in 1777. During 1778 he built new fortifications at West Point. He served under Gen. Anthony Wayne in the capture of Stony Point, July 16, 1779, and in subsequent campaigns. In January 1783 he was promoted to brigadier general. He had in 1780 bought a farm near Rutland, Massachusetts, and there he settled after the war, serving several terms in the legislature and taking part, as an aide to Gen. Benjamin Lincoln, in putting down Shays's Rebellion in 1787. In 1785 he was appointed by Congress a surveyor of western lands, and out of that post grew his interest in the Ohio country. In March 1786, with Benjamin Tupper, Manasseh Cutler, and others, he formed in Boston the Ohio Company of Associates with the aim of obtaining a land grant in the Ohio country for settlement by Revolutionary veterans. Cutler took charge of negotiations with Congress and at length obtained the right for the company to purchase 1.5 million acres at a very low price. Putnam, appointed a director of the company and superintendent of its colonizing activities, set out in the spring of 1788 at the head of the first party of settlers. On April 7 he established at the mouth of the Muskingum River the first settlement in the Northwest Territory; in July the name was changed from Adelphia to Marietta, honoring Marie Antoinette of France. In March 1790 President George Washington appointed him a judge of the Northwest Territory, a post he held for six years, and in May 1792 he was commissioned a brigadier general in the regular army, in which capacity he concluded a treaty in September at Vincennes (now in Indiana) with eight Indian tribes of the region. He resigned his commission in February 1793. In October 1796 Washington named him surveyor general of the United States, but his work was less than satisfactory owing to his deficiency in mathematics, and in September 1803 he was dismissed by President Thomas Jefferson. In 1802 he was a member of the first Ohio constitutional convention. Putnam remained an influential figure in Ohio until his death in Marietta on May 4, 1824, at which time he was the last surviving general officer of the Revolution except for Lafayette.

Pyle, Ernest Taylor (1900–1945), journalist. Born on August 3, 1900, near Dana, Indiana, Ernie Pyle served briefly in the navy in World War I and then studied journalism at Indiana University. In 1923 he took a job with a local newspaper shortly before graduation. He served in many journalistic capacities in Washington and New York City, finally securing an assignment as aviation editor for the Scripps-Howard newspaper chain in 1928. From 1932 to 1935 he was managing editor of the Washington *Daily News,* but in 1935 he returned to the life of roving reporter. The daily experiences of his travels up and down the country, to South America, Alaska, Hawaii, and elsewhere, were recorded in a column that was enthusiastically received and eventually syndicated to nearly 200 newspapers. His columns attracted wide readership by their focus on and sympathy for the minor and often obscure figures behind the news. His sensitive reports of the bombing of London in 1940 attracted still wider attention. When the United States entered World War II Pyle accompanied troops to Great Britain and later in the campaigns in North Africa, Sicily, Italy, and France. He went into Normandy the day after D-Day. His columns became immensely popular, in large part because of his comradeship with and understanding of the ordinary soldier in war. In 1944 he won a Pulitzer Prize for the stories he sent back home. Collections of his pieces were published as *Ernie Pyle in England,* 1941; *Here is Your War,* 1943; and *Brave Men,* 1944. Early in 1945 he traveled to the Pacific theater and attached himself to the forces assaulting the islands of Iwo Jima and Okinawa. During that campaign he visited the 77th Infantry Division on a neighboring island, Ie Shima, and there on April 18, 1945, he was felled by enemy machine-gun fire. He became a national hero, his last articles being published posthumously in *Last Chapter,* 1946. A collection of his prewar columns appeared in 1947 as *Home Country.*

Q

Quanah (1845?–1911), Indian leader. Born probably in north Texas about 1845, Quanah was the son of Nokoni, a Comanche chief, and Cynthia Ann Parker, a white woman abducted from Parker's Fort on the Navasota River in Lime Stone County, Texas, in May 1836, at the age of ten. (She was recaptured in 1860 by the Texas Rangers and returned to white civilization.) In later life he adopted the name Quanah Parker. In his youth a bold fighter and leader, he was made chief of the fierce Kwahadi band of the Comanche in 1867. He refused to accept confinement to a reservation as provided in the Treaty of Medicine Lodge of that year and for the next eight years led an alliance of Comanche, Kiowa, Apache, and Southern Cheyenne warriors in a series of raids on frontier settlements that culminated on June 27, 1874, in an attack on Adobe Walls, a hunter's fort and trading post on the South Canadian River in the Texas Panhandle. The Indians, 700 strong, were repulsed by 28 defenders (one of them the famed scout Billy Dixon) but continued their resistance to white incursions until the next year, when all surrendered to the army authorities (Col. Ronald S. Mackenzie and Col. Nelson A. Miles), Quanah being the last chief to do so. Somehow escaping the "accidental death" that was the fate of so many Indian warriors in captivity, he instead immediately set about learning the ways of the victors, became fluent in Spanish and fairly fluent in English, studied the agricultural methods employed by the whites in the arid Southwest, and soon had gained a reputation as a "white man's Indian." He was not only persuaded of the benefits of civilization, but also was widely successful in persuading his fellow Indians, especially after he managed to lease to cattlemen the surplus tribal pasturelands on his reservation for some $100,000 a year, greatly increasing tribal income. He established numerous Indian schools in the belief that the only chance for survival of the Indians lay in education. A shrewd businessman, he was said to be the wealthiest Indian in the country and for the last 25 years of his life was the general manager of almost all business dealings of the Comanche, Kiowa, and Apache tribes. He traveled widely and rode in the inaugural procession of President Theodore Roosevelt in 1905, seated next to Geronimo. He died in his large house near Fort Sill, Oklahoma, on February 23, 1911.

Quantrill, William Clarke (1837–1865), guerrilla leader. Born in Canal Dover (now Dover), Ohio,

on July 31, 1837, Quantrill taught school briefly in Ohio, Indiana, and Illinois, but by the age of twenty he was determined to seek a more adventurous life. He went to Kansas in 1857 and filed a land claim, but farming did not suit his restless spirit and he joined an army provision train bound for Utah. At Fort Bridger and Salt Lake City during the next few years he was a professional gambler under the pseudonym of Charley Hart. He returned to Kansas in the fall of 1859, and although he taught school again that year he was by that time a thoroughly bad character, living near Lawrence after the end of the school term, again under the name of Hart, and getting into trouble often and severely enough to be charged with horse stealing, theft, and murder. Posing as an abolitionist, he wormed his way into the confidence of a group of whites who were plotting to free some slaves in Missouri; but he then betrayed them to the slaves' owner, and three of the plotters were shot. His sympathies were with the South when the Civil War began, and as early as 1861 he was already the chief of a band of guerrilla fighters, only irregularly attached to the Confederate army, that raided communities in Kansas and Missouri, robbed mail coaches, and summarily executed supposed Union partisans. In September 1861 he was with Gen. Sterling Price in the siege of Lexington, Missouri. He was declared an outlaw by Union authorities in 1862, and a price was put upon his head. After he had aided the Confederates in the capture of Independence, Missouri, on August 11, 1862, he, as captain, and his men were formally mustered into the Confederate service. His most notorious action occurred at Lawrence, Kansas, on August 21, 1863, when he rode into town at dawn at the head of some 450 men and sacked the place, killing some 180 men, women, and children and burning most of the buildings. The sack of Osceola, Missouri, by Gen. James H. Lane in September 1861 was given as reason for the Lawrence massacre, although personal animosity may well have played a part. On October 6 of the same year he defeated a Union detachment at Baxter Springs, Kansas, and afterwards executed all of his captives, including many noncombatants. In 1864 he lost control of his band, which broke up into several groups, and he went to Kentucky. On May 10, near Taylorsville, Kentucky, he was surprised by a Union force and captured after being severely wounded. He died in a Louisville, Kentucky, prison on June 6, 1865. His reputation as "the bloodiest man in American history" lived after him as did a number of desperadoes who first learned outlawry as members of his raiders—Jesse and Frank James, Cole Younger, and (story has it) Belle Shirley, later notorious as Belle Starr.

Quesada, Elwood Richard (1904–   ), air force officer and public official. Born on April 13, 1904, in Washington, D.C., Quesada studied at the University of Maryland and at Georgetown University before enlisting in the army in 1924. He was assigned to the Air Service and on completing flight training in September 1925 was commissioned a second lieutenant in the reserves. In January 1927 he was similarly commissioned in the Air Corps of the regular army. In April 1928, while stationed at Bolling Field, D.C., he flew Gen. James E. Fechet, chief of the Air Corps, to the site in Labrador of the crash of the German *Bremen*, the first aircraft to cross the Atlantic east to west. In January 1929 he was a relief pilot under Maj. Carl Spaatz and Capt. Ira C. Eaker in the record endurance flight of the *Question Mark*. Promoted to first lieutenant in November 1932, Quesada was flying aide to the assistant secretary of war for air in 1932–1933 and chief pilot of the New York–Cleveland airmail route in 1933–1934. He advanced to temporary captain in April 1935, graduated from Command and General Staff School, Fort Leavenworth, Kansas, in 1937, and after commanding the 1st Bombardment Squadron at Mitchel Field, New York, in 1937–1938 was sent to Argentina as technical adviser to that nation's air force. In 1939 he was an air observer in London, and in 1940 he was attached to the General Staff, becoming temporary major in December 1940. In July 1941 he took command of the 33rd Pursuit Group at Mitchel Field. He was promoted to temporary lieutenant colonel in January 1942, temporary colonel in March, and temporary brigadier general in December, becoming then commander of the 1st Air Defense Wing. Early in 1943 he went to North Africa to command the 12th Fighter Command and serve as deputy commander of the Northwest African Coastal Air Force. In October 1943 he was named commander of the 9th Fighter Command in England. Promoted to temporary major general in April 1944, he commanded from then the 9th Tactical Air Command, flying cover and support missions in preparation for the Allied invasion on D-Day and subsequently during the battle into Germany. In June 1945 he was named assistant chief of the air staff for intelligence, and in March 1946 he briefly commanded the Third Air Force at Tampa, Florida, before becoming chief of the Tactical Air Command. He was promoted to temporary lieutenant general in October 1947. In November 1948 he was named a special assistant to the chief of staff of the air force, and in August 1949 he was chosen to head Joint Task Force III, the combined army, air force, navy, and Atomic Energy Commission group

conducting the first hydrogen bomb experiments at Eniwetok atoll. In October 1951 Quesada retired from the air force. He was vice-president of Olin Industries in 1951–1953 and of Lockheed Aircraft in 1953–1955, and he had numerous other business interests. In 1957 he was appointed special assistant for aviation facilities planning by President Dwight D. Eisenhower and later named chairman of the Airways Modernization Board. In January 1959 he became first administrator of the newly established Federal Aviation Administration. He held that post until January 1961, when he returned to private life. His business interests included the presidency in 1961–1962 of the company owning the Washington Senators baseball team.

Quitman, John Anthony (1798–1858), public official and army officer. Born in Rhinebeck, New York, on September 1, 1798, Quitman received an excellent private education and in 1818 was appointed adjunct professor of English at Mount Airy College in Germantown, Pennsylvania. He soon moved to Ohio, studied law, and in 1821 was admitted to the bar, moving in that year to Natchez, Mississippi, to enter practice. He was elected to the legislature in 1827, served as chancellor of the state superior court from 1827 to 1835, and in 1832 was chairman of the judiciary committee of the state constitutional convention. He early identified himself with campaigns against gambling and duelling and in the early 1830s was well ahead of most Mississippians in supporting the states'-rights doctrine of nullification. In 1835 he was elected to the state senate, of which he was chosen president, and during December 1835–January 1836 he was acting governor. He was defeated in a congressional election in 1836. In that year he led a volunteer company of "Fencibles" to Texas, but saw no action in the revolution. On his return to Mississippi he was appointed brigadier general of militia. In July 1846 he was appointed brigadier general of U.S. volunteers, and he joined Gen. Zachary Taylor in Mexico in time to take part in the battle of Monterrey, September 20–24. He was in the assault on Veracruz under Gen. Winfield Scott in March and in the entire campaign to Mexico City, leading a division composed mainly of Pennsylvania volunteers and marines. He was brevetted major general for his action during the capture of Puebla on May 15, and he distinguished himself on numerous occasions. On September 13 his division stormed the castle of Chapultepec, braving an uphill charge against heavy fire, carrying the fortress and later in the day the Belen gate of Mexico City, and thus becoming the first troops to enter the city. He was appointed civil and military governor of the city by Scott; subsequently he was promoted to major general of volunteers. In November 1849 he was elected governor of Mississippi. He strongly opposed the Compromise of 1850 and raised the possibility of secession. He was deeply interested in the notion of annexing Cuba, and in 1850, although he had declined an offer from Gen. Narciso López of command of the Cuban filibuster-revolutionary forces, he was indicted by a federal grand jury for violating neutrality laws. He resigned as governor in February 1851, but the case against him was eventually dropped. He withdrew midway in the gubernatorial compaign of 1851, but in 1854 he was elected to Congress. Reelected in 1856, he died at his home near Natchez, Mississippi, on July 17, 1858.

R

Radford, Arthur William (1896–1973), naval officer. Born in Chicago on February 27, 1896, Radford graduated from the Naval Academy in 1916. During World War I, while serving on the *South Carolina* in the 6th Battle Squadron with the British Grand Fleet, he advanced to temporary lieutenant. During 1919–1920 he served with the Pacific Fleet, receiving promotions to permanent lieutenant (junior grade) in the former year and lieutenant in the latter. In 1920 he completed aviation training at the Pensacola, Florida, Naval Air Station. During 1921–1923 he was attached to the Bureau of Aeronautics, and from 1923 to 1927 he served with aviation units aboard the *Aroostook*, the *Colorado*, and the *Pennsylvania*, all of the Battle Fleet. He was at the San Diego Naval Air Station in 1927–1929 and briefly in command of an Alaskan aerial survey operation in 1929. During 1929–1931 he was aboard the carrier *Saratoga*, and in 1931–1932 he was aide and flag secretary to the commander of aircraft, Battle Fleet. Radford was again in the Bureau of Aeronautics in 1932–1935; then served briefly on the *Wright* and in 1936–1937 again on the *Saratoga;* commanded the naval air station in Seattle, Washington, in 1937–1940; was executive officer of the carrier *Yorktown* in 1940–1941; and commanded the naval air station in Trinidad for a few months in 1941. Promoted to captain, he was named director of aviation training in the Bureau of Aeronautics in December 1941, a post he held until April 1943; during that period he served in various other staff capacities as well and received promotion to rear admiral. From July 1943 to May 1944 he commanded the Northern Carrier Group, comprising the *Enterprise, Belleau Wood,* and *Monterey,* of Adm. Raymond A. Spruance's Fifth Fleet, taking a notable part in the campaigns in the Gilbert and Marshall islands. In May 1944 he was named assistant deputy chief of naval operations for air, and during June–July he was acting deputy. In November 1944 he returned to the Pacific in command of Carrier Division 6, a unit of Adm. Marc A. Mitscher's Task Force 58 (38), and took part in operations around Iwo Jima, Okinawa, and the Japanese home islands. After a brief period as air commander of the Pacific Fleet, Radford was promoted to vice admiral in January 1946 (dating from December 1945) and named deputy chief of naval operations for air. In February 1947 he was given command of the Second Task Fleet in the Atlantic. He was appointed vice chief of naval operations in January 1948, and in April 1949, pro-

moted to admiral, he became commander of the Pacific Fleet and high commissioner of the Trust Territory of the Pacific Islands. Radford was a leading figure in the so-called "admirals' revolt" against what they perceived as a reduced role for the navy, particularly as against the air force, resulting from the unification of the services in the National Military Establishment. In July 1953 he turned over the Pacific Fleet to Adm. Felix B. Stump, and in August he succeeded Gen. Omar N. Bradley as chairman of the Joint Chiefs of Staff. Reappointed to that post in 1955, he held it until his retirement in August 1957. He continued to serve thereafter as a consultant to the Defense Department while pursuing private business interests. Radford died in Bethesda, Maryland, on August 17, 1973.

Radford, William (1809–1890), naval officer. Born in Fincastle, Virginia, on September 9, 1809, Radford grew up there, in Maysville, Kentucky, and in St. Louis, where in 1821 his widowed mother married Gov. William Clark. Through Clark's influence he was appointed a midshipman in the navy in March 1825, and he made his first cruise on the *Brandywine* bearing the Marquis de Lafayette home to France. He subsequently made cruises in the Mediterranean and the Pacific on various vessels, receiving promotion to lieutenant in February 1837. At the outbreak of the Mexican War he was in the Pacific aboard the sloop of war *Warren*. On September 7, 1846, he led a volunteer boat party into the harbor at Mazatlán and, under shore guns, cut out the Mexican brig *Malek Adhel*. He took part in other naval actions on the Mexican and California coasts and in the summer of 1847 made an eventful return home overland with his brother-in-law, Gen. Stephen W. Kearny. He was mainly on shore duty for the next decade, advancing to commander in September 1855 and serving as lighthouse inspector in New York in 1858–1859. In June 1860 he commanded the steam sloop *Dacotah* on a cruise to join the East India Squadron. At the outbreak of the Civil War he was ordered home and, because of his southern birth, assigned to minor duty until his loyalty had been established. In February 1862 he was given command of the sloop *Cumberland* at Hampton Roads, Virginia. He was ashore on court-martial duty when the *Cumberland*, temporarily under Lt. George U. Morris, was attacked and sunk by the *Virginia* on March 8. In May he was ordered to the New York navy yard, where he remained for two years, receiving promotions to captain in July 1862 and to commodore in April 1863. In May 1864 he was given command of the *New Ironsides*. In the two attacks on Fort Fisher at Wilmington, North Carolina, on December 24–25, 1864, and January 13–15, 1865, he commanded the ironclad division of Adm. David D. Porter's squadron and won high commendation, particularly in the second attack, for the accuracy and effectiveness of the naval gunfire directed by him in support of the infantry assaulting the works. Radford then commanded the James River Flotilla until the end of the war. During April–October 1865 he commanded the Atlantic Squadron, and he then took command of the Washington navy yard, becoming rear admiral in July 1866. In February 1869 he was named commander of the European Squadron. After his retirement in March 1870 he was on special duty with the Navy Department for two years. Radford died in Washington, D.C., on January 8, 1890.

Rains, Gabriel James (1803–1881), Confederate army officer. Born in Craven County, North Carolina, on June 4, 1803, Rains graduated from West Point in 1827 and was commissioned in the infantry. Over the next 20 years he saw action against Indians in the West and in Florida, receiving promotion to captain in December 1837 and being brevetted major in April 1840 for gallantry in a skirmish with Seminole Indians near Fort King, Florida. Early in 1846 he was ordered to Texas, where on May 3 he took part in the defense of Fort Texas (later Fort Brown) against attacking Mexican forces. He joined Gen. Zachary Taylor in the field in time to take part also in the battle of Resaca de la Palma, May 9. He was then ordered to recruiting duty. He later returned to the frontier, receiving promotion to major in March 1851. In 1853 he was ordered to Washington Territory, where during 1855–1858 he took part in suppressing the uprising of the Yakima Indians and their allies, receiving in 1855 the rank of brigadier general of the territorial volunteer militia. Promoted to lieutenant colonel in June 1860, he resigned his commission in July 1861 and immediately entered Confederate service and was appointed brigadier general in September. While commanding the garrison at Yorktown, Virginia, he devised a primitive land mine with a percussion detonator that he used during the retreat from Yorktown in May 1862 and at the battle of Williamsburg, May 5. The devices raised a considerable controversy in both the North and the South; such Confederate commanders as Gen. James Longstreet and Gen. Joseph E. Johnston opposed the use of mines, although Johnston was later won over. After taking a distinguished part in the battle of Fair Oaks (Seven Pines), May 31, Rains was removed from field service. He headed the Bureau of Conscription in Richmond, Virginia, while policy regarding his devices was worked out, and finally in June 1864 a Torpedo Bureau was organized under him. He developed a system of underwater mines (known as torpedoes) for the protection of vital points and deployed them at Richmond, Charleston, Mobile (where Adm. David G. Farragut damned them), and Savannah and in the James River. On August 9, 1864, two demolitionists of his bureau successfully blew up two supply barges and an ammunition warehouse at City Point, Virginia, in a spectacular demonstration of the military value of his work. After the war Rains lived in Atlanta, Georgia, and from 1877 in Charleston, South Carolina. He died in Aiken, South Carolina, on August 6, 1881. His brother, George Washington Rains (1817–1898), a former U.S. army engineer, built and operated the Confederate powder mill and armory works at Augusta, Georgia, throughout the Civil War and attained the rank of brigadier general.

Ramseur, Stephen Dodson (1837–1864), Confederate army officer. Born on May 31, 1837, in Lincolnton, North Carolina, Ramseur graduated from West Point in 1860 and was commissioned in the artillery. In April 1861 he resigned and accepted a commission as first lieutenant of artillery in the Confederate army. He advanced quickly to captain and early in 1862 was attached to the command of Gen. John B. Magruder on the Yorktown Peninsula. During the slow retreat from Gen. George B. McClellan's army he was given command of all the artillery on the right wing and the rank of major. In April he was chosen colonel of the 49th North Carolina Infantry, which he commanded with distinction through the Seven Days' Battles in June–July; he was severely wounded at Malvern Hill, July 1. In November he was promoted to brigadier general and given a brigade in Gen. Daniel H. Hill's division. He took part in the battles of Chancellorsville, where he was again wounded, Gettysburg, and the Wilderness. At Spotsylvania, May 8–12, 1864, he again distinguished himself in leading a charge against federal forces at the "Bloody Angle" on May 12. In June he was promoted to major general. After commanding a division at Cold Harbor, June 1–3, he joined Gen. Jubal A. Early in the Shenandoah valley. He fought gallantly at Winchester, September 19, but at Cedar Creek, October 19, while rallying his men against a Union counterattack, he fell mortally wounded. He died the next day, October 20, 1864, at the headquarters of his opponent, Gen. Philip H. Sheridan, in Winchester, Virginia.

Ransom, Thomas Edward Greenfield (1834–1864), army officer. Born on November 29, 1834, in Norwich, Vermont, Ransom was the son of a distinguished army officer who was later president of Norwich University. The son graduated from Norwich

University with an engineering degree in 1851 and moved to Illinois, where he practised civil engineering and developed business interests. In April 1861 he raised a volunteer company that became part of the 11th Illinois Infantry, and in July he was commissioned lieutenant colonel of the regiment. He took part in an attack on Confederate forces at Charleston, Missouri, on August 19, 1861, and was wounded; and he commanded his regiment in the operations under Gen. Ulysses S. Grant against Fort Henry and Fort Donelson in February 1862, receiving a serious wound during the latter. Promoted to colonel, he again distinguished himself and was again wounded at Shiloh (Pittsburg Landing), April 6–7, and in June was attached to the staff of Gen. John A. McClernand. Subsequently he was inspector general of the Army of the Tennessee, and in January 1863 he was promoted to brigadier general of volunteers. He impressed Grant during the Vicksburg campaign, following which he commanded a successful expedition to occupy Natchez. In October 1863 he was ordered to the Gulf coast of Texas, where he operated successfully against Confederate forces, and in March 1864 he was given command of the XIII Corps, succeeding the ailing McClernand. He was in command of the advance forces of the Red River campaign under Gen. Nathaniel P. Banks and on April 8 suffered a sharp repulse by Gen. Richard Taylor at Sabine Crossroads, being wounded badly once again. In August he took command of a division of Gen. Grenville M. Dodge's XVI Corps, and he succeeded to command of the corps later in the month when Dodge was wounded in the siege of Atlanta. On the fall of Atlanta on September 1 Ransom was brevetted major general of volunteers for his part in the campaign. He then took command of the XVII Corps, but while pursuing Gen. John B. Hood's army through Georgia he fell ill; he died near Rome, Georgia, on October 29, 1864.

Read, Albert Cushing (1887–1967), naval officer and airman. Born on March 29, 1887, in Lyme, New Hampshire, Read graduated from the Naval Academy in 1906. He was commissioned ensign in September 1908, following a world cruise on the *Decatur*, and he subsequently served on various other vessels, receiving promotions to lieutenant (junior grade) in September 1911 and to lieutenant in July 1913. During 1913–1915 he was at the Naval Torpedo Station, Newport, Rhode Island, and he then entered flight training at Pensacola Naval Air Station, Florida, receiving pilot certification in March 1916. After another year of sea duty and promotion to lieutenant commander in August 1917 he commanded naval air stations at Bay Shore, New York, and Miami, Florida, during World War I, flying numerous submarine-search missions over coastal waters. In March 1919 he was assigned to command one of four NC (Navy-Curtiss) seaplanes in an attempted transatlantic flight. One of the planes being eliminated in trials, the three remaining took off from Rockaway, Long Island, on May 8. The NC-1 was piloted by Lt. Patrick N. L. Bellinger and Lt. Marc A. Mitscher; the NC-3 carried Commander John H. Towers, overall commander of the flight; and Read piloted the NC-4. After stops in Halifax, Nova Scotia, and Trepassey, Newfoundland, they departed the latter place on May 16, flying a course marked by navy destroyers. The NC-1 and NC-3 both went down at sea near the Azores, but Read and the NC-4 reached Horta on the island of Faial safely on May 17. Ten days later he flew on to Lisbon, completing the first transatlantic flight in a total of 53 hours 58 minutes flying time. On May 31 he landed at Plymouth, England, the final goal of the flight. On his return home Read was promoted to commander in September 1919. During 1920–1922 he commanded the seaplane tender *Harding* and then served on the *Shawmut*. He graduated from the Naval War College in 1923, taught there a year, and in 1924–1925 commanded the *Ajax* and Aircraft Squadron 20, Asiatic Fleet. From 1926 to 1929 he commanded the naval air station at Hampton Roads, Virginia, and during 1929–1931 he was aboard the carrier *Saratoga*. Over the next several years he served two tours, 1931–1934 and 1936–1938, in the Bureau of Aeronautics and commanded the *Wright*, 1934–1936, and the *Saratoga*, 1938–1940. In the latter year he became commander of the Pensacola Naval Air Station, advancing to rear admiral in 1941, and from 1942 to 1944 he was chief of air technical training in Chicago. In January 1944 he was named commander of Fleet Air, Atlantic Fleet, at Norfolk, Virginia, and from December 1945 until his retirement in May 1946 he was attached to the air staff of the chief of naval operations. Read died in Miami, Florida, on October 10, 1967.

Read, Charles William (1840–1890), Confederate naval officer. Born in Yazoo County, Mississippi, on May 12, 1840, Read graduated from the Naval Academy in 1860. After brief service on the steamers *Pawnee* and *Powhatan* he resigned in March 1861 and entered the Confederate service as acting midshipman. Assigned to the steamer *McRae*, he took part in an expedition against Ship Island near the mouth of the Mississippi in July 1861 and in the successful attack of Commodore George N. Hollins's "Mosquito Fleet" on the federal squadron in the Mississippi passes on October 12. Made acting lieutenant in February 1862, he took part in the unsuccessful defense of Island No. 10 and New Madrid against Union army-navy forces under Gen. John Pope and Flag-Officer Andrew H. Foote in March–April 1862 and then joined the Confederate squadron defending New Orleans. During the battle with Commodore David G. Farragut's attacking squadron on April 24

Read succeeded to command of the *McRae* and performed gallantly in a losing contest. Later he served on the *Arkansas,* harassing Farragut's squadron and Col. Charles Ellet's gunboats around Vicksburg. Promoted to second lieutenant in October, he sailed under Capt. John N. Maffitt on the raider *Florida* from November until May 1863, when Maffitt put him in command of a converted prize, the brig *Clarence.* In a month's cruise Read took the amazing total of 22 prizes, transferring his crew in turn to the *Tacony* (his fifth prize) and late in June to the *Archer* (his twentieth). On June 27 he sailed boldly into the harbor of Portland, Maine, and captured the revenue cutter *Caleb Cushing.* The wind failed as he was making off, however, and the next day, having blown up the *Caleb Cushing,* he was forced to surrender the *Archer* to a hastily assembled flotilla from Portland and Fort Preble. He was promoted to first lieutenant in January 1864, while still in prison. Exchanged in October 1864, he took command in January 1865 of the torpedo boat division of the James River Flotilla under Adm. Raphael Semmes. In March he traveled to Shreveport, Louisiana, to take command of the ram *William H. Webb,* with which he attempted to run the blockade. He was blockaded by the *Richmond* and, after beaching the *Webb* and attempting to escape into the swamps, was captured and held until July. After the war he was a merchant captain, a Mississippi River pilot, and a harbor master at New Orleans. Read died in Meridian, Mississippi, on January 25, 1890.

Read, George Campbell (1787–1862), naval officer. Born in Ireland in 1787, Read came to America at a time unknown and settled in Pennsylvania. He entered the navy as a midshipman in April 1804 and advanced to lieutenant in April 1810. At the outbreak of the War of 1812 he was serving under Capt. Isaac Hull on the *Constitution,* and at the conclusion of the famous victory of August 19, 1812, over the *Guerrière* he boarded the British ship to receive her surrender from Capt. Dacres. Subsequently he was on the *United States,* Commodore Stephen Decatur, and had a share in the capture of the *Macedonian* on October 25. In the Algerine War of 1815 he commanded the brig *Chippewa* in Commodore William Bainbridge's squadron. He was promoted to commander in April 1816. During 1818–1821 he commanded the sloop *Hornet* off the coast of Africa, where he captured a slave ship, and in the West Indies. Promoted to captain in March 1825, Read commanded the *Constitution* in 1826 and the *Constellation* in 1832–1834. In May 1838 he sailed eastward from Hampton Roads, Virginia, on a world cruise in command of the frigate *Columbia* and the sloop *John Adams.* At Bombay he learned of the plundering of the American merchant vessel *Eclipse* by natives at Meuke, Sumatra. He proceeded there immediately; on December 25 he bombarded the town of Quallah Battoo (Kualabatee), where Capt. John Downes had demonstrated almost three years earlier, and on January 1, 1839 he landed a party that razed Meuke. He then sailed to Canton, China, and helped soothe the anxieties of foreigners over the actions of Chinese officials against the opium trade. He arrived in Boston in June 1840, having performed useful diplomatic services in the Sandwich (Hawaiian) Islands and in Tahiti. Read commanded the Philadelphia navy yard until 1846, in 1845 contributing to the organization of the Naval Academy, and in 1846–1849 he was commodore of the Africa Squadron, thereafter returning to the Philadelphia navy yard until 1853. He was placed on the reserve list in September 1855 and in May 1861 was appointed governor of the Naval Asylum in Philadelphia. He was promoted to rear admiral on the retired list in July 1862, and he died in Philadelphia on August 22, 1862.

Read, George Windle (1860–1934), army officer. Born on November 19, 1860, in Indianola, Iowa, Read graduated from West Point in 1883 and was commissioned in the infantry, transferring to the cavalry three months later. After six years of frontier duty with the 5th Cavalry he taught military science and tactics at the University of Iowa from 1889 to 1893, receiving promotion to first lieutenant in March 1891. From 1893 to 1897 he was in Texas. He went to Cuba with his regiment in 1898 and worked with the evacuation commission into 1899, advancing to captain in March of that year. During 1901–1902 he saw action in the Philippine Insurrection, and during a four-year assignment, 1905–1909, with the General Staff he was detached to serve with the provisional government in Cuba in 1906–1908, acting as governor of Pinar del Rio Province in the latter year. Promoted to major in April 1910, he was inspector general of the Department of Mindanao in the Philippines until 1912 and then spent two years on border duty in Arizona. On graduating from the Army War College in 1914 he was promoted to lieutenant colonel and in September assigned to the adjutant general's department. He advanced to colonel in July 1916. In August 1917 he was promoted to temporary brigadier general; in November he was promoted to temporary major general, and the next month he took command of a special cavalry division at El Paso, Texas. In April 1918 he was ordered to France in command of the 30th Infantry Division, and in June he moved up to command of the II Corps, with which he remained until its inactivation in February 1919. The II Corps, comprising the 27th and 30th Divisions, was attached to the British army and saw its main action in the Somme offensive in August–October 1918, in which the German Hindenburg line was penetrated. Read commanded the embarkation center at Le Mans, France, from February to April 1919 and then commanded Camp Jackson, South Carolina. In September 1920 he took command of the V Corps area at Fort Hayes, Ohio, and in March 1921 he was made permanent major general. From September 1922 until his retirement in November 1924 he commanded the Department of the Philippines. Read died in Washington, D.C., on November 6, 1934.

Red Cloud (1822–1909), Indian leader. Born in 1822 on Blue Creek in what is now north-central Nebraska, Mahpiua Luta, or Red Cloud, grew to be an outstanding warrior and chief of the important Bad Face band of the Oglala Sioux, and by 1860 he had become a principal chief of the entire Oglala nation. In July 1865 an army column under Gen. Patrick E. Connor was sent into the Powder River country of Wyoming to suppress Indian hostilities and begin the building of an army road to the newly opened mining region of western Montana. The Sioux, under Red Cloud, joined by Cheyenne lately outraged by the Chivington Massacre, resisted stoutly and even held a construction party prisoner for two weeks. The proposed Powder River Road, following the older Bozeman Trail, cut through the heart of the Bighorn country, the finest Indian hunting territory of the northern plains and a vital resource. Red Cloud, spokesman for the Sioux and Cheyenne, refused even to meet with a government commission in the autumn of 1865. In June 1866 a second commission was sent out; Red Cloud met with the commissioners, refused to grant permission for the road, and stalked out when it was learned that construction parties and supply trains were already entering the disputed territory under command of Col. Henry B. Carrington. "Red Cloud's War" ensued, a period of unremitting and often savage resistance. For two years his warriors fought and harassed the army at every turn and kept Fort Reno, Fort Phil Kearny, and Fort C. F. Smith, the defensive posts on the Powder River Road, under virtual siege. The road was rendered useless. Of the scores of skirmishes and fights, the principal ones were the massacre of 80 soldiers led by Capt. William J. Fetterman outside Fort Phil Kearny on December 21, 1866, and the inconclusive Hayfield Fight, near Fort C. F. Smith, on August 1, 1867, and Wagon Box Fight near Fort Kearny the next day. In April 1868 a new commission arrived at Fort Laramie and negotiated a treaty in which the Powder River Road was abandoned and the territory north of the North Platte was recognized as unceded Indian land closed to white settlement or passage. Red Cloud declined to sign until November, after troops had actually been withdrawn and the three forts burned. He then agreed to settle at the Red Cloud Agency in Nebraska, having become the only Indian leader to win, in a limited sense, a war with the United States. He was thereafter an advocate of peace with the white man and took no part in the Sioux–Cheyenne wars of the 1870s, in which such younger warriors as Sitting Bull, Crazy Horse, and Gall came to the fore. In 1878 he and his people moved to the Pine Ridge Agency in South Dakota. He traveled several times to Washington, D.C., and other eastern cities to present the Indian case, but over the years suffered a decline in prestige among his own people. In 1881 he was deposed as chief, largely through the machinations of a jealous Indian agent, one McGillycuddy. He again attempted to restrain the Sioux outburst of 1889–1891, the Ghost Dance uprising that culminated in the Wounded Knee Massacre. In his late years Red Cloud's health failed and he became blind; he was also baptized in the Roman Catholic Church. He died at Pine Ridge, South Dakota, on December 10, 1909.

Red Eagle (1780?–1824), Indian leader. Born about 1780 among the Upper Creek Indians in what is now Alabama, Red Eagle was of more European than Indian ancestry. There are various accounts of his parentage, and he may well have been a nephew of Alexander McGillivray. He was in any case known to whites as William Weatherford. He was stirred by a visit of Tecumseh in 1811 but resisted making war on whites until 1813. On August 30, 1813, he led the Upper Creeks—"Red Sticks"—in a sudden attack on Fort Mims at the confluence of the Alabama and Tombigbee rivers, an attack in which, perhaps over Red Eagle's protest, some 500 settlers in the fort were massacred. He and his followers then took up a strong position at Econochaca, on the Alabama River in present-day Lowndes County, from which raids were launched against the surrounding countryside. On December 23, 1813, a force of about 1000 mounted Mississippi volunteers under Gen. Ferdinand L. Claiborne attacked and burned the town. Most of the Creeks escaped, and after regrouping they launched a successful surprise attack on a large body of Georgia militia at Calabee Creek on January 27, 1814. The Creek War ended when they were finally defeated by Gen. Andrew Jackson at the Horseshoe Bend of the Tallapoosa River (a battle also known as Tohopeka) on March 27, 1814. Red Eagle was absent from that battle but surrendered himself to Jackson at Fort Toulouse, near the site of present-day Montgomery, shortly thereafter. He settled on a farm near Little River, Baldwin County, Alabama, where he died on March 9, 1824.

Reeves, Joseph Mason (1872–1948), naval officer. Born on November 20, 1872, in Tampico, Illinois, Reeves graduated from the Naval Academy in 1894 and was assigned to the engineering corps. In 1898, then a lieutenant (junior grade), he distinguished himself in the engineering performance of the *Oregon* during its famous run from San Francisco to Key

West under Capt. Charles E. Clark. The next year Reeves transferred from the engineers to the line of the navy. From 1904 to 1906 he was fleet gunnery officer, Asiatic Fleet, and after two years at the Naval Academy he held the same post with the Atlantic Fleet in 1909–1910. In 1913 he received his first command, the experimental electric-drive collier *Jupiter*. Promoted to captain, he commanded the battleships *Maine* and *Kansas* in the Atlantic during World War I and from 1919 to 1921 was naval attaché in Rome. After two years in command of the *North Dakota* he spent two years as instructor and student at the Naval War College, graduating in 1925. In October of that year, having completed aviation observer training at the age of fifty-two, he took command of Aircraft Squadrons, Battle Fleet. Working with the *Langley*, the navy's first flight-deck carrier (converted from the *Jupiter*), and from 1928 with the great carriers *Lexington* and *Saratoga*, he molded the navy's air wing into a trained tactical strike force. Promoted to rear admiral in June 1927, Reeves served that year as an adviser to the U.S. delegation at the Geneva Disarmament Conference. Except for a period on the General Board in 1929 he remained chief of the air arm until 1931. In 1932 he briefly commanded the Mare Island navy yard, California, and in 1933 he was named commander of the Battle Fleet with the rank of admiral. From June 1934 until his retirement (at his permanent rank of rear admiral) in December 1936 he was commander in chief of the U.S. Fleet, the first aviation officer to hold that post. In May 1940 he was recalled to active duty to serve on the Lend-Lease and munitions boards; he served until 1946, receiving permanent rank of admiral in June 1942. Following the Pearl Harbor attack he was a member of the commission under Justice Owen J. Roberts assigned to investigate the disaster; he was harshly critical of Adm. Husband E. Kimmel. Reeves died in Bethesda, Maryland, on March 25, 1948.

Reid, Samuel Chester (1783–1861), seaman. Born in Norwich, Connecticut, on August 25, 1783, Reid went to sea at eleven and during the undeclared naval war with France in the late 1790s was captured by a French privateer and imprisoned for six months on Guadaloupe. After his release he entered the navy and served on the *Baltimore* in Commodore Thomas Truxtun's squadron in the West Indies. He later returned to the merchant service for a time, and by the age of twenty he was master of a ship. In 1814 he was at sea in command of the privateer *General Armstrong,* and on September 26 he put in at Faial in the Azores. Immediately after him a British flotilla arrived, comprising the *Plantagenet,* 74 guns, the *Rota,* 38, and the *Carnation,* 18, with a total complement of about 2000 men. Reid, with 90 men and 9 guns, prepared to be attacked. In the evening four armed boat parties approached the *General Armstrong* and ig-

nored Reid's warnings to keep off. He then opened fire to great effect. At midnight a second, heavier attack was made, and the fighting was hand-to-hand on the deck of the *General Armstrong,* but the British were at length driven off with considerable losses. At dawn the next morning the *Carnation* let go a broadside, but the guns of the *General Armstrong,* particularly the 42-pounder "Long Tom," kept the British off while inflicting much damage. Then, expecting a general attack, Reid abandoned ship, scuttling and burning her, and took refuge ashore. Portuguese authorities finally forced the British to cease hostilities in their neutral port. Reid's losses were 2 killed and 7 wounded to the British 300 casualties. More important, the delay necessitated by repairs following the fight kept the British flotilla from reinforcing the fleet in the West Indies on schedule and thus allowed Gen. Andrew Jackson time to fortify New Orleans before the expected attack there. (The neutrality violation produced a set of claims and counterclaims involving three nations and both Reid and his son that at one point caused a breach of diplomatic relations between the United States and Portugal and that was not ultimately settled until 1897.) Reid was greeted as a hero on his return home. He received appointment as harbor master and warden of the port of New York, and in 1843 he received the equivalent of a naval pension with appointment as sailing master. In 1818 he proposed a new design for the American flag in which 13 stripes representing the original colonies would remain constant, while a new star would be added for each new state admitted. Congress adopted the plan in April 1818, and on April 12 a flag made by Mrs. Reid was raised on the Capitol. Reid later devised a method of rapid signaling over land and established a lightship off Sandy Hook, New Jersey. He died in New York City on January 28, 1861.

Remey, George Collier (1841–1928), naval officer. Born on August 10, 1841, in Burlington, Iowa, Remey graduated from the Naval Academy in 1859 and made his first cruise on the *Hartford* in the Asian Squadron. On his return late in 1861 with the rank of lieutenant he was assigned to the gunboat *Marblehead,* which was on blockade duty and helped support Gen. George B. McClellan's operations on the Peninsula in the spring of 1862. In April 1863 he transferred to the steam sloop *Canandaigua* in the South Atlantic Blockading Squadron. In August–September 1863 he took part in Adm. John A. B. Dahlgren's operations against Charleston, South Carolina. He briefly commanded the *Marblehead* in an attack on Fort Wagner, then commanded a naval battery on Morris Island, and on September 7 commanded a boat division in an unsuccessful attack on Fort Sumter in which he was captured. He was imprisoned for more than a year, and he saw no further action in the war. He was promoted to lieutenant commander in June 1865, and for two years he served on the *Mohongo* in the Pacific. From 1867 to 1869 he was an instructor at the Naval Academy, and during 1869–1870 he was on the *Sabine*. He took part in the survey of a canal route in the Tehuantepec Isthmus of Mexico in 1870–1871 and after a year at the Naval Observatory was promoted to commander in November 1872. Later assignments included duty with the Bureau of Yards and Docks in 1874–1877 and 1879–1881, command of the *Enterprise,* 1877–1878, and duty at navy yards in Washington, D.C., 1884–1886, and Norfolk, Virginia, 1886–1889. Promoted to captain in October 1885, he commanded the *Charleston,* flagship of the Pacific Squadron, in 1889–1892. He was at the Portsmouth, New Hampshire, navy yard in 1892–1895 and commanded it from 1896 to 1900 (advancing to commodore in June 1897), except for the period of the Spanish–American War in 1898, when he commanded the vital naval base at Key West, Florida. In that post he was responsible for the supply and maintenance of all the vessels engaged in the Cuban campaign and in the convoy of troops. Promoted to rear admiral in November 1898, Remey was named commander of the Asiatic Squadron in April 1900, and he directed naval operations during the final stages of the Philippine Insurrection. During July–October 1900 he patrolled the China coast off Taku during the Peking Relief Expedition. In 1902 he became chairman of the Lighthouse Board, and he retired in August 1903. Remey died in Washington, D.C., on February 10, 1928.

Reno, Jesse Lee (1823–1862), army officer. Born in Wheeling, Virginia (now West Virginia), on June 20, 1823, Reno graduated from West Point in 1846 and was commissioned in the Ordnance Corps. In the Mexican War he was brevetted first lieutenant for gallantry at Cerro Gordo, April 18, 1847, and captain for Chapultepec, September 13. For several months in 1849 he was an instructor at West Point. He was on ordnance duty in 1849–1852 and engaged in survey work in Minnesota in 1853–1854. He was chief ordnance officer in the Mormon expedition of 1857–1858 under Col. Albert S. Johnston and then commanded the federal arsenal in Mount Vernon, Alabama, until its seizure by Confederates in January 1861. He was promoted to captain in July 1860. After a period at Fort Leavenworth, Kansas, he was appointed brigadier general of volunteers in November 1861. He commanded a brigade in Gen. Ambrose E. Burnside's expedition against Confederate strongholds on the North Carolina coast in January–February 1862 and in April was given command of a division in the Department of North Carolina. In July he was promoted to major general of volunteers, and in August he took command of the IX Corps. He took part in the second battle of Bull Run (Manassas),

August 29–30, and the battle at Chantilly, September 1. A few days later he occupied Frederick, Maryland, where he heard a story about one Barbara Frietschie (or Frietchie, as it was to become under the pen of John Greenleaf Whittier), who had kept a Union flag waving while Gen. Thomas J. Jackson's Confederate troops marched through the town. He sought out and talked with Mrs. Frietschie, who refused to sell him the flag in question but gave him another, handmade by herself. The next day, September 14, 1862, he was killed leading a charge at South Mountain, Maryland; the Frietschie flag draped his coffin.

Reno, Marcus Albert (1834–1889), army officer. Born in December 1834 in Carrollton, Illinois, Reno graduated from West Point in 1857 and was commissioned in the 1st Dragoons. After serving on the western frontier he was promoted to first lieutenant in April 1861 and to captain in November. He took part in the battles of the Peninsula campaign and the Maryland campaign in 1862 and was brevetted major for his actions at Kelly's Ford, Virginia, March 17, 1863, and lieutenant colonel for Cedar Creek, October 19, 1864. During January–July 1865, as colonel of volunteers, he commanded the 12th Pennsylvania Cavalry, and in March he was brevetted brigadier general of volunteers and colonel of regulars for his war services. After the war he was an instructor at West Point for a time and was then attached to the Freedmen's Bureau in New Orleans. In December 1868 he was appointed major of the 7th Cavalry, commanded by Lt. Col. George A. Custer. In 1876 he took part with the 7th in the campaign against the Sioux mounted by Gen. Alfred H. Terry. When Custer decided to attack the Sioux-Cheyenne camp on the Little Bighorn River on June 25, he divided the regiment into three columns, sending one to scout the left under Capt. Frederick W. Benteen, one ahead under Reno, and taking the remainder himself downstream to the right. Reno led his three companies across a ford above the Indian camp, his orders being to attack the southern flank. Benteen disappeared from the scene for a time, and Reno, after meeting stout resistance, fell back, recrossed the river, and dug in before a line of bluffs. Their failures left Custer's column to the full fury of the Indians. Benteen later rejoined Reno and their combined forces—more than half the regiment—held out until relief arrived on June 27. Reno was accused of cowardice, but a court of inquiry held in Chicago in 1879 cleared him. Many later commentators held him and Benteen culpable for having remained in defensive positions for more than an hour while Custer was under attack. Reno was court-martialed on various minor charges brought by his commander, Col. Samuel D. Sturgis (whose son had died at Little Bighorn), and dishonorably discharged in April 1880. He died in Washington, D.C., on April 1, 1889. In 1967 a board of review altered his discharge to honorable; he was subsequently reburied at the Little Bighorn cemetery.

Revere, Joseph Warren (1812–1880), naval and army officer. Born in Boston on May 17, 1812, Revere was a grandson of Paul Revere. He entered the navy as a midshipman in April 1828, and his assignments included three years in the Pacific on the frigate *Guerrière* and cruises in the West Indies, on the African coast, in the Mediterranean, and to China. He was promoted to lieutenant in February 1841. At the outbreak of the Mexican War he was serving on the *Portsmouth* on the California coast, and on July 9, 1846, he led a party ashore and raised the flag over Sonoma. He took part in the subsequent conquest of California and in naval operations on the west coast of Mexico. After a period in California as a timber agent for the navy he resigned in September 1850 and developed a ranch near Sonoma. For a few months in 1851–1852 he served as colonel in the Mexican army, organizing the artillery branch. Later he lived in Morristown, New Jersey, and traveled widely. Soon after the start of the Civil War, unable to reenter the navy, he was appointed in August 1861 colonel of the 7th New Jersey Volunteers. He saw action in the Peninsula campaign in March–July 1862 and in the Maryland campaign in September, and in October 1862 he was promoted to brigadier general of volunteers. At Fredericksburg, December 13, he commanded a brigade of Gen. Daniel E. Sickles's division of Gen. George Stoneman's III Corps. At Chancellorsville on May 3, 1864, he succeeded to command of the division and without orders led it to the rear when ammunition ran low. For that he was relieved of command by Sickles, then III Corps commander, and he was promptly court-martialed and dismissed. In September 1864 President Abraham Lincoln revoked the sentence, and Revere was allowed to resign. His later years were spent largely in travel. Revere published *A Tour of Duty in California*, 1849, and *Keel and Saddle: A Retrospect of Forty Years of Military and Naval Service*, 1872. He died in Hoboken, New Jersey, on April 20, 1880.

Revere, Paul (1735–1818), silversmith and Revolutionary patriot. Born on January 1, 1735, in Boston, the son of a silversmith, Revere attended local schools and pursued his father's trade. In 1756 he took part in an expedition against Crown Point as a lieutenant of artillery. Afterward he returned to Boston and began his own silversmithing business. By 1765 his silver shop was also a purveyor of copper engravings of portraits, music sheets, surgical instruments, carved picture frames (many for John Singleton Copley's portraits), and dental plates. His inaccurate but effective engraving depicting the Boston Massacre in 1770 was a valuable piece of propaganda for Samuel Adams, John Hancock, and others of Revere's political friends. Later he was to engrave the first Continental money, the official seal of the united colonies, and the seal still used by Massachusetts. Active in local patriotic activities, especially in recruiting volunteer political workers, he was appointed one of three advisers in the crisis caused by the Tea Act of 1773 and was a leader of the Sons of Liberty in holding the Boston Tea Party. He was the principal express rider for the Boston committee of safety, and, when formally appointed a messenger to Congress for the Massachusetts provincial assembly in 1774, he was already a celebrated figure in the colonies. In December 1773 he carried news of the Boston Tea Party to New York City and in September 1774 the "Suffolk Resolves" to Philadelphia. In December 1774 he rode to Portsmouth, New Hampshire, to warn patriot leaders that Gen. Thomas Gage planned to capture stores at Fort William and Mary. On April 18, 1775, having arranged to receive the famed lantern signal from the steeple of the North Church, he rowed across the Charles River with muffled oars, mounted a horse in Charlestown, and rode to Lexington to warn Adams and Hancock that British forces were on the way to arrest them. He then set out for Concord in company with William Dawes and Dr. Samuel Prescott. They were detained by a British patrol, and only Prescott reached Concord to rouse the minutemen. Revere made his way afoot back to Lexington, but it is he who is remembered for his ride that night, later immortalized in Longfellow's poem, *Paul Revere's Ride*. He was a member of the Massachusetts committee of correspondence from March 1776, and his military services included management of a powder mill in Canton, Massachusetts, and in 1778–1779 command of Castle William, a fortification in Boston harbor. As a lieutenant colonel of artillery he took part in the unsuccessful expeditions to Rhode Island in 1778 under Gen. John Sullivan and to Penobscot Bay in July 1779 under Gen. Solomon Lovell with Commodore Dudley Saltonstall. The latter expedition was such a disaster as to tarnish for some years even Revere's reputation. After the Revolution he returned to his many crafts. His silverware was among the finest in the colonial and post-Revolutionary periods and is highly prized today. He was also involved in the manufacture of gunpowder, copper bells, and cannons; in copper plating; and in making hardware for frigates, including the *Constitution*—"Old Ironsides." He worked with Robert Fulton in developing copper boilers for steamboats. He daily wore uniforms of the Revolution until his death in Boston on May 10, 1818.

Reynolds, John Fulton (1820–1863), army officer. Born in Lancaster, Pennsylvania, on September 20, 1820, Reynolds graduated from West Point in 1841 and was commissioned in the artillery. He served at various posts in the South, and in 1846, promoted to first lieutenant, he was ordered to Texas. He took part in the defense of Fort Texas (later Fort Brown) on May 3 and won brevets to captain at Monterrey, September 20–24, and major at Buena Vista, February 22–23, 1847. After several more years of garrison duty in the East and the South and promotion to captain in March 1855 he began a period of service in the West, taking part in an expedition against the Rogue River Indians in Oregon in 1856 and in the Mormon expedition under Col. Albert S. Johnston in 1857–1858. After a year at Fort Vancouver, Washington Territory, he was named commandant of cadets at West Point in September 1860. In May 1861 he was promoted to lieutenant colonel and assigned to recruit and organize the 14th Infantry. In August he was appointed brigadier general of volunteers in command of the Pennsylvania reserves, and in May 1862 he was made military governor of Fredericksburg, Virginia. Later he was engaged in the Peninsula campaign, and following the battle of Gaines' Mill, June 27, he was taken prisoner. He was exchanged in August and was in the field at the second battle of Bull Run (Manassas), August 29–30, where he performed with great gallantry in rallying his division. At the request of the governor, Reynolds was then placed in command of the Pennsylvania militia in anticipation of Gen. Robert E. Lee's invasion. Promoted to major general of volunteers in November, he succeeded Gen. Joseph Hooker in command of the I Corps. He saw action at Fredericksburg, December 13, and Chancellorsville, May 2–4, 1863. Late in June, commanding the I, III, and XI corps as the left wing of the Army of the Potomac, he was ordered by Gen. George G. Meade to occupy Gettysburg, Pennsylvania. He arrived there ahead of his men on July 1, 1863, and found Gen. John Buford's cavalry sorely pressed by advance units of Lee's army. He rushed back to hurry his own advance troops and then returned to the battlefield at the head of the 2nd Wisconsin Regiment. He was killed at that moment by a sharpshooter's bullet.

Rhind, Alexander Colden (1821–1897), naval

officer. Born in New York City on October 31, 1821, Rhind entered the navy as a midshipman in September 1838. After several cruises he attended the naval school at Philadelphia in 1844–1845, and in the Mexican War he served in the squadron under Commodore David Conner and Commodore Matthew C. Perry on the east coast of Mexico. He was promoted to lieutenant in February 1854. While aboard the *John Adams* off the coast of Africa in 1855 he was courtmartialed for insubordination and sent home; later in the year he was dropped from the service. He was reinstated, however, in 1860, and at the outbreak of the Civil War he was given command of the steamer *Crusader* in the South Atlantic Blockading Squadron. He was commended for a series of operations conducted in Edisto Sound, South Carolina, and in July 1862 was promoted to lieutenant commander and put in command of the gunboat *Seneca*. Later in the year he took command of the ironclad *Keokuk*, and in January 1863 he advanced to commander. In the attack on Charleston harbor by Adm. Samuel F. Du Pont on April 7, 1863, the *Keokuk* brought up the rear. Rhind ran to within 550 yards of Fort Sumter and took 90 hits, 19 at or below the water line, before returning. He managed to keep the *Keokuk* afloat until next morning and got his crew off safely. Subsequently he commanded the *Paul Jones*, the *Wabash*, flagship of Adm. John A. B. Dahlgren in the South Atlantic Squadron, and the gunboat *Agawam* in the James River. He was again commended for actions at Deep Bottom, Virginia, on August 13, 1864. In the first attack on Fort Fisher, at Wilmington, North Carolina, on December 24, 1864, Rhind commanded the *Louisiana*, an old vessel packed with 215 tons of explosives. Fully expecting to be killed in the attempt, he maneuvered the vessel to within 300 yards of the fort; he and his crew then made a hasty escape, and the ship was detonated by a clockwork device. Although Fort Fisher was not damaged, Rhind was highly commended by Adm. David D. Porter for the exploit. He was promoted to captain in June 1870 and commodore in September 1876. Among his largely routine assignments in later years were command of the *Congress* in the European Squadron in 1872 and duty as lighthouse inspector in 1876–1878 and as president of the Board of Inspection in 1880–1882. He was promoted to rear admiral in October 1883 and retired a day later. Rhind died in New York City on November 8, 1897.

Richardson, Wilds Preston (1861–1929), army

officer. Born on March 20, 1861, in Hunt County, Texas, Richardson graduated from West Point in 1884 and was commissioned in the infantry. He was stationed for several years in the West, receiving promotion to first lieutenant in December 1889, and during 1891–1892 was aide-de-camp to the commander of the Department of the Columbia. From 1892 to 1897 he was an instructor at West Point, and in the latter year he began 20 years of almost uninterrupted duty in Alaska, during which he was promoted to captain in April 1898, major in April 1904, lieutenant colonel in March 1911, and colonel in April 1914. During 1902–1904 he was engaged in the building of Fort William H. Seward, and in 1905 he was named first president of the Alaska Roads Commission. His principal work in that post was opening the route from Valdez on the coast to Fairbanks in the interior. The "Richardson Trail" was surveyed in 1907 and opened to sled traffic; by 1910 it was negotiable by wagon, and in 1913 the first automobile made the 371-mile trip over the Richardson Highway. In August 1917 Richardson was promoted to temporary brigadier general. Put in command of a brigade of the 39th Infantry Division, he arrived in France with it in September 1918 and saw limited action before the armistice. In April 1919 he arrived to take command of U.S. forces, composed of infantry and engineers from the 85th Division, stationed at Murmansk in northern Russia as part of an Allied operation aimed at protecting ports and supplies against Bolshevist forces. He remained there until the final withdrawal of American troops in August 1919. Richardson reverted to permanent rank of colonel on his return to the United States, and he retired in October 1920. He died in Washington, D.C., on May 20, 1929.

Rickenbacker, Edward Vernon (1890–1973), army officer, aviator, and businessman. Born on October 8, 1890, in Columbus, Ohio, Rickenbacker adopted his middle name and dropped the Germanic spelling of his surname, Rickenbacher, during World War I. With little formal schooling and a succession of jobs behind him, be began working for a railroad-car manufacturing firm in 1905 and there developed a deep interest in internal-combustion engines and engine-powered vehicles. He began driving racing cars at sixteen (he became a regular at the Indianapolis 500 from its first year, 1911). By the time the United States entered World War I he was internationally famous as a daredevil speed driver and held a world speed record of 134 miles per hour. In May 1917 he enlisted in the army and went to France as a member of Gen. John J. Pershing's motor car staff. With help from Col. William Mitchell he secured a transfer to the Air Service in August, took pilot's training, and early in 1918, with the rank of captain, was assigned to the 94th Aero Pursuit Squadron. The 94th, which adopted the famous hat-in-the-ring insignia, was the first U.S. flying unit to participate actively at the front, fighting the "flying circus" commanded by the German ace, Baron Manfred von Richthofen. After the death of Maj. Raoul Lufbery in May 1918 Rickenbacker succeeded to command of the 94th in the temporary rank of major. By the end of the war the 94th had downed 69 enemy craft, of which Rickenbacker, the "ace of aces," accounted for 26 (22 airplanes, 4 observation balloons). He earned nearly every decoration possible, including the Medal of Honor, awarded (in 1931) for his lone attack on seven German planes, two of which he downed, on September 25, 1918. His *Fighting the Flying Circus* appeared in 1919. Returning to the United States a hero, he organized in Detroit the Rickenbacker Motor Company. The company was dissolved in 1926, and the next year he bought a controlling interest in the Indianapolis Speedway, which he retained until 1945. He later worked for the Cadillac division of General Motors Corporation and then was associated with a number of aircraft manufacturers and airlines. In 1935 he became general manager and vice-presi-

dent of Eastern Airlines, and three years later he became president and director of the line. His experience and technical knowledge prompted his appointment as special representative of Henry L. Stimson, secretary of war, to inspect air bases in the Pacific theater of war in 1942. In October 1942, on his second mission over the Pacific, his B-17 was forced down some 600 miles north of Samoa, and he and seven men (one of whom died) were set adrift on rubber rafts with only fish and rain water to sustain them. After 23 days he was rescued, and after a two-week rest he resumed his tour. In 1943 he published *Seven Came Through*, the story of the raft exploit. A film biography, *Captain Eddie*, was released in 1946. After the war he returned to Eastern Airlines, where he remained, from 1954 as chairman of the board, until his retirement in 1963. In 1967 he published *Rickenbacker: An Autobiography*. He died in Zurich, Switzerland, on July 23, 1973.

Rickover, Hyman George (1900–   ), naval officer. Born in Maków, Russia (now in Poland), on January 27, 1900, Rickover came to the United States with his parents in 1906 and settled in Chicago. He graduated from the Naval Academy in 1922 and saw service over the next several years in various types of ships, qualifying for submarine duty in 1930. Meanwhile he pursued graduate studies in electrical engineering at Annapolis and at Columbia, where he took an M.S. in 1929. He had his first sea command on the minesweeper *Finch* in 1937. His specialized knowledge led then to a post with the electrical division of the Bureau of Ships, of which he served as chief during World War II. Rickover's subsequent importance in U.S. naval history is analogous to that of George W. Melville during the navy's transition to steam power at the end of the nineteenth century. After a six-month tour as assistant director of operations of the Manhattan Engineering District at Oak Ridge, Tennessee, during the second half of 1946, Rickover became convinced of the feasibility and the military necessity of developing an atomic-powered submarine. He promoted the idea tirelessly, at length convincing Adm. Chester W. Nimitz, chief of naval operations. Rickover then, in 1947, engineered for himself the dual post of chief of the nuclear power division, Bureau of Ships, and head of the naval reactors branch of the Atomic Energy Commission. He was thus in a position to direct and coordinate a joint development program. During the next several years he worked unceasingly, often in the face of apathy and never without criticism, to achieve his goal. The naval reactor, known as Submarine Thermal Reactor Mark I, was successfully land-tested in March 1953. When the *Nautilus*, the world's first nuclear-powered submarine, was launched in January 1954 it was Rickover, more than any other single man, who was responsible for its overall design and development.

He also supervised the construction of the subsequent *Seawolf* and was instrumental in the development of an atomic reactor for powering an aircraft carrier. In 1956–1957 he helped develop the experimental nuclear electric-power plant at Shippingport, Pennsylvania. When he was passed over for promotion in the early 1950s public outcry and congressional pressure led to his advancement to rear admiral in July 1953 and to vice admiral in October 1958 and to extension of his active service beyond the mandatory retirement age in 1961. In the late 1950s Rickover established nuclear-power schools for the navy in Connecticut and California. Long a controversial figure in naval circles for his outspokenness and his devotion to the use of nuclear power, upon the publication of *Education and Freedom* in 1959 he attracted widespread attention as a critic of American educational practices. Further publications followed in the 1960s, including *Swiss Schools and Ours; Why Theirs are Better*, 1962, and *American Education; A National Failure*, 1963, as he contributed to the discussion of the need to train more and better engineers and scientists for the sake of the national defense. In January 1964 he was retired and immediately recalled to active duty in the same posts; he received regular extensions in active service thereafter. In 1965 he received the AEC's Fermi Award for his work in atomic science. In September 1973 he was promoted to the rank of admiral. Rickover was nearly as remarkable for his enduring influence with Congress as for his engineering ability, and his many accomplishments rested on both faculties.

Ridgway, Matthew Bunker (1895–   ), army officer. Born in Fort Monroe, Virginia, on March 3, 1895, Ridgway graduated from West Point in 1917 and was commissioned in the infantry. He was promoted to first lieutenant in May 1917 and to temporary captain in August. He served with the 3rd Infantry in Texas until September 1918, when he returned to West Point as an instructor and athletics officer. He became permanent captain in July 1919. After completing a course in 1925 at the Infantry School, Fort Benning, Georgia, he served tours successively in China, Texas, Nicaragua, the Canal Zone, and the Philippines, in the meanwhile graduating from the Infantry School advanced course in 1930 and receiving promotion to major in October 1932. On graduating from Command and General Staff School, Fort Leavenworth, Kansas, in 1935 he served on the staffs of the VI Corps area and the Second Army in Chicago. In 1937 he graduated from the Army War College, and after a period on the staff of the Fourth Army in San Francisco he joined the War Plans Division in the War Department in September 1939. He was promoted to lieutenant colonel in July 1940, to temporary colonel in December 1941, and to temporary brigadier general in January 1942. In March 1942

he was appointed deputy to Gen. Omar N. Bradley, commander of the 82nd Infantry Division at Camp Claiborne, Louisiana. He succeeded to command in June and oversaw conversion of the division to an airborne unit in August, advancing to temporary major general in that month. After months of training in North Africa the 82nd entered combat in the invasion of Sicily by Gen. George S. Patton's Seventh Army. Elements of the 82nd, mainly Col. James M. Gavin's 505th Regimental Combat Team, parachuted in behind enemy lines at Gela on July 9–10, 1943, in the army's first major airborne assault. On September 13, 1943, units of the 82nd joined the assault on Salerno, Italy. The 82nd was later withdrawn to training sites in Great Britain. Ridgway parachuted with his troops into Normandy on D-Day, June 6, 1944, and in August moved up to command of the XVIII Airborne Corps, which saw action in the Netherlands, Belgium, and northern Germany. His troops played a significant role in stemming the German offensive known as the Battle of the Bulge in December 1944. In June 1945 he was promoted to temporary lieutenant general. For three months in 1945–1946 he commanded the Mediterranean theater. In January 1946 he was appointed to the Military Staff Committee of the United Nations, and in March he joined the Inter-American Defense Board. In July 1948 he was named commander of the Caribbean Defense Command, and in August 1949 he became deputy chief of staff of the army. In December 1950 he succeeded Gen. Walton H. Walker as commander of the Eighth Army in Korea. He moved immediately to revitalize the seriously demoralized army and succeeded so well that by late January 1951 the Eighth took the offensive again. By mid-March the South Korean capital of Seoul was recaptured. When Gen. Douglas MacArthur was recalled in April, Ridgway succeeded him as head of the Far East Command and the United Nations command, receiving promotion to general in May. Under his leadership the Korean armistice talks were begun in July 1951. In May 1952 Ridgway succeeded Gen. Dwight D. Eisenhower as supreme commander of Allied forces in Europe, receiving in addition command of all U.S. forces in Europe in July. In August 1953 he was named chief of staff of the army, and he served in that post until his retirement in June 1955. Ridgway published *Soldier*, his war memoirs, in 1956. In later years he was an executive or director of various business firms.

Riley, Bennet (1787–1853), army officer. Born in St. Marys County, Maryland, on November 27, 1787, Riley was commissioned an ensign of riflemen in the army in January 1813. He was promoted to lieutenant two months later and saw service on the New York border in the War of 1812. He was subsequently sent to the western frontier. He advanced to captain in August 1818 and in 1821 was transferred into the infantry. Following a fight with Arikara Indians in Dakota Territory in 1823 he was brevetted major. He took part in Col. Henry Atkinson's Yellowstone expedition in 1825, and in 1829 he convoyed a wagon train to Santa Fe. He saw action in the Black Hawk War of 1831–1832. He was promoted to major in September 1837 and to lieutenant colonel in December 1839, and while serving against the Seminoles in Florida in 1839–1842 he was brevetted colonel for gallantry at Chakotta in June 1840. In the Mexican War he commanded the 2nd Infantry and then a brigade under Gen. David E. Twiggs, taking part in the capture of Veracruz in March 1847 and being brevetted brigadier general for gallantry at Cerro Gordo, April 18. At Contreras on August 20 he led his brigade in a spectacular charge down a slope on the rear of the Mexican position, carrying all before him. He was brevetted major general for that deed. After the war he served in Louisiana and Missouri, and late in 1848 he was made commander of the Department of the Pacific, becoming thereby military governor of California. He convened a constitutional convention at Monterey in September 1849 and turned over executive authority to the new state government in December. He was promoted to colonel in command of the 1st Infantry in January 1850, but illness soon forced him to settle in Buffalo, New York, where he died on June 9, 1853. Fort Riley, Kansas, built in that year, was named for him.

Ringgold, Cadwalader (1802–1867), naval officer. Born in Washington County, Maryland, on August 20, 1802, Ringgold entered the navy as a midshipman in March 1819. During 1823–1824 he served under Commodore David Porter in pirate patrol in the West Indies, and, promoted to lieutenant in May 1828, he later commanded the *Vandalia*, 1828–1832, and the *Adams*, 1834–1835. In 1838 he was given command of the brig *Porpoise* in the South Seas Exploring Expedition under Lt. Charles Wilkes. He took part in a skirmish with Fiji islanders in August 1840 following the murder of two officers. In July 1849 he was promoted to commander, and during 1849–1850 he conducted surveys in California coastal and harbor waters. In June 1853 he sailed from Norfolk, Virginia, on the *Vincennes* in command of the North Pacific Exploring and Surveying Expedition. After charting numerous islands the squadron reached China in March 1854. Four months later Ringgold, suffering from a severe illness, was relieved of command by Commodore Matthew C. Perry and sent home, command of the expedition passing to Lt. John Rodgers. In September 1855, over his objection, he was placed on the reserve list, but two years later he succeeded in winning reinstatement along with promotion to captain dating from April 1856. He remained in Washington, D.C., preparing the charts of the North Pacific expedition, until September 1861,

when he took command of the frigate *Sabine* in the South Atlantic Blockading Squadron. On November 2, when a gale scattered Flag-Officer Samuel F. Du Pont's squadron off Port Royal, Ringgold distinguished himself in rescuing a battalion of marines off the disabled steamer *Governor*. He was promoted to commodore in July 1862, and from October of that year until June 1863 he patrolled the Cape Verde Islands in unsuccessful search of the Confederate raider *Alabama*. Retired in August 1864, he was promoted to rear admiral on the retired list in July 1866. Ringgold died in New York City on April 29, 1867.

Ripley, Eleazar Wheelock (1782–1839), army officer. Born in Hanover, New Hampshire, on April 15, 1782, Ripley was a grandson of Eleazar Wheelock, founder of Dartmouth College. He graduated from Dartmouth in 1800 and took up the study of law, entering practice in Portland, Massachusetts (now Maine), and sitting in the Massachusetts legislature in 1807–1809. In March 1812 he was appointed lieutenant colonel in the army for service against Great Britain and placed in command of the 21st Infantry. He was occupied in training for a year and in March 1813 was advanced to colonel. He took part in the attack and capture, under Gen. Zebulon M. Pike, of York (now Toronto) on April 27, 1813, and in the capture by Gen. Henry Dearborn of Fort George on the Niagara River on May 27. In October–November he was in Gen. James Wilkinson's abortive expedition against Montreal. In April 1814 he was promoted to brigadier general, and he saw action under Gen. Jacob J. Brown at Fort Erie, July 3, Chippewa, July 5, and Lundy's Lane, July 25. With both Brown and Gen. Winfield Scott wounded following Lundy's Lane, Ripley led the American army back to Fort Erie, joining Gen. Edmund P. Gaines in holding it during the British siege in August–September and being severely wounded in a sortie out of the fort on September 17. During the campaign he was often at odds with Brown, who blamed him for the incomplete success of Lundy's Lane. Ripley was nonetheless voted a gold medal by Congress, and calls for a court of inquiry came ultimately to nothing. He continued in the army until 1820, when he resigned to resume the practice of law in New Orleans. He later moved to West Feliciana Parish. He was elected to the legislature in 1832 and from March 1835 until his death served in Congress as a Democrat. Ripley died in West Feliciana Parish, Louisiana, on March 2, 1839.

Robert, Henry Martyn (1837–1923), army officer, engineer, and parliamentarian. Born in Robertville, Jasper County, South Carolina, on May 2, 1837, Robert graduated from West Point in 1857 and, after spending a year as an instructor in military engineering there, was commissioned a second lieutenant of engineers and assigned to duty in the Northwest. He supervised the construction of defenses for Washington, D.C., Philadelphia, and other places during the Civil War, being promoted to first lieutenant in August 1861 and to captain in March 1863. After two years as an instructor at West Point and promotion to major in March 1867, he was ordered in that year to the staff of the Division of the Pacific. After 1871 he was engaged in river and harbor and defense projects in the Northwest, on the Great Lakes, and elsewhere, receiving promotion to lieutenant colonel in January 1883. In 1890–1891 he was engineer commissioner of the District of Columbia. Promoted to colonel in February 1895, he served as president of the Board of Fortifications during the Spanish–American War. He retired in May 1901 in the rank of brigadier general, having served two days as chief of engineers. He continued to be a consulting engineer after his retirement, receiving important commissions, including the supervision of the building of the seawall for Galveston, Texas. He wrote several books describing his engineering work, but none is as famous as a little volume he quickly wrote when he was twenty-five and several times enlarged and revised. About 1862 he was asked to preside over a meeting. He did not know how, and so he looked for a simple book or manual that would describe his duties. He soon discovered that none existed and decided to write one himself. *Pocket Manual of Rules of Order* was first published (although it had previously circulated in manuscript) in 1876, was revised in 1893 and 1904, and was greatly enlarged and systematized in 1915 and reissued under the title *Robert's Rules of Order Revised.* In time the book became the authority on parliamentary procedures for almost all organizations in the United States. Robert also published *Parliamentary Practice*, 1921, and *Parliamentary Law*, 1923, both standard works. He died in Hornell, New York, on May 11, 1923.

Robinson, John Cleveland (1817–1897),

army officer. Born in Binghamton, New York, on April 10, 1817, Robinson left West Point in 1838 after three years and took up the study of law, but he was nonetheless appointed second lieutenant of the 5th Infantry by President Martin Van Buren in October 1839. In the Mexican War he saw action at Palo Alto and Resaca de la Palma, May 8–9, 1846, was promoted to first lieutenant in June, and took part in the battle of Monterrey, September 20–24. Promoted to captain in August 1850, he saw action against Indians in Florida and Texas and in 1857–1858 was a member of the Mormon expedition under Col. Albert S. Johnston. At the outbreak of the Civil War he was in command of Fort McHenry in Baltimore, and he successfully defended it against pro-Southern rioters and city officials in April 1861. In September he was elected colonel of the 1st Michigan Volunteers, and the following April he was promoted to brigadier

general of volunteers in command of a brigade of Gen. Philip Kearny's division of the III Corps, Army of the Potomac. He fought through the Peninsula campaign and the Seven Days' Battles in 1862 and by the time of the battle of Fredericksburg, December 13, 1862, was in command of a division. He was at Chancellorsville, May 2–4, 1863, and was brevetted lieutenant colonel of regulars at Gettysburg, July 1–3. In the Wilderness campaign in May 1864 he won a brevet to colonel of regulars, and at Spotsylvania he was severely wounded while leading a gallant charge on the Confederate works. In June he was brevetted major general of volunteers. He commanded military districts in New York until the end of the war, receiving in March 1865 brevets of brigadier and major general of regulars for services. From then until late in 1866 he was military commander and commissioner of the Freedmen's Bureau of North Carolina, receiving permanent regular rank of colonel in July 1866. He commanded the Department of the South in 1867 and the Department of the Lakes in 1868 and in May 1869 was retired in the rank of major general. From 1872 to 1874 he served as lieutenant governor of New York under Gov. John A. Dix. In 1877–1878 he was national commander of the Grand Army of the Republic, and in 1887–1888 he was president of the Society of the Army of the Potomac. In 1894 he was awarded the Medal of Honor for gallantry at Laurel Hill, Virginia, in the Spotsylvania campaign. Robinson died in Binghamton, New York, on February 18, 1897.

Rochambeau, Comte de (1725–1807),

Revolutionary army officer. Born at Vendôme, France, on July 1, 1725, Jean Baptiste Donatien de Vimeur, Comte de Rochambeau, was originally destined for the church; but he entered the army at seventeen and, after service in the War of the Austrian Succession, was made a colonel at the age of twenty-two. Further service in the Seven Years' War, notably in Minorca in 1756 and at Crefeld in 1758, led to his promotion to brigadier general in 1761 and later to major general and in March 1780 to lieutenant general. In May 1780 he sailed from Brest in command of the troops sent by France to the American colonies to aid the Revolution. After languishing in Newport, Rhode Island, for nearly a year waiting for French naval vessels to be available for support, he led his 5500 soldiers to join Gen. George Washington's forces at White Plains, New York, early in July 1781. A Virginia campaign against Gen. Charles Cornwallis had been urged on Washington by Rochambeau at several earlier meetings; now they led the combined force of about 10,-000 swiftly southward to Yorktown (leaving behind a small force under Gen. William Heath to occupy the British in New York), where they joined other Continental forces and the French troops led by the Marquis de Lafayette, who had been harassing the

British in the vicinity. Aided by a blockade by French naval forces under Admiral de Grasse, the force of allies settled down to the siege of Yorktown on September 28; Cornwallis surrendered on October 19, 1781, an event that to all intents and purposes ended the Revolutionary War. Unlike many other European officers who served in the Revolution, Rochambeau was distinguished by the grace with which he accepted Washington's authority as commander in chief, at the same time maintaining commendable discipline among his own troops. For his services he was given the thanks of Congress. Remaining in Virginia until January 1783, Rochambeau returned then to France, where he was military commander of a succession of districts. He served in the Assembly of Notables in 1788. Made a marshal of France in December 1791, he fell out with the Robespierre regime and only escaped the guillotine because of the death of Robespierre himself in 1794. He was later, in 1804, created a grand officer of the Legion of Honor and pensioned by Napoleon. He died at Thoré, France, on May 10, 1807.

Rockwell, Kiffin Yates (1892–1916), airman. Born on September 20, 1892, in Newport, Tennessee, Rockwell entered Virginia Military Institute in 1908, transferred to the Naval Academy a year later, and soon thereafter transferred again to Washington and Lee University. A restless and romantic youth, he traveled west in 1912, worked for a time in San Francisco, and settled in Atlanta, Georgia, in 1914. At the outbreak of World War I in Europe in that year his earlier dreams of military glory were reawakened. He made his way to France and joined the Foreign Legion, seeing much action during the winter of 1914–1915 and being wounded in the attack of the 1st Foreign Regiment on La Targette in May 1915. In September of that year he transferred to the aviation service, and on completing training in April 1916 he was assigned to the newly organized Escadrille Américaine No. 124 (eight months later renamed the Lafayette Escadrille) with the rank of sergeant. On March 18, 1916, over Thann, he became the first pilot of the Escadrille to bring down an enemy aircraft. He flew numerous other missions during the summer and had a total score of four victories when, on September 23, 1916, while piloting one of the first of the new Nieuport 160 aircraft, he was shot down and killed over Luxeuil, France.

Rodes, Robert Emmett (1829–1864), Confederate army officer. Born in Lynchburg, Virginia, on March 29, 1829, Rodes graduated from the Virginia Military Institute in 1848 and for three years thereafter was an assistant professor there. In 1851 he took up civil engineering and seven years later became chief engineer of the N.E. and S.W. Alabama Railroad. In May 1861 he was appointed colonel of the 5th Alabama Infantry. He distinguished himself at Manassas (Bull Run), July 21, and in October was promoted to brigadier general. His brigade formed part of Gen. Daniel H. Hill's division of Gen. Thomas J. Jackson's corps, and he distinguished himself through the Peninsula campaign in 1862, particularly at Fair Oaks (Seven Pines), May 31, where he was badly wounded, and at Gaines' Mill, June 27, following which he was incapacitated for some months. He again performed gallantly at South Mountain, September 14, and Sharpsburg (Antietam), September 17, in the Maryland campaign, and in January 1863 he succeeded to command of Hill's division. At Chancellorsville on May 2 his division led Jackson's flank attack on Gen. Oliver O. Howard's XI Corps. A few days later Rodes was promoted to major general. He was commended by Gen. Robert E. Lee for his actions at Gettysburg, July 1–3. In the Wilderness and at Spotsylvania in May 1864 he was conspicuous in his success, and in June he was sent with his division to join Gen. Jubal A. Early in the Shenandoah valley. He took part in the battle at the Monocacy, July 9, in the raid on Washington, D.C., on July 11, and in battles at Castleman's Ferry, July 18, and Kernstown, July 24. At Winchester, Virginia, on September 19, 1864, Rodes arrived on the field as the Confederate position was weakening and launched a vigorous counterattack on Gen. Philip H. Sheridan's forces. He was killed in that battle.

Rodgers, Christopher Raymond Perry (1819–1892), naval officer. Born in Brooklyn, New York, on November 14, 1819, Rodgers was a son of Commander George W. Rodgers and an elder brother of the junior George W. Rodgers. He entered the navy as a midshipman in October 1833 and made his first cruise on the *Brandywine* in the Pacific. After a year, 1836–1837, at the New York navy yard he served on the *Fairfield* in the Brazil Squadron. During the Seminole War, 1839–1842, he served in Florida coastal waters on the *Flirt* and the *Wave* and in 1840–1841 commanded the *Phoenix*. He served on the *Saratoga* in the Africa Squadron in 1842–1843 and on the *Cumberland* in the Mediterranean in 1843–1845, receiving promotion to lieutenant in September 1844. In the Mexican War he took active part in the siege of Veracruz and in the capture of Tabasco and Tuxpan by Commodore Matthew C. Perry in the summer of 1847. After three years with the Coast Survey he served on the *Congress* in the Brazil Squadron, on the *Constitution* in the Africa Squadron, again with the Coast Survey in 1856–1858, and on the *Wabash* in the Mediterranean. During 1860–1861 he was commandant of midshipmen at the Naval Academy, which he helped transfer to Newport, Rhode Island, in the latter year. In September 1861 he was given command of the *Wabash,* Flag-Officer Samuel F. Du Pont's flagship in the South Atlantic Blockading

Squadron. He was promoted to commander in November and in that month took part in the squadron attack on Port Royal, South Carolina. During 1862 he engaged in numerous operations on the coast, receiving himself the surrender of St. Augustine, Florida, on March 11 and taking part in the assault on Fort Pulaski at Savannah, Georgia, in April. In August he was named fleet captain of the squadron, and in April 1863 he served on Du Pont's new flagship *New Ironsides* in the first attack on Charleston, South Carolina. From October 1863 until the end of the war he commanded the *Iroquois*, patrolling against Confederate raiders in the Atlantic and Pacific. Promoted to captain in July 1866, Rodgers commanded the *Franklin* in the Mediterranean in 1868–1870 and advanced to commodore in August 1870. During 1871–1874 he was chief of the Bureau of Yards and Docks, and, promoted to rear admiral in June 1874, he served as superintendent of the Naval Academy from then until 1878. As in his period as commandant of midshipmen, he made numerous distinctive contributions to the course and to the discipline of the Academy. During 1878–1880 he commanded the Pacific Squadron, and he then resumed the superintendency at the Academy until his retirement in November 1881. In 1884 he was president of the international conference in Washington, D.C., which fixed the prime (Greenwich) meridian and the universal day. Rodgers died in Washington, D.C., on January 8, 1892. Two of his sons attained the rank of rear admiral.

Rodgers, George Washington (1787–1832), naval officer. Born in Cecil County, Maryland, on February 22, 1787, Rodgers was a younger brother of John Rodgers (1773–1838). He entered the navy as a midshipman in April 1804 and made his first cruise in the Mediterranean on the *President*, seeing the conclusion of the Tripolitan War. He served subsequently on the *Essex*, the *Vixen*, and the *United States*, receiving promotion to lieutenant in April 1810. He was assigned to the *Wasp* under Commander Jacob Jones in 1811 and took part in the capture of the *Frolic* on October 18, 1812, and the subsequent surrender to the *Poictiers*. From December 1812 to April 1814 he was aboard the *Macedonian*, blockaded in New London, Connecticut. Later in 1814 he was on the *Mohawk* in the Lake Ontario squadron. In March 1815 he was given command of the brig *Firefly* in the squadron assembled in New York under Commodore Stephen Decatur for service against Algiers, but she was damaged in a gale soon after sailing in May and although repairs were made she rejoined the squadron too late to see any action. Rodgers was promoted to master commandant in April 1816. He commanded the *Peacock* in the Mediterranean from 1816 to 1819 and then spent six years at the New York navy yard. Promoted to captain in March 1825, he was inactive

for a time thereafter. He served on the Board of Examiners in 1828–1830 and in November 1831 was put in command of the Brazil Squadron aboard the flagship *Warren*. Soon after taking up his duties he died in Buenos Aires, Argentina, on May 21, 1832. Of the first generation of the navy's most remarkable family, he and his wife, a sister of Matthew C. and Oliver H. Perry, had two sons of naval note, Christopher R. P. Rodgers and George W. Rodgers.

Rodgers, George Washington (1822–1863), naval officer. Born in Brooklyn, New York, on October 30, 1822, Rodgers was a son of Commander George W. Rodgers and a younger brother of Christopher R. P. Rodgers. He entered the navy as a midshipman in April 1836 and made his first cruise on the *Boston* in the West Indies. He served subsequently on the *Constellation* and in 1839–1841 on the *Brandywine* and then attended the naval school in Philadelphia, becoming a passed midshipman in July 1842. For three years he served on the *Saratoga* in the Africa Squadron, and in the Mexican War he was on the *Colonel Harney* and later the *John Adams* in the squadron on the east coast of Mexico under Commodore David Conner and Commodore Matthew C. Perry (Rodgers's uncle). After two years with the Coast Survey he was promoted to lieutenant in June 1850; there followed service on the *Germantown* of the Home and later Africa Squadrons, 1850–1853; at the New York navy yard, 1853–1856; on the *Falmouth* of the Brazil Squadron, 1856–1859; and again at New York. In September 1860 he was put in command of the *Constitution*, then serving as the school ship of the Naval Academy. After the outbreak of the Civil War he evacuated the midshipmen's corps from Annapolis to Newport, Rhode Island, meanwhile thwarting a plot of a few secessionists to capture the *Constitution*. In September 1861 he succeeded his brother, Lt. C. R. P. Rodgers, as commandant of midshipmen. In May 1862 he joined the James River Flotilla under Commodore Louis M. Goldsborough and commanded the *Tioga* in operations there, receiving promotion to commander in July. A short time later he was transferred to command of the monitor *Catskill* in Adm. Samuel F. Du Pont's South Atlantic Blockading Squadron before Charleston (where his cousin, Capt. John Rodgers, commanded the *Weehawken*). He took part in the fruitless attack on Charleston on April 7, 1863, and in July was named chief of staff to the new squadron commander, Adm. John A. B. Dahlgren. He resumed command of the *Catskill* to take part in an attack on Fort Wagner in support of Gen. Quincy A. Gillmore's troops ashore on Morris Island on August 17, 1863, the *Catskill* serving as flagship of the force of four monitors (also the *Nahant*, *Montauk*, and *Weehawken*) participating. Early in the engagement Rodgers was killed by a shot striking the pilot house.

Rodgers, John (1773–1838), naval officer. Born near the present Havre de Grace, Maryland, in 1773, Rodgers was the son of John Rodgers, a Scotsman who had emigrated to America about 1760 and who, after serving as a colonel of militia in the Revolution, founded one of the most celebrated naval families in U.S. history. After spending some 11 years in the merchant service the younger Rodgers entered the navy as second lieutenant aboard the *Constellation* in March 1798 and in June went to sea on her under the command of Capt. Thomas Truxtun. He served as executive officer of the ship during her victorious engagement with the *Insurgente* on February 9, 1799. He was rewarded by being promoted the next month to captain, the first lieutenant to be raised to this rank in the newly reorganized United States navy. After a period of routine duty and a leave of absence he returned to active service in 1802, commanding the *John Adams* in the squadron sent out under Commodore Richard V. Morris to reinforce the blockade of Tripoli. In May 1803 he captured the *Mashuda* attempting to run the blockade. In June 1803 he was briefly acting commander of the squadron after the departure of Morris and before the arrival of Commodore Edward Preble. He returned home in December 1803 but rejoined the Tripolitan squadron in the summer of 1804 in command of the *Congress*. In May 1805 he succeeded Commodore James Barron in command of the squadron, and in June he completed a treaty with Tripoli abolishing the payment of tribute. In September Rodgers exacted a similar agreement from the bey of Tunis and then returned home. From July 1807 to February 1809 he commanded the gunboat flotilla and the naval station at New York, and he was then transferred to command of the Home Squadron. On May 16, 1811, while cruising off Cape Henry aboard the frigate *President*, he engaged what proved after a 15-minute fight to be the smaller British sloop *Little Belt* and inflicted heavy damage and many casualties. The action, coming after the *Chesapeake-Leopard* affair, was commended by his superiors and made him a popular hero. During the War of 1812 he was the ranking active officer of the navy, and again he performed effectively, particularly against British merchant shipping. Aboard his flagship *President* he commanded squadron patrols sweeping the Atlantic from the Indies to the Cape Verdes, making four such cruises before the end of the war. In 1815 he was chosen by President James Madison to head the newly established Board of Naval Commissioners (the other commissioners being Commodores Isaac Hull and David Porter). He retained the post until 1837, except for the period 1824–1827, when he was again on sea duty in command of the Mediterranean Squadron from aboard the *North Carolina*. He was senior officer of the navy from 1821, and in 1823 he served for a short period as secretary of the navy. He resigned as a naval com-

missioner in May 1837 and died in Philadelphia on August 1, 1838. His younger brother, George Washington Rodgers (1787–1832), was also a naval officer.

Rodgers, John (1812–1882), naval officer. Born near Havre de Grace, Maryland, on August 8, 1812, Rodgers was the son of naval hero John Rodgers (1773–1838). Appointed midshipman in April 1828, he saw his first service aboard the *Constellation* in the Mediterranean. He was certified passed midshipman in June 1834, and after studying for a year at the University of Virginia he was briefly with the Coast Survey and then on the *Dolphin* of the Brazil Squadron in 1836–1839. During the Seminole War he commanded the *Wave* and later the *Jefferson* in the waters of Florida, receiving promotion to lieutenant in January 1840. During 1842–1844 he commanded the *Boxer* in the Home Squadron, and after a three-year cruise with the Africa and Mediterranean squadrons he was again attached to the Coast Survey in 1849–1852. In October 1852 he was given command of the *John Hancock* of the North Pacific Exploring and Surveying Expedition, and in July 1854 he succeeded Commander Cadwalader Ringgold in command of the expedition. He was promoted to commander in September 1855, while surveying the Arctic Ocean on the *Vincennes*. In May 1861 he was put in charge of assembling a flotilla of ironclad steamers for service on western rivers. In October he took command of the *Flag* in Flag-Officer Samuel F. Du Pont's South Atlantic Blockading Squadron. In the attack on Port Royal, November 7, Rodgers led the occupation of Fort Walker. Early in 1862 he commanded a gunboat flotilla on the Savannah River and then the *Galena* on the James, on the latter leading a force up the James to Drewry's Bluff in May in support of Gen. George B. McClellan's Peninsula campaign. He was promoted to captain in July. In November he returned to the South Atlantic Squadron as commander of the monitor *Weehawken*, which on April 7, 1863, led Du Pont's attack at Charleston, pushing a "boot-jack" raft invented by John Ericsson to catch submarine mines and obstructions. In the battle the *Weehawken* was struck 53 times. On June 17, in Wassaw Sound, Georgia, he engaged and captured the Confederate ironclad *Atlanta*, widely believed to be invincible, and was promptly promoted to commodore. Subsequently he commanded the *Canonicus* and the *Dictator*. In 1865–1866 he commanded a small squadron in the Pacific, and in 1866–1869 the Boston navy yard. He was promoted to rear admiral in December 1869. From 1870 to 1872 he commanded the Asiatic Squadron, in which post he was obliged in June 1871 to land a force of seamen and marines near the Han River, Korea, in retaliation for unprovoked attacks during diplomatic talks. In 1872 he became president of the navy's Examining and Retiring boards. During 1873–1877 he commanded the

Mare Island navy yard, California, and during 1877–1882 he was superintendent of the Naval Observatory. He served also on various other boards and commissions. When he died in Washington, D.C., on May 5, 1882, he was senior rear admiral on the active list. He had a son, William L. Rodgers, who also rose to the rank of rear admiral.

Rodgers, John (1881–1926), naval officer and aviator. Born in Washington, D.C., on January 15, 1881, Rodgers was the son of a rear admiral, and a great-grandson of both Commodore John Rodgers (1773–1838) and Commodore Matthew C. Perry. He served on the auxiliary cruiser *Columbia* in the Spanish–American War while still a schoolboy. He graduated from the Naval Academy in 1903 and after service on various ships in the Asiatic Squadron was commissioned ensign in 1905. While assigned to the *Nebraska* he was promoted to lieutenant in 1908. In 1911 he attended the flying school conducted by the Wright brothers at Dayton, Ohio, and was the second naval officer to be qualified as a pilot. In 1912 he helped organize the naval air station at San Diego, California. Subsequently he served on the *Illinois*, the *Nebraska*, and the *Paducah* and then took submarine training on the *Columbia* and the *Fulton*. During 1916–1917 he commanded Submarine Division 1, Atlantic Fleet; promoted to lieutenant commander in 1917, he commanded the submarine base at New London, Connecticut, in 1917–1918, and, with temporary rank of commander, Submarine Division 10 in 1918–1919. Promoted to commander in November 1920, he commanded the naval air station at Pearl Harbor, Hawaii, from 1922 to 1925. In the latter year he was selected to command one of two navy seaplanes attempting to fly nonstop from San Francisco to Hawaii. He took off from San Francisco in his PN-9 biplane on August 31 with a crew of four. The companion plane was forced down at sea 300 miles out. Rodgers ran out of fuel 400 miles short of his destination the next day and ditched; for nine days he drifted on the open sea, his fate unknown, a makeshift canvas sail enabling the plane and crew to make for Hawaii. They were picked up on September 10 by a submarine about 15 miles out. Though incomplete, the flight set a distance record for seaplane navigation. Rodgers was appointed assistant chief of the Bureau of Aeronautics immediately thereafter. In August 1926 he took command of an experimental seaplane squadron. On August 27, 1926, a land plane he was flying between Washington, D.C., and Philadelphia fell into shallow Delaware River waters, and Rodgers was killed. With his death the U.S. navy was without a John Rodgers of his family on active duty for the first time since it was formed in 1798.

Rodman, Hugh (1859–1940), naval officer. Born on January 6, 1859, in Frankfort, Kentucky, Rodman graduated from the Naval Academy in 1880 and was commissioned ensign (junior grade) in March 1883. He advanced to ensign in June 1884, to lieutenant (junior grade) in October 1893, and to lieutenant in July 1897. During the Spanish–American War he served aboard the cruiser *Raleigh* of the Asiatic Squadron under Commodore George Dewey and took part in the battle of Manila Bay, May 1, 1898. Subsequently he served aboard the *New Orleans*, the *Cincinnati*, and the *Wisconsin*, advancing to lieutenant commander in March 1903; he commanded the *El Cano* in 1905–1907 and the *West Virginia* in 1907, receiving promotion to commander in July of that year. He was lighthouse inspector for the Sixth district in 1907–1908 and captain of the *Cleveland* in 1909–1910. He was stationed at Mare Island navy yard, California, from 1910 to 1912, commanding it with the rank of captain from 1911. He was captain of the *Connecticut* in 1912 and of the *Delaware* in 1912–1913, was assigned to duty at the Panama Canal in 1914–1915, was captain of the *New York* in 1915–1916, and was a member of the General Board of the navy in 1916–1917. In May 1917 he was promoted to rear admiral and given command of Division 3, Atlantic Fleet. In September he moved to command of a battleship squadron, and in November he took command of Battleship Division 9, which was attached to the British Grand Fleet and functioned as Battle Squadron 6. Comprising the battleships *New York, Wyoming, Florida, Delaware, Arkansas,* and *Texas,* the squadron was the principal heavy combat force of the U.S. navy at sea in the war; it helped patrol the North Sea against the German High Seas Fleet, escorted convoys between Britain and Norway, and supported Allied minelaying work in the North Sea. In April 1918 Rodman was named commander of U.S. battleships in European waters, continuing also in command of the 6th Squadron until the end of the war in November 1918. In July 1919 he was promoted to admiral and put in command of the Pacific Fleet. From 1921 he commanded the Fifth Naval District at Hampton Roads, Virginia. He retired in January 1923 and died in Washington, D.C., on June 7, 1940.

Rodman, Thomas Jackson (1815–1871), army officer and inventor. Born near Salem, Indiana, on July 30, 1815, Rodman graduated from West Point in 1841 and was assigned to the Ordnance Department. While stationed at the Alleghany arsenal in Pittsburgh, 1841–1848, he carried on numerous experiments in gun casting and construction, traveling in 1846 to Boston to study Col. George Bomford's 12-inch columbiads. By 1847 he had devised a new method of casting guns, using a hollow core through which cooling water was circulated, thereby shrinking each layer of metal onto those below. The strength gained by the compression thus achieved was far greater than that usual in previous methods, producing a gun of superior endurance. The government failed to avail itself of Rodman's work, however, and he remained in routine assignments. During the Mexican War he commanded ordnance depots in northern Mexico. He later commanded the Alleghany arsenal, receiving promotion to captain in July 1855. During 1855–1856 he commanded the arsenal in Baton Rouge, Louisiana. During these years he experimented with new forms of gunpowder and developed a perforated-cake and a mammoth (large-grain) form for use in large guns. By 1858 he had developed an improved configuration for columbiads cast by his method, and by 1860 his powder inventions were being adopted by Russia, Great Britain, and other nations. In that year, his work finally being accepted by the U.S. government, he began manufacturing 15-inch Rodman guns at the Watertown, Massachusetts, arsenal, of which he was commander. During the Civil War he turned out 12-, 15-, and 20-inch smoothbore and 12-inch rifled Rodman guns, and they were used for field and coast artillery and as naval guns on monitors of the John Ericsson type. He was promoted to major in June 1863. From 1864 the Rodman hollow-core cooling method was applied as well to the manufacture of shells. In March 1865 he was brevetted lieutenant colonel, colonel, and brigadier general for his services in the Ordnance Department. In August 1865 he was put in command of the Rock Island, Illinois, arsenal, and in March 1867 he was promoted to lieutenant colonel. Rodman died in Rock Island, Illinois, on June 7, 1871.

Rogers, Bernard William (1921–   ), army officer. Born on July 16, 1921, in Fairview, Kansas, Rogers attended Kansas State College (now University) for a year before entering West Point, from which he graduated, after an accelerated course, in 1943. For a year he served with the 275th Infantry Regiment, 70th Division, at Camp Adair, Oregon, receiving promotion to first lieutenant in December 1943; and during 1944–1946 he was an instructor and assistant to the superintendent at West Point, advancing to captain in February 1945. In 1946 he was appointed aide-de-camp to Gen. Mark W. Clark, then U.S. high commissioner in Austria and from June 1947 commander of the Sixth Army in San Francisco. Later in 1947 Rogers entered Oxford University, from which in 1950 he took B.A. and M.A. degrees in philosophy, politics, and economics. During 1950–1951 he was aide to the chief of Army Field Forces at Fort Monroe, Virginia. Promoted to major in July 1951, he graduated from the Infantry School, Fort Benning, Georgia, in 1952. From June to December 1952 he commanded a battalion of the 9th Infantry Regiment in combat in Korea, and he was then named aide for intelligence to Gen. Clark, now commander of the United Nations and U.S. Far Eastern commands. In August 1953 he was promoted to lieutenant colonel. He returned to the United States in 1954, graduated from the Command and General Staff College, Fort Leavenworth, Kansas, in 1955, and for a year commanded a battalion of the 23rd Infantry Regiment, 2nd Division, at Fort Lewis, Washington. In June 1956 he was assigned to duty in the office of the chief of staff, and during 1958–1959 he was executive and senior aide to the chief of staff, Gen. Maxwell D. Taylor. Rogers was promoted to colonel in September 1959, and in 1960 he graduated from the Army War College. He then joined the 24th Infantry Division in Augsburg, Germany, commanding the 1st Battle Group, 19th Infantry Regiment, for a few months and then serving as chief of staff of the division. In September 1962 he returned to Washington, D.C., as military assistant to the chairman of the Joint Chiefs of Staff, Gen. Taylor; he later became executive officer to Taylor and held the same post under the next chairman, Gen. Earle G. Wheeler. Promoted to temporary brigadier general in October 1966, Rogers was ordered to Vietnam as assistant commander of the 1st Infantry Division. In September 1967 he was named commandant of cadets at West Point. Two years later he took command of the 5th Infantry Division (Mechanized) and of Fort Carson, Colorado, receiving promotion to temporary major general in February 1970. In January 1971 he was appointed chief of legislative liaison for the army, and in November 1972, promoted to temporary lieutenant general, he was named deputy chief of staff for personnel. In November 1974 he was promoted to temporary general and made commander of the Army Forces Command at Fort McPherson, Georgia, and in July 1976 he was appointed by President Gerald R. Ford to succeed Gen. Frederick C. Weyand as chief of staff of the army. A highly decorated officer, Rogers brought an unusually scholarly background to the post.

Rogers, Robert (1731–1795), frontiersman and soldier. Born in Methuen, Massachusetts, on November 7, 1731, Rogers grew up in New Hampshire. He obtained what education he had from Indians and from his companions on hunting and exploring expeditions. He got into his first trouble in New Hampshire about 1755, when he was charged with counterfeiting; he got out of it in a way that he would many times later adopt, by volunteering for the expedition under Gen. (later Sir) William Johnson against the French at Crown Point. His daring and ingenuity in various scouting forays led to his promotion to captain of a company of rangers by Gov. William Shirley in March 1756. Two years later he was appointed by Gen. James Abercrombie major in command of nine ranger companies. He was at Halifax in 1757; at Ticonderoga with Abercrombie in 1758, a campaign in which, in the Battle on Snowshoes on March 13, 1758, at Lake George, he sustained heavy losses and escaped only by deceiving the Indians at what became known as Rogers' Rock; and at Crown Point with Gen. Jeffrey Amherst in 1759. In September–October 1759 he led a daring and harrowing expedition from Crown Point against the St. Francis Indians, an exploit marked by great courage, endurance, and ingenuity. Of the 180 or so men who set out with him, 142 lived to attack and destroy the St. Francis village on October 5, and 93 returned. After taking part in the Montreal campaign he was sent west to accept the surrender of French posts there, arriving at Detroit in November 1760. All in all, with his many daring raids and his sweeping excursions into enemy territory to obtain information and to ambush small detachments of troops, he emerged from the French and Indian War the most renowned and romantic military figure in the colonies. Rogers's Rangers, successful because of their adoption of the Indian tactics of secret march, ambush, and woodcraft, were nearly as famous for their rowdy humor as for their courage. Among those who received their early military training with Rogers were John Stark and Israel Putnam. Rogers's personal troubles returned with the peace. He was a bad administrator in the various frontier appointments given him by South Carolina and New York and a greedy trader who engaged in illicit dealings with the Indians, and when his debts reached unmanageable proportions he fled to England in 1765. There he published his *Journals* and his *Concise Account of North America*, both more renowned for their descriptions of frontier experience and adventure than for their accuracy, and a play, *Ponteach: or the Savages of America*, 1766. Lionized as a hero, he was appointed commander of the fort at Maclanac (Michilimackinac) in present-day Michigan and lived there for two years, during which he dispatched Jonathan Carver to explore the country that became Minnesota. His maladministration and outright dishonesty in his post led to charges being made against him by Sir William Johnson and Gen. Thomas Gage, and he was thrown into debtors' prison in England in 1769 after making further vain pleas for a lucrative position in the service. He was arrested by George Washington soon after his return to America in 1775, but he escaped and organized two Loyalist "Queen's Rangers" companies; in battles of the New York campaign, around White Plains, he failed to win military success, however, and he was removed from command. Proscribed by New Hampshire and plagued by his own dishonesty and dissipation, he sailed back to England in 1780 and lived out the rest of his life in dire poverty. He died in London on May 18, 1795.

Roosevelt, Theodore (1858–1919), twenty-sixth president of the United States. Born in New York City on October 27, 1858, Roosevelt came of a well-to-do family long established in New York. In his youth he set methodically about overcoming his physical weakness and developed his lifelong taste for the vigorous, rugged life. He graduated from Harvard in 1880 after winning election to Phi Beta Kappa and entered the Columbia University School of Law but soon withdrew to run successfully for the state assembly in 1881. During three one-year terms in that body he was nominally a Republican, but he acted and voted as an outspoken independent. During these years he also undertook the writing of history as a serious and continuing avocation, beginning with *The Naval War of 1812*, 1882. With the defeat of his progressive faction that opposed James G. Blaine at the Republican national convention of 1884, following upon the death of his wife in the same year, Roosevelt retired to a ranch in the Dakota Territory where he remained until called back to New York City for the mayoral election of 1886, in which he ran third to the Single-Tax candidate, Henry George, and the victorious Democrat, Abram S. Hewitt. He again retired from politics and devoted himself largely to writing, publishing *Hunting Trips of a Ranch Man*, 1885; *Ranch-Life and the Hunting Trail*, 1888; biographies of Thomas Hart Benton and Gouverneur Morris; and in 1889 the first two volumes of *The Winning of the West* (the third and fourth volumes followed in 1894 and 1896). In May 1889 he was appointed civil service commissioner by President Benjamin Harrison, and he served in that position, which he characteristically made a dramatic and much publicized one, until 1895, when he became president of New York City's Board of Police Commissioners. Continuing to battle corruption whenever he found it, he maintained his reputation as a reformer and this, together with his strong support of William McKinley in the 1896 presidential election, won him appointment in 1897 as assistant secretary of the navy. In that post he advocated a strong military stance for the United States and acted to achieve his aim, sometimes circumventing or assuming the authority of his superior. In May 1898 he resigned to join Col. Leonard Wood in organizing the 1st U.S. Volunteer Cavalry for service in Cuba during the Spanish–American War. Roosevelt succeeded to command of the regiment soon after its arrival—at half strength and without horses—in Cuba in June and as usual attracted great publicity to himself and the colorful "Rough Riders." He cut a spectacular figure and led the much-publicized charge up Kettle Hill (on the right wing of the general assault known as the battle of San Juan Hill) near Santiago de Cuba on July 1. That exploit, together with the publicity attending the "round-robin" letter to Gen. William R. Shafter on camp conditions, made him a national figure. (Of his book *The Rough Riders*, 1899, "Mr. Dooley" said it ought to have been called "Alone in Cubia.") Immediately upon his return home he was nominated and elected governor of New York. In two years in Albany his reformist views and insistence on competence in officeholders so exasperated Sen. Thomas C. Platt and other Republican machine leaders that, in order to remove him from New York politics, they pushed for his nomination for vice-president in 1900. He accepted the bid, but soon after the election he found himself so bored with the job that he considered returning to the study of law or joining a university faculty. Six months after his inauguration, on September 14, 1901, McKinley died of an assassin's bullet and Roosevelt, not yet forty-three, became President. While pledging a continuation of his predecessor's policies, he in fact pursued a course more suggestive of Western populist ideas than of the business-oriented views of the late protégé of Mark Hanna. Faced with a conservative, hostile Congress, however, the President, an excellent administrator and a subtle politician, chose to work through an expansion of the ill defined power of executive authority. He began by revitalizing the Sherman Anti-Trust Act of 1890 and, through Attorney General Philander C. Knox, hauled more than 30 corporations into court on antitrust charges. The most notable of the "trust-busting" cases were those against the Northern Securities Company and the Standard Oil Company of New Jersey, ordered dissolved by the Supreme Court in 1904 and 1911 respectively. When the anthracite miners' strike of 1902 began to cause massive coal shortages, he forcefully persuaded the recalcitrant operators to negotiate with the miners' union by threatening to use the army to work the mines. In February 1903, on his recommendation, the cabinet-level Department of Commerce and Labor was created by Congress. In foreign affairs he exercised power even more vigorously. He supported Secretary of State John Hay's "Open Door" initiatives in regard to China and was firm in his insistence that the United States be the dominant power in the Pacific. In 1902 and 1903, when first Venezuela and then the Dominican Republic were faced with intervention by European nations because of defaulted debts, he assumed for the United States responsibility for the payment of debts by Latin American nations; in December 1904, with soon-to-be Secretary of State Elihu Root, he announced what came to be known as the "Roosevelt corollary" to the Monroe Doctrine, stating that the United States would be, in effect, the armed policeman and defender of the Western Hemisphere. In the Dominican Republic the United States took full control of national finance in 1905 through an appointed comptroller. In 1903 the government of Colombia rejected a treaty allowing construction of a canal through a U.S.-controlled section of the Isthmus of Panama; but Roosevelt saw to it that a revolutionary secession by the territory involved was encouraged and protected by the presence of U.S. warships, and shortly thereafter, in November 1903, the Canal Zone

was ceded to the United States by the new nation of Panama. "I took the Isthmus, started the Canal," he explained years later, "and then left Congress—not to debate the Canal, but to debate me." The President maintained a close interest in the construction of the canal and, in visiting the site later, became the first incumbent president to leave U.S. soil. His later dispatch of a part of the U.S. Fleet on a world cruise in 1907–1909 (under Adm. Robley D. Evans and then Adm. Charles S. Sperry) perfectly exemplified his fundamental dictum in foreign policy: "Speak softly and carry a big stick." In 1904 he was reelected easily over Democratic candidate Alton B. Parker by 336 electoral votes to 140; he subsequently announced that he would regard his first three years in the White House as constituting a first term and would therefore not run again in 1908. In 1905 he took the initiative in arranging negotiations to end the Russo-Japanese War, culminating in the peace conference at Portsmouth, New Hampshire, in August, a service for which he was awarded the Nobel Peace Prize in 1906. In June 1906 he secured passage of both the Pure Food and Drug Act and the Hepburn Act, which greatly strengthened the Interstate Commerce Commission. Throughout his seven years as president, he worked (with and through such conservationists as Gifford Pinchot and John Muir) for an expanded government role in the conservation of natural resources, increasing the extent of national preserves nearly fivefold, and he was responsible for the New-lands Reclamation Act of 1902, which provided for federal sponsorship of irrigation and reclamation projects. As 1908 approached he began to regret his promise not to run, but he promoted the nomination of his close friend William Howard Taft, then secretary of war, as his successor. Soon after leaving office he set out on an extended African safari, followed by a tour of Europe during which he consulted with many heads of state. Returning in 1910, he immediately resumed his political activity. As Taft slowly allied himself with the conservative wing of the Republican party, Roosevelt's views moved leftward, and the breach between the two men was mirrored in the party ranks. He elaborated his earlier ideas of a "Square Deal" for all citizens, particularly for working men, and on a Western speaking tour that year delivered his famed "New Nationalism" address (at Osawatomie, Kansas, on August 31) that enunciated the principles later found in his 1912 platform. As the 1912 Republican national convention approached, he began to gather delegate votes for a showdown with Taft; he won several state primaries, but Taft controlled the party machinery and the convention. Rejected by the Republicans, Roosevelt immediately formed the Progressive party—soon dubbed the "Bull Moose" party after a comment by Roosevelt on his physical fitness—and, displacing Senator Robert M. La Follette, he accepted its nomination in August, with Gov. Hiram Johnson of California in second place on the ticket. The Republican split caused by the Progressive defection allowed Democrat Woodrow Wilson to win the election, with Taft running third (the electoral vote split 435 to 88 to 8). Roosevelt took an active dislike to Wilson and his policies, particularly that of neutrality toward the European war, and in 1916, although he again lost the Republican nomination, campaigned against him. He took the lead in promoting military preparedness and in 1915 joined his old friend Gen. Wood in establishing a summer training camp for civilians at Plattsburg, New York. When the United States entered World War I, Roosevelt unsuccessfully sought a military command and spoke widely in support of the war effort. He continued to publish books, among them *Progressive Principles*, 1913; *History as Literature*, 1913; *An Autobiography*, 1913; and *America and the World War*, 1915, as well as articles, for a total of more than 2000 titles. He still had hopes for the Republican nomination in 1920 when, weakened by a lingering illness contracted during a South American exploring journey in 1914, he died suddenly on January 6, 1919, at his home, Sagamore Hill, near Oyster Bay, Long Island, New York. One of the most colorful men ever to occupy the presidency, Roosevelt was widely admired for his boundless gusto, his devotion to the "strenuous life," his nearly jingoistic nationalism, and his manifest integrity. Remarkably foresighted in seeing the need for political adjustment to a new economic age, he succeeded mainly in setting the stage for changes to come.

Roosevelt, Theodore, Jr. (1887–1944), businessman, sportsman, and army officer. Born on September 13, 1887, at the family home in Oyster Bay, Long Island, New York, Roosevelt was the eldest son of (later President) Theodore Roosevelt. He graduated from Harvard in 1908, worked for the Hartford Carpet Company for four years, and then entered banking in New York. In 1915 he joined his father and Gen. Leonard Wood in organizing the summer training camp at Plattsburg, New York, as part of a preparedness campaign, and on the entry of the United States into World War I in April 1917 he took a commission as major in the 26th Infantry. He went to France in June and saw action with the 1st Division at Cantigny and Soissons, being wounded in both battles, and in the St. Mihiel and Meuse–Argonne offensives. He was promoted to lieutenant colonel in September 1918, and in 1919 he transferred into the army reserve as a colonel. He helped organize the American Legion in 1919 and in the same year was elected to the New York legislature; he was reelected in 1920. In 1921 he was appointed assistant secretary of the navy by President Warren G. Harding, and in 1922 he was an adviser to the U.S. delegation at the Limitation of Arms Conference in Wash-

ington. In October 1924 he resigned his post to campaign unsuccessfully against Alfred E. Smith for the governorship of New York. In 1925 and again in 1928–1929 he and his younger brother Kermit organized and led, for the Field Museum of Natural History in Chicago, zoological expeditions into central and eastern Asia, collecting numerous rare specimens, including the first giant panda seen in America. The two collaborated in writing *East of the Sun and West of the Moon*, 1926. Other writings of his included *Rank and File*, 1928, *Trailing the Giant Panda*, 1929, and *Taps* (with Grantland Rice), 1932. In 1929 he was appointed governor of Puerto Rico by President Herbert Hoover, and in 1932 he was named governor-general of the Philippines; in both posts he contributed significantly to the improvement of education and health care. He resigned the Philippines post in 1933. In 1934 he was named chairman of the board of the American Express Company, and he had various other business interests as well. He was also active in the national council of the Boy Scouts of America. In April 1941 he was recalled to active duty in the army as colonel of the 26th Infantry, and in December he was promoted to brigadier general. He took part with the 1st Division in the Tunisian and Sicilian campaigns in 1942–1943 and on June 6, 1944, led it ashore at Utah Beach, Normandy, the only general officer in the first wave of the assault. While serving as military governor of Cherbourg, he died suddenly on July 12, 1944. He was awarded the Medal of Honor posthumously in September.

Root, Elihu (1845–1937), lawyer, public official, and diplomat. Born in Clinton, New York, on February 15, 1845, Root graduated from Hamilton College in 1864 and after a year teaching school entered the law school of the University of the City of New York (now New York University). He graduated in 1867, was admitted to the bar, and, soon forming his own law firm in New York City, became within a few years one of the nation's leading corporation lawyers. Although not actively involved in politics, he was identifiably a Republican with leanings toward the party's conservative wing. He nonetheless became a close friend and adviser to Theodore Roosevelt while Roosevelt was in New York state politics, and he maintained the association for many years. In March 1883 he was appointed U.S. attorney for the southern district of New York, serving until July 1885. In 1894 he played a leading role in the state constitutional convention. He became secretary of war in August 1899 at President William McKinley's invitation and in four years in that office directed the department's activities more effectively than had any of his predecessors since the Civil War. Charged with the administration of territories acquired in the Spanish-American War, Root quickly arranged for an effective, conservative management of Puerto Rico through the Foraker Act of 1900, granting the island dependency much-needed tariff advantages, and then turned to the more difficult problem of Cuba. He chose Gen. Leonard Wood as military governor and in 1901 drafted the Platt Amendment, outlining safeguards for U.S. interests in Cuba that were to be included in the island's new constitution, to take effect with independence the following year. In the Philippines there was open insurrection against U.S. occupation; Root dispatched more troops there and in 1900 sent a governing commission, headed by William Howard Taft, with detailed instructions that amounted to a constitution and a legal and judicial code. The instructions were affirmed by Congress in 1902. Of the War Department itself Root effected a reorganization that greatly improved its efficiency and the army's readiness. Moving slowly in the face of entrenched bureau chiefs, he accepted the recommendation of an army board headed by Gen. William Ludlow and established in November 1901 the War College Board, which two years later became the Army War College. A long campaign of congressional lobbying preceded the establishment in August 1903 of a General Staff, with a chief of staff replacing the post of commanding general; the change was scheduled tactfully to follow the retirement of Gen. Nelson A. Miles. The Militia (Dick) Act of January 1903 constituted the various state National Guards as a national reserve militia and set federal standards for training. The principle of rotating staff and line assignments was established, and the total strength of the army was raised to over 88,000. Root resigned from the cabinet in January 1904 and returned to his law practice, only to be recalled by President Theodore Roosevelt to succeed the late Secretary of State John M. Hay in July 1905. He managed, despite Roosevelt's interventionist diplomacy, to improve greatly U.S. relations with Latin America during a tour in 1906; U.S.-Japanese affairs were smoothed by the "gentleman's agreement" of February 1907, whereby Japanese emigration to the United States was halted, and the Root-Takahira Agreement of November 1908, mutually supporting the Open Door, the status quo in the Pacific, and other formal points; and he negotiated numerous arbitration treaties with European nations. He brought the protracted dispute over North Atlantic fisheries to an end and strengthened U.S.-Canadian relations. For these accomplishments and for his earlier success in constructing an enlightened policy for U.S. possessions he was awarded the Nobel Peace Prize in 1912. He also made considerable progress in professionalizing the diplomatic corps. Root resigned his post in January 1909 and was immediately elected from New York to the Senate, where he remained until 1915, a Taft Republican and a leading opponent of President Woodrow Wilson. In 1910 he was named to the Permanent Court of Arbitration at The Hague. His long

friendship with Roosevelt ended in 1912 when he presided over the Republican national convention that rejected the bid of the former President and renominated Taft, to whom Root had earlier promised his backing. Out of the Senate Root continued to oppose Wilson until the United States entered World War I. In April 1917 he was sent by Wilson to Russia in a futile attempt to bolster the government of Alexander Kerensky. He supported, with minor reservations, the Treaty of Versailles and the Covenant of the League of Nations, breaking with Henry Cabot Lodge on the issue. In 1920 he was appointed to a commission of jurists charged with framing the statute for the Permanent Court of International Justice (World Court), and in 1929 he helped revise the statute; he was a constant though unsuccessful advocate of U.S. membership in the Court. President Warren G. Harding appointed him one of the U.S. delegates to the 1921 Washington arms-limitation conference. In his later years he was active in the direction of a number of Andrew Carnegie's philanthropic activities, particularly the Carnegie Endowment for International Peace, of which he was president from 1910 to 1925. Among Root's published works were *Experiment in Government and the Essentials of the Constitution*, 1913; *Military and Colonial Policy of The United States*, 1916; *Russia and The United States*, 1917; and *Men and Policies*, 1924. He died in New York City on February 7, 1937.

Rosecrans, William Starke (1819–1898), army officer and public official. Born in Kingston, Ohio, on September 6, 1819, Rosecrans graduated from West Point in 1842 and was commissioned in the engineers. He was assigned first to work on fortifications at Hampton Roads, Virginia, and later, after a period as an instructor at West Point in 1843–1847, he served at various posts in New England. He resigned his commission in April 1854, having attained the rank of first lieutenant, to enter business. The outbreak of the Civil War brought him back into the service as a volunteer aide to Gen. George B. McClellan in April 1861 and in June as colonel of the 23rd Ohio Volunteers and then as a regular brigadier general. He served under McClellan in western Virginia, and, succeeding him in July as commander of the Department of Western Virginia, he oversaw the operations that led to the complete expulsion of Confederate forces and the formation of the state of West Virginia. His most notable victories were over Col. John Pegram at Rich Mountain, July 11, and over Gen. John B. Floyd at Carnifex Ferry, September 10. In April 1862 he was ordered west, and he commanded the left wing of Gen. John Pope's Army of the Mississippi during the Corinth campaign. In June he succeeded to command of the army. On September 19 he managed to drive Gen. Sterling Price out of Iuka, Mississippi, and on October 3–4 repelled, with heavy losses on both sides, Gen. Earl Van Dorn's attacks on Corinth. Appointed major general of volunteers, he then succeeded Gen. Don Carlos Buell in command of the Department of the Cumberland, reorganizing his field forces as the Army of the Cumberland. Two months later he moved against Gen. Braxton Bragg and attacked him at Murfreesboro (Stones River), Tennessee, on December 31. Bragg retreated on January 3. In June 1863, after months of delay that exasperated his superiors, Rosecrans moved again, in the direction of Chattanooga. He masterfully outmaneuvered Bragg for three months, making great territorial gains without battle in what was called the Tullahoma campaign, but at Chickamauga Creek on September 18–20 Bragg, reinforced by Gen. James Longstreet's corps, attacked furiously. Faulty orders confused Union movements, and both sides retreated exhausted from the battle. Only the tactics of Gen. George H. Thomas, the "Rock of Chickamauga," had averted total destruction of Rosecrans's army. Rosecrans fell back and allowed himself to be shut up in Chattanooga, and in October he was relieved of command by Gen. Ulysses S. Grant. After a year in command of the Department of Missouri he was sent in December 1864 to await orders in Cincinnati. He at length resigned his commission in March 1867, having in March 1865 been brevetted major general in the regular army for his services at Murfreesboro. Later he was U.S. minister to Mexico, 1868–1869; he engaged in mining operations in Mexico and California for the next decade and served as a member from California in the House of Representatives from 1881 to 1885. From 1885 to 1893 he was register of the U.S. treasury. He died near Redondo Beach, California, on March 11, 1898.

Rowan, Andrew Summers (1857–1943), army officer. Born on April 23, 1857, in Gap Mills, Virginia (now West Virginia), Rowan graduated from West Point in 1881 and was commissioned in the infantry. He spent eight years in frontier duty from Texas to the Dakotas, was promoted to first lieutenant in November 1890, and in 1891–1892 performed survey work in Central America with the Intercontinental Railway Commission. From 1893 to 1898 he was in the adjutant general's office in Washington, D.C. In April 1898 he was appointed military attaché to Chile, but he was detached from that assignment shortly thereafter and given a secret assignment to secure information about the strength of Cuban insurrectionary forces from their leader, Gen. Calixto Garcia. He landed in Cuba from an open sailboat on April 24, the day Spain declared war on the United States, and he was thus the first American officer on hostile soil in the Spanish–American War. He located Garcia in Oriente province, secured the necessary information, and left Cuba on May 5. He had already been promoted to captain during his sojourn in Cuba,

and in May he was appointed lieutenant colonel of volunteers on the staff of Gen. Nelson A. Miles. He took part in the brief Puerto Rico campaign in July and later served in the Cuban occupation forces. Mustered out of volunteer service in March 1899, he served in the Philippines until 1902. During 1902–1903 he taught military science at Kansas State Agricultural College (now Kansas State University), and he then served briefly at Fort Riley, Kansas, at West Point, Kentucky, and at American Lake, Washington. In 1905 he returned to the Philippines, receiving promotion to major in October. He returned to the United States in 1907 and until his retirement in October 1909 was stationed at Fort Douglas, Utah. He died in San Francisco on January 10, 1943. Lt. Rowan is remembered for his Cuban exploit, as freely adapted and moralized in 1899 by Elbert Hubbard in the ceaselessly reprinted "A Message to Garcia." In actuality Rowan bore information and messages *from* Garcia.

Rowan, Stephen Clegg (1808–1890), naval officer. Born near Dublin, Ireland, on December 25, 1808, Rowan came to the United States in 1819, joining his family, who had preceded him, in Piqua, Ohio. He entered the navy as a midshipman in February 1826 and made his first cruise on the *Vincennes,* on which he circumnavigated the globe in 1826–1830. After two years on a revenue cutter in New York harbor he was ordered to the West India Squadron, where he served on the schooner *Shark* and the sloop *Vandalia* and in 1836–1837 took part in several river operations against the Seminole Indians of Florida. Promoted to lieutenant in March 1837, he was attached to the Coast Survey in 1838–1840, served on the *Delaware* in the Brazil and Mediterranean squadrons from 1841 to 1844, and in 1845 was assigned to the *Cyane* in the Pacific Squadron. In 1846 the *Cyane,* then under Capt. Samuel F. Du Pont, took part in Commodore John D. Sloat's operations in California. Rowan participated in the capture of Monterey on July 7 by sailors and marines under Capt. William Mervine and directed the building of earthworks, stockades, and other defenses. On July 29 he commanded a landing party from the *Cyane* that took possession of San Diego. Rowan later joined his small force to the army under Commodore Robert F. Stockton and Gen. Stephen W. Kearny and took part in the battles of San Gabriel and Mesa, January 9–10, 1847. On November 20 he commanded the boats in a combined land-water attack on Mexican forces inland from Mazatlán, and on February 14, 1848, he led a landing party to the relief of a small American garrison near San José. Rowan later was on ordnance duty at the New York navy yard, 1850–1853 and again 1858–1861, and filled other routine assignments, receiving promotion to commander in September 1855. Early in 1861 he took command of the steam sloop *Pawnee,* which for a time after the outbreak of the Civil War was nearly the only naval protection for Washington, D.C. He took part in the unsuccessful effort to relieve Fort Sumter in April, and on May 25 he attacked Confederate batteries on Aquia Creek, firing the first shot of the war from a naval vessel. He took part in the attack of the Potomac Flotilla, under Flag-Officer James H. Ward, on Aquia Creek on June 1. The *Pawnee* was in Flag-Officer Silas H. Stringham's squadron in the attack on Fort Clark and Fort Hatteras on August 27–29. In February 1862 he took part in the joint army-navy operation at Roanoke Island under Gen. Ambrose E. Burnside and Flag-Officer Louis M. Goldsborough. Commanding the army and navy gunboat squadrons from the steamer *Delaware,* he covered Burnside's landing and on February 8 attacked the Confederate gunboat squadron under Flag-Officer William F. Lynch. Rowan drove Lynch back to shelter at Elizabeth City, where the next day he renewed the attack and destroyed three of Lynch's six gunboats. He then occupied Elizabeth City and Edenton. He continued to operate in and out of the North Carolina sounds and cooperated with Burnside in the capture of New Bern on March 14 and Beaufort on April 25. In July he was promoted to captain and commodore on the same day. He was later put in command of the *New Ironsides* of the South Atlantic Blockading Squadron. The *New Ironsides* was Adm. John A. B. Dahlgren's flagship during the numerous attacks on Charleston in July–September 1863 and took more than 150 hits. Early in 1864 he was acting commander of the squadron in Dahlgren's absence, but in August he was detached to command naval forces in the North Carolina sounds. He ended the war on waiting orders. Promoted to rear admiral in July 1866, Rowan commanded the Norfolk navy yard in 1866–1867, the Asiatic Squadron in 1867–1870, being promoted to vice admiral in August 1870, and the New York navy yard in 1872–1879. He was president of the Board of Examiners in 1879–1881, governor of the Naval Asylum at Philadelphia in 1881, superintendent of the Naval Observatory in 1882, and chairman of the Lighthouse Board from 1883 until his retirement in 1889. He died in Washington, D.C., on March 31, 1890.

Ruffin, Edmund (1794–1865), agriculturalist. Born on January 5, 1794, in Prince George County, Virginia, Ruffin entered the College of William and Mary in 1809 but remained only briefly. He served for six months in the army during the War of 1812 and in 1813 returned home to take charge of his late father's farm. As was true of much of Virginia at the time, the soil on Ruffin's farm had been depleted by one-crop cultivation and overuse. He set about experimenting with various treatments and methods to revitalize the soil; by 1818 he was able to announce

considerable success in using marl (an earth containing a large proportion of calcium carbonate) on the soil, together with fertilizing, crop rotation, and improved patterns of plowing and drainage. A published article detailing his results in 1821 grew into a widely influential book, *An Essay on Calcareous Manures,* 1832, and continued to expand through several editions. He was elected as a Whig to the Virginia senate in 1823 and remained in that body for three years. From 1833 to 1842 he published the *Farmer's Register,* a journal promoting scientific agriculture. In 1842 he became agricultural surveyor for the state of South Carolina; two years later he refused to become the first president of the Virginia State Agricultural Society, but he accepted the presidency in 1852. He continued to publish articles and books on the improvement of agriculture, notably *Essays and Notes on Agriculture,* 1855, and was a much sought lecturer. In his later years he changed his political affiliation from the Whigs to the Democratic party as, with the crisis between North and South worsening, he became an outspoken defender of slavery and states' rights and an early advocate—a "fire-eater"—of Southern secession. His views were given wide circulation in Southern newspapers, in *De Bow's Review,* and in his many pamphlets. Finally, as the oldest member of the Palmetto Guards of Charleston, he was granted the honor of firing the first shot on Fort Sumter on April 12, 1861. He served sporadically in the Confederate army during the Civil War. Despondent over the South's defeat, he took his own life on June 18, 1865, at his plantation, Redmoor, in Amelia County, Virginia.

Russell, John Henry (1872–1947), marine officer. Born on November 14, 1872, at Mare Island, California, Russell was the son of a naval officer. He graduated from the Naval Academy in 1892 and two years later was commissioned a second lieutenant in the marine corps. He served aboard the *Massachusetts* of Commodore Winfield S. Schley's Flying Squadron in the Spanish–American War and received promotions to first lieutenant in November 1898 and to captain in March 1899. Later he was stationed at Guam and then aboard the *Oregon* in 1902–1904. He commanded a marine officers' school at Annapolis, Maryland, for a time, advancing to major in July 1906, and after tours in Hawaii and the Canal Zone was on the staff of the Naval War College in 1908–1910. He was attached to the U.S. legation in Peking, China, in 1910–1913 and in April–December 1914 took part with the 3rd Marine Regiment in the occupation of Veracruz, Mexico. For three years thereafter he was in the office of naval intelligence in Washington, D.C. In 1917, by then a colonel, he took command of the 3rd Marine Regiment in Santo Domingo, Dominican Republic; a short time later the regiment was ordered to Haiti and Russell became commander of all marines, constituting the 1st Provisional Brigade, on the island. Promoted to brigadier general in January 1922, he was appointed high commissioner to Haiti with rank of ambassador in February. With his aid much progress was made in developing the country, improving health and sanitation facilities, and establishing a stable political and economic order. He remained in Haiti until U.S. forces were withdrawn in 1931. He then commanded the marine barracks at Quantico, Virginia, until February 1933, when he became assistant to Gen. Ben H. Fuller, commandant of the marine corps, receiving promotion to major general in September. In March 1934 he was named to succeed Fuller as commandant of the corps, and he held that post until his retirement in November 1936. He died in Coronado, California, on March 6, 1947.

Rutherford, Griffith (1731?–1800?), Revolutionary militia officer. Born about 1731 in Ireland, Rutherford emigrated to America at some time and settled in the vicinity of Salisbury, North Carolina. In 1775 he was elected to the provincial congress, and in June 1776 he was appointed by the congress brigadier general of the North Carolina militia. In September he set out at the head of 2400 men to suppress the Cherokee Indians who, aided by Loyalists, had been ravaging the frontier settlements. He was reinforced in that campaign by some 2000 men led by Col. Andrew Williamson of South Carolina. In all, 36 Indian villages were destroyed, crops were burned, and the Cherokee were driven west into the Great Smoky Mountains. According to tradition Daniel Boone took part in the final battle of the campaign at Nantahala (or Wayah) Gap. On the day of the disastrous battle of Camden, South Carolina, August 16, 1780, Rutherford commanded a brigade of North Carolina militia at nearby Sanders Creek and was taken prisoner. Held first in Charleston and then in St. Augustine, Florida, until exchanged in June 1781, he reoccupied Wilmington when that city was evacuated by the British following Yorktown in October. After the Revolution Rutherford served occasionally in the North Carolina legislature. Sometime after 1786 he moved west to Tennessee, and in September 1794 he was appointed president of the legislative council of the Territory of Tennessee. He died in Tennessee about 1800.

Ryan, John Dale (1915–   ), air force officer. Born on December 10, 1915, in Cherokee, Iowa, Ryan graduated from West Point in 1938 and was assigned to the Air Corps. The following year he completed pilot training at Kelly Field, Texas, remaining there as an instructor for two years. He was promoted to first lieutenant in October 1940, to temporary captain a year later, and to temporary major and lieutenant colonel in March and July 1942. From February 1944 to April 1945 he saw duty with the Fifteenth Air Force (Gen. Nathan F. Twining) in Italy, commanding the 2nd Bombardment Group, later serving on the staff of the 5th Bombardment Wing, and advancing to temporary colonel in August 1944. From 1946 to 1948 he was assigned to the 58th Bombardment Wing. He commanded the 509th Bombardment Wing at Walker Air Force Base, New Mexico, in 1948–1951 and the 97th at Biggs Air Force Base, Texas, in 1951–1952. Promoted to permanent colonel in July 1952 and to temporary brigadier general in September, Ryan commanded the 810th Air Division at Biggs in 1952–1953 and the 19th Air Division at Carswell Air Force Base, Texas, in 1953–1956. Promoted to temporary major general in October 1956, he served as director of matériel of the Strategic Air Command, Offutt Air Force Base, Nebraska, from that year to 1960. In the latter year he was named commander of the Sixteenth Air Force, based at Torrejon Air Force Base in Spain, and in July 1961, promoted to temporary lieutenant general, he took command of the Second Air Force, a major SAC component, at Barksdale Air Force Base, Louisiana. In 1963–1964 he was inspector general of the air force, and in August 1964 he became vice commander and then, in December, with the temporary rank of general, commander of SAC, with headquarters at Offutt. In February 1967 he moved to command of the Pacific Air Forces, at Hickam Air Force Base, Hawaii. In August 1968 he became vice chief of staff of the air force, and in August 1969 he succeeded Gen. John P. McConnell as chief of staff, serving until his retirement in July 1973. He was succeeded as chief of staff of the air force by Gen. George S. Brown.

S

St. Clair, Arthur (1736–1818), army officer and public official. Born in Thurso, Caithness, Scotland, on March 23 (old style), 1736, St. Clair entered the British army in May 1757 and served in the American colonies and Canada, advancing to lieutenant in April 1759, until April 1762. He then resigned his commission to settle on an estate in western Pennsylvania, where he engaged in farming and the fur trade. From 1771 to 1775 he served in the colonial government of Pennsylvania, from 1773 as justice of Westmoreland County, a post that thrust him into the center of the rival claims of Pennsylvania and Virginia to the territory surrounding Fort Pitt. His just treatment of the Indians doubtless saved Pennsylvania from involvement in Lord Dunmore's War in 1774. St. Clair was appointed colonel of militia in July 1775; in January 1776 he resigned his civil offices and was commissioned colonel of the 2nd Pennsylvania Infantry in Continental service. He took part in Gen. John Sullivan's retreat from Canada and as brigadier general (from August 1776) in command of New Jersey militia was at Trenton, December 26, and Princeton, January 3, 1777. Promoted to major general in February, he was placed in command of Fort Ticonderoga and the northern defenses. On the approach of Gen. John Burgoyne in the summer he found himself outnumbered (9000 to 2300) and threatened on the flanks, so on July 6 he secretly abandoned Fort Ticonderoga. The pursuing British defeated a portion of his command under Gen. Seth Warner at Hubbardton, July 7, but the remnants of his forces reached safety at Fort Edward on July 12 and formed the nucleus of the army that would later defeat Burgoyne. At the time his actions were widely criticized, and although St. Clair served as an aide to Gen. George Washington at Brandywine, September 11, he saw little more action in the war, notwithstanding a complete acquittal in a court-martial in September 1778. After the war he settled again in Pennsylvania and became involved in state politics. For two years, 1785 to 1787, he was a delegate to Congress under the Articles of Confederation, serving as president of the body in 1787. When the Northwest Ordinance of July 1787 created the Northwest Territory, he was made its governor. The seat of the territorial government was at Marietta from July 1788; he moved it in 1790 to Losantiville, which he renamed Cincinnati. His tenure in office worked neither to his advantage nor to that of the territory. He was particularly unfortunate in his dealings with the Indians. The tribes west of the Alleghenies had been in a state of agitation since the French and Indian War because of the accelerating loss of their lands. The advance of white men into the Ohio valley after the Revolution heightened their fears, and they were determined, with the aid of their British allies, to resist further encroachments. On January 9, 1789, St. Clair presided over the signing of the treaty of Fort Harmar, which was highly unfavorable to the Indians. Within the year the treaty, plus raids made by frontier whites, had started a new Indian war. An expedition under Gen. Josiah Harmar in 1790 ended disastrously, and in March 1791 St. Clair was commissioned major general (making him the senior officer of the U.S. army) and ordered to mount another expedition. Recruiting and training were very poorly handled, and it was September before St. Clair was able to march from Fort Washington at Cincinnati for the Maumee country to the north. En route he built Fort Hamilton and Fort Jefferson. About 22 miles north of the latter, on November 4, 1791, he was attacked in his camp by a body of Indians led by Little Turtle; St. Clair's troops, superior in numbers but largely untrained militia, were badly defeated. (With this victory the Indians redoubled their efforts to drive the whites out of Ohio, and the war was not ended until their defeat by Gen. Anthony Wayne's troops in 1794.) Although exonerated of blame for his defeat, St. Clair resigned from the army in March 1792, continuing to serve as governor, however. In addition to failing against the Indians, St. Clair did little to win the confidence of settlers in the territory. He was an aristocrat and a Federalist, while most of the frontiersmen were poor and inclined toward Jeffersonian democracy. He also intrigued for several years to prevent statehood for Ohio, but the move for statehood nevertheless succeeded in 1802. When he denounced the enabling act, President Thomas Jefferson removed him from office in November of that year. The rest of his life was spent at his home near Ligonier, Pennsylvania, where, after losing his wealth, he passed his last years in poverty. He died in Greensburg, Pennsylvania, on August 31, 1818.

Saltonstall, Dudley (1738–1796), Revolutionary naval officer. Born in New London, Connecticut, on September 8, 173ª, Saltonstall was of a family long influential in colonal affairs. He went to sea at an early age and was in the merchant service until the Revolution, except for a period during the French and

Indian War when he sailed as a privateer. On December 22, 1775, he was appointed by Congress captain of the ship *Alfred*, flagship of the Continental fleet under Commodore Esek Hopkins. In February the fleet sailed for the Bahamas, and on March 3 a landing party of 250 marines under Capt. Samuel Nicholas went ashore at New Providence from the *Alfred* and captured the town, the fort, and quantities of valuable military stores. On the return voyage the *Alfred* captured the brig *Bolton* and two merchant prizes near Block Island on April 5. Early in the morning of April 6 the fleet encountered the large British ship *Glasgow*, but after a four-hour battle it escaped, attesting to the yet-untrained condition of the Continental crews. Hopkins was later to suffer for the failure to subdue the *Glasgow*, but Saltonstall survived inquiry to be appointed fourth on the navy captains' list in October 1776. He later commanded the *Trumbull* with some success. In July 1779 he was given command of an expedition mounted by the state of Massachusetts to Penobscot Bay, where in June a British force from Halifax had taken possession of Castine. Sailing on the frigate *Warren* with the brig *Diligent*, sloop *Providence*, and 16 other armed vessels, in all more than 200 guns, along with 24 transports carrying a force of 900 militiamen under Gen. Solomon Lovell, Saltonstall arrived at Penobscot Bay on July 25. He refused to enter the harbor and engage the 3 British sloops defending Castine with 56 guns, and gave no support to the militia after landing it. The fort could not be taken without either Saltonstall's aid, which he continued to refuse, or reinforcements, which were not to be had. Finally, on August 13, a British squadron led by the 64-gun *Raisonable* arrived, and Saltonstall's fleet fled up the Penobscot River, taking the militia along. Two American vessels were captured; the rest were destroyed by their crews. The disaster cost Massachusetts virtually its entire fleet and a great deal of scarce currency. Saltonstall was dismissed from the service in October 1779. Later in the war he commanded the privateer *Minerva*, and afterwards he returned to the merchant service. He died in Haiti sometime in 1796.

Sampson, Deborah (1760–1827), Revolutionary soldier. Born on December 17, 1760, in Plympton, Massachusetts, Deborah Sampson was put into service at the age of ten by her widowed mother, and she lived thereafter in Middleborough. About 1779 she left service and became a school teacher. In 1782 she decided to join the fight for independence. After one attempt was discovered, she succeeded in disguising herself as a man—she was tall, strong, and well coordinated—and enlisted in May at Uxbridge, Massachusetts, as a private in Capt. George Webb's company of the 4th Massachusetts Regiment under the name Robert Shurtleff. For over a year she served capably and without detection. Soon after the regi-

ment was ordered to West Point she received a saber wound in a skirmish near Tarrytown, New York, and a few weeks later she took a musket ball in a fight near East Chester. This second, fairly serious wound she dressed herself rather than risk exposure. She later served in western New York and then in Philadelphia. There she fell desperately ill and was hospitalized, whereupon her secret was revealed. In October 1783 she received her formal discharge and a sum of money from Gen. Henry Knox. She later published an account of her war experience as *The Female Review*, 1797. In April 1785 she married Benjamin Gannett and settled in Sharon, Massachusetts. In 1792 she was granted a sum of money by the Massachusetts General Court for her services in the Revolution. In 1805 she was granted a veteran's disability pension by Congress, and from September 1818 she received a full pension; she stands unique among women as a genuine Revolutionary veteran and pensioner. She died in Sharon, Massachusetts, on April 29, 1827; in July 1838 her widower, Gannett, was granted a survivor's pension.

Sampson, William Thomas (1840–1902), naval officer. Born in Palmyra, New York, on February 9, 1840, Sampson graduated from the Naval Academy first in his class in 1861. He remained for a time as an instructor at the Academy, which was shortly transferred to Newport, Rhode Island, and received promotion to lieutenant in July 1862. In 1864 he joined the monitor *Patapsco*, which was blown up by a torpedo in Charleston, South Carolina, harbor in January 1865. During 1865–1867 he served on the *Colorado* in the European Squadron, advancing to lieutenant commander in July 1866. He was again at the Academy in 1868–1871, and, after service on the *Congress* in 1872 and on European station in 1873 and promotion to commander in August 1874, he returned there for a third tour, 1874–1878, as head of the physics department. During 1879–1882 he commanded the *Swatara* in the Asiatic Squadron, and after two years as assistant superintendent of the Naval Observatory in Washington, D.C., during which time he was a delegate to the International Prime Meridian Conference in October 1884, he commanded the naval torpedo station at Newport from 1884 to 1886. In September 1886 he was named superintendent of the Naval Academy. Promoted to captain in March 1889, he left the Academy in 1890 to command the *San Francisco*. In 1893–1897 he was chief of the Bureau of Ordnance, where under his leadership much progress was made in such matters as the introduction of smokeless powder and the improvement of gunnery training. In June 1897 he was given command of the new battleship *Iowa*, joining the North Atlantic Squadron as senior captain. During February–March 1898 he served as president of the naval board investigating the sinking of the

Maine in Havana harbor. In the latter month he was advanced to acting rear admiral and named to succeed the ailing Adm. Montgomery Sicard in command of the North Atlantic Squadron. On the declaration of war against Spain in April he proceeded from Key West to institute a blockade of the northern coast of Cuba, his own plan to attack Havana directly having been overruled by the Navy Department. In May, while the location of the Spanish fleet under Adm. Cervera was yet unknown, Sampson made a cruise east to Puerto Rico and on May 12 bombarded San Juan. He then returned to the blockade and was joined by the "Flying Squadron" under Commodore Winfield S. Schley, who, though technically his senior, was placed under his command for the campaign. He sent Schley to reinforce the blockade of the southern coast, particularly at Cienfuegos and Santiago. Schley was tardy in his movements, and Cervera slipped undetected into the easily defended harbor at Santiago. When he was finally discovered there, Sampson concentrated his forces outside the harbor. He supported the landing of Gen. William R. Shafter's army at Daiquirí on June 22, the capture of Siboney the next day, and the advance to Santiago. Following the capture of the San Juan heights commanding the city on July 1 Sampson and Shafter arranged a shore conference to plan a coordinated land-sea assault. On the morning of July 3 Sampson, aboard the *New York*, headed for the conference point some miles to the east. Half an hour later the first of Cervera's ships appeared, steaming out of the harbor to the west. The blockade squadron, under the immediate command of Schley, went instantly into action and in less than four hours the entire Spanish fleet was sunk or run ashore. The battle took place entirely to the west of the harbor entrance, and the *New York* was out of it altogether. A considerable controversy ensued, with Schley, who had been present aboard the *Brooklyn*, quickly becoming the hero of the day in the newspapers, while the department and most knowledgeable observers credited Sampson's preparation, training, and standing orders with the squadron's success. The dispute, bitter at times, delayed promotions for both men for nearly a year. During September–December 1898 Sampson was in Cuba as one of three U.S. commissioners. Made permanent rear admiral in March, Sampson resumed command of his squadron until October 1899; he commanded the Boston navy yard until October 1901 and was on waiting orders from then until his retirement in February 1902. He died on May 6, 1902, in Washington, D.C.

Sands, Benjamin Franklin (1811–1883), naval officer. Born in Baltimore on February 11, 1811, Sands grew up in Louisville, Kentucky and entered the navy as a midshipman in April 1828. He served on the *Vandalia* in the Brazil Squadron, 1828–1831,

and the *St. Louis* in the West India Squadron, 1831–1832, and after a year at the Norfolk navy yard he was assigned to duty with the Coast Survey. He was promoted to lieutenant in March 1840. In 1842–1844 he was on the *Columbia* in the Mediterranean, and during 1844–1847 he was attached to the Depot of Charts and Instruments. In the Mexican War he served on the *Washington*, taking part in Commodore Matthew C. Perry's operations at Tabasco and Tuxpan. After a cruise in the Africa Squadron, 1848–1850, during which he succeeded to command of the *Porpoise*, he resumed survey work, advancing to commander in September 1855. In 1858 he was named chief of the Bureau of Construction. In February 1861 he was sent to Pensacola, Florida, with secret orders for the naval vessels based there, and in April he took part in the evacuation of the Norfolk navy yard. After another year of survey work he was promoted to captain in July 1862 and in October put in command of the steamer *Dacotah*. He was senior officer of the blockade division force before Wilmington, North Carolina, and the Cape Fear River until late in 1864, transferring from the *Dacotah* to the *Fort Jackson* in 1863. During that period his division captured some 53 would-be blockade-runners. He took part in the attacks on Fort Fisher on December 24–25, 1864, and January 13–15, 1865, under Adm. David D. Porter and then commanded a division of the West Gulf Blockading Squadron until July 1865. On June 2, 1865, he received the last formal surrender of Confederate troops and three days later raised the Union flag over Galveston, Texas. Promoted to commodore in July 1866, he was superintendent of the Naval Observatory from 1867 to 1874, advancing to rear admiral in April 1871. He retired in February 1874 and died in Washington, D.C., on June 30, 1883.

Schirra, Walter Marty, Jr. (1923–   ), naval officer and astronaut. Born on March 12, 1923, in Hackensack, New Jersey, Schirra learned to fly in his youth, and after a year at the Newark College of Engineering he entered the Naval Academy in 1942. He graduated in 1945, completed naval pilot training in 1948, and during the Korean War flew 90 combat missions with the air force's 154th Fighter Bomber Squadron. From 1952 to 1954 he took part in the development of the Sidewinder air-to-air missile at the Naval Ordnance Training Station, China Lake, California, and in 1954–1956 he was project pilot for the new F7U3 Cutlass jet fighter. After a year with the 124th Fighter Squadron aboard the carrier *Lexington* and a year of Naval Air Safety Officer School he entered test pilot training in 1958 at the Naval Air Test Center, Patuxent River, Maryland. In April 1959 he was among the first seven men chosen by the National Aeronautics and Space Administration for the astronaut corps. During the rigorous training period that followed he specialized in the development of life-support system technology. He also became noted as the most outspoken of the astronauts. His first spaceflight was the six-orbit mission of the Project Mercury capsule *Sigma 7*, the third orbital flight of the Mercury series, on October 3, 1962. Promoted to captain in 1965, he entered space again as pilot of *Gemini 6*, with copilot Thomas P. Stafford, on December 15, 1965. During the 26-hour flight he made the first rendezvous in space, maneuvering the capsule to within one foot of the already orbiting *Gemini 7* capsule (Frank Borman, James A. Lovell) and later flying formation for several hours and otherwise demonstrating space piloting capabilities. On October 11, 1968, Shirra again flew in command of *Apollo VII* (with Donn Eisele and Walter Cunningham), the first manned flight of the Apollo vehicle destined to go to the moon. The 11-day orbital mission thoroughly tested the vehicle's capabilities. Schirra resigned from NASA in 1969. Thereafter he developed a number of business interests in and around Denver, Colorado.

Schley, Winfield Scott (1839–1909), naval officer. Born in Frederick County, Maryland, on October 9, 1839, Schley graduated from the Naval Academy in 1860. After a routine cruise in the Pacific on the *Niagara* he was ordered in 1861 to the *Potomac* in the West Gulf Blockading Squadron. Later, on the gunboat *Winona* and sloops *Monongahela* and *Richmond*, he distinguished himself in operations before Mobile and took part in the campaign leading to the capture of Port Hudson. In July 1862 he was promoted to lieutenant. In 1864–1866 he was again in the Pacific on the *Wateree*. Promoted to lieutenant commander in July 1866, he taught at the Naval Academy from 1866 to 1869; served on the *Benicia* of the Asiatic Squadron in 1869–1873, taking part in the landing and capture of Korean forts at the Han River in June 1871 under Commodore John Rodgers; and was again at the Academy in 1873–1876, advancing to commander in June 1874. He commanded the *Essex* in the Brazil Squadron in 1876–1879 and was then lighthouse inspector in Boston, 1879–1883. In 1884 he was given command of an expedition to rescue the Arctic exploring party under Lt. Adolphus W. Greely, who had been out of touch in Greenland since 1881. With the vessels *Thetis*, flagship, *Bear*, and *Alert*, he pushed northward through perilous icy seas to Cape Sabine and there on June 22 discovered Greely and the six other survivors of the party. From 1884 to 1889 Schley was chief of the Bureau of Equipment and Recruiting, receiving promotion to captain in March 1888. In 1889 he took command of the cruiser *Baltimore* in the South Pacific. On October 16, 1891, a liberty party off the *Baltimore* was attacked by a mob in Valparaiso, Chile, and two sailors were killed. He maintained a firm but tactful presence in the harbor until relieved by the *Yorktown*, Capt. Robley D.

Evans, in November. He served as lighthouse inspector again in 1892–1895, commanded the *New York* in 1895–1897, and then was chairman of the Lighthouse Board in 1897–1898. Promoted to commodore in February 1898, he was put in command of the "Flying Squadron" based at Hampton Roads, Virginia, at the outbreak of the Spanish–American War in April. The squadron's mission was to be ready to meet any Spanish force in the Atlantic or Caribbean. In May, the Spanish fleet under Adm. Cervera having been detected making for Cuba, he was ordered to join his squadron to the main fleet under Adm. William T. Sampson, to whom he was technically superior in rank. Sampson ordered him on May 18 to blockade the southern Cuban ports, principally Cienfuegos and Santiago, but before he organized his forces Cervera slipped into Santiago on May 19. Schley took up a position outside Santiago on May 26, but a few hours later left, intending to return to the main naval base at Key West to refuel. He managed a refueling at sea, however, and resumed position outside Santiago on May 28, being joined by Sampson on June 1. On the morning of July 3, while Sampson was on his way to a conference ashore, Cervera's fleet attempted to run the blockade. Schley, though in immediate command, issued no special orders, and the squadron executed Sampson's standing orders to run down the Spanish fleet. The principal exception was the cruiser *Brooklyn*, Schley's flagship, which unaccountably turned in a direction opposite that of the rest of the squadron, causing considerable confusion and narrowly escaping collision with the *Texas*. The *Brooklyn* was nonetheless conspicuous in the battle, particularly against Cervera's flagship *Maria Teresa*, which was run ashore. Schley, senior officer present, was eager to accept credit for the victory, while newspapers and the public, to whom he was already a familiar and heroic figure, were eager to give it, ignoring the somewhat aloof Sampson. A public controversy quickly developed, delaying the promotions merited by both men until March 1899, when both were made rear admiral. Schley served on the Puerto Rico Evacuation Commission in September–October 1898, and after a brief period as president of the Retirement Board he was given command of the South Atlantic Squadron in 1899, a post he retained until his retirement in October 1901. By that time the Sampson–Schley controversy had become even more heated, at least on the parts of their respective partisans, and in July 1901 Schley requested and was granted a court of inquiry. In December a majority of the court, presided over by Adm. George Dewey, reported against Schley, particularly in the matters of his tardy movements, the outward turn of the *Brooklyn*, and other matters; Dewey himself, however, submitted a minority report in his favor. On appeal, President Theodore Roosevelt approved the majority report in January 1902. Schley's autobiography,

Forty-Five Years Under the Flag, appeared in 1904; he died in New York City on October 2, 1909.

Schofield, John McAllister (1831–1906), army

officer. Born in Gerry, New York, on September 29, 1831, Schofield grew up there and in Illinois, Iowa, and Missouri. He graduated from West Point in 1853 and was commissioned in the artillery. After service in Florida against the Seminole Indians he taught at West Point from 1855 to 1860, receiving promotion to first lieutenant in August 1855. In 1860 he took leave of absence and went to Washington University in St. Louis to teach and was there when the Civil War broke out. He was commissioned a major in the 1st Missouri Volunteer Infantry Regiment in April 1861 and in June became chief of staff to Gen. Nathaniel Lyon. In November he was appointed brigadier general of volunteers and brigadier general of the Missouri militia, which he commanded until October 1862, when he was put in command of the Army of the Frontier. In November he was nominated for major general, and he served in that rank until March 1863, when, the nomination not having been confirmed owing to political maneuvering in Missouri, he reverted. He was then given command of a division of the XIV Corps until May, when he was reappointed major general of volunteers and named commander of the Department of the Missouri. In February 1864 he was put in command of the Department and Army of the Ohio, the latter consisting mainly of the XXIII Corps. He was one of Gen. William T. Sherman's three army commanders in the Atlanta campaign. When Sherman began his march to the sea, Schofield's command was detached to screen Gen. George H. Thomas, commander of all western forces, at Nashville. Confederate forces under Gen. John B. Hood followed Schofield closely and, after an inconclusive encounter at Spring Hill, Tennessee, on November 29, attacked at Franklin the next day. Schofield drove them off with heavy losses and then joined Thomas in Nashville, taking part in the battle there on December 15–16. Promoted to brigadier general of regulars in November and brevetted major general in March 1865, Schofield then took command of the Department of North Carolina, and after landing by sea at Fort Fisher he met Sherman at Goldsboro and served under him until the end of the war in April. For a few months in 1865–1866 Schofield served in France as a confidential agent of the Department of State, negotiating the withdrawal of French interventionist forces from Mexico. On his return to the United States he was commander of the Department of the Potomac (later the First Military District), August 1866–June 1868, and was involved in implementing Reconstruction in the South. From June 1868 to March 1869, the final months of President Andrew Johnson's troubled administration, he was secretary of war. Promoted to major general in March 1869, he commanded the Department of the Missouri until May 1870, when he took command of the Division of the Pacific. In that post he traveled to Hawaii in 1872 to investigate its military value to the United States; his recommendations led to the acquisition of a naval base at Pearl Harbor. From September 1876 to January 1881 he served as commandant of West Point. He then commanded the Division of the Gulf briefly and, after a year's travel in Europe, the Division of the Pacific, October 1882–November 1883, and the Division of the Missouri to April 1886. On the death of Gen. Philip H. Sheridan in August 1888 Schofield became commanding general of the army, and he retained that post, from February 1895 as lieutenant general, until retiring in September 1895. He died in St. Augustine, Florida, on March 4, 1906.

Schuyler, Philip John (1733–1804), Revolution-

ary army officer and public official. Born in Albany, New York, on November 20, 1733, Schuyler was a member of a wealthy upstate New York family. After his father's death he eventually inherited sizable estates in the Mohawk valley and a substantial income. During the French and Indian War, 1755–1763, he was a captain (1755–1757) and major (1758–1761) in the provincial army and saw some action, notably under Gen. (later Sir) William Johnson at Lake George, September 8, 1755, but his main responsibility was provisioning troops. He spent two years, 1761–1763, in England trying to settle claims of Col. John Bradstreet, under whom he had served, and himself resulting from the conflict. He then spent most of his time until the outbreak of the Revolution improving his estates, engaging in the lumber business and foreign commerce, and in 1764 building the first flax mill in the colonies. He was elected to a term in the New York assembly in 1768, and from 1775 to 1777 he served as a delegate to the Second Continental Congress. When the Revolutionary War began Schuyler was named on June 15, 1775, one of the four major generals to serve under George Washington; he was put in command of the Northern, or New York, Department. His military service was not entirely beneficial to his reputation. He planned the invasion of Canada of that year, but illness at length forced him to relinquish field command to Gen. Richard Montgomery. The failure of that expedition fueled the constant bickering between Schuyler and various of his New England subordinates, notably Gen. David Wooster and Gen. Horatio Gates. Following Gen. Arthur St. Clair's abandonment of Fort Ticonderoga in July 1777 Schuyler directed an effective delaying retreat from Fort Edward, throwing all manner of obstacles in the path of Gen. John Burgoyne and allowing defenses to form to the south. Nonetheless he was relieved and replaced by Gates in August. He immediately requested a court-martial to examine his actions in the loss of Ticonderoga, and as a result the next year he was completely exonerated. He resigned his commission in April 1779. From 1778 to 1781 he was again in the Continental Congress. Elected a state senator in New York, he served from 1780 to 1784 and again from 1786 to 1790. A staunch supporter of the new Constitution in 1787, he helped gain its ratification in New York; and when the new federal government began functioning he was one of New York's first U.S. senators, serving as a Federalist from March 1789 to March 1791. During this short first term Schuyler strongly supported the monetary policies and other measures of benefit to large landholders proposed by his son-in-law, Alexander Hamilton. Then, defeated for reelection to the Senate, Schuyler returned to the state senate in 1792–1797, during which period he helped found Union College, Schenectady, New York. In March 1797 he again entered the U.S. Senate but was able to serve for less than a year. Poor health led to his resignation in January 1798. He died in Albany, New York, on November 18, 1804.

Scott, Charles (1739?–1813), Revolutionary army officer and public official. Born about 1739 in Goochland County (at a spot now in Powhatan County), Virginia, Scott served in the militia under Col. George Washington in Gen. Edward Braddock's campaign in 1755. At the beginning of the Revolution he raised several militia companies and led them to Williamsburg in July 1775. In February 1776 he was appointed lieutenant colonel of the 2nd Virginia Regiment; in May he became colonel of the 5th Virginia, and in August he transferred to the 3rd. He distinguished himself at the battle of Trenton, New Jersey, December 26, 1776, and in April 1777 was commissioned a brigadier general in the Continental army. He served subsequently at Germantown, Valley Forge, Monmouth, Stony Point, and Charleston, where he was captured in May 1780. Held prisoner almost until the end of the war, he saw no more active service but was brevetted major general in September 1783. He was a founding member of the Society of the Cincinnati. In 1785 he settled in what later became Woodford County, Kentucky, and represented the district in the Virginia legislature in 1789–1790. In 1790 he took part in Gen. Josiah Harmar's expedition against the Indians of the Ohio country, and in May–June 1791, as brigadier general of militia, he led an expedition to the Wabash River. Later in the year he joined Gen. Arthur St. Clair and was present at his defeat in November. In 1792 a region of Woodford County was designated Scott County in his honor. In 1794 he led a force of some 1500 mounted Kentucky volunteers in the campaign under Gen. Anthony Wayne culminating in the victorious Battle of Fallen Timbers, August 20. In August 1808 Scott was elected fourth governor of Kentucky. He

held that post for four years; one of his final acts was to commission William Henry Harrison major general of Kentucky militia in August 1812. Scott died in Clark County, Kentucky, on October 22, 1813.

Scott, Hugh Lenox (1853–1934), army officer. Born on September 22, 1853, in Danville, Kentucky, Scott grew up there and in Princeton, New Jersey. He graduated from West Point in 1876, was commissioned in the cavalry, and for some 20 years thereafter served on the frontier, chiefly with the 7th Cavalry. He saw action in the campaigns against the Sioux, Nez Percé, Cheyenne, and other Indians of the Plains, and became expert in their languages and ways of life. He was promoted to first lieutenant in June 1878. In 1890–1891 he was given responsibility for suppressing the "Ghost Dance" religious mania that swept the Indian reservations; he received official commendation for his work. In 1892 he organized Troop L of the 7th Cavalry, composed of Kiowa, Comanche, and Apache Indians, and commanded it until it was mustered out, the last Indian troop in the army, in 1897. During 1894–1897 he had charge of Geronimo's band of Chiricahua Apache prisoners at Fort Sill, Oklahoma. He advanced to captain in January 1895. In November 1897 he was attached to the Bureau of American Ethnology of the Smithsonian Institution, where he began preparing a work on Indian sign language. In May 1898, after the outbreak of the Spanish–American War, he was appointed major of volunteers and assistant adjutant general of the 2nd and 3rd divisions, I Corps. He saw no action in the war, but in March 1899 he went to Cuba as adjutant general of the Department of Havana with the rank of lieutenant colonel of volunteers. In May 1900 he moved up to adjutant general of the Division of Cuba (created the Department of Cuba in November 1900). He remained in that post until May 1902, served for a time as acting governor, and took an active part in the transfer of government into Cuban hands. Promoted to major of regulars in February 1903, he served as military governor of the Sulu Archipelago, Philippines, in 1903–1906 and also commanded troops there, taking part in various skirmishes, and reorganizing civil government and institutions. In August 1906 Scott was named superintendent of West Point, a post he held for four years with temporary rank of colonel. Promoted to lieutenant colonel in March 1911 and to colonel in August, he commanded the 3rd Cavalry in Texas, where he was engaged in settling various Indian troubles. In March 1913 he was promoted to brigadier general in command of the 2nd Cavalry Brigade, still posted to the Southwest. He won special commendation for his skillful handling of Navajo disturbances at Beautiful Mountain, Arizona, in November 1913. He was named assistant chief of staff in April 1914 and chief of staff of the army in November, and he was promoted to major general in April 1915. He continued to act in a diplomatic role with Indians and Mexican border officials in the Southwest, settling problems with the Piutes of Utah in March 1915 and recovering property "confiscated" by Pancho Villa in August. For a month, February–March 1916, he served as ad interim secretary of war. But his energy was directed more and more toward preparation for possible U.S. entry into World War I, and he was very influential in winning early acceptance among civil officials of the notion of conscription. He retired at the statutory age in September 1917 but was retained on active duty; he became commander of the 78th Division at Camp Dix, New Jersey, in December and of Camp Dix in March 1918. He retired finally in May 1919. Scott served on the Board of Indian Commissioners from 1919 to 1929 and was chairman of the New Jersey State Highway Commission from 1923 to 1933. In 1928 he published an autobiography, *Some Memories of a Soldier*. He died in Washington, D.C., on April 30, 1934.

Scott, Robert Lee, Jr. (1908–   ), army officer, aviator, and author. Born on April 12, 1908, in Macon, Georgia, Scott conceived a devotion to flying in his boyhood and narrowly survived several hair-raising escapades. After a poor academic record in high school and in brief periods at Mercer University and The Citadel, he enlisted in the army in 1927, attended the military academy preparatory school, and in 1928 entered West Point. He graduated in 1932, completed pilot training at Randolph Field, Texas, in 1933, and was assigned to the 99th Pursuit Squadron at Mitchel Field, New York. In 1934 he was on the New York–Chicago route of the army airmail service. After a tour of duty in the Canal Zone with the 78th Pursuit Squadron he became a flight instructor at Randolph Field and later at the California Aeronautics Academy. Early in World War II, unable to secure a combat post, he joined the American Volunteer Group ("Flying Tigers") under Gen. Claire L. Chennault. In June 1942 Scott returned to active duty with the Army Air Forces as a colonel and was given command of the 23rd Fighter Group (which absorbed much of the A.V.G.), operating in the China-Burma theater as part of Chennault's China Air Task Force and later the Fourteenth Air Force. By January 1943 he had achieved a score of 13 enemy aircraft shot down. He then returned to training duty in the United States, and in that year he published his first book, *God Is My Co-Pilot*, a vivid and popular account of his experiences that was later made into a successful motion picture. Later in 1943 he rejoined Chennault's staff as commander of fighters with the Fourteenth Air Force. In 1945 he became deputy chief of staff for operations of the Fourteenth, then based at Orlando, Florida. By that time he had published *Damned to Glory*, 1944, and *Runway to the Sun*, 1945. Subse-

quent assignments included command of the 36th Fighter-Bomber Wing in Germany in 1950–1953, and after graduating from the Army War College in 1954 Scott was named director of information services of the air force. He was promoted to brigadier general in 1955. From 1956 until his retirement in 1957 he commanded a training wing at Luke Air Force Base, Arizona. He devoted himself thereafter to writing; among his later books were *Between the Elephant's Eyes!*, 1954, *The Look of the Eagle*, 1955, *Flying Tiger: Chennault of China*, 1959, and *Boring a Hole in the Sky*, an autobiography, 1961. Scott also had various business interests in Phoenix, Arizona, where he lived in retirement.

Scott, Winfield (1786–1866), army officer. Born near Petersburg, Virginia, on June 13, 1786, Scott attended the College of William and Mary briefly in 1805 and then took up the study of law privately. In the flurry of war fever that followed the *Chesapeake-Leopard* affair in 1807 he enlisted in a local troop of cavalry. In May 1808, having personally petitioned President Thomas Jefferson, he was commissioned a captain of light artillery and ordered to New Orleans. For a year, 1809–1810, he was under suspension because of some disparaging remarks he had made about his commander, Gen. James Wilkinson, relating to Wilkinson's appearance in the 1807 trial of Aaron Burr, which Scott had attended. During 1811–1812 he was again at New Orleans on the staff of Gen. Wade Hampton. When an expansion of the army was authorized early in 1812 he made his way to Washington, D.C., where in July he learned of his promotion to lieutenant colonel. In October he joined the command of Gen. Alexander Smyth at Niagara. At the battle of Queenston, Ontario, on October 13, he led a small group of volunteers that crossed the river to aid Gen. Stephen Van Rensselaer's embattled troops, and he was captured. Paroled in November, he was promoted to colonel and named adjutant to Gen. Henry Dearborn in March 1813. He planned and led the capture of Fort George, May 27, with able assistance from Commander Oliver H. Perry and artillery support from Commodore Isaac Chauncey's fleet. After recovering from a wound received in that engagement he was made commander of the fort in the fall. In October he joined Gen. Wilkinson's army in the unsuccessful Montreal campaign. In March 1814 Scott was promoted to brigadier general, and after a period of training in Buffalo, New York, he led his troops as part of Gen. Jacob Brown's army across the Niagara River on July 3. On July 5 his 1300 men dealt a sharp defeat to the British at the Chippewa Creek. On July 25 he was severely wounded leading his brigade at the battle of Lundy's Lane, a hard fought battle in which his men bore the brunt of attacks by superior forces for two hours before the rest of Brown's army arrived. Immediately taken up as a national hero, he was brevetted major general and honored by Congress. He headed the board inquiring into Gen. William H. Winder's conduct at Bladensburg and another board writing the first standard drill for the army, and he virtually alone constituted the board of selection overseeing the huge reduction of the army at the end of the war. Making his headquarters in New York City as commander of the Northern Department, he devoted much of his time to the writing and revision of training manuals and to the improvement of discipline. He headed various boards and made two trips to Europe to study military methods. On the death of Gen. Brown in February 1828 Scott was passed over for the office of commanding general in favor of the formerly junior Gen. Alexander Macomb; he thereupon tendered his resignation, but it was not accepted. In 1829 he was named commander of the Eastern Division. In July 1832 he led some 950 troops to Wisconsin to take part in the Black Hawk War, but an epidemic of cholera prevented his reaching the scene before the war had ended. He helped negotiate the purchase of Sauk and Fox land in what is now Iowa in the treaty of Fort Armstrong, signed September 21, 1832. Later in the year he was sent by President Andrew Jackson to observe the activities of the Nullifiers in South Carolina; he managed the mission with great diplomatic skill, reinforcing the federal forts around Charleston without provoking local authorities. In 1835 Jackson, with whom he did not have good relations, sent him to command the forces in the field in Florida in the Second Seminole War. Arriving at St. Augustine in February 1836, Scott found a poor supply situation and an untrained short-term militia. He could do little, and he was further hampered by interference from Gen. Edmund P. Gaines and conflict with Gen. Thomas S. Jesup. At length he was recalled, Jesup succeeding him, but a court of inquiry in 1837 cleared him of all charges of failure to prosecute the war. In January 1838 he was sent by President Martin Van Buren to pacify the Maine–New Brunswick border, for decades the scene of the desultory "Aroostook War." His diplomacy was successful, and later in 1838 he met an even greater challenge in overseeing the forced removal of some 16,000 eastern Cherokee Indians from Georgia, South Carolina, and Tennessee to Indian Territory (now Oklahoma). In January 1839 he was again dispatched to Maine, where the border situation had deteriorated. Personal negotiation with the lieutenant governor of New Brunswick over several weeks eased the dispute and laid the groundwork for the permanent settlement achieved in the Webster-Ashburton Treaty of 1842. Following the death of Gen. Macomb, Scott became commanding general of the army with the rank of major general on July 5, 1841. At the outbreak of the Mexican War in 1846 he strongly supported Gen. Zachary Taylor for command of the army in the field, but he gradually became convinced that Taylor's northern campaign would not end the war. He developed an ambitious plan for a strike by a much larger army at Mexico's heart. President James K. Polk and the Democratic administration, wary of Scott as a possible political rival, refused for several months to approve such an undertaking, but by November it was clear that Taylor could accomplish little more where he was except to become an even greater public hero and equally dangerous rival. After meticulous planning Scott took the field, and by February 1847 he had assembled an army of more than 13,000—many drawn from the protesting Taylor—off the Mexican coast. Supported by a naval squadron commanded first by Commodore David Conner and subsequently by Commodore Matthew C. Perry, the first major amphibious operation ever attempted by the U.S. army took place below Veracruz on March 9. The city fell to siege and naval gunfire on March 27. On April 8 Scott began his march inland. The vanguard under Gen. David E. Twiggs halted in confusion at a narrow pass at Cerro Gordo commanded by Gen. Santa Anna's troops, but Scott's arrival galvanized the American army. A brilliant flanking movement directed by Capt. Robert E. Lee made the battle of April 18 a quick victory. Puebla was occupied on May 15. After a pause there Scott broke his supply line to the coast and moved out on August 7. On August 19–20 troops under Twiggs and Gen. Gideon J. Pillow overran Mexican troops on high ground at Contreras, and later on the second day the main army under Santa Anna, behind heavy fortifications, was attacked at Churubusco. The American assault inflicted extremely heavy casualties, totaling about a third of Santa Anna's army, in carrying the position. By early September Mexico City was reached. On September 8 the arsenal of Molino del Rey was taken in a costly battle. On September 13 Pillow's troops made a masterly assault on the heavily fortified castle of Chapultepec. The capture of that stronghold enabled Gen. William J. Worth and Gen. John A. Quitman to advance rapidly to the gates of Mexico City, which capitulated on September 14. Scott remained there as military governor until April 1848, when he returned to the United States to face a court of inquiry that grew out of false reports from Pillow and Worth and the eagerness of the Polk administration to discredit Scott. The inquiry redounded entirely to his favor, however, and he was again a popular hero. In 1852 he was nominated for the presidency by the Whigs (he had been considered as a candidate as early as 1839 and regularly since then); he lost the election to Democrat Franklin Pierce by 254 electoral votes to 42. In February 1855 the rank of lieutenant general, which had not existed since March 1799, was revived and awarded by brevet to Scott, to date from the fall of Veracruz. Despite his political troubles Scott was deeply respected by the men he commanded, to whom he was known, from his rather punctilious insistence on the finer points of decorum and military etiquette, as "Old Fuss and Feathers." In September 1859, aged seventy-three, he was sent to calm the dispute between the United States and Great Britain over possession of San Juan Island in Puget Sound. In 1860, in anticipation of civil war, he began urging the reinforcement of southern posts and armories to prevent their seizure. In January 1861 he moved his headquarters from New York City to Washington, D.C. He performed his final service in overseeing the recruitment and training of new troops and in advising, rather in vain, on strategy. On November 1, 1861, he retired, relinquishing command of the army to Gen. George B. McClellan. The preeminent military figure in the nation for nearly half a century, Scott died at West Point, New York, on May 29, 1866.

Seagrave, Gordon Stifler (1897–1965), physician.

Born on March 18, 1897, in Rangoon, Burma, Seagrave was the son, grandson, and great-grandson of American missionaries to Burma. From 1909 he grew up in Granville, Ohio. He graduated from Denison University in 1917 and from the Johns Hopkins Medical School in 1921. In 1922 he returned to Burma to take charge of a hospital at Namhkam, three miles from the Chinese border in Shan State, which was supported by the American Baptist Foreign Missions. With little money and little in the way of equipment or surgical tools beyond what he had salvaged during his internship and brought with him, he immediately set about enlarging and improving the hospital and training a native staff. Over the years the Namhkam establishment grew from a single hovel-like structure to a 22-building complex with a fully qualified nursing staff, treating upwards of 6000 in-patients each year. Much of the financial support for the expansion derived from Seagrave's books, *Waste-basket Surgery*, 1930, and *Tales of a Waste-basket Surgeon*, 1938. (The term "waste-basket" referred to the source of his original salvaged surgical instruments.) Shortly before the Japanese overran Burma in World War II Seagrave moved his work to a more secure location at Loiwing, just over the border into China. At the outbreak of war he set up virtually overnight a 400-bed hospital at Prome, Burma, to treat casualties. For a time his facilities and staff were loosely attached to the British Liaison Mission in Burma, but early in 1942 he transferred everything to the U.S. army, taking a commission as major in the Medical Corps and joining the staff of Gen. Joseph W. Stilwell. With Stilwell he made the exhausting retreat into India, performing prodigies of endurance as chief medical officer of the command. The story of those days helped make his next book, *Burma Surgeon*, 1943, one of the best-selling books of the war. Early in 1945 he returned to liberated Namhkam to begin the heart-breaking work of rebuilding his hospital. Having advanced to lieutenant colonel in the army Medical Corps, he served in 1945–1946 as chief medical officer of Shan State in the British military government. After the war his connection with the Baptist mission was severed, and support came from the American Medical Center for Burma. In 1950 he was arrested and convicted of various charges stemming from his having provided medical aid and supplies to rebel northern tribesmen. Sentenced to 6 years in prison, he spent 16 months in jail or under house arrest before his conviction was overturned by the supreme court of Burma. He then returned to his hospital; the work of later years was described in *Burma Surgeon Returns*, 1945, and *My Hospital in the Hills*, 1955. Seagrave died at Namhkam, Burma, on March 28, 1965.

Sedgwick, John (1813–1864), army officer.

Born in Cornwall Hollow, Connecticut, on September 13, 1813, Sedgwick graduated from West Point in 1837 and was commissioned in the artillery. Over the next several years he saw action in the Seminole War in Florida, took part in supervising the removal of the Cherokee Indians west beyond the Mississippi, and served on the Maine–Canada border, advancing to first lieutenant in April 1839. He served under Gen. Zachary Taylor and Gen. Winfield Scott in the Mexican War, winning brevets to captain at Contreras and Churubusco, August 19–20, 1847, and major at Chapultepec, September 13. Promoted to captain in January 1849, he returned to routine duties and in March 1855 was appointed major of the newly organized 1st Cavalry Regiment. He took part in the Mormon expedition under Col. Albert S. Johnston in 1857–1858 and saw considerable action against various Indian tribes in the West. In March 1861 he was promoted to lieutenant colonel of the 2nd Cavalry and in April to colonel of the 4th. In August he was appointed brigadier general of volunteers. He served with the Army of the Potomac, leading a division of Gen. Edwin V. Sumner's II Corps through the Peninsula campaign, and was badly wounded at Frayser's Farm, June 30, 1862. He was conspicuous on the field and was twice wounded at Antietam (Sharpsburg), September 17. In December he was promoted to major general of volunteers, to date from July. In February 1863 he took command of the VI Corps. In the Chancellorsville campaign Sedgwick commanded both the VI and the V Corps at Fredericksburg, a diversionary force intended to cover Gen. Joseph Hooker's encircling move toward Chancellorsville. Sedgwick crossed the Rappahannock on April 29 and held his position until May 2 when, the battle at Chancellorsville having begun with Gen. Thomas J. Jackson's surprise attack on Hooker's flank, he was called to support. He stormed Marye's Heights at Fredericksburg on May 3, carrying it against Gen. Jubal A.

Early's division, but at Salem Heights, on the road to Chancellorsville, he was struck and turned back by Gen. Robert E. Lee's entire force. He retired over the Rappahannock on May 4. He took part in the battle of Gettysburg, arriving on the second day, July 2, after a remarkable forced march by the VI Corps. He commanded the V and VI Corps, constituting the right wing of the Army of the Potomac, in the crossing of the Potomac and the Rapidan in November and in the confrontation with Lee at Mine Run, November 29–30. Following service in the Wilderness campaign in early May 1864 he was shot and killed by a Confederate sharpshooter while directing artillery emplacements at Spotsylvania, Virginia, on May 9, 1864.

Seeger, Alan (1888–1916), poet and soldier. Born on June 22, 1888, in New York City, Seeger graduated from Harvard in 1910. While in college he had contributed verse to the *Harvard Monthly*, of which he was in his final year an editor. A romantic as well as an aesthete and something of a sensualist, he found little in postgraduate life that pleased him, and in 1912 he left America for Paris. At the outbreak of World War I in August 1914 he enlisted in the French Foreign Legion. For nearly two years he served in the trenches, often volunteering for hazardous details to escape the monotony. He also continued writing poetry and sent back sketches of trench life to various American journals. During the battle of the Somme in the summer of 1916 he was in the first wave over the top in the attack on the village of Belloy-en-Santerre on July 4; he was cut down by machine gun fire almost instantly. Later in the year *The Poems of Alan Seeger* was published, containing his most famous verses, "Ode in Memory of the American Volunteers Fallen for France," "Champagne 1914–15," and the poem written almost in prophecy shortly before he died, "I Have a Rendezvous with Death." The volume was honored by the French Academy, and Seeger was awarded a Croix de Guerre posthumously. *Letters and Diary of Alan Seeger* appeared in 1917.

Selfridge, Thomas Oliver (1836–1924), naval officer. Born in Charlestown, Massachusetts, on February 6, 1836, Selfridge was the son of a noted naval officer who rose to rear admiral. He graduated from the Naval Academy in 1854 and saw his first sea duty in the Pacific aboard the *Independence*. He served later on the *Vincennes* of the Africa Squadron. Promoted to lieutenant in February 1860, he returned home and in September was ordered to the sloop *Cumberland* at Hampton Roads, Virginia. He was present at the abandonment and destruction of the Norfolk navy yard in April 1861, took part in the expedition under Flag-Officer Silas H. Stringham against Hatteras Inlet in August, and distinguished

himself in the defense of the *Cumberland* against the ironclad *Virginia* on March 8, 1862. In that fight Selfridge, second ranking officer present (under Lt. George U. Morris), commanded the forward guns, where the raking fire from the *Virginia* bore heaviest. He was ordered to command of the *Monitor* after its epic battle of March 9 but immediately thereafter transferred to duty with the North Atlantic Blockading Squadron. In June he commanded the *Alligator*, an experimental submarine torpedo boat that failed. Promoted to lieutenant commander in July, he took command of the gunboat *Cairo* in the Mississippi Squadron under Adm. David D. Porter. On the destruction of the *Cairo* during operations on the Yazoo River on December 12, he took command of the gunboat *Conestoga*. During the final siege of Vicksburg in June–July 1863 he commanded a land battery of naval guns. He then returned to the *Conestoga* and commanded a gunboat flotilla that captured two Confederate steamers. When the *Conestoga* sank in March 1864 he assumed command of the *Osage*, on which he took part in the Red River expedition, under Porter, in conjunction with Gen. Nathaniel P. Banks. In October 1864 he accompanied Porter east and, commanding the gunboat *Huron*, took part in the attacks on Fort Fisher on December 24–25, 1864, and January 13–15, 1865. During the second attack he commanded one of four divisions of the sailor-marine landing force. Selfridge was promoted to commander in December 1869 and put in charge of a naval party surveying routes for an interoceanic canal across the Isthmus of Darien. Several such routes were discussed in his final report of 1874. While commanding the steamer *Enterprise* in 1877–1880 he conducted explorations in the Amazon and Madeira rivers. In January 1881 he was put in command of the Naval Torpedo Station at Newport, Rhode Island, receiving promotion to captain the next month. During 1885–1887 he commanded the *Omaha* in the Asiatic Squadron. The death of four natives on the island of Ie Shima following a mishap during torpedo practice in prohibited waters led to a court-martial in 1888, but he was acquitted. He served on the Board of Inspection in 1889–1890, commanded the Boston navy yard in 1890–1893, and, promoted to commodore in April 1894, was president of the Board of Inspection in 1894–1895. During 1895–1897 he commanded the European Squadron, receiving promotion to rear admiral in February 1896. Selfridge retired in February 1898. He died in Washington, D.C., on February 4, 1924.

Semmes, Raphael (1809–1877), Confederate naval officer and lawyer. Born in Charles County, Maryland, on September 27, 1809, Semmes was appointed a midshipman in the navy in April 1826. He saw occasional sea duty in the next dozen years but also found enough free time to study law and be admitted to the bar in 1834. He was given the rank of lieutenant in February 1837 and spent the next nine years on routine tours of duty. At the outbreak of the Mexican War in 1846 he was attached to the squadron under Commodore David Conner. In October he took command of the brig *Somers*, which, while chasing a blockade-runner off Veracruz on December 8, capsized and sank in a sudden squall with the loss of about 40 men. Semmes, cleared by a court of inquiry, was made Conner's flag-lieutenant, and in that post he took part in the landing of U.S. troops at Veracruz and joined Gen. Winfield Scott's forces as they marched inland to Mexico City. From the end of the Mexican War until the start of the Civil War Semmes spent most of his time awaiting orders at his home near Mobile, Alabama, and practising law. He was for a time lighthouse inspector for the Gulf district. He was raised to the rank of commander in September 1855 but resigned his commission in February 1861 when Alabama seceded from the Union. With the start of the Civil War he was given a commander's commission in the Confederate States navy in March, and in April he was placed in command of the *Sumter* (formerly the merchant steamer *Havana*) with orders to harry Union shipping. Blockaded on the Mississippi, Semmes made a celebrated escape through the blockade at Pass à L'Outre on June 30. For several months he cruised the West Indies, the East Coast as far north as Maine, and the Atlantic, taking numerous prizes. Early in 1862 he put into Gibraltar, where he was promptly blockaded. Unable to escape, he at length sold the *Sumter* in April. On his way back to America he received orders to go to England to take possession and command of the British-built cruiser *Alabama*, with which he resumed his attacks on Union vessels in the Atlantic from Canada to Brazil. In August 1862 he was promoted to captain. In 1863 he took the ship around the world via Capetown and the Indian Ocean in his quest. In all he captured or destroyed 64 ships before, on June 19, 1864, the *Alabama* met the Union sloop *Kearsarge*, Capt. John A. Winslow, in the English Channel near Cherbourg, France, and was defeated and sunk. Semmes was rescued by an observing British yacht and, contrary to the rules of war, was carried off to safety. In January 1865 he returned to the Confederacy a hero. Promoted to rear admiral in February, he was put in charge of the warships on the James River in defense of Richmond; when Richmond fell he burned his ships. With the end of the war he returned to Mobile. He was arrested in December 1865 and spent a few months as a prisoner in Washington, D.C., but was released and returned to Mobile to the practice of law. He taught briefly in 1866 at Louisiana State Seminary (now Louisiana State University) and for a time edited the *Memphis Daily Bulletin*. He was a popular lecturer as well and made numerous tours of the South. During his career

Semmes wrote books and articles based on his war experiences, including *Service Afloat and Ashore During the Mexican War*, 1851, and *Memoirs of Service Afloat During the War Between the States*, 1869. He died at Point Clear, on Mobile Bay, Alabama, on August 30, 1877. His Civil War exploits with the *Alabama* provided a focus for a complex of claims by the United States against Great Britain, which had violated neutrality laws by supplying the Confederacy with ships and other aid. The whole claim became known as the "*Alabama* claims," for, although Semmes's ship was only one of eleven vessels involved, it had inflicted some $6.5 million of the total $19 million in damages to U.S. shipping. Eventually, in 1872, the U.S. government was awarded $15.5 million in damages by a joint U.S.–British tribunal.

Serrell, Edward Wellman (1826–1906), civil and military engineer. Born in London on November 5, 1826, Wellman was the son of American parents, and from the age of four he grew up in New York City. He followed his father into civil engineering, becoming in 1845 assistant engineer with the Erie Railroad and serving later in a similar capacity with the Central Railroad of New Jersey. In 1848, attached to the army's Corps of Topographical Engineers, he assisted in the railroad survey of Panama. He subsequently conducted railroad surveys in New Hampshire and designed and built a bridge over the Niagara River at Lewiston, New York, and another over the St. John River at St. John, New Brunswick. In 1853 he was in charge of construction of the Hoosac Tunnel in western Massachusetts, and later he was engaged in the building of the Bristol Bridge over the River Avon in England. At the outbreak of the Civil War he organized the 1st New York Volunteer Engineers and was appointed lieutenant colonel commanding the regiment; a short time later he advanced to colonel. By 1863 he had become chief engineer of the X Corps under Gen. Quincy A. Gillmore, and by 1864 he was chief engineer and chief of staff of Gen. Benjamin F. Butler's Army of the James. During the siege of Charleston, South Carolina, he designed and at great hazard supervised the construction of a battery known as the "Swamp Angel." Located in what had been considered from an engineering standpoint an impossibly treacherous swamp, the battery consisted of an 8-inch, 200-pounder Parrott rifle whose platform literally floated on mud. It was able to shell Charleston, five miles away, until it burst on the 36th round on August 24. Serrell ended the war as chief engineer of the Department of the South. Mustered out in February 1865, in March he was brevetted brigadier general of volunteers. After the war he resumed his work with railroad and bridge engineering and was consulting engineer to several firms, including the American Isthmus Ship Canal Company. He died in New York City on April 25, 1906.

Sevier, John (1745–1815), frontiersman, Revolutionary militia officer, and public official. Born near the present New Market, Virginia, on September 23, 1745, Sevier grew up on the frontier; what formal education he received was largely at the academy in Fredericksburg. As was common with pioneer families, he moved from place to place, mainly as a farmer and land speculator. In 1772 he settled on the Watauga River and in that year joined other settlers in forming the Watauga Association for mutual protection; in 1773 he took his family to the Holston River region in what is now eastern Tennessee. He served as a captain of militia (appointed in 1772) in the campaign against the Indians called Lord Dunmore's War, taking part in the final battle at Point Pleasant, October 10, 1774. He served on the local committee of safety and in 1776–1777, as representative of the "Washington District" organized by the Watauga and Nolichucky settlers, in the provincial legislature of North Carolina. From 1777 to 1780 he was a county clerk and a district judge and from 1777 a lieutenant colonel of militia. In 1780 he led a battalion of some 240 frontiersmen to join forces under Col. Isaac Shelby, Col. William Campbell, Maj. Joseph Mac-Dowell, and Maj. Joseph Winston at the battle of Kings Mountain, October 7, a victory over Loyalist forces that made him one of the heroes of the war. For the next two years he conducted raids against the Cherokee Indians, and after defeating them he forced them to cede more tribal lands. After the Revolution North Carolina, among other seaboard states that claimed land in the West, ceded its claims to the federal government. With news of the North Carolina cession, frontiersmen met at Jonesboro to plan for an independent state in August 1784. North Carolina hurriedly repealed its act of cession, but the Westerners disregarded it and proclaimed the State of Franklin. Sevier at first opposed and then joined the statehood movement, seeing in it a chance for profiting by land speculation, using a scheme he had concocted for developing a colony at Muscle Shoals. He was chosen governor of the new state in March 1785. But Congress refused to recognize Franklin and reversed certain policies regarding Indian lands on which Sevier and other promoters had counted. Gradually the State of Franklin began to disintegrate, and by 1788 it was defunct. Sevier was discredited and lived for a time almost as an outlaw. He soon became involved in what is known as the "Spanish Conspiracy" as a means of fostering his old plans for Muscle Shoals. The conspiracy was a grandiose but ill conceived series of plots in which a number of Americans cooperated secretly with Spanish colonial officials to detach the West from the United States. Nothing ever came of the affair, and Sevier soon lost interest. He returned to respectability, was pardoned for his involvement in the Franklin fiasco, and was elected to the North Carolina senate in 1789 and ap-

pointed brigadier general of the militia of the western district. He also took part in the state's convention to ratify the Constitution, and when the new national government began to function he was elected to the House of Representatives from the state's western district (1789–1791). In 1791, when the trans-Allegheny lands were organized as the Southwest Territory, Sevier was made a brigadier general of militia. When the territory became the state of Tennessee five years later, he became its first governor and served three consecutive terms, 1796–1801. In 1798–1799, during the undeclared war with France, he was a brigadier general in the Provisional Army. From 1803 to 1809 he served again as governor of Tennessee, and in 1810–1811 he was a member of the state senate. He was elected to Congress again in 1810 and served in the House from March 1811 until his death. In 1812 he spoke in favor of a declaration of war against Britain and thereafter urged the vigorous prosecution of war, particularly against Indians. In 1815 he was appointed one of the commissioners to survey the boundary between Georgia and the Creek Indian territory in Alabama. While engaged in that expedition Sevier died near Fort Decatur, Alabama, on September 24, 1815.

Shafter, William Rufus (1835–1906), army officer. Born on October 16, 1835, in Galesburg, Michigan, Shafter had been teaching school for three years when he enlisted and took a commission as a first lieutenant in the 7th Michigan Infantry in August 1861. He took part in the battle at Ball's Bluff, Virginia, October 21, and in the Peninsula campaign of 1862, distinguishing himself at Fair Oaks (Seven Pines), May 31. In September 1862 he was appointed major in the 19th Michigan Infantry. At Thompson's Station, Tennessee, on March 9, 1863, he was taken prisoner; exchanged in May, he was promoted to lieutenant colonel in June. In April 1864 he was appointed colonel of the 17th (Colored) Infantry, which he led at Nashville, December 15–16. In March 1865 he was brevetted brigadier general of volunteers. Mustered out of volunteer service in November 1865, he entered the regular army as lieutenant colonel of the 41st Infantry in January 1867. In March 1867 he received a brevet to colonel for his actions at Fair Oaks in 1862. In April 1869 he was transferred to the 24th Infantry, with which he served on the frontier. In March 1879 he was promoted to colonel of the 1st Infantry, and in May 1897 he advanced to brigadier general in command of the Department of California. On the outbreak of the Spanish–American War he was appointed major general of volunteers in May 1898 and ordered to Tampa, Florida, where he organized the expeditionary force destined for Cuba. He sailed on June 14 in command of the 15,000-man V Corps, comprising the bulk of the regular army, and was conveyed by Adm. William T. Sampson to the south coast of Cuba. On June 22 landings began at Daiquirí, and they continued the next day at Siboney after the occupation of that port by Gen. Henry W. Lawton. The V Corps then advanced on Santiago, fighting an engagement at Las Guásimas on June 24, and, with Gen. Jacob F. Kent's infantry on the left and Gen. Joseph Wheeler's dismounted cavalry on the right, attacked the city's defenses along the San Juan Heights on July 1. They were reinforced by Lawton's division after his seizure of the village of El Caney to the northeast. The corpulent Shafter was unable to command in the field because of the tropical heat. With the carrying of the San Juan Heights (and of Kettle Hill by Lt. Col. Theodore Roosevelt's Rough Riders) the V Corps paused before the more heavily fortified inner defenses of Santiago. The defenders' position became desperate with the destruction of Adm. Cervera's fleet on July 3, and by July 16 they were willing to surrender to Shafter. By that time the American army was suffering from epidemics of typhoid, malaria, and yellow fever, compounded by poor rations. A much celebrated "round-robin" letter sent by Roosevelt and Col. Leonard Wood and signed by all the division and brigade commanders in V Corps was sent to Shafter to arouse his concern for the rapidly deteriorating condition of the army, but its prior publication by the Associated Press touched off what was to prove a very long-lived public outcry over the conduct of the war. During August 8–25 Shafter embarked some 25,000 troops for Montauk Point, Long Island, where the army had hastily established an isolated medical detention camp. Nearly 80 percent of the men were ill. In October 1898 Shafter was named commander of the Department of the East and a few days later transferred to command of the Department of California and the Columbia. He retired from the regular army in October 1899 but continued in his volunteer commission until June 1901. In July he was promoted to major general on the retired list. He settled on a ranch near Bakersfield, California, and died there on November 12, 1906.

Shaw, John (1773–1823), naval officer. Born in 1773 in Mountmellick, Queen's County (now Laoighis), Ireland, Shaw, son of an English army officer, came to America in December 1790 and settled in Philadelphia. He entered the merchant service and by 1797 had risen to master of a vessel engaged in trade in the West Indies. In August 1798, the naval war with France having put an end to his trade, he was commissioned a lieutenant in the navy. He served for a time aboard the *Montezuma,* convoying merchant vessels in the West Indies, and in December 1799 was given command of the schooner *Enterprise,* a fast, lightly armed vessel built mainly for service against privateers. In an 8-month cruise Shaw captured 8 French privateers—including the notorious *L'Aigle,*

taken July 4, 1800, and the *Flambeau,* of superior armament, July 23—and recaptured 11 American prizes. Later in the year illness forced him to relinquish command of the *Enterprise* to Lt. Andrew Sterrett. In 1801 he commanded the *George Washington* to Algiers. In 1802, on furlough, he sailed a merchant vessel to China. Promoted to master commandant in May 1804 while still on leave of absence, he returned to active duty in 1805 and commanded the *John Adams* to the Mediterranean, joining the squadron at Tripoli after peace had been established. In 1806 he was ordered to New Orleans to assemble a gunboat squadron for coastal defense and the protection of commerce; the squadron eventually numbered 20 vessels. He was promoted to captain in August 1807. From 1808 to 1810 Shaw commanded the Norfolk, Virginia, navy yard, and from 1811 to 1814 he was again stationed at New Orleans, commanding the naval force that cooperated with Gen. James Wilkinson in the capture of Mobile, Alabama, in April 1813. In 1814 he assumed command of the squadron blockaded by the British in the Thames River at New London, Connecticut. In 1815 he joined the squadron commanded by Commodore William Bainbridge in the Mediterranean. On the conclusion of peace with Algiers in September he was left to command a token Mediterranean force, comprising the frigates *United States* and *Constellation* and the sloops *Erie* and *Ontario.* He returned to the United States on the *Constellation* in December 1817 and saw no more sea duty. He commanded the navy yard at Boston and later the yard at Charleston, South Carolina. Shaw died in Philadelphia on September 17, 1823.

Shaw, Robert Gould (1837–1863), army officer. Born in Boston on October 10, 1837, Shaw was of a distinguished Boston family. He attended Harvard in 1856–1859 and then entered a mercantile house in New York City. In April 1861 he enlisted as a private in the 7th New York Regiment, and in May he was commissioned a second lieutenant in the 2nd Massachusetts, advancing to first lieutenant in July. In August 1862 he was promoted to captain. He had seen action in numerous engagements when, in April 1863, he was appointed colonel of the 54th Massachusetts Regiment, the first regiment of black troops from a free state to be mustered into federal service. The 54th left Boston in May and went into combat as part of Gen. Quincy A. Gillmore's X Corps at James Island near Charleston, South Carolina, on July 16. On July 18 Shaw led his men in an assault on Fort Wagner on Morris Island, at the entrance to Charleston harbor. Having reached the rampart, sword in hand, he fell mortally wounded. He was buried, along with nearly half the regiment, in the fort. A subscription fund begun in Boston in 1865 was used to commission a memorial. Placed on Boston Common opposite the Massachusetts State House in

1897, the monument consisted of a bronze bas-relief sculpture by Augustus Saint-Gaudens set in a granite frame designed by Charles F. McKim.

Shays, Daniel (1747?–1825), Revolutionary soldier and post-Revolutionary rebel. Shays was born, probably in Hopkinton, Massachusetts, about 1747, although the town's records do not mention his name. Little is known of his early life, but he responded to the call for volunteers at the outbreak of the Revolution and served with distinction at Bunker Hill, Ticonderoga, Saratoga, and Stony Point, being commissioned captain in the 5th Massachusetts at the beginning of 1777. He resigned from the army in 1780 and settled in Pelham, Massachusetts, where he held several town offices. The post-Revolutionary prosperity soon gave way to a severe country-wide depression. The Massachusetts legislature ignored demands for redress of grievances arising from the economic situation, demands which were especially urgent in western Massachusetts, and the situation deteriorated there in 1786 to the point of armed rebellion. Shays was but one of several leaders, but his name became associated with the revolt, mainly because of a confrontation in Springfield on September 26 between a group of about 800 armed farmers and about the same number of militia under Gen. William Shepard. The immediate question was whether the state supreme court should be allowed to sit, for the farmers feared that it would return indictments against them. An agreement was reached and the court adjourned, but a period of chaotic relations between the two sides ensued, and actual fighting broke out during the winter when the rebels marched on the arsenal at Springfield on January 25, 1787, and were scattered by state troops. After confused rallyings, a band under Shays was defeated by Gen. Benjamin Lincoln at Petersham on February 2, 1787. He fled to Vermont and was one of the few who were exempted from a general pardon issued later in the year. He was condemned to death in absentia, but in February 1788 he petitioned for pardon and was granted it on June 13. He later moved to New York State, where he lived until his death in Sparta on September 29, 1825. In his later years he was given a pension for his service in the Revolution; and he always insisted that he had fought then and in the rebellion for exactly the same principles. Shays's Rebellion had the effect of hastening not only the specific reforms in taxation and judicial procedure demanded by the rebels but also the movement for a stronger central government capable of dealing swiftly with such uprisings.

Shelby, Evan (1719–1794), colonial and Revolutionary militia officer and public official. Born in 1719, presumably in Tregaron, Cardiganshire, Wales (where, at least, he was baptized in October of that year), Shelby came to America with his family about 1734, settling in Franklin County, Pennsylvania. In 1739 they moved to Frederick County, Maryland. Shelby acquired considerable holdings in land and engaged in the fur trade. In 1755 he served in Gen. Edward Braddock's campaign. In 1758, as captain of a company of Maryland rangers, he led the advance force in Gen. John Forbes's expedition against Fort Duquesne and distinguished himself on more than one occasion. By the end of the French and Indian War he had risen to major. Much of his property was lost during the Indian depredations in Pontiac's War, and about 1773 Shelby removed to Fincastle County in southwest Virginia, a spot near the present site of Bristol, where he soon rebuilt his fortune. He commanded a militia company from Fincastle in Lord Dunmore's War in 1774, taking conspicuous part in the final battle of Point Pleasant, October 10, where he succeeded to command of the Virginia forces. In 1776 he was appointed a major of militia, and in December of that year he became colonel of the militia of the newly organized Washington County. He concerned himself principally with defense of the frontier and in 1779 led some 2000 men in a successful campaign against the Chickamauga Indians (a branch of the Cherokee tribe). The extension of the Virginia–North Carolina border placed his residence in North Carolina, and in 1781 he was elected to the legislature of that state. In 1786 he was appointed brigadier general of North Carolina militia. He became involved in the complicated events that led to the formation of the short-lived state of Franklin and in August 1787 declined election as governor of the state to succeed John Sevier. Shelby died near what is now Bristol, Tennessee, on December 4, 1794. His son was Isaac Shelby.

Shelby, Isaac (1750–1826), Revolutionary militia officer and public official. Born in Washington County (then part of Frederick County), Maryland, on December 11, 1750, Shelby, the son of Evan Shelby, grew up in a frontier environment. In 1773 he and his family moved to the Holston River region of what is now eastern Tennessee. For the next eight years he was engaged mainly in soldiering, taking part in Lord Dunmore's War as a lieutenant in his father's company, and in surveying the western lands for settlement. He saw continuous service during the Revolutionary War, mostly against various Indian tribes in the Kentucky and Tennessee regions, and in 1779 he served in the Virginia legislature as well. Appointed colonel of North Carolina militia in the spring of 1780, he saw action in several skirmishes in eastern South Carolina in 1780. When Gen. Horatio Gates's defeat at Camden, August 16, left the region open to the depredations of Maj. Patrick Ferguson's Loyalists, Shelby organized a volunteer force to stop him. Reinforced by militia forces under Lt. Col. John

Sevier, Col. William Campbell, Maj. Joseph Mac-Dowell, and Maj. Joseph Winston, he met Ferguson at Kings Mountain, North Carolina, on October 7 and wiped out his command. After serving on the western Indian frontier early in 1781 he returned to the field in October at the head of 500 militia to serve under Gen. Francis Marion. At the end of the year he was elected to the North Carolina legislature. After the war Shelby settled in Kentucky and took part in making the political arrangements that led to statehood. In April 1792 he was a delegate to the convention that drew up Kentucky's constitution, and the next month he was elected the state's first governor. He served one four-year term, then retired to private life until being elected governor again in August 1812. His main duties during this term of office had to do with the prosecution of the War of 1812. He assembled and led 4000 volunteers in Gen. William Henry Harrison's invasion of Canada and took part in the battle of the Thames, October 5, 1813, at which the British were defeated. After his term of office expired Shelby was offered in 1817 the post of secretary of war in President James Monroe's cabinet, but he declined. In 1818 he joined Gen. Andrew Jackson in negotiating a treaty with the Chickasaw Indians. He died on July 18, 1826, at his home, Traveller's Rest, in Lincoln County, Kentucky.

Shelby, Joseph Orville (1830–1897), Confederate army officer. Born in Lexington, Kentucky, on December 12, 1830, Shelby attended Transylvania University in 1846–1849 and soon thereafter began a cordage business in Lexington. In 1852 he moved to Missouri, settling finally in Waverly, where he followed the same business. He led a company of proslavery Kentuckians in the Kansas–Missouri border war, and by the outbreak of the Civil War he was a prominent slaveholder in Missouri. With the coming of war he raised a company of cavalry, joined the irregular force under Gen. Sterling Price, and took part in the battle of Wilson's Creek, August 10. In September he took part in the siege of Lexington. In leading daring cavalry raids against federal posts and capturing great quantities of stores, Shelby quickly became a dashing heroic figure both to his men and to Confederate sympathizers throughout the region. He was prominent at the battle of Elkhorn Tavern (Pea Ridge), March 7–8, 1862. Commissioned colonel in the Confederate army in 1862, he was given command of a three-regiment cavalry force known as the "Iron Brigade." Raiding Missouri from camps in Arkansas, the brigade took part in countless skirmishes and battles during 1862–1863. In December 1862 Shelby's forces seized the outer defenses of Springfield. He was again with Price in the attack on Helena, Arkansas, on July 4, 1863. In September–October 1863 he led a long raid into Missouri, capturing Booneville, Neosho, Warsaw, Tipton, and other towns. In March 1864, with about 1000 men, he successfully held off Gen. Frederick Steele's 15,000 men near Prescott, Arkansas. By that time promoted to brigadier general, Shelby accompanied Price in his last invasion of Missouri in September 1864. On October 15 he captured Glasgow; he took part in the battle of Westport, October 21–23, and effectively covered Price's retreat. With Price he fell back to Arkansas and thence to Texas. On learning of Gen. Robert E. Lee's surrender he and his men crossed into Mexico in July 1865 and offered their services to Maximilian. Maximilian gave them some land for a Confederate colony, but after the emperor's fall in 1866 Shelby returned to Missouri and settled in Bates County, where he engaged in farming. An enormously popular figure, Shelby made a dramatic appearance as a defense witness in the trial of Frank James, the outlaw, in Gallatin, Missouri, in 1882 and by his testimony won an acquittal. In 1893 he was appointed by President Grover Cleveland to the post of U.S. marshal for western Missouri. Shelby died in Adrian, Missouri, on February 13, 1897.

Shepard, Alan Bartlett, Jr. (1923–   ), naval officer and astronaut. Born on November 18, 1923, in East Derry, New Hampshire, Shepard graduated from the Naval Academy in 1944. After service on the destroyer *Cogswell* in the Pacific he entered flight training. Qualified as a pilot in March 1947, he served with Fighter Squadron 42 until 1949 and in 1950 took test pilot training at Patuxent River, Maryland. From 1953 to 1955 he was with Fighter Squadron 193, based first in California and later on the carrier *Oriskany* in the Pacific. In 1955–1957 he was again at the Patuxent River facility as a test pilot in various projects and for a time as an instructor. On graduating from the Naval War College in 1958 he was attached to the staff of the Atlantic Fleet commander. In April 1959, by then a lieutenant commander, he was chosen one of the original seven Project Mercury astronauts. Two years of rigorous training followed, and on May 5, 1961, Shepard became the first American to enter space in a 15-minute suborbital flight in his Mercury capsule *Freedom 7*, a flight that attained an altitude of 115 miles above the earth. A short time later he was promoted to commander. In 1963 a minor medical problem with his ear that affected his equilibrium caused him to be removed from active status. In 1965 Shepard was named chief of the Astronaut Office of the National Aeronautics and Space Administration. In 1967 he was promoted to captain. Following surgical correction of the ear problem he returned to full astronaut status in 1969, and on January 31, 1971, he again entered space as commander of the *Apollo XIV* mission (with Stuart A. Roosa and Edgar D. Mitchell). On February 5 he piloted the lunar landing module *Antares* to a landing just 60 feet from the nominal target, and a short time later he became the fifth man to walk on the moon. During two periods of activity on the surface scientific instruments were set up, samples of soil and rock collected, and a televised first lunar "golf shot" was executed by Shepard. The astronauts splashed down in the Pacific in the command module *Kitty Hawk* on February 9. Promoted to rear admiral in August 1971, he was designated in September of that year a delegate to the United Nations General Assembly by President Richard M. Nixon. He retired from the navy and NASA in August 1974 to pursue private interests. Shepard was elected to the National Space Hall of Fame in August 1969.

Shepard, William (1737–1817), Revolutionary army officer. Born in Westfield, Massachusetts, on December 1, 1737, Shepard served in the militia for six years during the French and Indian War, rising from private to captain. He then took up farming in his native town. In May 1775 he was appointed lieutenant colonel of a Massachusetts regiment, with which he served through the siege of Boston. In January 1776 he was commissioned lieutenant colonel of the 3rd Infantry Regiment of the Continental army, and in October he was promoted to colonel, dating from May, and put in command of the 4th Massachusetts. In all he saw action in more than a score of battles in the Revolution. Mustered out in January 1783, he returned to Westfield. He served in the legislature in 1785–1786 and in the latter year was appointed major general of militia for Hampshire County. In September 1786 he was compelled to call out the militia to defend the federal armory and district court in Springfield against Daniel Shays and his rebels. Four months later the rebels reappeared and this time were not dissuaded; on January 25, 1787, Shepard and the militia repulsed an attack on the arsenal by rebels hoping to obtain arms. That defeat, followed by Gen. Benjamin Lincoln's mopping up, ended the rebellion. Shepard was a member of the governor's council from 1792 to 1796, and from March 1797 to March 1803 he was a member of the House of Representatives. He died in Westfield, Massachusetts, on November 16, 1817.

Shepherd, Lemuel Cornick, Jr. (1896–   ), marine officer. Born on February 10, 1896, in Norfolk, Virginia, Shepherd graduated from Virginia Military Institute in 1917 and in April of that year was commissioned a second lieutenant in the marine corps. He was ordered to France in June and served with the 5th Marine Regiment in the army's 2nd Division through the Aisne–Marne, St. Mihiel, and Meuse–Argonne operations. He received promotions to first lieutenant in August 1917 and captain in July 1918. He returned from occupation duty in 1919 and during 1920–1922 was an aide to Gen. John A. Le-

jeune, commandant of the corps. He then saw sea duty with marine detachments aboard the *Nevada* and the *Idaho*. After two years at the marine barracks at Norfolk, Virginia, he spent two years, 1927–1929, with the 4th Marine Regiment in China. He graduated from the field officers course of the Marine Corps Schools, Quantico, Virginia, in 1930 and until 1934 was stationed in Haiti, receiving promotion to major in April 1932. He was on the staff of the Marine Corps Institute until 1936, advancing to lieutenant colonel in July 1935, and on graduating from the Naval War College in 1937 he took command of a battalion of the 5th Marines assigned to Fleet Marine Force. In 1939 he was attached to the staff of the Marine Corps Schools. Promoted to colonel in August 1940, Shepherd was named commander of the 9th Marine Regiment in March 1942, and in January 1943 he was moved up to assistant commander of the 1st Marine Division, under Gen. Alexander A. Vandegrift, receiving promotion to brigadier general in July 1943. In December 1943 the 1st Division entered combat at Cape Gloucester, New Britain. In April 1944 Shepherd took command of the 1st Provisional Marine Brigade, and in July 1944 he took part in the assault on Guam. In September he was promoted to major general in command of the 6th Marine Division (an element of Gen. Roy S. Geiger's III Amphibious Corps), which he led in the capture of Okinawa in April–June 1945 and which was sent to China in October. In November 1946 he was named assistant commandant and chief of staff of the corps. In April 1948 he became commandant of the Marine Corps Schools. In June 1950 he was promoted to lieutenant general and appointed commander of the Fleet Marine Force, Pacific. He was on the staff of Gen. Douglas MacArthur, supreme commander of United Nations forces in Korea, during the amphibious landing at Inch'on in September, and he was among the first officers flown into the liberated Kimpo Airfield. In January 1952 Shepherd became commandant of the marine corps with the rank of general. He held that post until his retirement in January 1956. Later in that year he was named chairman of the Inter-American Defense Board. He was succeeded as commandant of the marine corps by Gen. Randolph M. Pate.

Sheridan, Philip Henry (1831–1888), army officer. Born on March 6, 1831, Sheridan at various times in his life gave his birthplace as Albany, New York; Boston; and Somerset, Ohio. In any case he was appointed to West Point from the last, graduated in 1853 after having been suspended for a year for fighting, and was commissioned in the infantry. He served with the 1st Infantry on the Rio Grande frontier of Texas and with the 4th Infantry in Oregon Territory, seeing much action against Indians. Promoted to first lieutenant in March 1861 and to captain in May, he began his Civil War service as a staff officer under Gen. Samuel R. Curtis in Missouri and then under Gen. Henry W. Halleck in the Corinth campaign of 1862. In May 1862 he finally received a line assignment with his appointment as colonel of the 2nd Michigan Cavalry. He distinguished himself at Booneville, Mississippi, on July 1, where he led a brigade in a raid on the town and engaged Gen. William J. Hardee's cavalry, and was promoted to brigadier general of volunteers later in the month. He performed brilliantly in command of a division under Gen. Don Carlos Buell at Perryville, October 8, and under Gen. William S. Rosecrans at Stones River (Murfreesboro), December 31–January 3, 1863, where he stubbornly held the center of the Union line against heavy attack by Gen. Leonidas Polk. Not yet thirty-two years old, he was promoted to major general of volunteers to date from December 31. Continuing with the Army of the Cumberland, he took part in the Tullahoma campaign in the summer of 1863, and at Chickamauga, September 18–20, when Rosecrans's mistaken order left Gen. George H. Thomas's corps virtually alone on the field, Sheridan quickly rallied the XX Corps to his support. At Chattanooga he led a charge up and over Missionary Ridge on November 25, his division carrying all before it; that exploit brought him to the attention of Gen. Ulysses S. Grant. In April 1864 Grant called him east to take command of the 12,000-man cavalry corps of the Army of the Potomac. During the advance toward Richmond in May 1864, Sheridan conducted raids against Confederate supply depots and lines of communication. He defeated the Confederate cavalry under Gen. J. E. B. Stuart at Todd's Tavern, May 7, and again during the Spotsylvania campaign at Yellow Tavern, May 11, where Stuart was mortally wounded. He was engaged at Hawes's Shop, May 28, and while conducting an operation against the Virginia Central Railroad toward Charlottesville he fought an inconclusive battle with Gen. Wade Hampton at Trevilian Station, June 11–12. In August Grant sent Sheridan to take command of all Union forces in the Shenandoah valley from Gen. David Hunter. After more than a month of careful preparation he moved against Gen. Jubal A. Early, defeating him at Winchester (Opequon) September 19, and Fisher's Hill, September 22. Following the latter battle he was promoted to brigadier general of regulars. Instead of pursuing Early, Sheridan then undertook a scorched-earth campaign, devastating the resources of the valley that had supported an entire Confederate army, along with numerous bands of guerrillas and irregulars, for so long. On October 19 his encamped army was attacked by the regrouped Early at Cedar Creek. Sheridan was just returning from Washington, D.C., and at the beginning of the battle was in Winchester, 15 miles distant. His dash to join the army was later immortalized in verse in Thomas Buchanan Read's "Sheridan's Ride." His arrival on the field rallied the Union forces, who were being soundly defeated, and the counterattack shattered Early's army. In November Sheridan was promoted to major general of regulars and in February 1865 was voted the thanks of Congress. In February 1865 he rejoined Grant in central Virginia, destroying en route all communications to the north of besieged Petersburg. He then concentrated his forces southwest of Petersburg. Repulsed by Gen. George E. Pickett at Dinwiddie Court House on March 31, he regrouped at Five Forks and defeated Pickett on April 1. His command of the only railroad out of Petersburg forced Gen. Robert E. Lee at last to abandon that stronghold on April 2 and race westward. Sheridan took part in the battle at Sayler's Creek, April 6, and then dashed ahead to block Lee at Appomattox Court House. Lee then surrendered on April 9. From May 1865 to March 1867 Sheridan commanded the Military Division (later Department) of the Gulf, where he provided moral and material support to the liberal forces in Mexico in their struggle with the French-imposed government of Maximilian. In March 1867 he was given command of the Fifth Military District, comprising Texas and Louisiana, but his harsh enforcement of Reconstruction measures led to his transfer in September to command of the Department of the Missouri. During 1868–1869 he directed a campaign against Cheyenne, Comanche, and Kiowa Indians in the Washita valley of Kansas and Indian Territory (Oklahoma). The campaign was marked by Maj. George A. Forsyth's battle at Beecher's Island in November and Col. George A. Custer's attack on Black Kettle's village in December 1868. (It was during this campaign that he summarized his attitude: "The only good Indian is a dead Indian.") In January 1869 Sheridan established Camp Wichita, later renamed Fort Sill, as the principal fort in Indian Territory. In March 1869 he was promoted to lieutenant general in command of the Division of the Missouri. During 1870–1871 he was an observer with the Prussian armies in the Franco-Prussian War. On his return to his headquarters in Chicago he directed the major campaign against the Indians of the Southern Plains, conducted by Col. Nelson A. Miles, Col. Ranald S. Mackenzie, and others on the Red River, and that against the northern tribes, carried on by Gen. Alfred H. Terry, Col. George Crook, and others in the Bighorn valley. In 1878 he moved to command of the Military Divisions of the West and Southwest. In November 1883 he succeeded Gen. William T. Sherman as commanding general of the army. In June 1888 he was promoted to the rank of general of the army. He had just completed his *Personal Memoirs of P. H. Sheridan*, 1888, when he died in Nonquitt, Massachusetts, on August 5, 1888. Although not a gifted strategist, Sheridan became a great commander through aggressiveness, astute use of military intelligence, and the loyalty he inspired in his men.

Sherman, Forrest Percival (1896–1951), naval officer. Born on October 30, 1896, in Merrimack, New Hampshire, Sherman attended the Massachusetts Institute of Technology for a year before entering the Naval Academy, from which he graduated in 1917. He served on the *Murray* and the *Nashville* in European waters during 1917–1919, receiving temporary promotion to lieutenant and becoming permanent in that grade in 1920. He commanded the *Barry* in the Atlantic Fleet in 1921. He completed flight training at the Pensacola, Florida, Naval Air Station in 1922, and in 1923–1924 he was attached to Fighting Plane Squadron 2 aboard the carrier *Aroostook*. He was on the training staff at Pensacola in 1924–1926, and after graduating from the Naval War College in 1927 he served tours on the carriers *Lexington* and *Saratoga*. In 1930–1931 he was an instructor at the Naval Academy, returning to the *Saratoga* in 1931 and assuming command of Fighting Squadron 1 in 1932. He commanded the Fighting Wing in 1932–1933. After three years as chief of aviation ordnance in the Bureau of Ordnance he was assigned to the *Ranger* in 1936, and in 1937, promoted to commander, he was made fleet aviation officer on the staff of the commander of the U.S. Fleet. Early in 1940 he was assigned to the office of the chief of naval operations. In May 1942, by then a captain, he took command of the carrier *Wasp* of Adm. Frank J. Fletcher's carrier force. On September 15 the *Wasp* was sunk by Japanese torpedoes during the Guadalcanal campaign. Sherman then became aide and chief of staff to the commander of the Pacific Fleet Air Force, Adm. John H. Towers. He was promoted to rear admiral in April 1943. In November he became deputy chief of staff under Adm. Chester W. Nimitz. He took command of Carrier Division 1 in October 1945 and two months later was named deputy chief of naval operations with the rank of vice admiral. In that post he played a major role in the negotiations preceding the unification of the armed services and in the establishment of the postwar network of U.S. naval bases around the world. He and Gen. Lauris Norstad were the principal authors of the National Security Act of 1947. In January 1948 he was put in command of U.S. naval forces in the Mediterranean, which were reorganized in June as the Sixth Fleet; and in November 1949 he became chief of naval operations with the rank of admiral. He was still in that post when he died on July 22, 1951, in Naples, Italy, during a round of discussions on European defense.

Sherman, Thomas West (1813–1879), army officer. Born in Newport, Rhode Island, on March 26, 1813, Sherman won appointment to West Point by a personal appeal to President Andrew Jackson. He graduated in 1836, was commissioned in the artillery, and served until 1838 in the Seminole War in Florida. Promoted to first lieutenant in March 1838, he was then ordered to duty in Indian Territory (Oklahoma) for a time, after which he was again in Florida. In May 1846 he advanced to captain. During the Mexican War he served under Gen. Zachary Taylor, winning a brevet to major at Buena Vista, February 22–23, 1847. From 1848 to 1853 he was stationed at Fort Trumbull, Connecticut, and then at Fort Adams, Rhode Island; from 1853 to 1861 he was on the frontier, seeing garrison duty and action against Indians in Minnesota and helping suppress the Kansas border disturbances. On the outbreak of the Civil War he was called to Washington, D.C.; he received promotions to major in April 1861 and to lieutenant colonel in May and was appointed brigadier general of volunteers in the latter month. After commanding artillery units in the defenses of Washington and of Baltimore, he commanded a force of nearly 13,000 army troops in the expedition to Port Royal, South Carolina, by Flag-Officer Samuel F. Du Pont's squadron in November 1861. After the reduction of most Confederate strongholds by naval gunfire, Sherman's troops took possession of Fort Walker on Hilton Head, Fort Beauregard on Bay Point opposite, and other points. Subsequently troops of that force also occupied Bull's Bay, South Carolina, and Fort Clinch at Fernandina, Florida. In April 1862 Sherman was given command of a division of the Army of the Tennessee, then engaged in the Corinth campaign. From September 1862 to January 1863 he commanded a division in the Department of the Gulf, and from January to May he was engaged in the defense of New Orleans. He took part in Gen. Nathaniel P. Banks's unsuccessful expedition against Port Hudson, Louisiana, in May and in the second assault, on May 27, received a wound that necessitated the amputation of his right leg. In February 1864 he returned to duty in command of a reserve brigade of artillery at Fort Jackson and Fort St. Philip below New Orleans. From June 1864 to February 1865 he commanded the Division of New Orleans. In March 1865 he was brevetted brigadier general of regulars for Port Hudson and major general of volunteers for his war services. Mustered out of volunteer service in 1866, he served as colonel of the 3rd Artillery at Fort Adams, Rhode Island, and elsewhere until November 1870. He was retired for disability in December 1870 under his brevet commission of major general, and he died in Newport, Rhode Island, on March 16, 1879.

Sherman, William Tecumseh (1820–1891), army officer. Born in Lancaster, Ohio, on February 8, 1820, Sherman, son of a state supreme court judge and an elder brother of John Sherman, statesman, grew up from the age of nine in the home of Sen. Thomas Ewing. He graduated from West Point in 1840, was commissioned in the artillery, and while serving in Florida against the Seminoles was promoted to first lieutenant in November 1841. He subsequently served at various posts in the South, and on the outbreak of the Mexican War in 1846 he was sent around the Horn to California, where he was on the staff of Gen. Stephen W. Kearny and later that of Gen. Persifor F. Smith. In 1850 he returned east, receiving promotion to captain in the commissary department in September. Three years later he resigned and took a partnership in a San Francisco bank. He later represented the firm, whose headquarters were in St. Louis, in New York City, but on its bankruptcy in 1857 he took up the practice of law in Leavenworth, Kansas. He failed to secure reappointment to the army, and from October 1859 to January 1861 he was superintendent of a military academy (a forerunner of Louisiana State University) in Alexandria, Louisiana. On the secession of Louisiana he returned to St. Louis, where he was briefly president of a street railway company. In May 1861 he returned to the army as colonel of the new 13th Infantry. He commanded a brigade under Gen. Irvin McDowell at Bull Run (Manassas), July 21, and in August was appointed brigadier general of volunteers. Ordered to Kentucky, he succeeded Gen. Robert Anderson in command there in October; in November he was relieved by Gen. Don Carlos Buell and ordered to report to Gen. Henry W. Halleck in the Western Department. He commanded the District of Cairo (Illinois) until the conclusion of Gen. Ulysses S. Grant's campaign against Fort Henry and Fort Donelson in February 1862, when he was given a division of Grant's Army of the Tennessee. He was conspicuous in the battle of Shiloh (Pittsburg Landing), April 6–7, and in May was promoted to major general of volunteers. He took part in the Corinth campaign until July, when Grant ordered him to Memphis, Tennessee, to secure that city as a Union base. In December Grant ordered him to move against Vicksburg, Mississippi, the major Confederate stronghold on the Mississippi. Raiding by Gen. Earl Van Dorn and Gen. Nathan B. Forrest on his extended line of communication, together with Grant's failure to keep Gen. John C. Pemberton bottled up, weakened his position, and after being decisively repulsed at Chickasaw Bluffs, December 29, he was forced to abandon the campaign; a short time later he was superseded in command by Gen. John A. McClernand. Sherman commanded the XV Corps in McClernand's Army of the Mississippi and took part in the capture of Arkansas Post, January 11. He retained command of the XV Corps when it became part of Grant's reorganized Army of the Tennessee later in the month. In March he demonstrated before Vicksburg and, with Adm. David D. Porter's gunboats, on the Yazoo waterways to cover the movement of McClernand and Gen. James B. McPherson (both under Grant) to the south, and on April 29–30 he feinted toward Hawes's Bluff above Vicksburg to divert attention from Porter's running of the batteries to join Grant below. He then rejoined

Grant's main army for the movement against Jackson, Mississippi, taking it from Gen. Joseph E. Johnston on May 14 and holding it while Grant turned back to Vicksburg. At the conclusion of the campaign in July Sherman was promoted to brigadier general of regulars. In the autumn of 1863 he took part in the relief of Gen. William S. Rosecrans's Army of the Cumberland besieged in Chattanooga, succeeding Grant as commander of the Army of the Tennessee in October. Following the battle of Chattanooga, November 24–25, he moved on to Knoxville, where his approach early in December forced Gen. James Longstreet to give up his siege of the city and of Gen. Ambrose E. Burnside. He then returned to winter headquarters in the west, first on the Tennessee River and later at Vicksburg. In February he led an inconclusive expedition toward Meridian, Mississippi, where an arsenal and various other installations were destroyed. In March 1864, when Grant became Union commander in chief, Sherman again succeeded him in the west as commander of the Military Division of the Mississippi, his forces consisting of Gen. George H. Thomas's Army of the Cumberland, Gen. McPherson's Army of the Tennessee, and Gen. John M. Schofield's Army of the Ohio. Sherman concentrated at Chattanooga the three armies of some 100,-000 men, and on May 4, a date coordinated with Grant's (Army of the Potomac) move to the Rapidan in the eastern theater, he set out toward Atlanta. Gen. Joseph E. Johnston, with about 65,000 men, retired slowly before him. In a campaign of position and maneuver Sherman took 74 days to cover the hundred miles to Atlanta, his only error being in frontally attacking Johnston, well entrenched at Kennesaw Mountain, on June 27. Running battles were fought at Dalton, May 8–12, Resaca, May 13–16, New Hope Church, May 24–28, and Dallas, May 25–28. On July 20, while completing his encirclement of Atlanta, he beat back a sortie out of the city by Gen. John B. Hood's army at Peach Tree Creek. On July 28 Gen. Stephen D. Lee's corps of Hood's army was beaten back at Ezra Church. Atlanta was occupied on September 2. Sherman sent Thomas back to protect the base at Nashville, and after briefly following Hood into northwest Georgia he detached Schofield to join Thomas in dealing with him. From Atlanta, which he burned to the ground, Sherman moved out on November 16, abandoning his supply line. On a 60-mile front his army devastated the richest agricultural resource of the Confederacy. The famous, or infamous, "march to the sea," was less attended by looting than has often been charged, although Sherman's strict orders and efficient discipline did not extend to the many stragglers accompanying or following the march. Savannah was reached on December 10 and occupied December 21; from then on a supply line by sea was open to him. On February 1 he started north through the Carolinas, his forces then consisting of the Army of the Tennessee under Gen. Oliver O. Howard and the Army of Georgia under Gen. Henry W. Slocum; Schofield later rejoined him. On February 17 he drove Gen. Wade Hampton out of Columbia, South Carolina, and that night, without orders from him, the city was burned. He continued north, his forces irresistible, and on April 17–18 met with Gen. Johnston to arrange surrender terms. Johnston formally surrendered to Sherman on April 26 near Durham Station, North Carolina. In June Sherman took command of the Division of the Missouri, receiving in July 1866 promotion to lieutenant general. Later in that year he was sent on an unsuccessful diplomatic mission to meet with President Benito Juárez of Mexico. In March 1869 he became commanding general of the army, a post he held with the rank of general of the army until resigning it in November 1883; he retired from the army in February 1884. A strong movement to give him the Republican presidential nomination in 1884 was thwarted when he wired the convention: "If nominated, I will not accept. If elected, I will not serve." His more famous statement that "war … is all hell" occurred in a speech at Columbus, Ohio, on August 11, 1880. In 1885 he published two volumes of *Memoirs.* Sherman lived in St. Louis until 1886; he then moved to New York City, where he died on February 14, 1891. The rank of general of the army expired with him and was not revived until December 1944. It has been claimed that Sherman's Georgia campaign, which remained bitterly controversial for decades, was the first application of the modern concept of "total war," aimed at the enemy's civilian morale and productive capacity as much as at his arms.

Shields, James (1806–1879), army officer and public official. Born in Altmore, County Tyrone, Ireland, on May 12, 1806, Shields received a good education and was a tutor for a time in Scotland before making his way to the United States about 1826. He settled in Kaskaskia, Illinois, where in 1832, after serving in the militia in the Black Hawk War, he undertook the practice of law. He was elected to the legislature in 1836, elected state auditor in 1839, appointed to the state supreme court in 1843, and appointed commissioner of the general land office by President James K. Polk in 1845. In July 1846 he was commissioned brigadier general of Illinois volunteers for service in the Mexican War. At Cerro Gordo, April 18, 1847, he led his brigade around the Mexican position and was conspicuous in routing the enemy; he was severely wounded in the battle and was brevetted major general for his actions. He again distinguished himself leading a memorable charge at Churubusco, August 20. Mustered out in July 1848, Shields was appointed governor of the Oregon Territory a short time later. After only a few months he resigned to enter the Senate as a Democrat from Il-

linois in March 1849. The Senate declared his election void because he had not been a citizen the required number of years, but he was reelected to the seat and served from October 1849 to March 1855, failing of reelection. He then moved to Minnesota, was active in organizing the territory, and in May 1858 was elected one of Minnesota's first senators, serving the short term to March 1859 and again failing to be reelected. He then moved to San Francisco and developed mining interests in Mexico. In August 1861 he was appointed brigadier general of volunteers. Early in 1862 he was in the Shenandoah valley, and he succeeded in March to command of a division of Gen. Nathaniel P. Banks's V Corps. He distinguished himself in repulsing an attack by Gen. Thomas J. Jackson at Kernstown, Virginia, on March 23, receiving a wound in the battle, and was prominent in Banks's victory at Winchester on May 25. At Port Republic, June 9, he was defeated by Jackson. Shields resigned his commission in March 1863 and returned to San Francisco. In 1866 he moved again, to Carrollton, Missouri, where he resumed the practice of law. He was elected to the legislature in 1874 and 1879 and served terms as state railroad commissioner and adjutant general. In January 1879 he was elected to fill an unexpired term in the Senate, where he sat until March. He died in Ottumwa, Iowa, on June 1, 1879.

Shipp, Scott (1839–1917), Confederate army officer and educator. Born in Warrenton, Virginia, on August 2, 1839, Shipp grew up from 1849 in Boone County, Missouri. After three years at Westminster College, Fulton, Missouri, he went to work for a railroad, but soon thereafter he entered Virginia Military Institute, from which he graduated in 1859. He remained at VMI as an assistant professor until April 1861, when, as lieutenant of the provisional army of Virginia, he was ordered to conduct the cadet corps to Camp Lee, near Richmond. In July he was commissioned major of the 21st Virginia Infantry. He saw action in West Virginia and in the Shenandoah valley. In January 1862 he was ordered to the reopened VMI as commandant of cadets with the rank of lieutenant colonel. He served also as professor of mathematics and instructor in tactics. On five occasions during the war he led the cadet corps into the field, most notably under Gen. John C. Breckinridge in battle with Gen. Franz Sigel at New Market, Virginia, on May 15, 1864, where he was wounded leading the 260 cadets, formed as an infantry battalion, in a gallant charge. After the war he continued as commandant, also taking a degree in 1866 from the Lexington Law School (later part of Washington and Lee University). In 1880 he declined the presidency of the new Virginia Agricultural and Mechanical College (now Virginia Polytechnic Institute). In January 1890 he was raised to the post of superintendent at VMI, and he held it until his retirement in June 1907. During his long tenure the physical plant, course of instruction, and level of achievement at VMI were all greatly improved. He served on the board of visitors of the U.S. Military Academy in 1890 and on that of the Naval Academy in 1894. Shipp died in Lexington, Virginia, on December 4, 1917.

Short, Walter Campbell (1880–1949), army officer. Born on March 30, 1880, in Fillmore, Illinois, Short graduated from the University of Illinois in 1901 and in March 1902 took a commission as second lieutenant of infantry. After five years at the Presidio in San Francisco and in the Southwest he was promoted to first lieutenant and ordered to the Philippines in 1907. Later he served in Alaska, and in 1913 he was attached to the staff of the School of Musketry at Fort Sill, Oklahoma. He took part in the Mexican Punitive Expedition under Gen. John J. Pershing in 1916, advancing to captain in July, and in June 1917 was ordered to France with the 1st Infantry Division. He held numerous training posts and served on Pershing's headquarters staff and as chief of staff of the Third Army; he reached the temporary rank of colonel before returning to the United States in 1919. While an instructor at the General Staff School, Fort Leavenworth, Kansas, in 1919–1921, he wrote a textbook, *Employment of Machine Guns,* 1922. He was promoted to major in July 1920, and after graduating from the School of the Line, Fort Leavenworth, in 1921 he joined the General Staff. He advanced to lieutenant colonel in 1923, graduated from the Army War College in 1925, and then served three years with the 65th Infantry in Puerto Rico. After two years as an instructor again at Fort Leavenworth he served in the Bureau of Indian Affairs of the War Department from 1930 to 1934 and then, promoted to colonel, commanded the 6th Infantry at Jefferson Barracks, Missouri, from 1934 to 1936. In the latter year he was named assistant commandant of the Infantry School, Fort Benning, Georgia, receiving promotion to brigadier general in December. In 1937 he took command of a brigade of the 1st Division at Fort Ontario, New York, and from July 1938 to October 1940 he commanded the 1st Division at Fort Hamilton, New York. After commanding a provisional army corps in maneuvers earlier in 1940, he was promoted to major general and given command of the I Corps. In January 1941 he was put in command of the Hawaiian Department, and he was promoted to temporary lieutenant general in February. Ten days after the Japanese attack on Pearl Harbor on December 7, 1941, he was removed from that post. A commission headed by Supreme Court Justice Owen J. Roberts investigated the circumstances of the attack and the lack of preparedness in the army and navy forces in Hawaii and in January 1942 reported poor judgment and dereliction of duty by Short and Adm. Husband E. Kimmel. Short was retired in February. An army

hearing in 1944 reached no conclusion as to blame. A congressional investigating committee heard his testimony, early in 1946, that he had indeed erred in not instituting an alert prior to the attack but that vital information had been withheld in Washington, D.C., and that his error was one of judgment rather than dereliction. The committee's report of July 1946 substantially upheld that interpretation. Despite all official findings, Short's and Kimmel's responsibility for the success of the surprise attack was long an item of active controversy. Ill health forced him to give up in 1946 the post he had held since 1942 with the Ford Motor Company; he died in Dallas, Texas, on September 3, 1949.

Shoup, David Monroe (1904–   ), marine officer. Born on December 30, 1904, in Battle Ground, Indiana, Shoup graduated from DePauw University in 1926 and in June of that year took a commission as second lieutenant in the marine corps. His various assignments over the next several years included duty aboard the *Maryland,* 1929–1931; with the 4th Marine Regiment in Shanghai and Peking, China, 1934–1936; at the Marine Corps Schools, Quantico, Virginia, as student and instructor, 1936–1938; and with the 6th Marines in Iceland, 1941. Shortly after the outbreak of war in the Pacific he took command of a battalion of the 6th, which was withdrawn from Iceland early in 1942; later in 1942 he was attached to the staff of the 2nd Marine Division. He observed the marine operations on New Georgia in the Solomon Islands in July 1943. During November 20–22, by then a colonel, he commanded the marine force assaulting Betio Island, part of the general operations against Makin and Tarawa in the Gilberts, and won the Medal of Honor for valorous conduct (presented in January 1945) in what proved to be one of the bloodiest operations of the war. In January 1944 Shoup became chief of staff of the 2nd Marine Division, which was in action in the Marianas in that year. At the end of the year he was transferred to corps headquarters in Washington, D.C., as a logistics officer. In 1947 he was put in command of the Service Command, Fleet Marine Force, Pacific. Two years later he became chief of staff of the 1st Marine Division at Camp Pendleton, California, and from 1950 to 1952 he was commandant of the Basic School at Quantico, Virginia. In July 1953 he was named fiscal director of the corps, receiving promotion to brigadier general in September. In May 1956 he was named inspector general of recruit training, a post created following the deaths of six recruits in training at Parris Island, South Carolina. In September he became inspector general of the corps. In May 1957 he was ordered to Okinawa, where he commanded the 1st Marine Expeditionary Force and later the 3rd Marine Division; he advanced to major general in February 1958. In May 1959 he became commander of the recruit depot at Parris Island. Later in the year he was briefly chief of staff, receiving promotion to lieutenant general in September, and in January 1960 he was appointed commandant of the marine corps with the rank of general. He remained in that post until his retirement in December 1963. He was succeeded as commandant of the corps by Gen. Wallace M. Greene, Jr.

Shubrick, John Templer (1788–1815), naval officer. Born on Bull's Island, South Carolina, on September 12, 1788, Shubrick, elder brother of William B. Shubrick, abandoned the study of law to enter the navy as a midshipman in June 1806. His first cruise was on the *Chesapeake* under Capt. James Barron, and he was present at the ignominious surrender to the *Leopard* on June 22, 1807. Subsequently he served under Capt. Stephen Decatur on the *Chesapeake* and the *Argus*, and then on the *Viper*, the *Siren*, and, after his promotion to lieutenant in May 1812, under Capt. Isaac Hull on the *Constitution*. He commanded the quarter-deck guns in the victory over the *Guerrière*, August 19, 1812, and took part as third lieutenant in the defeat of the *Java*, December 29. Transferred in January 1813, he was acting first lieutenant on the *Hornet* under Capt. James Lawrence in the victory over the *Peacock*, February 24. After a period of relative inactivity he sailed in January 1815 as second lieutenant on the *President* under Decatur. He distinguished himself in the fight with the British squadron on January 15, succeeded to second-in-command before the fight ended in capture, and was held prisoner in Bermuda until the end of the war. In May 1815 he sailed again as first lieutenant on the *Guerrière*, Decatur's flagship in the Algerine War, and was conspicuous in the capture of the *Mashuda*, flagship of the Algerian fleet, on June 17. On the conclusion of a treaty with the dey, Shubrick was ordered to bear the treaty home on the brig *Epervier*. The ship is known to have passed Gibraltar about July 10, but it was never seen again.

Shubrick, William Branford (1790–1874), naval officer. Born on Bull's Island, South Carolina, on October 31, 1790, Shubrick, a younger brother of John T. Shubrick, attended Harvard for a year and then entered the navy as a midshipman in June 1806. He made his first cruise on the *Wasp*, and after serving on various other vessels he was in 1810 again on the *Wasp*, then under Capt. James Lawrence, and shipmate to James Fenimore Cooper, with whom he formed a lasting friendship. Soon after his promotion to lieutenant in January 1813 he was ordered to the *Constellation*, then blockaded at Norfolk, Virginia. On June 22 he led a land party of sailors defending Craney Island against a British boat attack. Transferred to the *Constitution*, Commodore Charles Stewart, later in the year, he was third lieutenant aboard

her in the victory over the *Cyane* and the *Levant* on February 20, 1815, receiving a medal from Congress for his part in the battle. He made a world cruise on the *Washington* in 1815–1818, was promoted to master commandant in March 1820, and after several years at the Charleston and New York navy yards he commanded the *Lexington* and then the *Natchez* between 1826 and 1829. He was promoted to captain in February 1831. He was stationed for some years at the Washington, D.C., navy yard, and in 1838–1840 he commanded the West India Squadron. From 1840 to 1843 he commanded the Norfolk navy yard, and he was chief of the Bureau of Provisions and Clothing in 1845–1846. Shortly after the outbreak of the Mexican War he obtained command of the Pacific Squadron, and he arrived on the West Coast late in December 1846 aboard the *Independence*, relieving Commodore John D. Sloat. A week later his command was superseded by that of Commodore James Biddle, arriving on the *Columbus* from the East India Squadron. In April he instituted a blockade at Mazatlán and Guaymas, and in July he succeeded Biddle as commander of the Pacific coast naval forces. Naval operations during the rest of the war included the occupation of Guaymas by landing parties from the *Congress* and *Portsmouth* on October 19, the capture of Mazatlán by sailors and marines from the *Independence*, *Congress*, *Cyane*, and *Erie* on November 11, and the occupation of San Blas by men of the *Lexington* on January 12, 1848. In May 1848 he returned east, taking command of the Philadelphia navy yard in 1849 and later heading the Bureau of Construction and Repair. In 1852 he was appointed chairman of the Lighthouse Board, a post he retained until 1870, and he served on various other boards as well. Briefly in 1853 he commanded a squadron protecting east coast fisheries. In October 1858 he sailed in command of a squadron of 19 ships and 2500 men to Paraguay to exact redress for the unprovoked attack on the surveying steamer *Water-Witch*, Lt. Thomas Jefferson Page, in February 1855. The squadron took up a position in the La Plata River and conspicuously made ready for action while Shubrick and a special commission went on to Asunción for negotiations. Satisfactory adjustments were reached diplomatically in February 1859, and the squadron returned home. Shubrick refused to support the Confederacy in 1861. Retired in December of that year, he was promoted to rear admiral on the retired list in July 1862. Shubrick died in Washington, D.C., on May 27, 1874.

Shufeldt, Robert Wilson (1822–1895), naval officer. Born in Red Hook, New York, on February 21, 1822, Shufeldt entered the navy as a midshipman in May 1839 and made his first cruise on the *Potomac* in the Pacific. He studied at the naval school in Philadelphia in 1844–1845, was attached to the Coast Survey for a year, and between 1846 and 1848 served on the *Marion* and the *United States* on the African coast and in the Mediterranean. He was chief officer of the mail steamers *Atlantic* and *Georgia* in 1849–1851. Promoted to lieutenant in October 1853, he resigned from the navy in June 1854 and entered commercial service, first with Collins Line steamers on the New York–Liverpool run and later on ships operating between New York and New Orleans. In April 1861, having commanded a New York–Havana steamer, he was appointed U.S. consul general in Cuba. In April 1863 he reentered the navy with the rank of commander, dating from November 1862. He commanded the *Conemaugh* in the South Atlantic Blockading Squadron and took part in several actions at Charleston, South Carolina. During 1864–1865 he commanded the *Proteus* in the East Gulf Blockading Squadron. After the war he commanded the *Hartford* in the East India Squadron, 1865–1866, the *Wachusett* of the Asiatic Squadron, 1866–1868, and, after his promotion to captain in December 1869, the monitor *Miantonomah* in 1870. During 1870–1871 he was in charge of an expedition surveying a canal route through the Isthmus of Tehuantepec and in Nicaragua. He commanded the *Wabash*, flagship of the European Squadron, in 1871–1872, and after a period at the New York navy yard he was chief of the Bureau of Equipment and Recruiting from 1875 to 1878, receiving promotion to commodore in September 1876. Late in 1878 he sailed on the *Ticonderoga* on a diplomatic mission. After settling problems in Liberia and Anjouan (or Johanna—one of the Comoro Islands), he reached Japan in April 1880 and sought Japanese help in securing a treaty with Korea, then widely known as the "Hermit Kingdom." He also sought similar mediatory aid from Li Hung-chang, viceroy of China. He returned home briefly and then sailed back to China in June 1881 with credentials as naval attaché and authority from President Chester A. Arthur to negotiate a treaty. The treaty with Korea, that nation's first with a Western country, was negotiated and drawn up at Tientsin, China; Shufeldt then proceeded to Korea aboard the *Swatara* and went ashore at the mouth of the Han River on May 22, 1882, and signed the document along with representatives of the king. On his return home he was named president of the Naval Advisory Board, which played a leading role in the design of the new steel cruisers of the "White Fleet" and in the evolution of the "new navy." He was promoted to rear admiral in May 1883, and he served also as superintendent of the Naval Observatory from that year until his retirement in February 1884. Shufeldt died in Washington, D.C., on November 7, 1895.

Sibert, William Luther (1860–1935), army officer and engineer. Born on October 12, 1860, in Gadsden, Alabama, Sibert attended the University of Alabama from 1878 to 1880 and then entered West Point. On graduating in 1884 he was commissioned in the engineers, and after 3 years at the Engineer School of Application at Willett's Point, New York (now Fort Totten), he spent 11 years in river and harbor improvement work in Kentucky, on the Great Lakes, and in Arkansas, receiving promotions to first lieutenant in April 1888 and captain in March 1896. In September 1898 he became an instructor at Willett's Point, and in August 1899 he was ordered to the Philippines; a short time later he became chief engineer of the VIII Corps on the staff of Gen. Elwell S. Otis. His work there was concerned principally with railroad reconstruction and operation. From April 1900 to March 1907 he was again engaged in navigation improvement work on the Ohio, Alleghany, and Monongahela rivers, advancing to major in April 1904. His experience in lock and dam construction contributed to his appointment by President Theodore Roosevelt to the Isthmian Canal Commission in March 1907. For a year he concerned himself with the locks and dams of the Panama Canal, and in June 1908 he was put in charge of the entire Atlantic Division, embracing all of the canal and its works north of Gatun Lake. The Gatun dam and locks provided one of the greatest challenges of the canal project, and his mastery of it, not without friction with the chief engineer, Col. George W. Goethals, was a widely celebrated achievement. He advanced to lieutenant colonel in 1909. The Canal Commission was dissolved in April 1914, and Sibert was then sent to China to advise on flood control on the Huai River. In March 1915 he received promotion to brigadier general in recognition of his work in Panama, a promotion that removed him from the Corps of Engineers to the line of the army. After a time in command of the coast artillery on the Pacific he was promoted to major general in May 1917 and in June given command of the 1st Infantry Division and sent to France. In December he was recalled to command the Southeastern Department at Charleston, South Carolina. In May 1918 he was ordered to organize the Chemical Warfare Service in the Corps of Engineers. The service was formally activated in June, with Sibert named chief as of July 1. Under his direction the activities of research, manufacture, detection, and combat deployment, formerly divided among the Medical Corps, Signal Corps, Engineers, and other branches, were unified and coordinated, and the 1st Gas Regiment of the American Expeditionary Forces in France conducted 152 operations from the Marne–Vesle through the Meuse–Argonne. Sibert retired in April 1920. From 1923 to 1929 he served as chairman and chief engineer of the Alabama State Docks Commission, overseeing the construction of ocean terminal facilities at Mobile; and from 1928 to 1932 he was, on appointment of President Calvin Coolidge, chairman of the Boulder (later Hoover) Dam Commission. He died in Bowling Green, Kentucky, on October 16, 1935.

Sibley, Henry Hastings (1811–1891),

merchant, public official, and army officer. Born in Detroit on February 20, 1811, son of a Michigan Territory congressman and supreme court judge, Sibley became a clerk at Sault Ste. Marie in 1828 and the next year entered the employ of John Jacob Astor's American Fur Company. After five years as a clerk he went west as an agent in 1834, settling at what is now Mendota, near Fort Snelling on the Minnesota River, and there built the first stone house in what is now Minnesota. He soon had considerable influence among both the settlers and the Sioux Indians of the region. In October 1848 he was elected delegate to Congress from the area of the former Wisconsin Territory not included in the state, a region between the Mississippi and St. Croix rivers. Following a convention at Stillwater in the previous August he had been sent to Washington, D.C., to urge creation of a Minnesota Territory, and although it had not yet been organized, he was seated in Congress in January. He was active in the organization of Minnesota Territory and in July 1849 entered Congress again as its delegate, serving until March 1853. He sat in the territorial legislature in 1855, was president of the constitutional convention in 1857, and in May 1858 took office as first governor of the state of Minnesota. He served until 1860. In August 1862, following the sudden outbreak of violence by a band of Sioux led by Little Crow, Sibley was commissioned colonel of a volunteer militia force raised at Fort Snelling. On September 3 he relieved a burial detachment of army regulars who had been besieged at Birch Coulee, near Fort Ridgely, for over a day. On September 23, after fortuitously discovering an ambush laid by Little Crow, he decisively defeated the Sioux at Wood Lake. Six days later he was commissioned brigadier general of volunteers; the commission expired in March 1863 but he was promptly recommissioned in the same rank. In June 1863 he set out from Camp Pope, near Fort Ridgely, at the head of a large force in a campaign against the Sioux in the Dakotas in conjunction with Gen. Alfred Sully. He met and defeated Sioux bands at Big Mound in what is now Kidder County, North Dakota, on July 24; at Dead Buffalo Lake (Burleigh County) on July 26; and at Stony Lake (Burleigh County) on July 28. After waiting at Apple Creek, near present-day Bismarck, for news of Sully, Sibley marched back to Fort Abercrombie, Minnesota, in August. He was again in the field briefly in 1864. Brevetted major general of volunteers in November 1865, he was mustered out in April 1866. In 1865–1866 he was a commissioner in treaty negotiations with the Sioux. He then settled in St. Paul, where he developed extensive business interests. He served a term in the legislature in 1871 and in 1880 ran unsuccessfully for Congress. Sibley died in St. Paul, Minnesota, on February 18, 1891.

Sibley, Henry Hopkins (1816–1886),

Confederate army officer. Born on May 25, 1816, in Natchitoches, Louisiana, Sibley graduated from West Point in 1838 and was commissioned in the 2nd Dragoons. He was promoted to first lieutenant in March 1840 while serving against the Seminole Indians in Florida. Later his regiment took part in the occupation of Texas. Promoted to captain in February 1847, he served through the Mexican War and was brevetted for gallantry at Medelin, near Veracruz, March 25, 1847. He later served in Texas and Kansas and took part in the Mormon expedition under Col. Albert S. Johnston in 1857–1858 and the Navajo campaign of 1860. He was promoted to major in May 1861, but on the same day he resigned from the army and in June was commissioned a brigadier general in the Confederate army. In July he was assigned to command the Department of New Mexico. He raised a regiment mainly of Texans at San Antonio and marched to El Paso and then toward Fort Craig, headquarters of Col. Edward R. S. Canby, Union commander of New Mexico. At Valverde on February 21, 1862, Sibley's 2000 men attacked Canby's 3800, driving him over the Rio Grande and into Fort Craig. Sibley left him locked up there and marched on to occupy Albuquerque and, on March 10, Santa Fe. He then moved against Fort Union. A part of Canby's force had followed, however, and Sibley was checked at Apache Canyon on March 27 by a column composed mainly of Colorado volunteers under Maj. John M. Chivington, and he was heavily hit by a larger federal force at Glorieta Pass the next day. Although he dealt as many casualties as he took, his supply train was destroyed, and he was compelled to fall back. He abandoned Santa Fe on April 8, was hurried on his way by a skirmish at Peralta on April 15, and, dodging through the mountains to avoid Canby's army, he withdrew into Texas early in July, having lost over 500 men dead or captured. The Confederate campaign for New Mexico was never renewed. Sibley later commanded a brigade under Gen. Richard Taylor and Gen. Edmund Kirby-Smith. In December 1869 he accepted a commission as chief of artillery in the army of Khedive Ismail I of Egypt with the rank of brigadier general. He returned to the United States in 1874. In later years, his health precarious, he lectured on Egypt occasionally and sought unsuccessfully to recover royalties on the Sibley tent, invented while he was in the army and adopted by it before the Civil War; contractual payments had been stopped when he entered Confederate service. He died in Fredericksburg, Virginia, on August 23, 1886.

Sickles, Daniel Edgar (1825–1914),

army officer and public official. Born in New York City on October 20, 1825, Sickles attended the University of the City of New York (now New York University) for a time and later studied law. Admitted to the bar in 1846, he was soon involved in politics and was elected to the state legislature for a term in 1847. As corporation counsel for New York City in 1853 he was part of the commission that acquired the site of Central Park for the city. From 1853 to 1855 he was in London serving as secretary of the U.S. legation. He served terms in the New York state senate in 1856 and 1857 and was also elected as a Democrat in the House of Representatives in 1856, serving two terms there from March 1857 to March 1861. In 1859, on the then-novel grounds of temporary insanity, he was acquitted of a charge of murder arising from his shooting to death the son of Francis Scott Key for what he believed were improper attentions to his wife. With the start of the Civil War, Sickles, an officer of New York militia since 1852, raised troops for the "Excelsior Brigade" in New York and in June 1861 was appointed colonel in command of one of its five regiments, the 17th. In September he was advanced to brigadier general of volunteers, and he commanded a brigade under Gen. Joseph Hooker in the Peninsula campaign in 1862. He performed well there and at Antietam (Sharpsburg), September 17, following which battle he succeeded Hooker in command of the division. He was also at Fredericksburg, December 13. He received promotion to major general of volunteers in March 1863, to date from November 1862, and was put in command of the III Corps, which he led effectively at Chancellorsville, May 2–4. He arrived at Gettysburg on the second day of battle, July 2, and was ordered to occupy Round Top and Little Round Top, hills forming the left anchor of the Union line. He chose to move much of his corps forward to an exposed salient at the Peach Orchard, and in Gen. James Longstreet's furious attack that day the III Corps lost half its men. Sickles was wounded in the battle, and it was necessary to amputate his right leg on the spot. His active military service ended there. After a confidential diplomatic mission to South America in 1865 he was military governor of the Carolinas. In July 1866 he was commissioned colonel of the 42nd Infantry of regulars; in March 1867 he was brevetted brigadier and major general for Fredericksburg and Gettysburg, and in January 1868 he was mustered out of volunteer service. He retired from the regular army as a major general in April 1869. From May 1869 until December 1873 he was U.S. minister to Spain; he resigned from that post when his actions during the controversy over Spain's seizure of the American-registered ship *Virginius*, which had been caught carrying arms to Cuban rebels, proved unnecessarily belligerent. He remained in Europe for seven years. Back in the United States, he made his home in New York City, where he held various local offices during the 1880s.

In 1892 he was elected again to the House of Representatives and served one term. Having lost in the congressional election of 1894, Sickles retired to private life. He died in New York City on May 3, 1914.

Sieber, Al (1844–1907), scout. Born on February 29, 1844, in the Grand Duchy of Baden, Germany, Sieber came to America about 1849 and settled with his family in Lancaster, Pennsylvania. In 1856 he followed an elder sister to Minnesota. In March 1862 he enlisted as a private in the 1st Minnesota Volunteers, and he served through the Civil War, being severely wounded at Gettysburg. He traveled west to the mining territory of Nevada and California in 1866 and two years later settled in Arizona. He worked as a ranch hand and Indian fighter until 1871, when he was enrolled as an army scout under Col. George Crook. A man of great physical strength and endurance, boundless courage, and inflexible honor, he quickly became renowned not only for his own abilities as a scout but even more for his ability to command Apache scouts in the campaigns against Geronimo's and other renegade bands. The Indians respected him thoroughly as the "man of iron" and were secure in the knowledge of his devotion to them, although he never hesitated to shoot if crossed. He served as chief of scouts at San Carlos reservation for 20 years under such famed commanders as Crook, Oliver O. Howard, and Nelson A. Miles. He was wounded at least 29 times in that service. After his dismissal in December 1890 by an Indian agent whom he had accused of dishonest dealings, he lived in Globe, Arizona, and worked at odd jobs. During the construction of the Roosevelt Dam on the Salt River he supervised a gang of Apache road workers. On February 19, 1907, the blasting of a rocky point left a large boulder poised precariously; when the boulder suddenly began to roll, Sieber, hobbled by old wounds, was crushed while rescuing some of his workmen from its path. At the news of his death the Arizona legislature adjourned in respect. Monuments to his memory were erected at the site of his death and in Globe.

Sigel, Franz (1824–1902), army officer and editor. Born in Sinsheim, Grand Duchy of Baden, Germany, on November 18, 1824, Sigel graduated from the military academy of Karlsruhe in 1843 and entered the ducal army as a lieutenant. He resigned in 1847 following a duel that grew out of his liberal politics, and in 1848 he was twice defeated leading a revolutionary army against Freiburg. He escaped to Switzerland but returned to Baden in May 1849 to become minister of war in the liberal government. He again led the army against the Prussians and after several defeats again fled to Switzerland in July. In 1851 he was deported by Swiss authorities; he lived in England until May 1852, when he sailed for the United

States and settled in New York City. There he taught school and joined the 5th New York militia regiment, becoming a major. In 1857 he moved to St. Louis and took a post in the German-American Institute; subsequently he was chosen a director of the city's public schools. On the outbreak of the Civil War he organized the 3rd Missouri Infantry and received a commission as colonel in May 1861. He cooperated with Capt. Nathaniel Lyon in the capture of Camp Jackson that month, and, appointed brigadier general of volunteers in command of the 2nd Missouri Brigade, in June he marched to Rolla and then to Neosho in pursuit of the state Confederate forces under Gov. Claiborne F. Jackson and Gen. Sterling Price. At Carthage on July 5 he attacked Jackson and was defeated by greatly superior numbers. He then fell back to Springfield. After Lyon joined him there they launched a combined attack on Price and Gen. Ben McCulloch at Wilson's Creek on August 10. Sigel was defeated by McCulloch while attempting a flanking movement and then, following Lyon's death, retreated to Rolla. He commanded two divisions under Gen. Samuel R. Curtis at Pea Ridge (Elkhorn), March 7–8, 1862, performing with distinction and winning promotion to major general of volunteers. In June he was ordered east to command the I Corps, Army of Virginia, under Gen. John Pope, and he took part in the campaign culminating in the second battle of Bull Run (Manassas), August 29–30, where he commanded the right wing. In September his command was attached to the Army of the Potomac as the XI Corps. Under Gen. Ambrose E. Burnside's reorganization of the army he commanded the reserve grand division, comprising the XI and XII Corps; he reverted to command of the XI Corps alone in February 1863. In the spring of that year ill health forced him to turn the corps over to Gen. Oliver O. Howard, and on his return to active duty in June he was put in command of the Pennsylvania reserve. In March 1864 he took command of the Department and Army of West Virginia. He conducted operations in the Shenandoah valley until he was defeated by Gen. John C. Breckinridge and Gen. John D. Imboden at New Market on May 15, following which he was transferred to the garrison command of Harpers Ferry. He was successful in delaying Gen. Jubal A. Early's raid on Washington, D.C., in July, but soon afterward he was relieved of all command. He resigned his commission in May 1865. He then settled in Baltimore, where for two years he edited the German-language *Baltimore Wecker.* In 1867 he moved to New York City. He served as a pension agent until 1869, in May 1871 was appointed collector of internal revenue, and in October 1871 was elected register of the city. Later he published and edited the *New Yorker Deutsches Volksblatt* for some years, and from 1897 to 1900 he edited the *New York Monthly.* Sigel died in New York City on August 21, 1902.

Sigsbee, Charles Dwight (1845–1923), naval officer. Born in Albany, New York, on January 16, 1845, Sigsbee graduated from the Naval Academy in 1863. During 1863–1864 he served on the *Monongahela* and the *Brooklyn* of Adm. David G. Farragut's West Gulf Blockading Squadron, taking part aboard the latter, under Capt. James Alden, in the battle of Mobile Bay, August 5, 1864. He was later transferred to duty with the North Atlantic Blockading Squadron, and he participated in the attacks on Fort Fisher by Adm. David D. Porter on December 24–25, 1864, and January 13–15, 1865. From 1865 to 1869 he was with the Asiatic Squadron, receiving promotions to lieutenant in February 1867 and lieutenant commander in March 1868. In 1869–1871 he was an instructor at the Naval Academy. During 1871–1873 he commanded the *Worcester,* and after a year with the navy's Hydrographic Office he was attached to the Coast Survey in 1874. While in command of the survey ship *Blake* in 1875–1878, he made extensive explorations of the Gulf of Mexico in association with Harvard zoologist Alexander Agassiz and discovered the Sigsbee Deep, the deepest (12,425 feet) point in the Gulf. He also invented a number of deep-sea sounding and sampling devices. From 1878 to 1882 he was again in the Hydrographic Office; promoted to commander in May 1882, he was again at the Academy from then until 1885. He commanded the *Kearsarge* in the European Squadron in 1885–1886, and from 1887 to 1890 he was once again at the Academy, serving also on various boards. After two years in command of the training ship *Portsmouth* Sigsbee was chief of the Hydrographic Office from 1893 to 1897. In March 1897 he was promoted to captain and in April given command of the battleship *Maine.* In January 1898 he brought the *Maine* into the harbor of Havana, Cuba. On the evening of February 15 an explosion in the forward part of the ship touched off the magazines. The ship was utterly wrecked and sank quickly, 260 officers and men being killed or mortally injured in the disaster. The sinking of the *Maine* was immediately taken up by those sections of the press and those politicians eager for war with Spain, and Sigsbee's calm dispatches from Havana went far to prevent a general stampede of public opinion. A Spanish inquiry blamed spontaneous combustion in the coal bunkers for the first explosion, while a naval court of inquiry found evidence that it had been external to the hull and probably caused by a mine, although no evidence survived to point blame at either Spanish authorities or Cuban revolutionaries. Nonetheless the *Maine* became a potent symbol of the movement for war with Spain, and "Remember the *Maine*" was the best known catchphrase of the Spanish–American War. During the war Sigsbee commanded the *St. Paul,* which on May 25 captured the British collier *Restormel* bound for Adm. Cervera's fleet and on June 22 defeated the destroyer *Terror* and the cruiser *Isabella II* off San Juan, Puerto Rico. During 1900–1903 he was chief intelligence officer of the navy. Promoted to rear admiral in August 1903, he commanded the League Island navy yard at Philadelphia in 1903–1904, the South Atlantic Squadron in 1904–1905, and the 2nd division of the North Atlantic Fleet in 1905–1906. In June–July 1905 he commanded a special squadron detailed to carry the remains of John Paul Jones from Cherbourg, France, to the Naval Academy aboard the *Brooklyn*. Sigsbee retired in January 1907. He was the author of *Deep Sea Sounding and Dredging*, 1880, and *The Maine, an Account of her Destruction in Havana Harbor*, 1899. He died in New York City on July 19, 1923.

Silliman, Gold Selleck (1732–1790), Revolutionary army officer. Born on May 7, 1732, in Fairfield, Connecticut, Silliman, son of a prominent judge in the colony, graduated from Yale in 1752 and after studying law became a crown attorney in Fairfield County. He also was active in the colonial militia and was a colonel of cavalry at the outbreak of the Revolution. He and his regiment were mustered into Continental service in time to take part in the battle of Long Island and the Manhattan campaign in August–September 1776. He was also at White Plains, October 28. Promoted to brigadier general, he was later put in command of the defense of southwestern Connecticut, an area with a particularly vulnerable coastline. On April 25, 1777, Col. William Tryon (formerly royal governor of New York) and a force of about 2000 British regulars and Loyalists landed at Compo Point (in what is now Westport, Connecticut) and proceeded to Danbury, where they destroyed valuable stores and burned much of the town. The militia soon gathered to oppose him, and he began retreating to his ships, harried by militia under Silliman, Gen. Benedict Arnold, and Gen. David Wooster, who was killed. Silliman and Arnold combined to inflict heavy losses on Tryon at Ridgefield, April 27. In May 1779 he was captured in his own house in Fairfield by a British raiding party, and he was held captive on Long Island for a year before being exchanged. Silliman died in Fairfield on July 21, 1790. Benjamin Silliman, scientist, was his son.

Simpson, James Hervey (1813–1883), army officer and explorer. Born in New Brunswick, New Jersey, on March 9, 1813, Simpson graduated from West Point in 1832 and was commissioned in the artillery. After a period of service in the Seminole War in Florida he was promoted to first lieutenant in July 1838 and transferred into the newly organized Corps of Topographical Engineers. For ten years he was engaged in various duties in the East and the South, but in 1849 he was ordered to the Southwest to explore a route from Fort Smith, Arkansas, to Santa Fe, New

Mexico. While in New Mexico as chief topographical engineer for that department he also conducted the explorations later reported in his *Journal of a Military Reconnaisance from Santa Fe, N. Mex., to the Navajo Country*, 1852. Simpson is credited with the official discovery of Inscription Rock in what is now Valencia County, New Mexico, and of the Canyon de Chelly in Arizona, both later (1906 and 1931) created national monuments. Promoted to captain in March 1853, Simpson spent several years in Minnesota and two years with the Coast Survey and in 1857–1858 accompanied Col. Albert S. Johnston's Mormon expedition to Utah. He went on in 1859 to explore a new route from Salt Lake City to the Pacific coast. At the outbreak of the Civil War he was appointed chief topographical engineer of the Department of the Shenandoah, receiving promotion to major in August 1861, and later that month he was appointed colonel of the 4th New Jersey Volunteers. He was taken prisoner during the Peninsula campaign in 1862. He resigned his volunteer commission in August 1862 and for a year was chief topographical engineer and chief engineer of the Army of the Ohio. Promoted to lieutenant colonel in June 1863, he was in charge of fortifications and other engineering projects in Kentucky until the end of the war. In March 1865 he was brevetted colonel and brigadier general for services. He then served as chief engineer of the Department of the Interior until 1867, with particular responsibility for overseeing the activities of the Union Pacific Railroad. He was promoted to colonel in March 1867. From then until his retirement in March 1880 he was engaged in fortification, river and harbor, and road construction work in the South and the Midwest. During that period he published *The Shortest Route to California*, 1869, *Coronado's March in Search of the Seven Cities of Cibola*, 1871, and *Exploration Across the Great Basin of the Territory of Utah*, 1876. Simpson died in St. Paul, Minnesota, on March 2, 1883.

Simpson, William Hood (1888–   ), army officer. Born on May 19, 1888, in Weatherford, Texas, Simpson graduated from West Point in 1909 and was commissioned in the infantry. After a few months at Fort Lincoln, North Dakota, he served two years, 1910–1912, in the Philippines with the 6th Infantry. From 1912 to 1914 he was at the Presidio, San Francisco, after which he was ordered to duty in Texas. In 1916 he took part in the Mexican Punitive Expedition under Gen. John J. Pershing. Promoted to captain in May 1917, he served with the 33rd Division through World War I, receiving temporary promotions to major and lieutenant colonel and advancing to divisional chief of staff. After occupation duty he became in May 1919 chief of staff of the 6th Division at Camp Grant, Illinois; in June 1920 he reverted to captain and was promoted to major. After two years in the War Department he entered the Infantry

School, Fort Benning, Georgia, from which he graduated in 1924. A year later he graduated from the Command and General Staff School, Fort Leavenworth, Kansas, and after two years commanding a battalion of the 12th Infantry in Maryland he entered the Army War College, graduating in 1928. He served with the General Staff until 1932 and taught military science and tactics at Pomona College, California, from 1932 to 1936. He was promoted to lieutenant colonel in October 1934, and he advanced to colonel in September 1938 while an instructor, 1936–1940, at the Army War College. During August–September 1940 he commanded the 9th Infantry at Fort Sam Houston, Texas; promoted to temporary brigadier general in October, he became assistant commander of the 2nd Division there. From April to October 1941 he commanded Camp Wolters, Texas, receiving promotion to temporary major general in September, and in October he took command of the 35th Division, taking it from Camp Robinson, Arkansas, to a training site in California shortly after U.S. entry into World War II. During May–July 1942 he commanded the 30th Division at Fort Jackson, South Carolina. In September he took command of the newly activated XII Corps at that base. In October 1943, promoted to temporary lieutenant general, he took command of the Fourth Army at San Jose, California, and he moved with it to Fort Sam Houston in January 1944. In May Simpson and most of his staff went to England to organize the Eighth Army, which a few days later was redesignated the Ninth. The Ninth became operational as part of Gen. Omar N. Bradley's 12th Army Group on September 5 at Brest, France, which was liberated on September 20. After a month in the Ardennes Forest the army was moved north, and in November it broke through the Siegfried Line and advanced through some of the heaviest fighting of the war to the Roer River. (The Ninth was for short periods attached to Field Marshal Montgomery's 21st Army Group.) The Rhine was crossed on March 24, 1945, north of the Ruhr industrial area, and on April 1 the Ninth made contact with Gen. Courtney H. Hodges's First Army, making a complete encirclement of the Ruhr. The Ninth was the first American army across the Elbe on April 12. After brief occupation duty Simpson returned to the United States in June. He undertook a mission to China a month later, and in October he took command of the Second Army at Memphis, Tennessee. He retained that command, transferred to Baltimore in June 1946, until his retirement in November 1946. In July 1954 he was promoted to general on the retired list.

Sims, William Sowden (1858–1936), naval officer. Born on October 15, 1858, in Port Hope, Ontario, of an American father, Sims moved with his family to Orbisonia, Pennsylvania, in 1872. In 1876, after one rejection, he was admitted to the Naval Academy and graduated four years later. From 1880 to 1897 he was almost continuously on sea duty on the North Atlantic, Pacific, and China stations; during that period he wrote a navigation text that was long used by both the navy and the merchant marine. From 1897 to 1900 he was naval attaché at the U.S. embassies in Paris and, briefly, St. Petersburg. By the time he resumed sea duty on the China station in 1900 he had become convinced of the relative inferiority of the U.S. navy in matters of ship design, tactics, and gunnery, the victories of the Spanish–American War notwithstanding. In the Orient he met Capt. (later Adm. Sir) Percy Scott of the Royal Navy, developer of the new technique of continuous-aim firing. Sims wrote a series of memoranda to the Navy Department describing and advocating the adoption of this method but received no satisfactory reply. Finally, in 1901 and again in 1902, he wrote directly to President Theodore Roosevelt—technically an act of insubordination—and as a result was brought to Washington in November 1902 as inspector of target practice with the rank of lieutenant commander. Remaining in that post until February 1909, and after November 1907 serving additionally as naval aide to the President, he brought about an almost revolutionary improvement in the state of naval gunnery—big-gun firing time, for example, was reduced from five minutes to a half-minute, with improved accuracy. At his instigation a commission was appointed to investigate and make recommendations on the organization of the Navy Department, but this, like an earlier congressional investigation into faulty battleship design for which he was also indirectly responsible, led to no important reform. Sims advanced to commander in July 1907. In March 1909 he took command of the battleship *Minnesota*. In December 1910 he made an unauthorized speech in England pledging the full support of the United States in the event of an attack on the British Empire and was reprimanded by President William Howard Taft. Promoted to captain in March 1911, he was stationed at the Naval War College from that time until June 1913. He was then named commander of the Atlantic Torpedo Flotilla, with which he developed a tactical doctrine for the deployment of the newly introduced naval destroyers. From November 1915 to January 1917 he commanded the battleship *Nevada*, and in the latter month he was promoted to rear admiral and appointed president of the Naval War College. When the United States declared war on Germany in April 1917, Sims was at sea en route to London, where he was originally to have served in an informal liaison capacity with the British admiralty. In May he was promoted to temporary vice admiral, and in June he was placed in command of U.S. naval forces operating in European waters. Working closely with the naval departments of Allied nations at his headquarters in London, he argued effectively to secure the adoption of the convoy system. The navy's contribution to the war consisted, aside from Adm. Hugh Rodman's battleship division serving with the British Grand Fleet, principally in convoy-escort and mine-laying work. In December 1918 Sims was made temporary admiral, and in March 1919, on being relieved as commander of U.S. naval forces in Europe, he reverted to permanent rank of rear admiral and returned to the Naval War College. Because of the award of honors in a manner he considered arbitrary, he refused in December 1919 to accept the Distinguished Service Medal. His long and detailed report on mismanagement in the conduct of naval affairs during the war led to another congressional investigation, but 1920, like 1908, was an election year, and the results were partisan and inconclusive. Despite such disappointments, Sims was acknowledged to be the most influential officer in U.S. naval history. His book, *The Victory at Sea,* 1920, written with Burton J. Hendrick, was awarded a Pulitzer Prize for history. He retired as rear admiral in October 1922 but continued to write and speak on topics of public and military interest. In 1930 he was promoted by congressional action to admiral on the retired list. He died in Boston on September 28, 1936.

Sitting Bull (1831?–1890), Indian leader. Born about 1831 into the Hunkpapa Sioux, a Dakota Sioux tribe, on the Grand River in what is now South Dakota, Tatanka Iyotake, or Sitting Bull, son of Jumping Bull, was a warrior by the age of fourteen, and about 1856 he became head of the Strong Heart warrior society. He was first involved in conflict with the U.S. army in 1863 in the retaliatory actions that followed the Minnesota uprising of 1862, in which a band of Sioux under Little Crow protested white encroachments by killing more than 350 settlers. Sitting Bull took part in the battle against Gen. Alfred Sully at Killdeer Mountain, in what is now North Dakota, July 28, 1864. In 1866 he became chief of the northern hunting Sioux, with Crazy Horse, leader of the Oglala Sioux, as his subordinate chief. In 1868 he accepted peace with the U.S. government on the basis of the Fort Laramie treaty's guaranteed reservation north of the North Platte River, with the right to hunt off the reservation. But in 1874 gold was discovered in the Black Hills region, a country not merely vital but sacred to the northern plains tribes, and miners and settlers poured into the Indian territory. Enraged by the incursions, Sioux, Arapaho, and Cheyenne assembled at Sitting Bull's encampment in Montana, eventually growing to a force estimated at 2500 to 4000 men, and in 1875 he was made head of the war council of the confederacy. He defied the army's order of late 1875 that the Sioux return to their reservations by the end of January 1876. He was said to have beheld visions of the coming battles in a Sun Dance that he performed in June 1876. On the

17th of that month forces under the command of Gen. George Crook were defeated by Crazy Horse at the battle of the Rosebud; on the 25th Col. George A. Custer was killed and his immediate command destroyed at the battle of the Little Bighorn by warriors led by Crazy Horse and Gall, Sitting Bull's chief lieutenant and war chief. Sitting Bull, as was his function, "made medicine" during the battle and took no part in the fighting. When the Indians' encampment at Little Bighorn broke up Sitting Bull led his remaining people to Canada in May 1877, but he could not obtain assistance from the Canadian government. Suffering from famine and disease, he and 187 tribesmen returned to the United States and finally surrendered to the army at Fort Buford, Dakota Territory (in what is now North Dakota), in July 1881. He was imprisoned at Fort Randall (South Dakota) for two years, then in May 1883 moved to the Standing Rock Reservation. For a year, 1885–1886, he toured in Buffalo Bill's Wild West Show. A legendary figure, he never acquiesced in white rule or considered himself other than leader of the Sioux. He encouraged the religious agitation that swept a number of tribes about 1889 and led to the Ghost Dance uprising of the Sioux. In the tense atmosphere generated by the Ghost Dance mania he was ordered arrested on a pretext by the resident Indian agent. As Sioux warriors attempted to rescue him, he was shot by Indian police at Grand River on December 15, 1890. A few days later the U.S. 7th Cavalry engaged in the so-called "battle," in reality a massacre of Sioux, at Wounded Knee, ending the resistance fostered by the Ghost Dance.

Slayton, Donald Kent (1924–   ), air force officer and astronaut. Born on March 1, 1924, in Sparta, Wisconsin, Slayton, known as Deke, enlisted in the Army Air Forces on graduating from high school in 1942. He became a B-25 pilot and flew 63 combat missions in Europe and Japan. Discharged in 1946, he was a student at the University of Minnesota in 1947 –1949, taking a degree in aeronautical engineering, and after two years with the Boeing Aircraft Company he was recalled to active duty with the air force in 1951 with the rank of captain. During 1952–1955 he was stationed in Germany, and in 1955 he entered test pilot school at Edwards Air Force Base, California. He remained there as a test pilot until April 1959, when, promoted to major, he was chosen one of the original seven astronauts for Project Mercury by the National Aeronautics and Space Administration. He was scheduled to fly the second Project Mercury orbital mission in May 1962 when the discovery of a minor heart irregularity caused him to be removed from the active list. In November 1963, in order to avoid test pilot medical restrictions, he resigned from the air force and rejoined NASA as a civilian. He served as assistant director, 1963–1966, and director, from 1966, of flight crew operations, playing a major ground role in the Apollo program. Early in 1973, the heart irregularity having disappeared, he was restored to active astronaut status. Chosen for the crew of the joint U.S.–Soviet Apollo–Soyuz orbital mission, he underwent special training that included periods of study at the Russian space center, Star City. On July 15, 1975, at fifty-one the oldest astronaut ever to do so, he finally entered space in the Apollo spacecraft, along with Thomas Stafford and Vance Brand. The Soyuz spacecraft, carrying Aleksei A. Leonov and Valery N. Kubasov, had already lifted from Baikonur Cosmodrome, U.S.S.R., and entered orbit. On July 17 the two craft made rendezvous and docked. For two days crew exchanges, joint scientific experiments, and interplanetary hospitality were carried on before a television camera in the world's first international manned spaceflight. After undocking on July 19 and five days of further experiments, Apollo splashed down on July 24. Slayton then resumed work as flight crew operations director at the NASA Manned Spacecraft Center in Houston, Texas, where the Apollo–Soyuz experience aided in the development of the space shuttle.

Slemmer, Adam Jacoby (1828–1868), army officer. Born in Montgomery County, Pennsylvania, in 1828, Slemmer graduated from West Point in 1850 and was commissioned in the artillery. He served against the Seminole Indians in Florida, spent four years in California, and from 1855 to 1859 was an instructor at West Point. He was then ordered to garrison duty at Fort Moultrie, South Carolina, and in 1860 he was transferred to Fort Barrancas at Pensacola, Florida. On learning of the secession of Florida on January 10, 1861, Slemmer led 40 soldiers (aboard the navy storeship *Supply*, Commander Henry Walke) secretly across the bay to Santa Rosa Island, where they occupied the disused Fort Pickens. He soon found himself under virtual siege and short of food and ammunition. Slemmer contrived to hold out until relieved by the arrival of the *Powhatan*, commanded by Lt. David D. Porter, on April 13. Because of his action Fort Pickens remained in federal hands and was a key base for the naval blockade throughout the war. In May Slemmer was promoted two grades to major of the 16th Infantry. After a period as inspector general of the Department of the Ohio he was ordered to service in the field in May 1862 with the Army of the Ohio. He took part in operations at Corinth, Louisville, and Nashville. In November he was appointed brigadier general of volunteers. He was severely wounded on December 31 at Murfreesboro (Stones River) and saw little further active service in the war. He was promoted to lieutenant colonel of regulars in February 1864 and in March 1865 brevetted colonel and brigadier general. Mustered out of volunteer service in August 1865, he

was ordered to Fort Laramie, Kansas, where he died on October 7, 1868.

Sloat, John Drake (1781–1867), naval officer. Born in Goshen, New York, on July 26, 1781, Sloat was appointed a midshipman in the navy in February 1800. After brief service aboard Commodore Thomas Truxtun's flagship *President* in the Caribbean during the undeclared naval war with France (1798–1800) he was discharged from the navy in the reduction of 1801. For the next 11 years he was captain of a merchant vessel, but in January 1812, just before the second war with Great Britain broke out, he was called back into the navy with the rank of master. He served on the *United States* under Commodore Stephen Decatur and in July 1813 was raised to the rank of lieutenant. After the war he spent a year's leave in France, then returned to the United States and sea duty for most of the next 30 years. He received his first command in 1823, when he sailed on the schooner *Grampus* to suppress piracy in the region of the Windward Islands, and in March 1837 he was promoted to captain. In 1840–1844 he commanded the Portsmouth, New Hampshire, navy yard, and in August 1844 he became commander of the Pacific Squadron. From November 1845 until June 1846 he cruised off the west coast of Mexico; during that time he received orders from Secretary of the Navy George Bancroft to proceed to California if hostilities should break out with Mexico. On May 16, 1846, he learned from the U.S. consul at Mazatlán that fighting had begun along the Rio Grande in Texas (war had actually been declared by Congress on May 13). On June 7 Sloat ordered his squadron to sail for Monterey, California, where they arrived on July 2. Meanwhile settlers in the Sacramento valley had carried out their Bear Flag Revolt against Mexico and set up the short-lived Republic of California at Sonoma. Capt. John C. Frémont's forces had then taken over; Frémont declared California to be under martial law and added the insurgents to his command, naming the combined force the California Battalion. After several days of uncertainty, and unaware of most of what was going on in California, Sloat decided to occupy Monterey, which he did on July 7, sending ashore a detachment of marines and sailors under Capt. William Mervine, who read Sloat's proclamation taking possession of California for the United States. He also dispatched one of his officers to occupy San Francisco (then known as Yerba Buena). He notified Frémont of what he had done, and when Frémont arrived at Monterey, Sloat dismissed him and refused to accept his forces as a U.S. military unit. Sloat, in poor health, was relieved of command at Monterey by Commodore Robert Stockton on July 23 and returned to Washington, D.C., arriving in November 1846. His conduct in California was variously praised, notably by Bancroft, and condemned on the contradictory grounds that he was dilatory in taking action and that he had exceeded his authority. He spent the next nine years of his navy service on shore duty as commander of the navy yard at Norfolk, Virginia, 1848–1851, and with the Bureau of Construction and Repair at Hoboken, New Jersey. He was placed on the reserve list in September 1855 and on the retired list in December 1861; he was promoted to commodore in July 1862 and to rear admiral in July 1866. He died on Staten Island, New York, on November 28, 1867.

Slocum, Henry Warner (1827–1894), army officer. Born in Delphi, Onondaga County, New York, on September 24, 1827, Slocum graduated from West Point in 1852 and was commissioned in the artillery. He served in Florida and from 1853 at Fort Moultrie, South Carolina, receiving promotion to first lieutenant in March 1855. He studied law at the same time and in October 1856 resigned from the army to take it up full time. He won admission to the New York bar in 1858 and established his practice in Syracuse. He was elected to the legislature in 1859 and secured appointment as colonel in the militia. In May 1861 he was appointed colonel of the 27th New York Volunteer Infantry. He was badly wounded at Bull Run (Manassas), July 21, and in August was promoted to brigadier general of volunteers. He commanded a brigade in Gen. William B. Franklin's division in the Peninsula campaign, and after taking part in the siege of Yorktown and the battle of West Point, May 7, he succeeded to command of the division when Franklin moved up to the VI Corps. He performed with distinction at Gaines' Mill, June 27, and at Malvern Hill, July 1. In July he was promoted to major general of volunteers. He commanded the division at the second battle of Bull Run, August 29–30, and through the Maryland campaign—South Mountain and Antietam (Sharpsburg), September 14 and 17—and in October was given command of the XII Corps. He was heavily engaged at Chancellorsville, May 2–4, 1863. At Gettysburg he commanded the right wing, from Culp's Hill southward, and until Gen. George G. Meade's arrival early on July 2 he was senior officer on the field. In September the XII Corps and Gen. Oliver O. Howard's XI Corps were sent west to reinforce Gen. William S. Rosecrans's Army of the Cumberland at Chattanooga; they were placed together under the command of Gen. Joseph Hooker, between whom and Slocum there was considerable friction. In April 1864 Slocum was put in command of the District of Vicksburg as the two corps were merged into the XX Corps under Hooker's direct command. When Hooker was relieved in July Slocum returned to take over the XX Corps. He took part in the Atlanta campaign, and troops of his command were the first to enter the city on September 2. During the march through Georgia and the campaign in the Carolinas

Slocum commanded the left wing of Gen. William T. Sherman's army; his wing, comprising the XIV and XX Corps, gradually assumed separate status as the Army of Georgia. From the end of the war he commanded the Department of the Mississippi at Vicksburg until resigning in September 1865. He settled in Brooklyn, New York, in 1866, resumed the practice of law, and was elected to Congress as a Democrat in 1868 and 1870. He was commissioner of public works in Brooklyn in 1876 and in 1882 was elected to a third term in Congress. Slocum died in New York City on April 14, 1894.

Smalls, Robert (1839–1915), naval hero and public official. Born a slave in Beaufort, South Carolina, on April 5, 1839, Smalls had the benefit, uncommon for slaves, of rudimentary schooling. In 1851 he followed his master to Charleston, where he worked for wages and, in a short time, married. Impressed into the Confederate navy at the outbreak of the Civil War, he served as wheelman on the *Planter*, an armed frigate stationed in Charleston harbor. Smalls gained widespread fame in the North when during the early hours of May 13, 1862, taking advantage of the absence of white crewmen, he commandeered the *Planter*, slipped through the Confederate fortifications, and delivered the ship into Union hands. He thus gained freedom for himself and his wife, two children, and a dozen slave crewmen who accompanied him, in addition to prize money for his exploit. Appointed a pilot in the Union navy by President Abraham Lincoln, he served on the monitor *Keokuk* in the attack on Charleston by Adm. Samuel F. Du Pont in April 1863 and was given the rank of captain in December 1863 for his bravery under fire. From 1863 to 1866 he served as the highest ranking black officer in the Union navy. After the war his fame and moderate views helped him launch a successful career in South Carolina politics. Elected as a Republican to the state house of representatives in 1868, he went to the South Carolina senate in 1871 and to the U.S. House of Representatives in March 1875. He served in the House, except during 1879–1881, until March 1887, achieving some prominence as an advocate of civil-rights legislation. Smalls spent his last years in Beaufort, where he held the appointive post of collector of the port during 1889–1893 and 1897–1913; the lapse was owing to the incumbency of a Democrat, Grover Cleveland, as president. As a delegate to the state constitutional convention in 1895 he unsuccessfully fought the final erosion of the black political rights that had been won during Reconstruction. He died on February 22, 1915, in Beaufort, South Carolina.

Smallwood, William (1732–1792), Revolutionary army officer. Born in 1732 in Charles County, Maryland, Smallwood served in the militia in the

French and Indian War. In 1761 he was elected to the colonial assembly, and he was an early leader of Whig sentiment in the state. In January 1776 he was elected colonel of Maryland troops, eventually organized as a battalion of nine companies, and in July he marched them north to join Gen. George Washington's army. He was absent from the battle of Long Island in August, but the Maryland line distinguished itself. He was wounded at White Plains, October 28, shortly after he was voted by Congress a commission as brigadier general of the Continental army. The Maryland troops again fought valorously at Fort Washington, November 16, and took conspicuous part in the battles of Trenton, December 26, and Princeton, January 3, 1777. They performed especially well at Germantown, October 4, 1777. During 1778–1779 Smallwood and his troops were on defensive and garrison duty around Wilmington, Delaware. In April 1780 he was ordered to join the southern army, and the Maryland line was singled out for the thanks of Congress for its actions at Camden, South Carolina, August 16, where it was part of Gen. Johann Kalb's wing. In September Smallwood was promoted to major general. When the reorganization that followed the removal of Gen. Horatio Gates placed him subordinate to the Baron von Steuben, he threatened to resign. Against Washington's displeasure and the refusal of Congress to backdate his commission he submitted, however, and was ordered to recruiting and supply duty in Maryland; he remained in the army until November 1783. In December 1784 the Maryland legislature elected him to the Continental Congress, but he declined. In 1785 he was elected governor, and he served three consecutive one-year terms in that office. Smallwood died in Prince Georges County, Maryland, on February 12, 1792.

Smith, Andrew Jackson (1815–1897), army officer. Born in Bucks County, Pennsylvania, on April 28, 1815, Smith graduated from West Point in 1838 and was commissioned in the 1st Dragoons. After garrison duty at Carlisle Barracks, Pennsylvania, he was ordered west in 1840. He saw action against Indians in Missouri and Kansas, took part in the Mexican War, and later served in California and in the Northwest. He was promoted to first lieutenant in March 1845, to captain in February 1847, and to major in May 1861. In October 1861 he was appointed colonel of the 2nd California Cavalry, but he resigned that commission in November; from February to March 1862 he was chief of cavalry of the Department of the Missouri under Gen. Henry W. Halleck, and in the latter month he was appointed brigadier general of volunteers. He then served as chief of cavalry of the Department of the Mississippi through the campaign against Corinth. He commanded a division in Gen. William T. Sherman's forces in the Yazoo River expe-

dition and the battle of Chickasaw Bluffs at Vicksburg, December 29, 1862, and under Gen. John A. McClernand in the capture of Arkansas Post, January 11, 1863. In the final Vicksburg campaign of 1863 he commanded a division of the XIII Corps under McClernand and later Gen. Edward O. C. Ord. In the Red River campaign under Gen. Nathaniel P. Banks he led a division of the XVI Corps, winning a brevet to colonel of regulars at Pleasant Hill, April 9, 1864. In May he was promoted to major general of volunteers. Assigned to the Army of the Cumberland under Gen. George H. Thomas, Smith took part in operations in Tennessee and Mississippi. When Gen. Nathan B. Forrest attempted to interrupt lines of communication to Sherman, then at Atlanta, Smith followed him to Tupelo, Mississippi, in July, sending Gen. Benjamin H. Grierson ahead to destroy the Mobile and Ohio Railroad and on July 14 defeating Forrest soundly. Later he was sent to Missouri, only to be recalled by Thomas to take part in the battle at Nashville, December 15–16. In February 1865 he took command of the XVI Corps, and in March he was brevetted brigadier and major general of regulars for his actions at Tupelo and Nashville. During the final months of the war he was engaged in the siege and capture of Mobile, Alabama. Mustered out of volunteer service in January 1866, he reverted to lieutenant colonel, but in July he was appointed colonel of the 7th Cavalry (which he did not actually command in the field; it was led by Lt. Col. George A. Custer.) In September 1867 he was named commander of the Department of the Missouri, a post he held until March 1868. In May 1869 he resigned from the army to take the position of postmaster of St. Louis. From 1877 to 1889 he was auditor of the city. In January 1889, under a special law of 1888, he was appointed colonel of cavalry on the retired list. Smith died in St. Louis on January 30, 1897.

Smith, Charles Ferguson (1807–1862), army officer. Born in Philadelphia on April 24, 1807, Smith graduated from West Point in 1825 and was commissioned in the artillery. After four years of garrison duty he became an instructor at West Point in 1829, and he served also as adjutant there from 1831 to 1838 and as commandant of cadets, 1838–1842. He was promoted to first lieutenant in May 1832 and to captain in July 1838. From 1842 to 1845 he was again on garrison duty in New York and Pennsylvania, and he then joined Gen. Zachary Taylor's army in Texas. Commanding four companies of artillery acting as infantry and known variously as the "red-legged infantry" and "Smith's light battalion," he won a brevet to major at Palo Alto and Resaca de la Palma, May 8–9, 1846. At Monterrey, September 20–24, he led his battalion in storming the key position on Loma Federación and was brevetted lieutenant colonel. Transferred to Gen. Winfield Scott's army, he served in the campaign from Veracruz to Mexico City, winning a third brevet to colonel at Contreras and Churubusco, August 19–20, 1847. From 1849 to 1851 Smith served on a board that wrote a system of instruction for all forms of artillery. Promoted to major in November 1854, he was appointed lieutenant colonel of the new 10th Infantry in March 1855. He led an expedition to the Red River of the North in 1856 and in 1857–1858 took part in the Mormon expedition under Col. Albert S. Johnston. During 1860–1861 he commanded the Department of Utah. At the outbreak of the Civil War he was assigned to duty in Washington, D.C. Appointed brigadier general of volunteers in August 1861, he was put in command of the District of Western Kentucky. He commanded a division under Gen. Ulysses S. Grant in the campaigns against Fort Henry and Fort Donelson in February 1862, and for his actions in leading an assault that gained a critical position inside Donelson's defenses he was promoted to major general of volunteers in March. He was sent in command of an expedition up the Tennessee River to Savannah, and there he fell ill and died on April 25, 1862.

Smith, Gustavus Woodson (1822–1896),

Confederate army officer. Born in Georgetown, Kentucky, in March 1822, Smith graduated from West Point in 1842 and was commissioned in the engineers. After two years of fortification work at New London, Connecticut, he returned to West Point as an instructor. During the Mexican War he commanded, the captain being disabled, the sappers and miners comprising the only company of engineers in the war. The engineers were of notable service, and Smith was brevetted first lieutenant for Cerro Gordo, April 18, 1847, and captain for Contreras, August 19–20. After the war he returned to West Point. In December 1854 he resigned from the army and settled in New Orleans, where he was engaged as chief engineer in the repair of the U.S. Mint and the construction of a marine hospital. In 1856 he took the post of chief engineer in Peter Cooper and Abram S. Hewitt's Trenton Iron Works in New Jersey. From 1858 to 1861 he was street commissioner in New York City. In the summer of 1861, while traveling in the South for his health, he was declared disloyal to the Union and ordered arrested; he immediately went to Richmond, Virginia, and in September was appointed major general in the Confederate army. He commanded a corps under Gen. Joseph E. Johnston in the Peninsula campaign, and when Johnston was carried wounded from the field at Seven Pines, May 31, 1862, he succeeded to command of the entire army in the field until the arrival of Gen. Robert E. Lee the next day. In August he was given command of a defensive sector extending from the Rappahannock to the Cape Fear River and including Richmond. For three days in November he was acting secretary of

war. A long-standing dispute with Confederate President Jefferson Davis resulted finally in Smith's resignation in February 1863. After a brief period as a volunteer aide on the staff of Gen. P. G. T. Beauregard he became superintendent of the Etowah Mining and Manufacturing Company in Georgia. In June 1864 he was appointed major general in command of the 1st Division of the Georgia militia, attached to Gen. John B. Hood's Army of Tennessee. His command took part in the unsuccessful defense of Atlanta and then fell back through Georgia and into the Carolinas before the advance of Gen. William T. Sherman. He surrendered at Macon, Georgia, on April 20, 1865. From 1866 to 1870 he was general manager of the Southwestern Iron Company at Chattanooga, Tennessee, and from 1870 to 1875 insurance commissioner of the state of Kentucky. In 1876 he moved to New York City. Smith wrote *Confederate War Papers*, 1884, *The Battle of Seven Pines*, 1891, and other books. He died in New York City on June 24, 1896.

Smith, Holland McTyeire (1882–1967), marine

officer. Born on April 20, 1882, in Seale, Alabama, Smith graduated from Alabama Polytechnic Institute (now Auburn University) in 1901 and took a law degree from the University of Alabama in 1903. After two years in practice in Montgomery he took a commission as second lieutenant in the marine corps in March 1905. He served in the Philippines in 1906–1908, Panama in 1909–1910, the Philippines again in 1912–1914, and the Dominican Republic in 1916–1917, advancing to captain and earning the nickname that persisted through his career, "Howlin' Mad" Smith. In June 1917 he went to France in command of a machine gun company of the 5th Marine Regiment, and after attending staff school he served as adjutant of the 4th Marine Brigade, attached to the army's 2nd Division. In July 1918 he was assigned to the staff of the I Corps. He saw action in the Aisne–Marne, St. Mihiel, Oise, and Meuse–Argonne operations, and at war's end was on the staff of the Third Army. After occupation duty in Germany he graduated from the Naval War College in 1921, served in the War Plans Office of the navy in 1921–1923, was chief of staff of the marine brigade in Haiti in 1924–1925, and chief of staff of the 1st Marine Brigade, 1925–1926. From 1927 to 1931 he was at the marine barracks, Philadelphia navy yard. He was force marine officer on the staff of the commander of Battle Force in 1931–1933, and, by that time a colonel, commander of the marine barracks in Washington, D.C., in 1934–1935. In 1935–1937 he was chief of staff in the Department of the Pacific and in 1937–1939 director of the Division of Operations and Training, receiving promotion to brigadier general in 1938. In April 1939 he was named assistant to the commandant of the corps, Gen. Thomas Holcomb, in which post he began developing a new amphibious doctrine and the equipment required for modern assault warfare. In September of that year he took command of the 1st Marine Brigade, taking it to Guantánamo, Cuba, a year later for thorough training in the new amphibious techniques. He was promoted to major general in February 1941, and in May the brigade became the 1st Marine Division. Later in the year the division became the nucleus of the Amphibious Force, Atlantic Fleet, which he commanded, working with Adm. R. Kelly Turner in developing a combat-ready force. In September 1942 his headquarters company was transferred west to organize the Amphibious Force, Pacific Fleet, later redesignated 5th Amphibious Force, comprising the 2nd and 5th and later the 3rd and 4th divisions. Working with Adm. Chester W. Nimitz and later Adm. Raymond A. Spruance, Smith helped plan every marine assault operation in the central Pacific from that date: Tarawa and Makin in the Gilbert Islands in November 1943; the Marshalls, including Eniwetok and Kwajalein, February–March 1944; Saipan, Tinian, and Guam in the Marianas, June–August 1944; Iwo Jima, February 1945; Okinawa and the Ryukyus, March–June 1945. He personally led troops ashore at Tarawa, Saipan, and Iwo Jima. He was promoted to lieutenant general in February 1944. With the formation of Fleet Marine Force, Pacific, in July 1944 he was moved up to that command. In July 1945 he was named commander of the training base at Camp Pendleton, California. He retired in August 1946, becoming on the same day the third marine officer ever to attain the rank of general. In 1949 he published, with Percy Finch, a record of his war experiences as *Coral and Brass*. In 1956 the headquarters of Fleet Marine Force, Pacific, at Pearl Harbor was named Camp H. M. Smith in his honor. Smith died in San Diego, California, on January 12, 1967.

Smith, John (1580?–1631), soldier, explorer, and colonizer. Born about 1580 in Willoughby, Lincolnshire, England, Smith attended school until the age of fifteen, then was apprenticed to a wealthy merchant. He began to travel in Europe at the age of sixteen and four years later joined the fighting in Transylvania, where he won promotion to captain and was taken prisoner and made a slave by the Turks. He escaped, traveled further in Russia and Europe, and returned to England in 1604. In London he learned of the London (or South Virginia) Company and actively promoted its plan to found a colony in America. He sailed in December 1606 and arrived with the first settlers, numbering 105 of the 144 who sailed, on the ships *Susan Constant, Godspeed,* and *Discovery* in Chesapeake Bay on April 26, 1607. An acknowledged leader of the group, he took a leading part in the founding of Jamestown, Virginia, on May 14. He was appointed to the governing council after a short time

and began to explore the region. Soon the dominant figure in Jamestown, he ventured alone many times into Indian territory to obtain food. On one occasion that has become one of the best known tales of the early colonies he was captured by Indians and was sentenced to death by their chief, Powhatan, and escaped death only by the intervention of Powhatan's daughter, Pocahontas. On his return to Jamestown in 1608 he found the government in the hands of personal enemies, and he was sentenced to be hanged for having lost the men of his exploring party. New settlers and needed supplies arrived at the straitened colony shortly thereafter, and he was released and restored to his position on the council. In that year he published in England his *True Relation of Such Occurrences and Accidents of Noate as Hath Hapned in Virginia since the First Planting of That Colony.* In September 1608 he was elected president of the colony and with great resourcefulness brought it through many hardships. In particular he organized an effective system of fortifications and trained militia. He was constantly involved in quarrels over leadership, however, and after suffering a severe injury he finally returned to England in October 1609. In 1614 he returned to America and for Sir Fernando Gorges and the Plymouth (North Virginia) Company explored the coast of the region he named New England, returning to Britain with a cargo of fish and furs. He became a strong advocate of colonization of New England and publicized its attractions widely. In 1615, on his way again to New England, he was captured by pirates, with whom he was forced to remain for several months. During this time he wrote *A Description of New England,* published in 1616, which included in its pages the most accurate map of the region yet produced. It provided a rosy picture of New England and was later instrumental in attracting settlers. When released, he returned to England and offered his services as a guide to the Pilgrims, but they felt his books and maps would be sufficient (and perhaps less troublesome) guidance. He remained in England thereafter, actively promoting colonization and persuading settlers to emigrate. In 1624 he published a *Generall Historie of Virginia, New England and the Summer Isles* and in 1630 *The True Travels, Adventures, and Observations of Captaine John Smith in Europe, Asia, Africa and America.* He died in London in June 1631.

Smith, Melancton (1810–1893), naval officer. Born on May 24, 1810, in New York City, Smith entered the navy as a midshipman in March 1826. After cruises in the Pacific on the *Brandywine* and the *Vincennes* he attended the naval school in Philadelphia in 1830–1832. From 1832 to 1841 he served principally with the West India Squadron, except for a period in 1835 at the New York navy yard, and was promoted to lieutenant in March 1837; during 1839–

1840 he saw action in the Seminole War on the Florida coast. Subsequently he served in the Mediterranean, 1841–1843; aboard the *Vandalia* of the Home Squadron, 1844–1846; at Pensacola navy yard, Florida, 1846–1848; and aboard the *Constitution* in the Mediterranean Squadron, 1848–1851. For the next ten years he was for the most part on waiting orders, receiving promotion to commander in September 1855. At the outbreak of the Civil War he was put in command of the *Massachusetts* and dispatched to patrol the mouth of the Mississippi. On July 9, 1861, he exchanged fire with Confederate batteries on Ship Island, and on October 19 he fought an inconclusive engagement with the cruiser *Florida*. On December 31 he forced the surrender of a fort at Biloxi, Mississippi. On the organization of Flag-Officer David G. Farragut's squadron in February 1862 Smith took command of the side-wheeler *Mississippi*. During the passage of Fort Jackson and Fort St. Philip on April 24 the *Mississippi* was rammed by the *Manassas* but drove the Confederate vessel ashore and destroyed her. He was promoted to captain in July 1862. In the running of Port Hudson on March 14, 1863, the *Mississippi* grounded, and Smith ordered her burned to prevent her capture. He commanded the *Monongahela* for a time and was then transferred to the James River, where he commanded a division of the squadron from the monitor *Onondaga*. In May 1864 he was put in command of a small squadron of eight light vessels including his flagship, the side-wheeler *Mattabesett*, in Albemarle Sound and sent against the Confederate armored ram *Albemarle*, which had been perforating the blockade of the North Carolina sounds at will for several months. On May 5 the *Albemarle* and her companion, the captured steamer *Bombshell*, attacked; the *Bombshell* was retaken, and Smith's squadron drove the *Albemarle* up the Roanoke River to Plymouth, where she remained thereafter. In the attacks by Adm. David D. Porter's squadron on Fort Fisher on December 24–25, 1864, and January 13–15, 1865, Smith commanded the steam frigate *Wabash* and won commendations. Promoted to commodore in July 1866, Smith was chief of the Bureau of Equipment and Recruiting in 1866–1870, and, receiving promotion to rear admiral in July 1870, commanded the New York navy yard until his retirement in May 1871. In 1871–1872 he was governor of the Naval Asylum in Philadelphia. He died in Green Bay, Wisconsin, on July 19, 1893.

Smith, Morgan Lewis (1821–1874), army officer. Born on March 8, 1821, in Mexico, New York, Smith grew up there and in neighboring Jefferson County. In 1842 he moved to Pennsylvania and a short time later to Indiana. In July 1845 he enlisted as a private in the army, and during his five years' service he advanced to sergeant, being for the most part engaged in drill and training duties in Newport,

Kentucky. From 1850 to 1861 he worked on riverboats on the Ohio and Mississippi. Soon after the Civil War began he raised the 8th Missouri Volunteer Infantry, recruited largely among riverboatmen in St. Louis, and in July 1861 he was appointed colonel of the regiment. Attached to the forces of Gen. Ulysses S. Grant, he took part in the campaign of February 1862 against Fort Henry and Fort Donelson, at the latter commanding a brigade in the division of Gen. Lew Wallace and distinguishing himself in storming a Confederate position. He subsequently took part in an expedition up the Tennessee River, in the Shiloh and Corinth campaigns, and at the battle of Russell's House, May 17, 1862, where he won commendation from Gen. William T. Sherman. Appointed brigadier general of volunteers in July, he served under Sherman through the campaigning in Tennessee and around Vicksburg; and on December 28, while reconnoitering at Chickasaw Bluffs, he received a wound that kept him from active service for ten months. In October 1863 he took command of a division of the XV Corps under Gen. Francis P. Blair, Jr. He again distinguished himself at Missionary Ridge, November 25, in the relief of Knoxville, and in the Atlanta campaign of 1864, commanding the XV Corps for a few days in July. Weakened by exertion and the lingering effects of his wound, he relinquished field command in August and in September was put in command of the District of Vicksburg, where his stern administration of military rule quickly restored public order. He resigned in July 1865. From 1866 to 1868 he was U.S. consul general in Honolulu. Thereafter he engaged in various business pursuits in Washington, D.C. Smith died in Jersey City, New Jersey, on December 28, 1874.

Smith, Oliver Prince (1893–   ), marine officer. Born on October 26, 1893, in Menard, Texas, Smith graduated from the University of California at Berkeley in 1916 and in May of the next year took a commission as a second lieutenant in the marines. He was stationed on Guam in 1917–1919, at Mare Island, California, in 1919–1921, and aboard the *Texas* as commander of the marine detachment in 1921–1924. During 1924–1928 he was assigned to duty at corps headquarters in Washington, D.C., and for three years thereafter he was in Haiti serving as assistant chief of staff of the gendarmerie. He graduated from the army's Infantry School, Fort Benning, Georgia, in 1932 and then was an instructor at the Marine Corps Schools at Quantico, Virginia, for a year. He was attached to the staff of the naval attaché at the U.S. embassy in Paris in 1934–1936, and in 1936–1939 he was again an instructor at Quantico. After a year on the staff of Fleet Marine Force, Pacific, he took command of a battalion of the 6th Marine Regiment in 1940 and from May 1941 to March 1942 was with the regiment in Iceland. After two years on the headquarters staff he was given a combat assignment in January 1944 as commander of the 5th Marine Regiment, 1st Division. He led the regiment through the Cape Gloucester, New Britain, campaign and in April, promoted to brigadier general, became assistant commander of the division. After seeing action on Peleliu in September–October he was named in November marine deputy chief of staff of the Tenth Army, Gen. Simon B. Buckner, to which the 1st Division was attached. After taking part in the Okinawa campaign in April–June 1945 Smith returned to the United States to become commandant of the Marine Corps Schools at Quantico. In April 1948 he was named assistant commandant and chief of staff of the corps under Gen. Clifton B. Cates. Promoted to major general, he took command of the 1st Marine Division in June 1950 and was ordered with it to Korea. He commanded the division, which constituted about half of Gen. Edward M. Almond's X Corps, through the Inch'on assault in September and the capture of Seoul, the amphibious move to Wonsan on the west coast, and the advance to the Yalu River. Smith's division was hit hard in the sudden massive counterattack by Chinese forces in November, particularly at the Changjin Reservoir on November 27. While the units in the center and on the right flank of X corps managed a withdrawal to the port of Hungnam with little difficulty, the marines, under constant attack, fought a bitter 13-day retreat against eight enemy divisions in winter weather. After the abandonment of Hungnam late in December Smith's division was incorporated into the Eighth Army. In May 1951 he returned to the United States and took command of Camp Pendleton, California. Promoted to lieutenant general, he commanded the Fleet Marine Force, Atlantic, from July 1953 until September 1955. He lived thereafter in quiet retirement, out of the public eye.

Smith, Persifor Frazer (1798–1858), army officer. Born in Philadelphia on November 16, 1798, Smith graduated from the College of New Jersey (now Princeton) in 1815 and took up the study of law. In 1819 he settled in New Orleans and began practice, quickly achieving a position of prominence and filling numerous local political offices. He was also active in the militia, becoming adjutant general of the state. In 1836 he raised a regiment of Louisiana volunteers and as its colonel served under Gen. Edmund P. Gaines in the Seminole War in Florida, 1836–1838. In May 1846 he was appointed colonel of volunteers for service in the Mexican War. He saw action under Gen. Zachary Taylor at Monterrey, September 20–24, where he commanded a brigade and distinguished himself and won a brevet to brigadier general. He then served under Gen. Winfield Scott from Veracruz to Mexico City. On the second day of the battle of Contreras, August 20, 1847, he took command of a three-brigade force and in a boldly conceived action extricated it from a dangerous position and destroyed a large Mexican force. He was again prominent in the capture by Gen. John A. Quitman's division of the Belen Gate of Mexico City. In October 1847 he was a member of the armistice commission. Subsequently he commanded the 2nd Division of the army, and as military governor of Veracruz in May 1848 he oversaw the embarkation of the army. Brevetted major general in 1849, he commanded in that rank the Division of the Pacific in 1849–1850, the Department of Texas in 1850–1856, and the Western Department at St. Louis in 1856–1858. He was promoted to brigadier general in December 1856. In April 1858 he was put in command of the Department of Utah, where Mormon disturbances were still unsettled, but while organizing his forces at Fort Leavenworth, Kansas, he died on May 17, 1858.

Smith, Walter Bedell (1895–1961), army officer and diplomat. Born on October 5, 1895, in Indianapolis, Indiana, Smith entered an army reserve officers training course from the Indiana National Guard in August 1917 and in November was given a reserve commission as second lieutenant in the 39th Infantry. During April–August 1918 he served in France and was wounded. Promoted to temporary first lieutenant in September, he was attached to the Bureau of Military Intelligence in Washington, D.C., for a time. In July 1920 he was given a regular commission as first lieutenant. He held staff positions with the 2nd Infantry, VI Corps, in Chicago, and the 12th Infantry Brigade at Fort Sheridan, Illinois, until 1925, when he was ordered to the War Department's Bureau of Budget. Promoted to captain in September 1929, he served in the Philippines in 1929–1931. He graduated from Infantry School, Fort Benning, Georgia, in 1932, remained there for a year as an instructor, and returned for another year after graduating from Command and General Staff School, Fort Leavenworth, Kansas, in 1935. In 1937 he graduated from the Army War College and was once again assigned to the faculty of the Infantry School. Smith was promoted to major in January 1939 and later in the year was assigned to duty with the General Staff. He became temporary lieutenant colonel in April 1941, was made permanent in that grade in May, and advanced to temporary colonel in July. In August he was named secretary of the General Staff. In February 1942 he was promoted to temporary brigadier general and named secretary of the U.S.–British Combined Chiefs of Staff and of the Joint Board. His position was a crucial one in the period when joint strategy was being hammered out. In September 1942 he became chief of staff, under Gen. Dwight D. Eisenhower, of U.S. army forces in the European theater. Two months later he was chosen by Eisenhower to serve as chief of staff of the Allied North African campaign and was promoted to temporary major general. In January 1944 he was promoted to temporary lieutenant general and named chief of staff, again under Eisenhower, of the Supreme Headquarters, Allied Expeditionary Force (SHAEF), and of U.S. forces in the European theater. As chief planner and executive officer for the entire European war from that date, Smith was called on to perform prodigies of administration. He also had the honor of signing, on Eisenhower's behalf, the instruments of surrender of Italy on September 3, 1943, and of Germany on May 7, 1945. He continued in his post until December 1945, advancing to the permanent rank of major general in August. In February 1946 he was appointed by President Harry Truman to be U.S. ambassador to the Soviet Union. He held that post, retaining his military rank, until March 1949 and during that time helped to negotiate peace treaties with Bulgaria, Rumania, Finland, Hungary, and Italy. He then took command of the First Army at Governors Island, New York. In 1950 he published *My Three Years in Moscow*. In September 1950 Smith became director of the Central Intelligence Agency, succeeding the first director, Adm. Roscoe H. Hillenkoetter. He was promoted to general in July 1951. In February 1953 he was appointed by President Eisenhower undersecretary of state under John Foster Dulles. In 1954 he headed the U.S. delegation at the Geneva conference on the war in Indochina. He resigned that post and retired in October 1954, devoting himself thereafter to various business interests and serving as an occasional governmental adviser. In 1956 he published *Eisenhower's Six Great Decisions*. Smith died in Washington, D.C., on August 9, 1961.

Smith, William Farrar (1824–1903), army officer. Born in St. Albans, Vermont, on February 17, 1824, Smith graduated from West Point in 1845 and was commissioned in the topographical engineers. After a year of survey work on the Great Lakes he returned to West Point as an instructor from 1846 to 1848. He did further survey work in Texas, including the Mexican boundary, 1849–1851, on a Florida ship canal, and elsewhere, receiving promotion to first lieutenant in 1853. In 1855–1856 he was again an instructor at West Point, and from 1856 to 1861 he was a member and from 1859 secretary of the Lighthouse Construction Board. He was promoted to captain in July 1859. In June 1861 he was attached to the staff of Gen. Benjamin F. Butler at Fort Monroe, Virginia. In July he was appointed colonel of the 3rd Vermont Volunteers, which he led at the battle of Bull Run (Manassas), July 21. In August he was promoted to brigadier general of volunteers in command of a division of the IV Corps, which, under Gen. Erasmus D. Keyes, he led in the Peninsula campaign, taking prominent part in the battle of Williamsburg,

May 5, 1862, and the Seven Days' Battles, June 26–July 2, and winning a brevet to lieutenant colonel of regulars at White Oak Swamp, June 30. Promoted to major general of volunteers in July, he commanded a division of Gen. William B. Franklin's VI Corps in the Maryland campaign and won a brevet to colonel of regulars at Antietam (Sharpsburg), September 17. He commanded the VI Corps at Fredericksburg, December 13, and in the recriminations that followed that disaster he sided with Franklin against Gen. Ambrose E. Burnside, the Union commander in chief, and barely escaped congressional censure and dismissal. In February 1863 he was transferred to the IX Corps, and in March, his commission as major general having failed of ratification in the Senate, he reverted to brigadier general of volunteers. In the summer of 1863 he was with the Department of the Susquehannah. He became chief engineer of the Department of the Cumberland in October and of the Military Division of the Mississippi in November. His primary responsibility in those posts was to open and maintain lines of supply to Gen. George H. Thomas's Army of the Cumberland besieged in Chattanooga, Tennessee. He planned and directed the surprise assault by Gen. William B. Hazen on Brown's Ferry on October 27 and the construction there of a pontoon bridge that first opened up what became known as the "cracker line" to Chattanooga. He played the major role in planning troop movements and bridge and works construction for the battle of Missionary Ridge, November 25. In March 1864 he was again promoted to major general of volunteers. Brought back to the eastern theater of war by Gen. Ulysses S. Grant, Smith was given command of the XVIII Corps in Gen. Benjamin F. Butler's Army of the James. Following Butler's landing at Bermuda Hundred he advanced and met Gen. P. G. T. Beauregard at Drewry's Bluff, May 12–16, a battle marked by Smith's successful use of wire entanglements on the field. Smith was subsequently transferred to the Army of the Potomac. He was prominent in the bloody battles at Cold Harbor, June 1–3, and led the assault on Petersburg on June 15–18. His criticism of superior commanders led, however, to his relief from command a few days later. Brevetted brigadier and major general of regulars in March 1865, he resigned his volunteer commission in that year and resigned from the army in 1867. From 1865 to 1873 he was president of the International Ocean Telegraph Company and from 1875 to 1881 president of the New York City Board of Police Commissioners. Thereafter he worked as an engineer. In such writings as *Military Operations Around Chattanooga*, 1886, *The Relief of the Army of the Cumberland*, 1891, and *From Chattanooga to Petersburg*, 1893, he recounted his experiences and kept up a controversy with the partisans of Gen. William S. Rosecrans, who in later years was credited with planning, before his relief by Gen. Thomas, some of the operations subsequently undertaken by Smith at Chattanooga. Smith died in Philadelphia on February 28, 1903.

Smith, William Stephens (1755–1816), Revolutionary army officer and public official. Born in New York City on November 8, 1755, Smith graduated from the College of New Jersey (now Princeton) in 1774 and took up the study of law. Soon after the outbreak of the Revolution he joined the Continental army, becoming in August 1776 an aide to Gen. John Sullivan with the rank of major. He took part in the battle of Long Island in that month, and on October 18 he performed a gallant service in destroying a bridge at Throgs Neck (Pelham Manor) and thus preventing the British army from flanking the Americans. He saw action at White Plains, October 28, in the retreat across New Jersey, and at Trenton, December 26, where he distinguished himself. In 1777 he was with Gen. Rufus Putnam in New York, and in 1778 he took part in the battle of Monmouth, June 27, and in Sullivan's expedition against Newport, Rhode Island, in August. In November 1778 he became lieutenant colonel in command of the 13th Massachusetts Regiment; he remained in command until March 1779. He was with Sullivan in the Indian expedition of 1779, later served under Lafayette, and in July 1781 was named an aide to Gen. George Washington, with whom he was present at Yorktown in October. In 1785 he was appointed secretary of the U.S. legation in London, where he met and married the daughter of the American minister, John Adams. Before his return to New York in 1788 he formed a connection with the soldier of fortune and later dictator of Venezuela, Francisco Miranda. From 1788 to 1798 Smith held various public offices in New York and engaged heavily in land speculation. From 1795 to 1797 he was president of the Society of the Cincinnati. He was nominated by his father-in-law, then President, to be adjutant general of the Provisional Army raised for war with France in 1798, but his name was rejected by the Senate and he served as colonel of the 12th Infantry. In 1805 he aided Miranda in raising a body of some 200 recruits, who sailed from New York in February 1806 on an ill fated filibustering expedition to South America. For his part in the scheme Smith was prosecuted but acquitted. He retired from public life until 1812, when he won election to Congress. His reelection in 1814 was successfully contested, and he retired to his farm in Lebanon, New York, where he died on June 10, 1816.

Smyth, Alexander (1765–1830), army officer and public official. Born in 1765 on the island of Rathlin, part of County Antrim, Ireland, Smyth was brought to America as a child by his family and grew up in Botetourt County, Virginia. In 1785 he was appointed deputy clerk of the county, and in 1789 he was admitted to the bar. He practised in Abingdon until 1792 and thereafter in Wythe County. He served in the legislature in 1792, 1796, 1801–1802, and 1804–1809. In July 1808 he was appointed by President Thomas Jefferson colonel of the Southwest Virginia Rifle Regiment. In July 1812 he was appointed inspector general of the U.S. army with the rank of brigadier general, and he published in that year *Regulations for the Field Exercise, Manoeuvres, and Conduct of the Infantry of the United States.* He secured a field command for himself and was ordered to the Niagara frontier. Posted at Buffalo in command of about 1650 regulars and 400 militiamen, he quickly fell out with the senior area commander, Gen. Stephen van Rensselaer, whose troops numbered 2300 militiamen and 900 regulars. When Van Rensselaer ignored Smyth's preference for an attack across the Niagara River above the falls and instead crossed below the falls on October 13 and began his campaign against Queenston, Smyth refused to support him. When the campaign failed as a consequence, Smyth succeeded to command of the district on October 24. He issued a bombastic statement concerning the imminent conquest of Canada but did little but march his army up and down. A crossing of the Niagara was attempted on November 28 but called back when it was discovered there were too few boats. Another attempt was abandoned on December 1. The disgusted militia quickly dispersed, leaving the regulars to go into winter quarters. Smyth's request for leave to visit his family was granted, and in March 1813 a congressional reorganization of the army dropped his name from the rolls. In 1816 he was again elected to the Virginia legislature and in the same year to Congress, where he served four successive terms, from March 1817 to March 1825; he was in the House again from March 1827 and was elected a sixth time in 1828. During his absence from Congress he was again in the legislature in 1826–1827. Smyth died in Washington, D.C., on April 17, 1830.

Snelling, Josiah (1782–1828), army officer. Born in Boston in 1782, Snelling was commissioned a first lieutenant in the 4th Infantry in 1808. He was promoted to captain in June 1809. He took part in the battle of Tippecanoe under Gen. William Henry Harrison, November 7, 1811, and was brevetted major for his actions at the battle of Brownstown, August 9, 1812, during Gen. William Hull's abortive invasion of Canada. He was in Detroit when that post was surrendered by Hull on August 16. On being exchanged he was appointed major and assistant inspector general in April 1813. He served the rest of the war under Gen. Winfield Scott on the Niagara frontier, advancing to lieutenant colonel of the 4th Riflemen in February 1814 and to colonel and inspector general in April and taking part in the battles of Chippewa and Lundy's Lane, July 5 and 25. At the end of the war he was appointed lieutenant colonel of the 6th Infantry in May 1815. In June 1819 he was promoted to colonel of the 5th Infantry (formerly the 4th), and sent to Council Bluffs, Missouri Territory, with orders to establish army posts on the upper Mississippi River. In that year he dispatched Lt. Col. Henry Leavenworth to the confluence of the Mississippi and Minnesota rivers (a site originally chosen by Lt. Zebulon M. Pike in 1805), to begin construction of Fort St. Anthony. In September 1820 Snelling arrived to begin construction of a permanent garrison complex completed in 1823. He remained commandant of the fort, and the principal authority in the territory, until January 1828. In 1825 Gen. Scott ordered the fort renamed Fort Snelling in his honor. Snelling died while on leave of absence in Washington, D.C., on August 20, 1828.

Somers, Richard (1778–1804), naval officer. Born in Somers Point, New Jersey, on September 15, 1778, Somers grew up in Philadelphia and in Burlington, New Jersey. He had already gained experience in the merchant service when he entered the navy as a midshipman in April 1798. He made his first cruise in the West Indies on the *United States* under Commodore John Barry and advanced to lieutenant in May 1799. In 1801 he was made first lieutenant on the *Boston,* aboard which he sailed to France and the Mediterranean. Late in 1802 he returned and was given command of the schooner *Nautilus* in Commodore Edward Preble's squadron, which sailed in the spring of 1803 to reinforce the blockade of Tripoli. In August 1804 Somers was put in command of one of the two divisions of gunboats Preble had obtained from the king of the Two Sicilies, and he distinguished himself for coolness under fire in the several attacks on Tripoli harbor in August–September. In August Somers received word of his promotion, as of February 1804, to master commandant. On September 4 the ketch *Intrepid,* famed for Lt. Stephen Decatur's raid into the harbor to burn the *Philadelphia* in February, was packed with about 100 barrels of powder (about 15,000 pounds), 150 shells, and quantities of shot and miscellaneous iron. The plan, perhaps originated by Somers, was to drift the vessel into the harbor among the Tripolitan fleet and then blow it up, damaging the fleet and perhaps the town. Somers and a crew of 12 volunteered for the exploit. For two hours in the darkness of the evening the *Intrepid* drifted in with the tide, but it was apparently discovered and fired upon by Tripolitan guns, for at ten o'clock it blew up prematurely, killing all aboard. No damage was done the Tripolitan fleet.

Somervell, Brehon Burke (1892–1955), army officer. Born on May 9, 1892, in Little Rock, Arkan-

sas, Somervell grew up there and in Washington, D.C. He graduated from West Point in 1914 and was commissioned in the engineers. He was engaged in survey work on the Texas border when Pancho Villa began his raids from Mexico, and he served in the Mexican Punitive Expedition under Gen. John J. Pershing in 1916. In August 1917, promoted to temporary major, he was ordered to France, where he was involved in building numerous depots and other installations. From November 1918 to May 1919 he was on the staff of the 89th Division, and he was assistant chief of staff of the army of occupation until October 1920. He graduated from the Engineer School, Fort Belvoir, Virginia, in 1921, from Command and General Staff School, Fort Leavenworth, Kansas, in 1925, and from the Army War College in 1926, meanwhile serving in the office of the chief of engineers and in the engineer district of New York. In 1925 he assisted in a League of Nations survey of navigation on the Rhine and Danube rivers. He was district engineer in Washington, D.C., in 1926–1930; in Memphis, Tennessee, in 1931–1933; and in Ocala, Florida, supervising construction of the Florida Ship Canal, in 1935–1936, spending 1933–1934 in an economic survey of Turkey. He was promoted to lieutenant colonel in 1935. In August 1936 he was appointed administrator for New York of the Works Progress Administration, in which post he oversaw construction of La Guardia Airport, thousands of miles of roads, and numerous parks, playgrounds, and smaller works. In November 1940 he was recalled to duty in the office of the inspector general, and in December he was named chief of the construction division, Quartermaster Corps. In that post he directed the construction of some $2 billion worth of camps, barracks, and other facilities. In November 1941, by then a brigadier general, he was made assistant chief of staff for supply. With the creation of the Services of Supply in March 1942 he moved up to take on the expanded responsibilities of that post, receiving promotion to lieutenant general. He held that post, one of the army's three major commands (Army Ground Forces and Air Forces being the others), until his retirement in January 1946. The Services of Supply was redesignated Army Service Forces in March 1943. The unified service combined the formerly separate functions of procurement, inventory, and distribution and was the logistical support for the entire army. In March 1945 Somervell was promoted to temporary general. After his retirement in the rank of lieutenant general he became president and chairman of the Koppers Company. He died in Ocala, Florida, on February 13, 1955.

Sousa, John Philip (1854–1932), conductor and composer. Born on November 6, 1854, in Washington, D.C., Sousa early showed a marked aptitude for music. He studied violin at first and in 1867 took up the trombone. During 1868–1871 he played with the United States Marine Band, but in 1872 he returned to the violin and played in and conducted a number of theater orchestras during the next few years. In 1876 he played in Jacques Offenbach's orchestra at the Centennial Exposition in Philadelphia. In September 1880 he was appointed conductor of the U.S. Marine Band, and in his 12 years in that post he effected a great improvement in its standard of performance. He remained with it until August 1892, when he left to form his own band. During this period with the Marine Band—the President's official band, which he conducted for five presidents—he began to compose the marches that won him the title of "the March King"—"Semper Fidelis," which later became the official march of the marine corps, in 1888, "The Washington Post March" in 1889, and "The Liberty Bell" in 1893. From 1892 he toured the United States and Europe with his own band and met outstanding success. He appeared at virtually every major exposition held in the United States, from the 1893 World's Columbian in Chicago onward. In 1897 he wrote "The Stars and Stripes Forever," his most popular piece, and in 1899 "Hands Across the Sea." During the Spanish–American War he was music director for the army's VI Corps, and during World War I he became director, with the rank of lieutenant commander, of all navy bands. After the war's end he resumed his tours. In all he composed more than 100 marches, celebrated for their rhythm and ingenious orchestration, 10 comic operas, the most successful of which were *El Capitan*, 1896, *The Bride-Elect*, 1897, *The Charlatan*, 1898, and *The Free Lance*, 1906, and many other songs and miscellaneous works. He compiled a potpourri of songs of foreign nations for the Navy Department and wrote three novels, dissertations on the trumpet and violin, and an autobiography, *Marching Along*, 1928. He died in Reading, Pennsylvania, on March 6, 1932.

Spaatz, Carl (1891–1974), army and air force officer. Born on June 28, 1891, in Boyertown, Pennsylvania, Spaatz (originally Spatz—he added an "a" in 1937) graduated from West Point in 1914 and was commissioned in the infantry. After a year at Schofield Barracks, Hawaii, he entered aviation training at San Diego, California, becoming one of the army's first pilots in 1916 and winning promotion to first lieutenant in June. He advanced to captain in May 1917 and was ordered to France in command of the 31st Aero Squadron. He organized and directed the aviation training school at Issoudon and by the end of the war had managed to get just under three weeks' combat duty, during which he shot down three German aircraft. In June 1918 he was promoted to temporary major. During 1919–1920 he served as assistant air officer for the Western Department; he reverted to captain in February 1920 and received

promotion to permanent major in July. Spaatz served as commander of Mather Field, California, in 1920; as commander of Kelly Field, Texas, in 1920–1921; as air officer, VIII Corps, in 1921; as commander of the 1st Pursuit Group at Selfridge Field, Michigan, in 1922–1924; in the office of the chief of the Air Corps in 1925–1929; as commander of the 7th Bombardment Group at Rockwell Field, California, and subsequently of Rockwell Field in 1929–1931; and as commander of the 1st Bombardment Wing at March Field, California, in 1931–1933. During January 1–7, 1929, Spaatz and Capt. Ira C. Eaker established a flight endurance record of 150 hours, 40 minutes, in a Fokker aircraft, the *Question Mark*, over Los Angeles. After two years as chief of the training and operations division in the office of the chief of Air Corps and promotion to lieutenant colonel in September 1935, he entered the Command and General Staff School, Fort Leavenworth, Kansas, graduating in 1936. He was executive officer of the 2nd Wing at Langley Field, Virginia, until 1939 and then again joined the staff of the chief of the Air Corps. After a tour of observation in England in 1940 he was promoted to temporary brigadier general and named to head the matériel division of the Air Corps, and in July 1941 he became chief of air staff under Gen. Henry H. Arnold, chief of the (renamed) Army Air Forces. In January 1942 he was appointed chief of the Air Force Combat Command. Later in that year he returned to England to begin planning the American air effort in Europe. In May he became commander of the Eighth Air Force, and in July he was designated commander of U.S. Army Air Forces in Europe. In November he went to North Africa to reorganize the Allied air forces there for Gen. Dwight D. Eisenhower, becoming commander of the Allied Northwest African Air Forces (NWAAF) in February 1943. In March he was promoted to temporary lieutenant general. From March to December 1943 he was also commander of the U.S. Twelfth Air Force, a unit of the NWAAF, which took part in both the North Africa and the Sicily campaigns. In January 1944 Spaatz was named commander of the Strategic Air Force in Europe; his command included the Eighth Air Force under Gen. James H. Doolittle, based in England, and the Fifteenth Air Force under Gen. Nathan F. Twining, based in Italy, and had responsibility for all deep bombing missions against the German homeland. In March 1945 he was promoted to temporary general, and in July, war in Europe having ended, he took command of the Strategic Air Force in the Pacific. The atomic bombing of Hiroshima and Nagasaki took place under his command. In March 1946 he succeeded Gen. Arnold as commander in chief of the Army Air Forces, and he became the first chief of staff of the independent air force in September 1947. He held that post until retiring in July 1948 in the rank of general (he had been permanent major general since June 1946). He served subsequently as chairman of the Civil Air Patrol and for a time contributed a column to *Newsweek* magazine. Spaatz died in Washington, D.C., on July 14, 1974.

Spencer, Joseph (1714–1789), Revolutionary army officer. Born on October 3, 1714, in Haddam (now East Haddam), Connecticut, Spencer, member of a prominent local family, was commissioned a lieutenant of militia in 1747. As a major (from 1757) he took part in Gen. James Abercrombie's expedition to Ticonderoga in 1758, and, promoted to lieutenant colonel in 1759, he saw action through the end of the French and Indian War in 1763. In 1766 he became colonel of militia. In the meanwhile he had been chosen a probate judge in 1753 and elected several times to the colonial assembly before being chosen an assistant in 1766. On the outbreak of the Revolution he was promoted to brigadier general of Connecticut forces and in May 1775 ordered to Roxbury, Massachusetts. In June he was commissioned brigadier general in the Continental army, but the commissioning of Israel Putnam, who was junior to him in the militia, as major general outraged him and he left without notice and went home. He was eventually persuaded by a delegation from the governor and legislature to return to duty, and he served through the siege of Boston and the New York campaign, receiving promotion to major general in August 1776. In December 1776 he established headquarters in Providence, Rhode Island. There he planned, but failed to make, a move against British forces at Newport. Following a court of inquiry late in 1777, by which he was cleared, he resigned from the army in June 1778. In 1778 and 1779 he was elected a delegate to the Continental Congress, and he was a member of the Connecticut council of safety in 1778 and 1780–1781. He died in East Haddam, Connecticut, on January 13, 1789.

Sperry, Charles Stillman (1847–1911), naval officer. Born on September 3, 1847, in Brooklyn, New York, Sperry graduated from the Naval Academy in 1866 and was commissioned ensign in March 1868. Until after the Spanish–American War he saw routine duty at sea and ashore, advancing to lieutenant in March 1870, lieutenant commander in March 1885, and commander in June 1894. In 1899, then at the Brooklyn navy yard, he was given command of the cruiser *Yorktown* and ordered to the Philippines. He aided in the blockade of Lingayen Gulf to prevent the supply of insurgent forces during the northern Luzon campaign under Gen. Arthur MacArthur, and later he landed forces in the rear of the insurrectionists to help cut off their retreat. Sperry was promoted to captain in July 1900. From 1903 to 1906 he was president of the Naval War College, and he served on the General Board in 1903 and on the National Coast

Defense Board in 1905. Promoted to rear admiral in May 1906, he was a delegate in June of that year to the Geneva conference on the rules of war. In June 1907 he was a delegate to an international conference at The Hague on prize law. In December 1907 he sailed aboard the *Alabama* from Hampton Roads, Virginia, in command of the 4th division of the fleet of 16 battleships ordered on a world cruise under Adm. Robley D. Evans. At San Francisco in May 1908 Sperry succeeded the ailing Evans in command of the cruise. The fleet left San Francisco on July 7 and on its westward cruise called at Honolulu; Auckland, New Zealand; Sydney and Melbourne, Australia; Manila, Philippines; and Yokohama, Japan, where it arrived on October 18. The Battle Fleet completed its circumnavigation by way of China, the Indian Ocean, the Suez Canal, and the Mediterranean, arriving again at Hampton Roads on February 22, 1909. A skilled diplomat as well as an efficient officer, Sperry everywhere made a strongly favorable impression, and the world cruise of the Battle Fleet was a great success. He retired from the navy in September 1909 and died in Washington, D.C., on February 1, 1911.

Sprague, Clifton Albert Furlow (1896–1955), naval officer. Born on January 8, 1896, in Dorchester, Massachusetts, Sprague graduated from the Naval Academy in 1917. Over the next 25 years he rose to the rank of captain. In World War II he commanded the fleet carrier *Wasp* (successor in that name to Capt. Forrest P. Sherman's *Wasp*, sunk in 1942) at Marcus, Wake, the Marianas, and Guam, and in the first battle of the Philippine Sea in June 1944. Promoted to rear admiral in that year, he was put in command of an escort carrier group known as Taffy 3, an element of Adm. Thomas C. Kinkaid's Seventh Fleet. In addition to his flagship *Fanshaw Bay* he had five other escort carriers—"baby flattops"—three destroyers, and four destroyer escorts, none of which had guns larger than five-inchers. On October 25, 1944, patrolling off Samar Island in the Philippines during the assault on Leyte, Taffy 3 suddenly encountered the previously undetected Japanese Center Force—four battleships, six heavy cruisers, and a number of destroyers, with 14-inch guns on the battleships. Against these overwhelming odds Sprague fought perhaps the most remarkable naval battle of the war. His tactics were masterly, the more so for the lack of forewarning. Some support came in the form of aircraft from two distant Taffy groups. Battle was joined shortly before 7 A.M., was carried on through a rain storm, and was broken shortly after 9, when Adm. Kurita retired northward. Sprague lost two carriers, a destroyer, and a destroyer escort but sank three heavy cruisers and, most importantly, removed the Center Force from the all-important battle of Leyte. In 1946 he commanded the naval units taking part in the atomic bomb tests at Bikini atoll. From 1949 to 1950 he commanded the naval air bases of the 11th and 12th Naval Districts, and in 1950–1951 he commanded the 17th Naval District and the Alaska Sea Frontier. Sprague retired as a vice admiral in 1951, and he died in San Diego, California, on April 11, 1955.

Springs, Elliot White (1896–1959), airman, businessman, and author. Born in Lancaster, South Carolina, on July 31, 1896, Springs graduated from Culver Military Academy in 1913 and from Princeton University in 1917. Later in that year, as a private in the army Signal Corps attached to the aviation section, he began studying military aviation at Oxford University, where he trained with the Royal Flying Corps. He saw much combat in World War I, advancing to the rank of captain and squadron commander, and during service with the British 85th Squadron and the American 148th Aero Squadron compiled a record of 12 German aircraft shot down. In 1919 he flew in the first cross-country air race, from New York City to Toronto. He then turned down the opportunity to work in family-owned textile mills in favor of settling in New York City to pursue a career as an author. He produced many short stories and several books and novels, the best known of which was the best-selling *Warbirds—The Diary of an Unknown Aviator,* which he edited and ascribed to J. M. Grider, 1926; others included *Nocturne Militaire,* 1927; *Contact,* 1930; *Warbirds and Ladybirds,* 1931; and *Clothes Make the Man,* 1948. When his father died in 1931 Springs took over and consolidated the family's cotton mills in North and South Carolina. As head of the Springs Cotton Mills Company he became known as an innovative, daring, and occasionally eccentric entrepreneur. He was particularly noted for a style of advertising that was considered startling for its time—so much so that some ads, with their racy pictures and double-entendre captions, were banned by major magazines. But he made "Springmaid" sheets virtually a household word. By the end of his life Springs had made his company one of the largest of its kind in the nation, with a work force of more than 12,000 in 1958. Early in World War II Springs, still an officer in the Air Corps Reserve, served as executive officer of the air base at Charlotte, North Carolina, advancing to lieutenant colonel before his retirement in 1942. He died on October 15, 1959, in New York City.

Spruance, Raymond Ames (1886–1969), naval officer and diplomat. Born on July 3, 1886, in Baltimore, Spruance grew up there, in East Orange, New Jersey, and in Indianapolis. He graduated from the Naval Academy in 1906, served briefly on the *Iowa,* and made the world cruise of the Battle Fleet in 1907–1909 on the *Minnesota,* receiving his commission as

ensign in 1908. After service on various other ships and a period in command of the destroyer *Bainbridge,* he was ordered in 1914 to assist in fitting out the *Pennsylvania,* then building at Newport News, Virginia, and he sailed with her in 1916. Later in that year he was ordered to the New York navy yard. After World War I he assisted in the fitting out of the destroyer *Aaron Ward* and then took command of her. After a time in command of the *Perceval* he was attached to the Bureau of Engineering in 1921–1924. During 1924–1925 he was on the staff of the commander of U.S. naval forces in Europe, and after graduating from the Naval War College in 1927 he was assigned to the Office of Naval Intelligence. During 1929–1931, then a commander, he served on the *Mississippi.* He was an instructor at the Naval War College in 1931–1932, receiving promotion to captain in June 1932, and was on the staff of the commander, Scouting Force, in 1933–1935. Following three more years at the War College he took command of the *Mississippi* in 1938. Promoted to rear admiral in December 1939, Spruance was placed in command of the 10th Naval District at San Juan, Puerto Rico, in February 1940; he remained there until late 1941 and served also in July–August 1941 as commander of the Caribbean Sea Frontier. In 1941 he was given command of Cruiser Division 5 of the Pacific Fleet, from December under Adm. Chester W. Nimitz. As part of Task Force 16, under Adm. William F. Halsey, his destroyers protected the carrier *Hornet* during Col. James H. Doolittle's daring raid on Tokyo in April 1942. At the battle of Midway, June 3–6, he was in temporary command of the Task Force, centered on the carriers *Enterprise* and *Hornet,* and acted under Adm. Frank J. Fletcher on the *Yorktown.* In a tactically masterly battle, Spruance's force sank four Japanese carriers, a crippling loss. Spruance was then named chief of staff under Nimitz, and in September 1942 he became deputy commander of the Pacific Fleet and Pacific Ocean Areas. Promoted to vice admiral in May 1943, he was named commander of the Central Pacific Area and Force (subsequently also known as the Fifth Fleet) in August. In that post he directed the operations against Makin and Tarawa in the Gilbert Islands, November 1943. He landed Gen. Holland M. Smith's 5th Amphibious Force there and at Eniwetok and Kwajalein in the Marshalls in February–March 1944; the Marianas, notably Saipan, Tinian, and Guam, were similarly taken in June–August 1944. The battle of the Philippine Sea, June 19–21, was fought principally by Adm. Marc A. Mitscher's Task Force 58 operating under Fifth Fleet (Fifth Fleet and Adm. Halsey's Third Fleet consisted to a large degree of the same forces). Spruance, promoted to admiral in February 1944, and Gen. Smith conducted the assaults on Iwo Jima in February 1945 and on Okinawa in March–May 1945. In November 1945 Spruance became commander of the Pacific Fleet, succeeding Nimitz, but the next month he relinquished that command to Adm. John H. Towers to become president of the Naval War College. He retired in July 1948. From 1952 to 1955 he served as U.S. ambassador to the Philippines. Spruance died in Pebble Beach, California, on December 13, 1969.

Standish, Miles (1584?–1656), soldier and colonist. Born about 1584 in Lancashire, England, Miles (or Myles) Standish carved out a military career for himself as a soldier of fortune in the Netherlands during the Dutch wars for independence from Spain. While in Holland he met the English Puritans who were living in exile in Leiden. In 1620 he was hired by them to join their colonizing expedition to the New World, a fortunate choice for them, for he became one of the mainstays of their small colony during its early years of near-starvation and illness. He was one of the first party ashore from the *Mayflower* at Plymouth on December 11 (old style), 1620. Standish became the military leader of the Plymouth Colony and the chief negotiator with the New England Indian tribes. He was the first of the colonists to learn the Indian languages, and he was their chief strategist of defense. His expertise in Indian relations was such that after the first few years the colony had no real Indian troubles for half a century. In 1625–1626 he went to England as agent for the colony to secure new loans and purchase supplies. In 1627 he was one of a group of colonists that bought out the London merchant adventurers who had invested in the venture, thus enabling the Pilgrims to assume title to their land in New England. In June 1628 Standish led the expedition that arrested Thomas Morton (who referred to Standish uncharitably as "Captaine Shrimp") at his unpuritanical Merry Mount Colony and sent him back to England. In 1644–1649 he was assistant governor and treasurer of the colony. In 1631 Standish and John Alden founded the town of Duxbury, where Standish settled in 1637 and remained until his death on October 3, 1656. Until then he remained one of the influential men in the growing colony, serving in various posts and amassing considerable property. He is probably best remembered through Henry Wadsworth Longfellow's narrative poem, *The Courtship of Miles Standish,* but there is no historical evidence for his purported offer of marriage through John Alden to Priscilla Mullins.

Standley, William Harrison (1872–1963), naval officer and diplomat. Born on December 18, 1872, in Ukiah, California, Standley graduated from the Naval Academy in 1895 and was commissioned an ensign two years later. He saw active service during the Philippine Insurrection, was attached to the Coast and Geodetic Survey in 1901–1902, and, by then a lieutenant, was on duty in American Samoa in 1904–1905. Duty aboard the *Adams,* the *Albany,* the

Pennsylvania, the *New Jersey* in 1914, and, with the rank of commander, the *Yorktown* followed; and from 1916 to 1919 he was on the staff of the Naval Academy, becoming commandant of midshipmen and in 1919 receiving promotion to captain. In 1919–1920 he commanded the *Virginia,* and after graduating from the Naval War College in 1921 he was attached to the staff of the commander of the Battle Fleet. He headed the War Plans Division of the Bureau of Operations from 1923 to 1926, commanded the *California* in 1926–1927, and, promoted to rear admiral in November 1927, was named director of fleet training. He became assistant chief of naval operations in May 1928. From October 1930 to November 1931 he commanded the destroyer squadrons, Battle Fleet, and he then commanded the cruiser divisions, Scouting Force and U.S. Fleet, receiving promotion to vice admiral in January 1932. In May 1933 he became commander of the Battle Force aboard the *California* with the rank of admiral, and in July he was named chief of naval operations. Standley retired from the navy in January 1937. In 1939 he was made a special adviser to the secretary of the navy and to the President. He was also, in 1939–1941, a director of and consultant to the Electric Boat Company in Groton, Connecticut, and a director of Pan American Airways from 1940. In March 1941 he was recalled briefly to active service on the Production Planning Board of the Office of Production Management. In January 1942 he served on the commission under Justice Owen J. Roberts investigating the Pearl Harbor disaster. In February 1942 he was appointed U.S. ambassador to the Soviet Union, a post he held until September 1943. During 1944–1945 he was again on active service with the Office of Strategic Services. Standley died in San Diego, California, on October 25, 1963.

Stansbury, Howard (1806–1863), army officer and explorer. Born in New York City on February 8, 1806, Stansbury studied civil engineering and in October 1828 was given charge of a project to survey canal routes by which Lake Erie, Lake Michigan, and the Wabash River might be united. In 1832–1835 he was engaged in surveying the route of the Mad River & Lake Erie Railroad and other projects in Ohio and Indiana. He surveyed the lower James River in Virginia in 1836, rivers in Illinois in 1837, and a railroad route from Milwaukee to the Mississippi in 1838. In July 1838 he was commissioned a first lieutenant in the newly established Corps of Topographical Engineers of the army; he was promoted to captain in July 1840. From 1842 to 1845 he conducted a highly detailed survey of the harbor at Portsmouth, New Hampshire. In 1847 he took charge of building a lighthouse on Carysfort Reef, Florida. In 1849 he was sent to survey the Great Salt Lake, then known only sketchily from Lt. John C. Frémont's observations in

1843. He assembled a party of 18 men at Fort Leavenworth, Kansas, (his second-in-command being Lt. John W. Gunnison, destined to die in an infamous Indian massacre) and in May set out for Utah by way of South Pass and Fort Bridger, where he engaged Jim Bridger as a guide. He explored new routes to the Great Salt Lake and then spent several months in the vicinity of the lake, during which he completed the first circuit of the lake. Midway through 1850 he began the return journey, stopping in September at Fort Bridger to hire Jim Bridger again to seek out a new route eastward. The route he followed, though not unknown, was little used before the Stansbury expedition, but afterwards it became the route of the Overland Trail, of Ben Holladay's Overland Stage, and later of much of the Union Pacific Railroad. His report, printed as a Senate document under the title "Exploration and Survey of the Valley of the Great Salt Lake of Utah, Including a Reconnoissance of a New Route through the Rocky Mountains" in 1852 and published commercially in the same year as *An Expedition to the Valley of the Great Salt Lake of Utah,* was widely read. For ten years thereafter Stansbury was again engaged in river and road surveys, mainly in the Great Lakes region and in Minnesota. He retired in the rank of major in September 1861, but he later returned to active service as a recruiting officer in Madison, Wisconsin. He died there on April 17, 1863.

Stapp, John Paul (1910–   ), physician and air force officer. Born on July 11, 1910, in Salvador, Brazil, of American missionary parents, Stapp was educated from the age of twelve in the United States and in 1931 graduated from Baylor University. He took a master's degree there the next year, taught in 1932–1934 at Decatur (Texas) Baptist College, and entered the University of Texas in 1934, taking a Ph.D. in biophysics in 1939. He then attended the medical school of the University of Minnesota, graduating in 1943. After his internship he was commissioned a first lieutenant in the army Medical Corps in October 1944. Following study at the School of Aviation Medicine he was assigned in 1945 to the Aero Medical Laboratory at Holloman Field, New Mexico. There, and subsequently at Edwards Air Force Base, California, in 1947–1951, and at Wright-Patterson Air Force Base, Ohio, in 1951–1953, he carried on a highly fruitful program of research into the limits of endurance of the human body, specifically its ability to withstand high acceleration forces. Working with a series of rocket-powered sleds capable of increasingly higher speeds and more sudden stops and often using himself as the experimental subject, he found that far higher forces were endurable than had been believed. He himself experienced acceleration forces of up to 35g (g being the force of gravity), nearly twice the assumed human limit, and in December

1954 he set a land speed record of 632 miles per hour on his latest rocket sled. Tests were also conducted on the effect of high-speed wind blasts, such as those encountered in bailing out of jet aircraft, and on other physiological responses to high altitude conditions. From 1953 to 1958 Stapp was chief of the laboratory at Holloman, advancing to the rank of colonel by 1957, and in 1958–1960 he headed the Wright-Patterson laboratory. In 1960, his work having helped open the way for the manned exploration of space, he joined the aerospace medicine team at Brooks Air Force Base, Texas, becoming chief scientist of the program in 1962. From 1965 to 1967 he was attached to the Armed Forces Institute of Pathology in Washington, D.C., where he conducted studies on crash injuries and prevention—his earlier work had already led to the development of shoulder harness restraints for pilots—and in 1967 he transferred his research to the National Highway Safety Bureau. After his retirement in 1970 he continued as a consultant to the Department of Transportation and in 1973 was appointed to the faculty of the University of Southern California. Stapp was the recipient of numerous honors, including the John Jeffries Award in 1953, the Air Power Award in 1954, the Cheney Award in 1955, and the Cresson Medal in 1973.

Stark, Harold Raynsford (1880–1972), naval officer. Born on November 12, 1880, in Wilkes-Barre, Pennsylvania, Stark graduated from the Naval Academy in 1903 and was commissioned an ensign two years later. He served in various assignments at sea and ashore and in 1917, following U.S. entry into World War I, commanded the transfer of a torpedo flotilla from station in the Philippines to the Mediterranean. Later he was an aide to Adm. William S. Sims, 1917–1919. After the war he served on the *North Dakota* and the *West Virginia* and in 1924–1925 commanded the *Nitro.* During 1925–1928 he was inspector in charge of ordnance at the Naval Proving Ground, Dahlgren, Virginia. From 1928 to 1930 he was on the staff of the commander of destroyer squadrons, Battle Fleet, ultimately becoming chief of staff, and from 1930 to 1933 he was aide to the secretary of the navy. He again commanded the *West Virginia* in 1933–1934 and, promoted to rear admiral in November 1934, was chief of the Bureau of Ordnance from 1934 to 1937. In September 1937 he was given command of Cruiser Division 3, Battle Force, and in July 1938 he moved up to command of all cruiser divisions, Battle Force, with the rank of vice admiral. In August 1939 he became chief of naval operations with the rank of admiral, having been selected by President Franklin D. Roosevelt over more than 50 senior officers. He held that post until March 1942, when, in the reorganization that followed the Pearl Harbor disaster, he was replaced by Adm. Ernest J. King. Stark was given the largely administrative post of commander of U.S. naval forces in Europe, a post he retained until August 1945. He retired in April 1946. He suffered severe criticism for alleged failure to forward key intelligence to Adm. Husband E. Kimmel at Pearl Harbor before the Japanese attack of December 7, 1941, and was censured in a naval investigation in 1945; that judgment was mitigated in later years. Stark died on August 20, 1972, in Washington, D.C.

Stark, John (1728–1822), Revolutionary army officer. Born on August 28, 1728, in Londonderry, New Hampshire, Stark grew up on the New England frontier. In 1755 he was appointed a lieutenant in Maj. Robert Rogers's battalion of rangers. He took part in the battle at Crown Point, September 8, 1755, and in the assaults on Fort Ticonderoga by Gen. James Abercrombie in 1758 and Gen. Jeffrey Amherst in 1759. He left the service a captain in the latter year and took up farming in Derryfield (now Manchester), New Hampshire. As soon as news of the fighting at Lexington and Concord came in April 1775, Stark set out for Boston at the head of nearly 2000 New Hampshire volunteers. He was appointed colonel of a New Hampshire regiment, and at Bunker Hill, June 17, his men, marksmen all, manned the rail fence on the American left; in response to Stark's celebrated order, "Boys, aim at their waistbands," they laid down a galling fire. He participated in the defense of New York City, the retreat of the ill fated expedition of December 1775 from Canada, and in the battles of Trenton and Princeton, December 26, 1776, and January 3, 1777, in New Jersey. Angered by the promotion of junior officers over him, in March 1777 he resigned his commission and returned home, but by July he was back in the fray when Gen. John Burgoyne's British forces invaded New York and threatened Vermont. The General Court of New Hampshire appointed Stark to raise and command a defense force, with the rank of brigadier general. Near Bennington, Vermont, on August 16 he attacked a foraging contingent of 700 Hessian soldiers and Tories under Lt. Col. Friedrich Baum, later reinforced by another 600 men from Burgoyne, and captured most of them in an important victory of the Saratoga campaign. His own brigade numbered some 1500, augmented during the fight by Col. Seth Warner's 350. Stark's supposed rallying cry was long remembered: "My men, yonder are the Hessians. They were bought for seven pounds and ten pence a man. Are you worth more? Prove it! Tonight, the American flag floats from yonder hill, or Molly Stark sleeps a widow!" He was commended for his action by the Continental Congress and in October given the rank of brigadier general in the Continental army. He helped bring about the surrender of Burgoyne in New York, and twice he was put in command of the Northern Department. He also saw service in Rhode Island and at the battle of Springfield, New Jersey, in June 1780 and sat on the court-martial of Maj. John André, Benedict Arnold's British contact. In September 1783 he was brevetted a major general. Following the war Stark retired to his home in New Hampshire and declined several opportunities to hold office. He died in Manchester, New Hampshire, on May 8, 1822, at the age of ninety-three.

Steele, Frederick (1819–1868), army officer. Born in Delhi, New York, on January 14, 1819, Steele graduated from West Point in 1843 and was commissioned in the infantry. He served with the 2nd Infantry through the Mexican War, winning brevets to first lieutenant at Contreras, August 19–20, 1847, and to captain at Churubusco, August 20. He was promoted to first lieutenant in June 1848 and served in California from that year to 1853 and thereafter in Minnesota, Kansas, and Nebraska; he advanced to captain in February 1855. In May 1861 he was appointed major of the new 11th Infantry, and in June he took command of a brigade in Missouri, which he led at Wilson's Creek, August 10, and in other battles in that state. In September he was appointed colonel of the 8th Iowa Infantry; in January 1862 he was promoted to brigadier general of volunteers, and he was put in command of southeastern Missouri the next month. In the spring of 1862 he took command of a division in Gen. Samuel R. Curtis's Army of the Southwest. He saw action at Cache (Cotton Plant), July 7, and took part in the occupation of Helena and in other operations in the Arkansas campaign of that year. He was promoted to major general of volunteers in November. Transferred to the XIII Corps under Gen. John A. McClernand, he led a division at Chickasaw Bluffs, December 29, and in the capture of Arkansas Post, January 11, 1863. He then transferred to Gen. William T. Sherman's XV Corps and led one of its divisions through the capture of Vicksburg in July. He was brevetted colonel of regulars for his services in that campaign. In that month he was given command of Union forces in Arkansas. He successfully cleared the remaining Confederate forces from most of the state, occupying Little Rock on September 10. In March 1864 he was ordered to support Gen. Nathaniel P. Banks in the Red River campaign. The two forces were to rendezvous on the Red River somewhere above Alexandria, Louisiana, and move on Shreveport. He was held up for a full day by Gen. Joseph O. Shelby's relatively tiny force at Prescott, and before the junction was effected Banks was defeated by Gen. Richard Taylor at Sabine Crossroads and Pleasant Hill, April 8–9. On hearing of Banks's defeat Steele began to retire northward back to Little Rock. At Jenkins Ferry on the Saline River (near Leola, Arkansas) on April 30 he was attacked by Gen. Edmund Kirby-Smith and Gen. Sterling Price and repulsed them with heavy losses. Early in 1865 he was ordered to Alabama to take part in Gen. Edward R. S. Canby's campaign against Mobile. In March he was brevetted brigadier and major general of regulars. After a brief period in Texas at the end of the war he commanded the Department of the Columbia from December 1865 to November 1867, being mustered out of volunteer service in March 1867 and reverting to permanent rank of colonel (since July 1866). He was on leave at the time of his death on January 12, 1868, in San Mateo, California.

Stephen, Adam (1730?–1791), Revolutionary militia officer. Born about 1730 in Virginia, Stephen was captain of a militia company in the expedition to Fort Duquesne under Lt. Col. George Washington in 1754. By 1758 he was a lieutenant colonel, and in that year, in Washington's absence, he led an expedition against the Creek Indians. He commanded the defense of the Virginia frontier in 1763. At the outbreak of the Revolution he was a colonel of militia, and in September 1776 he was promoted to brigadier general. He took part in the battle of Trenton, December 26, and in February 1777 was advanced to major general in command of the entire Virginia militia force in the field. He saw action at Brandywine, September 11. At Germantown, October 4, he commanded the militia column advancing along the Schuylkill River, one of four converging columns in Washington's complex battle plan. The battle was at the point of an American victory when Stephen, arriving late in a fog, mistook the brigade under Gen. Anthony Wayne, the vanguard of one of the two columns of regulars, for a British force and opened fire. Wayne's men, already taking some mistaken fire from the second regular column on their left, fell back, throwing other brigades into confusion, and soon the Americans were in general retreat. The battle would have been a blow more serious than Trenton for the British. Stephen was accused of being intoxicated and a short time later was dismissed. He died in November 1791 in Virginia, possibly in the vicinity of Martinsburg (now in West Virginia), where he lived in his last years.

Stephenson, Benjamin Franklin (1823–1871), physician and army officer. Born in Wayne County, Illinois, on October 3, 1823, Stephenson took up the study of medicine under an older brother in Mount Pleasant, Iowa, and later attended Rush Medical College in Chicago, from which he graduated in 1850. He established a practice in Petersburg, Illinois, and during 1855–1857 was a lecturer in the medical department of the State University of Iowa in Keokuk. In June 1861 he was elected surgeon of the recently organized 14th Illinois Volunteer Regiment, with which he served for three years in the western campaigns under Gen. Ulysses S. Grant and Gen. William T. Sherman, advancing to the rank of major. Mus-

tered out in June 1864, he became a partner in a drug firm and resumed medical practice in Springfield, Illinois. During his army service he had conceived the idea of a national organization of veterans of the Union armies, and early in 1866 he drafted a constitution, a set of regulations, and a ritual for a proposed Grand Army of the Republic. The first post of the GAR was activated at Decatur, Illinois, on April 6, 1866, with Stephenson taking the office of commander of the department of Illinois. In July a convention of representatives of the 39 then-active posts met at Springfield and elected another man to that position. In the similarly assumed role of national commander in chief he issued a call for a national convention to meet at Indianapolis on November 20, 1866. Ten states and the District of Columbia were represented at that first "national encampment," and Stephenson was again bitterly disappointed when he was passed over for commander in chief in favor of Stephen A. Hurlbut. He was given the post of adjutant general, but his conduct of that office was such that he was not reelected at the second national encampment at Philadelphia on January 15, 1868. Stephenson moved to Rock Creek, Illinois, in the winter of 1870–1871 and died there on August 30, 1871. The GAR went on to become a powerful organization, with a peak membership in 1890 of over 409,000. Mutual aid, support of soldiers' widows and orphans, and, increasingly, political influence were its major work. After 1900 the GAR declined rapidly in national importance.

Sterett, Andrew (1778–1807), naval officer. Born in Baltimore on January 27, 1778, Sterett was of a prosperous family and entered the navy as a lieutenant in March 1798. He made his first cruise on the *Constellation* under Commodore Thomas Truxtun and took part in the victory over the French frigate *Insurgente,* February 9, 1799; in that battle he was compelled to kill one of his own men for cowardice in the heat of battle. He was again prominent in the victory over the *Vengeance* on February 2, 1800. Later in that year he succeeded the ailing Lt. John Shaw in command of the schooner *Enterprise.* In December he fought an inconclusive two-hour battle with a heavily armed privateer off St. Bartholomew Island, and later in the month he captured the privateer *L'Amour de la Patrie.* In 1801 he sailed the *Enterprise* to the Mediterranean in Commodore Richard Dale's squadron. On August 1 he encountered the *Tripoli,* a Tripolitan polacca of slightly superior armament (14 guns). In a three-hour fight, during which the Tripolitans' renown for boarding tactics was rendered empty by Sterett's skillful seamanship and marksmanship, he riddled the *Tripoli* and forced her to surrender. For that victory he was awarded a sword by Congress and was promoted to master commandant on his return home. He was then given command of a frigate under construction at Baltimore, but in June 1805, possibly in protest of the promotion of Stephen Decatur over him, he resigned from the navy and entered the merchant service. He died in Lima, Peru, on January 9, 1807.

Steuben, Baron von (1730–1794), Revolutionary army officer. Born in Magdeburg, Prussia (now Germany), on September 17, 1730, Friedrich Wilhelm Ludolf Gerhard Augustin von Steuben was the son of a lieutenant of engineers in the army of Frederick William I. About his early years very little is known; at seventeen he entered military service, and he served throughout the Seven Years' War, 1756–1763, emerging with the rank of captain. He was discharged from the Prussian army in 1763, and thereafter he served as chamberlain in the court of Hohenzollern-Hechingen. Sometime between 1764 and 1775 it appears that he was given the title of baron, but no documents survive to confirm this. After trying unsuccessfully from 1775 to 1777 to resume his military career in Europe, he learned of the American war for independence while in Paris. He obtained letters of introduction to Gen. George Washington from the American agents in France, Silas Deane and Benjamin Franklin. For the sake of gaining ready acceptance in America he promoted himself to "lieutenant general in the King of Prussia's service" (although captain had been his highest rank) and set sail for the United States. He arrived in December 1777 and reported to Washington at Valley Forge on February 23, 1778. Impressed with von Steuben's credentials, Washington appointed him acting inspector general of the Continental army and put him in charge of training the Continental troops. As drillmaster, von Steuben proved extremely effective, bringing to the ragged colonial citizen army a discipline and effectiveness it had hitherto lacked. His work brought him appointment from Congress as inspector general with the rank of major general at Washington's urging in May 1778, and he later proved his worth as a staff officer as well by performing valuable service at Monmouth Court House, June 27, 1778. During the following winter he prepared the *Regulations for the Order and Discipline of the Troops of the United States,* a manual of military regulations that remained in use until 1812. Although anxious for a field command and occasionally exasperating to Washington on that topic, he nonetheless worked faithfully in his staff post, continuing his training duties and instituting a system of accounting for supplies. Finally in 1780 he was sent to the Southern theater of war to get the Virginia militia into fighting shape, and he there became Gen. Nathanael Greene's aide. During Greene's absence in the Carolina campaign, von Steuben was in command in Virginia. In 1781 he served under the Marquis de Lafayette during Gen. Charles Cornwallis's

invasion of South Carolina. At Yorktown in October 1781 he successfully commanded a division, and he remained a divisional commander until the war's end. Following the war he continued as a military adviser to Washington, by whom he was publicly commended, until he was finally discharged from the army on March 24, 1784. He had, by act of the Pennsylvania legislature, become an American citizen in March 1783. Von Steuben then took up residence in New York City, where an extravagant social life brought him to the verge of bankruptcy. He had served throughout the Revolution without pay, but in 1790 Congress granted him a lifetime annual pension of $2800. He divided his time between the city and his farm, granted him by the State of New York, near Remsen, New York. He was active in the Society of the Cincinnati; a founder in July 1783, he served as president of the New York branch. He died at his Remsen farm on November 28, 1794.

Stevens, Isaac Ingalls (1818–1862), army officer and public official. Born in Andover, Massachusetts, on March 25, 1818, Stevens graduated from West Point in 1839 and was commissioned in the engineers. He was engaged in coastal fortification work in New England for several years, advancing to first lieutenant in July 1840. In the Mexican War he served as engineer adjutant on the staff of Gen. Winfield Scott and won brevets to captain at Churubusco, August 20, 1847, and to major at Chapultepec, September 13. He was severely wounded in the capture of Mexico City, September 13–14. In 1848–1849 he returned to his former work in New England and in September 1849 was attached to the Coast Survey office in Washington, D.C., as assistant to Superintendent Alexander D. Bache. In 1851 he published *Campaigns of the Rio Grande and of Mexico.* In March 1853 he was appointed first governor of the new Territory of Washington by President Franklin Pierce, and he resigned from the army to accept the post. A short time later he was also appointed to direct the exploration of a northern route for a Pacific railroad, extending from St. Paul, Minnesota, to the mouth of the Columbia River. The field work of the survey was conducted by a number of young officer volunteers, notably Capt. George B. McClellan, and Stevens exerted all his energy and influence in favor of the northern route (several others being surveyed and considered at the same time) and depleted his own modest wealth in financing the completion of the work. During 1854–1855 he made a series of treaties with the Indians of the territory, culminating in the treaty of October 1855 by which the Blackfoot confederations (Blackfeet, Bloods, Piegans) accepted designated hunting grounds north of the Missouri River in what is now Montana. In January 1856 Indian discontent erupted into violence, and for three months Stevens led a force of nearly a thousand volunteers against them. In that campaign he was often in conflict with Gen. John E. Wool, army commander in the area, who refused to give aid. In a dispute between Stevens and the chief judge of the territory over the imprisonment of alleged sympathizers with the Indians, each had the other arrested. In 1857 Stevens resigned as governor and was elected territorial delegate to Congress, where he remained until March 1861. Shortly after the outbreak of the Civil War he was appointed colonel of the 79th New York Volunteers, the "Highlanders," a regiment shattered at Bull Run and successfully rebuilt by Stevens. In September 1861 he was promoted to brigadier general of volunteers. He took part in the expedition under Gen. Thomas W. Sherman against Port Royal in November and in the Peninsula campaign in the spring of 1862. Promoted to major general of volunteers in July 1862, he was transferred to Gen. John Pope's Army of Virginia. He was killed leading a charge against Gen. Thomas J. Jackson's forces at Chantilly, Virginia, on September 1, 1862.

Stevens, Thomas Holdup (1819–1896), naval officer. Born in Middletown, Connecticut, on May 27, 1819, Stevens, son of a noted naval officer, entered the navy as a midshipman in December 1836. After a cruise on the *Independence* of the Brazil Squadron in 1838–1841 he attended the naval school in Philadelphia, receiving promotion to passed midshipman in July 1842, and for a short time afterward he served as aide to President John Tyler. He then performed survey work in the Gulf of Mexico, served on the *Michigan* in Lake Erie in 1843–1844, and from 1845 to 1848 was naval storekeeper in Honolulu. Surviving the wreck of a Chilean ship at Christmas Island while returning to the United States, he was at Sackett's Harbor, New York, in 1849, and, promoted to lieutenant in May of that year, on the *Michigan* again in 1849–1851. During 1852–1855 he commanded the schooner *Ewing*, engaged in survey work on the Pacific Coast, and in 1858–1860 he commanded the *Colorado* of the Home Squadron. At the outbreak of the Civil War he was given the gunboat *Ottawa*, which he commanded in Flag-Officer Samuel F. Du Pont's squadron in the expedition against Port Royal, South Carolina. The *Ottawa* took part with the other gunboats under Commodore John Rodgers in crossing Port Royal bar and driving off the Confederate flotilla under Flag-Officer Josiah Tattnall on November 4, 1861, and in the attack on Fort Walker three days later. Stevens engaged Tattnall again in the Savannah River on January 1, 1862, and in March took part in an expedition up the St. Mary's River that captured Fort Clinch and St. Mary's, Georgia. In March–April he was in the expedition up the St. John's River in Florida that captured Jacksonville and other towns as well as the Confederate yacht *America*. During May–July he was engaged in operations on the Pamunkey and the James rivers in Virginia, in command of the *Maratanza* and then the *Monitor*, receiving promotion to commander in July shortly after his capture of the gunboat *Teazer*. In September he took command of the *Sonoma* in the "Flying Squadron" under Commodore Charles Wilkes operating in the Caribbean. He captured five prizes while pursuing the Confederate raider *Florida*. In August 1863 he took command of the monitor *Patapsco* and took part in Adm. John A. B. Dahlgren's operations at Charleston in August–September. He led the boat attack on Fort Sumter on September 8. In 1864 he transferred to the *Oneida* of the West Gulf Blockading Squadron; in July of that year he temporarily took command of the monitor *Winnebago*, on which he took part in the battle of Mobile Bay, August 5, under Adm. David G. Farragut. He later returned to the *Oneida* off the coast of Texas. Promoted to captain in July 1866, Stevens was a lighthouse inspector from 1867 to 1870 and commanded the *Guerrière* of the European Squadron in 1870–1871. He advanced to commodore in November 1872. He was at Norfolk navy yard from 1873 to 1880, receiving promotion to rear admiral in October 1879, and commanded the Pacific Squadron in 1880–1881. He retired in May 1881 and died in Rockville, Maryland, on May 15, 1896.

Stewart, Alexander Peter (1821–1908), Confederate army officer and educator. Born in Rogersville, Tennessee, on October 2, 1821, Stewart graduated from West Point in 1842 and was commissioned in the artillery. After a year at Fort Macon, North Carolina, he returned to West Point as assistant professor of mathematics in 1843. He resigned from the army in May 1845 and joined the faculty of Cumberland University in Lebanon, Tennessee, as professor of mathematics and natural and experimental philosophy. He remained there until 1849, and in 1854 he resumed the post in the relocated and renamed University of Nashville (an ancestor of the George Peabody College for Teachers). In 1855 he left to become city surveyor of Nashville. In May 1861 he was appointed major of artillery in the provisional army of Tennessee. Mustered into the Confederate army in the same grade, he was promoted to brigadier general the day after taking part in the battle of Belmont, Missouri, on November 7, 1861, and he commanded a brigade in Gen. Benjamin F. Cheatham's division at Pittsburg Landing (Shiloh), April 6–7, Perryville, October 8, and Murfreesboro (Stones River), December 31–January 3, 1863. In June 1863 he was promoted to major general in command of a division under Gen. William J. Hardee, and he served through the Tullahoma campaign, June–August, the battle of Chickamauga, September 18–20, and the siege of Chattanooga, September–November. At Lookout Mountain and Missionary Ridge, November

24–25, his division was part of Gen. John C. Breckinridge's wing of Gen. Braxton Bragg's army. He served under Gen. Joseph E. Johnston in the retreat before Gen. William T. Sherman's advance from Dalton to Atlanta, commanding a division of Gen. John B. Hood's corps; and in June 1864, shortly after the death of Gen. Leonidas Polk, he was promoted to lieutenant general and given command of the latter's corps. He continued with the Army of Tennessee, under Hood and Johnston, through the battle of Nashville, December 15–16, and the Carolinas campaign in February–March 1865. In 1868 he was appointed professor of mathematics at the University of Mississippi, and from 1874 to 1886 he was chancellor of the university. In 1890 he was appointed to the board of commissioners overseeing the Chickamauga and Chattanooga National Military Park, and he spent several years developing the site. He settled in Biloxi, Mississippi, in 1906 and died there on August 30, 1908.

Stewart, Charles (1778–1869), naval officer. Born in Philadelphia on July 28, 1778, Stewart entered the merchant service at thirteen and rose quickly from cabin boy to master. In March 1798 he was commissioned a lieutenant in the navy, and after a cruise in the West Indies on the *United States* under Commodore John Barry he took command of the schooner *Experiment* in July 1800. In September he captured the privateer *Deux Amis* near Guadeloupe and in October the *Diana;* during that period he also recaptured a number of American merchant vessels. In December he rescued some 60 women and children who had been shipwrecked while fleeing a rebellion in Santo Domingo. In 1802 he sailed as first lieutenant on the *Constellation* in the squadron under Commodore Richard V. Morris sent to reinforce the blockade of Tripoli. He returned home in 1803 and sailed again to Tripoli in command of the brig *Siren* under Commodore Edward Preble. The *Siren* provided cover for Lt. Stephen Decatur and the *Intrepid* in the burning of the *Philadelphia* on February 16, 1804. During the blockade Stewart captured a British and a Greek vessel attempting to run through. In September 1805 he commanded the *Essex* in Commodore John Rodgers's demonstration at Tunis. Promoted to captain in April 1806, he was at the New York navy yard supervising the construction of coastal gunboats in 1806–1807, and from 1808 to 1812 he took leave of absence and returned to the merchant service. At the outbreak of the War of 1812 he returned to active duty. In June he was put in command of the brig *Argus* and the sloop *Hornet,* but their planned expedition to the West Indies was canceled, and in December he took command of the *Constellation,* blockaded in Norfolk, Virginia. In the summer of 1813 he transferred to the *Constitution* at Boston and in December sailed out of the harbor.

Before his return in April 1814 he destroyed a number of British vessels. In December 1814 he again escaped the blockade of Boston and sailed for Bermuda, where he captured a merchantman, and then across the Atlantic to Madeira. On February 20, 1815, he engaged and captured the frigate *Cyane,* 34 guns, and the sloop *Levant,* 20, in a sharp fight of four hours. He maneuvered the *Constitution* so skillfully that he was able to gain a raking position on both ships. On the return voyage the *Levant* was retaken by a British squadron, but Stewart arrived in Boston with the *Cyane* and was given a hero's welcome, including a gold medal and the thanks of Congress. From 1816 to 1820 he commanded the European Squadron aboard the *Franklin,* and from 1820 to 1824 he commanded the Pacific Squadron on the same ship. In 1829 he was president of the Examining Board and in 1830–1832 a member of the Board of Naval Commissioners. Stewart commanded the Philadelphia navy yard in 1838–1841, the Home Squadron in 1842–1843, and the Philadelphia navy yard again in 1846 and 1854–1861. In March 1859 he was promoted by Congress to the special rank of senior flag-officer, and in July 1862 he was made rear admiral on the retired list. Stewart died in Bordentown, New Jersey, on November 6, 1869. His grandson was Charles Stewart Parnell, Irish nationalist leader.

Stilwell, Joseph Warren (1883–1946), army officer. Born on March 19, 1883, in Palatka, Florida, Stilwell grew up in Yonkers, New York. He graduated from West Point in 1904 and was commissioned in the infantry. From 1904 to 1906 he was in the Philippines, where he saw some action against Moro rebels, and from 1906 to 1910 he was an instructor at West Point. He was again in the Philippines in 1911–1912, receiving promotion to first lieutenant in March 1911, and after a year at the Presidio in Monterey, California, he returned to West Point, 1913–1917, advancing to captain in July 1916. Promoted to temporary major in August 1917, he was ordered to France in December. He served briefly with the British and French forces and in June 1918 became assistant chief of staff for intelligence in Gen. Joseph T. Dickman's IV Corps. By the end of the war he held temporary rank as colonel. After a year studying Chinese at the University of California and promotion to major in July 1920 he was sent to Peking, where he continued his studies while serving as an intelligence officer. His work with the International Red Cross relief agency and in various engineering projects brought him into close contact with Chinese life. Stilwell returned to the United States in 1923, graduated from the Infantry School, Fort Benning, Georgia, in 1924 and from the Command and General Staff School, Fort Leavenworth, Kansas, in 1926 and then joined the 15th Infantry at Tientsin, China. In February 1928 he was named chief of staff of U.S. forces in China. Promoted to lieutenant colonel, he was on the staff of the Infantry School in 1929–1933, where he made a strongly favorable impression on Gen. George C. Marshall, and from 1933 to 1935 he was assigned to reserve training duty in San Diego, California. He was promoted to colonel in August 1935 and from then until 1939 was military attaché in China and Siam (Thailand). He returned to the United States in May 1939 and was promoted to brigadier general and put in command of the 3rd Infantry Brigade at Fort Sam Houston, Texas. In July 1940 he activated the 7th Infantry Division at Fort Ord, California. He was promoted to temporary major general in October, and in July 1941 he took command of the III Corps at Monterey, California. In February 1942 he was promoted to temporary lieutenant general and in March named commander of U.S. army forces (then consisting only of air units) in the China-Burma-India theater and chief of staff to Generalissimo Chiang Kai-shek, leader of the Kuomintang (Nationalist) forces in China, with headquarters at Chungking, China. His assignment was to train Chinese forces to resist Japanese expansion, to build and hold bases in China for the American effort against Japan, and to coordinate American, British, and Chinese strategy and operations in the theater. Chiang also gave him command of the Chinese V and VI army corps. Following the final conquest of Burma by Japan in May Stilwell personally led the remnants of his force in a torturous 140-mile trek through jungle to the Indian border. While he began rebuilding the Chinese army in India, air units under his command, principally the Tenth Air Force under Gen. Lewis H. Brereton and later Gen. Clayton L. Bissel and the Fourteenth Air Force under Gen. Claire L. Chennault mounted an airlift of supplies "over the hump" of the Himalayas to isolated China; when an Air Transport Command was organized for that function, the Tenth and Fourteenth flew escort, support, and some strategic missions. Late in 1942 work was begun on the Ledo Road supply line that eventually joined the old Burma Road and ended the burden of air transport. This epic of endurance, combat, and engineering progressed with painful slowness through northern Burma, led by the spectacular exploits of Gen. Frank D. Merrill's "Marauders" and culminating in the capture of the key point of Myitkyina in August 1944. From mid-1943 Stilwell also held the post of deputy supreme Allied commander in the China-Burma-India theater under Adm. Lord Louis Mountbatten. His relations with Chiang were never better than formal. Stilwell, entirely forthright, had long since earned the nickname "Vinegar Joe" for his caustic comments on incompetents, and Chiang's stubborn resistance to reform in the corruption-ridden Kuomintang command gave him ample ground for explicit characterization. The efficiency of the Nationalist forces was further hampered by Chiang's attempt to make war on the Chinese Communists as well as the Japanese. In August 1944 Stilwell was promoted to temporary general, and President Franklin D. Roosevelt strongly urged that he be given full command of Chinese armed forces. The conflict with Chiang quickly came to a head, and in October Stilwell was recalled; the China-Burma-India theater was then divided into the India-Burma, under Gen. Daniel I. Sultan, and the China, first under Gen. Chennault and subsequently Gen. Albert C. Wedemeyer. From January to May 1945 Stilwell was in Washington, D.C., as chief of Army Ground Forces, and in June he succeeded Gen. Simon B. Buckner, Jr., in command of the Tenth Army on Okinawa. During July–September he was acting military governor of the Ryukyu Islands. He remained with the Tenth until its deactivation in October, and from December 1945 to March 1946 he was commander of the Western Defense Command. He commanded the Sixth Army at the Presidio, San Francisco, from March 1946 until his death there on October 12, 1946.

Stimson, Julia Catherine (1881–1948), nurse. Born on May 26, 1881, in Worcester, Massachusetts, Miss Stimson was a cousin of Henry L. Stimson, later secretary of war and of state. She grew up in Worcester and later in St. Louis and New York City. She graduated from Vassar College in 1901. After three years of further study at Columbia University she entered the New York Hospital Nurses Training School in 1904 and graduated in 1908. She was superintendent of nursing at Harlem Hospital in 1908–1911 and then joined the hospital staff at Washington University in St. Louis, where she served as administrator of hospital social service in 1911–1912. From 1913 to 1917 she was superintendent of nurses training at Barnes Hospital and at St. Louis Children's Hospital. In 1917 she received a master's degree from Washington University. In May 1917 she sailed for France as chief nurse of American Red Cross Hospital Unit No. 21, which became Base Hospital 21, attached to British forces at Rouen. In April 1918 she was named chief nurse of the American Red Cross in France, and in November she became director of nursing for the American Expeditionary Forces with responsibility for some 10,000 nurses serving in Europe. Her experiences in the war were recorded in *Finding Themselves*, 1918. In July 1919 she was appointed acting superintendent of the Army Nurse Corps and dean of the Army School of Nursing (the latter post she held until the closing of the school in 1933.) Her superintendency was made permanent in December, and pursuant to the National Defense Act of June 1920 she was given the (relative) rank of major, the first nurse to hold that rank. She held that post until retiring in May 1937. She was president of the American Nurses Association from 1938 to 1944 and chairman of the Nursing Council on National Defense in 1940–1942. She was recalled briefly to active duty for recruiting work in 1942–1943. Promoted to colonel on the retired list in August 1948, she died in Poughkeepsie, New York, on September 30, 1948.

Stirling, Lord *see* Alexander, William

Stockton, Robert Field (1795–1866), naval officer. Born on August 20, 1795, in Princeton, New Jersey, Stockton attended the College of New Jersey (now Princeton) for a time before joining the navy as a midshipman in October 1811. During the War of 1812 he served on the *President* under Commodore John Rodgers in the North Atlantic and in the defenses of Baltimore and Washington, receiving promotion to lieutenant in September 1814. Aboard the *Guerrière* and later the *Spitfire* in Commodore Stephen Decatur's squadron in 1815 he participated in the Algerine War against the Barbary pirates. From 1816 to 1821 he was with the Mediterranean Squadron, on the *Washington* and then the *Erie*, eventually becoming captain of the latter. In 1821 he conveyed officials of the American Colonization Society to Africa on the *Alligator* and helped negotiate the cession of Liberia. (He was also a founder and first president of the New Jersey Colonization Society.) From 1822 to 1824 he was engaged in pirate patrol in the West Indies and in survey work. He remained on duty with the navy until 1828, then was on inactive status until 1838. In this decade he settled at the family home in Princeton and followed civilian occupations. He invested a good deal of money in the construction of the Delaware and Raritan Canal and served as the canal company's president. He invested as well in the Camden & Amboy Railroad operated by the Stevens family of Hoboken, New Jersey. In December 1838 Stockton left the life of a country gentleman to return to active naval duty with the rank of captain. He sailed to the Mediterranean in command of Commodore Isaac Hull's flagship *Ohio* and, while on furlough in England, became involved with John Ericsson in the design of a steam vessel. On behalf of the navy he commissioned the building of the *Princeton*, the navy's first screw-propeller-driven ship. He stayed on sea duty for most of the next seven years, except for time off in 1840 to campaign for William Henry Harrison; he rejected an offer from President John Tyler in 1841 to become secretary of the navy. He helped supervise the construction of the *Princeton* and commanded it on a demonstration cruise on the Potomac on February 28, 1844, with the President and other official guests aboard. When he attempted to fire the "Peacemaker," a 12-inch gun of his own devising, it burst, killing Secretary of the Navy Thomas W. Gilmer, Secre-

tary of State Abel P. Upshur, and others. In 1845, when the U.S. annexation of Texas made war with Mexico seem inevitable, Stockton was sent to Texas with the resolution of annexation. In October he sailed for California aboard the *Congress* to take command of the Pacific Squadron. He arrived at Monterey on July 15, 1846, about a week after Commodore John D. Sloat's operations against the Mexican authorities had begun in California. He relieved Sloat on July 23 and by proclamation assumed command of both land and sea forces, including the men of the Bear Flag revolt and Capt. John C. Frémont's California Battalion, determined to bring all of California under U.S. sovereignty. He occupied Santa Barbara on August 4 and San Pedro on August 6, and with Frémont he entered Los Angeles on August 13. On August 17 Stockton declared California a territory of the United States and set up a civil government, naming himself as temporary governor. He hoped to achieve the complete pacification of California before he set off for the war zone in Mexico. During his absence in the north, Californian (Mexican) forces retook most of the southern towns in September–October. Stockton dispatched troops to oppose them and, in December, to reinforce Gen. Stephen W. Kearny's Army of the West, which had arrived from New Mexico. Early in January 1847 Stockton and Kearny joined forces in San Diego and quickly retook Los Angeles on January 10. Shortly thereafter a heated dispute broke out between Stockton and Kearny as to supreme authority in California, their respective orders being vague and contradictory. Stockton appointed Frémont governor in mid-January, and he carried on the quarrel with Kearny. Kearny was finally upheld by Washington. Stockton turned over command of the Pacific Squadron to Commodore William B. Shubrick and returned overland to the East in the fall of 1847 and spent three more years in the navy before resigning in May 1850. Stockton served a brief term in the U.S. Senate as a Democrat from New Jersey, from March 1851 to January 1853, during which he urged the improvement of harbor defenses and the abolition of flogging in the navy. He then returned to New Jersey and spent the last 13 years of his life as president of the Delaware and Raritan Canal Company. In 1850 the name of the town of Tuleburg, California, was changed to Stockton. He died in Princeton, New Jersey, on October 7, 1866.

Stoddard, Amos (1762–1813), army officer. Born in Woodbury, Connecticut, on October 26, 1762, Stoddard grew up in Lanesborough, Massachusetts. In June 1779 he enlisted in the Continental army, and he served until the end of the Revolution in the infantry and later the artillery. In 1784 he was appointed assistant clerk of the Massachusetts supreme court, and at the same time he began the study of law in a Boston office. He took part in the suppression of Shays's Rebellion in 1787. In 1791 he traveled to England on family business, and he may have been the author of *The Political Crisis: or, A Dissertation on the Rights of Man*, published in London while he was there. Back in Massachusetts he was admitted to the bar in 1793, and until 1798 he practised in Hallowell (now in Maine), serving also in the legislature in 1797. In 1796 he joined the Massachusetts militia, and in June 1798 he took a commission as captain of engineers and artillery in the army. He was serving in the West at the time of the purchase of Louisiana, and he was designated agent and commissioner by France and the United States to enact the transfer at St. Louis. On March 9, 1804, nearly three months after the transfer of Lower Louisiana, he formally received Upper Louisiana from the Spanish governor on behalf of France and raised the French flag; and on March 10 he received the territory in the name of the United States from France, raising the American flag and assuming civil and military authority for the territory. He continued as commandant until September 30, 1804, and the civil government of the District of Louisiana took power the next day. His administration of the territory for seven months was unanimously approved. He continued on duty in Lower Louisiana and spent much of his time in gathering records and information and preserving archives; he was promoted to major in June 1807. In July 1812 he was made deputy quartermaster. His *Sketches, Historical and Descriptive, of Louisiana* was published that year. Early in the War of 1812 he helped build and organize Fort Meigs on the Maumee River in Ohio, and during the siege of the fort by Gen. Procter's British and Tecumseh's Indians he was wounded and died on May 11, 1813.

Stoddert, Benjamin (1751–1813), public official. Born in Charles County, Maryland, in 1751, Stoddert in his youth was apprenticed to a merchant. In January 1777 he joined a Pennsylvania militia regiment with the rank of captain and served in the Revolution until April 1779, when he resigned over a question of seniority. In September of that year he was appointed secretary to the Board of War of the Continental Congress, a post he filled capably until February 1781. He then settled in Georgetown, Maryland, and bought a partnership in a small mercantile firm. As he had foreseen, Georgetown soon flourished as a Potomac port, and as his fortune grew he made extensive investments in real estate in the region around the city. When the area was chosen as the site for the proposed federal city, Stoddert was asked confidentially by George Washington and others to act as agent in purchasing large tracts of land; his circumspect fulfillment of the commission prevented a frenzy of land speculation in what was to become the District of Columbia. In 1794 he

helped found and later served as president of the Bank of Columbia. Under pressure of French depredations on American commerce, the Department of the Navy was created by Congress on April 30, 1798, (naval affairs had until then been administered by the War Department) and on May 18 President John Adams appointed Stoddert the first secretary of the navy. Stoddert brought all his considerable energy to the post and added some fifty vessels to the navy over the next two years. By early 1799 a considerable naval presence was established in the privateer-infested West Indies, under such commanders as John Barry and Thomas Truxton. In July 1798 he drafted the bill that provided for the organization of the marine corps. He pushed for the construction of dock and naval yard facilities, acquiring properties for that purpose in Washington, D.C.; Norfolk, Virginia; Portsmouth, New Hampshire; Philadelphia; Brooklyn, New York, and other places. He also promoted the construction of a naval hospital at Newport. He retired to private life in April 1801. His later years were marked by serious financial difficulties as the Georgetown trade declined precipitously, and he was deeply in debt at his death in Bladensburg, Maryland, on December 18, 1813.

Stone, Charles Pomeroy (1824–1887), army officer. Born in Greenfield, Massachusetts, on September 30, 1824, Stone graduated from West Point in 1845 and was commissioned in the Ordnance Corps. He served in Gen. Winfield Scott's army throughout the Mexican War and won brevets to first lieutenant at Molino del Rey, September 8, 1847, and captain at Chapultepec, September 13. After the war he was stationed at the federal arsenal at Watervliet, New York, until 1848. After nearly two years leave of absence, during which he studied ordnance practices in Europe, he resumed his post at Watervliet in 1850; he later transferred to Fort Monroe, Virginia, and in 1851 conducted an ordnance detachment to California and became chief ordnance officer at Benicia. He resigned from the army in November 1856, and during 1857–1860 he was chief of a private commission surveying the state of Sonora in Mexico. In 1861 he published *Notes on the State of Sonora*. In January 1861 he was appointed colonel and inspector general of the District of Columbia militia, becoming colonel of the District volunteers in April and colonel of the 14th Infantry of regulars in July. In August he was promoted to brigadier general of volunteers. He took part in several minor skirmishes in northern Virginia during the summer. On October 20 he was ordered by Gen. George B. McClellan to make a demonstration at the Potomac River opposite Ball's Bluff. Col. Edward D. Baker, commanding one of Stone's brigades, impetuously crossed the river and on October 21 was surprised by a superior Confederate force. Baker, a popular officer and former Senator, was killed, and a public uproar quickly developed. The sharp and needless defeat at Ball's Bluff and Baker's death, compounded with a general anxiety about the Union's failure to make headway so far in the war, soon gave rise to a search for a scapegoat, and Stone was the obvious choice. On February 8, 1862, he was arrested and held in solitary confinement in Fort Lafayette in New York harbor. Congressional investigation of the Ball's Bluff affair became a witch-hunt into Stone's possible disloyalty, an investigation in which incredibly far-fetched and unfounded charges and suggestions were countenanced. Nonetheless, no formal charges were ever brought, and once the hysteria had spent itself Stone was ordered released on August 16. He was without orders until May 1863, when he joined the command of Gen. Nathaniel P. Banks, with whom he served at Port Hudson and, as chief of staff from July 1863, on the Red River. In April 1864, for reasons unknown, he was mustered out of volunteer service and left again without orders. He resigned his regular commission in September. From 1865 to 1869 he was superintendent and engineer of a mining company in Goochland County, Virginia. In 1870 he accepted a commission in the army of Khedive Ismail I of Egypt, in which he eventually became chief of staff with the rank of lieutenant general. He served in that army longer than any of the other Civil War veterans who had come to Egypt, resigning finally in March 1883. After his return to the United States he worked for a year as engineer with the Florida Ship Canal Company. In April 1886 he was appointed chief engineer of the construction of the pedestal for the Statue of Liberty. Stone died in New York City on January 24, 1887.

Stoneman, George (1822–1894), army officer.

Born on August 8, 1822, in Busti, New York, Stoneman graduated from West Point in 1846 and was commissioned in the 1st Dragoons. He served as quartermaster of the "Mormon Battalion" under Col. Philip St. G. Cooke in Gen. Stephen W. Kearny's Army of the West in 1846–1847 and remained on the Pacific coast for eight years after the Mexican War. Promoted to captain in March 1855, he served with the 2nd Cavalry, mainly in Texas, until 1861. In February 1861, then in command of Fort Brown, he refused to surrender the fort to his superior, Gen. David E. Twiggs, who had joined the secessionists. He later made his way east with most of his command. In May he was promoted to major in the 1st Cavalry, and he took part in the occupation of Alexandria, Virginia, and in Gen. George B. McClellan's operations in West Virginia. In August he was appointed brigadier general of volunteers, and McClellan made him chief of cavalry of the Army of the Potomac. The cavalry then being split up among corps and divisions and even brigades, Stoneman's

job was largely a staff and advisory one. He served through the Peninsula campaign and in September 1862 took command of the slain Gen. Philip Kearny's division. Early in November he succeeded Gen. Samuel P. Heintzelman in command of the III Corps, receiving promotion to major general of volunteers a few days later, and he commanded it at Fredericksburg, December 13, where he was brevetted colonel of regulars. Soon after Gen. Joseph Hooker took over the army of the Potomac in January 1863, he reorganized the cavalry into a unified corps of three divisions, constituting a full combat arm of the army, and put Stoneman in command. Late in April, as a preliminary to Hooker's Chancellorsville campaign, Stoneman set out on a rapid cavalry raid into Virginia, his task being to divert the Confederate cavalry and disrupt Gen. Robert E. Lee's communications with Richmond. Crossing the Rapidan on May 1 with three brigades—about 4300 men—Stoneman divided his force into detachments that in six days succeeded in capturing a quantity of stores, destroying more, cutting railroads in several places, and reaching as far south as the South Anna River; the main objectives were not met, however. In July Stoneman relinquished command of the corps to Gen. Alfred Pleasonton and became chief of the Cavalry Bureau in Washington, D.C. In January 1864 he took command of the XXIII Corps of the Army of the Ohio, and in April he took command of that army's cavalry corps. During the Atlanta campaign Gen. William T. Sherman ordered him to conduct a raid around Atlanta on the east in conjunction with an advance on the west by Gen. Edward M. McCook; the two forces were to meet at Lovejoy's Station, a major railroad depot south of Jonesboro. Stoneman secured permission to go on from there to attempt to release federal prisoners being held in Macon and Andersonville. He failed to meet McCook, and on July 31 at Clinton, north of Macon, he encountered a strong Confederate force. Holding them with less than a brigade while the rest of his men made their escape, he was then taken prisoner. After he was exchanged in October he was sent by Gen. George H. Thomas in December on another raid into Virginia from eastern Tennessee to drive Gen. John C. Breckinridge out of the mountain passes and accomplish what destruction he could. Between December 11 and 22 he took some 900 prisoners, captured 3000 horses and mules along with other supplies, destroyed the important salt works at Saltville, destroyed the towns of Bristol, Abingdon, and Wytheville along with much railroad trackage and stock, and fought Breckinridge at Marion, December 18. Between March 22 and April 15, 1865, he conducted his final raid, during which the Virginia Central Railroad was destroyed from Wytheville almost to Lynchburg, cutting off a possible escape route for the Army of Northern Virginia, and great quantities of stores and public property were captured or destroyed in western North Carolina, particularly at Salem, Salisbury, and Asheville. In March 1865 Stoneman was brevetted brigadier and major general of regulars. After the war he commanded at Richmond and Petersburg for four years. He was mustered out of volunteer service in July 1866 and appointed colonel of the 21st Infantry. He was with the regiment and was also commander of the Department of Arizona until his retirement for disability in August 1871. He settled near Los Angeles. In 1879 he was appointed railroad commissioner of California. He won a large following for his opposition to the growing political power of the railroads, and in 1883, on resigning his commission, he was elected Democratic governor of California; he served until 1887. In 1891 he was restored to the army retirement list. Stoneman died in Buffalo, New York, on September 5, 1894.

Stratton, Dorothy Constance (1899–), educator, naval officer, and public official. Born on March 24, 1899, in Brookfield, Missouri, Miss Stratton grew up in various towns in Kansas and Missouri. She graduated from Ottawa University in 1920, and while teaching and holding administrative posts in public schools in Renton, Washington, and from 1923 in San Bernardino, California, she took a master's degree from the University of Chicago in 1924 and a doctorate from Columbia University in 1932. In 1933 she was appointed dean of women and associate professor of psychology at Purdue University; she advanced to full professor in 1940. In June 1942 she served on the Women's Army Auxiliary Corps selection board for the V Corps area, and later in the year she enlisted in the Women Accepted for Volunteer Emergency Service (WAVES) of the navy and was given a lieutenant's commission. In November 1942 she was ordered to duty in the office of the commandant of the Coast Guard, where she developed plans and guidelines for a proposed women's reserve corps. By the end of the month she had devised a name for the corps, SPARS, derived from the Coast Guard motto Semper Paratus (Always Ready), and, with the rank of lieutenant commander, had been appointed director of the corps, which was authorized by Congress on November 23. She continued in that post, rising to the rank of captain, until 1946, and the SPARS grew during that period to some 10,000 officers and enlisted. From 1947 to 1950 she was director of personnel for the International Monetary Fund in Washington, D.C., and from 1950 to 1960 national executive director of the Girl Scouts of America. From 1962 she was a member of the President's Commission on the Employment of the Handicapped and a consultant on vocational rehabilitation to the Department of Health, Education and Welfare.

Streeter, Ruth Cheney (1895–), marine officer. Born on October 2, 1895, in Brookline, Massachusetts, Ruth Cheney attended Bryn Mawr College in 1914–1916 and in 1917 married Thomas W. Streeter. They settled in Morristown, New Jersey, where she became involved in a broad range of civic activities. She had also a long standing interest in aviation and the armed forces; in memory of her brother, a World War I pilot, she and her mother sponsored an annual Cheney Award for an outstanding member of the Army Air Corps, and in 1940 Mrs. Streeter began taking flying lessons herself. She earned a commercial license in 1942. She was active in the Civil Air Patrol and various national defense committees. On February 13, 1943, a Women's Reserve of the marine corps was formally established, and Ruth Streeter was named director with the rank of major. The women's reserve corps successfully resisted being nicknamed, an improvement over the World War I term *marinettes*; the corps was generally abbreviated WR. As with other women's reserve corps, the WR marines and officers were used in clerical and office work, communications, aviation support, cryptography, machine assembly and repair, and scores of other jobs that released thousands of male marines for duty overseas and combat. Trained at first in WAVES (navy) or SPARS (coast guard) camps and later in specifically marine camps, the WR reached a peak strength of 1000 officers and 18,000 enlisted by June 1944. Streeter was promoted to lieutenant colonel in November 1943 and in 1945 to colonel, and she retired in December 1945. After the war she returned to Morristown, where she continued active in civic affairs. During 1948–1952 she was national president of the Society of Colonial Dames, and in 1968–1970 she was a member of the New Jersey Historical Sites Council.

Stribling, Cornelius Kinchiloe (1796–1880), naval officer. Born on September 22, 1796, in Pendleton, South Carolina, Stribling entered the navy as a midshipman in June 1812. In 1815 he was aboard the frigate *Mohawk* on Lake Ontario, where he took part in the blockade of Kingston, Ontario. He then served two years in the Mediterranean Squadron, receiving promotion to lieutenant in April 1818. He was with the Brazil Squadron in 1819–1820 and subsequently took part in the operations of the West India Squadron in suppressing piracy. During 1833–1835 he was assistant inspector of ordnance, and in 1835–1837 he commanded the sloop *Peacock* in the East India Squadron. Two years' leave of absence was followed by promotion to commander in January 1840. He had command of the *Cyane* and the *United States* in the Pacific between 1842 and 1844; aboard the former he took part in the occupation by Commodore Thomas ap Catesby Jones of Monterey, California, in October 1842. After two years at the Norfolk navy yard, Virginia, he took command of the *Ohio* and was fleet captain of the Pacific Squadron in 1847–1850. From 1850 to 1853 Stribling was superintendent of the Naval Academy, advancing to captain in August 1853. He commanded the steam sloop *San Jacinto* in 1854–1855, served on the retiring board in 1855–1857, commanded the Pensacola, Florida, navy yard in 1857–1859, and was flag-officer of the East India Squadron in 1859–1861. He remained in the navy at the outbreak of the Civil War and was retained on active service beyond his normal retirement date in December 1861; he served for a time on a board of compensation and was on the Lighthouse Board in 1862. Promoted to commodore in July 1862, he commanded the Philadelphia navy yard until 1864, and during February–July 1865 he commanded the East Gulf Blockading Squadron. He was again on the Lighthouse Board until 1872, and he received promotion on the retired list to rear admiral in July 1866. Stribling died in Martinsburg, West Virginia, on January 17, 1880.

Stringfellow, Benjamin Franklin (1840–1913), Confederate scout. Born in Culpeper County, Virginia, on June 18, 1840, Stringfellow, known throughout life as Frank, attended schools in Albemarle County and in Alexandria and then became a schoolteacher in Shuqualak, Mississippi. Early in 1861 he returned to Virginia to offer his services for the Civil War, but his doubtful health and diminutive size made it difficult for him to find a post. In May he finally succeeded in enlisting as a private in the 4th Virginia Cavalry. He distinguished himself carrying dispatches at Manassas (Bull Run) in July and in consequence was appointed to the staff of Gen. J. E. B. Stuart. In 1863, following Gettysburg, Stringfellow was attached to the staff of Gen. Robert E. Lee as a scout and secret agent. During the remaining 20 months of war he rendered highly valuable service and performed numerous daring exploits, often going into Union lines, infiltrating headquarters in sundry disguises, and ferreting out vital information for Lee. Stringfellow's work lay behind Lee's near defeat of Gen. Ulysses S. Grant in the Wilderness campaign of May 1864. Imprisoned at the end of the war, he escaped from Old Capitol Prison just before the assassination of President Abraham Lincoln; the unfortunate coincidence of his stopping in his flight at the home of Mrs. Mary Surratt, later convicted of complicity in the assassination plot, led to his remaining in exile in Canada for several years. After his return to Virginia he settled in Fairfax County. He graduated from the Episcopal Seminary in Alexandria in 1876 and served thereafter in various parishes in the state. In later years he was also a popular lecturer on the many perilous adventures of his scouting days. Stringfellow was pastor in Mechanicsville, Virginia, at his death on June 8, 1913.

Stringham, Silas Horton (1797–1876), naval officer. Born in Middletown, New York, on November 7, 1797, Stringham entered the navy as a midshipman in November 1809. During his first cruise, on the *President* under Capt. John Rodgers, he took part in the fight with the *Little Belt* in May 1811. He remained on the *President* through the War of 1812, becoming a lieutenant in December 1814, and during the Algerine War of 1815 he was aboard the brig *Spark* in Commodore Isaac Chauncey's squadron. He distinguished himself in 1816 in the rescue of the crew of a French brig that foundered in a storm at Gibraltar. In 1818–1820 he was aboard the *Cyane*, which remained on antislavery patrol on the African coast after convoying the first boatload of Liberian colonists. While sailing two captured slavers back to the United States, he captured two others. In 1822–1824 he was on the *Hornet* in Commodore James Biddle's West India Squadron engaged in piracy suppression. From 1825 to 1830 he was at the New York navy yard. He was promoted to commander in March 1831. After various duties ashore and with the Mediterranean Squadron he was put in command of the New York navy yard in 1837. Promoted to captain in September 1841, he commanded the *Independence* of the Home Squadron in 1842 and the New York navy yard again in 1844–1846. In 1847 he commanded the *Ohio* under Commodore David Conner and Commodore Matthew C. Perry during the bombardment and capture of Veracruz, Mexico. Stringham commanded the Brazil Squadron in 1847–1848, the Norfolk navy yard in 1848–1852, the Mediterranean Squadron in 1853–1855, and the Boston navy yard in 1856–1860. In March 1861 he was called to Washington, D.C., to advise Secretary of the Navy Gideon Welles on the situation at Fort Sumter; he urged and began planning a strong relief expedition that never took place. In May he was put in command of the Atlantic Blockading Squadron. In August he commanded an expedition against Hatteras Inlet, North Carolina, the principal gateway to the privateer-infested Pamlico Sound. With the flagship *Minnesota* and five other large vessels, along with several transports bearing 860 soldiers under Gen. Benjamin F. Butler, he reached Hatteras Inlet on August 27 and the next morning began a heavy bombardment of the defending Fort Hatteras and Fort Clark. Stringham's heavy guns enabled him to stay out of range of the shore batteries, and the forts surrendered on August 29 without assault by the army troops and without a single Union casualty. Although this was the first major naval victory of the war, Stringham was unjustly criticized in some quarters for not advancing into Pamlico Sound (his orders did not call for it and the draft of his ships made it impossible), and in September 1861 he requested relief from duty. He retired in December, and in July 1862 he was promoted to rear admiral on the retired list. He returned to duty to¹ command the Boston navy yard in 1864–1865. He was port admiral in New York City in 1871–1872, and he died in Brooklyn, New York, on February 7, 1876.

Strong, James Hooker (1814–1882), naval officer. Born in Canandaigua, New York, on April 26, 1814, Strong entered the navy as a midshipman in February 1829. He made his first cruise in 1831 on the *Lexington* of the Brazil Squadron, and in 1832 he commanded a boat expedition that went ashore in the Falkland Islands to put an end to the seizing of American whaling vessels there. He served on the *Enterprise* in 1834, in New York in 1835, on the *Constellation* in 1836–1839, and on the *Independence,* again in the Brazil Squadron, from 1839 to 1844 and was promoted to lieutenant in September 1841. In 1844–1846 he served on the *Columbus* of the East India Squadron, and for the next 15 years he alternated service at the New York navy yard and in the Mediterranean Squadron. Promoted to commander in April 1861, he commanded the *Mohawk* in the Gulf Blockading Squadron until 1862, when he transferred to command of the steamer *Flag* of the South Atlantic Blockading Squadron. In 1863 he transferred again to the steamer *Monongahela* of the West Gulf Blockading Squadron. In October of that year, commanding also the *Owasco* and the *Virginia,* he conveyed Gen. Nathaniel P. Banks and 9000 troops to the mouth of the Rio Grande, from which they marched to capture Brownsville, Corpus Christi, and other points on the coast. On November 2 he supported a portion of that force, under Gen. Napoleon J. T. Dana, in the capture of Brazos Island, and on November 17 he landed more troops and provided naval artillery support at Mustang Island, Corpus Christi. At the battle of Mobile Bay under Adm. David G. Farragut on August 5, 1864, Strong distinguished himself in maneuvering the *Monongahela* out of line to attack the monitor *Tennessee,* which he rammed twice and effectively kept from the weaker vessels of the Union squadron. Promoted to captain in August 1865, Strong was inspector at the New York navy yard in 1866–1867, commanded the steamer *Canandaigua* in the Mediterranean Squadron in 1868–1869, and, with the rank of commodore from March 1870, was lighthouse inspector in 1871–1873. He was promoted to rear admiral in September 1873, and he commanded the South Atlantic Squadron until 1875. He retired in April 1876 and died in Columbia, South Carolina, on November 28, 1882.

Struble, Arthur Dewey (1894–   ), naval officer. Born in Portland, Oregon, on June 28, 1894, Struble graduated from the Naval Academy in 1915. For the next 25 years he served on a number of battleships, cruisers, and destroyers; was an instructor at the Academy in 1921–1923; and held staff assignments with the commander of Battleship Divisions, Battle Fleet, and of Battle Fleet in 1925–1927, with the Office of Navy Communications in 1927–1930, at the 12th Naval District headquarters in San Diego, California, in 1933–1935, and in the office of the chief of naval operations in 1939–1940. In January 1941, by that time a captain, he took command of the *Trenton,* and he was cruising in the Southeast Pacific at the time of the Pearl Harbor attack. In May 1942 he was once again attached to the office of the chief of naval operations as director of the central division, receiving promotion to rear admiral in October 1942. In November 1943 he returned to sea as chief of staff of Task Force 122, Twelfth Fleet, which in June 1944 provided naval cover for the Normandy landings. In August 1944 he was transferred to the Pacific to command Amphibious Group 2 (later redesignated 9) in Adm. Daniel E. Barbey's VII Amphibious Force. On December 7 Struble commanded the landing of troops at Ormoc Bay for the final operation on Leyte in the Philippines. On December 13, while convoying troops through the Visayan Sea toward Mindoro Island, his flagship *Nashville* was attacked by a kamikaze pilot; over a hundred men were killed, including Struble's and the commanding general's chiefs of staff. On January 29, 1945, he put the XI Corps ashore at Subic Bay, north of Manila, and he subsequently took part in directing amphibious operations at Corregidor, Negros, Panay, and elsewhere in the Philippines. In September 1945 he was given command of minecraft, Pacific Fleet, with the delicate task of clearing the western Pacific of mines. In June 1946 he took command of Amphibious Force, Pacific Fleet, and in April 1948 he was named deputy chief of naval operations with the rank of vice admiral. In May 1950 Struble took command of the Seventh Fleet in the Pacific. A month later the invasion of South Korea by northern forces brought the Seventh Fleet into action under the general command of Adm. C. Turner Joy, chief of United Nations naval forces. Naval support and blockade were maintained along the coasts of Korea, and a protective cordon was established around Formosa. Elements of the Seventh landed and supported Gen. Edward M. Almond's X Corps at Inch'on on September 15 and at Wonsan on October 20. In March 1951 Struble was transferred to command of the First Fleet. From 1952 to 1956 he was chairman of the U.S. military staff commission at the United Nations. After a year as commander of the Eastern Sea Frontier he retired with the rank of admiral in July 1956. He was associated thereafter with the Hamilton Watch Company in Lancaster, Pennsylvania.

Stuart, James Ewell Brown (1833–1864), Confederate army officer. Born in Patrick County, Virginia, on February 6, 1833, Stuart attended Emory and Henry College for two years before entering

West Point in 1850. He graduated in 1854, was commissioned in the Mounted Rifles (he later transferred to the 1st Cavalry), and for six years served mainly in Texas and Kansas. He saw some action against the Cheyenne and was promoted to first lieutenant in December 1855. In October 1859, while on leave in Washington, D.C., he served as aide to Col. Robert E. Lee in the capture of John Brown and his followers at Harpers Ferry. Promoted to captain in April 1861, Stuart resigned his commission in May and in that month was appointed successively lieutenant colonel of Virginia infantry and captain of Confederate cavalry. In July, promoted to colonel, he took command of a troop of some 350 cavalrymen (later designated the 1st Virginia Cavalry) at Harpers Ferry; and at Manassas (Bull Run), July 21, having successfully screened the approach of Gen. Joseph E. Johnston's Army of the Shenandoah, he performed gallantly in the battle. In September he was promoted to brigadier general. On December 20, while holding the high ground before Washington, he suffered one of his few defeats, at the hands of Gen. Edward O. C. Ord at Dranesville, Virginia. In the Peninsula campaign Stuart's cavalry covered the retreat from Yorktown and opened the battle of Williamsburg, May 5, 1862; Stuart personally won commendation from Gen. James Longstreet at Seven Pines (Fair Oaks), May 31. From June 12 to 15 he led 1200 cavalry in a daring ride out of Richmond, completely around Gen. George B. McClellan's Army of the Potomac, and back, bringing invaluable information on the disposition of Union forces to Gen. Robert E. Lee. During the Seven Days' Battles, June 26–July 2, he harried the Union rear and kept Lee posted on McClellan's movements. He was promoted to major general in command of all the cavalry of the Army of Northern Virginia in July. Ordered back to northern Virginia, he raided Gen. John Pope's headquarters at Catlett's Station on August 22 and captured several staff officers, raided the Union supply depot at Manassas Station on the 27th, and took part under Gen. Thomas J. Jackson in the second battle of Manassas, August 29–30. He screened Jackson's advance into Maryland and performed brilliantly at South Mountain, September 14, and Sharpsburg (Antietam), September 17. At the latter he made highly effective use of his mobile artillery to blunt the attack of Gen. Edwin V. Sumner's II Corps. During October, after Lee's withdrawal, Stuart led a cavalry raid into Pennsylvania, capturing over a thousand badly needed horses and the town of Chambersburg. At Fredericksburg, December 13, he held the extreme right of the Confederate line. Functioning as Lee's valued "eyes of the army," Stuart had by this time molded his cavalry into an incomparable tool for outpost and scouting work. He was personally one of the most popular Confederate commanders, though his turn for flamboyance in dress and demeanor dismayed some. Before the battle of Chancellorsville he sent a brigade to track Gen. George Stoneman's diversionary raid while holding the bulk of his force to watch the Army of the Potomac, then under Gen. Joseph Hooker. At the opening of the battle on May 2 a cavalry brigade under Gen. Fitzhugh Lee discovered Hooker's vulnerable right flank, making possible Jackson's smashing attack. The death of Jackson and disabling of Gen. Ambrose P. Hill brought Stuart temporary command of the II Corps. During Lee's northern advance in June Stuart met Gen. Alfred Pleasonton at Brandy Station, Virginia, in one of the passes out of the Shenandoah valley and on June 9 fought one of the few purely cavalry battles of the war to a standoff. Several more skirmishes followed, and then Lee ordered him forward to screen the Confederate army's move into Pennsylvania and scout the Union army. He attempted an overambitious raid into Pennsylvania and was unexpectedly delayed by scattered Union cavalry detachments, with the result that Lee received no word of the presence of a Union force at Gettysburg before July 1. Stuart's failure in that operation was long a topic of controversy. The next several months were occupied by screening, scouting, and foraging details, arduous work that bore heavily on Stuart's men. A few skirmishes were fought, notably the rout of a small Union cavalry force near Buckland Mills, Virginia, on October 19, 1863, an action known derisively as the "Buckland Races." At the opening of Gen. Ulysses S. Grant's campaign in May 1864 the cavalry again came to the fore. Stuart discovered and attempted to delay Grant's flanking movement toward Spotsylvania on May 7, engaging Gen. Philip H. Sheridan at Todd's Tavern. On May 9 Union cavalry under Sheridan set out on a raid in force toward Richmond. Stuart raced ahead and took up a position in front of Sheridan at Yellow Tavern, outnumbered 12,000 to 4500; Stuart was mortally wounded in the battle there on May 11 and died the next day, May 12, 1864, in Richmond, Virginia.

Stump, Felix Budwell (1894–1972), naval officer. Born on December 15, 1894, in Clarksburg, West Virginia, Stump graduated from the Naval Academy in 1917. He served briefly on the gunboat *Yorktown* and then on the cruiser *Cincinnati* on escort duty in the Atlantic during World War I, and in 1920 he completed aviation training at the Pensacola Naval Air Station, Florida. Various assignments followed, and in 1924 he took an M.S. degree in aeronautical engineering from the Massachusetts Institute of Technology. During 1924–1927 he served with Torpedo Squadron 2 aboard the carrier *Langley,* and in 1927–1930 he was stationed at Hampton Roads Naval Air Station, Virginia. He commanded scouting squadrons on various cruisers in 1930–1932 and in 1932–1934 was attached to the Bureau of Aeronautics. In 1934–1936 he commanded Scouting Squadron

2 on the *Saratoga*, and after a year aboard the *Lexington* he was again in the Bureau of Aeronautics in 1937–1940. He was executive officer of the *Enterprise* in 1940–1941, and for a few months in 1941–1942 he commanded the seaplane tender *Langley*. He joined the staff of Adm. Thomas C. Hart of the Asiatic Fleet in January 1942. Stump remained on Hart's staff as director of operations and intelligence of the Allied ABDACOM (American-British-Dutch-Australian Command) until May. After six months as air officer of the Western Sea Frontier in 1942 Stump returned to sea duty in February 1943 in command of the new carrier *Lexington*, which in March became a major unit of the new Fifth Fleet under Adm. Raymond A. Spruance. The *Lexington* took part in operations against the Gilbert and Marshall Islands late in 1943 until torpedo damage forced it to return to the United States in December. In April 1944 Stump, by then a rear admiral, took command of Carrier Division 24. His carriers provided escort support for the campaign against Saipan, Tinian, and Guam in the Marianas in June–August 1944. Later in the year his division was temporarily attached to Adm. Thomas C. Kinkaid's Seventh Fleet, becoming the "Taffy 2" unit of the Escort Carrier Group, to aid in the naval air support of the assault on Leyte—and subsequently other points—in the Philippines. During March–April 1945 his group was engaged in the Okinawa campaign. In June 1945 Stump became chief of naval air technical training. Promoted to vice admiral in November 1948, he became commander of Air Force, Atlantic Fleet, the next month and of the Second Fleet in April 1951. In June 1953 he advanced to admiral, and in July he took command of the Pacific Fleet. That post included overall command of all U.S. forces, army, navy, and air force, in the Pacific outside the army's Far East Command and Alaskan Department. The command was reorganized in 1957 as the Joint Pacific Command, and Stump remained at its head, even after relinquishing command of the Pacific Fleet in January 1958, until his retirement in July 1958. He died in Bethesda, Maryland, on June 13, 1972.

Sturgis, Samuel Davis (1822–1889), army officer. Born in Shippensburg, Pennsylvania, on June 11, 1822, Sturgis graduated from West Point in 1846 and was commissioned in the 2nd Dragoons. In the Mexican War he saw action at Palo Alto and Resaca de la Palma, May 8–9, 1846, and while reconnoitering before the battle of Buena Vista, February 22–23, 1847, he was captured and held for eight days. After the war he was on duty in the West, receiving promotions to first lieutenant in July 1853 and to captain in March 1855. He was in command of Fort Smith, Arkansas, at the outbreak of the Civil War. On his own responsibility he evacuated the fort and brought off most of the stores and equipment after all his officers

joined the Confederacy. Promoted to major in May 1861, he took part in the battle at Wilson's Creek, Missouri, August 10, and succeeded to command of the Union force there on the death of Gen. Nathaniel Lyon. He was then appointed brigadier general of volunteers. After brief periods with the Army of the Tennessee and in command of the Department of Kansas he was called to Washington, D.C., in mid-1862 to take command of the city's defenses. As commander of the reserves of Gen. John Pope's Army of Virginia he took part in the second battle of Bull Run (Manassas), August 29–30, and he commanded a division of the IX Corps under Gen. Ambrose E. Burnside at South Mountain, September 14, Antietam (Sharpsburg), September 17, and Fredericksburg, December 13; he was brevetted colonel of regulars at the last. During April–July 1863 he was with the IX Corps in Kentucky, and from July 1863 to April 1864 he commanded the cavalry of the Army of the Ohio. He suffered a sharp defeat at the hands of Gen. Nathan B. Forrest at Brice's Cross Roads (Guntown), Mississippi, on June 10, 1864. In March 1865 he was brevetted brigadier and major general of regulars. Having been promoted to lieutenant colonel of regulars in October 1863, he was mustered out of volunteer service in August 1865 and assigned to the 6th Cavalry. In May 1869 he succeeded Col. Andrew J. Smith as colonel of the 7th Cavalry (which, however, was usually commanded in the field by Lt. Col. George A. Custer). Sturgis was in the field in the Nez Percé War of 1877 and was defeated by Joseph and his warriors at Canyon Creek, Montana, September 13. Sturgis was governor of the Soldiers' Home in Washington, D.C., from 1881 to 1885, and he retired in June 1886. He died in St. Paul, Minnesota, on September 28, 1889.

Sullivan, John (1740–1795), Revolutionary army officer and public official. Born in Somersworth, New Hampshire, on February 17, 1740, Sullivan took up the study of law and entered practice in Durham about 1760. In 1772 he was appointed a major in the New Hampshire militia. During September–November 1774 he was a representative in the first Continental Congress. In December he returned to New Hampshire and, warned by Paul Revere of an impending British move, he raised a force and participated in the capture of Fort William and Mary, with its valuable stores, at Portsmouth on December 14. In May 1775 he entered the second Continental Congress, by which he was commissioned brigadier general in June. He served in the siege of Boston from July to March 1776. During June–July 1776 he was in command of the northern army, then recuperating from the disastrous Quebec campaign at Fort Chambly on the Richelieu River; the period was marked by the defeat of Gen. William Thompson at Three Rivers, June 8. Sullivan offered his resignation on being superseded by Gen. Horatio Gates in July but was persuaded to remain in the army by John Hancock. Promoted to major general early in August, he was sent to command the forces on Long Island. By the time of the British landing on August 22 he had yielded command to Gen. Israel Putnam. In the fighting on August 27 he was captured. Exchanged a short time later, he rejoined Gen. George Washington's army in Westchester County, New York, and took part in the campaign in New Jersey and the battles of Trenton, December 26, where he commanded the right wing, and Princeton, January 3, 1777. On August 21–22, 1777, he conducted a raid on British posts on Staten Island that failed to accomplish much. He again commanded the American right at Brandywine, September 11, and Germantown, October 4. After wintering at Valley Forge Sullivan was given command of Rhode Island in the spring of 1778. He planned an expedition against the British base at Newport to be carried out jointly with the French fleet under Adm. d'Estaing. Sullivan surrounded Newport in August, but d'Estaing's fleet was overtaken by Adm. Lord Howe's, and both were scattered in a sudden gale. D'Estaing then made for Boston to make repairs. Sullivan, his militia forces deserting, concentrated north of Newport, where the British attacked him furiously on August 29. He repelled the attack, but news of approaching British reinforcements made it necessary for him to withdraw. He remained at Providence until the following spring. As a result of the activities of Indians and Tories in western New York and Pennsylvania, notably Col. John Butler's Rangers and Joseph Brant's warriors in the Wyoming Valley and the Cherry Valley, Sullivan was ordered to lead an expedition into the region. At Easton, Pennsylvania, he assembled a force of about 2500 under Gen. Edward Hand, Gen. William Maxwell, and Gen. Enoch Poor. He marched toward the Wyoming Valley, Hand attacking en route the Indian village of Chemung, and at Tioga built Fort Sullivan. On August 22 he was joined by Gen. James Clinton and 1500 more men, and the combined force swept through Indian territory, burning crops and villages. The principal fight of the campaign was at Newtown, near present-day Elmira, New York, on August 29. Soon after the conclusion of the expedition Sullivan fell ill, and on November 30, 1779, he resigned his commission. He again sat in the Continental Congress in 1780–1781. He was a member of the New Hampshire constitutional convention in 1782, and he was state attorney general in 1782–1786, serving also in the legislature during that time. He was elected president of New Hampshire for two terms, 1786–1788. He served as chairman of the state convention that ratified the federal Constitution in 1788; he was speaker of the assembly in the same year, and president again in 1789. He was federal district judge for New Hampshire from 1789 until his death in Durham, New Hampshire, on January 23, 1795.

Sully, Alfred (1821–1879), army officer. Born in 1821 in Philadelphia, Sully graduated from West Point in 1841 and was commissioned in the infantry. He saw action against the Seminoles in Florida in 1841–1842 and was then on garrison duty at Sackett's Harbor, New York, until the Mexican War. After taking part in the siege of Veracruz in March 1847 he was recalled to recruiting duty. He was promoted to first lieutenant in March 1847 and to captain in February 1852 while stationed in California. He took part in an expedition against the Rogue River Indians in 1853 and later served in Minnesota, Nebraska, and the Dakotas. During 1860–1861 he saw action against the Cheyenne Indians. For some months after the outbreak of the Civil War he was in northern Missouri; he was called to Washington, D.C., in November 1861. Appointed colonel of the 1st Minnesota Volunteers in February 1862, he served through the Peninsula campaign, winning brevets to lieutenant colonel of regulars at Fair Oaks (Seven Pines), May 31, and colonel at Malvern Hill, July 1. He commanded a brigade at Chantilly, September 1, and after distinguishing himself at South Mountain, September 14, and Antietam (Sharpsburg), September 17, he was promoted later in the month to brigadier general of volunteers. He took part in the battles of Fredericksburg, December 13, and Chancellorsville, May 2–4, 1863, and was then given command of the Department of Dakota. From his headquarters at Sioux City, Iowa, Sully set out in June to campaign against the Sioux in cooperation with Gen. Henry H. Sibley. He missed a rendezvous with Sibley in August, but on September 3 he dealt a sharp defeat to the Sioux at Whitestone Hill, in what is now North Dakota, and destroyed their camp and supplies. In July 1864 he conducted another expedition. He ascended the Missouri River from Sioux City to the mouth of the Cannonball River, some 30 miles south of present-day Bismarck, and near there established Fort Rice. From there he marched northwest into the Badlands and on July 28 defeated a large Sioux force at Killdeer Mountain (Tahkahokuty). After a circuit to the Yellowstone River and back down the Missouri he returned to Fort Rice in early September. In 1865 he conducted a third field expedition, circling around to Devils Lake, Fort Berthold, and back to Fort Rice. Brevetted brigadier general of regulars and major general of volunteers in March 1865, Sully was mustered out of volunteer service in August 1866; in July of that year he had been appointed lieutenant colonel of the 10th Infantry. In November 1868, during Gen. Philip Sheridan's campaign against the Cheyenne, Comanche, and Kiowa tribes, Sully established Camp Supply on the Canadian River in what is now northwest Oklahoma. He was promoted to colonel of the 21st Infantry in December 1873. He died at Fort Vancouver, Washington Territory, on April 27, 1879.

Sultan, Daniel Isom (1885–1947), army officer. Born on December 9, 1885, in Oxford, Mississippi, Sultan attended the University of Mississippi in 1901–1903 and then entered West Point. He graduated in 1907 and took his commission in the engineers. He was stationed at Fort Leavenworth, Kansas, for a year and then in Washington, D.C., until 1912, and he was promoted to first lieutenant upon completing the Engineer School at Washington Barracks (now Fort Belvoir) in 1910. During 1912–1916 he was an instructor at West Point, advancing to captain in February 1914, and in 1916–1918 he was in the Philippines, where he had a part in the construction of the fortifications on Corregidor Island. Promoted to major in May 1917 and temporary lieutenant colonel in August, he was attached to the General Staff from 1918 to 1922 except for a few months spent in France with the occupation forces in 1919. After graduating from Command and General Staff School, Fort Leavenworth, in 1923 he was district engineer in Savannah, Georgia, for two years. He graduated from the Army War College in 1926 and remained in the District of Columbia until 1929 as a member of the Board of Engineers for Rivers and Harbors. During 1929–1931 he commanded U.S. army troops in Nicaragua and supervised a survey for an interoceanic canal. He was promoted to lieutenant colonel in October 1930. Following the Nicaragua earthquake of March 1931 he directed army relief activities. After a year on the Interoceanic Canal Board in Washington and a period as district engineer in Chicago, 1932–1934, during which he was also civil works administrator for Cook County, he was named engineering commissioner of the District of Columbia. He was promoted to colonel in October 1935. In August 1938 Sultan took command of the 2nd Engineers at Fort Logan, Colorado, becoming commander of the post with the rank of brigadier general in December. In June 1939 he took command of the 22nd Infantry Brigade at Schofield Barracks, Hawaii; he moved up to command of the Hawaiian Division a month before his promotion to temporary major general and transfer to command of the 38th Infantry Division at Camp Shelby, Mississippi, in April 1941. In April 1942 he was put in command of the VIII Corps. In January 1943 he was named deputy to Gen. Joseph W. Stilwell, commander of the China-Burma-India theater. There his principal concern was the building of supply lines to China, primarily the Burma Road and the Ledo Road. In September 1944 he was promoted to temporary lieutenant general. In October 1944, following Stilwell's recall, Sultan was named commander of the India-Burma portion of the Far Eastern theater. (China came under the command of Gen. Claire L.

Chennault and then Gen. Albert C. Wedemeyer.) In that capacity he commanded two Chinese armies in Burma and the British 36th Division in addition to American troops. The Ledo–Burma highway, renamed in Stilwell's honor, was finally completed to Wan-ting, China, in late January 1945. In March Sultan's Chinese First Army recaptured Lashio, Burma. In July he was recalled to Washington and appointed inspector general of the army. In August he became the first army officer to be awarded a fourth Distinguished Service Medal. Sultan died in Washington, D.C., on January 14, 1947.

Summerall, Charles Pelot (1867–1955), army officer. Born on March 4, 1867, in Lake City, Florida, Summerall graduated from West Point in 1892 and was commissioned in the infantry; he transferred to the artillery a few months later. After tours of garrison duty at the Presidio, San Francisco, and Fort Hamilton, New York, he was assigned to the staff of the commander of the Department of the Gulf at the outbreak of the Spanish–American War in 1898. Promoted to first lieutenant in March 1899, he saw action in the Philippine insurrection in 1899–1900 and in the Peking Relief Expedition in 1900–1901 and distinguished himself more than once. In July 1901 he was promoted to captain. In 1902 he located the site for and began construction of Fort Seward, Alaska. From 1905 to 1911 he was an instructor at West Point, advancing to major in March 1911, and in the latter year he took command of a battalion of the 3rd Field Artillery posted in Texas. In 1913 he selected and negotiated the purchase of the site for the army's field artillery training center at Tobyhanna, Pennsylvania. From 1913 to 1917 he was an instructor at the Army War College, receiving promotions to lieutenant colonel in June 1916 and colonel in May 1917. During 1914–1917 he served also as assistant to the bureau chief in charge of National Guard field artillery, and in 1916 he was a member of the army advisory board on arms and munitions manufacture. In 1917 he selected and negotiated the purchase of sites for field artillery training at Anniston, Alabama, and Monterey, California. During April–July 1917 he was a member of a military mission to Great Britain and France. He was promoted to temporary brigadier general in August and the next month given command of the 67th Field Artillery Brigade. Shortly after his arrival in France in October he took command of the 1st Field Artillery Brigade of the 1st Division, with which he saw action at Cantigny in May 1918. Promoted to permanent brigadier general in January 1918 and to temporary major general in June, Summerall succeeded Gen. Robert L. Bullard in command of the 1st Division in July and led it through the Aisne–Marne, St. Mihiel, and Meuse–Argonne operations until October, when he was moved up to command of the V Corps. He remained with that unit through the end of the Meuse–Argonne offensive in November and in occupation duty until February 1919; he subsequently commanded the IX Corps until April and the IV Corps until June. He later served on an Allied commission sent to investigate conditions in the disputed territory of Fiume in July–August 1919 and was an adviser to the American delegation at the Versailles peace conference. In September 1919 Summerall returned to the United States and took command of the 1st Division at Camp Zachary Taylor, Kentucky. He was promoted to permanent major general in April 1920. In November 1926 he was appointed chief of staff of the army, and he received the statutory rank of general by congressional action in February 1929. He remained chief of staff until November 1930, when he was succeeded by Gen. Douglas MacArthur, and he retired with the rank of general in March 1931. From that year until June 1953 Summerall was president of The Citadel military college in Charleston, South Carolina. He died in Washington, D.C., on May 14, 1955.

Sumner, Edwin Vose (1797–1863), army officer. Born in Boston on January 30, 1797, Sumner was appointed a second lieutenant in the 2nd Infantry in March 1819. He was promoted to first lieutenant in January 1823 and, after service in the Black Hawk War of 1832, he became captain in the 1st Dragoons in March 1833. He served mainly on the frontier except for a period in 1838 when he was commander of the School of Cavalry Practice at Carlisle Barracks, Pennsylvania. Promoted to major of the 2nd Dragoons in June 1846, Sumner served in Gen. Winfield Scott's army in the Mexican War. He was detached from his regiment for a time to command the newly organized and inexperienced Mounted Rifle Regiment (later the 3rd Cavalry). He was wounded leading a charge at Cerro Gordo, April 18, 1847, for which he was brevetted lieutenant colonel; and he again distinguished himself at Molino del Rey, September 8, receiving a brevet to colonel. Sumner was promoted to lieutenant colonel, 1st Dragoons, in July 1848. He commanded the Department of New Mexico in 1851–1853 and served briefly as acting governor of the territory in 1852. In the summer of 1851 he established the important military post of Fort Union in Mora County, New Mexico. After a tour of study of European cavalry practices he was promoted to colonel of the 1st Cavalry in March 1855. As commander of Fort Leavenworth he played a major role in suppressing the violence produced by the Free-Soil struggle in Kansas from 1856, and during that period he also conducted expeditions against the Indians. In 1858 he became commander of the Department of the West at St. Louis. For some reason he came to be suspected in St. Louis of secessionist sympathies, but Gen. Scott's confidence in him was demonstrated by the selection of Sumner to command the military

escort accompanying President-elect Abraham Lincoln from Springfield, Illinois, to Washington, D.C., in March 1861. Later in that month he was promoted to brigadier general and ordered to succeed Gen. Albert S. Johnston as commander of the Department of the Pacific. Early in 1862 he was recalled east to command the II Corps, Army of the Potomac, in Gen. George B. McClellan's Peninsula campaign. He distinguished himself at Seven Pines (Fair Oaks), May 31, and in all the operations on the Chickahominy; and at Savage Station, June 29, he defeated Gen. John B . Magruder. In July he was appointed major general of volunteers. He was wounded while commanding the II Corps at Antietam (Sharpsburg), September 17, and he commanded Gen. Ambrose E. Burnside's Right Grand Division (comprising the II and IX Corps) at Fredericksburg, December 13. A short time later he was relieved of his command at his own request. On his way to take command of the Department of Missouri he died in Syracuse, New York, on March 21, 1863.

Sumner, Jethro (1733?–1785), Revolutionary army officer. Born in Nansemond County, Virginia, about 1733, Sumner served in the Virginia militia from 1755 to 1761 during the French and Indian War, becoming a lieutenant in command of Fort Bedford (formerly Fort Raystown) in 1760. Sometime before late 1764 he moved to North Carolina and settled in Bute (now Warren) County. He became prominent in local affairs, served as sheriff from 1772 to 1777, and represented the county in the provincial congress in August–September 1775. There he was elected major of minutemen for his district. In April 1776 he was elected colonel of a battalion of North Carolina troops raised for service in the Continental army. He took part in various operations in the Southern Department and in the spring of 1777 led his troops north to join Gen. George Washington's army. He took part in the battles of Brandywine and Germantown and wintered at Valley Forge. In 1778, while on sick leave in North Carolina, he performed recruiting services. In January 1779 Sumner was commissioned brigadier general by the Continental Congress. He led a brigade at Stono Ferry, South Carolina, on June 20. He was then again on recruiting duty for several months. He commanded North Carolina militia troops in resistance to Gen. Charles Cornwallis's invasion in 1780, until the elevation of Gen. William Smallwood over him caused him to retire from active service in October. The following year, however, he raised still more troops and in July marched to reinforce Gen. Nathanael Greene, taking a distinguished part in the battle of Eutaw Springs, September 8, 1781. Thereafter he commanded troops in North Carolina until the end of the war. Sumner died at his home in Warren County sometime between March 15 and 19, 1785.

Sumter, Thomas (1734–1832), Revolutionary militia officer and public official. Born near Charlottesville, Virginia, on August 14, 1734, Sumter grew up on the frontier with little opportunity for schooling. During the French and Indian War he served, perhaps as an irregular, in the expeditions of 1755 and 1758 under Gen. Edward Braddock and Gen. John Forbes. In 1765 he settled near Eutaw Springs, South Carolina, and opened a country store. He was elected to the first and second provincial congresses in 1775–1776, and while taking part in a campaign against the Cherokees in Georgia and Florida he was appointed lieutenant colonel of the 2nd South Carolina Riflemen Regiment in Continental service in March 1776. He had risen to colonel by the time he resigned in September 1778 and returned home. The British conquest of South Carolina in May 1780 set off what amounted to a civil war within the region between Whigs and Tories. At that juncture, having fled to Charlotte, North Carolina, Sumter again took up arms and led raids against the British and Tories throughout the remainder of the war, contributing materially to the eventual victory at Yorktown. He defeated a mixed body of British and Tories at Hanging Rock, South Carolina, on August 6, 1780, but had his small command wiped out at Fishing Creek on August 18 by the main British force in the interior under Col. Banastre Tarleton. He was commissioned brigadier general of South Carolina militia, then little more than an armed partisan force, in October 1780. Only Gen. Daniel Morgan was left to oppose Tarleton until Sumter regrouped and took the field again in October under his formal commission. He defeated a detachment of Tarleton's force at Fishdam Ford, November 9, and heavily defeated his main body at Enoree (or Blackstock's Hill), November 20. For that he was voted the thanks of Congress. He operated independently of the nearly nonexistent state government and, with considerable friction, of Gen. Horatio Gates, commander of the southern theater of war. After recovering from a wound received at Enoree he was again in action during much of 1781, harrying British outposts and detachments and generally supporting Gen. Nathanael Greene's campaign. He joined Greene finally in July. At length Greene attempted to discipline the "gamecock of South Carolina," and that conflict led to Sumter's resignation early in 1782. Following the war Sumter founded the town of Stateburg, South Carolina, and established his home, South Mount, nearby. He engaged in tobacco raising, horse breeding, and land speculation. He served several terms in the state legislature and was an anti-Federalist at the South Carolina convention to ratify the Constitution. Under the new Federal government he served in the House of Representatives from 1789 to 1793 and again from 1797 to 1801. In December 1801 he was elected to the U.S. Senate, where he remained until resigning in December 1810. He then retired to his home near Stateburg, where he spent the rest of his life. Often harried by debts and creditors, he was finally relieved in 1830 when the state legislature granted him a lifetime moratorium from his debt to the state bank. He died at his plantation on June 1, 1832, in his ninety-eighth year, the last surviving general officer of the Revolution. Fort Sumter, South Carolina, was named in his honor, as were the city and county of Sumter.

T

Talbot, Silas (1751–1813), Revolutionary army and naval officer. Born in Dighton, Massachusetts, on January 11, 1751, Talbot was in his youth a stonemason before he went to sea in the merchant service. Early in the Revolutionary period he raised a company of volunteers, and in June 1775 he was commissioned captain in the Rhode Island militia; he received a similar commission in the Continental army a few days later. He took part in the siege of Boston and in most of the operations in and around New York City in 1776. His daring attempt to destroy the British ship *Asia* by drifting a fireship down the Hudson River into New York harbor brought him promotion to major in October 1777. He was severely wounded in an engagement at Hog Island in the Delaware River during the British naval campaign up the river toward Philadelphia in October–November 1777. In August 1778 he took part in Gen. John Sullivan's campaign in Rhode Island. In October of that year he fitted out a small sloop, the *Hawke*, and with it captured the British schooner *Pigot*, part of the force blockading Newport. Promoted to lieutenant colonel in November, he continued to patrol the coast between Long Island and Nantucket aboard the *Pigot* and later the *Argo*, capturing several British vessels. In September 1779 he was commissioned a captain in the Continental navy, but, there being no ship for him, he sailed early in 1780 aboard the privateer *General Washington*. He was quickly captured off New York; held on a prison ship and later in England, he made several attempts to escape and suffered terrible privations. His exchange was won at length by Benjamin Franklin and John Jay, and he landed in France in December 1781. He then sailed for America, but his voyage was interrupted by the capture of his French brig by a British privateer. After a period in Philadelphia spent in litigating his prize claims he settled in Fulton County, New York, and took up farming. He sat in the New York legislature in 1792–1793, and he was elected to the 3rd Congress, 1793–1795. In June 1794 he was commissioned captain, third on the list, in the newly organized navy, and later in the year he was sent to superintend the construction of the new frigate *President* in New York City. He was inactive from 1796 to May 1798, when President John Adams again commissioned him captain for service in the undeclared naval war with France. During 1799–1800 he commanded a squadron in the West Indies from aboard the *Constitution*. On May 11, 1800, Lt. Isaac Hull and marine Capt. Daniel

Carmick led a party from the *Constitution* to capture, illegally as it turned out, the French privateer *Sandwich* at Puerto Plata, Santo Domingo (Dominican Republic). Talbot resigned in September 1801, in part because of a dispute with Commodore Thomas Truxtun over seniority proceeding from Talbot's double commission. He died in New York City on June 30, 1813.

Taliaferro, William Booth (1822–1898), Confederate army officer. Born in Gloucester County, Virginia, on December 28, 1822, Taliaferro graduated from the College of William and Mary in 1841 and for a time studied law at Harvard. During the Mexican War he served in the army, being commissioned captain in the 11th Infantry in April 1847 and receiving promotion to major in August. He was mustered out in August 1848 and resumed his law practice in Gloucester County. He was a member of the Virginia legislature in 1850–1853. In November 1859, following the capture of John Brown, he took command of the militia guard at Harpers Ferry. In May 1861 Taliaferro was commissioned colonel in the Virginia provisional army and a short time later was mustered into Confederate service. He took part in several small engagements in northern Virginia, including those at Gloucester Point, May 1, 1861, and Carrick's Ford, July 13, and in March 1862 he was promoted to brigadier general. He served under Gen. Thomas J. Jackson in the Shenandoah valley campaign of that year, seeing action at Winchester, May 25, Cross Keys, June 8, Port Republic, June 9, and Cedar Mountain, August 9, where he succeeded to command of his division and managed its withdrawal so expertly that he retained command thenceforward. He was badly wounded at Groveton, August 28–29, but returned to active service in time to distinguish himself at Fredericksburg, December 13. In February 1863 he was ordered to Savannah, Georgia, and shortly thereafter to Charleston, South Carolina, where from July 18, with fewer than 1200 men, he defended Fort Wagner (or Battery Wagner) on Morris Island against nearly 5000 under Gen. Quincy A. Gillmore. In August he took command of the defenses on James Island, from which he successfully defended Charleston against all attempts to capture it. During February 1864 he commanded a division in Florida, and in December of that year, as commander of the District of South Carolina, he covered the withdrawal of the garrison at Savannah from Gen. William T.

Sherman's advancing forces. Promoted to major general in January 1865, he evacuated James Island in February but continued to fight Sherman through the Carolinas, notably at Bentonville, March 19–21, until surrendering with Gen. Joseph E. Johnston's army on April 26. Taliaferro served again in the Virginia legislature in 1874–1879, was judge of the Gloucester County court in 1891–1897, and served on the boards of visitors of the College of William and Mary, Virginia Military Institute, and other institutions. He died at his home near Belleville, Gloucester County, Virginia, on February 27, 1898.

Tanner, James (1844–1927), soldier and public official. Born in Richmondville, New York, on April 4, 1844, Tanner was a teacher in a local school when, in September 1861, he enlisted in the 87th New York Volunteer Infantry. He served as a corporal through the Peninsula campaign, April–July 1862, and at the second battle of Bull Run (Manassas), August 29–30, received wounds necessitating the amputation of both legs just below the knees. He learned to walk with artificial legs and in 1863 secured appointment as under-doorkeeper of the New York legislature. In 1864 he obtained a clerkship in the War Department. He took up the study of law in New York at the end of the war and in 1869 was admitted to the bar. From 1869 to 1877 he held posts in the New York customhouse, and from 1877 to 1885 he was tax collector in Brooklyn. He was also active in Republican politics and in the Grand Army of the Republic. As state GAR commander in 1876 he organized a letter-writing campaign that moved the legislature to establish a soldiers' home. Subsequently he was frequently called on to lobby Congress on behalf of veterans, and between 1886 and 1888 he made several national tours on the stump for Benjamin Harrison's presidential candidacy. In reward he was appointed in March 1889 commissioner of pensions. Declaring it his intention to secure the maximum possible benefit to "every old comrade that needs it," "Corporal" Tanner, as he was known, proceeded to make hash of administrative procedures and his office's budget. He was honest in his ineptness, but many subordinates were not, a fact that added to the confusion. At length Secretary of the Interior John W. Noble, of whose department the Pension Office was a part, was forced to step in, and Tanner resigned in September 1889. From then until 1904 he was a private pension attorney engaged in prosecuting various claims against the government. In April 1904 President Theodore Roosevelt appointed him register of wills for the District of Columbia. During 1905–1906 he was national commander of the GAR. Tanner died in Washington, D.C., on October 2, 1927.

Tattnall, Josiah (1795–1871), Confederate naval officer. Born on November 9, 1795, near Savannah,

Georgia, Tattnall was orphaned at nine and for six years thereafter lived with a grandfather in London. He returned to the United States in 1811 and in March 1812 entered the navy as a midshipman. He was ordered to duty on the *Constellation,* then blockaded at Hampton Roads, Virginia, but saw action ashore at Craney Island, June 22, 1813, and at Bladensburg, Maryland, August 24, 1814. In the latter year he was transferred to the *Epervier* at Savannah, and he served on her in Commodore Stephen Decatur's squadron in the Algerine War of 1815. Promoted to lieutenant in April 1818, he served on the *Macedonian* in the Pacific, 1818–1821, briefly attended Capt. Alden Partridge's military academy in Norwich, Vermont, and in 1823–1824 was on the *Jackal* in Commodore David Porter's squadron suppressing piracy in the West Indies. After a cruise in the Mediterranean in 1825–1826 he served on the *Erie* in the West Indies in 1828–1829, and he commanded a boat party that captured the Spanish privateer *Federal* off St. Bartholomew. In 1829 he was assigned to command of the survey of the Tortugas reefs and keys. He cruised the Gulf of Mexico in command of the *Grampus* in 1831–1832 with orders to protect American commerce, and he captured the Mexican schooner *Montezuma* in August of the latter year. After a period of shore duty he returned to sea in 1835 in command of the *Pioneer,* aboard which in 1837 he conveyed Gen. Antonio de Santa Anna, captured by Gen. Sam Houston at San Jacinto, back to Mexico and landed him at Veracruz. Promoted to commander in February 1838, Tattnall commanded the Boston navy yard for a time and later the *Fairfield* in the Mediterranean Squadron and the *Saratoga* in the African Squadron. He displayed great seamanship in saving the latter ship in a hurricane off Cape Ann, Massachusetts, in 1843. In the Mexican War he commanded the "mosquito division" of the squadron under Commodore David Conner and later Commodore Matthew C. Perry. Aboard his flagship *Spitfire* he took part in the capture of Tampico on November 14, 1846, and led a raid on Mexican stores and ordnance up the Tabasco River to Panuco on November 19. During the bombardment of Veracruz in March 1847 Tattnall took the *Spitfire* under the guns of the fortified castle of San Juan de Ulúa and inflicted considerable damage. In April he took part in the capture of Tuxpan. After two more years at the Boston navy yard he was promoted to captain in February 1850. Then, in command of the *Saranac,* he was ordered to Cuban waters to protect American shipping against Spanish actions arising from the Cuban insurrection. He subsequently commanded the Pensacola, Florida, navy yard until 1854 and the *Independence* in the Pacific Squadron in 1854–1855. After two years at Sackett's Harbor, New York, he was named commander of the East India Squadron in 1857. While in that station he assisted in the negotiation of a new treaty with China. On June 25, 1859, he compromised American neutrality by giving aid to a British squadron hard-pressed during its attack on the Taku forts at the mouth of the Pai (Pei-ho) River. His explanation for his conduct was the adage "blood is thicker than water," and he was upheld by the government. In 1860 he returned home on the *Powhatan*, carrying as passengers the first Japanese mission to the United States. He was again in command at Sackett's Harbor until February 1861, when he resigned his commission to become senior flag-officer of the Georgia navy. In March he was commissioned captain in the Confederate States navy and given responsibility for the coastal defenses of Georgia and South Carolina. During November 4–7, 1861, hopelessly outnumbered, he fought the Union squadron under Flag-Officer Samuel F. Du Pont at Port Royal Sound, South Carolina, from which he was driven off by Commander John Rodgers's gunboat flotilla. Early in 1862 he was engaged in the defense of Fort Pulaski at Savannah, and in March he took over command of the ironclad *Virginia* from the wounded Franklin Buchanan. With a small flotilla of steamers he occupied the Elizabeth River, commanding Hampton Roads and preventing the Union squadron under Flag-Officer Louis M. Goldsborough in Chesapeake Bay from providing naval support to Gen. George B. McClellan's advance up the Peninsula. On April 11 he dashed into Hampton Roads and captured three small vessels. The naval situation quickly became a standoff, but the Union capture of Norfolk on May 10 rendered Tattnall's position untenable. After an unsuccessful attempt to lighten the ship enough to run up the James River to Richmond, he burned the *Virginia* at Craney Island on May 11. He again commanded Georgia coastal defenses until March 1863 and Savannah's defenses until December 1864, when the city was occupied by Gen. William T. Sherman. He surrendered with Gen. Joseph E. Johnston in April 1865. In June 1866 he moved to Halifax, Nova Scotia. He returned to Savannah in January 1870 and was appointed inspector of the port. He died in Savannah, Georgia, on June 14, 1871.

Taylor, David Watson (1864–1940), naval officer and marine architect. Born in Louisa County, Virginia, on March 4, 1864, Taylor graduated from Randolph-Macon College in 1881. He then entered the Naval Academy and graduated in 1885 with the highest academic record ever achieved up to that time, a feat he repeated at the Royal Naval College in England, from which he graduated in 1888. Appointed an assistant naval constructor in 1886, in 1888 he began work on designing new ships (including the *Oregon*, *Indiana*, and *Massachusetts* of the "new navy") and quickly perceived that the lack of reliable scientific guidance available to designers sharply hindered the progress of the art. He became

concerned in particular with the rule-of-thumb—even haphazard—approach to estimating the power requirements of ships, and from the publication of his first book, *Resistance of Ships and Screw Propulsion*, 1893, he devoted himself to developing an experimental program to provide solid data. In 1892 he had been promoted to constructor. His campaign for a testing basin for ship models finally bore fruit in 1899, and from that year until 1914 he remained in charge of the testing facility at the Washington, D.C., navy yard. He was commissioned captain in March 1901. His systematic experiments with various hull configurations resulted in the publication of *The Speed and Power of Ships*, 1910, in which he outlined what became known internationally as the Taylor Standard Series, the first practical method of matching engine power to a given hull design. Named chief naval constructor and head of the navy's Bureau of Construction and Repair in December 1914 and promoted to rear admiral two years later, Taylor oversaw the feverish and markedly successful shipbuilding program of World War I. At the same time he was concerned in the design of the navy's early aircraft, including the famed NC seaplanes built by Glenn H. Curtiss, one of which became in 1919 the first aircraft to fly the Atlantic. Taylor remained head of the bureau until July 1922. From 1917 until his retirement from active naval service in January 1923 he served on the National Advisory Committee for Aeronautics, and immediately thereafter he was reappointed to that body as a civilian member, serving as vice-chairman from 1927 to 1930. During 1925–1932 he was also a member of a commercial shipbuilding firm. Widely honored both at home and abroad for his contributions to marine architecture, Taylor was a virtual invalid for several years before his death in Washington, D.C., on July 28, 1940.

Taylor, Maxwell Davenport (1901–   ), army officer and diplomat. Born on August 26, 1901, in Keytesville, Missouri, Taylor graduated from West Point in 1922 and was commissioned in the engineers. After a year of advanced study at the Engineer School, Camp Humphreys (now Fort Belvoir), Virginia, and tours of duty in Maryland, Hawaii, and Washington, he transferred to the field artillery in 1926. Promoted to first lieutenant in February 1927, he became an instructor at West Point later that year and remained there until 1932. He graduated from the Field Artillery School, Fort Sill, Oklahoma, in 1933 and from the Command and General Staff School, Fort Leavenworth, Kansas, in 1935, and, promoted to captain in the latter year, he was then attached to the U.S. embassy in Tokyo to study the Japanese language and, more secretly, the Japanese army. For three months at the end of 1937 he was assistant military attaché at the U.S. embassy in Peking. He returned to the United States in 1939, graduated from the Army War College in 1940, received promotion to major in July of that year, and was put in command of the 12th Field Artillery Battalion at Fort Sam Houston, Texas. In July 1941 he was attached to the General Staff as assistant secretary, advancing to temporary lieutenant colonel in December. In July 1942 Taylor was appointed chief of staff of the 82nd Infantry Division at Camp Claiborne, Louisiana, and he assisted Gen. Matthew B. Ridgway in the task of converting the division to an airborne one. He advanced to temporary brigadier general in December and accompanied the division to North Africa in March 1943. He took part with it in the landings in Sicily in July and Italy in September. In the latter month he undertook a highly dangerous mission to Rome, then still behind German lines, to establish contact with Italian authorities, who had already secretly surrendered, and to arrange with them the opening of the city to an airborne occupation; his discovery of greatly increased German strength in the city led to the cancellation of the airborne plan. After a period as senior U.S. member of the Allied Control Commission in occupied Italy Taylor was ordered to England in March 1944 to take command of the 101st Airborne Division. He advanced to temporary major general in May. The 101st dropped into Normandy behind Utah Beach on D-Day, June 6, 1944, and six days later captured the important town of Carentan. After a period of rest in England the 101st became part of Gen. Lewis H. Brereton's First Allied Airborne Army and in Operation Market-Garden were dropped into the Netherlands on September 17 and liberated the city of Eindhoven. In December, while Taylor was in the United States, the division was surrounded at Bastogne and Taylor's deputy commander, Gen. Anthony C. McAuliffe, made his celebrated stand. Taylor rejoined the division at the end of December and commanded it, through campaigns in Alsace and the Ruhr valley and the capture of Berchtesgaden on May 7, until September 1945, when he was named superintendent of West Point. In January 1949 he was appointed chief of staff of U.S. forces in Europe, becoming commander of the U.S. military government in Berlin in September. In August 1951 he became deputy chief of staff of the army. In February 1953 he succeeded Gen. James A. Van Fleet as commander of the Eighth Army in Korea, a post in which he directed the last months of bitter fighting and saw the signing of the armistice in July 1953. In November 1954 he moved up to command of all U.S. army forces in the Far East, and in April 1955, promoted to general, he was named commander of all U.S. and United Nations forces in the Far East. In June of that year he was appointed chief of staff of the army, and he retained that post until his retirement in July 1959. In that year he published *The Uncertain Trumpet*, a sharp criticism of U.S. defense policy during the Eisenhower administration, particularly the reliance on the strategy of "massive retaliation" at the expense of conventional warfare capabilities. After periods as president of the Mexican Light and Power Company in 1959–1960 and of the Lincoln Center for the Performing Arts in New York City in 1961 he reentered government service first as head of an investigation into the role of the Central Intelligence Agency in the abortive Bay of Pigs invasion of Cuba in April 1961 and then, from July, as military representative of President John F. Kennedy. He returned to active duty as chairman of the Joint Chiefs of Staff in October 1962. He resigned the post and retired from the army again to become, at the appointment of President Lyndon B. Johnson, U.S. ambassador to South Vietnam in July 1964. A year later he was succeeded in that post by Henry Cabot Lodge. From 1965 to 1969 Taylor continued as a special consultant to the President and was a member (later chairman) of the President's Foreign Intelligence Advisory Board. From 1966 to 1969 he was president of the Institute for Defense Analysis. He then retired to private life, publishing *Swords and Plowshares*, 1972. His *Responsibility and Response* had appeared earlier in 1967.

Taylor, Richard (1826–1879), Confederate army officer. Born near Louisville, Kentucky, on January 27, 1826, Taylor was the son of Lt. Col. (later President) Zachary Taylor. He grew up at various frontier posts, attended schools in Scotland and France, and studied at Harvard (briefly) and Yale, graduating from the latter in 1845. He was present with his father at the battles of Palo Alto and Resaca de la Palma, May 8–9, 1846. After recovering from a prolonged illness he managed the family cotton plantation in Mississippi in 1848–1849 and then established his own sugarcane plantation in Saint Charles Parish, Louisiana. He became active in Democratic politics, serving in the Louisiana legislature in 1856–1861 and attending the 1860 national convention at Charleston, South Carolina. He was a delegate to the Louisiana secession convention in January 1861 and soon afterward was appointed colonel of the 9th Louisiana Infantry. In July he went to Virginia, but he arrived too late to take part in the battle of Manassas (Bull Run). In October he was promoted to brigadier general (giving rise to some discontent among older officers who noted that he was Confederate President Jefferson Davis's brother-in-law). He served under Gen. Thomas J. Jackson in the Shenandoah valley in the spring of 1862 and then rejoined Gen. Robert E. Lee's army to take part in the Seven Days' Battles in June–July. In the latter month he was promoted to major general and put in command of the District of West Louisiana. Although often beset by illness, he succeeded in organizing a considerable military force there, bringing much of the state under Confederate control and launching numerous raids against Union depots and outposts. He was also successful in keeping Gen. Benjamin F. Butler bottled up in New Orleans. The fall of Vicksburg on July 4, 1863, cut him off from the East altogether. His principal victories in Louisiana were in stopping Gen. Nathaniel P. Banks's advance up the Red River toward the Confederate capital at Shreveport. On April 8, 1864, Taylor repelled Banks at Sabine Cross Roads; the next day he attacked Banks again in an entrenched position at Pleasant Hill and was in turn thrown back, but the Red River campaign was at an end. Following that success he engaged in a brief controversy with his superior officer, Gen. Edmund Kirby-Smith, and retired for a time to his home. In August he was promoted to lieutenant general and put in command of the Department of East Louisiana, Mississippi, and Alabama. In January 1865 he added to his command what remained of the Army of Tennessee of Gen. John B. Hood; a month later most of those forces were transferred east to Gen. Joseph E. Johnston in the Carolinas. On May 4, 1865, he surrendered his command, the last Confederate force east of the Mississippi, to Gen. Edward R. S. Canby at Citronelle, Alabama. After the war he lived in New Orleans and in New York City. In 1879 he published *Destruction and Reconstruction*. Taylor died in New York City on April 12, 1879.

Taylor, Zachary (1784–1850), army officer and twelfth president of the United States. Born on November 24, 1784, in Orange County, Virginia, Taylor grew up near Louisville, Kentucky. He received little formal education. His first military service was as a short-term volunteer in 1806. In May 1808 he received a commission as a first lieutenant in the 7th Infantry of the regular army. He advanced to captain in 1810 and in 1811 was put under the command of Gen. William Henry Harrison, who placed him in charge of Fort Knox, Indiana Territory. He was subsequently transferred to Fort Harrison on the Wabash River above Vincennes, and his defense of that post against a strong Indian attack on September 4, 1812, earned him a brevet to major. He continued in various duties on the frontier, receiving promotion to major in May 1814. In the summer of 1814 he led an expedition up the Mississippi to assert the federal authority. On the site of present-day Warsaw, Illinois, he built Fort Johnson (soon destroyed and later replaced by Fort Edwards), and on September 5–6 he was turned back by an Indian attack at Credit Island, at what is now Davenport, Iowa. He again commanded Fort Knox from December 1814, but when, in the reduction of the army in June 1815, he was retained in the reduced rank of captain, he resigned. In 1816 President James Madison restored him to major. He saw garrison duty with the 3rd Infantry at Green Bay (Wisconsin, but then still part of Michi-

gan Territory) and then commanded Fort Winnebago for two years, and after promotion to lieutenant colonel, 4th Infantry, in April 1819 he was transferred to Louisiana. In 1822 he built Fort Jesup 25 miles west of Natchitoches. During 1829–1832 he was stationed at Fort Snelling (then Michigan Territory, now Minnesota), commanding the post and acting as Indian superintendent. In April 1832 he was promoted to colonel of the 1st Infantry and transferred to Fort Crawford (Prairie du Chien). During Black Hawk's War he served under Gen. Henry Atkinson and took part in the final battle at Bad Axe River, August 2, 1832; he subsequently had custody of the captured Black Hawk. In July 1837, while en route to Fort Jesup, Taylor was ordered to Florida to take command of a field force. He defeated a Seminole band at Lake Okeechobee on December 25, a victory that was to prove decisive in the course of the long war with that tribe, and was brevetted brigadier general. In May 1838 he succeeded Gen. Thomas S. Jesup in command of the Department of Florida. He was unable to bring the war to a conclusion, however, and in April 1840, at his own request, he was relieved of that post. By that time he had acquired the affectionate sobriquet "Old Rough and Ready." After a year at Baton Rouge, Louisiana, he became commander of the Second Department, Western Division, at Fort Smith, Arkansas, in May 1841. In May 1844 he was ordered to the frontier at Fort Jesup, and in June 1845, with the annexation of Texas about to be completed and some reaction by Mexico expected, he was ordered into that territory. He established camp at Corpus Christi and by October had some 4000 men with him, including some volunteers and a company of Texas Rangers for scouts. In February 1846 he was ordered to advance to the Rio Grande, and the next month he established his main camp at Port Isabel and a forward post some 20 miles upriver at Fort Texas (later Fort Brown) opposite Matamoros. Hostilities with Mexican forces under Gen. Mariano Arista began quickly with a skirmish near Fort Texas on April 25. Taylor then publicly called for volunteers. On May 8, advancing with 2200 men from Port Isabel to Fort Texas, he met more than 4000 Mexicans at Palo Alto and in a battle marked by an artillery duel broke their ranks. The next day Arista regrouped in a series of dry river beds at Resaca de la Guerra; Taylor, attacking from Resaca de la Palma (which gave its name to the battle), overcame stubborn Mexican resistance in a battle of hand-to-hand fighting. Mexican casualties for the two battles exceeded 1200; the Americans' were 180. News of these victories and of the occupation of Matamoros on May 18 arrived in Washington, D.C., soon after the declaration of war on May 13, and Taylor, instantly a public hero, was brevetted major general and named commander of the Army of the Rio Grande. In July he moved his base farther up the Rio Grande to Camargo, and in

September he set out at the head of 6200 troops, half regulars and half volunteers, for Monterrey (thousands of untrained, unequipped volunteers were in camps along the river and coast or had already been sent home). He attacked the heavily fortified city, defended by more than 7000 troops, on September 20; hammered at it relentlessly; and on September 24 allowed the Mexican troops to surrender and depart peacefully under an eight-week armistice. On learning of Taylor's actions President James K. Polk repudiated the armistice and ordered Taylor to advance. He occupied Saltillo in mid-November but then learned that Gen. Winfield Scott was commandeering nearly all of his regulars, some 4000, and an equal number of volunteers to begin an entirely new campaign at Veracruz. He was ordered by Scott to remain on the defensive in Monterrey. Correctly judging that politics had entered into the conduct of the war (Polk feared both Taylor and Scott as potential presidential candidates), he chose to interpret Scott's orders as advice, and in February 1847 he moved farther south with 4650 troops. Unknown to him until February 21, Gen. Santa Anna had marched north from San Luis Potosí with 15,000 men. On February 22 Taylor, his army positioned at Buena Vista, refused a surrender demand; preliminary skirmishing occurred in the afternoon. The main battle took place the next day and was the most bitterly fought of the campaign; the tide was carried for the Americans by Maj. Braxton Bragg's artillery, Col. Jefferson Davis's Mississippi Rifles, and Taylor's inspiring presence. Santa Anna's army retreated with a loss of nearly 2000 men, and the war in the northern theater was over. Taylor was ordered to remain in Mexico until November. By that time he was beginning to receive serious consideration by the Whigs as a presidential candidate. He was already something of a Whig by inclination, although he had never voted in a presidential election, and his status as a slaveholder was an advantage as it would attract Southern support for a party suspected of Northern sympathies. At the Whig convention in Philadelphia in June 1848 he was nominated over Henry Clay, Daniel Webster, and Gen. Scott, and, aided by a Democratic split, was elected President in November (with Vice-President Millard Fillmore) with 163 electoral votes over Lewis Cass (127) and Martin Van Buren (running as a Free-Soiler, 0). He took office in March 1849 with virtually no knowledge of the political process but determined to preside over a neutral, nonpartisan administration. Although he adapted himself to the patronage system, he soon came into conflict with other party leaders over the admission of California and New Mexico to the Union. He strongly resented opposition to his own policy of encouraging admission of new states without reference to the status of slavery in them, and he opposed the injection of sectionalism into the issue. He was contemptuous of

Southern leaders who threatened secession should California enter the Union as a free state, and he referred with disdain to the proposals of the later Compromise of 1850 as the "Omnibus Bill." The signal achievement of his administration was the conclusion in April 1850 of the Clayton-Bulwer Treaty with England, providing for joint control of any canal built across the Central American isthmus. In mid-1850 he was troubled by a scandal involving three of his cabinet advisers and decided to reorganize the entire cabinet; before any of these matters was resolved, however, he became seriously ill following a July 4th celebration and died on July 9, 1850, in Washington, D.C.

Tecumseh (1768–1813), Indian leader. Born in 1768 in the Shawnee village of Old Piqua near present-day Springfield, Ohio, Tecumseh (Tecumtha or Tikamthi) was reared by a chief, Blackfish, after the death of his father in the battle of Point Pleasant at the end of Lord Dunmore's War in October 1774. During and after the period of the Revolution he was a prominent warrior in the raids and skirmishes that kept the frontier of white settlement in the Old Northwest in a state of virtual siege. At the same time he took a strong and effective stand against the common Indian practices of torture and killing of captives. He was a leader at the defeat of the Indians by Gen. Anthony Wayne at Fallen Timbers, August 20, 1794, but refused to take part in the negotiation of the Treaty of Greenville in August 1795 on the ground that Indian lands belonged to all Indians of all tribes in common and could not be sold or ceded by any number of chiefs. In propounding his views in councils Tecumseh gained a wide reputation for oratory, sometimes being compared with young Henry Clay. In 1808 he moved from Ohio to the Indiana country and settled near the mouth of Tippecanoe Creek on the Wabash with his brother, Tenskwatawa, who became known as "the Prophet" on his claim to have had a revelation from the "Master of Life." Together they preached a return to old ways, instructing their followers to give up intermarriage and white habits, particularly whiskey, and to seek to regain the purity of Indian life. Armed with the mystical appeal of the Prophet's visions and his own eloquence, Tecumseh began carrying his message to distant tribes, and he slowly forged a general confederation of tribes that, he believed, could successfully oppose further white expansion. He traveled as far as Iowa in the West and New York and Florida in the East, and he was particularly successful in influencing the Creeks and their allies in the South. His principal opponent in this work was William Henry Harrison, governor of Indiana Territory, who kept pressure on the fragile confederacy by making a series of treaties with individual tribes, notably the Treaty of Fort Wayne of September 1809 by which 2.5 million acres on the upper Wabash were ceded by a few tribes. Tecumseh thereupon redoubled his efforts to nullify such arrangements. By the summer of 1811 he had returned to the Southeastern tribes to rally their support, and he had some hope of aid from the British in Canada. In his absence Gov. Harrison took the initiative, leading a force of about 1000 men to the Indian village at Tippecanoe. He camped nearby and opened negotiations, but on the morning of November 7, 1811, the Prophet, contrary to Tecumseh's orders, led an attack on Harrison's camp. The Indians were repulsed, their village was burned, and Harrison marched back to Vincennes. On his return Tecumseh found the heart of his confederacy scattered. With war between the United States and Great Britain imminent he led his remaining followers to Canada and joined the British forces at Fort Malden. He commanded a large force of Indians and whites in the campaign against Detroit in August 1812, receiving a British commission as brigadier general for his part in the battle of Maguaga, August 9, against Col. James Miller and the 4th U.S. Infantry. He also took part, under Gen. Henry Proctor, in the invasion of Ohio and the sieges of Fort Meigs and Fort Stephenson in April–August 1813. During the British withdrawal through Upper Canada (Ontario) Tecumseh and his 2000 men covered the rear. At the Thames River on October 5, 1813, they were attacked by 3500 men under Gen. Harrison; in the battle Tecumseh was killed, reputedly by Col. Richard M. Johnson.

Terry, Alfred Howe (1827–1890), army officer. Born in Hartford, Connecticut, on November 10, 1827, Terry attended Yale Law School for a year, leaving on being admitted to the bar in 1849. He entered private practice and from 1854 to 1860 served as clerk of the New Haven County court. From 1854 he was colonel of the 2nd Regiment of Connecticut militia, which was mustered into federal service for a three-month period at the outbreak of the Civil War and which he commanded at the battle of Bull Run (Manassas), July 21, 1861. Later he raised the 7th Connecticut Volunteers, receiving a commission as colonel in September 1861. He commanded that regiment in Gen. Thomas W. Sherman's occupation of Port Royal, South Carolina, in November 1861 and in the capture of Fort Pulaski, Georgia, in April 1862, receiving promotion to brigadier general of volunteers in the latter month. Until late 1863 he was engaged in operations at Charleston, South Carolina, particularly those on Morris Island and the sieges of Fort Wagner and Fort Sumter. He was then transferred to the Army of the James under Gen. Benjamin F. Butler. He took part in operations on the James River and around Richmond and Petersburg, receiving a brevet as major general of volunteers in August 1864, and in October–December commanded the X

Corps. After Butler's failure to capture Fort Fisher at Wilmington, North Carolina, in December, Gen. Ulysses S. Grant gave the task to Terry. With naval support from Adm. David D. Porter, he carried the fort by assault on January 15, 1865. For that accomplishment he was commissioned brigadier general of regulars and in March brevetted major general. After occupying Wilmington he marched inland with the X Corps and joined Gen. William T. Sherman near Goldsboro, North Carolina, in April. In that month he was promoted to major general of volunteers. In 1866, mustered out of volunteer service, he was given command of the Department of Dakota. During 1869–1872 he commanded the Department of the South, and in the latter year he returned to command of the Department of Dakota at Fort Snelling, Minnesota. Following the invasion by whites of the treaty-reserved Black Hills in 1874–1875 and the failure of Sitting Bull and Crazy Horse and their followers to obey an order to settle on reservations by the end of January 1876, Gen. Philip H. Sheridan, commander of the Division of the Missouri, ordered a three-pronged expedition against the Sioux. Terry was to march west from Fort Abraham Lincoln (opposite Bismarck, in what is now North Dakota) and join columns coming north under Gen. George Crook and east under Col. John Gibbon. Crook was turned back at the Rosebud, but Terry and Gibbon rendezvoused on the Yellowstone in mid-June 1876. Terry sent his main force, the 7th Cavalry under Lt. Col. George A. Custer, to reconnoiter toward the Bighorn River. The battle of Little Bighorn ensued on June 25, and the survivors of Custer's regiment were relieved by the arrival of Terry on June 27. (Terry took no part in the long-lived controversy over whether Custer had obeyed the letter of his orders.) Despite that disaster the campaign continued, and the victories of Crook at Slim Buttes on September 9, Col. Ranald S. Mackenzie at Crazy Woman Creek on November 25, and Col. Nelson A. Miles at Wolf Mountain on January 7, 1877, largely ended Sioux resistance; the diehards under Sitting Bull escaped to Canada. In October 1877 Terry met with Sitting Bull at Fort Walsh in Canada in an unsuccessful attempt to persuade him to return to the United States. Promoted to major general in March 1886, Terry continued to command the Department of Dakota until April of that year, when he became commander of the Division of the Missouri. He retired in April 1888 and died in New Haven, Connecticut, on December 16, 1890.

Thatcher, Henry Knox (1806–1880), naval officer. Born in Thomaston, Maine (then a part of Massachusetts), on May 26, 1806, Thatcher was a grandson of Gen. Henry Knox. He entered West Point in 1822 but left a few months later and in March 1823 was appointed a midshipman in the navy. After a year in Commodore David Porter's squadron in the West

Indies he served in 1824–1827 on the *United States*, Commodore Isaac Hull's flagship in the Pacific Squadron. Over the next several decades he made cruises in the West Indies on the *Erie* in 1831 and the *Falmouth* in 1834, in the Mediterranean on the *Brandywine* in 1839–1841, in the Africa Squadron on the *Jamestown* in 1847–1850, and with the Brazil Squadron in command of the *Relief* in 1851–1852, serving betweentimes several tours at the Boston navy yard and other shore stations and receiving promotion to lieutenant in February 1833. After a year as executive officer of the Naval Asylum in Philadelphia he was promoted to commander in September 1855, and in 1857–1859 he commanded the *Decatur* of the Pacific Squadron. At the outbreak of the Civil War he was once again at the Boston navy yard, whence he proceeded in November 1861 to Portsmouth, New Hampshire, to take command of the corvette *Constellation*. While cruising that vessel in the Mediterranean, he was promoted two grades to commodore in July 1862, and a year later he was called home to command the frigate *Colorado* in the North Atlantic Blockading Squadron. He commanded the first division of the squadron during the attacks by Adm. David D. Porter on Fort Fisher, December 24–25, 1864, and January 13–15, 1865. In the latter month he was named acting rear admiral to succeed Adm. David G. Farragut in command of the West Gulf Blockading Squadron. His squadron cooperated with Gen. Edward R. S. Canby in the final capture of Mobile, Alabama, in April and captured the remaining Confederate naval forces there after a chase up the Tombigbee River. He then occupied the defenses before Galveston and other points on the Texas coast and on June 5 the city of Galveston itself. He commanded the combined Gulf Squadron until May 1866, when he took command of the North Pacific Squadron aboard the flagship *Pensacola*. He was promoted to rear admiral in July 1866, and he retired in May 1868. During 1869–1870 he served as port admiral of Portsmouth, New Hampshire. Thatcher died in Boston on April 5, 1880.

Thayer, Sylvanus (1785–1872), army officer and educator. Born in Braintree, Massachusetts, on June 9, 1785, Thayer attended Dartmouth College in 1807 and graduated from West Point in 1808. He was commissioned in the engineers and until 1812 was engaged in coastal fortification work in New York and New England, serving also for a time as an instructor at West Point. Promoted to first lieutenant in July 1812, he served on the staffs of Gen. Henry Dearborn and Gen. Wade Hampton on the northern frontier in the early part of the War of 1812 and was later at Norfolk, Virginia. He advanced to captain in October 1813 and was brevetted major in February 1815 for his services during the war. During 1815–1817 he made a tour of inspection of European military in-

stallations and schools, and on his return he was appointed in July 1817 superintendent of the Military Academy at West Point. The Academy was then in a state of near-chaos under the inept administration of Capt. Alden Partridge. Thayer immediately set about reforming the entire institution. Incompetents in the cadet body and faculty were weeded out; the cadets were organized into disciplined tactical companies and into classes based on instructional level, and all were put under a commandant of cadets; and a rigorous and regular four-year curriculum was established under an Academic Board. Regular examinations, weekly reports, and merit listings kept academic standards high, and tactical exercises under cadet officers and summer encampments for field exercises developed proficiency in purely military activities. Under Thayer's leadership the Academy developed from little better than a secondary school into a college whose liberal arts program was distinguished and whose engineering training, for many years unique in the United States, was on a par with the best European schools. The acquisition of such professors as Dennis Hart Mahan ensured that the military education would be the broadest and most useful offered anywhere. Thayer, justifiably called "the father of West Point," was brevetted lieutenant colonel in March 1823, promoted to major in May 1828, and brevetted colonel in March 1833. The course of his 16-years' superintendency was not entirely smooth, however; particularly in the early years there was much resentment among cadets of Thayer's strict discipline, and outbreaks in 1818 and 1826 challenged his authority. He was regularly upheld by his superiors, notably Secretary of War John C. Calhoun, until the period of Andrew Jackson's presidency. Jackson did not like Thayer personally, and he profoundly distrusted the notion of a professional regular army cadre as essentially antidemocratic. After numerous disagreements, including Jackson's reinstatement of several cadets dismissed by Thayer, Thayer was relieved of the superintendency at his own request in July 1833. For the next 25 years he was engaged in harbor improvement and fortification work in New England, and he served also as president of the Board of Engineers from December 1838 and on other boards. He was promoted to lieutenant colonel of engineers in July 1838 and colonel in March 1863. On leave of absence owing to ill health from 1858, he retired with the brevet rank of brigadier general in June 1863. In 1867 he endowed the Thayer School of Engineering at Dartmouth and drew up its curriculum and requirements. Thayer died in Braintree, Massachusetts, on September 7, 1872.

Thomas, George Henry (1816–1870), army officer. Born in Southampton County, Virginia, on July 31, 1816, Thomas graduated from West Point in 1840 and was commissioned in the artillery. After two years of service in the field against the Seminole Indians of Florida, during which he was brevetted first lieutenant in 1841, he served at various garrison posts in the South and was promoted to first lieutenant in 1844. In 1845 he was attached to the artillery battery under Maj. Braxton Bragg in Gen. Zachary Taylor's army in Texas, and in the Mexican War he was brevetted captain at Monterrey, September 20–24, 1846, and major at Buena Vista, February 22–23, 1847. During 1849–1851 he was again in Florida, and from 1851 to 1854 he was an instructor at West Point, receiving promotion to captain in December 1853. In May 1855, after a year in California and Arizona with the 3rd Artillery, he was appointed major in the newly organized 2nd Cavalry under Col. Albert S. Johnston. He served with that regiment in Texas until November 1860, when he took leave of absence. He returned to active duty as a lieutenant colonel in April 1861 and took command at Carlisle Barracks, Pennsylvania, of the remains of his regiment, which had been surrendered in Texas by Gen. David E. Twiggs and shorn of most of its officers, who had gone over to the Confederacy—Johnston, Robert E. Lee, William J. Hardee, John B. Hood, Fitzhugh Lee, Earl Van Dorn. In May Thomas was promoted to colonel of the 2nd Cavalry, and after preliminary operations in the Shenandoah valley at the head of a brigade of Pennsylvania volunteers he was appointed brigadier general of volunteers in August. In November he took command of the 1st Division, Army of the Ohio, and on January 19, 1862, he defeated a force of 4000 Confederates commanded by Gen. George B. Crittenden and led by Gen. Felix K. Zollicoffer (who was killed) at Mill Springs, Kentucky. After taking part in the battle of Shiloh (Pittsburg Landing), April 6–7, he was promoted to major general of volunteers later in that month and given command of the right wing of Gen. Henry W. Halleck's advance on Corinth, Mississippi. In June he resumed command of a division in Gen. Don Carlos Buell's Army of the Ohio. By the end of September Buell had lost favor in Washington, and Thomas was offered his command, but he declined out of loyalty to Buell and served as second-in-command at Perryville, October 8. He at first protested and then acquiesced in serving under a former junior when Buell was replaced by Gen. William S. Rosecrans. Under a reorganization Thomas gained command of the XIV Corps in Rosecrans's Army of the Cumberland. At Stones River (Murfreesboro), December 31–January 3, 1863, he proved himself a stubborn and capable fighter. He ably supported Rosecrans through the Tullahoma campaign in the summer of 1863. At Chickamauga he commanded the left from the opening of the battle on September 18 and bore the brunt of Bragg's attack on September 20; when an error by Rosecrans left a hole in the Union line and Gen.

James Longstreet drove through, the Union right melted away and Thomas was left unsupported on the field, his line bent double but not broken. For his stout resistance there, which ultimately discouraged Bragg, he earned the nickname "the Rock of Chickamauga," which he shared with the 19th Infantry, the central unit in his defense. Thomas withdrew his forces back to Chattanooga and rejoined Rosecrans, and Bragg's siege ensued. In October he succeeded Rosecrans in command of the Army of the Cumberland, receiving promotion to brigadier general of regulars in the same month. With the aid of reinforcements under Gen. Joseph Hooker, Thomas reopened his supply lines and gradually secured positions outside the city. The arrival of more troops under Gen. William T. Sherman and of Gen. Ulysses S. Grant as overall commander led to the lifting of the siege in the battles of Lookout Mountain and Missionary Ridge, November 24–25, in which Thomas's troops distinguished themselves in a gallant charge to the ridge. In the spring and summer of 1864 Thomas took part as second-in-command in Sherman's Atlanta campaign, in which his Army of the Cumberland constituted over half of Sherman's troops. He bore the weight of Gen. John B. Hood's attack at Peachtree Creek, July 20. After the occupation of Atlanta in September Sherman reorganized his army and gave Thomas two infantry and one cavalry corps with which to return to and protect the vital supply base at Nashville. Using Gen. John M. Schofield's two corps to delay Hood, he reached Nashville in November and began slowly building his forces for a decisive strike against Hood. His delay exasperated Grant, who twice was at the point of removing him, but on December 15–16 he executed a tactically masterful attack that completely shattered Hood's Army of Tennessee. He was promptly promoted to major general of regulars. He commanded the Division of the Tennessee through the rest of the war and the Departments of the Tennessee and the Cumberland afterwards. He was transferred to command of the Division of the Pacific in June 1869. Thomas died in San Francisco on March 28, 1870. The slowness of his advancement during the Civil War, stemming at first from his Southern birth and later from his diffidence concerning personal glory, partly hides a record of victories unexcelled by any other Union commander.

Thomas, John (1724–1776), colonial and Revolutionary army officer. Born on November 9, 1724, in Marshfield, Massachusetts, Thomas studied medicine and established a practice in Kingston, Massachusetts. In March 1746 he was appointed surgeon to a provincial regiment that was sent the next year to Nova Scotia. In February 1755 he was commissioned lieutenant and surgeon's mate. He again served in Nova Scotia in that year and yet again in 1759–1760, and in 1760 he rose to command of a regiment under

Gen. Jeffrey Amherst at Crown Point and Montreal. He then resumed his private practice. He was active in the Sons of Liberty before the outbreak of the Revolution and in February 1775 was appointed a brigadier general of Massachusetts militia. In May he was promoted to lieutenant general in command of the militia, and in June he was commissioned a brigadier general in the Continental army. He and his brigade occupied Roxbury during the siege of Boston, and on March 4, 1776, he led 3000 men in the occupation of Dorchester Heights, commanding Boston from the south. The successful fortification of that site forced the British to abandon Boston. Thomas was promoted to major general a few days later and ordered north to take command of the broken American army at Quebec. He arrived there on May 1 and discovered an army of fewer than 1000 effectives and rapidly dwindling supplies. He ordered a withdrawal. During the retreat he fell ill and died near Fort Chambly, Quebec, on June 2, 1776.

Thomas, Lorenzo (1804–1875), army officer. Born in New Castle, Delaware, on October 26, 1804, Thomas graduated from West Point in 1823 and was commissioned in the infantry. He served continuously in Florida from then until 1831. Promoted to captain in September 1836, he was again in Florida in 1836–1837 and saw action against the Seminole Indians. In July 1838 he was appointed an assistant adjutant general with brevet rank of major, and he served in that capacity in Washington, D.C., except for a brief period in 1839–1840 as chief of staff to Gen. Zachary Taylor in Florida, until the outbreak of the Mexican War in 1846. In that war he served as chief of staff to Gen. William O. Butler and won a brevet to lieutenant colonel for gallantry at Monterrey, September 20–24, 1846. He then returned to staff duty in Washington, receiving permanent rank of major in 1848. In 1853 he was appointed chief of staff to Gen. Winfield Scott, commanding general of the army. In March 1861 he was promoted to colonel and named adjutant general of the army. He was brevetted brigadier general in May and made permanent in that rank in August. As adjutant general he was responsible for recruitment, conscription, and other matters relating to the manning of the army, and he carried out his duties, as did most bureau chiefs of the day, as best he could, having had no preparation for the demands war would make. In March 1863, possibly as a cure for his administrative shortcomings, he was sent to the Mississippi valley to recruit troops for black regiments. Other similar duties kept him out of Washington until after the war. In March 1865 he was brevetted major general for services. In February 1868 he was recalled to Washington from inspection duty around the country by President Andrew Johnson, who a week later appointed him ad interim secretary of war to replace Edwin M. Stanton. Stanton had refused for months to give up his post and had carried his point with Gen. Ulysses S. Grant, who had been ad interim secretary from August 1867 until Stanton requested him to relinquish the office to him in January 1868. Thomas was another sort, however, and he proclaimed that he would oust Stanton by force if need be. Stanton, backed by Congress, promptly had Thomas arrested for violation of the Tenure of Office Act, the act over which Johnson was subsequently impeached. Thomas resumed his duties as adjutant general until retiring from the army in February 1869. He died in Washington, D.C., on March 2, 1875.

Thompson, John Taliaferro (1860–1940), army officer and inventor. Born on December 30, 1860, in Newport, Kentucky, Thompson entered Indiana University in 1877 but a year later transferred to West Point. He graduated in 1882, was commissioned in the artillery, and after completing the torpedo course at the Engineering School of Application at Willett's Point (now Fort Totten), New York, in 1884 he served at a succession of armories and garrison posts. He was promoted to first lieutenant in January 1889 and transferred to the Ordnance Department in December 1890. During 1896–1898 he was an instructor at West Point, and, promoted to captain in June 1898, he served with the rank of lieutenant colonel of volunteers as chief ordnance officer of the IV Corps at Tampa, Florida, and in Cuba during the Spanish–American War. From 1899 to 1907 he was stationed at the arsenals at Rock Island, Illinois, and Springfield, Massachusetts, advancing to major in June 1906; and from 1907 to 1914 he was chief assistant to Gen. William Crozier, chief of army ordnance. He was promoted to lieutenant colonel in January 1909 and to colonel in October 1913, and he served also during that period as a lecturer at the Army War College. He retired from the army in November 1914 and became a consulting engineer with the Remington Arms-Union Metallic Cartridge Company, for which he built a huge new plant at Eddystone, Pennsylvania, to manufacture rifles for the Allied armies in World War I. Shortly after the entry of the United States into the war in April 1917 he returned to active service, and he was promoted to temporary rank of brigadier general in August 1918. Put in charge of design and manufacture of small arms and ammunition for the army, he quickly discovered that the model 1903 Springfield rifle then being manufactured at Rock Island and Springfield could not be produced quickly enough, while the .303-caliber Enfield rifle being produced privately for the Allies was actually being turned out in surplus. He redesigned the Enfield to take army standard .30-caliber ammunition, and by the armistice in November 1918 American plants had turned out 2.5 million of the American Enfield, designated M1917, more than

Britain and France combined and at a lower cost. In 1919 Thompson returned to private consulting, mainly with the Auto-Ordnance Corporation, and in 1920 he patented the Thompson submachine gun, a light, fully automatic shoulder weapon firing .45-caliber ammunition with great reliability. The "tommy gun," as it became known, was adopted by the army in 1928 for use with mechanized cavalry, and it was also used by the navy and the marine corps and bought in quantity by other nations. It became notorious in the 1920s as the weapon of choice for warring gangsters and for the FBI. In 1930 he severed his connection with Auto-Ordnance; from 1939 his guns were produced by the Thompson Automatic Arms Company, headed by his son, Marcellus H. Thompson. The elder Thompson died in Great Neck, New York, on June 21, 1940.

Thompson, William (1736–1781), Revolutionary army officer. Born in 1736 in Ireland, Thompson emigrated to America and settled near Carlisle, Pennsylvania. He served as captain of a mounted militia company during the French and Indian War, 1755–1763, during which he took part in the expedition under Lt. Col. John Armstrong against Kittanning in September 1756. He was active before the Revolution in the local committees of correspondence and safety, and when word of the battle of Bunker Hill reached southeastern Pennsylvania he was appointed colonel of the 2nd Pennsylvania Regiment, mustered into Continental service in August 1775 as the 1st Continental Infantry. He and the regiment served with distinction through the siege of Boston, repelling an attempted British landing at Lechmere Point on November 9. In March 1776 he was promoted to brigadier general, and in April he was ordered to Canada with 2000 reinforcements for the army at Quebec. He succeeded the ailing Gen. John Thomas as commander of the northern army but relinquished command early in June to Gen. John Sullivan. On June 7, on orders from Sullivan, he marched on the British garrison at Three Rivers; the treachery of his guide, along with the garrison's unexpected strength, turned the attack early on June 8 into a disaster in which Thompson was taken prisoner. Paroled to Pennsylvania in August, he was not exchanged until October 1780. During that time he entered into a public dispute with Congressman Thomas McKean, to whom he lost a libel judgment. Thompson died in Carlisle, Pennsylvania, on September 3, 1781.

Tilghman, Tench (1744–1786), Revolutionary army officer. Born on December 25, 1744, in Talbot County, Maryland, Tilghman was educated at the College, Academy, and Charitable School of Philadelphia (forerunner of the University of Pennsylvania), and on graduating in 1761 he became a merchant in Philadelphia. At the outbreak of the

Revolution he sold his business and became a lieutenant in a local company of light infantry. In July 1775 he served as secretary of the commission sent by the Continental Congress to treat with the Indians of the Six Nations, and in 1776, as captain of an independent Pennsylvania infantry company, he joined the Flying Camp commanded by Gen. Hugh Mercer. In August 1776 he was appointed military secretary and aide to Gen. George Washington, with whom he served throughout the rest of the war. He served for the most part without pay and earned Washington's highest regard by his tireless efforts. In May 1781, at Washington's urging, Congress awarded Tilghman a commission as lieutenant colonel to date from April 1777. When Gen. Charles Cornwallis surrendered at Yorktown on October 19, 1781, Washington gave Tilghman the honor of carrying the news to Congress in Philadelphia, a task he accomplished in four days, riding into the city on October 23 crying "Cornwallis is taken!" He then resumed mercantile pursuits in Baltimore, where he died on April 18, 1786.

Tilton, James (1745–1822), physician. Born on June 1, 1745, in Kent County, Delaware (then still a part of Pennsylvania), Tilton studied medicine privately and then in the College of Philadelphia (now the University of Pennsylvania), from which he graduated in 1768. He established a practice in Dover, Delaware, and returned to the college in 1771 to obtain an advanced degree. He held the rank of lieutenant in the local militia at the outbreak of the Revolution, and on the organization of the first Delaware Regiment in January 1776 he was appointed regimental surgeon. He served with the regiment in the New York and New Jersey campaigns, at Trenton (December 26, 1776), and at Princeton (January 3, 1777), where it was decimated. From then until October 1780 he had charge of military hospitals in Trenton, Princeton, and New Windsor, Maryland. His novel system, first tried at Trenton, of replacing hospital tents with dry, well ventilated log huts holding only six patients worked a vast improvement in hospital sanitation and the recovery rate for patients. In September 1780 he was promoted to senior hospital physician and surgeon, and he succeeded in establishing a seniority system for the Medical Corps. In that year he declined a professorship at the University of Pennsylvania. He supervised a hospital at Williamsburg, Virginia, during the Yorktown campaign of October 1781. Resuming his private practice in Dover, he sat in the Continental Congress in 1783–1785 and on several occasions in the Delaware legislature. From 1785 to 1801 he was state commissioner of loans. He then retired from medical practice and took up farming near Wilmington. In February 1813 he published *Economical Observations on Military Hospitals: and the Prevention and Cure of Diseases Incident to an Army*, thereby contributing his Revolutionary experience to the second war with Great Britain. Congress created in March 1813 the post of physician and surgeon general to the army, and in June Tilton was appointed to the post. He immediately undertook a tour of camps on the Niagara frontier, where appalling sanitary conditions prevailed, most notoriously at Sackett's Harbor. As a result of his observations there he issued in December 1814 *Regulations for the Medical Department,* clearly outlining the duties of Medical Corps officers. His post passed out of existence in June 1815, and he retired to his home near Wilmington, Delaware, where he died on May 14, 1822.

Tompkins, Sally Louisa (1833–1916), humanitarian and philanthropist. Born in Poplar Grove, Mathews County, Virginia, on November 9, 1833, Miss Tompkins grew up there and in Richmond. Coming from a wealthy family, she devoted most of her time to philanthropic undertakings. When the Civil War began, she turned a large house in Richmond into a hospital at her own expense and operated it as the Robertson Hospital throughout the war, until June 1865. In September 1861, following the building of several military hospitals around Richmond, President Jefferson Davis of the Confederate States issued an order discontinuing all private hospitals, but to circumvent his order in her case he commissioned Miss Tompkins a captain in the Confederate cavalry, making her the only woman to hold a Confederate commission. As "Captain Sally" (a title she carried the rest of her life) she was thereafter able to operate her hospital more efficiently than before and with the cooperation of the military. In the nearly four years her hospital was in operation, it cared for more than a thousand patients, of whom only 73 died, an amazing record unapproached by any other hospital in the war. After the war she continued her various philanthropies until financial reverses destroyed the family fortune. She died in Richmond on July 25, 1916, and was buried with military honors.

Torbert, Alfred Thomas Archimedes (1833–1880), army officer and diplomat. Born in Georgetown, Delaware, on July 1, 1833, Torbert graduated from West Point in 1855 and was commissioned in the infantry. Over the next several years he served in New Mexico, in Florida, in the Mormon expedition under Col. Albert S. Johnston in 1857–1858, and again in New Mexico, receiving promotion to first lieutenant in February 1861. In April of that year he was ordered to New Jersey to muster in volunteers for Civil War service, and he was appointed colonel of the 1st New Jersey Volunteer Infantry in September and promoted to captain of regulars in the same month. He led his regiment through the Peninsula campaign of March–July 1862 and in August was given a brigade in Gen. William B. Franklin's VI Corps. He led the brigade at second Bull Run (Manassas), August 29–30, Antietam (Sharpsburg), September 17, Fredericksburg, December 13, Chancellorsville, May 2–4, 1863, and Gettysburg, July 1–3, and was promoted to brigadier general of volunteers in November 1862. In April 1864 Torbert took command of the 1st Cavalry Division under Gen. Philip H. Sheridan. During Sheridan's campaigns in central Virginia Torbert distinguished himself particularly at Hawes's Shop, May 28, where he won a brevet to lieutenant colonel of regulars; Matadequin Creek, May 30; Cold Harbor, which he captured on May 31 and held until relieved by infantry troops; Trevilian Station, June 11–12, where he defeated Gen. Wade Hampton; and Darbytown, July 28. With the move of Sheridan's forces to the Shenandoah valley in August he was named commander of the cavalry of the middle military division, constituting three cavalry divisions; he received brevet rank of major general of volunteers early in September. He saw action at Winchester, September 19, where he successfully flanked the Confederate left and won brevet to colonel of regulars; Tom's Brook, October 9; and Cedar Creek, October 19, where his division was one of two in the Army of the Shenandoah that held the line until Sheridan's arrival on the field. From December 1864 to February 1865 Torbert was on leave of absence. In March he was brevetted brigadier general of regulars for Cedar Creek and major general of regulars for services, and from April to July he commanded the Army of the Shenandoah. After commanding military districts in Virginia he was mustered out of volunteer service in January 1866, and in October he resigned from the regular army. President Ulysses S. Grant appointed Torbert U.S. minister to El Salvador in April 1869. In December 1871 he became U.S. consul general in Havana, Cuba, and two years later he transferred to a similar post in Paris. He resigned in 1878 and returned to the United States. He sailed from New York in August 1880 to visit business interests in Mexico; his ship, the *Vera Cruz,* sank off the coast of Florida on August 29.

Totten, Joseph Gilbert (1788–1864), army officer and engineer. Born on August 23, 1788, in New Haven, Connecticut, Totten was appointed a cadet at West Point in November 1802; and in July 1805, the tenth graduate of the Academy, he was commissioned a second lieutenant of engineers. After a year as secretary to the surveyor general of the Northwest Territory (an uncle who was also his guardian and a mathematics professor at West Point) he resigned his commission in March 1806, but two years later he reentered the Corps of Engineers at the same rank. While engaged in the construction of Castle William and Fort Clinton in New York harbor, 1808–1812, he was promoted to first lieutenant in July 1810. Advanced to captain in July 1812, he served as chief engineer of the army on the Niagara frontier during the War of 1812, winning brevets to major in June 1813 and lieutenant colonel in September 1814. For the next 24 years he was engaged in coastal defense and river and harbor work, from 1818 to 1830 in association with Gen. Simon Bernard. He was especially closely connected with the construction of Fort Adams at Newport, Rhode Island. He advanced to major in 1818 and to lieutenant colonel in 1828, and with his promotion to colonel in December 1838 he became chief engineer of the army and inspector at West Point. He held those posts until his death, a period far longer than any predecessor or successor. He continued to serve on various engineering boards, and during the Mexican War he served as chief engineer of Gen. Winfield Scott's army, earning a brevet to brigadier general in March 1847 for his successful planning of the siege of Veracruz. He was a regent of the Smithsonian Institution from its founding in 1846. From its establishment in 1851 until 1858 and again in 1860–1864 he was a member of the Lighthouse Board, and he contributed signally to the solution of several difficult problems of lighthouse construction, notably for those at Seven-Foot Knoll near Baltimore and Minot's Ledge near Cohasset, Massachusetts. He also carried on experiments in the construction of emplacements for heavy ordnance. During 1859–1861 he conducted a detailed inspection of the defense requirements of the Pacific coast. He continued as chief of engineers after the outbreak of the Civil War, receiving promotion to brigadier general in March 1863 when the Corps of Engineers and the Topographical Engineers were merged. He was brevetted major general in April 1864, but he died the following day, April 22, in Washington, D.C. Willett's Point, New York, home of the Engineer School of Application from 1885 to 1901, was renamed Fort Totten in his honor in the latter year on its conversion to a coast artillery fort.

Towers, John Henry (1885–1955), naval officer and airman. Born on January 30, 1885, in Rome, Georgia, Towers entered the Georgia School (now Institute) of Technology in 1901 but transferred to the Naval Academy a year later. He graduated in 1906, and during a cruise on the *Kentucky* he was commissioned an ensign in February 1908. He served subsequently on the *Kearsarge*, the *Indiana*, and the *Michigan* until 1911, when he took pilot instruction from Glenn Curtiss at Hammondsport, New York. In August of that year he became the third naval officer to qualify as an aviator. Promoted to lieutenant, he was stationed for two years at the navy's first air station, at Annapolis, Maryland, where in October 1912 he set a world endurance record for seaplanes. He later assisted in the establishment of the air station at San Diego, California, and the air station and

flying school at Pensacola, Florida. In April 1914 he commanded the small naval aviation unit attached to the occupation forces at Veracruz, Mexico. Later in that year he was named assistant naval attaché in London. From 1916 to 1919 he was executive officer of the aviation division in the office of the chief of naval operations, and he served also on a joint army-navy board on military aircraft specifications and on the National Advisory Committee for Aeronautics. He was promoted to commander in June 1918. During World War I he conceived a plan for a transatlantic flight of naval seaplanes, and after extensive preparations (and the end of the war) he commanded the flight of three NC (Navy-Curtiss) aircraft in May 1919. He flew the NC-3, which was forced down in heavy weather off Faial in the Azores; he rigged a sail and made harbor at Ponta Delgada two days later on May 19. (The NC-4, Lt. Cmdr. Albert C. Read, completed the crossing.) From 1919 to 1921 Towers served on the *Aroostook* and the *Mugford* in the Pacific, and from 1921 to 1923 he was at Pensacola. In 1923 he was appointed assistant naval attaché in London again, with additional duties that took him to many other European capitals. In 1925 he was again attached to the air wing of the Pacific Fleet, and in 1926 he joined the carrier *Langley*, of which he became captain in 1927. In 1928 he was ordered to the Bureau of Aeronautics, of which he became assistant chief in April 1929, receiving promotion to captain. In June 1931 he was named chief of staff to the aircraft commander, Battle Fleet. During 1933–1934 he was an instructor at the Naval War College, and in 1934–1936 he commanded the naval air station at San Diego. From 1936 to 1937 he was again chief of staff to the aircraft commander, Battle Fleet, and after a year as commander of the carrier *Saratoga* and another as assistant chief of the Bureau of Aeronautics he was promoted to rear admiral and made chief of the bureau in June 1939. He held that post until October 1942, during which time he oversaw a nearly twenty-fold increase in the navy's aircraft strength. In October 1942 he became commander of the Air Force, Pacific Fleet, with the rank of vice admiral and with responsibility for naval and marine aviation training, supply, organization, and operations in that theater. In February 1944 he was named deputy to Adm. Chester W. Nimitz, commander of Pacific Ocean Areas and the Pacific Fleet. During 1945 he held sea commands briefly with the 2nd Carrier Task Force of Task Force 38 (58), succeeding Adm. Marc A. Mitscher in command of 38 in September, and with the Fifth Fleet in November. Promoted to admiral in the latter month, he succeeded Adm. Raymond A. Spruance as commander of the Pacific Fleet and the Pacific Ocean Areas in December. He retired from the navy in December 1947. During 1948–1949 he was assistant to the president of Pan-American World Airways; he became a vice-president of the firm in

1949 and held the post until 1953. Towers died in St. Albans, Queens, New York, on April 30, 1955.

Towle, Katherine Amelia (1898–), educator and marine officer. Born on April 30, 1898, in Towle, California, Katherine Towle graduated from the University of California at Berkeley in 1920, and after a year as assistant admissions officer at the school she spent a year, 1922–1923, in advanced study at Columbia University. She then rejoined the administrative staff at Berkeley. In 1927 she was named resident dean of a private girls' school in Piedmont, California, and she became headmistress in 1929. In 1933 she resumed studies in political science at Berkeley, receiving a master's degree in 1935. From that year to 1942 she was assistant to the manager and a senior editor of the University of California Press. In February 1943 she took a commission as captain in the newly established Women's Reserve (WR) of the marine corps. Until September 1944 her duties were divided between corps headquarters in Washington, D.C., and the women's training centers at Hunter College, New York City, and, from June 1943, at Camp Lejeune, North Carolina. Promoted to major in February 1944, she became in September assistant director of the WR, advancing to lieutenant colonel in March 1945, and in December 1945 she was promoted to colonel and named director to succeed Col. Ruth C. Streeter. Towle remained in that post until June 1946, when the WR was inactivated. During 1946–1947 she served as administrative assistant to the vice-president and provost of the University of California, and in July 1947 she was appointed assistant dean of women. With the passage of the Women's Armed Forces Integration Act of June 12, 1948, the women's reserve of the marine corps, like those of the other arms, was integrated into the active line. Col. Towle was recalled to active duty as director in October. She retired from that post in May 1953. She then served as dean of women and associate dean of students at the University of California at Berkeley from 1953 to 1962 and as dean of students from 1962 until her retirement.

Travis, William Barret (1809–1836), lawyer and Texas army officer. Born near Red Banks, Edgefield County, South Carolina, on August 9, 1809, Travis grew up there and in Conecuh County, Alabama, where the family moved when he was nine. He attended a military academy in South Carolina for a while, then returned to Alabama and studied law privately. He was admitted to the bar before he was twenty years old. An unhappy marriage impelled him to leave Alabama in 1831, and he made his way to Texas and opened a law office first in Anahuac and in October 1832 in San Felipe. Almost from the day he arrived in Texas he was partial to the "war party," that minority of Anglo-Texans who wanted inde-

pendence from Mexico. In May 1832 the Mexican authorities declared Anahuac, the port of Galveston, under martial law, and Travis was arrested along with other Anglo-Texans. After a near-rebellion the prisoners were released. The crisis in Texas affairs abated, although the war party remained active. In October 1835 the crisis was renewed when the president of Mexico, Gen. Antonio de Santa Anna, abolished all local legislatures, dissolved the Congress, and became a virtual dictator. The war party redoubled its activities. When Anahuac was garrisoned in January 1835, Travis gathered two dozen followers and forced the surrender of the Mexican soldiers on June 30. This unnecessary gambit on the part of the war hawks aroused much Mexican resentment and was denounced even by the majority of Anglo-Texans. Events moved toward a confrontation between the Anglo-Texan and Mexican forces, and on December 10, after a brief siege, Mexican forces surrendered San Antonio to the Texans. This surrender enraged Santa Anna, who moved northward with a large army to put an end to the Texas problem once and for all. Travis was now enrolled in the Texas cavalry with the rank of lieutenant colonel. As the Texans prepared themselves for war, Travis was sent to the fortified mission called the Alamo in San Antonio with a few reinforcements on February 3. Col. James Bowie commanded the volunteers at the Alamo and Travis the regulars, and between them they had altogether slightly more than 150 men. For reasons which are unclear both men were determined to hold out, even in the face of the overwhelming numbers—6000 to 7000—of Santa Anna's approaching army. Since none of the Alamo defenders survived the siege, the situation is not well documented, but it is known that the entire garrison could have escaped even after Santa Anna's army arrived on February 23. Bowie fell ill shortly thereafter, leaving Travis in full command. On March 6, 1836, the Alamo fell in a final assault and all 187 or 188 defenders (32 men had secretly entered during the siege) died, Travis, Bowie, and Davy Crockett among them. The toll among the Mexican forces was far higher, with nearly 1600 dead and a larger number wounded. The battle was lost, but Travis, in losing, had given the newly declared Republic of Texas a rallying cry—"Remember the Alamo!"—and desperately needed time to prepare for the defeat of Santa Anna, which was accomplished some weeks later by Gen. Sam Houston at San Jacinto.

Tregaskis, Richard William (1916–1973), journalist. Born on November 28, 1916, in Elizabeth, New Jersey, Tregaskis graduated from Harvard in 1938. From that year until 1941 he was a feature writer for the *Boston American*, with which he had formed a connection while still in college. In 1941 he joined the International News Service, by which he was sent to

Hawaii following the Japanese attack at Pearl Harbor. He became the chief INS correspondent with the Pacific Fleet, and he covered the battle of the Coral Sea, Col. James H. Doolittle's raid on Tokyo, the battle of Midway, and the Solomons campaign. On August 7, 1942, he went ashore at Guadalcanal with the first boatload of marines from the 1st Marine Division. He remained in the thick of the fighting for the island until September, when he returned to Honolulu and quickly produced a manuscript that was published early in 1943 as *Guadalcanal Diary*. The book soon became one of the best-selling books about World War II and by the end of the year had been turned into a perennially popular motion picture. In 1943 he was sent to the Mediterranean theater, where he covered the campaigns in Sicily and Italy, receiving a serious head wound in the latter; in 1944 he joined the Allied armies in France. In 1945 he returned to the war in the Pacific for the *Saturday Evening Post*. From 1946 he was a freelance foreign correspondent. His experiences filled such books as *Invasion Diary*, 1944, *Stronger than Fear*, 1945, *Seven Leagues to Paradise*, 1951, *X-15 Diary*, 1961, *Last Plane to Shanghai*, 1961, *John F. Kennedy and PT-109*, 1962, and *Vietnam Diary*, 1963. He also wrote a number of motion-picture screenplays, including *The Wide Blue Yonder*, 1951, and *Mission over Korea*, 1953, as well as novels and a volume of poetry. Tregaskis covered nine wars in his long career as foreign correspondent. He died in Honolulu, Hawaii, on August 15, 1973.

Trumbull, Joseph (1737–1778), Revolutionary army officer. Born in Lebanon, Connecticut, on March 11, 1737, Trumbull was the son of Jonathan Trumbull, governor of Connecticut in 1769–1784, and the elder brother of the younger Jonathan, also governor and senator, and of John, painter of the Revolutionary period. He graduated from Harvard in 1756 and for a decade concerned himself with managing the family farm. He sat in the colonial assembly almost continuously from 1767 to 1773. In May 1773 he was named to the Connecticut committee of correspondence and in August 1774 chosen as Roger Sherman's alternate in the First Continental Congress. In April 1775 he was appointed commissary general to the Connecticut troops serving at Boston. His ability impressed Gen. George Washington, at whose urging Congress named Trumbull commissary general of the Continental army with the rank of colonel on July 19, 1775. The army's situation around Boston was such that provisioning was a simple matter, but during the year 1776 serious problems began to arise. British occupation of forts, difficult transportation, the inefficiency of Congress, recalcitrance on the part of state officials, and occasionally the corruption of subordinates made Trumbull's position increasingly less pleasant. He came into conflict with Gen. Philip J. Schuyler in 1776 over author-

ity to control provisioning of the northern army, and late in the year he retired to Connecticut, leaving Washington's army to winter near Morristown under the care of a deputy commissary later shown to be corrupt. In the spring of 1777 Congress and Washington agreed on a division of the commissary function into separate purchasing and issuing authorities, with Trumbull to retain the former. By this time his sensitivity to criticism was contributing to the breakdown of his health. In November 1777 he resigned his post, leaving the department in the still-chaotic condition that was to produce the terrible Valley Forge winter of 1777–1778. From November 1777 to April 1778 Trumbull was a member of the Board of War, but ill health prevented him from taking an active part. He died in Lebanon, Connecticut, on July 23, 1778.

Truscott, Lucian King, Jr. (1895–1965), army officer. Born on January 9, 1895, in Chatfield, Texas, Truscott grew up there and in Oklahoma. From 1911 he was a teacher in various small schools in Oklahoma. On the entry of the United States into World War I in 1917 he enlisted in the army, and after attending an officers' training camp in Arkansas he was commissioned a reserve second lieutenant of cavalry in August and commissioned in the regular cavalry and promoted to first lieutenant in October. From 1919 to 1921 he was stationed at Schofield Barracks, Hawaii, advancing to captain in 1920, and from 1922 to 1925 he was with the 1st Cavalry at Camp Douglas, Arizona. He graduated from the Cavalry School, Fort Riley, Kansas, in 1926 and, promoted to major, remained there as an instructor for five years. In 1931–1934 he was with the 3rd Cavalry at Fort Myer, Virginia. By 1936 he was a lieutenant colonel, and after his graduation from the Command and General Staff School, Fort Leavenworth, Kansas, in that year he again remained as an instructor. In September 1940 he was assigned to the 13th Armored Regiment at Fort Knox, Kentucky, and in July 1941 he was attached to the staff of the IX Corps area at Fort Lewis, Washington. Promoted to temporary colonel in December 1941 and temporary brigadier general in May 1942, he was assigned in the latter month to the Allied combined staff under Lord Louis Mountbatten. After studying the training methods used by British commandos, he recruited and trained a brigade of Rangers along the same lines, developing a small corps of tough, highly motivated shock troops. On August 19, 1942, he led his Rangers in a joint cross-Channel raid with commandos on the French port of Dieppe, an action that cost heavy casualties and taught vital lessons in amphibious techniques. In November, promoted to temporary major general, he led a special task force in the capture of Port Lyautey (now Kenitra), French Morocco, from Vichy French forces during the Allied invasion of North Africa. After a period as field deputy to Gen. Dwight D. Eisenhower he took command of the 3rd Infantry Division in March 1943. The 3rd landed in Sicily on July 10 as part of Gen. George S. Patton's Seventh Army and led in the capture of Palermo and Messina. On September 18 it went ashore to reinforce the Allied beachhead at Salerno, Italy. On January 22, 1944, as part of the VI Corps under Gen. John P. Lucas, the 3rd Division assaulted the beach at Anzio. In February Truscott succeeded Lucas in command of the VI Corps. After withstanding furious German counterattacks the VI Corps finally broke out of the Anzio beachhead in May and drove toward Rome. After rest and retraining, the VI Corps, then consisting of the 3rd, 36th, and 45th divisions, formed part of Gen. Alexander M. Patch's Seventh Army in the landings at St. Tropez and St. Raphaël on the French south coast on August 15. Promoted to temporary lieutenant general in September, Truscott remained with the VI Corps until December, when he returned to Italy to take command of the Fifth Army from Gen. Mark W. Clark. Under his command the Fifth, part of Clark's 15th Army Group, launched a final major attack in the spring of 1945 across the Po valley, taking Bologna on April 21 and driving on until the German surrender of May 2. The Fifth Army was inactivated in October 1945 and Truscott then succeeded Gen. Patton in command of the Third Army in occupation duty in Bavaria. He returned to the United States in May 1946 and retired from the army in October 1947. In May 1951 he was named an adviser to the U.S. high commissioner for West Germany. In 1954 he published *Command Missions*, and in July of that year he was given an honorary promotion to general, retired, by act of Congress. Truscott died in Washington, D.C., on September 12, 1965.

Truxtun, Thomas (1755–1822), naval officer. Born near Hempstead, on Long Island, New York, on February 17, 1755, Truxtun had little formal schooling before he went to sea on a merchant ship at the age of twelve. His abilities were such that eight years later, having served a time as an impressed seaman on a British man-of-war, he was in command of his own ship. During the Revolution he sailed as a privateer against British shipping in the Atlantic, first as lieutenant on the *Congress* and from 1777 to 1782 in command of, in turn, the *Independence*, the *Mars*, and the *St. James,* capturing a large number of prizes. He returned to merchant shipping for 12 years after the war. He sailed in command of one of the first U.S. ships to engage in the China trade, the *Canton* out of Philadelphia in 1786. In June 1794 he was appointed a captain in the newly organized U.S. navy. He supervised the construction of the frigate *Constellation,* 36 guns, at Baltimore and sailed in command of her in June 1798 at the beginning of a two-year period of undeclared naval war with France. During that time

he served as commodore of a squadron based at St. Christopher in the Leeward Islands. On February 9, 1799, he captured after an hour's fight the French frigate *Insurgente*, 38, which was subsequently refitted as an American ship and sailed under Capt. John Rodgers. Truxtun returned home in May and sailed again for the West Indies in December. In a spectacular five-hour engagement on the night of February 1–2, 1800, near Guadaloupe, the *Constellation* outfought the frigate *La Vengeance* of much heavier armament; the French vessel escaped when it was discovered that the *Constellation*'s mainmast had been sheared. On his return home in March Truxtun received a hero's welcome. After commanding the *President* for a few months in 1800 he returned home to Perth Amboy, New Jersey. In 1801 he was designated to command a squadron bound for the Tripolitan War, but when his request that a captain be assigned to his intended flagship, the *Chesapeake,* was refused by the Jefferson administration, apparently on political grounds, he remonstrated, and the protest was gladly seized upon as a resignation. He then lived in retirement in Perth Amboy and, from 1806, in Philadelphia. He ran unsuccessfully as a Federalist for a seat in the House of Representatives in 1810 but was elected sheriff of Philadelphia in 1816 for a four-year term. Truxtun contributed to the science of navigation with his books *Remarks, Instructions, and Examples Relating to Latitude and Longitude,* 1794, and *Instructions, Signals, and Explanations Offered for the U.S. Fleet,* 1797. In 1806 he published an anthology of writings on naval tactics. He died in Philadelphia on May 5, 1822.

Tucker, John Randolph (1812–1883), Confederate naval officer. Born in Alexandria, Virginia (then within the District of Columbia), on January 31, 1812, Tucker entered the navy as a midshipman in June 1826. Over the next several decades he made cruises with the Home, East India, and Mediterranean squadrons, served ashore at the Norfolk navy yard, and during the Mexican War was aboard the bombship *Stromboli* in Commodore Matthew C. Perry's operations against Tuxpan and Tabasco, later succeeding to command of the ship. He was promoted to lieutenant in December 1837 and commander in September 1855. He was ordnance officer at Norfolk when his native state seceded from the Union, and in April 1861 he resigned from the navy. He was immediately commissioned in the Virginia state navy and in June in the Confederate States navy with the rank of commander. Given charge of the naval defense of the James River, Tucker commanded from the cruiser *Patrick Henry* (converted from the steamer *Yorktown*) on station at Mulberry Island, actually a peninsula on the north bank of the James. During the Peninsula campaign he protected the right flank of Confederate forces ashore and on March 8–9, 1862, took part in the naval fighting in Hampton Roads, engaging shore batteries and inflicting considerable damage on the *Minnesota* while Flag-Officer Franklin Buchanan cut a swath with the ironclad *Virginia*. The *Patrick Henry* took part in the naval demonstration in Hampton Roads by Flag-Officer Josiah Tattnall on April 11, and, following the capture of Norfolk navy yard by Union forces, Tucker commanded the withdrawal of the small flotilla up the James to Drewry's Bluff, where on May 15, aided by shore fire, he sharply repulsed the pursuing Union flotilla under Commander John Rodgers. In August Tucker was transferred to command of the ironclad ram *Chicora* at Charleston, South Carolina. On January 31, 1863, the *Chicora* took part in the raid under Flag-Officer Duncan N. Ingraham on the Union blockade outside Charleston harbor. In March Tucker succeeded Ingraham in command of the flotilla in the harbor, and in May he was promoted to captain. On the evacuation of Charleston in February 1865 he returned to Drewry's Bluff, where he reformed his crews as a naval brigade that operated ashore in support of Adm. Raphael Semmes's forces afloat. The brigade was attached as a rearguard to Gen. Robert E. Lee's army on the abandonment of Richmond in April and took a distinguished part in the battle of Sayler's Creek, April 6, where he was captured. Tucker was imprisoned until July 1865. He lived in Raleigh, North Carolina, until 1866, when he accepted a commission as rear admiral in the Peruvian navy. He commanded the combined navies of Peru and Chile in their war with Spain; the war concluded in 1869, however, with no naval action having taken place. He then directed a hydrographic survey of the upper Amazon River, a task of great difficulty and danger. In 1877, while he was in New York City overseeing the preparation of the charts thus made, his commission was withdrawn by Peru. Tucker died in Petersburg, Virginia, on June 12, 1883.

Tucker, Samuel (1747–1833), Revolutionary naval officer. Born in Marblehead, Massachusetts, on November 1, 1747, Tucker went to sea at the age of eleven and by the age of twenty-one had risen to master. In January 1776 he was commissioned by Gen. George Washington captain of the schooner *Franklin* in "Washington's Fleet" of army vessels under Commodore John Manley. While the *Franklin* was fitting out Tucker sailed in another schooner and captured a British vessel carrying troops and valuable stores. In March 1776 he was transferred to the larger schooner *Hancock*. During 1776 he captured, alone or in company with another ship, more than 30 British vessels, notably the *Peggy* on July 29 and the *Lively* on October 29, and thereby secured large quantities of supplies for Washington's army. In March 1777 he was commissioned captain in the Continental navy. After some months of waiting he took command of

the frigate *Boston*. In February 1778 he conveyed John Adams to France on the *Boston,* capturing a prize en route. He took four more before making the return voyage in company with the *Providence*, Capt. Abraham Whipple, and the *Ranger*, Capt. John Paul Jones. In May–June 1779 the *Boston* was part of Commodore Samuel Nicholson's expedition out of the Delaware, and on June 6 the *Boston* and the *Confederacy*, Capt. Seth Harding, captured the privateer *Pole*, the armed schooner *Patsey*, and an unarmed prize. In July the *Boston* and the *Deane*, Capt. Nicholson, sailed from Chesapeake Bay with a convoy of merchantmen. In five weeks they took eight prizes, including the sloop of war *Thorn*. In November he sailed the *Boston* to Charleston, South Carolina, where, part of Commodore Whipple's squadron, he anchored in the Cooper River to help defend the city from siege. On the fall of Charleston on May 12, 1780, he was taken prisoner. After exchange and a leave of absence he sailed aboard the *Thorn* as a privateer. He made several cruises and took seven prizes before July 1781, when he was captured by the frigate *Hind* near the mouth of the St. Lawrence River. Released in an open boat to make his way from Prince Edward Island to Halifax, Nova Scotia, he instead sailed to Boston. From 1783 to 1786 Tucker was again in the merchant service. He then lived in Marblehead until 1792, when he took up farming in Bristol, Maine (then still part of Massachusetts). In 1813, when British vessels were regularly harrying the coast of Maine, he outfitted a schooner with improvised and borrowed armament and chased and captured the privateer *Crown*. He sat in the Massachusetts legislature in 1814–1818, was a member of the Maine constitutional convention in 1819, and sat in the Maine legislature in 1820–1821. In March 1821 he was granted a pension by Congress for his naval services. Tucker died in Bremen, Maine, on March 10, 1833.

Turner, Richmond Kelly (1885–1961), naval officer. Born on May 27, 1885, in Portland, Oregon, Turner graduated from the Naval Academy in 1908 and after his first cruise was commissioned ensign in June 1910. Routine duties over the next several years included service on the *Stewart*, his first command, in 1913–1915, attendance at the Naval Ordnance School in 1915–1916, service on several battleships during World War I, and command of the *Mervine* in 1924–1925. In 1926 he entered aviation training at the Pensacola Naval Air Station, and he won his pilot rating in 1927. During 1928–1929 he commanded the *Jason* and at the same time served as commander of aircraft squadrons, Asiatic Fleet. In July 1929 he was named chief of the planning division of the Bureau of Aeronautics. From December 1931 to December 1932 he was an aviation adviser to the U.S. delegation at the Geneva Disarmament Conference, and in the latter month he became executive officer of the carrier *Saratoga*. In June 1934 he was appointed chief of staff to the commander of aircraft, Battle Force. Promoted to captain in July 1935, he then spent three years on the staff of the Naval War College. In September 1938 he took command of the cruiser *Astoria*, and in October 1940 he was named director of the War Plans Division in the Navy Department; he advanced to rear admiral in January 1941. In July 1942 he was ordered to the South Pacific to command the amphibious forces in the area, under the general command of Adm. Robert L. Ghormley and later Adm. William F. Halsey. Turner's forces launched the grueling Guadalcanal campaign with the landing on August 7 of Gen. Alexander A. Vandegrift's 1st Marine Division at Cape Esperance and nearby islands. Early in the morning of August 9 Turner's forces (he being the senior commander present while Adm. Frank J. Fletcher was at some distance) were suddenly attacked by a Japanese task group near Savo Island. In half an hour four heavy cruisers were sunk or put in sinking condition, after which the Japanese group escaped unscathed from one of the worst defeats ever inflicted on the U.S. navy. Turner directed the continual reinforcement of the forces on Guadalcanal, and he was forced to fight off several more Japanese attacks through December. In June–July 1943 he directed amphibious operations in the Central Solomons, particularly the landings at Rendova Island opposite the Japanese airbase of Munda on New Georgia; his flagship *McCawley* was sunk in that action. In August he was transferred to command of the V Amphibious Force, Central Pacific area, under Adm. Raymond A. Spruance. He planned and directed the landing of amphibious troops under Gen. Holland M. Smith at Makin and Tarawa in the Gilberts on November 20; Kwajalein, January 31, 1944, and Eniwetok, February 17, in the Marshalls; Saipan, June 15, Guam, July 21, and Tinian, July 24, in the Marianas; Iwo Jima, February 19, 1945; and Okinawa, April 1. In April he became commander of Amphibious Forces, Pacific, comprising the III and V forces. He was promoted to vice admiral in February 1944 and to admiral in May 1945. From December 1945 to April 1947 Turner was the U.S. naval representative on the United Nations Military Staff Committee. He retired from the navy in July 1947 and died in Monterey, California, on February 12, 1961.

Twiggs, David Emanuel (1790–1862), army officer and Confederate army officer. Born in 1790 in Richmond County, Georgia, Twiggs was appointed a captain in the 8th Infantry in March 1812. He saw minor service in the War of 1812, advancing to major in September 1814, but with the disbanding of his regiment in June 1815 he was left without a position. In May 1825 he reentered the service as major of the 1st Infantry. Posted on the frontier, in 1828 he estab-

lished Fort Winnebago at the Fox-Wisconsin portage, and in 1831–1832 he saw action against Black Hawk. He was promoted to lieutenant colonel in July 1831 and to colonel of the 2nd Dragoons in June 1836. In 1846 the 2nd Dragoons was ordered to join the force in Texas under Gen. Zachary Taylor. After his arrival there he engaged in an indecorous dispute over rank with Col. William J. Worth, who was junior to him in regular rank but was then serving as brevet brigadier general. After performing well in command of Taylor's 1st Division at Palo Alto and Resaca de la Palma, May 8–9, Twiggs was promoted to brigadier general in June. Owing to illness he took no part in the battle of Monterrey in September but was nonetheless brevetted major general. Shortly thereafter he was transferred to Gen. Winfield Scott's army. He took part in the siege and capture of Veracruz in March 1847 and commanded the vanguard of the army on the march inland. On April 12 he encountered Gen. Santa Anna's army at the hamlet of Cerro Gordo. Guided by Capt. Robert E. Lee, he sent his artillery through rough country, flanking the Mexican position; on April 18 Santa Anna was quickly driven out of Cerro Gordo. Twiggs distinguished himself again in command of the 2nd Division in the assault on Mexico City, September 13–14. From December 1847 to March 1848 he was military governor of Veracruz. He later commanded the Department of the West until 1857 and then the Department of Texas with headquarters at San Antonio. On February 16, 1861, he voluntarily surrendered his entire command to Confederate Gen. Ben McCulloch. He was immediately dismissed from the army. In May he was commissioned major general of Confederate forces and placed in command of the District of Louisiana. He was for a short time the ranking general in the Confederate army. He died on July 15, 1862, in Augusta, Georgia.

Twining, Nathan Farragut (1897–   ), army and air force officer. Born on October 11, 1897, in Monroe, Wisconsin, Twining grew up there and in Portland, Oregon. He served as a corporal with the Oregon National Guard on the Mexican border in 1916 and in June 1917 entered West Point; he graduated from the accelerated wartime course in November 1918 and received a commission in the infantry. After brief occupation duty in Germany he attended the Infantry School, Fort Benning, Georgia, in 1919–1920, and the army's Primary Flying School at Brooks Field, Texas, in 1923–1924. In November 1926 he was formally transferred to the Air Service. Twining was a flight instructor at March Field, California, in 1929–1930 and was stationed with the 18th Pursuit Group at Schofield Barracks, Hawaii, in 1930–1932 and with the 3rd Attack Group at Fort Crockett, Texas, in 1932–1935. Promoted to captain in August 1935, he graduated from Air Corps Tactical School, Maxwell Field,

Alabama, in 1936 and from the Command and General Staff School, Fort Leavenworth, Kansas, in 1937. He was stationed at Duncan Field, Texas, until August 1940, when, promoted to major, he was attached to the staff of the chief of the Air Corps. He served in the operations division of headquarters until August 1942, when, by that time a temporary brigadier general, he became chief of staff of army forces in the South Pacific. In January 1943 he was named commander of the newly activated Thirteenth Air Force with headquarters on New Caledonia, receiving promotion to temporary major general in February. The Thirteenth's assignment was to provide air support for various operations in the area, including the occupation of Guadalcanal (where Henderson Field became headquarters in July), the Middle Solomons, Munda, and Bougainville; from July Twining also held the post of commander, aircraft, Solomon Islands. In January 1944 he was transferred to command of the Fifteenth Air Force (succeeding Gen. James H. Doolittle), also taking command of the Allied Strategic Air Forces, Mediterranean. Flying from bases in southern Italy, the Fifteenth provided support for Gen. Mark W. Clark's Fifth Army on the ground, flew strategic missions into Germany, Austria, and the Balkans, notably the raids on the Ploesti oilfields in Rumania, and in August 1944 pro-

vided air cover for the Seventh Army's landing in southern France. In May 1945 Twining was recalled to Washington; he was promoted to temporary lieutenant general in June, and in August he succeeded Gen. Curtis E. LeMay in command of the Twentieth Air Force in the Pacific. Strategic bombing of the Japanese homeland, including the atomic bombing of Hiroshima and Nagasaki, August 6 and 9, was carried on by the Twentieth until the end of the war. In October 1945 Twining returned to Washington, and in December he was named chief of the Air Matériel Command at Wright Field, Ohio. In September 1947 he was transferred into the independent air force. In November 1947 he became commander of the unified Alaskan Command at Fort Richardson. In May 1950 he was named a deputy chief of staff, and in October he was promoted to temporary general and made vice-chief of staff of the air force. In June 1953 he succeeded Gen. Hoyt S. Vandenberg as chief of staff. He moved up to chairman of the Joint Chiefs of Staff on appointment by President Dwight D. Eisenhower in August 1957, and he served in that post until retiring in September 1960. Thereafter he concerned himself with various business interests, including the vice-chairmanship of the board of Holt, Rinehart & Winston, publishers.

U

Underhill, John (1597?–1672), colonial official and militia officer. Born in England, probably in Warwickshire, about 1597, Underhill grew up in the Netherlands, where his father was a mercenary soldier. He received military training himself, and when he came to Massachusetts Bay in 1630 it was to organize the colonial militia. In his first few years in America he was readily accepted as a member of the colony; he was appointed a captain of the militia, voted arms and money, and granted a parcel of land. The only real annoyance he suffered was the colonists' general lack of interest in their own defense. During the Pequot War in Connecticut Underhill led a score of men early in 1637 to reinforce Capt. Lion Gardiner at Saybrook Fort. In May he took part under Capt. John Mason in the expedition culminating in the massacre of the Pequots at the Mystic River. His return to Boston afterward marked the beginning of 20 years of unsettled life, as he found himself thereafter on bad terms with the Massachusetts officials. In the religious controversy raging in the late 1630s he took the part of the Antinomians Anne Hutchinson and John Wheelwright against the Puritan administration. He was consequently charged with sedition and in November 1637 deprived of his militia rank and of his right to vote. After spending a few months in England in 1637–1638, during which he published *Newes from America*, 1638, an account of the Pequot War, he returned to Boston only to be put on trial for his religious attitudes and in September 1638 was banished from the colony. After fleeing to Dover, New Hampshire, to avoid trial on charges of adultery, Underhill became governor of the Dover settlement and defied the Massachusetts authorities. He was excommunicated for a brief period during 1640 and was finally reconciled with the officials at Boston in 1641. About 1643, after living for a time at Stamford, Connecticut, he went into the service of the Dutch colony of New Netherland as an Indian fighter. But again his success as a soldier was negated by his political ineptitude. After the outbreak of war between England and the Netherlands (1652), Underhill, acting on a dubious privateer's warrant from Providence colony, seized in June 1653 the vestigial Dutch post of Fort Good Hope (or House of Hope) on the Connecticut River within present-day Hartford. In 1658 he settled at Oyster Bay on Long Island, New York. During the Anglo-Dutch war in 1664–1665 he helped the British to extend their rule over New Amsterdam, and thereafter he served in various public capacities in the colony, now called New York. He retired to his Long Island home in 1667 and lived there until his death on September 21, 1672.

Upton, Emory (1839–1881), army officer. Born near Batavia, New York, on August 27, 1839, Upton attended Oberlin College for a year before entering West Point in 1856. He graduated in May 1861, was commissioned in the artillery and promptly promoted to first lieutenant, and was wounded at Bull Run (Manassas), July 21. He served with the Army of the Potomac through the Peninsula campaign and in Maryland in 1862, receiving appointment as colonel of the 121st New York Volunteers in October. He commanded a brigade in Gen. John Sedgwick's VI Corps through most of 1863 and was brevetted major of regulars at Rappahannock Station, November 7. At Spotsylvania on May 10, 1864, he was wounded while leading a gallant charge and was promoted to brigadier general of volunteers on the spot by Gen. Ulysses S. Grant and subsequently brevetted lieutenant colonel of regulars. Transferred to the Shenandoah valley later in the year, he was severely wounded at Winchester, September 19, but he nonetheless succeeded to command of his division and directed its movements from a stretcher; he was brevetted colonel of regulars and major general of volunteers for that action. Early in 1865 he was transferred to the southwestern theater at the request of Gen. James H. Wilson, and on April 2 he led a division of dismounted cavalry in the capture by storm of Selma, Alabama. In March he had been brevetted brigadier and major general of regulars. He commanded the District of Colorado from August 1865 to April 1866, when he was mustered out of volunteer service and reverted to his permanent rank of captain (from February 1865). In July he was appointed lieutenant colonel of the 25th Infantry. In 1867 he published *A New System of Infantry Tactics*, on which he had been working for some time and which reflected the experience of the Civil War by taking into account the vastly superior firepower of the breechloading rifle and detailing the countertactic of advance by columns and the use of skirmish groups in advance. The work attracted the attention of Gen. William T. Sherman, who in July 1870 appointed Upton commandant of cadets at West Point and instructor in tactics. He held those posts until June 1875, when Sherman appointed him to a three-man commission sent to inspect military organization in Asia and Europe. He was particularly struck by the Prussian efficiency of the German army and on his return discussed it at length in *The Armies of Asia and Europe*, 1878, a book that contained a proposal that the U.S. army be made a strictly professional body, with volunteers in future wars filling out a skeletal organization under regular officers instead of forming a separate army as in the Civil War. From 1877 to 1880 Upton was an instructor at the Artillery School, Fort Monroe, Virginia. In 1880 he was promoted to colonel of the 4th Artillery at the Presidio, San Francisco. A progressive disease, possibly a cerebral tumor, led to his resignation in March 1881 and his death by suicide the next day, March 15, 1881. He left an incomplete manuscript on "The Military Policy of the United States from 1775," in which the idea of a professional, expansible regular army was treated at length. He also proposed the establishment of military schools and a general staff corps, both on German models. The manuscript circulated among senior officers for several years, was consulted by Secretary of War Elihu Root in 1903 and helped shape his reorganization plans, and was at length published in 1904.

Usher, Nathaniel Reilly (1855–1931), naval officer. Born in Vincennes, Indiana, on April 7, 1855, Usher graduated from the Naval Academy in 1875 and, while serving on the *Tennessee* on Asiatic station, was commissioned ensign in July 1876. After a year on the *Kearsarge* he was a member of the U.S. naval delegation at the Paris Exposition of 1878. Subsequently he served aboard the *Independence,* 1878–1879, and the *Jamestown,* 1879–1881, was promoted to lieutenant (junior grade) in February 1882, and was aboard the *Bear* and later the *Alert* in the expedition under Commander Winfield S. Schley sent to the relief of Lt. Adolphus W. Greely in 1884. During a world cruise in 1886–1889 on the *Juniata* he was promoted to lieutenant in October 1888. After various other assignments he took command of the torpedo boat *Ericsson* in 1894. During the Spanish–American War he was credited with capturing the first Spanish prize taken. The *Ericsson* helped convoy Gen. William R. Shafter's army to Cuba, and at the battle of Santiago, July 3, 1898, Usher distinguished himself in rescuing Spanish sailors off the burning *Vizcaya.* Promoted to lieutenant commander in March 1899, he served on the *Kearsarge* in 1899–1901 and on the *Illinois* in 1901–1903. In 1903 he sat on the General Board of the navy. He advanced to commander in February 1904 and from that year to 1906 was attached to the Bureau of Navigation. Usher commanded the *St. Louis* in 1906–1908, receiving promotion to captain in April 1908, and, after another year in the Bureau of Navigation, commanded the *Michigan* in 1909–1911. Under his command the *Michigan* won the first battle efficiency pennant ever awarded. In September 1911 he was promoted to rear admiral. After a year as president of the Examining and Retiring boards he commanded various divisions of the Atlantic Fleet in 1912–1913, the Norfolk navy yard in 1913–1914, and the Brooklyn navy yard in 1914–1918. In the latter post he was responsible for the efficient embarkation of 80 percent of U.S. troops sent to France in World War I and a quarter of all the supplies and equipment. Foresight had led him to make preparations even before the American declaration of war in April 1917, and during the period of war he also maintained observation balloon, minesweeping, and antisubmarine patrols and established a secret service, known as the Commandant's Aide for Information. In 1918 Usher was named commander of the 3rd Naval District. He retired in April 1919 and died in Potsdam, New York, on January 9, 1931.

V

Vallejo, Mariano Guadalupe (1808–1890),
California provincial official and army officer. Born
in Monterey, California, on July 7, 1808, Vallejo took
up soldiering at the age of fifteen. He served the
Mexican provincial government in a military capacity until the United States took over California in
1846. Under the Mexican regime he was one of a
generation of younger, native-born Californians affected by the ideas of the Enlightenment and hostile
to the authority of the Roman Catholic church and
of the far-away government at Mexico City. He favored the rule of native-born officialdom in the
province and hoped to help bring about political independence for California comparable to its economic self-reliance. In 1827 he was stationed at the Presidio in San Francisco, and two years later he helped
put down an Indian uprising at the nearby San Jose
mission. In 1831–1832 and 1835–1836 he supported
revolts against authoritarian Mexican governors that
succeeded in obtaining the appointment of governors
more attuned to the political aspirations of Californians. In 1833–1834 he was put in charge of a military
expedition to reconnoiter the Russian colony at Fort
Ross to see if it posed a threat to the government at
Monterey. Having decided that the Russians were
too weak to be a danger, he proceeded to improve the
defenses around Sonoma against hostile Indians of
the area, forming also for that purpose a fruitful alliance with Solano, chief of the friendly Suisun. Vallejo's nephew, Juan Bautista Alvarado, who led the
1836 revolt that established California as a virtually
free state, became governor of California and in 1838
appointed Vallejo commandant of the provincial
military forces. He spent most of his time at Sonoma
until 1846. During the early 1840s, when Anglos
from the East were arriving in numbers in California,
Vallejo recognized the inevitability of the migration
and aided the new arrivals in getting settled. He was
ill rewarded for his goodwill; when the Bear Flag
Revolt took place in June 1846, Vallejo and his brother were both taken captive by the insurgents and held
for two months. Soon after U.S. military forces
claimed California for the United States, he was
released. In 1849 he was a delegate to the state constitutional convention, and he was then elected to the
senate of the first legislature. For many years after
that, as the old Spanish-Mexican families saw their
influence decline, he was involved in lawsuits to salvage some of his property. Land claims by newcom-
ers took much of it, but he continued to live at Sono-

ma. In 1851 he offered the state a tract of land on his
estate, site of the city of Vallejo, for a state capital.
The offer was accepted, but the city was California's
capital for only a week in January 1852 and again for
a month in 1853. During the 1860s and 1870s he
compiled materials for a history of California. He
died at his home in Sonoma on January 18, 1890.

Vandegrift, Alexander Archer (1887–1973),
marine officer. Born on March 13, 1887, in Charlottesville, Virginia, Vandegrift attended the University of Virginia during 1906–1908 and then enlisted
in the marine corps. After completing basic and field
officers' training he was commissioned a second lieutenant in January 1909. He saw varied service over
the next decades: He was ordered from Cuba to
Nicaragua in 1912 and took part in the bombardment
and occupation of Coyotepe in October of that year;
served in the Canal Zone in 1913; took part in the
occupation of Veracruz, Mexico, in April 1914;
fought Caco rebels in Haiti in 1915, by which time
he was a first lieutenant; and, after graduating from
Advanced Base School, Quantico, Virginia, served in
the Haitian Constabulary in 1916–1918 and 1919–
1923. After three years on the staff at Quantico,
where he also completed the field officers' course in
1926, he served in the marine expeditionary force in
China under Gen. Smedley D. Butler in 1927–1929.
From 1929 to 1935 he held staff posts at corps headquarters in Washington, D.C., and during the latter
two years he served as assistant chief of staff, Fleet
Marine Force. He was again in China in 1935–1937,
advancing to command of the marine detachment at
the U.S. embassy in Peking, and between 1937 and
1941 he was secretary and then assistant to the marine commandant, Gen. Thomas Holcomb, receiving
promotion to brigadier general in 1940. In 1941 he
was named assistant commander of the 1st Marine
Division; he was promoted to major general in March
1942, and in April he moved up to command of the
division. In May the 1st was ordered to the Pacific
theater, and on August 7 it was put ashore—19,000
strong—at Cape Esperance on Guadalcanal and on
nearby Tulagi by Adm. R. Kelly Turner's amphibious
forces. A beachhead was secured without much opposition, but the jungle campaign for the rest of Guadalcanal soon became one of the hardest-fought of
the war. Naval support was withdrawn to meet
strong Japanese sea forces, which succeeded in reinforcing the defending garrison, and vicious coun-

terattacks on the ground dragged the battle out for months. By late November the tide had turned, however, and on December 9 Vandegrift and the 1st Division were relieved by Gen. Alexander M. Patch's Americal Division. In February 1943 Vandegrift was awarded the Medal of Honor for his service on Guadalcanal. In July he was promoted to lieutenant general (the second marine, after Holcomb, to attain that rank) and given command of the I Marine Amphibious Corps. In that post he led in planning and oversaw the landing of the corps on Bougainville on November 1 by Adm. Theodore S. Wilkinson's Third Amphibious Force. Eight days later he relinquished command of the corps to Gen. Roy S. Geiger. In January 1944 Vandegrift succeeded Holcomb as commandant of the marine corps. In March 1945 he became the first marine officer to hold the rank of general while still on active duty, and he was made permanent in that grade in September. He was succeeded as commandant by Gen. Clifton B. Cates in January 1948 and retired in March 1949. Vandegrift died in Bethesda, Maryland, on May 8, 1973.

Vandenberg, Hoyt Sanford (1899–1954), army and air force officer. Born on January 24, 1899, in Milwaukee, Wisconsin, Vandenberg was a nephew of Sen. Arthur H. Vandenberg. He graduated from West Point in 1923 and was commissioned in the Air Service. After completing the Primary Flying School, Brooks Field, Texas, in that year and Advanced Flying School, Kelly Field, Texas, in 1924, he was attached to the 3rd Attack Group at Kelly and later at Crockett Field, Texas. Late in 1927 he became a flight instructor at March Field, California, receiving promotion to first lieutenant in August 1928. During 1929–1931 he was with the 6th Pursuit Squadron at Schofield Barracks, Hawaii, where he served as squadron commander for most of that period. After two years as an instructor at Randolph Field, Texas, he entered the Air Corps Tactical School, Maxwell Field, Alabama, he graduated in 1935, was promoted to captain, and in 1936 graduated from the Command and General Staff School, Fort Leavenworth, Kansas. He was an instructor at the Tactical School in 1936–1938, graduated from the Army War College in 1939, and then served in the plans division of the office of the chief of the Air Corps. In July 1941 he was promoted to major and attached to the staff of Gen. Henry H. Arnold, with whom he helped develop strategic plans for Army Air Corps deployment in a war. He was promoted to temporary lieutenant colonel in November 1941 and temporary colonel in January 1942, and in March he was named operations and training officer of the Air Staff. Later in the year he was sent to England to help prepare combined air plans for the North Africa campaign, and in October he was appointed chief of staff of the Twelfth Air Force under Gen. James H. Doolittle. In December he

was promoted to temporary brigadier general. In March 1943 he became chief of staff, again under Doolittle, of the Northwest Africa Strategic Air Force, and in that capacity he flew numerous combat missions over Tunisia, Sardinia, Sicily, and Italy. In August he was appointed a deputy chief of the Air Staff in Washington, D.C. Vandenberg accompanied Ambassador W. Averell Harriman on a diplomatic mission to the Soviet Union in September. In March 1944 he was promoted to temporary major general and ordered back to England as deputy commander of the Allied Expeditionary Air Forces, under Air Chief Marshal Sir Arthur W. Tedder, and commander of the U.S. air component. Having led in planning the tactical air support program for the European invasion, he took command of the Ninth Air Force from Gen. Lewis H. Brereton in August 1944. The Ninth was charged with flying close tactical support missions in conjunction with ground forces, particularly Gen. George S. Patton's Third Army, and it also flew escort missions with the strategic bombers of the Eighth Air Force. In March 1945 Vandenberg was promoted to temporary lieutenant general. In May he returned to Washington, D.C., and in July he was named assistant chief of staff for operations of the Army Air Forces. In January 1946 he was appointed chief of the intelligence division of the General Staff, becoming in June director of the Central Intelligence Group, a predecessor of the Central Intelligence Agency formed in 1947. In April 1947 he became deputy commander and chief of staff of the AAF. On the establishment of the air force as an independent branch in September 1947 he became vice chief of staff, and in July 1948 he succeeded Gen. Carl Spaatz as chief of staff. He held that post through the critical periods of the Berlin airlift, 1948–1949, and the Korean War, 1951–1953, until his retirement in June 1953. Vandenberg died in Washington, D.C., on April 2, 1954.

Van Dorn, Earl (1820–1863), Confederate army officer. Born near Port Gibson, Mississippi, on September 17, 1820, Van Dorn graduated from West Point in 1842 and was commissioned in the infantry. He took part with the 7th Infantry in the military occupation of Texas in 1845–1846 and was stationed at Fort Texas (later Fort Brown) at the outbreak of the Mexican War in the latter year. Transferred to Gen. Winfield Scott's army, he was promoted to first lieutenant in March 1847 and brevetted captain for gallantry at Cerro Gordo, April 18, and major for Contreras and Churubusco, August 19–20. He was wounded in the storming of the Belen Gate of Mexico City, September 13. In 1849–1850 he saw action against the Seminoles in Florida. After three years as secretary and treasurer of the military asylum at Pascagoula, Mississippi, he was promoted to captain of the 2nd Cavalry in March 1855. He saw action against Indians in Texas and Indian Territory and was wounded several times between 1855 and 1860. Promoted to major in June 1860, he resigned his commission in January 1861 and was appointed brigadier general of Mississippi state troops; in February he succeeded Jefferson Davis as major general of state troops. In March he was commissioned colonel in the Confederate army and given command of a body of Texas volunteers. In April–May he received the surrender of the Union forces remaining in Texas following the capitulation of Gen. David E. Twiggs. He was promoted to brigadier general in June and to major general in September, and in January 1862 he was appointed commander of the Trans-Mississippi Department. At Elkhorn Tavern (Pea Ridge), Arkansas, March 7–8, he and Gen. Sterling Price's Missouri volunteers met and were defeated by Gen. Samuel R. Curtis and the Army of the Southwest. He was relieved of his command later in the year by Gen. Theophilus H. Holmes and ordered to the Army of Mississippi under Gen. Braxton Bragg. When Bragg later moved north, Van Dorn remained in command of Confederate forces in Mississippi. His command was subsequently referred to as the Army of West Tennessee. On October 3 he launched a heavy attack on Gen. William S. Rosecrans at Corinth, Mississippi, and was repulsed with heavy losses. On October 5, while retreating across the Hatchie River, he was heavily attacked by a Union force under Gen. Stephen A. Hurlbut, who was superseded a short time later by Gen. Edward O. C. Ord. On December 20 he raided Holly Springs, Mississippi, and captured a major supply depot on which Gen. Ulysses S. Grant's first campaign against Vicksburg had been depending; that campaign was thereupon abandoned. On April 10, 1863, he fought a skirmish with Gen. Gordon Granger at Franklin, Tennessee. While sitting in his headquarters in Spring Hill, Tennessee, on May 8, 1863, he was shot and killed by a personal enemy.

Van Fleet, James Alward (1892–   ), army officer. Born on March 19, 1892, in Coytesville, New Jersey, Van Fleet graduated from West Point in 1915 and was commissioned in the infantry. In 1916–1917 he was on duty with the 3rd Infantry on the Mexican border. By July 1918, when he was ordered to France, he had advanced to temporary major in command of the 17th Machine Gun Battalion, 6th Infantry Division. He saw action in the Meuse–Argonne offensive. After occupation duty he spent several years as a reserve training instructor at Kansas State College, South Dakota State College, and the University of Florida. In 1925–1927, then a permanent major, he commanded a battalion of the 42nd Infantry in the Canal Zone, and after a year as an instructor he graduated from the senior course at the Infantry School, Fort Benning, Georgia, in 1929. He was again at the University of Florida from 1929 to 1933, and after

two years with the 5th Infantry at Fort Williams, Maine, he was promoted to lieutenant colonel and assigned as an instructor of reservists in San Diego, California. In 1939–1941 he was with the 29th Infantry at Fort Benning. Promoted to temporary colonel, he commanded the 8th Infantry at various training sites from 1941 to January 1944, when he took it to England for final preparation. On June 6, 1944, the 8th went ashore on Utah Beach, Normandy, in the van of the 4th Division and ahead of most of the rest of the Allied invasion force, and by the end of the month it had helped capture Cherbourg. From July to September Van Fleet, as temporary brigadier general, was assistant commander of the 2nd Division, and during that period he took part in the siege of Brest. In October he became commander of the 90th Division, receiving promotion to temporary major general in November. The 90th, attached variously to the First and Third armies, took part in the siege of Metz, crossed the Moselle on November 9, took part in the Ardennes counteroffensive in January 1945, and broke through the Siegfried Line in February. During February–March 1945 Van Fleet commanded the XXIII Corps in England, and in March he moved to command of the III Corps, which spearheaded the First Army's advance from the Remagen bridgehead across Germany. He remained with the corps in occupation duty and then at Camp Polk, Louisiana, until February 1946, when he took over the 2nd Service Command at Governors Island, New York. In June he became deputy commander of the First Army at the same post. In December 1947 he was named deputy chief of staff of the army's European Command in Frankfurt, Germany. In February 1948, promoted to temporary lieutenant general, he was appointed by President Harry S. Truman to direct the military adviser missions to Greece and Turkey under the terms of the Truman Doctrine. He continued in that assignment through 1950, contributing to the eventual defeat of armed Communist partisans in both countries. In April 1951 he was named to succeed Gen. Matthew B. Ridgway as commander of the Eighth Army in Korea, and he commanded it through months of bitter fighting for small tactical advantages while the armistice negotiations dragged on; he was promoted to general in July 1951. In February 1953 he was succeeded by Gen. Maxwell D. Taylor, and he retired the next month. Thereafter he was engaged in various business pursuits. In 1961–1962 he was a consultant on guerrilla warfare to the secretary of defense.

Van Lew, Elizabeth L. (1818–1900), Union agent. Born on October 17, 1818, in Richmond, Virginia, Miss Van Lew was the daughter of a prosperous family of Northern antecedents. She was educated in Philadelphia. She grew up to hold strong antislavery views, and during the 1850s, under her influence, the family's domestic servants were freed.

At the outbreak of the Civil War she remained firmly and publicly loyal to the United States. She made numerous visits to Union prisoners in Libby Prison, carrying in food, clothing, and other items and often carrying away military information that she was able to transmit to federal authorities. On occasion escaped prisoners were hidden in her house. In March 1864, following Gen. Hugh J. Kilpatrick's unsuccessful attempt to open Libby Prison during a cavalry raid on Richmond (a raid apparently planned in response to information gathered by Elizabeth Van Lew that the prisoners were soon to be moved farther south), she and her agents daringly spirited out of the city the body of Col. Ulric Dahlgren, Kilpatrick's second-in-command and the son of Adm. John A. B. Dahlgren, who had been killed in the raid and whose remains had suffered indignities at the hands of an outraged Richmond citizenry. During the year-long siege of Richmond and Petersburg in 1864–1865 she performed invaluable services in intelligence gathering. Her contacts reached even into Jefferson Davis's home, where she had placed one of her former servants; and her assumed manner of mental aberration, which gained her the indulgent nickname of "Crazy Bet" around Richmond, enabled her to carry on unsuspected. Agents carried coded messages by way of various relay stations to the Union headquarters beyond the city. After the fall of Richmond in April 1865 she was personally thanked and given protection by Gen. Ulysses S. Grant. Under President Grant she held the post of postmistress of Richmond from 1869 to 1877. She worked subsequently as a clerk in the Post Office Department in Washington, D.C., until the late 1880s. She then returned in poverty to Richmond, where she was still a social outcast because of her wartime activities. She lived in the family mansion in Richmond, Virginia, until her death on September 25, 1900.

Van Rensselaer, Stephen (1764–1839), militia officer and public official. Born in New York City on November 1, 1764, Van Rensselaer graduated from Harvard in 1782. Since at the age of five he had inherited his father's entire estate—an enormous manor in upstate Rensselaer and Albany counties of which he became the eighth patroon (by then merely an honorific title)—he was, on reaching maturity, one of the wealthiest residents of New York State and one of its major landholders. A Federalist in politics, Van Rensselaer was a member of the state assembly in 1789–1791, in 1798, and again in 1818. He served in the state senate from 1791 to 1796. In 1795 he was elected lieutenant governor; reelected in 1798, he served in that post until 1801. He sat in the state constitutional convention of 1801 and later in that of 1821. Along with inherited political position had come high rank in the state militia; he was a major in 1786, aged twenty-two, colonel in 1788, and major

general in 1801. Shortly after the outbreak of the War of 1812 he was ordered by Gov. Daniel D. Tompkins to defend the northern border of the state. By October he had some 2300 militia and 900 regular army troops under his command at Lewiston on the Niagara frontier. After one false start he crossed the Niagara River on October 13. Fewer than 500 of the first assault wave landed at the designated spot, owing to the current of the river, but the surprise of the attack enabled him quickly to gain possession of the Queenston Heights. The Americans repulsed a minor counterattack by British troops under Gen. Isaac Brock, who was killed in the fight, but were pinned down by artillery fire and unable to advance. Van Rensselaer's force eventually reached 1300; the rest of the militia refused, under the law, to cross the border, and the regular army commander, Gen. Alexander Smyth, declined to assist. Rapid British reinforcements turned the tide. A heavy counterattack drove the Americans back across the river with 300 casualties and nearly 1000 captured. Van Rensselaer promptly resigned his commission and resumed his political career. He strongly favored the building of a canal to connect the Hudson River with the Great Lakes, and he promoted this cause as a member of state's canal commission in 1810 and 1816; from 1825, when the Erie Canal was opened, to 1839 he was president of the commission. He was a regent of the University of the State of New York from 1819 until 1839 and served as chancellor after 1835. In November 1824 he founded at Troy, New York, the school that became in 1826 Rensselaer Polytechnic Institute. He was elected to the House of Representatives from New York in February 1822 to fill a vacancy and, twice reelected, he served until March 1829. His most significant achievement during his congressional years was casting the deciding vote for the election of John Quincy Adams as president after the election of 1824 was thrown into the House. Van Rensselaer did not seek reelection in 1828 but instead retired to look after his huge manor. He died in Albany, New York, on January 26, 1839.

Varnum, James Mitchell (1748–1789), Revolutionary army officer and public official. Born in Dracut, Massachusetts, on December 17, 1748, Varnum attended Harvard for a time and in 1769 graduated from Rhode Island College (now Brown University). He taught school briefly and then took up the study of law; he was admitted to the Rhode Island bar in 1771 and rapidly gained prominence in his practice at East Greenwich. In October 1774 he was elected colonel of a local militia troop, the Kentish Guards, whose officers also included Nathanael Greene. In May 1775 Varnum was appointed colonel of the 1st Rhode Island Infantry, which the next year was mustered into Continental service as the 9th Infantry. He commanded the regiment through the siege of Boston and through the battles on Long Island and Manhattan and at White Plains, and in December 1776 he was appointed by the legislature brigadier general of Rhode Island troops in the Continental line. In February 1777 he was promoted to brigadier general in the Continental army. In November 1777 he was ordered by Gen. George Washington to command Fort Mercer, on the east bank of the Delaware River, and Fort Mifflin, on Fort Island in the river directly opposite. His defense of these posts, in cooperation with the river fleet under Commodore John Hazelwood, against heavy British attack was ultimately unsuccessful but helped delay the consolidation of the British occupation of Philadelphia farther upriver. In 1778 Varnum was engaged in various operations in Rhode Island, including Gen. John Sullivan's campaign in August, and in January 1779 he was named commander of the Rhode Island district. He resigned from the Continental army two months later to resume his law practice, but in April 1779 he accepted appointment as major general of Rhode Island militia. In May 1780 he was elected to the Continental Congress, and he served in that body in 1780–1782, 1786, and 1787. In August 1787 he was elected a director of the Ohio Company of Associates, and in October he was appointed by Congress a judge of the Northwest Territory. Resigning as commander of the Rhode Island militia in May 1788, he set out for Marietta, Ohio, to take up his new duties. He died in Marietta on January 10, 1789.

Vickery, Howard Leroy (1892–1946), naval officer.

Born in Bellevue, Ohio, on April 20, 1892, Vickery graduated from the Naval Academy in 1915 and saw his first duty aboard the cruiser *Charleston*, on which he served through World War I. Promoted to lieutenant in 1918, he was transferred to the Construction Corps and sent to the Massachusetts Institute of Technology, from which he graduated in 1921 with a degree in naval architecture. During 1922–1925 he was new construction superintendent, docking superintendent, and outside superintendent at the Boston navy yard; and from 1925 to 1928 he was on loan to the government of Haiti, which he served as director of the Shop, Supply, and Transportation Division. He was attached to the navy's Bureau of Construction and Repair in 1928–1929 and was technical adviser on shipping to the governor-general of the Philippines in 1929–1933. After attending the Army Industrial College in 1933–1934 he was named head of the war plans section, design branch, of the Bureau of Construction and Repair. Following the disastrous burning of the liner *Morro astle* off the New Jersey coast in September 1934, in which 134 lives were lost, Vickery was named to head an investigating board; the board's findings and recommendations led to legislation requiring such safety devices as asbestos insulation and fire-sealing doors on

civil vessels. In 1937, by then a commander, he joined the staff of and in 1938 he became assistant to the chairman of the U.S. Maritime Commission, and by 1939 he had assumed responsibility for all ship design and construction carried on under the commission's authority. In September 1940, on the passage of special enabling legislation required because of his naval commission, he became a member of the commission. He became vice chairman of the commission in February 1942, receiving promotion to rear admiral in April, and in June he was named also deputy administrator of the War Shipping Administration. Under his direction between 1939 and 1945 nearly 40 million gross tons of merchant shipping was turned out of American shipyards. The number of yards was greatly increased, their efficiency was doubled and redoubled by innovative use of preassembly and production line techniques and standardized designs, notably the famous "Liberty" and "Victory" ships, and the entire industry was integrated into a working whole by Vickery's forceful administration. From August 1943 he served also as chairman of the Postwar Planning Committee. He was promoted to vice admiral in October 1944. Ill health restricted his activities in the final months of the war, and he retired from all posts in December 1945. He died in Palm Springs, California, on March 21, 1946.

Von Braun *see* Braun, Wernher von

Von Kármán *see* Kármán, Theodore von

Von Steuben *see* Steuben, Baron von

Voorhees, Philip Falkerson (1792–1862), naval officer.

Born in New Brunswick, New Jersey, in 1792, Voorhees entered the navy as a midshipman in November 1809. During the War of 1812 he served on the *United States,* Commodore Stephen Decatur, on which he took part in the capture of the *Macedonian,* and on the *Peacock,* Capt. Lewis Warrington, on which he participated in the capture of the *Epervier.* Routine duties followed, highlighted by cruises in the Mediterranean on the *North Carolina* in 1825–1827 and in command of the *John Adams* in 1831–1834. He was promoted to commander in April 1828 and captain in February 1838. In July 1842 he sailed for the Mediterranean in command of the *Congress,* the next year taking her to join the Brazil Squadron. On September 28, 1844, he helped rescue the stranded British steamer *Gorgon* in the Río de la Plata, Argentina. The next day an Argentinian cruiser, the *Sancala,* fired on an American brig, *Rosalba,* lying by the *Congress.* Voorhees promptly captured the *Sancala* and the rest of the Argentinian squadron blockading Montevideo, Uruguay. The squadron was soon released, but the *Sancala* was retained for a time until ordered released by the American squadron commander, Commodore Daniel Turner. In March 1845 Voorhees arrived home, and in June he was court-martialed for his actions in Argentinian waters. Despite the support of Turner and the administration, he was reprimanded and sentenced to a 3-year suspension from duty and another 18-month suspension on a more minor charge. Secretary of the Navy George Bancroft reconvened the court, which in August raised the sentence to dismissal. President James Polk mitigated the sentence to five years' suspension and in January 1847 restored Voorhees to duty. During 1848–1851 he commanded the East India Squadron, an assignment called by Attorney General Caleb Cushing a token of the complete rehabilitation of Voorhees's honor and reputation. In 1855 he was placed on the reserve list, and after several appeals and reviews he won upgrading in pay in 1858, then-Attorney General Jeremiah S. Black declaring that Voorhees had been the victim of an unprecedented series of administrative blunders. In December 1860 he appealed to Congress in vain for active service. Voorhees died in Annapolis, Maryland, on February 23, 1862.

W

Waddell, Hugh (1734?–1773), colonial militia officer. Born in Lisburn, County Down, Ireland, probably in 1734, Waddell was brought to Boston at an early age by his father. In 1753 he removed to North Carolina, where he quickly became active in public affairs as clerk of the provincial council in 1754–1755 and a member of the militia. He served as a lieutenant in a North Carolina regiment sent to aid Virginia against the French in 1754, was promoted to captain in 1755, and in the latter year was sent to build Fort Dobbs on the Indian frontier near present-day Statesville; he commanded that post until 1757. In 1756 he negotiated a treaty of alliance with the Cherokee and Catawba Indians of the frontier. He was a major in command of three companies sent from North Carolina to assist Col. John Forbes in the expedition of 1758 against Fort Duquesne, and in 1759–1760, by then a colonel, he was active against the Indians on the frontier. Waddell was also a frequent member of the colonial assembly, representing Rowan County each year from 1757 to 1760 and Bladen County in 1762, 1766, 1767, and 1771. During the popular resistance to the Stamp Act in 1765–1766 he was a leading figure in the mass actions—seizing the stamps and terrorizing the appointed stamp agent —that effectively nullified the act. Despite his defiance of Gov. William Tryon in that matter he kept Tryon's confidence. In May 1771 the governor ordered Waddell to raise and command, as major general of militia, a force to suppress the frontier disturbances of the Regulators, armed bands of backcountrymen protesting various measures of the colonial government and particularly the corrupt administration of law by officials appointed to govern the districts concerned. Waddell gathered about 1000 men at Hillsborough. He was intercepted by a Regulator band while away from his forces and prevented from taking part in the two-hour battle of Alamance River, May 16, 1771, in which a force of some 2000 Regulators was routed, effectively ending the disturbances. Released, he subsequently made a tour of pacification of the frontier districts. Waddell died in Castle Hayne, near Wilmington, North Carolina, on April 9, 1773.

Waddell, James Iredell (1824–1886), Confederate naval officer. Born in Pittsboro, North Carolina, on July 13, 1824, Waddell, a great-grandson of Gen. Hugh Waddell, joined the navy as a midshipman in September 1841. In 1846, during the Mexican War, he saw action aboard the *Somers* in the squadron at Veracruz. For two years after the war he studied at the naval school at Annapolis, Maryland, forerunner of the Naval Academy. Over the years sea duty took him to various parts of the world, and he became a lieutenant in September 1855. In 1857–1859 he taught at the Academy, and subsequently he undertook a mission to China. Upon returning home from the Far East in January 1862 he resigned his commission and in March went into the Confederate navy as a lieutenant. After a year's duty with forces on the Mississippi and the James and at Charleston he sailed for Europe, and in October 1864 he took command of the Confederate cruiser *Shenandoah* (ex-*Sea King*), which had been purchased in England, and brought her to Madeira for refitting. He sailed for the Pacific and spent most of the ensuing year harassing Union shipping. He virtually wiped out the New England whaling fleet in the Pacific, capturing 38 prizes, commandeering some ships and burning others while ranging from Australia, where he made repairs in January–February 1865, to the Bering Sea. Not knowing that the Union had won the war in April 1865, he continued his depredations until August. He even planned an attack upon San Francisco. When he learned from a British ship that the Civil War was indeed over, he sailed instead for England, rounding the Horn and becoming the only Confederate commander to carry his flag around the world. He docked at Liverpool on November 6, 1865, after a voyage of some 58,000 miles, during which he had put into port only once, at Melbourne. Legally he and his crew had been engaged in acts of piracy since the end of the war, and they therefore remained in England until an amnesty was granted. After returning to the United States, Waddell sailed for private shipping companies for the rest of his life. On May 16, 1877, his ship, the *San Francisco*, on the Pacific Mail's San Francisco –Yokohama run, struck a reef and went down with no loss of life. Waddell died in Annapolis, Maryland, on March 15, 1886.

Wadsworth, Peleg (1748–1829), Revolutionary militia officer. Born in Duxbury, Massachusetts, on May 6, 1748, Wadsworth graduated from Harvard in 1769 and then opened a private school. In 1774 he became captain of a company of minutemen in Plymouth, Massachusetts. He took the field immediately on learning of the battle at Lexington, April 19, 1775, and soon joined a Roxbury regiment at Boston, where he assisted Gen. John Thomas in laying out fortifications on Dorchester Heights and elsewhere. In February 1776 he became aide-de-camp to Gen. Artemas Ward. He took part in the Long Island and Manhattan campaigns under Gen. George Washington in 1776 and in Gen. John Sullivan's expedition to Rhode Island in 1778. He served also on the Massachusetts board of war and from May 1777 to May 1778 in the legislature. He was appointed adjutant general of Massachusetts militia in August 1778 and brigadier general in July 1779. In the latter month he was second-in-command under Gen. Solomon Lovell of the militia forces cooperating with Commodore Dudley Saltonstall in the disastrous expedition to Penobscot Bay, during which he was captured. In March 1780 Wadsworth took command of the eastern militia department of Massachusetts at Thomaston (now in Maine). He was taken prisoner in his home by a British raiding party in February 1781 and held captive in Fort George, at Castine, until he escaped in June. In 1784 he settled in Falmouth (now Portland, Maine) and developed various business interests. He sat in the legislature in 1792 and in Congress from March 1793 to March 1807. In the latter year he moved to Oxford County and established the town of Hiram (now in Maine), where he died on November 12, 1829. A grandson was Henry Wadsworth Longfellow.

Waesche, Russell Randolph (1886–1946), Coast Guard officer. Born on January 6, 1886, in Thurmont, Maryland, Waesche attended Purdue University in 1903–1904 and then transferred to the Revenue Cutter Service cadet school at Arundel Cove near Baltimore. On graduating he was commissioned a third lieutenant in October 1906, and for the next ten years he was a line officer on various cutters and destroyers in the Atlantic, Pacific, and Arctic, advancing to second lieutenant in 1907. Under a law of January 28, 1915, the Revenue Cutter Service and the Life Saving Service were merged as the U.S. Coast Guard, which continued to operate under the Department of the Treasury. In 1916 Waesche was named head of the newly created Division of Communications, in which post he helped develop the Guard's new radio network as well as its land line system. He was promoted to first lieutenant in 1917. In 1920–1921 he commanded the cutter *Bothwell* in the Bering Sea. He advanced to lieutenant commander in 1923 and in 1924–1926 commanded the destroyer *Beale* on patrol in coastal waters against rumrunners; in 1926–1927, from the destroyer *Tucker*, he commanded a division of destroyers on similar duty. Waesche, promoted to commander in 1926, served in 1927–1928 as force gunnery officer on the staff of the destroyer force commander and was then named chief ordnance officer of the Coast Guard. He instituted a reorganization of the Guard's field forces in 1931 and

the next year became aide to the commandant, serving also as budget officer and chief of finance. In June 1936 he was appointed commandant of the Coast Guard with the rank of rear admiral by President Franklin D. Roosevelt; he was reappointed to the post in June 1940 and June 1944. During that time the Coast Guard took over the Lighthouse Service in July 1939 and the Bureau of Marine Inspection and Navigation in February 1942. From September 1939 the Guard had responsibility, under the neutrality laws, for monitoring shipments from U.S. ports to belligerent nations for contraband. In November 1941, shortly before the United States entered World War II, the Coast Guard was transferred to the Department of the Navy and given vastly increased responsibility: patrol of waters around Greenland (the Greenland Patrol even operated occasionally on land, capturing a number of Nazi radio bases); air and surface antisubmarine patrol, which accounted for 12 U-boats during the war; coastal defense, port security, and sabotage prevention; sea rescue; maintenance of coastal communications and navigation systems including the new LORAN radio navigation system; and, owing to its great experience with small craft and surf seamanship, participation in all major amphibious combat operations in the Atlantic and Pacific theaters. During the war the Guard expanded from about 10,000 to nearly 172,000 men, operating roughly 350 naval vessels and 290 army vessels in addition to its own 760 cutters and 3500 smaller craft. A women's reserve, the SPARS, was established in November 1942 and under Commander Dorothy C. Stratton grew to a strength of 10,000 by the end of the war. Waesche was promoted to temporary vice admiral in March 1942 and temporary admiral in April 1945, the first Coast Guard officer to hold those ranks, and he retired as permanent admiral on December 31, 1945. (The following day the Coast Guard was turned back to the Treasury.) He died in Bethesda, Maryland, on October 17, 1946.

Wagner, Arthur Lockwood (1853–1905), army officer and educator. Born on March 16, 1853, in Ottawa, Illinois, Wagner graduated from West Point in 1875 and was commissioned in the infantry. During 1876–1877 he served with the 6th Infantry in the campaigns against the Sioux Indians in Montana and the Dakotas, and in 1880–1881 he saw action against the Utes in Utah. Promoted to first lieutenant in October 1882, he was assigned as professor of military science and tactics to East Florida Seminary (now the University of Florida) from that year until 1885. After a year at Fort Douglas, Utah, he was appointed instructor in the art of war at the Infantry and Cavalry School (from 1881 to 1886 known as the School of Application for Infantry and Cavalry) at Fort Leavenworth, Kansas. Wagner's was the principal influence in the rapid development of the institution into a fully professional training school. Permanent regulations and a program were established for the first time in 1888, and a two-year course of theoretical and practical instruction was perfected. During his years there he also published influential studies of *The Campaigns of Königgrätz*, 1889, *The Service of Security and Information*, 1893, *Organization and Tactics*, 1895, and *A Catechism of Outpost Duty*, 1896. Promoted to captain in April 1892 and major and assistant adjutant general in November 1896, Wagner had charge of the military information division of the War Department from April 1897 to May 1898, advancing to lieutenant colonel in February 1898. He served on the staff of Gen. Henry Lawton during the Santiago campaign in Cuba in June–July 1898 and on that of Gen. Nelson A. Miles in Puerto Rico in July–August. After a brief period as adjutant general of the Department of the Dakotas he was ordered to the Philippines in December 1899. He served there in various staff capacities, including adjutant general for the northern department from November 1901, until March 1902. He advanced during that period to colonel. Subsequently he was adjutant general of the Department of the Lakes at Chicago until 1904, when he was named to the staff of the newly organized Army War College at Washington Barracks (later Fort Humphreys and then Fort Lesley J. McNair), D.C. He died in Asheville, North Carolina, on June 17, 1905, the day his commission as brigadier general was signed.

Wainwright, Jonathan Mayhew (1883–1953), army officer. Born on August 23, 1883, at Fort Walla Walla, Washington, Wainwright was the son of an army officer and a descendant of a line of distinguished naval officers. He graduated from West Point in 1906, was commissioned in the cavalry, and over the next several years served with the 1st Cavalry in Texas, 1906–1908; in the Philippines, where he saw action against Moro rebels, 1908–1910; and at various posts in the West. He graduated from the Mounted Service School, Fort Riley, Kansas, in 1916, was promoted to captain, and in 1917 was on the staff of the first officers training camp at Plattsburg, New York. In February 1918 he was ordered to France. In June he became assistant chief of staff of the 82nd Infantry Division, with which he took part in the St. Mihiel and Meuse–Argonne offensives. Promoted to temporary lieutenant colonel in October, Wainwright remained on occupation duty in Germany with the Third Army until 1920, in which year, having reverted to captain, he was promoted to major. After a year as an instructor at the renamed Cavalry School at Fort Riley he was attached to the General Staff during 1921–1923 and was assigned to the 3rd Cavalry at Fort Myer, Virginia, in 1923–1925. Other routine assignments followed: He was promoted to lieutenant colonel in 1929, and he graduated from the Command and General Staff School, Fort

Leavenworth, Kansas, in 1931 and from the Army War College in 1934. Promoted to colonel in 1935, he commanded the 3rd Cavalry at Fort Myer until 1938, when he advanced to brigadier general in command of the 1st Cavalry Brigade at Fort Clark, Texas. In September 1940, promoted to temporary major general, he returned to the Philippines to take command of the Philippines Division. As senior field commander of American and Filipino forces under Gen. Douglas MacArthur, Wainwright had tactical responsibility for resisting the Japanese invasion that began in late December 1941. Pushed back from beachheads in the Lingayen Gulf, the Philippine forces withdrew into the Bataan Peninsula early in January 1942, where they occupied well prepared defensive positions and commanded the entrance to Manila Bay. In throwing back a major Japanese assault in January the defenders earned the name of "battling bastards of Bataan." When MacArthur was ordered off Bataan in March 1942 Wainwright, promoted to temporary lieutenant general, succeeded to command of U.S. Army Forces in the Far East, a command immediately afterward redesignated U.S. Forces in the Philippines. Japanese attacks resumed in earnest in April. A small core of the now starving, ill, and unsupplied garrison pulled farther back onto the island fortress of Corregidor, leaving the 70,000 defenders on Bataan to surrender on April 9. The Japanese gained a foothold on Corregidor on May 5 against a furious defense, and the next day Wainwright was forced to surrender the 3500 men on the island. Under orders that he was forced to broadcast, local commanders elsewhere in the Philippines surrendered one by one, and on June 9 the American command in the Philippines ceased to exist. Wainwright was held in prison camps in northern Luzon, on Formosa, and in Manchuria until liberated by Russian troops in August 1945. After witnessing the Japanese surrender aboard the *Missouri* on September 2 he returned to the Philippines to receive the surrender of the local Japanese commander. A hero's welcome in the United States was accompanied by promotion to general and the Medal of Honor. His memoir, *General Wainwright's Story*, was published in 1945. In January 1946 he took command of the Fourth Army at Fort Sam Houston, Texas. Wainwright retired in August 1947 and died in San Antonio, Texas, on September 2, 1953.

Wainwright, Richard (1849–1926), naval officer. Born in Washington, D.C., on December 17, 1849, Wainwright was the son of a naval officer who later commanded Flag-Officer David G. Farragut's flagship *Hartford* at New Orleans. The younger Wainwright graduated from the Naval Academy in 1868 and after a two-year cruise on the *Jamestown* of the Pacific Squadron was promoted to master in July 1870. He served on the *Colorado* of the Asiatic Squadron in 1870–1873, was promoted to lieutenant in September 1873, and after four years with the Hydrographic Office and the Coast Survey was again attached to the Asiatic Squadron in 1877–1880. From 1880 to 1884 he was in the Bureau of Navigation, and from 1884 to 1887 he served on the *Tennessee* and the *Galena* in the North Atlantic. He served as an instructor at the Naval Academy in 1888–1890, aboard the *Alert* in 1890–1893, and again in the Hydrographic Office in 1893–1896, advancing to lieutenant commander in September 1894. After a year as chief of the office of naval intelligence he joined the battleship *Maine* as executive officer late in 1897. Sternly resisting interference by Spanish authorities, he directed the recovery of bodies and preliminary inspection of the wreck after the *Maine* was blown up in Havana harbor on February 15, 1898. In the Spanish–American War he commanded the *Gloucester*, converted from J. Pierpont Morgan's yacht *Corsair*, in Adm. William T. Sampson's squadron. At the battle of Santiago, July 3, the *Gloucester* braved fire from the Spanish cruisers exiting the harbor to wait for the destroyers *Pluton* and *Furor*. When they appeared the *Gloucester* attacked furiously, supported by fire from other American vessels, and in short order the *Pluton* was forced to beach (she subsequently blew up) and the *Furor* was sunk. Wainwright then maneuvered to rescue 200 men, including Adm. Cervera, from the burning Spanish flagship *Maria Teresa*. He was duly recognized for his gallantry. The *Gloucester* led the expedition bearing Gen. Nelson A. Miles and his troops to Puerto Rico and captured the port of Guánica unassisted on July 25. Promoted to commander in March 1899, Wainwright was put in command of the ships of the Naval Academy, and in 1900 he became superintendent. During 1902–1904 he commanded the *Newark*, advancing to captain in August 1903, and after three years on the General Board he commanded the *Louisiana* in 1907–1908. Promoted to rear admiral in July 1908, he commanded Division 2, Atlantic Fleet, in 1908–1909 and Division 3 in 1909–1910. After a period as aide to the secretary of the navy he retired in December 1911. Wainwright died on March 6, 1926, in Washington, D.C.

Walke, Henry (1808–1896), naval officer. Born in Princess Anne County, Virginia, on December 24, 1808, Walke grew up in Chillicothe, Ohio, from the age of two. He entered the navy as a midshipman in February 1827 and after service in various routine assignments advanced to lieutenant in February 1839. During 1840–1843 he circumnavigated the globe on the *Boston*. In the Mexican War he served on the bomb-brig *Vesuvius*, which took part in operations at Veracruz, Tuxpan, Frontera, and Tabasco under Commodore Matthew C. Perry. Promoted to commander in September 1855, he commanded the storeship *Supply* in 1858–1861 in African and West Indian waters. Aboard that vessel on January 10, 1861, he ferried Lt. Adam J. Slemmer's small command from Fort Barrancas at Pensacola, Florida, across the bay to Fort Pickens on Santa Rosa Island. He then carried the garrison of the navy yard at Pensacola, which had been occupied by secessionist forces, to New York. His court-martial, required in that his actions involved disobedience to prior orders, ended with a very complimentary reprimand from Secretary of the Navy Gideon Welles. Ordered to duty on the upper Mississippi, he commanded the gunboats *Tyler* and *Lexington* of Flag-Officer Andrew H. Foote's flotilla at the battle of Belmont, Missouri, November 7, 1861, where he helped transport and cover Gen. Ulysses S. Grant's force. In January 1862 he took command of the armored gunboat *Carondelet*, which was one of four such vessels that attacked and forced the surrender of Fort Henry on the Tennessee River on February 6, with Grant's army standing by. On February 13 the *Carondelet* took part in an unsuccessful attack on Fort Donelson and on March 17 in the first bombardment of the heavily defended Island No. 10 in the Mississippi below New Madrid, Missouri. On the night of April 4, during a lightning storm that provided the only guidance in the narrow, twisting channel, Walke ran the *Carondelet* past the batteries on Island No. 10, a feat that was believed by most, including the Confederate defenders, to be impossible. His achievement opened the way for Gen. John Pope's capture of that stronghold and for the subsequent neutralization of Fort Pillow downstream. At the latter post on May 10 the *Carondelet* led the repulse of an attack by a Confederate flotilla (the Union flotilla was then commanded by Flag-Officer Charles H. Davis). She was in the forefront of another battle above Memphis on June 6, where Davis's flotilla and Col. Charles Ellet's army rams defeated a Confederate flotilla, and on July 15 she suffered much damage in an engagement with the ram *Arkansas* on the Yazoo River. Promoted to captain in July 1862, Walke took command of the converted ironclad ram *Lafayette* in February 1863, and he had a part in Adm. David D. Porter's running of the Vicksburg batteries, April 16, and the battle at Grand Gulf, April 29. In September 1863 he was put in command of the sloop *Sacramento* in the Atlantic and ordered to seek out the *Alabama* and other Confederate raiders. He held the raider *Rappahannock* blockaded in the harbor at Calais, France, for 15 months. In March 1865 he was with Commodore Thomas T. Craven when the latter declined battle with the raider *Stonewall*. Walke was promoted to commodore in July 1866 and to rear admiral in July 1870, and he served in various shore assignments until his retirement in April 1871. In 1877 he published *Naval Scenes and Reminiscences of the Civil War*. He died in Brooklyn, New York, on March 8, 1896.

Walker, John Grimes (1835–1907), naval officer. Born in Hillsboro, New Hampshire, on March 20, 1835, Walker lived from the age of eleven with his uncle, James W. Grimes, later (1854–1858) governor of Iowa. Walker entered the navy as a midshipman in October 1850, and after a Pacific cruise on the *Falmouth* he studied for a year at the Naval Academy, graduating in 1856. After two more years on various vessels in the Pacific and Brazil squadrons he was promoted to lieutenant in January 1858. He was an instructor at the Academy in 1859–1860. He served on the *Susquehannah* in 1860–1861 and the *Connecticut* in 1861, and in November 1861 he was assigned to the *Winona* of the West Gulf Blockading Squadron. He took part in the attack on Fort Jackson and Fort St. Philip and the capture of New Orleans by Flag-Officer David G. Farragut in April 1862 and in the subsequent advance to Vicksburg. Promoted to lieutenant commander in July, he later commanded the ironclad *Baron De Kalb* (ex-*St. Louis*) of the Mississippi Squadron under Adm. David D. Porter. On that vessel he led the attack on Arkansas Post, January 10–11, 1863, and took part in five expeditions up the Yazoo River to Haynes' Bluff and beyond in March–July in which much Confederate shipping was captured and vital support was rendered to land operations under Gen. William T. Sherman, Gen. Ulysses S. Grant, and Gen. Francis J. Herron. During the campaign to capture Yazoo City the *De Kalb* was sunk on July 13. In January 1864 Walker took command of the gunboat *Saco* of the North Atlantic Blockading Squadron and in January 1865 of the gunboat *Shawmut,* with which he took part in the capture of Wilmington, North Carolina. Promoted to commander in July 1866, he was on the staff of the Naval Academy in 1866–1869 and in 1869–1870 commanded the *Sabine* on a European cruise with a class of midshipmen. From 1873 to 1878 he was secretary of the Lighthouse Board, receiving promotion to captain in June 1877. After a two-year leave of absence, during which he was associated with the Chicago, Burlington & Quincy Railroad, Walker was head of the Bureau of Navigation from 1881 to 1889. He was promoted to commodore in February 1889 and in that year given command of the "White Squadron" comprising the *Atlanta, Boston, Chicago* (flagship), and *Dolphin,* the navy's first steel cruisers and the beginning of the "new navy." He also commanded the South Atlantic station during 1891–1892 and the North Atlantic station in 1892–1893. He was promoted to rear admiral in January 1894, and for a few months in that year he was commander of the Pacific Squadron during the period of unrest accompanying the establishment of the Republic of Hawaii. He then served as chairman of the Lighthouse Board until his retirement in March 1897. In July 1897 he was appointed to the Nicaragua Canal Commission by President William McKinley, and in June 1899 he was named president of the Isthmian Canal Commission, charged with evaluating both the Nicaragua and Panama routes. He took a leading part in the negotiations with French canal interests and headed the commission administering the Canal Zone until its dissolution in April 1905. Walker died at York Beach, Maine, on September 15, 1907.

Walker, Mary Edwards (1832–1919), physician and reformer. Born on a farm near Oswego, New York, on November 26, 1832, Mary Walker was of a family of singular individuals. She overcame numerous obstacles in graduating from the Syracuse Medical College in 1855, and after a few months in Columbus, Ohio, she established a practice in Rome, New York. In the same year she married one Albert Miller, also a physician, with whom she practiced but whose name she did not take; the marriage was not a happy one and they separated in 1859 and were finally divorced ten years later. She had from an early age been interested in dress reform and was an ardent follower of Amelia Bloomer in the cause, and that interest led her also to related reforms. At the outbreak of the Civil War she traveled to Washington, D.C., to offer her services. She worked as a volunteer nurse in the Patent Office Hospital there while attempting to gain a regular appointment to the army medical service. In 1862 she took time away from Washington to earn a degree from the New York Hygeio-Therapeutic College. In that year she began working in the field, and in September 1863 she finally was appointed assistant surgeon in the Army of the Cumberland by Gen. George H. Thomas. She was apparently the only woman so engaged in the Civil War. She was assigned to the 52nd Ohio Regiment in Tennessee, and she quickly adopted standard officers' uniform, suitably modified. During April–August 1864 she was a prisoner in Richmond, Virginia. In October she was given a contract as "acting assistant surgeon," but she saw no more field service, being instead assigned to a women's prison hospital and then to an orphanage. She left government service in June 1865 and a short time later was awarded a Medal of Honor. She was elected president of the National Dress Reform Association in 1866 and for some years thereafter was closely associated with Belva A. Lockwood in various reform movements. Feminist organizations widely publicized her Civil War service, but she became estranged from them over the years because of her growing eccentricity. She wore full male attire, complete to wing collar, bow tie, and top hat. Often arrested for masquerading as a man, she claimed—and the claim was given currency—that she had been granted permission to dress so by Congress; no record of any such action exists. Her view of the suffrage question was that the Constitution had already given the vote to women and that the legislation sought by organized suffragists was therefore pointless. She is said to have invented at some time in her Washington years the idea of attaching a postcard receipt to registered mail. She published two books, the partly autobiographical *Hit*, 1871, and *Unmasked, or the Science of Immorality*, 1878. From 1887 she exhibited herself in dime museum sideshows on several occasions. She lived in Oswego from 1890, increasingly eccentric although generally harmless. She wore her Medal of Honor constantly, even after it was revoked by an army board in 1917 (as were hundreds of others) because there was no record of the occasion of its award. A fall on the steps of the Capitol in Washington left her infirm, and she died in Oswego, New York, on February 21, 1919.

Walker, Walton Harris (1899–1950), army officer. Born on December 3, 1899, in Belton, Texas, Walker attended Virginia Military Institute in 1907–1908 and then entered West Point, graduating in 1912 and receiving his commission in the infantry. After garrison duty at Fort Sheridan, Illinois, Fort Sill, Oklahoma, and Galveston, Texas, he took part in the occupation of Veracruz, Mexico, in April 1914. More routine garrison assignments followed, and in July 1916 he was promoted to first lieutenant. Advanced to captain in May 1917, he went to France in April 1918 with the 13th Machine Gun Battalion, 5th Division. He saw action in the St. Mihiel and Meuse–Argonne offensives and was promoted to temporary major in June 1918 and, while on occupation duty, to temporary lieutenant colonel in May 1919. He graduated from the Field Artillery School, Fort Sill, in 1920, was promoted to permanent major in July of that year, and became an instructor at the Infantry School at Fort Benning, Georgia, where he graduated from the senior course in 1923. During 1923–1925 he was on the staff at West Point, and in 1926 he graduated from the Command and General Staff School, Fort Leavenworth, Kansas. After a time as an instructor at the Coast Artillery School, Fort Monroe, Virginia, he served three years, 1930–1933, with the 15th Infantry at Tientsin, China. Promoted to lieutenant colonel in August 1935, he graduated from the Army War College in 1936 and in 1937–1940 was attached to the War Plans Division of the General Staff. He was promoted to temporary colonel in February 1941 and put in command of the 36th Infantry at Camp Polk, Louisiana, and in July he advanced to temporary brigadier general in command of the 3rd Armored Brigade. In January 1942 he took command of the 3rd Armored Division, receiving promotion to temporary major general the next month. In September he took over the IV Armored Corps at Camp Young, California, and in November he was named also commander of the Desert Training Center on the California–Arizona border. In April 1943 he led the IV Armored Corps to Camp Campbell, Kentucky; the unit was

redesignated the XX Corps in October 1943, and in February 1944 it was ordered to England. The XX Corps landed in France in July 1944 and, as an element of Gen. George S. Patton's Third Army, captured Reims, crossed the Moselle in November, reduced the fortress complex at Metz and broke through the Siegfried Line in February 1945, earning the nickname of the "Ghost Corps" for the speed of its advance, and in April liberated the Buchenwald concentration camp in Austria. In that month Walker was promoted to temporary lieutenant general. In June 1945 he took over the 8th Service Command at Dallas, Texas, and in June 1946 he was named commander of the reactivated Fifth Army at Chicago. In September 1948 he was transferred to Japan to command of the Eighth Army, which constituted the ground arm of Gen. Douglas MacArthur's Far East Command. Following the North Korean attack on South Korea on June 25, 1950, various units drawn from the Eighth Army were dispatched to South Korea by MacArthur. As the American commitment quickly expanded, control of those units reverted to the Eighth Army, which transferred its headquarters to Taegu, South Korea, on July 13. Walker also received command of the army of the Republic of Korea and of other United Nations forces as they arrived. With most of his U.S. units understrength and his ROK forces demoralized and with insufficient tactical air support, Walker was forced to fight a stubborn withdrawal into the southeast corner of the Korean peninsula, his defensive line centered on the port of Pusan. The arrival of reinforcements, heavy armaments, and increased air support enabled him to establish a 140-mile "Pusan Perimeter," and he declared that "there will be no Dunkirk, there will be no Bataan." His skill in shifting reserves to blunt North Korean attacks on the perimeter held the line and gained time for the organization of the X Corps under Gen. Edward M. Almond and its landing at Inch'on on September 15. With the pressure thus relieved Walker assumed the offensive and pushed north. He made contact with the X Corps on September 26, and together they pushed into North Korean territory. The ROK I Corps took Wonsan on October 10, and the U.S. I Corps captured the North's capital, Pyongyang, on October 19. Heavy attacks by Chinese forces on the UN line at the Ch'ongch'on River beginning on November 25 reversed the tide quickly. Falling back under extreme pressure, Walker abandoned Pyongyang on December 5 and ten days later developed a new line roughly on the 38th parallel. On December 23, 1950, he was killed in a jeep accident on the road between Seoul and the front. Walker was succeeded by Gen. Matthew B. Ridgway.

Walker, William Henry Talbot (1816–1864), Confederate army officer. Born in Augusta, Georgia, on November 26, 1816, Walker graduated from West

Point in 1837 and was commissioned in the infantry. He was ordered to Florida for service against the Seminole Indians and at the battle of Okeechobee, December 25, 1837, was severely wounded; he was brevetted first lieutenant for his actions in that fight. He resigned from the army in October 1838 but was reappointed to his regiment, the 6th Infantry, as a first lieutenant in November 1840. He saw further service in Florida and was promoted to captain in November 1845. In the Mexican War he won brevets to major at Contreras, August 19–20, 1847, and lieutenant colonel at Molino del Rey, September 8, at the latter again being very seriously wounded. Until 1852 he was on sick leave and then recruiting duty, and in 1852–1854 he was deputy governor of the military asylum in East Pascagoula, Mississippi. During 1854 –1856 he was commandant of cadets and an instructor at West Point, receiving promotion to major in 1855, and he later served briefly in Minnesota. He resigned from the army in December 1860 after an extended period of sick leave and in April 1861 was appointed major general of Georgia volunteers. In that month he received the surrender of the federal arsenal in Augusta from Capt. Arnold Elzey. In May he was commissioned brigadier general in the Confederate army. After six months' service at Pensacola, Florida, and in northern Virginia he resigned for health reasons in October. Nonetheless in November he was again appointed major general of Georgia state troops by Gov. Joseph E. Brown, who throughout the Civil War attempted to conduct military affairs independent of the Confederate government. Walker reentered Confederate service as a brigadier general in March 1863. He commanded a division in Mississippi and later in Georgia and the reserve corps at Chickamauga, September 18–20, 1863. In January 1864 he was promoted to major general. He commanded a division of Gen. William J. Hardee's corps in Gen. Joseph E. Johnston's Army of Tennessee during the Atlanta campaign, and while leading a sortie out of the city against Gen. James B. McPherson's Army of the Tennessee at Peachtree Creek he was killed on July 22, 1864.

Wallace, Lewis (1827–1905), lawyer, army officer, diplomat, and author. Born in Brookville, Indiana, on April 10, 1827, Lew Wallace grew up there and in Indianapolis. He had some formal schooling but was basically self-taught. In 1846, when he was nineteen, he raised a volunteer company for the Mexican War and as a second lieutenant served with it in Mexico as part of the 1st Indiana Infantry. Following the war he returned to Indianapolis and, having read law in his father's law office, was admitted to the bar in 1849. He moved to Covington shortly thereafter and in 1850 and 1852 was elected prosecuting attorney. By 1853 he had settled in Crawfordsville, where he kept his interest in the military by organizing and training a local militia company. He continued his law practice during the 1850s and was active in state politics. In 1856 he won election to the state senate. In April 1861 he was appointed state adjutant general and then colonel of the 11th Indiana Infantry. After seeing minor action at Romney and Harpers Ferry, West Virginia, he was promoted to brigadier general of volunteers in September. He commanded a division under Gen. Ulysses S. Grant in the capture of Fort Donelson, February 16, 1862, and in March was promoted to major general of volunteers. He helped relieve Grant at Shiloh (Pittsburg Landing) on April 7 and took part in the advance to Corinth. In September 1862, in command of the defenses of Cincinnati, he staved off a threat from Gen. Edmund Kirby-Smith's raiders in Kentucky. In November he was president of a commission investigating the conduct of Gen. Don Carlos Buell. Early in 1864 he was given command of the VIII Corps and the Middle Division at Baltimore. On July 9, 1864, he led his fewer than 6000 men against Gen. Jubal A. Early's 11,000 at the Monocacy River; he was defeated, but the delay enabled Gen. Horatio G. Wright to rush reinforcements to Washington, D.C., to bolster the city's defenses against Early. In May and June of 1865 Wallace sat on the military court that tried the conspirators in the assassination of Abraham Lincoln, and in August he presided over the court that convicted Capt. Henry Wirz, commandant of the infamous Andersonville prison. After a brief period of service in Mexico in 1865 he returned to live in Indiana and resumed his law practice. In 1878 President Rutherford B. Hayes appointed him governor of the New Mexico Territory in the hope that he could settle the fierce "Lincoln County War" that was raging there. This cattle war, a complex feud between rival political and economic factions in which Billy the Kid (William H. Bonney) was but one of many hired gunmen, had been going on for some time with a great deal of violence and little prospect of an end. After Wallace arrived in Santa Fe in August he issued a proclamation of amnesty, listened to the stories of the participants, and eventually restored order. (Billy the Kid, however, refused amnesty and continued his bloody career.) He remained in New Mexico until 1881, when President James Garfield appointed him U.S. minister to Turkey. Leaving that post in 1885, he returned to live in Crawfordsville. Wallace's military and public careers notwithstanding, he is far better known for his novels. His first, *The Fair God*, 1873, dealt with the conquest of Mexico by Hernando Cortes and was based on William H. Prescott's history. *Ben Hur; A Tale of the Christ*, 1880, about Christians in the early Roman Empire, was one of the most popular novels ever published in the United States; continuously in print since its publication, it was later twice made into film extravaganzas. Less well known works were *The Boyhood of Christ*, 1888, and *The Prince of India*,

1893. Wallace died in Crawfordsville, Indiana, on February 15, 1905. *Lew Wallace, An Autobiography,* which he had left incomplete at his death, was published in 1906.

Waller, Littleton Waller Tazewell (1856–1926), marine officer.

Born on September 26, 1856, in York County, Virginia, Waller was commissioned a second lieutenant of marines in June 1880. In 1882, while serving with the European Squadron, he took part in the relief of the besieged embassies in Alexandria, Egypt. He advanced to first lieutenant in September 1885 and captain in June 1896 and in the latter year took command of the marine detachment on the new battleship *Indiana.* During the Spanish–American War he took part with the *Indiana* in the naval battle of Santiago, July 3, 1898. Promoted to major in July 1899, he was stationed at the Cavite naval base near Manila, Philippines, and in June 1900 he commanded a battalion of marines dispatched to Tientsin, China. Several small engagements with rebel Chinese forces around Tientsin in July and August finally secured that port as a base, and Waller then took part, with Maj. William P. Biddle and under Gen. Adna R. Chaffee, in the relief expedition to Peking. He was brevetted lieutenant colonel for his part in the battle of Tientsin, July 13–14. Back in the Philippines in 1900–1902, he saw considerable action against Moro rebels on Samar. After a period of recruiting duty in Pennsylvania in 1902–1903 he was promoted to lieutenant colonel in March 1903. In early 1904 he commanded a regiment in Gen. George F. Elliott's Provisional Marine Brigade in Panama following that nation's revolt against Colombia and during the early stages of U.S. occupation of the Canal Zone. Promoted to colonel in March 1905, Waller commanded the marine expeditionary force of two regiments sent to Cuba in October 1906 to quell unrest, and he was there again in August 1911 in command of a provisional brigade sent for the same purpose. In 1911–1914 he commanded the marine barracks at the Mare Island, California, navy yard. In April 1914 he was sent to succeed Col. John A. Lejeune in command of the 1st Marine Brigade occupying Veracruz, Mexico, under the overall command of Gen. Frederick Funston; and in July 1915 he commanded a force of nearly 2000 marines that landed in Haiti, put down a revolt that had degenerated into simple anarchy, and supervised the election of a new government in September. Waller was promoted to brigadier general in August 1916 and put in command of the Advanced Base Force at the League Island navy yard, Philadelphia, in January 1917. He advanced to major general in August 1918 and retired in June 1920; he was reputed to have taken part in more actions than any other marine officer of the period. He died on July 13, 1926, in Atlantic City, New Jersey.

Walthall, Edward Cary (1831–1898), Confederate army officer and public official.

Born in Richmond, Virginia, on April 4, 1831, Walthall grew up from the age of ten in Holly Springs, Mississippi. He won admission to the bar in 1852 and entered practice in Coffeeville, where he was elected district attorney in 1856 and 1859. He was elected first lieutenant of a local volunteer company shortly after the outbreak of the Civil War. The company became part of the 15th Mississippi Infantry, and Walthall became lieutenant colonel of the regiment in mid-1861. He distinguished himself in command of the 15th, under Gen. George B. Crittenden, at the battle of Mill Springs, Kentucky, January 19, 1862, and in April he was promoted to colonel of the 29th Mississippi Infantry. A year later, after heavy campaigning in Mississippi, Tennessee, and Kentucky, he advanced to brigadier general, dating from December 1862. He led a brigade of Gen. Benjamin F. Cheatham's division at Chickamauga, September 18–20, 1863, and in the siege of Chattanooga. His brigade suffered heavy casualties at Lookout Mountain, November 24; and at Missionary Ridge, November 25, numbering only 600, it made a heroic rearguard stand. Promoted to major general in June 1864, he served under Gen. John B. Hood in the defense of Atlanta and the campaign against Gen. George H. Thomas in Georgia and Tennessee in 1864, covering Hood's retreat after Nashville, December 15–16. After the war Walthall resumed his law practice in Coffeeville, briefly in partnership with Lucius Q. C. Lamar, and in 1871 he moved to nearby Grenada. Active in Democratic politics, Walthall was elected to Lamar's seat in the Senate in March 1885. He resigned because of ill health in January 1894, but in March 1895 he resumed his seat. He died in Washington, D.C., on April 21, 1898.

Ward, Artemas (1727–1800), Revolutionary army officer and public official.

Born in Shrewsbury, Massachusetts, on November 26, 1727, Ward graduated from Harvard in 1748 and two years later opened a general store in his native town. He held a variety of town offices and was active in the militia, receiving promotion to colonel during the expedition under Gen. James Abercrombie to Fort Ticonderoga in 1758. He was elected several times to the Massachusetts General Court from 1757. His support of Samuel Adams in the popular agitation against the Stamp Act and other such measures led to the revoking of his militia commission by the royal governor, (later Sir) Francis Bernard, in 1766 and to the veto of his election to the provincial council in 1768 and 1769. Under Gov. Thomas Hutchinson he took a seat on the council in 1770. He was a member of the first provincial congress in October 1774 and was appointed by it to several committees concerned with the preparedness of the militia. He also sat in the second provincial congress, February 1775, and under its authority he rose from his sickbed and rode to Cambridge in April, following receipt of news of the battle of Lexington, to assume command of the gathering colonial forces. On May 19 he was commissioned general in command of Massachusetts troops, and he was by common consent chief of the informal council of commanders from the several colonies. Under him the first steps toward organizing an army were taken, and in June he issued the order to fortify Bunker Hill in Charlestown, dispatching Col. William Prescott for the task. Ward remained in Cambridge through the battle that followed on June 17. With the appointment by the Continental Congress of George Washington as commander in chief of the army on June 15, Ward was commissioned senior major general and second-in-command. From Washington's arrival at Cambridge on July 2, Ward commanded the right wing of the army in the siege of Boston. In March 1776 he tendered his resignation owing to poor health; it was accepted in April, but at Washington's request he remained on duty in command of forces in Massachusetts until relieved by Gen. William Heath in March 1777. From that year to 1779 he was president of the executive council of Massachusetts, and from January 1780 to May 1782 he was a delegate to the Continental Congress. From 1782 to 1787 he was almost continuously a member of the General Court. In 1790, overcoming the unpopularity that had earlier resulted from his support of the federal Constitution and his opposition to Shays's Rebellion, he was elected to Congress, where he sat from March 1791 to March 1795. Ward died in Shrewsbury, Massachusetts, on October 28, 1800.

Ward, James Harmon (1806–1861), naval officer. Born on September 25, 1806, in Hartford, Connecticut, Ward graduated from Capt. Alden Partridge's military academy (later Norwich University) in Norwich, Vermont, in 1823 and in March of that year entered the navy as a midshipman. During 1824–1828 he was aboard the *Constitution* in the Mediterranean Squadron, and he then spent a year in scientific study at Washington (now Trinity) College in Hartford. Promoted to lieutenant in March 1831, he subsequently saw duty in the Mediterranean, Africa, and West India squadrons. Ward was recognized as one of the most scholarly officers in the navy, and after delivering a series of lectures in 1844–1845 at the naval school in Philadelphia and publishing them in the latter year as *An Elementary Course of Instruction on Ordnance and Gunnery* he became executive officer (later commandant of cadets) and head of the ordnance and gunnery department at the new Naval School (subsequently the Naval Academy) at Annapolis, Maryland, when it opened in October 1845. (His textbook was adopted by the Academy in 1852.) In 1847 he commanded the *Cumberland*, flagship of Commodore Matthew C. Perry, in the squadron on

the east coast of Mexico. He commanded the steamer *Vixen* of the Home Squadron in 1849–1850, was promoted to commander in September 1853, and in 1856–1857 commanded the *Jamestown* of the Africa Squadron. In 1859 he published *A Manual of Naval Tactics* and in 1860 *Steam for the Million.* In May 1861 he was put in command of the Potomac Flotilla for the defense of Washington, D.C., and surrounding areas of Chesapeake Bay. On May 31 the flotilla, consisting of three small steamers, the *Freeborn, Anacostia,* and *Resolute,* attacked the Confederate batteries at Aquia Creek; reinforced by the *Pawnee,* Commander Stephen C. Rowan, the flotilla attacked again on June 1 and silenced the batteries. On June 27 the flotilla attacked another battery at Matthias Point; in a counterattack by Confederate forces Ward, aboard the *Freeborn,* was shot and killed.

Warner, Seth (1743–1784), Revolutionary militia and army officer. Born in Woodbury (now Roxbury), Connecticut, on May 17, 1743, Warner moved with his family to Bennington in what was then known as the New Hampshire Grants (now Vermont) in 1763. Along with Ethan Allen he became a leader of the resistance to New York's claims to the region. He was elected captain of the Bennington company of "Green Mountain Boys" in 1770 and was declared an outlaw by New York in March 1774. He took part as second-in-command in Allen's capture of Fort Ticonderoga on May 10, 1775, and two days later led in the capture of Crown Point. With Allen he prevailed upon the Continental Congress to authorize the raising of a Vermont regiment for the Continental army and in July was elected lieutenant colonel of the Green Mountain Boys. Succeeding to command of the Green Mountain Boys after Allen's capture in September, Warner took part in the expedition under Gen. Richard Montgomery against Montreal and Quebec, during which he defeated a British relief column on its way to besieged St. John's, New Brunswick, on October 31. In July 1776 he was given a colonel's commission by Congress; he spent most of that year organizing troops in Vermont. During Gen. John Burgoyne's campaign down the Hudson valley in the summer of 1777 Warner commanded the rearguard of the American army under Gen. Arthur St. Clair. Following St. Clair's abandonment of Fort Ticonderoga, Warner fought a sharp action at Hubbardton on July 7. At the battle of Bennington, August 16, he and his regiment arrived on the field in time to secure the victory for Gen. John Stark's militia. He served under Gen. Horatio Gates through the rest of the northern campaign. In March 1778 he was commissioned brigadier general of militia by the newly organized Vermont legislature. He remained in the army until 1782 but owing to failing health saw little action. He died in Roxbury, Connecticut, on December 26, 1784.

Warren, Gouverneur Kemble (1830–1882),

army officer. Born in Cold Spring, New York, on January 8, 1830, Warren graduated from West Point in 1850 and was commissioned in the topographical engineers. For four years he was engaged in survey work on the Mississippi delta, the Ohio River, and the upper Mississippi at Des Moines. In 1854 he worked with Capt. Andrew A. Humphreys in the compilation of the reports of the five Pacific railroad surveys. In 1855 he was chief topographical engineer in Col. William S. Harney's expedition against the Sioux. Promoted to first lieutenant in July 1856, he was on survey duty in Nebraska and Dakota territories until 1859 and then taught mathematics at West Point. In May 1861 he was appointed lieutenant colonel of the 5th New York Volunteers. He saw action at Big Bethel, Virginia, under Gen. Benjamin F. Butler on June 10, and while engaged in preparing the defenses of Washington, D.C., and Baltimore he was promoted to colonel of his regiment in August and to captain of topographical engineers in September. He served through the Peninsula campaign in April–July 1862, commanding a brigade of Gen. Fitz-John Porter's V Corps from May and receiving a wound at Gaines' Mill, June 27, for which battle he was brevetted lieutenant colonel of regulars. He led a brigade through the Seven Days' Battles, at the second battle of Bull Run (Manassas), August 29–30, at Antietam (Sharpsburg), September 17, and, promoted to brigadier general of volunteers in September, at Fredericksburg, December 13. In February 1863 he was appointed chief topographical engineer of the Army of the Potomac, then commanded by Gen. Joseph Hooker; following the consolidation of the engineers and topographical engineers in March, he served as chief engineer of the Army of the Potomac during June–August, receiving promotion to major general of volunteers in June. At Gettysburg he discovered on the second day of battle, July 2, that the commanding position on Little Round Top at the extreme left of the Union line was virtually unoccupied. Obtaining two brigades of infantry and some artillery from the V Corps (Gen. George Sykes) and other troops from Gen. Daniel E. Sickles's III Corps, he established a line on the hill just in time to repel a heavy attack by Confederate troops of Gen. James Longstreet's corps. He was brevetted colonel of regulars for his actions that day. From August until March 1864 he commanded the II Corps. On October 14, 1863, he repulsed Gen. Ambrose P. Hill's corps, the vanguard of Gen. Robert E. Lee's advance toward Washington, at Bristoe Station. During Gen. George G. Meade's Rappahannock campaign of November 1863 he attempted unsuccessfully to flank Lee's left at Mine Run, November 28–29. From March 1864 he commanded the V Corps. He took part in the campaign through the Wilderness in early May, and his corps was the vanguard of the Army of the Potomac's advance to Spotsylvania. There his forces met Gen. Richard H. Anderson's entrenched corps and, attacking together with Gen. John Sedgwick's VI Corps, were thrown back by Anderson on May 8. The V Corps took part in the battle at Cold Harbor and in establishing the siege of Petersburg. In March 1865 Warren was brevetted brigadier and major general of regulars. At Five Forks, April 1, 1865, he acted promptly and to great effect in spite of conflicting orders, but he was nonetheless summarily relieved of command by Gen. Philip H. Sheridan. After two weeks in command of the Department of Mississippi he resigned his volunteer commission late in May 1865 and reverted to major of engineers. He served thereafter in routine surveying and engineering duties. He spent many years on various works in the upper Mississippi valley, including supervision of the construction of the Mississippi bridge at Rock Island, Illinois, in 1869–1870. He was promoted to lieutenant colonel in March 1879. After years of requests he was granted in December 1879 a court of inquiry into the manner of his relief at Five Forks. The court found fully in his favor against Sheridan's charges, but the report was not published until shortly after Warren's death in Newport, Rhode Island, on August 8, 1882.

Warren, Joseph (1741–1775),

Revolutionary patriot and militia officer and physician. Born in Roxbury, Massachusetts (now part of Boston), on June 11, 1741, Warren, the eldest brother of noted physician John Warren (1753–1815), graduated from Harvard in 1759. He taught at the Roxbury Grammar School for a year before taking up the study of medicine. He established a good practice in Boston in 1764, but his interest in the Whig cause led him to neglect medicine for politics. With the passage of the Stamp Act in 1765 he became active with Samuel Adams and other prominent Whigs in their political clubs. His frequent writings in the press and his speeches made him a leader of the popular party, and he was a member of the Boston committee of safety from its organization. He helped prepare the Suffolk Resolves of September 9, 1774, that denounced the coercive measures passed by Parliament after the Boston Tea Party, called Massachusetts to arms, and recommended economic sanctions against Britain. On their adoption by the convention of the towns of Suffolk County at Milton, Paul Revere carried the Resolves to the Continental Congress in Philadelphia, where they were endorsed. Warren was a member of the first three provincial congresses held in Massachusetts, was president of the third, convened in May 1775, and actively served the committee of safety. On April 18, 1775, he dispatched Paul Revere and William Dawes to Lexington to warn Adams and John Hancock of the approach of British troops. Warren was named a major general of militia by the provincial congress on June 14, 1775, but before receiving his commission he took part as a volunteer in the battle of Bunker Hill and was killed by enemy fire there on June 17, 1775.

Warrington, Lewis (1782–1851), naval officer. Born on November 3, 1782, in Williamsburg, Virginia, Warrington attended William and Mary College before entering the navy as a midshipman in January 1800. He made his first cruise on the *Chesapeake* in the West Indies and from 1802 to 1807 served in turn on the *President*, the *Vixen*, the *Siren*, and the *Enterprise*, all engaged in the Tripolitan War. He became acting lieutenant of the *Siren* in 1805 and received promotion to lieutenant in February 1807. In 1809 he was attached again to the *Siren*, and from 1811 to 1813 he was aboard the *Essex*, the *Congress*, and then the *United States*. He was promoted to master commandant in July 1813 and shortly afterward given command of the sloop *Peacock*, 22 guns. He sailed out of New York in March 1814 and off Cape Canaveral, Florida, on April 29 encountered the British brig *Epervier*, 18. In a 45-minute fight he inflicted heavy casualties and damage on the enemy and took her captive. Leaving the prize in Savannah, he sailed again in June, and after a voyage to the Grand Banks, Ireland, the Faroe and Shetland islands, Portugal, and Barbados, he returned to New York at the end of October, having taken 14 prizes. Promoted to captain in November, he made a cruise around the Cape of Good Hope to the Indian Ocean, accompanied for a time by the *Hornet*, Capt. James Biddle. Warrington took several more prizes, all after the War of 1812 had actually ended, and concluded his war service with the capture of the East Indiaman *Nautilus* in the Strait of Sunda on June 30, 1815. He commanded the *Macedonian* in 1816–1818, the *Java* in 1819–1820, and the *Guerrière* in 1820–1821, all in the Mediterranean Squadron. From 1821 to 1824 he was at the Norfolk navy yard, and in the latter year he succeeded Commodore David Porter as commander of the "Mosquito Fleet" engaged in piracy suppression in the West Indies. During 1826–1830 he was a member of the navy's Board of Commissioners, and from 1830 to 1840 he commanded the Norfolk navy yard. After two more years as a naval commissioner he became chief of the Bureau of Yards and Docks in 1842. He served as acting secretary of the navy for a brief time in 1844 and in 1846 became chief of the Bureau of Ordnance. Warrington died in Washington, D.C., on October 12, 1851.

Washington, George (1732–1799), Revolutionary army officer and first president of the United States. Born on February 22, 1732, in Westmoreland County, Virginia, Washington grew up on the family plantation, Wakefield. Little is known of his childhood, and much that was later written about it—

notably Mason Locke Weems's cherry tree story—is apocryphal. In 1743 his father died, and, after living for periods of time with various relatives, he came into the care of his older half-brother Lawrence, who was connected by marriage to the powerful Fairfax family and who owned a plantation known as Mount Vernon. His irregular schooling came to an end at fifteen, and he turned to surveying as a profession. In 1748 he joined a surveying party sent by Lord Fairfax into the Shenandoah valley, and the next year he was appointed official surveyor of Culpeper County. In 1751 he accompanied Lawrence, then suffering from tuberculosis, to Barbados; the deaths of Lawrence and Lawrence's daughter in 1752 left George in possession of Mount Vernon, one of the finest estates in the colony, at the age of twenty. Shortly thereafter he was named adjutant for the southern district of Virginia, with the rank of major, by Lt. Gov. Robert Dinwiddie. In 1753 he became adjutant of the Northern Neck and Eastern Shore. In October of that year he volunteered to carry a warning from Dinwiddie to French forces encroaching on the Ohio valley region claimed by England. The winter journey, on which he was guided by Christopher Gist, was extremely perilous, and Washington's account of it, emphasizing the refusal of the French to leave after he finally reached Fort Le Boeuf (at what is now Waterford, Pennsylvania), was published by the governor and widely read. In 1754 he was commissioned lieutenant colonel of a Virginia regiment and in April sent with 150 men back to the Ohio territory, where Dinwiddie had meantime sent a party to build a fort at the forks of the Ohio, the site of present-day Pittsburgh. Near the fort, which the French had seized and named Fort Duquesne, Washington built Fort Necessity at Great Meadows, and on May 28 he surprised and defeated a small French detachment under Coulon de Jumonville, who was killed. The battle was the first of the French and Indian War. Defending Fort Necessity with 360 men after the arrival of reinforcements, Washington was nonetheless compelled to surrender on liberal terms to a much superior enemy force of 500 French and 400 Indians on July 3; he and his men were allowed to march back to Virginia. In October he resigned his commission, largely because of conflicts with British regular officers who, although of inferior rank, assumed authority over provincial officers because they held king's commissions. Early in 1755 Gen. Edward Braddock arrived in Virginia from England with a fresh supply of regular troops and offered Washington a position as aide-de-camp. An expedition was mounted against Fort Duquesne, and Washington, who had fallen ill, joined the vanguard just one day before the column was ambushed and dispersed by French and Indians on July 9. Braddock was mortally wounded, and Washington, although holding no formal command position, rallied the colonial troops and succeeded in turning the rout into an orderly retreat, having two horses shot under him in the fray. After Braddock's death a few days later he returned home and in August was commissioned colonel in command of all Virginia forces. For the next three years of the French and Indian War he was primarily concerned with defense of the frontier against constant raids, a mission in which he was given insufficient support by the colonial government. With the title of brigadier he commanded a force of two Virginia regiments in the expedition under Gen. John Forbes that built Fort Pitt on the site of the abandoned and razed Fort Duquesne in November 1758. He resigned his commission shortly after his election to the Virginia House of Burgesses in December 1758. Early the next year he married Martha Dandridge Custis, a wealthy widow, and settled down to farming. He remained in the House of Burgesses and from 1760 to 1774 was a justice of the peace for Fairfax County. Mount Vernon and other properties waxed in value as he devoted himself to managing the estate and enjoying the social life of a country gentleman. He also pursued various land schemes in the Ohio country, acquiring eventually some 45,000 acres, over half of it in the valley of the Great Kanawha River. As tension between the colonies and Britain grew, he sided unequivocally with his native country. He took part in the unauthorized meetings of the burgesses at the Raleigh Tavern in Williamsburg in May 1770 and May 1774, sat in the first provincial congress in Williamsburg in August 1774, where he declared himself in favor of armed resistance to unlawful authority, and in September 1774 took his seat in the First Continental Congress in Philadelphia. He was also placed in command of the militia companies of several Virginia counties. (He was to retain his Fairfax County militia uniform throughout the Revolutionary War.) The next year he was a delegate to the Second Continental Congress, and on June 15, as part of a compromise between Virginia and Massachusetts, leaders respectively of the Southern and Northern factions, he was unanimously chosen commander in chief of the Continental army. He had under him four major generals (Artemas Ward, Charles Lee, Israel Putnam, and Philip J. Schuyler), eight brigadier generals (including Richard Montgomery, Horatio Gates, Nathanael Greene, and John Sullivan), and an untrained, undisciplined mob gathered at Cambridge, Massachusetts. He arrived at Boston after the battle of Bunker Hill, June 17, 1775, formally took command on July 3, and spent several months training the ill equipped troops, mostly short-term militia. In March 1776 he dispatched Gen. John Thomas to seize Dorchester Heights, which commanded Boston from the south. The site was fortified by Col. Richard Gridley with cannon captured earlier at Fort Ticonderoga by Ethan Allen and brought to Boston by Col. Henry Knox. Gen. Sir William Howe was thus forced to evacuate the city on March 17. Washington then moved south to New York, where he made a major error in attempting to defend the virtually indefensible city. Howe had 30,000 troops at his disposal on Staten Island when the campaign opened. On August 22 he sent about 20,000 across to Long Island to deal with Gen. Putnam's 9000. The Americans' forward line under Gen. William Alexander and Gen. Sullivan was quickly breached and flanked and pushed back within fortified Brooklyn Heights on August 27. Two nights later Washington managed to withdraw his forces under cover of fog to Manhattan in spite of the unchallenged presence of a strong British fleet under Adm. Richard Howe, Sir William's brother. The British army moved slowly, not crossing to Manhattan until September 15, when Howe made a landing on the flank at Kip's Bay; Connecticut militia posted there broke and ran. Howe moved too slowly to split the American army in southern Manhattan, and Washington, unable to rally his panicked troops, withdrew northward to Harlem Heights, where a sharp engagement was fought on September 16. After a month Washington was forced by another British landing in his rear, at Pell's Point, to abandon southernmost New York, except for garrison forces at Fort Washington on the Manhattan bank of the Hudson and Fort Lee on the New Jersey shore opposite. Howe continued his slow pursuit. At White Plains in Westchester County Washington fought off a probing attack on October 28 and withdrew further to Peekskill on the Hudson. From there he dispatched Gen. Greene to command the forts on the lower river and, leaving some 8000 men under Gen. Lee and Gen. William Heath to hold the upper river, he led his remaining 5000 over the Hudson and into New Jersey. Howe's capture of Fort Washington and 3000 prisoners on November 16, followed by Greene's abandonment of Fort Lee, concluded the New York campaign in virtually complete disaster. Washington fought a delaying retreat across New Jersey and into Pennsylvania, where late in December he was able to assemble about 7000 men, many of whose enlistments would expire at the end of the month. At that moment he dealt a brilliant stroke. On Christmas night he ferried the army back across the ice-filled Delaware River to surprise the British encampments at Trenton and Bordentown. The militia force sent to Bordentown failed in its task, but on the morning of December 26 Washington's main force converged in two columns under Greene and Sullivan and overwhelmed the Hessians under Lt. Col. Johann Rall at Trenton; 1000 were captured and Rall was killed. Gen. Charles Cornwallis rushed to Trenton with 8000 more troops; a skirmish took place at Assunpink River, but on the night of January 2 Washington, deceptively leaving his campfires burning, slipped away, flanked Cornwallis, and at dawn routed the garrison at Princeton. Washington then went into winter quarters at Morristown, and Cornwallis rejoined Howe in New York City. The year 1777 was marked by the constant struggle to maintain the army despite short-term enlistments, desertions, and lack of congressional and state support in money and supplies; by the desperate battle at Brandywine, September 11, and the subsequent loss of Philadelphia; and by the Conway Cabal, an apparent plan by several of Washington's military rivals (notably Lee, Thomas Conway, and Thomas Mifflin) and their allies in Congress to have him replaced by Gen. Horatio Gates, who had been victorious over Burgoyne at Saratoga. After a final unsuccessful attack on the British at Germantown, October 4, where Washington's elaborate tactical plan overtaxed his subordinates' abilities, the army encamped at Valley Forge. The winter of 1777–1778 was perhaps the darkest moment of the Revolution, as the army starved and dwindled, Congress meddled, and only the personal strength of the commander held the tatters together. The efforts of Baron von Steuben to instill military discipline into the troops that winter, however, boded well for the renewed campaign. In early 1778 an alliance between the colonies and France was sealed, and, in anticipation of the arrival of a French fleet, the British army, now under Gen. Sir Henry Clinton, abandoned Philadelphia and withdrew toward New York City. Washington hurried to cut off part of Clinton's army and on June 27 engaged it at Monmouth, New Jersey, only to be kept from a major victory by the incompetence and probable treachery of Gen. Charles Lee, commander of the American advance column. Clinton proceeded to occupy New York, and American forces surrounded the city. Aside from Gen. John Sullivan's unsuccessful attempt to attack Newport, Rhode Island, jointly with Adm. d'Estaing's French fleet in August 1778, his expedition against the Iroquois in 1779, and Gen. Anthony Wayne's capture of Stony Point on the Hudson, July 15, 1779, little action occurred in the Northern Department for the remainder of the war. The year 1780 was marked by Gen. Benedict Arnold's treason in the North and the decline and rebirth of the patriot cause in the South under Gates and Greene. In August 1781 Washington, reinforced by French troops that had arrived in Rhode Island in the previous year under the Comte de Rochambeau, learned that the French fleet under Adm. De Grasse was bound from the West Indies to Chesapeake Bay. The combined American-French army embarked in Delaware Bay, landed at Williamsburg, Virginia, in late September, and joined the small southern army under Gen. Greene and the Marquis de Lafayette, facing Gen. Cornwallis, who had entrenched himself at Yorktown, Virginia. In this climactic campaign Washington commanded some 5500 Continental regulars, 3500 Virginia militia, and 5000 French regulars against Cornwallis's 7000. By September 30 Yorktown was completely invested; the siege proceeded according to classic principles under the direction of the French engineer Gen. Louis L. Duportail, and on October 19, escape blocked by De Grasse's fleet, Cornwallis surrendered. The Revolutionary War was effectively ended. Nonetheless for many months Washington remained in command of the army, continued to plead with Congress to pay the soldiers, and put down a scheme concocted by certain officers to displace Congress and make their commander king. He settled his army at Newburgh, New York, in 1782 and for more than a year awaited the peace. Articles of peace were signed in November, effective as of January 20, 1783; the treaty of peace was signed September 3, 1783. Soon after the reoccupation of New York City in November 1783 he bid his officers farewell at Fraunces Tavern on December 4, returned his commission to Congress on December 23 (leaving Gen. Henry Knox the senior officer of the Continental army), and on Christmas Eve returned to Mount Vernon. Much of his own money had gone into the war effort, and he had accepted no compensation for the work of eight years; in addition, his properties had suffered greatly during the war, and he now devoted his energies to restoring them to prosperity. He also resumed his interest in the development of western lands. Washington shared in the rapidly growing concern that the Articles of Confederation were incapable of providing the unity and security necessary for the new nation. In March 1785 a meeting was held at his home between representatives of Virginia and Maryland to settle problems concerning the navigation of the Potomac. That conference led to the larger Annapolis Convention of September 1786, which in turn produced the Federal Constitutional Convention held in Philadelphia in May–September 1787. Sent as a Virginia delegate, Washington was unanimously chosen to preside over the convention. He took no part in the debates but approved of the Constitution and played a prominent role in securing its ratification in Virginia. When the state electors met in February 1789 to select the first president, they ratified without exception the long-obvious choice of George Washington, to which he acceded with reluctance. On April 30, 1789, he was inaugurated at Federal Hall in New York City. As the first president of a new and unsure government, he understood that not the least of his responsibilities was to avoid creating potentially harmful precedents. He constructed his cabinet with an eye to sectional and ideological balance (Thomas Jefferson, secretary of state; Alexander Hamilton, secretary of the treasury; Henry Knox, secretary of war; Edmund Randolph, attorney general), strove to the utmost to maintain cordial relations with and among all his governmental officers, and conducted himself with republican decorum and restraint. His first term passed without major crisis, but his second (he was reelected, again unanimously and again with John Adams as vice-president, in December 1792) witnessed an inevitable and heated clash between Jefferson and Hamilton and the consequent polarization of politics into party camps. While seeking to steer a middle course, Washington more often than not found himself aligned with the Hamiltonian Federalists, particularly when he issued his proclamation of neutrality in April 1793 upon the outbreak of war between England and France, precipitating Jefferson's resignation; when he sent troops under Hamilton to suppress the Whisky Rebellion in western Pennsylvania in 1794; and when he presented for ratification Jay's Treaty with England, concluded in November 1794. The treaty provoked a particularly bitter attack from the opposition, and the President resisted an attempt by the House of Representatives to gain a share of the treaty-making power. In 1796 he firmly rejected pleas that he accept a third term (setting a precedent that endured for 144 years, until Franklin D. Roosevelt's election in 1940, and that was later made law) and in September he arranged the publication of his "Farewell Address," which owed much to Hamilton and in which he advised his country on its future course. In March 1797 he returned once again to Mount Vernon. The apparent imminence of war with France in 1798 led to his appointment by President John Adams on July 3 as lieutenant general in command of a Provisional Army, but the crisis passed without his having to take the field. He died at Mount Vernon on December 14, 1799. He has remained in the century and three-quarters since his death, in the words of Henry Lee's famous eulogy, "first in war, first in peace, and first in the hearts of his countrymen."

Washington, John Macrae (1797–1853), army

officer. Born in Stafford County, Virginia, in October 1797, Washington, whose middle name is sometimes given as Marshall, was a distant cousin of George Washington and a nephew of William Washington. He graduated from West Point in 1817 and was commissioned in the artillery. He was stationed with the 3rd Artillery in Charleston, South Carolina, for three years and then, promoted to first lieutenant in May 1820, ordered to Florida. During 1821–1822 he was with the 4th Artillery at Savannah, Georgia; in 1822–1824 he was at Fort Moultrie in Charleston; and after a brief period at Augusta, Georgia, he was an instructor at the artillery school at Fort Monroe, Virginia, in 1824–1826. Following another year in Florida he was ordnance officer at Fort Monroe from 1827 to 1833, receiving a brevet as captain for service in May 1830 and regular promotion in May 1832. From 1833 to 1838 he was once again in Florida, this time actively engaged against the Creeks and Seminoles. He served on the staff of Gen. Winfield Scott during the removal of the Cherokee Indians to Indian Territory in

1838–1839 and in the pacification of the Maine–New Brunswick border in 1839. Various routine garrison assignments then occupied him until the outbreak of the Mexican War in 1846, when he was given command of a light battery in the division under Gen. John E. Wool. In February 1847 he was promoted to major, but he had not yet learned of the fact when the battle of Buena Vista took place on February 22–23. On the first day his battery was assigned the task of holding the key point, a mountain spur known as La Angostura. On the second day he held La Angostura, forming the anchor of the American right, against repeated attacks, and when a strong advance of fresh Mexican reserves scattered the Illinois and Kentucky volunteers on that wing he held fast, covering their retreat and doubtless saving hundreds of them while decimating the attacking force. Washington was brevetted lieutenant colonel for his actions that day. From June to December 1847 he was military governor of Saltillo, and until May 1848 he was chief of artillery of the army of occupation. Later ordered to Santa Fe, he was civil and military governor of New Mexico from October 1848 to October 1849. After two years at Fort Constitution, New Hampshire, 1850–1852, he was ordered to the Pacific Coast with the 3rd Artillery in 1853. In a violent storm on December 24, 1853, off Cape Henlopen, Delaware, he was swept off the steamer *San Francisco* along with 181 other men and drowned.

Washington, William (1752–1810), Revolution-

ary army officer. Born in Stafford County, Virginia, on February 28, 1752, Washington was a cousin of George Washington. Little is known of him prior to 1775, when he was commissioned a captain in the 3rd Virginia Infantry. In 1776 he served through the Long Island-Manhattan campaign, in which he was wounded, and the retreat across New Jersey and distinguished himself at Trenton, December 26, in charging and capturing a Hessian battery. In 1778 he was transferred to the dragoons and the following year ordered south to join Gen. Benjamin Lincoln's army. In March 1780 he was promoted to lieutenant colonel in command of a regiment of dragoons. Serving under Gen. Isaac Huger, he was surprised and defeated by the infamous Col. Banastre Tarleton at Monk's Corner, South Carolina, on April 14, and again at Lanneau's Ferry on May 6. On December 4, acting as part of Gen. Daniel Morgan's force, he employed the stratagem of a painted log (a "Quaker gun") to capture a Tory force at Rudgely's (or Rugley's) Mills. At the battle of the Cowpens under Morgan, January 17, 1781, Washington commanded the cavalry reserve that struck Tarleton's left at the critical moment; in the battle Washington and Tarleton had a personal encounter in which both were wounded. Under Gen. Nathanael Greene he took part in the battles of Guilford Court House, March 15, Hobkirk's Hill, April 25, and Eutaw Springs, September 8, at the last of which he was captured. After the Revolution he settled near Charleston, South Carolina, and occasionally sat in the legislature. In July 1798 he was commissioned brigadier general in the Provisional Army for possible war with France. He died in Charleston, South Carolina, on March 6, 1810.

Waterbury, David (1722–1801), Revolutionary militia officer. Born on February 12, 1722, in Stamford, Connecticut, Waterbury served in the militia in the French and Indian War, and he took part in the expedition to Crown Point under Gen. (later Sir) William Johnson in 1755 and in that to Ticonderoga under Gen. James Abercrombie in 1758. At the outbreak of the Revolution in 1775 he was appointed lieutenant colonel of the 9th Connecticut Regiment. He took part in the expedition into Canada under Gen. Richard Montgomery in that year. In June 1776 he was commissioned brigadier general of Connecticut troops in the Northern Department. Stationed at Skenesborough, New York, he assisted Gen. Benedict Arnold, who was in command of the American retreat from Canada, in building a small fleet for use on Lake Champlain. The British, halted in their pursuit of Arnold, also built a fleet at the north end of the lake and in October resumed their advance southward. The two fleets—the American of 15 tiny craft, the British of 25 led by the *Inflexible*, by far the largest vessel on either side—met near Valcour Island on October 11. Waterbury, second-in-command of the American fleet aboard the *Washington*, put up a stiff resistance and was wounded while his ship took several hits. The American fleet was badly battered but still for the most part afloat after a sharp battle, and Arnold ordered a retirement under cover of darkness. Two days later a second battle was fought. The *Washington*, covering the rear, was captured; the rest of the fleet, including Arnold's flagship *Congress*, was destroyed by the British or by the abandoning American crews. Waterbury was held prisoner until mid-1781, and after his exchange he continued to serve in command of a brigade under Gen. George Washington. After the Revolution he settled in Stamford. He sat in the legislature in 1783, 1794, and 1795. He died in Stamford, Connecticut, on June 29, 1801.

Waters, Daniel (1731–1816), Revolutionary naval officer. Born in Charlestown, Massachusetts, on June 20, 1731, Waters went to sea at an early age. From 1771 he made his home in Malden, where he was a member of the local company of minutemen. He took part in the fighting from Lexington to Boston on April 19, 1775 and later in the year he commanded a gunboat in the Charles River at besieged Boston. In January 1776 he was appointed captain of the schooner *Lee* in "Washington's fleet" under Commodore John Manley, and during that year he took several prizes. In March 1777 he was commissioned a captain in the Continental navy. He served for a time as a volunteer aboard Manley's *Hancock* and commanded the prize *Fox* from June until its recapture in July. Exchanged in 1778, he cruised the West Indies in command of the sloop *General Gates* in the spring of 1779 and in July commanded the Massachusetts ship *General Putnam* in the disastrous Penobscot expedition under Commodore Dudley Saltonstall. On December 25, 1779, in command of the Boston privateer *Thorn*, he fought a two-hour action against two British privateers, *Governor Tryon* and *Sir William Erskine*, each of about equal armament, and defeated them, although he was unable to prevent the *Tryon's* escape later. In January he brought the *Erskine* to port along with another prize, the *Sparlin*. In 1781 he made his final cruise on the Massachusetts privateer *Friendship*. After the Revolution Waters took up farming in Malden, Massachusetts; he died there on March 26, 1816.

Watie, Stand (1806–1871), Indian leader and Confederate army officer. Born on December 12, 1806, near present-day Rome, Georgia, Stand Watie was of the Cherokee Indian tribe. His given name, Degataga, was roughly translated as "stand," and his father's name, Oowatie or Uweti, became contracted into his common surname. He was a younger brother of Elias Boudinot, editor of the *Cherokee Phoenix* from 1824 to 1835. Stand Watie was educated in a mission school, later worked with Boudinot on the newspaper, and became a supporter of the idea of Indian removal to western lands. He was a signer of the Treaty of New Echota, December 29, 1835, by which the Cherokee were committed to give up all lands east of the Mississippi. The majority of the tribe opposed removal, which was carried out in 1838–1839 under the supervision of Gen. Winfield Scott, and Stand Watie narrowly escaped assassination, the fate of Boudinot and the other signers. He lived quietly in Indian Territory (now part of Oklahoma) until the outbreak of the Civil War, when, espousing the Confederate cause, he raised a company of home guards, of which he was captain. In August 1861 Cherokee, under Chief John Ross, reluctantly gave in to the persuasion of Gen. Albert Pike, gave up neutrality, and allied themselves with the Confederacy. Stand Watie was given a commission as colonel in October and put in command of the regiment of Mounted Rifles raised among the Cherokee. The regiment took part in numerous skirmishes in Indian Territory and occasionally in battles in Arkansas and Missouri, notably Pea Ridge (Elkhorn Tavern), March 7–8, 1862, under Gen. Earl Van Dorn. The majority of the Cherokee tribe repudiated the Confederate alliance in 1863, but Stand Watie continued in Southern service. He was later given command of a brigade by Gen. Samuel B. Maxey, Pike's successor, and he received promotion to brigadier general in May 1864. At its peak his command consisted of two regiments of Cherokee Mounted Rifles and three battalions of Cherokee, Seminole, and Osage infantry. He finally surrendered in June 1865, and he died in Indian Territory on September 9, 1871.

Wayne, Anthony (1745–1796), army officer. Born at Wayneborough, near Wayne, Chester County, Pennsylvania, on January 1, 1745, Wayne left school after two years at the Philadelphia Academy. He worked as a surveyor for several years and helped his father run the family farm and tannery. He served in the Pennsylvania assembly in 1774–1775 and on the provincial committee of safety in 1775 and in January 1776 was commissioned colonel of the 4th Pennsylvania Regiment. In March he accompanied Gen. William Thompson's relief force to Canada and on June 8 was at the head of the attack on the British army at Three Rivers. His regiment covered the rear of the American withdrawal to Fort Ticonderoga, of which he was then made commander. In February 1777 he was commissioned a brigadier general. During 1777 he took part in the defense of Philadelphia, notably the battle of Brandywine, September 11. Nine days later he was surprised and roughly handled by a British detachment at Paoli, but a court-martial cleared him of negligence, and he distinguished himself at Germantown, October 4. His brigade formed part of Gen. Charles Lee's vanguard at Monmouth Court House, June 27, 1778. Some months later he was given command of a new corps of light infantry. With 1300 men, many armed only with the bayonets on their unloaded muskets, on July 16, 1779, he stormed and took Stony Point, the northernmost British defense post on the Hudson River, in a brilliantly executed maneuver that gave a huge boost in morale to the American army. In September 1780 he forestalled British seizure of West Point after Benedict Arnold's attempted betrayal of the post by moving in reinforcements. Because of his tactical boldness and his personal courage in the field (which some fellow officers called recklessness), Wayne was often called "Mad Anthony," but his worth was recognized on all sides, and for his Stony Point exploit he received the congratulations of Gen. George Washington and the Continental Congress, which had a medal struck in his honor. In 1781 he was ordered south with some 800 men to reinforce the Marquis de Lafayette facing Gen. Charles Cornwallis's army near Williamsburg, Virginia. On July 6, mistaking the main British army for a detachment, he attacked 5000 men with his 800 at Green Spring, but he discovered his error in time to fall back adroitly. After Cornwallis's surrender at Yorktown on October 19, he served under Gen. Nathanael Greene and

was largely responsible for liberating Georgia from the British, receiving the surrender of the garrison at Savannah on July 12, 1782, and occupying Charleston, South Carolina, on December 14. He also helped pacify the Creek and Cherokee Indians of the region. Brevetted major general in October 1783, he shortly afterward retired to private life and divided his time between Pennsylvania and Georgia, where the grateful state had given him an 847-acre rice plantation. He served in the Pennsylvania assembly during 1784–1785, then settled on his Georgia plantation, which proved to be a losing venture for him. He voted for the new Constitution as a member of the Pennsylvania ratifying convention in 1788, and, after moving South, he was elected to the House of Representatives from Georgia in 1790 but served only until March 21, 1792, when his seat was declared vacant owing to irregularities in the election. On April 13, 1792, President Washington called Wayne back into military service with the rank of major general; he succeeded Gen. Arthur St. Clair as senior officer in the army. His principal task, one at which St. Clair and, before him, Gen. Josiah Harmar had failed, was to deal with Indian troubles in the Ohio valley. The Indians had been on the warpath intermittently since the close of the French and Indian War, and incitements to fresh hostilities were given them by the continued existence of British forts in the West. Wayne spent months preparing for his campaign. He marched his troops (at that time organized as the "Legion") from Fort Fayette (in what is now Pittsburgh) into the Ohio country in 1793, establishing a camp near Fort Washington (Cincinnati). Months of training followed, and in the fall he moved 80 miles north and built Fort Greenville. In December he sent out a detachment to build Fort Recovery on the site of St. Clair's defeat. On June 30, 1794, the Indians began hostilities by laying brief siege to Fort Recovery. Wayne pursued them northward, building Fort Defiance ("I defy the English, Indians, and all the devils in hell to take it," he declared) at the confluence of the Maumee and Auglaize rivers. Farther down the Maumee, at a place where a tornado had lately flattened the trees, occurred the decisive engagement of the campaign, the brief Battle of Fallen Timbers, on August 20. Much of the Indians' will to fight was lost when they realized the British at nearby Fort Miamis would not aid them. Gradually Wayne pacified the whole region and built Fort Wayne in present-day Indiana in October 1794. In 1795 he gathered together the chiefs of the several tribes and dictated the terms of the Treaty of Greenville, signed August 3, 1795, which opened part of the Old Northwest to settlement. He spent the winter of 1795–1796 in Philadelphia, then was sent west again to take possession for the United States of the forts the British were abandoning according to the terms of Jay's Treaty. He died at Presque Isle (now

Erie), Pennsylvania, on December 15, 1796, while returning from this mission.

Weatherford, William *see* Red Eagle

Webb, Alexander Stewart (1835–1911), army

officer and educator. Born in New York City on February 15, 1835, Webb graduated from West Point in 1855 and was commissioned in the artillery. After field service against the Seminoles in Florida in 1856 and garrison duty at Fort Independence, Massachusetts, and Fort Snelling, Minnesota Territory, he was appointed an instructor in mathematics at West Point late in 1857. In April 1861 he was promoted to first lieutenant and in May to captain, and after a brief time at Fort Pickens, Florida, he took part in the battle of Bull Run (Manassas), July 21, and was then named assistant chief of artillery of the Army of the Potomac. In September he was appointed major of volunteers. From the beginning of the Peninsula campaign in March 1862 until November of that year he was inspector general on the staff of the chief of artillery, Gen. William F. Barry, and he saw action on the Peninsula and, with Gen. Fitz-John Porter's V Corps, in the Maryland campaign in August–September. In January 1863 he was appointed assistant inspector general of the V Corps (from February under Gen. George G. Meade), and in May he took command of a brigade of Gen. John Gibbon's 2nd Division, II Corps, receiving promotion to brigadier general of volunteers in June. His brigade occupied the point of the "Bloody Angle" and bore the brunt of Pickett's Charge on the third day of the battle of Gettysburg, July 3. He was brevetted major of regulars for his actions that day and in 1891 was awarded a Medal of Honor. Moved up to command of a division of the II Corps, he served through the Rappahannock campaign and in the offensive of May 1864 until he was seriously wounded at Spotsylvania; for his actions in that battle he was brevetted colonel of regulars. Brevetted major general of volunteers in December 1864, he returned to field service in January 1865 as chief of staff of Meade's Army of the Potomac. In March he was brevetted brigadier and major general of regulars, and from June 1865 to February 1866 he was assistant inspector general of the Division of the Atlantic. Mustered out of volunteer service in February 1866, he was again an instructor at West Point until August 1868, receiving promotion in July 1866 to lieutenant colonel, and in 1868–1869 he commanded the 44th Infantry. From April 1869 until his resignation in December 1870 he commanded the 1st Military District (Virginia) with the rank of brevet major general. He had already, in July 1869, been elected president of the College of the City of New York, a position he retained until retiring in December 1902. During his long tenure the enrollment of the college grew from fewer than 800

to nearly 2000 students. Webb died in New York City on February 12, 1911.

Wedemeyer, Albert Coady (1897–   ), army

officer. Born on July 9, 1897, in Omaha, Nebraska, Wedemeyer graduated from West Point in 1918 and was commissioned in the infantry. Shortly before completing the course at the Infantry School, Fort Benning, Georgia, he was promoted to first lieutenant in February 1920. He remained at Fort Benning until 1922, and after brief periods at Fort Sill, Oklahoma, and Fort Sam Houston, Texas, he spent two years in the Philippines. During 1925–1927 he was at Fort Washington, Maryland, and from 1927 to 1930 he was on the staff of the commander of the military district of Washington, D.C. After two years at Tientsin, China, during which he studied the language, he returned to the Philippines, remaining there in various staff positions until 1934. Promoted to captain in August 1935, he graduated from Command and General Staff School, Fort Leavenworth, Kansas, in 1936, and after a few weeks attached to the Intelligence Division of the General Staff he was sent to attend the Kriegsakademie, the German general staff school, becoming the first American officer to do so since World War I. From his graduation in 1938 until 1940 he was again stationed at Fort Benning. In July 1940, while attached to the 94th Antitank Battalion at Fort Benning, he was promoted to major. Later that year he was called to duty with the General Staff, and in May 1941 he joined the War Plans Office under Gen. Dwight D. Eisenhower. He advanced to temporary lieutenant colonel in September 1941 and temporary colonel in February 1942, and in June 1942 he was named assistant to Gen. Thomas T. Handy, director of the Plans and Operations Division. In July he was promoted to temporary brigadier general. During this period he also served on the Joint Strategic Committee and later as chief of the Strategy and Policy Group, and he sat in on the principal joint and combined (Allied) strategy conferences as aide to or representative of the U.S. chief of staff, Gen. George C. Marshall. Promoted to temporary major general in September 1943, he was named the following month deputy chief of staff under Adm. Lord Louis Mountbatten, supreme Allied commander in Southeast Asia. When Gen. Joseph W. Stilwell, U.S. commander of the China-Burma-India theater, was recalled in October 1944, the theater was split into two commands, and Wedemeyer was named commander of the China theater (Gen. Daniel I. Sultan took over the India-Burma theater). He became at the same time chief of staff to Generalissimo Chiang Kai-shek, leader of the Kuomintang, or Chinese Nationalist, forces. He held that delicate and difficult post through the rest of the war and until May 1946, receiving promotion to temporary lieutenant general in January 1945. From June 1946 to

October 1947 he commanded the Second Army, first at Baltimore and then at Fort George Meade, Maryland, and from October 1947 to November 1948 he was director of the Plans and Operations Division of the General Staff. He then commanded the Sixth Army at the Presidio, San Francisco, until his retirement in July 1951. In July 1954 he was promoted to general on the retired list. In 1958 he published *Wedemeyer Reports*. After his retirement from the army he served as an officer or director of numerous major corporations.

Weitzel, Godfrey (1835–1884), army officer.
Born in Cincinnati, Ohio, on November 1, 1835, Weitzel graduated from West Point in 1855 and was commissioned in the engineers. For four years he was engaged in work on fortifications at New Orleans, and in 1859 he was appointed an instructor at West Point. He was promoted to first lieutenant in July 1860. In January 1861 he was ordered to engineering duty in Washington, D.C., and in April he took part, under Capt. Montgomery C. Meigs, in the relief expedition to Fort Pickens, Florida. In October 1861 he was named chief engineer on the staff of Gen. Ormsby M. Mitchel, commander of the Department of Ohio, and he concerned himself with the fortification of Cincinnati. In April 1862 he was made chief engineer on the staff of Gen. Benjamin F. Butler in the expedition against New Orleans, and following the surrender of the city he was its assistant military commander. Weitzel was appointed brigadier general of volunteers in August 1862. He took the field in the autumn of that year and saw action in numerous engagements in Louisiana and, in command of a division, in the assaults on Port Hudson on May 27 and June 14, 1863, receiving brevets through lieutenant colonel of regulars. In May 1864 he became chief engineer of Butler's Army of the James, receiving a brevet to major general of volunteers in August for his services, which included the construction of the defenses at Bermuda Hundred. In September he was given command of the XVIII Corps. He took part in the capture of Fort Harrison, Virginia, September 29–30, being brevetted colonel of regulars, and in November was promoted to major general of volunteers. In December he was transferred to command of the XXV Corps, which he led as second-in-command under Butler in the unsuccessful attack on Fort Fisher, North Carolina, on December 24–25; during that operation he was in immediate command of the troops ashore. He took part in the final operations against Petersburg and Richmond in March–April 1865 and on April 3 took possession of Richmond. He was brevetted brigadier and major general of regulars for his services in that campaign. A short time later he was put in command of the District of the Rio Grande in Texas. Mustered out of volunteer service in March 1866, he resumed his engineering duties

and in August of that year was promoted to major. From 1867 to 1873 he was in charge of the construction of a ship canal around the Falls of the Ohio at Louisville, and from 1873 he supervised the building of a similar canal at Sault Sainte Marie, Michigan, a project that required the construction of what was then the largest lock in the world. Later he also built the Stannard's Rock lighthouse in Lake Superior. Promoted to lieutenant colonel in June 1882, Weitzel was transferred to Philadelphia, where he died on March 19, 1884.

Westmoreland, William Childs (1914–   ),
army officer. Born on March 26, 1914, in Spartanburg County, South Carolina, Westmoreland graduated from West Point in 1936 and was commissioned in the field artillery. He served with various field artillery units at Fort Sill, Oklahoma, in Hawaii, and at Fort Bragg, North Carolina, before the outbreak of World War II. In April 1942 he advanced to major in command of a field artillery battalion, and he took part with it in the North Africa and Sicily campaigns. He went ashore at Utah Beach, Normandy, with the 9th Infantry Division (Gen. J. Lawton Collins's VII Corps, First Army) on June 10, 1944, and in July, promoted to colonel, he became chief of staff of the division. He served with the 9th through the rest of the war and then commanded the 60th Infantry Regiment in occupation duty in Germany. During January–March 1946 he was acting chief of staff and then acting commander of the 71st Infantry Division. After parachute training at Fort Benning, Georgia, Westmoreland took command of the 504th Parachute Infantry Regiment and in August 1947 was named chief of staff of the 82nd Airborne Division at Fort Bragg. During 1950–1952 he was an instructor at the Command and General Staff School, Fort Leavenworth, Kansas, and then at the Army War College. In August 1952 he was given command of the 187th Airborne Regimental Combat Team, which he led into combat in Korea later in the year. In November he was promoted to brigadier general. From 1953 to 1958 he was attached to the General Staff, serving as secretary from July 1955 and receiving promotion to major general in December 1956. From April 1958 to July 1960 he commanded the 101st Airborne Division at Fort Campbell, Kentucky, and he then became superintendent at West Point. He remained in that post for three years. After a year as commander of the XVIII Airborne Corps at Fort Bragg and promotion to lieutenant general in 1963 he was named in June 1964 to command the U.S. Military Assistance Command in South Vietnam. Two months later he was promoted to general. The direct involvement of U.S. forces, in other than advisory and support roles, in the struggle between North and South Vietnam began after the alleged incident of attacks by Northern gunboats on U.S. destroyers in the Gulf of Tonkin in August

1964. Combat troops from the United States began to arrive in numbers during 1965, and their reinforcement accelerated until a peak of 510,000 ground troops, army and marine, were present in 1968. Military operations on the ground were of the "sweep and clear" and then "search and destroy" order, unsuccessfully attempting to draw an enemy using guerrilla and insurgent tactics with vast strategic patience into conventional forms of combat. Huge amounts of artillery and air bombardment, along with such novel weapons as chemical defoliants to deny jungle cover and such controversial ones as antipersonnel bombs and napalm, failed to stop the infiltration of regular troops and supplies from North to South, an infiltration that was both steady and steadily denied by the North. During the Tet (lunar new year) holiday in January–February 1968 Northern troops and Vietcong guerrillas staged heavy attacks on 40 cities in the South; during March–April a major marine base at Khe Sanh was under siege. In June Westmoreland was succeeded as U.S. commander by Gen. Creighton W. Abrams. He returned to the United States to become in July chief of staff of the army, a post he held until his retirement in July 1972. In 1976 he published *A Soldier Reports.* In later years he pursued private interests in South Carolina.

Westover, Oscar (1883–1938), army officer and airman. Born on July 23, 1883, in Bay City, Michigan, Westover enlisted as a private in the army in 1901 and the next year won appointment to West Point. He graduated in 1906 and was commissioned in the infantry. He served in the Philippines in 1908–1910 and later at Fort Wright, Washington, and Fort Gibbon, Alaska, and was an instructor at West Point in 1910–1913 and again in 1916–1917, advancing during that time to captain. Transferred to the Signal Corps in September 1917 and promoted to temporary major, he served for a time as signal officer at the army's port of embarkation at Hoboken, New Jersey, and was then assigned to duty with the aviation section. In August 1918 he was promoted to temporary lieutenant colonel, and in May 1919 he advanced to temporary colonel. In June 1920 he reverted to permanent captain and was then promoted to major. From 1921 to 1928 he was director of aircraft production of the Air Service. During that period he also served as chief of the balloon and airship division in 1921–1922, won ratings as airship pilot at Langley Field, Virginia, in 1922 and as airplane pilot at Brooks and Kelly fields, Texas, in 1923, commanded Langley Field and the Air Corps Tactical School in 1924–1926, and graduated from the Tactical School in 1927 and from the Command and General Staff School, Fort Leavenworth, Kansas, in 1928. In May 1922 he won the national elimination free balloon race, covering 866 miles from Milwaukee to Lake St. John, Quebec, in 16½ hours, and in August he was the army's entrant

in the international Bennett Cup race in Switzerland. His flight ended some 90 miles from Budapest when Hungarian peasants seized his drag rope and helpfully, so they believed, pulled him to earth. From 1928 to 1932 Westover was an instructor at the Command and General Staff School, receiving promotion to lieutenant colonel in January 1930. In January 1932 he was appointed assistant chief of the Air Corps with the rank of brigadier general, and in December 1935 he succeeded Gen. B. D. Foulois as chief of the Air Corps with the rank of major general. He remained in that post until his death in the crash in Burbank, California, of a Northrop attack plane he was piloting himself on September 21, 1938. Westover Field, Massachusetts, was later named for him.

Weyand, Frederick Carlton (1916–   ), army officer. Born on September 15, 1916, in Arbuckle, California, Weyand graduated from the University of California at Berkeley in 1939. He had been commissioned a second lieutenant in the coast artillery reserve in the year before, and in December 1940 he was called to active duty. After service with the 6th Artillery Regiment he attended the Command and General Staff School, Fort Leavenworth, Kansas, in the summer of 1942. By November 1942 he had advanced to temporary rank of major. He was assigned to harbor defense service in San Francisco in 1942–1943, and after a few months with the General Staff he became in May 1944 assistant chief of staff of army forces in the China-Burma-India theater under Gen. Joseph W. Stilwell. Promoted to temporary lieutenant colonel in March 1945, he was attached to the Military Intelligence Service in 1945–1946 and was on the staff of U.S. Army Forces, Middle Pacific, in 1946–1949. After graduating from the Infantry School, Fort Benning, Georgia, in 1950 he was ordered to staff duty with the 3rd Infantry Division in Korea. During January–July 1951 he commanded a battalion of the 7th Infantry in combat, returning to the divisional staff thereafter. He was on the staff of the Infantry School in 1952–1953 and in the latter year graduated from the Armed Forces Staff College in Norfolk, Virginia. From 1954 to 1957 he was military assistant to the secretary of the army, advancing to temporary colonel in July 1955, and after graduating from the National War College in 1958 he was stationed in Berlin until 1960, receiving promotion to temporary brigadier general in July 1960. In 1962–1964 Weyand was chief legislative liaison officer for the army in Washington, D.C., advancing to temporary major general in November 1962. He commanded the 25th Infantry Division at Schofield Barracks, Hawaii, in 1964–1966, and in March of the latter year he took the division to South Vietnam. In May 1967 he became acting commander and in July commander of the II Field Force; he was the senior U.S. commander in the Saigon area during the North

Vietnamese–Vietcong Tet (lunar new year) offensive of January–February 1968. In August 1968 he returned to Washington as chief of the Office of Reserve Components, receiving promotion to temporary lieutenant general (and permanent brigadier and major general). From March 1969 to June 1970 he was the chief military adviser to the U.S. delegation at the Vietnam peace negotiations in Paris. In September 1970 he was named deputy commander of the U.S. Military Assistance Command in Vietnam under Gen. Creighton W. Abrams, receiving promotion to temporary general in October, and in June 1972 he succeeded to command of MACV when Abrams became chief of staff. Weyand remained in that post until the withdrawal of U.S. combat forces early in 1973. From March to July 1973 he was commander of U.S. army forces in the Pacific, and in August 1973 he became vice chief of staff. He became acting chief of staff on the death of Abrams in September 1974 and was formally appointed to the post by President Gerald R. Ford in October. In March 1975 he flew to South Vietnam to observe the rapidly deteriorating military situation there, and he remained as senior U.S. officer during the final evacuation of U.S. and Vietnamese personnel in April. Weyand stepped down as chief of staff in July 1976 and retired in October. He was succeeded as chief of staff of the army by Gen. Bernard W. Rogers.

Wharton, Franklin (1767–1818), marine officer. Born in Philadelphia on July 23, 1767, Wharton entered the marine corps as a captain in August 1798. Until 1801 he commanded the marine detachment aboard the *United States,* Commodore John Barry. He then commanded the marine barracks in Philadelphia until being appointed lieutenant colonel and commandant of the corps in March 1804, succeeding Lt. Col. William W. Burrows. He retained that post until his death, contributing to the establishment of corps traditions in discipline, dress, and ceremony. In the War of 1812, during which the corps was considerably expanded and saw much action at sea and on all fronts on land, he appears to have contributed little. During the British attack on Washington, D.C., he fled with the corps paymaster to Frederick, Maryland. His failure to take the field—100 or so marines were among the mixed force under Capt. Joshua Barney at Bladensburg—outraged a number of fellow officers; dissatisfaction with him grew and finally culminated in a court-martial in 1817, by which he was acquitted of all charges. Wharton died in New York City on September 1, 1818.

Wheaton, Frank (1833–1903), army officer. Born in Providence, Rhode Island, on May 8, 1833, Wheaton entered Brown University in 1849 but left the next year to take a job with the U.S.–Mexican boundary commission in California. In March 1855 he was appointed a first lieutenant in the 1st Cavalry. He served principally in Missouri, Kansas, and Indian Territory (Oklahoma) over the next six years and took part in several actions against the Indians and in the Mormon expedition under Col. Albert S. Johnston in 1857–1858. Promoted to captain in March 1861, he was appointed lieutenant colonel of the 2nd Rhode Island Volunteers in July. He distinguished himself at Bull Run (Manassas), July 21, where the regiment was heavily engaged, and succeeded to command of the 2nd with the rank of colonel. He served with the Army of the Potomac through the Peninsula and Maryland campaigns in 1862, receiving promotion to brigadier general of volunteers in November. At Fredericksburg, December 13, he led a brigade of Gen. William F. Smith's VI Corps, and he took part in the fighting on the third day of Gettysburg, July 3, 1863. He led the same brigade through the battles of Spotsylvania, May 8–12, and Cold Harbor, June 1–3, and in the first assaults on Petersburg later in June. Moved up to command of a division of VI Corps, Wheaton was subsequently in the Shenandoah valley, and in July he was rushed to Washington, D.C., to help defend the city against Gen. Jubal A. Early. He engaged and repulsed Early at Fort Stevens on July 11–12. He then returned to Petersburg, where he served to the end of the war, receiving brevets to major general of both regulars and volunteers. He was mustered out of volunteer service in April 1866, reverting to major (as of November 1863), and was promoted to lieutenant colonel of the 39th Infantry in July. During the Modoc War in northern California he led the first attack, January 16–17, 1873, on Captain Jack's stronghold in the lava beds at Tule Lake. He advanced to colonel of the 2nd Infantry in December 1874 and to brigadier general in 1892, when he was put in command of the Department of Texas. In 1894 he became commander of the Department of Colorado. He retired in May 1897, shortly after his promotion to major general, and he died in Washington, D.C., on June 18, 1903.

Wheaton, Loyd (1838–1918), army officer. Born on July 15, 1838, in Pennfield, Michigan, Wheaton enlisted as a sergeant in the 8th Illinois Infantry in April 1861. At the expiration of his three-month enlistment in July he was commissioned a first lieutenant in the same regiment. He served through the Civil War and advanced to captain in March 1862, major in August 1863, and lieutenant colonel in November 1864; he was wounded at Shiloh (Pittsburg Landing), April 6–7, 1862, and distinguished himself in the siege of Vicksburg in July 1863 and in the assault on and capture of Fort Blakely at Mobile, Alabama, on April 9, 1865. Brevetted colonel in March 1865, he was mustered out of volunteer service in May 1866 and in July was appointed a captain in the 34th Infantry of regulars. In March 1867 he received brevets to major and lieutenant colonel for Civil War services. While serving mainly on the frontier he received promotions to major in October 1891 and lieutenant colonel in May 1895. On the outbreak of the Spanish–American War he was appointed brigadier general of volunteers in May 1898, and in August he was sent to the Philippines with Gen. Wesley Merritt's (subsequently Gen. Elwell S. Otis's) VIII Corps. He took part in all the field operations in the Philippines, earning a brevet to major general of volunteers for gallantry in a battle at Imus in June 1899. In the autumn 1899 campaign against the insurrectionists under Aguinaldo, Wheaton led a division on the left of the American drive in northern Luzon. He won a battle at San Jacinto and, together with the other columns under Gen. Arthur MacArthur and Gen. Henry W. Lawton, fragmented the insurrectionist forces. Promoted to major general of volunteers in June 1900, he commanded the departments of Northern Luzon and the Northern Philippines until 1902. He was discharged from volunteer service in February 1901, having meanwhile been promoted to colonel of the 20th Infantry of regulars in February 1899 and to brigadier general earlier in February 1901. He was promoted to major general in March 1901 and retired in July 1902. Wheaton died on September 17, 1918, in Chicago.

Wheeler, Earle Gilmore (1908–1975), army officer. Born on January 13, 1908, in Washington, D.C., Wheeler graduated from West Point in 1932 and was commissioned in the infantry. After four years at Fort Benning, Georgia, during which he advanced to first lieutenant in August 1935 and graduated from the Infantry School in 1937, he served a year at Tientsin, China, with the 15th Infantry. In 1938–1940 he was at Fort Lewis, Washington, with the same regiment, and in 1940–1941 he was an instructor at West Point, receiving promotion to temporary captain. In 1942 he graduated from the Command and General Staff School, Fort Leavenworth, Kansas, and advanced to temporary major in February and colonel in November. After various training assignments, mainly in the South, he was sent to Europe in November 1944 as chief of staff of the 63rd Infantry Division, which landed at Marseilles, France, and joined Gen. Alexander M. Patch's Seventh Army. Late in 1945 Wheeler returned to the United States and for a year was an instructor at the Field Artillery School, Fort Sill, Oklahoma. In 1946 he returned to Europe, and from 1947 to 1949 he was on the staff of the U.S. Constabulary (formerly the VI Corps) in occupied Germany. He graduated from the National War College in 1950. Promoted to brigadier general in November 1952, he served in staff posts with NATO forces in southern Europe until 1955, when he was attached to the General Staff in Washington, D.C., receiving promotion to temporary major general in

December of that year. In October 1958 he took command of the 2nd Armored Division at Fort Hood, Texas, moving up to command also the III Corps in March 1959. In April 1960, promoted to temporary lieutenant general, he was named director of the joint staff of the Joint Chiefs of Staff. In March 1962 he was promoted to temporary general and made deputy commander of U.S. forces in Europe under Gen. Lauris Norstad, and in October of that year he became chief of staff of the army. In July 1964 he succeeded Gen. Maxwell D. Taylor as chairman of the Joint Chiefs of Staff. He held that post, through a period of rapid modernization of the armed forces and the trying era of the war in Vietnam, until his retirement in July 1970. In 1973 he revealed that he had, on personal orders of President Richard M. Nixon, directed secret and, when made public, highly controversial bombing missions over Cambodia in 1969–1970. Wheeler died in Frederick, Maryland, on December 18, 1975.

Wheeler, George Montague (1842–1905), army officer and explorer. Born in Hopkinton, Massachusetts, on October 9, 1842, Wheeler graduated from West Point in 1866 and was commissioned in the engineers. For five years he was stationed in California, where until 1868 he was engaged in the survey of Point Lobos and the construction of defenses in San Francisco harbor and thereafter served on the staff of the commander of the Department of California. He advanced to first lieutenant in March 1867. In 1871 he took charge of the survey of United States territory west of the 100th meridian. He directed the field work of that huge project until March 1879, when the organization developed for it was absorbed into the newly established U.S. Geological Survey under Clarence King. Wheeler's 14 field trips, each of several months' duration, covered the land as far south and east as south-central Texas and as far north and west as central Washington, and included the mountains and valleys of some of the most challenging country in North America. The survey produced not only topographical maps, many of them of previously unexplored, even untrod territory, but also great quantities of information on the geology, climate, flora and fauna, and archaeology of the country. Wheeler, promoted to captain in March 1879, devoted himself thereafter to collating the data and writing the official report of the survey, which appeared as the *Report upon United States Geographical Surveys West of the One Hundredth Meridian* in eight volumes plus two atlases between 1875 and 1889. In 1881 he represented the United States at the Third International Geographical Congress and Exhibition in Venice. Failing health led to his retirement in June 1888, and in September 1890 he was promoted to major on the retired list dating from July 1888. Wheeler died in New York City on May 3, 1905.

Wheeler, Joseph (1836–1906), Confederate army officer and public official. Born near Augusta, Georgia, on September 10, 1836, Wheeler graduated from West Point in 1859 and was commissioned in the dragoons. He saw action in various Indian campaigns in Kansas and New Mexico before resigning in April 1861 to become a first lieutenant of artillery in the Confederate army. In September he was appointed colonel of the 19th Alabama Infantry. He commanded a brigade at Pittsburg Landing (Shiloh), April 6–7, 1862, where he covered the Confederate retreat on the second day, and in July he was given command of the cavalry of Gen. Braxton Bragg's Army of Mississippi. He was thereafter almost continually in the field; during the remainder of the war he was to be wounded 3 times and have 16 horses shot under him. After leading Bragg's advance into Kentucky in August–September, distinguishing himself at Perryville, October 8, and covering the retreat from that battle, he was promoted to brigadier general at the end of October. At Stones River (Murfreesboro), December 31–January 3, 1863, he again distinguished himself after having skillfully delayed Gen. William S. Rosecrans's advance. In January 1863 he was promoted to major general. He took a prominent part in the battle of Chickamauga, September 18–20, 1863, and after Rosecrans was shut up in Chattanooga he undertook a spectacular cavalry raid to the Union rear in which he and his men destroyed railroad lines by which Rosecrans might be supplied and inflicted upward of $3 million in damage to supply depots and other resources in and around Murfreesboro and central Tennessee. In November he cooperated with Gen. James Longstreet in the siege of Knoxville, and following Bragg's defeat at Lookout Mountain and Missionary Ridge, November 24–25, he helped cover the latter's retreat, taking part under Gen. Patrick R. Cleburne in the rearguard action at Ringgold, November 27. In 1864 he was active in opposing Gen. William T. Sherman's advance toward Atlanta, engaging the Union cavalry of Gen. George Stoneman on several occasions. In August–September he led a long raid to Sherman's rear that reached as far as central Tennessee and northern Alabama and interrupted his communications and destroyed his supplies. During Sherman's march to the sea Wheeler fell back slowly in advance of him; he kept a close watch on Union raiders and foragers on the flanks and thereby confined the destruction to as narrow a front as possible. In February 1865 (aged twenty-eight) he was promoted to lieutenant general. He fought under Gen. Joseph E. Johnston against Sherman in the Carolinas, and shortly after Johnston's surrender he was captured near Atlanta. After the war Wheeler entered business in New Orleans; he moved in 1868 to Wheeler, Alabama, to practice law and plant cotton. He entered Congress in March 1881, but in June 1882 his seat was successfully contested. His successor soon died, however, and he was elected to the same seat in January 1883 for the last two months of the term. He was again elected to Congress in 1884 and served from March 1885 until his resignation in April 1900. As he rose to the chairmanship of the Ways and Means Committee, the high rank and personal popularity he had achieved in the Civil War made him something of a symbol of the reunion of North and South in that period. On the outbreak of the Spanish–American War he offered his services and was appointed major general of volunteers by President William McKinley in May 1898 and given command of the cavalry division (largely unmounted) in Gen. William R. Shafter's V Corps for the Cuban campaign. Troops under Wheeler's command (including Col. Leonard Wood's and Lt. Col. Theodore Roosevelt's Rough Riders) won the battle of Las Guásimas, June 24, and took part in the assault of July 1 on the San Juan heights before Santiago, where they formed the American right while Gen. Jacob F. Kent's infantry division formed the left. At the conclusion of that campaign he commanded the army convalescent camp at Montauk Point, Long Island, and briefly commanded a brigade in the Philippines, August 1899–January 1900. Mustered out of volunteer service, he was appointed a brigadier general of regulars in June 1900, and he commanded the Department of the Lakes until his retirement in September of that year. Wheeler died in Brooklyn, New York, on January 25, 1906.

Whipple, Abraham (1733–1819), Revolutionary naval officer. Born in Providence, Rhode Island, on September 26, 1733, Whipple entered the merchant service at an early age. In 1759–1760, during the French and Indian War, he commanded the privateer *Game Cock*, which took 23 French prizes in a 6-month cruise. In March 1772 the British revenue cutter *Gaspée*, under a Lt. Dudingston, was posted in Narragansett Bay in an attempt to control the widespread smuggling made possible by the bay's innumerable inlets, coves, and islands. Local resentment mounted rapidly, and on June 9, 1772, when the *Gaspée* ran aground near Warwick while chasing the *Hannah*, a packet boat out of Providence, an angry meeting at a Providence tavern resolved to take action. A group of about 50, led by Whipple and in boats supplied by local merchant John Brown (later benefactor of Brown University), captured the *Gaspée* on June 10, shooting Lt. Dudingston and burning the vessel to the water. This exploit is cited among the very earliest overt acts of rebellion in the colonies. Despite the efforts of British officials and the general public knowledge of the deed, no prosecutions resulted. In the summer of 1775 Rhode Island outfitted two armed vessels for coastal defense, and Whipple was appointed commodore of the fleet. Aboard the *Katy* he captured a British tender, the first prize of the war taken under official commission. On December 22, 1775, he was commissioned a captain in the new Continental navy and given command of the *Columbus* in Commodore Esek Hopkins's fleet. He took part in the capture of New Providence, Bahamas, in March 1776 and on the return voyage captured the British schooner *Hawk* on April 4. The *Columbus* was the last vessel of the fleet to give up the pursuit of the *Glasgow* in the inglorious fight of April 6. Later he commanded the schooner *Providence*, which took a large number of prizes before being captured. In 1778 he sailed the frigate *Providence* to France with dispatches, and in 1779 he sailed out of Boston as commodore of a squadron that comprised his flagship *Providence*, the *Queen of France*, and the *Ranger*. In July he fell in with a convoy of richly laden merchantmen; operating quietly, he captured 11 of them, 8 of which actually reached Boston bearing cargo worth an estimated one million dollars. Late in 1779 his squadron, reinforced by the *Boston*, was sent to help Gen. Benjamin Lincoln defend Charleston, South Carolina. He captured a number of transports and other British vessels in the harbor, but later three of the ships under his command were stripped of arms so that the guns could be emplaced in shore batteries. On the fall of Charleston to Gen. Sir Henry Clinton in May 1780 Whipple was taken prisoner. He was paroled to Chester, Pennsylvania, where he remained until the end of the war. He farmed in Cranston, Rhode Island, until 1788, making one voyage during that time in command of a merchant vessel to England; he then removed to Marietta, Ohio. He made another voyage in 1801 but otherwise devoted himself to farming. He received a pension from Congress in 1811, and he died near Marietta, Ohio, on May 27, 1819.

Whipple, Amiel Weeks (1816–1863), army officer and explorer. Born in Greenwich, Massachusetts, probably in the autumn of 1816 (many sources say 1818), Whipple attended Amherst College briefly before entering West Point. He graduated in 1841 and was commissioned in the artillery, but he transferred to the topographical engineers a short time later. After brief assignments to make hydrographic surveys of the Patapsco River in Maryland, the approaches to New Orleans, and the harbor at Portsmouth, New Hampshire, he spent the period 1844–1849 engaged in the survey of the northeast boundary of the United States. From 1849 to 1853 he was involved in the work of the U.S.–Mexican boundary commission, receiving promotion to first lieutenant in 1851, and from 1853 to 1856 he directed the survey of a transcontinental railroad route along the 35th parallel from Fort Smith, Arkansas, to Los Angeles. Promoted to captain in 1855, he was engaged in supervising lighthouse and navigation improvements on the southern Great Lakes from 1856

until the outbreak of the Civil War. He was then appointed chief topographical engineer on the staff of Gen. Irvin McDowell, and he drew the Union army's first maps of the northern Virginia theater of war; he also took part in the battle of Bull Run (Manassas), July 21. He remained with McDowell, receiving promotion to major in September, until March 1862, when he was made chief topographical engineer of the Army of the Potomac under Gen. George B. McClellan. He was appointed brigadier general of volunteers in April and recalled to Washington, D.C., where he commanded a brigade in the defense of the city. In September he moved up to command of a division, and in October he was ordered to duty in the field as commander of a division of Gen. George Stoneman's III Corps. He saw some action at Fredericksburg, December 13. At Chancellorsville, May 2–4, 1863, the III Corps, then under Gen. Daniel E. Sickles, was heavily engaged, and on May 3 Whipple was mortally wounded. He was evacuated to Washington, D.C., where he died on May 7, 1863; his promotion to major general of volunteers was signed shortly before his death. Later in 1863 Fort Whipple was erected at his old headquarters near Alexandria, Virginia; Fort Myer now includes the site.

White, Thomas Dresser (1901–1965), air force officer. Born on August 6, 1901, in Walker, Minnesota, White graduated from West Point in 1920 and was commissioned in the infantry, receiving immediate promotion to first lieutenant. After graduating from the Infantry School, Fort Benning, Georgia, in 1921 he served a time in the Canal Zone, and in 1925 he completed aviation training at Kelly Field, Texas. He was with the 99th Observation Squadron, Bolling Field, D.C., in 1925–1927, and after a period of study he was language officer at the U.S. embassy in Peking, China, until 1931. Staff duty in Washington was followed in 1934 by appointment as military attaché for air at the U.S. embassy in Moscow. Promoted to captain in August 1935, he held a similar post in Rome, accredited to both Italy and Greece, in 1935–1937. In 1938 he graduated from the Air Corps Tactical School, Maxwell Field, Alabama, and in 1939 from the Command and General Staff School, Fort Leavenworth, Kansas, receiving promotion to major in the latter year and being assigned to duty in Air Corps headquarters. In 1940 he was named military attaché in Rio de Janeiro, Brazil. Promoted to lieutenant colonel in July 1941, White was attached to the staff of the Third Air Force at McDill Field, Florida, early in 1942; he became chief of staff of the Third later in the year and in November was promoted to temporary brigadier general. In January 1944 he was named assistant chief of staff for intelligence on the Army Air Forces staff. In September 1944 he secured a combat post as deputy commander of the

Thirteenth Air Force, then preparing to support the reconquest of the Philippines. In June 1945 he assumed command of the Seventh Air Force, which took part in the campaigns on Iwo Jima and Okinawa and against the Japanese home islands. In January 1946 the Seventh returned to its prewar base at Hickam Field, Hawaii. Promoted to temporary major general in July 1946, White became chief of staff of the Far East Air Forces in Tokyo in October. From January to October 1948 he commanded the Fifth Air Force at Nagoya Air Force Base, Japan. In October he was named director of legislation and liaison in the office of the secretary of the air force. In May 1950 he was appointed the air force member of the Joint Strategic Survey Committee, and in July 1951 he became air force deputy chief of staff for operations with the rank of lieutenant general. Promoted to general in June 1953, he was vice chief of staff from then until July 1957, when he succeeded Gen. Nathan F. Twining as chief of staff of the air force. He held that post through a period of intensive development of advanced missile-based strategic systems and radar defenses. White retired in June 1961 and pursued various business interests until his death on December 22, 1965, in Washington, D.C.

Whiting, William Henry Chase (1824–1865), Confederate army officer. Born in Biloxi, Mississippi (of Massachusetts parents), on March 22, 1824, Whiting graduated from Georgetown College (now University) in 1840 and from West Point in 1845. He was commissioned in the engineers, and for 16 years he was engaged in fortification and river and harbor work in the South and in California, receiving promotions to first lieutenant in March 1853 and to captain in December 1858. In February 1861 he resigned from the army and in March was commissioned a major of engineers in the Confederate service. After a short time engaged in planning new works for Charleston harbor he served in June–July as chief engineer of Gen. Joseph E. Johnston's Army of the Shenandoah. His success in transporting the army to Manassas Junction, Virginia, and his actions in the battle of July 21 earned him immediate promotion to brigadier general. He succeeded to command of a division during the Peninsula campaign in the spring of 1862 and particularly distinguished himself at West Point, May 7, and at Gaines' Mill, June 27, where his division was part of Gen. Thomas J. Jackson's corps. In November 1862 he was appointed commander of the District of Wilmington, North Carolina, where he built Fort Fisher and other works and made the Cape Fear River one of the South's most active havens for blockade-runners. He was promoted to major general in February 1863. In May 1864 he was called into the field as commander at Petersburg, Virginia, whence he was directed to move in conjunction with Gen. P. G. T. Beauregard against

Gen. Benjamin F. Butler's Army of the James at Drewry's Bluff. He failed to execute his orders promptly and was soon returned to Fort Fisher. On December 24–25 the fort repelled an attack by a Union squadron under Adm. David D. Porter and army troops under Butler. Shortly thereafter Whiting's authority was superseded by Gen. Braxton Bragg in Wilmington. Porter's squadron returned on January 13, 1865, and landed 8000 army troops under Gen. Alfred H. Terry along with numbers of marines and seamen. With the outer walls shattered by naval gunfire, the fort was captured on January 15 and Whiting, badly wounded, was taken prisoner. He was taken to Fort Columbus on Governors Island in New York harbor, where he died on March 10, 1865.

Whittlesey, Charles White (1884–1921), lawyer and army officer. Born on January 20, 1884, in Florence, Wisconsin, Whittlesey graduated from Williams College in 1905 and in 1908 took a law degree from Harvard. He took a position in a New York City law firm in the latter year and in 1911, with a partner, formed his own firm. In 1917 he enlisted in the army for service in World War I; he received a captain's commission and was assigned to the 308th Infantry Regiment of the 77th Division. The 77th arrived in France in April 1918 and took part in various operations of the I Corps, Gen. Hunter Liggett, during the summer. On October 1 the 77th was stopped in its northward progress through the Ardennes Forest by heavy German resistance. A concentrated attack on October 2 gained little ground except on a narrow front northeast of Binarville, where six companies of the 308th and parts of two companies of the 306th Machine Gun Battalion broke through and pushed forward half a mile. Unsupported on the flanks and in the rear, the small force was quickly isolated by German forces closing in behind; at the last moment a company of the 307th Infantry broke through to join the advanced force. Whittlesey, by then a major, found himself in command of between 550 and 600 men (sources vary), entirely surrounded and clinging to a position on an exposed hillside. For five days his small command, soon famous as the "Lost Battalion," held out against repeated heavy attacks. Rations ran out on October 3, water was scarce, and soon ammunition was being scavenged from German casualties; there was no medical officer. Attempts to supply the battalion by air failed. Nonetheless, Whittlesey refused even to answer a surrender demand on the afternoon of October 6, whereupon the starving and exhausted soldiers were forced to repulse the heaviest attack yet, with machine gun fire, trench mortars, and flame-throwers pouring in from all sides. On the evening of October 7 a determined push by elements of the 77th Division on the east at last reached the "Lost Battalion"; only 194 men were able to walk at that point.

Whittlesey was promoted to lieutenant colonel a few days later, and on his return to the United States in November he was awarded the Medal of Honor. He resumed his law practice in New York in 1920. On November 11, 1921, he served as one of the pallbearers at the ceremonial interment of the Unknown Soldier at Arlington National Cemetery, Virginia. The event evidently caused or exacerbated a mood of depression, and on the night of November 25–26, 1921, Whittlesey threw himself into the sea from the deck of a New York-to-Cuba steamer.

Wickes, Lambert (1735?–1777), Revolutionary naval officer. Born on Eastern Neck Island, part of Kent County, Maryland, probably in 1735, Wickes went to sea at an early age and by 1774 had risen through the ratings to master and part owner of the merchant vessel *Neptune.* In that year he attracted the notice of patriots by refusing in London a cargo of tea bound for Annapolis. In April 1776 he was commissioned a captain in the Continental navy and given command of the *Reprisal.* In July he convoyed 13 merchant vessels out of the Delaware River and then sailed for Martinique carrying the Continental commercial and naval agent to that island. En route he took three prizes and fought an inconclusive battle with the British sloop *Shark* on July 27. He then carried a cargo of munitions and other supplies back to Philadelphia. In October, ranked 11th on the list of 24 Continental captains by Congress, he sailed for France bearing Benjamin Franklin and took two prizes before reaching Brittany late in November. Under Franklin's direction he sailed from St.-Nazaire, France, in January 1777 on a commerce-raiding mission. He took five prizes in the English channel and brought them to port at L'Orient, where he sold them secretly even as the British ambassador protested such an illegal use of neutral ports. In May he sailed forth in command of a squadron, having been joined by the *Dolphin,* Capt. Samuel Nicholson, and the *Lexington,* Capt. Henry Johnson. After weathering a gale the three ships circled Ireland and took 18 prizes. On June 26, reaching the Channel again from the Irish Sea, they encountered the British 74-gun ship of the line *Burford,* and after a 12-hour chase during which Wickes threw all his guns overboard the *Reprisal* finally broke away. He put in at Saint-Malo and, with the British again protesting strongly, resisted French authorities, who tried first to sequester the vessel and then to prod him into leaving, until the *Reprisal* was thoroughly refitted. He sailed for America in mid-September. On October 1, 1777, the *Reprisal* foundered in a gale off the Newfoundland banks and all aboard were drowned except the cook.

Wilcox, Cadmus Marcellus (1824–1890), Confederate army officer. Born on May 29, 1824, in Wayne County, North Carolina, Wilcox grew up there and in Tipton County, Tennessee. He graduated from West Point in 1846, was commissioned in the infantry, and joined Gen. Zachary Taylor's army in northern Mexico in time to take part in the battle of Monterrey, September 20–24, 1846. Transferred to Gen. Winfield Scott's army, he distinguished himself several times in the campaign to Mexico City, particularly at Chapultepec, September 13, 1847, and at the Belen Gate, September 14, and from July of that year was an aide to Gen. John A. Quitman. After serving in Indian campaigns in Texas and Florida, during which he was promoted to first lieutenant in August 1851, he was appointed an instructor at West Point in 1852, and he remained there for five years. After a year's travel in Europe on sick leave in 1858 he published *Rifles and Rifle Practice,* 1859, the first American text on that topic, which was adopted at West Point. In 1859 he was ordered to Fort Fillmore, Arizona Territory. Promoted to captain in December 1860, he resigned from the army in June 1861 and took a commission as colonel of the 9th Alabama Infantry. He was in the field in time to take part in the battle of Manassas (Bull Run), July 21, and, promoted to brigadier general in October 1861, he served with the Army of Northern Virginia throughout the war. His brigade was heavily engaged in the Peninsula campaign in 1862 and made a particularly good show against Gen. George G. Meade at Frayser's Farm, June 30. At the second battle of Manassas, August 29–30, he commanded three brigades. He performed valuable service at Chancellorsville, May 2–4, 1863, and at Gettysburg he led a charge on the Union center on the second day, July 2, and took part in Pickett's Charge the next day. In January 1864 he was promoted to major general, dating from August 1863; and from the Wilderness and Spotsylvania campaigns of May 1864 to Appomattox he commanded the division formerly led by Gen. William D. Pender. In the summer of 1865 Wilcox, along with numerous other ex-Confederate leaders, followed Gen. Joseph O. Shelby to Mexico, but he returned to the United States the next year and settled in Washington, D.C. He declined high commissions offered by Egypt and Korea and engaged in the insurance business until 1886, when President Grover Cleveland appointed him head of the railroad division of the General Land Office. Wilcox died in Washington, D.C., on December 2, 1890. His *History of the Mexican War,* edited by a niece, appeared in 1892.

Wilkes, Charles (1798–1877), naval officer and explorer. Born in New York City on April 3, 1798, Wilkes entered the merchant service in 1815 and in January 1818 was commissioned a midshipman in the navy. For several years he alternated routine sea cruises in the Mediterranean and the Pacific with periods of shore duty and study, the last for a time under Ferdinand R. Hassler of the Coast Survey. In

April 1826 he was promoted to lieutenant, and in 1830 he was placed in charge of the navy's Depot of Charts and Instruments in Washington, D.C. In 1838, despite his junior rank, he was appointed to command a naval scientific expedition to the South Seas. Setting out from Hampton Roads, Virginia, in August with six ships—flagship *Vincennes*, sloop *Peacock*, brig *Porpoise*, schooners *Sea Gull* (which was later lost) and *Flying Fish*, storeship *Relief*—he was accompanied by a team of scientists in various fields. After calls on both coasts of South America, islands of the South Pacific, and Australia, the squadron left Sydney in December 1839 and sailed through the Antarctic Ocean, where several sightings of land were made. Wilkes claimed on the basis of these observations to have discovered Antarctica as a continent; although long disputed, his claim was later substantiated, and the large region he had seen was named Wilkes Land. The expedition then sailed northward, visited the Fiji (May–August 1840) and Hawaiian (October 1840–April 1841) islands, and made explorations along the North American coast that served to bolster U.S. claims to the Oregon Territory. (The *Peacock* was lost off Cape Disappointment, but all hands were saved.) After sailing westward via Honolulu, Manila, Cape Town, and Brazil to complete his circling of the globe, Wilkes and his party returned to the port of New York in June 1842. In matters of discipline he was something of a martinet, and soon after his return he was court-martialed and publicly reprimanded for having improperly administered punishment to some of his crew, but in July 1843 he was nonetheless promoted to commander. From 1844 to 1861 he was engaged in preparing the report of the expedition; he edited all of the 19 volumes and wrote the 5-volume *Narrative of the United States Exploring Expedition*, 1844, and the single volumes on *Meteorology*, 1851, and *Hydrography*, 1861. He was made a captain in September 1855. In April 1861 he was ordered to take command of the *Merrimac*, then fitting out at Norfolk navy yard; he arrived just after the ship had been scuttled and burned and the yard abandoned. He was then sent to command the *San Jacinto* on station in African waters. On November 8, 1861, in the Bahama Channel, he stopped the British mail ship *Trent* and forcibly removed two Confederate commissioners en route to Europe, James M. Mason and John Slidell; although publicly acclaimed, his action in the Trent Affair was officially disavowed, and Mason and Slidell were ordered released to end tension between Britain and the United States. In July 1862 Wilkes was promoted to commodore and placed in command of the James River Flotilla. A short time later he was transferred to the Potomac Flotilla, and in September, appointed acting rear admiral, he took command of a squadron sent to suppress Confederate raids on commerce in the West Indies. The mission was largely a failure

and aroused considerable diplomatic difficulties. He was recalled in June 1863. There followed a period of considerable friction between him and the Navy Department, during which his promotion to commodore was rescinded and he was placed on the retired list. In March 1864 he was court-martialed for insubordination and suspended from duty. The period of suspension was later reduced from three years to one, and in July 1866 he was given the rank of rear admiral (retired). He died in Washington, D.C., on February 8, 1877.

Wilkinson, James (1757–1825), army officer and adventurer. Born in 1757 in Calvert County, Maryland, Wilkinson was studying medicine in Philadelphia when the Revolution began in the spring of 1775. He enlisted in the Continental army, served in the siege of Boston, and in September 1775 set out as a member of Col. Benedict Arnold's expedition to Quebec. Early in 1776 he was commissioned captain, dating from September 1775, and by the end of the year he had advanced to major and aide-de-camp to Gen. Horatio Gates. He took part in the battles of Trenton, December 26, 1776, and Princeton, January 3, 1777, was promoted to lieutenant colonel a short time later, and in May 1777 was named deputy adjutant general for the Northern Department. He served under Gates through the Saratoga campaign. Just before the second battle of Bemis Heights, October 7, he was asked by Lt. Col. John Hardin to pass on to Gates information on the British position that Hardin had scouted; Wilkinson passed the information on, but as his own. Partly as a result, Gates delegated to him the honor of carrying news of Burgoyne's surrender (October 17) to Congress, along with his recommendation that Wilkinson be promoted to brigadier general. The dilatory Wilkinson reached Congress in 18 days, a week after the news, and his promotion was held up until late November, when it was voted him by brevet. In January 1778 he became secretary of the Board of War, and in that post he was a central figure in the Conway Cabal aimed at elevating Gates to commander in chief. Forced to resign later in the year on exposure of the plot, which came about through his own indiscretion (in September 1778 he and Gates fought a bloodless duel over that point), he secured in 1779 the post of clothier general, but in March 1781 he was obliged to give up that job as well owing to serious deficiencies in his accounts. He then settled in Bucks County, Pennsylvania, where he was appointed brigadier general of militia and in 1783 elected to the legislature. In 1784 he removed to the Kentucky country, where by facile pen and impressive oratory he worked to displace George Rogers Clark and other leaders of the region and co-opt the movement for separate statehood to his own purposes. In 1786 he moved from the village of Lexington, where he had operated a small store, and founded the town of Frankfort. In 1787 he made a voyage down the Mississippi to New Orleans, where, by swearing allegiance to Spain, he obtained from Gov. Esteban Miró a monopoly on trade down the river to that vital port. While representing to the Spanish that he would work for the separation of the western settlements from the United States, a service for which he collected a $2000 pension annually until 1800, he continued while at home to lead agitation for statehood for Kentucky. He used his trade monopoly and New Orleans connections to work on the Kentuckians' fears of commercial isolation and sent Miró greatly exaggerated accounts of his activities on Spain's behalf. On a second journey to New Orleans in 1789 he obtained the first of several large loans or gifts to finance his activities. By 1791 his machinations had come to nothing and his monopoly had been rendered useless by the opening of the Mississippi to various other agents. After leading a volunteer expedition against the Indians in the Ohio country early in the year he secured a commission as lieutenant colonel in the regular army in October. In March 1792 he was promoted to brigadier general. While serving under Gen. Anthony Wayne he conducted both open and covert campaigns to discredit him. In July 1796 he took possession of Detroit on its abandonment by the British, and on the death of Wayne on December 15, 1796, he became the senior officer in the army. (He was technically superseded in that post on the appointment of George Washington as lieutenant general of the Provisional Army on July 13, 1798, and by that reckoning Wilkinson again became senior officer on June 15, 1800, on the expiration of Alexander Hamilton's commission as provisional major general.) He returned to Detroit in 1797, and in 1798 he was ordered to the southwestern frontier. There he carried on negotiations with the Indians; concluded among others the treaty of Fort Adams, December 12, 1801, with the Choctaws, a treaty that secured the right-of-way for the Natchez Trace; and maintained good public and private relations with Spanish authorities. He also carried on private speculations in land and army contracts. On December 20, 1803, he and Gov. William C. C. Claiborne of Mississippi Territory received possession of the Louisiana Purchase from the French prefect at New Orleans. On the creation of the Territory of Louisiana (the portion of the Purchase north of 33° N.) in 1805 Wilkinson was appointed governor with headquarters at St. Louis. His major contribution in the period of his governorship was the dispatch of a number of exploring parties to various parts of the West, most notably those of Lt. Zebulon M. Pike. During 1804–1805, in Washington, D.C., Ohio, and St. Louis, Wilkinson met with Aaron Burr on several occasions. What precise part Wilkinson was intended to play in the mysterious Burr Conspiracy is unknown, although his continuing contact with Span-

ish authorities was doubtless central, but when Burr began his descent of the Mississippi in 1806 Wilkinson, apparently fearing exposure, notified President Thomas Jefferson and the Spanish viceroy in Mexico of impending danger (once again requesting money from the latter) and in November occupied and declared martial law in New Orleans. He arrested scores of persons in the next few months for alleged complicity in Burr's scheme. Burr's men and eventually the fleeing Burr himself were arrested, and in May 1807 Wilkinson, already replaced as governor by Meriwether Lewis, was called east as the principal prosecution witness in Burr's treason trial before Chief Justice John Marshall. He narrowly escaped indictment himself and was subsequently tried and acquitted of wrongdoing by a military court of inquiry. Ordered back to New Orleans, he was again called east for a congressional investigation of his activities in 1809 and for a court-martial in 1811. He was officially cleared though generally held in bad repute, and he resumed command in New Orleans in 1812. In April 1813 he seized Mobile and Fort Charlotte in what was then Spanish West Florida on the ground that the city was being used by British forces. Promoted to major general, he was ordered to the St. Lawrence frontier later in 1813, and he established his headquarters at Sackett's Harbor, New York, in August. Early in November he set out with about 7000 men for Montreal. A second column under Gen. Wade Hampton, between Wilkinson and whom there was much animosity, failed to support him, and on November 11 his army suffered heavy casualties in a drawn battle with British forces at Chrysler's Field. He then followed Hampton into winter quarters at Plattsburg. He was defeated again on March 30, 1814, when a force of some 4000 troops under his command was sharply repulsed by 200 British in a stone mill at Lacolle Mill, just over the Canadian border above Lake Champlain. Another court-martial later in 1814 on a variety of serious charges ended in acquittal, but in 1815 he was honorably discharged from the army. In 1816 he published the curious *Memoirs of My Own Times* in three volumes. He lived near New Orleans until 1821, when he went to Mexico to obtain a land grant in Texas. He died near Mexico City on December 28, 1825.

Wilkinson, John (1821–1891), Confederate naval officer. Born in Norfolk, Virginia, on November 6, 1821, Wilkinson, son of a naval officer, entered the navy as a midshipman in December 1837. He made cruises on the *Independence* in the South Atlantic in 1838–1840 and the *Boston* in the Pacific in 1840–1842, attended the naval school in Philadelphia in 1843, and as passed midshipman from June 1843 served on the *Oregon* in 1844–1845 and the *Portsmouth* in 1845–1846. A long period of illness kept him from service in the Mexican War. Promoted to lieutenant in November 1850, he saw mainly shore and Home Squadron duty thereafter, except for service on the *Southern Star* in the expedition under Commodore William B. Shubrick to Paraguay in 1858–1859. He was in command of the Coast Survey vessel *Corwin* from 1859 to the outbreak of the Civil War, and in April 1861 he resigned his commission. He then took a commission as lieutenant in the Confederate States navy and for a year was on shore battery duty on the James River and on Aquia Creek in Virginia. Early in 1862 he was put in command of the uncompleted ram *Louisiana* on the lower Mississippi; he destroyed the vessel on the fall of Fort Jackson, Fort St. Philip, and New Orleans late in April and was taken prisoner. Exchanged in August 1862, he traveled to England to purchase and fit out the blockade-runner *Robert E. Lee* (ex-*Giraffe*). Making his base in Wilmington, North Carolina, he made the *Lee* one of the most successful blockade-runners of the war, carrying cotton to Nassau and munitions and other supplies back. Many techniques of deception that became standard practice among blockade-runners were originated by Wilkinson. In October 1863 he led a daring attempt to capture and arm a northern lake steamer and free the thousands of Confederate prisoners on Johnson's Island in Lake Erie; the plot was broken up by Canadian authorities. In October 1864 he took command in Wilmington of the blockade-runner and commerce raider *Chickamauga*. In November he took federal prizes within sight of Montauk Point, Long Island, and in December he broke the blockade of Wilmington to secure supplies for Gen. Robert E. Lee's starving army, but the fall of Fort Fisher in January prevented his return. A short time later he took command of the raider *Chameleon*, which he took to Liverpool, England, at the end of the war. He lived in Nova Scotia for some years thereafter and then settled in Amelia County, Virginia. In 1877 he published *Narrative of a Blockade-Runner*. Wilkinson died in Annapolis, Maryland, on December 29, 1891.

Wilkinson, Theodore Stark (1888–1946), naval officer. Born on December 22, 1888, in Annapolis, Maryland, Wilkinson graduated from the Naval Academy in 1909 and was commissioned an ensign two years later. In the occupation of Veracruz, Mexico, in April 1914 he led a landing party from the *Florida* that captured the customhouse, an exploit for which he was awarded the Medal of Honor. During World War I he was attached to the Bureau of Ordnance, where he helped perfect antisubmarine depth charges and the Mark VI naval mine that was heavily used in the mine screen laid across the North Sea. Various routine assignments followed, including command of a destroyer and in 1931–1934 secretaryship of the General Board of the navy. He was promoted to captain in 1937. In October 1941, after a few

months in command of the battleship *Mississippi*, he was named director of the Office of Naval Intelligence, and in that post he was responsible for the gathering (but not interpreting or forwarding to the field) of intelligence relating particularly to Japanese intentions for war. In November he was promoted to rear admiral. From August 1942 to January 1943 Wilkinson commanded Battleship Division 2, and in the latter month he was named deputy commander of the South Pacific Force under Adm. William F. Halsey. After holding that post through the campaign in the Central Solomons, Wilkinson succeeded Adm. R. Kelly Turner as commander of the Third Amphibious Force (III 'Phib) in July 1943. Destroyer forces under his command won the naval battle of Vella Gulf, August 6–7, and he directed the landing of troops on Vella Lavella beginning on August 15 and the naval battles around that island through October. On November 1, in a major jump of the "leapfrog" strategy employed in the Pacific islands, he landed 14,000 men of Gen. Alexander A. Vandegrift's I Amphibious Corps at Empress Augusta Bay on Bougainville. In September 1944, after directing the long-planned assault on Peleliu in the Palau Islands on the 15th and Ulithi Atoll on the 23rd, he quickly shifted his forces from the canceled Yap campaign to the recently moved up Philippines invasion, redeploying brilliantly to make the scheduled landing of Gen. John R. Hodge's XXIV Corps at Dulag, Leyte, on October 20. Promoted to vice admiral following that accomplishment, he overcame heavy opposition, including furious kamikaze attacks, to put a corps of Gen. Walter Krueger's Sixth Army ashore at Lingayen Gulf, Luzon, in January 1945, cooperating with Adm. Daniel E. Barbey in that operation. In September III 'Phib conveyed Gen. Robert L. Eichelberger's Eighth Army to Japan for occupation duty. In January 1946 Wilkinson was named to the Joint Strategic Survey Committee of the Joint Chiefs of Staff, but on February 21, 1946, he drowned in an automobile mishap in Norfolk, Virginia.

Williams, Ephraim (1714–1755), colonial militia officer. Born in Newton, Massachusetts, on March 7, 1714, Williams evidently went to sea in his early years. In 1739 he settled in Stockbridge, Massachusetts, and he may later have represented the town in the General Court. In 1745 he was commissioned a captain of militia and placed in command of the three "Province Forts" built for the protection of the northern border. He was absent from the principal fort, Fort Massachusetts, when it was destroyed by a band of French and Indians on August 30, 1746, but he resumed his headquarters there when it was rebuilt the following year. Another attack on August 2, 1748, was repulsed. In 1750 Williams was granted land adjacent to the fort. He was promoted to major in 1753 and colonel in 1755, and in the latter year he commanded a regiment in the expedition under Gen. (later Sir) William Johnson against Crown Point. He was killed in an ambush on September 8 while leading a large reconnaissance force at Lake George. His will, made only a few weeks before, left most of his estate to establish a free school in what was then called West Township, or West Hoosac, near Fort Massachusetts, provided the town be renamed Williamstown. Funds were allowed to accumulate for 30 years before action was taken, but in April 1785 a free school was created in Williamstown, although it did not actually open until 1790, and in June 1793 it was chartered as Williams College.

Williams, John Foster (1743–1814), Revolutionary naval officer. Born in Boston on October 12, 1743, Williams early went to sea and in May 1776 was commissioned captain of the sloop *Republic* of the Massachusetts navy. Later he commanded the state ship *Massachusetts,* the privateers *Wilkes* and *Active,* and in 1778–1779 the state brig *Hazard,* 14 guns. Aboard the last he captured numerous prizes and on March 16, 1779, defeated the British brig *Active,* 18. He took part in the ill fated Penobscot expedition under Commodore Dudley Saltonstall in July–August 1779 and was forced to burn the *Hazard.* In 1780 he sailed in command of the *Protector,* the state's largest vessel, and on June 9, southeast of Newfoundland, destroyed the privateer *Admiral Duff* after an action of 90 minutes. He took several more prizes in a cruise in the West Indies before being captured by a superior British force off Nantasket in the spring of 1781. After a period of imprisonment in England he was exchanged, and in early 1783 he sailed from Boston in command of the privateer *Alexander.* In 1790 he was appointed captain of the revenue cutter *Massachusetts* by President George Washington. He held that post until his death in Boston on June 24, 1814.

Williams, Jonathan (1750–1815), public official and army officer. Born in Boston on May 26, 1750, Williams was educated from 1770 in London, where he was under the eye of his granduncle, Benjamin Franklin. He formed various business connections there but severed them in 1776 to accompany Franklin to France. He became an agent of American interests at Nantes, where his responsibilities included the inspection and forwarding of supplies bought by Franklin and other commissioners for the colonies and the disposition of marine prizes. He became caught up in the quarrels among Silas Deane, Arthur Lee, and other representatives, however, and eventually had to give up his post. He improved his time in France by studying fortifications and military engineering. He returned to America with Franklin in 1785 and eventually settled in Philadelphia, where in 1796 he was appointed a judge of the court of com-

mon pleas. He gained a reputation as a scientist, in part through his assistance in various of Franklin's experiments, and in that context came into contact with Thomas Jefferson. In February 1801 President Jefferson appointed him major in the 2nd Artillery and Engineers and in December made him inspector of fortifications and commander of the post at West Point. In April 1802, under an act of March 16, the United States Military Academy was established at West Point, and Williams, as ranking engineer, became the first superintendent. The Academy opened formally in July with ten cadets. In June 1803 he resigned his commission in a conflict concerning his authority over cadets not assigned to the Corps of Engineers, but in April 1805 he was persuaded to accept recommissioning as a lieutenant colonel and the superintendency again. He remained in that post until July 1812, and during that time he also supervised the construction of fortifications in New York harbor, including Fort Columbus and Castle Williams on Governors Island, Fort Gansevoort, and Fort Clinton (Castle Garden). The Military Academy during that period advanced little beyond its original narrow scope owing largely to neglect by the War Department. Williams was generally at odds, politically and professionally, with the secretary of war; and in July 1812, on being refused command of Castle Williams for the duration of the war with England, he resigned from the army. A short time later he was appointed brigadier general of New York militia, but he soon returned to Philadelphia. In 1814 he was elected to Congress, but before he took his seat he died in Philadelphia on May 16, 1815.

Williams, Otho Holland (1749–1794), Revolutionary army officer. Born in Prince Georges County, Maryland, in March 1749, Williams took a post in the office of the county clerk in Frederick at thirteen, and from 1767 to 1774 he was similarly employed in Baltimore. The outbreak of the Revolution found him engaged in a mercantile enterprise in Frederick. Appointed first lieutenant of a Maryland rifle company in June 1775, he advanced to captain in command of the company while serving in the siege of Boston. In June 1776 he was promoted to major of a combined Maryland-Virginia rifle regiment. He took part in the unsuccessful defense of Fort Washington in northern Manhattan and was wounded and captured in its fall on November 16, 1776. While a prisoner, he was appointed colonel of the 6th Maryland Regiment in December 1776. After 15 months he was exchanged in January 1778, and he rejoined Gen. George Washington's army in time to see action at Monmouth Court House, June 27. In 1780 he was sent to reinforce the southern army under Gen. Horatio Gates and took part in the battles at Camden, August 16, and King's Mountain, October 7. Gates's successor, Gen. Nathanael Greene, named Williams adjutant general of the southern army. Williams commanded a light corps as the rearguard in Greene's retreat across North Carolina and was conspicuous in the battles of Guilford Court House, March 15, 1781, Hobkirk's Hill, April 25, and especially Eutaw Springs, September 8, where he led a bayonet charge that cleared the field. Greene detailed him to bear dispatches to Congress, and in May 1782 he was promoted to brigadier general. After the war he settled in Baltimore and was appointed district naval officer under the state authority. In 1789 President Washington named him federal collector of the port. Owing to failing health Williams declined appointment in May 1792 as senior brigadier general of the army under Gen. Anthony Wayne. He died in Miller's Town, Virginia, on July 15, 1794.

Wilson, Henry Braid (1861–1954), naval officer. Born on February 23, 1861, in Camden, New Jersey, Wilson graduated from the Naval Academy in 1881, and after a cruise in the Atlantic on the *Tennessee* he was commissioned ensign (junior grade) in July 1883. He was promoted to ensign in June 1884, lieutenant (junior grade) in February 1894, and lieutenant in September 1897. During those years he saw routine sea duty, service with the Coast Survey in the Bering Sea and in the survey of the San Francisco–Honolulu submarine cable, and two years of advanced study at the Naval War College. During the Spanish–American War he served on the *Bancroft* and then the *Indiana* of Commodore Winfield S. Schley's squadron. For a time he was assigned to inspect the construction of the *Alabama* and the new *Maine* at a civilian shipyard, and he later served on the *Kentucky* in the Asiatic Squadron. Promoted to lieutenant commander in March 1903, he was attached to the Bureau of Navigation in 1904–1908, advancing to commander in July 1907. In 1908–1909 he commanded the *Chester*, and after a short time as a member of the Board of Inspection and Survey in 1909 he returned to the Bureau of Navigation as assistant chief in 1910–1911. In March 1911 he was promoted to captain, and he commanded the *North Dakota* in 1911–1913. From 1913 to 1916 he was president of the Board of Inspection and Survey, and in 1916–1917 he commanded the *Pennsylvania*. In July 1917, shortly after the United States entered World War I, he was promoted to rear admiral, and until November he commanded the Patrol Force, Atlantic, engaged in escorting troop and cargo convoys through waters infested with German submarines. He then took command of U.S. naval forces on the French coast. In January 1918 he was named commander of all U.S. naval forces in France, and he held that post for the rest of the war, being responsible for patrol and escort work on the coast and navigable inland waters. In September 1918 he was promoted to vice admiral. Through an indiscretion, Wilson allowed unverified news of the ar-

mistice to leak to the press four days in advance of the official date of November 11, 1918. In June 1919, promoted to admiral, he took command of the Atlantic Fleet, and from July 1921 until his retirement in February 1925 he was superintendent of the Naval Academy. Wilson died on January 30, 1954, in New York City.

Wilson, James Harrison (1837–1925), army officer. Born on September 2, 1837, near Shawneetown, Illinois, Wilson attended McKendree College for a year before entering West Point in 1855. He graduated in 1860, was commissioned in the topographical engineers, and was stationed at Fort Vancouver, Washington Territory, until the summer of 1861. After a brief period of recruiting duty in Boston and promotion to first lieutenant in September 1861, he served as chief topographical engineer under Gen. Thomas W. Sherman in the expedition against Port Royal, South Carolina, in November and in a similar post under Gen. David Hunter in the siege of Fort Pulaski, Georgia, in March–April 1862. As a volunteer aide to Gen. George B. McClellan he took part in the battles of South Mountain and Antietam (Sharpsburg), September 14 and 17, and in November he was appointed a lieutenant colonel of volunteers and made chief engineer of Gen. Ulysses S. Grant's Army of the Tennessee. He became inspector general as well early in 1863 and in May was promoted to captain of regular engineers. He took part in the Vicksburg campaign that summer and in October was promoted to brigadier general of volunteers. He saw action in the Chattanooga campaign, particularly the battle of Missionary Ridge, November 25, and was chief engineer of the relief expedition to Knoxville. In January 1864 he was named chief of the Cavalry Bureau in the War Department, and at the beginning of Grant's spring offensive he was given command of the 3rd Division of Gen. Philip H. Sheridan's cavalry corps. His division led the advance from the Rapidan through the Wilderness, was conspicuous at Yellow Tavern, May 11, took part in laying the siege of Petersburg, and then followed Sheridan to the Shenandoah valley to fight at Opequon (Winchester), September 19. In October Wilson was named chief of cavalry of Gen. William T. Sherman's Military Division of the Mississippi with the rank of brevet major general of volunteers. When Sherman set out from Atlanta on his march to the sea Wilson sent a division of cavalry under Gen. Hugh J. Kilpatrick with him, keeping the remainder of his corps to support Gen. John M. Schofield and Gen. George H. Thomas. On November 29 he skirmished with Confederate cavalry under Gen. Nathan B. Forrest at Spring Hill, Tennessee, and engaged it heavily the next day at Franklin, throwing a screen between Schofield and Gen. John B. Hood and enabling Schofield to reach Thomas at Nashville. Wilson's cavalry was prominent in the battle of Nashville, December 15–16. In March 1865 he was brevetted brigadier and major general of regulars. In the renewed campaign of 1865 he led a spectacularly successful raid. He again defeated Forrest at Ebenezer Church on April 1, stormed the defenses of Selma, Alabama on April 2, occupied Montgomery on April 12, took Columbus, Georgia, by assault on April 16, and reached Macon on April 20. Early in May he was promoted to major general of volunteers. On May 10 a detachment of his cavalry captured Jefferson Davis near Irwinville, Georgia. In January 1866 Wilson was mustered out of volunteer service, and in July he was appointed lieutenant colonel of the 35th Infantry. He was assigned to engineering duty on the Mississippi, but he resigned in December 1870 to engage in railroad construction in the Mississippi valley and New England. In 1883 he settled in Wilmington, Delaware. In May 1898, on the declaration of war against Spain, Wilson offered his services and was appointed major general of volunteers in command of the VI Corps, which was never organized. In July he commanded the 1st Division, I Corps, in Gen. Nelson A. Miles's campaign in Puerto Rico. Later he commanded the I Corps in Georgia and led a division of it to occupation duty in Cuba, becoming commander of the Matanzas and later the Santa Clara departments. In April 1899 his rank was reduced to brigadier general of volunteers. He served as second-in-command under Gen. Adna R. Chaffee of the Peking Relief Expedition in 1900. In February 1901 he was appointed by special act of Congress brigadier general of regulars, and the next month he retired in that rank. In March 1915 he was promoted to major general on the retired list. He was the author of numerous books, including *The Life of Ulysses S. Grant*, 1868, *China; Travels and Investigations in the "Middle Kingdom"*, 1887, and *Under the Old Flag*, 1912. Wilson died in Wilmington, Delaware, on February 23, 1925.

Wilson, Louis Hugh (1920–   ), marine officer. Born on February 11, 1920, in Brandon, Mississippi, Wilson graduated from Millsaps College in 1941 and shortly thereafter was commissioned a second lieutenant in the marine corps. From 1943 to 1944 he saw action in the Pacific with the 9th Marine Regiment, 3rd Marine Division, taking part in the campaigns on Guadalcanal and Bougainville and in the Solomons and advancing to captain in April 1943. On Guam on July 25–26, 1944, he was wounded several times and won the Medal of Honor in leading a small force in the capture and holding of a vital point while under extremely heavy enemy fire. In December 1944 he took command of a marine detachment in Washington, D.C., receiving promotion to major in March 1945. From 1946 to 1948 he was aide-de-camp to the commander of the Fleet Marine Force, Pacific, and in 1949–1951 he was in charge of marine

recruiting in New York City. From 1951 to 1954 he held various staff posts and was a senior student at the training and school center at Quantico, Virginia, advancing to lieutenant colonel in November 1951. For a time in 1954–1955 he was on the staff of the 1st Marine Division stationed in the Republic of Korea, and in 1956–1958 he was attached to marine corps headquarters in Washington. In 1958 he returned to Quantico, becoming commander of the Basic School in 1960. In 1961 he entered the National War College, and on graduating in 1962 he was attached to the headquarters staff again. During 1964–1966 he was assistant chief of staff of the 1st Marine Division, and he served with it in South Vietnam in 1965–1966. After a few months as commander of the 6th Marine Corps District in Atlanta, Georgia, and promotion to brigadier general in November 1966, he was named legislative assistant to Gen. Wallace M. Greene, commandant of the corps, in January 1967. From July 1968 to March 1970 he was chief of staff of the Fleet Marine Force, Pacific, and, promoted to major general in the latter month, he then commanded the I Marine Amphibious Force/3rd Marine Division on Okinawa until April 1971. After a year as director of the marine education center at Quantico and promotion to lieutenant general in August 1972, Wilson took command of the Fleet Marine Force, Pacific, in September 1972. In July 1975, following appointment by President Gerald R. Ford, he became commandant of the marine corps with the rank of general, succeeding the retiring Gen. Robert E. Cushman.

Winchester, James (1752–1826), army officer. Born in Carroll County, Maryland, on February 6, 1752, Winchester served in the Maryland militia battalion of Gen. Hugh Mercer's Flying Camp early in the Revolution and was taken prisoner in Gen. John Sullivan's attack on Staten Island on August 22, 1777. By the time he was exchanged a year later he had been commissioned, in May 1778, a lieutenant in the 3rd Maryland Regiment. In the fall of Charleston, South Carolina, May 12, 1780, he was again taken prisoner and held until December. Promoted to captain, he served under Gen. Nathanael Greene until the end of the war at Yorktown in October 1781. In 1785 he removed from Maryland to what is now central Tennessee, then a frontier district of North Carolina, and he rose through the local militia organization to the rank of brigadier general. He was elected to the first legislature on the organization of Tennessee's state government in 1796, and he was both politically and privately one of the state's most influential citizens. In March 1812 he was commissioned brigadier general in the United States army in anticipation of war with England, and by August he had several regiments encamped at Cincinnati. In that month William Henry Harrison, acting under a militia commission from the state of Kentucky, commandeered his troops for an expedition to Fort Wayne. Winchester managed to secure confirmation of his command of the Army of the Northwest early in September, but a few days later he was compelled once again to yield to Harrison, now commissioned major general of regulars. In that month Winchester led one wing of the army to Fort Defiance, and by December, after a few minor skirmishes with British troops and Indians, he was encamped at the Maumee Rapids (above the site of present-day Toledo, Ohio). In mid-January 1813 he dispatched a force to recapture Frenchtown (now Monroe, Michigan). On January 22, at the River Raisin, he was attacked by a large British-Indian force under Col. Henry Procter. After the first onslaught and the capture of Winchester and many others, the remaining American troops surrendered, whereupon the Indians under Procter's command broke a pledge of protection and massacred hundreds of disarmed soldiers. The River Raisin Massacre subsequently became an American rallying cry. After more than a year of imprisonment in Canada Winchester was exchanged, and he commanded the District of Mobile until the end of the war. He resigned his commission in March 1815. In 1819 he served on the commission appointed to run the Tennessee–Mississippi boundary. He died at his home near Gallatin, Tennessee, on July 26, 1826.

Winder, John Henry (1800–1865), Confederate army officer. Born in Somerset County, Maryland, on February 21, 1800, Winder was the son of (later Gen.) William H. Winder. The younger Winder graduated from West Point in 1820 and was commissioned in the artillery. After various routine assignments, including a period as an instructor at West Point, he resigned in 1823, but in 1827 he reentered the army. He was stationed in Maine, Florida, and elsewhere over the next several years and in October 1842 was promoted to captain. During the Mexican War he served under Gen. Winfield Scott and won brevets to major at Contreras and Churubusco, August 19–20, 1847, and lieutenant colonel at Chapultepec, September 13. More routine duty followed, along with promotion to major in November 1860, but in April 1861 he resigned to offer his services to the Confederacy. In July he was appointed provost marshal and commander of military prisons in Richmond, Virginia, with the rank of brigadier general. With the arrival of the first large body of Union prisoners following the battle of Manassas (Bull Run), July 21, he commandeered a number of tobacco warehouses in the city and established the Libby Prison, soon second only to Andersonville in notoriety. Winder was responsible for maintaining order in the crowded and often chaotic city as well, and as conditions deteriorated toward the end of the war Libby Prison grew more rigorous. Food shortages from December 1863 led to partially successful mass-escape attempts in January,

and in February and March Union cavalry forces under Gen. Hugh J. Kilpatrick attempted twice to liberate the prison. In May 1864 most prisoners were moved from Libby to Macon, Georgia, and Winder was put in charge of all prisons in Alabama and Georgia. In November 1864 he was appointed commissary general for all prisons east of the Mississippi. He died in Florence, South Carolina, on February 8, 1865.

Winder, William Henry (1775–1824), army officer. Born in Somerset County, Maryland, on February 18, 1775, Winder attended the University of Pennsylvania, took up the study of law, and from 1802 practised in Baltimore. In March 1812 he was appointed lieutenant colonel of the 14th Infantry, and in July he was promoted to colonel of that regiment. Ordered to service on the northern front, he led a raid on November 28 from Black Rock, New York, to the Canadian shore opposite. In March 1813 he was promoted to brigadier general. On June 6, 1813, his command of some 1400 troops at Stoney Creek, near Burlington Heights, Ontario, was attacked by a British force half the size, and he was taken prisoner. Sent home on parole, he resumed duty in May 1814 as inspector general and adjutant general of the army and was put in command of a military district comprising Maryland and Virginia. On August 19 a British force of 4000 soldiers under Gen. Robert Ross landed at the Patuxent River and marched on Washington, D.C. Winder hastily called together a motley force of about 6000, mostly militia with a few regulars and a small naval contingent. No serious preparations for the defense of the city had been made, and the forces available were unskillfully deployed in three unsupported lines. The presence on the field of Secretary of War John Armstrong and Secretary of State James Monroe, both issuing orders, as well as President James Madison, merely complicated matters. On August 24 the British attacked the defensive lines at Bladensburg, Maryland. The regulars made a brief stand, as did Commodore Joshua Barney's sailors and marines, who fired 18-pounders brought up from their abandoned river flotilla, but with few exceptions the militia broke and ran before the British advance, even though they incurred far fewer casualties than the British. Winder managed to instill some order into a general retreat back through Washington and on to Georgetown, while British troops were left free to burn the Capitol, the White House, the Treasury, the State and War buildings, and others. In subsequent congressional and army investigations all concerned in the affair were exculpated except Armstrong, who was forced to resign. Winder remained in the army until being honorably discharged in June 1815. He resumed his law practice in Baltimore, served in the legislature, and died in Baltimore on May 24, 1824.

Winship, Blanton (1869–1947), army officer and public official. Born on November 23, 1869, in Macon, Georgia, Winship graduated from Mercer University in 1889 and in 1893 took a law degree from the University of Georgia. He practised in Macon until the outbreak of the Spanish–American War in 1898, when he took a commission as captain in the 1st Georgia Volunteer Infantry. The next year he was appointed a first lieutenant in the Judge Advocate Corps of the regular army, and until 1901 he served in the Philippines. By 1904 he had advanced to major, and in 1906 he served on the commission under Gen. Enoch H. Crowder sent to Cuba to draw up a new constitution and code of laws for the island. He remained there until 1909 as judge advocate of the Army of Cuban Pacification. Following the occupation of Veracruz, Mexico, by U.S. forces in April 1914, Winship was given responsibility for the administration of civil affairs in the city. During World War I, as a lieutenant colonel, he served briefly as judge advocate of the 42nd Division and later commanded the 110th Infantry, 28th Division, in combat. Following a special mission to Switzerland in 1918 he was named director general of the Army Claims Settlement Commission. In 1919–1920 he was judge advocate of U.S. army occupation forces in Germany, and, promoted to colonel in 1920, he was a member of the Reparations Commission until 1923. In 1925 he was legal counsel to the court-martial that tried Col. William Mitchell. From May 1927 to January 1928 he was military aide to President Calvin Coolidge, and from 1928 to 1930 he was legal adviser to Henry L. Stimson, governor general of the Philippines. In March 1931 Winship was appointed judge advocate general of the army with the rank of major general. He held the post until his retirement in November 1933. In January 1934, on appointment by President Franklin D. Roosevelt, he became civil governor of Puerto Rico. He proved to be a stern and unpopular governor, and rapidly growing unrest on the island culminated in an unsuccessful assassination attempt in the summer of 1938. In September 1939 he resigned. During World War II he was recalled to active duty as coordinator of the Inter-American Defense Board from 1941 to 1944. Winship died in Washington, D.C., on October 9, 1947.

Winslow, John Ancrum (1811–1873), naval officer. Born in Wilmington, North Carolina, on November 19, 1811, Winslow entered the navy as a midshipman in February 1827. During various routine assignments over the next several years he advanced to passed midshipman in June 1833 and lieutenant in February 1839. In 1842 he sailed for Europe aboard the *Missouri*, which burned at Gibraltar on August 26, 1843. Late in 1845 he sailed for Mexico on the *Cumberland*, and during the Mexican War he took part in the actions of the squadron under Commodore Matthew C. Perry, who rewarded him with the command of the captured and recommissioned schooner *Morris*. That ship foundered in a gale off Tampico on December 16, 1846. Later he served on the *Saratoga* in the Gulf of Mexico in 1848–1849, at the Boston navy yard for a year, and on the *St. Lawrence* of the Pacific Squadron in 1851–1855, receiving promotion to commander in September 1855. He then served in shore posts, principally in Boston, until the outbreak of the Civil War. In 1861 he was ordered to the Western River Squadron under Commodore Andrew H. Foote; after assisting in the construction and fitting-out of the squadron he commanded the steamer *Benton* until December, when a severe injury sustained in an accident forced him to convalesce at home. He returned to the squadron in June 1862 and was promoted to captain in July. His outspokenness in criticizing Union strategy led to his being placed on waiting orders for several months and then to his assignment to command the *Kearsarge*, a sloop of war that would ordinarily have been given to a more junior officer. Nonetheless Winslow accepted command with a will and was ordered to seek out Confederate raiders, particularly the *Florida* and the *Alabama*, the latter of which under Capt. Raphael Semmes had become the terror of federal shipping. Winslow patrolled the waters from the Azores to the English Channel through 1863 and into 1864 before receiving word in June that the *Alabama* was in port at Cherbourg, France. On June 14, after entering the harbor and notifying Semmes of his presence, he took up a position in neutral waters offshore; on June 19 Semmes, not having made his planned overhaul, accepted the challenge and sailed out to meet the *Kearsarge*. The action lasted 90 minutes, during which the superior weight of arms of the *Kearsarge*, together with her superior sailing against the foul-hulled *Alabama*, inflicted a heavy toll. While thousands watched from shore and from pleasure craft, the *Alabama* went down soon after noon. Winslow stood by as the English yacht *Deerhound* rescued Semmes and 41 other Confederate sailors and, contrary to the rules of war, made off with them; he took 70 others aboard the *Kearsarge*. On his return home he was promoted to commodore as of the date of the battle. He commanded the Gulf Squadron in 1866–1867, served on the Board of Examiners in 1868–1869, and, promoted to rear admiral in March 1870, commanded the Pacific Squadron in 1870–1872. Winslow died in Boston on September 29, 1873.

Winslow, Josiah (1629?–1680), colonial official. Born in Plymouth County (now Massachusetts), probably in 1629, Winslow was the son of Gov. Edward Winslow. The younger Winslow attended Harvard for a time and later settled in Marshfield, where in 1652 he became captain of the town militia.

From 1657 to 1673 he was annually elected assistant governor, and in 1659 he was chosen military commander of Plymouth Colony, a post left vacant since the death of Miles Standish. He was one of six signers of the new articles of confederation of the United Colonies of New England, September 5, 1672. In 1673 he was elected governor of Plymouth, the first native New Englander to hold the post, and in it he saw established the first free school in the colony in 1674. With the outbreak of King Philip's War in 1675, Winslow was chosen commander in chief of the militia forces of the United Colonies. He commanded a force of more than 1000 from Plymouth, Massachusetts Bay, and Connecticut in the Great Swamp Fight of December 19, 1675, in which the great Narragansett village in what is now South Kingstown, Rhode Island, was completely destroyed and the tribe scattered. In February 1676 Winslow relinquished command to Capt. Benjamin Church. He continued to be elected governor annually until his death in Marshfield (Massachusetts) on December 18, 1680.

Winston, Joseph (1746–1815), Revolutionary militia officer. Born in Louisa County, Virginia, on June 17, 1746, Winston early became active in military affairs, and at seventeen he took part in an expedition against the Indians. In 1769 he removed to Surry County, North Carolina. He was a member of the provincial convention that met at Hillsboro on August 20, 1775, to organize an independent government, and in September he was appointed major of militia. He took part in Gen. Griffith Rutherford's expedition against the Cherokees in 1776, and in 1777 he was elected to the provincial legislature and appointed an Indian commissioner. He saw some action in the field early in 1780 and on October 7 commanded part of the right wing of the combined militia-partisan force (also under Col. Isaac Shelby, Col. William Campbell, Maj. John Sevier, and Maj. Joseph MacDowell) that defeated Maj. Patrick Ferguson's Loyalists at King's Mountain. Later he took part in the battle of Guilford Court House, March 15, 1781, under Gen. Nathanael Greene. After the war he returned home to Surry County. His home was in the part of the county later included in the newly created Stokes County, which he represented in the legislature in 1790 and 1791. In 1792 he was elected to Congress, serving from March 1793 to March 1795. He was again in the legislature in 1802, again in Congress for two terms from March 1803 to March 1807, and again in the legislature in 1807 and 1812. From the formation of Stokes County he was lieutenant colonel of the county militia. Winston died near Germantown, North Carolina, on April 21, 1815.

Wood, John Taylor (1830–1904), Confederate naval officer. Born at Fort Snelling, Minnesota (then part of Michigan Territory), on August 13, 1830, Wood was the son of an army surgeon and a grandson of Gen. Zachary Taylor. In June 1847 he entered the Naval School in Annapolis, Maryland, and after a brief period there and cruises on the *Brandywine* and the *Ohio* he was warranted a midshipman as of April 1847. Another short time at the school in 1850 was followed by a cruise in African waters on the *Germantown*, and in 1853 he formally graduated from the renamed Naval Academy. He served subsequently on the *Cumberland*, at the Academy, and on the *Wabash*, receiving promotion to lieutenant as of September 1855. In April 1861 he resigned from the navy (he was recorded as dismissed), but he did not enter Confederate service until October, when he was appointed a lieutenant in the Confederate States navy. He served for a time with a Potomac River shore battery and then was assigned to the *Virginia*, under Capt. Franklin Buchanan, on which he took part in the famous battle with the *Monitor*, March 9, 1862, and in subsequent actions. In October 1862 he led a night boat raid that burned the schooner *Frances Elmor* in the Potomac and the *Alleghanian* in Chesapeake Bay. In January 1863 Wood was appointed naval aide to President Jefferson Davis, his uncle, with statutory rank of colonel of cavalry. In August 1863 he led a second raid in the Chesapeake, capturing five federal schooners and winning promotion to commander. In February 1864 he led a third raid and destroyed the gunboat *Underwriter* at New Bern, North Carolina. In August 1864 he ran the blockade at Wilmington, North Carolina, on the *Tallahassee*, and in a spectacular 19-day cruise north to Halifax, Nova Scotia, and back he captured 33 vessels; he destroyed 26 of them and released the others. In February 1865 he was promoted to captain. He fled south from Richmond with President Davis in April 1865 but avoided capture and made his way to Cuba and thence to Halifax, Nova Scotia, where he engaged in business until his death on July 19, 1904.

Wood, Leonard (1860–1927), army officer. Born on October 9, 1860, in Winchester, New Hampshire, Wood grew up there and in Pocasset, Massachusetts. He entered the Harvard Medical School in 1880 and received his M.D. degree in 1884, and after two years of practice in Boston he secured appointment as an army assistant surgeon with the rank of first lieutenant in January 1886. Ordered to Arizona Territory, he took part in Capt. Henry W. Lawton's expedition against Geronimo that year. He served as both a medical and a line officer and distinguished himself in battle with the Apaches; in March 1898 he was awarded a Medal of Honor for his role in the expedition. Routine service in California and in the East followed, and in January 1891 he was promoted to captain and assistant surgeon. In 1895, while stationed in Washington, D.C., he became White House physician to President Grover Cleveland. He continued in that post under President William McKinley. By mid-1897 he had formed a close friendship with Theodore Roosevelt, then in Washington as assistant secretary of the navy. In May 1898 he and Roosevelt organized the 1st Volunteer Cavalry Regiment for service in the Spanish–American War; Wood received appointment as colonel of volunteers in command. After recruiting and training the "Rough Riders," as the regiment became known (largely through Roosevelt's talent for public relations), they led about half of them, minus horses, to Cuba in June. Wood commanded the regiment at Las Guásimas, June 24, and was then moved up to command of one of Gen. Joseph Wheeler's two cavalry brigades, consisting of the Rough Riders and the 1st and 10th Cavalry regiments of regulars, for the remainder of the campaign against San Juan Heights and Santiago. Promoted to brigadier general early in July, he was appointed military governor of the city after its surrender. He quickly instituted a number of reforms in sanitation and public order. In October he was named governor of Santiago Province, and in December he was promoted to major general of volunteers. In April 1899 he was retained in the volunteer service under a new commission of brigadier general, and in December of that year he was promoted again to major general of volunteers and named military governor of Cuba. During his term in that post great strides were taken in improving internal conditions, notably through the sanitation work of Maj. William C. Gorgas. Modern school, police, transportation, and communications systems were established, and a new constitution and body of laws were drawn up. On May 20, 1902, Wood relinquished the executive power to the popularly elected President Tomás Estrada Palma. He had been commissioned brigadier general of regulars in February 1901 and mustered out of volunteer service in June of that year. After an inspection tour of German army maneuvers in 1902 he was sent to the Philippines in March 1903 and in July appointed governor of the rebellious Moro Province. In August 1903 he was promoted to major general. (His rapid rise from a captaincy in a staff corps in just five years aroused some controversy.) In April 1906 Wood became commander of the Department of the Philippines at Manila. On his return to the United States in November 1908 he took command of the Department of the East. In April 1910 he was appointed chief of staff of the army, although he did not assume the duties of the office until July, after a special diplomatic mission to Argentina. The post of chief of staff had not yet been firmly established, and in asserting statutory authority Wood came into conflict with entrenched bureau chiefs, principally the adjutant general, Gen. Frederick C. Ainsworth, who was forced to retire. In April 1914 Wood resumed command of the Department of the East. Like Roosevelt he was an outspoken advocate of military preparedness, and he created hostility within the War Department and in the administration of President Woodrow Wilson by going outside official policy to foster the establishment of civilian training camps at Plattsburg, New York, and elsewhere in 1915. (The camps were an outgrowth of a summer camp program for college students originated by Wood in 1913.) By the time the United States entered World War I in April 1917 the "Plattsburg idea" had generated 16 camps and trained some 40,000 volunteers. Passed over for field command in the war, although he was senior officer in the army, Wood commanded the 89th Infantry Division in training at Camp Funston, Kansas, in April–June 1918 and subsequently trained other units for service in France. In January 1919 he was appointed commander of the Central Department at Chicago. In 1920 he was the leading candidate for the Republican presidential nomination going into the national convention, but he lost on the tenth ballot to Warren G. Harding. In 1921 he deferred accepting the presidency of the University of Pennsylvania in order to undertake a mission for President Harding to the Philippines. While there he accepted appointment in October as governor-general of the Philippines. He still held that post when he died on August 7, 1927, in Boston, following surgery for a cerebral tumor.

Woodford, William (1734–1780), Revolutionary army officer. Born on October 6, 1734, in Caroline County, Virginia, Woodford served in the Virginia militia during the French and Indian War. In 1774 he became a member of the Caroline County committee of correspondence, and in August 1775, while serving as Edmund Pendleton's alternate at the Virginia provincial convention, he was appointed colonel of the 3rd Virginia Regiment. On October 25 he defeated a band of Loyalists serving under the royal governor, Lord Dunmore, and on December 9, at Great Bridge, near Norfolk, he defeated a larger force of over 300 Loyalists and 200 British regulars and thereby compelled Dunmore to take to his ship in the bay. He occupied Norfolk on December 14. He was reinforced in these and subsequent operations by Col. Robert Howe's 2nd North Carolina Regiment. In February 1776 Woodford was commissioned colonel of the 2nd Virginia in Continental service, and in February 1777 he was promoted to brigadier general. He took part in the battles of Brandywine, September 11, 1777, Germantown, October 4, and Monmouth Court House, June 27, 1778. In December 1779 he was ordered by Gen. George Washington to lead 700 men to Charleston, South Carolina. He arrived there in April 1780, during the siege of the city and of Gen. Benjamin Lincoln's army by Sir Henry Clinton. On the fall of Charleston on May 12, Woodford was taken prisoner. He died on November 13, 1780, while being held in New York City.

Wool, John Ellis (1784–1869), army officer. Born in Newburgh, New York, on February 29, 1784, Wool grew up in Troy, New York, after the death of his parents. He worked as a clerk and in various other jobs until April 1812, when, having raised a company for service against England, he was commissioned a captain in the 13th Infantry. He distinguished himself and was wounded at Queenston Heights, Quebec, October 13, 1812, under Gen. Stephen Van Rensselaer, and was promoted to major of the 29th Infantry in April 1813. He was brevetted lieutenant colonel for gallantry at Plattsburg, September 11, 1814, where he fought under Gen. Alexander Macomb. He remained in the army after the war; he was transferred to the 6th Infantry in May 1815 and in April 1816 was promoted to colonel and appointed inspector general of the army, a post he held for a quarter of a century, longer than any other officer. In April 1826 he was brevetted brigadier general for ten years' service in grade. He made a tour of European military establishments in 1832 and in 1836 assisted Gen. Winfield Scott in supervising the westward removal of the Cherokee Indians. Wool was promoted to brigadier general in June 1841. Immediately following the declaration of war against Mexico in May 1846 he was ordered to supervise the training of volunteers. After six weeks of prodigious labor he had mustered in and organized and forwarded to Gen. Zachary Taylor on the Texas front some 12,000 volunteers. He arrived in San Antonio in August and in September set out at the head of about 2500 men for Chihuahua. On arriving at Parras early in December he learned that Chihuahua had already been abandoned by the Mexican army, so instead he moved east to Saltillo and joined Taylor's army there. The troops under his command were by that time thoroughly trained and disciplined, having marched through 900 miles of inhospitable country. At the beginning of the battle of Buena Vista, February 22, 1847, Wool chose the ground and deployed the army before Taylor's arrival from Saltillo; he continued as Taylor's second-in-command through both days of fighting and for his actions was brevetted major general. He returned to Troy, New York, in July 1848 and from there commanded the Division of the East in 1848–1853. In October 1853 he took command of the Department of the East in Baltimore, and from 1854 to 1857 he commanded the Department of the Pacific. In the latter post he had responsibility for conducting the Yakima Indian War. From 1857 he again commanded the Department of the East. By timely reinforcement he saved Fort Monroe, Virginia, for the Union in the spring of 1861, and in August he was made commander of the Department of Virginia. Wool was promoted to major general in May 1862. In

June he took command of the Middle Department at Baltimore, and in January 1863 he again took command of the Department of the East. He retired in August 1863. Wool died in Troy, New York, on November 10, 1869.

Wooster, Charles Whiting (1780–1848), naval officer. Born in New Haven, Connecticut, in 1780, Wooster was a grandson of Gen. David Wooster. He went to sea at the age of eleven and within ten years had risen to command of a vessel. During the War of 1812 he commanded the privateer *Saratoga*, with which he took 22 British prizes. In 1814 he was appointed captain in a battalion of volunteer "sea fencibles" raised for the protection of New York harbor; he was later promoted to major in command of the battalion. From 1815 to 1817 he was again engaged in the merchant service, but in October 1817 he accepted a commission as captain in the newly created Chilean navy from Bernardo O'Higgins, who had recently become dictator of that country after leading the forces of revolution against Spanish rule. Wooster bought the bark *Columbus* and sailed her with a cargo of munitions from New York to Valparaiso, arriving in April 1818; the *Columbus* was subsequently recommissioned the *Araucano*. In October 1818, commanding the *Lautaro*, he trapped and captured the Spanish ship *Maria Isabel* at Talcahuano. In January 1819 he resigned from Chilean service in a dispute with the commander of the navy, Adm. Thomas Cochrane. In March 1822, after Cochrane had left Chile for Brazil, he reentered Chilean service as commander of the navy. On January 11, 1826, he led Chilean naval forces in a joint land-sea assault on the final Spanish stronghold in Chile, the island of Chiloé. In November 1829 Wooster was appointed rear admiral. He continued to command the small navy through numerous changes of government until late in 1835, when he resigned and returned to the United States. In 1847 he went to California to try his luck at gold mining; he died in San Francisco in 1848.

Wooster, David (1711–1777), Revolutionary army officer. Born on March 2, 1711, in Stratford (at a site now in Huntington), Connecticut, Wooster graduated from Yale in 1738. In 1741 he was appointed a lieutenant in the provincial militia, and the next year he was made captain of the armed sloop *Defence* for the protection of the Connecticut coast. He was a captain of militia in the capture of Louisbourg by Gen. (later Sir) William Pepperrell in 1745, and after conveying prisoners to England he was commissioned a captain in Pepperrell's regiment of regulars. He served with the regiment until it was reduced and then returned to New Haven, Connecticut, although he continued to draw half-pay until 1774. He served as colonel of the 3rd Connecticut Regiment of militia from the beginning of the French and Indian War in

1755, receiving promotion to brigadier general by 1763. In 1763 he was appointed collector of customs at New Haven. In April 1775 he was appointed major general of Connecticut militia and colonel of the 1st Regiment. He led Connecticut troops to New York in May and performed garrison duty in Harlem and Long Island through the summer. In June he was appointed brigadier general in the Continental army by Congress. In September he was ordered to the Northern Department, and he took part in Gen. Richard Montgomery's expedition into Canada. He remained in command of the captured Montreal while Montgomery moved on to Quebec, and after Montgomery's death in the assault on Quebec on December 31 Wooster succeeded to command of the American army in Canada (although the wounded Col. Benedict Arnold was more prominent). He took personal command at Quebec in April 1776 and remained there until the arrival of Gen. John Thomas in May. By that time his lack of military ability had become notorious; he was recalled by Congress and kept on waiting orders. In the autumn of 1776 he was reappointed major general of militia in Connecticut. When Col. William Tryon (formerly royal governor of New York) landed with a force of some 2000 British regulars and Loyalists at Compo Point (now Westport), Connecticut, on April 25, 1777, and moved rapidly on Danbury to destroy a Continental supply depot, Wooster assembled 200 militiamen and took a position near Ridgefield, between Danbury and the coast. The retiring British were attacked by this tiny force twice on April 27, and in the second attack Wooster was mortally wounded. He lingered while other militia forces under Arnold and Gen. Gold S. Silliman continued to harry the British back to their ships. Wooster died in Danbury, Connecticut, on May 2, 1777.

Worden, John Lorimer (1818–1897), naval officer. Born in Westchester County, New York, on March 12, 1818, Worden entered the navy as a midshipman in January 1834. Until 1837 he served on the *Erie* of the Brazil Squadron, and after two years with the Mediterranean Squadron he attended the naval school in Philadelphia for a few months, being made passed midshipman in July 1840. He served with the Pacific Squadron in 1840–1842, at the Naval Observatory in Washington, D.C., in 1844–1846, and, promoted to lieutenant in November 1846, with the squadron on the California coast in 1847–1850. In 1850–1852 he was again at the Observatory, and subsequently he saw duty with the Mediterranean and Home squadrons and at the New York navy yard. In April 1861 he requested sea duty in the Civil War and was given the assignment of bearing secret dispatches to the squadron lying off Fort Pickens at Pensacola, Florida. Arrested by Confederate authorities near Montgomery, Alabama, during his return,

he was held prisoner for seven months. In January 1862 he was given command of the new ironclad *Monitor*, then being completed in New York by John Ericsson. He sailed the still-experimental and untried vessel through heavy seas to Hampton Roads, Virginia, in March, and during the voyage he was compelled to overcome numerous mechanical difficulties while training a crew in the operation of the novel vessel. The *Monitor* arrived at Hampton Roads on the evening of March 8, just after the destruction of the *Cumberland* by the ironclad *Virginia* (ex-*Merrimac*), and Worden made last-minute preparations for the coming battle. At 8 o'clock on the morning of March 9 Lt. Catesby ap Roger Jones of the *Virginia* began the attack. The *Monitor*—lighter, faster, lower in the water—outmaneuvered the *Virginia* and was able to make use of shallower parts of the channel. On the other hand, while it carried two huge 11-inch guns, it was far inferior in rate of fire, the gun crews were poorly trained, and the shot itself, although heavy, was of poor quality. The battle had raged at close quarters for nearly three hours when the *Virginia* managed at last to get in position to ram the *Monitor*, but the blow did little damage owing to the *Virginia*'s loss of its iron prow the day before. Moments later a shell struck the *Monitor*'s pilothouse and flying iron fragments temporarily blinded Worden, who was forced to relinquish command to Lt. Samuel D. Greene. By that time, however, the *Virginia* was retiring from the ebbing tide toward Norfolk and the battle had ended. In July Worden was voted the thanks of Congress. In October he took command of the monitor *Montauk* of the South Atlantic Blockading Squadron. As part of Adm. Samuel F. Du Pont's testing of the capabilities of monitor-type vessels, Worden engaged in a four-hour duel with the guns of Fort McAllister near Savannah, Georgia, on January 27, 1863; little damage was inflicted on either side in that or in a second duel on February 1. Promoted to captain early in February, he destroyed the cruiser *Nashville* during another action before Fort McAllister on February 28, the *Montauk* being considerably damaged this time by an underwater torpedo (mine). The *Montauk* was prominent in Du Pont's futile attack on Charleston, South Carolina, on April 7, 1863. After that operation Worden passed the rest of the war supervising the construction of ironclads in New York. In 1866–1867 he commanded the *Pensacola* in the Pacific Squadron. Promoted to commodore in May 1868, he became superintendent of the Naval Academy in 1869, remaining there until 1874 and advancing to rear admiral in November 1872. From 1875 to 1877 he commanded the European Squadron, and he served on the Examining Board and as president of the Retiring Board from 1877 until his own retirement in December 1886. Worden died in Washington, D.C., on October 18, 1897.

Worth, William Jenkins (1794–1849), army officer. Born on March 1, 1794, in Hudson, New York, Worth worked as a clerk in an Albany store until the War of 1812. He entered the army as a first lieutenant of the 23rd Infantry in March 1813 and served on the staffs of Gen. Morgan Lewis and Gen. Winfield Scott. He distinguished himeslf as Scott's aide-de-camp at the battles of Chippewa, July 5, 1814, for which he was brevetted captain, and Lundy's Lane, July 25, in which he was seriously wounded and for which he was brevetted major. He remained in the army after the war and from 1820 to 1828 was commandant of cadets at West Point. He was brevetted lieutenant colonel in July 1824 for ten years' service in grade. He was on the staff of the Coast Artillery School at Fort Monroe, Virginia, in 1829–1830, and in 1832 he was promoted to major in the Ordnance Corps. In July 1838 he was appointed colonel of the 8th Infantry, which he commanded on the Canadian border in 1838–1839 and in Florida in action against the Seminoles in 1841–1842. He defeated the Indians in a battle at Palatka on April 19, 1842, and was brevetted brigadier general for that action. His ceaseless campaigning, aimed particularly at the Indians' food supply, brought the seven-year Second Seminole War to an official end in August 1842. He remained in Florida until 1846, when he was named second-in-command of the army in Texas under Gen. Zachary Taylor. After the arrival of Col. David E. Twiggs later in 1846 the two engaged in an unseemly conflict over seniority that damaged their reputations and for a time threatened the army's morale. Worth led the vanguard of Taylor's advance to the Rio Grande, took part in the battles of Palo Alto and Resaca de la Palma, May 8 and 9, 1846, and led a vigorous assault on Monterrey on September 23, for which he was brevetted major general. Transferred to Gen. Winfield Scott's army, he commanded a division from the capture of Veracruz in March 1847 to the end of the war. After the battle of Cerro Gordo, April 18, he commanded the advance force that received the capitulation of Puebla on May 15, took part in the battles of Contreras and Churubusco, August 19–20, stormed Molino del Rey against heavy opposition on September 8, and in the assault on Mexico City seized the San Cosmé Gate, September 13–14. A vain and ambitious officer, Worth engaged in a considerable amount of scheming and grumbling against Scott, some of it public. In November 1848 he was given command of the Department of Texas. He died in San Antonio, Texas, on May 7, 1849.

Wotherspoon, William Wallace (1850–1921), army officer. Born on November 16, 1850, in Washington, D.C., Wotherspoon enlisted in the navy in 1870. After three years of various routine assignments he transferred to the army, receiving appointment as second lieutenant in the 12th Infantry in

October 1873. For many years he served mainly in the West; he saw action against the Indians and received promotion to first lieutenant in March 1879. He had charge of a large body of Apache prisoners, including Geronimo, at Mt. Vernon Barracks, Alabama, in 1889–1894, during which time he advanced to captain in April 1893. From 1895 to 1898 he was professor of military science at the Rhode Island College of Agriculture and Mechanic Arts (now Rhode Island College), Providence. He was with the 12th Infantry in Georgia during the Spanish–American War, and from 1899 to 1903 he was in the Philippines, receiving promotion to major in February 1901. After a year on the faculty of the General Service and Staff College, Fort Leavenworth, Kansas, and promotion to lieutenant colonel in July 1904, he served two years as director of the newly established Army War College. From October 1906 to February 1907 he was chief of staff of the Army of Cuban Occupation, and he then served as president of the Army War College until April 1912, receiving promotion to brigadier general in October 1907 and serving also as assistant to Gen. J. Franklin Bell, army chief of staff, in 1909–1910. Promoted to major general in May 1912, he commanded the Department of the Gulf until September, when he was named assistant to Gen. Leonard Wood, chief of staff. In April 1914 he succeeded Wood as chief of staff of the army, and he held the post until his retirement in November of the same year. During 1915–1919 he served as superintendent of public works of New York state. Wotherspoon died in Washington, D.C., on October 21, 1921.

Wright, Horatio Gouverneur (1820–1899), army officer. Born on March 6, 1820, in Clinton, Connecticut, Wright graduated from West Point in 1841 and was commissioned in the engineers. He was an instructor at West Point from 1842 to 1844, and from 1846 to 1856 he was engaged in river and harbor work and construction of fortifications in Florida and the Keys, receiving promotions to first lieutenant in 1848 and to captain in July 1855. In 1856 he became assistant to Col. Joseph G. Totten, the chief of engineers, in Washington, D.C. On the outbreak of the Civil War he took part in the destruction of the Norfolk navy yard on April 20, 1861, and was captured while attempting to burn the dry dock. He was quickly released, and in May, declining a major's commission in the 13th Infantry, he undertook the construction of fortifications in Washington, D.C., including Fort Ellsworth. He served as chief engineer of Gen. Samuel P. Heintzelman's 3rd Division at Bull Run (Manassas), July 21, and in August was promoted to major of engineers. In September he was appointed brigadier general of volunteers, and in November he served as chief engineer in Gen. Thomas W. Sherman's expedition against Port Royal, South Carolina; in that operation he commanded the landing force that occupied Fort Walker at Hilton Head on November 7. In February–June 1862 he commanded the army troops in the expedition under Flag-Officer Samuel F. Du Pont that captured Jacksonville, St. Augustine, and other points on the Florida coast. From August 1862 to March 1863 he commanded the Department of the Ohio and the new Army of the Ohio (the old one, under Gen. William S. Rosecrans, having become the Army of the Cumberland). Relinquishing that post to Gen. Ambrose E. Burnside, he took command of a division of Gen. John Sedgwick's VI Corps, Army of the Potomac, in May 1863. He saw much action in the Mine Run campaign of November 1863 and in the spring offensive of 1864. With the death of Sedgwick during the battle of Spotsylvania in May 1864, Wright succeeded to command of the VI Corps, which bore the brunt of the hand-to-hand fighting at the "Bloody Angle," on May 12. Wright was promoted to major general of volunteers as of that date and brevetted colonel of regulars. In July he and the VI Corps were hurriedly sent to defend Washington against Gen. Jubal A. Early; they arrived just in time to engage Early at the outskirts of the city. He took part in Gen. Philip H. Sheridan's campaign in the Shenandoah valley in the autumn of 1864 and was in command of the army at Cedar Creek, October 19, before Sheridan's arrival on the field. Troops of the VI Corps were the first to breach the Confederate line at Petersburg on April 2, 1865, and the corps led the attack at Sayler's Creek, April 6, that forced the surrender of Gen. Richard S. Ewell. For his actions at Petersburg Wright was brevetted major general of regulars. From July 1865 to August 1866 he commanded the Department of Texas. Having been promoted to lieutenant colonel of engineers in November 1865, he resumed engineering duties on being mustered out of volunteer service. Among the projects he was later associated with were the East River Bridge in New York City, the Sutro Tunnel in Nevada, and the Washington Monument. He was promoted to colonel in March 1879 and named chief of engineers with the rank of brigadier general in June of that year. He held that post until his retirement in March 1884. Wright died in Washington, D.C., on July 2, 1899.

Wright, William Mason (1863–1943), army officer. Born on September 24, 1863, in Newark, New Jersey, Wright attended Yale for a time before entering West Point in 1882. He left after a few months, but in January 1885 he was appointed a second lieutenant of infantry. After service on the frontier and at Fort Omaha, Nebraska, he graduated from the Infantry and Cavalry School, Fort Leavenworth, Kansas, in 1891 and was promoted to first lieutenant in December of that year. Further routine service followed until the outbreak of the Spanish–American War. In May 1898 he was appointed captain and

assistant adjutant general of volunteers; he took part in the Santiago campaign in Cuba, and, promoted to captain of regulars in March 1899 and mustered out of volunteer service in May, he then saw action in the suppression of the Philippine insurrection. From 1905 to 1908 he was attached to the General Staff, serving as secretary from August 1907 to April 1908, and he advanced to major in March 1908 and to lieutenant colonel in November 1913. In April 1914, with the 19th Infantry, he took part under Gen. Frederick Funston in the occupation of Veracruz, Mexico. He was promoted to colonel in July 1916. After the entry of the United States into World War I he was quickly promoted to brigadier general in May 1917 and temporary major general in August. In the latter month he took command of the newly activated 35th Infantry Division and after a month of training with it was transferred to command of Camp Doniphan at Fort Sill, Oklahoma. In December he resumed command of the 35th and in May 1918 took it to France. He commanded and trained in rapid succession the III Corps in June–July, the V Corps in July–August, and the VII Corps in August–September, before entering the line in command of the 89th Division in September. He took part in the reduction of the St. Mihiel salient and in the Meuse–Argonne offensive. From November to March 1919 he commanded the I Corps in occupation duty. After his return to the United States he was again attached to the General Staff, serving from September 1920 to June 1921 as assistant chief of staff in charge of purchase, storage, and traffic. Promoted to permanent major general in March 1921, he was given command of the IX Corps area in July, and from February to September 1922 he commanded the Department of the Philippines. He retired in December 1922 and was later promoted to lieutenant general on the retired list. Wright died in Washington, D.C., on August 16, 1943.

Wyman, Robert Harris (1822–1882), naval officer. Born in Portsmouth, New Hampshire, on July 12, 1822, Wyman, son of a naval officer, entered the navy as a midshipman in March 1837. He made cruises on the *Independence* of the Brazil Squadron, the *Fairfield*, and in 1838–1840 the *John Adams*, commanded by his father, of the East India Squadron. After attending the naval school in Philadelphia he was made passed midshipman in June 1843. From 1843 to 1846 he was on the *Brandywine*, and in the Mexican War he served in the squadron under Commodore David Conner and Commodore Matthew C. Perry. He was attached to the Naval Observatory in 1848–1850, receiving promotion to lieutenant in July 1850, and was there again in 1853–1854. After the outbreak of the Civil War he was given command in succession of the steamer *Yankee* in July 1861, of the *Pocahontas* of the Potomac Flotilla in September, and of the steam sloop *Pawnee* of the South Atlantic

Blockading Squadron in October. He took part in Flag-Officer Samuel F. Du Pont's expedition against Port Royal, South Carolina, in November, and a short time later he was put in command of the Potomac Flotilla. In April 1862 he led an expedition up the Rappahannock River that destroyed bridges and a large number of small craft and captured nine larger vessels. Promoted to commander in July 1862, he commanded the gunboat *Sonoma* on the James River briefly and then the *Wachusett* on the Potomac before being assigned to command the *Santiago de Cuba* on special blockade duty in the West Indies. In 1864 he was attached to the Navy Department staff in Wash-

ington, D.C. From 1865 to 1867 he commanded the *Colorado*, flagship of the European Squadron, receiving promotion to captain in July 1866, and in 1867–1869 he commanded the *Ticonderoga* at the same station. In 1871 he was appointed chief of the Hydrographic Office in Washington; during his eight years in that post he published numerous books on the navigation of various waters. Promoted to commodore in July 1872 and to rear admiral in April 1878, he commanded the North Atlantic Squadron in 1879 –1882. In June 1882 he became chairman of the Lighthouse Board. Wyman died in Washington, D.C., on December 2, 1882.

Y

Yeager, Charles Elwood (1923–   ), air force officer. Born on February 13, 1923, in Myra, West Virginia, Yeager enlisted in the army in September 1941, shortly after graduating from high school, and was assigned to the Army Air Corps. After aviation training he was commissioned a reserve flight officer in March 1943. In November of that year he went to England with the 357th Fighter Group, and as a pilot in the fighter command of the Eighth Air Force he flew a total of 64 missions over Europe, mainly in P-51 Mustangs; he shot down 13 German aircraft and was shot down once himself (he escaped capture through the aid of the French underground). After the war he became a flight instructor at Perrin Field, Texas, and then a test pilot at Wright Field, Ohio. He secured a regular commission as captain in February 1947. From among several volunteers he was chosen later in that year to test-fly the secret experimental X-1 aircraft, built by the Bell Aircraft Company to test the capabilities of the human pilot and fixed-wing aircraft against the severe aerodynamic stresses of sonic flight. On October 14, 1947, over Rogers Dry Lake in southern California, he rode the X-1, attached to a B-29 mother ship, to an altitude of 25,000 feet and then rocketed to 40,000 feet; at that altitude he became the first man to exceed the speed of sound in level flight, breaking the sound barrier at about 662 miles per hour. Following the public announcement of his feat in mid-1948 Yeager was awarded the Mackay Trophy and shared the Collier Trophy with the designer and builder of the X-1. In 1951 he was promoted to major. On December 12, 1953, he established a world speed record of 1650 miles per hour in an X-1A rocket plane. He was awarded the 1954 Harmon Air Trophy for that achievement. In October 1954 he left his post as assistant chief of test flight operations at Edwards Air Force Base, California, to join the staff of the Twelfth Air Force in Germany. Following other routine assignments he returned to Edwards in 1962 as commandant of the Aerospace Research Pilot School with the rank of colonel. In March 1968 Yeager took command of the 4th Tactical Fighter Wing. He retired from the air force in the rank of brigadier general in February 1975. Among honors paid him was the issue in 1976 by the U.S. Mint of a medal commemorating his first flight through the sound barrier.

York, Alvin Cullum (1887–1964), soldier. Born in Pall Mall, Fentress County, Tennessee, on Decem-ber 13, 1887, York had little formal education, for he left school in the third grade to work in a blacksmith shop. In 1911 he underwent a religious conversion at a revival meeting, and when the United States entered World War I in 1917 he declared himself a conscientious objector. His petition for exemption from the draft was twice denied, however, and he was inducted into the army and sent to France with the 328th Infantry Regiment, 82nd Division. While taking part in the battle of the Argonne Forest on October 8, 1918, York, then a private first class, demonstrated outstanding heroism by leading a 17-man patrol in an attack on a German machine gun nest. The patrol surprised and captured a small number of German soldiers, including the commander of a machine gun battalion. They were suddenly pinned down, however, by extremely heavy rifle and machine gun fire from high ground on their left. Leaving the rest of the patrol to guard the prisoners, York attacked alone; he took the position, killing 25 enemy soldiers in doing so (he was a remarkable marksman). More prisoners were taken on the march back to American lines, and York was finally credited with capturing 132. When asked how he had done this all by himself, he replied "I surrounded 'em." On November 1, 1918, shortly before the armistice, he was promoted to sergeant, and later he was awarded the Medal of Honor and the French Croix de Guerre. Altogether he received some 50 other decorations and became one of the most celebrated heroes of the war. After the war, however, he refused to capitalize on his fame; he returned to Tennessee to live on a farm granted him by the state. In 1928 he published his autobiography and in 1940 allowed the movie *Sergeant York*, starring Gary Cooper, to be made. Cooper won an Academy Award in 1941 for his performance. York himself lived very modestly, giving away the bulk of the proceeds from his book and the movie to a foundation organized to support an industrial school and a Bible school in Tennessee. That generosity led to difficulty when it was discovered he had not kept enough money to pay income taxes; Congressman Sam Rayburn of Texas led a public fundraising drive to settle the account. York died in Nashville, Tennessee, on December 2, 1964.

Young, Samuel Baldwin Marks (1840–1924), army officer. Born on January 9, 1840, in Pittsburgh, Pennsylvania, Young enlisted as a private in the 12th Pennsylvania Infantry in April 1861. After the expiration of his term he was commissioned a captain in the 4th Pennsylvania Volunteer Cavalry in September. He served with distinction with the Army of the Potomac throughout the Civil War, receiving promotions to major in September 1862, lieutenant colonel in October 1864, and colonel in December 1864 and in April 1865 being brevetted brigadier general of volunteers for his services during the final campaign from Petersburg to Appomattox. He was mustered out of volunteer service in July 1865 and in May 1866 was appointed a second lieutenant in the 12th Infantry, receiving promotion to captain in the 8th Cavalry in July of that year. He served thereafter principally on the frontier and saw action against the Indians on several occasions. In March 1867 he was brevetted major for Civil War service at Sulphur Springs, Virginia, October 12, 1863; lieutenant colonel for Amelia Spring, Virginia, April 5, 1865; and colonel for Sayler's Creek, April 6. He was regularly promoted to major in April 1883, lieutenant colonel in August 1892, and colonel of the 3rd Cavalry in June 1897. On the outbreak of the Spanish–American War in May 1898 he was appointed brigadier general of volunteers. He commanded a brigade of Gen. Joseph Wheeler's cavalry division in the Santiago campaign in Cuba and in July was promoted to major general of volunteers. In April 1899 his volunteer commission expired, and he was reappointed brigadier general of volunteers. From July 1899 to March 1901 he saw action against the Philippine insurrectionists. He commanded a succession of brigades in Gen. Henry Lawton's 1st Division of the VIII Corps under Gen. Elwell S. Otis, led the advance forces in the final campaign in northern Luzon, and then served as military governor of that district. In January 1900 he was promoted to brigadier general of regulars and in February 1901 to major general. From then until March 1902 he commanded the Department of California. In November 1901 he was named president of the War College Board, a forerunner of the actual college and of the General Staff, and in July 1902 he was appointed the first president of the Army War College. In August 1903 he was promoted to lieutenant general and appointed the first chief of staff of the army under the newly adopted General Staff system. He held that post until his retirement in January 1904. In 1909–1910 he was president of a board of inquiry that investigated the alleged riot of black soldiers of the 25th Infantry in Brownsville, Texas, on August 13, 1906, and affirmed the subsequent dishonorable discharge of 159 men by order of President Theodore Roosevelt. From 1910 to 1920 he was governor of the Soldiers Home in Washington, D.C. Young died on September 1, 1924, in Helena, Montana.

Z

Zeilin, Jacob (1806–1880), marine officer. Born in Philadelphia on July 16, 1806, Zeilin entered West Point in 1822 but did not remain to graduate. In October 1831 he was commissioned a second lieutenant in the marine corps. After brief assignments at marine barracks in Washington, D.C., Philadelphia, Boston, and Norfolk, Virginia, he saw his first sea duty aboard the *Erie* of the Brazil Squadron in 1835–1837, receiving promotion to first lieutenant in September 1836. After a tour of duty at the Boston navy yard he returned to the Brazil station in 1843 on the *Columbia,* on which he later served also in the Mediterranean. He was stationed at Washington and then Philadelphia from 1845 until sailing for the Pacific coast on the *Congress,* Commodore Robert F. Stockton, in the spring of 1846. He commanded the marine detachments that took possession of Santa Barbara on August 4 and San Pedro on August 6 and served as adjutant of Stockton's battalion of marines and sailors that took Los Angeles on August 13. He led a small force of marines in a relief expedition sent by Stockton from San Diego to the American forces under Gen. Stephen W. Kearny besieged at Agua Caliente (Warren's Ranch); he arrived on December 11 and broke the siege. Zeilin commanded the marines and acted as Stockton's adjutant in the campaign to recapture Los Angeles and distinguished himself in the battle of San Gabriel, January 8–9, 1847, for which he won a brevet to major. In September 1847 he was promoted to captain, and on November 11 he commanded the marines in the landing party from the *Congress, Independence, Cyane,* and *Erie,* all under Commodore William B. Shubrick, that captured Mazatlán. From 1848 to 1852 Zeilin was stationed at Norfolk and then New York City. In 1852 he was given command of the marines of the squadron dispatched to Japan under Commodore Matthew C. Perry; he sailed on the flagships *Mississippi* and later *Susquehannah* and took prominent part, with the squadron marine force formed as a battalion, in the ceremonials attending Perry's diplomacy. From 1854 to 1861 Zeilin served at various marine barracks, and in 1859 he commanded the marines of the Mediterranean Squadron from aboard the *Wabash.* At the outbreak of the Civil War he was stationed in Washington. He commanded one of four companies of marines that took part in the battle of Bull Run (Manassas), July 21, 1861, and was wounded. Promoted to major a few days later, he was put in command of the marine barracks at New York and saw no further

action until August 1863, when he led a battalion of marines to join Adm. John A. B. Dahlgren's South Atlantic Blockading Squadron before Charleston, South Carolina. He commanded a regiment on Morris Island until ill health forced him to return to garrison duty at Portsmouth, New Hampshire. In June 1864 he was appointed colonel commandant of the marine corps, the several officers senior to him being simultaneously retired. In March 1867 he was promoted to brigadier general, the first marine officer to hold that rank. He retired in November 1876 and died in Washington, D.C., on November 18, 1880.

Zollicoffer, Felix Kirk (1812–1862), journalist, public official, and Confederate army officer. Born on May 19, 1812, in Maury County, Tennessee, Zollicoffer attended Jackson College in Columbia, Tennessee, for a year before entering a newspaper office at the age of sixteen. Later he was a journeyman printer in Knoxville, and from 1834 he helped edit a number of small newspapers in the area. He was appointed state printer in 1835. He served as a lieutenant in the Seminole War in Florida in 1836. In 1842 he became editor of the powerful *Republican Banner* in Nashville, and he played a key role in the defeat of James K. Polk's candidacy for governor in 1843. From 1845 to 1849 he served as state adjutant general and comptroller, and from 1849 to 1852 he was in the legislature. Having resumed editorship of the *Republican Banner* in 1850, he used it effectively to support Gen. Winfield Scott's presidential campaign of 1852 and in that year was himself elected to Congress, where he served three terms as a States' Rights Whig from March 1853 to March 1859. An opponent of secession, he was a member of the futile peace conference in Washington, D.C., in February 1861, but on the outbreak of war in April he declared for the Confederacy. In July he was appointed brigadier general in the Confederate army and put in command of the important and as yet uncommitted district of eastern Tennessee. He suffered a minor defeat by Union forces at Camp Wild-Cat in Laurel County, Kentucky, on October 21. Late in 1861 he was ordered to establish a strongpoint at Mill Springs, Kentucky, to close the Cumberland Gap. Gen. George B. Crittenden arrived there later and assumed command, and on January 19, 1862, he ordered Zollicoffer to attack a Union camp manned by troops under Col. George H. Thomas at nearby Fishing Creek. Zollicoffer inadvertently rode beyond his line in the battle and in a minor skirmish was shot and killed. The battle of Mill Springs was an important Union victory in Kentucky, while the early death of Zollicoffer was mourned throughout the South.

Zumwalt, Elmo Russell, Jr. (1920–   ), naval officer. Born on November 29, 1920, in Tulare, California, Zumwalt graduated from the Naval Academy in 1942 and during World War II served on destroyers in the Pacific, advancing to lieutenant by 1945. Various routine assignments followed, including a period, 1948–1950, as a Naval Reserve Officers Training Corps instructor at the University of North Carolina. In 1950–1951, by then a lieutenant commander, he had his first command aboard the *Tills,* and after graduating from the Naval War College in 1953 he was attached for two years to the Bureau of Personnel. In 1955–1957, then a commander, he commanded the destroyer *Arnold J. Isbell,* and from 1957 to 1959 he held various staff posts in Washington, D.C. In 1959–1961 he commanded the missile frigate *Dewey,* and in 1962, by then a captain, he graduated from the National War College. After a year in the office of the assistant secretary of defense he was named executive assistant and senior aide to the secretary of the navy in 1963. Promoted to rear admiral in July 1965, in 1965–1966 Zumwalt was again at sea in command of Cruiser-Destroyer Flotilla 7. From 1966 to 1968 he was attached to the office of the chief of naval operations, where he established and directed a new division of systems analysis. In September 1968 he became commander of U.S. naval forces in Vietnam and head of the naval wing of the Military Assistance Command there under Gen. Creighton W. Abrams. In October he was promoted to vice admiral. In July 1970 he succeeded Adm. Thomas H. Moorer as chief of naval operations, receiving promotion to admiral. His term in that post was marked by a purposeful liberalization of a number of naval practices regarding personal liberty and expression among enlisted personnel, a largely successful effort to stem a rapid drop in the enlistment rate. Zumwalt retired in July 1974 and later in the year was named a visiting professor at Vanderbilt University. In 1976 he campaigned unsuccessfully as a Republican to unseat Sen. Harry F. Byrd of Virginia. In that year he published *On Watch; a Memoir.* He continued thereafter to be an outspoken critic of proposals to reduce defense expenditures.

ADDENDA

The following pages contain a number of lists and tables that are intended to aid the reader in gaining access to the information contained in the biographies and at the same time to provide some additional information on the nation's wars and its military and naval commanders. The lists and tables fall into six groups, as follows:

1. Secretaries of war, 1789–1947   page 500
   Secretaries of the navy, 1798–1947   page 501
   Secretaries of defense, 1947–   page 502
   Chairmen of the Joint Chiefs of Staff, 1949–   page 502
   Commanders of NATO forces, 1950–   page 503

2. Army
   Chief officers   page 503
   Chronology and commanders   page 504

3. Navy
   Chief officers   page 528
   Chronology and commanders   page 529

4. Marine Corps
   Chief officers   page 540
   Chronology and commanders   page 540

5. Air Force
   Chief officers   page 542
   Commanders   page 543

6. Career categories   page 544

The lists in the first group are self-explanatory. Those in the sixth group display under various occupational headings the names of many biographical subjects who, often because they were not combatants or major commanders, are not otherwise indexed.

The four groups concerning the four branches of the armed forces provide three sorts of information. First in each case is a list of the chief officers of that service. When, as is particularly the case with the army and the air force, the title of the chief officer has changed several times in the course of history, each such change is noted; succeeding officers retained that title until a further change was made. Following the lists of chief officers in the army, navy, and marine corps groups are chronological lists of wars, battles, expeditions, and other notable events. The third column of those lists gives references to persons in whose biographies that event is given *substantial* mention. Thus, in the case of a major Civil War battle, for example, references will be given for up to 25 participants; in the biographies of those participants the reader will find information on that battle. Where a biography notes only that a particular person was present, giving no other information, no reference has been entered on the chronological list. In a few cases, where the additional information seemed useful for balance or completeness, references have been entered for persons who are not treated in a biography; these references are printed in small capitals. (This does not apply to the lists of civilian secretaries, most of whom are not entered.) Where references are made for both sides in a battle (chiefly Indian wars, some Revolutionary battles, and the Civil War), the names are ranged in two parallel columns separated by a bullet •. The left column contains references for the colonial, patriot, or Union sides, the right column for the Indian, Loyalist, or Confederate sides.

A third kind of information is contained in boxed tables inserted into the chronological lists following the sections dealing with the Civil War, the two World Wars, and certain others. These show the commanders of various major components of the armed services in that war.

In the case of the air force, there is no chronological list because of the very small number of discrete major events in air war. The tables of air commanders in the World Wars and Korea will lead the reader to all appropriate references.

Secretaries of War

Henry Knox	Sept. 1789–Dec. 1794
Timothy Pickering	Jan. 1795–Dec. 1795
James McHenry	Jan. 1796–May 1800
Samuel Dexter	June 1800–Jan. 1801
Henry Dearborn	March 1801–March 1809
William Eustis	March 1809–Jan. 1813
John Armstrong	Jan. 1813–Sept. 1814
James Monroe	Sept. 1814–March 1815
William H. Crawford	Aug. 1815–Oct. 1816
George Graham (ad interim)	Oct. 1816–Oct. 1817
John C. Calhoun	Oct. 1817–March 1825
James Barbour	March 1825–May 1828
Peter B. Porter	May 1828–March 1829
John H. Eaton	March 1829–June 1831
Lewis Cass	Aug. 1831–Oct. 1836
Benjamin F. Butler	Oct. 1836–March 1837
Joel R. Poinsett	March 1837–March 1841
John Bell	March 1841–Sept. 1841
John C. Spencer	Oct. 1841–March 1843
James M. Porter	March 1843–Jan. 1844
William Wilkins	Feb. 1844–March 1845
William L. Marcy	March 1845–March 1849
George W. Crawford	March 1849–July 1850
Charles M. Conrad	Aug. 1850–March 1853
Jefferson Davis	March 1853–March 1857
John B. Floyd	March 1857–Dec. 1860
Joseph Holt	Jan. 1861–March 1861
Simon Cameron	March 1861–Jan. 1862
Edwin M. Stanton	Jan. 1862–May 1868
Ulysses S. Grant (ad interim)	August 1867–Jan. 1868 May 1868–June 1868
John M. Schofield	June 1868–March 1869
John A. Rawlins	March 1869–Sept. 1869
William T. Sherman (ad interim)	Sept. 1869–Oct. 1869
William W. Belknap	Oct. 1869–March 1876
Alphonso Taft	March 1876–May 1876
James D. Cameron	May 1876–March 1877
George W. McCrary	March 1877–Dec. 1879
Alexander Ramsey	Dec. 1879–March 1881
Robert T. Lincoln	March 1881–March 1885
William C. Endicott	March 1885–March 1889
Redfield Proctor	March 1889–Nov. 1891
Stephen B. Elkins	Dec. 1891–March 1893
Daniel S. Lamont	March 1893–March 1897
Russell A. Alger	March 1897–Aug. 1899
Elihu Root	Aug. 1899–Jan. 1904
William H. Taft	Feb. 1904–June 1908

Luke E. Wright	July 1908–March 1909
Jacob M. Dickinson	March 1909–May 1911
Henry L. Stimson	May 1911–March 1913
Lindley K. Garrison	March 1913–Feb. 1916
Hugh L. Scott (ad interim)	Feb. 1916–March 1916
Newton D. Baker	March 1916–March 1921
John W. Weeks	March 1921–Oct. 1925
Dwight F. Davis	Oct. 1925–March 1929
James W. Good	March 1929–Nov. 1929
Patrick J. Hurley	Dec. 1929–March 1933
George H. Dern	March 1933–Aug. 1936
Henry H. Woodring	Sept. 1936–June 1940
Henry L. Stimson	July 1940–Sept. 1945
Robert P. Patterson	Sept. 1945–July 1947
Kenneth C. Royall	July 1947–Sept. 1947

Secretaries of the Navy

Benjamin Stoddert	May 1798–March 1801
Robert Smith	July 1801–March 1809
Paul Hamilton	May 1809–Dec. 1812
William Jones	Jan. 1813–Dec. 1814
Benjamin W. Crowninshield	Jan. 1815–Sept. 1818
Smith Thompson	Jan. 1819–Aug. 1823
Samuel L. Southard	Sept. 1823–March 1829
John Branch	March 1829–May 1831
Levi Woodbury	May 1831–June 1834
Mahlon Dickerson	July 1834–June 1838
James K. Paulding	July 1838–March 1841
George E. Badger	March 1841–Sept. 1841
Abel P. Upshur	Oct. 1841–July 1843
David Henshaw	July 1843–Feb. 1844
Thomas W. Gilmer	Feb. 1844
John Y. Mason	March 1844–March 1845
George Bancroft	March 1845–Sept. 1846
John Y. Mason	Sept. 1846–March 1849
William B. Preston	March 1849–July 1850
William A. Graham	Aug. 1850–June 1852
John P. Kennedy	July 1852–March 1853
James C. Dobbin	March 1853–March 1857
Isaac Toucey	March 1857–March 1861
Gideon Welles	March 1861–March 1869
Adolph E. Borie	March 1869–June 1869
George M. Robeson	June 1869–March 1877
Richard W. Thompson	March 1877–Dec. 1880
Nathan Goff, Jr.	Jan. 1881–March 1881
William H. Hunt	March 1881–April 1882
William E. Chandler	April 1882–March 1885
William C. Whitney	March 1885–March 1889

Benjamin F. Tracy	March 1889–March 1893
Hilary A. Herbert	March 1893–March 1897
John D. Long	March 1897–April 1902
William H. Moody	May 1902–June 1904
Paul Morton	July 1904–June 1905
Charles J. Bonaparte	July 1905–Dec. 1906
Victor H. Metcalf	Dec. 1906–Nov. 1908
Truman H. Newberry	Dec. 1908–March 1909
George von L. Meyer	March 1909–March 1913
Josephus Daniels	March 1913–March 1921
Edwin Denby	March 1921–March 1924
Curtis D. Wilbur	March 1924–March 1929
Charles F. Adams	March 1929–March 1933
Claude A. Swanson	March 1933–July 1939
Charles Edison	Jan. 1940–June 1940
Frank Knox	June 1940–April 1944
James V. Forrestal	May 1944–Sept. 1947

Secretaries of Defense

James V. Forrestal	Sept. 1947–March 1949
Louis A. Johnson	March 1949–Sept. 1950
George C. Marshall	Sept. 1950–Sept. 1951
Robert A. Lovett	Sept. 1951–Jan. 1953
Charles E. Wilson	Jan. 1953–Oct. 1957
Neil H. McElroy	Oct. 1957–Dec. 1959
Thomas S. Gates	Dec. 1959–Jan. 1961
Robert S. McNamara	Jan. 1961–March 1968
Clark M. Clifford	March 1968–Jan. 1969
Melvin R. Laird	Jan. 1969–Jan. 1973
Elliot L. Richardson	Jan. 1973–May 1973
James R. Schlesinger	July 1973–Nov. 1975
Donald H. Rumsfeld	Nov. 1975–Jan. 1977
Harold Brown	Jan. 1977–

Chairmen, Joint Chiefs of Staff

Omar N. Bradley	Aug. 1949–Aug. 1953
Arthur W. Radford	Aug. 1953–Aug. 1957
Nathan F. Twining	Aug. 1957–Sept. 1960
Lyman L. Lemnitzer	Sept. 1960–Oct. 1962
Maxwell D. Taylor	Oct. 1962–July 1964
Earle G. Wheeler	July 1964–July 1970
Thomas H. Moorer	July 1970–July 1974
George S. Brown	July 1974–

Commander, North Atlantic Treaty Organization forces

Dwight D. Eisenhower	Dec. 1950–May 1952
Matthew B. Ridgway	May 1952–July 1953
Alfred M. Gruenther	July 1953–Nov. 1956
Lauris Norstad	Nov. 1956–Jan. 1963
Lyman L. Lemnitzer	Jan. 1963–July 1969
Andrew J. Goodpaster	July 1969–Dec. 1974
Alexander M. Haig	Dec. 1974–

ARMY
Chief officers

George Washington	(commander in chief, Continental army, from June 17, 1775)	June 1775–Dec. 1783
Henry Knox	(senior officer)	Dec. 1783–June 1784
John Doughty		June 1784–Aug. 1784
Josiah Harmar		Aug. 1784–March 1791
Arthur St. Clair		March 1791–March 1792
Anthony Wayne		April 1792–Dec. 1796
James Wilkinson		Dec. 1796–July 1798
George Washington	(commanding general, Provisional Army, from July 13, 1798)	July 1798–Dec. 1799
ALEXANDER HAMILTON	(senior officer)	Dec. 1799–June 1800
James Wilkinson		June 1800–Jan. 1812
Henry Dearborn		Jan. 1812–June 1815
Jacob Brown	(senior officer to June 1, 1821; thereafter commanding general)	June 1815–Feb. 1828
Alexander Macomb	(commanding general)	May 1828–June 1841
Winfield Scott		July 1841–Nov. 1861
George B. McClellan		Nov. 1861–March 1862
Henry W. Halleck		July 1862–March 1864
Ulysses S. Grant		March 1864–March 1869
William T. Sherman		March 1869–Nov. 1883
Philip H. Sheridan		Nov. 1883–Aug. 1888
John M. Schofield		Aug. 1888–Sept. 1895
Nelson A. Miles		Oct. 1895–Aug. 1903
Samuel B.M. Young	(chief of staff)	Aug. 1903–Jan. 1904
Adna R. Chaffee		Jan. 1904–Jan. 1906
John C. Bates		Jan. 1906–April 1906
J. Franklin Bell		April 1906–April 1910

Leonard Wood	April 1910–April 1914
William W. Wotherspoon	April 1914–Nov. 1914
Hugh L. Scott	Nov. 1914–Sept. 1917
Tasker H. Bliss	Sept. 1917–May 1918
Peyton C. March	May 1918–June 1921
John J. Pershing	July 1921–Sept. 1924
John L. Hines	Sept. 1924–Nov. 1926
Charles P. Summerall	Nov. 1926–Nov. 1930
Douglas MacArthur	Nov. 1930–Oct. 1935
Malin Craig	Oct. 1935–Aug. 1939
George C. Marshall	Sept. 1939–Nov. 1945
Dwight D. Eisenhower	Nov. 1945–Feb. 1948
Omar N. Bradley	Feb. 1948–Aug. 1949
J. Lawton Collins	Aug. 1949–Aug. 1953
Matthew B. Ridgway	Aug. 1953–June 1955
Maxwell D. Taylor	June 1955–June 1959
Lyman L. Lemnitzer	June 1959–Sept. 1960
George H. Decker	Sept. 1960–Oct. 1962
Earle G. Wheeler	Oct. 1962–July 1964
Harold K. Johnson	July 1964–July 1968
William C. Westmoreland	July 1968–July 1972
Creighton W. Abrams	July 1972–Sept. 1974
Frederick C. Weyand	Oct. 1974–July 1976
Bernard W. Rogers	July 1976–

Chronology and commanders

Pequot War	1636–1637	J. Underhill, J. Mason
Mystic, Conn.	May 26, 1637	L. Gardiner, J. Mason, J. Underhill
Fort Good Hope, Conn.	June 1653	J. Underhill
King Philip's War	1675–76	• Philip
Swansea, Mass.	June 18, 1675	
Deerfield (Bloody Brook), Mass.	Sept. 18, 1675	
Great Swamp Fight, R.I.	Dec. 19, 1675	J. Winslow • Canonchet
capture of Philip	Aug. 12, 1676	B. Church
Bacon's Rebellion	1676	N. Bacon
Pueblo revolt	Aug. 1680	• Popé
King William's War	1689–1697	
Port Royal, Nova Scotia	May 11, 1690	W. Phips
Queen Anne's War	1702–1713	
Port Royal, N.S.	1704	B. Church
Port Royal, N.S.	1710	F. NICHOLSON, S. VETCH
Lovewell's Fight	May 9, 1725	J. Lovewell
War of Jenkins' Ear	1739–1743	

King George's War	1744–1748	
siege of Louisbourg, N.S.	April 30–June 15, 1745	W. Pepperrell, J. Bradstreet, R. Gridley
Fort Massachusetts, Mass.	Aug. 30, 1746	E. Williams
French and Indian War	1755–1763	
Fort LeBoeuf, Pa.	Dec. 1753	G. Washington, C. Gist
Fort Necessity, Great Meadows, Pa.	May–July 1754	G. Washington
Braddock's defeat	July 9, 1755	E. BRADDOCK, G. Washington
Lake George (Crown Point), N.Y.	Sept. 8, 1755	W. Johnson, S. Pomeroy, E. Williams
Kittanning, Pa.	Sept. 8, 1756	J. Armstrong
Fort William Henry, N.Y.	Aug. 9, 1757	G. MONRO
Battle on Snowshoes	March 13, 1758	R. Rogers
Forbes expedition	May–Nov. 1758	J. FORBES, H. Bouquet, J. Armstrong, E. Shelby
Grant's Hill, Pa.	Sept. 14, 1758	J. GRANT
Loyalhanna, Pa.	Oct. 12, 1758	J. BURD
Fort Duquesne, Pa., occupied	Nov. 25, 1758	J. FORBES, H. Bouquet, G. Washington
Ticonderoga, N.Y.	July 8, 1758	J. ABERCROMBIE
Louisbourg, N.S.	July 26, 1758	J. AMHERST
Fort Frontenac, Ont.	Aug. 27, 1758	J. Bradstreet
Fort Niagara, N.Y.	July 25, 1759	W. Johnson
Plains of Abraham, Que.	Sept. 13, 1759	J. WOLFE, R. Gridley
St. Francis, Que.	Oct. 5, 1759	R. Rogers
Montreal, Que.	Sept. 8, 1760	J. AMHERST
Havana, Cuba	June–Aug. 1762	G. KEPPEL
Pontiac's War	1763–1764	
siege of Detroit	May 1763–Aug. 1764	H. Gladwin • Pontiac
Bloody Run	July 31, 1763	J. DALZELL • Pontiac
Bouquet expedition	1763–1765	H. Bouquet
Bushy Run, Pa.	Aug. 5–6, 1763	H. Bouquet
Fort Pitt, Pa.	Aug. 10, 1763	H. Bouquet
Bradstreet expedition	1764	J. Bradstreet
Boston Massacre	March 5, 1770	C. Attucks
Alamance, N.C.	May 16, 1771	H. Waddell, R. Caswell
Cresap's War	1774	M. Cresap • J. Logan
Yellow Creek Massacre (O.)	April 30, 1774	D. GREATHOUSE
Lord Dunmore's War	1774	J. MURRAY, J. Gibson
Point Pleasant (W. Va.)	Oct. 10, 1774	A. Lewis • Cornstalk E. Shelby
REVOLUTION		
Fort William and Mary, N.H.	Dec. 14, 1774	P. Revere, J. Sullivan
Paul Revere's ride	April 18, 1775	P. Revere, W. Dawes, S. Prescott, J. Warren
Lexington, Mass.	April 19, 1775	J. Nixon, J. Parker
Concord, Mass.	April 19, 1775	J. Buttrick

Fort Ticonderoga, N.Y.	May 10, 1775	E. Allen, B. Arnold, S.H. Parsons
Crown Point, N.Y.	May 12, 1775	S. Warner
Bunker Hill, Boston	June 17, 1775	I. Putnam, W. Prescott, T. Knowlton, R. Gridley, S. Pomeroy, J. Stark, A. Ward, J. Warren
siege of Boston	June 1775–Mar. 17, 1776	G. Washington, H. Knox, A. Ward
siege of St. John's, Que.	Sept. 17–Nov. 2, 1775	R. Montgomery
Fort Chambly, Que.	Oct. 18, 1775	R. Montgomery
St. John's, Que.	Oct. 31, 1775	S. Warner
Lechmere Pt., Mass.	Nov. 9, 1775	W. Thompson
Montreal, Que.	Nov. 13, 1775	R. Montgomery, D. Wooster
Great Bridge, Va.	Dec. 9, 1775	W. Woodford
Quebec	Dec. 31, 1775	R. Montgomery, B. Arnold, D. Morgan
Charlestown, Mass., raid	Jan. 8, 1776	T. Knowlton
Moore's Creek Bridge, N.C.	Feb. 27, 1776	R. Caswell, J. Moore
Dorchester Heights, Mass.	March 4, 1776	J. Thomas, R. Gridley
Three Rivers, Que.	June 8, 1776	W. Thompson, A. Wayne
Chambly, Que.	June 16, 1776	J. Sullivan
Fort Moultrie, S.C.	June 28, 1776	W. Moultrie, W. Jasper
Long Island, N.Y.	Aug. 27–29, 1776	G. Washington, I. Putnam, J. Sullivan, W. Alexander, J. Glover
Harlem Heights, N.Y.	Sept. 16, 1776	T. Knowlton
Valcour Island, Lake Champlain, N.Y.	Oct. 11–13, 1776	B. Arnold, D. Waterbury
Throgs Neck (Pelham Manor), N.Y.	Oct. 18, 1776	W.S. Smith
White Plains, N.Y.	Oct. 28, 1776	G. Washington
Fort Washington, N.Y.	Nov. 16, 1776	N. Greene, M. Corbin
Fort Lee, N.J.	Nov. 18, 1776	N. Greene
Trenton, N.J.	Dec. 26, 1776	G. Washington, J. Sullivan, N. Greene, H. Knox, H. Mercer, J. Glover
Princeton, N.J.	Jan. 3, 1777	G. Washington, H. Mercer, I. Putnam
Somerset Court House, N.J.	Jan. 20, 1777	P. Dickinson
Danbury and Ridgefield, Conn.	Apr. 25–27, 1777	B. Arnold, G.S. Silliman, D. Wooster
Fort Ticonderoga, N.Y.	July 5–6, 1777	P.J. Schuyler, A. St. Clair
Hubbardton, Vt.	July 7, 1777	S. Warner
capture of Gen. Prescott	July 9, 1777	W. Barton
siege of Fort Stanwix, N.Y.	Aug. 3–20, 1777	P. Gansevoort, B. Arnold
Oriskany, N.Y.	Aug. 6, 1777	N. Herkimer • J. Brant P. Gansevoort J. Butler
Bennington, Vt.	Aug. 16, 1777	J. Stark, S. Warner
Staten Island, N.Y.	Aug. 21–22, 1777	J. Sullivan
Cooch's Bridge, N.J.	Sept. 3, 1777	W. Maxwell

Brandywine, Pa.	Sept. 11, 1777	G. Washington, Lafayette, J. Sullivan
Bemis Heights (Freeman's Farm, Stillwater), N.Y.	Sept. 19, 1777	H. Gates, D. Morgan, B. Arnold, B. Lincoln
Paoli, Pa.	Sept. 20, 1777	A. Wayne
Philadelphia occupied	Sept. 26, 1777	
Germantown, Pa.	Oct. 4, 1777	G. Washington, A. Wayne, J. Sullivan, F. Nash, A. Stephen
Fort Montgomery, N.Y.	Oct. 6, 1777	G. Clinton
Fort Clinton, N.Y.	Oct. 6, 1777	J. Clinton
second Bemis Heights, N.Y.	Oct. 7, 1777	H. Gates, B. Arnold, J. Hardin, J. Wilkinson, E. Poor
Burgoyne surrender, Saratoga, N.Y.	Oct. 17, 1777	H. Gates, T. Kosciuszko
Fort Mercer, N.J.	Oct.–Nov. 1777	C. GREENE, J.M. Varnum
Fort Mifflin, Pa.	Oct.–Nov. 1777	J.M. Varnum
"Battle of the Kegs"	Jan. 7, 1778	D. Bushnell
West Point, N.Y.	Jan. 20, 1778	S.H. Parsons
"Squaw campaign" (O.)	Feb. 1778	E. Hand
Barren Hill, Pa.	May 18, 1778	Lafayette
Philadelphia reoccupied	June 19, 1778	
Monmouth Court House, N.J.	June 27, 1778	G. Washington, C. Lee, A. Wayne, W. Alexander, Lafayette, M. McCauley
Wyoming massacre, Pa.	July 3, 1778	Z. Butler • J. Butler
Kaskaskia (Ill.)	July 4, 1778	G.R. Clark
Vincennes (Ind.)	July 5, 1778	G.R. Clark
Rhode Island (Quaker Hill)	Aug. 29, 1778	J. Sullivan, J. Hancock
Egg Harbor, N.J.	Oct. 15, 1778	K. Pulaski
Cherry Valley massacre, N.Y.	Nov. 11, 1778	I. Alden • W.N. Butler J. Brant
Vincennes (Ind.) recaptured	Dec. 17, 1778	
Savannah, Ga., occupied	Dec. 29, 1778	R. Howe
Augusta, Ga., occupied	Jan. 29, 1779	
Kettle Creek, Ga.	Feb. 14, 1779	A. Pickens
Vincennes (Ind.)	Feb. 25, 1779	G.R. Clark
Briar Creek, Ga.	March 4, 1779	J. Ashe
Charleston, S.C.	May 1779	B. Lincoln, K. Pulaski, W. Moultrie
Stono Ferry, S.C.	June 20, 1779	B. Lincoln, J. Sumner
Stony Point, N.Y.	July 16, 1779	A. Wayne
Penobscot expedition (Me.)	July–Aug. 1779	S. LOVELL, P. Revere, P. Wadsworth
Paulus Hook, N.J.	Aug. 19, 1779	H. Lee
Newtown (Elmira, N.Y.)	Aug. 29, 1779	J. Sullivan • J. Butler J. Clinton E. Poor
siege of Savannah, Ga.	Sept. 23–Oct. 19, 1779	B. Lincoln

Savannah, Ga., assault	Oct. 9, 1779	B. Lincoln, K. Pulaski, W. Jasper, I. Huger, L. McIntosh
siege of Charleston, S.C.	March 29–May 12, 1780	B. Lincoln
Monk's Corner, S.C.	April 14, 1780	I. Huger, W. Washington
Lanneau's Ferry, S.C.	May 6, 1780	W. Washington
Waxhaws, S.C.	May 29, 1780	A. Buford
Hanging Rock, S.C.	Aug. 6, 1780	T. Sumter
Camden, S.C.	Aug. 16, 1780	H. Gates, R. Caswell, J. Kalb, W. Smallwood
Fishing Creek, S.C.	Aug. 18, 1780	T. Sumter
Charlotte, N.C.	Sept. 26, 1780	W.R. Davie
King's Mountain, N.C.	Oct. 7, 1780	I. Shelby, W. Campbell, J. Sevier, J. McDowell, J. Winston
Fishdam Ford, S.C.	Nov. 9, 1780	T. Sumter
Enoree (Blackstock's Hill), S.C.	Nov. 20, 1780	T. Sumter
Virginia raid	Dec. 1780	• B. Arnold
Rudgely's Mills, S.C.	Dec. 4, 1780	W. Washington
Cowpens, S.C.	Jan. 17, 1781	D. Morgan, J.E. Howard, A. Pickens, W. Washington, J. McDowell
Haw River, N.C.	Feb. 25, 1781	H. Lee
Guilford Court House, N.C.	March 15, 1781	N. Greene, I. Huger
Georgetown, S.C.	April 1781	F. Marion
siege of Augusta, Ga.	April 16–June 5, 1781	H. Lee, A. Pickens
Hobkirk's Hill, S.C.	April 25, 1781	N. Greene, I. Huger
siege of Ninety-Six, S.C.	May–June, 1781	N. Greene, A. Pickens
Green Spring, Va.	July 6, 1781	Lafayette, A. Wayne
New London, Conn.	Sept. 6, 1781	• B. Arnold
Fort Griswold massacre, Conn.	Sept. 6, 1781	J. Ledyard, A.W. Bailey
Eutaw Springs, S.C.	Sept. 8, 1781	N. Greene, F. Marion, J. Sumner, O.H. Williams
siege of Yorktown, Va.	Oct. 6–19, 1781	G. Washington, B. Lincoln, L.L. Duportail, Lafayette, Rochambeau, T. Tilghman, H. Knox
siege of Charleston, S.C.	Dec. 1781–Dec. 1782	N. Greene, A. Wayne
Shays's Rebellion	1786–1787	D. Shays, B. Lincoln, W. Shepard
Harmar's defeat	Oct. 18, 22, 1790	J. Harmar • Little Turtle J. Armstrong J. Hardin
St. Clair's defeat	Nov. 4, 1791	A. St. Clair • Little Turtle
Fallen Timbers	Aug. 20, 1794	A. Wayne • Tecumseh
Whisky Rebellion	July–Nov. 1794	H. Lee, W. Irvine, D. Morgan
Provisional Army (quasi-war with France)	July 1798–Sept. 1800	G. Washington, E. Hand, J.E. Howard, J. Sevier
receipt of Louisiana Purchase	Dec. 20, 1803	J. Wilkinson
receipt of Upper Louisiana	March 10, 1804	A. Stoddard

Lewis and Clark expedition	May 1804–Sept. 1806	W. Clark, M. Lewis
Derna, Libya	April 27, 1805	W. Eaton
Pike expedition (Minnesota)	Aug. 1805–April 1806	Z.M. Pike
Pike expedition (Southwest)	July 1806–July 1807	Z.M. Pike
Tippecanoe River, Ind.	Nov. 7, 1811	W.H. Harrison • Tecumseh
WAR OF 1812		
Fort Michilimackinac (Mich.)	July 17, 1812	
Maguaga (Mich.)	Aug. 9, 1812	J. Miller • Tecumseh
Fort Dearborn (Ill.)	Aug. 15, 1812	
Fort Detroit	Aug. 16, 1812	W. Hull • Tecumseh
Fort Harrison, O.	Sept. 4, 1812	Z. Taylor
Ogdensburg, N.Y.	Oct. 3, 1812	J.J. Brown
Queenston, Que.	Oct. 13, 1812	S. Van Rensselaer, W. Scott, A. Smyth
Raisin River massacre, (Mich.)	Jan. 22, 1813	J. Winchester, W.O. Butler
Mobile, Ala.	April 1813	J. Wilkinson
York (Toronto), Ont.	April 27, 1813	H. Dearborn, Z.M. Pike
siege of Fort Meigs, O.	April 28–May 9, 1813	• Tecumseh
Sackett's Harbor, N.Y.	May 26–27, 1813	J.J. Brown
Fort George, Ont.	May 27, 1813	H. Dearborn, W. Scott
Stoney Creek, Ont.	June 6, 1813	W.H. Winder
Fort Stephenson, O.	Aug. 1–2, 1813	G. Croghan
Thames River, Ont.	Oct. 5, 1813	W.H. Harrison • Tecumseh R.M. Johnson J. Johnson S. Kenton O.H. Perry I. Shelby
Chateaugay, Que.	Oct. 26, 1813	W. Hampton
Chrysler's Field, Que.	Nov. 11, 1813	J. Wilkinson, E.P. Gaines
burning of Newark, Que.	Dec. 10, 1813	G. McClure
Lacolle Mill, Que.	March 30, 1814	J. Wilkinson
Fort Erie, Ont.	July 3, 1814	J.J. Brown
Chippewa Creek, Ont.	July 5, 1814	W. Scott
Lundy's Lane, Ont.	July 25, 1814	W. Scott, J.J. Brown, J. Miller, E.W. Ripley
siege of Fort Erie, Ont.	Aug. 1–Sept. 21, 1814	E.P. Gaines, E.W. Ripley
Bladensburg, Md.	Aug. 24, 1814	W.H. Winder
Credit Island, (Iowa)	Sept. 5–6, 1814	Z. Taylor
Plattsburg, N.Y.	Sept. 11, 1814	A. Macomb
Fort McHenry, Md.	Sept. 13–14, 1814	G. Armistead
Villere's Plantation, La.	Dec. 23, 1814	A. Jackson, W.O. Butler
New Orleans, La.	Jan. 8, 1815	A. Jackson, J. Laffite
Creek War	1813–1814	
Fort Mims massacre (Ala.)	Aug. 30, 1813	D. BEASLEY • Red Eagle
Talladega (Ala.)	Nov. 8, 1813	A. Jackson
Auttose (Ala.)	Nov. 29, 1813	J. Floyd, W. McIntosh
Econochaca (Ala.)	Dec. 23, 1813	F.L. CLAIBORNE • Red Eagle
Calabee Creek (Ala.)	Jan. 27, 1814	• Red Eagle

Horseshoe Bend (Tohopeka) (Ala.)	March 27, 1814	A. Jackson, W. McIntosh
Seminole War	1817–1818	A. Jackson
capture of Pensacola, Fla.	May 24, 1818	A. Jackson
Arikara expedition	1823	H. Leavenworth
Black Hawk's War	April–Sept. 1832	
Wisconsin Heights (Wis.)	July 21, 1832	H. Dodge • Black Hawk
Bad Axe River (Wis.)	Aug. 2, 1832	H. Atkinson • Black Hawk Z. Taylor
Second Seminole War	1835–1842	W. Scott • Osceola E.P. Gaines T.S. Jesup Z. Taylor W.K. ARMISTEAD W.J. Worth
Dade massacre	Dec. 28, 1835	F. Dade
Withlacoochee River, Fla.	Feb.–March 1836	E.P. Gaines
Lake Okeechobee, Fla.	Dec. 25, 1837	Z. Taylor
Palatka, Fla.	April 19, 1842	W.J. Worth
Texas Revolution	1835–1836	
Anahuac, Tex.	June 30, 1835	W.B. Travis
Gonzalez, Tex.	Oct. 2, 1835	
Mission Concepción, Tex.	Oct. 28, 1835	J. Bowie, J.W. Fannin
siege of San Antonio, Tex.	Oct.–Dec. 9, 1835	S.F. AUSTIN, B. MILAM
siege of the Alamo	Feb. 23–March 6, 1836	W.B. Travis, J. Bowie, D. Crockett
Goliad massacre	March 27, 1836	J.W. Fannin
San Jacinto, Tex.	April 21, 1836	S. Houston, M.B. Lamar
Plum Creek, Tex.	Aug. 1840	J.C. Hays
Mier expedition	Nov. 1842	A. SOMERVELL, G.B. Crittenden
Oregon Trail expedition	1842	J.C. Frémont, K. Carson
Frémont expedition	1843–1844	J.C. Frémont, K. Carson
MEXICAN WAR		
Matamoros, Mex.	April 25, 1846	S.B. THORNTON
Fort Texas (Brown), Tex.	May 3–9, 1846	J. BROWN, J.K.F. Mansfield
Palo Alto, Mex.	May 8, 1846	Z. Taylor, A. Elzey, C.F. Smith
Resaca de la Palma, Mex.	May 9, 1846	Z. Taylor, C.A. May
Los Angeles, Cal.	Aug. 13, 1846	J.C. Frémont, R.F. Stockton
Santa Fe, N.M., occupied	Aug. 18, 1846	S.W. Kearny, P.St.G. Cooke, A. Doniphan
Monterrey, Mex.	Sept. 20–24, 1846	Z. Taylor, C.F. Smith, W.J. Worth
San Pasqual, Cal.	Dec. 6, 1846	S.W. Kearny, K. Carson
San Diego, Cal.	Dec. 10, 1846	S.W. Kearny
Brazito, N.M.	Dec. 25, 1846	A. Doniphan
El Paso, Tex.	Dec. 27, 1846	A. Doniphan
San Gabriel, Cal.	Jan. 8–9, 1847	S.W. Kearny, J.C. Frémont, R.F. Stockton
Los Angeles, Cal.	Jan. 10, 1847	S.W. Kearny, J.C. Frémont, R.F. Stockton, K. Carson
Buena Vista, Mex.	Feb. 22–23, 1847	Z. Taylor, J.E. Wool, J.M. Washington

Sacramento River, Mex.	Feb. 28, 1847	A. Doniphan
Chihuahua, Mex.	March 1, 1847	A. Doniphan
Veracruz, Mex.	March 9–27, 1847	W. Scott, J.G. Totten
Cerro Gordo, Mex.	April 18, 1847	D.E. Twiggs, W.S. Harney, R.E. Lee, J. Shields
Puebla, Mex.	May 15, 1847	W.J. Worth
Contreras, Mex.	Aug. 19–20, 1847	W. Scott, B. Riley, G.J. Pillow, P.F. Smith
Churubusco, Mex.	Aug. 20, 1847	W. Scott, J. Shields
Molino del Rey, Mex.	Sept. 8, 1847	W.J. Worth
Chapultepec, Mex.	Sept. 13, 1847	G.J. Pillow, J.A. Quitman, S. Casey, J.W. Geary, G.E. Pickett
Mexico City, Mex.	Sept. 13–14, 1847	W. Scott
Belen Gate	Sept. 13, 1847	J.A. Quitman
San Cosme Gate	Sept. 13, 1847	W.J. Worth
Santa Cruz de Rosales, Mex.	March 16, 1848	S. Price
Salt Lake expedition	1849–1850	H. Stansbury, J.W. Gunnison
Gunnison massacre	Oct. 26, 1853	J.W. Gunnison
Sioux expedition	1855–1856	W.S. Harney
Ash Hollow	Sept. 3, 1855	W.S. Harney • LITTLE THUNDER
"Wakarusa War"	Dec. 1855	J.H. Lane
Mormon expedition	1857–1858	A.S. Johnston, J. Buford, P.St.G. Cooke, R.B. Marcy
Four Lakes, Wash.	Sept. 1, 1858	J. Mullan
Harpers Ferry, Va.	Oct. 18, 1859	R.E. Lee, J.E.B. Stuart
CIVIL WAR		
Fort Pickens, Fla.	January 10, 1861	A.J. Slemmer • W.H. Chase
San Antonio, Tex.	Feb. 16, 1861	D.E. Twiggs • B. McCulloch G. Stoneman
Fort Sumter, S.C.	April 12–14, 1861	R. Anderson • P. Beauregard A. Doubleday E. Ruffin G.V. Fox S.D. Lee
Camp Jackson, Mo.	May 10, 1861	N. Lyon • D.M. FROST F. Sigel
Alexandria, Va., occupied	May 24, 1861	S.P. Heintzelman, E.E. Ellsworth
Philippi, Va.	June 3, 1861	B.F. Kelley • G.A. PORTERFIELD
Big Bethel, Va.	June 10, 1861	B.F. Butler • J.B. Magruder
Jefferson City, Mo.	June 15, 1861	N. Lyon
Boonville, Mo.	June 17, 1861	N. Lyon • C.F. JACKSON
Carthage, Mo.	July 5, 1861	F. Sigel • C.F. JACKSON
Rich Mountain (W. Va.)	July 11, 1861	W.S. Rosecrans • J. Pegram G.B. McClellan
Blackburn's Ford, Va.	July 18, 1861	D. TYLER • J. Longstreet
Bull Run (Manassas), Va.	July 21, 1861	I. McDowell • P. Beauregard D. Hunter J.E. Johnston J.E.B. Stuart J. Longstreet T.J. Jackson B.E. Bee A. Elzey J.D. Imboden E. Kirby-Smith

Dug Springs, Mo.	Aug. 2, 1861	N. Lyon • J.S. RAINS
Wilson's Creek, Mo.	Aug. 10, 1861	N. Lyon • B. McCulloch F. Sigel S. Price S.D. Sturgis
Hatteras Inlet, N.C. (Fort Hatteras, Fort Clark)	Aug. 28–29, 1861	B.F. Butler • W.S.G. ANDREWS W.F. MARTIN
Carnifex Ferry, W. Va.	Sept. 10, 1861	W.S. Rosecrans • J.B. Floyd
Lexington, Mo.	Sept. 12–20, 1861	J.A. MULLIGAN • S. Price
Santa Rosa Island, Fla.	Oct. 8, 1861	W. WILSON • R.H. Anderson
Ball's Bluff, Va.	Oct. 21, 1861	C.P. Stone • N.G. EVANS E.D. Baker
Romney, Va.	Oct. 26, 1861	B.F. Kelley • A. MC DONALD
Belmont, Mo.	Nov. 7, 1861	U.S. Grant • L. Polk G.J. Pillow
Port Royal, S.C.	Nov. 7, 1861	T.W. Sherman • T.F. DRAYTON
Blackwater, Mo.	Dec. 18, 1861	J. Pope • S. Price J.C. Davis
Dranesville, Va.	Dec. 20, 1861	E.O.C. Ord • J.E.B. Stuart
Mount Zion, Mo.	Dec. 28, 1861	B.M. Prentiss
Mill Springs, Ky.	Jan. 19, 1862	G.H. Thomas • G.B. Crittenden S.P. Carter F.K. Zollicoffer
Fort Henry, Tenn.	Feb. 6, 1862	U.S. Grant • L. TILGHMAN
Roanoke Island, N.C.	Feb. 7, 1862	A.E. Burnside • H.A. WISE
Fort Donelson, Tenn.	Feb. 16, 1862	U.S. Grant • J.B. Floyd C.F. Smith G.J. Pillow M.L. Smith S.B. Buckner N.B. Forrest
Valverde, N.M.	Feb. 21, 1862	E.R.S. Canby • H.H. Sibley K. Carson
New Madrid, Mo.	March 3–14, 1862	J. Pope, J.A. Mower
Fort Clinch (Fernandina), Fla.	March 7, 1862	T.W. Sherman
Pea Ridge (Elkhorn), Ark.	March 7–8, 1862	S.R. Curtis • E. Van Dorn E.A. Carr S. Price F. Sigel B. McCulloch S. Watie
Leesburg, Va.	March 8, 1862	J.W. Geary
St. Augustine, Fla.	March 11, 1862	H.G. Wright
New Bern, N.C.	March 14, 1862	A.E. Burnside • L.O. BRANCH
Kernstown, Va.	March 23, 1862	J. Shields • T.J. Jackson N. KIMBALL
Apache Canyon, N.M.	March 27, 1862	E.R.S. Canby • H.H. Sibley J.M. Chivington
Glorietta Pass, N.M.	March 28, 1862	E.R.S. Canby • H.H. Sibley
Peninsula campaign, Va.	March–July 1862	G.B. McClellan • J.B. Magruder J.E. Johnston R.E. Lee
siege of Yorktown, Va.	April 4–May 4, 1862	S. Heintzelman • J.E. Johnston J.B. Magruder
Shiloh (Pittsburg Landing), Tenn.	April 6–7, 1862	U.S. Grant • A.S. Johnston D.C. Buell B. Bragg B.M. Prentiss L. Polk L. Wallace J. Wheeler W. Nelson P. Beauregard W.J. Hardee

Island No. 10, Tenn.	April 7, 1862	J. Pope • W.W. MACKALL
Huntsville, Ala.	April 11, 1862	O.M. Mitchel
Fort Pulaski, Ga.	April 11, 1862	Q.A. Gillmore • C.H. OLMSTEAD D. Hunter
General raid	April 12, 1862	J.J. Andrews
Peralta, N.M.	April 15, 1862	E.R.S. Canby • H.H. Sibley
Beaufort, N.C.	April 25, 1862	A.E. Burnside
New Orleans, La., occupied	May 1, 1862	B.F. Butler • M. Lovell
Williamsburg, Va.	May 5, 1862	S. Heintzelman • J. Longstreet J. Hooker G.J. Rains J.E.B. Stuart
McDowell, Va.	May 8, 1862	R.H. MILROY • T.J. Jackson
capture of Norfolk, Va.	May 10, 1862	G.B. McClellan
Front Royal, Va.	May 23, 1862	N.P. Banks • T.J. Jackson
Winchester, Va.	May 24–25, 1862	N.P. Banks • T.J. Jackson J. Shields R.S. Ewell
Hanover Court House, Va.	May 27, 1862	J.W. Barlow • L.O. BRANCH
Fair Oaks (Seven Pines), Va.	May 31, 1862	G.B. McClellan • J.E. Johnston S. Heintzelman D.H. Hill G.W. Smith
surrender of Memphis, Tenn.	June 6, 1862	C.R. Ellet • J.E. MONTGOMERY
Cross Keys, Va.	June 8, 1862	J.C. Frémont • R.S. Ewell
Port Republic, Va.	June 9, 1862	J. Shields • T.J. Jackson
Stuart's ride	June 12–15, 1862	• J.E.B. Stuart
Seven Days' Battles	June 26–July 2, 1862	G.B. McClellan • R.E. Lee
Mechanicsville, Va.	June 26, 1862	F.-J. Porter • A.P. Hill J. Longstreet
Gaines' Mill, Va.	June 27, 1862	F.-J. Porter • R.E. Lee A.P. Hill
Savage Station, Va.	June 29, 1862	E.V. Sumner • J.B. Magruder
Frayser's Farm (Glendale), Va.	June 30, 1862	G.B. McClellan • J. Longstreet A.P. Hill C.M. Wilcox
White Oak Swamp, Va.	June 30, 1862	W.B. Franklin • T.J. Jackson
Malvern Hill, Va.	July 1, 1862	G.B. McClellan • R.E. Lee F.-J. Porter
Booneville, Miss.	July 1, 1862	P.H. Sheridan • W.J. Hardee
Cache (Cotton Plant), Ark.	July 7, 1862	S.R. Curtis • A. RUST F. Steele
Cedar Mountain, Va.	Aug. 9, 1862	N.P. Banks • T.J. Jackson R.S. Ewell A.P. Hill J.H. Winder
Catlett's Station, Va.	Aug. 22, 1862	J. Pope • J.E.B. Stuart
Manassas Station, Va., raid	Aug. 27, 1862	J. Pope • J.E.B. Stuart
Groveton, Va.	Aug. 28–29, 1862	J. Pope • T.J. Jackson
second Bull Run (Manassas), Va.	Aug. 29–30, 1862	J. Pope • T.J. Jackson F.-J. Porter J. Longstreet I. McDowell F. Sigel
Richmond, Ky.	Aug. 30, 1862	M.D. MANSON • E. Kirby-Smith
Chantilly, Va.	Sept. 1, 1862	J. Pope • T.J. Jackson

South Mountain, Md.	Sept. 14, 1862	G.B. McClellan • D.H. Hill A.E. Burnside T.R.R. COBB W.B. Franklin J.L. Reno
siege of Mumfordville, Ky.	Sept. 14–17, 1862	J.T. WILDER • B. Bragg
Harpers Ferry, W. Va.	Sept. 15, 1862	D.H. MILES • T.J. Jackson
Antietam (Sharpsburg), Md.	Sept. 17, 1862	G.B. McClellan • R.E. Lee A.P. Hill J. Longstreet J.E.B. Stuart
Iuka, Miss.	Sept. 19, 1862	W.S. Rosecrans • S. Price E.O.C. Ord
Corinth, Miss.	Oct. 3, 1862	W.S. Rosecrans • E. Van Dorn J.B. McPherson S. Price J.A. Mower
Hatchie River, Miss.	Oct. 5, 1862	S.A. Hurlbut • E. Van Dorn E.O.C. Ord J. Wheeler M. Lovell
Perryville, Ky.	Oct. 8, 1862	D.C. Buell • B. Bragg G.H. Thomas L. Polk J. Wheeler
Chambersburg, Pa., raid	Oct. 9–13, 1862	• J.E.B. Stuart
Hartsville, Tenn.	Dec. 7, 1862	A.B. MOORE • J.H. Morgan
Prairie Grove (Fayetteville), Ark.	Dec. 7, 1862	J.G. BLUNT • T.C. HINDMAN F.J. Herron
Fredericksburg, Va.	Dec. 13, 1862	A.E. Burnside • R.E. Lee E.V. Sumner J. Longstreet J. Hooker G.E. Pickett W.B. Franklin J.E.B. Stuart W.F. Smith
Holly Springs, Miss.	Dec. 20, 1862	R.C. MURPHY • E. Van Dorn
Chickasaw Bluffs, Miss.	Dec. 29, 1862	W.T. Sherman • J.C. Pemberton S.D. Lee
Murfreesboro (Stones River) Tenn.	Dec. 31–Jan. 3, 1863	W.S. Rosecrans • B. Bragg T.L. Crittenden J. Wheeler A.M. McCook P.H. Sheridan
capture of Galveston, Tex.	Jan. 1, 1863	W.B. RENSHAW • J.B. Magruder
White House, Va.	Jan. 7, 1863	E.D. Keyes
Arkansas Post (Fort Hindman), Ark.	Jan. 11, 1863	J.A. McClernand • T.J. CHURCHILL
Queen of the West **runs Vicksburg, Miss.**	Feb. 2, 1863	C.R. Ellet
Red River raid, Ark.	Feb. 3–16, 1863	C.R. Ellet
Fairfax Court House, Va.	March 9, 1863	E.H. STOUGHTON • J.S. Mosby
Steele's Bayou expedition, Miss.	March 14–27, 1863	W.T. Sherman
Kelly's Ford, Va.	March 17, 1863	W.W. Averell • F. Lee J. Pelham
Somerset, Ky.	March 30, 1863	Q.A. Gillmore • J. Pegram
Grierson's raid	April 1863	B.H. Grierson
Franklin, Tenn.	April 10, 1863	G. Granger • E. Van Dorn
Imboden's raid	April 20–May 14, 1863	• J.D. Imboden W.E. JONES
Hawes's Bluff, Miss.	April 29–30, 1863	W.T. Sherman

Stoneman's raid	April–May 1863	G. Stoneman • J.J. Pettigrew J. Buford
Port Gibson, Miss.	May 1, 1863	J.A. McClernand • J.S. BOWEN
Stoneman's Virginia raid	May 1–7, 1863	G. Stoneman • J.E.B. Stuart
Chancellorsville, Va.	May 2–4, 1863	J. Hooker • R.E. Lee O.O. Howard T.J. Jackson J. Buford R.E. Rodes A. Pleasonton F. Lee J.W. Revere J.E.B. Stuart J. Sedgwick
Marye's Heights, Fredericksburg, Va.	May 3, 1863	J. Sedgwick • J.A. Early
West Point, Va., raid	May 7, 1863	E.D. Keyes
Raymond, Miss.	May 12, 1863	J.B. McPherson • J. GREGG
Jackson, Miss.	May 14, 1863	W.T. Sherman • J.E. Johnston J.B. McPherson
Champion's Hill, Miss.	May 16, 1863	U.S. Grant • J.C. Pemberton S.D. Lee
Black River Bridge, Miss.	May 17, 1863	U.S. Grant • J.C. Pemberton
siege of Vicksburg, Miss.	May 18–July 4, 1863	U.S. Grant • J.C. Pemberton E.A. Carr J.A. Mower
siege of Port Hudson, La.	May 22–July 9, 1863	N.P. Banks • F.K. GARDNER H.C. Merriam
Tullahoma campaign, Tenn.	June–Aug. 1863	W.S. Rosecrans • B. Bragg
Brandy Station (Beverly Ford), Va.	June 9, 1863	A. Pleasonton • J.E.B. Stuart
Winchester, Va.	June 13–15, 1863	R.H. MILROY • R.S. Ewell J.A. Early
Gettysburg, Pa.	July 1–3, 1863	G.G. Meade • R.E. Lee J.F. Reynolds R.S. Ewell J. Buford A.P. Hill J.L. Chamberlain J. Longstreet A. Doubleday R.H. Anderson G.S. Greene C.M. Wilcox W.S. Hancock J.E.B. Stuart D.E. Sickles J.D. Imboden H.W. Slocum G.K. Warren
Pickett's Charge	July 3, 1863	W.S. Hancock • G.E. Pickett J. Gibbon W.D. Pender A.S. Webb J.J. Pettigrew L.A. Armistead E.P. Alexander
Helena, Ark.	July 4, 1863	B.M. Prentiss • T.H. Holmes S. Price
Morgan's raid	July 9–19, 1863	• J.H. Morgan
Fort Wagner, Morris I., S.C.	July 10–Sept. 7, 1863	Q.A. Gillmore • W. Taliaferro
Yazoo City, Miss.	July 13, 1863	F.J. Herron
Falling Waters, W. Va.	July 14, 1863	H.J. Kilpatrick • J.J. Pettigrew
Fort Wagner, S.C.	July 18, 1863	R.G. Shaw • L.M. KEITT T. SEYMOUR
Lawrence, Kan., massacre	Aug. 21, 1863	• W.C. Quantrill
"Swamp Angel" at Charleston, S.C.	Aug. 21–24, 1863	E.W. Serrell
capture of Fort Wagner, S.C.	Sept. 7, 1863	Q.A. Gillmore • W. Taliaferro T. SEYMOUR

Sabine Pass, Tex.	Sept. 8, 1863	W.B. Franklin • R. DOWLING
Little Rock, Ark.	Sept. 10, 1863	F. Steele • S. Price
Chickamauga, Ga.	Sept. 18–20, 1863	W.S. Rosecrans • B. Bragg G.H. Thomas J. Longstreet G. Granger S.B. Buckner A.M. McCook N.B. Forrest P.H. Sheridan
siege of Chattanooga, Tenn.	Sept. 24–Nov. 25, 1863	W.S. Rosecrans • B. Bragg U.S. Grant
Shelby's raid	Sept.–Oct. 1863	• J.O. Shelby
Baxter Springs, Kan., raid	Oct. 6, 1863	J.G. BLUNT • W.C. Quantrill
Farmington, Tenn.	Oct. 7, 1863	G. Crook • J. Wheeler
Bristoe Station, Va.	Oct. 14, 1863	G.K. Warren • A.P. Hill
"Buckland Races," Va.	Oct. 19, 1863	H.J. Kilpatrick • J.E.B. Stuart
Pine Bluff, Ark.	Oct. 25, 1863	P. CLAYTON • S. Price
Brown's Ferry, Tenn.	Oct. 27, 1863	W.B. Hazen, W.F. Smith
Droop Mountain, W. Va.	Nov. 6, 1863	W.W. Averell • J. ECHOLS
siege of Knoxville, Tenn.	Nov. 7–29, 1863	A.E. Burnside • J. Longstreet O.M. Poe W.T. Sherman

Lookout Mountain (Battle
  Above the Clouds),
  Tenn.
	Nov. 24, 1863	U.S. Grant • B. Bragg
		J. Hooker

Missionary Ridge, Tenn.	Nov. 25, 1863	U.S. Grant • B. Bragg G.H. Thomas J.C. Breckinridge P.H. Sheridan W.J. Hardee W.F. Smith E.C. Walthall
Ringgold Gap, Ga.	Nov. 27, 1863	J. Hooker • P.R. Cleburne J. Wheeler
Mine Run, Va.	Nov. 28–29, 1863	G.K. Warren • R.E. Lee J. Sedgwick
Libby Prison raid, Va.	Feb. 28–March 1, 1864	H.J. Kilpatrick • J.H. Winder
Red River campaign, La.	March–May 1864	N.P. Banks • E. Kirby-Smith A.J. Smith R. Taylor T.E.G. Ransom J. Bailey
Sabine Crossroads, La.	April 8, 1864	N.P. Banks • R. Taylor T.E.G. Ransom W.B. Franklin
Pleasant Hill, La.	April 9, 1864	N.P. Banks • R. Taylor
Fort Pillow, Tenn.	April 12, 1864	L.F. BOOTH • N.B. Forrest
Poison Springs, Ark.	April 18, 1864	F. Steele • S.B. Maxey
Jenkins Ferry, Ark.	April 30, 1864	F. Steele • E. Kirby-Smith S. Price
Atlanta campaign	May 4–Sept. 2, 1864	W.T. Sherman, J.B. McPherson G.H. Thomas, J.M. Schofield
Richmond campaign	May 4–April 2, 1865	U.S. Grant, G.G. Meade
Wilderness, Va.	May 5–7, 1864	U.S. Grant • R.E. Lee G.G. Meade R.S. Ewell A.P. Hill J. Longstreet
Todd's Tavern, Va.	May 7, 1864	P.H. Sheridan • J.E.B. Stuart

Spotsylvania, Va.	May 8–12, 1864	U.S. Grant • R.E. Lee	
		G.G. Meade	R.H. Anderson
		F.C. Barlow	R.S. Ewell
		G.K. Warren	S.D. Ramseur
		H.G. Wright	
Dalton, Ga.	May 8–12, 1864	W.T. Sherman • J.E. Johnston	
Yellow Tavern, Va.	May 11, 1864	P.H. Sheridan • J.E.B. Stuart	
		J.H. Wilson	
Drewry's Bluff, Va.	May 12–16, 1864	B.F. Butler • P. Beauregard	
		W.F. Smith	
Resaca, Ga.	May 13–16, 1864	W.T. Sherman • J.E. Johnston	
New Market, Va.	May 15, 1864	F. Sigel • J.D. Imboden	
		H.A. Du Pont	J.C. Breckinridge
			S. Shipp
North Anna River, Va.	May 22–27, 1864	U.S. Grant • R.E. Lee	
New Hope Church, Ga.	May 24–28, 1864	W.T. Sherman • J.E. Johnston	
Dallas, Ga.	May 25–28, 1864	W.T. Sherman • J.E. Johnston	
Hawes's Shop, Va.	May 28, 1864	P.H. Sheridan • J.E.B. Stuart	
		A.T.A. Torbert	
Matadequin Creek, Va.	May 30, 1864	A.T.A. Torbert	
Cold Harbor, Va.	June 1–3, 1864	U.S. Grant • R.E. Lee	
		G.G. Meade	
		A.T.A. Torbert	
Piedmont, Va.	June 5, 1864	D. Hunter • W.E. JONES	
Brices Cross Roads, Miss.	June 10, 1864	S.D. Sturgis • N.B. Forrest	
Trevilian Station, Va.	June 11–12, 1864	P.H. Sheridan • W. Hampton	
		A.T.A. Torbert	F. Lee
		G.A. Custer	
Lynchburg, Va.	June 16–18, 1864	D. Hunter • J.A. Early	
siege of Petersburg, Va.	June 18–April 2, 1865	U.S. Grant • R.E. Lee	
		G.L. Hartsuff	
Kenesaw Mountain, Ga.	June 27, 1864	W.T. Sherman • J.E. Johnston	
Monocacy R., Md.	July 9, 1864	L. Wallace • J.A. Early	
Early's raid	July 11, 1864	F. Wheaton • J.A. Early	
Tupelo, Miss.	July 14, 1864	A.J. Smith • N.B. Forrest	
		B.H. Grierson	
Peachtree Creek, Ga.	July 20–21, 1864	W.T. Sherman • J.B. Hood	
		G.H. Thomas	
	July 22, 1864	J. McPherson • W.J. Hardee	
			W.H.T. Walker
Stoneman's Macon, Ga., raid	July 27–31, 1864	G. Stoneman	
Lovejoy's Station, Ga.	July 27–31, 1864	E.M. McCook	
Darbytown, Va.	July 28, 1864	A.T.A. Torbert	
Ezra Church, Ga.	July 28, 1864	W.T. Sherman • J.B. Hood	
			S.D. Lee
Chambersburg, Pa., burned	July 30, 1864	• J. McCausland	
		J.A. Early	
Battle of the Crater	July 30, 1864	A.E. Burnside • S. ELLIOTT	
Cumberland, Md.	Aug. 1, 1864	B.F. Kelley • J. McCausland	
Fort Morgan (Mobile), Ala.	Aug. 5–23, 1864	G. Granger • R.L. Page	
			D.H. MAURY
Moorfield, Va.	Aug. 7, 1864	W.W. Averell • J. McCausland	
Mobile (Forts Gaines & Morgan), Ala.	Aug. 8, 1864	G. Granger • R.L. Page	

City Point, Va.	Aug. 9, 1864	• G.J. Rains
raid around Atlanta, Ga.	Aug. 18–22, 1864	H.J. Kilpatrick
Atlanta, Ga., occupied	Sept. 2, 1864	W.T. Sherman • J.B. Hood H.W. Slocum
Winchester (Opequon), Va.	Sept. 19, 1864	P.H. Sheridan • J.A. Early A.T.A. Torbert R.E. Rodes F. Lee
Fisher's Hill, Va.	Sept. 22, 1864	P.H. Sheridan • J.A. Early
Pilot Knob, Mo.	Sept. 27, 1864	T. EWING • S. Price
Allatoona Pass, Ga.	Oct. 5, 1864	J.M. Corse • J.B. Hood S.G. FRENCH
Jefferson City, Mo.	Oct. 8, 1864	A. Pleasonton • S. Price
Tom's Brook, Va.	Oct. 9, 1864	A.T.A. Torbert • T.L. ROSSER L.L. LOMAX
Glasgow, Mo.	Oct. 15, 1864	• J.O. Shelby
Cedar Creek, Va.	Oct. 19, 1864	H.G. Wright • J.A. Early P.H. Sheridan S.D. Ramseur A.T.A. Torbert L.A. Grant
Westport, Mo.	Oct. 21–23, 1864	S.R. Curtis • S. Price A. Pleasonton J.O. Shelby
Marais des Cygnes, Kan.	Oct. 25, 1864	A. Pleasonton • S. Price
March to the Sea	Nov. 16–Dec. 12, 1864	W.T. Sherman
Adobe Walls, Tex.	Nov. 25, 1864	K. Carson
Spring Hill, Tenn.	Nov. 29, 1864	J.H. Wilson • J.B. Hood N.B. Forrest B.F. Cheatham
Franklin, Tenn.	Nov. 30, 1864	J.M. Schofield • J.B. Hood J.H. Wilson N.B. Forrest P.R. Cleburne W.W. Loring
Stoneman's Tennessee raid	Dec. 11–22, 1864	G. Stoneman
Fort McAllister, Ga.	Dec. 13, 1864	W.B. Hazen • G.W. ANDERSON
Nashville, Tenn.	Dec. 15–16, 1864	G.H. Thomas • J.B. Hood J.M. Schofield J. Breckinridge J.H. Wilson N.B. Forrest S.D. Lee W.W. Loring A.P. Stewart
Savannah, Ga., occupied	Dec. 21, 1864	W.T. Sherman • W.J. Hardee W. Taliaferro
Fort Fisher, N.C.	Dec. 24–25, 1864	B.F. Butler • W.H.C. Whiting G. Weitzel W. LAMB
Carolinas campaign	Jan.–March 1865	W.T. Sherman, O.O. Howard, J.M. Schofield, H.W. Slocum
Fort Fisher, N.C.	Jan. 13–15, 1865	A.H. Terry • W.H.C. Whiting W. LAMB
burning of Columbia, S.C.	Feb. 17, 1865	W.T. Sherman
Waynesboro, Va.	March 2, 1865	P.H. Sheridan • J.A. Early
Fayetteville, N.C.	March 11, 1865	H.J. Kilpatrick, W.T. Sherman
Bentonville, N.C.	March 19–21, 1865	W.T. Sherman • J.E. Johnston W.B. Taliaferro
Stoneman's Lynchburg, Va., raid	March 22–April 15, 1865	G. Stoneman
Fort Stedman, Va.	March 25, 1865	J.G. PARKE • J.B. Gordon
Quaker Road, Va.	March 29, 1865	J.L. Chamberlain • R.E. Lee

Dinwiddie Court House, Va.	March 31, 1865	P.H. Sheridan • G.E. Pickett
Five Forks, Va.	April 1, 1865	P.H. Sheridan • G.E. Pickett G.K. Warren
Ebenezer Church, Ala.	April 1, 1865	J.H. Wilson • N.B. Forrest
Selma, Ala.	April 2, 1865	J.H. Wilson • N.B. Forrest E. Upton
assault on Petersburg, Va.	April 2, 1865	U.S. Grant • R.E. Lee E.O.C. Ord H.G. Wright L.A. Grant
occupation of Richmond, Va.	April 3, 1865	G. Weitzel
Sayler's Creek, Va.	April 6, 1865	H.G. Wright • R.S. Ewell P.H. Sheridan R.H. Anderson J.B. Gordon
High Bridge, Farmville, Va.	April 7, 1865	F.C. Barlow • W. MAHONE
Appomattox, Va.	April 9, 1865	U.S. Grant • R.E. Lee J.L. Chamberlain E.S. Parker
Fort Blakely, Ala.	April 9, 1865	F. Steele • ST.J. LIDDELL H.C. Merriam
Mobile, Ala.	April 12, 1865	E.R.S. Canby • D.H. MAURY G. Granger
Salisbury, N.C.	April 12, 1865	G. Stoneman • G. Andrews
Montgomery, Ala.	April 12, 1865	J.H. Wilson • W. ADAMS
Columbus, Ga.	April 16, 1865	J.H. Wilson • H. COBB
capture of Jefferson Davis	May 10, 1865	J.H. Wilson

UNION COMMANDERS

Commander in chief	Winfield Scott	April 1861–Nov. 1861
	George B. McClellan	Nov. 1861–March 1862
	Henry W. Halleck	July 1862–March 1864
	Ulysses S. Grant	March 1864–April 1865
Army of the Potomac	George B. McClellan	Aug. 1861–Nov. 1862
	Ambrose E. Burnside	Nov. 1862–Jan. 1863
	Joseph Hooker	Jan. 1863–June 1863
	George G. Meade	June 1863–April 1865
Army of the Ohio *redesignated*	Don Carlos Buell	Nov. 1861–Oct. 1862
Army of the Cumberland	William S. Rosecrans	Oct. 1862–Oct. 1863
	George H. Thomas	Oct. 1863–April 1865
Army of the Southwest	Samuel R. Curtis	Dec. 1861–Aug. 1862
Army of the Mississippi	John Pope	March 1862–June 1862
	William S. Rosecrans	June 1862–Oct. 1862
became XIII Corps in *Oct. 1862*		
Army of the Rappahannock *merged into*	Irvin McDowell	April 1862–July 1862
Army of Virginia	John Pope	July 1862–Sept. 1862

Army of the Ohio	**Horatio G. Wright**	Aug. 1862–March 1863
	Ambrose E. Burnside	March 1863–Nov. 1863
	John G. Foster	Nov. 1863–Feb. 1864
	John M. Schofield	Feb. 1864–April 1865
Army of the Mississippi	**John A. McClernand**	Jan. 1863
Army of the Tennessee	**Ulysses S. Grant**	March 1862–Oct. 1863
	William T. Sherman	Oct. 1863–March 1864
	James B. McPherson	March 1864–July 1864
	John A. Logan	July 1864
	Oliver O. Howard	July 1864–April 1865
Army of the Mountain Dept.	**John C. Frémont**	March 1862–June 1862
Army of the Frontier	**John M. Schofield**	Oct. 1862–March 1863
	Francis J. Herron	March 1863–May 1863
Army of West Virginia	**Benjamin F. Kelley**	June 1863–March 1864
	Franz Sigel	March 1864–May 1864
	David Hunter	May 1864–Aug. 1864
	George Crook	Aug. 1864
merged into		
Army of the Shenandoah	**Philip H. Sheridan**	Aug. 1864–Feb. 1865
	Alfred T.A. Torbert	April 1865–July 1865
Military Division of the Mississippi	**Ulysses S. Grant**	Oct. 1863–March 1864
	William T. Sherman	March 1864–April 1865
Army of the James	**Benjamin F. Butler**	April 1864–Dec. 1864
	Edward O.C. Ord	Jan. 1865–April 1865
Army of Georgia	**Henry W. Slocum**	Nov. 1864–April 1865

CONFEDERATE COMMANDERS

Senior officer	**Samuel Cooper**	Aug. 1861–April 1865
Commander in chief	**Robert E. Lee**	Feb. 1865–April 1865
Army of the Shenandoah	**Joseph E. Johnston**	May 1861–Aug. 1861
Army of the Potomac	**P.G.T. Beauregard**	May 1861–Aug. 1861
Army of Kentucky	**Albert S. Johnston**	Aug. 1861–March 1862
Army of Mississippi	**Albert S. Johnston**	March 1862–April 1862
	P.G.T. Beauregard	April 1862–June 1862
	Braxton Bragg	June 1862–Nov. 1862
reorganized as		
Army of Tennessee	**Braxton Bragg**	Nov. 1862–Dec. 1863
	Joseph E. Johnston	Dec. 1863–July 1864
	John B. Hood	July 1864–Jan. 1865
	Richard Taylor	Jan. 1865–Feb. 1865
	Joseph E. Johnston	Feb. 1865–April 1865
Army of Northern Virginia	**Joseph E. Johnston**	Aug. 1861–June 1862
	Robert E. Lee	June 1862–April 1865
I Corps	**James Longstreet**	Sept. 1862–April 1865

	Richard H. Anderson (acting)	May 1864–Oct. 1864
II Corps	Thomas J. Jackson	Sept. 1862–May 1863
	Richard S. Ewell	May 1863–April 1865
	John B. Gordon	April 1865
III Corps	Ambrose P. Hill	May 1863–April 1865
Cavalry	J.E.B. Stuart	July 1862–May 1864
	Wade Hampton	May 1864–April 1865
Trans-Mississippi Dept.	Earl Van Dorn	Jan. 1862–Sept. 1862
	Theophilus H. Holmes	Sept. 1862–Feb. 1863
	Edmund Kirby-Smith	Feb. 1863–May 1865

Apache War	Feb. 1861–Sept. 1871	• Cochise
Apache Pass	July 1862	J.H. CARLTON • Cochise
capture of Cochise	Sept. 1871	G. Crook
Sioux War	1862–1865	
Fort Ridgely, Minn.	Aug. 18–24, 1862	• Little Crow
New Ulm, Minn., massacre	Aug. 24, 1862	• Little Crow
Birch Coulee, Minn.	Sept. 2–3, 1862	H.H. Sibley • Little Crow
Wood Lake, Minn.	Sept. 23, 1862	H.H. Sibley • Little Crow
Big Mound, N.D.	July 24, 1863	H.H. Sibley
Dead Buffalo Lake, N.D.	July 26, 1863	H.H. Sibley
Stony Lake, N.D.	July 28, 1863	H.H. Sibley
Whitestone Hill, N.D.	Sept. 3, 1863	A. Sully
Killdeer Mountain, N.D. (Tahkahokuty)	July 28, 1864	A. Sully
Cheyenne, Arapaho War	1863–1865	
Sand Creek massacre, Colo.	Nov. 29, 1864	J.M. Chivington • BLACK KETTLE
Red Cloud's War	1865–1868	
Fetterman massacre, Wyo.	Dec. 21, 1866	W.J. Fetterman • Red Cloud H.B. Carrington Crazy Horse
Hayfield fight, Mont.	Aug. 1, 1867	
Wagon Box fight, Wyo.	Aug. 2, 1867	H.B. Carrington • Red Cloud Crazy Horse
Cheyenne, Arapaho, Kiowa, Comanche War	1867–1869	W.S. Hancock, P.H. Sheridan
1867 expedition		W.S. Hancock
Plum Creek, Neb.	Aug. 17, 1867	F.J. North
Beecher Island, Colo.	Sept. 17, 1868	G.A. Forsyth • ROMAN NOSE F.H. Beecher
Washita River massacre, I.T. (Okla.)	Nov. 27, 1868	G.A. Custer • BLACK KETTLE M.E. Milner
Summit Springs, Colo.	July 11, 1869	F.J. North, E.A. Carr
Modoc War, Cal.	1872–1873	E.R.S. Canby • Captain Jack J.C. Davis F. Wheaton

Cheyenne, Comanche, Kiowa War	1874–1875	N.A. Miles • Quanah
Adobe Walls, Tex.	June 27, 1874	W. Dixon • Quanah
Palo Duro Canyon, Tex.	Sept. 24, 1874	R.S. Mackenzie
Sioux, Cheyenne campaign	1876–1877	A.H. Terry, G. Crook, J. Gibbon
Rosebud Creek, Mont.	June 17, 1876	G. Crook • Crazy Horse
Little Bighorn River, Mont.	June 25–27, 1876	G.A. Custer • Crazy Horse M.A. Reno Gall F. BENTEEN Sitting Bull
War Bonnet Creek, Neb.	July 17, 1876	W. Merritt • YELLOW HAND W.F. Cody
Slim Buttes, S.D.	Sept. 9, 1876	G. Crook • AMERICAN HORSE
Crazy Woman Creek, Wyo.	Nov. 25, 1876	R.S. MacKenzie • DULL KNIFE F.J. North
Wolf Mountain, Mont.	Jan. 7, 1877	N.A. Miles • Crazy Horse
Nez Percé War	June–Oct. 1877	
White Bird Canyon, Ida.	June 17, 1877	O.O. Howard • Joseph
Clearwater River, Ida.	July 11, 1877	O.O. Howard • Joseph
Big Hole River, Mont.	Aug. 9, 1877	J. Gibbon • Joseph
Canyon Creek, Mont.	Sept. 13, 1877	S.D. Sturgis • Joseph
Joseph's surrender	Oct. 5, 1877	N.A. Miles
Greely Arctic expedition	July 1881–June 1884	A.W. Greely, W.B. Hazen
Apache War	1885–1886	G. Crook • Geronimo N.A. Miles
capture of Geronimo	Sept. 4, 1886	C.B. GATEWOOD, H.W. Lawton, L. Wood
Sioux (Pine Ridge) War	1890–1891	
Wounded Knee massacre, S.D.	Dec. 29, 1890	J.W. Forsyth • BIG FOOT
SPANISH–AMERICAN WAR		
"message to Garcia"	April 24–May 5, 1898	A.S. Rowan
Daiquirí landing, Cuba	June 22, 1898	W.R. Shafter, H.W. Lawton
Siboney, Cuba	June 23, 1898	H.W. Lawton, J.C. Bates
Las Guásimas, Cuba	June 24, 1898	J. Wheeler
siege of Santiago, Cuba	June 24–July 17, 1898	W.R. Shafter
El Caney, Cuba	July 1, 1898	H.W. Lawton, J.C. Bates, A.R. Chaffee
San Juan Hill, Cuba	July 1, 1898	J. Wheeler, J.F. Kent, L. Wood, S.B.M. Young
Kettle Hill, Cuba	July 1, 1898	T. Roosevelt
Cavite, P.I.	July 17, 1898	T.M. Anderson
Puerto Rico campaign	July 25–Aug. 13, 1898	N.A. Miles, J.H. Wilson
Manila, P.I.	July 31–Aug. 13, 1898	W. Merritt, T.M. Anderson
Philippine Insurrection	1899–1903	E.S. Otis, A. MacArthur, H.W. Lawton, L. Wheaton, H.T. Allen, J.C. Bates, J.F. Bell, S.B.M. Young
Santa Cruz	April 10, 1899	H.W. Lawton
San Isidro	May 15, 1899	H.W. Lawton
Battle of the Clouds	Dec. 2, 1899	P.C. March
Rosario	Jan. 19, 1900	C.H. Muir
capture of Aguinaldo	March 23, 1901	F. Funston

Peking Relief expedition	July–Aug. 1900	A.R. Chaffee, J.H. Wilson
occupation of Cuba	1906–1909	
Veracruz occupation	April 1914	F. Funston
Mexican Punitive expedition	March 1916–Feb. 1917	J.J. Pershing
WORLD WAR I		
Seicheprey	April 20–21, 1918	
Aisne campaign	May 27–June 5, 1918	
Cantigney	May 28–29, 1918	R.L. Bullard
Château-Thierry	May 31–July 18, 1918	O. Bundy, J.T. Dickman
Belleau Wood	June 6–25, 1918	O. Bundy, J.G. Harbord, J.A. Lejeune
Montdidier-Noyon campaign	June 9–13, 1918	
Champagne–Marne campaign	July 15–18, 1918	J.T. Dickman, W.G. Haan, H. Liggett, C.H. Muir
"Rock of the Marne"		U.G. McAlexander
Aisne–Marne campaign	July 18–Aug. 6, 1918	H. Liggett, C.H. Muir, C.P. Summerall
Oise–Aisne campaign	Aug. 7–Nov. 11, 1918	W.G. Haan
Somme offensive	Aug. 8–Nov. 11, 1918	G.W. Read
Ypres–Lys campaign	Aug. 19–Nov. 11, 1918	
St. Mihiel campaign	Sept. 12–16, 1918	J.J. Pershing, H.T. Allen, G.H. Cameron, J.T. Dickman, H. Liggett, C.P. Summerall, W.M. Wright
Meuse–Argonne campaign	Sept. 26–Nov. 11, 1918	J.J. Pershing, H.T. Allen, C.C. Ballou, R.L. Bullard, G.H. Cameron, A. Cronkhite, J.T. Dickman, J.L. Hines, R.L. Howze, H. Liggett, C.T. Menoher, C.H. Muir, C.P. Summerall, W.M. Wright
"Lost Battalion"	Oct. 2–7, 1918	C.W. Whittlesey
Blanc Mont Ridge	Oct. 3, 1918	J.A. Lejeune
Siberia expedition	Aug. 1918–April 1920	W.S. Graves
Archangel expedition	Sept. 1918–Aug. 1919	W.P. Richardson

WORLD WAR I COMMANDERS

American Expeditionary Forces	John J. Pershing	May 1917–Nov. 1918
First Army	John J. Pershing	Aug. 1918–Oct. 1918
	Hunter Liggett	Oct. 1918–Nov. 1918
Second Army	Robert L. Bullard	Oct. 1918–Nov. 1918
Third Army	John T. Dickman	Nov. 1918
became Army of Occupation		Dec. 1918–Jan. 1923

I Corps	H. Liggett	Jan. 1918–Oct. 1918
	J.T. Dickman	Oct. 1918–Nov. 1918
II Corps	G.W. Read	June 1918–Nov. 1918
III Corps	W.M. Wright	June 1918–July 1918
	R.L. Bullard	July 1918–Oct. 1918
	J.L. Hines	Oct. 1918–Nov. 1918
IV Corps	J.T. Dickman	Aug. 1918–Oct. 1918
	C.H. Muir	Oct. 1918–Nov. 1918
V Corps	W.M. Wright	July 1918–Aug. 1918
	G.H. Cameron	Aug. 1918–Oct. 1918
	C.P. Summerall	Oct. 1918–Nov. 1918
VI Corps	O. Bundy	Aug. 1918–Sept. 1918
	C.C. Ballou	Oct. 1918–Nov. 1918
	C.T. Menoher	Nov. 1918
VII Corps	W.M. Wright	Aug. 1918–Sept. 1918
	O. Bundy	Sept. 1918–Oct. 1918

WORLD WAR II

Pearl Harbor, Hawaii	Dec. 7, 1941	W.C. Short
Philippines	Dec. 7, 1941	D. MacArthur, L.H. Brereton
Bataan	Jan.–April 9, 1942	J.M. Wainwright
Corregidor	April–May 6, 1942	J.M. Wainwright
Doolittle raid	April 18, 1942	J.H. Doolittle
Unalaska Island, Alaska	June 1942	S.B. Buckner
Dieppe raid, France	Aug. 19, 1942	L.K. Truscott
Papua New Guinea	Sept. 1942–Jan. 1943	R.L. Eichelberger
Gona	Dec. 9, 1942	R.L. Eichelberger
Buna	Jan. 2, 1943	R.L. Eichelberger
Guadalcanal	Oct. 13, 1942	A.M. Patch, J.L. Collins
North Africa	Nov. 1942–May 1943	D.D. Eisenhower, O.N. Bradley, L.H. Brereton, C. Spaatz, F.M. Andrews, J.H. Doolittle
French Morocco assault	Nov. 7, 1942	G.S. Patton, E.N. Harmon, L.K. Truscott
Oran, Algeria	Nov. 8, 1942	T. Allen
Algiers, Algeria	Nov. 8, 1942	R.P. HARTLE
Kasserine Pass, Tunisia	Feb. 14–22, 1943	L.R. FREDENALL
Bizerte, Tunisia	May 8, 1943	O.N. Bradley
Aleutian Islands	May–Aug. 1943	S.B. Buckner
Sicily	July 10–Aug. 17, 1943	G.S. Patton, O.N. Bradley, L.K. Truscott, T. Allen, M.B. Ridgway, J.M. Gavin
Palermo, Sicily	July 22, 1943	O.N. Bradley

Trobriand Islands (Kiriwina, Woodlark)	July 1943	W. Krueger
Ploesti, Rumania, raids	Aug. 1943	L.H. Brereton
Italy	Sept. 9, 1943–May 2, 1945	M.W. Clark, J.P. Lucas, L.K. Truscott, E.M. Almond, M.B. Ridgway
Naples, Italy	Oct. 1, 1943	M.W. Clark, J.P. Lucas
Anzio, Italy, assault	Jan. 22, 1944	J.P. Lucas, E.N. Harmon, L.K. Truscott
Admiralty Islands	Feb. 29–May 1944	D. MacArthur, I.P. SWIFT, W.C. Chase
Hollandia, New Guinea	April 22–May 3, 1944	W. Krueger
Biak Island	May 27–Aug. 20, 1944	W. Krueger
Rome, Italy	June 4, 1944	M.W. Clark
Normandy invasion, France	June 6, 1944	D.D. Eisenhower, O.N. Bradley, L.T. Gerow, J.L. Collins, M.B. Ridgway, J.M. Gavin, T. Roosevelt Jr., M.D. Taylor
Carentan, France	June 12, 1944	M.D. Taylor
St. Lô, France	July 25, 1944	O.N. Bradley, J.L. Collins
Myitkyina, Burma	Aug. 4, 1944	J.W. Stilwell, F.D. Merrill
southern France assault	Aug. 15, 1944	A.M. Patch, L.K. Truscott
Paris, France	Aug. 25, 1944	L.T. Gerow
Marseilles and Toulon, France	Aug. 28, 1944	A.M. Patch
Morotai Island	Sept. 15, 1944	W. Krueger
Market-Garden	Sept. 17–26, 1944	L.H. Brereton, J.M. Gavin, M.D. Taylor
Brest, France	Sept. 20, 1944	W.H. Simpson
Leyte assault, Philippines	Oct. 20, 1944	W. Krueger, J.R. Hodge, F.C. SIBERT
Metz, France	Nov. 19, 1944	G.S. Patton, W.H. Walker
Ardennes counteroffensive (Battle of the Bulge) Bastogne, Belgium	Dec. 16–Jan. 25, 1945	A.C. McAuliffe, G.S. Patton, C.W. Abrams
Lingayen Gulf assault, Philippines	Jan. 9, 1945	W. Krueger
Ledo–Burma road opened	Jan. 22, 1945	D.I. Sultan
Manila, Philippines	Feb. 3, 1945	W.C. Chase
Köln, Germany	March 5, 1945	T. Allen
Lashio, Burma	March 7, 1945	D.I. Sultan
Remagen Bridge captured	March 8, 1945	C.H. Hodges
first Rhine crossing	March 22, 1945	G.S. Patton
Okinawa	April 1–July 3, 1945	S.B. Buckner, J.R. Hodge, J.W. Stilwell, E. Pyle
first Elbe crossing	April 12, 1945	W.H. Simpson
Bologna, Italy	April 21, 1945	L.K. Truscott
Genoa, Italy	April 27, 1945	E.M. Almond
Berchtesgaden, Germany	May 7, 1945	M.D. Taylor
Tokyo, Japan	Sept. 8, 1945	W.C. Chase

WORLD WAR II COMMANDERS

Alaska Defense Command	**Simon B. Buckner**	Feb. 1941–Oct. 1943
redesignated		
Alaskan Department	**Simon B. Buckner**	Nov. 1943–March 1944
	Delos C. Emmons	June 1944–June 1946
Hawaiian Department	**Walter C. Short**	Jan. 1941–Dec. 1941
	Delos C. Emmons	Dec. 1941–May 1943
	ROBERT C. RICHARDSON	June 1943–Aug. 1943
Far East	**Douglas MacArthur**	July 1941–March 1942
	Jonathan M. Wainwright	March 1942–June 1942
Central Pacific Area	ROBERT C. RICHARDSON	Aug. 1943–Aug. 1944
merged into		
Pacific Ocean Areas	ROBERT C. RICHARDSON	Aug. 1944–June 1945
South Pacific Area	**Millard F. Harmon**	Jan. 1942–Aug. 1944
Southwest Pacific Area	**Douglas MacArthur**	April 1942–Sept. 1945
Pacific	**Douglas MacArthur**	April 1945–Dec. 1946
China-Burma-India	**Joseph W. Stilwell**	March 1942–Oct. 1944
split into		
China	**Claire L. Chennault**	Oct. 1944
	Albert C. Wedemeyer	Oct. 1944–May 1946
and		
India-Burma	**Daniel I. Sultan**	Oct. 1944–June 1945
European Theater	**Dwight D. Eisenhower**	June 1942–Feb. 1943
	Frank M. Andrews	Feb. 1943–May 1943
	WILLIAM S. KEY	May 1943
	Jacob L. Devers	May 1943–Jan. 1944
	Dwight D. Eisenhower	Jan. 1944–July 1945
redesignated		
U.S. Forces, European Theater	**Dwight D. Eisenhower**	July 1945–Nov. 1945
	George S. Patton	Nov. 1945
	Joseph T. McNarney	Nov. 1945–March 1947
North African Theater	**Dwight D. Eisenhower**	Feb. 1943–Jan. 1944
	Jacob L. Devers	Jan. 1944–Oct. 1944
	Joseph T. McNarney	Oct. 1944–Nov. 1944
redesignated		
Mediterranean Theater	**Joseph T. McNarney**	Nov. 1944–Nov. 1945
	John C.H. Lee	Dec. 1945–Sept. 1947
Supreme Headquarters, Allied Expeditionary Force	**Dwight D. Eisenhower**	Feb. 1944–July 1945
First U.S. Army Group	**Omar N. Bradley**	Oct. 1943–Aug. 1944
superseded by		
12th Army Group	**Omar N. Bradley**	Aug. 1944–July 1945
15th Army Group	SIR H.R.L.G. ALEXANDER	July 1943–Dec. 1944
	Mark W. Clark	Dec. 1944–July 1945
6th Army Group	**Jacob L. Devers**	Sept. 1944–June 1945

First Army	Omar N. Bradley	Jan. 1944–Aug. 1944
	Courtney H. Hodges	Aug. 1944–March 1949
Third Army	Courtney H. Hodges	Feb. 1943–Jan. 1944
	George S. Patton	Jan. 1944–Nov. 1945
	Lucian K. Truscott	Nov. 1945–May 1946
Fourth Army	John L. DeWitt	Dec. 1941–Sept. 1943
	William H. Simpson	Oct. 1943–April 1944
	John P. Lucas	April 1944–July 1945
	Alexander M. Patch	July 1945–June 1946
Fifth Army	Mark W. Clark	Dec. 1942–Dec. 1944
	Lucian K. Truscott	Dec. 1944–Oct. 1945
Sixth Army	Walter Krueger	Feb. 1943–Jan. 1946
Seventh Army	George S. Patton	July 1943–Jan. 1944
	Mark W. Clark	Jan. 1944–March 1944
	Alexander M. Patch	March 1944–June 1945
Eighth Army	Robert L. Eichelberger	Sept. 1944–Sept. 1948
Ninth Army	William H. Simpson	May 1944–Oct. 1945
Tenth Army	Simon B. Buckner	June 1944–June 1945
	Roy S. Geiger (USMC)	June 1945
	Joseph W. Stilwell	June 1945–Oct. 1945
Fifteenth Army	Leonard T. Gerow	Jan. 1945–Oct. 1945
	George S. Patton	Nov. 1945–Dec. 1945
First Allied Airborne Army	Lewis H. Brereton	Aug. 1944–May 1945
Women's Army Corps	Oveta C. Hobby	May 1942–July 1945
	WESTRAY B. BOYCE	July 1945–May 1947

Berlin airlift	June 24, 1948–May 12, 1949	L.D. Clay
Korean War	June 25, 1950–July 27, 1953	
Taejon	July 20–21, 1950	W.F. Dean
Inch'on assault	Sept. 15, 1950	E.M. Almond

KOREAN WAR COMMANDERS

U.S., UN commander	Douglas MacArthur	July 1950–April 1951
	Matthew B. Ridgway	April 1951–May 1952
	Mark W. Clark	May 1952–Oct. 1953
Eighth Army	Walton H. Walker	Sept. 1948–Dec. 1950
	Matthew B. Ridgway	Dec. 1950–April 1951
	James A. Van Fleet	April 1951–Feb. 1953
	Maxwell D. Taylor	Feb. 1953–Nov. 1954
X Corps	Edward M. Almond	Sept. 1950–July 1951

Vietnam War   1964–1973

U.S. COMMANDERS
Military Assistance
  Command, Vietnam   **William Westmoreland**   June 1964–June 1968
                        Creighton W. Abrams   June 1968–June 1972
                        Frederick C. Weyand   June 1972–March 1973

NAVY
Chief officers

(the navy had no senior commander until 1915; Farragut, Porter, and Dewey were senior by virtue of special ranks created for them)

David G. Farragut	(admiral, senior officer)	July 1866–Aug. 1870
David D. Porter		Aug. 1870–Feb. 1891
George Dewey	(admiral of the navy)	March 1899–Jan. 1917
William S. Benson	(chief of naval operations)	May 1915–Sept. 1919
Robert E. Coontz		Oct. 1919–July 1923
Edward W. Eberle		July 1923–Nov. 1927
Charles F. Hughes		Nov. 1927–Sept. 1930
William V. Pratt		Sept. 1930–July 1933
William H. Standley		July 1933–Jan. 1937
William D. Leahy		Jan. 1937–July 1939
Harold R. Stark		Aug. 1939–March 1942
Ernest J. King		March 1942–Dec. 1945
Chester W. Nimitz		Dec. 1945–Dec. 1947
Louis E. Denfeld		Dec. 1947–Oct. 1949
Forrest P. Sherman		Nov. 1949–July 1951
William M. Fechteler		Aug. 1951–Aug. 1953
Robert B. Carney		Aug. 1953–Aug. 1955
Arleigh A. Burke		Aug. 1955–Aug. 1961
George W. Anderson		Aug. 1961–Aug. 1963
David L. McDonald		Aug. 1963–Aug. 1967
Thomas H. Moorer		Aug. 1967–July 1970
Elmo R. Zumwalt		July 1970–July 1974
James L. Holloway		July 1974–

Chronology and commanders

REVOLUTION

Unity–Margaretta	June 12, 1775	J. O'Brien
Liberty–Diligent, *Tapnaquish*	July 14, 1775	J. O'Brien
Washington's Fleet	July 1775	J. Manley
Continental fleet	Dec. 1775	E. Hopkins, J. Barney, N. Biddle, D. Saltonstall, A. Whipple, J.B. Hopkins
New Providence, Bahamas	March 3, 1776	E. Hopkins
Columbus–Hawk	April 4, 1776	A. Whipple
Alfred–Bolton	April 5, 1776	D. Saltonstall
Cabot–Glasgow	April 5–6, 1776	J.B. Hopkins
Lexington–Edward	April 7, 1776	J. Barry
Reprisal–Shark	July 27, 1776	L. Wickes
Hancock–Peggy	July 29, 1776	S. Tucker
Tyrannicide cruise	July 1776	J. Fiske
American Turtle–Eagle	Aug. 1776	D. Bushnell, E. Lee
Providence cruise	Aug.–Sept. 1776	J.P. Jones
Valcour Island, Lake **Champlain, N.Y.**	Oct. 11–13, 1776	B. Arnold, D. Waterbury
Hancock–Lively	Oct. 29, 1776	S. Tucker
Alfred cruise	Nov.–Dec. 1776	J.P. Jones
Reprisal cruise	Jan. 1777	L. Wickes
Hancock–Fox	June 7, 1777	J. Manley
Reprisal–Burford	June 26, 1777	L. Wickes
Hancock–Rainbow, Victor	July 8, 1777	J. Manley
Revenge cruise	July–Dec. 1777	G. Conyngham
Delaware River	Oct.–Nov. 1777	J. Hazelwood
Fort Mercer, N.J.	Oct. 22, 1777	J. Hazelwood
Fort Mifflin, Pa.	Oct. 23, 1777	J. Hazelwood
Randolph–Yarmouth	March 7, 1778	N. Biddle
Ranger–Drake	April 24, 1778	J.P. Jones
Raleigh–Experiment, Unicorn	Sept. 27, 1778	J. Barry
Hazard–Active	March 16, 1779	J.F. Williams
Boston, Confederacy– *Pole, Patsey*	June 6, 1779	S. Tucker, S. Harding
Providence squadron cruise	July 1779	A. Whipple
Penobscot (Me.) expedition	July–Aug. 1779	D. Saltonstall
Deane, Boston cruise	July–Aug. 1779	S. Nicholson, S. Tucker
Bonhomme Richard–Serapis	Sept. 23, 1779	J.P. Jones, R. Dale, N. Fanning
Thorn–Governor Tryon, Sir *William Erskine*	Dec. 25, 1779	D. Waters
Providence squadron captured	May 1780	A. Whipple, S. Tucker
Protector–Admiral Duff	July 9, 1780	J.F. Williams
Confederacy–Roebuck, *Orpheus*	April 15, 1781	S. Harding
Alliance–Atalanta, Trepassy	May 29, 1781	J. Barry
Hyder-Ally–General Monk	April 8, 1782	J. Barney

Hague cruise	Sept. 1782–Jan. 1783	J. Manley
Alliance–Alarm, Sybil	March 10, 1783	J. Barry, S. Harding
Quasi-war with France	1798–1800	
Retaliation–Insurgente, Volontaire	Sept. 1798	W. Bainbridge
Constellation–Insurgente	Feb. 9, 1799	T. Truxtun, A. Sterett
Constellation–Vengeance	Feb. 1–2, 1800	T. Truxtun
Constitution–Sandwich	May 11, 1800	S. Talbot, I. Hull
Enterprise cruise	June–July 1800	J. Shaw
Experiment–Deux Amis	Sept. 1800	C. Stewart
Boston–Berceau	Oct. 12, 1800	G. Little
Tripolitan War	May 1801–June 1805	
Enterprise–Tripoli	Aug. 1, 1801	A. Sterett
John Adams–Mashuda	May 1803	J. Rodgers
Philadelphia grounded	Oct. 31, 1803	W. Bainbridge
Intrepid raid	Feb. 16, 1804	S. Decatur, C. Morris, J. Lawrence, C. Stewart
bombardment of Tripoli	Aug. 3, 7, 24, 28, Sept. 3, 1804	E. Preble
Intrepid bomb	Sept. 4, 1804	R. Somers
capture of Derna, Libya	April 27, 1805	I. Hull

TRIPOLI SQUADRON COMMANDERS

	Richard Dale	July 1801–March 1802
	Richard V. Morris	June 1802–June 1803
	John Rodgers	(acting) June 1803
	Edward Preble	June 1803–Sept. 1804
	SAMUEL BARRON	Sept. 1804–May 1805
	John Rodgers	May 1805–June 1805

Chesapeake–Leopard	June 22, 1807	J. Barron, W.H. Allen
President–Little Belt	May 16, 1811	J. Rodgers
WAR OF 1812		
President–Belvidera	June 23, 1812	J. Rodgers
Essex–Alert	Aug. 13, 1812	D. Porter
Constitution–Guerrière	Aug. 19, 1812	I. Hull, C. Morris, J.T. Shubrick, G.C. Read
capture of *Caledonia, Detroit*	Oct. 8, 1812	J.D. Elliott, N. TOWSON
Wasp–Frolic	Oct. 18, 1812	J. Jones, J. Biddle
United States–Macedonian	Oct. 25, 1812	S. Decatur, W.H. Allen
Constitution–Java	Dec. 29, 1812	W. Bainbridge
Hornet–Peacock	Feb. 24, 1813	J. Lawrence
York (Toronto), Ont.	April 27, 1813	I. Chauncey

Mobile, Ala.	April 1813	J. Shaw
Fort George, Ont.	May 26–27, 1813	I. Chauncey
Chesapeake–Shannon	June 1, 1813	J. Lawrence
Craney Island, Va.	June 22, 1813	W.B. Shubrick
capture of *Eagle*	July 5, 1813	J. Percival
Argus–Pelican	Aug. 14, 1813	W.H. Allen
Enterprise–Boxer	Sept. 5, 1813	W. Burrows
Lake Erie	Sept. 10, 1813	O.H. Perry, J.D. Elliott
York Bay, Lake Ontario	Sept. 28, 1813	I. Chauncey
Nuku Hiva, Marquesas Islands	Nov. 27, 1813	J. Downes
Essex–Phoebe, Cherub	March 28, 1814	D. Porter, J. Downes
Peacock–Epervier	April 29, 1814	L. Warrington, J. Percival
Wasp–Reindeer	June 28, 1814	J. Blakely
Bladensburg, Md.	Aug. 24, 1814	J. Barney
Wasp–Avon	Sept. 1, 1814	J. Blakely
Lake Champlain (Plattsburg, N.Y.)	Sept. 11, 1814	T. Macdonough, S. Cassin
Baratara raid, La.	Sept. 16, 1814	D.T. Patterson • J. Lafitte
Wasp–Atalanta	Sept. 21, 1814	J. Blakely
General Armstrong at Faial, Azores	Sept. 26–27, 1814	S.C. Reid
Lake Borgne, La.	Dec. 14, 1814	T.ap C. Jones
Villere's Plantation, La.	Dec. 23, 1814	D.T. Patterson
New Orleans, La.	Jan. 8, 1815	D.T. Patterson
President–Endymion	Jan. 15, 1815	S. Decatur
Constitution–Cyane, Levant	Feb. 20, 1815	C. Stewart
Hornet–Penguin	March 23, 1815	J. Biddle
Algerine War	1815–1816	S. Decatur, I. Chauncey
capture of *Mashuda*	June 17, 1815	J. Downes, J.T. Shubrick
operations against Gulf pirates	1815–1819	D.T. Patterson
possession of Oregon	Aug. 19, 1818	J. Biddle
operations against West Indian pirates	1822–1826	J. Biddle, D. Porter, L. Warrington, S. Cassin
Dolphin at Honolulu, Hawaii	Jan.–May 1826	J. Percival
Peacock at Tahiti and Hawaii	Aug.–Oct. 1826	T.ap C. Jones
Potomac bombards Quallah Battoo, Sumatra	Feb. 6, 1832	J. Downes
South Seas (Wilkes) Expedition	1838–1842	C. Wilkes, J. Alden
Columbia bombards Quallah Battoo, Sumatra	Dec. 25, 1838	G.C. Read
Columbia burns Mukkee, Sumatra	Jan. 1, 1839	G.C. Read
Texas navy	July 1839–May 1843	E.W. Moore
St. Louis at Monterey, Cal.	June 1840	F. Forrest
occupation of Monterey, Cal.	Oct. 19, 1842	T.ap C. Jones, C.K. Stribling
Constellation, Boston at Canton, China	1842	L. Kearny
Somers mutiny	Nov. 1842	A.S. Mackenzie
Congress–Sancala	Sept. 29, 1844	P.F. Voorhees

MEXICAN WAR

Point Isabel, Tex.	May 8, 1846	D. Conner
occupation of Monterey, Cal.	July 7, 1846	J.D. Sloat, W. Mervine, S.C. Rowan
Sonoma, Cal.	July 9, 1846	J.W. Revere
occupation of San Diego, Cal.	July 29, 1846	S.F. Du Pont, S.C. Rowan
Santa Barbara, Cal.	Aug. 4, 1846	R.F. Stockton
San Pedro, Cal.	Aug. 6, 1846	R.F. Stockton
Los Angeles, Cal.	Aug. 13, 1846	R.F. Stockton, J.C. Frémont
Mazatlán, Mex.	Sept. 7, 1846	W. Radford
Frontera, Mex.	Oct. 23, 1846	M.C. Perry, F. Forrest
Tabasco, Mex.	Oct. 26, 1846	M.C. Perry, F. Forrest
Tampico, Mex.	Nov. 14, 1846	M.C. Perry
Panuco, Mex.	Nov. 19, 1846	J. Tattnall
Laguna, Mex.	Dec. 1846	M.C. Perry
San Gabriel, Cal.	Jan. 8–9, 1847	R.F. Stockton, S.W. Kearny, J.C. Frémont
Los Angeles, Cal.	Jan. 10, 1847	R.F. Stockton, S.W. Kearny, J.C. Frémont
Veracruz, Mex.	March 9–27, 1847	D. Conner, M.C. Perry, F. Forrest, A.S. Mackenzie, R. Semmes, J. Tattnall
Tuxpan, Mex.	April 18, 1847	M.C. Perry
Frontera, Mex.	June 14, 1847	M.C. Perry
Tabasco, Mex.	June 15, 1847	M.C. Perry
Guaymas, Mex.	Oct. 19, 1847	W.B. Shubrick
Mazatlán, Mex.	Nov. 11, 1847	W.B. Shubrick, S.F. Du Pont, T.P. Greene
San Blas, Mex.	Jan. 12, 1848	T. Bailey
San Jose, Mex.	Feb. 14, 1848	S.C. Rowan
River Jordan, Dead Sea expedition	Nov. 1847–Dec. 1848	W.F. Lynch
Preble at Nagasaki, Japan	April 1849	J. Glynn
Grinnell Arctic expedition	May 1850–Sept. 1851	E.J. De Haven, E.K. Kane
St. Louis at Smyrna, Turkey (Koszta affair)	July 1853	D.N. Ingraham
Japan expedition	1853–1854	M.C. Perry, F. Buchanan
second Grinnell expedition	May 1853–Aug. 1855	E.K. Kane
North Pacific Surveying Expedition	1853–1856	C. Ringgold, J. Rodgers
Cyane bombards Greytown, Nicaragua	July 13, 1854	G.N. Hollins
Water-Witch at Paraguay	Feb. 1855	T.J. Page
bombardment of barrier forts, Canton, China	Nov. 1856	A.H. Foote
St. Mary's at Nicaragua	May 1857	C.H. Davis
La Plata River	Jan.–Feb. 1859	W.B. Shubrick
Powhatan at Taku, China	June 25, 1859	J. Tattnall

CIVIL WAR

Fort Pickens, Fla.	Jan. 10, 1861	H. Walke
burning of Norfolk, Va., navy yard	April 20, 1861	C.S. McCauley, H. Paulding
Yankee at Gloucester Point, Va.	May 7, 1861	T.O. Selfridge
Aquia Creek, Va.	May 25, 1861	S.C. Rowan
Aquia Creek, Va.	May 31–June 1, 1861	J.H. Ward • W.F. Lynch S.C. Rowan
Perry–Savannah	June 3, 1861	E.G. Parrott
Matthias Point, Va.	June 27, 1861	J.H. Ward
Hatteras Inlet (Fort Hatteras, Fort Clark), N.C.	Aug. 27–29, 1861	S.H. Stringham • S. Barron
Mississippi passes, La.	Oct. 12, 1861	J. POPE • G.N. Hollins
Port Royal, S.C.	Nov. 4, 1861	J. Rodgers • J. Tattnall
Belmont, Mo.	Nov. 7, 1861	H. Walke
Port Royal, S.C.	Nov. 7, 1861	S.F. Du Pont • J. Tattnall C.H. Davis C. Ringgold
Fort Walker, S.C.	Nov. 7, 1861	J. Rodgers
Galveston, Tex., raid	Nov. 7–8, 1861	J.E. Jouett
Trent affair	Nov. 8, 1861	C. Wilkes
Biloxi, Miss.	Dec. 31, 1861	M. Smith
Fort Henry, Tenn.	Feb. 6, 1862	A.H. Foote, H. Walke
Roanoke Island, N.C.	Feb. 7, 1862	L.M. Goldsborough, S.C. Rowan
Croatan Sound, N.C.	Feb. 8, 1862	S.C. Rowan • W.F. Lynch
Elizabeth City, N.C.	Feb. 9, 1862	S.C. Rowan • W.F. Lynch
Fort Donelson, Tenn.	Feb. 14–16, 1862	A.H. Foote, H. Walke
Fernandina, Fla.	March 7, 1862	S.F. Du Pont
Cumberland–Merrimac	March 8, 1862	G.U. Morris • F. Buchanan C. Heywood J.R. Tucker T.O. Selfridge
Monitor–Merrimac	March 9, 1862	J.L. Worden • C.ap R. Jones
St. Augustine, Fla.	March 11, 1862	S.F. Du Pont, C.R.P. Rodgers
New Bern, N.C.	March 14, 1862	S.C. Rowan
Carondelet runs Island No. 10, Tenn.	April 4, 1862	H. Walke
occupation of Island No. 10, Tenn.	April 7, 1862	A.H. Foote • G.N. Hollins
Hampton Roads, Va.	April 11, 1862	• J. Tattnall J.R. Tucker
passing of Fort Jackson and Fort St. Philip, La.	April 24, 1862	D. Farragut • J.K. MITCHELL T. Bailey T.T. Craven S.P. Lee M. Smith
Beaufort, N.C.	April 25, 1862	S.C. Rowan
New Orleans, La.	April 25, 1862	T. Bailey
Fort Jackson and Fort St. Philip, La., surrender	April 28, 1862	D.D. Porter • E. HIGGINS

Fort Pillow, Tenn.	May 10, 1862	H. Walke
burning of *Virginia*	May 11, 1862	• J. Tattnall
capture of *Planter*	May 13, 1862	R. Smalls
Drewry's Bluff, Va.	May 15, 1862	J. Rodgers • J.R. Tucker
battle above Memphis, Tenn.	June 6, 1862	C.H. Davis • J.E. MONTGOMERY C. Ellet H. Walke
running of Vicksburg, Miss.	June 28, 1862	D.G. Farragut, J.S. Palmer, T.T. Craven
Malvern Hill, Va.	July 1, 1862	J. Rodgers
Carondelet–Arkansas	July 15, 1862	H. Walke • I.N. BROWN
Florida cruise	Jan.–Aug. 1863	• J.N. Maffitt C.W. Read
Arkansas Post (Fort Hindman), Ark.	Jan. 10–11, 1863	D.D. Porter, J.G. Walker
Fort McAllister, Ga.	Jan. 27, Feb. 1, 1863	J.L. Worden • G.W. ANDERSON
Charleston, S.C., sortie	Jan. 31, 1863	H.S. STELLWAGEN • D.N. Ingraham W.E. LEROY J.R. Tucker
Queen of the West runs Vicksburg, Miss.	Feb. 2, 1863	C.R. Ellet
Red River raid, La.	Feb. 3–16, 1863	C.R. Ellet
Montauk–Nashville	Feb. 28, 1863	J.L. Worden
running of Port Hudson, La.	March 14, 1863	D.G. Farragut, J.S. Palmer
Steele's Bayou, Miss.	March 16–23, 1863	D.D. Porter
Charleston, S.C., attack	April 7, 1863	S.F. Du Pont, J. Rodgers, A.C. Rhind
running of Vicksburg, Miss.	April 16, 1863	D.D. Porter
Grand Gulf, Miss.	April 29–May 3, 1863	D.D. Porter
Clarence cruise	May–June 1863	• C.W. Read
bombardment of Vicksburg, Miss.	May 22, 1863	D.D. Porter
Weehawken–Atlanta	June 17, 1863	J. Rodgers • W. WEBB
Caleb Cushing–Archer	June 27, 1863	• C.W. Read
Morris Island, S.C.	July 10, 1863	J.A.B. Dahlgren
Yazoo River expedition, Miss.	July 12–13, 1863	J.G. Walker
Fort Wagner, S.C.	Aug. 17, 1863	G.W. Rodgers
Fort Moultrie, S.C.	Sept. 7, 1863	J.A.B. Dahlgren
Fort Sumter, S.C.	Sept. 8, 1863	J.A.B. Dahlgren, T.H. Stevens
Brazos Island, Tex.	Nov. 2, 1863	J.H. Strong
Mustang Island, Tex.	Nov. 17, 1863	J.H. Strong
Red River campaign, La.	March–May 1864	D.D. Porter
Mattabesett–Albemarle	May 5, 1864	M. Smith
Kearsarge–Alabama	June 19, 1864	J.A. Winslow • R. Semmes
Tallahassee cruise	Aug. 1864	J.T. Wood
Mobile Bay, Ala.	Aug. 5, 1864	D.G. Farragut • F. Buchanan J. Alden T.A.M. Craven J.H. Strong J.E. Jouett
Shenandoah cruise	Oct. 1864–Nov. 1865	J.I. Waddell
Wachusett–Florida	Oct. 7, 1864	N. Collins • C.M. MORRIS

sinking of *Albemarle*	Oct. 27, 1864	W.B. Cushing
Fort Fisher, N.C.	Dec. 24–25, 1864	D.D. Porter, W. Radford, A.C. Rhind, H.K. Thatcher
Fort Fisher, N.C.	Jan. 13–15, 1865	D.D. Porter, W. Radford, W.B. Cushing, R.D. Evans, T.O. Selfridge, H.K. Thatcher
Niagara, Sacramento– *Stonewall*	March 24, 1865	T.T. Craven • T.J. Page H. Walke
Fort Blakely, Ala.	April 9, 1865	H.K. Thatcher • E. FARRAND
Mobile, Ala.	April 12, 1865	H.K. Thatcher • E. FARRAND
occupation of Galveston, Tex.	June 5, 1865	H.K. Thatcher, B.F. Sands

UNION COMMANDERS

Western river gunboat squadron	John Rodgers	May 1861–Aug. 1861
	Andrew H. Foote	Aug. 1861–June 1862
	Charles H. Davis	June 1862–Sept. 1862
succeeded by Mississippi Squadron	David D. Porter	Oct. 1862–Oct. 1864
	Samuel P. Lee	Oct. 1864–April 1865
Atlantic Blockading Squadron	Silas H. Stringham	May 1861–Sept. 1861
	Louis M. Goldsborough	Sept. 1861
North Atlantic Blockading Squadron	Louis M. Goldsborough	Sept. 1861–Sept. 1862
	Samuel P. Lee	Sept. 1862–Oct. 1864
	David D. Porter	Oct. 1864–April 1865
South Atlantic Blockading Squadron	Samuel F. Du Pont	Sept. 1861–July 1863
	John A.B. Dahlgren	July 1863–April 1865
Gulf Blockading Squadron	William Mervine	May 1861–Sept. 1861
West Gulf Blockading Squadron	William W. McKean	Oct. 1861–Feb. 1862
	David G. Farragut	Feb. 1862–Sept. 1864
	James S. Palmer (acting)	Sept. 1864–Jan. 1865
	Henry K. Thatcher	Jan. 1865–June 1865
East Gulf Blockading Squadron	James L. Lardner	June 1862–Nov. 1862
	Theodorus Bailey	Nov. 1862–Sept. 1864
	Theodore P. Greene	Sept. 1864–Feb. 1865
	Cornelius K. Stribling	Feb. 1865–July 1865
West Indies Squadron	Charles Wilkes	Sept. 1862–June 1863
	James L. Lardner	June 1863–Nov. 1864
Potomac Flotilla	James H. Ward	May 1861–June 1861
	Thomas T. Craven	June 1861–Nov. 1861
	Robert H. Wyman	Nov. 1861–July 1862
	Andrew A. Harwood	July 1862–Jan. 1864
	Foxhall A. Parker	Jan. 1864–April 1865

CONFEDERATE COMMANDERS

James River (Virginia and North Carolina coastal waters, Chesapeake Bay)	Samuel Barron	April 1861–Aug. 1861
	William F. Lynch	Aug. 1861–Feb. 1862
	Franklin Buchanan	Feb. 1862–March 1862
	Josiah Tattnall	March 1862–May 1862
	Samuel Barron	Nov. 1862–March 1863
	French Forrest	March 1863–May 1864
	JOHN K. MITCHELL	May 1864–Feb. 1865
	Raphael Semmes	Feb. 1865–April 1865
Mississippi	George N. Hollins	July 1861–April 1862
	JOHN K. MITCHELL	
	William F. Lynch	March 1862–Oct. 1862
	J. EDWARD MONTGOMERY	
Charleston, S.C.	Duncan N. Ingraham	Nov. 1861–March 1863
	John R. Tucker	March 1863–Feb. 1865
Confederate naval forces in Europe	Samuel Barron	Nov. 1863–Feb. 1865

Wyoming at Shimonoseki, Japan	July 16, 1863	D.S. McDougal
Han River, Korea	June 10, 1871	J. Rodgers
Virginius rescue	Nov. 1873	W.B. Cushing
DeLong Arctic expedition	July 1879–Oct. 1881	G.W. DeLong, G.W. Melville
Korean treaty	May 22, 1882	R.W. Shufeldt
Greely relief expedition	1884	W.S. Schley, F.W. Melville
Panama	April 1885	J.E. Jouett, B.H. McCalla
Valparaiso, Chile	Oct.–Nov. 1891	W.S. Schley, R.D. Evans
SPANISH–AMERICAN WAR		
Maine sunk	Feb. 15, 1898	C.D. Sigsbee
Oregon run	March–May 1898	C.E. Clark, J.M. Reeves
Manila Bay, Philippines	May 1, 1898	G. Dewey, C.V. Gridley, B.A. Fiske
bombardment of San Juan, P.R.	May 12, 1898	W.T. Sampson
Guantánamo, Cuba	June 8, 1898	B.H. McCalla
St. Paul–Terror, Isabella II	June 22, 1898	C.D. Sigsbee
Santiago, Cuba	July 3, 1898	W.T. Sampson, W.S. Schley, R. Wainwright, N.R. Usher, R.D. Evans, R.P. Hobson, J.W. Philip
Guánica, P.R.	July 25, 1898	R. Wainwright
Philippine insurrection	1899–1901	C.S. Sperry
Vigan, Philippines	Dec. 5, 1899	B.H. McCalla
Boxer Rebellion, China	1900–1901	L. Kempff, B.H. McCalla

Battle Fleet cruise	Dec. 1907–Feb. 1909	R.D. Evans, C.S. Sperry
North Pole reached	April 6, 1909	R.E. Peary
Nicaragua expedition	1909–1910	W.W. Kimball
Tampico, Mex., incident	April 9, 1914	H.T. Mayo
Veracruz, Mex.	April 21, 1914	F.F. Fletcher, P. Bellinger, W.A. Moffett, J.H. Towers
Port-au-Prince, Haiti	July 28, 1915	W.B. Caperton
Santo Domingo	May 1916	W.B. Caperton

WORLD WAR I COMMANDERS

Atlantic Fleet	**Henry T. Mayo**
U.S. naval forces in Europe	**William S. Sims**
Battleships (Battle Squadron 6)	**Hugh Rodman**
Patrol Force, later U.S. naval forces in France	**Henry B. Wilson**
Convoys	**Albert Gleaves**
Asiatic Fleet	**Austin M. Knight**

NC Atlantic flight	May 1919	A.C. Read, P. Bellinger, M.A. Mitscher, J.H. Towers
North Pole flight	May 9, 1926	R.E. Byrd, F. Bennett
South Pole flight	Nov. 29, 1929	R.E. Byrd, B. Balchen
WORLD WAR II		
Pearl Harbor	Dec. 7, 1941	H.E. Kimmel, P. Bellinger
Philippines	Dec. 1941–April 1942	T.C. Hart, J.D. Bulkeley
Kwajalein, Marshall Islands, raid	Feb. 1, 1942	W.F. Halsey, T.C. Kinkaid
Lexington air battle	Feb. 20, 1942	E.H. O'Hare
Java Sea	Feb. 27, 1942	K. DOARMAN
evacuation of MacArthur	Mar. 11, 1942	J.D. Bulkeley
Doolittle raid	April 18, 1942	J.H. Doolittle, M.A. Mitscher, W.F. Halsey, R.A. Spruance
Coral Sea	May 7–8, 1942	F.J. Fletcher, A.W. Fitch, T.C. Kinkaid
Midway Island	June 3–6, 1942	F.J. Fletcher, R.A. Spruance, T.C. Kinkaid
Guadalcanal assault	Aug. 7, 1942	R.L. Ghormley, F.J. Fletcher, R.K. Turner
Savo Island	Aug. 9, 1942	R.K. Turner
Eastern Solomons	Aug. 24, 1942	F.J. Fletcher, T.C. Kinkaid
Cape Esperance, Guadalcanal	Oct. 11–12, 1942	R.L. Ghormley, N. SCOTT
Santa Cruz Islands	Oct. 26–27, 1942	W.F. Halsey, T.C. Kinkaid
French Morocco landing	Nov. 7, 1942	H.K. Hewitt

Guadalcanal	Nov. 12–15, 1942	W.F. Halsey, R.K. Turner, D.J. Callaghan
Trobriand Islands landing	June 30, 1943	D.E. Barbey
New Georgia Island landing	July 1, 1943	R.K. Turner
Sicily landing	July 10, 1943	H.K. Hewitt, A.G. Kirk
Vella Gulf	Aug. 6–7, 1943	T.S. Wilkinson
Vella Lavella Island landing	Aug. 15, 1943	T.S. Wilkinson
Lae, New Guinea, landing	Sept. 6, 1943	D.E. Barbey
Salerno, Italy, landing	Sept. 9, 1943	H.K. Hewitt
Vella Lavella	Oct. 6–7, 1943	T.S. Wilkinson
Bougainville landing	Nov. 1, 1943	T.S. Wilkinson
Empress Augusta Bay	Nov. 2, 1943	A.A. Burke
Tarawa and Makin Island landings	Nov. 20–24, 1943	R.K. Turner
Kwajalein Island landing	Jan. 31, 1944	R.K. Turner, R.A. Spruance
Truk Island raid	Feb. 4–5, 1944	M.A. Mitscher, R.A. Spruance
Eniwetok Island landing	February 17, 1944	R.K. Turner, R.A. Spruance
Admiralty Islands landing	Feb. 29, 1944	D.E. Barbey
Hollandia, New Guinea, landing	April 22, 1944	D.E. Barbey, W.M. Fechteler
Biak Island landing	May 27, 1944	W.M. Fechteler
capture of U-505	June 4, 1944	D.V. Gallery
Normandy (France) landing	June 6, 1944	A.G. Kirk, J.D. Bulkeley
Saipan Island landing	June 15, 1944	R.K. Turner, R.A. Spruance, F.B. Stump
Philippine Sea	June 19–21, 1944	R.A. Spruance, M.A. Mitscher
"Great Marianas Turkey Shoot"	June 19, 1944	M.A. Mitscher
Guam Island landing	July 21, 1944	R.K. Turner, R.A. Spruance, F.B. Stump
Tinian Island landing	July 24, 1944	R.K. Turner, R.A. Spruance, F.B. Stump
Sansapor Island landing	July 30, 1944	W.M. Fechteler
southern France landing	Aug. 15, 1944	H.K. Hewitt, J.D. Bulkeley
Morotai Island landing	Sept. 15, 1944	D.E. Barbey
Peleliu Island landing	Sept. 15, 1944	T.S. Wilkinson
Ulithi atoll landing	Sept. 23, 1944	T.S. Wilkinson
Formosa raid	Oct. 12–14, 1944	M.A. Mitscher
Leyte, Philippines, landing	Oct. 20, 1944	D.E. Barbey, T.S. Wilkinson
Leyte Gulf (second battle of Philippine Sea)	Oct. 24–26, 1944	T.C. Kinkaid, W.F. Halsey
Sibuyan Sea	Oct. 24, 1944	M.A. Mitscher
Surigao Strait	Oct. 24–25, 1944	T.C. Kinkaid
Samar	Oct. 25, 1944	C.A.F. Sprague, F.B. Stump
Cape Engaño	Oct. 25–26, 1944	W.F. Halsey, M.A. Mitscher
Ormoc Bay, Leyte, landing	Dec. 7, 1944	A.D. Struble
Mindoro, Philippines, landing	Dec. 15, 1944	A.D. Struble
Lingayen Gulf landing	Jan. 9, 1945	T.C. Kinkaid, D.E. Barbey, T.S. Wilkinson
South China Sea raid	Jan. 10–20, 1945	W.F. Halsey
Subic Bay, Philippines, landing	Jan. 29, 1945	A.D. Struble

Iwo Jima Island landing	Feb. 19, 1945	R.K. Turner,
Okinawa Island landing	April 1, 1945	R.A. Spruance
		R.K. Turner,
		R.A. Spruance

WORLD WAR II COMMANDERS

U.S. Fleet	Husband E. Kimmel	Feb. 1941–Dec. 1941
	Ernest J. King	Dec. 1941–Oct. 1945
Atlantic Fleet	Ernest J. King	Feb. 1941–Jan. 1942
	Royal E. Ingersoll	Jan. 1942–Nov. 1944
	Jonas H. Ingram	Nov. 1944–April 1947
Amphibious Force	H. Kent Hewitt	April 1942–Feb. 1943
	Alan G. Kirk	Feb. 1943–Oct. 1944
Pacific Fleet	Husband E. Kimmel	Feb. 1941–Dec. 1941
	Chester W. Nimitz	Dec. 1941–Nov. 1945
Asiatic Fleet	Thomas C. Hart	July 1939–Jan. 1942
merged into		
American-British-Dutch-Australian Command (ABDACOM)	Thomas C. Hart	Jan. 1942–Feb. 1942
U.S. Naval Forces, Europe	Harold R. Stark	March 1942–Aug. 1945
Pacific Ocean Areas	Chester W. Nimitz	April 1942–Sept. 1945
North Pacific Area	Thomas C. Kinkaid	Jan. 1943–Nov. 1943
Central Pacific Area *subsequently* Fifth Fleet	Raymond A. Spruance	Aug. 1943–Sept. 1945
V Amphibious Force	R. Kelly Turner	Aug. 1943–April 1945
Task Force 58 (38)	Marc A. Mitscher	Jan. 1944–July 1945
South Pacific Area	Robert L. Ghormley	April 1942–Oct. 1942
	William F. Halsey	Oct. 1942–June 1944
Amphibious Force	R. Kelly Turner	July 1942–July 1943
	Theodore S. Wilkinson	July 1943–June 1944
subsequently Third Fleet	William F. Halsey	June 1944–Sept. 1945
III Amphibious Force	Theodore S. Wilkinson	June 1944–Sept. 1945
Task Force 38 (58)	Marc A. Mitscher	Jan. 1944–July 1945
Southwest Pacific Area	ARTHUR S. CARPENDER	March 1943–Nov. 1943
subsequently Seventh Fleet	Thomas C. Kinkaid	Nov. 1943–Sept. 1945
VII Amphibious Force	Daniel E. Barbey	Jan. 1943–Sept. 1945
Eighth Fleet	H. Kent Hewitt	Feb. 1943–Aug. 1945
Tenth Fleet	Ernest J. King	May 1943–June 1945
Construction Battalions (Seabees)	Ben Moreell	Dec. 1941–Sept. 1945
Women Accepted for Volunteer Emergency Service (WAVES)	Mildred H. (McAfee) Horton	Aug. 1942–Feb. 1946
Coast Guard	Russell R. Waesche	Nov. 1941–Dec. 1945
Coast Guard Auxiliary (SPARS)	Dorothy C. Stratton	Nov. 1942–Feb. 1946

Korean War	1950–1953	C.T. Joy
Inch'on landing	Sept. 15, 1950	A.D. Struble
Lebanon	July 1958	G.W. Anderson
Vietnam War	1964–1973	J.L. Holloway, E.R. Zumwalt

MARINE CORPS
Chief officers

Samuel Nicholas	(commandant, Continental marines)	Nov. 1775–Aug. 1781
William W. Burrows	(commandant, U.S. Marine Corps)	July 1798–March 1804
Franklin Wharton		March 1804–Sept. 1818
Anthony Gale		March 1819–Oct. 1820
Archibald Henderson		Oct. 1820–Jan. 1859
John Harris		Jan. 1859–May 1864
Jacob Zeilin		June 1864–Nov. 1876
Charles G. McCawley		Nov. 1876–Jan. 1891
Charles Heywood		Jan. 1891–Oct. 1903
George F. Elliot		Oct. 1903–Nov. 1910
William P. Biddle		Feb. 1911–Feb.·1914
George Barnett		Feb. 1914–June 1920
John A. Lejeune		June 1920–March 1929
Wendell C. Neville		March 1929–July 1930
Ben H. Fuller		July 1930–March 1934
John H. Russell		March 1934–Nov. 1936
Thomas Holcomb		Nov. 1936–Dec. 1943
Alexander A. Vandegrift		Jan. 1944–Jan. 1948
Clifton B. Cates		Jan. 1948–Jan. 1952
Lemuel C. Shepherd		Jan. 1952–Jan. 1956
Randolph M. Pate		Jan. 1956–Jan. 1960
David M. Shoup		Jan. 1960–Dec. 1963
Wallace M. Greene		Jan. 1964–Jan. 1968
Leonard F. Chapman		Jan. 1968–Jan. 1972
Robert E. Cushman		Jan. 1972–June 1975
Louis H. Wilson		June 1975–

Chronology and commanders

REVOLUTION

New Providence, Bahamas	March 3, 1776	S. Nicholas
Trenton, N.J.	Dec. 26, 1776	S. Nicholas
Puerto Plata, Santo Domingo	May 11, 1800	D. Carmick
Derna, Libya	April 27, 1805	P.N. O'Bannon

WAR OF 1812

New Orleans, La.	Jan. 8, 1815	D. Carmick
Seminole War	1836–1838	A. Henderson, J. Harris

MEXICAN WAR

Monterey, Cal.	July 7, 1846	W. Mervine
Santa Barbara, Cal.	Aug. 4, 1846	J. Zeilin
San Pedro, Cal.	Aug. 6, 1846	J. Zeilin
Los Angeles, Cal.	Aug. 13, 1846	J. Zeilin
San Gabriel, Cal.	Jan. 8–9, 1847	J. Zeilin
Mazatlán, Mex.	Nov. 11, 1847	J. Zeilin
Japan expedition	1853–1854	J. Zeilin

CIVIL WAR

Bull Run (Manassas), Va.	July 21, 1861	J. Zeilin
Cumberland–Merrimac	March 8, 1862	C. Heywood
reoccupation of Norfolk, Va.	May 10, 1862	C.G. McCawley
Fort Sumter, S.C.	Sept. 8, 1863	C.G. McCawley
Mobile, Ala.	Aug. 1864	C. Heywood
Panama	April 1885	C. Heywood
Seoul, Korea	1894	G.F. Elliott
Tientsin, China	June 1900	L.W.T. Waller
Peking, China	May–Aug. 1900	J.T. Meyers
Peking Relief Expedition	July–Aug. 1900	W.P. Biddle, L.W. Waller, S.D. Butler
Panama	Nov. 1903	J.A. Lejeune, G.F. Elliott
Cuba	Oct. 1906	L.W. Waller, W.C. Neville
Nicaragua	Aug.–Nov. 1912	S.D. Butler, J.H. Pendleton
Coyotepe Hill, Nicaragua	Oct. 4, 1912	J.H. Pendleton
Veracruz, Mexico	April 1914	J.A. Lejeune, L.W. Waller, S.D. Butler, W.C. Neville
Haiti	July 1915	L.W. Waller
Fort Riviere, Haiti	Nov. 1915	S.D. Butler
Santo Domingo	June–July 1916	J.H. Pendleton

WORLD WAR I

4th Marine Brigade	Oct. 1917–Nov. 1918	J.G. Harbord, J.A. Lejeune, W.C. Neville, J.T. Boone (USN), T. Holcomb
Tientsin, China	1927–1929	S.D. Butler

WORLD WAR II

Guadalcanal assault	Aug. 7, 1942	A. Vandegrift, C.B. Cates
Makin Island raid	Aug. 1942	E.F. Carlson
Henderson Field, Guadalcanal	Oct. 23–25, 1942	L.B. Puller
Guadalcanal air war	Oct.–Nov. 1942	J.J. Foss
Bougainville	Nov. 1, 1942	A. Vandegrift, R.S. Geiger
Cape Gloucester, New Britain	Dec. 26, 1942	
Central Solomons air war	Aug. 1943–Jan. 1944	G. Boyington
Tarawa	Nov. 20–23, 1943	H.M. Smith
Betio	Nov. 20–22, 1943	D.M. Shoup
Makin atoll	Nov. 22–24, 1943	H.M. Smith
Kwajalein	Jan. 31–Feb. 7, 1944	H.M. Smith
Eniwetok	Feb. 17–21, 1944	H.M. Smith

Saipan	June 15, 1944	H.M. Smith, C.B. Cates
Guam assault	July 21, 1944	R.S. Geiger
Tinian assault	July 24, 1944	H.M. Smith, C.B. Cates
Peleliu	Sept. 15, 1944	R.S. Geiger
Iwo Jima	Feb. 19–March 27, 1945	H.M. Smith, C.B. Cates, I.H. Hayes
Okinawa	April 1–July 3, 1945	R.S. Geiger

Women's Reserve (WR)	**Ruth C. Streeter**	Feb. 1943–Dec. 1945

Korean War	1950–1953	L.C. Shepherd
Inch'on	Sept. 15, 1950	O.P. Smith, L.B. Puller
Vietnam War	1964–1973	R.E. Cushman

AIR FORCE
Chief officers

JAMES ALLEN	(Chief Signal Officer, ex officio head of Aeronautical Division created Aug. 1, 1907)	Aug. 1907–Feb. 1913
GEORGE P. SCRIVEN	(Chief Signal Officer; Aviation Section, Signal Corps, created July 18, 1914)	Feb. 1913–Feb. 1917
GEORGE O. SQUIER	(Chief Signal Officer)	Feb. 1917–May 1918
WILLIAM L. KENLY	(director of Bureau of Military Aeronautics, created May 20, 1918; director of Air Service, comprising Bureau of Military Aeronautics and Bureau of Aircraft Production, from Aug. 28, 1918)	May 1918–Dec. 1918
Charles T. Menoher	(director of Air Service; chief of reorganized Air Service, line of the army, from June 4, 1920)	Jan. 1919–Oct. 1921
Mason M. Patrick	(chief of Air Service; chief of Army Air Corps from July 2, 1926)	Oct. 1921–Dec. 1927
JAMES E. FECHET	(chief, AAC)	Dec. 1927–Dec. 1931
BENJAMIN D. FOULOIS		Dec. 1931–Dec. 1935
Oscar Westover		Dec. 1935–Sept. 1938

Henry H. Arnold	(chief, AAC; chief, Army Air Forces from July 20, 1941; commanding general, AAF, from March 9, 1942)	Sept. 1938–March 1946
Carl Spaatz	(commanding general, AAF; chief of staff Air Force, from Sept. 17, 1947)	March 1946–July 1948
Hoyt S. Vandenberg	(chief of staff)	July 1948–June 1953
Nathan F. Twining		June 1953–July 1957
Thomas D. White		July 1957–June 1961
Curtis E. LeMay		June 1961–Feb. 1965
John P. McConnell		Feb. 1965–July 1969
John D. Ryan		Aug. 1969–July 1973
George S. Brown		July 1973–July 1974
David C. Jones		July 1974–

Commanders

WORLD WAR I

Lafayette Escadrille	V.E. Chapman, T. Hitchcock, R.G.V. Lufbery, K.Y. Rockwell	April 1916–Jan. 1918
Commander, Air Service, AEF	William Mitchell	June 1917–May 1918
	Mason M. Patrick	May 1918–Oct. 1918

See also **V. Castle, F. Lahm, F. Luke, J.T. McNarney, E.V. Rickenbacker, E.W. Springs**

WORLD WAR II

American Volunteer Group (Flying Tigers)	C.L. Chennault, G. Boyington, R.L. Scott	
Fifth Air Force	Lewis H. Brereton	Nov. 1941–Jan. 1942
	GEORGE H. BRETT	Feb. 1942–Aug. 1942
	George C. Kenney	Sept. 1942–June 1944
	ENNIS C. WHITEHEAD	June 1944–Dec. 1945
Seventh Air Force	FREDERICK L. MARTIN	Nov. 1940–Dec. 1941
	CLARENCE L. TINKER	Dec. 1941–June 1942
	HOWARD C. DAVIDSON	June 1942
	WILLIS H. HALE	June 1942–April 1944
	ROBERT W. DOUGLASS	April 1944–June 1945
	Thomas D. White	June 1945–Oct. 1946
Eighth Air Force	ASA N. DUNCAN	Jan. 1942–May 1942
	Carl Spaatz	May 1942–Dec. 1942
	Ira C. Eaker	Dec. 1942–Jan. 1944
	James H. Doolittle	Jan. 1944–May 1945
	WILLIAM E. KEPNER	May 1945–June 1945
	WESTSIDE T. LARSON	June 1945–July 1945
	James H. Doolittle	July 1945–Sept. 1945

Ninth Air Force	**Lewis H. Brereton**	June 1942–Aug. 1944
	Hoyt S. Vandenberg	Aug. 1944–May 1945
Tenth Air Force	**Lewis H. Brereton**	March 1942–June 1942
	EARL L. NAIDEN	June 1942–Aug. 1942
	CLAYTON L. BISSELL	Aug. 1942–Aug. 1943
	HOWARD C. DAVIDSON	Aug. 1943–Aug. 1945
	ALBERT F. HEGENBERGER	Aug. 1945–Nov. 1945
Eleventh Air Force	EVERETT S. DAVIS	Feb. 1942
	LIONEL H. DUNLAP	Feb. 1942–March 1942
	WILLIAM O. BUTLER	March 1942–Sept. 1943
	DAVENPORT JOHNSON	Sept. 1943–July 1945
	JOHN B. BROOKS	July 1945–Nov. 1945
Twelfth Air Force	**James H. Doolittle**	Sept. 1942–March 1943
	Carl Spaatz	March 1943–Dec. 1943
	JOHN K. CANNON	Dec. 1943–April 1945
	BENJAMIN W. CHIDLAW	April 1945–May 1945
Thirteenth Air Force	**Nathan F. Twining**	Jan. 1943–Dec. 1943
	RAY L. OWENS	Dec. 1943–Jan. 1944
	HUBERT R. HARMON	Jan. 1944–June 1944
	GEORGE L. USHER	June 1944
	ST. CLAIR STREETT	June 1944–Feb. 1945
	PAUL B. WURTSMITH	Feb. 1945–July 1946
Fourteenth Air Force	**Claire L. Chennault**	March 1943–Aug. 1945
	CHARLES B. STONE	Aug. 1945–Jan. 1946
Fifteenth Air Force	**James H. Doolittle**	Nov. 1943–Jan. 1944
	Nathan F. Twining	Jan. 1944–May 1945
Twentieth Air Force	**Henry H. Arnold**	April 1944–July 1945
	Curtis E. LeMay	July 1945–Aug. 1945
	Nathan F. Twining	Aug. 1945–Oct. 1945
WAC director, AAF	**Geraldine P. May**	March 1943–Oct. 1946
Women's Airforce Service Pilots (WASP)	**Jacqueline Cochran**	July 1943–December 1944

See also **F.M. Andrews, R.I. Bong, B.O. Davis, T. Hitchcock, T.B. McGuire, L. Norstad, E.E. Partridge, E.R. Quesada**

KOREA

| Fifth Air Force | **E.E. Partridge, D.E. Hess** |

Adventurers

Burnham, Frederick R.
Chaillé-Long, Charles
Dye, William M.
Ingraham, Prentiss
Jones, John Paul
Jordan, Thomas
Kearny, Philip
Laffite, Jean
Lea, Homer
Lee, Charles

Loring, William W.
McGiffin, Philo N.
Magruder, John B.
O'Hara, Theodore
Porter, David
Sibley, Henry H.
Smith, William S.
Stone, Charles P.
Tucker, John R.
Wooster, Charles W.

Aircraft and marine designers and builders

Braun, Wernher von
Bushnell, David
Curtiss, Glenn H.
De Seversky, Alexander P.
Douglas, Donald W.
Ellet, Charles
Ericsson, John
Fulton, Robert
Gibbs, William F.
Griffiths, John W.
Grumman, Leroy R.
Holland, John P.
Hovgaard, William
Humphreys, Joshua
Hunley, Horace L.
Hunsaker, Jerome C.
Isherwood, Benjamin F.
Johnson, Clarence L.
Kármán, Theodore von
Lake, Simon
Lowe, Thaddeus S.C.
Melville, George W.
Northrop, John K.
Porter, John L.
Rickover, Hyman G.
Taylor, David W.
Vickery, Howard L.

Astronauts, test pilots

Anders, William A.
Armstrong, Neil A.
Borman, Frank
Collins, Michael
Crossfield, A. Scott
Glenn, John H.
Lovell, James A.
Schirra, Walter M.
Shepard, Alan B.
Slayton, Donald K.
Yeager, Charles E.

Authors, cartoonists, journalists

Baker, George
Beach, Edward L.
Caniff, Milton A.
De Seversky, Alexander P.

Ellsberg, Edward
Empey, Arthur G.
Hess, Dean E.
Ingraham, Prentiss
Kilmer, Joyce
Mackenzie, Alexander S.
Mauldin, William H.
O'Hara, Theodore
Pike, Albert
Pyle, Ernest T.
Robert, Henry M.
Ruffin, Edmund
Scott, Robert L.
Seeger, Alan
Sousa, John P.
Springs, Elliot W.
Tregaskis, Richard W.
Wallace, Lewis

Cartoonists *see* Authors

Educators, historians, scientists

Crozet, Claude
Chamberlain, Joshua L.
Gilliss, James M.
Lieber, Francis
Luce, Stephen B.
Mahan, Alfred T.
Mahan, Dennis H.
Maury, Matthew F.
Mitchel, Ormsby M.
Morison, Samuel E.
Newcomb, Simon
Otis, Elwell S.
Parker, William H.
Partridge, Alden
Perry, Matthew C.
Polk, Leonidas
Pratt, Richard H.
Shipp, Scott
Thayer, Sylvanus
Upton, Emory
Wagner, Arthur L.
Ward, James H.
Williams, Ephraim
Williams, Jonathan

Engineers

Abbot, Henry L.

Bailey, Joseph
Bernard, Simon
Bullard, William H.G.
Bush, Vannevar
Casey, Thomas L.
Crozet, Claude
Dodge, Grenville M.
Du Coudray, Philippe C.
Duportail, Louis L.
Ellet, Charles
Ellsberg, Edward
Ericsson, John
Gaillard, David D.
Gillmore, Quincy A.
Goethals, George W.
Gridley, Richard
Groves, Leslie R.
Humphreys, Andrew A.
Hunsaker, Jerome C.
Isherwood, Benjamin F.
Jadwin, Edgar
Kármán, Theodore von
Kosciuszko, Tadeusz
Ludlow, William
McCallum, Daniel C.
Mansfield, Joseph K.F.
Meigs, Montgomery C.
Moreell, Ben
Patrick, Mason M.
Poe, Orlando M.
Putnam, Rufus
Richardson, Wilds P.
Rickover, Hyman G.
Robert, Henry M.
Serrell, Edward W.
Sibert, William L.
Smith, Gustavus W.
Somervell, Brehon B.
Sultan, Daniel I.
Totten, Joseph G.
Warren, Gouverneur K.
Weitzel, Godfrey
Whiting, William H.C.
Wright, Horatio G.

Explorers, frontiersmen, scouts, surveyors

Abert, John J.
Armstrong, John (1755–1816)
Atkinson, Henry

Balchen, Bernt
Barlow, John W.
Bennett, Floyd
Bonneville, Benjamin L.E. de
Burnham, Frederick R.
Byrd, Richard E.
Carson, Kit
Carver, Jonathan
Chaillé-Long, Charles
Clark, William
Cody, William F.
Crockett, David
De Haven, Edwin J.
De Long, George W.
Dixon, William
Erskine, Robert
Frémont, John C.
Girty, Simon
Gist, Christopher
Greely, Adolphus W.
Gunnison, John W.
Hays, John C.
Hood, Washington
Humphreys, Andrew A.
Hutchins, Thomas
Kane, Elisha K.
Kelly, Luther S.
Kenton, Simon
Lewis, Meriwether
Long, Stephen H.
Lynch, William F.
McArthur, William P.
Marcy, Randolph B.
Melville, George W.
Milner, Moses E.
Mullan, John
North, Frank J.
Page, Thomas J.
Peary, Robert E.
Pike, Zebulon M.
Richardson, Wilds P.
Ringgold, Cadwalader
Sieber, Al
Sigsbee, Charles D.
Simpson, James H.
Smith, John
Standish, Miles
Stansbury, Howard
Wheeler, George M.
Whipple, Amiel W.

Wilkes, Charles

Frontiersmen *see* Explorers

Heroes, patriots

Attucks, Crispus
Bailey, Anna W.
Corbin, Margaret
Cushing, William B.
Darragh, Lydia B.
Dawes, William
Edmonds, Sarah E.E.
Hale, Nathan
Hayes, Ira H.
Jasper, William
Lindbergh, Charles A.
Ludington, Sybil
Ludwick, Christopher
McCauley, Mary L.H.
Murphy, Audie
Prescott, Samuel
Revere, Paul
Rowan, Andrew S.
Sampson, Deborah
Smalls, Robert
York, Alvin C.

Historians *see* Educators

Indian leaders

Black Hawk
Brant, Joseph
Canonchet
Captain Jack
Cochise
Cornstalk
Crazy Horse
Gall
Geronimo
Joseph
Little Crow
Little Turtle
Logan, James
McGillivray, Alexander
McIntosh, William
Osceola
Parker, Ely S.
Philip
Pontiac
Popé

Quanah
Red Cloud
Red Eagle
Sitting Bull
Tecumseh
Watie, Stand

Journalists *see* Authors

Marine architects
see Aircraft and marine designers

Nurses *see* Physicians

Ordnance inventors, manufacturers

Anderson, Joseph R.
Benton, James G.
Bomford, George
Bowie, James
Braun, Wernher von
Brooke, John M.
Browning, John M.
Bush, Vannevar
Colt, Samuel
Crozier, William
Dahlgren, John A.B.
Davison, Gregory C.
Dyer, Alexander B.
Fiske, Bradley A.
Garand, John C.
Gatling, Richard J.
Gleaves, Albert
Gorgas, Josiah
Griffiths, John W.
Howell, John A.
Kemble, Gouverneur
Kimball, William W.
Lewis, Isaac N.
Maxim, Hiram S.
Maxim, Hudson
Norden, Carl L.
Parrott, Robert P.
Rains, Gabriel J.
Rodman, Thomas J.
Thompson, John T.

Panama Canal

Abbot, Henry L.
Gaillard, David D.

Goethals, George W.
Gorgas, William C.
Hodges, Harry F.
Jadwin, Edgar
Sibert, William L.

Patriots *see* Heroes

Physicians, nurses

Ashford, Bailey K.
Barton, Clara
Beaumont, William
Bickerdyke, Mary Ann B.
Blanchfield, Florence A.
Boone, Joel T.
Dauser, Sue S.
Dooley, Thomas A.
Gorgas, William C.
Hopkins, Juliet A.O.
Hume, Edgar E.
Kean, Jefferson R.
Letterman, Jonathan
Lovell, Joseph
Seagrave, Gordon S.
Stapp, John P.
Stimson, Julia C.
Tilton, James
Tompkins, Sally L.
Walker, Mary E.

Scientists *see* Educators

Scouts *see* Explorers

Spies, intelligence agents

Boyd, Belle
Donovan, William J.
Hale, Nathan
Hillenkoetter, Roscoe H.
Stringfellow, Benjamin F.
Van Lew, Elizabeth L.

Staff officers

Ainsworth, Frederick C.
Crowder, Enoch H.
De Witt, John L.
Dix, John A.
Fry, James B.
Handy, Thomas T.

Harbord, James G.
Hershey, Lewis B.
Hitchcock, Ethan A.
Hume, Edgar E.
Jesup, Thomas S.
Johnson, Hugh S.
Kean, Jefferson R.
Lee, John C.H.
Lewis, Morgan
Ludlow, William
McCallum, Daniel C.
McNair, Lesley J.
Meigs, Montgomery C.
Mifflin, Thomas
Mitchell, William
Moffett, William A.
Myer, Albert J.
Otis, Elwell S.
Pickering, Timothy
Reeves, Joseph M.
Remey, George C.
Root, Elihu
Scott, Hugh L.
Sibert, William L.
Sims, William S.
Smith, Walter B.
Somervell, Brehon B.
Steuben, Baron von
Thomas, Lorenzo
Tilghman, Tench
Trumbull, Joseph
Usher, Nathaniel R.
Vickery, Howard L.
Winder, John H.
Winship, Blanton

Surveyors *see* Explorers

Test pilots *see* Astronauts

Veterans officials

Burnside, Ambrose E.
Hurlbut, Stephen A.
Lee, Stephen D.
Logan, John A.
Knox, Henry
Robinson, John C.
Stephenson, Benjamin F.
Tanner, James

A CATALOGUE OF SELECTED DOVER BOOKS
IN ALL FIELDS OF INTEREST

A CATALOGUE OF SELECTED DOVER
BOOKS IN ALL FIELDS OF INTEREST

CONDITIONED REFLEXES, Ivan P. Pavlov. Full translation of most complete statement of Pavlov's work; cerebral damage, conditioned reflex, experiments with dogs, sleep, similar topics of great importance. 430pp. 5⅜ x 8½.   60614-7 Pa. $4.50

NOTES ON NURSING: WHAT IT IS, AND WHAT IT IS NOT, Florence Nightingale. Outspoken writings by founder of modern nursing. When first published (1860) it played an important role in much needed revolution in nursing. Still stimulating. 140pp. 5⅜ x 8½.   22340-X Pa. $3.00

HARTER'S PICTURE ARCHIVE FOR COLLAGE AND ILLUSTRATION, Jim Harter. Over 300 authentic, rare 19th-century engravings selected by noted collagist for artists, designers, decoupeurs, etc. Machines, people, animals, etc., printed one side of page. 25 scene plates for backgrounds. 6 collages by Harter, Satty, Singer, Evans. Introduction. 192pp. 8⅞ x 11¾.   23659-5 Pa. $5.00

MANUAL OF TRADITIONAL WOOD CARVING, edited by Paul N. Hasluck. Possibly the best book in English on the craft of wood carving. Practical instructions, along with 1,146 working drawings and photographic illustrations. Formerly titled *Cassell's Wood Carving.* 576pp. 6½ x 9¼.
23489-4 Pa. $7.95

THE PRINCIPLES AND PRACTICE OF HAND OR SIMPLE TURNING, John Jacob Holtzapffel. Full coverage of basic lathe techniques—history and development, special apparatus, softwood turning, hardwood turning, metal turning. Many projects—billiard ball, works formed within a sphere, egg cups, ash trays, vases, jardiniers, others—included. 1881 edition. 800 illustrations. 592pp. 6⅛ x 9¼.   23365-0 Clothbd. $15.00

THE JOY OF HANDWEAVING, Osma Tod. Only book you need for hand weaving. Fundamentals, threads, weaves, plus numerous projects for small board-loom, two-harness, tapestry, laid-in, four-harness weaving and more. Over 160 illustrations. 2nd revised edition. 352pp. 6½ x 9¼.
23458-4 Pa. $6.00

THE BOOK OF WOOD CARVING, Charles Marshall Sayers. Still finest book for beginning student in wood sculpture. Noted teacher, craftsman discusses fundamentals, technique; gives 34 designs, over 34 projects for panels, bookends, mirrors, etc. "Absolutely first-rate"—E. J. Tangerman. 33 photos. 118pp. 7¾ x 10⅝.   23654-4 Pa. $3.50

AN AUTOBIOGRAPHY, Margaret Sanger. Exciting personal account of hard-fought battle for woman's right to birth control, against prejudice, church, law. Foremost feminist document. 504pp. 5⅜ x 8½.
20470-7 Pa. $5.50

MY BONDAGE AND MY FREEDOM, Frederick Douglass. Born as a slave, Douglass became outspoken force in antislavery movement. The best of Douglass's autobiographies. Graphic description of slave life. Introduction by P. Foner. 464pp. 5⅜ x 8½.
22457-0 Pa. $5.50

LIVING MY LIFE, Emma Goldman. Candid, no holds barred account by foremost American anarchist: her own life, anarchist movement, famous contemporaries, ideas and their impact. Struggles and confrontations in America, plus deportation to U.S.S.R. Shocking inside account of persecution of anarchists under Lenin. 13 plates. Total of 944pp. 5⅜ x 8½.
22543-7, 22544-5 Pa., Two-vol. set $12.00

LETTERS AND NOTES ON THE MANNERS, CUSTOMS AND CONDITIONS OF THE NORTH AMERICAN INDIANS, George Catlin. Classic account of life among Plains Indians: ceremonies, hunt, warfare, etc. Dover edition reproduces for first time all original paintings. 312 plates. 572pp. of text. 6⅛ x 9¼.
22118-0, 22119-9 Pa.. Two-vol. set $12.00

THE MAYA AND THEIR NEIGHBORS, edited by Clarence L. Hay, others. Synoptic view of Maya civilization in broadest sense, together with Northern, Southern neighbors. Integrates much background, valuable detail not elsewhere. Prepared by greatest scholars: Kroeber, Morley, Thompson, Spinden, Vaillant, many others. Sometimes called Tozzer Memorial Volume. 60 illustrations, linguistic map. 634pp. 5⅜ x 8½.
23510-6 Pa. $10.00

HANDBOOK OF THE INDIANS OF CALIFORNIA, A. L. Kroeber. Foremost American anthropologist offers complete ethnographic study of each group. Monumental classic. 459 illustrations, maps. 995pp. 5⅜ x 8½.
23368-5 Pa. $13.00

SHAKTI AND SHAKTA, Arthur Avalon. First book to give clear, cohesive analysis of Shakta doctrine, Shakta ritual and Kundalini Shakti (yoga). Important work by one of world's foremost students of Shaktic and Tantric thought. 732pp. 5⅜ x 8½. (Available in U.S. only)
23645-5 Pa. $7.95

AN INTRODUCTION TO THE STUDY OF THE MAYA HIEROGLYPHS, Syvanus Griswold Morley. Classic study by one of the truly great figures in hieroglyph research. Still the best introduction for the student for reading Maya hieroglyphs. New introduction by J. Eric S. Thompson. 117 illustrations. 284pp. 5⅜ x 8½.
23108-9 Pa. $4.00

A STUDY OF MAYA ART, Herbert J. Spinden. Landmark classic interprets Maya symbolism, estimates styles, covers ceramics, architecture, murals, stone carvings as artforms. Still a basic book in area. New introduction by J. Eric Thompson. Over 750 illustrations. 341pp. 8⅜ x 11¼.
21235-1 Pa. $6.95

HOUSEHOLD STORIES BY THE BROTHERS GRIMM. All the great Grimm stories: "Rumpelstiltskin," "Snow White," "Hansel and Gretel," etc., with 114 illustrations by Walter Crane. 269pp. 5⅜ x 8½.
21080-4 Pa. $3.50

SLEEPING BEAUTY, illustrated by Arthur Rackham. Perhaps the fullest, most delightful version ever, told by C. S. Evans. Rackham's best work. 49 illustrations. 110pp. 7⅞ x 10¾.
22756-1 Pa. $2.50

AMERICAN FAIRY TALES, L. Frank Baum. Young cowboy lassoes Father Time; dummy in Mr. Floman's department store window comes to life; and 10 other fairy tales. 41 illustrations by N. P. Hall, Harry Kennedy, Ike Morgan, and Ralph Gardner. 209pp. 5⅜ x 8½.
23643-9 Pa. $3.00

THE WONDERFUL WIZARD OF OZ, L. Frank Baum. Facsimile in full color of America's finest children's classic. Introduction by Martin Gardner. 143 illustrations by W. W. Denslow. 267pp. 5⅜ x 8½.
20691-2 Pa. $3.50

THE TALE OF PETER RABBIT, Beatrix Potter. The inimitable Peter's terrifying adventure in Mr. McGregor's garden, with all 27 wonderful, full-color Potter illustrations. 55pp. 4¼ x 5½. (Available in U.S. only)
22827-4 Pa. $1.25

THE STORY OF KING ARTHUR AND HIS KNIGHTS, Howard Pyle. Finest children's version of life of King Arthur. 48 illustrations by Pyle. 131pp. 6⅛ x 9¼.
21445-1 Pa. $4.95

CARUSO'S CARICATURES, Enrico Caruso. Great tenor's remarkable caricatures of self, fellow musicians, composers, others. Toscanini, Puccini, Farrar, etc. Impish, cutting, insightful. 473 illustrations. Preface by M. Sisca. 217pp. 8⅜ x 11¼.
23528-9 Pa. $6.95

PERSONAL NARRATIVE OF A PILGRIMAGE TO ALMADINAH AND MECCAH, Richard Burton. Great travel classic by remarkably colorful personality. Burton, disguised as a Moroccan, visited sacred shrines of Islam, narrowly escaping death. Wonderful observations of Islamic life, customs, personalities. 47 illustrations. Total of 959pp. 5⅜ x 8½.
21217-3, 21218-1 Pa., Two-vol. set $12.00

INCIDENTS OF TRAVEL IN YUCATAN, John L. Stephens. Classic (1843) exploration of jungles of Yucatan, looking for evidences of Maya civilization. Travel adventures, Mexican and Indian culture, etc. Total of 669pp. 5⅜ x 8½.
20926-1, 20927-X Pa., Two-vol. set $7.90

AMERICAN LITERARY AUTOGRAPHS FROM WASHINGTON IRVING TO HENRY JAMES, Herbert Cahoon, et al. Letters, poems, manuscripts of Hawthorne, Thoreau, Twain, Alcott, Whitman, 67 other prominent American authors. Reproductions, full transcripts and commentary. Plus checklist of all American Literary Autographs in The Pierpont Morgan Library. Printed on exceptionally high-quality paper. 136 illustrations. 212pp. 9⅛ x 12¼.
23548-3 Pa. $12.50

UNCLE SILAS, J. Sheridan LeFanu. Victorian Gothic mystery novel, considered by many best of period, even better than Collins or Dickens. Wonderful psychological terror. Introduction by Frederick Shroyer. 436pp. 5⅜ x 8½.   21715-9 Pa. $6.00

JURGEN, James Branch Cabell. The great erotic fantasy of the 1920's that delighted thousands, shocked thousands more. Full final text, Lane edition with 13 plates by Frank Pape. 346pp. 5⅜ x 8½.
23507-6 Pa. $4.50

THE CLAVERINGS, Anthony Trollope. Major novel, chronicling aspects of British Victorian society, personalities. Reprint of Cornhill serialization, 16 plates by M. Edwards; first reprint of full text. Introduction by Norman Donaldson. 412pp. 5⅜ x 8½.   23464-9 Pa. $5.00

KEPT IN THE DARK, Anthony Trollope. Unusual short novel about Victorian morality and abnormal psychology by the great English author. Probably the first American publication. Frontispiece by Sir John Millais. 92pp. 6½ x 9¼.   23609-9 Pa. $2.50

RALPH THE HEIR, Anthony Trollope. Forgotten tale of illegitimacy, inheritance. Master novel of Trollope's later years. Victorian country estates, clubs, Parliament, fox hunting, world of fully realized characters. Reprint of 1871 edition. 12 illustrations by F. A. Faser. 434pp. of text. 5⅜ x 8½.   23642-0 Pa. $5.00

YEKL and THE IMPORTED BRIDEGROOM AND OTHER STORIES OF THE NEW YORK GHETTO, Abraham Cahan. Film *Hester Street* based on *Yekl* (1896). Novel, other stories among first about Jewish immigrants of N.Y.'s East Side. Highly praised by W. D. Howells—Cahan "a new star of realism." New introduction by Bernard G. Richards. 240pp. 5⅜ x 8½.   22427-9 Pa. $3.50

THE HIGH PLACE, James Branch Cabell. Great fantasy writer's enchanting comedy of disenchantment set in 18th-century France. Considered by some critics to be even better than his famous *Jurgen*. 10 illustrations and numerous vignettes by noted fantasy artist Frank C. Pape. 320pp. 5⅜ x 8½.   23670-6 Pa. $4.00

ALICE'S ADVENTURES UNDER GROUND, Lewis Carroll. Facsimile of ms. Carroll gave Alice Liddell in 1864. Different in many ways from final Alice. Handlettered, illustrated by Carroll. Introduction by Martin Gardner. 128pp. 5⅜ x 8½.   21482-6 Pa. $2.50

FAVORITE ANDREW LANG FAIRY TALE BOOKS IN MANY COLORS, Andrew Lang. The four Lang favorites in a boxed set—the complete *Red, Green, Yellow* and *Blue* Fairy Books. 164 stories; 439 illustrations by Lancelot Speed, Henry Ford and G. P. Jacomb Hood. Total of about 1500pp. 5⅜ x 8½.   23407-X Boxed set, Pa. $15.95

PRINCIPLES OF ORCHESTRATION, Nikolay Rimsky-Korsakov. Great classical orchestrator provides fundamentals of tonal resonance, progression of parts, voice and orchestra, tutti effects, much else in major document. 330pp. of musical excerpts. 489pp. 6½ x 9¼. 21266-1 Pa. **$7.50**

TRISTAN UND ISOLDE, Richard Wagner. Full orchestral score with complete instrumentation. Do not confuse with piano reduction. Commentary by Felix Mottl, great Wagnerian conductor and scholar. Study score. 655pp. 8⅛ x 11. 22915-7 Pa. $13.95

REQUIEM IN FULL SCORE, Giuseppe Verdi. Immensely popular with choral groups and music lovers. Republication of edition published by C. F. Peters, Leipzig, n. d. German frontmaker in English translation. Glossary. Text in Latin. Study score. 204pp. 9⅜ x 12¼.
23682-X Pa. $6.00

COMPLETE CHAMBER MUSIC FOR STRINGS, Felix Mendelssohn. All of Mendelssohn's chamber music: Octet, 2 Quintets, 6 Quartets, and Four Pieces for String Quartet. (Nothing with piano is included). Complete works edition (1874-7). Study score. 283 pp. 9⅜ x 12¼.
23679-X Pa. **$7.50**

POPULAR SONGS OF NINETEENTH-CENTURY AMERICA, edited by Richard Jackson. 64 most important songs: "Old Oaken Bucket," "Arkansas Traveler," "Yellow Rose of Texas," etc. Authentic original sheet music, full introduction and commentaries. 290pp. 9 x 12. 23270-0 Pa. **$7.95**

COLLECTED PIANO WORKS, Scott Joplin. Edited by Vera Brodsky Lawrence. Practically all of Joplin's piano works—rags, two-steps, marches, waltzes, etc., 51 works in all. Extensive introduction by Rudi Blesh. Total of 345pp. 9 x 12. 23106-2 Pa. $14.95

BASIC PRINCIPLES OF CLASSICAL BALLET, Agrippina Vaganova. Great Russian theoretician, teacher explains methods for teaching classical ballet; incorporates best from French, Italian, Russian schools. 118 illustrations. 175pp. 5⅜ x 8½. 22036-2 Pa. $2.50

CHINESE CHARACTERS, L. Wieger. Rich analysis of 2300 characters according to traditional systems into primitives. Historical-semantic analysis to phonetics (Classical Mandarin) and radicals. 820pp. 6⅛ x 9¼.
21321-8 Pa. $10.00

EGYPTIAN LANGUAGE: EASY LESSONS IN EGYPTIAN HIERO-GLYPHICS, E. A. Wallis Budge. Foremost Egyptologist offers Egyptian grammar, explanation of hieroglyphics, many reading texts, dictionary of symbols. 246pp. 5 x 7½. (Available in U.S. only)
21394-3 Clothbd. $7.50

AN ETYMOLOGICAL DICTIONARY OF MODERN ENGLISH, Ernest Weekley. Richest, fullest work, by foremost British lexicographer. Detailed word histories. Inexhaustible. Do not confuse this with *Concise Etymological Dictionary*, which is abridged. Total of 856pp. 6½ x 9¼.
21873-2, 21874-0 Pa., Two-vol. set $12.00

HOLLYWOOD GLAMOUR PORTRAITS, edited by John Kobal. 145 photos capture the stars from 1926-49, the high point in portrait photography. Gable, Harlow, Bogart, Bacall, Hedy Lamarr, Marlene Dietrich, Robert Montgomery, Marlon Brando, Veronica Lake; 94 stars in all. Full background on photographers, technical aspects, much more. Total of 160pp. 8⅜ x 11¼. 23352-9 Pa. $6.00

THE NEW YORK STAGE: FAMOUS PRODUCTIONS IN PHOTO-GRAPHS, edited by Stanley Appelbaum. 148 photographs from Museum of City of New York show 142 plays, 1883-1939. *Peter Pan, The Front Page, Dead End, Our Town,* O'Neill, hundreds of actors and actresses, etc. Full indexes. 154pp. 9½ x 10. 23241-7 Pa. $6.00

DIALOGUES CONCERNING TWO NEW SCIENCES, Galileo Galilei. Encompassing 30 years of experiment and thought, these dialogues deal with geometric demonstrations of fracture of solid bodies, cohesion, leverage, speed of light and sound, pendulums, falling bodies, accelerated motion, etc. 300pp. 5⅜ x 8½. 60099-8 Pa. $4.00

THE GREAT OPERA STARS IN HISTORIC PHOTOGRAPHS, edited by James Camner. 343 portraits from the 1850s to the 1940s: Tamburini, Mario, Caliapin, Jeritza, Melchior, Melba, Patti, Pinza, Schipa, Caruso, Farrar, Steber, Gobbi, and many more—270 performers in all. Index. 199pp. 8⅜ x 11¼. 23575-0 Pa. $7.50

J. S. BACH, Albert Schweitzer. Great full-length study of Bach, life, background to music, music, by foremost modern scholar. Ernest Newman translation. 650 musical examples. Total of 928pp. 5⅜ x 8½. (Available in U.S. only) 21631-4, 21632-2 Pa., Two-vol. set $11.00

COMPLETE PIANO SONATAS, Ludwig van Beethoven. All sonatas in the fine Schenker edition, with fingering, analytical material. One of best modern editions. Total of 615pp. 9 x 12. (Available in U.S. only) 23134-8, 23135-6 Pa., Two-vol. set $15.50

KEYBOARD MUSIC, J. S. Bach. Bach-Gesellschaft edition. For harpsichord, piano, other keyboard instruments. English Suites, French Suites, Six Partitas, Goldberg Variations, Two-Part Inventions, Three-Part Sinfonias. 312pp. 8⅛ x 11. (Available in U.S. only) 22360-4 Pa. $6.95

FOUR SYMPHONIES IN FULL SCORE, Franz Schubert. Schubert's four most popular symphonies: No. 4 in C Minor ("Tragic"); No. 5 in B-flat Major; No. 8 in B Minor ("Unfinished"); No. 9 in C Major ("Great"). Breitkopf & Hartel edition. Study score. 261pp. 9⅜ x 12¼. 23681-1 Pa. $6.50

THE AUTHENTIC GILBERT & SULLIVAN SONGBOOK, W. S. Gilbert, A. S. Sullivan. Largest selection available; 92 songs, uncut, original keys, in piano rendering approved by Sullivan. Favorites and lesser-known fine numbers. Edited with plot synopses by James Spero. 3 illustrations. 399pp. 9 x 12. 23482-7 Pa. $9.95

THE ANATOMY OF THE HORSE, George Stubbs. Often considered the great masterpiece of animal anatomy. Full reproduction of 1766 edition, plus prospectus; original text and modernized text. 36 plates. Introduction by Eleanor Garvey. 121pp. 11 x 14¾.   23402-9 Pa. $6.00

BRIDGMAN'S LIFE DRAWING, George B. Bridgman. More than 500 illustrative drawings and text teach you to abstract the body into its major masses, use light and shade, proportion; as well as specific areas of anatomy, of which Bridgman is master. 192pp. 6½ x 9¼. (Available in U.S. only)
22710-3 Pa. $3.50

ART NOUVEAU DESIGNS IN COLOR, Alphonse Mucha, Maurice Verneuil, Georges Auriol. Full-color reproduction of *Combinaisons ornementales* (c. 1900) by Art Nouveau masters. Floral, animal, geometric, interlacings, swashes—borders, frames, spots—all incredibly beautiful. 60 plates, hundreds of designs. 9⅜ x 8-1/16.   22885-1 Pa. $4.00

FULL-COLOR FLORAL DESIGNS IN THE ART NOUVEAU STYLE, E. A. Seguy. 166 motifs, on 40 plates, from *Les fleurs et leurs applications decoratives* (1902): borders, circular designs, repeats, allovers, "spots." All in authentic Art Nouveau colors. 48pp. 9⅜ x 12¼.
23439-8 Pa. $5.00

A DIDEROT PICTORIAL ENCYCLOPEDIA OF TRADES AND INDUSTRY, edited by Charles C. Gillispie. 485 most interesting plates from the great French Encyclopedia of the 18th century show hundreds of working figures, artifacts, process, land and cityscapes; glassmaking, papermaking, metal extraction, construction, weaving, making furniture, clothing, wigs, dozens of other activities. Plates fully explained. 920pp. 9 x 12.
22284-5, 22285-3 Clothbd., Two-vol. set $40.00

HANDBOOK OF EARLY ADVERTISING ART, Clarence P. Hornung. Largest collection of copyright-free early and antique advertising art ever compiled. Over 6,000 illustrations, from Franklin's time to the 1890's for special effects, novelty. Valuable source, almost inexhaustible.
Pictorial Volume. Agriculture, the zodiac, animals, autos, birds, Christmas, fire engines, flowers, trees, musical instruments, ships, games and sports, much more. Arranged by subject matter and use. 237 plates. 288pp. 9 x 12.
20122-8 Clothbd. $14..50

Typographical Volume. Roman and Gothic faces ranging from 10 point to 300 point, "Barnum," German and Old English faces, script, logotypes, scrolls and flourishes, 1115 ornamental initials, 67 complete alphabets, more. 310 plates. 320pp. 9 x 12.   20123-6 Clothbd. $15.00

CALLIGRAPHY (CALLIGRAPHIA LATINA), J. G. Schwandner. High point of 18th-century ornamental calligraphy. Very ornate initials, scrolls, borders, cherubs, birds, lettered examples. 172pp. 9 x 13.
20475-8 Pa. $7.00

THE COMPLETE WOODCUTS OF ALBRECHT DURER, edited by Dr. W. Kurth. 346 in all: "Old Testament," "St. Jerome," "Passion," "Life of Virgin," Apocalypse," many others. Introduction by Campbell Dodgson. 285pp. 8½ x 12¼.   21097-9 Pa. $7.50

DRAWINGS OF ALBRECHT DURER, edited by Heinrich Wolfflin. 81 plates show development from youth to full style. Many favorites; many new. Introduction by Alfred Werner. 96pp. 8⅛ x 11.   22352-3 Pa. $5.00

THE HUMAN FIGURE, Albrecht Dürer. Experiments in various techniques—stereometric, progressive proportional, and others. Also life studies that rank among finest ever done. Complete reprinting of *Dresden Sketchbook*. 170 plates. 355pp. 8⅜ x 11¼.   21042-1 Pa. $7.95

OF THE JUST SHAPING OF LETTERS, Albrecht Dürer. Renaissance artist explains design of Roman majuscules by geometry, also Gothic lower and capitals. Grolier Club edition. 43pp. 7⅞ x 10¾   21306-4 Pa. $3.00

TEN BOOKS ON ARCHITECTURE, Vitruvius. The most important book ever written on architecture. Early Roman aesthetics, technology, classical orders, site selection, all other aspects. Stands behind everything since. Morgan translation. 331pp. 5⅜ x 8½.   20645-9 Pa. $4.50

THE FOUR BOOKS OF ARCHITECTURE, Andrea Palladio. 16th-century classic responsible for Palladian movement and style. Covers classical architectural remains, Renaissance revivals, classical orders, etc. 1738 Ware English edition. Introduction by A. Placzek. 216 plates. 110pp. of text. 9½ x 12¾.   21308-0 Pa. $10.00

HORIZONS, Norman Bel Geddes. Great industrialist stage designer, "father of streamlining," on application of aesthetics to transportation, amusement, architecture, etc. 1932 prophetic account; function, theory, specific projects. 222 illustrations. 312pp. 7⅞ x 10¾.   23514-9 Pa. $6.95

FRANK LLOYD WRIGHT'S FALLINGWATER, Donald Hoffmann. Full, illustrated story of conception and building of Wright's masterwork at Bear Run, Pa. 100 photographs of site, construction, and details of completed structure. 112pp. 9¼ x 10.   23671-4 Pa. $5.50

THE ELEMENTS OF DRAWING, John Ruskin. Timeless classic by great Viltorian; starts with basic ideas, works through more difficult. Many practical exercises. 48 illustrations. Introduction by Lawrence Campbell. 228pp. 5⅜ x 8½.   22730-8 Pa. $3.75

GIST OF ART, John Sloan. Greatest modern American teacher, Art Students League, offers innumerable hints, instructions, guided comments to help you in painting. Not a formal course. 46 illustrations. Introduction by Helen Sloan. 200pp. 5⅜ x 8½.   23435-5 Pa. $4.00

THE EARLY WORK OF AUBREY BEARDSLEY, Aubrey Beardsley. 157 plates, 2 in color: *Manon Lescaut, Madame Bovary, Morte Darthur, Salome,* other. Introduction by H. Marillier. 182pp. 8⅛ x 11. 21816-3 Pa. $4.50

THE LATER WORK OF AUBREY BEARDSLEY, Aubrey Beardsley. Exotic masterpieces of full maturity: *Venus and Tannhauser, Lysistrata, Rape of the Lock, Volpone,* Savoy material, etc. 174 plates, 2 in color. 186pp. 8⅛ x 11. 21817-1 Pa. $5.95

THOMAS NAST'S CHRISTMAS DRAWINGS, Thomas Nast. Almost all Christmas drawings by creator of image of Santa Claus as we know it, and one of America's foremost illustrators and political cartoonists. 66 illustrations. 3 illustrations in color on covers. 96pp. 8⅜ x 11¼.
23660-9 Pa. $3.50

THE DORÉ ILLUSTRATIONS FOR DANTE'S DIVINE COMEDY, Gustave Doré. All 135 plates from Inferno, Purgatory, Paradise; fantastic tortures, infernal landscapes, celestial wonders. Each plate with appropriate (translated) verses. 141pp. 9 x 12. 23231-X Pa. $4.50

DORÉ'S ILLUSTRATIONS FOR RABELAIS, Gustave Doré. 252 striking illustrations of *Gargantua and Pantagruel* books by foremost 19th-century illustrator. Including 60 plates, 192 delightful smaller illustrations. 153pp. **9 x 12.** 23656-0 Pa. $5.00

LONDON: A PILGRIMAGE, Gustave Doré, Blanchard Jerrold. Squalor, riches, misery, beauty of mid-Victorian metropolis; 55 wonderful plates, 125 other illustrations, full social, cultural text by Jerrold. 191pp. of text. 9⅜ x 12¼. 22306-X Pa. **$7.00**

THE RIME OF THE ANCIENT MARINER, Gustave Doré, S. T. Coleridge. Dore's finest work, 34 plates capture moods, subtleties of poem. Full text. Introduction by Millicent Rose. 77pp. 9¼ x 12. 22305-1 Pa. $3.50

THE DORE BIBLE ILLUSTRATIONS, Gustave Doré. All wonderful, detailed plates: Adam and Eve, Flood, Babylon, Life of Jesus, etc. Brief King James text with each plate. Introduction by Millicent Rose. 241 plates. 241pp. 9 x 12. 23004-X Pa. $6.00

THE COMPLETE ENGRAVINGS, ETCHINGS AND DRYPOINTS OF ALBRECHT DURER. "Knight, Death and Devil"; "Melencolia," and more—all Dürer's known works in all three media, including 6 works formerly attributed to him. 120 plates. 235pp. 8⅜ x 11¼.
22851-7 Pa. $6.50

MECHANICK EXERCISES ON THE WHOLE ART OF PRINTING, Joseph Moxon. First complete book (1683-4) ever written about typography, a compendium of everything known about printing at the latter part of 17th century. Reprint of 2nd (1962) Oxford Univ. Press edition. 74 illustrations. Total of 550pp. 6⅛ x 9¼. 23617-X Pa. $7.95

SECOND PIATIGORSKY CUP, edited by Isaac Kashdan. One of the greatest tournament books ever produced in the English language. All 90 games of the 1966 tournament, annotated by players, most annotated by both players. Features Petrosian, Spassky, Fischer, Larsen, six others. 228pp. 5⅜ x 8½. 23572-6 Pa. $3.50

ENCYCLOPEDIA OF CARD TRICKS, revised and edited by Jean Hugard. How to perform over 600 card tricks, devised by the world's greatest magicians: impromptus, spelling tricks, key cards, using special packs, much, much more. Additional chapter on card technique. 66 illustrations. 402pp. 5⅜ x 8½. (Available in U.S. only) 21252-1 Pa. $4.95

MAGIC: STAGE ILLUSIONS, SPECIAL EFFECTS AND TRICK PHO-TOGRAPHY, Albert A. Hopkins, Henry R. Evans. One of the great classics; fullest, most authorative explanation of vanishing lady, levitations, scores of other great stage effects. Also small magic, automata, stunts. 446 illus-trations. 556pp. 5⅜ x 8½. 23344-8 Pa. $6.95

THE SECRETS OF HOUDINI, J. C. Cannell. Classic study of Houdini's incredible magic, exposing closely-kept professional secrets and revealing, in general terms, the whole art of stage magic. 67 illustrations. 279pp. 5⅜ x 8½. 22913-0 Pa. $4.00

HOFFMANN'S MODERN MAGIC, Professor Hoffmann. One of the best, and best-known, magicians' manuals of the past century. Hundreds of tricks from card tricks and simple sleight of hand to elaborate illusions involving construction of complicated machinery. 332 illustrations. 563pp. 5⅜ x 8½. 23623-4 Pa. $6.00

MADAME PRUNIER'S FISH COOKERY BOOK, Mme. S. B. Prunier. More than 1000 recipes from world famous Prunier's of Paris and London, specially adapted here for American kitchen. Grilled tournedos with anchovy butter, Lobster a la Bordelaise, Prunier's prized desserts, more. Glossary. 340pp. 5⅜ x 8½. (Available in U.S. only) 22679-4 Pa. $3.00

FRENCH COUNTRY COOKING FOR AMERICANS, Louis Diat. 500 easy-to-make, authentic provincial recipes compiled by former head chef at New York's Fitz-Carlton Hotel: onion soup, lamb stew, potato pie, more. 309pp. 5⅜ x 8½. 23665-X Pa. $3.95

SAUCES, FRENCH AND FAMOUS, Louis Diat. Complete book gives over 200 specific recipes: bechamel, Bordelaise, hollandaise, Cumberland, apri-cot, etc. Author was one of this century's finest chefs, originator of vichyssoise and many other dishes. Index. 156pp. 5⅜ x 8.

23663-3 Pa. $2.75

TOLL HOUSE TRIED AND TRUE RECIPES, Ruth Graves Wakefield. Authentic recipes from the famous Mass. restaurant: popovers, veal and ham loaf, Toll House baked beans, chocolate cake crumb pudding, much more. Many helpful hints. Nearly 700 recipes. Index. 376pp. 5⅜ x 8½. 23560-2 Pa. $4.50

HISTORY OF BACTERIOLOGY, William Bulloch. The only comprehensive history of bacteriology from the beginnings through the 19th century. Special emphasis is given to biography-Leeuwenhoek, etc. Brief accounts of 350 bacteriologists form a separate section. No clearer, fuller study, suitable to scientists and general readers, has yet been written. 52 illustrations. 448pp. 5⅝ x 8¼.   23761-3 Pa. $6.50

THE COMPLETE NONSENSE OF EDWARD LEAR, Edward Lear. All nonsense limericks, zany alphabets, Owl and Pussycat, songs, nonsense botany, etc., illustrated by Lear. Total of 321pp. 5⅜ x 8½. (Available in U.S. only)   20167-8 Pa. $3.95

INGENIOUS MATHEMATICAL PROBLEMS AND METHODS, Louis A. Graham. Sophisticated material from Graham *Dial*, applied and pure; stresses solution methods. Logic, number theory, networks, inversions, etc. 237pp. 5⅜ x 8½.   20545-2 Pa. $4.50

BEST MATHEMATICAL PUZZLES OF SAM LOYD, edited by Martin Gardner. Bizarre, original, whimsical puzzles by America's greatest puzzler. From fabulously rare *Cyclopedia*, including famous 14-15 puzzles, the Horse of a Different Color, 115 more. Elementary math. 150 illustrations. 167pp. 5⅜ x 8½.   20498-7 Pa. $2.75

THE BASIS OF COMBINATION IN CHESS, J. du Mont. Easy-to-follow, instructive book on elements of combination play, with chapters on each piece and every powerful combination team—two knights, bishop and knight, rook and bishop, etc. 250 diagrams. 218pp. 5⅜ x 8½. (Available in U.S. only)   23644-7 Pa. $3.50

MODERN CHESS STRATEGY, Ludek Pachman. The use of the queen, the active king, exchanges, pawn play, the center, weak squares, etc. Section on rook alone worth price of the book. Stress on the moderns. Often considered the most important book on strategy. 314pp. 5⅜ x 8½.
20290-9 Pa. $4.50

LASKER'S MANUAL OF CHESS, Dr. Emanuel Lasker. Great world champion offers very thorough coverage of all aspects of chess. Combinations, position play, openings, end game, aesthetics of chess, philosophy of struggle, much more. Filled with analyzed games. 390pp. 5⅜ x 8½.
20640-8 Pa. $5.00

500 MASTER GAMES OF CHESS, S. Tartakower, J. du Mont. Vast collection of great chess games from 1798-1938, with much material nowhere else readily available. Fully annotated, arranged by opening for easier study. 664pp. 5⅜ x 8½.   23208-5 Pa. $7.50

A GUIDE TO CHESS ENDINGS, Dr. Max Euwe, David Hooper. One of the finest modern works on chess endings. Thorough analysis of the most frequently encountered endings by former world champion. 331 examples, each with diagram. 248pp. 5⅜ x 8½.   23332-4 Pa. $3.75

GEOMETRY, RELATIVITY AND THE FOURTH DIMENSION, Rudolf Rucker. Exposition of fourth dimension, means of visualization, concepts of relativity as Flatland characters continue adventures. Popular, easily followed yet accurate, profound. 141 illustrations. 133pp. 5⅜ x 8½.
23400-2 Pa. $2.75

THE ORIGIN OF LIFE, A. I. Oparin. Modern classic in biochemistry, the first rigorous examination of possible evolution of life from nitrocarbon compounds. Non-technical, easily followed. Total of 295pp. 5⅜ x 8½.
60213-3 Pa. $4.00

PLANETS, STARS AND GALAXIES, A. E. Fanning. Comprehensive introductory survey: the sun, solar system, stars, galaxies, universe, cosmology; quasars, radio stars, etc. 24pp. of photographs. 189pp. 5⅜ x 8½. (Available in U.S. only)
21680-2 Pa. $3.75

THE THIRTEEN BOOKS OF EUCLID'S ELEMENTS, translated with introduction and commentary by Sir Thomas L. Heath. Definitive edition. Textual and linguistic notes, mathematical analysis, 2500 years of critical commentary. Do not confuse with abridged school editions. Total of 1414pp. 5⅜ x 8½.
60088-2, 60089-0, 60090-4 Pa., Three-vol. set $18.50

Prices subject to change without notice.

Available at your book dealer or write for free catalogue to Dept. GI, Dover Publications, Inc., 31 East Second Street, Mineola, N.Y. 11501. Dover publishes more than 175 books each year on science, elementary and advanced mathematics, biology, music, art, literary history, social sciences and other areas.